American Government

Power and Purpose

NINTH EDITION

American Government

Power and Purpose

NINTH
EDITION

Theodore J. Lowi
Cornell University

Benjamin Ginsberg
The Johns Hopkins University

and

Kenneth A. Shepsle
Harvard University

W • W • NORTON & COMPANY NEW YORK • LONDON

W. W. Norton & Company has been independent since its founding in 1923, when William Warder Norton and Mary D. Herter Norton first published lectures delivered at the People's Institute, the adult education division of New York City's Cooper Union. The Nortons soon expanded their program beyond the Institute, publishing books by celebrated academics from America and abroad. By mid-century, the two major pillars of Norton's publishing program—trade books and college texts—were firmly established. In the 1950s, the Norton family transferred control of the company to its employees, and today—with a staff of four hundred and a comparable number of trade, college, and professional titles published each year—W. W. Norton & Company stands as the largest and oldest publishing house owned wholly by its employees.

The text of this book is composed in Berling Roman
with the display set in Bawdy.
Composition by TSI Graphics
Manufacturing by Quebecor World Versailles

Editor: Peter Lesser
Electronic media editor: Denise Shanks
Manuscript editor: Candace Levy
Managing editor, College: Marian Johnson
Assistant editor: Birgit Larsson
Graphic artist: John McCausland
Book designer: Sandra Watanabe
Production manager: Diane O'Connor

Library of Congress Cataloging-in-Publication Data

Lowi, Theodore J.
   American government: power and purpose / Theodore J. Lowi, Benjamin Ginsberg, and Kenneth A. Shepsle.—9th ed.
       p. cm.
   Includes bibliographical references and index.
             ISBN 0-393-92716-4
   1. United States—Politics and government. I. Ginsberg, Benjamin. II. Shepsle, Kenneth
A. III. Title.

JK275.L68 2006
320.473—dc22

                                                                   2005055474

W. W. Norton & Company, Inc.
500 Fifth Avenue, New York, NY 10110
www.wwnorton.com
W. W. Norton & Company Ltd.
Castle House, 75/76 Wells Street, London W1T 3QT
1 2 3 4 5 6 7 8 9 0

Contents

Preface   xix

PART 1   FOUNDATIONS

1 | Five Principles of Politics   2

Making Sense of Government and Politics   4

What Is Government?   5

Forms of Government   5

Foundations of Government   5

Why Is Government Necessary?   7

Influencing the Government: Politics   9

Principle 1: All Political Behavior Has a Purpose   10

Principle 2: All Politics Is Collective Action   11

Principle 3: Institutions Routinely Solve Collective-Action
Problems   15

Principle 4: Political Outcomes Are the Products of Individual
Preferences and Institutional Procedures   19

Principle 5: History Matters   21

APPLYING THE FIVE PRINCIPLES OF POLITICS: The Politics of
Prescription Drugs   22

The Principles of Politics in Action   24

The Rationality Principle   27

The Collective-Action Principle   27

The Institution Principle   28

The Policy Principle   29

The History Principle   29

Summary   32

For Further Reading   33

POLITICS IN THE NEWS: Competing Interests and
Prescription Drugs   34

2 Constructing a Government: The Founding and the Constitution 36

The First Founding: Interests and Conflicts   39
British Taxes and Colonial Interests   39
Political Strife and the Radicalizing of the Colonists   41
The Declaration of Independence   42
The Articles of Confederation   42

The Second Founding: From Compromise to Constitution   43
International Standing and Balance of Power   43
The Annapolis Convention   44
Shays's Rebellion   44
The Constitutional Convention   45

The Constitution   49
APPLYING THE FIVE PRINCIPLES OF POLITICS: Were the Framers Rational Actors?   50
The Legislative Branch   52
The Executive Branch   53
The Judicial Branch   54
National Unity and Power   55
Amending the Constitution   55
Ratifying the Constitution   56
Constitutional Limits on the National Government's Power   56

The Fight for Ratification: Federalists versus Antifederalists   59
Representation   62
The Threats Posed by the Majority   63
Governmental Power   64

Changing the Institutional Framework: Constitutional Amendment   65
Amendments: Many Are Called, Few Are Chosen   66
The Twenty-seven Amendments   67

Reflections on the Founding: Principles or Interests?   72

Summary   74

For Further Reading   75
POLITICS IN THE NEWS: The Challenges Faced by Constitutional Amendments   76

3 **The Constitutional Framework: Federalism and the Separation of Powers** **78**

The Dynamics of the Framework: A Case Study **80**

Federalism and the Separation of Powers as Political Institutions **82**

Who Does What? Stability and Change in the Federal Framework **83**

Federalism in the Constitution 84

The Slow Growth of the National Government's Power 89

Cooperative Federalism and Grants-in-Aid 92

Regulated Federalism and National Standards 97

New Federalism and the National-State Tug-of-War 99

APPLYING THE FIVE PRINCIPLES OF POLITICS: Federalism and the No Child Left Behind Act 102

The Separation of Powers **105**

Checks and Balances 106

Legislative Supremacy 106

The Role of the Supreme Court 108

Altering the Balance of Power: What Are the Consequences? **111**

Summary **114**

For Further Reading **115**

POLITICS IN THE NEWS: Fiscal Federalism in the Twenty-first Century 116

4 **The Constitutional Framework and the Individual: Civil Liberties and Civil Rights** **118**

Civil Liberties: Nationalizing the Bill of Rights **121**

Dual Citizenship 122

The Fourteenth Amendment 123

The Constitutional Revolution in Civil Liberties 127

Rehnquist and Beyond: A De-nationalizing Trend? 130

Civil Rights **133**

Plessy v. Ferguson: "Separate but Equal" 133

APPLYING THE FIVE PRINCIPLES OF POLITICS: Rights, Liberties, and the World Wide Web 134

Racial Discrimination after World War II 136

Civil Rights after *Brown v. Board of Education* 138

The Rise of the Politics of Rights 144

Affirmative Action 149

Summary **154**

For Further Reading **157**

POLITICS IN THE NEWS: Data Mining and Personal Privacy 158

PART 2   INSTITUTIONS   161

5 | Congress: The First Branch   162

Representation   165
House and Senate: Differences in Representation   167
The Electoral System   169

Problems of Legislative Organization   178
Cooperation in Congress   179
Underlying Problems and Challenges   180

The Organization of Congress   182
Party Leadership and Organization in the House and the
    Senate   182
The Committee System: The Core of Congress   185
The Staff System: Staffers and Agencies   191
Informal Organization: The Caucuses   192

Rules of Lawmaking: How a Bill Becomes a Law   192
Committee Deliberation   193
Debate   193
Conference Committee: Reconciling House and Senate Versions
    of a Bill   194
Presidential Action   195
Normal and Abnormal Procedures in Congress   195
The Distributive Tendency in Congress   197
APPLYING THE FIVE PRINCIPLES OF POLITICS: Why Congress Cannot
    Get Things Done   198

How Congress Decides   200
Constituency   200
Interest Groups   201
Party Discipline   202
Weighing Diverse Influences   207

Beyond Legislation: Additional Congressional Powers   208
Advice and Consent: Special Senate Powers   208
Impeachment   210

Power and Representation   211

Summary   212

For Further Reading   214
POLITICS IN THE NEWS: Differences Between the House
    and Senate   216

6 | The Presidency as an Institution   218

The Constitutional Basis of the Presidency   220

The Constitutional Powers of the Presidency   222
Expressed Powers   223
APPLYING THE FIVE PRINCIPLES OF POLITICS: A Veto-less
      Presidency?   234
Delegated Powers   237

The Rise of Presidential Government   239
The Legislative Epoch, 1800–1933   240
The New Deal and the Presidency   242

Presidential Government   245
What Are the Formal Resources of Presidential Power?   246
The Contemporary Bases of Presidential Power   252
The Administrative State   259

Summary   266

For Further Reading   266
POLITICS IN THE NEWS: Presidential Power and the Press
      Conference   268

7 | The Executive Branch: Bureaucracy in a Democracy   270

Why Bureaucracy?   275
Bureaucratic Organization Enhances Efficiency   278
Bureaucracies Allow Governments to Operate   278
Bureaucrats Fulfill Important Roles   279
Politics   281

How Is the Executive Branch Organized?   282
Clientele Agencies Serve Particular Interests   284
Agencies for Maintenance of the Union Keep the Government
      Going   285
Regulatory Agencies Guide Individual Conduct   287
Agencies of Redistribution Implement Fiscal/Monetary and Welfare
      Policies   288

The Problem of Bureaucratic Control   289
Bureaucrats Have Their Own Motivational Considerations   290
Control of the Bureaucracy Is a Principal-Agent Problem   292
The President as Chief Executive Can Direct Agencies   294
Congress Can Promote Responsible Bureaucracy through Oversight
      and Incentives   296
APPLYING THE FIVE PRINCIPLES OF POLITICS: The Politics of
      Disaster—Terror and Hurricane Katrina   298

How Can Bureaucracy Be Reduced?   302

Termination   303

Devolution   306

Privatization   308

Summary   309

For Further Reading   311

POLITICS IN THE NEWS: U.S. Politics and Natural Disasters   312

8 | The Federal Courts: Structure and Strategies   314

The Judicial Process   316

The Organization of the Court System   319

Types of Courts   319

Federal Jurisdiction   320

Federal Trial Courts   324

Federal Appellate Courts   324

The Supreme Court   324

How Judges Are Appointed   325

How Do Courts Work as Political Institutions?   329

Dispute Resolution   329

Coordination   330

Rule Interpretation   331

The Power of Judicial Review   333

Judicial Review of Acts of Congress   333

Judicial Review of State Actions   333

Judicial Review of Federal Agency Actions   335

Judicial Review and Presidential Power   337

Judicial Review and Lawmaking   338

The Supreme Court in Action   341

How Cases Reach the Supreme Court   341

Controlling the Flow of Cases   346

The Case Pattern   347

The Supreme Court's Procedures   349

Judicial Decision Making   353

The Supreme Court Justices   353

Other Institutions of Government   358

Implementation of Supreme Court Decisions   359

Strategic Behavior in the Supreme Court   361

APPLYING THE FIVE PRINCIPLES OF POLITICS: Judicial Decision
     Making   362

Judicial Power and Politics   366

Traditional Limitations on the Federal Courts   367

Two Judicial Revolutions   367

Summary   370

For Further Reading   373

POLITICS IN THE NEWS: John Roberts and the Constitution   374

PART 3   POLITICS   377

9 | **Public Opinion**   378

What Are the Origins of Public Opinion?   382

Common Fundamental Values   383

Political Socialization   385

Political Ideology   395

Public Opinion and Political Knowledge   397

APPLYING THE FIVE PRINCIPLES OF POLITICS: America the
    Moderate?   400

**Shaping of Opinion: The Influence of Political Leaders, Private
Groups, and the Media**   402

Government and the Shaping of Public Opinion   402

Private Groups and the Shaping of Public Opinion   404

The Media and Public Opinion   406

Measuring Public Opinion   407

Constructing Public Opinion from Surveys   408

Public Opinion, Political Knowledge, and the Political Uncertainty
    Principle   414

How Does Public Opinion Influence Government Policy?   414

Summary   417

For Further Reading   419

POLITICS IN THE NEWS: Deliberative Polling   420

10 | Elections 422

How Does Government Regulate the Electoral Process? 426

Electoral Composition 426

Translating Voters' Choices into Electoral Outcomes 432

Insulating Decision-Making Processes 437

Direct Democracy: The Referendum and Recall 442

How Do Voters Decide? 444

Partisan Loyalty 444

Issues 446

Candidate Characteristics 450

The 2004 Elections 452

Democratic Opportunities 452

Republican Strategies 454

The End Game 455

APPLYING THE FIVE PRINCIPLES OF POLITICS: The 2004 Election—The Minimax Regret Strategy of Presidential Campaigning 456

Campaign Finance 458

Sources of Campaign Funds 458

Campaign Finance Reform 461

Implications for Democracy 464

Do Elections Matter? 466

Why Is There a Decline in Voter Turnout? 466

Why Do Elections Matter as Political Institutions? 469

Summary 471

For Further Reading 471

POLITICS IN THE NEWS: Voting and Rational Behavior 474

11 | Political Parties 476

Why Do Political Parties Form? 479

To Facilitate Collective Action in the Electoral Process 480

To Resolve Collective Choice in the Policy-Making Process 480

To Deal with the Problem of Ambition 481

What Functions Do Parties Perform? 481

Recruiting Candidates 481

Nominations 482

Getting Out the Vote 484

Facilitating Mass Electoral Choice 485

Influencing National Government 486

APPLYING THE FIVE PRINCIPLES OF POLITICS: The Causes and Effects of Party Polarization in the United States 488

Parties and the Electorate   491

Group Affiliations   491

Party Systems   494

The First Party System: Federalists and
   Democratic-Republicans   498
The Second Party System: Democrats and Whigs   498
The Third Party System: Republicans and Democrats,
   1860–96   500
The Fourth Party System, 1896–1932   502
The Fifth Party System: The New Deal Coalition, 1932–68   503
The Sixth Party System?   504
American Third Parties   506

How Strong Are Political Parties Today?   510

High-Tech Politics and the Rise of Candidate-Centered and
   Capital-Intensive Politics   510
Labor-Intensive to Capital-Intensive Politics   513
Contemporary Party Organizations   513
The Contemporary Party as Service Provider to Candidates   517
Parties and Democracy   517

Summary   518

For Further Reading   521
POLITICS IN THE NEWS: ACT and the Post-Party World   522

12 | Groups and Interests   524

What Are the Characteristics of Interest Groups?   526

Interest Groups Enhance Democracy . . .   527
. . . But Also Represent the Evils of Faction   527
Organized Interests Are Predominantly Economic   528
All Groups Require Money and Leadership, and Most Need
   Members   529
Group Membership Has an Upper-Class Bias   530
Groups Form in Response to Changes in the Political
   Environment   530

How and Why Do Interest Groups Form?   533

Interest Groups Facilitate Cooperation   534
Selective Benefits: A Solution to the Collective-Action Problem   537
Political Entrepreneurs Organize and Maintain Groups   539
APPLYING THE FIVE PRINCIPLES OF POLITICS: Can the Internet Help
   Americans "Meet Up" and Cooperate?   541

How Do Interest Groups Influence Policy?   **543**

Direct Lobbying   543

Using the Courts   549

Mobilizing Public Opinion   550

Using Electoral Politics   553

Interest Groups: Are They Effective?   556

Groups and Interests: The Dilemma of Reform   **557**

Summary   **559**

For Further Reading   **561**

POLITICS IN THE NEWS: The Politics of Same-Sex Marriage   562

---

13 | The Media   564

The Media Industry and Government   566

Types of Media   567

Regulation of the Broadcast and Electronic Media   570

Freedom of the Press   572

APPLYING THE FIVE PRINCIPLES OF POLITICS: The Press and Politicians—
    Caught in a Prisoner's Dilemma   574

Organization and Ownership of the Media   576

Nationalization of the News   577

What Affects News Coverage?   580

Journalists   580

Politicians   582

Consumers   587

What Are the Sources of Media Power in American Politics?   589

Agenda Setting   590

Priming   590

Framing   591

The Media and Elections   592

The Rise of Adversarial Journalism   593

Media Power and Responsibility   595

Summary   596

For Further Reading   597

POLITICS IN THE NEWS: Freedom of the Press   598

PART 4 GOVERNANCE 601

14 Government in Action: Public Policy and the Economy 602

How Does Government Make a Market Economy Possible? 605
Prerequisites for a Market Economy 606
The Bases of Government Involvement 608

What Are the Goals, Tools, and Politics of Economic Policy? 611
Public Order and Private Property 611
Business Development 613
Maintaining a Stable and Strong Economy 620
APPLYING THE FIVE PRINCIPLES OF POLITICS: The Federal Reserve Board as a Political Institution 628

Summary 633

Further Reading 635
POLITICS IN THE NEWS: Tax Reform and Special Interests 636

15 Government and Society 638

The Politics of Social Policy 640

The History of the Social Welfare System 644

What Are the Foundations of the Social Welfare System? 647
Social Security 647
Medicare 651
Welfare: Means-Tested Public Assistance Policy 653

Analyzing the Welfare System 657
Arguments against It 657
Arguments for It 659
APPLYING THE FIVE PRINCIPLES OF POLITICS: Social Welfare and the Politics of Collective Action 662

How Can Government Create Opportunity? 664
Education Policies and Their Politics 664
Health Policies and Their Politics 668

Who Is Poor? What Can Government Do? 669

Summary 671

Further Reading 672
POLITICS IN THE NEWS: The Politics of Social Security Reform 674

16 | Foreign Policy and Democracy   676

Who Makes and Shapes American Foreign Policy?   680
The President   680
The Bureaucracy   683
Congress   685
Interest Groups   686
The Media   688
Putting It Together   690

What Are the Values in American Foreign Policy?   691
Legacies of the Traditional System   692
The Great Leap to World Power   693

What Are the Instruments of Modern American Foreign Policy?   694
Diplomacy   694
The United Nations   696
The International Monetary Structure   699
Economic Aid   700
Collective Security   702
Military Deterrence   705
APPLYING THE FIVE PRINCIPLES OF POLITICS: The Bush Doctrine—
Unilateralism in a Unipolar World   706

Roles Nations Play   710
Choosing a Role   710
Choice of Roles for America Today   712

Summary   714

For Further Reading   717
POLITICS IN THE NEWS: Country Coalitions and
U.S. Foreign Policy   718

APPENDIX   A1

The Declaration of Independence   A3
The Articles of Confederation   A7
The Constitution of the United States of America   A13
Amendments to the Constitution   A25
Federalist Papers   A35
No. 10   A35
No. 51   A40

Glossary of Terms   A45
Index   A63

Preface

Someone once asked if it is difficult for scholars to "write down" to introductory students. No. It is difficult to "write up" to them. Introductory students, of whatever age or reading level, need more, require more, and expect more of a book. A good teaching book, like a good novel or play, is written on two levels. One is the level of the narrative, the story line, the characters in action. The second is the level of character development, of the argument of the book or play. We would not be the first to assert that theater is an aspect of politics, but our book may be unusual to the extent that we took that assertion as a guide. We have packed it full of narrative—with characters and with the facts about the complex situations in which they find themselves. We have at the same time been determined not to lose sight of the second level, yet we have tried to avoid making the second level so prominent as to define us as preachers rather than teachers.

Our collective one-hundred-plus years of teaching have taught us not to underestimate students. Their raw intelligence is not satisfied until a second level provides a logic linking the disparate parts of what we were asserting was a single system of government. And these linkages have to be made in ordinary language. We hope we brought this to the book.

We hope also that we brought over from our teaching experience a full measure of sympathy for all who teach the introductory course, most particularly those who teach the course from departmental necessity rather than voluntarily as a desired part of their career. We hope our book will help them appreciate the course as we do—as an opportunity to make sense of a whole political system, usually one's own, and one of the largest, most durable, and most consequential ever. Much can be learned about the system from a reexamination of the innumerable familiar facts under the still more challenging condition that the facts be somehow interesting, significant, and, above all, linked.

All Americans are to a great extent familiar with the politics and government of their own country. No fact is intrinsically difficult to grasp, and in such an open society, facts abound. In America, many facts are commonplace that are suppressed elsewhere. The ubiquity of political commonplaces is a problem, but it can be turned into a virtue. These very commonplaces give us a vocabulary that is widely shared, and such a vocabulary enables us to communicate effectively at the first level of the book, avoiding abstract concepts and professional language (jargon). Reaching beyond the commonplaces to the second level also identifies what is to us the single most important task of the teacher of political science—to confront the million commonplaces and to choose from among them the small number of really significant concepts. Students give us proportion; we must in turn give the students priorities. Virtually everything we need to know about the institutions and processes of government and politics is readily at hand. But to choose a few commonplaces from the millions—there's the rub.

THE APPROACH OF THE BOOK

This book was written for faculty and students who are looking for a little more than just "nuts and bolts" and who are drawn to an analytical perspective. Although we don't specifically address political-science methodology, the book serves as an integration of the historical-institutional and rational-choice perspectives and as a set of tools (the "Five Principles of Politics") that students can use to think analytically about politics. The feedback we have received thus far from students and fellow professors gives us confidence that the most appealing feature of the book is the analytical framework based on the principles of politics. With this Ninth Edition, we hope to broaden our appeal among political scientists and their students by incorporating new applications of the principles of politics in action and new pedagogy that keeps students focused on the main points of each chapter. The book is based on the idea that the best way to teach students is to expose them to repeated applications of a small number of the core ideas of the discipline in a presentation devoid of the usual clutter. We hope that students will get from this book more than just a bunch of facts about American government; we hope that they will develop a way of thinking about and analyzing politics.

The book's analytical approach is incorporated in the following ways:

Emphasis on five fundamental, underlying principles of politics provides students with the "tools" for analysis. Politics is messy, complex, and contentious. How do we make sense of what seems too large and impossible to explain? In answering this question throughout each chapter, we repeatedly draw on five fundamental principles of politics:

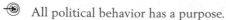 All political behavior has a purpose.

All politics is collective action.

Institutions routinely solve collective-action problems.

Political outcomes are the products of individual preferences and institutional procedures.

History matters.

The application of the five principles to each chapter's topic is first introduced in a **"Previewing the Principles"** box at the beginning of the chapter. Each time one of these principles is used in the analysis, a marginal icon appears, reminding students of the core principle. These principles are also summarized in a **"Principles of Politics in Review"** box toward the conclusion of every chapter. Our goal is to equip students with the tools to evaluate the political world that they observe around them.

Four new applications of the "Five Principles of Politics." Merely knowing a principle is different from understanding it. For students to analyze politics, they need a framework (the five principles) and models of how to use the framework. Students also need to be prompted to use the framework on their own. In the Ninth Edition, four applications show students how to apply the framework and then use it on their own in in-class simulations and Web-based exercises.

1. **"Applying the Five Principles of Politics" boxed case studies** (one per chapter). These case studies go beyond the text and apply one or more of the five principles to a central topic such as Bush's veto-less presidency, or whether the two Americas—red and blue—actually exist.
2. **"Politics in the News: Reading between the Lines"** (one per chapter). These two-page spreads show students how to use the five principles to better understand political situations reported in the news, such as FEMA and the response to Hurricane Katrina or the nomination of John Roberts to the Supreme Court. This feature consists of an excerpt from a *New York Times* article, a bulleted summary of the article's central issues, and a bulleted "political analysis" using the five principles.
3. *Playing Politics* **game theory–based simulations workbook** (by Tobin Grant, Southern Illinois University—Carbondale). Active involvement is an essential part of effective learning. These role-playing simulations will allow students to put themselves in the shoes of strategic political actors responding to a wide range of political situations. The simulations are designed to take from 30 to 45 minutes in class and include an out-of-class written analysis by students. They are a perfect supplement for discussion sections.
4. **Web-site exercises based on "Applying the Five Principles of Politics" and "Politics in the News."** Another "active learning" component, these exercises help students build their analytical skills and demonstrate that the principles of politics can be used to interpret current political events. To preview these exercises, go to wwnorton.com/lowi.

An "analytic narrative" that ties the five principles together. As teachers and scholars, we believe that it is easiest to understand the system of American government by looking at political institutions (Principle 3). In every chapter, we look at an institution's source and its historical development (Principle 5). Along the way, we offer accounts of important historical events and analysis of the individual decisions and choices by political actors (Principle 1). Throughout, we analyze political conflict and compromise (Principle 2) and the outcomes of these conflicts and compromises (Principle 4). History gives each chapter a narrative flow, making the book engaging. The focus on individual decisions and choices and the conflicts between them explains not only political outcomes such as policy, but also how and why institutions develop and change. For example, in discussing the presidency, we evaluate how presidents have used the threat of a veto and "going public" to build power vis-à-vis Congress. By the time students get to the end of this chapter, they will understand why some policies get adopted while others don't. And they will also have a richer sense of why today's institutions function as they do and how they interact with each other.

THE ORGANIZATION OF THE BOOK

The book is divided into three parts, reflecting the historical process by which Americans have used governmental power. Part 1, "Foundations," comprises the chapters concerned with the bases of political analysis and the writing of the rules of the "game." The founding of 1787–89 put it all together, but that was actually a second effort after a first failure. The original contract, the Articles of Confederation, did not achieve an acceptable balance—too much freedom and not enough power. The second founding, the Constitution ratified in 1789, was itself an imperfect effort to establish the rules, and within two years new terms were added—the first ten amendments, called the Bill of Rights. And for the next century and a half following the ratification of the Bill of Rights in 1791, the courts played umpire and translator in the struggle to interpret those terms. Chapter 1 introduces our five principles of politics. Chapter 2 concentrates on the founding itself. Chapters 3 and 4 chronicle the long struggle to establish what was meant by the three great principles of limited government: federalism, separation of powers, and individual liberties and rights.

Part 2, "Institutions," includes the chapters sometimes referred to as the "nuts and bolts." But none of these pieces of government means anything except in the larger context of the goals governments must meet and the limits, especially of procedure, that have been imposed upon them. Chapter 5 is an introduction to the fundamental problem of representative government as this has been institutionalized in the U.S. Congress. Congress, with all its problems, is the most creative legislative body in the world. But how well does Congress function as a meeting ground between consent and governing? How are society's demands taken into account in debates on the floor of Congress and deliberations by its committees? What interests are most effectively "represented" in Congress? What is the modern Congress's constituency?

Chapter 6 explores the same questions for the presidency. Although Article II of the Constitution provides that the president should see that the laws made by Congress are "faithfully executed," the presidency was always part of our theory of representative government, and the modern presidency has increasingly become a law *maker* rather than merely a law implementer. What effect, then, does the strong presidency have on the conduct and the consequences of representative government? Chapter 7 treats the executive branch as an entity separate from the presidency, but one that ultimately has to be brought back into the general process of representative government. That, indeed, is the overwhelming problem of what we call "bureaucracy in a democracy." After spelling out the organization and workings of "the bureaucracy" in detail, we then evaluate the role of Congress and the president in imposing some political accountability on an executive branch composed of roughly 5 million civilian and military personnel.

Chapter 8 on the judiciary should not be lost in the shuffle. Referred to by Hamilton as "the least dangerous branch," the judiciary truly has become a co-equal branch to such an extent that if Hamilton were alive today, he would probably eat his words.

Part 3 we simply call "Politics" because politics encompasses all the efforts by any and all individuals and groups inside as well as outside the government to determine what government will do and on whose behalf it will be done. Our chapters take the order of our conception of how politics developed since the Age of Revolution and how politics works today: Chapter 9, "Public Opinion," Chapter 10, "Elections," Chapter 11, "Political Parties," Chapter 12, "Groups and Interests," and Chapter 13, "The Media."

In the full edition, Part 4 is entitled "Governance." These are chapters primarily about public policies, which are the most deliberate and goal-oriented aspects of the still-larger phenomenon of "government in action." We begin Chapter 14, "Government in Action: Public Policy and the Economy," by looking at policies that are concerned with the conduct of business, the obligations of employers, the rights and limits of workers to organize, and the general ability of the economy to operate without coming apart. Chapter 15, "Government and Society," looks at policies that affect society at large, outside and beyond the economic marketplace. Since ours is a commercial society, many policies aimed at society have direct economic consequences. For example, many aspects of what we call the welfare system are social policies, but they have a profound effect on the economy because welfare, as we put it, changes the rules governing who shall be poor. Chapter 16, "Foreign Policy and Democracy," turns to the international realm and America's place in it. Our concern here is to understand American foreign policies and why we have adopted them. Given the traditional American fear of "the state" and the genuine danger of international involvements to domestic democracy, a chapter on foreign policy is essential to a book on American government and also reveals a great deal about America as a culture.

ACKNOWLEDGMENTS

Our students at Cornell, Johns Hopkins, and Harvard have already been identified as an essential factor in the writing of this book. They have been our most immediate intellectual community, a hospitable one indeed. Another part of our community, perhaps a large suburb, is the discipline of political science itself. Our debt to the scholarship of our colleagues is scientifically measurable, probably to several decimal points, in the footnotes of each chapter. Despite many complaints that the field is too scientific or not scientific enough, political science is alive and well in the United States. It is an aspect of democracy itself, and it has grown and changed in response to the developments in government and politics that we have chronicled in our book. If we created a time line on the history of political science, it would show a close association with developments in "the American state." Sometimes the discipline has been out of phase and critical; at other times, it has been in phase and perhaps apologetic. But political science has never been at a loss for relevant literature, and without that literature, our job would have been impossible.

There have, of course, been individuals on whom we have relied in particular. Of all writers, living and dead, we find ourselves most in debt to two—James Madison and Alexis de Tocqueville. Many other great authors have shaped us as they have shaped all political scientists. But Madison and Tocqueville have stood for us not only as the bridge to all timeless political problems but also as representations of the ideal of political science itself—that political science must be steadfastly scientific in the search for what is, yet must keep alive a strong sense of what ought to be, recognizing that democracy is neither natural nor invariably good, and must be fiercely dedicated to constant critical analysis of all political institutions in order to contribute to the maintenance of a favorable balance between individual freedom and public power.

We are pleased to acknowledge our debt to the many colleagues who had a direct and active role in criticism and preparation of the manuscript. The First Edition was read and reviewed by Gary Bryner, Brigham Young University; James F. Herndon, Virginia Polytechnic Institute and State University; James W. Riddlesperger, Jr., Texas Christian University; John Schwarz, University of Arizona; Toni-Michelle Travis, George Mason University; and Lois Vietri, University of Maryland. We also want to reiterate our thanks to the four colleagues who allowed us the privilege of testing a trial edition of our book by using it as the major text in their introductory American Government courses: Gary Bryner, Brigham Young University; Allan J. Cigler, University of Kansas; Burnet V. Davis, Albion College; and Erwin A. Jaffe, California State University—Stanislaus.

For subsequent editions, we relied heavily on the thoughtful manuscript reviews we received from David Canon, University of Wisconsin; Russell Hanson, Indiana University; William Keech, Carnegie Mellon University; Donald Kettl, University of Wisconsin; Anne Khademian, University of Wisconsin;

William McLauchlan, Purdue University; J. Roger Baker, Wittenburg University; James Lennertz, Lafayette College; Allan McBride, Grambling State University; Joseph Peek, Jr., Georgia State University; Grant Neeley, Texas Tech University; Mark Graber, University of Maryland; John Gilmour, College of William and Mary; Victoria Farrar-Myers, University of Texas at Arlington; Timothy Boylan, Winthrop University; Robert Huckfeldt, University of California—Davis; Mark Joslyn, University of Kansas; Beth Leech, Rutgers University; Charles Noble, California State University, Long Beach.

For the Eighth Edition, we benefited from the comments of Scott Ainsworth, University of Georgia; Thomas Brunell, Northern Arizona University; Daniel Carpenter, Harvard University; Brad Gomez, University of South Carolina; Paul Gronke, Reed College; Marc Hetherington, Bowdoin College; Gregory Huber, Yale University; Robert Lowry, Iowa State University; and Anthony Nownes, University of Tennessee; Scott Adler, University of Colorado—Boulder; John Coleman, University of Wisconsin—Madison; Richard Conley, University of Florida; Keith Dougherty, University of Georgia; John Ferejohn, Stanford University; Douglas Harris, Loyola College; Brian Humes, University of Nebraska—Lincoln; Jeffrey Jenkins, Northwestern University; Paul Johnson, University of Kansas; Andrew Polsky, Hunter College—CUNY; Mark Richards, Grand Valley State University; Charles Shipan, University of Iowa; Craig Volden, Ohio State University; and Garry Young, George Washington University.

Most recently, for the Ninth Edition, we benefited from the comments of John Baughman; Lawrence Baum, Ohio State University; Chris Cooper, Western Carolina State University; Charles Finocciaro, State University of New York—Buffalo; Lisa Garcia-Bellorda, University of California—Irvine; Sandy Gordon, New York University; Steven Greene, North Carolina State University; Richard Herrera, Arizona State University; Ben Highton, University of California—Davis; Trey Hood, University of Georgia; Andy Karch, University of Texas—Austin; Glen Krutz; University of Oklahoma; Paul Labedz, Valencia Community College; Brad Lockerbie, University of Georgia; Wendy Martinek, State University of New York—Binghamton; Nicholas Miller, University of Maryland Baltimore County; Russell Renka, Southeast Missouri State University; Debbie Schilkraut, Tufts University; Charles Shipan, University of Iowa; Chris Shortell, California State University, Northridge; John Sides, University of Texas—Austin; Sean Theriault, University of Texas—Austin; and Lynn Vavreck, University of California, Los Angeles.

We are also extremely grateful to a number of colleagues who were kind enough to lend us their classrooms. During the past eight years, we had the opportunity to lecture at a number of colleges and universities around the country and to benefit from discussing our book with those who know it best—colleagues and students who used it. We appreciate the gracious welcome we received at Austin Community College, California State University—Fullerton, University of Central Oklahoma, Emory University, Gainesville College, Georgia Southern University, Georgia State University, Golden West College, Grambling

State University, University of Houston—University Park, University of Illinois—Chicago, University of Illinois—Urbana-Champaign, University of Maryland—College Park, University of Massachusetts—Amherst, Morgan State University, University of North Carolina—Chapel Hill, University of North Texas, University of Oklahoma, Oklahoma State University, Pasadena City College, University of Richmond, Sam Houston State University, San Bernadino Valley College, Santa Barbara City College, Santa Monica College, University of Southern California, Temple University, University of Texas—Austin, Texas Tech University, Virginia Commonwealth University, and University of Wisconsin—Madison.

We owe thanks to Greg Wawro of Columbia University, who served as an intellectual bridge between the Sixth and Seventh Editions, and helped us set our sights for future editions of the book. We owe a special debt to Paul Gronke of Reed College for authoring the "Applying the Five Principles of Politics" and "Politics in the News" features. We also are grateful for the talents and hard work of several research assistants, whose contribution can never be adequately compensated: Mingus Mapps, Douglas Dow, John Forren, Michael Harvey, Doug Harris, Brenda Holzinger, Steve McGovern, Melody Butler, Nancy Johnson, Noah Silverman, Rebecca Fisher, David Lytell, Dennis Merryfield, Rachel Reiss, Nandini Sathe, Rob Speel, Jennifer Waterston, and Daniel Wirls. For the Seventh Edition, Israel Waismel-Manor devoted a great deal of time and energy and original ideas.

Jacqueline Discenza not only typed several drafts of the manuscript, but also helped to hold the project together. We thank her for her hard work and dedication.

Theodore Lowi would like to express his gratitude to the French-American Foundation and the Gannett Foundation, whose timely invitations helped him prepare for his part of this enterprise.

Perhaps above all, we wish to thank those who kept the production and all the loose ends of the book coherent and in focus. Peter Lesser has been a talented editor, offering numerous suggestions for this edition. Candace Levy has been a superb manuscript editor, following in the great tradition of her predecessors. Diane O'Connor has been an efficient production manager and Birgit Larsson has been an excellent assistant editor. Denise Shanks brought a vision to the Web site and spent countless hours making it a reality. For their work on previous editions of the book, we want to thank Steve Dunn, who edited five previous editions of the book, Jan Hoeper, Kathy Talalay, Scott McCord, Margaret Farley, Traci Nagle, Margie Brassil, Stephanie Larson, Sarah Caldwell, Nancy Yanchus, Jean Yelovich, Sandra Smith, Sandy Lifland, Amy Cherry, Roby Harrington, and especially Ruth Dworkin.

We are more than happy, however, to absolve all these contributors from any flaws, errors, and misjudgments that this book contains. We wish it could be free of all production errors, grammatical errors, misspellings, misquotes, missed citations, etc. From that standpoint, a book ought to try to be perfect. But substantively we have not tried to write a flawless book; we have not tried to write a book to please everyone. We have again tried to write an effective book, a book that cannot be taken lightly. Our goal was not to make every reader a political scientist. Our goal was to restore politics as a subject of vigorous and enjoyable discourse, releasing it from the bondage of the thirty-second sound bite and the thirty-page technical briefing. Every person can be knowledgeable because everything about politics is accessible. One does not have to be a television anchorperson to profit from political events. One does not have to be a philosopher to argue about the requisites of democracy, a lawyer to dispute constitutional interpretations, an economist to debate public policy. We will be very proud if our book contributes in a small way to the restoration of the ancient art of political controversy.

Theodore J. Lowi
Benjamin Ginsberg
Kenneth A. Shepsle
February 2006

American Government

Power and Purpose

NINTH EDITION

PART

one

Foundations

CHAPTER

1

Five Principles of Politics

Most Americans are mystified by government and politics. As we shall see in Chapter 9, on public opinion, many have difficulty making sense of major political issues and know little about the nation's basic political institutions. But perhaps it is not surprising that Americans are bewildered. American government and politics are quite confusing!

To begin with, America's institutional arrangements are extraordinarily complex. The United States has many levels of government—federal, state, county, city, and town, to say nothing of a host of special and regional authorities. Each of these governments operates under its own rules and statutory authority and is related to the others in complex ways. In many nations, regional and local governments are largely appendages of the national government. This is not true in the United States. America's fifty states possess a considerable measure of sovereign authority. The American Constitution, as it has been interpreted by the courts, protects the states from becoming mere vassals of the federal government. In recent years, as Chapter 3 illustrates, the U.S. Supreme Court has placed strict limits on the federal government's powers vis-à-vis the states.

Each level of government, moreover, consists of a complex array of departments, agencies, offices, and bureaus undertaking what often seem to be overlapping tasks. The framers of the Constitution created a complex national government, apportioning governmental powers among three different sets of institutions (see Chapters 2 and 3). In the more than two centuries since the Constitution's ratification, Congress has added to the national government's complexity by creating fifteen cabinet departments, such as the Departments of Treasury, Defense, and Agriculture; a host of bureaus and agencies in the executive branch (Chapter 7); hundreds of general-purpose and specialized courts (Chapter 8); and a staff system and staff agencies within the national legislature (Chapter 5).

Each of the cabinet departments is a gigantic enterprise consisting of hundreds of thousands of workers (the government's civilian employees are colloquially known as "feds") engaged in myriad activities. America's oldest cabinet departments, created in 1789, are the Departments of State, Treasury, Justice, and Defense (the latter was originally called the War Department). America's newest cabinet department is the Department of Homeland Security (DHS), which was established in 2002 to coordinate the nation's defenses against terrorism. DHS consists of twenty-two agencies and 170,000 employees, and it is responsible for 2,800 power plants, 800,000 bridges, 190,000 miles of natural gas pipelines, and 20,000 miles of border. To create the DHS, Congress and the president combined a number of existing agencies such as the Coast Guard, the Customs Service, and the Federal Emergency Management Agency (FEMA). Many of these agencies have a long history of professional antagonism and are not eager to cooperate with one another—something tragically demonstrated in fall 2005 when Hurricane Katrina struck New Orleans and other parts of the Gulf Coast. Bureaucratic rivalries add to the difficulties the government faces in carrying out its tasks and the difficulties the citizen faces in trying to understand what the government is doing.

If America's government seems complex, its politics can be utterly bewildering. Like the nation's governmental structure, its political processes have numerous components. For most Americans, the focal point of politics is the electoral process. As we will see in

CHAPTER OUTLINE

Making Sense of Government and Politics

• What Is Government?

• Forms of Government

• Foundations of Government

• Why Is Government Necessary?

• Influencing the Government: Politics

• Principle 1: All Political Behavior Has a Purpose

• Principle 2: All Politics Is Collective Action

• Principle 3: Institutions Routinely Solve Collective-Action Problems

• Principle 4: Political Outcomes Are the Products of Individual Preferences and Institutional Procedures

• Principle 5: History Matters

The Principles of Politics in Action

• The Rationality Principle

• The Collective-Action Principle

• The Institution Principle

• The Policy Principle

• The History Principle

Chapter 10, tens of millions of Americans participate in a host of national, state, and local elections during which they listen to thousands of candidates debate a perplexing array of issues. Candidates inundate the media with promises, charges, and countercharges while an army of pundits and journalists, whom we discuss in Chapter 13, adds its own clamor to the din.

Politics, however, does not end on Election Day. Indeed, given the growing tendency of losers to challenge election results in the courts, even elections do not end on Election Day. Long after the voters have spoken, political struggles continue in Congress, the executive branch, and the courts (Chapters 5, 6, 7, and 8) and embroil political parties, interest groups, and the mass media (Chapters 11, 12, and 13). In some instances, the participants in political struggles and their goals seem fairly obvious. For example, it is no secret that business and upper-income wage earners strongly support programs of tax reduction; farmers support maintenance of agricultural price supports; labor unions oppose "outsourcing" of production. Each of these forces has created or joined organized groups to advance its cause. We examine some of these groups in Chapter 12.

In other instances, though, the participants in political struggles and their goals are not so clear. Sometimes corporate groups hide behind environmental causes to surreptitiously promote their economic interests. Other times groups claiming to want to help the poor and downtrodden seek only to help themselves. And, to make matters worse, many of the government's policies are made behind closed doors, away from the light of publicity. For example, as we see in Chapter 6, after Congress refused to enact his environmental agenda, President Bill Clinton implemented his goals through executive orders and an obscure technique known as "regulatory review." Recent presidents, including Reagan, Clinton, and both Bushes have used regulatory review to circumvent the Congress and achieve their objectives through the bureaucratic rule-making process, a process whose importance we address in Chapter 7.

Ordinary citizens can hardly be blamed for failing to understand bureaucratic rule making and regulatory review. For the most part, these are topics that even experienced journalists have failed to comprehend fully. Take, for example, a presidential office called the OIRA (Office of Information and Regulatory Affairs). This office, within the White House Office of Management and Budget (OMB) is responsible for the president's regulatory agenda. The OIRA has become an important instrument of presidential power but has largely gone unnoticed by the press. Can you recall reading a story about the OIRA? Search online to see how often the media mention the OIRA and its mission. Then read Chapters 6 and 7.

MAKING SENSE OF GOVERNMENT AND POLITICS

Can we find order in the apparent chaos of politics? The answer is that we can, and that is precisely the purpose of this text. In this chapter, we offer a number of concepts and principles that should clarify the nature of government and the logic of the political process. In later chapters, we apply the principles presented here to the government and politics of the United States.

What Is Government?

Government is the term generally used to describe the formal institutions through which a land and its people are ruled. To govern is to rule. *Government is composed of institutions and processes that rulers establish to strengthen and perpetuate their power or control over a land and its inhabitants.* A government may be as simple as a tribal council that meets occasionally to advise the chief or as complex as our own vast establishment with its forms, rules, and bureaucracies. This more complex government is sometimes referred to as "the state," an abstract concept referring to the source of all public authority.

Forms of Government

Governments vary in their institutional structure, in their size, and in their modes of operation. Two questions are of special importance in determining how governments differ from each other: Who governs? How much government control is permitted?

In some nations, governing is done by a single individual—a king or dictator, for example. This state of affairs is called *autocracy*. When a small group of landowners, military officers, or wealthy merchants controls most of the governing decisions, that government is said to be an *oligarchy*. If more people participate and if the populace is deemed to have some influence over decision making, that government is tending toward *democracy*.

Governments also vary considerably in terms of how they govern. In the United States and a small number of other nations, governments are severely limited as to *what* they are permitted to control (substantive limits), as well as *how* they go about it (procedural limits). Governments that are so limited are called *constitutional*, or liberal, governments. In other nations, including many in Europe as well as in South America, Asia, and Africa, although the law imposes few real limits, a government is nevertheless kept in check by other political and social institutions that the government is unable to control but must come to terms with—such as autonomous territories, an organized church, organized business groups, or organized labor unions. Such governments are generally called *authoritarian*. In a third group of nations, including the Soviet Union under Joseph Stalin, Nazi Germany, and perhaps pre–World War II Japan and Italy, governments not only are free of legal limits but seek to eliminate those organized social groupings that might challenge or limit their authority. These governments typically attempt to dominate or control every sphere of political, economic, and social life and, as a result, are called *totalitarian*.

Foundations of Government

Whatever their makeup, governments historically have included two basic components: a means of coercion, such as an army or police force, and a means of

government
Institutions and procedures through which a land and its people are ruled.

autocracy A form of government in which a single individual rules.

oligarchy A form of government in which a small group of landowners, military officers, or wealthy merchants controls most of the governing decisions.

democracy A system of rule that permits citizens to play a significant part in the governmental process, usually through the selection of key public officials.

constitutional government A system of rule in which formal and effective limits are placed on the powers of the government.

authoritarian government A system of rule in which the government recognizes no formal limits but may nevertheless be restrained by the power of other social institutions.

totalitarian government A system of rule in which the government recognizes no formal limits on its power and seeks to absorb or eliminate other social institutions that might challenge it.

collecting revenue. These two components have been the essential foundations of government—the building blocks that all individuals and groups who ever sought to rule have been compelled to construct if they were to secure and maintain a measure of control over their territory and its people. Groups aspire to govern for a variety of reasons. Some have the most high-minded aims, whereas others are little more than ambitious robbers. But whatever their motives and character, those who aspire to rule must be able to secure obedience and fend off rivals as well as collect the revenues needed to accomplish these tasks.[1] Some governments, including many of those in the less developed nations today, have consisted of little more than an army and a tax-collecting agency. Other governments, especially those in the developed nations, have attempted to provide services as well as to collect taxes in order to secure popular consent and control. For some, power is an end in itself. For most, power is necessary for the maintenance of public order. For all, power is needed to permit governments to provide the collective goods and services that citizens want and need but cannot provide for themselves.

The Means of Coercion Government must have the power to order people around, to get people to obey its laws, and to punish them if they do not. Coercion takes many different forms, and each year millions of Americans are subject to one form of government coercion or another. Table 1.1 is an outline of the uses of coercion by federal and state governments in America.

conscription
Compulsory military service, usually for a prescribed period or for the duration of a war; the draft.

One aspect of coercion is *conscription,* whereby government requires certain involuntary services of citizens. The best-known example of conscription is military conscription, which is called "the draft." Although there has been no draft since 1974, there were drafts during the Civil War, World War I, World War II, and the wars in Korea and Vietnam. With these drafts, our government compelled millions of men to serve in the armed forces; half a million of these soldiers made the ultimate contribution by giving their lives in their nation's service. If the need arose, military conscription would undoubtedly be reinstituted. All eighteen-year-old males are required to register today, just in case.

Military conscription, however, is not the only form of involuntary service that government can compel Americans to perform. We can, by law, be compelled to serve on juries; to appear before legal tribunals when summoned; to file a great variety of official reports, including income tax returns; and to attend school or to send our children to school.

The Means of Collecting Revenue Each year American governments collect enormous sums from their citizens to support their institutions and programs. Taxation has grown steadily over the years. In 2001, the national government

---

[1]For an excellent discussion, see Charles Tilly, "Reflections on the History of European State-Making," in *The Formation of National States in Western Europe*, ed. Charles Tilly (Princeton, NJ: Princeton University Press, 1975), pp. 3–83. See also Charles Tilly, "War Making and State Making as Organized Crime," in *Bringing the State Back In*, ed. Peter B. Evans, Dietrich Rueschemeyer, and Theda Skocpol (New York: Cambridge University Press, 1985), pp. 169–91.

TABLE 1.1

The Means of Coercion		
FORMS	**INSTANCES**	**LEVEL OF GOVERNMENT**
Arrests	11,231,000	Federal, state, and local (1998)
Prison inmates	1,194,581	Federal and state (1997)
Jail inmates	605,943	County and municipal (1999)
Executions	98	State (1999)

SOURCE: U.S. Bureau of the Census, *Statistical Abstract of the United States: 2000* (Washington, D.C.: U.S. Department of Commerce, 2000).

alone collected $972 billion in individual income taxes, $195 billion in corporate income taxes, $682 billion in social insurance taxes, $77 billion in excise taxes, $21 billion in custom duties, and another $40 billion in miscellaneous revenue. The grand total amounted to more than $2 trillion, or almost $7,000 from every living soul in the United States. And of course, while some groups receive more in benefits from the government than they pay in taxes, others get less for their tax dollar. One of the perennial issues in American politics is the distribution of tax burdens versus the distribution of program benefits. Every group would like more of the benefits while passing more of the burdens of taxation onto others.

Why Is Government Necessary?

As we have just seen, control is the basis for government. But what forms of government control are justifiable? To answer this question, we begin by examining the ways in which government makes it possible for people to live together in harmony.

To Maintain Order   Human beings usually do not venture out of their caves (or the modern counterpart) unless there is a reasonable probability that they can return safely. But for people to live together peacefully, law and order are required, the institutionalization of which is called government. From the standpoint of this definition, the primary purpose of government is to maintain order. But order can come about only by controlling a territory and its people. This may sound like a threat to freedom until you ponder the absence of government, or anarchy—the absence of rule. According to Thomas Hobbes (1588–1679), author of the first masterpiece of political philosophy in English, anarchy is even worse than the potential tyranny of government because anarchy, or life outside "the state," is one of "continual fear, and danger of violent death [where life is] solitary, poor, nasty, brutish and short."[2] Governmental power can be a threat to freedom, yet we need government to maintain order so that we can enjoy our freedom.

To Protect Property   After safety of persons comes security of a person's labor, which we call property, or private property. Protection of property is almost universally recognized as a justifiable function of government. John Locke (1632–1704), the worthy successor to Hobbes, was the first to assert clearly that whatever we have removed from nature and also mixed our labor with is considered our property. But even Locke recognized that although the right to own what we have produced by our own labor is absolute, it means nothing if someone with greater power than ours decides to take it or trespass on it. As Locke puts it,

> If man . . . be absolute Lord of his own person and possessions . . . why will he part with his freedom . . . ? To which, it is obvious to answer, that the enjoyment of it is very uncertain. . . . This makes him willing to quit this condition, which, however free, is full of fears and continual danger; and it is not without reason that he seeks out and is willing to join in society with others . . . for the mutual preservation of their lives, liberties, and estates.[3]

So, something we call our own *is ours only as long as the laws against trespass* improve the probability that we can enjoy it, use it, consume it, trade it, or sell it. In reality, then, property can be defined as *all the laws against trespass* that permit us not only to call something our own but also to make sure that our claim sticks. In other words, property—that is, private property—is virtually meaningless without a government of laws and policies that makes trespass prohibitive.

To Provide Public Goods   David Hume (1711–1776), another worthy successor to Hobbes, observed that although two neighbors may agree voluntarily to cooperate in draining a swampy meadow, the more neighbors there are, the more difficult it will be to cooperate to get the task done. A few neighbors might clear the swamp because they understand the benefits each of them will receive. But as you expand the number of neighbors who benefit from clearing the swamp, many neighbors will realize that all of them can get the same benefit if only a few clear the swamp and the rest do nothing. This is an example of *free riding*. A *public* (or collective) *good* is, therefore, a benefit that neighbors or members of a group cannot be kept from enjoying once any individual or small minority of members have provided the benefit for themselves—the clearing of the swamp, for example, or national defense, for another example. National defense

free riding
Enjoying the benefits of some good or action and letting others bear the costs.

public good   A good (1) that may be enjoyed by anyone if it is provided and (2) that may not be denied to anyone once it has been provided.

---

[2]Thomas Hobbes, *Leviathan* (New York: Macmillan, 1947), p. 82.
[3]This quote is from John Locke's masterpiece, *Two Treatises of Government* (London: Everyman, 1993), pp. 178 and 180.

is one of the most important public goods—especially when the nation is threatened by war or terrorism. Without government's coercive powers through a policy (backed by taxation) to build a bridge, produce an army, or provide a swamp-free meadow, "legal tender," or uniform standards of weights and measures, there is no incentive—in fact, very often there is a *dis*incentive—for even the richest, most concerned members to provide the benefit.[4]

Influencing the Government: Politics

Although public order, the protection of property, and the provision of public goods are justifications for government, they are not justifications for all its actions. A government's actions can be justified only by the people being governed. This is why government would be intolerable without politics. With politics, we have at least a faint hope that a government's actions can be influenced in some way.

In its broadest sense, the term *politics* refers to conflicts over the character, membership, and policies of any organization to which people belong. As Harold Lasswell, a famous political scientist, once put it, politics is the struggle over "who gets what, when, how."[5] Although politics is a phenomenon that can be found in any organization, in this book politics will refer only to conflicts and struggles over the leadership, structure, and policies of *governments*. The goal of politics, as we define it, is to have a share or say in the composition of the government's leadership, how the government is organized, or what its policies are going to be. Having a share is called *power* or *influence*. Most people are eager to have some say in matters affecting them; witness the willingness of so many individuals over the past two centuries to risk their lives for voting rights and representation. In recent years, Americans have become more skeptical about their actual "say" in government, and many do not bother to vote. This increased skepticism, however, does not mean that Americans no longer want to have a share in the governmental process. Rising levels of skepticism mean, rather, that many Americans doubt the capacity of the political system to provide them with influence.

It is one thing to define politics, quite another to understand the complexities of political life. But although politics is complex, political activity does possess an underlying logic, a logic that can be understood in terms of five key principles:

Principle 1: All political behavior has a purpose.
Principle 2: All politics is collective action.
Principle 3: Institutions routinely solve collective-action problems.
Principle 4: Political outcomes are the products of individual preferences and institutional procedures.
Principle 5: History matters.

---

[4]The most instructive treatment of the phenomenon of public goods and the free rider is Mancur Olson, *The Logic of Collective Action: Public Goods and the Theory of Groups* (Cambridge: Harvard University Press, 1965 and 1971), pp. 33–43, esp. n. 53.

[5]Harold D. Lasswell, *Politics: Who Gets What, When, How* (New York: Meridian Books, 1958).

Principle 1: All Political Behavior Has a Purpose

Rationality Principle

All political behavior has a purpose.

One compelling reason why governments do what they do is that all people have goals and they work to achieve those goals through their political behavior. For many citizens, political behavior is as simple as reading a headline or editorial in the newspaper while drinking their morning coffee or discussing the latest local political controversy with a neighbor over the back fence. Though political, these actions are basically routines of everyday life. Beyond these almost perfunctory acts, citizen political behavior broadens to include still relatively modest activities like watching a political debate on television, arguing about politics with a co-worker, signing a petition, or attending a city council meeting. These are understood to be explicitly political activities that require some forethought and advanced reflection—these are discretionary *choices* rather than mechanical *acts* like accidentally catching a political headline in the newspaper on your way to the sports section, the comics, or the movie listings. Political behavior requiring even more "premeditation"—even calculation—includes going to the polls and casting a vote in the November election (having first registered in a timely manner), writing one's legislative representatives about a political issue, contributing time or money to a political campaign, or even running for local office.

Some of these acts require effort, time, financial resources, and courage, whereas others place small, even insignificant, demands on a person. Nevertheless, all of these acts are done for specific reasons. They are not random; they are not entirely automatic or mechanical, even the smallest of them. Sometimes they are engaged in for the sake of entertainment (reading the front page in the morning) or just to be sociable (chatting about politics with a neighbor, co-worker, or family member). At other times, they take on considerable personal importance explicitly because of their political content—because an individual cares about, and wants to influence, an issue, a candidate, a party, or a cause. We will treat all of this political activity as *purposeful*, as having a point. Indeed, our attempts to discern the point of various political activities will help us understand them better.

We've just noted that many political activities of ordinary citizens are hard to distinguish from conventional everyday behavior—reading newspapers, watching television news, discussing politics, and so on. For the professional politician on the other hand—legislator, executive, judge, party leader, bureau chief, or agency head—nearly everything he or she does is political. The legislator's decision to introduce a particular piece of legislation, to give a speech in the legislative chamber, to move an amendment to a pending bill, to vote for or against that bill, or to accept a contribution from a PAC[6] requires the politician's careful attention. There are pitfalls and dangers, and the slightest miscalculation can have huge consequences. Introduce a bill that appears to be too pro-labor in the eyes of your constituents, for example, and before you know it you're charged with being in bed

---

[6]A PAC (political action committee) is a group established by an interest group, labor union, or some other organization to collect donations and distribute them as campaign contributions to candidates and political parties.

with the unions during the next election campaign. Give a speech against job quotas for minorities, and you set yourself up to have your words turned against you by an electoral opponent, risking your standing with the minority communities in your state or district. Accept campaign contributions from local businesspeople, and environmentalists think you are no friend of the earth. Nearly every move a legislator makes is fraught with risks. And because of these risks, legislators think about their moves before they make them—sometimes carefully, sometimes not; sometimes correctly, sometimes not. But whatever actions they take, or decide against taking, they do so with forethought, with deliberation, with calculation. Their actions are not knee-jerk, but are, in a word, *instrumental.* Individuals think through the benefits and the costs of a decision, speculate about future effects, and weigh the risks of their decision. Making decisions is all about weighing probabilities of various events and determining the personal value of various outcomes.

instrumental
Done with purpose, sometimes forethought and even calculation.

As an example of instrumental behavior, consider the electoral politician. Most politicians want to keep their positions or move up the political ladder to even more important positions. They like their jobs for a variety of reasons—salary, privileges, prestige, stepping-stones, and accomplishments in the job, just to name a few. So we can go a long way in trying to understand why politicians do what they do by thinking of their behavior as instrumental, as trying to keep their jobs. This is quite straightforward when thinking about elected politicians. They often see no further than the next election, and think mainly about how to prevail in that contest. To understand their routines and behaviors, it is essential to figure out who can help them win. "Retail" politics involves dealing directly with constituents, as when a politician helps you navigate a federal agency, helps you find a misplaced Social Security check, or helps your child apply to a service academy. "Wholesale" politics involves appealing to collections of constituents, as when a legislator introduces a bill that would benefit a group active back home (say, veterans), secures money for a bridge or public building in his or her state or district, or intervenes in an official proceeding on behalf of an interest group that will, in turn, contribute to the next campaign. Politicians may do any and all of these things just because it is "right" or makes them feel good. But we institute elections and provide incentives for politicians to do such things as a means to winning elections, just in case their generosity of spirit and sense of doing good are insufficient. Elections and electoral politics are thus premised on instrumental behavior by politicians.

Principle 2: All Politics Is Collective Action

The second factor that helps explain why governments do what they do is that political action is collective, involving the building, combining, mixing, and amalgamating of the individual goals of people. They join together to achieve these goals. But, as we shall see, collective action can be very difficult to orchestrate because the individuals involved in the decision-making process often have somewhat different goals and preferences. The result is mixed motives for cooperation. Conflict is inevitable; the question is how it can be resolved. The most typical and widespread means is bargaining, involving a small number

Collective-Action Principle
All politics is collective action.

of individuals. But when the number of parties involved is too large to engage in face-to-face bargaining, incentives must be provided to get everyone to act collectively.

Informal Bargaining   Political bargaining is a process that may be highly formal or entirely informal. Relations among neighbors, for example, are usually based on informal give-and-take. To present a personal example, one of this book's authors has a neighbor with whom he shares a privet hedge on the property line. First one takes responsibility for trimming the hedge and then the other, alternating from year to year. This arrangement is merely an "understanding," not a legally binding agreement, and it was reached amicably and without much fuss or fanfare after a brief conversation. No organizational effort was required—like hiring lawyers, drafting an agreement, having it signed, witnessed, notarized, filed at the county courthouse, and so on.

Bargaining in politics can also be informal and unstructured. Whether called horse trading, back-scratching, logrolling, or wheeling and dealing, it has much the same flavor as the casual, over-the-fence negotiations among neighbors just described. Deals will be struck depending on the preferences and beliefs of the participants. If preferences are too incompatible or beliefs too inconsistent with one another, then a deal simply may not be in the cards. On the other hand, if preferences and beliefs are not too far out of line, then there will be a range of possible bargaining outcomes, some of which slightly advantage one party, others of which advantage other parties. But all deals in this range are at least acceptable to all the parties involved.

In fact, much of politics *is* informal, unstructured bargaining. First, many disputes subjected to bargaining are of sufficiently low impact that it is just not worth establishing elaborate formal machinery for dealing with them. Rules of thumb often develop as a benchmark—such as "split the difference" or "take turns" (the outcome of the hedge-trimming example given earlier). Second, there is repetition. If a small group engages in bargaining today over one matter and tomorrow over another—as neighbors bargain over draining a meadow one day, fixing a fence another, and trimming a hedge on still another occasion—then patterns develop. If one party constantly tries to extract maximal advantage, then the other parties will undoubtedly cease doing business with her. If, on the other hand, each party "gives a little" to "get a little," reciprocating kindness at one point with kindness at another, then a pattern of cooperation develops over time. It is the repetition of mixed-motive occasions that allows this pattern to emerge without formal trappings. Many political circumstances are either amenable to rules of thumb like those mentioned or are repeated with sufficient frequency so as to allow cooperative patterns to emerge.

Formal Bargaining   Formal bargaining entails interactions among bargainers that are governed by rules. The rules describe such things as who gets to make the first offer, how long the recipient parties have to consider it, whether recipient parties must "take it or leave it" or can make counteroffers, the method by which they convey their assent or rejection, what happens when all (or some decisive subset) of the others accept or reject, what transpires next if the proposal is rejected, and so on. One could not imagine two neighbors deciding how to trim their common hedge under procedures as explicit and formal as these. One could, however, imagine a bargaining session over wages and working conditions between labor and management at the local manufacturing plant proceeding in just this manner. This suggests that some parties are more appropriately suited to formal proceedings, whereas others get on well enough without them. The same may be said about situations. A husband and wife are likely to divide household chores by informal bargaining, but this same couple would employ a formal procedure if it were household assets they were dividing (in a divorce settlement).

Formal bargaining is often associated with events that take place in official institutions—legislatures, courts, party conventions, administrative and regulatory agencies. These are settings in which mixed-motive situations arise over and over again. Year in and year out, legislatures pass statutes, approve executive budgets, and oversee the administrative branch of government. Courts administer justice, determine guilt or innocence, impose sentences, resolve differences between disputants, and render interpretive opinions about the meaning of the law. Party conventions nominate candidates and approve the platforms on which they base their campaigns. Administrative and regulatory agencies implement policy and make rulings about its applicability. All of these are instances of mixed-motive circumstances where gains from cooperation are possible, but bargaining failures are also a definite possibility. Consequently, the formal bargaining that takes place under the aegis of institutions is governed by rules that regularize proceedings both to maximize the prospects of reaching agreement and to guarantee that procedural "wheels" don't have to be reinvented each time a similar bargaining problem arises.

Collective Action   The idea of political bargaining suggests an "intimate" kind of politics, involving face-to-face relations, negotiation, compromise, give-and-take, and so on. Such bargaining results from the combination of mixed motives and small numbers. When the numbers become large, bargaining may no longer be practical. If 100 people own property bordering a swampy meadow, or if a privet hedge runs the length of Main Street in a small town, insulating hundreds of households from the street, then how do these communities solve the swamp's mosquito problem or resolve to trim the hedge to a common height? How do these communities secure the dividends that arise from cooperation?

These are clearly mixed-motive situations. Everyone shares some common values—eliminating the mosquito habitat or giving the hedge a uniform look—but they may disagree on other matters. Some may want to use pesticides in the meadow, while others are concerned about the environmental impact. Some may want the hedge cut very short, allowing it to be maintained easily by each household; others may want it kept tall to shield homes from street noise. And in both situations there are bound to be disagreements over how to pay for the project. The collective-action problem arises, as in these examples, when there is something to be gained if the group can cooperate and assure group members that some do not get away with bearing less than their fair share of the effort. Face-to-face bargaining, however, is compromised by sheer numbers. The issue, then, is how to accomplish some common objective when explicit bargaining is not an option.

collective action The pooling of resources and coordination of effort and activity by a group of people (often a large one) to achieve common goals.

Groups of individuals intent on ***collective action*** will ordinarily establish some decision-making procedures—relatively formal arrangements by which to resolve differences, coordinate the group around a course of action, and sanction slackers, if necessary. Most groups will also require a structure of leadership, which is necessary even if all the members of the group are in agreement about how to proceed. This is due to a phenomenon that we saw in the swamp-draining example: free riding. Each owner of land bordering the swamp wants the area cleared. But if one or a few owners were to clear the swamp alone, their actions would benefit all the other owners as well, without any efforts on the part of those other owners. Those owners would be free riders. It is this prospect of free riding that risks undermining collective action. A leadership structure will have to be in place to threaten and, if necessary, inflict punishments to discourage individuals from reneging on the individual contributions required to enable the group to pursue its common goals.

by-product theory The idea that groups provide members with private benefits to attract membership; the possibility of group collective action emerges as a consequence.

Various solutions to the collective action problem have been proposed. The most famous is Mancur Olson's ***by-product theory.***[7] Briefly, Olson's idea is this: the nub of free riding derives from the fact that most individuals in a large group don't make much difference to the final result, and they know it. This is why they may comfortably abstain from participation—they know that in following their inclination to avoid the costs of participation, they do not damage their prospects (or anyone else's) for receiving benefits. The problem is that while no one person's free riding does much harm, if enough people free ride, then the purpose of the collective action will be compromised. What if, however, something of value were at stake that would be lost if the person abstained from participation? What if participants were given something special that non-participants were denied? That is, what if some benefits were contingent on contributing to the group effort? Many organizations use this tactic, giving dues-paying or effort-contributing members special insurance or education benefits, reduced-fare travel, free or subsidized subscriptions to magazines and newsletters, bowling and golf tournaments, soccer leagues, access to members-only social events, and so on. Olson argued that if members were prepared to "pay their dues" to join an organization partially (or even mainly) for these special benefits of which they would otherwise be deprived—what Olson called ***selective benefits***—then the collective cooperation would end up being provided as well, *as a by-product,* with whatever surplus the dues structure gener-

selective benefits Benefits that do not go to everyone, but rather are distributed selectively—only to those who contribute to the group enterprise.

---

[7]On the general subject of collective action, the interested reader should consult Kenneth A. Shepsle and Mark S. Bonchek, *Analyzing Politics: Rationality, Behavior, and Institutions* (New York: Norton, 1997), ch. 9, where Olson's work, among others, is taken up.

ated. A member's inclination to free ride would be alleviated, not because of feelings of obligation to his or her fellow members, not because of a moral imperative to participate, not even because of a desire for the collective benefit supplied by the group, but rather because of naked self-interest—the desire for selective benefits! Clearly this is an extreme version of the argument; the main point here is that the selective benefits available only to participants and contributors—and denied to nonparticipants and noncontributors—are the key to successful collective action. A group that appeals to its members *only* on the basis of its common collective purposes is a group that will have trouble achieving those purposes.[8]

One of the most notorious collective-action problems involves too much of a good thing. Known as "the tragedy of the commons," it is an acknowledgment of how unbridled self-interest can have damaging collective consequences. A party's reputation, for example, is not irreparably harmed if one of its legislators pushes her advantage by getting approval for a minor amendment helpful to a special interest in her district. But if lots of party members do it, the party comes to be known as the champion of special interests, and its reputation is tarnished. A pool of resources is not much depleted if someone takes a little of it. But it does become depleted if lots of people take from it—a forest is lost a pine tree at a time, an oil reserve declines a gallon at a time, the atmosphere is polluted a particle at a time.

To summarize, individuals try to accomplish things not only as individuals but also as members of larger collectivities—families, friendship groups, clubs and associations, political parties and in larger categories like economic class, ethnicity, and nationality. Principle 1 covers individual initiative. Principle 2 describes the paradoxes encountered, the obstacles that must be overcome, and the incentives necessary for individuals to combine with like-minded others to coordinate their energies, accomplish collective purposes, and secure the dividends of cooperation. Much of politics is about doing this or failing to do this. The next principle takes this argument to its logical conclusion, focusing on collective activities that are regularized because they are both important and frequently occurring. Institutions do the public's business while relieving communities of having to reinvent collective action each time it is required. Here we provide a rationale for government.

Principle 3: Institutions Routinely Solve Collective-Action Problems

In the last section, we looked at the conditions in which people engage in bargaining, cooperation, and collective action to solve some political problem. Because people, especially elected leaders and other government officials,

Institution Principle
Institutions routinely solve collective-action problems.

---

[8]Getting such an organizational effort up and running, however, is no small feat. Olson's argument appreciates what is necessary to keep a group going but underestimates what it takes to organize collective action in the first place. Put differently, a prior collective-action problem needs to be solved—an organizational problem. The solution is leadership, and the individuals imaginative enough to see this need are referred to as *political entrepreneurs*. That is, there must be a selective benefit available to those who bear organizational burdens, thereby facilitating the collective action; the selective benefits of leadership include perquisites of office, financial reward, and honor and status.

repeatedly are required to confront recurring problems, they develop routines and standard ways of dealing with things. In a word, responses to regularly recurring problems are *institutionalized*. Collective action results because standard procedures and rules are established that provide people with appropriate incentives to take the action necessary to solve the problems. Routinized, structured relations are what we call **institutions.** What interests students of politics most is how institutions discourage conflict, enable bargaining, and thus facilitate decision making, cooperation, and collective action.

institutions
Rules and procedures that provide incentives for political behavior, thereby shaping politics.

Consider publicly owned parks and land reserves that are today the object of great passion by those who place significant value on "green space." In an earlier time in Europe (and still today in various parts of the world), commons were valued for more practical reasons—notably as places to graze cattle and to forage. Today, examples of commons include not only green space and sites for grazing and foraging but also bodies of water used for commercial fishing, irrigation systems, urban water supplies, and, indeed, even the earth's atmosphere.[9]

A commons is, by definition, "owned" by everyone (in common) and therefore is the responsibility of no one. On a field owned by a village, each villager gets to graze his or her cattle "for free." If a villager is contemplating adding a head to his herd, he will take into account his personal costs of doing so, but this calculation will *not* include the cost of grazing. If the commons is large and the village demands on it minimal, this will not pose serious problems. But even if demands on the commons grow, no villager has an incentive to restrict his or her use of this free resource, resulting in "the tragedy of the commons."[10] The commons will be overgrazed and ultimately destroyed, inasmuch as its capacity to regenerate itself will have been disabled. As a metaphor, the tragedy of the commons suggests that individual purposes may sometimes clash with collective welfare: a collective reputation is tarnished, a commons is overgrazed, a common asset is depleted.

Institutions are part script and part scorecard. As scripts, they choreograph political activity. As scorecards, they list the players, their positions, what they want, what they can do, and when they can do it. While the Constitution sets the broad framework, much adaptation and innovation takes place as the institutions themselves are bent to the various political purposes of strategic political actors who want to win for their side and defeat the other side. Our focus here will be on the authority that institutions provide politicians for the pursuit of public policies. The discussion is divided into four broad subjects: jurisdiction, decisiveness, agenda and veto power, and delegation and transaction costs.

Jurisdiction   A critical feature of an institution is the designation of who has the authority to apply the rules or make the decisions; members recognize the juris-

---

[9]A most insightful discussion of "common pool problems," of which these are examples, is Elinor Ostrom, *Governing the Commons* (New York: Cambridge University Press, 1990).

[10]Garrett Hardin, "The Tragedy of the Commons," *Science* 162 (1968): 1243–48. This now-classic essay is must reading for the interested student.

diction of the main players and are quick to impose limits on those players if they feel jurisdictional authority has been exceeded. Political institutions are full of specialized jurisdictions. One of the most unusual features of the U.S. Congress is the existence of the "standing committee," whose jurisdictions are carefully defined in law. Some members of Congress are generalists, but most members become specialists in all aspects of the jurisdiction of their committees—and they often seek committee assignments based on the subject in which they want to specialize. Committee members are granted specific authority within their jurisdiction to set the agenda of the larger parent chamber. Thus the legislative institution in the United States is affected by the way its jurisdiction-specific committees are structured.

Decisiveness   Another crucial feature of an institution is its rules for making decisions. It might sound like a straightforward task to lay out what the rules for deciding are, but it really isn't so easy to do without a raft of conditions and qualifications. Every organization has rules of some sort, and the more an organization values participation by the broadest range of its members, the more it actually needs these rules: the requirement of participation must be balanced with the need to bring discussion and activity to a close at some point so that an actual decision can be made! This is why one of the most privileged motions that can be made on the floor of a legislature is "to move the previous question," a motion to close the debate and to move immediately to a vote.[11] It is no accident that *Deschler's Procedures*, a book of rules and interpretations about procedure in the House of Representatives, runs to more than 600 pages! Its companion for the U.S. Senate, *Jefferson's Manual*, is shorter but no less intricate.

Even juries have rules for decisiveness; if discussion goes on too long among the members, the judge may in fact declare a *hung jury*, leading to a new trial and another round of discussion (or the dropping of charges). In most organizations, including corporations, the decision to close discussion is left in the hands of the presiding officer, who might simply ask for a motion to vote on the issue in question. But even such a ruling by the chair can be appealed if the participants decide that they have not discussed the matter enough to decide.

Agenda Power and Veto Power   If decisiveness characterizes what it takes to win, then *agenda power* describes who determines what will be taken up for consideration in the first place. Those who exercise some form of agenda power are said to engage in *gatekeeping*. They determine which alternatives may pass through the gate onto the agenda and which ones have the gate slammed in their face. Gatekeeping, in other words, consists of the power to make proposals and the power to block proposals from being made. The ability to keep something off

agenda power
Control over what the group will consider for discussion.

---

[11]For a general discussion of motions to close debate and get on with the decision, see Henry M. Robert, *Robert's Rules of Order* (1876), items III, #21, and VI, #38. *Robert's* has achieved the status of an icon and now exists in an enormous variety of forms and shapes.

veto power
The ability to defeat something, even if it has made it onto the agenda of an institution.

an institution's agenda should not be confused with ***veto power.*** The latter is the ability to defeat something, *even if it does become part of the agenda.* In the legislative process, for example, the president has (limited) veto power. Congress cannot be prevented from taking up a particular bill—the president does not have agenda power in Congress. It cannot be prevented from passing such a measure—the president has no power to block in Congress. But a presidential veto can prevent the measure from becoming the law of the land.[12]

delegation
Transmitting authority to some other official or body for the latter's use (though often with the right of review and revision).

Delegation   Representative democracy is the quintessential instance of ***delegation*** in which citizens, through voting, delegate the authority to make decisions on their behalf to representatives—chiefly legislators and executives—rather than exercising political authority directly.[13] We think of our political representatives as our *agents*, just as we think of professionals and craftsmen whose services we retain—doctors, lawyers, accountants, plumbers, mechanics, and so on—as agents whom we hire to act on our behalf. Now, why would those with authority, whom we will call *principals*, delegate some of their authority to agents? In effect, we are asking about the virtues of decentralization and of a division and specialization of labor. The answer is that both principals and agents benefit from it. Principals benefit because they are able to off-load to experts and specialists tasks that they themselves are far less capable of performing. Ordinary citizens, for example, are not as well versed in the tasks of governance and other forms of collective action as are professional politicians. Thus, by delegating, citizens do not have to be specialists and can focus their energies on other things. This is the rationale for representative democracy.

This same rationale applies to the division and specialization of labor we often observe in specific political institutions. Legislators generally benefit from a decentralized arrangement in which they focus on those aspects of public policy for which they are best equipped—issue areas of special interest to their constituents or on which their prior occupational and life experiences give them familiarity and perspective. In exchange, they are freed from having to be policy generalists and can avoid areas of little interest or relevance to them. The legislative committee system accomplishes this by partitioning policy into different jurisdictions and allowing legislators to gravitate to those committees that most suit their purposes.

principal–agent relationship   The relationship between a principal and his or her agent; this relationship may be affected by the fact that each is motivated by self-interest, yet their interests may not be well aligned.

The delegation principle, in which a principal delegates authority to an agent, seems almost too good to be true. But there is a dark side to this ***principal-agent relationship.*** As the eighteenth-century economist Adam Smith noted in

[12]Article I, Section 7, of the Constitution specifies that a bill becomes a law in either of two ways: (1) a majority of the House and Senate approves it, and it is signed by the president or (2) a majority of each chamber approves a measure, the president *vetoes* it, and then—upon congressional reconsideration—at least two thirds of each chamber approves the measure. See Chapter 5.
[13]A surviving vestige of the direct exercise of political authority is the New England town meeting. This institution still exists in one form or another throughout states in the Northeast. Increasingly, however, town meetings occur only occasionally, with day-to-day governance delegated to an advisory committee and to an elected board of selectmen.

his classic *The Wealth of Nations*, economic agents are not motivated by the welfare of their customers to grow vegetables, make shoes, or weave cloth; rather, they do those things out of their own self-interest. Thus a principal must take care when delegating to agents that those agents are properly motivated to serve the principal's interests, either by sharing the principal's interests or by deriving something of value (reputation, compensation, etc.) for acting to advance those interests. Alternatively, the principal will need to have some instruments by which to monitor and validate what his or her agent is doing and then reward or punish the agent accordingly. Nevertheless, a principal will not bother to eliminate *entirely* the agent's prospective deviations from the principal's interests. The reason is **transaction costs.** The organizational effort necessary to negotiate and then police every aspect of a principal–agent relationship becomes, at some point, more costly than it is worth. In sum, the upside of delegation consists of the assignment of activities to precisely those agents who possess a comparative advantage in performing them. (A corollary is that those who are poorly prepared to conduct these activities are relieved of performing them.) The downside is the prospective misalignment of agent goals with the goals of principals, and thus the possibility of agents marching to the beat of their own drummer.

transaction costs
The cost of clarifying each aspect of a principal–agent relationship and monitoring it to make sure arrangements are complied with.

Characterizing institutions in terms of jurisdiction, decisiveness, agenda and veto power, and delegation and transaction cost, covers an immense amount of ground. Our purpose here has been to introduce the reader to the multiplicity of ways collectivities arrange their business and routinize it, thereby enabling cooperation, facilitating recurring requirements of bargaining, and solving collective-action problems. A second purpose has been to impress on the reader the potential diversity in institutional arrangements—there are so many ways to do things collectively—because this underscores the amazing sophistication and intelligence of the framers of the U.S. Constitution in the institutional choices they made more than two centuries ago. Finally, we want to make clear that institutions not only make rules for governing but also describe strategic opportunities for various political interests. As George Washington Plunkett, the savvy and candid political boss of Tammany Hall, said of the institutional situations in which he found himself, "I seen my opportunities, and I took 'em."[14]

Principle 4: Political Outcomes Are the Products of Individual Preferences and Institutional Procedures

At the end of the day, politics leads to collective decisions that emerge from the political process and these have consequences for individuals. A Nebraska farmer is not much interested in the various facets of institutions we've just described, even those concerning the House Agriculture Committee. What he does care

Policy Principle
Political outcomes are the products of individual preferences and institutional procedures.

[14]In the nineteenth century and well into the twentieth, Tammany Hall was the club that ran New York City's Democratic party like a machine.

about is how public laws and rulings affect his welfare and that of his family, friends, and neighbors. He cares about how export policies affect the prices his crops and livestock products earn in international markets and how monetary policy influences inflation and, as a result, the cost of purchasing fuel, feed, seed, and fertilizer; the funding of public and private research and development efforts, and their effect on the quality and reliability of scientific information he obtains; and the affordability of the state university where he hopes to educate his children. He also cares, eventually, about inheritance laws and their effect on his ability to pass his farm on to his kids without Uncle Sam taking a huge chunk of it in estate taxes. As students of American politics, we need to consider the link between institutional arrangements and policy outcomes. Do the organizational features of institutions leave their marks on policy? What biases, predilections, and tendencies manifest themselves in policies?

The linchpin connecting institutions to policy is the motivations of political actors. As we saw in our discussion of Principle 1, their ambitions—ideological, personal, electoral, and institutional—provide politicians with the incentives to craft policies in particular ways. In fact, most policies make sense only as reflections of individual politicians' interests, goals, and beliefs. Examples include

Personal interests: Congressman Xcitement is an enthusiastic supporter of subsidizing home heating oil (but opposes regulation to keep its price down) because some of his friends own heating-oil distributorships.[15]

Electoral ambitions: Senator Yougottabekidding, a well-known political moderate, has lately been introducing very conservative amendments to bills dealing with the economy to appeal to more conservative financial donors who might then contribute to her budding presidential campaign.

Institutional ambitions: Representative Zeal has promised his vote and given a rousing speech on the House floor supporting a particular amendment because he knows it is near and dear to the Speaker's heart. He hopes his support will earn him the Speaker's endorsement next year for an assignment to the prestigious Appropriations Committee.

These examples illustrate how policies are politically crafted according to institutional procedures and individual aspirations. The procedures, as we saw in a previous discussion, are a series of chutes and ladders that shape, channel, filter, and prune the alternatives from which ultimate policy choices are made. The politicians that populate these institutions, as we have just noted, are driven both by private objectives and by public purposes, pursuing their own private interests while working on behalf of their conception of the public interest.

[15]These friends would benefit from people having the financial means to buy home heating oil but would not want the price they charge for the oil restricted.

Because the institutional features of the American political system are complex and policy change requires success at every step, change is often impossibly difficult, meaning the status quo usually prevails. A long list of players must be satisfied with the change, or it won't happen. Most of these politicians will need some form of "compensation" to provide their endorsement and support.

Majorities are usually built by drafting bills so as to spread the benefits to enough members of the legislature to get the requisite number of votes for that particular bill. Derisively, this is called "pork-barrel legislation." It can be better understood by remembering that the overwhelming proportion of pork-barrel projects that are distributed to build policy majorities are justified to voters as valuable additions to the public good of the various districts. What may be "pork" to the critic are actual bridges, roads, and post offices.

Elaborate institutional arrangements, complicated policy processes, and intricate political motivations make for a highly combustible mixture. The policies that emerge are inevitably lacking in the neatness that citizens desire. But policies in the United States today are sloppy and slapdash for a clear reason—it is the tendency to spread the benefits broadly that results when political ambition comes up against a decentralized political system.

Principle 5: History Matters

History Principle
History matters.

There is one more aspect of our analysis that is important: we must ask how we have gotten to where we are. By what series of steps? When by choice, and when by accident? To what extent was the history of Congress, the parties, and the presidency a fulfillment of constitutional principle and when were the developments a series of dogged responses to economic necessity? Are the parties a product of democracy, or is democracy a product of the parties? Every question and problem we confront has a history. History will not tell the same story for every institution. Nevertheless, without history, there is neither a sense of causation nor a sense of how institutions are related to each other. In explaining the answer to why governments do what they do, we must turn to history to see what choices were available to political actors at a given time and what consequences resulted from these choices.

Imagine a tree growing from the bottom of the page. Its trunk grows upward from some root ball at the bottom, dividing into branches that continue to grow upward, further dividing into smaller branches. Imagine a "path" through this tree, from its very roots at the bottom of the page to the end of one of the highest branches at the top of the page. There are many such paths, beginning from the one point at the bottom to many possible points at the top. If instead of a tree, this were a "time diagram," then the root ball at the bottom would represent some specific beginning point and all of the top-branch endings would represent some terminal time. Each path is now a *history*, the delineation of movement from some specific beginning to some concluding time. Alternative histories, like paths through trees, entail *irreversibilities*. Once one starts down a historical path (or up a tree), one cannot always retrace one's

The Politics of Prescription Drugs

The Medicare Prescription Drug, Improvement, and Modernization Act of 2003 is the largest new federal entitlement program since the creation of Medicare in 1965. This massive social spending program—the drug benefit alone is estimated to cost nearly 1.2 trillion dollars in its first decade[1]—was passed by a Republican-controlled Senate and House and signed by Republican president George W. Bush on December 8, 2003.

Why did it take prescription drug coverage, a gap in coverage that was evident two years after passage of Medicare,[2] thirty-eight years to be added into the program? And why were the political planets aligned in 2003 when so many previous efforts to add a prescription drug benefit had failed? The principles of politics can help us understand why Medicare reform was unsuccessful in the past and why it finally was successful in 2003.

Many actors were involved in the Medicare debate, from ordinary citizens to large interest groups (AARP), the medical establishment (the AMA, hospital administrators), the pharmaceutical industry, and, of course, elected politicians and federal bureaucrats. Collective action is hindered as the number of actors grows. Still, most involved with this issue recognized that the program needed to address the combination of millions of aging baby boomers and the high costs of prescription drugs.[3]

However, even if most players agreed on the nature of the problem, they were far from agreeing on a solution. Medicare reform had become a microcosm of a deep national divide about the role of government. Advocates of the free market, including many Republicans and Libertarians, assert that government programs should be minimal and should use market incentives wherever possible. Medicare, as they saw it, was a "relic of the Great Society, a collection of government bureaucrats rigidly administering price."[4] Liberals, including many Democrats, believe that collective action via the government can solve many social problems. To Liberals, Medicare and Social Security are "enduring achievements" and conservative attacks on these programs are a "calculated attempt to starve the government."[5] In such a situation, with many players, competing interests, and different goals, collective action remains elusive.

Yet the Medicare prescription drug benefit *did* pass. What historical circumstances allowed Congress and the president to overcome the barriers to collective action that had prevented reform for nearly forty years?

First, the tenor of the nation's political debate changed dramatically after the 1994 election (which gave Republicans control of both houses of Congress), and this provided an opening for a reexamination of Medicare. For the first thirty years of Medicare, the divisive nature of medical reform led both parties to keep Medicare reform off the agenda. Starting in early 1995 (and following President Clinton's failed health care initiative), newly installed Republican Speaker of the House Newt Gingrich identified Medicare reform as a centerpiece of the Republican agenda. And because his party controlled the House of Representatives for the first time in forty years, it had the ability to put his idea into practice.

Still, though the Republicans controlled Congress, they did not hold the presidency. Clinton vetoed the first attempt at reform in 1995 and vowed to continue to do so. For

Collective-Action Principle

Though all agreed that Medicare posed a problem, reaching a solution was difficult in light of the many competing interests.

Institution Principle

Despite resistance to change, Medicare reform got on the agenda because the Republicans controlled both houses of Congress for the first time in decades.

Clinton, deficit reduction was the priority, and Republican willingness to shut down the government in 1995—and pay the political costs in 1996—took Medicare reform off the agenda. It did not help matters when James Jeffords bolted the party and Republicans lost control of the Senate soon after the 2000 election.

By 2002, however, Republicans controlled both Congress *and* the presidency. Two long-time advocates of Medicare reform were in the Republican leadership: Senator Bill Frist of Tennessee, a physician, and Bill Thomas, chair of the House Committee on Ways and Means.[6]

Still, most of the hurdles to reform remained. The majority party had to use every procedural mechanism at its disposal—even inventing some new ones—to push the legislation to passage. The Republican leadership in the House took the unprecedented step of holding open a roll-call vote, normally limited to fifteen minutes, to nearly three hours in order to avoid an embarrassing loss for the president in a chamber controlled by his own party.[7] Republicans continued to play hardball during the conference process, excluding all but two Democrats from the committee. And Bush was victorious in the 2004 election, pointing to Medicare reform as one of his most important domestic achievements.

Not surprisingly, the battle over the future of Medicare is far from over. A few months after the passage of the bill, it came to light that the administration's estimate of the costs of the program were too low—by nearly 50 percent—and that a Medicare actuary had been banned from telling Congress these details.[8] While AARP stunned the Washington establishment by supporting the president's program, 46 percent of seniors opposed the changes (as compared to only 26 percent who supported them).[9] And if conservatives were hoping that this bill would wean Americans from their dependence on Medicare and other government entitlements, the rising public backlash against the reforms may end up having the opposite effect.

History Principle

Despite Republican control of Congress, Republican clashes with Clinton took Medicare reform off the agenda.

Rationality Principle

Having Medicare reform advocates in key positions in Congress made passing a Medicare bill possible.

Policy Principle

Medicare reform resulted from the combination of Republican leadership and the party's use of unprecedented rules procedures in Congress.

[1]Ceci Connolly and Mike Allen, "Medicare Drug Benefit May Cost 1.2 Trillion," *Washington Post,* 9 February 2005.

[2]In May 1967, in response to a charge from President Lyndon Johnson, the government established a Task Force on Prescription Drugs. See Thomas Oliver, Philip R. Lee, and Helene L. Lipton, "A Political History of Medicare and Prescription Drug Coverage," *The Milbank Quarterly* 82.2 (2004).

[3]The baby boomer generation is defined as Americans born between 1946 and 1964. There are about 76 million boomers, representing 29 percent of the nation's population.

[4]The "Great Society" was defined in Johnson's 1965 State of the Union address as a package of government programs that would improve the lives of all Americans. The Great Society measures included Medicare, Head Start, food stamps, and the establishment of the Department of Housing and Urban Development.

[5]Robin Toner, "Hard to Swallow: Medicare, Battleground for a Bigger Struggle," *New York Times,* 20 July 2003.

[6]Oliver, Lee, and Lipton, p. 309.

[7]Carl Hulse, "Pass the Sour Grapes, Not Sweet Potatoes," *New York Times,* 27 November 2003.

[8]Robert Pear, "Medicare Official Testifies on Cost Figures," *New York Times,* 24 March 2004.

[9]Oliver, Lee, and Lipton, p. 284.

steps.[16] Once things happen, they cannot always "un-happen." One need not subscribe uncompromisingly to historical determinism to take the position that some futures are foreclosed by the choices people have already made or, if not literally foreclosed, then made extremely unlikely.

It is in this sense that we explain a current situation at least in part by alluding to the historical path by which we arrived at it. We say that the situation is *path dependent*, that various features of the current situation are what they are in part because of the path by which the situation occurred, and had a different path been taken, the features might well be different, too. Today's events and situations are a storehouse of the historical past. History provides contemporaries with an interpretive framework and a context in which to update beliefs. The principle of ***path dependency*** underscores the contingent nature of things: a particular unfolding of history precludes some things from happening. The historical record combines with the choices of contemporaries and the institutional arrangements they invent to produce final results or outcomes.

path dependency
The idea that certain possibilities are made more or less likely because of the historical path taken.

Finally, without history we cannot appreciate change. We are not concerned with history for its own sake. But history does allow us to analyze the consequences of institutional change in government, both intended and unintended. For example, the construction of democratic electoral institutions and popular representative bodies in the United States and other Western societies has had historic consequences that influence how government operates and what it does.

THE PRINCIPLES OF POLITICS IN ACTION

In just the first five years of the twenty-first century, several seismic events have changed many facets of American political life—the continuing consequences of the terrorist attacks of September 11, 2001, and the associated war on terrorism; the wars in Afghanistan and Iraq; the election of 2004; and the devastation of a turbulent hurricane season in the Gulf of Mexico during the summer and fall of 2005. These events have affected the objectives and strategies and attention of politicians and citizens (Rationality Principle); the deployment of political resources and the mobilization of activities (Collective-Action Principle); the agendas of our political institutions (Institution Principle); the policies of government, the ones pursued and the ones deferred (Policy Principle); and the ways in which history has shaped our responses and our responses will shape tomorrow's history (History Principle). In this section, we briefly examine these events and demonstrate how our five principles can help us organize our thinking about them. In a nutshell, this is what political scientists do: look at real events and, using principles, try to explain them.

---

[16]Clearly, with tree climbing this is not literally true, or once we started climbing a tree we would never get down! So the tree analogy is not perfect here.

To demarcate the scope of the discussion, let's set the stage in January 2003 with the convening of the 108th Congress. The just-held midterm elections in November 2002 had produced modest gains for the Republicans. In the long history of elections in the United States, this is a relatively unusual event. The typical pattern is for the party of the president to lose seats at midterm. Thus President George W. Bush began his run-up to re-election in 2004 with small majorities in both the House and the Senate. His leadership in the wake of the September 11 terrorist attacks, especially the creation of the Department of Homeland Security and his move against the Taliban regime in Afghanistan, had provided his party with the head of steam it needed to continue to control both legislative chambers after the midterm elections. In effect, the events of September 11, 2001, gave President Bush an opportunity to lead decisively, and that decisiveness paid off handsomely for the Republicans in the fall elections.

Flush with victory as 2003 unfolded, President Bush began a series of diplomatic and military moves aimed at the regime of Saddam Hussein in Iraq. Saddam and his Baathist party cronies had dominated Iraq for several decades, using oil revenues, police-state tactics, and military incursions against its neighbors (Iran and Kuwait, in particular) to quash domestic opposition, enrich themselves financially, and entrench themselves politically. Bush's father, President George H. W. Bush, had led an international coalition against Saddam a decade earlier—the Persian Gulf War of 1991—expelling Iraq from Kuwait, which it had invaded; destroying much of Iraq's army and military hardware; but leaving Saddam's regime intact. President George W. Bush was intent on diminishing the threat of Saddam in the Middle East. He sought acknowledgment from the Iraqi regime that it possessed weapons of mass destruction (WMDs) and its commitment to destroy existing stocks and capabilities and to end dealings with terrorist elements. Frustrated by lack of progress in securing these objectives, the administration increasingly focused on removing Saddam and deposing the Baathist regime, by diplomatic or collective military measures if possible and by (essentially) unilateral means if necessary.

Without much enthusiasm, the administration allowed UN weapons inspections to run their course over many months without uncovering any WMDs in Iraq. Saddam's intransigence in dealing with these inspectors, on more than one occasion forcing them out of the country, fueled the Bush administration's campaign for a military solution. Under pressure from the Democrats and domestic public opinion and lacking support for war from America's Western allies (as well as many in the American diplomatic and intelligence communities), President Bush agreed in the winter of 2003 to continue pursuing a diplomatic solution to the disagreement. He sent Secretary of State Colin Powell to the United Nations in February to lay out the administration's case against the Iraqi regime. But our nominal allies on the UN Security Council, especially France and Russia, refused to sanction military action. So, together with a "coalition of the willing" (several dozen countries, including Australia, Great Britain, Spain, and Japan), the United States launched a war against Iraq in March 2003.

Military results came quickly. The Iraqi army and police were defeated and disbanded; Saddam's sons, his heirs-apparent, were killed; and Saddam was ultimately captured. Other Baathist politicians were killed or captured, or disappeared into hiding, and Baghdad and other major cities were occupied. Indeed, at one point President Bush landed on an aircraft carrier in full flight gear beneath a banner reading "Mission Accomplished." Alas, only the initial *military* mission had been accomplished. The postwar reconstruction of a ravaged Iraqi infrastructure and economy was but the first of many headaches facing the victorious coalition. The task of what had been thought of as neutralizing "pockets of resistance" grew into the much bigger task of defeating a broad military resistance, especially in the Sunni Triangle of central Iraq.

As American casualties mounted, and the vast scope of what remained to be done to stabilize Iraq and transform it politically and economically became increasingly apparent, political repercussions began to be felt at home. The financial burdens of the war and reconstruction were immense (and the "coalition of the willing," unlike the Gulf War coalition of a decade earlier, provided an inadequate foundation for cost sharing). With domestic tax revenues already reduced by the combination of a shaky economy at home and huge tax cuts engineered by the Bush administration and the Republican Congress, Americans were facing historically unprecedented deficits that promised to burden the economy for years to come. Facing the combination of a war whose unpopularity grew with each military casualty, the increasing evidence of inadequate postwar planning, and an economy struggling with recession, job loss, and deficits, Republican politicians grew nervous as election-year 2004 approached.

In parallel to developments abroad—especially in Iraq and Afghanistan—a war on terrorism was waged at home. The newly created Department of Homeland Security and its head, former Pennsylvania governor Tom Ridge, orchestrated a vast governmental reorganization involving other agencies such as the Justice and State Departments. Ever since, American society has been on nearly a war footing, massive inconveniences are still tolerated (especially at airports), personal plans are affected (obtaining passports and visas, for example, has grown more complicated, especially for foreign students), and in some instances civil liberties are curtailed if not suspended (police have been granted considerable leeway in pursuing suspected terrorists). The war on terrorism provided *prime facie* evidence to Americans that the country since September 11, 2001, remained seriously at risk and that President Bush was not asleep at the switch. To some extent, it diminished the impact of the negative press the Iraq war was receiving, as President Bush played on the fears of citizens to persuade them of the necessity for inconvenience and sacrifice.

As the 2004 election season approached, war-on-terrorism activities encouraged voters to stay the course, stick with the president and his Republican team, and think twice before handing awesome responsibilities over to unproven leaders. The Democrats, on the other hand, would claim they had nominated an experienced legislator and war hero, Senator John Kerry, who could be trusted to wear the mantle of leadership with confidence. The war in Iraq and the war on terrorism cross-pressured the electorate and, therein, provided each party with issues around which to mount an election campaign. Democrats would promise to undo the mismanagement of postwar Iraq while hanging tough on the war on terrorism. Republicans would stress their continuing championing of the war on terrorism and what they presented as steady and sure progress toward a democratic Iraq.

The events of September 11 were bolts out of the blue: unimaginable events that required immediate and forceful response and that would prove central in assessing candidates in the 2004 election. The wars in Afghanistan and Iraq and the domestic war on terrorism were discretionary choices—perhaps wise, perhaps not—that allowed the incumbents to respond decisively to events over which they had had no control. All of this provided a context for the 2004 election. Discretionary choices by incumbent politicians about matters of war, security, and peace and responses by opposition politicians to those discretionary choices were affected by re-election ambitions. Each side did its best to portray its standard-bearer—Bush for the Republicans and Kerry for the Democrats—as a man of vision, responsibility, and courage. And there is no denying the fact that these portraits were intended for an audience that would soon be deciding whom to support in November.

Now that we have reviewed these important events, we can ask ourselves, Why did the people involved make the choices they did, and what were the consequences? Answering these questions becomes much easier using our five principles of politics. This discussion will take us through 2004. The year 2005 was not uneventful, and we will briefly cover some of its most significant points—the response to Hurricane Katrina and the major changes in the Supreme Court—at the conclusion of this chapter.

The Rationality Principle

Throughout these events, President Bush was highly focused on re-election. He was intent on avoiding the fate of his father: being a one-term president. His Republican brethren in the House and the Senate were also keen on staying in office and holding their majorities; they realized that their fates were intertwined with that of the president. Although it is unfair and inaccurate to accuse President Bush of being *single-minded* in his pursuit of re-election, it is clear that no action was taken without considering its ramifications for re-election.

The Collective-Action Principle

To succeed politically, the war on terrorism and the wars in Afghanistan and Iraq needed to produce results. The commitment of manpower and financial resources was essential. The orchestration of policy—through the Department of Homeland Security and Department of Justice on the home front and the Department of Defense overseas—was also essential. The need for coordination meant that some players gained strength and others were marginalized. The winners were Secretary

Donald Rumsfeld at Defense, National Security Adviser Condoleezza Rice in the White House, Secretary Tom Ridge at Homeland Security, and Attorney General John Ashcroft at Justice. The biggest loser was the Department of State and its secretary, Colin Powell (who was replaced after the 2004 elections by Rice). Other domestic agencies were also sidelined by this focus. (The No Child Left Behind education policy, one of President Bush's domestic centerpieces, was significantly underfunded, for example.) The bureaucratic sorting that took place was the product of results-oriented politics against the backdrop of the 2004 election.

The Institution Principle

The single biggest institutional manifestation of the war policies that were highlighted during George W. Bush's first term was the creation of the Department of Homeland Security. Coordinated collective action is crucial, of course, to produce major policy results. Wars, whether against amorphous terrorists or concrete opponents, are complex undertakings with many different "moving parts." But a continuing effort cannot depend on ad hoc, one-off arrangements; it needs to be *institutionalized*. It is still too early to judge whether the new department has successfully synchronized the many agencies that now fall under its control.[17] And it should be emphasized that institutional arrangements like the DHS are not set in stone. There will be incessant tinkering with its structure, jurisdiction, and budget—all in response to a changing environment, its initial track record, and bureaucratic maneuverings by politicians.

A related development illustrates the "it ain't over till it's over" corollary to the Institution Principle even more clearly. In November and December 2004, after the election, there were attempts to reorganize the intelligence services. The 9/11 Commission, an expert body formed to investigate the terrorist attacks of September 11, 2001, and recommend what the government should do to prevent future acts of terrorism, delivered a series of proposals in July 2004. One suggested creating an "intelligence czar" who would coordinate and oversee the activities of our various intelligence services, such as the Central Intelligence Agency, the National Security Agency, and the Defense Intelligence Agency. In response to this proposal, the House and Senate produced slightly different versions of a massive piece of legislation. After the House and Senate agreed on a compromise measure that had the support of President Bush, it was taken to each chamber for final approval. However, Speaker of the House Dennis Hastert prevented its being scheduled for a House vote before Congress recessed for Thanksgiving. Apparently, support was withdrawn by several conservative Republican legislators who chaired committees that oversaw agencies slated to lose power with the consolidation of intelligence agencies. Hastert felt he could not go forward with a vote under these circumstances. Various media, the *New York Times* in particular, accused Secretary of Defense Rumsfeld of being behind this bureaucratic maneuver. Defense would be one of the jurisdictional and

---

[17]Several of DHS's emergency response agencies did not function well in responding to the aftermath of Hurricane Katrina.

budgetary losers if the consolidation took place. After the election, this was all sorted out and, in the winter of 2005, an intelligence czar, former UN Ambassador and Ambassador to Iraq John Negroponte, was named by President Bush.

The Policy Principle

Policies are the result of political ambitions played out in a context of institutional processes. President Bush's seizing of the initiative after the horrors of September 11, first in fighting the Taliban in Afghanistan, then in developing the overall war against terrorism, and finally in destroying Saddam's regime in Iraq, reflected his ambition for a successful first term and a successful campaign for a second. This is, as noted earlier, an oversimplification; clearly President Bush aspired to accomplish much more. But his first nine months in office were unspectacular, and the challenges following September 11 gave his administration an opportunity to respond forcefully. Bush's ambitions, together with the powers both in principle and in actual practice of a chief executive faced with a security threat, were translated into policies, ranging from congressional authorization to use force in Afghanistan and Iraq, to the budgetary means to fight those wars, to legislation (for example, the Patriot Act, which empowered executive agencies to prosecute a domestic war against terrorism). Bush's political ambitions were a necessary ingredient, but so too was his effective mobilization of the political power of other institutions to produce the desired policies. The Bush administration transformed small majorities in each legislative chamber into winning coalitions on policies that enabled his ambitions to be realized.

Another illustration of the ambition–institutions nexus (ambition + institutions = policy) relates to a piece of domestic legislation that Congress passed in late 2004—a major farm bill. The Democratic minority in the Senate was unhappy with various aspects of its provisions and was prepared to filibuster the bill (that is, engage in delaying tactics that would prevent it from coming to a vote). To do this it needed nearly all Democrats to participate in this tactic. Of all people, however, the Democratic leader in the Senate, Tom Daschle of South Dakota, announced he would support the bill and would oppose any delaying tactic. The reason? Daschle was engaged in a tough re-election contest (one he ultimately lost by a slim margin). Agriculture is the major industry in South Dakota, and South Dakota farmers generally favored the farm bill's generous subsidies for the crops they grew as well as the financial backing for converting corn into ethanol. So Daschle's political ambitions, though they ran counter to the preferences of the party of which he was Senate leader, led him to play a pivotal institutional role in defeating the delaying tactics and, in the end, allowing passage of legislation that his constituents expected to be a boon to his state.

The History Principle

History matters a lot to President Bush. As is true of any president, he looks to his reputation and historical legacy. And he has the experience of his father's failed re-election bid as a burr under his saddle. When Bush addressed firefighters, police, and rescue workers at Ground Zero just after September 11, 2001, and spoke to Congress and the American people shortly after that, he surely had in mind the image of Franklin D. Roosevelt the day after the attack on Pearl Harbor. It was his opportunity to come across as a decisive leader, to rescue his faltering administration, to reinvigorate his re-election prospects, and to strike a pose for the history books.

It was a heroic moment in which he not only *made* history but also *drew on* history. Bush's decisive leadership after September 11 and his bold initiatives in Afghanistan and Iraq transformed him into a "war president" and put him in the same category, at least initially, with previous war presidents. Historically, being in this category is a double-edged sword. On the one hand, it contrasts favorably with instances of presidential weakness (such as his father's decision not to take the fighting all the way to Baghdad in the Persian Gulf War, or Jimmy Carter's ineffectual handling of the Iranian hostage crisis in 1979–80) and compares favorably with instances of presidential strength (Roosevelt after Pearl Harbor, Truman's bringing a conclusion to fighting in the Pacific theater during World War II). On the other hand, it risks one's actions being compared to instances of presidential failure (Truman in Korea, Johnson and Nixon in Vietnam). George W. Bush now has a second term in which to clarify which war president he will become.

We have given a glimpse of the principles at work in organizing the recent political history running up to the 2004 election. Elections, as we shall frequently emphasize in this book, provide a temporal rhythm to political life. Just after an election, the winners celebrate with the spoils of victory, the losers suffer "the agony of defeat" and lick their wounds, and everyone starts getting ready for the next electoral cycle.

Events, however, continue apace and politicians must respond. In 2005, some of these were continuing events. The wars in Iraq and Afghanistan continued, exhausting resources and taking lives. But the Iraqis approved a new constitution, allowing American politicians to hope for an exit strategy in the not-too-distant future. Beyond continuing events such as these, two major jolts commanded political attention, especially in the second half of 2005.

The Supreme Court had gone a decade without any personnel change, one of the longest such periods in history. Justice Stephen Breyer, appointed by President Clinton in 1994, was the newest member of the Court. In the summer of 2005, Justice Sandra Day O'Connor announced her retirement; shortly thereafter Chief Justice William Rehnquist died. President Bush nominated John Roberts, a sitting federal judge, to succeed the Chief Justice and Harriet Miers, White House Counsel, to succeed O'Connor. Roberts was confirmed, but Miers was forced to withdraw her candidacy—in part because she lacked the *gravitas* of a distinguished career, in part because of charges of cronyism, and in part because conservatives in the Republican base of support did not feel she was reliably conservative. President Bush then nominated Samuel Alito, a sitting federal judge with a distinguished career and sterling conservative credentials, and Alito was confirmed in February 2006.

Rationality is at work here as partisans (Democrats and Republicans) and ideologues (conservatives and liberals) have attempted to manipulate things to make the results of appointment politics come out closest to their preferences. Tensions within the administration—should we play to our conservative electoral base? should we nominate someone who can easily win Senate confirmation?—required making tradeoffs among competing objectives. The *collective action* principle is apparent in the big push made by Bush administration operatives to organize coalitions for confirmation of their candidates in the Senate and to bargain with pivotal legislators to secure their support. The *institutional* requirements of "advise and consent" politics dictated wooing moderate senators to their cause, and institutional procedures like the filibuster clearly mattered in the final result. (As we will see later in this book, the Senate may appear to be a simple majority-rule body, but it actually requires sixty votes to win passage for anything there.) *Policy* on the Court was at stake with these appointments, affecting both whom the president found acceptable and whom the Senate would ultimately confirm. Finally, *history* matters in terms both of setting bounds on what a president can expect out of the appointment process and of what a president will be remembered for long after he leaves office.

The second jolt in 2005 was Hurricane Katrina. Our five principles of politics would organize a nice case study of the political disaster that followed this natural disaster. But for present purposes we will emphasize primarily *failures* of collective action. Many of the agencies responsible for prior planning and post-emergency response simply weren't on the same page. At the federal level many of these agencies had been brought under the recently created Department of Homeland Security. Whether because of the newness of this department, the rivalries among some of its parts, or the lack of professional competence of its political appointees, the nation was unprepared for a disaster like the storm that devastated New Orleans and the Mississippi, Alabama, and Louisiana coasts. The institutional failure of collective action was exacerbated by federal-state malcoordination, state-local malcoordination, and a general sense that there were many chiefs and many followers but no clear lines of command or communication between or across levels of government. Katrina provides an exemplary illustration of the proposition that collective action is often most difficult at exactly the point when it is most needed.

The five principles of politics provide a useful analytical framework for thinking about contemporary politics. We will consistently employ this frame in the rest of the book. As you read—in fact, even when you encounter politics outside the classroom—keep this framework in mind. If you find yourself wondering why Republicans (who traditionally favor smaller government) argued for government involvement in the Terri Schiavo right-to-die case in 2005, or why the Democrats might (or might not) nominate Hillary Clinton for president in 2008, think about these principles. Ask yourself: What are the goals of the individuals involved? (Rationality Principle). What are the challenges to forming effective coalitions in this situation? (Collective-Action Principle). What institutional rules are in place that shape the debate? (Institution Principle). What consequences are likely to result, considering the people involved and rules they are working under? (Policy Principle). And how has this issue been shaped by past events? (History Principle). These are the questions that you (thinking like a political scientist) can ask and, using our five principles of politics, begin to answer.

Rationality Principle	Collective-Action Principle	Institution Principle	Policy Principle	History Principle
All political behavior has a purpose.	All politics is collective action.	Institutions routinely solve collective-action problems.	Political outcomes are the products of individual preferences and institutional procedures.	History matters.

SUMMARY

The enormous scope of national programs in the last century required the construction of a large and elaborate state apparatus and the transfer of considerable decision-making power from political bodies like Congress to administrative agencies. As a consequence, the development and implementation of today's public policies are increasingly dominated by complicated bureaucratic institutions, rules, and procedures that are not easily affected by the preferences that citizens express in the voting booth. Can citizens use the power of the institutions we have created? Or are we doomed simply to become their subjects?

In addition, as government has grown in size and power, the need for citizen action has diminished. Unlike their predecessors, many governments today have administrative, military, and police agencies that *can* curb disorder, collect taxes, and keep their foes in check without necessarily depending on popular involvement or approval. Will governments continue to bow to the will of the people even though public opinion may not be as crucial as it once was? Likewise, will citizens participate in the political process when few incentives are provided to do so? And by what means will citizens band together to accomplish their shared goals?

Our five principles of politics provide a focus and a means for answering these and other questions. Understanding the complexities of government might seem an overwhelming task, but these basic principles are where we need to begin. Throughout this book, we will refer to the five principles introduced in this chapter. When we do, an icon will appear in the margin to indicate which principle is involved and how that principle applies to the discussion. Again, try to keep these principles in mind beyond the reading of this book. They not only are the basis of political science as an academic enterprise but also are important tools for citizens to employ as participants in America's democratic process.

FOR FURTHER READING

Bianco, William T. *American Politics: Strategy and Choice*. New York: Norton, 2001.

Dahl, Robert A. *Who Governs? Democracy and Power in an American City*. New Haven, CT: Yale University Press, 1961.

Downs, Anthony. *An Economic Theory of Democracy*. New York: Harper & Row, 1957.

Lupia, Arthur, and Mathew D. McCubbins. *The Democratic Dilemma: Can Citizens Learn What They Need to Know?* New York: Cambridge University Press, 1998.

Olson, Mancur, Jr. *The Logic of Collective Action: Public Goods and the Theory of Groups*. Cambridge: Harvard University Press, 1965.

Putnam, Robert D. *Making Democracy Work: Civic Traditions in Modern Italy*. Princeton, NJ: Princeton University Press, 1993.

Riker, William H. *Liberalism against Populism: A Confrontation between the Theory of Democracy and the Theory of Social Choice*. San Francisco: Freeman, 1982.

Politics in the News— Reading between the Lines

Competing Interests and Prescription Drugs

Florida Elderly Feel Let Down by Medicare Drug Benefit

By ROBERT PEAR

In the condominiums and on the palm-shaded beaches here, where Medicare is a frequent topic of conversation, few people expect to get much help from the new drug benefit just approved by Congress.

They express disappointment but little surprise because, they say, they never had high hopes. They say they feel they were sold out, by Republicans and AARP, which endorsed a Medicare bill drafted mainly by Republicans. But the Democrats, they say, did not fight hard enough for a better drug benefit. . . .

The drug benefit has often been described as the biggest expansion of Medicare since its creation in 1965. Some people here, especially those who have been struggling to pay for prescription drugs, applauded the change. But Ernest D. DeBlasis, 73, echoed the view of many when he said the new coverage "amounts to peanuts."

"It's not going to help me," said Mr. DeBlasis, who spends half the year here and half in Marlboro, N.J., where he was an architect. "Let's hope Congress re-vises this thing before it takes effect in 2006." . . .

The new drug benefit would be voluntary. It would be offered to all 40 million Medicare beneficiaries, through government-subsidized private plans, in 2006. Federal officials say premiums would average $35 a month.

Under "standard prescription drug coverage," as defined in the Medicare bill, a beneficiary would be responsible for the first $250 in drug costs each year. Of the next $2,000, Medicare would cover 75 percent and the beneficiary would pay 25 percent, or $500. The beneficiary would then be responsible for all of the next $2,850 in drug costs.

The beneficiary would thus pay $3,600 for the first $5,100 worth of medicine in a year, and that does not include the premiums, estimated at $420 a year. Beyond that, Medicare would cover 95 percent of the cost of each prescription, after the patient had spent $3,600.

Several Medicare beneficiaries over the age of 75 said they would need

New York Times, 30 November 2003, section 1, p. 34.

lawyers to figure out the new benefits. The options could be even more complex than they realize. Under the bill, insurers could offer variations of the standard drug benefit.

A major reason for the convoluted shape of the drug benefit is that Congress and President Bush wanted to limit the cost to $400 billion over 10 years. . . .

"If they can send $87 billion to Iraq and Afghanistan this year, I think they could do a little better for our citizens, especially senior citizens who are on fixed incomes," said Tony J. Forzese, 71, a small-business man from Massachusetts who has had a condominium here for 20 years.

. . . Low-income people without any insurance for prescription drugs stand to gain most from the new Medicare benefit. They could receive extra assistance, reducing their premiums, deductibles and other costs. . . .

[Hyacinth] Rickman said that she and her husband lived mainly on a Social Security check of about $500 a month. More than $100 of that, she said, goes for drug costs not covered by her health maintenance organization.

"The $100 is a lot for us," said Mrs. Rickman. . . . "It would be great to get the government to pay some." . . .

The local member of Congress, Representative E. Clay Shaw Jr., a Republican, cited the assistance for low-income people as one of the main reasons he voted for the bill.

About three-fourths of Medicare beneficiaries have some kind of public or private insurance to help pay drug costs, but the coverage becomes more expensive and more limited every year.

AARP often comes up when people here discuss the new drug benefit.

Mr. Shapiro, a former New York City school principal and songwriter, said: "I'm going to resign from AARP. Its support of this drug plan tipped the balance. They're more sympathetic to the big drug and insurance companies

ESSENCE OF THE STORY

- Many elderly expressed disappointment at the prescription drug benefit provided in the Medicare modernization act. The new benefit is either too complicated or does not help the majority of seniors.

- Some questioned the government's priorities, comparing the costs of the Medicare bill with spending in Iraq and Afghanistan.

- Seniors also complained about the role of AARP, which worked with the Republican Party to pass this new benefit.

POLITICAL ANALYSIS

- Prescription drug benefits are unavoidably complex, because they balance government involvement in an area normally dominated by the private sector with private citizens' demands that the government help with an increasingly costly part of their health-care budget.

- Seniors are one of the most powerful political constituencies in the United States. They vote at a high rate; they are well-informed about government programs such as Social Security and Medicare; and large numbers of them live in battleground states.

- AARP is criticized in this article for working with the Republican majority. Perhaps this interest group, the largest in the country, recognizes the likelihood that Republicans will control Congress for the foreseeable future.

than to ordinary seniors who want a simple solution."

Mr. DeBlasis said, "I'm disappointed in AARP, but I can understand their argument for the new drug benefit as a first step."

Elsewhere, a 73-year-old man, sitting on the promenade of Hollywood Beach as a soft evening breeze fluttered the palm fronds on Thanksgiving Day, said: "I'm more angry at AARP than at Congress because they are supposed to support us. They sold us out."

CHAPTER

2

Constructing a Government: The Founding and the Constitution

"No taxation without representation" were words that stirred a generation of Americans long before they even dreamed of calling themselves Americans rather than Englishmen. In reaction to new English attempts to extract tax revenues to pay for the troops that were being sent to defend the colonial frontier, protests erupted throughout the colonies against the infamous Stamp Act of 1765. This act required that all printed and legal documents, including newspapers, pamphlets, advertisements, notes and bonds, leases, deeds, and licenses be printed on official paper stamped and sold by English officials. To show their displeasure with the act, the colonists conducted mass meetings, parades, bonfires, and other demonstrations throughout the spring and summer of 1765. In Boston, for example, a stamp agent was hanged and burned in effigy. Later, the home of the lieutenant governor was sacked, leading to his resignation and that of all of his colonial commission and stamp agents. By November 1765, business proceeded and newspapers were published without the stamp; in March 1766, Parliament repealed the detested law. Through their protest, the nonimportation agreements that the colonists subsequently adopted, and the Stamp Act Congress that met in October 1765, the colonists took the first steps that ultimately would lead to war and a new nation.

The people of every nation tend to glorify their own history and especially their nation's creation. Generally, through such devices as public-school texts and national holidays, governments encourage a heroic view of the nation's past as a way of promoting national pride and unity in the present. Great myths are part of the process of nation building and citizenship training in every nation, and the United States is no exception. To most contemporary Americans, the revolutionary period represents a brave struggle by a determined and united group of colonists against British oppression. The Boston Tea Party, the battles of Lexington and Concord, the winter at Valley Forge—these are the events that we emphasize in our history. Similarly, the U.S. Constitution—the document establishing the system of government that ultimately emerged from this struggle—is often seen as an inspired, if not divine, work, expressing timeless principles of democratic government. These views are by no means false. During the founding era, Americans did struggle against misrule. Moreover, the Constitution did establish the foundations for more than 200 years of democratic government.

To really understand the character of the American founding and the meaning of the American Constitution, however, it is essential to look beyond the myths and rhetoric.

The men and women who became revolutionaries were guided by principles, to be sure, but they also had interests. Most of them were not political theorists, but were hard-headed and

CHAPTER OUTLINE

The First Founding: Interests and Conflicts

- British Taxes and Colonial Interests
- Political Strife and the Radicalizing of the Colonists
- The Declaration of Independence
- The Articles of Confederation

The Second Founding: From Compromise to Constitution

- International Standing and Balance of Power
- The Annapolis Convention
- Shays's Rebellion
- The Constitutional Convention

The Constitution

- The Legislative Branch
- The Executive Branch
- The Judicial Branch
- National Unity and Power
- Amending the Constitution
- Ratifying the Constitution
- Constitutional Limits on the National Government's Power

The Fight for Ratification: Federalists versus Antifederalists

- Representation
- The Threats Posed by the Majority
- Governmental Power

Changing the Institutional Framework: Constitutional Amendment

- Amendments: Many Are Called, Few Are Chosen
- The Twenty-seven Amendments

Reflections on the Founding: Principles or Interests?

pragmatic in their commitments and activities. Although their interests were not identical, they did agree that a relationship of political and economic dependence on a colonial power, one that did not treat them as full-fledged citizens of the empire, was intolerable. In the end, the decision to break away and, over the succeeding decade, to fashion institutions of self-governance was the consequence.

Many of those most active in the initial days of the Revolution felt backed into a corner, their decisions forced. For years, the imperial center in London, preoccupied by a war with France that spread across several continents, had left the colonists to their own devices. These were years in which colonists enjoyed an immense amount of local control and home rule. But suddenly, as the war with France drew to a close in the 1760s, the British presence became more onerous and intrusive. This historical experience incited the initial reactions to taxes. Nearly a century of relatively light-handed colonial administration by London had produced a set of expectations in the colonists that later British actions unmistakably violated.

This is where we begin our story in the present chapter. We first assess the political backdrop of the American Revolution. Then we examine the Constitution that ultimately emerged—after a rather bumpy experience in self-government just after the Revolution—as the basis for America's government. We conclude with a reflection on the founding period by emphasizing a lesson to be learned from the founding that continues to be important throughout American history. The lesson is that politics, as James Madison said in *The Federalist*, generally involves struggles among conflicting interests. In 1776, the conflict was between prorevolutionary and antirevolutionary forces. In 1787, the struggle was between the Federalists and the Antifederalists. Today, the struggle is between the Democrats and the Republicans, each representing competing economic, social, and sectional interests. Often, political principles are the weapons developed by competing interests to further their own causes. The New England merchants who cried "no taxation without representation" cared more about lower taxes than expanded representation. Yet, today, representation is one of the foundations of American democracy.

What were the great principles that emerged from the conflicts during the founding period? How do these principles continue to shape our lives long after the Constitution's framers completed their work? These are the important questions that are addressed in this chapter.

THE FIRST FOUNDING: INTERESTS AND CONFLICTS

Competing ideals and principles often reflect competing interests, and so it was in revolutionary America. The American Revolution and Constitution were outgrowths and expressions of a struggle among economic and political forces within the colonies. Five sectors of society had interests that were important in colonial politics: (1) the New England merchants; (2) the southern planters; (3) the "royalists"—holders of royal lands, offices, and patents (licenses to engage in a profession or business activity); (4) shopkeepers, artisans, and laborers; and (5) small farmers. Throughout the eighteenth century, these groups were in conflict over issues of taxation, trade, and commerce. For the most part, however, the southern planters, the New England merchants, and the royal office and patent holders—groups that together made up the colonial elite—were able to maintain a political alliance that held in check the more radical forces representing shopkeepers, laborers, and small farmers. After 1750, however, by seriously threatening the interests of New England merchants and southern planters, British tax and trade policies split the colonial elite, permitting radical forces to expand their political influence, and set into motion a chain of events that culminated in the American Revolution.[1]

British Taxes and Colonial Interests

Beginning in the 1750s, the debts and other financial problems faced by the British government forced it to search for new revenue sources. This search rather quickly led to the Crown's North American colonies, which, on the whole, paid remarkably little in taxes to the mother country. The British government reasoned that a sizable fraction of its debt was, in fact, attributable to the expenses it had incurred in defense of the colonies during the recent French and Indian wars, as well as to the continuing protection that British forces were giving the colonists from Indian attacks, and that the British navy was providing for colonial shipping. Thus, during the 1760s, England sought to impose new, though relatively modest, taxes on the colonists.

Like most governments of the period, the British regime had at its disposal only limited ways to collect revenues. The income tax, which in the twentieth century became the single most important source of governmental revenue, had not yet been developed. For the most part, in the mid-eighteenth century, governments relied on tariffs, duties, and other taxes on commerce, and it was to such taxes, including the Stamp Act, that the British turned during the 1760s.

[1]The social makeup of colonial America and some of the social conflicts that divided colonial society are discussed in Jackson Turner Main, *The Social Structure of Revolutionary America* (Princeton, NJ: Princeton University Press, 1965).

The Stamp Act and other taxes on commerce, such as the Sugar Act of 1764, which taxed sugar, molasses, and other commodities, most heavily affected the two groups in colonial society whose commercial interests and activities were most extensive—the New England merchants and southern planters. Under the famous slogan "no taxation without representation," the merchants and planters together sought to organize opposition to the new taxes. In the course of the struggle against British tax measures, the planters and merchants broke with their royalist allies and turned to their former adversaries—the shopkeepers, small farmers, laborers, and artisans—for help. With the assistance of these groups, the merchants and planters organized demonstrations and a boycott of British goods that ultimately forced the Crown to rescind most of its new taxes. It was in the context of this unrest that a confrontation between colonists and British soldiers in front of the Boston customshouse on the night of March 5, 1770, resulted in what came to be known as the Boston Massacre. Nervous British soldiers opened fire on the mob surrounding them, killing five colonists and wounding eight others. News of this event quickly spread throughout the colonies and was used by radicals to fan anti-British sentiment.

From the perspective of the merchants and planters, however, the British government's decision to eliminate most of the hated taxes represented a victorious end to their struggle with the mother country. They were anxious to end the unrest they had helped arouse, and they supported the British government's efforts to restore order. Indeed, most respectable Bostonians supported the actions of the British soldiers involved in the Boston Massacre. In their subsequent trial, the soldiers were defended by John Adams, a pillar of Boston society and a future president of the United States. Adams asserted that the soldiers' actions were entirely justified, provoked by a "motley rabble of saucy boys, negroes and mulattoes, Irish teagues and outlandish Jack tars." All but two of the soldiers were acquitted.[2]

Despite the efforts of the British government and the better-to-do strata of colonial society, it proved difficult to bring an end to the political strife. The more radical forces representing shopkeepers, artisans, laborers, and small farmers, who had been mobilized and energized by the struggle over taxes, continued to agitate for political and social change within the colonies. These radicals, led by individuals like Samuel Adams, cousin of John Adams, asserted that British power supported an unjust political and social structure within the colonies, and they began to advocate an end to British rule.[3]

Organizing resistance to the British authorities, however, required widespread support. Collective action, as we saw in the previous chapter, may emerge *spontaneously* in certain circumstances, but the colonists' campaign against the British imperial power in late-eighteenth-century America was a series of en-

[2]George B. Tindall and David E. Shi, *America: A Narrative History*, 6th ed. (New York: Norton, 2004), p. 199.

[3]For a discussion of events leading up to the Revolution, see Charles M. Andrews, *The Colonial Background of the American Revolution: Four Essays in American Colonial History* (New Haven, CT: Yale University Press, 1924).

counters, maneuvers, and, ultimately, confrontations that required planning, coalition building, bargaining, compromising, and coordinating—all elements of the give-and-take of politics. Conflicts among the colonists had to be solved by bargaining, persuasion, and even force. Cooperation needed cultivation and encouragement. Leadership was clearly a necessary ingredient.

Collective-Action Principle

The colonists required strong leaders to resolve differences and to organize resistance to British authority.

Political Strife and the Radicalizing of the Colonists

The political strife within the colonies was the background for the events of 1773–74. In 1773, the British government granted the politically powerful East India Company a monopoly on the export of tea from Britain, eliminating a lucrative form of trade for colonial merchants. To add to the injury, the East India Company sought to sell the tea directly in the colonies instead of working through the colonial merchants. Tea was an extremely important commodity in the 1770s, and these British actions posed a mortal threat to the New England merchants. The merchants once again called on their radical adversaries for support. The most dramatic result was the Boston Tea Party of 1773, led by Samuel Adams.

This event was of decisive importance in American history. The merchants had hoped to force the British government to rescind the Tea Act, but they did not support any demands beyond this one. They certainly did not seek independence from Britain. Samuel Adams and the other radicals, however, hoped to provoke the British government to take actions that would alienate its colonial supporters and pave the way for a rebellion. This was precisely the purpose of the Boston Tea Party, and it succeeded. By dumping the East India Company's tea into Boston Harbor, Adams and his followers goaded the British into enacting a number of harsh reprisals. Within five months after the incident in Boston, the House of Commons passed a series of acts that closed the port of Boston to commerce, changed the provincial government of Massachusetts, provided for the removal of accused persons to England for trial, and, most important, restricted movement to the West—further alienating the southern planters who depended on access to new western lands. These acts of retaliation confirmed the worst criticisms of England and helped radicalize Americans.

The choice of this course of action by English politicians looks puzzling in retrospect, but at the time it appeared reasonable to those who prevailed in Parliament that a show of force was required. The toleration of lawlessness and the making of concessions, they felt, would only egg on the more radical elements in the colonies to take further liberties and demand further concessions. The English, in effect, drew a line in the sand. Their repressive reactions served as a clear point around which dissatisfied colonists could rally. Radicals like Samuel Adams had been agitating for more violent measures to deal with England. But ultimately they needed Britain's political repression to create widespread support for independence.

Thus the Boston Tea Party set into motion a cycle of provocation and retaliation that in 1774 resulted in the convening of the First Continental Congress—

an assembly consisting of delegates from all parts of the colonies—that called for a total boycott of British goods and, under the prodding of the radicals, began to consider the possibility of independence from British rule. The eventual result was the Declaration of Independence.

The Declaration of Independence

In 1776, the Second Continental Congress appointed a committee consisting of Thomas Jefferson of Virginia, Benjamin Franklin of Pennsylvania, Roger Sherman of Connecticut, John Adams of Massachusetts, and Robert Livingston of New York to draft a statement of American independence from British rule. The Declaration of Independence, written by Jefferson and adopted by the Second Continental Congress, was an extraordinary document both in philosophical and political terms. Philosophically, the Declaration was remarkable for its assertion that certain rights, called "unalienable rights"—including life, liberty, and the pursuit of happiness—could not be abridged by governments. In the world of 1776, a world in which some kings still claimed to rule by divine right, this was a dramatic statement. Politically, the Declaration was remarkable because, despite the differences of interest that divided the colonists along economic, regional, and philosophical lines, the Declaration identified and focused on problems, grievances, aspirations, and principles that might unify the various colonial groups. The Declaration was an attempt to identify and articulate a history and set of principles that might help to forge national unity.[4]

The Articles of Confederation

Articles of Confederation and Perpetual Union America's first written constitution. Adopted by the Continental Congress in 1777, the Articles of Confederation and Perpetual Union was the formal basis for America's national government until 1789, when it was supplanted by the Constitution.

Having declared their independence, the colonies needed to establish a governmental structure. In November of 1777, the Continental Congress adopted the *Articles of Confederation and Perpetual Union*—the United States' first written constitution. Although it was not ratified by all the states until 1781, it was the country's operative constitution for almost twelve years, until March 1789.

The Articles of Confederation was a constitution concerned primarily with limiting the powers of the central government. The central government, first of all, was based entirely in Congress. Because it was not intended to be a powerful government, it was given no executive branch. Execution of its laws was to be left to the individual states. Second, Congress had little power. Its members were not much more than delegates or messengers from the state legislatures. They were chosen by the state legislatures, their salaries were paid out of the state treasuries, and they were subject to immediate recall by state authorities. In addition, each state, regardless of its size, had only a single vote.

Congress was given the power to declare war and make peace, to make treaties and alliances, to coin or borrow money, and to regulate trade with Native

[4]See Carl L. Becker, *The Declaration of Independence: A Study in the History of Political Ideas* (New York: Vintage, 1942).

Americans. It could also appoint the senior officers of the United States Army. But it could not levy taxes or regulate commerce among the states. Moreover, the army officers it appointed had no army to serve in because the nation's armed forces were composed of the state militias. Probably the most unfortunate part of the Articles of Confederation was that the central government could not prevent one state from discriminating against other states in the quest for foreign commerce.

In brief, the relationship between Congress and the states under the Articles of Confederation was much like the contemporary relationship between the United Nations and its member states, a relationship in which virtually all governmental powers are retained by the states. It was properly called a "confederation" because, as provided under Article II, "each state retains its sovereignty, freedom, and independence, and every power, jurisdiction, and right, which is not by this Confederation expressly delegated to the United States, in Congress assembled." Not only was there no executive but there was also no judicial authority and no other means of enforcing Congress's will. If there were to be any enforcement at all, it would be done for Congress by the states.[5]

THE SECOND FOUNDING: FROM COMPROMISE TO CONSTITUTION

The Declaration of Independence and the Articles of Confederation were not sufficient to hold the nation together as an independent and effective nation-state. From almost the moment of armistice with the British in 1783, moves were afoot to reform and strengthen the Articles of Confederation.

International Standing and Balance of Power

There was a special concern for the country's international position. Competition among the states for foreign commerce allowed the European powers to play the states against each other, which created confusion on both sides of the Atlantic. At one point during the winter of 1786–87, John Adams of Massachusetts, a leader in the independence struggle, was sent to negotiate a new treaty with the British, one that would cover disputes left over from the war. The British government responded that, because the United States under the Articles of Confederation was unable to enforce existing treaties, it would negotiate with each of the thirteen states separately.

At the same time, well-to-do Americans—in particular the New England merchants and southern planters—were troubled by the influence that "radical" forces exercised in the Continental Congress and in the governments of several of the states. The colonists' victory in the Revolutionary War not only had meant

---

[5]See Merrill Jensen, *The Articles of Confederation* (Madison: University of Wisconsin Press, 1963).

the end of British rule but also had significantly changed the balance of political power within the new states. As a result of the Revolution, one key segment of the colonial elite—the royal land, office, and patent holders—was stripped of its economic and political privileges. In fact, many of these individuals, along with tens of thousands of other colonists who considered themselves loyal British subjects, left for Canada after the British surrender. And while the pre-revolutionary elite was weakened, the pre-revolutionary radicals were now better organized than ever before and were the controlling forces in such states as Pennsylvania and Rhode Island, where they pursued economic and political policies that struck terror into the hearts of the pre-revolutionary political establishment. In Rhode Island, for example, between 1783 and 1785, a legislature dominated by representatives of small farmers, artisans, and shopkeepers had instituted economic policies, including drastic currency inflation, that frightened businessmen and property owners throughout the country. Of course, the central government under the Articles of Confederation was powerless to intervene.

Institution Principle

Institutional arrangements matter, but there is no guarantee that they will be perfect, as the Articles of Confederation make apparent.

The Annapolis Convention

The continuation of international weakness and domestic economic turmoil led many Americans to consider whether their newly adopted form of government might not already require revision. Institutional arrangements are experiments in governance, and they don't always work out. Nearly a decade under the Articles had made amply clear the flaws it contained. In the fall of 1786, many state leaders accepted an invitation from the Virginia legislature for a conference of representatives of all the states. Delegates from five states actually attended. This conference, held in Annapolis, Maryland, was the first step toward the second founding. The one positive thing that came out of the Annapolis Convention was a carefully worded resolution calling on Congress to send commissioners to Philadelphia at a later time "to devise such further provisions as shall appear to them necessary to render the Constitution of the Federal Government adequate to the exigencies of the Union."[6] This resolution was drafted by Alexander Hamilton, a thirty-four-year-old New York lawyer who had played a significant role in the Revolution as George Washington's secretary and who would play a still more significant role in framing the Constitution and forming the new government in the 1790s. But the resolution did not necessarily imply any desire to do more than improve and reform the Articles of Confederation.

Shays's Rebellion

It is possible that the Constitutional Convention of 1787 in Philadelphia would never have taken place at all except for a single event that occurred during the winter after the Annapolis Convention: Shays's Rebellion. Like the Boston Tea

[6]Reported in Samuel Eliot Morrison, Henry Steele Commager, and William E. Leuchtenburg, *The Growth of the American Republic*, 6th ed., vol. 1 (New York: Oxford University Press, 1969), p. 244.

Party, this was a focal event. It concentrated attention, coordinated beliefs, produced widespread fear and apprehension, and thus convinced waverers that "something was broke and needed fixing." In short, it provided politicians who had long been convinced that the Articles were flawed and insufficient with just the ammunition they needed to persuade a much broader public of these facts.[7]

Daniel Shays, a former army captain, led a mob of farmers in a rebellion against the government of Massachusetts. The purpose of the rebellion was to prevent foreclosures on their debt-ridden land by keeping the county courts of western Massachusetts from sitting until after the next election. The state militia dispersed the mob, but for several days, Shays and his followers terrified the state government by attempting to capture the federal arsenal at Springfield, provoking an appeal to Congress to help restore order. Within a few days, the state government regained control and captured fourteen of the rebels (all were eventually pardoned). In 1787, a newly elected Massachusetts legislature granted some of the farmers' demands.

Although the incident ended peacefully, its effects lingered and spread. Washington summed it up: "I am mortified beyond expression that in the moment of our acknowledged independence we should by our conduct verify the predictions of our transatlantic foe, and render ourselves ridiculous and contemptible in the eyes of all Europe."[8]

Congress under the Confederation had been unable to act decisively in a time of crisis. This provided critics of the Articles of Confederation with precisely the evidence they needed to push Hamilton's Annapolis resolution through the Congress. Thus the states were asked to send representatives to Philadelphia to discuss constitutional revision. Delegates were eventually sent by every state except Rhode Island.

History Principle

Shays's Rebellion focused attention on the flaws of the Articles of Confederation, leading to the Constitutional Convention.

The Constitutional Convention

Twenty-nine of a total of seventy-three delegates selected by the state governments convened in Philadelphia in May 1787, with political strife, international embarrassment, national weakness, and local rebellion fixed in their minds. Recognizing that these issues were symptoms of fundamental flaws in the Articles of Confederation, the delegates soon abandoned the plan to revise the Articles and committed themselves to a second founding—a second, and ultimately successful, attempt to create a legitimate and effective national system. This effort occupied the convention for the next five months.

A Marriage of Interest and Principle For years, scholars have disagreed about the motives of the founders in Philadelphia. Among the most controversial views of the framers' motives is the "economic" interpretation put forward by historian

---

[7]For an easy-to-read argument that supports this view, see Keith L. Dougherty, *Collective Action under the Articles of Confederation* (New York: Cambridge University Press, 2001).

[8]Morrison et al., *The Growth of the American Republic*, p. 242.

Charles Beard and his disciples.[9] According to Beard's account, America's founders were a collection of securities speculators and property owners whose only aim was personal enrichment. From this perspective, the Constitution's lofty principles were little more than sophisticated masks behind which the most venal interests sought to enrich themselves.

Contrary to Beard's approach is the view that the framers of the Constitution *were* concerned with philosophical and ethical principles. Indeed, the framers sought to devise a system of government consistent with the dominant philosophical and moral principles of the day. But, in fact, these two views belong together; the founders' interests were reinforced by their principles. The convention that drafted the American Constitution was chiefly organized by the New England merchants and southern planters. Though the delegates representing these groups did not all hope to profit personally from an increase in the value of their securities, as Beard would have it, they did hope to benefit in the broadest political and economic sense by breaking the power of their radical foes and establishing a system of government more compatible with their long-term economic and political interests. Thus the framers sought to create a new government capable of promoting commerce and protecting property from radical state legislatures. They also sought to liberate the national government from the power of individual states and their sometimes venal and corrupt local politicians. At the same time, they hoped to fashion a government less susceptible than the existing state and national regimes to populist forces hostile to the interests of the commercial and propertied classes.

The Great Compromise   The proponents of a new government fired their opening shot on May 29, 1787, when Edmund Randolph of Virginia offered a resolution that proposed corrections and enlargements in the Articles of Confederation. The proposal, which showed the strong influence of James Madison, was not a simple motion. It provided for virtually every aspect of a new government. Randolph later admitted it was intended to be an alternative draft constitution, and it did in fact serve as the framework for what ultimately became the Constitution. (There is no verbatim record of the debates, but Madison was present during virtually all of the deliberations and kept full notes on them.)[10]

This proposal, known as the "Virginia Plan," provided for a system of representation in the national legislature based on the population of each state or the proportion of each state's revenue contribution, or both. (Randolph also proposed a second branch of the legislature, but it was to be elected by the members of the first branch.) Because the states varied enormously in size and wealth, the Virginia Plan was thought to be heavily biased in favor of the large states.

---

[9]Charles A. Beard, *An Economic Interpretation of the Constitution of the United States* (New York: Macmillan, 1913).

[10]Madison's notes along with the somewhat less complete records kept by several other participants in the convention are available in a four-volume set. See Max Farrand, ed., *The Records of the Federal Convention of 1787*, rev. ed., 4 vols. (New Haven, CT: Yale University Press, 1966).

While the convention was debating the Virginia Plan, additional delegates were arriving in Philadelphia and were beginning to mount opposition to it. Their resolution, introduced by William Paterson of New Jersey and known as the "New Jersey Plan," did not oppose the Virginia Plan point for point. Instead, it concentrated on specific weaknesses in the Articles of Confederation, in the spirit of revision rather than radical replacement of that document. Supporters of the New Jersey Plan did not seriously question the convention's commitment to replacing the Articles. But their opposition to the Virginia Plan's scheme of representation was sufficient to send its proposals back to committee for re-working into a common document. In particular, delegates from the less populous states, which included Delaware, New Jersey, Connecticut, and New York, asserted that the more populous states, such as Virginia, Pennsylvania, North Carolina, Massachusetts, and Georgia, would dominate the new government if representation were to be determined by population. The smaller states argued that each state should be equally represented in the new regime regardless of its population.

The issue of representation was one that threatened to wreck the entire constitutional enterprise. Delegates conferred, factions maneuvered, and tempers flared. James Wilson of Pennsylvania told the small-state delegates that if they wanted to disrupt the union they should go ahead. The separation could, he said, "never happen on better grounds." Small-state delegates were equally blunt. Gunning Bedford of Delaware declared that the small states might look elsewhere for friends if they were forced. "The large states," he said, "dare not dissolve the confederation. If they do the small ones will find some foreign ally of more honor and good faith, who will take them by the hand and do them justice." These sentiments were widely shared. The union, as Oliver Ellsworth of Connecticut put it, was "on the verge of dissolution, scarcely held together by the strength of a hair."

The outcome of this debate was the Connecticut Compromise, also known as the *Great Compromise.* Under the terms of this compromise, in the first branch of Congress—the House of Representatives—the representatives would be apportioned according to the number of inhabitants in each state. This, of course, was what delegates from the large states had sought. But in the second branch—the Senate—each state would have an equal vote regardless of its size; this was to deal with the concerns of the small states. This compromise was not immediately satisfactory to all the delegates. Indeed, two of the most vocal members of the small-state faction, John Lansing and Robert Yates of New York, were so incensed by the concession that their colleagues had made to the large-state forces that they stormed out of the convention. In the end, however, both sets of forces preferred compromise to the breakup of the union, and the plan was accepted.

Great Compromise Agreement reached at the Constitutional Convention of 1787 that gave each state an equal number of senators regardless of its population but linked representation in the House of Representatives to population.

The Question of Slavery: The Three-fifths Compromise

The story so far is too neat, too easy, and too anticlimactic. If it were left here, it would only contribute to American mythology. After all, the notion of a bicameral (two-chambered) legislature was very much in the air in 1787. Some of the states had had this for years. The Philadelphia delegates might well have gone straight to the adoption of two chambers based on two different principles of representation even without the dramatic interplay of conflict and compromise. But a far more fundamental issue had to be confronted before the Great Compromise could take place: the issue of slavery.

Many of the conflicts that emerged during the Constitutional Convention were reflections of the fundamental differences between the slave and the nonslave states—differences that pitted the southern planters and New England merchants against one another. This was the first premonition of a conflict that was almost to destroy the Republic in later years. In the midst of debate over large versus small states, Madison observed:

> The great danger to our general government is the great southern and northern interests of the continent, being opposed to each other. Look to the votes in Congress, and most of them stand divided by the geography of the country, not according to the size of the states.[11]

Over 90 percent of all slaves resided in five states—Georgia, Maryland, North Carolina, South Carolina, and Virginia—where they accounted for 30 percent of the total population. In some places, slaves outnumbered nonslaves by as much as 10 to 1. If the Constitution were to embody any principle of national supremacy, some basic decisions would have to be made about the place of slavery in the general scheme. Madison hit on this point on several occasions as different aspects of the Constitution were being discussed. For example, he observed:

> It seemed now to be pretty well understood that the real difference of interests lay, not between the large and small but between the northern and southern states. The institution of slavery and its consequences formed the line of discrimination. There were five states on the South, eight on the northern side of this line. Should a proportional representation take place it was true, the northern side would still outnumber the other: but not in the same degree, at this time; and every day would tend towards an equilibrium.[12]

Three-fifths Compromise
Agreement reached at the Constitutional Convention of 1787 stipulating that for purposes of the apportionment of congressional seats, every slave would be counted as three fifths of a person.

Northerners and southerners eventually reached agreement through the ***Three-fifths Compromise.*** The seats in the House of Representatives would be apportioned according to a "population" in which five slaves would count as three people. The slaves would not be allowed to vote, of course, but the number of representatives would be apportioned accordingly. This arrangement was supported by the slave states, which obviously included some of the biggest and some of the smallest states at that time. It was also accepted by many delegates from nonslave states who strongly supported the principle of property representation, whether that property was expressed in slaves or in land, money, or stocks. The concern exhibited by most

[11]Ibid., I, p. 476.
[12]Ibid., II, p. 10.

delegates was over how much slaves would count toward a state's representation rather than whether the institution of slavery would continue. The Three-fifths Compromise, in the words of political scientist Donald Robinson, "gave Constitutional sanction to the fact that the United States was composed of some persons who were 'free' and others who were not, and it established the principle, new in republican theory, that a man who lives among slaves had a greater share in the election of representatives than the man who did not. Although the Three-fifths Compromise acknowledged slavery and rewarded slave owners, nonetheless, it probably kept the South from unanimously rejecting the Constitution."[13]

The issue of slavery was the most difficult one faced by the framers, and it nearly destroyed the Union. Although some delegates believed slavery to be morally wrong, an evil and oppressive institution that made a mockery of the ideals and values espoused in the Constitution, morality was not the issue that caused the framers to support or oppose the Three-fifths Compromise. Whatever they thought of the institution of slavery, most delegates from the northern states opposed counting slaves in the distribution of congressional seats. Wilson of Pennsylvania, for example, argued that if slaves were citizens they should be treated and counted like other citizens. If on the other hand, they were property, then why should not other forms of property be counted toward the apportionment of Congress? But southern delegates made it clear that if the northerners refused to give in, they would never agree to the new government. William R. Davie of North Carolina heatedly said that it was time "to speak out." He asserted that the people of North Carolina would never enter the Union if slaves were not counted as part of the basis for representation. Without such agreement, he asserted ominously, "the business was at an end." Even southerners like Edmund Randolph of Virginia, who conceded that slavery was immoral, insisted on including slaves in the allocation of congressional seats. This conflict between the southern and northern delegates was so divisive that many came to question the possibility of creating and maintaining a union of the two. Pierce Butler of South Carolina declared that the North and South were as different as Russia and Turkey. Eventually, the North and South compromised on the issue of slavery and representation. Indeed, northerners even agreed to permit a continuation of the odious slave trade to keep the South in the Union. But, in due course, Butler proved to be correct, and a bloody war was fought when the disparate interests of the North and South could no longer be reconciled.

Collective-Action Principle
The framers preferred compromise to the breakup of the Union and thus accepted the Great Compromise and the Three-fifths Compromise.

THE CONSTITUTION

The political significance of the Great Compromise and Three-fifths Compromise was to reinforce the unity of the mercantile and planter forces that sought to create a new government. The Great Compromise reassured those who feared that the importance of their own local or regional influence would be reduced

---

[13]Donald L. Robinson, *Slavery in the Structure of American Politics, 1765–1820* (New York: Harcourt Brace Jovanovich, 1971), p. 201.

Were the Framers Rational Actors?

How can we use the principles of politics to interpret events that occurred centuries ago? The strategic decision making at the American Constitutional Convention has been a fertile area of study.

Many of the basic ingredients for a strategic politics analysis are present. The historical record is detailed and seemingly very accurate. The entire Constitutional Convention took place in secret, and the delegates took pains to ensure that the media and mass public were not aware of the decisions being made, the alternatives that were rejected, or the process that was being used.

Collective-Action Principle

Small groups often make collective action easier.

In line with the collective action principle, keeping the group small and homogeneous increased the chance of successful collective action. Participation was restricted to those delegates who were directly appointed by the state legislatures. Keeping the proceedings closed reduced the likelihood that outside parties could influence the discussion or that new issues could be introduced that would complicate the process.

At the same time, the convention allowed for extensive internal discussion. Most participants knew the preferences of the other participants. In the language of rational choice, the setting was close to "full information." When every player knows the goals and options of every other player, it is far easier to predict everyone's behavior.[1]

Rationality Principle

Many believe that the framers' self interests, more than their high moral values, influenced the Constitution.

In a famous article and book, historian Charles Beard advocated the view of the founders as strategic actors by making the provocative argument that the Constitution is a document written by wealthy elites to preserve their own economic and political power.[2] Beard focused on the secretive and elite-centered nature of the convention and the limited franchise found throughout the process. In Beard's analysis, the Constitution is not the grand design of political philosophers but the product of hard-nosed political bargaining and self-interests. An infamous example of this is the "three-fifths" rule for counting slaves. This was the result of a bargain between pro-slavery, anti-tariff southerners and northerners who were opposed to slavery yet wanted to retain protective tariffs.

Institution Principle

Morris manipulated the rules and procedures of the debate to achieve his desired outcome.

William Riker similarly shows how delegates, such as Gouverneur Morris, from Pennsylvania, manipulated the procedures at the convention to obtain his desired outcome. According to Riker, Morris and a few other Pennsylvanians were the only opponents of the Virginia Plan, whereby the executive would be elected by the national legislature (the two houses of Congress). If adopted, the Virginia Plan would have rendered states wholly subservient to the national government because the plan also allowed the national legislature to abrogate state laws.[3] In essence, Morris was able to change the order in which various provisions of the Virginia Plan were considered so that it became apparent that endorsing the Virginia Plan was tantamount to endorsing a lifetime presidency.[4]

Still, this interpretation of the founding remains controversial. Americans revere the founders as brilliant philosophers. Many object to a portrait of them as self-interested. Historian Robert Brown disputes Beard's account of the convention.[5] What Beard fails to appreciate, Brown argues, is that American society as a whole was in favor of the democratic changes enshrined in the Constitution. Americans did not perceive the Constitution as an elite vehicle being foisted on them. Brown adds that agrarian, commercial, and mercantile interests felt that they were well represented by the delegates.

Regardless of whether you believe that the founders were strategic actors or not, rational choice can help you understand how the convention proceeded the way it did. Keep the group small, keep control of rules and procedures, and you can readily control the outcome. Even when actors are motivated by altruistic concerns, institutional rules and procedures can be used to obtain a preferred outcome.

[1]These types of situations are rare in everyday life. Substantial research in political science and economics has focused on how individuals make do with "limited" information.

[2]Charles A. Beard, *An Economic Interpretation of the Constitution of the United States* (New York: Macmillan, 1913).

[3]This was precisely the goal of the supporters of the Virginia Plan. They believed that state legislatures were incompetent and that states should be governed by a national elite.

[4]The specifics are laid out in more detail in Chapter 4 of William H. Riker's *The Art of Political Manipulation* (New Haven, CT: Yale University Press, 1986).

[5]Robert E. Brown, *Charles Beard and the Constitution: A Critical Analysis of "An Economic Interpretation of the Constitution"* (New York: Norton, 1965).

by the new governmental framework. The Three-fifths Compromise temporarily defused the rivalry between the merchants and planters. Their unity secured, members of the alliance supporting the establishment of a new government moved to fashion a constitutional framework consistent with their economic and political interests.

In particular, the framers sought a new government that, first, would be strong enough to promote commerce and protect property from radical state legislatures such as Rhode Island's. This became the constitutional basis for national control over commerce and finance, as well as the establishment of national judicial supremacy and the effort to construct a strong presidency. Second, the framers sought to prevent what they saw as the threat posed by the "excessive democracy" of the state and national governments under the Articles of Confederation. This led to such constitutional principles as *bicameralism* (division of the Congress into two chambers), checks and balances, staggered terms in office, and indirect election (selection of the president by an electoral college rather than by voters directly). Third, the framers, lacking the power to force the states or the public at large to accept the new form of government, sought to

bicameralism
The division of a legislative assembly into two chambers or houses.

identify principles that would help secure support. This became the basis of the constitutional provision for direct popular election of representatives and, subsequently, for the addition of the Bill of Rights to the Constitution. Finally, the framers wanted to be certain that the government they created did not use its power to pose even more of a threat to its citizens' liberties and property rights than did the radical state legislatures they feared and despised. To prevent the new government from abusing its power, the framers incorporated principles such as the separation of powers and federalism into the Constitution.

The framers provided us with a grand lesson in instrumental behavior. They came to Philadelphia united by a common distaste for government under the Articles and animated by the agitation following Shays's Rebellion. They didn't always agree on what it was they disliked about the Articles. They certainly didn't agree on how to proceed—hence the necessity for the historic compromises we have just described. But they did believe that the fostering of commerce and the protection of property could better be served by an alternative set of institutional arrangements than that of the Articles. They agreed that the institutional arrangements of government mattered for their lives and those of their fellow citizens. They believed that both too much democracy and too much governmental power were threats to the common good, and they felt compelled to find instruments and principles that weighed against these. Let us assess the major provisions of the Constitution's seven articles to see how each relates to these objectives.

 Rationality Principle

The framers of the Constitution were guided by principles, but they also had interests.

 Institution Principle

The constitutional framework promoted commerce, protected property, prevented "excessive democracy," and limited the power of the national government.

The Legislative Branch

The first seven sections of Article I of the Constitution provided for a Congress consisting of two chambers—a House of Representatives and a Senate. Members of the House of Representatives were given two-year terms in office and were to be elected directly by the people. Members of the Senate were to be appointed by the state legislatures (this was changed in 1913 by the Seventeenth Amendment, which instituted direct election of senators) for six-year terms. These terms, moreover, were staggered so that the appointments of one-third of the senators would expire every two years. The Constitution assigned somewhat different tasks to the House and Senate. Though the approval of each body was required for the enactment of a law, the Senate alone was given the power to ratify treaties and approve presidential appointments. The House, on the other hand, was given the sole power to originate revenue bills.

The character of the legislative branch was directly related to the framers' major goals. The House of Representatives was designed to be directly responsible to the people to encourage popular consent for the new Constitution and to help enhance the power of the new government. At the same time, to guard against "excessive democracy," the power of the House of Representatives was checked by the Senate, whose members were to be appointed for long terms rather than be elected directly by the people. The purpose of this provision, according to Alexander Hamilton, was to avoid "an unqualified complaisance to every sudden breeze of passion, or to every transient impulse which the people may receive."[14] Staggered terms of service in the Senate, moreover, were intended to make that body even more resistant to popular pressure. Because only one third of the senators would be selected at any given time, the composition of the institution would be protected from changes in popular preferences transmitted by the state legislatures. This would prevent what James Madison called "mutability in the public councils arising from a rapid succession of new members."[15] Thus the structure of the legislative branch was designed to contribute to governmental power, to promote popular consent for the new government, and at the same time to place limits on the popular political currents that many of the framers saw as a radical threat to the economic and social order.

The issues of power and consent were important throughout the Constitution. Section 8 of Article I specifically listed the powers of Congress, which include the authority to collect taxes, to borrow money, to regulate commerce, to declare war, and to maintain an army and navy. By granting it these powers, the framers indicated clearly that they intended the new government to be far more influential than its predecessor. At the same time, by defining the new government's most important powers as belonging to Congress, the framers sought to promote popular acceptance of this critical change by reassuring citizens that their views would be fully represented whenever the government exercised its new powers.

As a further guarantee to the people that the new government would pose no threat to them, the Constitution implied that any powers not listed were not granted at all. This is the doctrine of **expressed power.** The Constitution grants only those powers specifically *expressed* in its text. But the framers intended to create an active and powerful government, and so they included the **necessary and proper clause,** sometimes known as the elastic clause, which signified that the enumerated powers were meant to be a source of strength to the national government, not a limitation on it. Each power could be used with the utmost vigor, but no new powers could be seized on by the national government without a constitutional amendment. In the absence of such an amendment, any power not enumerated was conceived to be "reserved" to the states (or the people).

The Executive Branch

The Constitution provided for the establishment of the presidency in Article II. As Alexander Hamilton commented, the presidential article aimed toward "energy in the Executive." It did so in an effort to overcome the natural stalemate that was built into the bicameral legislature as well as into the separation of powers among the legislative, executive, and judicial branches. The Constitution afforded the president a measure of independence from the people and from the other branches of government—particularly the Congress.

expressed power
The notion that the Constitution grants to the federal government only those powers specifically named in its text.

necessary and proper clause
Article I, Section 8, of the Constitution, which enumerates the powers of Congress and provides Congress with the authority to make all laws "necessary and proper" to carry them out; also referred to as the "elastic clause."

[14]E. M. Earle, ed., *The Federalist* (New York: Modern Library, 1937), No. 71.
[15]Ibid., No. 62.

In line with the framers' goal of increased power to the national government, the president was granted the unconditional power to accept ambassadors from other countries; this amounted to the power to "recognize" other countries. He was also given the power to negotiate treaties, although their acceptance required the approval of the Senate. The president was given the unconditional right to grant reprieves and pardons, except in cases of impeachment. And he was provided with the power to appoint major departmental personnel, to convene Congress in special session, and to veto congressional enactments. (The veto power is formidable, but it is not absolute because Congress can override it by a two-thirds vote.)

The framers hoped to create a presidency that would make the federal government rather than the states the agency capable of timely and decisive action to deal with public issues and problems. This was the meaning of the "energy" that Hamilton hoped to impart to the executive branch.[16] At the same time, however, the framers sought to help the president withstand (excessively) democratic pressures by making him subject to indirect rather than direct election (through his selection by a separate electoral college). The extent to which the framers' hopes were actually realized is the topic of Chapter 6.

The Judicial Branch

In establishing the judicial branch in Article III, the Constitution reflected the framers' preoccupations with nationalizing governmental power and checking radical democratic impulses, while guarding against potential interference with liberty and property from the new national government itself.

Under the provisions of Article III, the framers created a court that was to be literally a supreme court of the United States and not merely the highest court of the national government. The most important expression of this intention was granting the Supreme Court the power to resolve any conflicts that might emerge between federal and state laws. In particular, the Supreme Court was given the right to determine whether a power was exclusive to the federal government, concurrent with the states, or exclusive to the states. The significance of this was noted by Justice Oliver Wendell Holmes, who observed:

> I do not think the United States would come to an end if we lost our power to declare an act of Congress void. I do think the union would be imperilled if we could not make that declaration as to the laws of the several states.[17]

In addition, the Supreme Court was assigned jurisdiction over controversies between citizens of different states. The long-term significance of this was that as the country developed a national economy, it came to rely increasingly on the federal judiciary, rather than on the state courts, for resolution of disputes.

[16]Ibid., No. 70.
[17]Oliver Wendell Holmes, *Collected Legal Papers* (New York: Harcourt Brace, 1920), pp. 295–96.

Judges were given lifetime appointments to protect them from popular politics and from interference by the other branches. This, however, did not mean that the judiciary would actually remain totally impartial to political considerations or to the other branches, for the president was to appoint the judges and the Senate to approve the appointments. Congress would also have the power to create inferior (lower) courts, to change the jurisdiction of the federal courts, to add or subtract federal judges, even to change the size of the Supreme Court.

No direct mention is made in the Constitution of *judicial review*—the power of the courts to render the final decision when there is a conflict of interpretation of the Constitution or of laws between the courts and Congress, the courts and the executive branch, or the courts and the states. Scholars generally feel that judicial review is implicit in the very existence of a written Constitution and in the power given directly to the federal courts over "all Cases . . . arising under this Constitution, the Laws of the United States, and Treaties made, or which shall be made, under their Authority" (Article III, Section 2). The Supreme Court eventually assumed the power of judicial review. Its assumption of this power, as we shall see in Chapter 8, was not based on the Constitution itself but on the politics of later decades and the membership of the Court.

judicial review
Power of the courts to declare actions of the legislative and executive branches invalid or unconstitutional. The Supreme Court asserted this power in *Marbury v. Madison*.

National Unity and Power

Various provisions in the Constitution addressed the framers' concern with national unity and power, including Article IV's provisions for comity (reciprocity) among states and among citizens of all states.

Each state was prohibited from discriminating against the citizens of other states in favor of its own citizens, with the Supreme Court charged with deciding in each case whether a state had discriminated against goods or people from another state. The Constitution restricted the power of the states in favor of ensuring enough power to the national government to give the country a free-flowing national economy.

The framers' concern with national supremacy was also expressed in Article VI, in the *supremacy clause,* which provided that national laws and treaties "shall be the supreme Law of the Land." This meant that all laws made under the "Authority of the United States" would be superior to all laws adopted by any state or any other subdivision, and the states would be expected to respect all treaties made under that authority. This was a direct effort to keep the states from dealing separately with foreign nations or businesses. The supremacy clause also bound the officials of all state and local as well as federal governments to take an oath of office to support the national Constitution. This meant that every action taken by the U.S. Congress would have to be applied within each state as though the action were in fact state law.

supremacy clause
Article VI of the Constitution, which states that all laws passed by the national government and all treaties are the supreme laws of the land and superior to all laws adopted by any state or any subdivision.

Amending the Constitution

The Constitution established procedures for its own revision in Article V. Its provisions are so difficult that Americans have availed themselves of the amending process only seventeen times since 1791, when the first ten amendments were adopted. Many other amendments have been proposed in Congress, but fewer than forty of them have even come close to fulfilling the Constitution's requirement of a two-thirds vote in Congress, and only a fraction have gotten anywhere near adoption by three fourths of the states. The Constitution could also be amended by a constitutional convention. Occasionally, proponents of particular measures, such as a balanced-budget amendment, have called for a constitutional convention to consider their proposals. Whatever the purpose for which it was called, however, such a convention would presumably have the authority to revise America's entire system of government.

It should be noted that any body of rules, including a national constitution, must balance the need to respond flexibly to changes, on the one hand, with the caution not to be too flexible, on the other. An inflexible body of rules is one that cannot accommodate major change. It risks being rebelled against, a circumstance in which the slate is wiped clean and new rules designed, or ignored altogether. Too much flexibility, however, is disastrous. It invites those who lose in normal everyday politics to replay battles at the constitutional level. If institutional change is too easy to accomplish, the stability of the political system becomes threatened.

Ratifying the Constitution

The rules for ratification of the Constitution of 1787 were set forth in Article VII of the Constitution. This provision actually violated the amendment provisions of the Articles of Confederation. For one thing, it adopted a nine-state rule in place of the unanimity required by the Articles of Confederation. For another, it provided that ratification would occur in special state conventions called for that purpose rather than in the state legislatures. All the states except Rhode Island eventually did set up state conventions to ratify the Constitution.

Constitutional Limits on the National Government's Power

separation of powers The division of governmental power among several institutions that must cooperate in decision making.

federalism System of government in which a constitution divides power between a central government and regional governments.

Bill of Rights The first ten amendments to the U.S. Constitution, ratified in 1791. They ensure certain rights and liberties to the people.

As we have indicated, although the framers sought to create a powerful national government, they also wanted to guard against possible misuse of that power. To that end, the framers incorporated two key principles into the Constitution—the *separation of powers* and *federalism* (see Chapter 3). A third set of limitations, in the form of the *Bill of Rights,* was added to the Constitution to help secure its ratification when opponents of the document charged that it paid insufficient attention to citizens' rights.

The Separation of Powers   No principle of politics was more widely shared at the time of the 1787 founding than the principle that power must be used to balance power. The French political theorist Baron de Montesquieu (1689–1755) believed that this balance was an indispensable defense against tyranny, and his writings, especially his major work, *The Spirit of the Laws,* "were taken as political

FIGURE 2.1

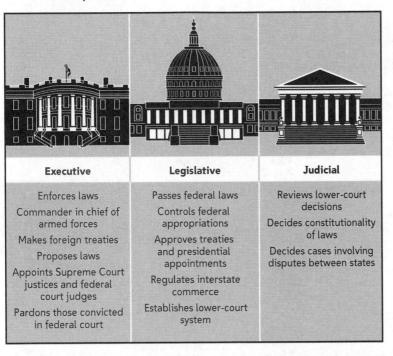

The Separation of Powers

Executive	Legislative	Judicial
Enforces laws	Passes federal laws	Reviews lower-court decisions
Commander in chief of armed forces	Controls federal appropriations	Decides constitutionality of laws
Makes foreign treaties	Approves treaties and presidential appointments	Decides cases involving disputes between states
Proposes laws		
Appoints Supreme Court justices and federal court judges	Regulates interstate commerce	
Pardons those convicted in federal court	Establishes lower-court system	

gospel" at the Philadelphia convention.[18] The principle of the separation of powers is nowhere to be found explicitly in the Constitution, but it is clearly built on Articles I, II, and III, which provide for the following:

1. Three separate and distinct branches of government (Figure 2.1).
2. Different methods of selecting the top personnel, so that each branch is responsible to a different constituency. This is supposed to produce a "mixed regime," in which the personnel of each department will develop different interests and outlooks on how to govern, and different groups in society will be ensured some access to governmental decision making.

[18]Max Farrand, *The Framing of the Constitution of the United States* (New Haven, CT: Yale University Press, 1962), p. 49.

FIGURE 2.2

Checks and Balances

LEGISLATIVE

Executive over Legislative
Can veto acts of Congress
Can call Congress into a special session
Carries out, and thereby interprets, laws passed by Congress
Vice president casts tie-breaking vote in the Senate

Legislative over Judicial
Can change size of federal court system and the number of Supreme Court justices
Can propose constitutional amendments
Can reject Supreme Court nominees
Can impeach and remove federal judges

Legislative over Executive
Can override presidential veto
Can impeach and remove president
Can reject president's appointments and refuse to ratify treaties
Can conduct investigations into president's actions
Can refuse to pass laws or to provide funding that president requests

Judicial over Legislative
Can declare laws unconstitutional
Chief justice presides over Senate during hearing to impeach the president

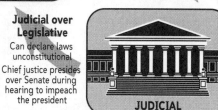

JUDICIAL

Executive over Judicial
Nominates Supreme Court justices
Nominates federal judges
Can pardon those convicted in federal court
Can refuse to enforce Court decisions

Judicial over Executive
Can declare executive actions unconstitutional
Power to issue warrants
Chief justice presides over impeachment of president

EXECUTIVE

---

checks and balances
Mechanisms through which each branch of government is able to participate in and influence the activities of the other branches.

3. *Checks and balances*—a system under which each of the branches is given some power over the others. Familiar examples are the presidential veto power over legislation, the power of the Senate to approve presidential appointments, and judicial review of acts of Congress (Figure 2.2).

One clever formulation of the separation of powers is that of a system not of separated powers but of "separated institutions sharing power,"[19] and thus diminishing the chance that power will be misused.

[19]Richard E. Neustadt, *Presidential Power: The Politics of Leadership* (New York: Wiley, 1960), p. 33.

Federalism Compared to the confederation principle of the Articles of Confederation, federalism was a step toward greater centralization of power. The delegates agreed that they needed to place more power at the national level, without completely undermining the power of the state governments. Thus they devised a system of two sovereigns—the states and the nation—with the hope that competition between the two would be an effective limitation on the power of both.

The Bill of Rights Late in the Philadelphia convention, a motion was made to include a bill of rights in the Constitution. After a brief debate in which hardly a word was said in its favor and only one speech was made against it, the motion to include it was almost unanimously turned down. Most delegates sincerely believed that because the federal government was already limited to its expressed powers, further protection of citizens was not needed. The delegates argued that the states should adopt bills of rights because their greater powers needed greater limitations. But almost immediately after the Constitution was ratified, there was a movement to adopt a national bill of rights. This is why the Bill of Rights, adopted in 1791, makes up the first ten amendments to the Constitution rather than being part of the body of it. We will have a good deal more to say about the Bill of Rights in Chapter 4.

THE FIGHT FOR RATIFICATION: FEDERALISTS VERSUS ANTIFEDERALISTS

The first hurdle faced by the new Constitution was ratification by state conventions of delegates elected by the people of each state. This struggle for ratification was carried out in thirteen separate campaigns. Each involved different men, moved at a different pace, and was influenced by local as well as national considerations. Two sides faced off throughout all the states, however, calling themselves Federalists and Antifederalists (Table 2.1).[20] The Federalists (who more accurately should have called themselves "Nationalists," but who took their name to appear to follow in the revolutionary tradition) supported the Constitution and preferred a strong national government. The Antifederalists opposed the Constitution and preferred a federal system of government that was decentralized; they took on their name by default, in reaction to their better-organized opponents. The Federalists were united in their support of the Constitution, while the Antifederalists were divided as to what they believed the alternative to the Constitution should be.

[20]An excellent analysis of these ratification campaigns—based on a quantitative assessment of the campaigners' own words as found in campaign documents, pamphlets, tracts, public letters, and the eighteenth-century equivalent of op-ed pieces (like the individual essays that make up the *Federalist Papers*)—is William H. Riker, *The Strategy of Rhetoric: Campaigning for the American Constitution* (New Haven, CT: Yale University Press, 1996).

TABLE 2.1

Federalists versus Antifederalists

	FEDERALISTS	ANTIFEDERALISTS
Who were they?	Property owners, creditors, merchants	Small farmers, frontiersmen, debtors, shopkeepers
What did they believe?	Believed that elites were best fit to govern; feared "excessive democracy"	Believed that government should be closer to the people; feared concentration of power in hands of the elites
What system of government did they favor?	Favored strong national government; believed in "filtration" so that only elites would obtain governmental power	Favored retention of power by state governments and protection of individual rights
Who were their leaders?	Alexander Hamilton James Madison George Washington	Patrick Henry George Mason Elbridge Gerry George Clinton

During the struggle over ratification of the proposed Constitution, Americans argued about great political issues and principles. How much power should the national government be given? What safeguards were most likely to prevent the abuse of power? What institutional arrangements could best ensure adequate representation for all Americans? Was tyranny to be feared more from the many or from the few?

In political life, of course, principles—even great principles—are seldom completely divorced from some set of interests. In 1787, Americans were divided along economic, regional, and political lines. These divisions inevitably influenced their attitudes toward the profound political questions of the day. Many well-to-do merchants and planters, as we saw earlier, favored the creation of a stronger central government that would have the capacity to protect property, promote commerce, and keep some of the more radical state legislatures in

Rationality Principle

The debate over ratification revealed the conflicting interests of the Federalists and Antifederalists.

check. At the same time, many powerful state leaders, like Governor George Clinton of New York, feared that strengthening the national government would reduce their own influence and status. Each of these interests, of course, justified its position with an appeal to principle.

Principles are often important weapons in political warfare, and seeing how and by whom they are wielded can illuminate their otherwise obscure implications. In our own time, dry academic discussions of topics such as "free trade" become easier to grasp once it is noted that free trade and open markets are generally favored by low-cost producers, whereas protectionism is the goal of firms whose costs of production are higher than the international norm.

Even if a principle is invented and initially brandished to serve an interest, however, once it has been articulated it can take on a life of its own and prove to have implications that transcend the narrow interests it was created to serve. Some opponents of the Constitution, for example, who criticized the absence of a bill of rights in the initial document did so simply with the hope of blocking the document's ratification. Yet, the Bill of Rights that was later added to the Constitution has proven for two centuries to be a bulwark of civil liberty in the United States.

Similarly, closer to our own time, support for the extension of voting rights and for massive legislative redistricting under the rubric of "one man, one vote" during the 1960s came mainly from liberal Democrats who were hoping to strengthen their own political base because the groups that would benefit most from these initiatives were overwhelmingly Democratic. The principles of equal access to the ballot and one man, one vote, however, have a moral and political validity that is independent of the political interests that propelled these ideas into the political arena.

These examples show us that truly great political principles surmount the interests that initially set them forth. The first step in understanding a political principle is understanding why and by whom it is espoused. The second step is understanding the full implications of the principle itself—implications that may go far beyond the interests that launched it. Thus, even though the great political principles about which Americans argued in 1787 *did* reflect competing interests, they also represented views of society, government, and politics that surmount interest and so must be understood in their own terms. Whatever the underlying clash of interests that may have guided them, the Federalists and Antifederalists presented important alternative visions of America.

During the ratification struggle, thousands of essays, speeches, pamphlets, and letters were presented in support of and in opposition to the proposed Constitution. The best-known pieces supporting ratification of the Constitution were the eighty-five essays written, under the name of "Publius," by Alexander Hamilton, James Madison, and John Jay between the fall of 1787 and the spring of 1788. These *Federalist Papers*, as they are collectively known today, defended the principles of the Constitution and sought to dispel fears of a national authority. The Antifederalists published essays of their own, arguing that the new Constitution betrayed the Revolution and was a step toward monarchy. Among the best of the Antifederalist works were the essays, usually attributed to New York Supreme Court justice Robert Yates, that were written under the name of "Brutus" and published in the *New York Journal* at the same time the *Federalist Papers* appeared. The Antifederalist view was also ably presented in the pamphlets and letters written by a former delegate to the Continental Congress and future U.S. senator, Richard Henry Lee of Virginia, using the pen name "the Federal Farmer." These essays highlight the major differences of opinion between Federalists and Antifederalists. Federalists appealed to basic principles of government in support of their nationalist vision. Antifederalists cited equally fundamental precepts to support their vision of a looser confederacy of small republics.

The two sides engaged in what was almost certainly the very first nationwide political campaign in the history of the world. Though each side was itself only loosely organized, a rudimentary form of coordination and cooperation was manifest—especially in the division of labor between Hamilton, Madison, and Jay as they alternately wrote under the "Publius" pseudonym on different aspects of the newly drafted Constitution in an effort to affect its ratification in the state of New York.

Representation

One major area of contention between the two sides was the question of representation. The Antifederalists asserted that representatives must be "a true picture of the people, . . . [possessing] the knowledge of their circumstances and their wants."[21] This could be achieved, argued the Antifederalists, only in small, relatively homogeneous republics such as the existing states. In their view, the size and extent of the entire nation precluded the construction of a truly representative form of government.

The absence of true representation, moreover, would mean that the people would lack confidence in and attachment to the national government and would refuse to obey its laws voluntarily. As a result, according to the Antifederalists, the national government described by the Constitution would be compelled to resort to force to secure popular compliance. The Federal Farmer averred that laws of the remote federal government could be "in many cases disregarded, unless a multitude of officers and military force be continually kept in view, and employed to enforce the execution of the laws, and to make the government feared and respected."[22]

Federalists, for their part, did not long for pure democracy and saw no reason that representatives should be precisely like those they represented. In their view, government must be representative *of* the people, but must also have a measure of autonomy *from* the people. Their ideal government was to be so con-

---

[21]Melancton Smith, quoted in Herbert J. Storing, *What the Anti-Federalists Were For: The Political Thought of the Opponents of the Constitution* (Chicago: University of Chicago Press, 1981), p. 17.

[22]"Letters from the Federal Farmer," No. 2, in *The Complete Anti-Federalist*, ed. Herbert J. Storing, 7 vols. (Chicago: University of Chicago Press, 1981).

structed as to be capable of serving the long-term public interest even if this conflicted with the public's current preference.

Federalists also dismissed the Antifederalist claim that the distance between representatives and constituents in the proposed national government would lead to popular disaffection and compel the government to use force to secure obedience. Federalists replied that the system of representation they proposed was more likely to produce effective government. In Hamilton's words, there would be "a probability that the general government will be better administered than the particular governments."[23] Competent government, in turn, should inspire popular trust and confidence more effectively than simple social proximity between rulers and ruled.

The Threats Posed by the Majority

A second important issue dividing Federalists and Antifederalists was the threat of *tyranny*—unjust rule by the group in power. Both opponents and defenders of the Constitution frequently affirmed their fear of tyrannical rule. Each side, however, had a different view of the most likely source of tyranny and, hence, of the way in which the threat was to be forestalled.

tyranny
Oppressive government that employs the cruel and unjust use of power and authority.

From the Antifederalist perspective, the great danger was the tendency of all governments—including republican governments—to become gradually more and more "aristocratic" in character, where the small number of individuals in positions of authority would use their stations to gain more and more power over the general citizenry. In essence, the few would use their power to tyrannize the many. For this reason, Antifederalists were sharply critical of those features of the Constitution that divorced governmental institutions from direct responsibility to the people—institutions such as the Senate, the executive, and the federal judiciary. The latter, appointed for life, presented a particular threat: "I wonder if the world ever saw . . . a court of justice invested with such immense powers, and yet placed in a situation so little responsible," protested Brutus.[24]

The Federalists, too, recognized the threat of tyranny. They were not naive about the motives and purposes of individuals and took them to be no less opportunistic and self-interested than the Antifederalists did. But the Federalists believed that the danger particularly associated with republican governments was not aristocracy, but instead, majority tyranny. The Federalists were concerned that a popular majority, "united and actuated by some common impulse of passion, or of interest, adverse to the rights of other citizens," would endeavor to "trample on the rules of justice."[25] From the Federalist perspective, it was precisely those features of the Constitution attacked as potential sources of tyranny by the Antifederalists that actually offered the best hope of averting the threat of

[23]*The Federalist*, No. 27.
[24]"Essays of Brutus," No. 15, in *The Complete Anti-Federalist*.
[25]*The Federalist*, No. 10.

oppression. The size and extent of the nation, for instance, was for the Federalists a bulwark against tyranny. In Madison's famous formulation,

> The smaller the society, the fewer probably will be the distinct parties and interests . . . the more frequently will a majority be found of the same party; and the smaller the number of individuals composing a majority, and the smaller the compass within which they are placed, the more easily will they concert and execute their plans of oppression. Extend the sphere, and you take in a greater variety of parties and interests; you make it less probable that a majority of the whole will have a common motive to invade the rights of other citizens; or if such a common motive exists, it will be more difficult for all who feel it to discover their own strength, and to act in unison with each other.[26]

The Federalists understood that, in a democracy, temporary majorities could abuse their power. The Federalists' misgivings about majority rule were reflected in the constitutional structure. The indirect election of senators, the indirect election of the president, the judicial branch's insulation from the people, the separation of powers, the president's veto power, the bicameral design of Congress, and the federal system were all means to curb majority tyranny. These design features in the Constitution suggest an awareness on the part of the framers of the problems of majority rule and the need for institutional safeguards. Except for the indirect election of senators (which was changed in 1913), these aspects of the constitutional structure remain in place today.[27]

Governmental Power

A third major difference between Federalists and Antifederalists was the issue of governmental power. Both the opponents and proponents of the Constitution agreed on the principle of limited government. They differed, however, on the fundamentally important question of how to place limits on governmental action. Antifederalists favored limiting and enumerating the powers granted to the national government in relation both to the states and to the people at large. To them, the powers given the national government ought to be "confined to certain defined national objects."[28] Otherwise, the national government would "swallow up all the power of the state governments."[29] Antifederalists bitterly attacked the supremacy clause and the necessary and proper clause of the Constitution as unlimited and dangerous grants of power to the national government.[30]

---

[26]Ibid.

[27]A classic development of this theme is found in James M. Buchanan and Gordon Tullock, *The Calculus of Consent: Logical Foundations of Constitutional Democracy* (Ann Arbor: University of Michigan Press, 1962). For a review of the voting paradox and a case study of how it applies today, see Kenneth A. Shepsle and Mark S. Bonchek, *Analyzing Politics: Rationality, Behavior, and Institutions* (New York: Norton, 1997), pp. 49–81.

[28]"Essays of Brutus," No. 7.

[29]"Essays of Brutus," No. 6.

[30]Storing, *What the Antifederalists Were For*, p. 28.

Antifederalists also demanded that a bill of rights be added to the Constitution to place limits on the government's exercise of power over the citizenry. "There are certain things," wrote Brutus, "which rulers should be absolutely prohibited from doing, because if they should do them, they would work an injury, not a benefit to the people."[31] Similarly, the Federal Farmer maintained that "there are certain unalienable and fundamental rights, which in forming the social compact . . . ought to be explicitly ascertained and fixed."[32]

Federalists favored the construction of a government with broad powers. They wanted a government that had the capacity to defend the nation against foreign foes, guard against domestic strife and insurrection, promote commerce, and expand the nation's economy. Antifederalists shared some of these goals but still feared governmental power. Hamilton pointed out, however, that these goals could not be achieved without allowing the government to exercise the necessary power. Federalists acknowledged, of course, that every power could be abused but argued that the way to prevent misuse of power was not by depriving the government of the powers needed to achieve national goals. Instead, they argued that the threat of abuse of power would be mitigated by the Constitution's internal checks and controls. As Madison put it, "the power surrendered by the people is first divided between two distinct governments, and then the portion allotted to each subdivided among distinct and separate departments. Hence a double security arises to the rights of the people. The different governments will control each other, at the same time that each will be controlled by itself."[33] The Federalists' concern with avoiding unwarranted limits on governmental power led them to oppose a bill of rights, which they saw as nothing more than a set of unnecessary restrictions on the government.

The Federalists acknowledged that abuse of power remained a possibility, but felt that the risk had to be taken because of the goals to be achieved. "The very idea of power included a possibility of doing harm," said the Federalist John Rutledge during the South Carolina ratification debates. "If the gentleman would show the power that could do no harm," Rutledge continued, "he would at once discover it to be a power that could do no good."[34]

CHANGING THE INSTITUTIONAL FRAMEWORK: CONSTITUTIONAL AMENDMENT

The Constitution has endured for two centuries as the framework of government. But it has not endured without change. Without change, the Constitution might have become merely a sacred relic, stored under glass.

---

[31]"Essays of Brutus," No. 9.
[32]"Letters from the Federal Farmer," No. 2.
[33]*The Federalist*, No. 51.
[34]Quoted in Storing, *What the Antifederalists Were For*, p. 30.

Amendments: Many Are Called, Few Are Chosen

The need for change was recognized by the framers of the Constitution, and the provisions for amendment incorporated into Article V were thought to be "an easy, regular and Constitutional way" to make changes, which would occasionally be necessary because members of Congress "may abuse their power and refuse their consent on the very account . . . to admit to amendments to correct the source of the abuse."[35] Madison made a more balanced defense of the amendment procedure in Article V: "It guards equally against that extreme facility, which would render the Constitution too mutable; and that extreme difficulty, which might perpetuate its discovered faults."[36]

> **Institution Principle**
>
> The procedures for amending the Constitution are difficult. As a result, the amendment route to political change is extremely limited.

Experience since 1789 raises questions even about Madison's more modest claims. The Constitution has proven to be extremely difficult to amend. In the history of efforts to amend the Constitution, the most appropriate characterization is "many are called, few are chosen." Between 1789 and 1993, 9,746 amendments were formally offered in Congress. Of these, Congress officially proposed only 29, and 27 of these were eventually ratified by the states. But the record is even more severe than that. Since 1791, when the first 10 amendments, the Bill of Rights, were added, only 17 amendments have been adopted. And two of them—Prohibition and its repeal—cancel each other out, so that for all practical purposes, only 15 amendments have been added to the Constitution since 1791. Despite vast changes in American society and its economy, only 12 amendments have been adopted since the Civil War amendments in 1868.

Four methods of amendment are provided for in Article V:

1. Passage in House and Senate by two-thirds vote; then ratification by majority vote of the legislatures of three fourths (thirty-eight) of the states.
2. Passage in House and Senate by two-thirds vote; then ratification by conventions called for the purpose in three fourths of the states.
3. Passage in a national convention called by Congress in response to petitions by two thirds of the states; ratification by majority vote of the legislatures of three fourths of the states.
4. Passage in a national convention, as in method 3; then ratification by conventions called for the purpose in three fourths of the states.

(Figure 2.3 illustrates each of these possible methods.) Because no amendment has ever been proposed by national convention, however, methods 3 and 4 have never been employed. And method 2 has been employed only once (the Twenty-first Amendment, which repealed the Eighteenth, or Prohibition, Amendment). Thus method 1 has been used for all the others.

[35]Observation by Colonel George Mason, delegate from Virginia, early during the convention period. Quoted in Farrand, *The Records of the Federal Convention of 1787*, I, pp. 202–3.

[36]Clinton Rossiter, ed., *The Federalist Papers* (New York: New American Library, 1961), No. 43, p. 278.

FIGURE 2.3

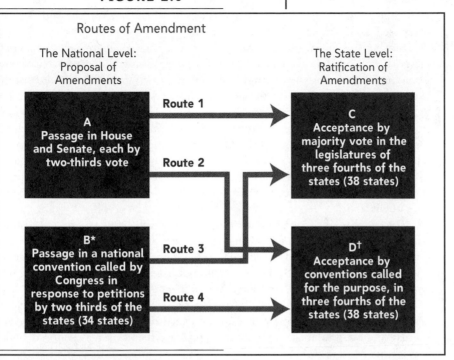

Routes of Amendment

The National Level:
Proposal of
Amendments

The State Level:
Ratification of
Amendments

A
**Passage in House
and Senate, each by
two-thirds vote**

Route 1

Route 2

C
**Acceptance by
majority vote in the
legislatures of
three fourths of the
states (38 states)**

B*
**Passage in a national
convention called by
Congress in
response to petitions
by two thirds of the
states (34 states)**

Route 3

Route 4

D†
**Acceptance by
conventions called
for the purpose, in
three fourths of the
states (38 states)**

*This method of proposal has never been employed. Thus amendment routes 3 and 4 have never been attempted.

†In each amendment proposal, Congress has the power to choose the method of ratification, the time limit for consideration by the states, and other conditions of ratification.

Now we should be better able to explain why it has been so difficult to amend the Constitution. The main reason is the requirement of a two-thirds vote in the House and the Senate, which means that any proposal for an amendment in Congress can be killed by only 34 senators *or* 146 members of the House. What is more, if the necessary two-thirds vote is obtained, the amendment can still be killed by the refusal or inability of only thirteen state legislatures to ratify it. Because each state has an equal vote regardless of its population, the thirteen hold-out states may represent a very small fraction of the total American population.

The Twenty-seven Amendments

Despite difficulties of the process, the Constitution has been amended twenty-seven times since the framers completed their work. The first ten of these amendments, known as the Bill of Rights, were added to the Constitution shortly after its ratification. As we saw, Federalists feared that a bill of rights would weaken the new government, but they were forced to commit themselves to the principle of an enumeration of rights when the Antifederalists charged that the proposed Constitution was a threat to liberty.

Most of the Constitution's twenty-seven amendments share a common characteristic: all but two are concerned with the structure or composition of government. This is consistent with the dictionary, which defines *constitution* as the "makeup or composition of a thing," anything. And it is consistent with the concept of a constitution as "higher law," because the whole point and purpose of a higher law is to establish *a framework within which government and the process of making ordinary law can take place*. Even those who would have preferred more changes in the Constitution would have to agree that there is great wisdom in this principle. A constitution ought to enable legislation and public policies to take place, but it should not determine what that legislation or those public policies ought to be.

The purpose of the ten amendments in the Bill of Rights was basically structural, *to give each of the three branches clearer and more restricted boundaries*. The First Amendment clarified the jurisdiction of Congress. Although the powers of Congress under Article I, Section 8, would not have justified laws regulating religion, speech, and the like, the First Amendment made this limitation explicit: "Congress shall make no law. . . ." The Second, Third, and Fourth Amendments similarly spelled out specific limits on the executive branch. This was seen as a necessity given the abuses of executive power Americans had endured under British rule.

The Fifth, Sixth, Seventh, and Eighth Amendments contain some of the most important safeguards for individual citizens against the arbitrary exercise of government power. And these amendments sought to accomplish their goal by defining the judicial branch more concretely and clearly than had been done in Article III of the Constitution. Table 2.2 analyzes the ten amendments included in the Bill of Rights.

Five of the seventeen amendments adopted since 1791 are directly concerned with expansion of the electorate (Table 2.3). These occasional efforts to expand the electorate were made necessary by the fact that the founders were unable to establish a national electorate with uniform voting qualifications. Stalemated on that issue, the delegates decided to evade it by providing in the final draft of Article I, Section 2, that eligibility to vote in a national election would be the same as "the Qualifications requisite for Electors of the most numerous Branch of the State Legislature." Article I, Section 4, added that Congress could alter state regulations as to the "Times, Places and Manner of holding Elections for Senators and Representatives." Nevertheless, this meant that any important *expansion* of the American electorate would almost certainly require a constitutional amendment.

Six more amendments are also electoral in nature, although not concerned directly with voting rights and the expansion of the electorate (Table 2.4). These six amendments are concerned with the elective offices themselves (the Twenti-

TABLE 2.2

The Bill of Rights: Analysis of Its Provisions

AMENDMENT	PURPOSE
I	*Limits on Congress:* Congress is not to make any law establishing a religion or abridging the freedom of speech, press, assembly, or the right to petition freedoms.
II, III, IV	*Limits on Executive:* The executive branch is not to infringe on the right of people to keep arms (II), is not to arbitrarily take houses for a militia (III), and is not to engage in the search or seizure of evidence without a court warrant swearing to belief in the probable existence of a crime (IV).
V, VI, VII, VIII	*Limits on Courts:* The courts are not to hold trials for serious offenses without provision for a grand jury (V), a petit (trial) jury (VII), a speedy trial (VI), presentation of charges, confrontation of hostile witnesses (VI), immunity from testimony against oneself (V), and immunity from trial more than once for the same offense (V). Neither bail nor punishment can be excessive (VIII), and no property can be taken without just compensation (V).
IX, X	*Limits on National Government:* All rights not enumerated are reserved to the states or the people.

eth, Twenty-second, and Twenty-fifth) or with the relationship between elective offices and the electorate (the Twelfth, Fourteenth, and Seventeenth).

Another five amendments have sought to expand or to delimit the powers of the national and state governments (Table 2.5).[37] The Eleventh Amendment protected the states from suits by private individuals and took away from the federal courts any power to take suits by private individuals of one state (or a foreign country) against another state. The other three amendments in Table 2.5 are obviously designed to reduce state power (Thirteenth), to reduce state power and

---

[37]The Fourteenth Amendment is included in this table as well as in Tables 2.2 and 2.3 because it not only seeks to define citizenship but *seems* to intend that this definition of citizenship include, along with the right to vote, all the rights of the Bill of Rights, regardless of the state in which the citizen resides. A great deal more will be said about this in Chapter 4.

TABLE 2.3

Amending the Constitution to Expand the Electorate

AMENDMENT	PURPOSE	YEAR PROPOSED	YEAR ADOPTED
XIV	Section I provided national definition of citizenship*	1866	1868
XV	Extended voting rights to all races	1869	1870
XIX	Extended voting rights to women	1919	1920
XXIII	Extended voting rights to residents of the District of Columbia	1960	1961
XXIV	Extended voting rights to all classes by abolition of poll taxes	1962	1964
XXVI	Extended voting rights to citizens aged 18 and over	1971	1971

*In defining *citizenship*, the Fourteenth Amendment actually provided the constitutional basis for expanding the electorate to include all races, women, and residents of the District of Columbia. Only the "eighteen-year-olds' amendment" should have been necessary because it changed the definition of citizenship. The fact that additional amendments were required after the Fourteenth suggests that voting is not considered an inherent right of U.S. citizenship. Instead it is viewed as a privilege.

expand national power (Fourteenth), and to expand national power (Sixteenth). The Twenty-seventh put a limit on Congress's ability to raise its own salary.

The two missing amendments underscore the meaning of the rest: the Eighteenth, or Prohibition, Amendment and the Twenty-first, its repeal. This is the only instance in which the country tried to *legislate* by constitutional amendment. In other words, the Eighteenth is the only amendment that was designed to deal directly with some substantive social problem. And it was the only amendment ever to have been repealed. Two other amendments—the Thirteenth, which abolished slavery, and the Sixteenth, which established the power to levy an income tax—can be said to have had the effect of legislation. But the purpose of the Thirteenth was to restrict the power of the states by forever forbidding them to treat any human being as property. As for the Sixteenth, it is certainly true that income-tax legislation followed immediately; nevertheless, the amendment concerns itself strictly with establishing the power of Congress to enact such legislation. The legislation came later; and if down the line a majority in Congress had wanted to abolish the

TABLE 2.4

	Amending the Constitution to Change the Relationship between the Elected Offices and the Electorate		
AMENDMENT	**PURPOSE**	**YEAR PROPOSED**	**YEAR ADOPTED**
XII	Provided separate ballot for vice president in the electoral college	1803	1804
XIV	Section 2 eliminated counting of slaves as three-fifths citizens for apportionment of House seats	1866	1868
XVII	Provided direct election of senators	1912	1913
XX	Eliminated "lame duck" session of Congress	1932	1933
XXII	Limited presidential term	1947	1951
XXV	Provided presidential succession in case of disability	1965	1967

income tax, they could also have done this by legislation rather than through the arduous path of a constitutional amendment repealing the income tax.

For those whose hopes for change center on the Constitution, it must be emphasized that the amendment route to social change is, and always will be, extremely limited. Through a constitution it is possible to establish a working structure of government; and through a constitution it is possible to establish basic rights of citizens by placing limitations and obligations on the powers of that government. Once these things have been accomplished, the real problem is how to extend rights to those people who do not already enjoy them. Of course, the Constitution cannot enforce itself. But it can and does have a real influence on everyday life because a right or an obligation set forth in the Constitution can become a *cause of action* in the hands of an otherwise powerless person.

Private property is an excellent example. Property is one of the most fundamental and well-established rights in the United States; but it is well established not because it is recognized in so many words in the Constitution but because legislatures and courts have made it a crime for anyone, including the government, to trespass or to take away property without compensation.

TABLE 2.5

Amending the Constitution to Expand or Limit the Power of Government

AMENDMENT	PURPOSE	YEAR PROPOSED	YEAR ADOPTED
XI	Limited jurisdiction of federal courts over suits involving the states	1794	1798
XIII	Eliminated slavery and eliminated the rights of states to allow property in persons	1865*	1865
XIV	(Part 2) Applied due process of Bill of Rights to the states	1866	1868
XVI	Established national power to tax incomes	1909	1913
XXVII	Limited Congress's power to raise its own salary	1789	1992

*The Thirteenth Amendment was proposed on January 31, 1865, and adopted less than a year later, on December 18, 1865.

REFLECTIONS ON THE FOUNDING: PRINCIPLES OR INTERESTS?

The final product of the Constitutional Convention would have to be considered an extraordinary victory for the groups that had most forcefully called for the creation of a new system of government to replace the Articles of Confederation. Antifederalist criticisms forced the Constitution's proponents to accept the addition of a bill of rights designed to limit the powers of the national government. In general, however, it was the Federalist vision of America that triumphed. The Constitution adopted in 1789 created the framework for a powerful national government that for more than 200 years has defended the nation's interests, promoted its commerce, and maintained national unity. In one notable instance, the national government fought and won a bloody war to prevent the nation from breaking apart.

Though the Constitution was the product of a particular set of political forces, the principles of government it established have a significance that goes far beyond the interests of its authors. As we have observed, political principles often take on lives of their own. The great political principles incorporated into the Constitution continue, more than two centuries later, to shape our political lives in ways that the Constitution's framers may not always have anticipated. For example, when they empowered the Congress of the United States to regulate commerce among the states in Article I, Section 8, of the Constitution, the framers could hardly have anticipated that this would become the basis for many of the federal government's regulatory activities in areas as diverse as the environment and civil rights.

Two great constitutional principles, federalism and civil liberties, will be discussed in Chapters 3 and 4. A third important constitutional principle that has affected America's government for the past 200 years is the principle of *checks and balances*. As we saw earlier, the framers gave each of the three branches of government a means of intervening in and blocking the actions of the others. Often, checks and balances have seemed to prevent the government from getting much done. During the 1960s, for example, liberals were often infuriated as they watched Congress stall presidential initiatives in the area of civil rights. More recently, conservatives were outraged when President Clinton thwarted congressional efforts to enact legislation promised in the Republican "Contract with America." At various times, all sides have vilified the judiciary for invalidating legislation enacted by Congress and signed by the president.

Over time, checks and balances have acted as brakes on the governmental process. Groups hoping to bring about changes in policy or governmental institutions seldom have been able to bring about decisive and dramatic transformations in a short period of time. Instead, checks and balances have slowed the pace of change and increased the need for compromise and accommodation.

Groups able to take control of the White House, for example, must bargain with their rivals who remain entrenched on Capitol Hill. New forces in Congress must reckon with the influence of other forces in the executive branch and in the courts. Checks and balances inevitably frustrate those who desire change, but they also function as a safeguard against rash action. During the 1950s, for example, Congress was caught up in a quasi-hysterical effort to unmask subversive activities in the United States, which might have led to a serious erosion of American liberties if not for the checks and balances provided by the executive and the courts. Thus a governmental principle that serves as a frustrating limitation one day may become a vitally important safeguard the next.

As we close our discussion of the founding, it is also worth reflecting on the Antifederalists. Although they were defeated in 1789, the Antifederalists present us with an important picture of a road not taken and of an America that might have been. Would we have been worse off as a people if we had been governed by a confederacy of small republics linked by a national administration with severely limited powers? Were the Antifederalists correct in predicting that a government given great power in the hope that it might do good would, through "insensible progress," inevitably turn to evil purposes? Two hundred plus years of government under the federal Constitution are not necessarily enough to definitively answer these questions. Only time will tell.

Policy Principle

The constitutional framework, such as the principle of checks and balances, can act as a brake on the policy process.

Rationality Principle	Collective-Action Principle	Institution Principle	Policy Principle	History Principle
The framers of the Constitution were guided by principles, but they also had interests.	The colonists required strong leaders to resolve differences and to organize resistance to British authority.	Institutional arrangements, such as the Articles of Confederation, can be flawed.	The constitutional framework, such as the principle of checks and balances, can act as a brake on the policy process.	The American colonists, used to self-governance, believed that the Stamp Act of 1765 threatened their autonomy.
The debate over ratification revealed the conflicting interests of the Federalists and Antifederalists.	The framers preferred compromise to the breakup of the Union, and thus accepted the Great Compromise and the Three-fifths Compromise.	The constitutional framework promoted commerce, protected property, prevented "excessive democracy," and limited the power of the national government.		Shays's Rebellion focused attention on the flaws of the Articles of Confederation, leading to the Constitutional Convention.
		The procedures for amending the Constitution are difficult. As a result, the amendment route to political change is extremely limited.		

SUMMARY

Political conflicts between the colonies and England, and among competing groups within the colonies, led to the first founding as expressed by the Declaration of Independence. The first constitution, the Articles of Confederation, was adopted one year later (1777). Under this document, the states retained their sovereignty. The central government, composed solely of Congress, had few powers and no means of enforcing its will. The national government's weakness soon led to the Constitution of 1787, the second founding.

In this second founding the framers sought, first, to fashion a new government sufficiently powerful to promote commerce and protect property from radical state legislatures. Second, the framers sought to bring an end to the "excessive democracy" of the state and national governments under the Articles of Confederation. Third, the framers introduced mechanisms that helped secure popular consent for the new government. Finally, the framers made certain that their new government would not itself pose a threat to liberty and property.

The Constitution consists of seven articles. In part, Article I provides for a Congress of two chambers (Sections 1–7), defines the powers of the national government (Section 8), and interprets the national government's powers as a source of strength rather than a limitation (necessary and proper clause). Article II describes the presidency and establishes it as a separate branch of government. Article III is the judiciary article. While there is no direct mention of judicial review in this article, the Supreme Court eventually assumed that power. Article IV addresses reciprocity among states and their citizens. Article V describes the procedures for amending the Constitution. Thousands of amendments have been offered, but only twenty-seven have been adopted. With the exception of the two Prohibition amendments, all amendments were oriented toward some change in the framework or structure of government. Article VI establishes that national laws and treaties are "the supreme Law of the Land." And finally, Article VII specifies the procedure for ratifying the Constitution of 1787.

The struggle for the ratification of the Constitution pitted the Antifederalists against the Federalists. The Antifederalists thought the proposed new government would be too powerful, and they fought against the ratification of the Constitution. The Federalists supported the Constitution and were able to secure its ratification after a nationwide political debate.

FOR FURTHER READING

Bailyn, Bernard. *The Ideological Origins of the American Revolution*. Cambridge: Harvard University Press, 1967.

Beard, Charles A. *An Economic Interpretation of the Constitution of the United States*. New York: Macmillan, 1913.

Farrand, Max, ed. *The Records of the Federal Convention of 1787*. Rev. ed. 4 vols. New Haven, CT: Yale University Press, 1966.

Hamilton, Alexander, James Madison, and John Jay. *The Federalist Papers*. Ed. Isaac Kramnick. New York: Viking Press, 1987.

Lipset, Seymour M. *The First New Nation: The United States in Historical and Comparative Perspective*. New York: Basic Books, 1963.

Main, Jackson Turner. *The Social Structure of Revolutionary America*. Princeton, NJ: Princeton University Press, 1965.

Riker, William H. *The Strategy of Rhetoric: Campaigning for the American Constitution*. New Haven, CT: Yale University Press, 1996.

Storing, Herbert J., ed. *The Complete Anti-Federalist*. 7 vols. Chicago: University of Chicago Press, 1981.

Wood, Gordon S. *The Creation of the American Republic, 1776–1787*. New York: Norton, 1982.

Politics in the News—
Reading between the Lines

The Challenges Faced by Constitutional Amendments

Senate Hears Testimony on a Gay Marriage Amendment

By CARL HULSE

Senate Republican leaders said Wednesday that they would aggressively pursue a constitutional amendment banning gay marriages despite Democratic arguments that the proposal is divisive, unnecessary and a distraction from more pressing issues.

"It is becoming increasingly clear that Congress must act," Senator Bill Frist, the majority leader, told members of a conservative group pushing for an amendment even as gay couples began marrying in Oregon. Congress would not let the courts "radically redefine what marriage is, and that is the union between a man and woman," Dr. Frist said.

But the obstacles facing an amendment quickly became clear at a Senate hearing on the issue, the first since President Bush endorsed the concept last week. Sharp partisan divisions emerged as Democrats accused Republicans of trying to generate momentum for an amendment by creating a false air of crisis.

"This is a divisive political exercise in an election year, plain and simple," said Senator Russell D. Feingold of Wis-

consin, the senior Democrat on the Senate Judiciary Subcommittee on the Constitution. Republican authors of an amendment will need substantial Democratic support if they hope to move forward because it requires approval by two-thirds of the members of the House and Senate.

Witnesses testifying before the panel, which was meeting in a packed hearing room, also disagreed on the need for an amendment. Advocates argued that the institution of marriage needed to be protected, while opponents said an amendment would be discriminatory and premature given that existing law on the subject had not been fully tested.

Chuck Muth, president of Citizen Outreach and a self-described conservative advocate of limited government, equated the proposal to calls early in the 1900's for an amendment banning interracial marriages, an idea that he said seemed wildly intolerant today.

"It is simply wrong for our generation to presume to dictate via a federal

New York Times, 4 March 2004, p. A26.

constitutional amendment how future generations of Americans address this social policy," Mr. Muth said. . . .

Senator Orrin G. Hatch, Republican of Utah and chairman of the Judiciary Committee, said he would support an amendment that has been introduced in Congress, though he said he would consider alternatives that left the issue more in the hands of state legislatures. . . .

Lawmakers and other supporters of the proposed amendment disputed the notion that it amounted to discrimination and said that accusation was offensive. They said their goal was to place in the Constitution a recognition of the traditional view of marriage and family.

"Children are raised expecting to have a biological mother and father," said the Rev. Richard Richardson, president of a child welfare agency in Boston and a leader of the Black Ministerial Alliance of Greater Boston. "It is not just society—it is biology, it is basic human instinct."

Maggie Gallagher, an author and president of the Institute for Marriage and Public Policy, in her testimony said, "Marriage is a national issue because marriage is a key social institution." She added, "Without a common, national definition of marriage, our marriage culture will be fragmented as judges and public officials impose their own definition of marriage."

But Hilary Shelton, director of the Washington Bureau of the N.A.A.C.P., said his organization was "greatly disappointed that President George Bush and others have decided to enter this election cycle by endorsing an amendment that would forever write discrimination into the U.S. Constitution, rather than focusing on the crucial problems and challenges that affect the lives of all of us."

A professor from Yale Law School, Lea Brilmayer, undermined a main rationale offered for an amendment, that the "full faith and credit" clause of the Constitution could force states that do not allow gay marriages to recognize

ESSENCE OF THE STORY

- Senate Republicans are pressing for a vote on a constitutional amendment defining marriage as between a man and a woman. The senators are acting in response to the issuing of marriage licenses to gay couples in several states and localities.

- The proponents of the amendment argue that marriage is a key social institution and deserves constitutional protection.

- Opponents argue that the amendment would write discrimination into the Constitution and that social norms about gay marriage may change substantially in the future.

POLITICAL ANALYSIS

- The Founders designed our system so that there would be a tension between the legislative and judicial branches, and the gay marriage amendment is only the most recent of many attempts by Congress to limit certain rights and freedoms.

- Taking a strong stance on this amendment is a no-brainer for many Republicans. Even if they have concerns about the measure, they are assured that Democrats will use the filibuster in the Senate to stop the amendment from proceeding, so the politically strategic position for Republicans is to support the measure.

- With the growing federal deficit and an ongoing and increasingly unpopular war in Iraq hurting Republican chances in upcoming elections, staking out a position on a moral issue such as gay marriage helps Republicans maintain the loyalty of some voters.

those from states where they are legal. Ms. Brilmayer said there had not been a single case of a state being put in that position, noting that states had long been able to refuse recognition of marriages between cousins and even recently divorced individuals.

"This problem is as old as the hills and, frankly, it is not much of a problem" she said, rejecting the notion of changing the Constitution to deal with it. . . .

CHAPTER

3

The Constitutional Framework: Federalism and the Separation of Powers

As an instrument of government, the Articles of Confederation had many virtues. Many considered it the second greatest constitution ever drafted. But as a confederation, it left too much power to the states, whose restrictions and boundaries interfered with national and international markets being sought by new economic interests. The Articles of Confederation had to be replaced, and a stronger national power had to be provided for, if the barriers to economic progress were to be lowered.[1]

There had to be a redistribution of powers between the states and the national government, and that would be accomplished only by negotiation because the states and the nation were equals. The former colonies were renamed *states*, which even then were defined as entities with autonomy and *sovereignty*. Then

sovereignty
Supreme and independent political authority.

[1]For two important realist interpretations of the rejection of the Articles in favor of the Constitution, see John P. Roche, "The Founding Fathers: A Reform Caucus in Action," *American Political Science Review* 55 (December 1961): 799–816, and the discussion of Charles Beard's economic interpretation in the text.

as now, when two autonomous entities (individuals or states) negotiate a deal, it's called a *contract*. The Constitution of 1789 was a contract in which the people in their respective states gave to the national government some of the powers they had enjoyed under the Articles of Confederation *on condition* that the national government accept certain strict limitations on its powers and how to exercise those powers. This contract of exchanging limitations for powers is the very definition of **constitutionalism.**

Three fundamental limitations were the basis of the contract between the American people and the framers of the Constitution: *federalism*, the *separation of powers*, and *individual rights*. Nowhere in the Constitution were these mentioned by name, but we know from the debates and writings that they were the primary framework of the Constitution. We can call them the *framework* because they were to be the structure, the channel through which governmental power would flow.

Federalism sought to limit government by dividing it into two levels—national and state—each with sufficient independence, or sovereignty, to compete with the other, thereby restraining the power of both.[2]

The *separation of powers* sought to limit the power of the national government by dividing government against itself—by giving the legislative, executive, and judicial branches separate functions, thus forcing them to share power.

Individual rights as embodied in the Bill of Rights sought to limit government by defining the people as separate from it—granting to each individual an identity in opposition to the government itself. Individuals are given rights, which are claims to identity, to property, and to personal satisfaction or to "the pursuit of happiness," that cannot

constitutionalism
A system of rule in which formal and effective limits are placed on the powers of the government.

CHAPTER OUTLINE

Federalism and the Separation of Powers as Political Institutions

The Dynamics of the Framework: A Case Study

Who Does What? Stability and Change in the Federal Framework

- Federalism in the Constitution

- The Slow Growth of the National Government's Power

- Cooperative Federalism and Grants-in-Aid

- Regulated Federalism and National Standards

- New Federalism and the National-State Tug-of-War

The Separation of Powers

- Checks and Balances

- Legislative Supremacy

- The Role of the Supreme Court

Altering the Balance of Power: What Are the Consequences?

[2]The notion that federalism requires separate spheres or jurisdictions in which lower and higher levels of government are uniquely decisive is developed fully in William H. Riker, *Federalism: Origin, Operation, Significance* (Boston: Little, Brown, 1964). This American version of federalism is applied to the emerging federal arrangements in the People's Republic of China during the 1990s in a paper by Barry R. Weingast, "The Economic Role of Political Institutions: Market-Preserving Federalism and Economic Development," *Journal of Law, Economics & Organization* 11 (1995): 1–32.

Although this chapter refers to all five principles of politics, the most salient principle is that institutions matter—that is, rules and procedures shape politics. As we learned in Chapter 1, institutions are part "script" and part "scorecard." Throughout American political history, the institutional script has determined whether states or the national government would exercise influence in a given policy area. Similarly, at the national level, the separation-of-powers system that delineates the role and authority of members of Congress, the president, and the courts provides the scorecard that allows political actors to predict who will be influential on a given political issue. And, in that they are consequential, these institutional structures channel and constrain the actions of political actors as they pursue their different goals.

be denied except by extraordinary procedures that demonstrate beyond doubt that the need of the government or the "public interest" is more compelling than the claim of the citizen.

This chapter is concerned with federalism and the separation of powers. The purpose here is to look at the evolution of each to understand how we got to where we are and what the significance of each in operation is. Together federalism and the separation of powers constitute a script and a scorecard for the exercise of governmental power. They characterize the way the different fragments of governmental machinery mesh together into a whole, and they provide a list and a description of the players in the game of politics. We conclude by reviewing the question "How do federalism and the separation of powers limit the power of the national government?" Individual rights is the topic of the next chapter. But all of this is for introductory purposes only. All three elements form the background and the context for every chapter in this book.

THE DYNAMICS OF THE FRAMEWORK: A CASE STUDY

Terri Schiavo, a native of Pinellas Park, Florida, had been in a coma since 1990, from brain damage that had left her in what neurologists diagnosed as a "persistent vegetative state." In 1998, her husband, as legal guardian, sought authorization to meet her wish for a "dignified death" by removing the feeding tube, her life support. But because she had not written a living will, her parents intervened to keep the tube in place with a lawsuit before the Pinellas County court. After a series of decisions denying the parents' petition, which had been up and down the state courts for seven years, the county judge in February 2005 set March 19 as the deadline for removing Ms. Schiavo's feeding tube.

The court's deadline galvanized popular support on the side of the parents, which quickly pushed the issue up to Florida governor Jeb Bush, who turned to Congress through his Republican congressional delegation. With only three weeks until the deadline, but with the help of a national conservative movement that had been building for two years, the full weight of the Republican congressional leadership (plus a goodly number of Democrats) was able to bring House and Senate members back to Washington during Easter recess. On Palm Sunday weekend they produced an unprecedented law to change the jurisdiction of the U.S. District Court to preempt the state courts. This enabled Terri Schiavo's parents (identified by name in the act) to bring their suit *de novo* ("from the start," with new evidence, new witnesses, new expert testimony, and so forth). In record time, the bill was enacted into law, and President George W. Bush flew from Texas to Washington on Sunday night to sign the bill shortly after midnight; he then returned to Texas to complete his Easter vacation.

Things had to move with extraordinary speed because the feeding tube had been removed the Friday before, giving no more than two weeks to prevent Ms. Schiavo's certain death from starvation. The federal judge in Tampa took two days to deny the petition to reinstate life support. Immediately, six days since the removal of the feeding tube, an appeal went to the U.S. Court of Appeals for the Eleventh Circuit in Atlanta. Overnight, the three-judge panel deliberated and denied the appeal by a 2–1 vote. This was followed within hours by a confirmation of their denial by a 10–2 vote of the full appellate court. The decision was appealed directly to the U.S. Supreme Court—the fifth time the case had been appealed to it—and with equal speed the Court denied the appeal, with no opinion and without a recorded vote. It was March 24, 2005.

Was that the end of the story? Not quite. Although the parents had exhausted their legal remedies, the state had two more cards to play. First, the state could request a court review based on what was alleged to be new evidence: the report of a neurologist (who was also a prominent member of the right-to-life coalition), compiled from a brief visit to Ms. Schiavo, and the review of an amateur video of her apparent responses to various stimuli. Was that sufficient for a new trial? The state was denied almost immediately. Second, the governor himself might have the power to order his Department of Children and Families to "take custody" of Ms. Schiavo on grounds of alleged abuse of the patient and deprivation of her Fourteenth Amendment due process rights. There was also a remote possibility of an appeal based on another Fourteenth Amendment argument, that Ms. Schiavo had been denied her due process right to a fair trial in the state courts, putting the case back into the federal courts!

But all efforts were closed down on the seventh day after life support was removed when the federal district court judge in Tampa denied the sixth appeal, despite the fact that it had been joined by Governor Bush himself, who put forward new allegations that Ms. Schiavo had been abused in 1991. This denial was followed by a teary reply from Governor Bush that he could not and would not use executive power to take custody of Terri Schiavo and circumvent the courts altogether.

For our purposes here, the outcome of the case is of less concern than the interplay of controversies within the institutions. The Schiavo case demonstrates just how relevant and effective the 1789 constitutional framework still is after 200-plus years. A summary of how that framework weighed in here may be helpful:

Federalism. A dispute between the husband and the parents over custody of Terri Schiavo took them to a Florida county court, the base of the state judiciary. Parents lose.

Separation of powers. Parents get public support and go to Congress. Congress breaches separation of powers *and* federalism with a law transferring jurisdiction from state judiciary to federal district court. Denial by federal district court. Appeal to federal appeals court. Denial. Appeal to U.S. Supreme Court on grounds of *individual rights*. Denial.

Federalism. Back to state court, reaffirming state jurisdiction.

State separation of powers. Parents appeal to governor for exceptional action, possibly an act by state health services agency to take custody and reconnect Ms. Schiavo to life support. Governor denies he has the power.

Case closed. Terri Schiavo dies after twenty-six court decisions.

The entire controversy was shaped by the federal structure, with Congress and the executive branch trying to make this an exceptional case, challenging both the division of powers between national and state government and the separation of powers between the legislative, executive, and judicial branches. In the end, the decisions by the state and federal courts reinforced both federalism and the separation of powers.

FEDERALISM AND THE SEPARATION OF POWERS AS POLITICAL INSTITUTIONS

The great achievement of American politics is the fashioning of an effective constitutional structure of political institutions. Although it is an imperfect and continuously evolving "work in progress," this structure of law and political practice has served its people well for more than two centuries by managing conflict, providing inducements for bargaining and cooperation, and facilitating collective action. There has been one enormous failure—the cruel practice of slavery, which ended only after a destructive civil war. But the basic configuration of institutions first formulated in Philadelphia in 1787 survived these debacles, though severely scarred by them, and has otherwise stood the test of time.

As we noted earlier, institutional arrangements like federalism and the separation of powers are part *script* and part *scorecard*. As two of the most important features of the constitutional structure, federalism and the separation of powers serve to channel and constrain political agents, first by limiting their jurisdictional authority and second by pitting them against one another as political competitors.

One of the ingenious features of the constitutional design adopted by the framers is the principle of dividing and separating. Leaving political authority unobstructed and undivided, it was thought, would invite intense competition of a winner-take-all variety. The winners would then be in a position to tyrannize, while the losers would either submit or, with nothing else to lose, be tempted to violent opposition. By adopting the divide-and-separate principle—implemented as federalism and the separation of powers, and consisting of checks and balances—the framers of the Constitution created *jurisdictional arrangements*. The Constitution reflects this in two distinct ways. First, it encourages diversity in the political actors occupying the various institutions of government by requiring that they be selected at different times, from different constituencies, by different modes of selection (chiefly various forms of election and appointment). This, it was believed, would prevent a small clique or narrow slice of the political elite from dominating all the institutions of government at the same time. Second, the Constitution allocates the consideration of different aspects of policy to different institutional arenas. Some explicitly mentioned activities, like the coinage of money or the declaration of war, were assigned to Congress. Matters relating to the execution and implementation of the law were delegated to the president and the executive bureaucracy. Other activities, like adjudicating disputes between states, were made the preserve of the judicial branch. Those activities not explicitly mentioned in the Constitution were reserved to the states. In short, through a jurisdictional arrangement, the Constitution sought a balance in which there was the capacity for action but in which power was not so concentrated as to make tyranny likely.

The amazing thing about these American political institutions is that they are not carved in granite (even if the official buildings that house them are!). While the Constitution initially set a broad framework for the division of authority between the national government and the states, and the division of labor among the branches of the national government, much adaptation and innovation took place as these institutions themselves were bent to the purposes of various political players. Politicians, remember, are goal-oriented and are constantly exploring the possibilities provided them by their institutional positions and political situations. Another political player that has helped shape the current jurisdictional arrangements and sharing of power is worth remembering as well. This is the U.S. Supreme Court. As former Supreme Court Justice Charles Evans Hughes once remarked, "We are under a Constitution, but the Constitution is what the judges say it is."[3] As we shall see in this chapter, the Court has been a central player in settling the ongoing debate over how power should be divided between the national government and the states and between Congress and the president.

Institution Principle
The Constitution created jurisdictional arrangements by encouraging diversity in the elected leaders and allocating the consideration of different aspects of policy to different institutional arenas.

Rationality Principle
As political institutions, federalism and the separation of powers have adapted to the purposes of various political players.

History Principle
Since the time of the founding, federalism has been shaped strongly by the Supreme Court.

WHO DOES WHAT? STABILITY AND CHANGE IN THE FEDERAL FRAMEWORK

Federalism can be defined with misleading ease and simplicity as the division of powers and functions between the national government and the state governments. Federalism sought to limit national and state power by creating two sovereigns—the national government and the state governments, each to a large extent independent of the other. As we saw in Chapter 2, the states had already existed as former

federalism
System of government in which a constitution divides power between a central government and regional governments.

[3]Charles Evans Hughes, speech at Elmira, New York, 3 May 1907.

colonies before independence, and for nearly thirteen years they were virtually autonomous units under the Articles of Confederation. In effect, the states had retained too much power under the Articles, a problem that led directly to the Annapolis Convention in 1786 and to the Constitutional Convention in 1787. Under the Articles, disorder within states was beyond the reach of the national government (see Shays's Rebellion, Chapter 2), and conflicts of interest between states were not manageable. For example, states were making their own trade agreements with foreign countries and companies that might then play one state against another for special advantages. Some states adopted special trade tariffs and further barriers to foreign commerce that were contrary to the interest of another state.[4] Tax and other barriers were also being erected between the states.[5] But even after the ratification of the Constitution, the states continued to be more important than the national government. For nearly a century and a half, virtually all of the fundamental policies governing the lives of Americans were made by the state legislatures, not by Congress.

Federalism in the Constitution

The United States was the first nation to adopt federalism as its governing framework. With federalism, the framers sought to limit the national government by creating a second layer of state governments. American federalism recognized two sovereigns in the original Constitution and reinforced the principle in the Bill of Rights by granting a few ***expressed powers*** to the national government and reserving all the rest to the states.

The Powers of the National Government   As we saw in Chapter 2, the "expressed powers" granted to the national government are found in Article I, Section 8, of the Constitution. These seventeen powers include the powers to collect taxes, to coin money, to declare war, and to regulate commerce (which, as we will see, became a very important power for the national government). Article I, Section 8, also contains another important source of power for the national government: the ***implied powers*** that enable Congress "to make all Laws which shall be necessary and proper for carrying into Execution the foregoing Powers." Not until several decades after the founding did the Supreme Court allow Congress to exercise the power granted in this ***necessary and proper clause;*** but, as we shall see later in this chapter, this doctrine allowed the national government to expand considerably the scope of its authority, although the process was a slow one. In addition to these expressed and implied powers, the Constitution affirmed the power of the national government in the supremacy clause (Article VI), which made all national laws and treaties "the supreme Law of the Land."

expressed power   The notion that the Constitution grants to the federal government only those powers specifically named in its text.

implied powers   Powers derived from the necessary and proper clause of Article I, Section 8, of the Constitution. Such powers are not specifically expressed but are implied through the expansive interpretation of delegated powers.

necessary and proper clause   Article I, Section 8, of the Constitution, which enumerates the powers of Congress and provides Congress with the authority to make all laws "necessary and proper" to carry them out; also referred to as the "elastic clause."

[4]For good treatment of these conflicts of interests between states, see Forrest McDonald, *E Pluribus Unum: The Formation of the American Republic, 1776–1790* (Boston: Houghton Mifflin, 1965), Chapter 7, especially pp. 319–38.
[5]See David M. O'Brien, *Constitutional Law and Politics,* 3rd ed., 2 vols. (New York: Norton, 1997), I, pp. 602–3.

The Powers of State Government   One way in which the framers sought to preserve a strong role for the states was through the Tenth Amendment to the Constitution. The Tenth Amendment states that the powers the Constitution does not delegate to the national government or prohibit to the states are "reserved to the States respectively, or to the people." The Antifederalists, who feared that a strong central government would encroach on individual liberty, repeatedly pressed for such an amendment as a way of limiting national power. Federalists agreed to the amendment because they did not think it would do much harm, given the powers of the Constitution already granted to the national government. The Tenth Amendment is also called the *reserved powers* amendment because it aims to reserve powers to the states.

The most fundamental power retained by the states is that of coercion—the power to develop and enforce criminal codes, to administer health and safety rules, to regulate the family via marriage and divorce laws. The states have the power to regulate individuals' livelihoods; if you're a doctor or a lawyer or a plumber or a barber, you must be licensed by the state. Even more fundamental, the states had the power to define private property—private property exists because state laws against trespass define who is and is not entitled to use a piece of property. If you own a car, your ownership isn't worth much unless the state is willing to enforce your right to possession by making it a crime for anyone else to drive your car. These are fundamental matters, and the powers of the states regarding these domestic issues are much greater than the powers of the national government, even today.

A state's authority to regulate these fundamental matters is commonly referred to as the *police power* of the state and encompasses the state's power to regulate the health, safety, welfare, and morals of its citizens. Policing is what states do—they coerce you in the name of the community in order to maintain public order. And this was exactly the type of power that the founders intended the states to exercise.

In some areas, the states share *concurrent powers* with the national government, wherein they retain and share some power to regulate commerce and to affect the currency—for example, by being able to charter banks, grant or deny corporate charters, grant or deny licenses to engage in a business or practice a trade, and regulate the quality of products or the conditions of labor. This issue of concurrent versus exclusive power has come up from time to time in our history, but wherever there is a direct conflict of laws between the federal and the state levels, the issue will most likely be resolved in favor of national supremacy.

State Obligations to One Another   The Constitution also creates obligations among the states. These obligations, spelled out in Article IV, were intended to promote national unity. By requiring the states to recognize actions and decisions taken in other states as legal and proper, the framers aimed to make the states less like independent countries and more like parts of a single nation.

Article IV, Section I, calls for "Full Faith and Credit" among states, meaning that each state is normally expected to honor the "public Acts, Records, and judicial Proceedings" that take place in any other state. So, for example, if a couple is

reserved powers
Powers, derived from the Tenth Amendment to the Constitution, that are not specifically delegated to the national government or denied to the states.

police power
Power reserved to the government to regulate the health, safety, and morals of its citizens.

concurrent powers
Authority possessed by *both* state and national governments, such as the power to levy taxes.

full faith and
credit clause
Provision from Article
IV, Section 1, of the
Constitution requir-
ing that the states
normally honor the
public acts and judi-
cial decisions that
take place in another
state.

married in Texas—marriage being regulated by state law—Missouri must also recognize that marriage, even though they were not married under Missouri state law.

This *full faith and credit clause* has recently become embroiled in the controversy over gay and lesbian marriage. In 1993, the Hawaii Supreme Court prohibited discrimination against gay and lesbian marriage except in very limited
circumstances. Many observers believed that Hawaii would eventually fully legalize gay marriage. In fact, after a long political battle, Hawaii passed a constitutional amendment in 1998 outlawing gay marriage. However, in December 1999,
the Vermont Supreme Court ruled that gay and lesbian couples should have the
same rights as heterosexuals. The Vermont legislature responded with a new law
that allowed gays and lesbians to form "civil unions." Although not legally considered marriages, such unions allow gay and lesbian couples most of the benefits of
marriage, such as eligibility for the partner's health insurance, inheritance rights,
and the right to transfer property. The Vermont statute could have broad implications for other states. More than thirty states have passed "defense of marriage
acts" that define marriage as a union between a man and a woman only. Anxious
to show its disapproval of gay marriage, Congress passed the Defense of Marriage
Act in 1996, which declared that states will *not* have to recognize a same-sex
marriage, even if it is legal in one state. The act also said that the federal government will not recognize gay marriage—even if it is legal under state law—and
that gay marriage partners will not be eligible for the federal benefits, such as
Medicare and Social Security, normally available to spouses.[6]

In 2004, a presidential election year, Alabama, Georgia, Kentucky, Michigan,
Montana, North Dakota, Ohio, Oklahoma, and Utah approved state constitutional amendments strictly defining marriage as between a man and a woman.
The large-scale approval of such amendments was probably prompted by a Massachusetts court decision permitting gays and lesbians to wed, which was to go
into effect in May 2004. In March 2005 a ruling by the San Francisco Superior
Court said that California's state law banning same-sex marriage was a violation
of the rights of gays and lesbians. This ruling also nullified the state's Proposition
22, approved by referendum in 2000 (by 61.4 to 38.6 percent), limiting marriage
to one man and one woman. This was all the more important because it was California and the judge was a registered Republican appointed in 1996 by a Republican governor. Finally, these developments put fire back into President George W.
Bush's pledge to support a constitutional amendment banning same-sex marriage,
even though polls have shown substantial majorities favoring some form of same-
sex union, whether marriage or "civil union."[7] In effect, although a great many
state laws are observed in a normal, routine way in sister states, laws that confront
what have come to be called "values" will be exempted from comity—or taken off
the table altogether by an amendment to that effect in the U.S. Constitution.

.[6]Ken I. Kersch, "Full Faith and Credit for Same-Sex Marriages?" *Political Science Quarterly* 112 (Spring
    1997): 117–36; Joan Biskupic, "Once Unthinkable, Now under Debate," *Washington Post*, 3 September
    1996, p. A1.
[7]This is a peculiar, albeit effective distinction because all marriages are "civil unions"—and nothing else.

Because of this controversy, the extent and meaning of the full faith and credit clause is sure to be considered by the Supreme Court. In fact, it is not clear that the clause requires states to recognize gay marriage because the Court's past interpretation of the clause has provided exceptions for "public policy" reasons: If states have strong objections to a law, they do not have to honor it. In 1997 the Court took up a case involving the full faith and credit clause. The case concerned a Michigan court order that prevented a former engineer for General Motors from testifying against the company. The engineer, who left the company on bad terms, later testified in a Missouri court about a car accident in which a woman died when her Chevrolet Blazer caught fire. General Motors challenged his right to testify, arguing that Missouri should give "full faith and credit" to the Michigan ruling. The Supreme Court ruled that the engineer could testify and that the court system in one state cannot hinder other state courts in their "search for the truth."[8]

Article IV, Section 2, known as the "comity clause," also seeks to promote national unity. It provides that citizens enjoying the ***privileges and immunities*** of one state should be entitled to similar treatment in other states. What this has come to mean is that a state cannot discriminate against someone from another state or give special privileges to its own residents. For example, in the 1970s, when Alaska passed a law that gave residents preference over nonresidents in obtaining work on the state's oil and gas pipelines, the Supreme Court ruled the law illegal because it discriminated against citizens of other states.[9] This clause also regulates criminal justice among the states by requiring states to return fugitives to the states from which they have fled. Thus, in 1952, when an inmate escaped from an Alabama prison and sought to avoid being returned to Alabama on the grounds that he was being subjected to "cruel and unusual punishment" there, the Supreme Court ruled that he must be returned according to Article IV, Section 2.[10] This example highlights the difference between the obligations among states and those among different countries. In the late 1990s, France refused to return an American fugitive because he might be subject to the death penalty, which does not exist in France.[11] The Constitution clearly forbids states from doing something similar.

Limitations on the States   Although most of the truly coercive powers of government are reserved to the states, the Constitution does impose some significant limitations. One example was already given in the discussion of the privileges and immunities clause: that one state cannot discriminate against a person residing in another state. But the most prominent application of this clause bears the name *extradition*; any person in any state "who shall flee from justice [to] another State, shall on Demand . . . be delivered up . . . to the State

privileges and immunities clause   Provision from Article IV, Section 2, of the Constitution that a state cannot discriminate against someone from another state or give its own residents special privileges.

---

[8]Linda Greenhouse, "Supreme Court Weaves Legal Principles from a Tangle of Legislation," *New York Times*, 30 June 1988, p. A20.

[9]*Hicklin v. Orbeck*, 437 U.S. 518 (1978).

[10]*Sweeny v. Woodall*, 344 U.S. 86 (1953).

[11]Marlise Simons, "France Won't Extradite American Convicted of Murder," *New York Times*, 5 December 1997, p. A9.

having jurisdiction . . ." (Article IV, Section 2). In the last section, we gave the example of the 1952 case of an Alabama inmate.

Another limitation on states that occasionally becomes significant is a clause in Article I, Section 10 that provides that "no state shall, without the Consent of Congress . . . enter in any Agreement or Compact with another state." Compacts are a way for two or more states to reach a legally binding agreement about how to solve a problem that crosses state lines. In the early years of the Republic, states turned to compacts primarily to settle border disputes. Today they are used for a wide range of issues but are especially important in regulating the distribution of river water, addressing environmental concerns, and operating transportation systems that cross state lines.[12] The most famous contemporary example is the Port of New York Authority, a compact formed between New York and New Jersey in 1921. Without the port authority, such public works as the bridges connecting Brooklyn and Staten Island as well as New Jersey and Staten Island, the Lincoln Tunnel, the completion of the George Washington Bridge, the expansion and integration of the New York port area, and the expansion and integration of the three major airports and countless approaches in transfer facilities could not have been financed or built.[13] In 1972, the name was changed to the Port Authority of New York and New Jersey.

Local Government and the Constitution Local government occupies a peculiar but very important place in the American system. In fact, the status of American local government is probably unique in world experience. First, it must be pointed out that local government has no status in the American Constitution. *State* legislatures created local governments, and *state* constitutions and laws permit local governments to take on some of the responsibilities of the state governments. Most states amended their own constitutions to give their larger cities *home rule*—a guarantee of noninterference in various areas of local affairs. But local governments enjoy no such recognition in the Constitution. Local governments have always been mere conveniences of the states.[14]

Local governments became administratively important in the early years of the Republic because the states possessed little administrative capability. They relied on local governments—cities and counties—to implement the laws of the state. Local government was an alternative to a statewide bureaucracy.

home rule
Power delegated by the state to a local unit of government to manage its own affairs.

---

[12]Patricia S. Florestano, "Past and Present Utilization of Interstate Compacts in the United States" *Publius* (Fall 1994): 13–26.

[13]A good discussion of the status in politics of the New York Port Authority is found in Wallace Sayre and Herbert Kaufman, *Governing New York City—Politics in the Metropolis* (New York: Russell Sage Foundation, 1960), Chapter 9.

[14]A good discussion of the constitutional position of local governments is in York Y. Willbern, *The Withering away of the City* (Bloomington: Indiana University Press, 1971). For more on the structure and theory of federalism, see Thomas R. Dye, *American Federalism: Competition among Governments* (Lexington, MA.: Lexington Books, 1990), Chapter 1; and Martha Derthick, "Up-to-Date in Kansas City: Reflections on American Federalism" (the 1992 John Gaus Lecture), *PS: Political Science & Politics* 25 (December 1992): 671–75.

The Slow Growth of the National Government's Power

Dual federalism, a two-layered system—national and state—in which the states and their local principalities do most of the governing, is demonstrated in Table 3.1. The items in each column (disregarding the local-level functions dealt with in the previous section) are the important types of public policies that governed America for the first century and a half under the Constitution. We refer to it here as the "traditional system" precisely because almost nothing about our pattern of government changed during two thirds of our history. That is, of course, with the exception of the four years of the Civil War, after which we returned to the traditional system.

But there was more to dual federalism than merely the existence of two tiers. The two tiers were functionally quite different from each other. There have been debates every generation over how to divide responsibilities between the two tiers. As we have seen in this chapter, the Constitution delegated a list of specific powers to the national government and reserved all the rest to the states. That left a lot of room for interpretation, however, because of the final "elastic" clause of Article I, Section 8. The three formal words *necessary and proper* amounted to an invitation to struggle over the actual distribution of powers between national and state governments. We will confront this struggle throughout the book. However, the most remarkable thing about the history of American federalism is that it remained *dual* for nearly two thirds of that history, with the national government remaining steadfastly within a "strict construction" of Article I, Section 8. The results are clear in Table 3.1.

The best example of the potential elasticity in Article I, Section 8 is in the *commerce clause,* which delegates to Congress the power "to regulate commerce with foreign nations, and *among the several states* and with the Indian tribes." It is obvious that this clause can be interpreted broadly or narrowly, and in fact the Supreme Court embraced the broad interpretation throughout most of the nineteenth century. Yet Congress chose not to take the Court's invitation to be expansive. The first and most important case favoring national power was *McCulloch v. Maryland.*[15] The issue was whether Congress had the power to charter a bank, in particular the Bank of the United States, because no power to create banks was found anywhere in Article I, Section 8. Chief Justice John Marshall, speaking for the Supreme Court, answered that such a power could be "implied" from the other specific powers in Article I, Section 8, plus the final clause enabling Congress "to make all Laws which shall be necessary and proper for carrying into Execution the foregoing Powers." Thus the Court created the potential for significant increases in national government power. Congress had created the Bank of the United States in 1791 (over Thomas Jefferson's constitutional opposition).

A second question of national power arose in *McCulloch v. Maryland* over whether Maryland's attempt to tax the bank was constitutional. Once again Marshall and the Supreme Court took the side of the national government, arguing that a legislature representing all the people (Congress) could not be taxed out of business by a state legislature (Maryland) representing only a small portion of the

dual federalism
The system of government that prevailed in the United States from 1789 to 1937 in which most fundamental governmental powers were shared between the federal and state governments.

 Institution Principle

In answering "Who does what?" federalism determines the flow of government functions and, through that, the political development of the country.

 Institution Principle

The national–state tug-of-war is an institutional feature of the federal system.

commerce clause
Article I, Section 8, of the Constitution, which delegates to Congress the power "to regulate Commerce with foreign Nations, and among the several States, and with the Indian Tribes." This clause was interpreted by the Supreme Court in favor of national power over the economy.

[15]*McCulloch v. Maryland,* 4 Wheaton 316 (1819).

TABLE 3.1

The Federal System: Specialization of Governmental Functions in the Traditional System (1789–1937)

NATIONAL GOVERNMENT POLICIES (DOMESTIC)	STATE GOVERNMENT POLICIES	LOCAL GOVERNMENT POLICIES
Internal improvements	Property laws (including slavery)	Adaptation of state laws to local conditions ("variances")
Subsidies	Estate and inheritance laws	Public works
Tariffs	Commerce laws	Contracts for public works
Public lands disposal	Banking and credit laws	Licensing of public accommodations
Patents	Corporate laws	Assessable improvements
Currency	Insurance laws	Basic public services
	Family laws	
	Morality laws	
	Public health laws	
	Education laws	
	General penal laws	
	Eminent domain laws	
	Construction codes	
	Land-use laws	
	Water and mineral laws	
	Criminal procedure laws	
	Electoral and political parties laws	
	Local government laws	
	Civil service laws	
	Occupations and professions laws	

Under the traditional system, the separate levels of government typically handled different types of policies. On the domestic front, the federal government focused on promoting commerce, whereas state and local policies dealt mainly with various forms of regulation.

American people. This was accompanied by Marshall's immortal dictum that "the power to tax is the power to destroy." It was also in this case that the Supreme Court recognized and reinforced the supremacy clause: Whenever a state law conflicts with a federal law, the state law should be deemed invalid because "the laws of the United States . . . shall be the supreme law of the land." (This was introduced in Chapter 2 and will return again in Chapter 8.)

This nationalistic interpretation of the Constitution was reinforced by another major case, that of *Gibbons v. Ogden* in 1824. The important but relatively narrow issue was whether the state of New York could grant a monopoly to Robert Fulton's steamboat company to operate an exclusive service between New York and New Jersey. Ogden had secured his license from Fulton's company, while Gibbons, a former partner of Ogden's, secured a competing license from the U.S. government. Chief Justice Marshall argued that Gibbons could not be kept from competing because the state of New York did not have the power to grant this particular monopoly. To reach this decision, it was necessary for Chief Justice Marshall to define what Article I, Section 8, meant by "Commerce . . . among the several States." Marshall insisted that the definition was "comprehensive" but added that the comprehensiveness was limited "to that commerce which concerns more states than one." This gave rise to what later came to be called "interstate commerce."[16] Although *Gibbons* was an important case, the precise meaning of interstate commerce would remain uncertain for several decades of constitutional discourse. However, one thing was certain: "Interstate commerce" was a source of power for the national government as long as Congress sought to improve commerce through subsidies, services, and land grants (Table 3.1, col. 1). But later in the nineteenth century, when the national government sought to use its power to *regulate* the economy rather than merely promote economic development, the concept of interstate commerce began to operate as a restraint rather than as a source of national power. Any effort by the federal government to regulate commerce in such areas as fraud, the production of impure goods, the use of child labor, or the existence of dangerous working conditions or long hours was declared unconstitutional by the Supreme Court as a violation of the concept of interstate commerce. Regulation in these areas would mean the federal government was entering the factory and workplace, areas inherently local because the goods produced there had not yet passed into commerce and crossed state lines. Any effort to enter these local workplaces was an exercise of police power—the power reserved to the states. No one questioned the power of the national government to regulate certain kinds of businesses, such as railroads, gas pipelines, and waterway transportation, because they intrinsically involved interstate commerce.[17] But well into the twentieth century, most other efforts by Congress to regulate commerce were blocked by the Supreme Court's interpretation of federalism, with the concept of interstate commerce as the primary barrier.

---

[16]*Gibbons v. Ogden*, 9 Wheaton 1 (1824).

[17]*In Wabash, St. Louis, and Pacific Railway Company v. Illinois*, 118 U.S. 557 (1886), the Supreme Court struck down a state law prohibiting rate discrimination by a railroad; in response, Congress passed the Interstate Commerce Act of 1887 creating the Interstate Commerce Commission (ICC), which was the first federal regulatory agency.

After 1937, the Supreme Court threw out the old distinction between interstate and intrastate commerce, converting the commerce clause from a barrier to a source of power. The Court began to refuse even to review appeals challenging acts of Congress protecting the rights of employees to organize and engage in collective bargaining, regulating the amount of farmland in cultivation, extending low-interest credit to small businesses and farmers, restricting the activities of corporations dealing in the stock market, and many other laws that contributed to the construction of the "regulatory state" and the "welfare state."[18]

Cooperative Federalism and Grants-in-Aid

If the traditional system of two sovereigns performing highly different functions could be called dual federalism, the system since the 1930s could be called *cooperative federalism*—which generally refers to supportive relations, sometimes partnerships, between the national government and the state and local governments. It comes in the form of federal subsidization of special state and local activities; these subsidies are called *grants-in-aid.* But make no mistake about it: Although many of these state and local programs would not exist without the federal grant-in-aid, the grant-in-aid is also an important form of federal influence. (Another form of federal influence, the mandate, is covered in the next section.)

A grant-in-aid is really a kind of bribe, or "carrot," whereby Congress appropriates money for state and local governments with the condition that the money be spent for a particular purpose as defined by Congress. Congress uses grants-in-aid because it does not have the political or constitutional power to command cities to do its bidding. When you can't command, a monetary inducement becomes a viable alternative. Grants-in-aid are also mechanisms that help coordinate the separate activities of all those state and local governments around a common set of standards or policy principles in circumstances when a multiplicity of these things would undermine the purposes of the policy.

The principle of the grant-in-aid goes back to the nineteenth-century land grants to states for the improvement of agriculture and farm-related education. Since farms were not in "interstate commerce," it was unclear whether the Constitution would permit the national government to provide direct assistance to agriculture. Grants-in-aid to the states, earmarked to go to farmers, presented a way of avoiding the constitutional problem while pursuing what was recognized in Congress as a national goal.

Beginning in the late 1930s, this same approach was applied to cities. Congress set national goals, such as public housing and assistance to the unemployed, and provided grants-in-aid to meet these goals. World War II temporarily stopped the distribution of these grants. But after the war, Congress resumed providing grants for urban development and school lunches. The value of such *categorical grants-in-aid* increased from \$2.3 billion in 1950 to \$406 billion in 2002 (Figure 3.1).

[18]This will come up again in Chapter 6, with the effect of the new role of the national government on presidential and congressional power.

FIGURE 3.1

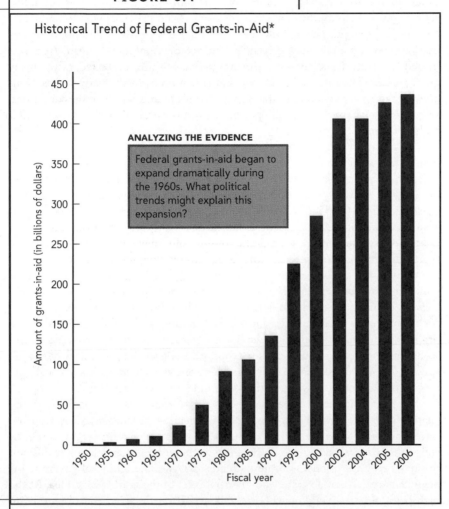

Historical Trend of Federal Grants-in-Aid*

ANALYZING THE EVIDENCE

Federal grants-in-aid began to expand dramatically during the 1960s. What political trends might explain this expansion?

Y-axis: Amount of grants-in-aid (in billions of dollars)

X-axis: Fiscal year — 1950, 1955, 1960, 1965, 1970, 1975, 1980, 1985, 1990, 1995, 2000, 2002, 2004, 2005, 2006

*Excludes outlays for national defense, international affairs, and net interest.

SOURCE: Office of Management and Budget, *Budget of the United States Government, Fiscal Year 2006, Analytical Perspectives* (Washington, DC: Government Printing Office, 2005), Table 8-3, p. 131.

Sometimes Congress requires the state or local government to match the national contribution dollar for dollar, but for some programs, such as the interstate highway system, the congressional grant-in-aid provides 90 percent of the cost of the program. The nationwide speed limit of fifty-five miles per hour was not imposed on individual drivers by an act of Congress. Instead, Congress bribed the state legislatures by threatening to withdraw the federal highway grants-in-aid if the states did not set that speed limit. In the early 1990s, Congress began to ease up on the states, permitting them, under certain conditions, to go back to the sixty-five mile per hour limit (or higher) without losing their highway grants.

For the most part, the categorical grants created before the 1960s simply helped the states perform their traditional functions such as education and policing.[19] In the 1960s, however, the national role expanded, and the number of categorical grants increased dramatically. For example, during the Eighty-ninth Congress (1965–66) alone, the number of categorical grant-in-aid programs grew from 221 to 379.[20] The grants authorized during the 1960s announced national purposes much more strongly than did earlier grants. Central to that national purpose was the need to provide opportunities to the poor.

project grants
Grant programs in which state and local governments submit proposals to federal agencies and for which funding is provided on a competitive basis.

formula grants
Grants-in-aid in which a formula is used to determine the amount of federal funds a state or local government will receive.

Many of the categorical grants enacted during the 1960s were *project grants,* which require state and local governments to submit proposals to federal agencies. In contrast to the older *formula grants,* which used a formula (composed of such elements as need and state and local capacities) to distribute funds, the new project grants made funding available on a competitive basis. Federal agencies would give grants to the proposals they judged to be the best. In this way, the national government acquired substantial control over which state and local governments got money, how much they got, and how they spent it.

The most important student of the history of federalism, Morton Grodzins, characterized the shift to post–New Deal cooperative federalism as a move from "layer cake federalism" to "marble cake federalism,"[21] in which intergovernmental cooperation and sharing have blurred the distinguishing line, making it difficult to say where the national government ends and the state and local governments begin. Figure 3.2 demonstrates the financial basis of the marble cake idea. At the high point of grant-in-aid policies in the late 1970s, federal aid contributed 25 to 30 percent of the operating budgets of all the state and local governments in the country (Figure 3.3). Table 3.2 presents some of the more extreme examples from 1977 and the severe drop since that time.

---

[19]Kenneth T. Palmer, "The Evolution of Grant Policies," *The Changing Politics of Federal Grants,* in ed. Lawrence D. Brown, James W. Fossett, and Kenneth T. Palmer (Washington, DC: Brookings Institution, 1984), p. 15.

[20]Ibid., p. 6.

[21]Morton Grodzins, "The Federal System," in *Goals for Americans,* ed. President's Commission on National Goals (Englewood Cliffs, NJ: Prentice-Hall, 1960), p. 265. In a marble cake, the white cake is distinguishable from the chocolate cake, but the two are streaked rather than in distinct layers.

FIGURE 3.2

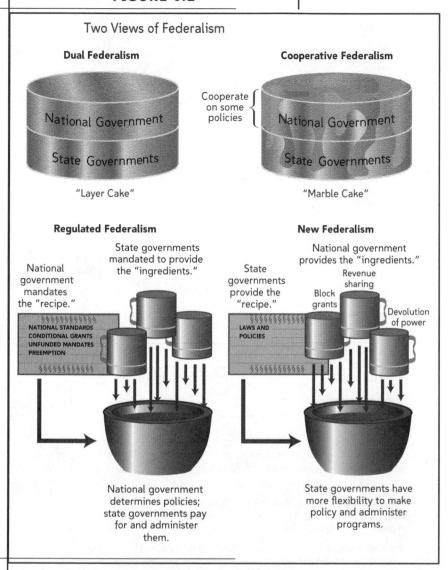

Two Views of Federalism

Dual Federalism

National Government

State Governments

"Layer Cake"

Cooperative Federalism

Cooperate on some policies

National Government

State Governments

"Marble Cake"

Regulated Federalism

National government mandates the "recipe."

State governments mandated to provide the "ingredients."

NATIONAL STANDARDS
CONDITIONAL GRANTS
UNFUNDED MANDATES
PREEMPTION

National government determines policies; state governments pay for and administer them.

New Federalism

National government provides the "ingredients."

State governments provide the "recipe."

Revenue sharing

Block grants

Devolution of power

LAWS AND POLICIES

State governments have more flexibility to make policy and administer programs.

In marble cake federalism, national policies, state policies, and local policies overlap in many areas. Under new federalism, states have much more leeway to experiment with various policies to achieve the goals of the national government.

FIGURE 3.3

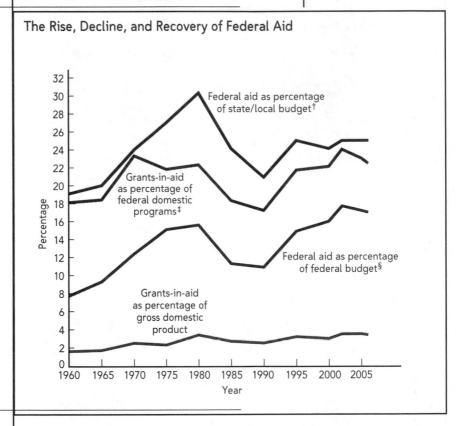

The Rise, Decline, and Recovery of Federal Aid

The extent to which grants to state and local governments use up the federal government's entire budget has fluctuated as the nature of federalism has changed. State and local governments have at times relied on federal funds for a substantial portion of their budget.

†Federal aid as a percentage of state and local expenditures after transfers.
‡Federal aid as a percentage of federal expenditures from its own funds.
§Excludes outlays for national defense, international affairs, and net interest.

SOURCE: Office of Management and Budget, *Budget of the United States Government, Fiscal Year 2006, Analytical Perspectives* (Washington, DC: Government Printing Office, 2005), Table 8-3, p. 131.

TABLE 3.2

Federal Aid as a Percentage of General Annual Expenditure							
CITY	1977	1999	2001	CITY	1977	1999	2001
Chicago	20	8	7	Houston	13	6	4
Cleveland	29	8	4	Indianapolis	21	3	3
Denver	14	2	1	Los Angeles	22	7	3
Detroit	31	9	7	San Antonio	28	2	2
Honolulu	30	9	8	Seattle	23	4	1

SOURCE: Department of Commerce, *Statistical Abstract of the United States, 2004–2005* (Washington, DC: Government Printing Office, 2004), Tables 449 and 450.

Regulated Federalism and National Standards

Developments from the 1960s to the present have moved well beyond cooperative federalism to what might be called "regulated federalism."[22] In some areas the national government actually regulates the states by threatening to withhold grant money unless state and local governments conform to national standards. One example is the establishment of a national highway speed limit of 55 mph for several years during and after the oil crisis of the late 1970s. Every state obeyed the new national standard in response to a federal threat to cut off their interstate highway subsidies if they refused to go along. (Congress repealed the penalties for higher speed limits in 1995.) However, the most notable instances of this kind of regulated federalism are in the areas of civil rights, poverty programs, and environmental protection. This reflects a general shift in federal regulation away from the oversight and control of strictly economic activities toward "social regulation"—interventions on behalf of individual rights and liberties, environmental protection, workplace safety, and so on. In these instances, the national government provides grant-in-aid financing but sets conditions the states must meet to keep the grants. The national government refers to these policies as "setting national standards." Important examples include the Asbestos Hazard Emergency Act of 1986, which requires school districts to inspect for asbestos hazards and to remove them from school buildings

[22] The concept and the best discussion of this modern phenomenon is found in Donald F. Kettl, *The Regulation of American Federalism* (Baltimore: Johns Hopkins University Press, 1983 and 1987), especially pp. 33–41.

when necessary, and the Americans with Disabilities Act of 1990, which requires all state and local governments to promote access for the handicapped to all government buildings. The net effect of these national standards is that state and local policies are more uniform from coast to coast. As we noted earlier about grants-in-aid, national regulations and standards provide coordination across states and localities and solve collective-action problems. However, there are a number of other programs in which the national government engages in regulated federalism by imposing national standards on the states *without providing any funding at all*. These have come to be called **unfunded mandates.** States complained that mandates took up so much of their budgets that they were not able to set their own priorities.[23]

unfunded mandates
National standards or programs imposed on state and local governments by the federal government without accompanying funding or reimbursement.

These burdens became a major part of the rallying cry that produced the famous Republican Congress elected in 1994, with its Contract with America. One of the first measures adopted by the 104th Republican Congress in 1995 was an act to limit unfunded mandates—the Unfunded Mandates Reform Act (UMRA). This was considered a triumph of lobbying efforts by state and local governments, and it was "hailed as both symbol and substance of a renewed congressional commitment to federalism."[24] Under this law, any mandate with an uncompensated state and local cost estimated at greater than $50 million a year, as determined by the Congressional Budget Office (CBO), can be stopped by a point of order raised on the House or Senate floor. This was called a "stop, look and listen" requirement, forcing Congress to take positive action to own up to the mandate and its potential costs. During 1996, its first full year of operation, only eleven bills included mandates that exceeded the $50 million threshold—from a total of sixty-nine estimates of actions in which mandates were included. Examples included minimum wage increase, parity for mental health and health insurance, mandated use of Social Security numbers on driver's licenses, and extension of federal Occupation Safety & Health standards to state and local employees. Most of them were modified in the House, to reduce their costs. However, as one expert put it, "The primary impact of UMRA came not from the affirmative blockage of [mandate] legislation, but rather from its effect as a deterrent to mandates in the drafting and early consideration of legislation."[25]

As indicated by the first year of its operation, the effect of UMRA will not be revolutionary. UMRA does not prevent congressional members from passing unfunded mandates; it only makes them think twice before they do. Moreover, the act exempts several areas from coverage by UMRA. And states must still enforce antidiscrimination laws and meet other requirements to receive federal assistance. But, on the other hand, UMRA does represent a serious effort to move the national–state relationship a bit further toward the state side.

[23]John J. DiIulio and Donald F. Kettl report that in 1980 there were thirty-six laws that could be categorized as unfunded mandates. And despite the concerted opposition of the Reagan and George H. W. Bush administrations, another twenty-seven laws qualifying as unfunded mandates were adopted between 1982 and 1991. See John DiIulio Jr., and Donald F. Kettl, *Fine Print: The Contract with America, Devolution, and the Administrative Realities of American Federalism* (Washington, DC: Brookings Institution, 1995), p. 41.

[24]Paul Posner, "Unfunded Mandate Reform: How Is It Working?" *Rockefeller Institute Bulletin* (Albany: Nelson A. Rockefeller Institute of Government, 1998): 35.

[25]Ibid., 36.

President George W. Bush made this a key feature of his electoral campaign of 2000 and his legislative agenda of 2001. Yet the most heralded item in his domestic policy agenda, the No Child Left Behind Act (NCLB), a concept going back to his successful program as governor of Texas, *is a very expensive unfunded mandate!* Signed into law in January 2002, it set a national standard for steady improvement in student performance on standardized tests and punishes schools whose students fail to improve. It also set rules for educating disabled students and presented detailed requirements that, as lobbyists for the states put it, "fail to recognize the tapestry of educational challenges faced by teachers in the nation's 15,000 school districts."[26] President Bush's promise that NCLB would provide the money for compliance brought him support from his leading Democratic opposition voice in the Senate, Senator Edward Kennedy. Republican leaders could only say that, while the law *authorized* as much as $80 billion for high-poverty schools alone, the Democrats surely understood that this was an authorization to be met by 2007 and not an amount to be appropriated for a single year or even during Bush's second term.

Opposition lobbying of Congress and the president by state government representatives became so intense that in 2004 the National Conference of State Legislatures began publishing the *Mandate Monitor*, which itemizes the "gap" in funding it claims is directly attributable to Congress's failure to appropriate the support necessary to comply with unfunded mandates. The first results of this analysis produced a list of fifteen major federal programs—the largest being education (No Child Left Behind and Independents with Disabilities), State Drug Costs for the Dual-Eligibles, and the Department of Homeland Security. These have contributed to a total "cost shift" from the federal government to the states. According to the National Conference of State Legislatures, the cost shift in federal funding to the states for fiscal years 2004 and 2005 collectively was $51 billion, and the estimate for 2006 alone is $30 billion. However, the NCSL insists that these are estimates and that "additional research . . . strongly suggests the cost shift to the states is double these amounts."[27] Though the measurement of these gaps can be criticized, the scale of "unfunded and under-funded mandates" is undeniable. Note also that the responsibility for this enormous shortfall is not attributable only to the party in power.

New Federalism and the National-State Tug-of-War

Federalism in the United States can best be understood today as a tug-of-war between those seeking more uniform national standards and those seeking more room for variability from state to state. This is a struggle over federalism's script and scorecard—over who does what and how the various activities are structured and sequenced. Presidents Nixon and Reagan called their efforts to reverse

---

[26]Sam Dillon, "Report from States Faults Bush's Education Initiative," *New York Times*, 24 February 2005, p. A18.

[27]*Mandate Monitor*, An Information Service of the NCSL Budgets and Revenue Committee, Vol. 2, Issue 1, 10 March 2005.

block grants
Federal funds given to state governments to pay for goods, services, or programs, with relatively few restrictions on how the funds may be spent.

the trend toward national standards and reestablish traditional policy making and implementation the "new federalism." They helped craft national policies whose purpose was to return more discretion to the states. Examples of these policies include Nixon's revenue sharing and Reagan's **block grants,** which consolidated a number of categorical grants into one larger category, leaving the state (or local) government more discretion to decide how to use the money. Presidents Nixon and Reagan, as well as former president Bush, were sincere in wanting to return somewhat to a traditional notion of freedom of action for the states. They called it new federalism, but their concepts and their goals were really much closer to the older, traditional federalism that predated the 1930s.

In effect, President Clinton adopted the "new federalism" of Nixon and Reagan even while expanding federal grant activity: he signed the Unfunded Mandates Reform Act of 1995 and the Personal Responsibility and Work Opportunity Reconciliation Act of 1996, which goes further than any other act of Congress in the past sixty years to relieve the states from national mandates, funded or unfunded. This new law replaced the sixty-one-year-old program of Aid to Families with Dependent Children (AFDC) and its education, work, and training program with block grants to states for Temporary Assistance to Needy Families (TANF). Although some national standards remain, the place of the states in the national welfare system has been virtually revolutionized through **devolution,** the strategy of delegating to the states more and more authority over a range of policies that had up until then been under national government authority, plus providing the states with a substantial portion of the cost of these programs. Since the mid-1990s, devolution has been quite consequential for the national–state tug-of-war.

devolution
A policy to remove a program from one level of government by deregulating it or passing it down to a lower level of government, such as from the national government to the state and local governments.

Collective-Action Principle
States compete with one another not only for new business, but also in terms of being less attractive to welfare recipients.

By changing welfare from a combined federal–state program into a block grant to the states, Congress gave the states more responsibility for programs that serve the poor. One argument in favor of devolution is that states can act as "laboratories of democracy" by experimenting with many different approaches to find one that best meets the needs of their citizens.[28] As states have altered their welfare programs in the wake of the new law, they have indeed designed diverse approaches. For example, Minnesota has adopted an incentive-based approach that offers extra assistance to families that take low-wage jobs. Other states, such as California, have more "sticks" than "carrots" in their new welfare programs.[29]

Policy Principle
Devolution has had an important influence on policy outcomes, particularly welfare.

President George W. Bush, though sometimes compared to Ronald Reagan, has not been an unwavering supporter of smaller national government, new federalism, and states' rights. On a number of very important matters dear to his heart, Bush has been closer to the spirit of the New Deal and "regulated federal-

---

[28]The phrase *laboratories of democracy* was coined by Supreme Court Justice Louis Brandeis in his dissenting opinion in *New State Ice Co. v. Liebman,* 285 U.S. 262 (1932).

[29]For assessments of the use of welfare grants to the states for increased regulation as a condition for welfare benefits, see Frances Fox Piven, "Welfare and Work," and Dorothy Roberts, "Welfare's Ban on Poor Motherhood," in *Whose Welfare?,* ed. Gwendolyn Mink (Ithaca, NY: Cornell University Press, 1999), pp. 83–99 and 152–167.

ism" in terms of both direct expansion of the national government and increasing imposition of national standards on the states. The former has gone by the name "compassionate conservatism," and it has not been altogether popular among his own partisan supporters. The latter is called "unfunded mandates," and such mandates not only rankle his supporters but go against strict rules established by his administration. Some of the expansions of national government under Bush are clearly attributable to 9/11 and the gigantic reaction to world terrorism, the creation of the Department of Homeland Security, and, after March 2003, the war in Iraq and the cost of Katrina, all complicated by failed implementation. But President Bush had other plans for the national government that he brought with him from his experience as a governor. His No Child Left Behind Act increased by 51 percent the budget of the Department of Education, a department that conservatives had vowed since the Reagan administration to abolish. Agriculture subsidies were increased by 40 percent. The 2005 Transportation Act incorporated a commitment of $286 billion, of which $24 billion was for "pork barrel projects" for favorite congressional districts. The prescription drug benefit that he added to Medicare was another enormous national government commitment; its estimated cost is $534 billion, the largest expansion of the welfare state since LBJ.[30]

The Supreme Court as Referee   For much of the nineteenth century, federal power remained limited. The Tenth Amendment was used to bolster arguments about ***states' rights,*** which in their extreme version claimed that the states did not have to submit to national laws when they believed the national government had exceeded its authority. These arguments in favor of states' rights were voiced less often after the Civil War. But the Supreme Court continued to use the Tenth Amendment to strike down laws that it thought exceeded national power, including the Civil Rights Act passed in 1875.

In the early twentieth century, however, the Tenth Amendment appeared to lose its force. Reformers began to press for national regulations to limit the power of large corporations and to preserve the health and welfare of citizens. The Supreme Court approved of some of these laws, but it struck others down, including a law combating child labor. The Court stated that the law violated the Tenth Amendment because only states should have the power to regulate conditions of employment. By the late 1930s, however, the Supreme Court had approved such an expansion of federal power that the Tenth Amendment appeared irrelevant. In fact, in 1941, Justice Harlan Fiske Stone declared that the Tenth Amendment was simply a "truism," that it had no real meaning.[31]

Recent years have seen a revival of interest in the Tenth Amendment and important Supreme Court decisions limiting federal power. Much of the interest in the Tenth Amendment stems from conservatives who believe that a strong federal

states' rights
The principle that states should oppose increasing authority of the national government. This view was most popular before the Civil War.

---

[30]The figures and judgments in this paragraph are provided by George F. Will, one of America's most distinguished conservative columnists/philosophers: "The Last Word," *Newsweek,* 27 October 2005, p. 78.
[31]*United States v. Darby Lumber Co.,* 312 U.S. 100 (1941).

Federalism and the No Child Left Behind Act

Education has traditionally been a responsibility of state and local governments, but in the past forty years has increasingly become a federal responsibility. Starting in the 1960s, the federal government tried to address inequities in educational attainment, particularly for poor and minority populations, using grants-in-aid and other programs. Without federal action, educational advocates argued, there was no way to coordinate state and local responsibilities. But the bulk of educational funding still came from local property taxes, and many local governments resisted federal encroachment on education. Still, via cooperative federalism, the national government's influence over local educational policies grew rapidly.

Fast-forward to the 2000 election. Republican candidate George W. Bush's strategy to counter his Democratic opponent, Al Gore, was to promote himself as a "compassionate conservative." Texas, especially the large Harris County school district, which included Houston, had been a laboratory for some well-publicized experiments with high-stakes testing.[1] Naturally, education reform was an important part of Bush's campaign plank. Once elected, Bush acted on this promise rapidly, pressing for the passage of No Child Left Behind.

On January 8, 2002, President George W. Bush proudly signed into law the No Child Left Behind Act (NCLB). This legislation, he promised, would raise academic standards, reward successful schools, penalize failing ones, and begin a new era of accountability in American education.[2] NCLB's most controversial provisions included regular "high-stakes" testing and significant financial and enrollment penalties for schools identified as "failing" via those tests.

Just a few years after the passage of NCLB, the National Education Association, along with school districts in Texas, Michigan, and Vermont, is suing the U.S. Department of Education, charging that NCLB constitutes a massive unfunded mandate.[3] The Utah state legislature passed a bill that gives local and state laws precedence over any federal mandate, including NCLB. And President Bush's own state of Texas was fined for failing to comply with the law.[4]

What happened in only two years to a bill that passed overwhelmingly in the House and Senate and enjoyed broad bipartisan support? The politics of NCLB illustrates many of the principles of politics as they apply to federal/state relations in the United States.

NCLB relies heavily on regulated federalism rather than on cooperative federalism. Under regulated federalism, Congress writes the rules but does not have to pay the bills. And given the burgeoning federal budget deficit, Congress is in no mood to be writing new checks. So even though no one opposes education standards, state and local governments, many of whose budgets are in the worst shape in decades, simply don't have the resources to implement major new programs. At the same time, if a state does not implement NCLB programs, it risks losing any federal funding it is receiving. State governments are between the federal rock and a budgetary hard place, and as a result are complaining bitterly.

History Principle

Education has always been funded largely by local governments, making those governments wary of federal involvement.

Rationality Principle

Candidate Bush's invocation of "compassionate conservatism" was an effort to counter the image that Republicans did not care about less-well-off Americans.

Policy Principle

Regulated federalism is a problem because it allows Congress to vote in favor of a policy but not have to find a way to pay for it.

NCLB also suffers from the "one size fits all" problem that bedevils many federal regulations. NCLB does not allow for local flexibility in meeting its standards. For example, schools with relatively high numbers of students with disabilities or students for whom English was a second language had to meet some of the same performance benchmarks as schools in suburban areas that had generous funding and a well-off student population. The outcome from the first few rounds of high-stakes testing has been that many of the troubled schools, where educators believe they have struggled mightily against forces that they cannot control, are now identified as "failing," and as a result stand to lose teachers, students, and funding.

Finally, NCLB, while it received bipartisan support in Congress, crosscuts many traditional Republican and Democratic party positions on federal spending and federal authority. As a result, it has created strange bedfellows. Neoconservatives complain that NCLB created an intrusive set of federal regulations. In this they were joined by the traditionally liberal National Education Association and teacher unions. Democrats, along with many local officials, complain that NCLB is a massive unfunded mandate. Republicans, who in their 1994 "Contract with America" pledged to end unfunded mandates, continue to defend NCLB.

Collective-Action Principle

Legislation like No Child Left Behind, which crosscut traditional partisan divisions, may be surprisingly easy to pass since it attracts support across the political spectrum.

[1]Roderick Paige, Bush's Secretary of Education, previously served as the superintendent of the Harris County school district.

[2]The main components of NCLB are (1) improving academic performance of disadvantaged students; (2) improving the quality of teachers and principals; (3) raising the standards of English-language proficiency programs; (4) promoting parental choice; and (5) improving the educational environment for Native Indian, Hawaiian, and Alaskan Americans. See www.ed.gov for the full text of the bill.

[3]An unfunded mandate is a requirement imposed by the federal government on state and local governments with no funding to pay for it.

[4]Ben Feller, "Educators Launch National Suit in Michigan over Education Law," Associated Press, 20 April 2005. Rob Hotakainen, "No State Left Untouched by Education Law; Fine against Texas Schools Highlights a Growing Rift," *Star Tribune* (Minneapolis, MN), 9 May 2005.

government encroaches on individual liberties. They believe such freedoms are better protected by returning more power to the states through the process of devolution. In 1996, Republican presidential candidate Bob Dole carried a copy of the Tenth Amendment in his pocket as he campaigned, pulling it out to read at rallies.[32] Around the same time, the Eleventh Amendment concept of *state sovereign immunity* was revived by the Court. This legal doctrine holds that states are immune from lawsuits by private persons or groups claiming that the state violated a statute enacted by Congress.

state sovereign immunity
Legal doctrine holding that states cannot be sued for violating an act of Congress.

[32]W. John Moore, "Pleading the 10th," *National Journal*, 29 July 1995, p. 1940.

The Supreme Court's ruling in *United States v. Lopez* in 1995 fueled further interest in the Tenth Amendment. In that case, the Court, stating that Congress had exceeded its authority under the commerce clause, struck down a federal law that barred handguns near schools. This was the first time since the New Deal that the Court had limited congressional powers in this way. The Court further limited the power of the federal government over the states in a 1996 ruling based on the Eleventh Amendment that prevented Native Americans from the Seminole tribe from suing the state of Florida in federal court. A 1988 law had given Indian tribes the right to sue a state in federal court if the state did not negotiate in good faith over issues related to gambling casinos on tribal land. The Supreme Court's ruling appeared to signal a much broader limitation on national power by raising new questions about whether individuals can sue a state if it fails to uphold federal law.[33]

Another significant decision involving the relationship between the federal government and state governments was the 1997 case *Printz v. United States* (joined with *Mack v. United States*), in which the Court struck down a key provision of the Brady Bill, enacted by Congress in 1993 to regulate gun sales. Under the terms of the act, state and local law enforcement officers were required to conduct background checks on prospective gun purchasers. The Court held that the federal government cannot require states to administer or enforce federal regulatory programs. Because the states bear administrative responsibility for a variety of other federal programs, this decision could have far-reaching consequences. Finally, in another major ruling from the 1996–97 term, in *City of Boerne v. Flores*, the Court ruled that Congress had gone too far in restricting the power of the states to enact regulations they deemed necessary for the protection of public health, safety, or welfare. These rulings signal a move toward a much more restricted federal government.

In 1999, the Court's ruling on another Eleventh Amendment case further strengthened the doctrine of state sovereign immunity, finding that "the federal system established by our Constitution preserves the sovereign status of the States. . . . The generation that designed and adopted our federal system considered immunity from private suits central to sovereign dignity."[34] As reported earlier, in 2000 in *United States v. Morrison*,[35] the Supreme Court invalidated an important provision of the 1994 Violence against Women Act, which permitted women to bring private damage suits if their victimization was "gender-motivated." Although the 1994 act did not add any new national laws imposing liability or obligations on the states, the Supreme Court still held the act to be "an unconstitutional exercise" of Congress's power. And, although *Morrison* is a quite narrow federalism decision, when it is coupled with *United States v. Lopez* (1995)—the first modern holding against national authority to use commerce power to reach into the states—there is a definite trend toward strict scrutiny of the federal intervention aspects of all national civil rights, social, labor, and gender laws.

[33] *Seminole Indian Tribe v. Florida*, 116 S. Ct. 1114 (1996).
[34] *Alden v. Maine.*
[35] *United States v. Morrison*, 529 U.S. 598 (2000).

This puts federalism and the Court directly in the line of fire. But there is nothing new in this. The Court under John Marshall was, on net, a nationalizing court. Marshall's successor, Chief Justice Taney, gave us the most extreme denationalizing period—virtually inventing the concept of "states' rights," as slavery and its extension were endangering the Union. The Court in place when FDR was first elected was extremely anti-national; it declared virtually all the novel New Deal programs unconstitutional. And, most notoriously, that same Court, after Roosevelt's landslide 1936 re-election, followed public opinion into the longest and most profound pro-nationalizing era. (It should be explained once again that the national government was permitted to expand *but not at the expense of the states*.) The only remarkable thing about the current era has been the moderation and patience of the Burger and Rehnquist Courts in turning the tendency back toward the states.

This tug-of-war between state and national levels of government will almost certainly continue. The Roberts Court will surely take us further back toward the state level, but how far back will depend on the number and character of justices as new presidents, new parties, and new vacancies on the Court arise.

THE SEPARATION OF POWERS

In his discussion of the separation of powers, James Madison quoted the originator of the principle, the French political thinker Baron de Montesquieu:

> There can be no liberty where the legislative and executive powers are united in the same person . . . [or] if the power of judging be not separated from the legislative and executive powers.[36]

Using this same reasoning, many of Madison's contemporaries argued that there was not *enough* separation among the three branches, and Madison had to backtrack to insist that the principle did not require complete separation:

Institution Principle

Checks and balances is a system of "separated institutions sharing power."

> . . . unless these departments [branches] be so far connected and blended as to give to each a constitutional control over the others, the degree of separation which the maxim requires, as essential to a free government, can never in practice be duly maintained.[37]

This is the secret of how we have made the separation of powers effective: we made the principle self-enforcing by giving each branch of government the means to participate in, and partially or temporarily to obstruct, the workings of the other branches.

[36]Clinton Rossiter, ed., *The Federalist Papers* (New York: New American Library, 1961), No. 47, p. 302.
[37]Ibid., No. 48, p. 308.

Checks and Balances

checks and balances
Mechanisms through which each branch of government is able to participate in and influence the activities of the other branches.

The means by which each branch of government interacts is known informally as *checks and balances.* The best-known examples are the presidential power to veto legislation passed by Congress; the power of Congress to override the veto by a two-thirds majority vote, to impeach the president, and (of the Senate) to approve presidential appointments; the power of the president to appoint the members of the Supreme Court and the other federal judges with Senate approval; and the power of the Supreme Court to engage in judicial review (discussed below). These and other examples are shown in Table 3.3. The framers sought to guarantee that the three branches would in fact use the checks and balances as weapons against each other by giving each branch a different political constituency: direct, popular election of the members of the House; indirect election of senators (until the Seventeenth Amendment, adopted in 1913); indirect election of the president (which still exists, at least formally, today); and appointment of federal judges for life. All things considered, the best characterization of the separation of powers principle in action is, as we said in Chapter 2, "separated institutions sharing power."[38]

Legislative Supremacy

legislative supremacy
The preeminent position assigned to Congress by the Constitution.

 Institution Principle
The framers provided for legislative supremacy by making Congress the preeminent branch.

Although each branch was to be given adequate means to compete with the other branches, it is also clear that within the system of separated powers the framers provided for *legislative supremacy* by making Congress the preeminent branch. Legislative supremacy made the provision of checks and balances in the other two branches all the more important.

The most important indication of the intention of legislative supremacy was made by the framers when they decided to place the provisions for national powers in Article I, the legislative article, and to treat the powers of the national government as powers of Congress. In a system based on the "rule of law," the power to make the laws is the supreme power. Section 8 provides in part that "*Congress* shall have Power . . . To lay and collect Taxes . . . To borrow Money . . . To regulate Commerce . . ." [emphasis added]. The founders also provided for legislative supremacy in their decision to give Congress the sole power over appropriations and to give the House of Representatives the power to initiate all revenue bills. Madison recognized legislative supremacy as part and parcel of the separation of powers:

> . . . It is not possible to give to each department an equal power of self-defense. In republican government, the legislative authority necessarily predominates. The remedy for this inconveniency is to divide the legislature into different branches; and to render them, by different modes of election and different principles of action, as little connected with each other as the nature of their common functions and their common dependence on the society will admit.[39]

[38]Richard E. Neustadt, *Presidential Power and the Modern Presidents: The Politics of Leadership from Roosevelt to Reagan* (New York: Free Press, 1960, rev. ed. 1990), p. 33.

[39]Rossiter, ed., *The Federalist Papers*, No. 51, p. 322.

TABLE 3.3

Checks and Balances

	LEGISLATIVE BRANCH CAN BE CHECKED BY	EXECUTIVE BRANCH CAN BE CHECKED BY	JUDICIAL BRANCH CAN BE CHECKED BY
LEGISLATIVE BRANCH CAN CHECK	—	Can overrule veto (two-thirds vote) Controls appropriations Controls by statute Impeachment of president Senate approval of appointments and treaties Committee oversight	Controls appropriations Can create inferior courts Can add new judges Senate approval of appointments Impeachment of judges
EXECUTIVE BRANCH CAN CHECK	Can veto legislation Can convene special session Can adjourn Congress when chambers disagree Vice president presides over Senate and votes to break ties	—	President appoints judges
JUDICIAL BRANCH CAN CHECK	Judicial review of legislation Chief justice presides over Senate during proceedings to impeach president	Judicial review over presidential actions Power to issue warrants Chief justice presides over impeachment of president	—

Checks and balances exist when each branch has the ability to participate in, and thus control, the activities of another branch.

In other words, Congress was so likely to dominate the other branches that it would have to be divided against itself, into House and Senate. One could say that the Constitution provided for four branches, not three.

Although "presidential government" seemed to supplant legislative supremacy after 1937, the relative power position of the executive and legislative branches since that time has not been static. The degree of conflict between the president and Congress has varied with the rise and fall of political parties, and it has been especially tense during periods of ***divided government,*** when one party controls the White House and another controls the Congress, as has been the case almost solidly since 1969.

divided government
The condition in American government when the presidency is controlled by one party while the opposing party controls one or both houses of Congress.

The Role of the Supreme Court

The role of the judicial branch in the separation of powers has depended on the power of judicial review (see Chapter 8), a power not provided for in the Constitution but asserted by Chief Justice Marshall in 1803:

> If a law be in opposition to the Constitution; if both the law and the Constitution apply to a particular case, so that the Court must either decide that case conformable to the law, disregarding the Constitution, or conformable to the Constitution, disregarding the law; the Court must determine which of these conflicting rules governs the case: This is of the very essence of judicial duty.[40]

Review of the constitutionality of acts of the president or Congress is relatively rare.[41]

For example, there were no Supreme Court reviews of congressional acts in the fifty plus years between *Marbury v. Madison* (1803) and *Dred Scott* (1857). In the century or so between the Civil War and 1970, eighty-four acts of Congress were held unconstitutional (in whole or in part), but there were long periods of complete Supreme Court deference to the Congress, punctuated by flurries of judicial review during times of social upheaval. The most significant of these was 1935–36, when twelve acts of Congress were invalidated, blocking virtually the entire New Deal program.[42] Then, after 1937, when the Court made its great reversals, no significant acts were voided until 1983, when the Court declared unconstitutional the legislative veto.[43] Another, in 1986, struck down the Gramm-Rudman Act mandating a balanced budget, which, the Court held, delegated too much power to the

---

[40]*Marbury v. Madison*, 1 Cranch 137 (1803).

[41]C. Herman Pritchett, *The American Constitution* (New York: McGraw-Hill, 1959), pp. 180–86.

[42]In response to New Deal legislation, the Supreme Court struck down eight out of ten New Deal statutes. For example, in *Panama Refining Co. v. Ryan*, 293 U.S. 388 (1935), the Court ruled that a section of the National Industrial Recovery Act was an invalid delegation of legislative power to the executive branch. And in *Schechter Poultry Co. v. United States*, 295 U.S. 495 (1935), the Court found the National Industrial Recovery Act itself to be invalid for the same reason. But since 1935, the Supreme Court has rarely confronted the president or Congress on constitutional questions.

[43]*Immigration and Naturalization Service v. Chadha*, 462 U.S. 919 (1983).

comptroller general to direct the president to reduce the budget.[44] The Supreme Court became much more activist (i.e., less deferential to Congress) after the elevation of Justice William H. Rehnquist to chief justice (1986), and "a new program of judicial activism"[45] seemed to be in place; but this could be a conservative one against Congress comparable to the liberal activism against the states during the Warren Court of the 1960s and 1970s. All of the cases in Table 3.4 altered some aspect of federalism by declaring unconstitutional all or an important portion of an act of Congress, and the end of this episode of judicial activism against Congress is not over. Between 1995 and 2002, at least twenty-six acts or parts of acts of Congress were struck down on constitutional grounds.[46]

Since the New Deal period, the Court has been far more deferential toward the president, with only five significant confrontations. One was the so-called *Steel Seizure* case of 1952, in which the Court refused to permit President Truman to use "emergency powers" to force workers back into the steel mills during the Korean War.[47] A second case was *United States v. Nixon*, in which the Court declared unconstitutional President Nixon's refusal to respond to a subpoena to make available the infamous White House tapes as evidence in a criminal prosecution. The Court argued that, although **executive privilege** did protect confidentiality of communications to and from the president, this did not extend to data in presidential files or tapes varying on criminal prosecutions.[48] During the heat of the Clinton scandal, the Supreme Court rejected the claim that the pressures and obligations of the office of president was so demanding that all litigation "but the most exceptional cases" should be deferred until his term ends.[49] But of far greater importance, the Supreme Court struck down the Line-Item Veto Act of 1996 on the grounds that it violated Article I, Section 7, which prescribed procedures for congressional enactment and presidential acceptance or veto of statutes. Any such change in the procedures of adopting laws would have to be made by amendment to the Constitution, not by legislation.[50]

The fifth confrontation came after the September 11, 2001, terrorist attacks. But because of the terrorism scare, this was the least restrictive of the five. It came in *Rasul v. Bush* 244 S. Ct. 2686 (2004), in which the Court held that the estimated 550 "enemy combatants" detained without formal charges at Guantánamo Bay Naval Base, Cuba, had the right to seek release through a **writ of habeas corpus.**[51] However, the *Rasul* decision left a very large escape hatch by relegating to the lower district courts the decision, case by case, whether to actually grant the writ. The first

executive privilege The claim that confidential communications between a president and close advisers should not be revealed without the consent of the president.

writ of habeas corpus A court order demanding that an individual in custody be brought into court and shown the cause for detention. *Habeas corpus* is guaranteed by the Constitution and can be suspended only in cases of rebellion or invasion.

[44]*Bowsher v. Synar,* 478 U.S. 714 (1986).
[45]Cass R. Sunstein, "Taking Over the Courts," *New York Times,* 9 November 2002, p. A19.
[46]Ibid.
[47]*Youngstown Sheet & Tube Co. v. Sawyer,* 343 U.S. 579 (1952).
[48]*United States v. Nixon,* 418 U.S. 683 (1974).
[49]*Clinton v. Jones,* 117 S.Ct. 1636 (1997).
[50]*Clinton v. City of New York,* 524 U.S. 417 (1998).
[51]*Rasul v. Bush,* 244 S. Ct. 2686 (2004).

TABLE 3.4

A New Federal System?
The Recent Case Record

CASE	DATE	COURT HOLDING
United States v. Lopez, 514 U.S. 549	1995	Voids federal law barring handguns near schools. Beyond Congress's power to regulate commerce.
Seminole Indian Tribe v. Florida, 517 U.S. 44	1996	Voids federal law giving tribes the right to sue a state in federal court. "Sovereign immunity" requires state permission to be sued.
Printz v. United States (and *Mack v. United States*), 117 S.Ct. 2365	1997	Voids key provision of Brady Law requiring states to make background checks on gun purchases. As "unfunded mandate," it violates state sovereignty under Tenth Amendment.
City of Boerne v. Flores, 521 U.S. 507	1997	Restricts Congress's power to regulate city zoning, health and welfare policies to "remedy" rights but not expand rights, under Fourteenth Amendment.
Alden v. Maine, 119 S.Ct. 2240	1999	State also "immune" from suits by their *own* employees for overtime pay under federal Fair Labor Standards Act. (See also *Seminole* case.)
United States v. Morrison, 529 U.S. 598	2000	Extends *Seminole* case by invalidating Violence against Women Act, holding that states are immune to suits by individuals to enforce federal laws.

application came in early 2005, when a federal district judge in Washington denied *habeas corpus* to seven detainees. Essential to the judge's reasoning was the resolution that Congress adopted on September 18, 2001, authorizing President Bush to use "all necessary and appropriate force" and that "unless Congress adopts legislation limiting the president's powers, there is nothing the courts can do."[52] One glint of hope for the detainees had come in a Supreme Court case handed down earlier in 2004 in which Justice Sandra Day O'Connor (in one of the several opinions in a disjointed Court) asserted that the requirements of due process could be met in a military tribunal. The Pentagon quickly embraced her invitation.[53]

Like federalism, the separation of powers is an ongoing struggle. Deference to the president is not necessarily a permanent condition, because it is a war phenomenon and not a partisan phenomenon. However, reversal will not be easy, even after the war is considered over. More and more executive branch activities are being put beyond the reach of the courts, and if the more conservative "strict constructionist" justices display the same deference as the liberal justices do, discretionary executive power will be increasingly difficult to harness as a constructive participant in the separation of powers, because eventually such deference unbalances the "checks and balances."

ALTERING THE BALANCE OF POWER: WHAT ARE THE CONSEQUENCES?

Federalism and the separation of powers are two of the three fundamental constitutional principles on which the U.S. system of limited government is based (the third is the principle of individual rights). By its very existence, federalism recognizes the principle of two sovereigns: the national government and the state government (hence the term *dual federalism*). In addition, the Constitution specifically restrained the power of the national government to regulate the economy. As a result, the states were free to do most of the fundamental governing for the first century and a half of American government. This began to change during and after the New Deal, as the national government began to exert more influence over the states through grants-in-aid and mandates. In the last decade, however, we have noticed a countertrend to the growth of national power as Congress has opted to devolve some of its powers to the states. The most recent notable instance of devolution was the welfare reform plan of 1996.

But the problem that arises with devolution is that programs that were once uniform across the country (because they were the national government's responsibility) can become highly variable, with some states providing benefits not

---

[52]Reported in Charles Lane and John Mintz, "Detainees Lose Bid for Release," *Washington Post*, 20 January 2005, p. A03.

[53]Reported in David B. Rivkin and Lee A. Casey, "Bush's Good Day in Court," *Washington Post*, 4 August 2004, p. A19. Though a military tribunal does not favor the defendant with a "presumption of innocence," it is far better than no trial at all.

available in other states. To a point, variation can be considered one of the virtues of federalism. But there are dangers inherent in large variations and inequalities in the provision of services and benefits in a democracy. For example, because the Food and Drug Administration has been under attack in recent years, could the problem be solved by devolving its regulatory tasks to the states? Would people care if drugs would require "caution" labels in some states and not in others? Would Americans want each state to set its own air and water pollution control policies without regard to the fact that pollution flows across state boundaries? Devolution, as attractive as it may be, is not an approach that can be applied across the board without analyzing carefully the nature of the program and of the problems it is designed to solve. Even the capacity of states to handle "devolved" programs will vary. According to the Washington research organization the Brookings Institution, the level of state and local government employment varies from state to state—from a low of 400 per 10,000 residents in some states to a high of 700 per 10,000 in others. "Such administrative diversity is bound to mediate the course and consequences of any substantial devolution of federal responsibility; no one-size-fits-all devolution [from federal to state and local government] can work."[54]

Moreover, the temptation is ever present for federal politicians to limit state discretion to achieve their own policy objectives. Indeed, the "devolution revolution" promised by congressional Republicans created much more rhetoric than action. Despite the complaints of Republican governors, Congress has continued to use its power to preempt state action and impose mandates on states. The No Child Left Behind Act sets some exacting national standards; and Bush's prescription drugs program and his welfare reform plans are strong additions to the national safety net. Looking ahead, one of the most ominous dangers in devolution is what has come to be called the "race to the bottom," where states in this age of globalization are free to compete with each other in giving concessions to foreign and interstate companies to attract new industry.

The second principle of limited government, separation of powers, is manifested in our system of checks and balances, whereby separate institutions of government share power with each other. Even though the Constitution clearly provided for legislative supremacy, checks and balances have functioned well. Some would say they have worked too well. The last fifty years have witnessed long periods of divided government, when one party has controlled the White House and the other party controlled Congress. During these periods, the level of conflict between the executive and legislative branches has been particularly divisive, resulting in what some analysts derisively call gridlock. Nevertheless, this is a genuine separation of powers, not so far removed from the intent of the framers. Go back to the Schiavo case, in which there was a historic struggle between the branches as well as between nation and state. And this drama sets the stage for more struggles between the president and Senate over the presi-

History Principle

The legacy of cooperative federalism and national standards has raised some doubts about devolution.

---

[54]Eliza Newlin Carney, "Power Grab," *National Journal*, 11 April 1998, p. 798.

Rationality Principle	Collective-Action Principle	Institution Principle	Policy Principle	History Principle
As political institutions, federalism and the separation of powers have adapted to the purposes of various political players.	Grants-in-aid allow the national government to coordinate state and local policies around a common set of national standards. States compete with one another not only for new businesses but also in terms of being less attractive to welfare recipients.	The Constitution created jurisdictional arrangements by encouraging diversity in the elected leaders and allocating the consideration of different aspects of policy to different institutional arenas. In answering "Who does what?" federalism determines the flow of government functions and, through that, the political development of the country. The national–state tug-of war is an institutional feature of the federal system. Checks and balances is a system of "separated institutions sharing power." The framers provided for legislative supremacy by making Congress the preeminent branch.	Devolution has had an important influence on policy outcomes, particularly welfare.	Since the time of the founding, federalism has been shaped strongly by the Supreme Court. In 1937, the Supreme Court converted the commerce clause from a source of limitations to a source of power for the national government. The legacy of cooperative federalism and national standards has raised some doubts about devolution.

dent's power of appointment to the federal courts, confronting also the Senate's own tradition of respect for the minority's power through the filibuster. And 2005 was just one more year in which there was an extensive fight between Congress and the Pentagon over who gets to decide which "surplus" military bases ought to be closed down. Meanwhile, during the months after September 11, and despite Congress's granting of almost complete discretion in the conduct of the war against terrorism, President Bush felt it necessary to organize an unprecedentedly large White House Office of Legislative Affairs—a euphemistic title for White House lobbying.

With the rise of political parties, Americans developed a parliamentary theory that "responsible party government" requires that the same party control both branches, including both chambers of the legislature. But that kind of parliamentary/party government is a "fusion of powers," not a separation of powers. Although it may not make for good government, having an opposition party in majority control of the legislature reinforces the separation and the competition that were built into the Constitution. We can complain about the inability of divided government to make decisions, and we can criticize it as stalemate or gridlock,[55] but even that is in accord with the theory of the framers of the Constitution that public policy is supposed to be difficult to make.

SUMMARY

In this chapter we have traced the development of two of the three basic principles of the U.S. Constitution—federalism and the separation of powers. Federalism involves a division between two layers of government: national and state. The separation of powers involves the division of the national government into three branches. These principles are limitations on the powers of government; Americans made these compromises as a condition for giving their consent to be governed. And these principles became the framework within which the government operates. The persistence of local government and the reliance of the national government on grants-in-aid to coerce local governments into following national goals were used as case studies to demonstrate the continuing vitality of the federal framework. Examples were also given of the intense competition among the president, Congress, and the courts to dramatize the continuing vitality of the separation of powers.

The purpose of a constitution is to organize the makeup or the composition of the government, the *framework within which* government and politics, including actual legislation, can take place. A country does not require federalism and the separation of powers to have a real constitutional government. And the country does not have to approach individual rights in the same manner as the American Constitution. But to be a true constitutional government, a government must have a few limits so that it cannot be manipulated by people in power merely for their own convenience. This is the essence of constitutionalism—limits on power that are above the reach of everyday legislators, executives, bureaucrats, and politicians, yet are not so far above their reach that they cannot be adapted to changing times.

[55]Not everybody will agree that divided government is much less productive than government in which both branches are controlled by the same party. See David R. Mayhew, *Divided We Govern: Party Control, Lawmaking, and Investigations, 1946–1990* (New Haven, CT: Yale University Press, 1991). For another good evaluation of divided government, see Charles O. Jones, *Separate but Equal Branches: Congress and the Presidency* (Chatham, NJ: Chatham House, 1995).

FOR FURTHER READING

Bensel, Richard F. *Sectionalism and American Political Development: 1880–1980*. Madison: University of Wisconsin Press, 1984.

Bernstein, Richard B., with Jerome Agel. *Amending America—If We Love the Constitution So Much, Why Do We Keep Trying to Change It?* (Lawrence: University Press of Kansas, 1993).

Black, Charles L., Jr. *Impeachment: A Handbook*. New Haven, CT: Yale University Press, 1974, 1998.

Caraley, Demetrios. "Dismantling the Federal Safety Net: Fictions Versus Realities." *Political Science Quarterly*, 8, no. 2 (Summer 1996): 225–58.

Corwin, Edward, and J. W. Peltason. *Corwin & Peltason's Understanding the Constitution*. 13th ed. Fort Worth, TX: Harcourt Brace, 1994.

Crovitz, L. Gordon, and Jeremy A. Rabkin, eds. *The Fettered Presidency: Legal Constraints on the Executive Branch*. Washington, DC: American Enterprise Institute, 1989.

Dye, Thomas R. *American Federalism: Competition among Governments*. Lexington, MA: Lexington Books, 1990.

Elazar, Daniel J. *American Federalism: A View from the States*. 3rd ed. New York: Harper & Row, 1984.

Ferejohn, John A., and Barry R. Weingast, eds. *The New Federalism: Can the States Be Trusted?* Stanford, CA: Hoover Institution Press, 1997.

Grodzins, Morton. *The American System: A New View of Government in the United States*. Chicago: Rand McNally, 1974.

Kahn, Ronald. *The Supreme Court and Constitutional Theory, 1953–1993*. Lawrence: University Kansas Press, 1994.

Kettl, Donald F. *The Regulation of American Federalism*. Baltimore: Johns Hopkins University Press, 1987.

Noonan, John T. *Narrowing the Nation's Power: The Supreme Court Sides with the States*. Berkeley: University of California Press, 2002.

Peterson, Paul E. *The Price of Federalism*. Washington, DC: Brookings Institution, 1995.

Smith, Rogers M. *Civic Ideals: Conflicting Visions of Citizenship in U.S. History*. New Haven, CT: Yale University Press, 1997.

Politics in the News—
Reading between the Lines

Fiscal Federalism in the Twenty-first Century

States Rejecting Demand
to Pay for Medicare Cost

By ROBERT PEAR

States are openly resisting a provision of the Medicare law that requires them to pay billions of dollars a year to the federal government to help finance the cost of the new Medicare drug benefit.

Texas is leading the charge against the requirement, which states see as more onerous than the mandates imposed on them by the 2002 education law, the No Child Left Behind Act.

Gov. Rick Perry, a Republican, has vetoed a $444 million appropriation covering the Texas contribution for the next two years.

In his veto message and in a letter to other governors, Mr. Perry said he objected to the federal requirement in principle and to the way it was being interpreted by the federal Medicare agency.

"For the first time," Mr. Perry said, "state governments would be expected to directly finance federal Medicare benefits with state tax dollars. In effect, states will be billed on a monthly basis for the cost of federal services."

Bush administration officials say the

federal Medicare law clearly requires states to make the payments, starting in January. One purpose of the 2003 Medicare law was to relieve states of prescription drug costs for low-income elderly people. But as states do the arithmetic, many have concluded that they will lose money because they must give back most of the savings and will incur new administrative costs. . . .

About seven million people are simultaneously eligible for Medicaid, the federal-state program for low-income people, and Medicare, the federally financed program for the elderly and disabled. Medicaid now covers drug costs for such "dual eligibles." On Jan. 1, Medicare will take over the responsibility.

But under the Medicare law, states must make monthly payments to the federal Treasury to help defray the cost. If a state fails to comply, the federal government can simply deduct the amount owed, plus interest, from its regular payments to the state's Medicaid program.

New York Times, 3 June 2005, p. A9.

The legislation was pushed through Congress by President Bush and Republican leaders. But at the state level, Republicans and Democrats alike express qualms about the costs and the precedent. . . .

When Medicaid recipients fill prescriptions, the federal government and the states share the costs, just as they do for other Medicaid benefits like doctors' services and hospital care. The Bush administration says states should save money under the 2003 law because the federal government will pay almost all drug costs for Medicaid recipients and most drug costs for retired state employees.

"Texas is going to come out ahead by many millions of dollars," said Gary R. Karr, a spokesman for the federal Centers for Medicare and Medicaid Services. "That's the intent of the law, to save states money as Medicare picks up the cost of prescription drugs for those on Medicare and Medicaid. States cannot withhold their payments simply because they'd like a larger windfall."

But the National Governors Association says the clawback requirement will cause many states to spend more on Medicaid than they would under prior law. In addition, state officials said, they will have new costs. Under the 2003 law, they must establish procedures to determine whether low-income people qualify for extra help with their drug expenses. . . .

Ms. Edwards, the Ohio Medicaid director, said the clawback costs were "a real blow to our ability to provide benefits to other people." To come up with the money in a tight budget, she said, Ohio is eliminating Medicaid coverage for 25,000 low-income parents and has reduced dental benefits for 800,000 adults.

ESSENCE OF THE STORY

- The new Medicare prescription drug plan includes a provision whereby the federal government pays for the benefit, but requires the state governments to reimburse the federal government for the expense. If they do not pay, the federal government will withhold the funds from regular Medicaid payments.

- This provision is called "reverse revenue sharing" by some governors.

- Texas governor Rick Perry, a Republican, vetoed a bill that authorized the payments; Ohio has had to cut some Medicaid coverage in order to cover Medicare payments to the government.

POLITICAL ANALYSIS

- The Supreme Court decided long ago that the federal government is preeminent. The federal government has tended to pass mandates onto the state governments without paying for them, but this is the first instance in which the federal government actually takes money back from the states.

- Reducing taxes at the federal level is politically popular; expanding political programs is also popular. The combination of these preferences at the federal level and the lack of rules holding Congress financially responsible for these mandates creates a situation in which the federal government can create new programs even though it cannot pay for them.

- Because many states operate under constitutional provisions that require a balanced budget, something not required at the federal level, fiscal federalism in an era of federal budget deficits will increase these institutional conflicts between governors and state legislatures on the one hand, and the president and the Congress on the other.

CHAPTER

4

The Constitutional Framework and the Individual: Civil Liberties and Civil Rights

When the First Congress under the new Constitution met in late April of 1789 (having been delayed since March 4 by lack of a quorum because of bad winter roads), the most important item of business was consideration of a proposal to add a bill of rights to the Constitution. Such a proposal by Virginia delegate George Mason had been turned down with little debate in the waning days of the Philadelphia Constitutional Convention in September 1787, not because the delegates were too tired or too hot or against rights, but because of arguments by Hamilton and other Federalists that a bill of rights was irrelevant in a constitution providing the national government with only delegated powers. How could the national government abuse powers not given to it in the first place? But when the Constitution was submitted to the states for ratification, Antifederalists, most of whom had *not* been delegates in Philadelphia, picked up on the argument of Thomas Jefferson (who also had not been a delegate) that the omission of a bill of rights was a major imperfection of the new Constitution. Whatever the merits of Hamilton's or Jefferson's positions, to gain ratification, the Federalists in Massachusetts, South Carolina, New Hampshire, Virginia, and

New York made an "unwritten but unequivocal pledge" to add a bill of rights and a promise to confirm (in what became the Tenth Amendment) the understanding that all powers not delegated to the national government or explicitly prohibited to the states were reserved to the states.[1]

James Madison, who had been a delegate at the Philadelphia convention and later became a member of Congress, may still have agreed privately that a bill of rights was not needed. But in 1789, recognizing the urgency of obtaining the support of the Antifederalists for the Constitution and the new government, he fought for the bill of rights, arguing that the principle it embodied would acquire "the character of fundamental maxims of free Government, and as they become incorporated with the national sentiment, counteract the impulses of interest and passion."[2] Madison and his fellow Virginian delegates were, if nothing else, practical men. Although they may have conceded on principle Hamilton's argument against the need for a bill of rights, *principle* was not what the debate was all about. They felt that, as a practical political matter, it was essential to put to rest the arguably unnecessary and exaggerated fears of the less-than-enthusiastic supporters of the new Constitution. It was also thought prudent to take off the table, so to speak, a possible issue—the absence of explicit protections a bill of rights would provide—that could be brandished by opponents of the new regime the first time a crisis occurred. Prudence, foresight, and practicality were behind Madison's support for these changes in the new Constitution.

"After much discussion and manipulation . . . at the delicate prompting of Washington and under the masterful prodding of Madison," the House adopted seventeen amendments; the Senate adopted twelve of these. Ten of the amendments

Collective-Action Principle

The Federalists supported a bill of rights because it would gain the support of the Antifederalists for the Constitution.

Rationality Principle

Madison believed a bill of rights would remove a potential source of opposition to the new government.

CHAPTER OUTLINE

Civil Liberties: Nationalizing the Bill of Rights

- Dual Citizenship

- The Fourteenth Amendment

- The Constitutional Revolution in Civil Liberties

- Rehnquist and Beyond: A De-nationalizing Trend?

Civil Rights

- *Plessy v. Ferguson:* "Separate but Equal"

- Racial Discrimination after World War II

- Civil Rights after *Brown v. Board of Education*

- The Rise of the Politics of Rights

- Affirmative Action

[1] Clinton L. Rossiter, *1787: The Grand Convention*, Norton Library Edition (New York: Norton, 1987), p. 302.

[2] Quoted in Milton Konvitz, "The Bill of Rights: Amendments I–X," in *An American Primer*, ed. Daniel J. Boorstin (Chicago: University of Chicago Press, 1966), p. 159.

were ratified by the states on December 15, 1791—from the start, these ten were called the Bill of Rights.[3]

The Bill of Rights—its history and the controversy of interpretation surrounding it—can be usefully subdivided into two categories: civil liberties and civil rights. This chapter is divided accordingly. **Civil liberties** are defined as *protections of citizens from improper government action*. When adopted in 1791, the Bill of Rights was seen as guaranteeing a private sphere of personal liberty free of governmental restrictions.[4] As Jefferson had put it, a bill of rights "is what people are entitled to *against every government on earth.* . . ." Note the emphasis—citizen *against* government. In this sense, we could call the Bill of Rights a "bill of liberties" because the amendments focus on what government must *not* do. For example (with emphasis added),

civil liberties
Protections of citizens from improper government action.

1. "Congress shall make *no* law . . ." (I)
2. "The right . . . to . . . bear Arms, shall *not* be infringed" (II)
3. "*No* Soldier shall . . . be quartered . . ." (III)
4. "*No* Warrants shall issue, but upon probable cause . . ." (IV)
5. "*No* person shall be held to answer . . . unless on a presentment or indictment of a Grand Jury . . ." (V)
6. "Excessive bail shall *not* be required . . . *nor* cruel and unusual punishments inflicted." (VIII)

Thus the Bill of Rights is a series of "thou shalt nots"—restraints addressed to governments. Some of these restraints are *substantive*, putting limits on *what* the government shall and shall not have power to do—such as establishing a religion, quartering troops in private homes without consent, or seizing private property without just compensation. Other restraints are *procedural*, dealing with *how* the government is supposed to act. For example, even though the government has the substantive power to declare certain acts to be crimes and to arrest and imprison persons who violate its criminal laws, it may not do so except by fairly meticulous observation of procedures designed to protect the accused person. The best-known procedural rule is that "a person is presumed innocent until proven guilty." This rule does not question the government's power to punish someone for committing a crime; it questions only the way the government determines *who* committed the crime. Substantive and procedural restraints together identify the realm of civil liberties.

civil rights Legal or moral claims that citizens are entitled to make on the government.

We define **civil rights** as obligations imposed on government to guarantee equal citizenship and to protect citizens from discrimination by other private cit-

---

[3]Rossiter, *1787: The Grand Convention*, p. 303, where he also reports that "in 1941 the States of Connecticut, Massachusetts, and Georgia celebrated the sesquicentennial of the Bill of Rights by giving their hitherto withheld and unneeded assent."

[4]Lest our interchangeable use of the words *liberty* and *freedom* be confusing, treat as synonyms. *Freedom* is from the German *Freiheit*. *Liberty* is from the French *liberté*. Both have to do with the absence of restraints on individual choices of action.

izens and other government agencies. Civil rights did not become part of the Constitution until 1868 with the adoption of the Fourteenth Amendment, which addressed the issue of who was a citizen and provided for each citizen "the equal protection of the laws." From that point on, we can see more clearly the distinction between civil liberties and civil rights, because civil liberties issues arise under the "due process of law" clause, and civil rights issues arise under the "equal protection of the laws" clause.

We turn first to civil liberties and to the long history of the effort to make personal liberty a reality for every citizen in America. The struggle for freedom against arbitrary and discriminatory actions by governments has continued to this day. And inevitably it is tied to the continuing struggle for civil rights, to persuade those same governments to take positive actions. We deal with that in the second section of this chapter, but we should not lose sight of the connection in the real world between civil liberties and civil rights. We should also not lose sight of the connection to the constitutional framework established in Chapter 3. Although individual liberties and rights were identified in Chapter 3 as making up the third of the three most important bases in the Constitution, the third cannot be understood except in the context of the other two, especially federalism.

PREVIEWING THE PRINCIPLES

We can conceive of both civil liberties and civil rights as the "rules" that govern government action and the responsibilities the government has to protect citizens from one another. History matters as well. The rules and procedures that are adopted in one era live on and shape the political reasoning, goals, and actions of political actors in subsequent eras. In many ways, debates over civil liberties and rights today are shaped by the historical development of these concepts and their interpretations by key political actors, most notably the members of the Supreme Court.

CIVIL LIBERTIES: NATIONALIZING THE BILL OF RIGHTS

The First Amendment provides that "Congress shall make no law respecting an establishment of religion . . . or abridging the freedom of speech, or of the press; or the right of [assembly and petition]." But this is the only amendment in the Bill of Rights that addresses itself exclusively to the national government. For example, the Second Amendment provides that "the right of the people to keep and bear Arms, shall not be infringed." The Fifth Amendment says, among other things, that *no person* "shall . . . be twice put in jeopardy of life or limb" for the same crime; that *no person* "shall be compelled in any criminal case to be a witness against himself"; that *no person* shall "be deprived of life, liberty, or property, without due process of law"; and that private property cannot be taken "without just compensation."[5] Because the First Amendment is the only part of the Bill of Rights that is explicit in its intention to put limits on the national government, a fundamental question inevitably arises: *Do the remaining amendments of the Bill of Rights put limits on state governments or only on the national government?*

Dual Citizenship

The question concerning whether the Bill of Rights also limits state governments was settled in 1833 in a way that seems odd to Americans today. The 1833 case was *Barron v. Baltimore*, and the facts were simple. In paving its streets, the city of Baltimore had disposed of so much sand and gravel in the water near Barron's wharf that the value of the wharf for commercial purposes was virtually destroyed. Barron brought the city into court on the grounds that it had, under the Fifth Amendment, unconstitutionally deprived him of his property. Barron had to take his case all the way to the Supreme Court, despite the fact that the argument made by his attorney seemed airtight. The following is Chief Justice John Marshall's characterization of Barron's argument:

> The plaintiff [Barron] . . . contends that it comes within that clause in the Fifth Amendment of the Constitution which inhibits the taking of private property for public use without just compensation. He insists that this amendment, being in favor of the liberty of the citizen, ought to be so construed as to restrain the legislative power of a state, as well as that of the United States.[6]

Then Marshall, in one of the most significant Supreme Court decisions ever handed down, disagreed:

> The Constitution was ordained and established by the people of the United States for themselves, for their own government, and not for the government of individual States. Each State established a constitution for itself, and in that constitution provided such limitations and restrictions on the powers of its particular government as its judgment dictated. . . . If these propositions be correct, *the fifth amendment must be understood as restraining the power of the General Government, not as applicable to the States.*[7]

In other words, if an agency of the *national* government had deprived Barron of his property, there would have been little doubt about Barron's winning his case. But if the constitution of the state of Maryland contained no such provision pro-

[5]It would be useful at this point to review all the provisions of the Bill of Rights (in the Appendix) to confirm this distinction between the wording of the First Amendment and the rest. Emphasis in the example quotations was not in the original. For a spirited and enlightening essay on the extent to which the entire Bill of Rights was about equality, see Martha Minow, "Equality and the Bill of Rights," in *The Constitution of Rights: Human Dignity and American Values*, ed. Michael J. Meyer and William A. Parent (Ithaca, NY: Cornell University Press, 1992), pp. 118–28.
[6]*Barron v. Baltimore*, 7 Peters 243 (1833).
[7]Ibid. [emphasis added].

tecting citizens of Maryland from such action, then Barron had no legal leg to stand on against Baltimore, an agency of the state of Maryland.

Barron v. Baltimore confirmed "dual citizenship"—that is, that each American was a citizen of the national government and *separately* a citizen of one of the states. This meant that the Bill of Rights did not apply to decisions or to procedures of state (or local) governments. Even slavery could continue, because the Bill of Rights could not protect anyone from state laws treating people as property. In fact, the Bill of Rights did not become a vital instrument for the extension of civil liberties for anyone until after a bloody civil war and a revolutionary Fourteenth Amendment intervened. And even so, as we shall see, nearly another century would pass before the Bill of Rights would truly come into its own.

Institution Principle

Dual citizenship meant that the Bill of Rights did not apply to decisions or to procedures of state governments.

The Fourteenth Amendment

From a constitutional standpoint, the defeat of the South in the Civil War settled one question and raised another. It probably settled forever the question of whether secession was an option for any state. After 1865 there was to be more "united" than "states" to the United States. But this left unanswered just how much the states were obliged to obey the Constitution and, in particular, the Bill of Rights. Just reading the words of the Fourteenth Amendment, anyone might think it was almost perfectly designed to impose the Bill of Rights on the states and thereby to reverse *Barron v. Baltimore*. The very first words of the Fourteenth Amendment point in that direction:

> All persons born or naturalized in the United States, and subject to the jurisdiction thereof, are citizens of the United States and of the State wherein they reside.

This provides for a *single national citizenship*, and at a minimum that means that civil liberties should not vary drastically from state to state. That would seem to be the spirit of the Fourteenth Amendment: *to nationalize the Bill of Rights by nationalizing the definition of citizenship.*

This interpretation of the Fourteenth Amendment is reinforced by the next clause of the Amendment:

> *No State* shall make or enforce any law which shall abridge the privileges or immunities of citizens of the United States; nor shall any State deprive any person of life, liberty, or property, without due process of law. [Emphasis added.]

All of this sounds like an effort to extend the Bill of Rights in its *entirety* to citizens *wherever* they might reside.[8] But this was not to be the Supreme Court's

---

[8]The Fourteenth Amendment also seems designed to introduce civil rights. The final clause of the all-important Section 1 provides that no state can "deny to any person within its jurisdiction the equal protection of the laws." It is not unreasonable to conclude that the purpose of this provision was to obligate the state governments as well as the national government to take *positive* actions to protect citizens from arbitrary and discriminatory actions, at least those based on race.

History Principle

Dual citizenship was upheld by the Supreme Court for nearly one hundred years after *Barron v. Baltimore* (1833).

interpretation for nearly a hundred years. Within five years of ratification of the Fourteenth Amendment, the Court was making decisions as though it had never been adopted. The shadow of *Barron* grew longer and longer. In an important 1873 decision known as *The Slaughter-House Cases*, the Supreme Court determined that the federal government was under no obligation to protect the "privileges and immunities" of citizens of a particular state against arbitrary actions by that state's government. The case had its origins in 1867, when a corrupt Louisiana legislature conferred upon a single corporation a monopoly of all the slaughterhouse business in the city of New Orleans. The other slaughterhouses, facing bankruptcy, all brought suits claiming, like Mr. Barron, that this was a taking of their property in violation of Fifth Amendment rights. But unlike Mr. Barron, they believed that they were protected now because, they argued, the Fourteenth Amendment incorporated the Fifth Amendment, applying it to the states. The suits were all rejected. The Supreme Court argued, first, that the primary purpose of the Fourteenth Amendment was to protect "Negroes as a class." Second, and more to the point here, the Court argued, without trying to prove it, that the framers of the Fourteenth Amendment could not have intended to incorporate the entire Bill of Rights.[9] Yet, when the Civil Rights Act of 1875 attempted to protect blacks from discriminatory treatment by proprietors of hotels, theaters, and other public accommodations, the Supreme Court disregarded its own primary argument in the previous case and held the act unconstitutional, declaring that the Fourteenth Amendment applied only to discriminatory actions by state officials, "operating under cover of law," and not to discrimination against blacks by private individuals, even though these private individuals were companies offering services to the public.[10] Such narrow interpretations raised the inevitable question of whether the Fourteenth Amendment had incorporated *any* of the Bill of Rights. The Fourteenth Amendment remained shadowy until the mid-twentieth century. The shadow was *Barron v. Baltimore* and the Court's unwillingness to "nationalize" civil liberties—that is, to interpret the civil liberties expressed in the Bill of Rights as imposing limitations not only on the federal government but also on the states.

It was not until the very end of the nineteenth century that the Supreme Court began to nationalize the Bill of Rights by incorporating its civil liberties provisions into the Fourteenth Amendment. Table 4.1 outlines the major steps in this process. The only change in civil liberties during the first sixty years after the adoption of the Fourteenth Amendment came in 1897, when the Supreme Court held that the due process clause of the Fourteenth Amendment did in fact prohibit states from taking property for a public use without just compensation.[11] This effectively overruled *Barron* because it meant that the citizen of Maryland or any state was henceforth protected from a "public taking" of property (eminent domain) even if the state constitution did not provide such protection. However,

[9]*The Slaughter-House Cases*, 16 Wallace 36 (1873).
[10]*The Civil Rights Cases*, 109 U.S. 3 (1883).
[11]*Chicago, Burlington, and Quincy Railroad Company v. Chicago*, 166 U.S. 226 (1897).

TABLE 4.1

Incorporation of the Bill of Rights into the Fourteenth Amendment

SELECTED PROVISIONS AND AMENDMENTS	NOT "INCORPORATED" UNTIL	KEY CASE
Eminent domain (V)	1897	*Chicago, Burlington, and Quincy Railroad Company v. Chicago*
Freedom of speech (I)	1925	*Gitlow v. New York*
Freedom of press (I)	1931	*Near v. Minnesota*
Freedom of assembly (I)	1939	*Hague v. CIO*
Freedom from warrantless search and seizure (IV) ("exclusionary rule")	1961	*Mapp v. Ohio*
Right to counsel in any criminal trial (VI)	1963	*Gideon v. Wainwright*
Right against self-incrimination and forced confessions (V)	1964	*Malloy v. Hogan; Escobedo v. Illinois*
Right to counsel and to remain silent (VI)	1966	*Miranda v. Arizona*
Right against double jeopardy (V)	1969	*Benton v. Maryland*
Right to privacy (III, IV, & V)	1973	*Roe v. Wade; Doe v. Bolton*

in a broader sense, *Barron* still cast a shadow because the Supreme Court had "incorporated" into the Fourteenth Amendment only the property protection provision of the Fifth Amendment and no other clause, let alone the other amendments of the Bill of Rights. In other words, although "due process" applied to the taking of life and liberty as well as property, only property was incorporated into the Fourteenth Amendment as a limitation on state power.

No further expansion of civil liberties through incorporation occurred until 1925, when the Supreme Court held that freedom of speech is "among the fundamental personal rights and 'liberties' protected by the due process clause of the Fourteenth Amendment from impairment by the states."[12] In 1931, the Court added freedom of the press to that short list of civil rights protected by the Bill of Rights from state action; in 1939, it added freedom of assembly.[13] But that was as far as the Court was willing to go. As late as 1937, the Supreme Court was still loath to nationalize civil liberties beyond the First Amendment. In fact, the Court in that year took one of its most extreme turns backward toward *Barron v. Baltimore*. The state of Connecticut had indicted a man named Palko for first-degree murder, but a lower court had found him guilty of only second-degree murder and sentenced him to life in prison. Unhappy with the verdict, the state of Connecticut appealed the conviction to its highest court, won the appeal, got a new trial, and then succeeded in getting Palko convicted of first-degree murder. Palko appealed to the Supreme Court on what seemed an open-and-shut case of **double jeopardy**—being tried twice for the same crime. Yet, though the majority of the Court agreed that this could indeed be considered a case of double jeopardy, they decided that double jeopardy was *not* one of the provisions of the Bill of Rights incorporated in the Fourteenth Amendment as a restriction on the powers of the states. Justice Benjamin Cardozo, considered one of the most able Supreme Court justices of the twentieth century, rejected the argument made by Palko's lawyer that "whatever is forbidden by the Fifth Amendment is forbidden by the Fourteenth also." Cardozo responded tersely, "There is no such general rule." As far as Cardozo and the majority were concerned, the only rights from the Bill of Rights that ought to be incorporated into the Fourteenth Amendment as applying to the states as well as to the national government were those that were "implicit in the concept of ordered liberty." He asked the questions: Does double jeopardy subject Palko to a "hardship so acute and shocking that our polity will not endure it? Does it violate those 'fundamental principles of liberty and justice which lie at the base of all our civil and political institutions?' . . . The answer must surely be 'no.'"[14] Palko was eventually executed for the crime, because he lived in the state of Connecticut rather than in some state whose constitution included a guarantee against double jeopardy.

Cases like *Palko* extended the shadow of *Barron* into its second century, despite adoption of the Fourteenth Amendment. The Constitution, as interpreted by the Supreme Court, left standing the framework in which the states had the power to determine their own law on a number of fundamental issues. It left states with the power to pass laws segregating the races—and thirteen southern states chose to exercise that power. The constitutional framework also left states with the power to engage in searches and seizures without a warrant, to indict accused persons without benefit of a grand jury, to deprive persons of trial by

double jeopardy
Being tried more than once for the same crime. The Constitution guarantees that no one shall be subjected to double jeopardy.

---

[12]*Gitlow v. New York*, 268 U.S. 652 (1925).
[13]*Near v. Minnesota*, 283 U.S. 697 (1931); *Hague v. CIO*, 307 U.S. 496 (1939).
[14]*Palko v. Connecticut*, 302 U.S. 319 (1937).

jury, to force persons to testify against themselves, to deprive accused persons of their right to confront adverse witnesses, and, as we have seen, to prosecute accused persons more than once for the same crime.[15] Few states chose the option to use that kind of power, but some states did, and the power to do so was there for any state whose legislative majority so chose.

The Constitutional Revolution in Civil Liberties

For nearly thirty years after the *Palko* case,[16] the nineteenth-century framework was sustained, but signs of change came after 1954, in *Brown v. Board of Education*, when the Supreme Court overturned the infamous *Plessy v. Ferguson*.[17] *Plessy* was a civil rights case involving the "equal protection" clause of the Fourteenth Amendment and was not an issue of applying the Bill of Rights to the states (dealt with in the next section). Nevertheless, even though *Brown* was not a civil liberties case, it indicated clearly that the Supreme Court was going to be expansive about civil liberties because with *Brown* the Court had effectively promised that it was *actively* going to subject the states and all actions affecting civil rights and civil liberties to *strict scrutiny*. In retrospect, one could say that this constitutional revolution was given a "jump start" by the *Brown* decision,[18] even though the results were not apparent until after 1961, when the number of civil liberties incorporated increased (Table 4.1).

Nationalizing the Bill of Rights   As with the federalism revolution, the constitutional revolution in civil liberties was a movement toward nationalization. But the two revolutions required opposite motions on the part of the Supreme Court. In the area of commerce (the first revolution), the Court had to decide to assume a *passive* role by not interfering as Congress expanded the meaning of the commerce clause of Article I, Section 8. This expansion has been so extensive that the national government can now constitutionally reach a single farmer growing twenty acres of wheat or a small neighborhood restaurant selling barbecues to local "whites only" without being anywhere near interstate commerce routes. In the second revolution—involving the Bill of Rights through the Fourteenth Amendment rather than the commerce clause—the Court had to assume an *active* role, which required close review not of Congress but of the laws of state legislatures and decisions of state courts, to apply a single national Fourteenth Amendment standard to the rights and liberties of all citizens.

[15]All of these were implicitly identified in the *Palko* case as "not incorporated" into the Fourteenth Amendment as limitations on the powers of the states.

[16]*Palko* was explicitly reversed in *Benton v. Maryland*, 395 U.S. 784 (1969), in which the Court said that double jeopardy was in fact incorporated in the Fourteenth Amendment as a restriction on the states.

[17]*Plessy v. Ferguson*, 163 U.S. 537 (1896).

[18]The First Constitutional Revolution began with *National Labor Relations Board v. Jones & Laughlin Steel Corporation* (1937).

Table 4.1 shows that until 1961, only the First Amendment had been fully and clearly incorporated into the Fourteenth Amendment.[19] After 1961, several other important provisions of the Bill of Rights were incorporated. Of the cases that expanded the Fourteenth Amendment's reach, the most famous was *Gideon v. Wainwright*, which established the right to counsel in a criminal trial, because it became the subject of a best-selling book and a popular movie.[20] In *Mapp v. Ohio*, the Court held that evidence obtained in violation of the Fourth Amendment ban on unreasonable searches and seizures would be excluded from trial.[21] This "exclusionary rule" was particularly irksome to the police and prosecutors because it meant that patently guilty defendants sometimes got to go free because the evidence that clearly damned them could not be used. In *Miranda*,[22] the Court's ruling required that arrested persons be informed of the right to remain silent and to have counsel present during interrogation. This is the basis of the **Miranda rule** of reading persons their rights, which has been made famous by TV police shows. By 1969, in *Benton v. Maryland*, the Supreme Court had come full circle regarding the rights of the criminally accused, explicitly reversing the *Palko* ruling and thereby incorporating double jeopardy.

During the 1960s and early 1970s, the Court also expanded another important area of civil liberties: rights to privacy. When the Court began to take a more activist role in the mid-1950s and 1960s, the idea of a "right to privacy" was revived. In 1958, the Supreme Court recognized "privacy in one's association" in its decision to prevent the state of Alabama from using the membership list of the National Association for the Advancement of Colored People (NAACP) in the state's investigations.[23]

The sphere of privacy was drawn in earnest in 1965, when the Court ruled that a Connecticut statute forbidding the use of contraceptives violated the right of marital privacy. Estelle Griswold, the executive director of the Planned Parenthood League of Connecticut, was arrested by the state of Connecticut for providing information, instruction, and medical advice about contraception to married couples. She and her associates were found guilty as accessories to the crime and fined $100 each. The Supreme Court reversed the lower court decisions and declared the Connecticut law unconstitutional because it violated "a right of privacy older than the Bill of Rights—older than our political parties, older than our school system."[24] Jus-

Miranda rule
Principles developed by the Supreme Court in the 1966 case of *Miranda v. Arizona* requiring that persons under arrest be informed of their legal rights, including their right to counsel, before police interrogation.

 Institution Principle
Most of the important provisions of the Bill of Rights were nationalized by the Supreme Court during the 1960s.

[19]The one exception was the right to public trial (the Sixth Amendment), but the 1948 case did not actually mention the right to public trial as such; it was cited in a 1968 case as a case establishing the right to public trial as part of the Fourteenth Amendment. The 1948 case was *In Re Oliver*, 33 U.S. 257, where the issue was put more generally as "due process" and public trial itself was not actually mentioned. Later opinions, such as *Duncan v. Louisiana*, 391 U.S. 145 (1968), cited the *Oliver* case as the precedent for incorporating public trials as part of the Fourteenth Amendment.

[20]*Gideon v. Wainwright*, 372 U.S. 335 (1963); Anthony Lewis, *Gideon's Trumpet* (New York: Random House, 1964).

[21]*Mapp v. Ohio*, 367 U.S. 643 (1961).

[22]*Miranda v. Arizona*, 384 U.S. 436 (1966).

[23]*NAACP v. Alabama ex rel. Patterson*, 357 U.S. 449 (1958).

[24]*Griswold v. Connecticut*, 381 U.S. 479 (1965).

tice William O. Douglas, author of the majority decision in the *Griswold* case, argued that this right of privacy is also grounded in the Constitution because it fits into a "zone of privacy" created by a combination of the Third, Fourth, and Fifth Amendments. A concurring opinion, written by Justice Arthur Goldberg, attempted to strengthen Douglas's argument by adding that "the concept of liberty . . . embraces the right of marital privacy though that right is not mentioned explicitly in the Constitution [and] is supported by numerous decisions of this Court . . . and *by the language and history of the Ninth Amendment* [emphasis added]."[25]

The right to privacy was confirmed—and extended—in 1973 in the most important of all privacy decisions, and one of the most important Supreme Court decisions in American history: *Roe v. Wade.*[26] This decision established a woman's right to have an abortion and prohibited states from making abortion a criminal act. The basis for the Supreme Court's decision in *Roe* was the evolving right to privacy. But it is important to realize that the preference for privacy rights and for their extension to include the rights of women to control their own bodies was not something invented by the Supreme Court in a political vacuum.

Most states did not begin to regulate abortions in any fashion until the 1840s; prior to then only six of the twenty-six existing states had any regulations governing abortion. By the end of the nineteenth century, some form of anti-abortion law was in place in most of the states, but abortion was still "a highly visible, frequently performed, commercial procedure. . . ."[27] During the 1960s, a number of states began to reform their original anti-abortion laws, and several of them actually repealed the law, making abortion an elective procedure.

This suggests that the 1973 *Roe* decision was another case of the tendency of the Supreme Court to follow public opinion. In the same spirit, in recent years a number of states have reinstated restrictions on abortion, testing the limits of *Roe.* One of the most widespread efforts to restrict abortions without violating *Roe* is state requirements that underage females must seek parental consent or show parental notification or, failing that, the notification of a local judge in order to receive an abortion. This, of course, is far short of satisfying the pro-life movement, which has been growing and becoming more assertive, especially with the distinctly more conservative Republican administration under George W. Bush. With the death of Chief Justice Rehnquist and the retirement of Justice Sandra Day O'Connor, the future of *Roe* and of abortion rights may have changed drastically. O'Connor's retirement is especially significant because she, though conservative, had been a "swing vote," willing to add the fifth vote for restriction on abortions but unwilling to provide the fifth vote to actually reverse *Roe.* Although conservative judge Samuel Alito has taken his place on the Court, it can be stated with confidence that no test of *Roe* will come until there is an actual test case, and

History Principle

Roe v. Wade was not decided in a political vacuum. Many states had already eased their restrictions on abortion before 1973.

[25]*Griswold v. Connecticut,* concurring opinion. In 1972, the Court extended the privacy right to unmarried women: *Eisenstadt v. Baird,* 405 U.S. 438 (1972).

[26]*Roe v. Wade,* 410 U.S. 113 (1973).

[27]Raymond Tatalovich and Byron Daynes, eds., *Moral Controversies in American Politics—Cases in Social Regulatory Policy* (Armonk, NY: Sharpe, 1998), pp. 4–5.

even so, there is no way to predict how the new justices will vote until the test case gets through the appeals process and the facts and arguments in that case have been presented to the Supreme Court.

Rehnquist and Beyond: A De-nationalizing Trend?

The issues, coming before the Roberts Court are far larger than abortion. Once privacy was established as a right—as anticipated and provided for by the Ninth Amendment of the Bill of Rights—the privacy right, like any important principle, took on a life all its own. In a number of important decisions, the Supreme Court and the lower federal courts opened the door to the expansion of rights, consistent with the Ninth Amendment, which provided that "the enumeration in the Constitution, of certain rights, shall not be construed to deny or disparage others as retained by the people." These new rights could not be found in the text of the Constitution but could be discovered through the study of philosophic sources and historical and cultural practices. Through this line of reasoning, the federal courts sought to protect sexual autonomy, lifestyle choices, sexual preferences, procreational choice, and various forms of intimate association.

Criticism and opposition mounted with every extension of this line of reasoning. The critics argued that the federal judiciary had displaced the judgments of legislatures and state courts with its own judgment of what is reasonable, without regard to local popular majorities or specific constitutional provisions. These new civil liberties cases came to be denounced as "judicial activism," as "legislating from the bench," and as evidence of the rise of an "imperial judiciary."[28] This movement had been growing well before the return of Republicans to power in 2000, but by 2004 there was a veritable national movement for a genuine conservative judiciary, sparked by President Bush's frequently repeated campaign promises. It took the form of a series of cases seeking "a new respect for the sovereignty of the states and . . . corresponding restrictions on the powers of Congress."[29] In 2000, the victory of state sovereignty" and the reversal of the New Deal's nationalizing trend seemed assured with *U.S. v. Morrison*, a 5–4 decision written by Chief Justice Rehnquist, striking down a central revision of the Violence Against Women Act authorizing victims of crimes "motivated by gender" to sue their attackers in federal court. The principle was that "intrastate" conduct not essentially economic was beyond Congress's "interstate commerce" power. But five years later, the same court (with the same members but a different 6–3 majority) held that federal law regulating cultivation and use of marijuana for medical purposes "trumps" the state laws *(Gonzales v. Raich)*. This was "irreconcilable" not only with *U.S. v. Morrison* but also with the important 1995 *U.S. v. Lopez*, which held that federal law couldn't regulate the possession of

---

[28]A good discussion will be found in Paul Brest and Sanford Levinson, *Processes of Constitutional Decision-Making: Cases and Materials,* 2nd ed. (Boston: Little, Brown, 1983), p. 660. See also Chapter 8.

[29]Linda Greenhouse, "The Rehnquist Court and Its Imperiled States' Rights Legacy," *New York Times,* 12 June 2005, Sec. 4, p. 3.

guns near schools. The opinion in the marijuana case virtually disregarded those inconsistent cases, leaving us only to guess as to the future of the movement to constrain national power and restore state sovereignty. One important judgment by a leading conservative think tank was that the "federalism boomlet [sparked by the conservatives] has fizzled." Conservatives may be more optimistic now that two new Bush appointments are on the Court.

This history of civil liberties in the United States is evidence that the Bill of Rights is not carved in stone. Subsequent constitutional amendments and the interpretations of the Supreme Court have made it so that the framers of the Constitution would be unlikely to recognize their original handiwork. But as we shall see, what the Supreme Court gives, the Supreme Court can also take away.

The preferences of individual Supreme Court justices have certainly been consequential throughout the history of our republic. Judicial power was at its pinnacle during the Court of Chief Justice John Marshall, but even then there was opposition to the Court's power, and that opposition has not diminished. Judicial power and opposition to it were definitely present during the long stretch of the Rehnquist Court. It is difficult to determine just how much influence Rehnquist had as Chief Justice, but it is undeniable that the Court has been moving in a more conservative, de-nationalizing direction during the past two decades or more (Figure 4.1).

The Supreme Court has moved in a conservative direction, for example, regarding the First Amendment's "establishment clause," which established a "wall of separation" between church and state. In the 1995 case of *Rosenberger v. University of Virginia*, the Court seemed to open a new breach in the wall between church and state when it ruled that the university had violated the free speech rights of a Christian student group by refusing to provide student activity funds to the group's magazine, although other student groups had been given funds for their publications. In the 1997 case of *Agostini v. Felton*, the Court again breached the wall between church and state, ruling that states could pay public school teachers to offer remedial courses at religious schools.[30]

The conservative trend has also extended to the burning question of abortion rights. In *Webster v. Reproductive Health Services*, the Court narrowly upheld by a 5–4 majority the constitutionality of restrictions on the use of public medical facilities for abortion.[31] And in 1992, in the most recent major decision on abortion, *Planned Parenthood v. Casey*, another 5–4 majority of the Court barely

 Institution Principle

As a political institution, the Bill of Rights has not been carved in stone. Through subsequent amendments, on the one hand, and constant updating of the original ten through judicial review, on the other, the balance between freedom and power has been transformed.

 Rationality Principle

The preferences of individual Supreme Court justices have been consequential for the development of civil liberties.

 Policy Principle

The civil liberties decisions of the Rehnquist Court during the 1990s revealed the conservative preferences of a majority of its justices.

---

[30]*Rosenberger v. University of Virginia*, 94-329 (1995); *Agostini v. Felton*, 96-522 (1997).

[31]In *Webster v. Reproductive Health Services*, 109 S.Ct. 3040 (1989), Chief Justice Rehnquist's decision upheld a Missouri law that restricted the use of public medical facilities for abortion. The decision opened the way for other states to limit the availability of abortion. The first to act was the Pennsylvania legislature, which adopted in late 1989 a law banning all abortions after pregnancy had passed twenty-four weeks, except to save the life of the pregnant woman or to prevent irreversible impairment of her health. In 1990, the pace of state legislative action increased, with new statutes passed in South Carolina, Ohio, Minnesota, and Guam. In 1991, the Louisiana legislature adopted, over the governor's veto, the strictest law yet. The Louisiana law prohibits all abortions except when the mother's life is threatened or when rape or incest victims report these crimes immediately.

FIGURE 4.1

ANALYZING THE
EVIDENCE

What does this
figure suggest
about the
members of
the Supreme
Court in the
1960s versus
the 1990s?

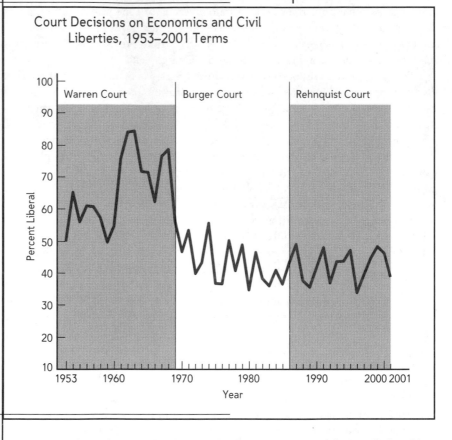

Court Decisions on Economics and Civil
Liberties, 1953–2001 Terms

SOURCES: Jeffrey A. Segal and Harold J. Spaeth, *The Supreme Court and the Attitudinal Model*
(New York: Cambridge University Press, 1993), p. 223.

upheld *Roe* but narrowed its scope, refusing to invalidate a Pennsylvania law that
significantly restricts freedom of choice. The decision defined the right to an
abortion as a "limited or qualified" right subject to regulation by the states as
long as the regulation does not impose an "undue burden."[32]

Will the Supreme Court, with a majority of conservatives, reverse the nationalization of the Bill of Rights? Possibly, but not necessarily. First of all, the Rehnquist Court did not actually reverse any of the decisions made during the 1960s

[32]*Planned Parenthood of Southeastern Pennsylvania v. Casey*, 112 S.Ct. 2791 (1992).

by the Warren or Burger Courts nationalizing most of the clauses of the Bill of Rights. As we have seen, the Rehnquist Court gave narrower and more restrictive interpretations of the earlier decisions, but it did not reverse any, not even *Roe v. Wade.* Second, President Bill Clinton's appointments to the Court, Ruth Bader Ginsburg and Stephen Breyer, helped strengthen centrist resistance to the movement toward complete de-nationalization, a movement that could otherwise be made possible by George W. Bush's two conservative appointments. But whatever the direction of the Roberts Court, the question of the contraction of the Bill of Rights and the Fourteenth Amendment is certain to be in the forefront of political debate for a long time to come.

Thus we end about where we began. *Barron v. Baltimore* has not been entirely put to rest; its spirit still hovers, casting a shadow over the Bill of Rights. A Court with the power to expand the Bill of Rights also has the power to contract it.[33]

CIVIL RIGHTS

With the adoption of the Fourteenth Amendment in 1868, civil rights became part of the Constitution, guaranteed to each citizen through "equal protection of the laws." These words launched a century of political movements and legal efforts to press for racial equality. The African American quest for civil rights, in turn, inspired many other groups, including members of other racial and ethnic groups, women, the disabled, and gays and lesbians, to seek new laws and constitutional guarantees of their civil rights.

Congress passed the Fourteenth Amendment and the states ratified it in the aftermath of the Civil War. Together with the Thirteenth Amendment, which abolished slavery, and the Fifteenth Amendment, which guaranteed voting rights for black men, it seemed to provide a guarantee of civil rights for the newly freed black slaves. But the general language of the Fourteenth Amendment meant that its support for civil rights could be far reaching. The very simplicity of the *equal protection clause* of the Fourteenth Amendment left it open to interpretation:

> No State shall make or enforce any law which shall . . . deny to any person within its jurisdiction the equal protection of the laws.

equal protection clause Provision of the Fourteenth Amendment guaranteeing citizens "the equal protection of the laws." This clause has served as the basis for the civil rights of African Americans, women, and other groups.

Plessy v. Ferguson: "Separate but Equal"

The Supreme Court was no more ready to enforce the civil rights aspects of the Fourteenth Amendment than it was to enforce the civil liberties provisions. The Court declared the Civil Rights Act of 1875 unconstitutional on the ground that the act sought to protect blacks against discrimination by *private* businesses,

[33]For a lively and readable treatment of the possibilities of restricting provisions of the Bill of Rights, without actually reversing Warren Court decisions, see David G. Savage, *Turning Right: The Making of the Rehnquist Supreme Court* (New York: Wiley, 1992).

Rights, Liberties, and the World Wide Web

The Bill of Rights was included in the Constitution at the urging of the anti-federalists, who believed it was necessary to explicitly protect certain fundamental individual rights and liberties. But "right" and "liberty," and even "justice," are words whose meanings have changed over time. The Supreme Court has also struggled with the meaning of "obscenity" as the larger society has loosened its standards of what constitutes "pornographic" versus "erotic" material. Even our understanding of something as fundamental as freedom of speech has changed significantly over the past hundred years. Early in the twentieth century, Eugene Debs, a socialist and labor organizer, was imprisoned for speaking out against World War I. By the 1960s, few challenged the right of individuals to protest the Vietnam War.

The Supreme Court has always had to strike a balance between an individual's personal rights and freedoms and society's interests in safety and stability. This balance has become much more difficult to maintain with the rise of the Internet and the war on terror.

The Internet has broken down state and national borders, thus complicating the Court's ability to rely on "community standards" as a way to establish the proper boundaries for speech. What do "community standards" mean when something comes from a computer located thousands of miles away?

The Communication Decency Act (CDA) of 1996 attempted to make it illegal to provide Web pages that let minors view indecent materials. Photographs and videos that are legal in the Netherlands may be illegal in Peoria—does that make it illegal to view these items on your computer? Who will be penalized if minors view pornographic material—the computer owner, the Internet service provider, or a common carrier such as your own college or university? Ultimately, the CDA, vigorously opposed by free-speech advocates, was overturned by the Court in 1997. But the battle over Internet porn will continue, and because the Internet does not respect state or national borders, any solution to Internet pornography will most likely be imposed by the federal government.

The Patriot Act of 2001—which was conditionally renewed in fall 2005[1]—has also raised the hackles of civil libertarians. The Patriot Act greatly expanded the federal government's power to monitor individuals and groups. Provisions of the act include expanded wiretapping powers and increased abilities to search student records. Advocates argued that these new measures were vital tools in the war on terror, and that most Americans were more than willing to give up some personal freedom if it meant a more secure and safe nation. The legislation, which might have seemed controversial at any other time, passed with overwhelming bipartisan support less than six weeks after the September 11 terrorist attacks.

Similar initiatives to fight terrorism include the Terrorism Information Awareness program, which promises to link electronic information from as many different sources as possible. The program is designed to bring together pre-existing and newly gathered information on nearly every individual and then "mine" that data using still undeveloped

History Principle

The meaning of legal rights and freedoms changes as societal norms and values change.

Institution Principle

Because the Internet is "borderless," regulation of Internet speech will involve national or even international institutions.

Rationality Principle

In a period of national crisis, citizens may be willing to forgo some rights and freedoms in exchange for security.

algorithms. Proponents of the system argue that it can help prevent terrorist attacks. Critics worry that the system will violate basic constitutional protections. The Supreme Court has not yet ruled on the constitutionality of such efforts. Ironically, much of this information is already available to anyone with some money and an Internet connection.

Many scholars, in fact, worry that the Internet, far from being an avenue for personal empowerment, may actually threaten individual rights and liberties.[2] Personal privacy is not enshrined in the Bill of Rights, but freedom from government intrusion into private matters has long been a part of American values and the American legal tradition (though most Americans associate the right to privacy with the 1973 *Roe v. Wade* decision legalizing abortion).[3]

Because the Internet allows the government to monitor your activities without physically entering your home or even installing a "tap" on your phone, government and corporate entities can assemble vast new storehouses of information about you with no oversight on its use.

The news on the Internet front is not all bad, however. In many totalitarian regimes, such as Iran, China, or Myanmar, the Internet is a tool for democratization. The same technology that has allowed terrorist groups to post streaming videos of beheadings in Iraq was used by the organizers of the "Orange Revolution" in Ukraine. Perhaps it is the very flexibility of the Internet that makes it both a powerful tool for individual empowerment and a potent threat to individual freedom.

[1]Uniting and Strengthening America by Providing Appropriate Tools Required to Intercept and Obstruct Terrorism Act of 2001. The legislation contained a "sunset" clause that required Congress to renew the act after four years.

[2]See Lawrence Lessig, *Code* (New York: Basic Books, 1999); Andrew Shapiro, *The Control Revolution* (New York: Public Affairs, 1999); and Cass Sunstein, *republic.com* (Princeton: Princeton University Press, 2001).

[3]The right is rooted in a famous article written in 1890 by Samuel D. Warren and Louis D. Brandeis in which they describe a "right to privacy" as a "right to be left alone." "The Right to Privacy," *Harvard Law Review,* 15 December 1890.

while the Fourteenth Amendment, according to the Court's interpretation, was intended to protect individuals from discrimination only against actions by *public* officials of state and local governments.

In 1896, the Court went still further, in the infamous case of *Plessy v. Ferguson*, by upholding a Louisiana statute that *required* segregation of the races on trolleys and other public carriers (and, by implication, in all public facilities, including schools). Homer Plessy, a man defined as "one-eighth black," had violated a

Louisiana law that provided for "equal but separate accommodations" on trains and a $25 fine for any white passenger who sat in a car reserved for blacks or any black passenger who sat in a car reserved for whites. The Supreme Court held that the Fourteenth Amendment's "equal protection of the laws" was not violated by racial distinction as long as the facilities were equal. People generally pretended they were equal as long as some accommodation existed. The Court said that although "the object of the [Fourteenth] Amendment was undoubtedly to enforce the absolute equality of the two races before the law, . . . it could not have intended to abolish distinctions based on color, or to enforce social, as distinguished from political, equality, or a commingling of the two races upon terms unsatisfactory to either."[34] What the Court was saying in effect was that the use of race as a criterion of exclusion in public matters was not unreasonable. This was the origin of the *"separate but equal" rule,* which was not reversed until 1954.

"separate but equal" rule
Doctrine that public accommodations could be segregated by race but still be equal.

Racial Discrimination after World War II

The Supreme Court had begun to change its position on racial discrimination before World War II by being stricter about the criterion of equal facilities in the "separate but equal" rule. In 1938, the Court rejected Missouri's policy of paying the tuition of qualified blacks to out-of-state law schools rather than admitting them to the University of Missouri Law School.[35]

After the war, modest progress resumed. In 1950, the Court rejected Texas's claim that its new "law school for Negroes" afforded education equal to that of the all-white University of Texas Law School; without confronting the "separate but equal" principle itself, the Court's decision anticipated *Brown v. Board of Education* by opening the question of whether *any* segregated facility could be truly equal.[36] The same was true in 1944, when the Supreme Court struck down the southern practice of "white primaries," which legally excluded blacks from participation in the nominating process. Here the Court simply recognized that primaries could no longer be regarded as the private affairs of the parties but were an integral aspect of the electoral process. This made parties "an agency of the State," and, therefore, any practice of discrimination against blacks was "state action within the meaning of the Fifteenth Amendment."[37] The most important pre-1954 decision was probably *Shelley v. Kraemer,*[38] in which the Court ruled against the widespread practice of "restrictive covenants," whereby the seller of a home added a clause to the sales contract requiring the buyers to agree not to sell their home to any non-white, non-Christian, and so on. The Court ruled that although private persons could sign

[34]*Plessy v. Ferguson,* 163 U.S. 537 (1896).
[35]*Missouri ex rel. Gaines v. Canada,* 305 U.S. 337 (1938).
[36]*Sweatt v. Painter,* 339 U.S. 629 (1950).
[37]*Smith v. Allwright,* 321 U.S. 649 (1944).
[38]*Shelley v. Kraemer,* 334 U.S. 1 (1948).

such restrictive covenants, they could not be judicially enforced because the Fourteenth Amendment prohibits any organ of the state, including the courts, from denying equal protection of its laws.

However, none of these pre-1954 cases had yet confronted head-on the principle of "separate but equal" as such and its legal and constitutional support for racial discrimination. Each victory by the Legal Defense Fund of the NAACP was celebrated for itself and was seen, it was hoped, as a trend; but each was still a small victory, not a leading case. The massive effort by the southern states to resist direct desegregation and to prevent further legal actions against it by making a show of equalizing the quality of white and black schools kept the NAACP pessimistic about the readiness of the Supreme Court for a full confrontation with the constitutional principle sustaining segregation. But the continued unwillingness of Congress after 1948 to consider fair employment legislation seemed to have convinced the NAACP that the courts were their only hope. Thus, by 1951, the NAACP finally decided to attack the principle of segregation itself as unconstitutional and, in 1952, instituted cases in South Carolina, Virginia, Kansas, Delaware, and the District of Columbia. The obvious strategy was that by simultaneously filing suits in different federal districts, inconsistent results between any two states would more quickly lead to Supreme Court acceptance of at least one appeal.[39] Of these, the Kansas case became the chosen one. It seemed to be ahead of the pack in its district court, and it had the special advantage of being located in a state outside the Deep South.[40]

Oliver Brown, the father of three girls, lived "across the tracks" in a low-income, racially mixed Topeka neighborhood. Every school-day morning, Linda Brown took the school bus to the Monroe School for black children about a mile away. In September 1950, Oliver Brown took Linda to the all-white Sumner School, which was actually closer to home, to enter her into the third grade in defiance of state law and local segregation rules. When they were refused, Brown took his case to the NAACP, and soon thereafter *Brown v. Board of Education* was born. In mid-1953, the Court announced that the several cases on their way up would be re-argued within a set of questions having to do with the intent of the Fourteenth Amendment. Almost exactly a year later, the Court responded to those questions in one of the most important decisions in its history.

In deciding the case, the Court, to the surprise of many, basically rejected as inconclusive all the learned arguments about the intent and the history of the

[39]The best reviews of strategies, tactics, and goals is found in John Hope Franklin, *From Slavery to Freedom: A History of Negro Americans*, 4th ed. (New York: Knopf, 1974), Chapter 22; and Richard Kluger, *Simple Justice: The History of Brown v. Board of Education and Black America's Struggle for Equality* (New York: Vintage, 1977), Chapters 21 and 22.

[40]The District of Columbia case came up too, but because the District of Columbia is not a state, this case did not directly involve the Fourteenth Amendment and its "equal protection" clause. It confronted the Court on the same grounds, however—that segregation is inherently unequal. Its victory in effect was "incorporation in reverse," with equal protection moving from the Fourteenth Amendment to become part of the Bill of Rights. See *Bolling v. Sharpe*, 347 U.S. 497 (1954).

Fourteenth Amendment and committed itself to considering only the consequences of segregation:

> Does segregation of children in public schools solely on the basis of race, even though the physical facilities and other "tangible" factors may be equal, deprive the children of the minority group of equal educational opportunities? We believe that it does. . . . We conclude that, in the field of public education, the doctrine of "separate but equal" has no place. Separate educational facilities are inherently unequal.[41]

 Institution Principle

The *Brown* decision altered the constitutional framework by giving the national government the power to intervene against the discriminatory actions of state and local governments and some aspects of the private sector.

The *Brown* decision altered the constitutional framework in two fundamental respects. First, after *Brown*, the states would no longer have the power to use race as a criterion of discrimination in law. Second, the national government would from then on have the constitutional basis for extending its power (hitherto in doubt, as we saw earlier) to intervene with strict regulatory policies against the discriminatory actions of state or local governments, school boards, employers, and many others in the private sector.

Civil Rights after *Brown v. Board of Education*

 History Principle

The *Brown* decision galvanized the modern civil rights movement.

***de jure* segregation**

Racial segregation that is a direct result of law or official policy.

***de facto* segregation**

Racial segregation that is not a direct result of law or government policy but is, instead, a reflection of residential patterns, income distributions, or other social factors.

Although *Brown v. Board of Education* withdrew all constitutional authority to use race as a criterion of exclusion, this historic decision was merely a small opening move. First, most states refused to cooperate until sued, and many ingenious schemes were employed to delay obedience (such as paying the tuition for white students to attend newly created "private" academies). Second, even as southern school boards began to cooperate by eliminating their legally enforced (*de jure*) school segregation, there remained extensive actual (*de facto*) school segregation in the North as well as in the South as a consequence of racially segregated housing that could not be reached by the 1954–55 *Brown* principles. Third, discrimination in employment, public accommodations, juries, voting, and other areas of social and economic activity were not directly touched by *Brown*.

A decade of frustration following *Brown* made it fairly obvious to all that adjudication alone would not succeed. The goal of "equal protection" required positive, or affirmative, action by Congress and by administrative agencies. And given massive southern resistance and a generally negative national public opinion toward racial integration, progress would not be made through courts, Congress, *or* agencies without intense, well-organized support. The number of peaceful civil rights demonstrations for voting rights and public accommodations increased greatly during the fourteen years following *Brown*.[42]

Organized civil rights demonstrations began to mount slowly but surely after *Brown v. Board of Education*. By the 1960s, the many organizations that made up

---

[41]*Brown v. Board of Education of Topeka, Kansas,* 347 U.S. 483 (1954).
[42]Jonathan D. Casper, *The Politics of Civil Liberties* (New York: Harper & Row, 1972), p. 90.

the civil rights movement had accumulated experience and built networks capable of launching massive direct-action campaigns against southern segregationists. The Southern Christian Leadership Conference, the Student Nonviolent Coordinating Committee, and many other organizations had built a movement that stretched across the South. The movement used the media to attract nationwide attention and support. In the massive March on Washington in 1963, the Reverend Martin Luther King Jr. staked out the movement's moral claims in his famous "I Have a Dream" speech. The image of protesters being beaten, attacked by police dogs, and set upon with fire hoses did much to win broad sympathy for the cause of black civil rights and to discredit state and local governments in the South. In this way, the movement created intense pressure for reluctant federal government to take more assertive steps to defend black civil rights.

Collective-Action Principle

Given the massive resistance to the *Brown* decision, the civil rights movement required large, well-organized protests.

One of the tenets of our five principles of politics from Chapter 1 is that individuals have little incentive to participate in mass-action politics. After all, what possible difference could one person make by taking part in a civil rights protest? Participation was costly in terms of time; and, in the case of civil rights marchers, even one's health or life was endangered. The risks outweighed the potential benefits, yet hundreds of thousands of people *did* participate. Why?

Even though little scholarly attention has been paid by those who apply this perspective to the civil rights movements,[43] a general answer is available. Most rational analysis takes behavior to be *instrumental*—to be motivated by and directed toward some purpose or objective. But behavior may also be *experiential*. People do things, on this account, because they like doing them—they feel good inside, they feel free of guilt, they take pleasure in the activity for its own sake. We maintain that this second view of behavior is entirely compatible with rational accounts. Instrumental behavior may be thought of as *investment activity*, whereas experiential behavior may be thought of as *consumption activity*. It is the behavior itself that generates utility, rather than the consequences produced by the behavior. To take a specific illustration of collective action, many people certainly attended the 1963 march on Washington because they cared about civil rights. But it is unlikely that many deluded themselves into thinking their individual participation made a large difference to the fate of the civil rights legislation in support of which the march was organized. Rather, they attended because they wanted to be a part of a social movement, to hear Martin Luther King speak, and to identify with the hundreds of thousands of others who felt the same way. Also—and this should not be minimized—they participated because they anticipated that the march would be fun, an adventure of sorts.

Collective-Action Principle

People participated in the civil rights movement for experiential as well as instrumental purposes.

So, experiential behavior is consumption-oriented activity predicated on the belief that the activity in question is fulfilling, apart from its consequences. Individuals, complicated things that they are, are bound to be animated both by the consumption value of a particular behavior that we just described *and* its

---

[43]One notable exception is Dennis Chong, *Collective Action and the Civil Rights Movement* (Chicago: University of Chicago Press, 1991).

instrumental value, the rational (investment) explanation that we have used throughout this book. To insist on only one of these complementary forms of rationality, and to exclude the other, is to provide but a partial explanation.

School Desegregation, Phase One   Although the District of Columbia and some of the school districts in the border states began to respond almost immediately to court-ordered desegregation, the states of the Deep South responded with a carefully planned delaying tactic called "massive resistance." Southern politicians stood shoulder to shoulder to declare that the Supreme Court's decisions and orders were without effect. The legislatures in these states enacted statutes ordering school districts to maintain segregated schools and state superintendents to terminate state funding wherever there was racial mixing in the classroom. Some southern states violated their own long traditions of local school autonomy by centralizing public school authority under the governor or the state board of education and by giving states the power to close the schools and to provide alternative private schooling wherever local school boards might be tending to obey the Supreme Court.

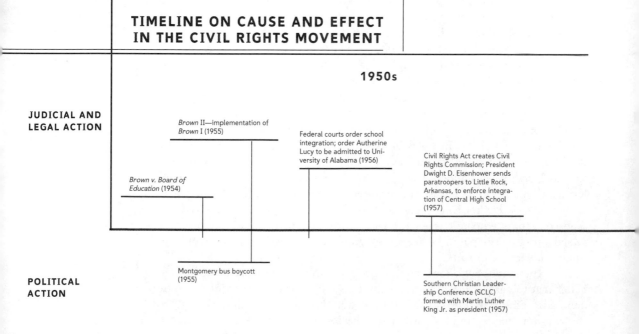

TIMELINE ON CAUSE AND EFFECT IN THE CIVIL RIGHTS MOVEMENT

1950s

JUDICIAL AND LEGAL ACTION

Brown II—implementation of *Brown* I (1955)

Federal courts order school integration; order Autherine Lucy to be admitted to University of Alabama (1956)

Civil Rights Act creates Civil Rights Commission; President Dwight D. Eisenhower sends paratroopers to Little Rock, Arkansas, to enforce integration of Central High School (1957)

Brown v. Board of Education (1954)

Montgomery bus boycott (1955)

POLITICAL ACTION

Southern Christian Leadership Conference (SCLC) formed with Martin Luther King Jr. as president (1957)

Most of these plans of "massive resistance" were tested in the federal courts and were struck down as unconstitutional.[44] But southern resistance was not confined to legislation. For example, in Arkansas in 1957, Governor Orval Faubus mobilized the National Guard to intercede against enforcement of a federal court order to integrate Little Rock's Central High School, and President Dwight D. Eisenhower was forced to deploy U.S. troops and literally place the city under martial law. The Supreme Court considered the Little Rock confrontation so historically important that the opinion it rendered in that case was not only agreed to unanimously but was, unprecedentedly, signed personally by each and every one of the justices.[45] The end of massive resistance, however, became simply the

[44]The two most important cases were *Cooper v. Aaron*, 358 U.S. 1 (1958), which required Little Rock, Arkansas, to desegregate; and *Griffin v. Prince Edward County School Board*, 377 U.S. 218 (1964), which forced all the schools of that Virginia county to reopen after five years of closing to avoid desegregation.

[45]In *Cooper*, the Supreme Court ordered immediate compliance with the lower court's desegregation order and went beyond that with a stern warning that it is "emphatically the province and duty of the judicial department to say what the law is."

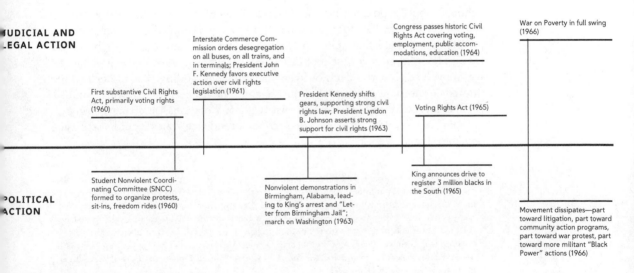

1960s

JUDICIAL AND LEGAL ACTION

Interstate Commerce Commission orders desegregation on all buses, on all trains, and in terminals; President John F. Kennedy favors executive action over civil rights legislation (1961)

Congress passes historic Civil Rights Act covering voting, employment, public accommodations, education (1964)

War on Poverty in full swing (1966)

First substantive Civil Rights Act, primarily voting rights (1960)

President Kennedy shifts gears, supporting strong civil rights law; President Lyndon B. Johnson asserts strong support for civil rights (1963)

Voting Rights Act (1965)

Student Nonviolent Coordinating Committee (SNCC) formed to organize protests, sit-ins, freedom rides (1960)

Nonviolent demonstrations in Birmingham, Alabama, leading to King's arrest and "Letter from Birmingham Jail"; march on Washington (1963)

King announces drive to register 3 million blacks in the South (1965)

POLITICAL ACTION

Movement dissipates—part toward litigation, part toward community action programs, part toward war protest, part toward more militant "Black Power" actions (1966)

beginning of still another southern strategy, "pupil placement" laws, which authorized school districts to place each pupil in a school according to a whole variety of academic, personal, and psychological considerations, never mentioning race at all. This put the burden of transferring to an all-white school on the nonwhite children and their parents, making it almost impossible for a single court order to cover a whole district, let alone a whole state. This delayed desegregation a while longer.[46]

As new devices were invented by the southern states to avoid desegregation, the federal courts followed with cases and decisions quashing them. Ten years after *Brown*, less than 1 percent of black school-age children in the Deep South were attending schools with whites.[47] It had become unmistakably clear well before that time that the federal courts could not do the job alone. The first modern effort to legislate in the field of civil rights was made in 1957, but the law contained only a federal guarantee of voting rights, without any powers of enforcement, although it did create the Civil Rights Commission to study abuses. Much more important legislation for civil rights followed, especially the Civil Rights Act of 1964. It is important to observe here the mutual dependence of the courts and legislatures—not only do the legislatures need constitutional authority to act, but the courts need legislative and political assistance, through the power of the purse and the power to organize administrative agencies to implement court orders, and through the focusing of political support. Consequently, even as the U.S. Congress finally moved into the field of school desegregation (and other areas of "equal protection"), the courts continued to exercise their powers, not only by placing court orders against recalcitrant school districts but also by extending and reinterpreting aspects of the "equal protection" clause to support legislative and administrative actions.

School Desegregation: Busing and Beyond   The most important judicial extension of civil rights in education after 1954 was probably the *Swann* decision (1971), which held that state-imposed desegregation could be brought about by busing children across school districts even where relatively long distances were involved. But the decision went beyond that, adding that under certain limited circumstances even racial quotas could be used as the "starting point in shaping a remedy to correct past constitutional violations," and that pairing or grouping of schools and reorganizing school attendance zones would also be acceptable (Figure 4.2).[48]

---

[46]*Shuttlesworth v. Birmingham Board of Education*, 358 U.S. 101 (1958), upheld a "pupil placement" plan purporting to assign pupils on various bases, with no mention of race. This case interpreted *Brown* to mean that school districts must stop explicit racial discrimination but were under no obligation to take positive steps to desegregate. For a while black parents were doomed to case-by-case approaches.

[47]For good treatments of that long stretch of the struggle of the federal courts to integrate the schools, see Brest and Levinson, *Process of Constitutional Decision-Making*, pp. 471–80; and Alfred Kelly, Winfred A. Harbison, and Herman Beltz, *The American Constitution: Its Origins and Development*, 7th ed. (New York: Norton, 1991), pp. 610–16.

[48]*Swann v. Charlotte-Mecklenburg Board of Education*, 402 U.S. 1 (1971).

FIGURE 4.2

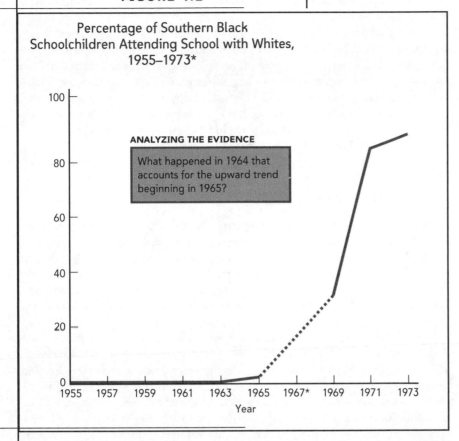

Percentage of Southern Black Schoolchildren Attending School with Whites, 1955–1973*

ANALYZING THE EVIDENCE

What happened in 1964 that accounts for the upward trend beginning in 1965?

*Dashed line indicates missing data.

SOURCE: Gerald N. Rosenberg, *Hollow Hope: Can Courts Bring about Social Change?* (Chicago: University of Chicago Press, 1991), pp. 50–51.

Three years later, however, the *Swann* case was severely restricted when the Supreme Court determined that only cities found guilty of deliberate and *de jure* racial segregation (segregation in law) would have to desegregate their schools.[49] This decision was handed down in the 1974 case of *Milliken v. Bradley* involving the city of Detroit and its suburbs. The *Milliken* ruling had the effect of exempting most northern states and cities from busing because school segregation in

[49]*Milliken v. Bradley*, 418 U.S. 717 (1974).

northern cities is generally *de facto* segregation (segregation in fact) that follows from segregated housing and from thousands of acts of private discrimination against blacks and other minorities.

Additional progress in the desegregation of schools is likely to be extremely slow unless the Supreme Court decides to permit federal action against *de facto* segregation and against the varieties of private schools and academies that have sprung up for the purpose of avoiding integration. The prospects for further school integration diminished with a series of Supreme Court decisions handed down in the 1990s. For example, in 1995 in *Missouri v. Jenkins*, the Court signaled to the lower courts that they should "disengage from desegregation efforts."[50] This is a direct and explicit threat to the main basis of the holding in the original 1954 *Brown v. Board*.

The Rise of the Politics of Rights

Outlawing Discrimination in Employment   Despite the agonizingly slow progress of school desegregation, there was some progress in other areas of civil rights during the 1960s and 1970s. Voting rights were established and fairly quickly began to revolutionize southern politics. Service on juries was no longer denied to minorities. But progress in the right to participate in politics and government dramatized the relative lack of progress in the economic domain, and it was in this area that battles over civil rights were increasingly fought.

The federal courts and the Justice Department entered this area through Title VII of the Civil Rights Act of 1964, which outlawed job discrimination by all private and public employers, including governmental agencies (such as fire and police departments), that employed more than fifteen workers. We have already seen that the Supreme Court gave "interstate commerce" such a broad definition that Congress had the constitutional authority to cover discrimination by virtually any local employers.[51] Title VII makes it unlawful to discriminate in employment on the basis of color, religion, sex, or national origin as well as race.

The first problem with Title VII was that the complaining party had to show that deliberate discrimination was the cause of the failure to get a job or a training

[50]*Missouri v. Jenkins*, 115 S.Ct. 2038 (1995). The quotation is from David M. O'Brien, *Supreme Court Watch—1996*, Annual Supplement to *Constitutional Law and Politics* (New York: Norton, 1996), p. 220.

[51]See especially Katzenbach v. McClung, 379 U.S. 294 (1964). Almost immediately after passage of the Civil Rights Act of 1964, a case challenged the validity of Title II, which covered discrimination in public accommodations. Ollie's Barbecue was a neighborhood restaurant in Birmingham, Alabama. It was located eleven blocks from an interstate highway and even farther from railroad and bus stations. Its table service was for whites only; there was only a takeout service for blacks. The Supreme Court agreed that Ollie's was strictly an intrastate restaurant, but since a substantial proportion of its food and other supplies were bought from companies outside Alabama, there was a sufficient connection to interstate commerce; therefore, racial discrimination at such restaurants would "impose commercial burdens of national magnitude upon interstate commerce." Although this case involved Title II, it had direct bearing on the constitutionality of Title VII.

opportunity. Rarely does an employer explicitly admit discrimination on the basis of race, sex, or any other illegal reason. Recognizing the rarity of such an admission, the courts have allowed aggrieved parties (the plaintiffs) to make their case if they can show that an employer's hiring practices had the *effect* of exclusion. A leading case in 1971 involved a "class action" by several black employees in North Carolina attempting to show with statistical evidence that blacks had been relegated to only one department in the Duke Power Company, which involved the least desirable, manual-labor jobs, and that they had been kept out of contention for the better jobs because the employer had added high school education and the passing of specially prepared aptitude tests as qualifications for higher jobs. The Supreme Court held that although the statistical evidence did not prove intentional discrimination and although the requirements were race neutral in appearance, their effects were sufficient to shift the burden of justification to the employer to show that the requirements were a "business necessity" that bore "a demonstrable relationship to successful performance."[52] The ruling in this case was subsequently applied to other hiring, promotion, and training programs.[53]

Gender Discrimination   Even before equal employment laws began to have a positive effect on the economic situation of blacks, something far more dramatic began happening—the universalization of civil rights. The right not to be discriminated against was being successfully claimed by the other groups listed in Title VII—those defined by sex, religion, or national origin—and eventually by still other groups defined by age or sexual preference. This universalization of civil rights has become the new frontier of the civil rights struggle, and women have emerged with the greatest prominence in this new struggle. The effort to define and end gender discrimination in employment has led to the historic joining of women's rights to the civil rights cause.

Despite its interest in fighting discrimination, the Supreme Court during the 1950s and 1960s paid little attention to gender discrimination. Ironically, it was left to the more conservative Burger Court (1969–1986) to establish gender discrimination as a major and highly visible civil rights issue. Although the Burger Court refused to treat gender discrimination as the equivalent of racial discrimination,[54] it did make it easier for plaintiffs to file and win suits on the basis of gender discrimination by applying an "intermediate" level of review to these cases.[55] This intermediate level of scrutiny is midway between traditional rules of evidence, which put the burden of proof on the plaintiff, and the doctrine of "strict scrutiny," which requires the defendant to show not only that a particular classification is reasonable but also that there is a need or compelling interest for

---

[52]*Griggs v. Duke Power Company*, 401 U.S. 24 (1971). See also Allan P. Sindler, *Bakke, DeFunis, and Minority Admissions: The Quest for Equal Opportunity* (New York: Longman, 1978), pp. 180–89.

[53]For a good treatment of these issues, see Charles O. Gregory and Harold A. Katz, *Labor and the Law*, 3rd ed. (New York: Norton, 1979), Chapter 17.

[54]See *Frontiero v. Richardson*, 411 U.S. 677 (1973).

[55]See *Craig v. Boren*, 423 U.S. 1047 (1976).

it. "Intermediate" scrutiny, therefore, shifts the burden of proof partially onto the defendant, rather than leaving it entirely on the plaintiff.

One major step was taken in 1992, when the Court decided in *Franklin v. Gwinnett County Public Schools* that violations of Title IX of the 1972 Education Act could be remedied with monetary damages.[56] Title IX forbade gender discrimination in education, but it initially sparked little litigation because of its weak enforcement provisions. The Court's 1992 ruling that monetary damages could be awarded for gender discrimination opened the door for more legal action in the area of education. The greatest impact has been in the areas of sexual harassment—the subject of the *Franklin* case—and in equal treatment of women's athletic programs. The potential for monetary damages has made universities and public schools take the problem of sexual harassment more seriously. Colleges and universities have also started to pay more attention to women's athletic programs. In the two years after the *Franklin* case, complaints to the Education Department's Office for Civil Rights about unequal treatment of women's athletic programs nearly tripled. In several high-profile legal cases, some prominent universities have been ordered to create more women's sports programs; many other colleges and universities have added more women's programs to avoid potential litigation.[57] In 1997, the Supreme Court refused to hear a petition by Brown University challenging a lower-court ruling that the university establish strict sex equity in its athletic programs. The Court's decision meant that in colleges and universities across the country, varsity athletic positions for men and women must now reflect their overall enrollment numbers.[58]

In 1996, the Supreme Court made another important decision about gender and education by putting an end to all-male schools supported by public funds. It ruled that the policy of the Virginia Military Institute not to admit women was unconstitutional.[59] Along with the Citadel, another all-male military college in South Carolina, VMI had never admitted women in its 157-year history. VMI argued that the unique educational experience it offered—including intense physical training and the harsh treatment of freshmen—would be destroyed if women students were admitted. The Court, however, ruled that the male-only policy denied "substantial equality" to women. Two days after the Court's ruling, the Citadel announced that it would accept women. VMI considered becoming a private institution to remain all-male, but in September 1996, the school board finally voted to admit women. The legal decisions may have removed formal barriers to entry, but the experience of the new female cadets at these schools was not easy. The first female cadet at the Citadel, Shannon Faulkner, won admission in 1995 under a federal court order but quit after four days. Although four women were admitted to the Citadel after the Supreme Court decision, two of

---

[56]*Franklin v. Gwinnett County Public Schools*, 503 U.S. 60 (1992).

[57]Jennifer Halperin, "Women Step Up to Bat," *Illinois Issues* 21 (September 1995): 11–14.

[58]Joan Biskupic and David Nakamura, "Court Won't Review Sports Equity Ruling," *Washington Post*, 22 April 1997, p. A1.

[59]*United States v. Virginia*, 116 S.Ct. 2264 (1996).

the four quit several months later. They charged harassment from male students, including attempts to set the female cadets on fire.[60]

Ever since sexual harassment was first declared a form of employment discrimination, employers and many employees have worried about the ambiguity of the issue. When can an employee bring charges, and when is the employer liable? In 1998, the Court clarified these questions in an important ruling. It said that if a company has an effective antiharassment policy in place, which the employee fails to use, the company cannot be held liable for sexual harassment. If no policy is in place, the company may be held legally responsible for harassment. In addition, the Court ruled that to pursue a suit on the grounds of sexual harassment, the employee does not have to show that she or he suffered a tangible loss, such as loss of promotion. Most important is whether an effective policy is in place and available to employees.[61]

The development of gender discrimination as an important part of the civil rights struggle has coincided with the rise of women's politics as a discrete movement in American politics. As with the struggle for racial equality, the relationship between changes in government policies and political action suggests a two-way pattern of causation, where changes in government policies can produce political action and vice versa. Today, the existence of a powerful women's movement derives in large measure from the enactment of Title VII of the Civil Rights Act of 1964 and from the Burger Court's vital steps in applying that law to protect women. The recognition of women's civil rights has become an issue that in many ways transcends the usual distinctions of American political debate. In the heavily partisan debate over the federal crime bill enacted in 1994, for instance, the section of the bill that enjoyed the widest support was the Violence against Women Act, whose most important feature was that it defined gender-biased violent crimes as a matter of civil rights and created a civil rights remedy for women who had been the victims of such crimes. But since the act was ruled unconstitutional by the Supreme Court in 2000, the struggle for women's rights will likely remain part of the political debate.

 History Principle

The civil rights and women's rights movements both suggest that changes in government policies can produce political action and vice versa.

Discrimination against Other Groups As gender discrimination began to be seen as an important civil rights issue, other groups arose demanding recognition and active protection of their civil rights. Under Title VII of the 1964 Civil Rights Act, any group or individual can try—and in fact is encouraged to try—to convert goals and grievances into questions of rights and the deprivation of those rights. A plaintiff must only establish that his or her membership in a group is an unreasonable basis for discrimination unless it can be proven to be a "job-related" or otherwise clearly reasonable and relevant decision. In America today, the list of individuals and groups claiming illegal discrimination is lengthy. The disabled,

---

[60]Judith Havemann, "Two Women Quit Citadel over Alleged Harassment," *Washington Post*, 13 January 1997, p. A1.

[61]*Burlington Industries v. Ellerth*, 118 S.Ct. 2257 (1998); *Faragher v. City of Boca Raton*, 118 S.Ct. 2275 (1998).

for instance, increasingly press their claim to equal treatment as a civil rights matter, a stance encouraged by the Americans with Disabilities Act of 1990.[62] Deaf Americans increasingly demand social and legal recognition of deafness as a separate culture, not simply as a disability.[63] One of the most familiar of these groups has been the gay and lesbian movement, which in less than forty years has emerged from invisibility to become one of the largest civil rights movements in contemporary America. Beginning with street protests in the 1960s, the movement has grown into a well-financed and sophisticated lobby. The Human Rights Campaign Fund is the primary national political action committee (PAC) focused on gay rights; it provides campaign financing and volunteers to work for candidates endorsed by the group. The movement has also formed legal rights organizations, including the Lambda Legal Defense and Education Fund.

Gay and lesbian rights drew national attention in 1993, when President Bill Clinton confronted the question of whether gays should be allowed to serve in the military. As a candidate, Clinton had said he favored lifting the ban on homosexuals in the military. The issue set off a huge controversy in the first months of Clinton's presidency. After nearly a year of deliberation, the administration enunciated a compromise: their "Don't ask, don't tell" policy. This policy allows gays and lesbians to serve in the military as long as they do not openly proclaim their sexual orientation or engage in homosexual activity. The administration maintained that the ruling would protect gays and lesbians against witch-hunting investigations, but many gay and lesbian advocates expressed disappointment, charging the president with reneging on his campaign promise.

But until 1996, there was no Supreme Court ruling or national legislation explicitly protecting gays and lesbians from discrimination. The first gay rights case that the Court decided, *Bowers v. Hardwick*, ruled against a right to privacy that would protect consensual homosexual activity.[64] After the *Bowers* decision, the gay and lesbian rights movement sought suitable legal cases to test the constitutionality of discrimination against gays and lesbians, much as the black civil rights movement did in the late 1940s and in the 1950s. As one advocate put it, "Lesbians and gay men are looking for their *Brown v. Board of Education*."[65] Among the cases tested were those stemming from local ordinances restricting gay rights (including the right to marry), job discrimination, and family law issues such as adoption and parental rights. In 1996, the Supreme Court, in *Romer v. Evans*, explicitly extended fundamental civil rights protections to gays and lesbians by declaring unconstitutional a 1992 amendment to the Colorado State

[62]In 1994, for instance, after pressure from the Justice Department under the terms of the Americans with Disabilities Act, one of the nation's largest rental-car companies agreed to make special hand controls available to any customer requesting them. See "Avis Agrees to Equip Cars for Disabled," *Los Angeles Times*, 2 September 1994, p. D1.

[63]Thus a distinction has come to be made between "deaf," the pathology, and "Deaf," the culture. See Andrew Solomon, "Defiantly Deaf," *New York Times Magazine*, 28 August 1994, pp. 40ff.

[64]*Bowers v. Hardwick*, 478 U.S. 186 (1986).

[65]Quoted in Joan Biskupic, "Gay Rights Activists Seek a Supreme Court Test Case," *Washington Post*, 19 December 1993, p. A1.

constitution that prohibited local governments from passing ordinances to protect gay rights.[66] The decision's forceful language highlighted the connection between gay rights and civil rights as it declared discrimination against gay people unconstitutional.

In *Lawrence v. Texas* (2003), the Court overturned *Bowers* and struck down a Texas statute criminalizing certain intimate sexual conduct between consenting partners of the same sex.[67] A victory for lesbians and gays every bit as significant as *Roe v. Wade* was for women, *Lawrence v. Texas* extends at least one aspect of civil liberties to sexual minorities: the right to privacy. However, this decision by itself does not undo the various exclusions that deprive lesbians and gays full civil rights, including the right to marry, which became a hot-button issue in 2004.

In early 2004, the Supreme Judicial Court of Massachusetts ruled that under that state's constitution, gay men and lesbians were entitled to marry. The state senate then asked the court to rule on whether a civil-union statute (avoiding the word *marriage*) would, as it did in Vermont, satisfy the court's ruling—to which the court ruled negatively, asserting that civil unions were too much like the "separate but equal" doctrine that maintained legalized racial segregation from 1896 to 1954. Meanwhile, in San Francisco hundreds of gays and lesbians responded to the opportunity provided by the mayor, who had directed the city clerk to issue marriage licenses to same-sex couples in defiance of California law. At the same time, signs were that Massachusetts might move toward a state constitutional amendment that would ban gay unions by whatever name. Voters in Missouri and Louisiana approved a ban on same-sex marriages, joining Alaska, Hawaii, Nebraska, and Nevada in implementing such a ban. Voters in eleven other states approved similar bans in the November 2004 elections.

Affirmative Action

The politics of rights not only spread to increasing numbers of groups in the society but also expanded its goal. The relatively narrow goal of equalizing opportunity by eliminating discriminatory barriers had been developing toward the far broader goal of *affirmative action*—compensatory action to overcome the consequences of past discrimination and to encourage greater diversity. An affirmative action policy tends to involve two novel approaches: (1) positive or benign discrimination in which race or some other status is actually taken into account, but for compensatory action rather than mistreatment, and (2) compensatory action to favor members of the disadvantaged group who themselves may never have been the victims of discrimination. Quotas may be, but are not necessarily, involved in affirmative action policies.

In 1965, President Lyndon Johnson attempted to inaugurate affirmative action by executive orders directing agency heads and personnel officers to pursue

affirmative action A policy or program designed to redress historic injustices committed against specific groups by making special efforts to provide members of these groups with access to educational and employment opportunities.

[66]*Romer v. Evans*, 116 S.Ct. 1620 (1996).
[67]*Lawrence v. Texas*, 123 S.Ct. 2472 (2003).

vigorously a policy of minority employment in the federal civil service and in companies doing business with the national government. But affirmative action did not become a prominent goal until the 1970s.

The Supreme Court and the Burden of Proof   As this movement spread, it also began to divide civil rights activists and their supporters. The whole issue of qualification versus minority preference was addressed in the case of Allan Bakke. Bakke, a white male with no minority affiliation, brought suit against the University of California at Davis Medical School on the grounds that in denying him admission the school had discriminated against him on the basis of his race (that year, the school had reserved 16 of 100 available slots for minority applicants). He argued that his grades and test scores had ranked him well above many students who had been accepted at the school and that the only possible explanation for his rejection was that those others accepted were black or Hispanic while he was white. In 1978, Bakke won his case before the Supreme Court and was admitted to the medical school, but he did not succeed in getting affirmative action declared unconstitutional. The Court rejected the procedures at the University of California because its medical school had used both a quota *and* a separate admissions system for minorities. The Court agreed with Bakke's argument that racial categorizations are suspect categories that place a severe burden of proof on those using them to show a "compelling public purpose." The Court went on to say that achieving "a diverse student body" was such a public purpose, but the method of a rigid quota of student slots assigned on the basis of race was incompatible with the equal protection clause. Thus the Court permitted universities (and other schools, training programs, and hiring authorities) to continue to take minority status into consideration but limited severely the use of quotas to situations in which (1) previous discrimination had been shown and (2) in which quotas were used more as a *guideline* for social diversity than as a mathematically defined ratio.[68]

For nearly a decade after *Bakke*, the Supreme Court was tentative and permissive about efforts by corporations and governments to experiment with affirmative action programs in employment.[69] But in 1989, the Court returned to the *Bakke* position that any "rigid numerical quota" is suspect. In *Wards Cove v. Atonio*, the Court further weakened affirmative action by easing the way for employers to prefer white males, holding that the burden of proof of unlawful discrimination should be shifted from the defendant (the employer) to the plaintiff (the person claiming to be the victim of discrimination).[70] This decision virtually overruled the Court's prior holding.[71] That same year, the Court ruled that any affirmative action program already approved by federal courts

[68]*Regents of the University of California v. Bakke*, 438 U.S. 265 (1978).
[69]*United Steelworkers v. Weber*, 443 U.S. 193 (1979); and *Fullilove v. Klutznick*, 100 S.Ct. 2758 (1980).
[70]*Wards Cove v. Atonio*, 109 S.Ct. 2115 (1989).
[71]*Griggs v. Duke Power Company*, 401 U.S. 24 (1971).

could be subsequently challenged by white males who alleged that the program discriminated against them.[72]

In 1995, the Supreme Court's ruling in *Adarand Constructors, Inc. v. Pena* further weakened affirmative action. This decision stated that race-based policies, such as preferences given by the government to minority contractors, must survive strict scrutiny, placing the burden on the government to show that such affirmative action programs serve a compelling government interest and are narrowly tailored to address identifiable past discrimination.[73] President Clinton responded to the *Adarand* decision by ordering a review of all government affirmative action policies and practices. Although many observers suspected that the president would use the review as an opportunity to back away from affirmative action, the conclusions of the task force largely defended existing policies. Reflecting the influence of the Supreme Court's decision in *Adarand*, President Clinton acknowledged that some government policies would need to change. But on the whole, the review found that most affirmative action policies were fair and did not "unduly burden nonbeneficiaries."[74]

Although Clinton sought to "mend, not end" affirmative action, developments in the courts and the states continued to restrict affirmative action in important ways. One of the most significant was the *Hopwood* case, in which white students challenged admissions practices in the University of Texas Law School, charging that the school's affirmative action program discriminated against whites. In 1996, a federal court (the U.S. Court of Appeals for the Fifth Circuit) ruling on the case stated that race could never be considered in granting admissions and scholarships at state colleges and universities.[75] This decision effectively rolled back the use of affirmative action permitted by the 1978 *Bakke* case. In *Bakke*, as discussed earlier, the Supreme Court had outlawed quotas but said that race could be used as one factor among many in admissions decisions. Many universities and colleges have since justified affirmative action as a way of promoting racial diversity among their student bodies. What was new in the *Hopwood* decision was the ruling that race could *never* be used as a factor in admissions decisions, even to promote diversity.

In 1996, the Supreme Court refused to hear a challenge to the *Hopwood* case. This meant that its ruling remains in effect in the states covered by the Fifth Circuit—Texas, Louisiana, and Mississippi—but does not apply to the rest of the country. The impact of the *Hopwood* ruling is greatest in Texas because Louisiana and Mississippi are under conflicting court orders to desegregate their

---

[72]*Martin v. Wilks*, 109 S.Ct. 2180 (1989). In this case, some white firefighters in Birmingham challenged a consent decree mandating goals for hiring and promoting blacks. This was an affirmative action plan that had been worked out between the employer and aggrieved black employees and had been accepted by a federal court. Such agreements become "consent decrees" and are subject to enforcement. Chief Justice William Rehnquist held that the white firefighters could challenge the legality of such programs even though they had not been parties to the original litigation.

[73]*Adarand Constructors, Inc. v. Pena*, 115 S.Ct. 2097 (1995).

[74]Ann Devroy, "Clinton Study Backs Affirmative Action," *Washington Post*, 19 July 1995, p. A1.

[75]*Hopwood v. State of Texas*, 78 F3d 932 (Fifth Circuit, 1996).

universities. In Texas, in the year after the *Hopwood* case, minority applications to Texas universities declined. Concerned about the ability of Texas public universities to serve the state's minority students, the Texas legislature quickly passed a new law granting students who graduate in the top 10 percent of their classes automatic admission to the state's public universities. State officials hoped that this measure would ensure a racially diverse student body.[76]

The weakening of affirmative action in the courts was underscored in a case the Supreme Court agreed to hear in 1998. A white schoolteacher in New Jersey who had lost her job had sued her school district, charging that her layoff was racially motivated: a black colleague hired on the same day was not laid off. Under former President George H. W. Bush, the Justice Department had filed a brief on her behalf in 1989, but in 1994 the Clinton administration formally reversed course in a new brief supporting the school district's right to make distinctions based on race as long as it did not involve the use of quotas. Three years later, the administration, worried that the case was weak and could result in a broad decision against affirmative action, reversed course again. It filed a brief with the Court urging a narrow ruling in favor of the dismissed worker. Because the school board had justified its actions on the grounds of preserving diversity, the administration feared that a broad ruling by the Supreme Court could totally prohibit the use of race in employment decisions, even as one factor among many designed to achieve diversity. But before the Court could issue a ruling, a coalition of civil rights groups brokered and arranged to pay for a settlement. This unusual move reflected the widespread fear of a sweeping negative decision. Cases involving dismissals, as the New Jersey case did, are generally viewed as much more difficult to defend than cases that concern hiring. In addition, the particular facts of the New Jersey case—two equally qualified teachers hired on the same day—were seen as unusual and unfavorable to affirmative action.[77]

This betwixt and between status of affirmative action was how things stood in 2003, when the Supreme Court took two cases against the University of Michigan that were virtually certain to clarify, if not put closure on, affirmative action. The first suit, *Gratz v. Bollinger* (the university president), was against the University of Michigan's undergraduate admissions policy and practices, alleging that by using a point-based ranking system that automatically awarded 20 points (out of 150) to African American, Latino, and Native American applicants, the university discriminated unconstitutionally against white students of otherwise equal or superior academic qualifications. The Supreme Court agreed, 6 to 3, arguing that something tantamount to a quota was involved because undergraduate admissions

[76]See Lydia Lum, "Applications by Minorities down Sharply," *Houston Chronicle*, 8 April 1997, p. A1; R. G. Ratcliffe, "Senate Approves Bill Designed to Boost Minority Enrollments," *Houston Chronicle*, 8 May 1997, p. A1.

[77]Linda Greenhouse, "Settlement Ends High Court Case on Preferences," *New York Times*, 22 November 1997, p. A1; Barry Bearak, "Rights Groups Ducked a Fight, Opponents Say," *New York Times*, 22 November 1997, p. A1.

lacked the necessary "individualized consideration," employing instead a "mechanical one," based too much on the favorable minority points.[78] The Court's ruling in *Gratz v. Bollinger* was not surprising, given *Bakke*'s (1978) holding against quotas and given recent decisions calling for strict scrutiny of all racial classifications, even those that are intended to remedy past discrimination or promote future equality.

The second case, *Grutter v. Bollinger*, broke new ground. Grutter sued the University of Michigan's law school on the grounds that it had discriminated in a race-conscious way against white applicants with equal or superior grades and law boards. A precarious vote of 5 to 4 aligned the majority of the Supreme Court with Justice Lewis Powell's lone plurality opinion in *Bakke* for the first time. In *Bakke*, Powell argued that diversity in education is a compelling state interest and that race could be constitutionally considered as a plus factor in admissions decisions. In *Grutter*, the Court reiterated Powell's holding and, applying strict scrutiny to the law school's policy, found that the law school's admissions process was narrowly tailored to the school's compelling state interest in diversity because it gave a "highly individualized, holistic review of each applicant's file" in which race counted but was not used in a "mechanical way."[79]

Throughout the 1990s, federal courts, including the Supreme Court, had subjected public affirmative action programs to strict scrutiny to invalidate them. *Adarand Constructors, Inc. v. Pena* (1995) definitively established the Supreme Court's view that constitutionally permissible use of race must serve a compelling state interest. Since *Korematsu v. United States* (1944) and until *Grutter*, no consideration of race had survived strict scrutiny. Such affirmative action plans as had survived constitutional review did so before 1995 under a lower standard of review reserved for policies intended to remedy racial injustice. For affirmative action to survive under the post-1995 judicial paradigm, the Court needed to find that sometimes racial categories can be deployed to serve a compelling state interest. That the Court found exactly this in *Grutter* puts affirmative action on stronger ground—at least if its specific procedures pass the Supreme Court's muster, and until the Court's majority changes.

Referendums on Affirmative Action   The courts have not been the only center of action: challenges to affirmative action have also emerged in state and local politics. One of the most significant state actions was the passage of the California Civil Rights Initiative, also known as Proposition 209, in 1996. Proposition 209 outlawed affirmative action programs in the state and local governments of California, thus prohibiting state and local governments from using race or gender preferences in their decisions about hiring, contracting, or university admissions. The political battle over Proposition 209 was heated, and supporters and defenders took to the streets and airwaves to make their cases. When the referendum was held, the measure passed with 54 percent of the vote, including 27 percent of the black vote, 30 percent of the Latino vote, and 45 percent of the

Policy Principle

Individual challenges in the courts as well as several state and local referenda have weakened affirmative action.

---

[78]*Gratz v. Bollinger*, 123 S.Ct. 2411 (2003).
[79]*Grutter v. Bollinger*, 123 S.Ct. 2325 (2003).

Asian American vote.[80] In 1997, the Supreme Court refused to hear a challenge to the new law.

Many observers predicted that the success of California's ban on affirmative action would provoke similar movements in states and localities across the country. But the political factors that contributed to the success of Proposition 209 in California may not exist in many other states. Winning a controversial state referendum takes leadership and lots of money. Popular California Republican governor Pete Wilson led with a strong anti–affirmative action stand (favoring Proposition 209), and his campaign had a lot of money for advertising. But those conditions did not exist elsewhere. Few prominent Republican leaders in other states were willing to come forward to lead the anti–affirmative action campaign. Moreover, the outcome of any referendum, especially a complicated and controversial one, depends greatly on how the issue is drafted and placed on the ballot for the voters. California's Proposition 209 was framed as a civil rights initiative: "the state shall not discriminate against, or grant preferential treatment to, any individual or group on the basis of race, sex, color, ethnicity, or national origin." Different wording can produce quite different outcomes, as a 1997 vote on affirmative action in Houston revealed. There, the ballot initiative asked voters whether they wanted to ban affirmative action in city contracting and hiring, not whether they wanted to end preferential treatment. In that city, 55 percent of voters decided in favor of affirmative action.[81]

SUMMARY

Civil liberties and *civil rights* are two different phenomena and have to be treated legally and constitutionally in two different ways. We have defined *civil liberties* as that sphere of individual freedom of choice created by restraints on governmental power. When the Constitution was ratified, it was already seen as inadequate in the provision of protections of individual freedom and required the addition of the Bill of Rights. The Bill of Rights explicitly placed a whole series of restraints on government. Some of these were *substantive*, regarding *what* government could do; and some of these restraints were *procedural*, regarding *how* the government was permitted to act. We call the rights in the Bill of Rights civil liberties because they are rights to be free from arbitrary government interference.

But *which* government? This was settled in the *Barron* case in 1833 when the Supreme Court held that the restraints in the Bill of Rights were applicable only to the national government and not to the states. The Court was recognizing "dual citizenship." At the time of its adoption in 1868, the Fourteenth

[80]Michael A. Fletcher, "Opponents of Affirmative Action Heartened by Court Decision," *Washington Post*, 13 April 1997, p. A21.

[81]See Sam Howe Verhovek, "Houston Vote Underlined Complexity of Rights Issue," *New York Times*, 6 November 1997, p. A1.

Rationality Principle	Collective-Action Principle	Institution Principle	Policy Principle	History Principle
Madison believed a bill of rights would remove a potential source of opposition to the new government.	The Federalists supported the addition of a bill of rights because it would gain the support of the Antifederalists for the Constitution.	Dual citizenship meant that the Bill of Rights did not apply to decisions or to procedures of state governments.	The civil liberties decisions of the Rehnquist Court during the 1990s revealed the conservative preferences of a majority of its justices.	Dual citizenship was upheld by the Supreme Court for nearly 100 years after *Barron v. Baltimore* (1833).
The preferences of individual Supreme Court justices have been consequential for the development of civil liberties.	Given the massive resistance to the *Brown* decision, the civil rights movement required large, well-organized protests.	Most of the important provisions of the Bill of Rights were nationalized by the Supreme Court during the 1960s.	Individual challenges in the courts as well as several state and local referenda have weakened affirmative action.	*Roe v. Wade* was not decided in a political vacuum. Many states had already eased their restrictions on abortion before 1973.
	People participated in the civil rights movement for experiential as well as instrumental purposes.	As a political institution, the Bill of Rights has not been carved in stone. Through subsequent amendments, on the one hand, and constant updating of the original ten through judicial review, on the other, the balance between freedom and power has been transformed.		The *Brown* decision galvanized the modern civil rights movement.
	Enforcement of civil rights law required courts and legislatures to work together.			The civil rights and women's rights movements both suggest that changes in government policies can produce political action and vice versa.
		The *Brown* decision altered the constitutional framework by giving the national government the power to intervene against the discriminatory actions of state and local governments and some aspects of the private sector.		

Amendment was considered by many a deliberate effort to reverse *Barron*, to put an end to dual citizenship, and to nationalize the Bill of Rights, applying its restrictions to state governments as well as to the national government. But the post–Civil War Supreme Court interpreted the Fourteenth Amendment otherwise. Dual citizenship remained almost as it had been before the Civil War, and the shadow of *Barron* extended across the rest of the nineteenth century and well into the twentieth century. The slow process of nationalizing the Bill of Rights began in the 1920s, when the Supreme Court recognized that at least the restraints of the First Amendment had been "incorporated" into the Fourteenth Amendment as restraints on the state governments. But it was not until the 1960s that most of the civil liberties in the Bill of Rights were incorporated into the Fourteenth Amendment. Almost exactly a century after the adoption of the Fourteenth Amendment, the Bill of Rights was nationalized. Citizens now enjoy close to the same civil liberties regardless of the state in which they reside.

As for the second aspect of protection of the individual, *civil rights*, stress has been put on the expansion of governmental power rather than restraints on it. If the constitutional base of civil liberties is the "due process" clause of the Fourteenth Amendment, the constitutional base of civil rights is the "equal protection" clause. This clause imposes a positive obligation on government to advance civil rights, and its original motivation seems to have been to eliminate the gross injustices suffered by "the newly emancipated negroes . . . as a class." But as with civil liberties, there was little advancement in the interpretation or application of the "equal protection" clause until after World War II. The major breakthrough came in 1954 with *Brown v. Board of Education*, and advancements came in fits and starts during the succeeding ten years.

After 1964, Congress finally supported the federal courts with effective civil rights legislation that outlawed a number of discriminatory practices in the private sector and provided for the withholding of federal grants-in-aid to any local government, school, or private employer as a sanction to help enforce the civil rights laws. From that point, civil rights developed in two ways. First, the definition of civil rights was expanded to include victims of discrimination other than African Americans. Second, the definition of civil rights became increasingly positive; affirmative action has become an official term. Judicial decisions, congressional statutes, and administrative agency actions all have moved beyond the original goal of eliminating discrimination and toward creating new opportunities for minorities and, in some areas, compensating today's minorities for the consequences of discriminatory actions not directly against them but against members of their group in the past. Because compensatory civil rights action has sometimes relied on quotas, there has been intense debate over the constitutionality as well as the desirability of affirmative action.

The story has not ended and is not likely to end. The politics of rights will remain an important part of American political discourse.

FOR FURTHER READING

Abraham, Henry J., and Barbara A. Perry. *Freedom and the Court: Civil Rights and Liberties in the United States.* 6th ed. New York: Oxford University Press, 1994.

Baer, Judith A. *Equality under the Constitution: Reclaiming the Fourteenth Amendment.* Ithaca, NY: Cornell University Press, 1983.

Drake, W. Avon, and Robert D. Holsworth. *Affirmative Action and the Stalled Quest for Black Progress.* Urbana: University of Illinois Press, 1996.

Garrow, David J. *Bearing the Cross: Martin Luther King, Jr., and the Southern Christian Leadership Conference: A Personal Portrait.* New York: William Morrow, 1986.

Glendon, Mary Ann. *Rights Talk: The Impoverishment of Political Discourse.* New York: Free Press, 1991.

Greenberg, Jack. *Crusaders in the Courts: How a Dedicated Band of Lawyers Fought for the Civil Rights Revolution.* New York: Basic Books, 1994.

Kelly, Alfred, Winfred A. Harbison, and Herman Beltz. *The American Constitution: Its Origins and Development.* 7th ed. New York: Norton, 1991.

Levy, Leonard W. *Freedom of Speech and Press in Early America: Legacy of Suppression.* New York: Harper & Row, 1963.

Lewis, Anthony. *Gideon's Trumpet.* New York: Random House, 1964.

Minow, Martha. *Making All the Difference—Inclusion, Exclusion, and American Law.* Ithaca, NY: Cornell University Press, 1990.

Nava, Michael, and Robert Dawidoff. *Created Equal: Why Gay Rights Matter to America.* New York: St. Martin's Press, 1994.

Rosenberg, Gerald N. *The Hollow Hope: Can Courts Bring about Social Change?* Chicago: University of Chicago Press, 1991.

Silverstein, Mark. *Constitutional Faiths: Felix Frankfurter, Hugo Black, and the Process of Judicial Decision Making.* Ithaca, NY: Cornell University Press, 1984.

Thernstrom, Abigail M. *Whose Votes Count? Affirmative Action and Minority Voting Rights.* Cambridge, MA: Harvard University Press, 1987.

Politics in the News—
Reading between the Lines

Data Mining and Personal Privacy

Behind-the-Scenes Battle on Tracking Data Mining

By ERIC LICHTBLAU

Bush administration officials are opposing an effort in Congress under the antiterrorism law known as the USA Patriot Act to force the government to disclose its use of data-mining techniques in tracking suspects in terrorism cases.

As part of the vote in the House this week to extend major parts of the antiterrorism law permanently, lawmakers agreed to include a little-noticed provision that would require the Justice Department to report to Congress annually on government-wide efforts to develop and use data-mining technology to track intelligence patterns. . . .

The government's use of vast public and private databases to mine for leads has produced several damaging episodes for the Bush administration, most notably in connection with the Total Information Awareness system developed by the Pentagon for tracking terror suspects and the Capps program of the Department of Homeland Security for screening airline passengers. Both programs were ultimately scrapped after public

outcries over possible threats to privacy and civil liberties, and some Republicans and Democrats in Congress say they want to keep closer tabs on such computer operations to guard against abuse.

"We have wasted millions and millions of dollars on implementing database-mining activities which, when they became public, produced such an outrage they were canceled," Representative Howard L. Berman, a California Democrat who sponsored the amendment requiring a report to Congress, said this week during the House debate.

"We do not want to tie the hands of our security agencies in gathering this information," Mr. Berman said. "We simply want to provide a logical mechanism to gather the information so that the American people can feel more comfortable that what is being done is protected."

Justice Department officials said they were very pleased that the House decided Thursday to reauthorize the Patriot Act and to leave intact virtually all of its main counterterrorism powers.

New York Times, 24 July 2005, section 1, p. 16.

But the department fought fiercely to persuade lawmakers not to include in the bill the reporting requirement on data-mining operations, Congressional officials said. . . .

Attorney General Alberto R. Gonzales has earned plaudits from lawmakers in both parties for publicly pledging his cooperation with Congressional oversight functions and for providing more information to Congress after frequent complaints that his predecessor, John Ashcroft, had been uncooperative. But the talking points suggested that the Congressional requests have become an annoyance for at least some Justice Department officials.

"These reporting requirements require the department to direct resources away from important law enforcement duties and functions," the document said. "We oppose overbroad, costly, unrealistic reporting requirements." It also said the reporting requirement would create an "impossible job" for the attorney general in requiring that he tell Congress what all federal agencies are doing in the way of data mining.

Republican leaders who opposed the amendment also said it could tip off terrorists to the sources and methods that federal officials are using to track intelligence. . . .

Supporters of the reporting requirement have received support from an unlikely corner: Representative F. James Sensenbrenner Jr., Republican of Wisconsin, the chairman of the Judiciary Committee and one of the administration's principal supporters in pushing for reauthorization of the antiterrorism law.

Mr. Sensenbrenner said that past data-mining programs by the F.B.I. and other agencies, even before the Sept. 11 attacks, had wasted tax dollars and "compromised the privacy of literally millions of Americans," and he said

members of Congress had a right to know when the government was planning to use such technology in the future.

Despite the opposition of other Republican leaders, the House approved the amendment by a vote of 261 to 165. . . .

ESSENCE OF THE STORY

- An amendment to the USA Patriot Act, which had to be renewed in 2005 (the act was made permanent six days after this story), required intelligence agencies to report to Congress on their use of "data mining."

- Proponents of the amendment argue that government use of data mining is a potential threat to personal privacy and that such activities have to be closely monitored by Congress.

- The Justice Department opposed the amendment, regarding it as nothing more than an overly burdensome reporting requirement, and one that could harm anti-terrorism efforts.

POLITICAL ANALYSIS

- Debate over the renewal of the Patriot Act highlighted the political tension between protection of personal freedoms, such as privacy, and the needs of law enforcement.

- Data mining is a new and powerful technology that takes advantage of cheap computing power to link vast storehouses of information on individuals. Use of this technology by the government is an example of a technological innovation that may force us to rethink the limits of governmental intrusions into personal privacy.

- Political disagreements on privacy issues are usually strictly partisan, though in this story, a conservative Republican, James Sensenbrenner, is opposed to data-mining techniques.

two

Institutions

CHAPTER

5

Congress: The First Branch

The U.S. Congress is the "first branch" of government under Article I of our Constitution and is also among the world's most important representative bodies. Congress is the only national representative assembly that can actually be said to govern. Many of the world's representative bodies only represent—that is, their governmental functions consist mainly of affirming and legitimating the national leadership's decisions. The only national representative body that actually possesses powers of governance is the U.S. Congress. For example, while the U.S. Congress never accedes to the president's budget proposals without making major changes, both the British House of Commons and the Japanese Diet always accept the budget exactly as proposed by the government.

In this chapter, we shall try to understand how the U.S. Congress is able to serve simultaneously as a representative assembly and a powerful agency of government. Congress controls a formidable battery of powers that it uses to shape policies and, when necessary, defend its prerogatives against the executive branch.

Congress has vast authority over the two most important powers given to any government: the power of force (control over the nation's military forces) and the power over money. Specifically, in Article I, Section 8, Congress can "lay and collect Taxes," deal with indebtedness and bankruptcy, impose duties, borrow and coin money, and generally control the nation's purse strings. It also may "provide for the common Defense and general welfare," regulate interstate commerce, undertake public works, acquire and control federal lands, promote science and "useful Arts" (pertaining mostly to patents and copyrights), and regulate the militia.

In the realm of foreign policy, Congress has the power to declare war, deal with piracy, regulate foreign commerce, and raise and regulate the armed forces and military installations. These powers over war and the military are supreme—even the president, as commander in chief of the military, must obey the laws and orders of Congress *if* Congress chooses to assert its constitutional authority. (In the past century, Congress has usually surrendered this authority to the president.) Further, the Senate has the power to approve treaties (by a two-thirds vote) and to approve the appointment of ambassadors. Capping these powers, Congress is charged to make laws "which shall be necessary and proper for carrying into Execution the foregoing Powers, and all other Powers vested by this Constitution in the Government of the United States, or in any Department or Officer thereof."

If it seems to the reader that many of these powers belong to the president, from war power to spending power, that is because modern presidents do exercise great authority in these areas. The modern presidency is a more powerful institution than it was 200 years ago, and much of that power has come from Congress, either because Congress has delegated the power to the president by

CHAPTER OUTLINE

Representation
- House and Senate: Differences in Representation
- The Electoral System

Problems of Legislative Organization
- Cooperation in Congress
- Underlying Problems and Challenges

The Organization of Congress
- Party Leadership and Organization in the House and the Senate
- The Committee System: The Core of Congress
- The Staff System: Staffers and Agencies
- Informal Organization: The Caucuses

Rules of Lawmaking: How a Bill Becomes a Law
- Committee Deliberation
- Debate
- Conference Committee: Reconciling House and Senate Versions of a Bill
- Presidential Action
- Normal and Abnormal Procedures in Congress
- The Distributive Tendency in Congress

How Congress Decides
- Constituency
- Interest Groups
- Party Discipline
- Weighing Diverse Influences

Beyond Legislation: Additional Congressional Powers
- Advice and Consent: Special Senate Powers
- Impeachment

Power and Representation

law or because Congress has simply allowed, or even urged, presidents to be more active in these areas. This also helps explain why the executive branch seems like a more important branch of government today than Congress. Still, the constitutional powers of Congress remain intact in the document. As we shall see, congressional power cannot be separated from congressional representation. Indeed, there is a reciprocal relationship between the two. Without its array of powers, Congress could do little to represent effectively the views and interests of its constituents. At the same time, the power of Congress is ultimately a function of its capacity to represent important groups and forces in American society effectively.

Questions of power and representation are also closely tied to the issue of congressional reform. Critics of Congress want it to be both more representative and more effective. On the one hand, Congress is frequently criticized for falling victim to "gridlock" and failing to reach decisions on important issues like Social Security reform, something on which President George W. Bush has placed great emphasis during his second term. This incapacity was one reason why, in 1995, the Republican House leadership reduced the number of committees and subcommittees in the lower chamber. Having fewer committees and subcommittees generally means greater centralization of

PREVIEWING THE PRINCIPLES

All five principles of politics are important to our understanding of Congress. Members of Congress, like all politicians, are ambitious and are thus eager to serve the interests of constituents to improve their own chances of re-election. In many ways, Congress works because its system of representation harnesses individual legislators' goals and puts them to use. Because the policy goals of members of Congress are many and varied, cooperation among members can be difficult to achieve. The internal organization of Congress seeks to remedy the problems of collective action by regularizing patterns of cooperation and creating a division of labor among members. Similarly, the legislative process and legislative parties try to provide coordination to a diverse institution, and in the legislative process it is clear that rules matter. The legislative process also reveals that political outcomes result from preferences and procedures. Finally, in the discussion of the evolution of the committee system and the influence of political parties in Congress, we see that history matters. In fact, the ebb and flow of Congress's power in the political system can be evaluated only in historical context.

power and more expeditious decision making. On the other hand, critics demand that Congress become more representative of the changing makeup and values of the American populace. In recent years, for example, some reformers have demanded limits on the number of terms that any member of Congress can serve. Term limits are seen as a device for producing more rapid turnover of members and hence a better chance for new political and social forces to be represented in Congress. The problem, however, is that while reforms such as term limits and greater internal diffusion of power may make Congress more representative, they may also make it less efficient and effective. By the same token, reforms that may make Congress better able to act, such as strong central leadership, reduction of the number of committees and subcommittees, and retention of members with seniority and experience, may make Congress less representative.

Congressional power cannot be separated either from the bases of congressional representation or from the precise form taken by its decision-making institutions. We begin our discussion with a brief consideration of representation. Then we examine the institutional structure of the contemporary Congress and the manner in which congressional powers are organized and employed. Throughout, we point out the connections between these two aspects—the ways in which representation affects congressional operations (especially through "the electoral connection") and the ways in which congressional institutions enhance or diminish representation (especially Congress's division- and specialization-of-labor committee system).

REPRESENTATION

Congress is the most important representative institution in American government. Each member's primary responsibility is to the district, to his or her *constituency,* not to the congressional leadership, a party, or even Congress itself. Yet the task of representation is not a simple one. Views about what constitutes fair and effective representation differ, and constituents can make very different kinds of demands on their representatives. Members of Congress must consider these diverse views and demands as they represent their districts (Figure 5.1). A representative claims to act or speak for some other person or group. But how can one person be trusted to speak for another? How do we know that those who call themselves our representatives are actually speaking on our behalf, rather than simply pursuing their own interests?

Legislators generally vary in the weight given to personal priorities and the things desired by campaign contributors and past supporters. Some see themselves as perfect agents of others; they have been elected to do the bidding of those that sent them to the legislature, and they act as *delegates.* Other legislators see themselves as being selected by their fellow citizens to do what the legislator thinks is "right," and they act as *trustees.* Most legislators are mixes of these two types.

As we discussed in Chapter 1, one person might be trusted to speak for another if the two are formally bound together so that the representative is in some way accountable to those he or she purports to represent. If representatives can somehow be punished or held to account for failing to speak properly for their constituents, then we know they have an incentive to provide good representation even if their own personal backgrounds, views, and interests differ from those they represent. This principle is called *agency representation*—the sort of representation that takes place when constituents have the power to hire and fire their representatives. Frequent competitive elections constitute an important means by which constituents hold their representatives to account and keep them responsive to constituency views and preferences. The idea of representative as agent is

constituency
The district making up the area from which an official is elected.

delegate A representative who votes according to the preferences of his or her constituency.

trustee A representative who votes based on what he or she thinks is best for his or her constituency.

agency representation
The type of representation by which representatives are held accountable to their constituents if they fail to represent them properly—that is, constituents have the power to hire and fire their representatives. This is the incentive for good representation when the personal backgrounds, views, and interests of the representatives differ from their constituents'.

 Institution Principle

According to the principle of agency representation, elections induce a member of Congress to act according to the preferences of his or her constituency.

FIGURE 5.1

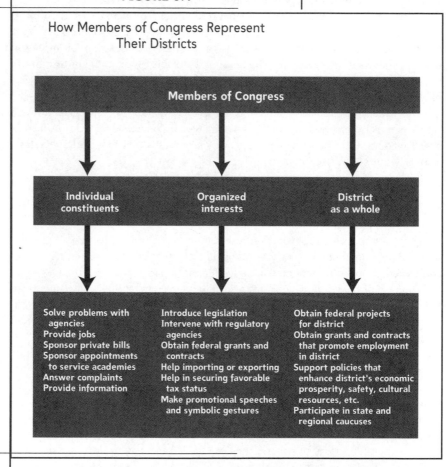

How Members of Congress Represent
Their Districts

Members of Congress

Individual constituents	Organized interests	District as a whole
Solve problems with agencies	Introduce legislation	Obtain federal projects for district
Provide jobs	Intervene with regulatory agencies	Obtain grants and contracts that promote employment in district
Sponsor private bills	Obtain federal grants and contracts	Support policies that enhance district's economic prosperity, safety, cultural resources, etc.
Sponsor appointments to service academies	Help importing or exporting	
Answer complaints	Help in securing favorable tax status	Participate in state and regional caucuses
Provide information	Make promotional speeches and symbolic gestures	

Legislative representation consists of elected officials taking care of individuals and groups in their constituency, solving problems, facilitating access to agencies and policy making, and delivering policy outputs to their states and districts.

similar to the relationship of lawyer and client. True, the relationship between the member of Congress and as many as 630,000 "clients" in the district or between the senator and millions of clients in the state is very different from that of the lawyer and client. But the criteria of performance are comparable.

One expects at the very least that each representative will constantly be seeking to discover the interests of the constituency and will be speaking for those interests in Congress and in other centers of government.[1] We expect this because we believe that members of Congress, like politicians everywhere, are ambitious. For many, this ambition is satisfied simply by maintaining a hold on their present office and advancing up the rungs of power in that legislative body. Some may be looking ahead to the next level—to higher legislative office, as when a representative seeks a Senate seat; or to an executive office, as when a legislator returns home to run for his or her state's governorship; or, at the highest level, when a legislator seeks the presidency.[2] We will return to this topic shortly in a discussion of elections. But we can say here that in each of these cases, the legislator is eager to serve the interests of constituents, either to enhance his or her prospects of contract renewal at the next election or to improve the chances of moving to another level. In short, the agency conception of representation works in proportion to the ambition of politicians (as "agents") and the capacity of constituents (as "principals") to reward or punish on the basis of their legislator's performance and reputation. This latter capacity depends on, among other things, the quality of political competition, which, in turn, is a product of the electoral and campaign finance systems.

Rationality Principle

Members of Congress, like all politicians, are ambitious and thus eager to serve the interests of constituents to improve their own chances of re-election.

House and Senate: Differences in Representation

The framers of the Constitution provided for a ***bicameral legislature***—that is, a legislative body consisting of two chambers. As we saw in Chapter 2, the framers intended each of these chambers, the House and Senate, to represent a different constituency. Members of the House were to be "close to the people," elected popularly every two years. Members of the Senate, on the other hand, were appointed by state legislatures for six-year terms and were to represent the elite members of society and to be more attuned to the interests of property than of population. Today, members of the House and Senate are elected directly by the people. The 435 members of the House are elected from districts apportioned according to population; the 100 members of the Senate are elected by state, with two senators from each. Senators continue to have much longer terms in office and usually represent much larger and more diverse constituencies than do their counterparts in the House of Representatives (Table 5.1).

bicameral legislature A legislative assembly composed of two chambers or houses.

The House and Senate play different roles in the legislative process. In essence, the Senate is the more deliberative of the two bodies—the forum in which any and all ideas can receive a thorough public airing. The House is the more centralized and organized of the two bodies—better equipped to play a routine role in the governmental process. In part, this difference stems from the different rules governing the two bodies. These rules give House leaders more control over the legislative process and provide for House members to specialize

---

[1]The classic description of interactions between politicians and "the folks back home" is given by Richard F. Fenno Jr., *Home Style: House Members in Their Districts* (Boston: Little, Brown, 1978).
[2]For more on "progressive ambition," see Joseph A. Schlesinger, *Ambition and Politics: Political Careers in the United States* (Chicago: Rand McNally, 1966).

TABLE 5.1

Differences between the House and the Senate		
	HOUSE	**SENATE**
Minimum age of member	25 years	30 years
U.S. citizenship	At least 7 years	At least 9 years
Length of term	2 years	6 years
Number per state	Depends on population: 1 per 30,000 in 1789; now 1 per 630,000	2 per state
Constituency	Tends to be local	Both local and national

in certain legislative areas. The rules of the much smaller Senate give its leadership relatively little power and discourage specialization. (On the relative *breadth* of senators versus the *depth* of the House members, it is said that a U.S. Senator is like the mouth of the North Platte River: a mile wide and an inch deep!)

Both formal and informal factors contribute to differences between the two chambers of Congress. Differences in the length of terms and requirements for holding office specified by the Constitution in turn generate differences in how members of each body develop their constituencies and exercise their powers of office. The result is that members of the House most effectively and frequently serve as the agents of well-organized local interests with specific legislative agendas—for instance, used-car dealers seeking relief from regulation, labor unions seeking more favorable legislation, or farmers looking for higher subsidies. The small size and relative homogeneity of their constituencies and the frequency with which they must seek re-election make House members more attuned to the legislative needs of local interest groups. This is what the framers intended when they drafted the Constitution—namely, that the House of Representatives would be "the people's house" and that its members would reflect and represent public opinion in a timely manner.

Senators, on the other hand, serve larger and more heterogeneous constituencies. As a result, they are somewhat better able than members of the House to serve as the agents for groups and interests organized on a statewide or national basis. Moreover, with longer terms in office, senators have the luxury of considering "new ideas" or seeking to bring together new coalitions of interests, rather

History Principle

The historical intentions of the founders for the House to represent current passions and the Senate to balance it by serving a more deliberative function are still manifest in these legislative bodies more than two centuries later.

than simply serving existing ones. This, too, was the intent of the Constitution's drafters—that the Senate should provide a balance to the more responsive House with its narrower and more homogenous constituencies. The Senate was said to be "the saucer that cools the tea," bringing deliberation, debate, inclusiveness, calm, and caution to policy formulation.

In recent years, the House has exhibited considerably more intense partisanship and ideological division than the Senate. Because of their diverse constituencies, senators are more inclined to seek compromise positions that will offend as few voters and interest groups as possible. Members of the House, in contrast, with their more homogeneous districts in which their own party is dominant, are less inclined to seek compromises and more willing to stick to their partisan and ideological guns. For instance, the House divided almost exactly along partisan lines on the 1998 vote to impeach President Clinton. In the Senate, by contrast, ten Republicans joined Democrats to acquit Clinton of obstruction of justice charges, and, in a separate vote, five Republicans joined Democrats to acquit Clinton of perjury.[3] Also, in October 2001, the Senate passed an airport security bill unanimously. The House, however, divided along partisan lines over whether new security personnel should be federal employees or private contractors. During the George W. Bush presidency, even the Senate has grown more partisan and polarized—especially on social issues and the war in Iraq.

The Electoral System

In light of their role as agents for various constituencies in their states and districts, and the importance of elections as a mechanism by which principals (constituents) reward and punish their agents, representatives are very much influenced by electoral considerations. Three factors related to the U.S. electoral system affect who gets elected and what he or she does once in office. The first set of issues concerns who decides to run for office and which candidates have an edge over others. The second issue is that of incumbency advantage. Finally, the way congressional district lines are drawn can greatly affect the outcome of an election. Let us examine more closely the impact that these considerations have on who serves in Congress.

Running for Office Voters' choices are restricted from the start by who decides to run for office. In the past, decisions about who would run for a particular elected office were made by local party officials. A person who had a record of service to the party, or who was owed a favor, or whose "turn" had come up might be nominated by party leaders for an office.[4] Today, few party organiza-

---

[3]Eric Pianin and Guy Gugliotta, "The Bipartisan Challenge: Senate's Search for Accord Marks Contrast to House," *Washington Post*, 8 January 1999, p. 1.

[4]In the nineteenth century, it was often an *obligation*, not an honor, to serve in Congress. The real political action was back home in the state capital or a big city, not in Washington. So the practice of "rotation" was devised, according to which a promising local politician was to do a tour of duty in Washington before being slated for an important local office.

tions have the power to slate candidates in that way. Instead, the decision to run for Congress is a more personal choice. One of the most important factors determining who runs for office is a candidate's individual ambition.[5] A potential candidate may also assess whether he or she can attract enough money to mount a credible campaign. The ability to raise money depends on connections with other politicians, interest groups, and national party organizations. Wealthy individuals may finance their own races. In 2000, for example, New Jersey Democrat and former investment banker Jon Corzine spent more than $60 million of his own money to win a U.S. Senate seat. (In 2005 he spent a similar amount of money to win the governorship of New Jersey.)

In the past, the difficulty of raising campaign funds posed a disadvantage to female candidates. Since the 1980s, however, a number of political action committees (PACs) and other organizations have emerged to recruit women and fund their campaigns. The largest of them, EMILY's List, has become one of the most powerful fund-raisers in the nation. Recent research shows that money is no longer the barrier it once was to women running for office.[6]

Features distinctive to each congressional district also affect the field of candidates. Among them are the range of other political opportunities that may lure potential candidates away. In addition, the way the congressional district overlaps with state legislative boundaries may affect a candidate's decision to run. A state-level representative or senator who is considering running for the U.S. Congress is more likely to assess his or her prospects favorably if his or her state district coincides with the congressional district (because the voters will already know him or her). For similar reasons, U.S. representatives from small states, whose congressional districts overlap with a large portion of their state, are far more likely to run for statewide office than members of Congress from large states. For example, John Thune was elected as the lone representative from South Dakota in 1996. His constituency thus completely overlapped those of Senator Tim Johnson and Senator Tom Daschle. In 2002 Thune challenged Johnson, losing by barely 500 votes. In 2004 he defeated Daschle, then the Democratic leader in the Senate. For any candidate, decisions about running must be made early because once money has been committed to already declared candidates, it is harder for new candidates to break into a race. Thus the outcome of a November election is partially determined many months earlier, when decisions to run are finalized.

incumbency

Holding a political office for which one is running.

Incumbency *Incumbency* plays a very important role in the American electoral system and in the kind of representation citizens get in Washington. Once in office, members of Congress typically are eager to remain in office and make poli-

---

[5]See Linda L. Fowler and Robert D. McClure, *Political Ambition: Who Decides to Run for Congress* (New Haven, CT: Yale University Press, 1989); and Alan Ehrenhalt, *The United States of Ambition: Politicians, Power, and the Pursuit of Office* (New York: Times Books, 1991).

[6]See Barbara C. Burrell, *A Woman's Place Is in the House: Campaigning for Congress in the Feminist Era* (Ann Arbor: University of Michigan Press, 1994), Chapter 6; and the essays in Elizabeth Adell Cook, Sue Thomas, and Clyde Wilcox, eds., *The Year of the Woman: Myths and Realities* (Boulder, CO: Westview, 1994).

FIGURE 5.2

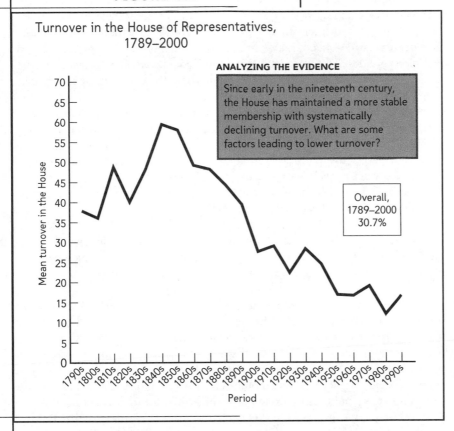

Turnover in the House of Representatives, 1789–2000

ANALYZING THE EVIDENCE

Since early in the nineteenth century, the House has maintained a more stable membership with systematically declining turnover. What are some factors leading to lower turnover?

Mean turnover in the House

Overall, 1789–2000 30.7%

Period

SOURCE: Revised from John Swain, Stephen A. Borelli, Brian C. Reed, and Sean F. Evans, "A New Look at Turnover in the U.S. House of Representatives, 1789–1998," *American Politics Quarterly* 28 (2000): 435–57.

tics a career. Throughout the twentieth century, Congress developed into a *professional legislature,* a legislature with members that serve full-time for multiple terms (see Figure 5.2).[7] The career ambitions of members of Congress are helped by an array of tools that they can use to stack the deck in favor of their re-election. Through effective use of this arsenal of weapons, an incumbent establishes a reputation for competence, imagination, and responsiveness—the attributes most principals look for in an agent. One well-known tool of incumbency is the franking privilege. Under a law enacted by the first U.S. Congress in 1789,

professional legislature
A legislature with members that serve full-time for multiple terms.

[7]Nelson W. Polsby, "The Institutionalization of the U.S. House of Representatives," *American Political Science Review* 63 (1968): 144–68.

members of Congress may send mail to their constituents free of charge to keep them informed of government business and public affairs. Under current law, members receive an average of about $100,000 in free postage for mailings to their constituents. Members may not use these funds to send mail outside their own districts or to send out mass mailings within ninety days of a primary or general election. Despite these restrictions, the franking privilege provides incumbents with a valuable resource for publicizing their activities and making themselves visible to voters.

A particularly important tool is the incumbent's reputation for constituency service: taking care of the problems and requests of individual voters. Through such services and their advertisement by word of mouth, the incumbent seeks to establish an attractive political reputation and a "personal" relationship with his or her constituents. Well over a quarter of the representatives' time and nearly two-thirds of the time of their staff members is devoted to constituency service (termed **casework**). This service is not merely a matter of writing and mailing letters. It includes talking to constituents, providing them with minor services, presenting special bills for them, and attempting to influence decisions by regulatory commissions on their behalf. Indeed, one might think of the member's legislative staff and office operation as a "congressional enterprise," much like a firm, with the member himself or herself as the CEO.[8]

One very direct way in which incumbent members of Congress serve as the agents of their constituencies is through the venerable institution of *patronage.* Patronage refers to a variety of forms of direct services and benefits that members provide for their districts. One of the most important forms of patronage is *pork-barrel legislation.* Through pork-barrel legislation, representatives seek to capture federal projects and federal funds for their own districts (or states in the case of senators) and thus to "bring home the bacon" for their constituents.

A common form of pork barreling is the "earmark," the practice through which members of Congress insert into otherwise pork-free bills language that provides special benefits for their own constituents.[9] For example, in 2005 a transportation bill was enacted, and it was weighed down by earmarks. Among the more outrageous was a bridge in Alaska costing more than $10 million to an island on which no one lives (the so-called "bridge to nowhere"). This proved so embarrassing to the Republicans once they began receiving adverse publicity that they rescinded the appropriation.

So why do legislators continue this exasperating practice? One answer is that each individual legislator can credibly and visibly claim personal responsibility, and thus take personal credit, for earmarked programs and special highway projects. This enhances the legislator's reputation back home as a Washington mover and

casework An effort by members of Congress to gain the trust and support of constituents by providing them with personal service. One important type of casework consists of helping constituents obtain favorable treatment from the federal bureaucracy.

patronage The resources available to higher officials, usually opportunities to make partisan appointments to offices and to confer grants, licenses, or special favors to supporters.

pork-barrel legislation Appropriations made by legislative bodies for local projects that are often not needed but that are created so that local representatives can carry their home district in the next election.

---

[8]For more on the congressional office as an "enterprise" that processes the casework demands of constituents, see Robert H. Salisbury and Kenneth A. Shepsle, "Congressman as Enterprise," *Legislative Studies Quarterly* 6 (1981): 559–76.

[9]For an excellent study of academic earmarking, see James D. Savage, *Funding Science in America: Congress, Universities, and the Politics of the Academic Pork Barrel* (New York: Cambridge University Press, 1999).

shaker, while also enhancing his or her re-election prospects. If the same money came to the states or districts through an existing program, like the Highway Trust Fund, the individual legislator would get little credit for being personally responsible. (As with the "bridge to nowhere," however, sometimes this can backfire.)

The incumbency advantage is evident in the high rates of re-election for congressional incumbents: over 95 percent for House members and nearly 90 percent for members of the Senate in recent years (see Figure 5.3).[10] In 2004, 98 percent of House incumbents running in the general election were successful and of the handful defeated, most lost because redistricting placed them in new and unfriendly districts. Only one incumbent senator was defeated. Democratic Senate Minority Leader Tom Daschle lost his bid for reelection in South Dakota. The advantage is also evident in what is called sophomore surge—the tendency for candidates to win a higher percentage of the vote when seeking their second term in office than in their initial election victory. Once in office, members of Congress find it much easier to raise campaign funds and are thus able to outspend their challengers (see Figure 5.4).[11] Over the past quarter century, and despite many campaign-finance regulations to level the playing field, the gap between incumbent and challenger spending has grown (House) or held steady (Senate). Members of the majority party in the House and Senate are particularly attractive to donors who want access to those in power.[12]

Incumbency can help a candidate by scaring off potential challengers. In many races, potential candidates may decide not to run because they fear that the incumbent simply has brought too many benefits to the district, has too much money, or is too well liked or too well known.[13] Potentially strong challengers may also decide that a district's partisan leanings are too unfavorable. The experience of Republican representative Dan Miller in Florida is instructive. When Miller first ran in 1992, he faced five opponents in the Republican primary and a bruising campaign against his Democratic opponent in the general election. In the 1994 election, by contrast, Miller faced only nominal opposition in the Republican primary, winning 81 percent of the vote. In the general election, the strongest potential challenger from the Democratic party decided not to run; the combination of the incumbency advantage coupled with the strongly

Policy Principle

Pork-barrel legislation exists because it allows members of Congress to claim credit for federally granted resources, thus improving their chances for re-election.

[10]Norman J. Ornstein, Thomas E. Mann, and Michael J. Malbin, *Vital Statistics on Congress, 1995–1996* (Washington, DC: Congressional Quarterly Press, 1996), pp. 60–61 (see also subsequent editions); Robert S. Erickson and Gerald C. Wright, "Voters, Candidates, and Issues in Congressional Elections," in *Congress Reconsidered*, ed. Lawrence C. Dodd and Bruce I. Oppenheimer, 5th ed. (Washington, DC: Congressional Quarterly Press, 1993), p. 99; John R. Alford and David W. Brady, "Personal and Partisan Advantage in U.S. Congressional Elections, 1846–1990," in *Congress Reconsidered*, ed. Dodd and Oppenheimer, pp. 141–57.

[11]Stephen Ansolabehere and James Snyder, "Campaign War Chests and Congressional Elections," *Business and Politics* 2 (2000): 9–34.

[12]Gary W. Cox and Eric Magar, "How Much Is Majority Status in the U.S. Congress Worth?" *American Political Science Review* 93 (1999): 299–309.

[13]Kenneth Bickers and Robert Stein, "The Electoral Dynamics of the Federal Pork Barrel," *American Journal of Political Science* 40 (November 1996): 1300–26.

FIGURE 5.3

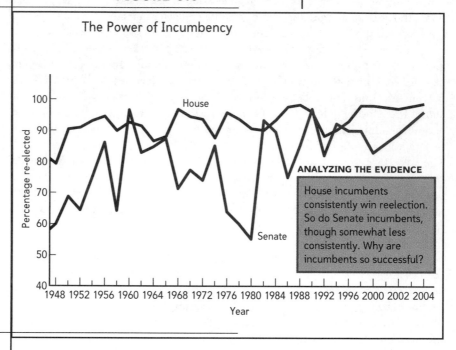

The Power of Incumbency

ANALYZING THE EVIDENCE

House incumbents consistently win reelection. So do Senate incumbents, though somewhat less consistently. Why are incumbents so successful?

SOURCE: Norman J. Ornstein, Thomas E. Mann, and Michael J. Malbin, eds., *Vital Statistics on Congress, 1995–1996* (Washington, DC: Congressional Quarterly Press, 1996), pp. 60–61 and authors' update.

Republican leanings of the district gave the Democrats little chance of winning. Miller was re-elected without a challenge.[14]

The advantage of incumbency thus tends to preserve the status quo in Congress by discouraging potentially strong challengers from running. When incumbents do face strong challengers, they are often defeated.[15] The reason is that strong challengers are willing to throw their hat in the ring only when they believe the incumbent is weak, out of touch, too preoccupied with national affairs, or plagued by scandal or declining capabilities. In the 2004 election, Tom Daschle (D-S.D.), leader of the Democrats in the Senate, lost to a very strong challenger (a former congressman) in part because his national responsibilities allowed him to be portrayed as out of touch with the values of the good folks of South Dakota.

[14]Kevin Merida, "The 2nd Time Is Easy; Many House Freshmen Have Secured Seats," *Washington Post*, 18 October 1994, p. A1.

[15]Gary C. Jacobson, *The Politics of Congressional Elections*, 6th ed. (New York: Longman, 2004).

FIGURE 5.4

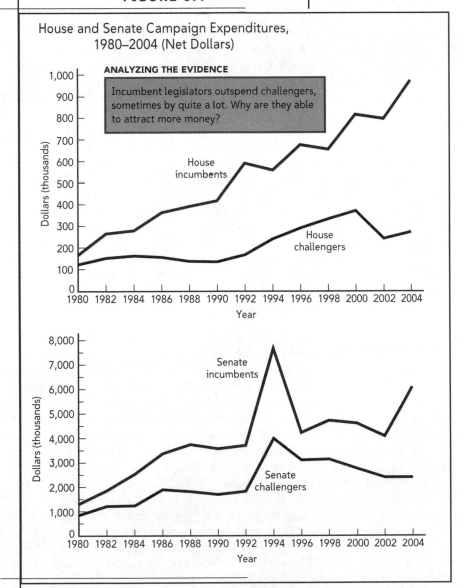

House and Senate Campaign Expenditures, 1980–2004 (Net Dollars)

ANALYZING THE EVIDENCE

Incumbent legislators outspend challengers, sometimes by quite a lot. Why are they able to attract more money?

SOURCE: Norman J. Ornstein, Thomas E. Mann, and Michael J. Malbin, eds., *Vital Statistics on Congress, 2001–2002* (Washington, DC: American Enterprise Institute, 2002), pp. 87, 93, and Campaign Finance Institute, www.cfinst.org.

The role of incumbency has implications for the social composition of Congress. For example, the incumbency advantage makes it harder for women to increase their numbers in Congress because most incumbents are men. Women who run for open seats (for which there are no incumbents) are just as likely to win as male candidates.[16] Supporters of term limits argue that such limits are the only way to get new faces into Congress. They believe that the incumbency advantage and the tendency of many legislators to view politics as a career mean that very little turnover will occur in Congress unless limits are imposed on the number of terms a legislator can serve.

But the tendency toward the status quo is not absolute. In recent years, political observers have suggested that the incumbency advantage may be declining. In the 1992 and 1994 elections, for example, voters expressed considerable anger and dissatisfaction with incumbents, producing a 25 percent turnover in the House in 1992 and a 20 percent turnover in 1994. Yet the defeat of incumbents was not the main factor at work in either of these elections; 88.3 percent of House incumbents who sought re-election were re-elected in 1992, and 90.2 percent won re-election in 1994. In 1992, it was an exceptionally high retirement rate (20 percent, as opposed to the norm of 10 percent) among members of Congress that created more open seats, which brought new faces into Congress.[17] In 1994, a large number of open seats combined with an unprecedented mobilization of Republican voters to shift control of Congress to the Republican party.

Congressional Districts   The final factor that affects who wins a seat in Congress is the way congressional districts are drawn. Every ten years, state legislatures must redraw congressional districts to reflect population changes. In 1929, Congress enacted a law fixing the total number of congressional seats at 435. As a result, when states with growing populations gain districts they do so at the expense of states whose populations have remained stagnant or declined. In recent decades, this has meant that the nation's growth areas in the South and West have gained congressional seats at the expense of the Northeast and Midwest (see Figure 5.5). After the 2000 Census, for example, Arizona, Texas, Florida, and Georgia each gained two seats while New York and Pennsylvania each lost two seats. Redrawing congressional districts is a highly political process: districts are shaped to create an advantage for the majority party in the state legislature, which controls the redistricting process. In this complex process, those charged with drawing districts use sophisticated computer technologies to come up with the most favorable district boundaries. Redistricting can create open seats and may pit incumbents of the same party against one another, ensuring that one of

---

[16]See Burrell, *A Woman's Place Is in the House;* and David Broder, "Key to Women's Political Parity: Running," *Washington Post*, 8 September 1994, p. A17.

[17]The reason for the high voluntary retirement rate that year is interesting. Congress had passed a reform making it no longer possible for members to pocket any money left in their office accounts when they retired. The last year in which this was permitted was 1992, and a number of members took this opportunity to retire, some enriching themselves by hundreds of thousands of dollars.

FIGURE 5.5

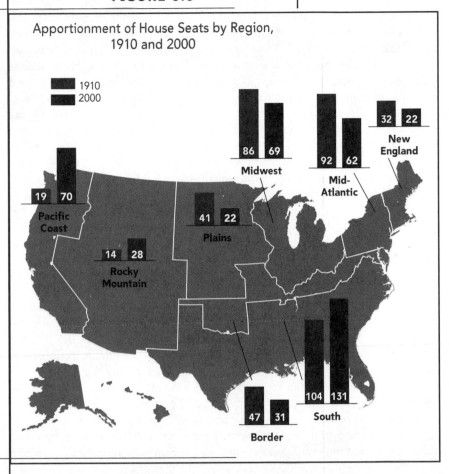

Apportionment of House Seats by Region, 1910 and 2000

■ 1910
■ 2000

Midwest 86 | 69

Mid-Atlantic 92 | 62

New England 32 | 22

Pacific Coast 19 | 70

Plains 41 | 22

Rocky Mountain 14 | 28

Border 47 | 31

South 104 | 131

The southern, mountain, and western states have gained congressional representation at the expense of other parts of the country.

SOURCE: Norman J. Ornstein, Thomas E. Mann, and Michael J. Malbin, eds., *Vital Statistics on Congress, 2001–2002* (Washington, DC: American Enterprise Institute, 2002), p. 59.

them will lose. Redistricting can also give an advantage to one party by clustering voters with some ideological or sociological characteristics in a single district, or by separating those voters into two or more districts. *Gerrymandering* can have a major effect on the outcomes of congressional elections. For example, before 1980, California House seats had been almost evenly divided between the two parties. After the 1980 census, a redistricting effort controlled by the Democrats,

gerrymandering
Apportionment of voters in districts in such a way as to give unfair advantage to one political party.

who held both houses of the state legislature as well as the governorship, resulted in Democrats taking control of two-thirds of the state's seats in the U.S. House of Representatives.[18] Another more recent case benefited the Republicans. The 2002 congressional election was the first one under the redistricting required by the 2000 census. In 2003, the Texas legislature, controlled by the Republicans, set to work drawing up a *new* set of congressional districts. Ordinarily this exercise is done once per decade after the constitutionally required census. But, argued Texas Republicans, nothing prohibits a state from doing it more frequently. Democrats in the Texas House were furious and twice staged walkouts, even fleeing across the border to Oklahoma to avoid a posse of Texas Rangers sent to retrieve them. These walkouts delayed proceedings by making it difficult to assemble enough legislators to meet the minimum requirements to do legislative business. Finally, however, the Republicans prevailed, redrawing the federal districts in a way very favorable to them. In 2004, the Republicans gained five seats in Texas, defeating four Democratic incumbents, in part the result of their redistricting maneuver.[19] Examples like these explain why the two parties invest substantial resources in state legislative and gubernatorial contests during the electoral cycle before the year that congressional district boundaries will be redrawn.

As we shall see in Chapter 10, since the passage of the 1982 amendments to the 1965 Voting Rights Act, race has become a major—and controversial—consideration in drawing voting districts. These amendments, which encouraged the creation of districts in which members of racial minorities have decisive majorities, have greatly increased the number of minority representatives in Congress. After the 1991–92 redistricting, the number of predominantly minority districts doubled, rising from twenty-six to fifty-two. Among the most fervent supporters of the new minority districts were white Republicans, who used the opportunity to create more districts dominated by white Republican voters.[20] These developments raise thorny questions about representation. Some analysts argue that the system may grant minorities greater sociological representation, but it has made it more difficult for minorities to win substantive policy goals.[21]

PROBLEMS OF LEGISLATIVE ORGANIZATION

The U.S. Congress is not only a representative assembly. It is also a legislative body. For Americans, representation and legislation go hand in hand. Many par-

---

[18]David Butler and Bruce Cain, *Congressional Redistricting: Comparative and Theoretical Perspectives* (New York: Macmillan, 1992).

[19]It is not over yet. In late 2004, the U.S. Supreme Court ordered a lower federal court to reconsider the "extra" Texas redistricting plan. See "Texas Redistricting Fight Not Over," 18 October 2004, available online (cbsnews.com).

[20]David Lublin, *The Paradox of Representation: Racial Gerrymandering and Minority Interests in Congress* (Princeton, NJ: Princeton University Press, 1997).

[21]Lani Guinier, *The Tyranny of the Majority: Fundamental Fairness in Representative Democracy* (New York: Free Press, 1995).

liamentary bodies, however, are representative without the power to legislate. It is no small achievement that the U.S. Congress both represents *and* governs.

Yet governing is a challenge. It is extraordinarily difficult for a large, representative assembly to formulate, enact, and implement laws. The internal complexities of conducting business within Congress—the legislative process—alone are daunting. In addition, there are many individuals and institutions that have the capacity to influence the legislative process. Because successful legislation requires the confluence of so many distinct factors, it is little wonder that most of the thousands of bills considered by Congress each year are defeated long before they reach the president.

The supporters of legislative proposals often feel that the formal rules of the congressional process are deliberately designed to prevent their own deserving proposals from ever seeing the light of day. But these rules allow Congress to play an important role in lawmaking. If it wants to be more than simply a rubber stamp for the executive branch, like so many other representative assemblies around the world, a national legislature like the Congress must develop a division of labor, set an agenda, maintain order through rules and procedures, and place limits on discussion. If it wants to accomplish these things in a representative setting in which a veritable diversity of political preferences exists, then it must find the ways and means to enable cooperation despite the variety of interests and coalitions, and compromises despite conflicts. We will first take up the general issues that face any legislature or decision-making group possessing diverse preferences—the problems of cooperation, coalitions, and compromises.

Cooperation in Congress

A popularly elected legislative assembly—the Boston city council, the Kansas legislature, the U.S. Congress, the French National Assembly, or the European Parliament—consists of politicians who harbor a variety of political objectives. Because they got where they are by winning an election, and many hope to stay where they are or possibly advance their political careers, these politicians are intimately aware of whom they must please to do so:

- Because campaigns are expensive propositions, most politicians are eager to please those who can supply resources for the next campaign—financial "fat cats," PACs, important endorsers, small contributors, party officials, volunteer activists.
- The most recent campaign—one that the politicians won—provides them with information about just why their victory was secured. It is sometimes quite difficult to sort out the myriad factors, but at the very least the politicians have a good sense of what categories of voters supported them and may be prepared to support them again, if performance is adequate.
- Many politicians not only aim to please campaign contributors and voters but also have an agenda of their own. Whether for virtuous reasons or evil ones, for private gain or public good, politicians come to the legislature with policy goals of personal importance.

Rationality Principle

The political opinions and policy goals of members of Congress are many and varied.

Congress consists of a heterogeneous group of legislators, and the specific public policies that they want to pursue are thus many and varied. First, owing to their different constituencies, legislators will give priority to different realms of public policy. A Cape Cod congressman will be interested in shipping, fishing, coastal preservation, harbor development, tourism, and shipbuilding. A Philadelphia congresswoman may not care much at all about those issues, focusing her attention instead on welfare reform, civil rights policy, aid to inner-city school systems, and job-retraining programs. Montana's sole member of Congress is probably not interested in coastal preservation or in inner-city schools, but rather in issues of ranching, agriculture, mining, and public land use. Evidently, Congress contains a mélange of legislative priorities.

Second, the opinions its members hold on any given issue are diverse. While interest in environmental protection, for example, ranges from high priority among those who count many Sierra Club members among their constituents to low priority among those who have other fish to fry, once environmental protection is on the agenda there is a broad range of preferences over specific environmental initiatives. Some want pollution discharges carefully monitored and regulated by a relatively powerful environmental watchdog agency. Others believe that more decentralized and less intrusive means, such as marketable pollution permits, are the way to go. Still others think the entire issue is overblown, that any proposed cure is worse than the disease, and that the republic would best be served by leaving well enough alone.

Diversity in both priorities and preferences among legislators is sufficiently abundant that the view of no group of legislators predominates. Legislative consensus must be built—this is what legislative politics is all about. Each legislator clamors to get his or her priority issue the attention he or she believes it deserves, or to make sure that his or her position on a given issue prevails. But neither effort is likely to succeed on its own merits. Support must be assembled, deals consummated, and promises and threats used. In short, legislators intent on achieving their objectives must cooperate, coalesce, and compromise. And these activities are facilitated by rules and procedures. This leads to legislative work being divided and specialized, procedures regularized, and agenda power created. All of these organizational features of Congress arise as part of a governance structure to allow for cooperation and coalition building that yield compromise policies.

Collective-Action Principle

Cooperation on recurring matters like congressional votes is facilitated by the institutionalization of legislative structures and procedures.

Underlying Problems and Challenges

Before we can understand why Congress selects particular ways to institutionalize its practices, we need a finer appreciation of other underlying problems with which legislators must grapple. Then we can turn to how the U.S. Congress deals with these problems.

Matching Influence and Interest Legislatures are highly egalitarian institutions. Each legislator has one vote on any issue coming before the body. Unlike a consumer, who has a cash budget that she may allocate in any way she wishes over categories of consumer goods, a legislator is not given a vote budget in quite the same sense. Instead, his budget of votes is "earmarked"—one vote for each motion before the assembly; he cannot aggregate the votes in his possession and cast them all, or some large fraction of them, for a motion on a subject near and dear to his heart (or those of his constituents). This is a source of frustration because, as we have noted, the premise of instrumental behavior means that legislators would, if they could, concentrate whatever resources they commanded on those subjects of highest priority to them.

Information   The egalitarian arrangement thus forces legislators to make deals with each other—"I'll support you on the motion before the legislature, if you support me on a future motion." Legislators do not vote for outcomes directly but rather for *instruments* (or policies) whose effects produce outcomes. Thus legislators, to vote intelligently, must know the connection between the instruments they vote for and the effects they desire. In short, they must have information and knowledge about how the world works.

Few legislators—indeed, few people in general—know how the world works in very many policy domains except in the most superficial of ways. Nearly everyone in the legislature would benefit from the production of valuable information—at the very least information that would allow legislators to eliminate policy instruments that make very little difference in solving social problems, or even make matters worse. Producing such information, however, is not a trivial matter. Simply to digest the knowledge that is being produced outside the legislature by knowledge-industry specialists (academics, scientists, journalists, interest groups) is a taxing task. Clearly, institutional arrangements that provide incentives to some legislators to produce, evaluate, and disseminate this knowledge for others will permit public resources to be used more effectively. Because legislatures are in competition with other branches of government—particularly the executive—informational requirements must be met just to keep up with the competition.

Compliance   The legislature is not the only game in town. The promulgation of public policies is a joint undertaking in which courts, executives, bureaucrats, and others participate alongside legislators. If the legislature develops no means to monitor what happens after a bill becomes law, then it risks public policies implemented in ways other than those intended when the law was passed. Cooperation does not end with the successful passage of a law. If legislators wish to have an impact on the world around them, especially on those matters to which their constituents give priority, then it is necessary to attend to policy *implementation*, not just policy *formulation*. But it is just not practical for all 435 representatives and all 100 senators to march down to this or that agency at the other end of Pennsylvania Avenue to ensure appropriate implementation by the executive bureaucracy. Compliance will not "just happen"; and, like the production and dissemination of reliable information at the policy-formulation stage, the need for oversight of the executive bureaucracy is but an extension of the cooperation that produced legislation in the first place. It, too, must be institutionalized.

What we have suggested in this abstract discussion about legislative institutions and practices is that, first and foremost, Congress is a place in which different kinds of representatives congregate and try to accomplish things so that they may reap the support of their respective constituents back home. This very diversity is problematic—it requires cooperation, coalitions, and compromise. In addition, there is a mismatch between influence and interest (owing to one person, one vote), information about the effectiveness of alternative policies is in short supply, and the legislature must worry about how its product—public laws—gets treated by other branches of government. These are the problems for which legislatures, of which the U.S. Congress is the preeminent example, devise institutional arrangements to mitigate, if not solve altogether.

THE ORGANIZATION OF CONGRESS

We will now examine the organization of Congress and the legislative process, particularly the basic building blocks of congressional organization: political parties, the committee system, congressional staff, the caucuses, and the parliamentary rules of the House and Senate. Each of these factors plays a key role in the organization of Congress and in the process through which Congress formulates and enacts laws. We will also look at other powers Congress has in addition to lawmaking and explore the future role of Congress in relation to the powers of the executive.

Party Leadership and Organization in the House and the Senate

Collective-Action Principle

Political parties in the legislature foster cooperation, coalitions, and compromise.

One significant aspect of legislative life is not even part of the *official* organization: political parties. The legislative parties—primarily Democratic and Republican in modern times, but numerous others over the course of American history—are exemplars of organizations that foster cooperation, coalitions, and compromise. They are the vehicles of collective action, both for legislators sharing common policy objectives inside the legislature and for those very same legislators as candidates in periodic election contests back home.[22] In short, political parties in Congress are the fundamental building blocks from which policy coalitions are fashioned to pass legislation and monitor its implementation, thereby providing a track record on which members build electoral support back home.

[22]For a historically grounded analysis of the development of political parties as well as a treatment of their general contemporary significance, see John H. Aldrich, *Why Parties? The Origin and Transformation of Political Parties in America* (Chicago: University of Chicago Press, 1995). For an analysis of the parties in the legislative process, see Gary W. Cox and Mathew D. McCubbins, *Legislative Leviathan: Party Government in the House* (Berkeley: University of California Press, 1993). A provocative essay questioning the role of parties is Keith Krehbiel, "Where's the Party?" *British Journal of Political Science* 23 (1993): 235–66.

Every two years, at the beginning of a new Congress, the members of each party gather to elect their House leaders. This gathering is traditionally called the *party caucus* (or *party conference* by the Republicans). The elected leader of the majority party is later proposed to the whole House and is automatically elected to the position of *Speaker of the House*, with voting along straight party lines. The House majority caucus (or conference) then also elects a *majority leader*. The minority party goes through the same process and selects the *minority leader*. Both parties also elect whips to line up party members on important votes and relay voting information to the leaders.

In December 2004, before the opening of the 109th Congress, Democrats and Republicans chose their leaders. House Republicans, who increased their slim majority in the chamber, retained J. Dennis Hastert of Illinois as Speaker, and Tom DeLay of Texas as majority leader. On the Democratic side, Nancy Pelosi of California, who had become the first woman to lead a major party in Congress when she was elected to replace Dick Gephardt in 2002, was retained as minority leader. Steny Hoyer of Maryland was retained as whip. In the summer of 2005, Majority Leader DeLay was indicted for campaign finance irregularities and was forced to step down from his leadership post. Roy Blunt of Missouri took over for him.

At one time, party leaders strictly controlled committee assignments, using them to enforce party discipline. Today, representatives expect to receive the assignments they want and resent leadership efforts to control committee assignments. For example, during the 104th Congress (1995–96) the then-chairman of the powerful Appropriations Committee, Robert Livingston (R-La.), sought to remove freshman Mark Neumann (R-Wisc.) from the committee because of his lack of party loyalty. The entire Republican freshman class angrily opposed this move and forced the leadership to back down. Not only did Neumann keep his seat on the Appropriations Committee but he was given a seat on the Budget Committee as well to placate the freshmen.[23] The leadership's best opportunities to use committee assignments as rewards and punishments come when a seat on the same committee is sought by more than one member.

Generally, representatives seek assignments that will allow them to influence decisions of special importance to their districts. Representatives from farm districts, for example, may request seats on the Agriculture Committee.[24] This is one method by which the egalitarian allocation of power in the legislature is overcome. Even though each legislator has just one vote in the full chamber on

party caucus
A normally closed meeting of a political or legislative group to select candidates, plan strategy, or make decisions regarding legislative matters.

Speaker of the House   The chief presiding officer of the House of Representatives. The Speaker is elected at the beginning of every Congress on a straight party vote. The Speaker is the most important party and House leader, and can influence the legislative agenda, the fate of individual pieces of legislation, and members' positions within the House.

majority leader
The elected leader of the party holding a majority of the seats in the House of Representatives or in the Senate. In the House, the majority leader is subordinate in the party hierarchy to the Speaker.

minority leader
The elected leader of the party holding less than a majority of the seats in the House or Senate.

[23]Linda Killian, *The Freshmen: What Happened to the Republican Revolution?* (Boulder, CO: Westview, 1998). A recent example went the other way. In December 2004, Speaker Hastert allowed a Colorado Republican to rotate off the House Ethics Committee, in part because of the committee member's role in investigating ethical breaches of majority leader DeLay. The member had hoped to remain on the committee.

[24]Fenno Jr., *Home Style*. For an extensive discussion of the committee assignment process in the U.S. House, see Kenneth A. Shepsle, *The Giant Jigsaw Puzzle: Democratic Committee Assignments in the Modern House* (Chicago: University of Chicago Press, 1978). See also E. Scott Adler, *Why Congressional Reforms Fail: Reelection and the House Committee System* (Chicago: University of Chicago Press, 2002).

Rationality Principle

Generally, members of Congress seek committee assignments that allow them to acquire more influence in areas important to their constituents.

each and every issue, he or she, by serving on the right committees, is able to acquire extra influence in areas important to constituents. Seats on powerful committees such as Ways and Means, which is responsible for tax legislation, and Appropriations are especially popular.

Turning to the Senate, the presidency pro tempore is a position designated in the Constitution that exercises mainly ceremonial leadership. Usually, the majority party designates the member with the greatest seniority to serve in this capacity. Real power is in the hands of the majority leader and minority leader, each elected by party caucus. The majority and minority leaders, together, control the Senate's calendar, or agenda for legislation. In addition, the senators from each party elect a whip.

The 2002 elections gave the Republican party a one-seat majority in the Senate. In the 2004 election, they gained an additional four seats for a 55–45-seat majority. Republicans re-elected Bill Frist of Tennessee as majority leader, while Democrats replaced recently defeated Tom Daschle of South Dakota with Harry Reid of Nevada as minority leader.

In recent years, party leaders have sought to augment their formal powers by reaching outside Congress for resources that might enhance their influence within Congress. One aspect of this external strategy is the increased use of national communications media, including televised speeches and talk-show appearances by party leaders. Former Republican House Speaker Newt Gingrich, for example, used television extensively to generate support for his programs among Republican loyalists.[25] As long as it lasted, Gingrich's support among the Republican rank and file gave him an added measure of influence over Republican members of Congress. Now no longer in the House, Gingrich has become a power inside the Beltway as the head of a very influential Republican consulting company.

A second external strategy involves fund-raising. In recent years, congressional leaders have frequently established their own political action committees. Interest groups are usually eager to contribute to these "leadership PACs" to curry favor with powerful members of Congress. The leaders, in turn, use these funds to support the various campaigns of their party's candidates to create a sense of obligation. For example, in the 1998 congressional election, House majority leader Dick Armey, who was running unopposed, raised more than $6 million, which he distributed to less well heeled Republican candidates. Armey's generosity served him well in the leadership struggle that erupted after the election.

Institution Principle

Party leaders have considerable agenda-setting powers.

In addition to the tasks of organizing Congress, congressional party leaders set the legislative agenda. Not only do party leaders have considerable sway over Congress's agenda "in the large" but also they regulate the fine-grained deliberation over specific items on the agenda. This aspect of agenda setting is multifaceted. For example, at the outset, when a bill is initially "dropped in the hopper" as a legislative proposal, the Speaker of the House determines which committee has jurisdiction over the proposal. Indeed, since the mid-1970s, the Speaker has been given additional bill-assignment powers, known as *multiple re-*

---

[25]Douglas Harris, "The Public Speaker" (Ph.D. diss., Johns Hopkins University, 1998).

ferral, permitting him to assign different parts of a bill to different committees or to assign the same parts sequentially or simultaneously to several committees.[26] The steering and agenda setting by party leaders work, however, within an institutional framework consisting of structures and procedures. Let's now turn to this "backbone" of Congress, the committee system, and the party leadership's role in guiding it.

The Committee System: The Core of Congress

If the system of leadership in each party and chamber constitutes the first set of organizational arrangements in the U.S. Congress, then the committee system provides it with a second set of organizational structures. But these are more a division- and specialization-of-labor system rather than the hierarchy-of-power system that determines leadership arrangements.

Congress began as a relatively unspecialized assembly, with each legislator participating equally in each and every step of the legislative process in all realms of policy. By the time of the War of 1812, if not earlier, Congress began employing a system of specialists, the committee system, because members with different interests and talents wished to play disproportionate roles in some areas of policy making while ceding influence in other areas in which they were less interested.[27]

The congressional committee system consists of a set of standing committees, each with its own jurisdiction, membership, and authority to act. Each **standing committee** is given a permanent status by the official rules, with a fixed membership, officers, rules, staff, offices, and, above all, a jurisdiction that is recognized by all other committees and usually the leadership as well (Table 5.2). The jurisdiction of each standing committee is defined by the subject matter of legislation. Except for the Rules Committee in the House and Senate, all the important committees receive proposals for legislation and process them into official bills. The House Rules Committee decides the order in which bills come up for a vote and determines the specific rules that govern the length of debate and opportunity for amendments. Standing committees' jurisdictions usually parallel those of the major departments or agencies in the executive branch. There are important exceptions—Appropriations and Rules in both chambers, for example—but by and large, the division of labor is self-consciously designed to parallel executive-branch organization.

 History Principle

The committee system evolved during the early nineteenth century as a means of allowing individual legislators disproportionate influence in areas of policy most important to them.

 Institution Principle

The committee system is a means of dividing labor and allowing members of Congress to specialize in certain policy areas.

standing committee A permanent legislative committee that considers legislation within its designated subject area; the basic unit of deliberation in the House and Senate.

---

[26]For a now-classic treatment of the ebbs and flows of parties and their leaders in the modern era, see David W. Rohde, *Parties and Leaders in the Postreform House* (Chicago: University of Chicago Press, 1991). For a historical look, see David W. Rohde and Kenneth A. Shepsle, "Leaders and Followers in the House of Representatives: Reflections on Woodrow Wilson's *Congressional Government*," *Congress and the Presidency* 14 (1987): 111–33.

[27]The story of the evolution of the standing committee system in the House and Senate in the early part of the nineteenth century is told in Gerald Gamm and Kenneth A. Shepsle, "Emergence of Legislative Institutions: Standing Committees in the House and Senate, 1810–1825," *Legislative Studies Quarterly* 14 (1989): 39–66.

TABLE 5.2

Standing Committees of Congress

HOUSE COMMITTEES

Agriculture	Judiciary
Appropriations	Resources
Armed Services	Rules
Budget	Science
Education and the Workforce	Small Business
Energy and Commerce	Standards of Official Conduct
Financial Services	Transportation and Infrastructure
Government Reform	Veterans' Affairs
House Administration	Ways and Means
International Relations	

SENATE COMMITTEES

Agriculture, Nutrition, and Forestry	Finance
Appropriations	Foreign Relations
Armed Services	Governmental Affairs
Banking, Housing, and Urban Affairs	Health, Education, Labor, and Pensions
Budget	Judiciary
Commerce, Science, and Transportation	Rules and Administration
Energy and Natural Resources	Small Business
Environment and Public Works	Veterans' Affairs

The committee systems of the House and Senate are the policy backbones of their respective chambers.

Jurisdiction   The world of policy is partitioned into policy jurisdictions, which become the responsibility of committees. The members of the Armed Services Committee, for example, become specialists in all aspects of military affairs, the subject matter defining their committee's jurisdiction. Legislators tend to have disproportionate influence in their respective committee jurisdictions, not only because they have become the most knowledgeable members of the legislature in that area of policy but also because they are given the opportunity to exercise various forms of agenda power—a subject we develop further in the next section.

Dividing up institutional activities among jurisdictions, thus encouraging participants to specialize, has its advantages. But it has costs, too. If the Armed Services Committee of the House of Representatives had no restraints, its members would undoubtedly shower their own districts with military facilities and contracts. In short, the delegation of authority and resources to specialist subunits exploits the advantages of the division and specialization of labor but risks jeopardizing collective objectives of the group as a whole. The monitoring of committee activities thus goes hand in hand with delegation.

Sometimes new issues arise that fit neatly into no jurisdiction. Some, like the issue of energy supplies that emerged during the 1970s, are so multifaceted that bits and pieces of them are spread across many committee jurisdictions. Thus the Energy and Commerce Committee of the U.S. House of Representatives had jurisdiction over the regulation of energy prices, the Armed Services Committee dealt with military implications, the Ways and Means Committee dealt with tax-related energy aspects, the Science and Technology Committee claimed jurisdiction over energy research, the Agriculture Committee dealt with grain-to-energy conversion matters, and several other committees picked off still other pieces of this Hydra-headed issue. Some issues, like that of regulating tobacco products, fall in the gray area claimed by several different committees—in this case the Energy and Commerce Committee, with its traditional claim over health-related issues, fought with the Agriculture Committee, whose traditional domain includes crops like tobacco, for jurisdiction over this issue. Turf battles between committees of the U.S. Congress are notorious.[28] These battles involve committee chairs, the Parliamentarian's Office, the political leadership of the chamber, and, from time to time, select committees appointed to realign committee jurisdictions.

Authority Committees may be thought of as *agents* of the parent body to whom jurisdiction-specific authority is provisionally delegated. In this section, we describe committee authority in terms of gatekeeping and after-the-fact authority.

Normally, any member of the legislature can submit a bill calling for changes in some policy area. Almost automatically, this bill is assigned to the committee of jurisdiction and, very nearly always, there it languishes. In a typical session in the House of Representatives, about 8,000 bills are submitted, fewer than 1,000 of which are acted on by the appropriate committee of jurisdiction. In effect, then, while any member is entitled to make proposals, committees get to decide whether or not to open the gates and allow the bill to be voted on by the full chamber. Related to **gatekeeping authority** is a committee's **proposal power.** After a bill is referred to a committee, the committee may take no further action on it, may amend the legislation in any way, or may even write its own legislation

gatekeeping authority The right and power to decide if a change in policy will be considered.

proposal power The capacity to bring a proposal to the full legislature.

[28]An outstanding description and analysis of these battles is found in David C. King, "The Nature of Congressional Committee Jurisdictions," *American Political Science Review* 88 (1994): 48-63. See also his *Turf Wars: How Congressional Committees Claim Jurisdiction* (Chicago: University of Chicago Press, 1997).

Institution Principle

Among the powers delegated to committees are gatekeeping authority, bargaining with the other chamber, and oversight.

after-the-fact authority The authority to follow up on the fate of a proposal once it has been approved by the full chamber.

conference committee A joint committee created to work out a compromise for House and Senate versions of a piece of legislation.

oversight The effort by Congress, through hearings, investigations, and other techniques, to exercise control over the activities of executive agencies.

before bringing the bill to a vote on the floor. Committees, then, are lords of their jurisdictional domains, setting the table, so to speak, for their parent chamber.[29]

A committee also has responsibilities for bargaining with the other chamber and for conducting oversight or *after-the-fact authority.* Because the U.S. Congress is bicameral, once one chamber passes a bill, it must be considered by the other chamber. If the other chamber passes a bill different from the one passed in the first chamber, and the first chamber refuses to accept the changes made, then the two chambers ordinarily meet in a *conference committee* in which representatives from each chamber hammer out a compromise. In the wide majority of cases, conferees are drawn from the committees that had original jurisdiction over the bill. For example, in a sample of Congresses in the 1980s, of the 1,388 House members who served as conferees for various bills during a three-year period, only 7 were not on the committee of original jurisdiction; similarly, in the Senate on only 7 of 1,180 occasions were conferees not drawn from the "right" committee.[30] The committee's effective authority to represent its chamber in conference-committee proceedings constitutes after-the-fact power that complements its before-the-fact gatekeeping and proposal powers.

A second manifestation of after-the-fact committee authority consists of the committee's primacy in legislative *oversight* of policy implementation by the executive bureaucracy. Even after a bill becomes a law, it is not always (indeed, it is rarely) self-implementing. Executive agents—bureaucrats in the career civil service, commissioners in regulatory agencies, political appointees in the executive branch—march to their own drummers. Unless legislative actors hold their feet to the fire, they may not do precisely what the law requires (especially in light of the fact that statutes are often vague and ambiguous). Congressional committees are "continuously watchful" of the manner in which legislation is implemented and administered. They play this after-the-fact role by allocating staff and resources to track what the executive branch is doing and, from time to time, holding oversight hearings in which particular policies and programs are given intense scrutiny. This, in turn, gives congressional committees an additional source of leverage over policy in their jurisdictions.

Subcommittees The standing committees of the U.S. House are divided into about a hundred, even more specialized *subcommittees*. These subcommittees serve their full committees in precisely the same manner the full committees serve the parent chamber. Thus, in their narrow jurisdictions, they have gate-

---

[29]This clearly gives committee members extraordinary power in their respective jurisdictions, allowing them to push policy into line with their own preferences. But only up to a point. If the abuse of their agenda power becomes excessive, the parent body has structural and procedural remedies available to counteract this—like stacking the committee with more compliant members, deposing a particularly obstreperous committee chair, or removing policies from a committee's jurisdiction. These are the "clubs behind the door" that only rarely have to be employed; their mere presence suffices to keep committees from the more outrageous forms of advantage taking.

[30]See Kenneth A. Shepsle and Barry R. Weingast, "The Institutional Foundations of Committee Power," *American Political Science Review* 81 (1987), pp. 85–104.

keeping, proposal, interchamber bargaining, and oversight powers. For a bill on wheat to be taken up by the full Agriculture Committee, for example, it first has to clear the Feedgrains Subcommittee. All of the issues involving assignments, jurisdictions, amendment control, and monitoring that we discussed earlier regarding full committees apply at the subcommittee level as well.

Hierarchy   At the committee level, the mantle of leadership falls on the committee chair. He or she determines, together with party leaders, the committee's agenda and then coordinates the committee's staff, investigatory resources, and subcommittee structure.[31] This includes scheduling hearings, "marking up" bills— that is, transforming legislative drafts into final versions—and scripting the process by which a bill goes from committee to floor proceedings to final passage. For many years, the Congress followed a rigid *seniority* rule for the selection of these chairs. The benefits of this rule are twofold. First, the chair will be occupied by someone knowledgeable in the committee's jurisdiction, familiar with interest-group and executive-branch players, and politically experienced. Second, the larger institution will be spared divisive leadership contests that often reduce the legislative process to efforts in vote grubbing by contenders. There are costs, however. Senior individuals may be unenergetic, out of touch, even senile.

The U.S. House operated according to a strict seniority principle from about 1910 (informally, even earlier) until the mid-1970s, when most members felt that the burdens of this arrangement were beginning to outweigh its advantages. Committee chairs are now elected by the majority-party members of the full legislature, though there remains a presumption (which may be rebutted) that the most senior committee member will normally assume the chair.[32]

Monitoring Committees   If unchecked, committees could easily take advantage of their authority. Indeed, what prevents committees from exploiting their before-the-fact proposal power and their after-the-fact bargaining and oversight authority? As we saw in Chapter 1 in our discussion of the principal-agent problem, principals must be certain that agents are *properly motivated* to serve the principal's interests, either by actually sharing the principal's interest themselves or by deriving something of value (reputation, compensation, etc.) for acting to advance that interest. Alternatively, the principal will need to have some instruments by which to monitor and validate what his or her agent is doing, rewarding or punishing the agent accordingly.

Consider again the example of congressional committees. The House or Senate delegates responsibility to its Committee on Agriculture to recommend legislative policy in the field of agriculture. Not surprisingly, legislators from farm districts are most eager to get onto this committee, and for the most part, their

seniority   Priority or status ranking given to an individual on the basis of length of continuous service on a congressional committee.

---

[31]Because subcommittee chairs do essentially the same things in their narrower jurisdictions, we won't provide a separate discussion of them.

[32]Beginning with the Republican takeover of the House in 1995, committee chairs are now term limited. After three terms, a chair must step down.

wishes are accommodated. The Committee on Agriculture, consequently, is composed mainly of these farm legislators. And non-farm legislators are relieved at not having to spend their time on issues of little material interest to themselves or their constituents. In effecting this delegation, however, the parent legislature is putting itself in the hands of its farm colleagues, benefiting from their expertise on farm-related matters, to be sure, but laying itself open to the danger of planting the fox squarely in the henhouse. The Committee on Agriculture will have become not only a collection of specialists but also a collection of *advocates* for farm interests. How can the parent body know for certain that a recommendation from that committee is not more a reflection of its advocacy than of its expertise? This is the risk inherent in delegation in principal-agent relationships.

And it is for this reason that the parent legislature maintains a variety of tools and instruments to protect itself from being exploited by its agents. First, it does not allow committees to make final decisions on agriculture policy; it allows only *recommendations*, which the parent legislature retains the authority to accept, amend, or reject. A committee has agenda power, but it is not by itself decisive. Second, the parent body relies on the committee's concern for its own reputation. Making a recommendation on a piece of legislation is not a one-shot action; the committee knows it will return to the parent body time and time again with legislative recommendations, and it will not want to tarnish its reputation for expertise by too much advocacy. Third, the parent body relies on *competing* agents—interest groups, expert members not on the committee, legislative specialists in the other chamber of the legislature, executive-branch specialists, and even academics—to keep its own agents honest. Finally, in the House there is an institutional "club behind the door"—the *discharge petition*. A committee that is sitting on a bill, not permitting it to be taken up by the full chamber, can be *discharged* of responsibility for the bill if a petition is signed by a majority of the chamber.

Nevertheless, a principal will not bother to eliminate *entirely* these prospective deviations from his or her interests by agents who have interests of their own. A principal will suffer some **agency loss** from having delegated authority to a "hired hand"; therefore, nearly all principal-agent relationships will be imperfect in some respects from the principal's perspective. Agents will be in a position to extract some advantage from the privileged relationship they have with their principal—not too much, or it will undermine the relationship altogether, but enough to diminish the benefits of the relationship a bit from the principal's point of view. The Committee on Agriculture, for example, cannot get away with spending huge proportions of the federal budget on agricultural subsidies to farmers. But they can insert small things into agriculture bills from time to time—an experimental grain-to-fuel conversion project in an important legislator's state or district, for example, or special funds to the U.S. trade representative to give priority to agriculture trade issues. The parent body, as we suggested, will find it worth its while to keep an eye on the Agriculture Committee, but it won't be worth its while to take action on every single instance of indulgence by the committee. The cost of doing that—the transaction cost of monitoring and overseeing committee performance—gets excessive if perfection is the objective.

Institution Principle

The House and Senate have methods of keeping committees in check.

agency loss The difference between what a principal would like an agent to do and the agent's actual performance.

Committee Reform Over the years, Congress has reformed its organizational structure and operating procedures. Most changes have been made to improve efficiency, but some reforms have also represented a response to political considerations. In the 1970s a series of reforms substantially altered the organization of power in Congress. Among the most important changes put into place at that time were an increase in the number of subcommittees, greater autonomy for subcommittee chairs, the opening of most committee deliberations to the public, and a system of multiple referral of bills that allowed several committees to consider one bill at the same time. One of the driving impulses behind these reforms was an effort to reduce the power of committee chairs.

As a consequence of the reforms of the 1970s, power became more fragmented, making it harder to reach agreement on legislation. In 1995, the Republican leadership of the 104th Congress sought to concentrate more authority in the party leadership. One of the ways the House achieved this was by abandoning the principle of seniority in the selection of a number of committee chairs, appointing them instead according to their loyalty to the party. This move tied committee chairs more closely to the leadership. In addition, the Republican leadership eliminated 25 of the House's 115 subcommittees and gave committee chairs more power over their subcommittees. The result was an unusually cohesive congressional majority, which pushed forward a common agenda. House Republicans also agreed to impose a three-term limit on committee and subcommittee heads. As a result, all the chairmen were replaced in 2001 when the 107th Congress convened. In many instances, chairmen were replaced by the most senior Republican committee member, but the net result was some redistribution of power in the House of Representatives.

The Staff System: Staffers and Agencies

A congressional institution ranking just below committees and parties in importance is the staff system. Every member of Congress employs a large number of staff members, whose tasks include handling constituency requests and, to a large and growing extent, dealing with legislative details and the activities of administrative agencies. Increasingly, staffers bear the primary responsibility for formulating and drafting proposals, organizing hearings, dealing with administrative agencies, and negotiating with lobbyists. Indeed, legislators typically deal with one another through staff, rather than through direct, personal contact. Representatives and senators together employ nearly 11,000 staffers in their Washington and home offices. In addition to the personal staffs of individual senators and representatives, Congress also employs roughly 2,000 committee staffers. These individuals make up the permanent staff, who often stay regardless of turnover in Congress and are attached to every House and Senate committee. They are responsible for organizing and administering the committee's work, including research, scheduling, organizing hearings, and drafting legislation.

Not only does Congress employ personal and committee staff but it has also established three *staff agencies* designed to provide the legislative branch with

staff agencies
Agencies responsible for providing Congress with independent expertise, administration, and oversight capability.

resources and expertise independent of the executive branch. These agencies enhance Congress's capacity to oversee administrative agencies and to evaluate presidential programs and proposals. They are the Congressional Research Service, which performs research for legislators who wish to know the facts and competing arguments relevant to policy proposals or other legislative business; the General Accounting Office, through which Congress can investigate the financial and administrative affairs of any government agency or program; and the Congressional Budget Office, which assesses the economic implications and likely costs of proposed federal programs, such as President George W. Bush's proposed revisions of the Social Security system in 2005.

Informal Organization: The Caucuses

In addition to the official organization of Congress, there also exists an unofficial organizational structure—the caucuses, formally known as legislative service organizations (LSOs). *Caucuses* are groups of senators or representatives who share certain opinions, interests, or social characteristics. They include ideological caucuses such as the liberal Democratic Study Group and the conservative Democratic Forum. At the same time, there are a large number of caucuses composed of legislators representing particular economic or policy interests, such as the Travel and Tourism Caucus, the Steel Caucus, the Mushroom Caucus, and the Concerned Senators for the Arts. Legislators who share common backgrounds or social characteristics have organized caucuses such as the Congressional Black Caucus, the Congressional Caucus for Women's Issues, and the Hispanic Caucus. All these caucuses seek to advance the interests of the groups they represent by promoting legislation, encouraging Congress to hold hearings, and pressing administrative agencies for favorable treatment.

caucus An association of members of Congress based on party, interest, or social characteristics such as gender or race.

RULES OF LAWMAKING: HOW A BILL BECOMES A LAW

The institutional structure of Congress is one key factor that helps shape the legislative process. A second and equally important set of factors are the rules of congressional procedure. These rules govern everything from the introduction of a bill through its submission to the president for signing. Not only do these regulations influence the fate of each and every bill but they also help determine the distribution of power in the Congress.[33]

---

[33]We should emphasize, though we don't mean to confuse the reader, that a legislature as often "suspends" its rules as it follows them. There are unorthodox ways to proceed in order to avoid procedural logjams, and the House—and especially the Senate—frequently resort to these unorthodox ways. See Barbara Sinclair, *Unorthodox Lawmaking*, 2nd ed. (Washington, DC: Congressional Quarterly Press, 2000).

Committee Deliberation

Even if a member of Congress, the White House, or a federal agency has spent months developing and drafting a piece of legislation, it does not become a bill until it is submitted officially by a senator or representative to the clerk of the House or Senate and referred to the appropriate committee for deliberation. No floor action on any bill can take place until the committee with jurisdiction over it has taken all the time it needs to deliberate.[34] During the course of its deliberations, the committee typically refers the bill to one of its subcommittees, which may hold hearings, listen to expert testimony, and amend the proposed legislation before referring it to the full committee for its consideration. The full committee may accept the recommendation of the subcommittee or hold its own hearings and prepare its own amendments. Or, even more frequently, the committee and subcommittee may do little or nothing with a bill and simply allow it to "die in committee." In a typical congressional session, 85 to 90 percent of the roughly 8,000 bills introduced die in committee—an indication of the power of the congressional committee system.

Once the bill's assigned committee or committees in the House of Representatives have acted affirmatively, the whole bill or various parts of it are transmitted to the Rules Committee, which determines the specific rules under which the legislation will be considered by the full House. Together with the Speaker, it influences when debate will be scheduled, for how long, what amendments will be in order, and in what order they will be considered. The Speaker also rules on all procedural points of order and points of information raised during the debate. A bill's supporters generally prefer what is called a *closed rule,* which puts severe limits on floor debate and amendments. Opponents of a bill usually prefer an *open rule,* which permits potentially damaging floor debate and makes it easier to add amendments that may cripple the bill or weaken its chances for passage.

Debate

Party control of the agenda is reinforced by the rule giving the Speaker of the House and the majority leader of the Senate the power of recognition during debate on a bill. Usually the chair knows the purpose for which a member intends to speak well in advance of the occasion. Spontaneous efforts to gain recognition are often foiled. For example, the Speaker may ask, "For what purpose does the member rise?" before deciding whether to grant recognition. In general, the party leadership in the House has total control over debate. In the Senate, each member has substantial power to block the close of debate. A House majority can

closed rule Provision by the House Rules Committee prohibiting the introduction of amendments during debate.

open rule Provision by the House Rules Committee that permits floor debate and the addition of amendments to a bill.

 Institution Principle

The Rules Committee's decision about whether to adopt a closed or open rule for floor debate greatly influences a bill's chances for passage.

---

[34]As noted earlier, a bill can be pulled from a committee by a discharge petition, but this is an extreme measure and is only rarely resorted to. There are also other parliamentary tricks that may be attempted, but it is fair to say that, most of the time at least, it is the committee of jurisdiction that influences the course of a bill.

override opposition, while it takes an *extraordinary* majority (a three-fifths vote) to close debate in the Senate; thus the Senate tends to be far more tolerant in debate, far more accommodating of various views, and far less partisan.

In the House, virtually all of the time allotted by the Rules Committee for debate on a given bill is controlled by the bill's sponsor and by its leading opponent. These two participants are, by rule and tradition, granted the power to allocate most of the debate time in small amounts to members who are seeking to speak for or against the measure.

In the Senate, other than the power of recognition, the leadership has much less control over floor debate. Indeed, the Senate is unique among the world's legislative bodies for its commitment to unlimited debate. Once given the floor, a senator may speak as long as he or she wishes, unless an extraordinary majority votes to end debate. On a number of memorable occasions, senators have used this right to prevent action on legislation that they opposed. Through this tactic, called the **filibuster,** small minorities or even one individual in the Senate can force the majority to give in to their demands. During the 1950s and 1960s, for example, opponents of civil rights legislation often sought to block its passage by adopting the tactic of filibuster. The votes of three-fifths of the Senate, or sixty votes, are needed to end a filibuster. This procedure is called **cloture.**

Although it is the best known, the filibuster is not the only technique used to block Senate action. Under Senate rules, members have a virtually unlimited ability to propose amendments to a pending bill. Each amendment must be voted on before the bill can come to a final vote. The introduction of new amendments can be stopped only by unanimous consent. This, in effect, can permit a determined minority to filibuster-by-amendment, indefinitely delaying the passage of a bill.

Senators can also place "holds," or stalling devices, on bills to delay debate. Senators place holds on bills when they fear that openly opposing them will be unpopular. Because holds are kept secret, the senators placing the holds do not have to take public responsibility for their actions.

Once a bill is debated on the floor of the House and the Senate, the leaders schedule it for a vote on the floor of each chamber. By this time, congressional leaders know what the vote will be; leaders do not bring legislation to the floor unless they are fairly certain it is going to pass. As a consequence, it is unusual for the leadership to lose a bill on the floor. On rare occasions, the last moments of the floor vote can be very dramatic, as each party's leadership puts its whip organization into action to make sure that wavering members vote with the party.

Conference Committee: Reconciling House and Senate Versions of a Bill

Getting a bill out of committee and through one of the houses of Congress is no guarantee that a bill will be enacted into law. Frequently, bills that began with similar provisions in both chambers emerge with little resemblance to each other. Alternatively, a bill may be passed by one chamber but undergo substan-

filibuster A tactic used by members of the Senate to prevent action on legislation they oppose by continuously holding the floor and speaking until the majority backs down. Once given the floor, senators have unlimited time to speak, and it requires a cloture vote of three-fifths of the Senate to end the filibuster.

cloture A rule allowing a supermajority of the members in a legislative body to set a time limit on debate over a given bill.

tial revision in the other chamber. In such cases, a conference committee composed of the senior members of the committees or subcommittees that initiated the bills may be required to iron out differences between the two pieces of legislation. Sometimes members or leaders will let objectionable provisions pass on the floor with the idea that they will get the change they want in conference. Conference agreement requires a majority of each of the two delegations. Legislation that emerges successfully from a conference committee is more often a compromise than a clear victory of one set of forces over another.

When a bill comes out of conference, it faces one more hurdle. Before a bill can be sent to the president for signing, the House-Senate conference report must be approved on the floor of each chamber. Usually such approval is given quickly. Occasionally, however, a bill's opponents use the conference report as one last opportunity to defeat a piece of legislation.

Collective-Action Principle
If a bill passes both the House and the Senate, the differences need to be ironed out in a conference committee.

Presidential Action

Once adopted by the House and Senate, a bill goes to the president, who may choose to sign the bill into law or **veto** it (Figure 5.6). The veto is the president's constitutional power to reject a piece of legislation. To veto a bill, the president returns it within ten days to the house of Congress in which it originated, along with his objections to the bill. If Congress adjourns during the ten-day period and the president has taken no action, the bill is also considered to be vetoed. This latter method is known as the **pocket veto.** The possibility of a presidential veto affects how willing members of Congress are to push for different pieces of legislation at different times. If they think a proposal is likely to be vetoed, they might shelve it for a later time. Alternatively, the sponsors of a popular bill opposed by the president might push for passage to force the president to pay the political costs of vetoing it.[35] For example, in 1996 and 1997, Republicans passed bills outlawing partial-birth abortions even though they knew President Clinton would veto them. The GOP calculated that Clinton would be hurt politically by vetoing legislation that most Americans favored.

A presidential veto may be overridden by a two-thirds vote in both the House and Senate. A veto override says much about the support that a president can expect from Congress, and it can deliver a stinging blow to the executive branch. Presidents will often back down from a veto threat if they believe that Congress will override the veto. These strategic interactions between the legislature and the executive branch are taken up in the next chapter.

veto The president's constitutional power to turn down acts of Congress. A presidential veto may be overridden by a two-thirds vote of each house of Congress.

pocket veto A method by which the president vetoes a bill by taking no action on it when Congress has adjourned.

Normal and Abnormal Procedures in Congress

We have noted that although there is a "normal" procedure in each chamber, it is often the case that the normal is abandoned and an abnormal or unorthodox

---

[35]John B. Gilmour, *Strategic Disagreement: Stalemate in American Politics* (Pittsburgh, PA: University of Pittsburgh Press, 1995).

FIGURE 5.6

A bill must pass through many stages and succeed at all of them in order to become a law. To prevent a bill from becoming a law, opponents need prevail at only one stage. What effects do the complications in the process have on policy outcomes?

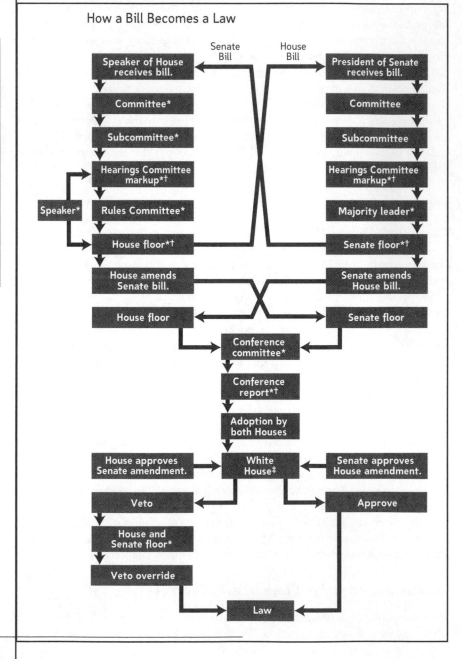

How a Bill Becomes a Law

*Points at which the bill can be amended.

†Points at which the bill can die.

‡If the president neither signs nor vetoes the bill within ten days, it automatically becomes law.

procedure devised. The treatment of appropriations bills in the period leading up to the November 2004 election provides an excellent example.

"Normally" the House passes thirteen separate appropriations bills after each has passed through an appropriations process, beginning with a subcommittee hearing, full Appropriations Committee deliberations, and passage by the full House. These thirteen measures are then transmitted to the Senate, which subjects each of them to its own "regular" appropriations process. Each of the bills (thirteen in all) now has a House version and a Senate version. Thirteen separate conference committees are set up to take each of these pairs and compromise on the differences between them. The thirteen compromised versions are then sent back to each chamber for final approval. And, in principle though rarely in practice, this entire process is completed before the October 1 start date for the new fiscal year.

But 2004 was an election year and members up for re-election really did not want to remind the voters that the appropriations bills they were passing were growing to produce the largest deficits in history. So an unorthodox procedure was invented. One of the thirteen appropriations bills passed the House and Senate through the normal process and was sent to conference. During the conference, the *other twelve* bills were tacked on, making a single omnibus appropriations bill. This was sent to each chamber for a single up-or-down vote. In voting for this omnibus measure, a member was "innoculated" against local objections from constituents. He or she could respond, "I know, I know. The omnibus bill is not ideal. But what was I to do? Defeating this would have shut the government down."

Bottom-line, take-home point: There are regular procedures, and they are often followed. But politicians are creative, and there are many ways to skin a cat.

The Distributive Tendency in Congress

To pass a policy, it is necessary to *authorize* the policy—that is, to provide statutory authority to a government agency to implement the legislation—and then to provide *appropriations* to fund the implementation. The list of politicians whose consent is required in these processes is extraordinarily long. At a minimum it includes majorities on the relevant committee and subcommittee of each chamber (almost certainly including their chairs), the appropriation subcommittee and Appropriation Committee in each chamber (including chairs), the House Rules Committee, chamber majorities (including majority party leaders), and the president. Some of them may go along without requiring much for their states or districts in the bill on the assumption that their turn will come on another bill. But most of these politicians will need some form of "compensation" to provide their endorsement and support.

With so many hurdles to clear for a legislative initiative to become a public law, the benefits must be spread broadly. It is as though a bill had to travel on a toll road past a number of tollbooths, each one containing a collector with his or her hand out for payment. On rare occasions, the required toll is in the form of a

Why Congress Cannot Get Things Done

If you want to know how to get something done, you need to know who can stop you. In the language of institutional analysis, "veto points" are wielded by individuals (but they may also be groups, committees, courts, etc.) who must approve any change to the status quo.[1] If a change from the status quo is a form of *collective action,* then it is possible to set rules that make change easier or harder. To take an extreme example, dictatorships have a distinct advantage over democracies: they can get things done quickly. A huge "electronic democracy," in comparison, could be highly egalitarian and participatory, but it's unlikely that in today's complex society, New England meetings on a grand scale could agree on anything.

Policy Principle

The institutional rules the framers set for Congress make it difficult to change the status quo.

In American democracy, we err on the side of making it hard to get things done. Our democracy privileges individual and minority rights. The Federalists were suspicious of governmental power and especially worried about legislative power, so they created a set of *rules and procedures* that would make it difficult to change the status quo.[2]

Our bicameral legislature promotes stability yet is problematic when major policy needs to be enacted. The slowing of the legislative process can prevent initially popular but potentially destructive policies and precedents from being enacted. Examples of this include Franklin Roosevelt's court-packing plan, the controversy following Harry Truman's dismissal of Douglas MacArthur, and Thomas Jefferson's attempt to impeach Justice Samuel Chase. The prerogative for unlimited debate can also turn the Senate into a graveyard for important bills. The most famous example might be the ability of southern senators to halt the passage of major civil rights legislation for nearly one hundred years. Originally, there was no procedural way to end debate, but since 1917 the Senate has adopted a cloture rule. Invoking cloture limits debate and can force a vote. However, cloture requires 60 votes, not a simple majority. This means that the operational majority required to pass legislation in the Senate is 60, not 51, votes.

In the language of *institutional analysis,* the U.S. Congress has many more veto points than any other advanced industrial democracy. Any piece of legislation, for example, must obtain a majority in both the House, whose members are from relatively homogeneous and small (half million) districts, and the Senate, whose members vary from those elected from California, Texas, and Florida to those who ran in districts contiguous to House districts (Delaware, Wyoming, South Dakota). Why was the Congress designed in this way? The Senate was designed to give disproportionate representation to minority interests. House seats are allotted in proportion to states' populations, but each state gets two senators, no more and no less.

Policy Principle

The way the House and Senate are elected helps equalize power between the majority and the minority.

The House was designed to be the "people's branch" of government, representing the will of the majority. Power is highly concentrated in the ruling party. Bills can be enacted quickly, and the majority can ride roughshod over the minority. This often leads to complaints from the minority that they are being ignored. After the Republicans took over the

House in 1994, they promised to end perceived abuses of majority power. But they have not followed through on many of these promises.

In contrast, the Senate is a bastion of minority power, but it can also be frustratingly devoted to its own institutional prerogatives. Over time, the Senate has never developed the elaborate rules and procedures of the House. There is no Senate equivalent to the House's Rules Committee. The Senate has a long tradition of unlimited debate. As illustrated in popular lore, such as the movie *Mr. Smith Goes to Washington*, this means that a heroic individual senator can stand up for truth, justice, and the American way. The modern filibuster, however, bears little resemblance to Jimmy Stewart speaking in the well of the Senate. Instead, senators propose an endless series of dilatory motions to stall the progress of the institution.

Some celebrate the U.S. legislative system. The American political system is heavily tilted toward the status quo. The government is unlikely to change in response to superficial changes in public sentiments. But this also creates the impression of gridlock. Another advantage of our system is greater representation of minority interests. But the accompanying disadvantage is the potential to frustrate the will of the majority. Conflict between the two chambers is exacerbated by the different sets of rules that they employ. The differences between the rules of the House and Senate reflect the different purposes of each.[3]

[1]George Tsebelis, *Veto Players: How Political Institutions Work* (Princeton, N.J.: Princeton University Press, 2002).

[2]See Clinton Rossiler, ed., *The Federalist Papers* (New York: New American Library, 1961), especially Nos. 10 and 51.

[3]For further comparisons, see Ross K. Baker, *House and Senate,* 3rd ed. (New York: Norton, 2002).

---

personal bribe—a contract to a firm run by a congressman's brother, a job for a senator's son, a boondoggle "military inspection" trip to some exotic Pacific isle for a legislator and companion. Occasionally, there is "a wink and a nod" understanding, usually given by the majority leader or committee chair, that support from a legislator today will result in reciprocal support for legislation of interest to him or her down the road. Most frequently, features of the bill are drafted initially or revised so as to be more inclusive, spreading the benefits widely among beneficiaries. This is the ***distributive tendency.***

The distributive tendency is part of the American system of representative democracy. Legislators, in advocating the interests of their constituents, are eager to advertise their ability to deliver for their state or district. They maneuver to put themselves in a position to claim credit for good things that happen there and to duck blame for bad things. This is the way they earn trust back home,

distributive tendency The tendency of Congress to spread the benefits of a policy over a wide range of members' districts.

deter strong challengers in upcoming elections, and defeat those who do run against them. This means that legislators must take advantage of every opportunity that presents itself. In some instances, the results may seem bizarre. For example, in April 2003, Senator Thad Cochran (R-Miss.) was able to insert language into the bill funding the war in Iraq that provided $250 million for "disaster relief" for southern catfish farmers.[36] Most Americans would never have guessed that driving Saddam Hussein from power would have an effect on catfish farmers in Mississippi.

Policy Principle

The distributive tendency in Congress results from the need for a broad base of support for a bill to be passed.

This system, which is practiced in Washington and most state capitals, means that political pork gets spread around; it is not controlled by a small clique of politicians or concentrated in a small number of states or districts. But it also means that public authority and appropriations are not targeted where they are most needed. The most impoverished cities do not get as much money as is appropriate because some of the money must be diverted elsewhere to buy political support. The most needy individuals often do not get tax relief, health care, or occupational subsidies for reasons unrelated to philosophy or policy grounds. It is the distributive tendency at work. It is one of the unintended consequences of the separation of powers and the multiple veto.

HOW CONGRESS DECIDES

Policy Principle

Multiple factors influence how a member of Congress votes on legislation. These include constituency, interest groups, party leaders, congressional colleagues, and the president.

What determines the kinds of legislation that Congress ultimately produces? According to the simplest theories of representation, members of Congress respond to the views of their constituents. In fact, the process of creating a legislative agenda, drawing up a list of possible measures, and deciding among them is very complex, one in which a variety of influences from inside and outside government play important roles. External influences include a legislator's constituency and various interest groups. Influences from inside government include party leadership, congressional colleagues, and the president. Let us examine each of these influences individually and then consider how they interact to produce congressional policy decisions.

Constituency

Because members of Congress, for the most part, want to be re-elected, we would expect the views of their constituents to have a key influence on the decisions that legislators make. Yet constituency influence is not so straightforward as we might think. In fact, most constituents do not even know what policies their representatives support. The number of citizens who *do* pay attention to such matters—the attentive public—is usually very small. Nonetheless, members of Congress spend a lot of time worrying about what their constituents think because these representatives realize that the choices they make may be scruti-

[36]Dan Morgan, "War Funding Bill's Extra Riders," *Washington Post*, 8 April 2003, p. A4.

nized in a future election and used as ammunition by an opposing candidate. Because of this possibility, members of Congress will try to anticipate their constituents' policy views.[37] Legislators are more likely to act in accordance with those views if they think that voters will take them into account during elections. In this way, constituents may affect congressional policy choices even when there is little direct evidence of their awareness.

Interest Groups

Interest groups are another important external influence on the policies that Congress produces. When members of Congress are making voting decisions, those interest groups that have some connection to constituents in particular members' districts are most likely to be influential. For this reason, interest groups with the ability to mobilize followers in many congressional districts may be especially influential in Congress. The small-business lobby, for example, played an important role in defeating President Clinton's proposal for comprehensive health-care reform in 1993–94. The mobilization of networks of small businesses across the country meant that virtually every member of Congress had to take their views into account.

Collective-Action Principle

Interest groups with the ability to mobilize followers in many congressional districts are especially influential in Congress.

In the 2004 electoral cycle, many millions of dollars in campaign contributions were given by interest groups and PACs to incumbent legislators and challengers. What does this money buy? A popular conception is that campaign contributions buy legislative votes. In this view, legislators vote for whichever proposal favors the bulk of their contributors. Although the vote-buying hypothesis makes for good campaign rhetoric, it has little factual support. Empirical studies by political scientists show little evidence that contributions from large PACs influence legislative voting patterns.[38]

If contributions don't buy votes, then what do they buy? Our claim is that campaign contributions influence legislative behavior in ways that are difficult for the public to observe and for political scientists to measure. The institutional structure of Congress provides opportunities for interest groups to influence legislation outside the public eye, which legislators and contributors prefer.

Committee proposal power enables legislators, if they are on the relevant committee, to introduce legislation that favors contributing groups. Gatekeeping power enables committee members to block legislation that harms contributing groups. The fact that certain provisions are *excluded* from a bill is as much an indicator of PAC influence as the fact that certain provisions are *included*. The difference is that it is hard to measure what you don't see. Committee oversight

---

[37]See John W. Kingdon, *Congressmen's Voting Decisions* (New York: Harper & Row, 1973). Chapter 3; and R. Douglas Arnold. *The Logic of Congressional Action* (New Haven, CT: Yale University Press, 1990).

[38]See Janet M. Grenke, "PACs and the Congressional Supermarket: The Currency Is Complex," *American Journal of Political Science* 33 (1989): 1–24. More generally, see Jacobson, *The Politics of Congressional Elections.*

powers enable members to intervene in bureaucratic decision making on behalf of contributing groups.

The point here is that voting on the floor, the alleged object of campaign contributions according to the vote-buying hypothesis, is a highly visible, highly public act, one that could get a legislator in trouble with his or her broader electoral constituency. The committee system, on the other hand, provides loads of opportunities for legislators to deliver "services" to PAC contributors and other donors that are more subtle and disguised from broader public view. Thus we suggest that the most appropriate places to look for traces of campaign contribution influence on the legislative process are in the manner in which committees deliberate, mark up proposals, and block legislation from the floor; outside public view, these are the primary arenas for interest-group influence.

Party Discipline

party vote A roll-call vote in the House or Senate in which at least 50 percent of the members of one party take a particular position and are opposed by at least 50 percent of the members of the other party. Party votes are rare today, although they were fairly common in the nineteenth century.

roll-call votes Votes in which each legislator's yes or no vote is recorded.

In both the House and the Senate, party leaders have a good deal of influence over the behavior of their party members. This influence, sometimes called "party discipline," was once so powerful that it dominated the lawmaking process. Let us define a vote for which 50 percent or more of the members of one party take one position while at least 50 percent of the members of the other party take the opposing position as a ***party vote.*** At the beginning of the twentieth century, most ***roll-call votes*** in the House of Representatives were party votes. The frequency of party votes declined through most of the twentieth century as legislative parties grew more ideologically diverse. Democrats included liberals from the big cities and conservatives from the South. Republicans included conservatives from the Midwest and West and moderates from the Northeast. The tail end of this decline in party voting can be observed in Figure 5.7 between 1955 and 1970. Beginning in the 1970s, however, legislative parties grew more homogeneous and polarized. Conservative southern districts began electing Republicans and liberal northeastern districts began sending Democrats to Congress. The data shown in the figure reflect this, with party votes ticking upward from the 1970s onward. Some of this is due to the intense partisan struggles that began during the Reagan and George H. W. Bush years. Straight party-line voting was also seen briefly in the 103rd Congress (1993–94) after Bill Clinton's election in 1992. The situation, however, soon gave way to the many long-term factors working against party discipline in Congress as seen in the decline in party voting over the most recent decade.[39]

In 2001, newly elected president George W. Bush called for an end to partisan squabbling in Congress. During the 2000 campaign, Bush claimed that as governor of Texas he had been able to build effective bipartisan coalitions, which, he said, should serve as a model for the conduct of the nation's business, as well.

[39]David Broder, "Hill Democrats Vote as One: New Era of Unity or Short-Term Honeymoon?" *Washington Post,* 14 March 1993, p. A1. See also Adam Clymer, "All Aboard: Clinton's Plan Gets Moving," *New York Times,* 21 March 1993, sec. 4, p. 1.

FIGURE 5.7

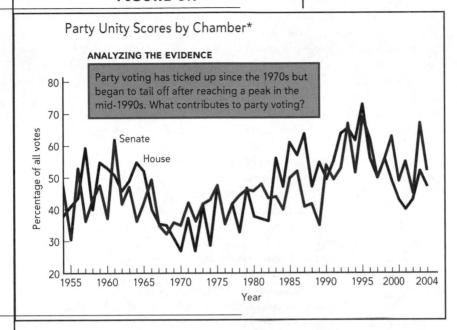

Party Unity Scores by Chamber*

ANALYZING THE EVIDENCE

Party voting has ticked up since the 1970s but began to tail off after reaching a peak in the mid-1990s. What contributes to party voting?

*The percentage of times that members voted with the majority of their party, based on recorded votes on which a majority of one party voted against the majority of the other party.

SOURCE: *Congressional Quarterly Weekly Report*, 11 December 2004, p. 2907.

September 11, 2001, prompted almost every member of Congress to rally behind President Bush's military response. But, as we read earlier, Democrats and Republicans in the House almost immediately divided sharply over the issue of airport security. Over the next several years, partisan differences emerged on a variety of issues, including taxation and foreign policy. On the issue of taxation, President Bush had sought to slash federal taxes by as much as $700 billion over a period of several years. Many Democrats, on the other hand, opposed most or all of Bush's tax-cut proposals and called for increased federal spending on social programs, especially health care. On issues of foreign policy, many Democrats were deeply troubled by the president's willingness to use military force on a unilateral basis when he deemed it necessary to do so. Before the 2003 Iraq War, Democratic leaders argued for giving UN weapons inspectors and diplomacy more time. Even after the quick conclusion of the active first phase of the war, some Democrats accused the president of undermining America's relations with its allies.

To some extent, party divisions are based on ideology and background. Republican members of Congress are more likely than Democrats to be drawn from rural or suburban areas. Democrats are likely to be more liberal on economic and social questions than their Republican colleagues. This ideological gap has been especially pronounced since 1980 (see Figure 5.8). Ideological differences certainly help explain roll-call divisions between the two parties.[40] Ideology and background, however, are only part of the explanation of party unity. The other part has to do with party organization and leadership. Although party organization has weakened since the beginning of the twentieth century, today's party leaders still have some resources at their disposal: (1) committee assignments, (2) access to the floor, (3) the whip system, (4) logrolling, and (5) the presidency. These resources are regularly used and are often effective in securing the support of party members. [41]

Committee Assignments   Leaders can create debts among members by helping them get favorable committee assignments. These assignments are made early in the congressional careers of most members and ordinarily cannot be taken from them if they later balk at party discipline. Nevertheless, if the leadership goes out of its way to get the right assignment for a member, this effort is likely to create a bond of obligation that can be called on without any other payments or favors.

In 2005, the Republicans removed several members from the House Ethics Committee because of their participation, in the previous Congress, in investigating House Republican Leader Tom DeLay. Inasmuch as the Ethics Committee is seen as a bipartisan watchdog, these actions were seen as muscle-flexing responses by the Republican leadership. Bipartisan or not, the leadership seemed to be saying, as noted above, there are some lines that should not be crossed.

Access to the Floor   The most important everyday resource available to the parties is control over access to the floor. With thousands of bills awaiting passage and most members clamoring for access to influence a bill or to publicize themselves, floor

---

[40]Keith T. Poole and Howard Rosenthal, *Congress: A Political-Economic History of Roll Call Voting* (New York: Oxford University Press, 1997).

[41]Legislative leaders may behave in ways that embellish their reputation for being willing to punish party members who stray from the party line. The problem for leaders of developing such credible reputations is analyzed in Randall Calvert, "Reputation and Legislative Leadership," *Public Choice* 55 (1987): 81–120, and is summarized in Kenneth A. Shepsle and Mark S. Boncheck, *Analyzing Politics: Rationality, Behavior, Institutions* (New York: Norton, 1997), pp. 397–403. The classic example of such punishment occurred after the 1964 election, in which two prominent House Democrats, John Bell Williams of Mississippi and Albert Watson of South Carolina, were disciplined for having supported the Republican presidential nominee, Barry Goldwater. The party leaders pushed for, and the Democratic caucus supported, a punishment in which each was demoted to the bottom of the seniority roster on the committees of which they were members. In Williams's case, the punishment was serious because he was the second-highest-ranking Democrat on the House Energy and Commerce Committee. Each resigned from the House in the wake of this punishment and ran for elective office (both successfully) as Republicans. The message was clear: there are some partisan lines that party members cross at their peril! Put slightly differently, the famous mid-twentieth-century House Speaker, Sam Rayburn (D-Tex.), is known to have believed that deviation from the party position would be tolerated for "reasons of conscience or constituency." Of one wayward Democrat he is alleged to have said that the departure from the party line "better be a matter of conscience, because it damn sight isn't because of his constituency." In short, there would be hell to pay!

FIGURE 5.8

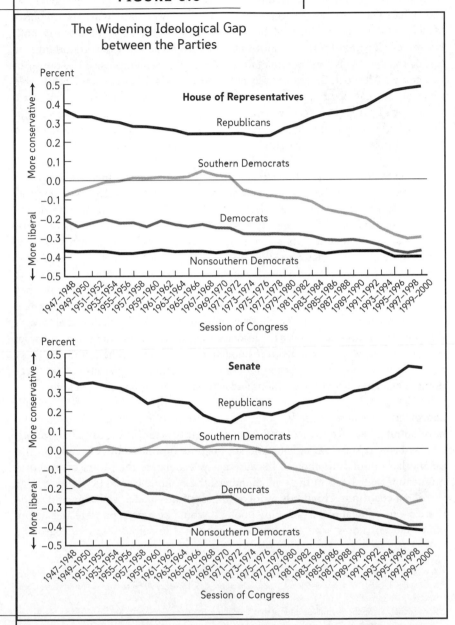

The ideological gap between Democrats and Republicans has widened, primarily due to a "sorting out" in the South, where Republicans have elected conservatives and Democrats liberals.

SOURCES: Data from Keith T. Poole and Howard Rosenthal, computed by Gary Jacobson, and reprinted in Poole and Rosenthal's *Congress: A Political-Economic History of Roll Call Voting* (New York: Oxford University Press, 1997); updates by Keith T. Poole.

time is precious. In the Senate, the leadership allows ranking committee members to influence the allocation of floor time—who will speak for how long; in the House, the Speaker, as head of the majority party (in consultation with the minority leader), allocates large blocks of floor time. Thus floor time is allocated in both houses of Congress by the majority and minority leaders. More important, the Speaker of the House and the majority leader in the Senate possess the power of recognition. Although this power may not appear to be substantial, it is a formidable authority and can be used to stymie a piece of legislation completely or to frustrate a member's attempts to speak on a particular issue. Because the power is significant, members of Congress usually attempt to stay on good terms with the Speaker and the majority leader to ensure that they will continue to be recognized.[42]

whip system A communications network in each house of Congress; whips poll the membership to learn their intentions on specific legislative issues and to assist the majority and minority leaders in various tasks.

Collective-Action Principle

The whip system helps maintain party unity in Congress.

logrolling A legislative practice wherein reciprocal agreements are made between legislators, usually in voting for or against a bill. In contrast to bargaining, logrolling unites parties that have nothing in common but their desire to exchange support.

The Whip System Some influence accrues to party leaders through the *whip system,* which is primarily a communications network. Between twelve and twenty assistant and regional whips are selected by geographic zones to operate at the direction of the majority or minority leader and the whip. They take polls of all the members to learn their intentions on specific bills. This enables the leaders to know if they have enough support to allow a vote and whether the vote is so close that they need to put pressure on a few swing votes. Leaders also use the whip system to convey their wishes and plans to the members, but only in very close votes do they actually exert pressure on a member. In those instances, the Speaker or a lieutenant will go to a few party members who have indicated they will switch if their vote is essential. The whip system helps the leaders limit pressuring members to a few times per session. The whip system helps maintain party unity in both houses of Congress, but it is particularly critical in the House of Representatives because of the large number of legislators whose positions and votes must always be accounted for.

Logrolling An agreement between two or more members of Congress who have nothing in common except the need for mutual support is called *logrolling.* The agreement states, in effect, "You support me on bill X and I'll support you on another bill of your choice." Because party leaders are the center of the communications networks in the two chambers, they can help members create large logrolling coalitions. Hundreds of logrolling deals are made each year, and while there are no official record-keeping books, it would be a poor party leader whose whips did not know who owed what to whom.[43] In some instances, logrolling

---

[42]A recent analysis of how floor time is allocated is found in Gary W. Cox and Matthew D. McCubbins, *Setting the Agenda: Responsible Party Government in the U.S. House of Representatives* (New York: Cambridge University Press, 2005).

[43]For an analysis of the formal problems that logrolling (or vote trading) both solves and creates, see Shepsle and Bonchek, *Analyzing Politics,* pp. 317–19. They argue that logrolling cannot be the entire solution to the problem of assembling majority coalitions out of the diverse preferences found in any political party. The reason is that, while party leaders can try to keep track of who owes what to whom, this is imperfect and highly complex bookkeeping at best. Nevertheless, if anyone is positioned to orchestrate a system of logrolls, it is the party leaders. And, of all those who have tried to facilitate such "cooperation," Robert Byrd of West Virginia, who served both as majority whip and as majority leader in the Senate, has been the acknowledged master.

produces strange alliances. A seemingly unlikely alliance emerged in Congress in June 1994, when 119 mainly conservative senators and representatives from oil-producing states met with President Clinton to suggest that they might be willing to support the president's health-care proposals in exchange for his support for a number of tax breaks for the oil industry. Senator J. Bennett Johnston of Louisiana, a leader of the oil-state representatives, contended that the issues of health care and oil production were closely related because both "affected the longterm economic security of the nation." Ironically, the oil-producing groups that promoted this alliance are generally among the most conservative forces in the nation. When asked what he personally thought of the president's health-care proposal, George Alcorn, a leading industry lobbyist involved in the logrolling effort, dismissed Clinton's plan as "socialized medicine." Another logrolling alliance of strange bedfellows was the 1994 "corn for porn" logroll, in which liberal urbanites supported farm programs in exchange for rural support for National Endowment for the Arts funding. Good logrolling, it would seem, is not hampered by minor ideological concerns.[44]

Collective-Action Principle

Logrolling is an informal means of facilitating cooperation in Congress.

The Presidency   Of all the influences that maintain the clarity of party lines in Congress, the influence of the presidency is probably the most important. Indeed, it is a touchstone of party discipline in Congress. Since the late 1940s, under President Truman, presidents each year have identified a number of bills to be considered part of their administration's program. By the mid-1950s, both parties in Congress began to look to the president for these proposals, which became the most significant part of Congress's agenda. The president's support is a criterion for party loyalty, and party leaders are able to use it to rally some members.

Weighing Diverse Influences

Clearly, many different factors affect congressional decisions. But at various points in the decision-making process, some factors are likely to be more influential than others. For example, interest groups may be more effective at the committee stage, when their expertise is especially valued and their visibility is less obvious. Because committees play a key role in deciding what legislation actually reaches the floor of the House or Senate, interest groups can often put a halt to bills they dislike, or they can ensure that the options that do reach the floor are those that the group's members support.

Once legislation reaches the floor and members of Congress are deciding among alternatives, constituent opinion will become more important. Legislators are also influenced very much by other legislators: many of their assessments about the substance and politics of legislation come from fellow members of Congress.

The influence of the external and internal forces described in the preceding section also varies according to the kind of issue being considered. On policies of

---

[44] Allen R. Meyerson, "Oil-Patch Congressmen Seek Deal with Clinton," *New York Times*, 14 June 1994, p. D2.

great importance to powerful interest groups—farm subsidies, for example—those groups are likely to have considerable influence. On other issues, members of Congress may be less attentive to narrow interest groups and more willing to consider what they see as the general interest.

Finally, the mix of influences varies according to the historical moment. The 1994 electoral victory of Republicans allowed their party to control both houses of Congress for the first time in forty years. The fact, combined with an unusually assertive Republican leadership, meant that party leaders became especially important in decision making. The willingness of moderate Republicans to support measures they had once opposed indicated the unusual importance of party leadership in this period. As House minority leader Richard Gephardt put it, "When you've been in the desert forty years, your instinct is to help Moses."[45]

BEYOND LEGISLATION: ADDITIONAL CONGRESSIONAL POWERS

In addition to the power to make the law, Congress has at its disposal an array of other instruments through which to influence the process of government.

Advice and Consent: Special Senate Powers

The Constitution has given the Senate a special power, one that is not based on lawmaking. The president has the power to make treaties and to appoint top executive officers, ambassadors, and federal judges—but only "with the Advice and Consent of the Senate" (Article II, Section 2). For treaties, two-thirds of those present must concur; for appointments, a majority is required.

The power to approve or reject presidential requests also involves the power to set conditions. The Senate only occasionally exercises its power to reject treaties and appointments. Only nine Supreme Court nominees have been rejected by the Senate during the past century, while hundreds have been approved.

More common than Senate rejection of presidential appointees is a senatorial "hold" on an appointment. By Senate tradition, any member may place an indefinite hold on the confirmation of a mid- or lower-level presidential appointment. The hold may be a signal of a senator's willingness to filibuster a nomination, but it is typically used by senators trying to wring concessions from the White House on matters having nothing to do with the appointment in question. Since Bush came to power in January 2001, the Democratic minority in the Senate has actively scrutinized judicial nominations. They have prevented final confirmation votes on a dozen especially conservative nominees, a matter about which President Bush frequently complained during the 2004 re-election campaign. In February 2005, President Bush resubmitted the nominees to the Senate.

[45]David Broder, "At 6 Months, House GOP Juggernaut Still Cohesive," *Washington Post*, 17 July 1995, p. A1.

Judicial nomination politics have loomed large during Bush's second term. In May of 2005 Senate Majority Leader Frist, responding to continual obstructionist tactics by the minority Democrats on confirming Bush nominees to the federal courts, threatened the "nuclear option." This was a procedural tactic to close down a filibuster that only required *majority* approval (instead of the "normal" three-fifths requirement). Had this occurred it is believed it would have constituted a procedural watershed in the Senate, making this chamber much more similar to the more majoritarian House. A group of fourteen senators, seven from each party, brokered a compromise in which the minority agreed to reserve the filibuster for "extraordinary circumstances" (leaving the latter imprecise). This permitted a number of previously controversial nominees for judgeships to be confirmed.

Into this highly charged environment, in the summer of 2005, came a number of bolts from the blue. Bush, who had not had a single opportunity to name a Supreme Court justice in his first term, was confronted with a flurry of opportunities during a few short months of his second term. During the summer, Justice Sandra Day O'Connor (the first woman to serve on the Court) announced her retirement. Bush nominated John Roberts, a sitting federal judge, as her replacement. But before he could be confirmed, Chief Justice William Rehnquist died. O'Connor agreed to remain on the Court till her replacement was confirmed, so President Bush withdrew Roberts's nomination and then *re-nominated* him, this time to replace Rehnquist as Chief Justice. Roberts was confirmed in time for the opening of the Court's term in October. Bush now turned to O'Connor's replacement, nominating Harriet Miers, the White House Counsel. However, in nominating a member of his own staff who had never served as a judge, Bush was accused of cronyism on the one hand and of failing to nominate someone of distinction on the other. Moreover, his conservative base refused to support Miers, claiming that she was not a true-blue conservative who would work against the liberal activism they believed dominated the Court. Ultimately, Miers withdrew and Bush nominated Samuel Alito, a sitting federal judge with a substantial conservative track record.

Most presidents make every effort to take potential Senate opposition into account in treaty negotiations and will frequently resort to *executive agreements* with foreign powers instead of treaties. The Supreme Court has held that such agreements are equivalent to treaties, but they do not need Senate approval.[46] In the past, presidents sometimes concluded secret agreements without informing Congress of the agreements' contents or even their existence. For example, American involvement in the Vietnam War grew in part out of a series of secret arrangements made between American presidents and the South Vietnamese during the 1950s and 1960s. Congress did not even learn of the existence of

executive agreement An agreement between the president and another country that has the force of a treaty but does not require the Senate's "advice and consent."

---

[46]*United States v. Pink*, 315 U.S. 203 (1942). For a good discussion of the problem, see James W. Davis, *The American Presidency: A New Perspective* (New York: Harper & Row, 1987), Chapter 8. A recent analysis is found in William Howell, *Power without Persuasion: The Politics of Direct Presidential Action* (Princeton, NJ: Princeton University Press, 2003).

these agreements until 1969. In 1972, Congress passed the Case Act, which requires that the president inform Congress of any executive agreement within sixty days of its having been reached. This provides Congress with the opportunity to cancel agreements that it opposes. In addition, Congress can limit the president's ability to conduct foreign policy through executive agreement by refusing to appropriate the funds needed to implement an agreement. In this way, for example, executive agreements to provide American economic or military assistance to foreign governments can be modified or even canceled by Congress.

Impeachment

impeachment
The charging of a governmental official (president or otherwise) with "Treason, Bribery, or other high Crimes and Misdemeanors" and bringing of him or her before Congress to determine guilt.

The Constitution also grants Congress the power of ***impeachment*** over the president, vice president, and other executive officials. Impeachment means the charging of a government official (president or otherwise) with "Treason, Bribery, or other high Crimes and Misdemeanors" and bringing of him or her before Congress to determine guilt. Impeachment is thus like a criminal indictment in which the House of Representatives acts like a grand jury, voting (by simple majority) on whether the accused ought to be impeached. If a majority of the House votes to impeach, the impeachment trial moves to the Senate, which acts like a trial jury by voting whether to convict and forcibly remove the person from office (this vote requires a two-thirds majority of the Senate).

Controversy over Congress's impeachment power has arisen over the grounds for impeachment, especially the meaning of "high Crimes and Misdemeanors." A strict reading of the Constitution suggests that the only impeachable offense is an actual crime. But a more commonly agreed on definition is that "an impeachable offense is whatever the majority of the House of Representatives considers it to be at a given moment in history."[47] In other words, impeachment, especially impeachment of a president, is a political decision.

The closest that the United States has come to impeaching and convicting a president came in 1867. President Andrew Johnson, a southern Democrat who had battled a congressional Republican majority over Reconstruction, was impeached by the House but saved from conviction by one vote in the Senate. At the height of the Watergate scandal in 1974, the House started impeachment proceedings against President Richard M. Nixon, but Nixon resigned before the House could proceed. The possibility of impeachment arose again in 1998, when President Clinton was accused of lying under oath and obstructing justice in the investigation into his sexual affair with White House intern Monica Lewinsky. In October 1998, the House voted to impeach President Clinton. At the conclusion of the Senate trial in 1999, Democrats, joined by a handful of Republicans, acquitted the president of both charges.

The impeachment power is a considerable one; its very existence in the hands of Congress is a highly effective safeguard against the executive tyranny so greatly feared by the framers of the Constitution.

[47]Carroll J. Doherty, "Impeachment: How It Would Work," *Congressional Quarterly Weekly Report*, 31 January 1998, p. 222.

POWER AND REPRESENTATION

Because they feared both executive and legislative tyranny, the framers of the Constitution pitted Congress and the president against one another. But for more than 100 years, the contest was unequal. During the first century of American government, Congress was the dominant institution. American foreign and domestic policy was formulated and implemented by Congress; and, generally, the most powerful figures in American government were the Speaker of the House and the leaders of the Senate—not the president. During the nineteenth century, Congress—not the president—dominated press coverage on "the affairs of government."[48] The War of 1812 was planned and fought by Congress. The great sectional compromises before the Civil War were formulated in Congress, without much intervention from the executive branch. Even during the Civil War, a period of extraordinary presidential leadership, a joint congressional committee on the conduct of the war played a role in formulating war plans and campaign tactics—and even had a hand in the promotion of officers. After the Civil War, when President Andrew Johnson sought to interfere with congressional plans for Reconstruction, he was summarily impeached, saved from conviction by only one vote. Subsequent presidents understood the moral and did not attempt to thwart Congress.

This congressional preeminence began to diminish after the turn of the twentieth century, so that by the 1960s, the executive had become, at least temporarily, the dominant branch of American government. The major domestic policy initiatives of the twentieth century—Franklin Roosevelt's "New Deal," Harry Truman's "Fair Deal," John F. Kennedy's "New Frontier," and Lyndon Johnson's "Great Society"—all included some congressional involvement but were essentially developed, introduced, and implemented by the executive. In the area of foreign policy, although Congress continued to be influential during the twentieth century, the focus of decision-making power clearly moved into the executive branch. The War of 1812 may have been a congressional war, but in the twentieth century, American entry into World War I, World War II, Korea, Vietnam, and a host of lesser conflicts was essentially a presidential—not a congressional—decision. In the last forty years, there has been a good deal of resurgence of congressional power vis-à-vis the executive. This has occurred mainly because Congress has sought to represent many important political forces, such as the civil rights, feminist, environmental, consumer, and peace movements, which in turn became constituencies for congressional power. During the mid-1990s, Congress became more receptive to a variety of new conservative political forces, including groups on the social and religious right as well as more traditional economic conservatives. After Republicans won control of both houses in the 1994 elections, Congress took the lead in developing programs and policies supported by these groups. These efforts won Congress the support of conservative forces in its battles for power against a Democratic White House.

> **History Principle**
> During the first century of American government, Congress was the dominant institution. In recent decades, members of Congress have sought to restore that dominance.

[48]Samuel Kernell and Gary C. Jacobson, "Congress and the Presidency as News in the Nineteenth Century," *Journal of Politics* 49 (1987): 1016–35.

To herald the new accessibility of Congress, Republican leaders instituted a number of reforms designed to eliminate many of the practices that they had criticized during their long years in opposition as examples of Democratic arrogance. Republican leaders reduced the number of committees and subcommittees, eliminated funding of the various unofficial caucuses, imposed term limits on committee chairmen, eliminated the practice of proxy voting, reduced committee staffs by one-third, ended Congress's exemption from the labor health and civil rights laws that it imposed on the rest of the nation, and prohibited members from receiving most gifts. With these reforms, Republicans hoped to make Congress both more effective and more representative. Term limits and gift bans were seen as increasing the responsiveness of Congress to new political forces and to the American people more generally. Simplification of the committee structure was seen as making Congress more efficient and thus potentially more effective and powerful. To some extent, unfortunately, the various reforms worked at cross-purposes. Simplification of the committee structure and elimination of funding for the caucuses increased the power of the leadership but reduced the representation of a variety of groups in the legislative process. For example, the Congressional Black Caucus, one of the major groups to lose its funding, had come to play an important role in representing African Americans. For their part, when term limits for committee and subcommittee chairmen were finally imposed in 2001, the result was confusion because experienced chairs were forced to step down. This is the dilemma of congressional reform. Efficiency and representation are often competing principles in our system of government, and we must be wary of gaining one at the expense of the other.

Thus we face a fundamental dilemma: a representative system that can undermine the government's very capacity to govern. In the next chapter, we turn to the second branch of American government, the presidency, to view this dilemma from a somewhat different angle.

SUMMARY

The U.S. Congress is one of the few national representative assemblies that actually govern. Members of Congress take their representative function seriously. They devote a significant portion of their time to constituent contact and service. Representation and power go hand in hand in congressional history.

The legislative process must provide the order necessary for legislation to take place amid competing interests. It depends on a hierarchical organizational structure within Congress. Six basic dimensions of Congress affect the legislative process: (1) the parties, (2) the committees, (3) the staff, (4) the caucuses (or conferences), (5) the rules, and (6) the presidency.

Because the Constitution provides for only for a presiding officer in each house, some method had to be devised for conducting business. Parties quickly assumed the responsibility for this. In the House, the majority party elects a leader every two years. This individual becomes Speaker. In addition, a majority leader

PRINCIPLES OF POLITICS IN REVIEW

Rationality Principle	Collective-Action Principle	Institution Principle	Policy Principle	History Principle
Members of Congress, like all politicians, are ambitious and thus eager to serve the interests of constituents to improve their own chances of re-election.	Cooperation on recurring matters like congressional votes is facilitated by the institutionalization of legislative structures and procedures.	According to the principle of agency representation, elections induce a member of Congress to act according to the preferences of his or her constituency.	Pork-barrel legislation exists because it allows members of Congress to claim credit for federally granted resources, thus improving their chances for re-election.	The historical intentions of the founders for the House to represent current passions and the Senate to balance it by serving a more deliberative function are still manifest in these legislative bodies more than two centuries later.
One of the most important factors determining who runs for office is each candidate's individual ambition. Access to money doesn't hurt either.	Political parties in legislature foster cooperation, coalitions, and compromise.	Party leaders have considerable agenda-setting powers.	The distributive tendency in Congress results from the need for a broad base of support for a bill to be passed.	The committee system evolved during the early nineteenth century as a means of allowing individual legislators disproportionate influence in areas of policy most important to them.
The opportunity to run for office is often more attractive to a small-state politician whose current constituency heavily overlaps the one for higher office.	If a bill passes both the House and the Senate, the differences need to be ironed out in a conference committee.	The committee system is a means of dividing labor and allowing members of Congress to specialize in certain policy areas.	Multiple factors influence how a member of Congress votes on legislation. These include constituency, interest groups, party leaders, congressional colleagues, and the president.	
The political opinions and policy goals of members of Congress are many and varied.	Interest groups with the ability to mobilize followers in many congressional districts are especially influential in Congress.	Among the powers delegated to committees are gatekeeping authority, bargaining with the other chamber, and oversight.		During the first century of American government, Congress was the dominant institution. In recent decades, members of Congress have sought to restore that dominance.
Generally, members of Congress seek committee assignments that allow them to acquire more influence in areas important to their constituents.	The whip system helps maintain party unity in Congress.	The House and Senate have methods of keeping committees in check.		
	Logrolling is an informal means of facilitating cooperation in Congress.	The Rules Committee's decision about whether to adopt a closed or open rule for floor debate greatly influences a bill's chances for passage.		

and a minority leader (from the minority party) and party whips are elected. Each party has a committee whose job it is to make committee assignments.

The committee system surpassed the party system in its importance in Congress during much of the twentieth century, although there has been a resurgence of the party system in the last two decades. Standing committees, however, are a fundamental aspect of Congress. They have, for the most part, evolved to correspond to executive-branch departments or programs and thus reflect and maintain the separation of powers.

The Senate has a tradition of unlimited debate, on which the various cloture rules it has passed have had little effect. Filibusters still occur. And the mere possibility of one deters the introduction of some legislation and alters the shape of others. The rules of the House, on the other hand, restrict talk and support committees; deliberation is recognized as committee business. The House Rules Committee has the power to control debate and floor amendments. The rules prescribe the formal procedure through which bills become law. Generally, the parties control scheduling and agenda, but the committees determine action on the floor. Committees, seniority, and rules all limit the ability of members to represent their constituents. Yet, these factors enable Congress to maintain its role as a major participant in government.

While voting along party lines remains strong, party discipline has declined. Still, parties do have several means of maintaining discipline. In most cases, party leaders accept constituency obligations as a valid reason for voting against the party position.

The power of the post–New Deal presidency does not necessarily signify the decline of Congress and representative government. During the 1970s, Congress again became the "first branch" of government. During the early years of the Reagan administration, some of the congressional gains of the previous decade were diminished, but in the last two years of Reagan's second term, and in President George H. W. Bush's term, Congress reasserted its role. At the start of the Clinton administration, congressional leaders promised to cooperate with the White House rather than confront it. But only two years later, confrontation was once again the order of the day. George W. Bush's presidency has witnessed close collaboration between the White House and Capitol Hill.

FOR FURTHER READING

Arnold, R. Douglas. *The Logic of Congressional Action*. New Haven, CT: Yale University Press, 1990.

Baker, Ross K. *House and Senate*. 3rd ed. New York: Norton, 2001.

Cox, Gary W., and Mathew D. McCubbins. *Legislative Leviathan: Party Government in the House*. Berkeley: University of California Press, 1993.

Dodd, Lawrence C., and Bruce I. Oppenheimer, eds. *Congress Reconsidered*. 7th ed. Washington, DC: Congressional Quarterly Press, 2001.

Fenno, Richard F., Jr. *Home Style: House Members in Their Districts*. Boston: Little, Brown, 1978.

Fiorina, Morris P. *Congress: Keystone of the Washington Establishment*. 2nd ed. New Haven, CT: Yale University Press, 1989.

Fowler, Linda L., and Robert D. McClure. *Political Ambition: Who Decides to Run for Congress*. New Haven, CT: Yale University Press, 1989.

Krehbiel, Keith. *Pivotal Politics: A Theory of U.S. Lawmaking*. Chicago: University of Chicago Press, 1998.

Mayhew, David R. *Congress: The Electoral Connection*. New Haven, CT: Yale University Press, 1974.

Rieselbach, Leroy N. *Congressional Reform*. Washington, DC: Congressional Quarterly Press, 1986.

Rohde, David W. *Parties and Leaders in the Postreform House*. Chicago: University of Chicago Press, 1991.

Sinclair, Barbara. *The Transformation of the U.S. Senate*. Baltimore: Johns Hopkins University Press, 1989.

Smith, Steven S., and Christopher J. Deering. *Committees in Congress*. 3rd ed. Washington, DC: Congressional Quarterly Press, 1997.

Sundquist, James L. *The Decline and Resurgence of Congress*. Washington, DC: Brookings Institution, 1981.

Politics in the News—
Reading between the Lines

Differences between the House and Senate

2 Chambers That Don't Understand Each Other

By CARL HULSE

Forget Republicans and Democrats. The lawmakers who seem least to understand each other are senators and representatives—no matter the party. . . .

Even with one-party control, the vast differences in the way the House and the Senate operate make policy blowups inevitable. Throughout history, the House and the Senate have clashed. But lately those clashes have been frequent—and loud.

The House is insisting on oil drilling in Alaska; the Senate has rejected the idea. The Senate blocked a Bush administration proposal to give public money to religious groups, compelling the House to go along. The House is ready to advance a Medicare overhaul; the Senate is taking it slower. And the latest dispute was on Friday. House Republicans pushed through a tax-cut package substantially at odds in size and content with the measure emerging in the Senate, setting up a nasty negotiation to reconcile the two.

"We expedite, they obstruct," a top House Republican aide said.

While differences in policy goals certainly exist, the problem can often be found in the very nature of the institutions. House rules severely restrain the power of the opposition, giving Mr. Hastert and Mr. DeLay iron-fisted control so they can—and do—rapidly ram through almost anything they want.

In the Senate, every member wields tremendous power through the ability to put blind "holds" on legislation, raise procedural obstacles on the floor and generally gum things up. That makes the Senate a place where the majority does not always rule.

The House leadership uses a Rules Committee to limit debate; the Senate routinely engages in interminable debates without limits. . . .

The power of the individual in the Senate was on vivid display again last week as Senator Olympia J. Snowe, Republican of Maine, single-handedly

New York Times, 12 May 2003, p. A18.

forced the Finance Committee to compromise on a tax-cutting plan that raised some taxes to pay for tax cuts elsewhere. That idea did not go down well in the House.

"I think the Capitol Police better check to see if someone's slipped something into the water over there," said Representative Mark Foley, Republican of Florida, adding that the Senate tax-writers were "not acting like Republicans."

Indeed. They were acting like senators. . . .

The framers of the Constitution envisioned the Senate as a legislative bulwark against the more populist House, and Washington famously and perhaps apocryphally described it to Jefferson as the saucer to "cool" the passions of the House members. . . .

In the early years of the nation, the House was where the action was, with the Senate a sleepy chamber caught up in confirmations. The Senate historian Richard A. Baker said that balance of power changed with the rising emphasis on slavery issues in the 19th century. With the Senate split between slave states and free states, politicians quickly realized that one lawmaker in the Senate could wield significant power.

"That is where the political talent of the nation went, where a single member could make a difference if only to stand up and say no," Mr. Baker said. . . .

Because Senators represent entire states, they often are less ideological and unyielding than House members, who are often elected from safe partisan districts and can afford to be less willing to compromise.

Things could well get worse before they get better in the current Congress, with coming negotiations over the tax bill, drug coverage under Medicare, energy policy and the usual list of spending measures. . . .

ESSENCE OF THE STORY

- For the first time since 1953, the Republicans had unified control of the House, Senate, and presidency after the 2002 election. Republicans want to promote their agenda.

- House members have made progress on a series of issues important to the White House, including drilling in the Arctic National Wildlife Refuge, a tax cut, and Medicare reform.

- The Senate has moved much more slowly on these issues, prompting complaints from their colleagues in the House.

- Individual members celebrate their own institution and complain about the other.

POLITICAL ANALYSIS

- Collective action (passage of a bill) is affected by both rules and member preferences. Member preferences, furthermore, are shaped by another set of rules (the electoral game).

- Structured rules for debate and participation in the House mean that Republican House leaders can push forward their legislation even if Democrats object. House leaders are less concerned with cross-party coalitions.

- In the Senate, individual members can slow down progress even though the Republicans are ostensibly in control. Senate leaders must build cross-party coalitions.

- Difference in the electoral calendar and the makeup of their constituencies exacerbate these differences. House members have to point to accomplishments in just two years. Partisans in their districts demand results. Senators can afford to move more slowly. Because states tend to be more heterogeneous and because Senate races are more competitive, senators have to be more attentive to a wider variety of demands.

- The relative influence of the two chambers has ebbed and flowed throughout U.S. history, mainly in response to real-world events such as the growth of the nation, increasing economic and governmental complexity, and foreign conflicts.

CHAPTER

6

The Presidency as an Institution

Although the first domestic effect of war is inevitably on civil liberties, war has ramifications throughout all governmental and political institutions as well as for public policies. For example, President Abraham Lincoln's 1862 declaration of martial law and Congress's 1863 legislation giving the president the power to make arrests and imprisonments through military tribunals amounted to a "constitutional dictatorship," which lasted through the war and Lincoln's reelection in 1864. But these measures were viewed as emergency powers that could be taken back once the crisis of union was resolved. In less than a year after Lincoln's death, Congress reasserted its power, leaving the presidency in many respects the same as, if not weaker than, it had been before.

During World War II, Franklin D. Roosevelt, like Lincoln, did not bother to wait for Congress but took executive action first and expected Congress to follow. Roosevelt brought the United States into an undeclared naval war against Germany a year before Pearl Harbor, and he ordered the unauthorized use of wiretaps and other surveillance as well as the investigation of suspicious persons for reasons not clearly specified. The most egregious (and revealing) of these was his segregation and eventual confinement of 120,000 individuals of Japanese descent, many of whom were American citizens. Even worse, the Supreme Court validated Roosevelt's treatment of the Japanese on the flimsy grounds of military necessity. One dissenter on the Court called the president's assumption of emergency powers "a loaded weapon ready for the hand of any authority that can bring forward a plausible claim of an urgent need."

The "loaded weapon" was seized again on September 14, 2001, when Congress defined the World Trade Center and Pentagon attacks as acts of war and proceeded to adopt a joint resolution authorizing the president to use "all necessary and appropriate force against those nations, organizations or persons he determines planned, authorized, committed or aided the terrorist attacks that occurred on September 11, 2001, or harbored such organizations or persons. . . ." Congress did attach a sunset provision to the authorization resolution and planned for congressional oversight during the war.

September 11 and its aftermath immensely accentuated the president's role and place in foreign policy. By 2002, foreign policy was the centerpiece of the Bush administration's agenda. In a June 1 speech at West Point, the "Bush Doctrine" of preemptive war was announced. Bush argued that "our security will require all Americans . . . to be ready for preemptive action when necessary to defend our liberty and to defend our lives." Bush's statement was clearly intended to justify his administration's plans to invade Iraq, but it had much wider implications, including the increasing power of the American president in guiding foreign policy.

National emergencies provide presidents a source of power, and the way presidents exercise these powers has profound consequences for the country. As we have seen, civil liberties are particularly threatened by what presidents do during times of war. In this chapter, we go beyond this and look at the long-term consequences of national emergencies on presidential power. What circumstances explain why some emergencies produced new and long-lasting powers for the president, while others did not? In the instances in which new powers were institutionalized, what was the long-term effect? The central task of this chapter is to explain why the American system of government could be described as presidential government and how it got to be that way. In doing so, we will see that it's the office that wields great power, not necessarily the person.

The power of the office has gradually developed over time. The framers, wanting "energy in the Executive," provided

CHAPTER OUTLINE

The Constitutional Basis of the Presidency

The Constitutional Powers of the Presidency

• Expressed Powers

• Delegated Powers

The Rise of Presidential Government

• The Legislative Epoch, 1800–1933

• The New Deal and the Presidency

Presidential Government

• What Are the Formal Resources of Presidential Power?

• The Contemporary Bases of Presidential Power

• The Administrative State

All presidents have goals and want to be influential, but presidential power is constrained by the constitutional and structural contours of the institution of the presidency. The Constitution endows the president with only a small number of expressed powers, so the presidency is an office whose powers are primarily delegated to it by Congress. Presidents have sought to broaden their inherent powers by their successful execution of the law. Presidential power can be enhanced through strategic interactions that a president has with other political actors and a president's ability to build and sustain popular support. Historical events requiring bold action and leadership from the president, such as the Great Depression, can also contribute to the president's power. The institution of the presidency has accumulated more and more power over time, but a president's ultimate success is based on the skillful use of those powers.

for a single-headed office with an electoral base independent of Congress. But by giving the presidency no explicit powers independent of Congress, each president would have to provide that energy by asserting the inherent powers of the office.

A tug-of-war between formal constitutional provisions for a president who is nominally rather weak and a theory of necessity favoring a strong executive has persisted for over two centuries. It was not until Franklin Roosevelt's election in 1932 that the tug-of-war seems to have been won for the strong executive presidency because, after FDR, as we shall see, every president has been strong, whether he was committed to the strong presidency or not.

Thus a strong executive, a genuine chief executive, was institutionalized in the twentieth century. But it continues to operate in a schizoid environment: As the power of the presidency has increased, popular expectations of presidential performance have increased at an even faster rate, requiring more leadership than was ever exercised by any but the greatest presidents in the past.

Our focus in this chapter is on the development of the institutional character of the presidency, the power of the presidency, and the relationship between the two. The chapter is divided into four sections. First and second, we review the constitutional origins and powers of the presidency. In particular, this involves an examination of the constitutional basis for the president's foreign and domestic roles. Third, we review the history of the American presidency to see how the office has evolved from its original status under the Constitution. We will look particularly at the ways in which Congress has augmented the president's constitutional powers by deliberately delegating to the presidency many of Congress's own responsibilities. Fourth, we assess the means by which presidents can enhance their own ability to govern.

THE CONSTITUTIONAL BASIS OF THE PRESIDENCY

The presidency was established by Article II of the Constitution. Article II begins by asserting, "The executive power shall be vested in a President of the United

States of America." It goes on to describe the manner in which the president is to be chosen and defines the basic powers of the presidency. By vesting the executive power in a single president, the framers were emphatically rejecting proposals for various forms of collective leadership. Some delegates to the Constitutional Convention had argued in favor of a multiheaded executive or an "executive council" to avoid undue concentration of power in the hands of one individual. Most of the framers, however, were anxious to provide for "energy" in the executive. They hoped to have a president capable of taking quick and aggressive action. The framers thought a unitary executive would be more energetic than some form of collective leadership. They believed that a powerful executive would help protect the nation's interests vis-à-vis other nations and promote the federal government's interests relative to the states.

Immediately following the first sentence of Article II, Section 1, of the Constitution, the manner in which the president is to be chosen is defined. This is an odd sequence, but it does say something about the struggle the delegates were having over how to provide great power of action or energy to the executive and at the same time balance that power with limitations. The struggle was between those delegates who wanted the president to be selected by, and thus responsible to, Congress and those delegates who preferred that the president be elected directly by the people. Direct popular election would create a more independent and more powerful presidency. With the adoption of a scheme of indirect election through an electoral college in which the electors would be selected by the state legislatures (and close elections would be resolved in the House of Representatives), the framers hoped to achieve a "republican" solution: a strong president responsible to state and national legislators rather than directly to the electorate. This indirect method of electing the president probably did dampen the power of most presidents in the nineteenth century.

The presidency was strengthened somewhat in the 1830s with the introduction of the national convention system of nominating presidential candidates. Until then, presidential candidates had been nominated by their party's congressional delegates. This was the *caucus* system of nominating candidates, and it was derisively called "King Caucus" because any candidate for president had to be beholden to the party's leaders in Congress to get the party's nomination and the support of the party's congressional delegation in the presidential election. The national nominating convention arose outside Congress to provide some representation for a party's voters who lived in districts where they weren't numerous enough to elect a member of Congress. The political party in each state made its own provisions for selecting delegates to attend the presidential nominating convention, and in virtually all states the selection was dominated by the party leaders (called "bosses" by the opposition party). Only in recent decades have state laws intervened to regularize the selection process and to provide (in all but a few instances) for open election of delegates. The convention system quickly became the most popular method of nominating candidates for all elective offices and remained so until well into the twentieth century, when it succumbed to the criticism that it was a nondemocratic method dominated by a few leaders in a "smoke-filled room." But in the nineteenth century, it was seen as a

History Principle

The framers created a unitary executive; they wanted an energetic president but also a limited one.

Institution Principle

By structuring the election of the president to be not by the people directly but by the electoral college, the framers sought to downplay presidential power.

caucus (political)

A normally closed meeting of a political or legislative group to select candidates, plan strategy, or make decisions regarding legislative matters.

victory for democracy against the congressional elite. And the national convention gave the presidency a base of power independent of Congress.

This additional independence did not immediately transform the presidency into the office we recognize today, but the national convention did begin to open the presidency to larger social forces and newly organized interests in society. In other words, it gave the presidency a mass popular base that would eventually support and demand increased presidential power. Improvements in telephone, telegraph, and other forms of mass communication allowed individuals to share their complaints and allowed national leaders—especially presidents and presidential candidates—to reach out directly to people to ally themselves with, and even sometimes to create, popular groups and forces. Eventually, though more slowly, the presidential selection process began to be further democratized, with the adoption of primary elections through which millions of ordinary citizens were given an opportunity to take part in the presidential nominating process by popular selection of convention delegates.

But despite political and social conditions favoring the enhancement of the presidency, the development of presidential government as we know it today did not mature until the middle of the twentieth century. For a long period, even as the national government began to grow, Congress was careful to keep tight reins on the president's power. The real turning point in the history of American national government came during the administration of Franklin Delano Roosevelt. Since FDR, the tug-of-war seems to have been won for the chief executive presidency, because after FDR every president has been strong, whether he was committed to the strong presidency or not.

THE CONSTITUTIONAL POWERS OF THE PRESIDENCY

While Article II, Section 1, explains how the president is to be chosen, Sections 2 and 3 outline the powers and duties of the president. These two sections identify two sources of presidential power. Some presidential powers are specifically established by the language of the Constitution. For example, the president is authorized to make treaties, grant pardons, and nominate judges and other public officials. These specifically defined powers are called the *expressed powers* of the office and cannot be revoked by the Congress or any other agency without an amendment to the Constitution. Other expressed powers include the power to receive ambassadors and to command the military forces of the United States.

In addition to the president's expressed powers, Article II declares that the president, "shall take Care that the Laws be faithfully executed." Because the laws are enacted by Congress, this language implies that Congress is to delegate to the president the power to implement or execute its will. Powers given to the president by Congress are called *delegated powers.* In principle, Congress delegates to the president only the power to identify or develop the means through which to carry out its decisions. So, for example, if Congress determines that air

expressed powers Specific powers granted to Congress under Article I, Section 8, of the Constitution.

delegated powers Constitutional powers assigned to one governmental agency that are exercised by another agency with the express permission of the first.

quality should be improved, it might delegate to a bureaucratic agency in the executive branch the power to identify the best means of bringing about such an improvement as well as the power to actually implement the cleanup process. In practice, of course, decisions about how to clean the air are likely to have an enormous effect on businesses, organizations, and individuals throughout the nation. As it delegates power to the executive, Congress substantially enhances the importance of the presidency and the executive branch. In most cases, Congress delegates power to bureaucratic agencies in the executive branch rather than to the president. As we shall see, however, contemporary presidents have found ways to capture a good deal of this delegated power for themselves.

Presidents have claimed a third source of power beyond expressed and delegated powers. These are powers not specified in the Constitution or the law but are said to stem from "the rights, duties and obligations of the presidency."[1] They are referred to as the **inherent powers** of the presidency and are most often asserted by presidents in times of war or national emergency. For example, after the fall of Fort Sumter and the outbreak of the Civil War, President Abraham Lincoln issued a series of executive orders for which he had no clear legal basis. Without even calling Congress into session, Lincoln combined the state militias into a ninety-day national volunteer force, called for 40,000 new volunteers, enlarged the regular army and navy, diverted $2 million in unspent appropriations to military needs, instituted censorship of the U.S. mails, ordered a blockade of southern ports, suspended the writ of habeas corpus in the border states, and ordered the arrest by military police of individuals whom he deemed to be guilty of engaging in or even contemplating treasonous actions.[2] Lincoln asserted that these extraordinary measures were justified by the president's inherent power to protect the nation.[3] Subsequent presidents, including Franklin D. Roosevelt and George W. Bush, have had similar views.

Expressed Powers

The president's expressed powers, as defined by Article II, Sections 2 and 3, fall into several categories:

1. *Military.* Article II, Section 2, provides for the power as "Commander in Chief of the Army and Navy of the United States, and of the Militia of the several States, when called in to the actual Service of the United States."

Institution Principle

The Constitution has established a presidency of expressed and delegated powers.

inherent powers

Powers claimed by a president that are not expressed in the Constitution but are inferred from it.

Rationality Principle

Occupants of the presidency have, from time to time, taken upon themselves additional authority to enable the pursuit of national objectives.

---

[1] In the case of *In re Neagle*, 135 U.S. 1 (1890), Neagle, a deputy U.S. marshal, had been authorized by the president to protect a Supreme Court justice whose life had been threatened by an angry litigant. When the litigant attempted to carry out his threat, Neagle shot and killed him. Neagle was then arrested by local authorities and tried for murder. His defense was that his act was "done in pursuance of a law of the United States.:" Although the law was not an act of Congress, the Supreme Court declared that it was an executive order of the president and that the protection of a federal judge was a reasonable extension of the president's power to "take Care that the Laws be faithfully executed."

[2] James G. Randall, *Constitutional Problems under Lincoln* (New York: Appleton, 1926), Chapter 1.

[3] Edward S. Corwin, *The President: Office and Powers*, 4th rev. ed. (New York: New York University Press, 1957), p. 229.

2. *Judicial.* Article II, Section 2, provides the power to "grant Reprieves and Pardons for Offences against the United States, except in Cases of Impeachment."
3. *Diplomatic.* Article II, Section 2, provides the power "by and with the Advice and Consent of the Senate to make Treaties." Article II, Section 3, provides the power to "receive Ambassadors and other public Ministers."
4. *Executive.* Article II, Section 3, authorizes the president to see to it that all the laws are faithfully executed. Section 2 gives the chief executive power to appoint, remove, and supervise all executive officers and to appoint all federal judges.
5. *Legislative.* Article I, Section 7, and Article II, Section 3, give the president the power to participate authoritatively in the legislative process.

commander in chief The power of the president as commander of the national military and the state national guard units (when called into service).

Military The president's military powers are among the most important exercised by the chief executive. The position of ***commander in chief*** makes the president the highest military authority in the United States, with control of the entire defense establishment. The president is also head of the nation's intelligence network, which includes not only the Central Intelligence Agency (CIA) but also the National Security Council (NSC), the National Security Agency (NSA), the Federal Bureau of Investigation (FBI), and a host of less well known but very powerful international and domestic security agencies.

WAR AND INHERENT PRESIDENTIAL POWER The Constitution, of course, gives Congress the power to declare war. Presidents, however, have gone a long way toward capturing this power for themselves. Congress has not declared war since December 1941, and yet, since then American military forces have engaged in numerous campaigns throughout the world under the orders of the president. When North Korean forces invaded South Korea in June 1950, Congress was actually prepared to declare war, but President Harry S Truman decided not to ask for congressional action. Instead, Truman asserted the principle that the president and not Congress could decide when and where to deploy America's military might. Truman dispatched American forces to Korea without a congressional declaration, and in the face of the emergency, Congress felt it had to acquiesce. Congress passed a resolution approving the president's actions and this became the pattern for future congressional–executive relations in the military realm. The wars in Vietnam, Bosnia, Afghanistan, and Iraq, as well as a host of lesser conflicts, were all fought without declarations of war.

War Powers Resolution A resolution of Congress that the president can send troops into action abroad only by authorization of Congress or if American troops are already under attack or serious threat.

In 1973, Congress responded to presidential unilateralism by passing the ***War Powers Resolution*** over President Nixon's veto. This resolution reasserted the principle of congressional war power, required the president to inform Congress of any planned military campaign, and stipulated that forces must be withdrawn within sixty days in the absence of a specific congressional authorization for their continued deployment. Presidents, however, have generally ignored the War Powers Resolution, claiming inherent executive power to defend the nation. Thus, for example, in 1989, President George H. W. Bush ordered an invasion of Panama without consulting Congress. In 1990, the same President Bush received congressional authorization to attack Iraq but had already made it clear that he was prepared to go to war with or without congressional assent. In 1995, President Bill Clinton ordered a massive bombing campaign against Serbian forces in the former nation of Yugoslavia without congressional authorization. And, of course, President George W. Bush responded to the 2001 attacks by Islamic terrorists by organizing a major military campaign to overthrow the Taliban regime in Afghanistan, which had sheltered the terrorists. In 2002, Bush ordered a major American campaign against Iraq, which he accused of posing a threat to the United States. U.S. forces overthrew the government of Iraqi dictator Saddam Hussein and occupied the country. In both instances, Congress passed resolutions approving the president's actions, but the president was careful to assert that he did not need congressional authorization. The War Powers Resolution was barely mentioned on Capitol Hill and was ignored by the White House.

Institution Principle

There is separation-of-powers tension between the president and Congress over policy related to war making.

MILITARY SOURCES OF DOMESTIC POWER   The president's military powers extend into the domestic sphere. Article IV, Section 4, provides that the "United States shall [protect] every State . . . against Invasion . . . and . . . domestic Violence," Congress has made this an explicit presidential power through statutes directing the president as commander in chief to discharge these obligations.[4] The Constitution restrains the president's use of domestic force by providing that a state legislature (or governor when the legislature is not in session) must request federal troops before the president can send them into the state to provide public order. Yet this proviso is not absolute. First, presidents are not obligated to deploy national troops merely because the state legislature or governor makes such a request. And, more important, the president may deploy troops in a state or city without a specific request from the state legislature or governor if the president considers it necessary to maintain an essential national service during an emergency, to enforce a federal judicial order, or to protect federally guaranteed civil rights.

One historic example of the unilateral use of presidential emergency power to protect the states against domestic disorder, even when the states do not request it, was the decision by President Dwight Eisenhower in 1957 to send troops into Little Rock, Arkansas, literally against the wishes of the state of Arkansas, to enforce court orders to integrate Little Rock's Central High School. The governor of Arkansas, Orval Faubus, had actually posted the Arkansas National Guard at the entrance of Central High School to prevent the court-ordered admission of nine black students. After an effort to negotiate with Governor Faubus failed, President Eisenhower reluctantly sent a thousand paratroopers to Little Rock; they stood watch while the black students took their places in the all-white classrooms. This case makes quite clear that the president does not have to wait for a request by a state legislature or governor before acting as a domestic commander in chief.[5]

---

[4]These statutes are contained mainly in Title 10 of the United States Code, Sections 331, 332, and 333.
[5]The best study covering all aspects of the domestic use of the military is that of Adam Yarmolinsky, *The Military Establishment* (New York: Harper & Row, 1971). Probably the most famous instance of a president's unilateral use of the power to protect a state "against domestic violence" was in dealing with the Pullman Strike of 1894. The famous Supreme Court case that ensued was *In re Debs*, 158 U.S. 564 (1895).

However, in most instances of domestic disorder—whether from human or from natural causes—presidents tend to exercise unilateral power by declaring a "state of emergency," thereby making available federal grants, insurance, and direct assistance. In 1992, in the aftermath of the devastating riots in Los Angeles and the hurricanes in Florida, American troops were very much in evidence, sent in by the president, but more as Good Samaritans than as military police. Such was also the case after the devastation of 9/11. Most recently, after the destructive hurricanes, Katrina and Rita, that struck the Gulf Coast in the fall of 2005, President Bush declared a state of emergency, using state militias and federal troops for rescue operations, to prevent looting and violence, and to deliver medical, health, and food services. The Coast Guard and the Army Corps of Engineers were especially evident. The Federal Emergency Management Agency (FEMA) coordinated many of these services.

Military emergencies have typically also led to expansion of the domestic powers of the executive branch. This was true during World War I and II and has been during the "war on terrorism" as well. Within a month of the September 11 attacks, the White House had drafted and Congress had enacted the Patriot Act, expanding the power of government agencies to engage in domestic surveillance activities, including electronic surveillance, and restricting judicial review of such efforts. The act also gave the attorney general greater authority to detain and deport aliens suspected of having terrorist affiliations. The following year, Congress created the Department of Homeland Security, combining offices from twenty-two federal agencies into one huge new cabinet department that would be responsible for protecting the nation from attack. The new agency, with a tentative budget of $40 billion, was to include the Coast Guard; Transportation Safety Administration; Federal Emergency Management Agency; Immigration and Naturalization Service; and offices from the departments of Agriculture, Energy, Transportation, Justice, Health and Human Services, Commerce, and the General Services Administration. The actual reorganization plan was drafted by the White House, but Congress weighed in to make certain that the new agency's workers had civil service and union protections.

Judicial   The presidential power to grant reprieves, pardons, and amnesties involves the power of life and death over all individuals who may be a threat to the security of the United States. Presidents may use this power on behalf of a particular individual, as did Gerald Ford when he pardoned Richard Nixon in 1974 "for all offenses against the United States which he . . . has committed or may have committed." Or they may use it on a large scale, as did President Andrew Johnson in 1868, when he gave full amnesty to all southerners who had participated in the "Late Rebellion," and President Jimmy Carter in 1977, when he declared an amnesty for all the draft evaders of the Vietnam War. President Clinton issued a number of controversial pardons during his last weeks in office. This power of life and death over others helped elevate the president to the level of earlier conquerors and kings by establishing him as the person before whom supplicants might come to make their pleas for mercy.

Diplomatic   The president is America's "head of state"—its chief representative in dealings with other nations. As head of state, the president has the power to make treaties for the United States (with the advice and consent of the Senate). When President George Washington received Edmond Genêt ("Citizen Genêt") as the formal emissary of the revolutionary government of France in 1793 and had his cabinet officers and Congress back his decision, he established a greatly expanded interpretation of the power to "receive Ambassadors and other public Ministers," extending it to the power to "recognize" other countries. That power gives the president the almost unconditional authority to review the claims of any new ruling groups to determine whether they indeed control the territory and population of their country, so that they can commit it to treaties and other agreements.

In recent years, presidents have expanded the practice of using executive agreements instead of treaties to establish relations with other countries.[6] An *executive agreement* is exactly like a treaty because it is a contract between two countries, but an executive agreement does not require a two-thirds vote of approval by the Senate. Ordinarily, executive agreements are used to carry out commitments already made in treaties or to arrange for matters well below the level of policy. But when presidents have found it expedient to use an executive agreement in place of a treaty, Congress typically has acquiesced.

executive agreement   An agreement between the president and another country that has the force of a treaty but does not require the Senate's "advice and consent."

Executive Power   The most important basis of the president's power as chief executive is found in Article II, Section 3, which stipulates that the president must see that all the laws are faithfully executed, and Section 2, which provides that the president will appoint, remove, and supervise all executive officers and appoint all federal judges (with Senate approval). The power to appoint the principal executive officers and to require each of them to report to the president on subjects relating to the duties of their departments makes the president the true chief executive officer (CEO) of the nation. In this manner, the Constitution focuses executive power and legal responsibility on the president. The famous sign on President Truman's desk, "The buck stops here," was not merely an assertion of Truman's personal sense of responsibility but was in fact recognition by him of the legal and constitutional responsibility of the president. The president is subject to some limitations, because the appointment of all such officers, including ambassadors, ministers, and federal judges, is subject to majority approval by the Senate. But these appointments are at the discretion of the president, and the loyalty and the responsibility of each appointee are presumed to be directed toward the president.

Another component of the president's power as chief executive is *executive privilege.* Executive privilege is the claim that confidential communications between a president and close advisers should not be revealed without the consent

executive privilege   The claim that confidential communications between a president and close advisers should not be revealed without the consent of the president.

---

[6]In *United States v. Pink*, 315 U.S. 203 (1942), the Supreme Court confirmed that an executive agreement is the legal equivalent of a treaty, despite the absence of Senate approval. This case approved the executive agreement that was used to establish diplomatic relations with the Soviet Union in 1933. An executive agreement, not a treaty, was used in 1940 to exchange "fifty over-age destroyers" for ninety-nine-year leases on some important military bases.

of the president. Presidents have made this claim ever since George Washington refused a request from the House of Representatives to deliver documents concerning negotiations of an important treaty. Washington refused (successfully) on the grounds that, first, the House was not constitutionally part of the treaty-making process and, second, that diplomatic negotiations required secrecy.

Executive privilege became a popular part of the "checks and balances" counterpoint between president and Congress, and presidents have usually had the upper hand when invoking it. The expansion of executive privilege into a claim of "uncontrolled discretion" to refuse Congress's request for information came when President Nixon was beginning to get into political trouble over the Vietnam War in 1971.[7] It was President Nixon's claim to an almost absolute immunity to congressional inquiry that led to a Supreme Court rejection of the doctrine as a constitutional feature of the presidency in *United States v. Nixon.*[8] Although the doctrine continued to be invoked by succeeding presidents, the occasions were usually when presidents had something to hide that was of questionable legality (Iran-Contra) or potentially scandalous (Clinton's alleged land purchases and sexual intrigues). The exercise of presidential power through the executive-privilege doctrine has been all the more frequent in the past twenty years, when we have been living nearly 90 percent of the time under conditions of "divided government," where the party not in control of the White House is in control of one or both of the chambers of Congress.

Rationality Principle

Under conditions of divided government, presidents may rationally want the protection of executive privilege from the partisan scrutiny of elements of Congress, and Congress may well suspect a president of hiding questionable activity behind a veil of executive privilege.

The President's Legislative Power   The president plays a role not only in the administration of government but also in the legislative process. Two constitutional provisions are the primary sources of the president's power in the legislative arena. The first of these is the provision in Article II, Section 3, providing that the president "shall from time to time give to the Congress Information of the State of the Union, and recommend to their Consideration such Measures as he shall judge necessary and expedient." The second of the president's legislative powers is of course the veto power assigned by Article I, Section 7.[9]

Delivering a "State of the Union" address might not appear to be of any great import. It is a mere obligation on the part of the president to make recommendations

Institution Principle

The president's constitutional role provides an opportunity for significant agenda setting by the executive for the Congress.

---

[7]Raoul Berger, *Executive Privilege: A Constitutional Myth* (Cambridge, MA: Harvard University Press), pp. 1–14.

[8]*United States v. Nixon,* 418 U.S. 683 (1974).

[9]There is a third source of presidential power implied in the provision for faithful execution of the laws. This is the president's power to impound funds—that is, to refuse to spend money Congress has appropriated for certain purposes. One author referred to this as a "retroactive veto power" (Robert E. Goosetree, "The Power of the President to Impound Appropriated Funds," *American University Law Review* [January 1962]). This impoundment power was used freely and to considerable effect by many modern presidents, and Congress occasionally delegated such power to the president by statute. But in reaction to the Watergate scandal, Congress adopted the Budget and Impoundment Control Act of 1974, an act designed to circumscribe the president's ability to impound funds by requiring the president to spend all appropriated funds unless both houses of Congress consent to an impoundment within forty-five days of a presidential request. Therefore, since 1974, the use of impoundment has declined significantly. Presidents have had either to bite their tongues and accept unwanted appropriations or to revert to the older and more dependable but politically limited method of vetoing the entire bill.

for Congress's consideration. But as political and social conditions began to favor an increasingly prominent role for presidents, each president, especially since Franklin Delano Roosevelt, began to rely on this provision to become the primary initiator of proposals for legislative action in Congress and the principal source for public awareness of national issues, as well as the most important single individual participant in legislative decisions. Few today doubt that the president and the executive branch together are the primary source for many important congressional actions.[10]

The **veto** is the president's constitutional power to turn down acts of Congress (Figure 6.1). It alone makes the president the most important single legislative leader.[11] No bill vetoed by the president can become law unless both the House and Senate override the veto by a two-thirds vote. In the case of a **pocket veto,** Congress does not even have the option of overriding the veto, but must reintroduce the bill in the next session. A pocket veto can occur when the president is presented with a bill during the last ten days of a legislative session. Usually, if a president does not sign a bill within ten days, it automatically becomes law. But this is true only while Congress is in session. If a president chooses not to sign a bill presented within the last ten days that Congress is in session, then the ten-day limit does not expire until Congress is out of session, and instead of becoming law, the bill is vetoed. In 1996, a new power was added to the president's lineup—the **line-item veto**—giving the president power to strike specific spending items from appropriations bills passed by Congress, unless reenacted by a two-thirds vote of both House and Senate. In 1997, President Clinton used this power eleven times to strike eighty-two items from the federal budget. But in 1998 the Supreme Court ruled that the Constitution does not authorize the line-item veto. Only a constitutional amendment would restore this power to the president.

The Games Presidents Play: The Veto   Use of the veto varies according to the political situation that each president confronts (Figure 6.2). During Bill Clinton's first two years in office, when Democrats controlled both houses of Congress, he vetoed no bills. After the congressional elections of 1994, however, Clinton confronted a Republican-controlled Congress with a definite agenda, and he began to use his veto power more vigorously. Likewise, George W. Bush vetoed no bill during his first term, a period in which his party controlled both

veto   The president's constitutional power to turn down acts of Congress. A presidential veto may be overridden by a two-thirds vote of each house of Congress.

pocket veto   A method by which a president vetoes a bill by taking no action on it when Congress has adjourned.

line-item veto   The power of the executive to veto specific provisions (lines) of a bill passed by the legislature.

 **Institution Principle**

The veto power makes the president the most important single legislative leader.

[10]For a different perspective, see William F. Grover, *The President as Prisoner: A Structural Critique of the Carter and Reagan Years* (Albany: State University of New York Press, 1989).

[11]Although the veto power is the most important legislative resource in the hands of the president, it can often end in frustration, especially when the presidency and Congress are held by opposing parties. George H. W. Bush vetoed forty-six congressional enactments during his four years, and only one was overridden. Ronald Reagan vetoed thirty-nine in his eight years, and nine were overridden. This compares to thirty-one during Jimmy Carter's four years, with two overridden. In 1993–94, Bill Clinton did not veto a single bill, a record unmatched since the days of President Millard Fillmore in 1853; both, of course, were working with Congresses controlled by their own political party. President George W. Bush has not vetoed a single bill in more than four years stretching over both of his terms, thus topping Clinton's record. For more on the veto, see Chapter 5 and Robert J. Spitzer, *The Presidential Veto: Touchstone of the American Presidency* (Albany: State University of New York Press, 1988).

FIGURE 6.1

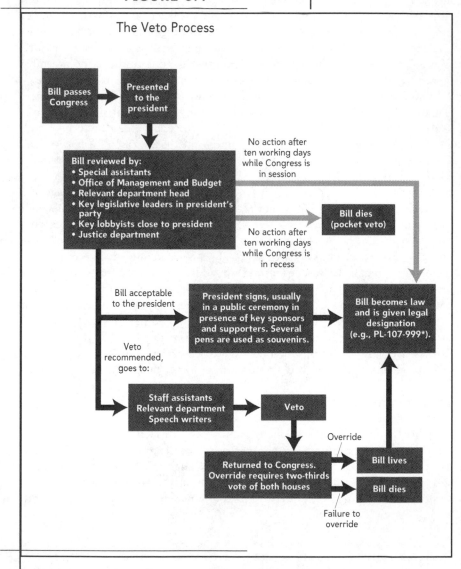

The Veto Process

*PL = public law; 107 = number of Congress (107th was 2000–2001); 999 = number of the law.

FIGURE 6.2

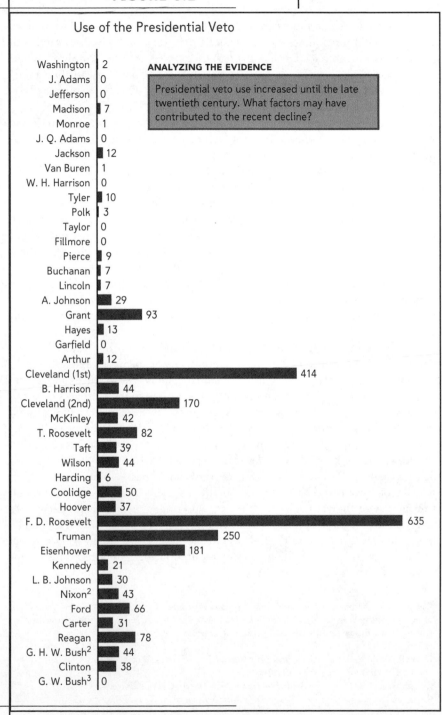

Use of the Presidential Veto

Washington	2
J. Adams	0
Jefferson	0
Madison	7
Monroe	1
J. Q. Adams	0
Jackson	12
Van Buren	1
W. H. Harrison	0
Tyler	10
Polk	3
Taylor	0
Fillmore	0
Pierce	9
Buchanan	7
Lincoln	7
A. Johnson	29
Grant	93
Hayes	13
Garfield	0
Arthur	12
Cleveland (1st)	414
B. Harrison	44
Cleveland (2nd)	170
McKinley	42
T. Roosevelt	82
Taft	39
Wilson	44
Harding	6
Coolidge	50
Hoover	37
F. D. Roosevelt	635
Truman	250
Eisenhower	181
Kennedy	21
L. B. Johnson	30
Nixon[2]	43
Ford	66
Carter	31
Reagan	78
G. H. W. Bush[2]	44
Clinton	38
G. W. Bush[3]	0

ANALYZING THE EVIDENCE

Presidential veto use increased until the late twentieth century. What factors may have contributed to the recent decline?

SOURCES: Gary L. Galemore, *Presidential Vetoes, 1789–Present: A Summary Overview*, Congressional Research Service Report for Congress, 98–148 GOV, 4 November 2000; and "Résumé of Congressional Activity: First Session of the One Hundred Seventh Congress," *Congressional Record Daily Digest*, 29 January 2002, D23.

Collective-Action Principle

Vetoes are usually part of an intricate bargaining process between the president and Congress.

Policy Principle

Because of the president's veto power, Congress will alter the content of a bill to make it more to a president's liking.

Rationality Principle

Bargaining between Congress and the president is strategic, as the president tries to influence the beliefs of the legislature about what they must do to keep him from using his veto power.

houses of Congress. In general, presidents have used the veto to equalize or perhaps upset the balance of power with Congress. While the simple power to reject or accept legislation in its entirety might seem like a crude tool for making sure that legislation adheres to a president's preferences, the politics surrounding the veto are complicated, and it is rare that vetoes are used simply as bullets to kill legislation. Instead, vetoes are usually part of an intricate bargaining process between the president and Congress, involving threats of vetoes, repassing legislation, and re-vetoes.[12]

Although presidents rarely veto legislation, this does not mean vetoes and veto bargaining have an insignificant influence over the policy process. The fact that presidents vetoed only 434 of the 17,000 public bills that Congress sent to them between 1945 and 1992 belies the centrality of the veto to presidential power. Many of these bills were insignificant and not worth the veto effort. Thus it is important to separate "significant" legislation, for which vetoes frequently occur, from insignificant legislation.[13] Vetoes can also be effective—even though they are rarely employed—because of a concept known as "the second face of power"—that is, individuals will condition their actions based on how they think others will respond.[14] With respect to vetoes, this means that members of Congress will alter the content of a bill to make it more to a president's liking to preempt a veto. Thus the veto power can be influential even when the veto pen rests in its inkwell. This the second face of power works to influence the content of legislation.

Rhetoric and reputation take on particular importance when vetoes become part of a bargaining process. The key to veto bargaining is uncertainty. Members of Congress are often unsure about the president's policy preferences and, therefore, don't know which bills the president would be willing to sign. When the policy preferences of the president and Congress diverge, as they typically do under divided government, the president tries to convince Congress that his preferences are more extreme than they really are to get Congress to enact something that is closer to what he really wants. If members of Congress knew the president's preferences ahead of time, they would pass a bill that was closest to what *they* wanted, subject to minimally satisfying the president. Through strategic use of the veto and veto threats, a president tries to shape Congress's beliefs about his policy preferences to gain greater concessions from Congress. Reputation is central to presidential effectiveness.[15] By influencing congressional beliefs, the president is building a policy reputation that will affect future congressional behavior.

[12]Charles M. Cameron, *Veto Bargaining: Presidents and the Politics of Negative Power* (New York: Cambridge University Press, 2000). Also see David W. Rohde and Dennis Simon, "Presidential Vetoes and Congressional Response: A Study of Institutional Conflict," *American Journal of Political Science* 29 (1985): 397–427.

[13]David R. Mayhew, *Divided We Govern: Party Control, Lawmaking, and Investigations, 1946–1990* (New Haven, CT: Yale University Press, 1991).

[14]Jack H. Nagel, *The Descriptive Analysis of Power* (New Haven, CT: Yale University Press, 1975).

[15]Richard E. Neustadt, *Presidential Power: The Politics of Leadership* (New York: Wiley, 1960).

The back-and-forth negotiating between the president and Congress was no more evident than in the events surrounding the creation of a cabinet-level Department of Homeland Security in 2002–03. As part of his decisive leadership in the wake of the terrorist attacks of September 11, 2001, President George W. Bush established a Department of Homeland Security in the Executive Office of the President. The president believed that his "terrorism czar," Tom Ridge, had ample authority to coordinate national policy in the fight against terrorism. Capitol Hill critics felt that a cabinet-level department should be created, partly because they felt that Ridge lacked the necessary resources and authority to do the job but also because they thought it would permit the House and Senate a more explicit role (through the appropriations process). Ultimately, President Bush relented, but the conflict between president and Congress did not end there as the executive and legislature negotiated, threatened, promised, and eventually settled on the details of this department. President Bush had veto power as his "club behind the door," while Senate Democrats (Bush's main opponents), even though in the minority, could threaten delay through dilatory tactics and the filibuster (see Chapter 5). Both sides "went public" in an effort to sway public opinion and brandished "blame" in attempts to weaken the credibility of the other side. Such public, high-visibility squabbling is unusual, but on matters of salient national policy that pits the two parties against one another, it occasionally emerges, giving us a picture of the full array of powers possessed by executive and legislature.

What about the relationship between mass public support for the president and the use of the veto? At least for the modern presidency, a crucial resource for the president in negotiating with Congress has been his public approval as measured by opinion polls.[16] In some situations, members of Congress pass a bill, not because they want to change policy but because they want to force the president to veto a popular bill that he disagrees with in order to hurt his approval ratings.[17] The key is that the public, uncertain of the president's policy preferences, uses information conveyed by vetoes to reassess what they know about his preferences. As a result, vetoes may come at a price to the president. A president must weigh the advantages of vetoing or threatening to do so—to gain concessions from Congress—against the hit he may take in his popularity. The president may be reluctant to use the veto or the threat of a veto to gain concessions from Congress if such vetoes will hurt him in the polls. But in some cases, the president will take a hit in his approval ratings if the bill is drastically inconsistent with his policies.

Legislative Initiative   Although not explicitly stated, the Constitution provides the president with the power of *legislative initiative.* To "initiate" means to originate, and in government that can mean power. The framers of the Constitution

 Rationality Principle

A president must weigh the advantages of vetoing legislation against the possible drop in his public approval.

legislative initiative   The president's inherent power to bring a legislative agenda before Congress.

[16]Theodore J. Lowi, *The Personal President: Power Invested, Promise Unfulfilled* (Ithaca, N.Y.: Cornell University Press, 1985).

[17]Timothy Groseclose and Nolan McCarty, "Presidential Vetoes: Bargaining, Blame-Game, and Gridlock," *American Journal of Political Science* 45 (2001): 100–19.

A Veto-less Presidency?

Inspector Gregory: "Is there any other point to which you would wish to draw my attention?"

Holmes: "To the curious incident of the dog in the night-time."

"The dog did nothing in the night-time."

"That was the curious incident," remarked Sherlock Holmes.

Arthur Conan Doyle, "The Adventure of Silver Blaze"

We know a lot about why presidents veto legislation. Vetoes are not simply weapons wielded by presidents to kill legislation they do not like. Vetoes—and more often the threat of a veto—is part of a complicated policy-making ballet.

But do we know why presidents *do not* cast vetoes? Like the dog that did not bark, sometimes the event that did not happen, or the bill that did not pass, is as revealing as those that did happen. The principles of politics can help us understand why presidents cast few vetoes and what this tells us about the strategic aspects of their administrations.

Only seven presidents never vetoed a bill: John Adams, Thomas Jefferson, John Quincy Adams, William Henry Harrison, Zachary Taylor, Millard Fillmore, and James A. Garfield. All these presidents were in office before the Civil War, when far fewer bills were introduced in Congress and the federal government was much smaller.

George W. Bush is poised to be the eighth president on this list. Why? Like the dog that does not bark, what does Bush's *non*-use of the veto tell us about his presidency?

The first reason that Bush has not had to veto much legislation is that he—and the country—have been focused on international issues. Foreign policy is an area where Congress has historically deferred to the executive branch, and this tendency became even more pronounced during and after World War II, since the stakes of international conflict were so much higher. Institutional rules place much of foreign policy decision-making authority in the president's hands. Thus, the policy principle helps us understand why Bush does not employ the veto.

The second reason that Bush has not had to veto bills is that he has spent much of his presidency with a unified Republican Congress (the Republicans have controlled the House of Representatives since the 1994 election and have held the Senate since the 2002 election). And after the terrorist attacks of September 11, Bush enjoyed widespread public support, making it even less likely that members of Congress would propose legislation that he disagreed with. This translated into a high level of policy agreement between the Bush administration and Congress. The collective-action principle helps us understand Bush's non-use of the veto. Bush and his congressional allies, largely in agreement over policy issues, find it easy to cooperate.

Contrast Bush's experience with that of Democratic presidents over the past fifty years. Lyndon Baines Johnson, in office from 1963 to 1968, enjoyed an overwhelming Democratic advantage in Congress, yet the Democratic Party in this period was so deeply

History Principle

Early presidents could not veto much legislation simply because the federal government was much smaller prior to the Civil War.

Policy Principle

Bush's non-use of the veto is explained by the country's focus on foreign affairs and the tendency of Congress to defer to the president on those issues.

Collective-Action Principle

When the president and Congress agree on policy grounds, they find it far easier to co-operate.

divided over race and foreign policy that many Southern Democrats voted more often with Republicans than with their own party.[1] Not surprisingly, Democratic presidents in the last half of the twentieth century were vigorous users of the veto even when their own party controlled Congress.

We have additional evidence that Bush has found it comparatively easy to work with Congress. Not only has Bush vetoed no bills, but he also lags in issuing executive orders.[2] In the post–World War II era, many scholars argue that presidents have come to rely more and more on executive orders as a way to bypass Congress. Executive orders have become a critical way for a president to assert authority.[3]

In his first four years, President Bush issued 171 executive orders, fewer than any of his recent predecessors except his own father and far fewer than the historic high-points reached by Roosevelt (3,728 executive orders during his more than three terms of office) or Hoover (1,011 executive orders during his single term).[4]

Like the dog that did not bark, Bush's neglect of the veto and relatively low use of executive orders in his first term tell us volumes about the political environment in which he governs. Bush focuses on foreign affairs, an area where the president has wide latitude. And since September 11, 2001, Bush has enjoyed fairly widespread public support for his policies.

But what of Bush's second term? A major natural disaster—Hurricane Katrina—has forced the president to refocus his energies in the domestic arena. Lingering public unhappiness with the war in Iraq has undercut his claim to foreign policy success. The principles of politics lead us to predict that Bush, though he governs in an era of unified Republican control of Congress, will face a less cooperative Congress and will more frequently use executive orders and vetoes in his second term.

 History Principle

Executive orders are one of many ways that the presidency has grown stronger relative to Congress since World War II.

[1]Nolan McCarty, Keith Poole, and Howard Rosenthal, *Polarized America: The Dance of Ideology and Unequal Riches* (Boston: MIT Press, 2006).

[2]An executive order is a president's or governor's ("executive's") declaration that has force of law. It is based on existing law or statute and requires no action from the legislature.

[3]Kenneth Mayer, *With the Stroke of a Pen: Executive Orders and Presidential Power* (Princeton: Princeton University Press, 2002).

[4]Information on executive orders can be found in the National Archives: www.archives.gov/federal-register/executive-orders/disposition.html.

clearly saw legislative initiative as one of the keys to executive power. Initiative obviously implies the ability to formulate proposals for important policies, and the president, as an individual with a great deal of staff assistance, is able to initiate decisive action more frequently than Congress, with its large assemblies that have to deliberate and debate before taking action. With some important exceptions, Congress banks on the president to set the agenda of public policy. And quite clearly, there is power in initiative; there is power in being able to set the terms of discourse in the making of public policy.

For example, during the weeks immediately following September 11, Bush took many presidential initiatives to Congress, and each was given almost unanimous support—from commitments to pursue al Qaeda to the removal of the Taliban, the reconstitution of the Afghanistan regime, all the way to almost unlimited approval for mobilization of both military power and power over the regulation of American civil liberties. After winning reelection in 2004, Bush sought to push forward his legislative domestic agenda, including changes in the nation's Social Security system and comprehensive tax reform. Bush also called on Congress to act quickly to limit lawsuit awards against doctors, and to push for tougher educational standards for high schools. Bush said, "I earned capital in this campaign, political capital, and now I intend to spend it. . . . There is a feeling that the people have spoken and embraced your point of view, and that's what I intend to tell the Congress."[18] The first year of Bush's second term, however, was difficult. Growing problems (and casualties) in Iraq, administrative scandals, and charges of incompetence in responding to the aftermath of Hurricanes Katrina and Rita plagued Bush during 2005. One could almost feel a shift in momentum, with Congress seizing back some of the initiative in dealing with the president. Presidential bargaining advantages ebb and flow—as presidential popularity ebbed in the polls in 2005, so too did Bush's agenda power.

The president's initiative does not end with policy making involving Congress and the making of laws in the ordinary sense of the term. The president has still another legislative role (in all but name) within the executive branch. This is designated as the power to issue *executive orders.* The executive order is first and foremost simply a normal tool of management, a power possessed by virtually any CEO to make "company policy"—rules setting procedures, etiquette, chains of command, functional responsibilities, and so on. But evolving out of this normal management practice is a recognized presidential power to promulgate rules that have the effect and the formal status of legislation. Most of the executive orders of the president provide for the reorganization of structures and procedures or otherwise direct the affairs of the executive branch—either to be applied across the board to all agencies or applied in some important respect to a single agency or department.

As the size and scope of the executive branch grew throughout the twentieth century, so did the president's use of executive orders. Presidential executive orders give the president the capacity to make policy on his own, but they do not abrogate the legislature's authority to legislate. So there are limits. In some Latin American democracies, on the other hand, presidents have the power of *executive decree*, effectively allowing them to govern without any participation of the legislature and essentially without constitutional limit. American presidential authority does not run this far. Nevertheless, the power to issue executive orders

executive orders
Rules or regulations issued by the president that have the effect and formal status of legislation.

---

[18]Quoted in Richard W. Stevenson, "Focus on Social Security and the Tax Code," *New York Times,* 5 November 2004, p. A1.

does illustrate that, although reputation and persuasion are typically required in presidential policy making, the practice of executive order, within limits, allows a president to govern without the necessity to persuade.[19]

One of the most important examples is Executive Order No. 8248, September 8, 1939, establishing the divisions of the Executive Office of the President. Another one of equal importance is President Nixon's executive order establishing the Environmental Protection Agency in 1970–71, which included establishment of the Environmental Impact Statement. President Reagan's Executive Order No. 12291 of 1981 provided a regulatory reform process that was responsible for more genuine deregulation in the past twenty years than was accomplished by any acts of congressional legislation. President Clinton's most important policy toward gays and gay rights in the military took the form of an executive order referred to as "Don't ask, don't tell."

This legislative or policy leadership role of the presidency is an institutionalized feature of the office that exists independent of the occupant of the office. That is to say, anyone duly elected president would possess these powers regardless of his or her individual energy or leadership characteristics.[20]

Delegated Powers

Many of the powers exercised by the president and the executive branch are not found in the Constitution but are the products of congressional statutes and resolutions. Over the past three-quarters of a century, Congress has voluntarily delegated a great deal of its own legislative authority to the executive branch. To some extent, this delegation of power has been an almost inescapable consequence of the expansion of government activity in the United States since the New Deal. Given the vast range of the federal government's responsibilities, Congress cannot execute and administer all the programs it creates and the laws it enacts. Inevitably, Congress must turn to the hundreds of departments and agencies in the executive branch or, when necessary, create new agencies to implement its goals. Thus, for example, in 2002, when Congress sought to protect America from terrorist attacks, it established a Department of Homeland Security and gave it broad powers in the realms of law enforcement, public health, and immigration. Similarly, in 1970, when Congress enacted legislation designed to improve the nation's air and water quality, it assigned the task of implementing its goals to a new Environmental Protection Agency (EPA) created by an executive order issued by President Nixon. Congress gave the EPA substantial power to set and enforce air and water quality standards.

[19]This point is developed both in Kenneth R. Mayer, *With the Stroke of a Pen: Executive Orders and Presidential Power* (Princeton, NJ: Princeton University Press, 2001), and in William G. Howell, *Power without Persuasion: The Politics of Direct Presidential Action* (Princeton, NJ: Princeton University Press, 2003).

[20]For a good review of President Clinton's legislative leadership in the first session of his last Congress, see *Congressional Quarterly Weekly*, 13 November 1999, especially the cover story by Andrew Taylor, "Clinton Gives Republicans a Gentler Year-End Beating," pp. 2698–700.

As they implement congressional legislation, federal agencies collectively develop thousands of rules and regulations and issue thousands of orders and findings every year. Agencies interpret Congress's intent; promulgate rules aimed at implementing that intent; and issue orders to individuals, firms, and organizations throughout the nation designed to impel them to conform to the law. When it establishes an agency, Congress sometimes grants it only limited discretionary authority, providing very specific guidelines and standards that must be followed by the administrators charged with the program's implementation. Take the Internal Revenue Service (IRS), for example. Most Americans view the IRS as a powerful agency whose dictates can have an immediate and sometimes unpleasant effect on their lives. Yet congressional tax legislation is very specific and detailed and leaves little to the discretion of IRS administrators.[21] The agency certainly develops numerous rules and procedures to enhance tax collection. It is Congress, however, that establishes the structure of tax liabilities, tax exemptions, and tax deductions that determine each taxpayer's burdens and responsibilities.

In most instances, however, congressional legislation is not very detailed. Often, Congress defines a broad goal or objective and delegates enormous discretionary power to administrators to determine how that goal is to be achieved. For example, the 1970 act creating the Occupational Safety and Health Administration (OSHA) states, as Congress's purpose, "to assure so far as is possible every working man and woman in the nation safe and healthful working conditions." The act, however, neither defines such conditions nor suggests how they might be achieved.[22] The result is that agency administrators have enormous discretionary power to draft rules and regulations that have the effect of law. Indeed, the courts treat these administrative rules like congressional statutes. For all intents and purposes, when Congress creates an agency like OSHA or the EPA, giving it broad mandate to achieve some desirable outcome, it transfers its own legislative power to the executive branch.

In the nineteenth and early twentieth centuries, Congress typically wrote laws that provided fairly clear principles and standards to guide executive implementation. For example, the 1923 tariff act empowered the president to increase or decrease duties on certain manufactured goods to reduce the difference in costs between domestically produced products and those manufactured abroad. The act authorized the president to make the final determination, but his discretionary authority was quite constrained. The statute listed the criteria the president was to consider, fixed the permissible range of tariff changes, and outlined the procedures to be used to calculate the cost differences between foreign and domestic goods. When an importer challenged a particular executive decision as an abuse of delegated power, the Supreme Court had no difficulty finding that the president was merely acting in accordance with Congress's directives.[23]

At least since the New Deal, however, Congress has tended to give executive agencies broad mandates and to draft legislation that offers few clear standards or

---

[21]Kenneth F. Warren, *Administrative Law*, 3rd ed. (Upper Saddle River, NJ: Prentice Hall, 1996), p. 250.
[22]Theodore J. Lowi, *The End of Liberalism*, 2nd ed. (New York: Norton, 1979), pp. 117–18.
[23]*J. W. Hampton & Co. v. U.S.*, 276 U.S. 394 (1928).

guidelines for implementation by the executive. For example, the 1933 National In-dustrial Recovery Act gave the president the authority to set rules to bring about *fair competition* in key sectors of the economy without ever defining what the term meant or how it was to be achieved.[24] Similarly, the 1938 Agricultural Adjustment Act, which led to a system of commodity price supports and agricultural produc-tion restrictions, authorized the secretary of agriculture to make agricultural mar-keting "orderly" without offering any guidance regarding the commodities to be affected, how markets were to be organized, or how prices should be determined. All these decisions were left to the discretion of the secretary and his or her agents.[25] This pattern of broad delegation became typical in the ensuing decades. The 1972 Consumer Product Safety Act, for example, authorizes the Consumer Product Safety Commission to reduce unreasonable risk of injury from household products but offers no suggestions to guide the commission's determination of what constitutes reasonable and unreasonable risks or how these are to be reduced.[26]

This shift from the nineteenth-century pattern of relatively well defined con-gressional guidelines to administrators to the more contemporary pattern of broad delegations of congressional power to the executive branch is, to be sure, partially a consequence of the great scope and complexity of the tasks that America's contemporary government has undertaken. During much of the nine-teenth century, the federal government had relatively few domestic responsibili-ties and Congress could pay close attention to details. Today, the operation of an enormous executive establishment and literally thousands of programs under varied and changing circumstances requires that administrators be allowed some considerable measure of discretion to carry out their jobs. Nevertheless, the end result is to shift power from Congress to the executive branch.

THE RISE OF PRESIDENTIAL GOVERNMENT

Most of the real influence of the modern presidency derives from the powers granted by the Constitution and the laws made by Congress. Thus any person properly elected and sworn in as president will possess almost all of the power held by the strongest presidents in American history. Even when they are "lame ducks," presidents still possess all the power of the office. For example, in the weeks after the election of 2000, lame-duck President Clinton took the opportu-nity to become the first U.S. president to visit a united Vietnam and to continue major diplomatic efforts to bring peace to the Middle East.

This case illustrates an extremely important fact about the presidency: *the popular base of the presidency is important less because it gives the president power*

[24]48 Stat. 200.

[25]David Schoenbrod, *Power without Responsibility: How Congress Abuses the People through Delegation* (New Haven, CT: Yale University Press, 1993), pp. 49–50.

[26]Lowi, *The End of Liberalism*, p. 117.

than because it gives him consent to use all the powers already vested by the Consti-tution in the office. Anyone installed in the office could exercise most of its pow-ers. But what variables account for a president's success in exercising these powers? Why are some presidents considered to be great successes and others colossal failures? This relates broadly to the very concept of presidential power. Is it a reflection of the attributes of the person or is it more characteristic of the political situations that a president encounters? The personal view of presiden-tial power dominated political scientists' view for several decades,[27] but recent scholars have argued that presidential power should be analyzed in terms of the strategic interactions that a president has with other political actors. The veto, which we reviewed earlier in this chapter, is one example of this sort of strategic interaction, but there are many other "games" that presidents play: the Supreme Court–nomination and treaty-ratification games with the Senate, the executive-order game, the agency-supervision-and-management game with the executive branch. As the political scientist Charles M. Cameron has argued, *"Understand-ing the presidency means understanding these games."*[28] Success in these "games" translates into presidential power.

We must not forget, however, the tremendous resources that a president can rely on in his strategic interactions with others. Remember that the presidency is a democratic institution with a national constituency. Its broad popular base is a strategic presidential resource that can be deployed in the various bargaining games just discussed. For example, political scientist Samuel Kernell suggests that presi-dents may rally public opinion and put pressure on Congress by "going public."[29] With the occasional exception, however, it took more than a century, perhaps as much as a century and a half, before presidents came to be seen as consequential players in these strategic encounters. A bit of historical review will be helpful in un-derstanding how the presidency has risen to its current level of influence.

Collective-Action Principle

The president can use public approval as a strategic resource.

The Legislative Epoch, 1800–1933

In 1885, a then-obscure political-science professor named Woodrow Wilson titled his general textbook *Congressional Government* because American government was just that, "congressional government." There is ample evidence that Wilson's description of the national government was consistent not only with nineteenth-century reality but also with the intentions of the framers. Within the system of three separate and competing powers, the clear intent of the Constitution was for *legislative supremacy.*

The strongest evidence of original intent is the fact that the powers of the national government were not placed in a separate article of the Constitution, but were in-stead listed in Article I, the legislative article. Madison had laid it out explicitly in *The*

---

[27]Neustadt, *Presidential Power.*

[28]Charles M. Cameron, "Bargaining and Presidential Power," in *Presidential Power: Forging the Presidency for the Twenty-first Century,* ed. Robert Y. Shapiro, Martha Joynt Kumar, and Lawrence R. Jacobs (New York: Columbia University Press, 2000), p. 47. [Emphasis in original.]

[29]Samuel Kernell, *Going Public: New Strategies of Presidential Leadership,* 3rd ed. (Washington, DC: Con-gressional Quarterly Press, 1998).

Federalist, No. 51: "In republican government, the legislative authority necessarily predominates." President Washington echoed this in his first inaugural address in 1789:

> By the article establishing the Executive Department, it is made the duty of the President "to recommend to your consideration, such measures as he shall judge necessary and expedient." The circumstances under which I now meet you, will acquit me from entering into that subject, farther than to refer to the Great Constitutional Charter . . . which, in defining your powers, designates the objects to which your attention is to be given. It will be more consistent with those circumstances . . . to substitute, in place of a recommendation of particular measures, the tribute that is due . . . the characters selected to devise and adopt them.

By President Jefferson's second term (1805), the executive branch was beginning to play the secondary role anticipated by the Constitution. The quality of presidential performance and then of presidential personality and character declined accordingly. The president during this era was seen by some observers as little more than America's "chief clerk." It was said of President James Madison, who had been principal author of the Constitution, that he knew everything about government except how to govern. Indeed, after Jefferson and until the beginning of the twentieth century, most historians agree that Presidents Jackson and Lincoln were the only exceptions to what had been a succession of weak presidents. And those two exceptions can be explained. Jackson was a war hero and founder of the Democratic party. Lincoln was also a founder of his party, the Republican party, and although not a war hero, he was a wartime president who exercised the extraordinary powers that are available to any president during war because during war the Constitution is put on hold. Both Jackson and Lincoln are considered great presidents because they used their great power wisely. But it is important in the history of the presidency that neither of these great presidents left their own powers as a new institutional legacy to their successors. That is to say, once Jackson and Lincoln left office, the presidency went back to the subordinate role that it played during the nineteenth century.

One of the reasons that so few great men became presidents in the nineteenth century is that there was only occasional room for greatness in such a weak office.[30] As Chapter 3 indicated, the national government of that period was not a particularly powerful entity. Moreover, most of the policies adopted by the national government were designed mainly to promote the expansion of commerce. These could be directed and administered by the congressional committees and political parties without much reliance on an executive bureaucracy.

Another reason for the weak presidency of the nineteenth century is that during this period the presidency was not closely linked to major national political and social forces. Indeed, there were few important *national* political or social

---

[30]For related appraisals, see Jeffrey Tulis, *The Rhetorical Presidency* (Princeton, NJ: Princeton University Press, 1987); Stephen Skowronek, *The Politics Presidents Make: Leadership from John Adams to George Bush* (Cambridge, MA: Harvard University Press, 1993); and Robert J. Spitzer, *President and Congress: Executive Hegemony at the Crossroads of American Government* (Philadelphia: Temple University Press, 1993).

forces to which presidents could have linked themselves even if they had wanted to. Federalism had taken very good care of this by fragmenting political interests and diverting the energies of interest groups toward the state and local levels of government, where most key decisions were being made.

As discussed earlier in the chapter, the presidency was strengthened in the 1830s when the national convention system of nominating presidential candidates was introduced. However, this additional independence did not change the presidency into the office we see today because the parties disappeared back into their states and Congress once the national election was over. In addition, as the national government grew, Congress kept tight rein on the president's power. For example, when Congress began to make its first efforts to exert power over the economy (beginning in 1887 with the adoption of the Interstate Commerce Act and in 1890 with the adoption of the Sherman Antitrust Act), it sought to keep this power away from the president and the executive branch by placing these new regulatory policies in "independent regulatory commissions" responsible to Congress rather than to the president (see also Chapter 7).

As discussed earlier, the key moment in the history of American national government came during Franklin Delano Roosevelt's administration. The New Deal was a response to political forces that had been gathering national strength and focus for fifty years. What is remarkable is not that they gathered but that they were so long gaining influence in Washington—and even then it took the Great Depression, a popular new president, and substantial working majorities for his party in both chambers of Congress to bring about a new shape to the national government. The New Deal combined the personal brilliance and persuasiveness of a new president, economic conditions that generated an agenda of political action and unified partisan government, and a bargaining circumstance that put a premium on coordination among kindred spirits in the Capitol and White House. Roosevelt seized the opportunity, and the shape of American government has never been the same since.

The New Deal and the Presidency

The "First Hundred Days" of the Roosevelt administration in 1933 had no parallel in U.S. history. But this period was only the beginning. The policies proposed by President Roosevelt and adopted by Congress during the first thousand days of his administration so changed the size and character of the national government that they constitute a moment in American history equivalent to the founding or to the Civil War. The president's constitutional obligation to see "that the laws be faithfully executed" became, during Roosevelt's presidency, virtually a responsibility to shape the laws before executing them.

New Programs Expand the Role of National Government Many of the New Deal programs were extensions of the traditional national-government approach, which was described in Chapter 3 (see especially Table 3.1). But the New Deal went well beyond the traditional approach, adopting types of policies never before tried on a large scale by the national government; it began intervening into economic life in ways that had hitherto been reserved to the states. In other words, the national government discovered that it, too, had "police power" and could directly regulate individuals as well as provide roads and other services.

The new programs were such dramatic departures from the traditional policies of the national government that their constitutionality was in doubt. The Supreme Court in fact declared several of them unconstitutional, mainly on the grounds that in regulating the conduct of individuals or their employers, the national government was reaching beyond "*inter*state" into "*intra*state," essentially local, matters. Most of the New Deal remained in constitutional limbo until 1937, five years after Roosevelt was first elected and one year after his landslide 1936 re-election.

The turning point came with *National Labor Relations Board v. Jones & Laughlin Steel Corporation*. At issue was the National Labor Relations Act, or Wagner Act, which prohibited corporations from interfering with the efforts of employees to organize into unions, to bargain collectively over wages and working conditions, and, under certain conditions, to go on strike and engage in picketing. The newly formed National Labor Relations Board (NLRB) had ordered Jones & Laughlin to reinstate workers fired because of their union activities. The appeal reached the Supreme Court because Jones & Laughlin had made a constitutional issue over the fact that its manufacturing activities were local and, therefore, beyond the national government's reach. The Supreme Court rejected this argument with the response that a big company with subsidiaries and suppliers in many states was innately in interstate commerce:

> When industries organize themselves on a national scale, making their relation to interstate commerce the dominant factor in their activities, how can it be maintained that their industrial labor relations constitute a forbidden field into which Congress may not enter when it is necessary to protect interstate commerce from the paralyzing consequences of industrial war?[31]

Since the end of the New Deal, the Supreme Court has never again seriously questioned the constitutionality of an important act of Congress broadly authorizing the executive branch to intervene into the economy or society.[32]

---

[31] *National Labor Relations Board v. Jones & Laughlin Steel Corporation*, 301 U.S. 1 (1937). Congress had attempted to regulate the economy before 1933, as with the Interstate Commerce Act and Sherman Antitrust Act of the late nineteenth century and with the Federal Trade Act and the Federal Reserve in the Wilson period. But these were rare attempts, and each was restricted very carefully to a narrow and acceptable definition of "interstate commerce." The big break did not come until after 1933.

[32] Some will argue that there are exceptions to this statement. One was the 1976 case declaring unconstitutional Congress's effort to supply national minimum wage standards to state and local government employees (*National League of Cities v. Usery*, 426 U.S. 833 [1976]). But the Court reversed itself on this nine years later, in 1985 (*Garcia v. San Antonio Metropolitan Transit Authority*, 469 U.S. 528 [1985]). Another was the 1986 case declaring unconstitutional the part of the Gramm-Rudman law authorizing the comptroller general to make "across the board" budget cuts when total appropriations exceeded legally established ceilings (*Bowsher v. Synar*, 478 U.S. 714 [1986]). In 1999, executive authority was compromised somewhat by the Court's decision to question the Federal Communication Commission's authority to supervise telephone deregulation under the Telecommunications Act of 1996. But cases such as these are few and far between, and they touch on only part of a law, not the constitutionality of an entire program.

History Principle

By the end of the New Deal, the practice of significant management of the economy by the executive, as broadly defined by Congress, was firmly established.

History Principle

The New Deal's expanded role for the national government enhanced presidential power.

Delegation of Power The most important constitutional effect of Congress's actions and the Supreme Court's approval of those actions during the New Deal was the enhancement of *presidential power*. Most major acts of Congress in this period involved significant exercises of control over the economy. But few programs specified the actual controls to be used. Instead, Congress authorized the president or, in some cases, a new agency to determine what the controls would be. Some of the new agencies were independent commissions responsible to Congress. But most of the new agencies and programs of the New Deal were placed in the executive branch directly under presidential authority.

Technically, this form of congressional act, as we noted earlier, is the "delegation of power." In theory, the delegation of power works as follows: (1) Congress recognizes a problem, (2) Congress acknowledges that it has neither the time nor expertise to deal with the problem, and (3) Congress therefore sets the basic policies and then delegates to an agency the power to "fill in the details." But, in practice, Congress was delegating not merely the power to "fill in the details" but actual and real *policy-making powers*—that is, real legislative powers—to the executive branch.

No modern government can avoid the delegation of significant legislative powers to the executive branch. But the fact remains that this delegation produced a fundamental shift in the American constitutional framework. During the 1930s, the growth of the national government through acts delegating legislative power tilted the American national structure away from a Congress-centered government toward a president-centered government.[33] Make no mistake, Congress continues to be the constitutional source of policy. Legislative supremacy remains a constitutional fact of life, even at the beginning of the twenty-first century, because delegations are *contingent*. And not all delegations are the same. A Democratic Congress, for example, is unwilling to empower a Republican president and vice versa; unified governments are more likely to engage in broad delegation than divided governments are.[34] In short, Congress can rescind these delegations of power, restrict them with later amendments, and oversee the exercise of delegated power through congressional hearings, oversight agencies, budget controls, and other administrative tools. However, it is fair to say that presidential government has become an administrative fact of life as government-by-delegation has expanded greatly over the past hundred years. The world of Woodrow Wilson's *Congressional Government* is forever changed. But Congress has many "clubs behind its

---

[33]The Supreme Court did in fact *dis*approve broad delegations of legislative power by declaring the National Industrial Recovery Act of 1933 unconstitutional on the grounds that Congress did not accompany the broad delegations with sufficient standards or guidelines for presidential discretion (*Panama Refining Co. v. Ryan*, 293 U.S. 388 [1935], and *Schechter Poultry Corp. v. United States*, 295 U.S. 495 [1935]). The Supreme Court has never reversed those two decisions, but it has also never really followed them. Thus broad delegations of legislative power from Congress to the executive branch can be presumed to be constitutional. See also Sotirios A. Barber, *The Constitution and the Delegation of Congressional Power* (Chicago: University of Chicago Press, 1975).

[34]David Epstein and Sharyn O'Halloran, *Delegating Powers: A Transaction Cost Politics Approach to Policy Making under Separate Powers* (New York: Cambridge University Press, 1999).

door" with which to influence the manner in which the executive branch exercises its newly won power.

PRESIDENTIAL GOVERNMENT

The locus of policy decision making shifted to the executive branch because, as we just noted, Congress made delegations of authority to the president. But this should not be construed as Congress having abdicated its constitutional position in policy making. Delegation is not abdication, and Congress retained many strings by which to oversee and regulate the executive's use of delegated authority.[35] Congress delegated to the executive for instrumental reasons, much as a principal delegates to an agent. An expanded agenda of political demands, necessitated first by economic crisis—the Great Depression—but also by an accumulation of the effects of nearly a century's worth of industrialization, urbanization, and greater integration into the world economy, confronted the national government, forcing Congress's hand. The legislature itself was limited in its ability to expand its own capacity to undertake these growing responsibilities, so delegation proved a natural administrative strategy. If you can't do it yourself, then hire agents to do it! The president, executive-branch bureaus, and the independent regulatory commissions constituted precisely this army of agents. They were (at least in part) *congressional* agents, however, because it was delegation with a catch—oversight, regulation, amendment, budgetary control, etc., from the legislative branch. Nevertheless, these delegations certainly gave a far greater role to the president, empowering this "agent" to initiate in his own right.

In the case of Franklin D. Roosevelt, it is especially appropriate to refer to his New Deal as launching an era of "presidential government." Congress certainly retained many "clubs behind its door" with which to threaten, cajole, encourage, and persuade its executive agent to do its bidding. But presidents in general, and Roosevelt in particular, are not *only* agents of the Congress and not *only* dependent on Congress for resources and authority. They are also agents of national constituencies before whom they are eager to demonstrate their capacity for leadership in executing constituency policy agendas.[36]

Likewise, congressional delegations of power are not the only resources available to a president. Presidents have at their disposal a variety of other formal and informal resources that have important implications for their ability to govern. Indeed, without these other resources, presidents would lack the ability—the tools of management and public mobilization—to make much use of the power

Rationality Principle

Congress delegates more power to the president as more demands are made on its agenda.

Institution Principle

Congress delegates authority to the president but also maintains the means to influence how the executive branch exercises that power.

---

[35]D. Roderick Kiewiet and Mathew D. McCubbins, *The Logic of Delegation: Congressional Parties and the Appropriations Process* (Chicago: University of Chicago Press, 1991).

[36]As the political scientist Terry Moe writes, "This is the rational basis for the institutional presidency. Throughout [the twentieth] century, presidents have struggled to provide themselves with a structural capacity for leadership by building institutions of their own." See Terry Moe, "Presidents, Institutions, and Theory," in *Researching the Presidency: Vital Questions, New Approaches*, ed. George C. Edwards III, John H. Kessel, and Bert A. Rockman (Pittsburgh: University of Pittsburgh Press, 1993), p. 367.

and responsibility given to them by Congress. Let us first consider the president's formal or official resources and then turn to the more informal resources that affect a president's capacity to govern, in particular the president's base of popular support.

What Are the Formal Resources of Presidential Power?

The Cabinet In the American system of government, the *cabinet* is the traditional but informal designation for the heads of all the major federal government departments (Figure 6.3). The cabinet has no constitutional status. Unlike in England and many other parliamentary countries, where the cabinet *is* the government, the American cabinet is not a collective body. It meets but makes no decisions as a group. Each appointment must be approved by the Senate, but cabinet members are not responsible to the Senate or to Congress at large. Cabinet appointments help build party and popular support, but the cabinet is not a party organ. The cabinet is made up of directors, but is not a true board of directors.

Aware of this fact, the president tends to develop a burning impatience with and a mild distrust of cabinet members; to make the cabinet a rubber stamp for actions already decided on; and to demand results, or the appearance of results, more immediately and more frequently than most department heads can provide. Because cabinet appointees generally have not shared political careers with the president or with each other, and because they may meet each other literally for the first time after their selection, the formation of an effective governing group out of this motley collection of appointments is unlikely. Although President Clinton's insistence on a cabinet diverse enough to resemble American society could be considered an act of political wisdom, it virtually guaranteed that few of his appointees had ever spent much time working together or even knew the policy positions or beliefs of the other appointees.[37]

Some presidents have relied more heavily on an "inner cabinet," the *National Security Council (NSC).* The NSC, established by law in 1947, is composed of the president, the vice president, the secretaries of state, defense, and the treasury, the attorney general, and other officials invited by the president. It has its own staff of foreign-policy specialists run by the special assistant to the president for national security affairs. For these highest appointments, presidents turn to people from outside Washington, usually longtime associates. George W. Bush's "inner cabinet" is composed largely of former and proven senior staffers and cabinet members of former Republican administrations, most particularly Vice President Dick Cheney, Defense Secretary Donald Rumsfeld, Secretary of State Condoleezza Rice, National Security Advisor Stephen Hadley, and Attorney General Alberto Gonzales.

Presidents have obviously been uneven and unpredictable in their reliance on the NSC and other subcabinet bodies because executive management is inherently a personal matter. Despite all the personal variations, however, one generalization

[37]*New York Times,* 23 December 1992, p. 1.

FIGURE 6.3

The Institutional Presidency

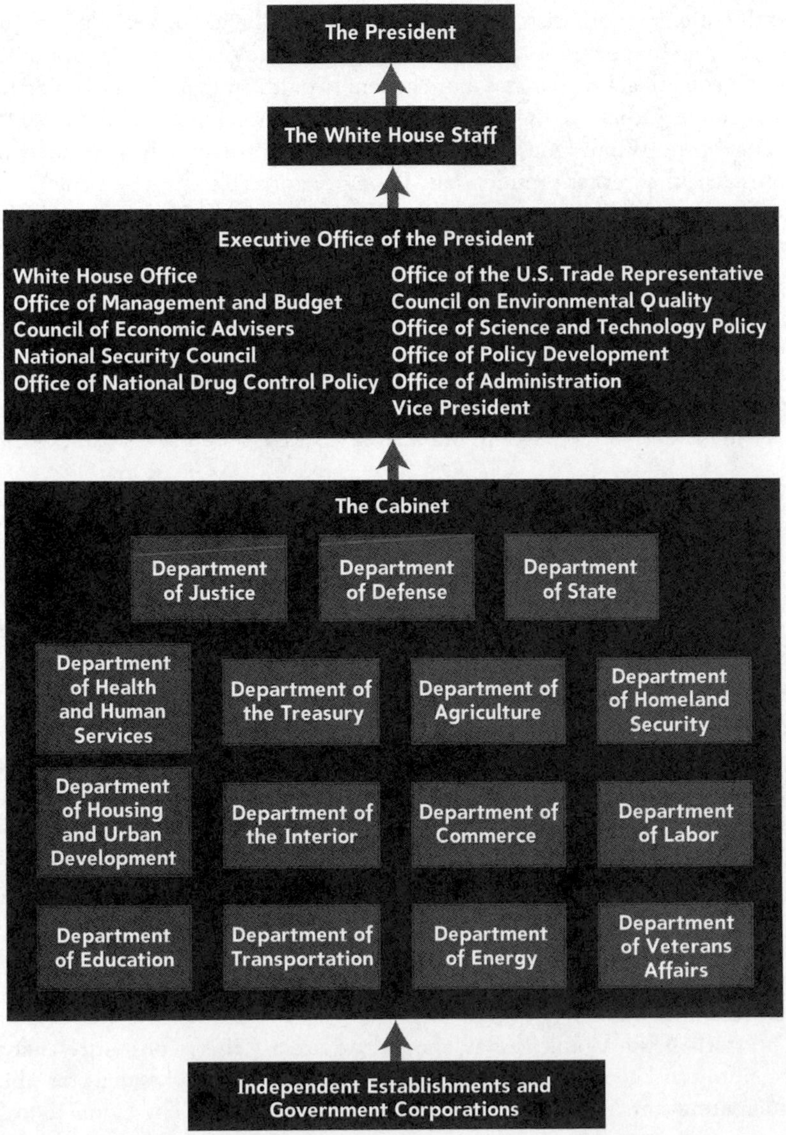

The President

↑

The White House Staff

↑

Executive Office of the President

White House Office
Office of Management and Budget
Council of Economic Advisers
National Security Council
Office of National Drug Control Policy

Office of the U.S. Trade Representative
Council on Environmental Quality
Office of Science and Technology Policy
Office of Policy Development
Office of Administration
Vice President

↑

The Cabinet

Department of Justice	Department of Defense	Department of State

Department of Health and Human Services	Department of the Treasury	Department of Agriculture	Department of Homeland Security
Department of Housing and Urban Development	Department of the Interior	Department of Commerce	Department of Labor
Department of Education	Department of Transportation	Department of Energy	Department of Veterans Affairs

↑

Independent Establishments and Government Corporations

The institutional presidency consists of *staff* agencies, mainly collected into the Executive Office of the President, and *line* agencies, whose heads together make up the president's cabinet.

can be made: Presidents have increasingly preferred the White House staff instead of the cabinet as their means of managing the gigantic executive branch.

White House staff Analysts and advisers to the president, often given the title "special assistant."

The White House Staff The *White House staff*[38] is composed mainly of analysts and advisers. Although many of the top White House staff members are given the title "special assistant" for a particular task or sector, the types of judgments they are expected to make and the kinds of advice they are supposed to give are a good deal broader and more generally political than those coming from the Executive Office of the President or from the cabinet departments. The members of the White House staff also tend to be more closely associated with the president than other presidentially appointed officials.

Kitchen Cabinet An informal group of advisers to whom the president turns for counsel and guidance. Members of the official cabinet may or may not also be members of the Kitchen Cabinet.

From an informal group of fewer than a dozen people (popularly called the *Kitchen Cabinet*), and no more than four dozen at the height of the domestic Roosevelt presidency in 1937, the White House staff has grown substantially with each successive president.[39] Richard Nixon employed 550 people in 1972. President Carter, who found so many of the requirements of presidential power distasteful and who publicly vowed to keep his staff small and decentralized, built an even larger and more centralized staff. President Clinton reduced the White House staff by 20 percent, but a large White House staff is still essential.

Executive Office of the President (EOP) The permanent agencies that perform defined management tasks for the president. Created in 1939, the EOP includes the Office of Management and Budget, the Council of Economic Advisers, the National Security Council, and other agencies.

The Executive Office of the President The development of the White House staff can be appreciated only in its relation to the still-larger *Executive Office of the President (EOP).* Created in 1939, the EOP is a major part of what is often called the "institutional presidency"—the permanent agencies that perform defined management tasks for the president. The most important and the largest EOP agency is the Office of Management and Budget (OMB). Its roles in preparing the national budget, designing the president's program, reporting on agency activities, and overseeing regulatory proposals make OMB personnel part of virtually every conceivable presidential responsibility. The status and power of the OMB have grown in importance with each successive president. The process of budgeting at one time was a "bottom-up" procedure, with expenditure and program requests passing from the lowest bureaus through the departments to "clearance" in OMB and hence to Congress, where each agency could be called in to reveal what its "original request" had been before OMB revised it. Now the budgeting process is "top-down"; OMB sets the terms of discourse for agencies as well as for Congress. The director of OMB is now one of the most powerful officials in Washington.

The staff of the Council of Economic Advisers (CEA) constantly analyzes the economy and economic trends and attempts to give the president the ability to anticipate events rather than to wait and react to events. The Council on En-

---

[38]A substantial portion of this section is taken from Lowi, *The Personal President*, pp. 141–50.

[39]All the figures since 1967, and probably 1957, are understated because additional White House staff members were on "detailed" service from the military and other departments (some secretly assigned) and are not counted here because they were not on the White House payroll.

vironmental Quality was designed to do the same for environmental issues as the CEA does for economic issues. The National Security Council (NSC) is composed of designated cabinet officials who meet regularly with the president to give advice on the large national security picture. The staff of the NSC assimilates and analyzes data from all intelligence-gathering agencies (the CIA, etc.). Other EOP agencies perform more specialized tasks.

Somewhere between 1,500 and 2,000 highly specialized people work for EOP agencies.[40] The importance of each agency in the EOP varies according to the personal orientation of each president. For example, the NSC staff was of immense importance under President Nixon, especially because it served essentially as the personal staff of presidential assistant Henry Kissinger. But it was of less importance to President George H. W. Bush, who looked outside the EOP altogether for military policy matters, turning much more to the Joint Chiefs of Staff and its chair at the time, General Colin Powell.

The Vice Presidency The vice presidency is a constitutional anomaly, even though the office was created along with the presidency by the Constitution. The vice president exists for two purposes only: to succeed the president in case of death, resignation, or incapacitation and to preside over the Senate, casting a tie-breaking vote when necessary.[41]

The main value of the vice presidency as a political resource for the president is electoral. Traditionally, a presidential candidate's most important rule for the choice of a running mate is that he or she bring the support of at least one state (preferably a large one) not otherwise likely to support the ticket. Another rule holds that the vice presidential nominee should provide some regional balance and, wherever possible, some balance among various ideological or ethnic subsections of the party. It is very doubtful that John Kennedy would have won in 1960 without his vice presidential candidate, Lyndon Johnson, and the contribution Johnson made to winning in Texas. George W. Bush's choice of Dick Cheney in 2000 was completely devoid of direct electoral value, since Cheney came from one of our least populous states (Wyoming, which casts only three electoral votes). But given Cheney's stalwart right-wing record both in Congress and as President George H. W. Bush's secretary of defense, coupled with his even more prominently right-wing wife, Lynne Cheney, his inclusion on the Republican ticket was clearly an effort to consolidate the support of the restive right wing of his party. In 2004, John Kerry chose Senator John Edwards of North Carolina as his vice-presidential running mate. Edwards was viewed as an effective campaigner and fund-raiser who might bolster the Democratic ticket's prospects in the South and in rural parts of the Midwest. In the end, the Democrats failed to carry a single Southern state, losing even North Carolina. Edwards also aroused

[40]The actual number is difficult to estimate because, as with the White House staff, some EOP personnel, especially those in national security work, are detailed to the office from outside agencies.

[41]Article I, Section 3, provides that "The Vice President . . . shall be President of the Senate, but shall have no Vote, unless they be equally divided." This is the only vote the vice president is allowed.

some controversy when, during his nationally televised debate with Vice President Cheney, he commented on the sexual orientation of Cheney's daughter.

As the institutional presidency has grown in size and complexity, most presidents of the past twenty-five years have sought to use their vice presidents as a management resource after the election. George H. W. Bush, as President Reagan's vice president, was "kept within the loop" of decision making because Reagan delegated so much power. A copy of virtually everything made for Reagan was made for Bush, especially during the first term, when Bush's close friend James Baker was chief of staff. Former President Bush did not take such pains to keep Vice President Dan Quayle "in the loop," but President Clinton relied greatly on his vice president, Al Gore, and Gore emerged as one of the most trusted and effective figures in the Clinton White House. Gore's most important task was to oversee the National Performance Review (NPR), an ambitious program to "reinvent" the way the federal government conducts its affairs. The presidency of George W. Bush has resulted in unprecedented power and responsibility for his vice president, Dick Cheney. Before becoming vice president, Cheney served as chief executive of Halliburton—the world's largest oil-and-gas services company—for five years (from 1995 to 2000) and developed the reputation, among supporters and critics, for being a "man who gets things done." Known as a hands-on vice president, he plays an active role in cabinet meetings and policy formation and directed the National Energy Policy Development Group, for which the Bush administration received some criticism when the Enron scandal unfolded in 2002. Cheney is widely viewed as one of the most influential, if not the most influential, vice presidents in American history.

The First Lady   The president serves as both chief executive and chief of state—the equivalent of Great Britain's prime minister and monarch rolled into one, simultaneously leading the government and serving as a symbol of the nation at official ceremonies and functions. For their part, most first ladies (all presidents so far have been men) limit their activities to the ceremonial portion of the presidency. First ladies greet foreign dignitaries, visit other countries, attend important national ceremonies, and otherwise act as America's "queen" when the president is called on to serve in a kingly capacity.

Because the first lady is generally associated exclusively with the head of state aspect of America's presidency, she is usually not subject to the same sort of media scrutiny or partisan attack as that aimed at the president. Yet this has changed in recent times as first ladies have begun to exert more influence over policy. Franklin Roosevelt's wife, Eleanor, was widely popular, but also widely criticized, for her active role in many elements of her husband's presidency. She was a tireless advocate for the poor, the working class, and African Americans. She was also the first first lady to hold a former government post—assistant director of the Office of Civil Defense. Lyndon Johnson's wife, Lady Bird, headed the national campaign to beautify America. More recently, Jimmy Carter's wife, Rosalynn, sat in on cabinet meetings and was considered a close adviser to her husband on policy matters. President Reagan's wife, Nancy, exercised great control over her husband's schedule and over who could and could not see him. Hillary Clinton played a major political and policy role in Bill Clinton's presidency. During the 1992 campaign, Bill Clinton often implied that she would be active in the administration by joking that voters would get "two for the price of one." After the election, Hillary took a leading role in many policy areas, most notably heading the administration's healthcare reform effort. Like Eleanor Roosevelt, Hillary Clinton was fiercely criticized for exercising too much influence over her husband's administration. She also became the first first lady to seek public office on her own when she ran for and won a seat in the U.S. Senate in New York in 2000. Laura Bush has maintained a relatively low policy profile, displaying particular interest in reading-related education programs (she is a trained librarian), as well as accompanying her husband on official trips and occasional campaign appearances.

The President and Policy   The president's powers and institutional resources, taken together, give the chief executive a substantial voice in the nation's policy-making processes. Strictly speaking, presidents cannot introduce legislation. Only members of Congress can formally propose new programs and policies. However, presidents often do send proposals to Congress. Congress, in turn, takes these proposals up by referring them to the relevant committee of jurisdiction. Sometimes these proposals are said to be "dead on arrival," an indication that presidential preferences are at loggerheads with those in the House or Senate. This is especially common during periods of divided government in which the president and at least one chamber majority are loyal to different parties. In such circumstances, presidents and legislators engage in *bargaining*, although at the end of the day the status quo may prevail. Presidents are typically in a weak position in this circumstance, especially if they have grand plans to change the status quo.[42] During periods of unified government, the president has fellow co-partisans in charge of each chamber; in these cases, the president may indeed seize the initiative, seeking to *coordinate* policy initiatives from the White House. Political scientist Charles M. Cameron suggests that the distinction between unified and divided government is quite consequential for presidential "style": it makes the chief executive either bargainer in chief or coordinator in chief.[43]

Collective-Action Principle

Whether government is divided or unified has a big influence on whether a president is a bargainer or a coordinator.

Congress has come to expect the president to propose the government's budget, and the nation has come to expect presidential initiatives to deal with major problems. Some of these initiatives have come in the form of huge packages of programs—Franklin Roosevelt's New Deal and Lyndon Johnson's Great Society. Sometimes presidents craft a single program they hope will have a significant effect on the nation and on their political fortunes. For example, George W. Bush made the "War on Terrorism" the centerpiece of his administration. To fight this war, Bush brought about the creation of a new cabinet department—the Department of Homeland Security—and the enactment of such pieces of legislation as the Patriot Act to give the executive branch more power to deal

[42]Kiewiet and McCubbins, *The Logic of Delegation*.
[43]Cameron, "Bargaining and Presidential Power."

with the terrorist threat. Going beyond terrorism, Bush also presided over the enactment of a huge expansion of the Medicare program to provide prescription drug benefits for senior citizens. All this from a president who was said to lack a popular *mandate* in the wake of the controversial 2000 election. Bush may have lacked a mandate, but the expressed and delegated powers of the office gave him the resources through which to prevail. Ironically, his 2004 reelection victory was more substantial than his victory in 2000, but it failed to provide him much leverage on new policy initiatives. His efforts to reshape and reinvigorate the social security system and to reform estate-tax policy have come to naught; the war in Iraq, the fight against terrorism, and the response to hurricane catastrophes have squeezed other domestic initiatives off the active "to do" list.

At one time, historians and journalists liked to debate the question of strong versus weak presidents. Today, *Every president is strong.* This strength is not so much a function of personal charisma or political savvy as it is a reflection of the increasing power of the institution of the presidency. Let us see how this came about.

mandate A claim by a victorious candidate that the electorate has given him or her special authority to carry out promises made during the campaign.

The Contemporary Bases of Presidential Power

In the nineteenth century, Congress was America's dominant institution of government whose members sometimes treated the president with disdain. Today, however, no one would assert that the presidency is an unimportant institution. Presidents seek to dominate the policy-making process and claim the inherent power to lead the nation in time of war. The expansion of presidential power over the course of the past century has not come about by accident but as the result of an ongoing effort by successive presidents to enlarge the powers of the office. Some of these efforts have succeeded and others have failed. As the framers of the Constitution predicted, presidential *ambition* has been a powerful and unrelenting force in American politics.

Generally, presidents can expand their power in three ways: party, popular mobilization, and administration. In the first instance, presidents may construct or strengthen national partisan institutions with which to exert influence in the legislative process and through which to implement their programs. Alternatively, or in addition to the first tactic, presidents may use popular appeals to create a mass base of support that will allow them to subordinate their political foes. This tactic has sometimes been called the strategy of "going public" or the "rhetorical" presidency.[44] Third, presidents may seek to bolster their control of established executive agencies or to create new administrative institutions and procedures that will reduce their dependence on Congress and give them a more independent governing and policy-making capability. Presidents' use of executive orders to achieve their policy goals in lieu of seeking to persuade Congress to enact legislation is, perhaps, the most obvious example.

[44]Samuel Kernell, *Going Public: New Strategies of Presidential Leadership*, 3rd ed. (Washington, DC: Congressional Quarterly Press, 1997); also, Jeffrey K. Tulis, *The Rhetorical Presidency* (Princeton, NJ: Princeton University Press, 1987).

Party as a Source of Power   All presidents have relied on the members and leaders of their own party to implement their legislative agendas. President George W. Bush, for example, has worked closely with congressional GOP leaders on such matters as energy policy and Medicare reform. But the president does not control his own party; party members have considerable autonomy. Moreover, in America's system of separated powers, the president's party may be in the minority in Congress and unable to do much for the chief executive's programs (Figure 6.4). Consequently, although their party is valuable to chief executives, it has not been a fully reliable presidential tool. The more unified the president's party is behind his legislative requests, the more unified the opposition party is also likely to be. Unless the president's party majority is very large, he must also appeal to the opposition to make up for the inevitable defectors within the ranks of his own party. Thus, the president often poses as being above partisanship to win "bipartisan" support in Congress. But to the extent he pursues a bipartisan strategy, he cannot throw himself fully into building the party loyalty and party discipline that would maximize the value of his own party's support in Congress. This is a dilemma for every president, particularly those faced with an opposition-controlled Congress.

> **Collective-Action Principle**
>
> The more unified the president's party is in Congress, the more unified the opposition is likely to be.

The role of the filibuster in the Senate should not be underestimated in this context. Even a president with a large House majority and a good working Senate majority may not have the 60 votes needed to shut down debate in the Senate. This is especially apparent in the case of presidential appointments, where individual senators can place a "hold" on the nomination, putting everyone on notice that if the president pursues this particular candidate, it will trigger a filibuster.[45] Filibuster power was especially prominent in 2005 as President Bush sought senate confirmation of federal judges and two Supreme Court justices. The Democratic minority was in a position to filibuster nominations they regarded as "extremist." This forced the president (and his majority partisans in the Senate) to negotiate. The Democrats lifted the filibuster threat in exchange for some moderation on the part of the president, and they have allowed up-or-down votes on some nominees. Because they cannot always rely on their party in Congress, contemporary presidents are more likely to use two other methods—popular mobilization and executive administration—to achieve their political goals.

Going Public   Popular mobilization as a technique of presidential power has its historical roots in the presidencies of Theodore Roosevelt and Woodrow Wilson and has, subsequently, become a weapon in the political arsenals of most presidents since the mid-twentieth century. During the nineteenth century, it was considered rather inappropriate for presidents to engage in personal campaigning on their own behalf or in support of programs and policies. When Andrew Johnson broke this unwritten rule and made a series of speeches vehemently seeking public support for his Reconstruction program, even some of Johnson's most ardent supporters were shocked at what was seen as his lack of decorum

---

[45]A powerful argument that invokes this logic is that of Keith Krehbiel in *Pivotal Politics: A Theory of U.S. Lawmaking* (Chicago: University of Chicago Press, 1998).

FIGURE 6.4

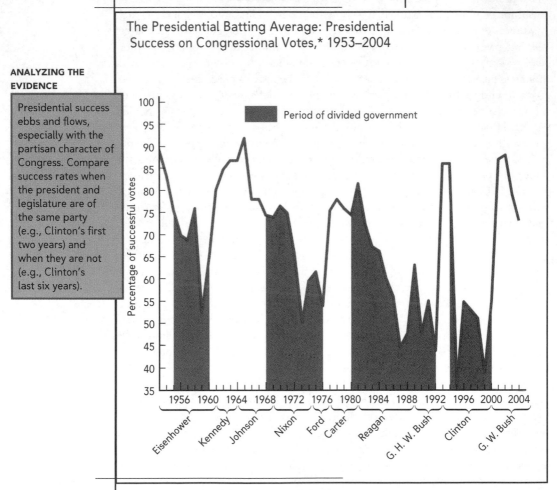

The Presidential Batting Average: Presidential Success on Congressional Votes,* 1953–2004

Period of divided government

*Percents based on votes on which presidents took a position.
SOURCE: *Congressional Quarterly Weekly Report*, 3 January 2004, p. 18.

and dignity. The president's opponents cited his "inflammatory" speeches in one of the articles of impeachment drafted by the Congress pursuant to the first effort in American history to oust a sitting president.[46]

The president who used public appeals most effectively was Franklin D. Roosevelt. Political scientist Sydney Milkis observes that FDR was "firmly persuaded

[46]Tulis, *The Rhetorical Presidency*, p. 91.

of the need to form a direct link between the executive office and the public."[47] FDR developed a number of tactics aimed at forging such a link. Like his predecessors, he often embarked on speaking trips around the nation to promote his programs. On one such tour, he told a crowd, "I regain strength just by meeting the American people."[48] In addition, FDR made limited but important use of the new electronic medium, the radio, to reach millions of Americans. In his famous "fireside chats," the president, or at least his voice, came into every living room in the country to discuss programs and policies and generally to assure Americans that Franklin Delano Roosevelt was aware of their difficulties and working diligently toward solutions. Another executive, Mayor Fiorello La Guardia of New York City, also "went public," using radio to read comic strips to Depression-era city children during a long newspaper strike. A brilliant political ploy, it deeply impressed voting-age citizens as well as entertained the young ones.

Roosevelt was also an innovator in the realm of what now might be called press relations. When he entered the White House, FDR faced a mainly hostile press typically controlled by conservative members of the business establishment. As the president wrote, "All the fat-cat newspapers—85 percent of the whole—have been utterly opposed to everything the Administration is seeking."[49] Roosevelt hoped to be able to use the press to mold public opinion, but to do so he needed to circumvent the editors and publishers who were generally unsympathetic to his goals. To this end, the president worked to cultivate the reporters who covered the White House. Roosevelt made himself available for biweekly press conferences during which he offered candid answers to reporters' questions and made certain to make important policy announcements that would provide the reporters with significant stories to file with their papers.[50] Roosevelt was the first president to designate a press secretary (Stephen Early) who was charged with organizing the press conferences and making certain that reporters observed the informal rules distinguishing presidential comments that were off the record from those that could be attributed directly to the president.

Every president since FDR has sought to craft a public relations strategy that would emphasize the incumbent's strengths and maximize his popular appeal. One Clinton innovation was to make the White House Communications Office an important institution within the EOP. In a practice continued by George W. Bush, the Communications Office became responsible not only for responding to reporters' queries but for developing and implementing a coordinated communications strategy—promoting the president's policy goals, developing responses to unflattering news stories, and making certain that a favorable image of the president would, insofar as possible, dominate the news. George W. Bush's first communications director, Karen Hughes, sought to put the office "ahead of the news," constantly developing stories that would dominate the headlines,

[47]Sidney M. Milkis, *The President and the Parties* (New York: Oxford, 1993), p. 97.
[48]James MacGregor Burns, *Roosevelt: The Lion and the Fox* (New York: Harcourt, Brace, 1956), p. 317.
[49]Burns, *Roosevelt*, p. 317.
[50]Kernell, *Going Public*, p. 79.

present the president in a favorable light, and deflect criticism. For example, after the administration responded to the September 11 terrorist attacks against the World Trade Center and Pentagon with a massive military campaign in Afghanistan, the Communications Office developed several stories that made it difficult for administration critics to gain much traction. One such story concerned the brutal treatment of women by Afghanistan's fundamentalist Taliban regime, and this treatment was underlined in several speeches by First Lady Laura Bush and communicated to the press in hundreds of news releases. The wave of publicity the Communications Office was able to generate concerning the Taliban's harsh and demeaning posture toward women was one factor that made it extremely difficult for the Bush administration's liberal critics to utter even a word of protest regarding America's determined effort to oust the Taliban from power.

In addition to using the media, recent presidents, particularly Bill Clinton, have reached out directly to the American public to gain its approval. President Clinton's enormously high public profile, as is indicated by the number of public appearances he made (see Figure 6.5), is only the most recent dramatic expression of the presidency as a ***permanent campaign*** for re-election. A study by political scientist Charles O. Jones shows that President Clinton engaged in campaignlike activity throughout his presidency and was the most-traveled American president in history. In his first twenty months in office, he made 203 appearances outside of Washington, compared to 178 for George H. W. Bush and 58 for Ronald Reagan. President George W. Bush might outdo them all. During his first hundred days, Bush gave speeches and other public appearances in twenty-six states; Clinton's and former president Bush's records during their first hundred days were fifteen states each. In light of the need to mobilize the American people after September 11, 2001, Bush's number of appearances outside of Washington far exceeded that of Bill Clinton's.

permanent campaign A description of presidential politics in which all presidential actions are taken with re-election in mind.

THE LIMITS OF GOING PUBLIC   Some presidents have been able to make effective use of popular appeals to overcome congressional opposition. Popular support, though, has not been a firm foundation for presidential power. To begin with, popular support is notoriously fickle. President George W. Bush maintained an approval rating of over 70 percent for more than a year after the September 11 terrorist attacks. By 2003, however, his approval rating had fallen nearly twenty points as American casualties in Iraq mounted; by the end of 2005 it had fallen almost another twenty points to the high-30s range. Such declines in popular approval during a president's term in office are nearly inevitable and follow a predictable pattern (see Figure 6.6).[51] Presidents generate popular support by promising to undertake important programs that will contribute directly to the well-being of large numbers of Americans. Almost inevitably, presidential performance falls short of promises and popular expectations, leading to a sharp decline in public support and ensuing collapse of presidential influence.[52]

[51]Lowi, *The Personal President*.
[52]Lowi, *The Personal President*, p. 11.

FIGURE 6.5

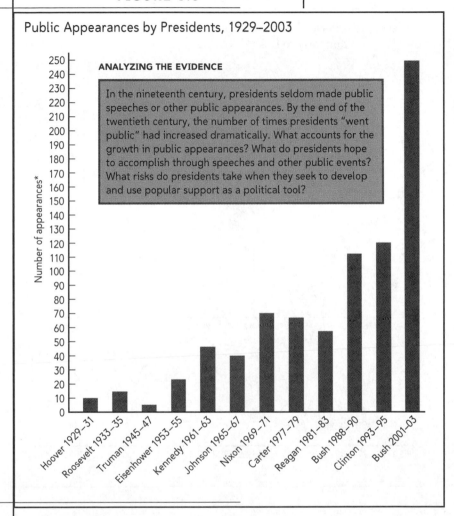

Public Appearances by Presidents, 1929–2003

ANALYZING THE EVIDENCE

In the nineteenth century, presidents seldom made public speeches or other public appearances. By the end of the twentieth century, the number of times presidents "went public" had increased dramatically. What accounts for the growth in public appearances? What do presidents hope to accomplish through speeches and other public events? What risks do presidents take when they seek to develop and use popular support as a political tool?

*Number of appearances**

Hoover 1929–31 · Roosevelt 1933–35 · Truman 1945–47 · Eisenhower 1953–55 · Kennedy 1961–63 · Johnson 1965–67 · Nixon 1969–71 · Carter 1977–79 · Reagan 1981–83 · Bush 1988–90 · Clinton 1993–95 · Bush 2001–03

SOURCE: Samuel Kernell, *Going Public*, 3rd ed. (Washington, DC: Congressional Quarterly Press, 1998), p. 118.

Presidents have certainly not abandoned "going public," but they no longer do so as frequently as they once did—there has been, for example, a decline in presidential appearances on prime-time television over the past four administrations.[53] Instead, presidents have employed institutionalized public and media

[53]Kernell, *Going Public*, p. 114.

FIGURE 6.6

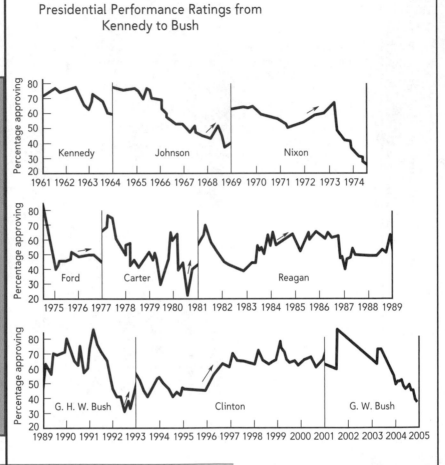

Presidential Performance Ratings from Kennedy to Bush

ANALYZING THE EVIDENCE

In the presidential performance rating poll, respondents are asked, "Do you approve of the way the president is handling his job?" The graphs show the percent of positive responses. Observe that presidents generally experience broad shifts in popular approval. What factors help explain changes in presidential approval ratings? Does popular approval really affect presidential power? How can popular feelings about the president affect the president's conduct and influence?

NOTE: Arrows indicate pre-election upswings.

SOURCE: Courtesy of the Gallup Organization and Louis Harris & Associates.

relations efforts more to create a generally favorable public image than to promote specific policies. Thus, in 2002, President George W. Bush made several speeches to boost the proposed creation of a Homeland Security department. At the same time, however, the White House Communications Office was engaged in a nonstop, seven-day-a-week effort to promote news and feature stories aimed at bolstering the president's more general public image. Stories emphasized the president's empathy for retirees hurt by the downturn of stock prices, the president's anger over corporate abuses, the president's concern for the environment, the president's determination to prevent terrorism, the president's support for Israel, and so forth. These are all examples of image-polishing rather than going public on behalf of specific programs. Confronted with the limitations of a strategy of popular mobilization, presidents have shifted from an offensive strategy to a more defensive mode in this domain. The limitations of going public as a route to presidential power have also led contemporary presidents to make use of a third technique: expansion of their administrative capabilities.

The Administrative State

Contemporary presidents have increased the administrative capabilities of their office in three ways. First, they have enhanced the reach and power of the EOP. Second, they have sought to increase White House control over the federal bureaucracy. Third, they have expanded the role of executive orders and other instruments of direct presidential governance. Taken together, these three components of what might be called the White House "administrative strategy" have given presidents a capacity to achieve their programmatic and policy goals even when they are unable to secure congressional approval. Indeed, some recent presidents have been able to accomplish quite a bit without much congressional, partisan, or even public support.

The Executive Office of the President The Executive Office of the President has grown from six administrative assistants in 1939 to today's 400 employees working directly for the president in the White House office along with some 1,400 individuals staffing the several (currently eight) divisions of the Executive Office.[54] The creation and growth of the White House staff gives the president an enormously enhanced capacity to gather information, plan programs and strategies, communicate with constituencies, and exercise supervision over the executive branch. The staff multiplied the president's eyes, ears, and arms, becoming a critical instrument of presidential power.[55]

In particular, the OMB serves as a potential instrument of presidential control over federal spending and hence a mechanism through which the White House has greatly expanded its power. The OMB has the capacity to analyze and approve all legislative proposals, not only budgetary requests, emanating from all federal agencies before being submitted to Congress. This procedure, now a matter of routine, greatly enhanced the president's control over the entire executive branch. All legislation emanating from the White House as well as all executive orders also go through the OMB.[56] Thus in one White House agency, the president has the means to exert major influence over the flow of money as well as the shape and content of national legislation.

---

[54]Harold W. Stanley and Richard G. Niemi, *Vital Statistics on American Politics, 2001–2002* (Washington, DC: Congressional Quarterly Press, 2001), pp. 250–51.

[55]Milkis, *The President and the Parties*, p. 128.

[56]Milkis, *The President and the Parties*, p. 160.

Regulatory Review A second tactic that presidents have used to increase their power and reach is the process of regulatory review, through which presidents have sought to seize control of rule making by the agencies of the executive branch (also see Chapter 14). Whenever Congress enacts a statute, its actual implementation requires the promulgation of hundreds of rules by the agency charged with administering the law and giving effect to the will of Congress. Some congressional statutes are quite detailed and leave agencies with relatively little discretion. Typically, however, Congress enacts a relatively broad statement of legislative intent and delegates to the appropriate administrative agency the power to fill in many important details.[57] In other words, Congress typically says to an administrative agency, "Here is the problem: deal with it."[58]

The discretion Congress delegates to administrative agencies has provided recent presidents with an important avenue for expanding their own power. For example, President Clinton believed the president had full authority to order agencies of the executive branch to adopt such rules as the president thought appropriate.

During the course of his presidency, Clinton issued 107 directives to administrators ordering them to propose specific rules and regulations. In some instances, the language of the rule to be proposed was drafted by the White House staff; in other cases, the president asserted a priority but left it to the agency to draft the precise language of the proposal. Presidential rule-making directives covered a wide variety of topics. For example, Clinton ordered the Food and Drug Administration (FDA) to develop rules designed to restrict the marketing of tobacco products to children. White House and FDA staffers then spent several months preparing nearly 1,000 pages of new regulations affecting tobacco manufacturers and vendors.[59] Republicans, of course, denounced Clinton's actions as a usurpation of power.[60] However, after he took office, President George W. Bush made no move to surrender the powers Clinton had claimed. Quite the contrary. Bush continued the Clinton era practice of issuing presidential directives to agencies to spur them to issue new rules and regulations.

Governing by Decree: Executive Orders A third mechanism through which contemporary presidents have sought to enhance their power to govern unilaterally is through the use of executive orders and other forms of presidential decrees, including executive agreements, national security findings and directives, proclamations, reorganization plans, the signing of statements, and a host of others.[61] Executive orders have a long history in the United States and have been the vehicles for a number of important government policies, including the purchase of Louisiana, the annexation of Texas, the emancipation of the slaves,

[57]The classic critique of this process is Lowi, *The End of Liberalism*.
[58]Kenneth Culp Davis, *Administrative Law Treatise* (St. Paul, MN: West Publishing, 1958), p. 9.
[59]Elena Kagan, "Presidential Administration," 114 *Harvard Law Review 2245* (2001), p. 2265.
[60]For example, Douglas W. Kmiec, "Expanding Power," in *The Rule of Law in the Wake of Clinton*, ed. Roger Pilon (Washington, DC: Cato Institute Press, 2000), pp. 47–68.
[61]A complete inventory is provided in Harold C. Relyea, "Presidential Directives: Background and Review," The Library of Congress, *Congressional Research Service Report 98–611*, 9 November 2001.

the internment of the Japanese, the desegregation of the military, the initiation of affirmative action, and the creation of important federal agencies, among them the EPA, FDA, and Peace Corps.[62]

While wars and national emergencies produce the highest volume of executive orders, such presidential actions also occur frequently in peacetime (see Figure 6.7). In the realm of foreign policy, unilateral presidential actions in the form of executive agreements have virtually replaced treaties as the nation's chief foreign policy instruments.[63] Presidential decrees, however, are often used for purely domestic purposes.

Presidents may not use executive orders to issue whatever commands they please. The use of such decrees is bound by law. If a president issues an executive order, proclamation, directive, or the like, in principle he does so pursuant to the powers granted to him by the Constitution or delegated to him by Congress, usually through a statute. When presidents issue such orders, they generally state the constitutional or statutory basis for their actions. For example, when President Truman ordered the desegregation of the armed services, he did so pursuant to his constitutional powers as commander in chief. In a similar vein, when President Johnson issued Executive Order 11246, he asserted that the order was designed to implement the 1964 Civil Rights Act, which prohibited employment discrimination. Where an executive order has no statutory or constitutional basis, the courts have held it to be void. The most important case on this point is *Youngstown Sheet & Tube Co. v. Sawyer*, the so-called steel seizure case of 1952.[64] Here, the Supreme Court ruled that President Truman's seizure of the nation's steel mills during the Korean War had no statutory or constitutional basis and was thus invalid.

A number of court decisions, though, have established broad boundaries that leave considerable room for presidential action. By illustration, the courts have held that Congress might approve presidential action after the fact or, in effect, ratify presidential action through "acquiescence"—for example, by not objecting for long periods of time or by continuing to provide funding for programs established by executive orders. In addition, the courts have indicated that some areas, most notably the realm of military policy, are presidential in character and have allowed presidents wide latitude to make policy by executive decree. Thus, within the very broad limits established by the courts, presidential orders can be and have been important policy tools.

President Clinton issued numerous orders designed to promote a coherent set of policy goals: protecting the environment, strengthening federal regulatory power, shifting America's foreign policy from a unilateral to a multilateral focus, expanding affirmative action programs, and helping organized labor in its struggles with employers.[65] As in his use of regulatory review, President Clinton was

---

[62]Terry M. Moe and William G. Howell, "The Presidential Power of Unilateral Action," *Journal of Law, Economics and Organization*, 15, no. 1 (January 1999), pp. 133–34.

[63]Moe and Howell, "The Presidential Power of Unilateral Action," p. 164.

[64]*Youngstown Sheet & Tube Co. v. Sawyer*, 346 U.S. 579 (1952).

[65]Todd Gaziano, "The New 'Massive Resistance,'" *Policy Review* (May–June 1998), p. 283.

FIGURE 6.7

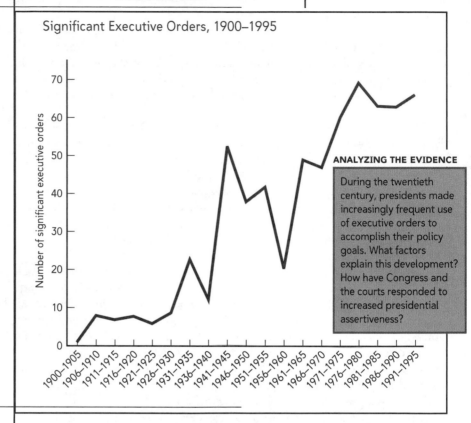

Significant Executive Orders, 1900–1995

ANALYZING THE EVIDENCE

During the twentieth century, presidents made increasingly frequent use of executive orders to accomplish their policy goals. What factors explain this development? How have Congress and the courts responded to increased presidential assertiveness?

SOURCE: William Howell, "The President's Powers of Unilateral Action: The Strategic Advantages of Acting Alone" (PhD diss., Stanford University, 1999).

able to craft a policy agenda through executive orders that he could not accomplish through legislation. Faced with a hostile Congress, Clinton turned to unilateral instruments of executive power including regulatory review, executive orders, and the like. Clinton certainly did not issue more executive orders than previous presidents. His innovation was to take an instrument that had been used sporadically and show that an activist president could develop and implement a significant policy agenda without legislation—a lesson that surely has not been lost on Clinton's successor.

Indeed, just as he continued the practice of using regulatory review as a policy instrument, President George W. Bush has not hesitated to use executive orders—issuing more than forty during his first year in office. During his first months in office, Bush issued orders prohibiting the use of federal funds to support international family planning groups that provided abortion-counseling services and placing limits on the use of embryonic stem cells in federally funded research projects. Subsequently, Bush made very aggressive use of executive orders in response to the threat of terrorism—which the president has declared to be his administration's most important policy agenda. In November 2001, for example, Bush issued a directive authorizing the creation of military tribunals to try noncitizens accused of involvement in acts of terrorism against the United States. The presidential directive also prohibits defendants from appealing their treatment to any federal or state court. In addition, the president issued orders freezing the assets of groups and individuals associated with terrorism, providing expedited citizenship for foreign nationals serving in the U.S. military, and ordering the CIA to use all means possible to oust President Saddam Hussein of Iraq, whom Bush accused of plotting terrorist actions.

While terrorism was certainly at the top of President Bush's agenda, he also issued a number of executive orders having to do with domestic policy. For example, the president was able to overcome congressional resistance to his efforts to increase domestic energy exploration and the rapid exploitation of domestic energy resources. Like Clinton, President Bush discovered that an executive order can often substitute for legislation. In May 2001, Bush signed an executive order that closely followed a recommendation from the American Petroleum Institute, an oil industry trade association, to free energy companies from a number of federal regulations.

The Advantages of the Administrative Strategy   Through the course of American history, party leadership and popular appeals have played important roles in presidential efforts to overcome political opposition. Both party and appeals to the people continue to be instruments of presidential power. Reagan's tax cuts and Clinton's budget victories were achieved with strong partisan support. George W. Bush, lacking the oratorical skills of a Reagan or a Roosevelt, nevertheless has made good use of sophisticated communications strategies to promote his agenda. Yet, as we saw, in the modern era parties have waned in institutional strength while the effects of popular appeals have often proven evanescent. The limitations of the alternatives have increasingly impelled presidents to try to expand the administrative capabilities of the office and their own capacity for unilateral action as means of achieving their policy goals. And in recent decades, the expansion of the Executive Office, the development of regulatory review, and the use of executive orders, the signing of statements, and the like have given presidents a substantial capacity to achieve significant policy results despite congressional opposition to their legislative agendas.

To be sure, the administrative strategy does not always succeed. In some instances over the years the federal courts have struck down unilateral actions by the president. And, occasionally, Congress acts to reverse presidential orders. For example, in 1999, Congress enacted legislation prohibiting the Department of Education from carrying out a presidential directive to administer national education

Rationality Principle	Collective-Action Principle	Institution Principle	Policy Principle	History Principle
Occupants of the presidency have, from time to time, taken upon themselves additional authority to enable the pursuit of national objectives.	Vetoes are usually part of an intricate bargaining process between the president and Congress.	By structuring the election of the president to be not by the people directly but by the electoral college, the framers sought to downplay presidential power.	Because of the president's veto power, Congress will alter the content of a bill to make it more to a president's liking.	The framers created a unitary executive; they wanted an energetic president but also a limited one.
Under conditions of divided government, presidents may rationally want the protection of executive privilege from the partisan scrutiny of elements of Congress, and Congress may well suspect a president of hiding questionable activity behind a veil of executive privilege.	Presidential power should be analyzed in terms of the strategic interactions that a president has with other political actors. The president can use public approval as a strategic resource.	The Constitution has established a presidency of expressed and delegated powers. There is a separation-of-powers tension beween the president and Congress over policy related to war making.	The outcomes of congressional policy making depend greatly on how much room executive agencies have to interpret policies.	The first decade of the new constitutional order was an amazing period of state building in which relations between the executive and the legislative branches were unusually cooperative.
Bargaining between Congress and the president is strategic, as the president tries to influence the beliefs of the legislature about what they must do to keep him from using his veto power.	Whether government is divided or unified has a big influence on whether a president is a bargainer or a coordinator.	The president's constitutional role provides an opportunity for significant agenda setting by the executive for the Congress.		The presidency was strengthened somewhat in the 1830s with the introduction of a national-convention system of nominating presidential candidates.
A president must weigh the advantages of vetoing legislation against the possible drop in his public approval.	The more unified the president's party is in Congress, the more unified the opposition is likely to be.	The veto power makes the president the most important single legislative leader.		By the end of the New Deal, the practice of significant management of the economy by the executive, as broadly defined by Congress, was firmly established.
Congress delegates more power to the president as more demands are made on its agenda.		Congress delegates authority to the president but also maintains the means to influence how the executive branch exercises that power.		The New Deal's expanded role for the national government enhanced presidential power.

tests.[66] In 2000, Congress went even a step further. In response to President Clinton's aggressive regulatory review program, the Republican-controlled Congress moved to strengthen its capacity to block the president's use of administrative directives by enacting the Congressional Review Act (CRA). This piece of legislation requires federal agencies to send all proposed regulations to Congress for review sixty days before they take effect. The act also creates a fast-track procedure to allow the House and Senate to enact a joint resolution of disapproval that not only would void the regulation but also would prohibit the agency from subsequently issuing any substantially similar rule. The first test of the act came after Clinton left office. In the early weeks of the Bush administration, Congress passed a joint resolution repealing an ergonomics standard that had been supported by the Clinton administration and adopted by OSHA. President Bush, who opposed the standard, signed the resolution and the ergonomics standard was voided. While this outcome may be seen as an effective effort by Congress to thwart a presidential directive, it seems clear that Congress was successful only because Clinton was out of office. Had his term not expired, Clinton would almost certainly have vetoed the resolution. Indeed, one reason Clinton was willing to sign CRA into law in the first place was that the president retained the power to veto any action undertaken by Congress under the statute's authority.

In principle, perhaps, Congress could respond more vigorously than it has to unilateral policy making by the president. Certainly a Congress willing to impeach a president should have the mettle to overturn his administrative directives. But the president has significant advantages in such struggles with Congress. In battles over presidential directives and orders, Congress is on the defensive, reacting to presidential initiatives. The framers of the Constitution saw "energy," or the ability to take the initiative, as a key feature of executive power.[67] When the president takes action by issuing an order or an administrative directive, Congress must initiate the cumbersome and time-consuming lawmaking process, overcome internal divisions, and enact legislation that the president may ultimately veto. Moreover, as Terry Moe has argued, in such battles Congress faces a significant collective-action problem insofar as members are likely to be more sensitive to the substance of a president's actions and its effects on their constituents than to the more general implications of presidential power for the long-term vitality of their institution.[68]

---

[66]Kagan, "Presidential Administration," p. 2351.

[67]Clinton Rossiter, ed., *The Federalist Papers, No. 70* (New York: Signet, 1961), pp. 423–30.

[68]Terry Moe, "The Presidency and the Bureaucracy: The Presidential Advantage," in *The Presidency and the Political System*, ed. Michael Nelson (Washington, DC: Congressional Quarterly Press, 2002), pp. 416–20.

SUMMARY

The foundations for presidential government were laid in the Constitution by providing for a unitary executive. The first sections of the chapter reviewed these powers, focusing on expressed, delegated, and inherent variations. But we noted that the presidency was subordinated to congressional government during the nineteenth century and part of the twentieth, when the national government was relatively uninvolved in domestic functions and inactive or sporadic in foreign affairs.

The next section of the chapter traced the rise of modern presidential government after the much longer period of congressional dominance. There is no mystery in the shift to government centered on the presidency. Congress built the modern presidency by delegating to it not only the power to implement the vast new programs of the 1930s but also by delegating its own legislative power to make the policies themselves. The cabinet, the other top appointments, the White House staff, and the Executive Office of the President are some of the impressive formal resources of presidential power.

The chapter then focused on the president's formal and informal resources, in particular his political party, the supportive group coalitions, and his access to the media and, through that, his access to the millions of Americans who make up the general public. But it was noted that these resources are not cost- or risk-free. The president's direct relation with the mass public is his most potent modern resource but also the most problematic.

FOR FURTHER READING

Brace, Paul, and Barbara Hinckley. *Follow the Leader: Opinion Polls and the Modern Presidents.* New York: Basic Books, 1992.

Cameron, Charles M. *Veto Bargaining: Presidents and the Politics of Negative Power.* New York: Cambridge University Press, 2000.

Drew, Elizabeth. *On the Edge: The Clinton Presidency.* New York: Simon & Schuster, 1994.

Kernell, Samuel. *Going Public: New Strategies of Presidential Leadership.* 3rd ed. Washington, DC: Congressional Quarterly Press, 1997.

Lowi, Theodore J. *The Personal President: Power Invested, Promise Unfulfilled.* Ithaca, NY: Cornell University Press, 1985.

Milkis, Sidney M. *The President and the Parties: The Transformation of the American Party System since the New Deal.* New York: Oxford University Press, 1993.

Nelson, Michael, ed. *The Presidency and the Political System.* 7th ed. Washington, DC: Congressional Quarterly Press, 2003.

Neustadt, Richard E. *Presidential Power and the Modern Presidents: The Politics of Leadership from Roosevelt to Reagan.* New York: Free Press, 1990.

Pfiffner, James P. *The Modern Presidency.* New York: St. Martin's Press, 1994.

Polsby, Nelson W., and Aaron Wildavsky. *Presidential Elections: Contemporary Strategies of American Electoral Politics.* 8th ed. New York: Free Press, 1991.

Skowronek, Stephen. *The Politics Presidents Make: Leadership from John Adams to Bill Clinton.* Cambridge, MA: Harvard University Press, 1997.

Spitzer, Robert J. *The Presidential Veto: Touchstone of the American Presidency.* Albany: State University of New York Press, 1988.

Tulis, Jeffrey. *The Rhetorical Presidency.* Princeton, NJ: Princeton University Press, 1987.

Politics in the News—
Reading between the Lines

Presidential Power and the Press Conference

After 99 Days, Testing Winds

By TODD S. PURDUM

With his presidency at best becalmed and at worst beset—just 99 days into his second term, President Bush seized the prime-time power of an East Room news conference for only the fourth time in his tenure in an effort to show that he could still do what he has always done in the face of storms around him: make his own weather.

But even after his hourlong encounter with reporters was over on Thursday night, the atmosphere remained unsettled. The changes he suggested to help keep Social Security solvent seemed unlikely to unfreeze the stalemate on Capitol Hill over revising the system. He acknowledged that he had no easy fix for high gasoline prices, nor any firm timetable for bringing American troops home from Iraq.

Mr. Bush called the news conference because his centerpiece domestic proposal—overhauling Social Security—is stalled despite 60 days of his personal barnstorming around the country to sell his plan for personal investment accounts; his effort to force an up-or-down Senate vote on his judicial nominees seems uncertain to succeed;

and his poll ratings equal the worst of his 51 months in office. But this president has never been one to dwell on the obstacles. . . .

Yet with gasoline prices and interest rates high and economic growth slowing; with some restive Republicans on Capitol Hill worried about their electoral fortunes, not his; with the whiff of reported ethical improprieties whirling around the House majority leader, Tom DeLay; and with lame-duck status stalking Mr. Bush with each passing month, the question now is whether he can prevail by simply persevering, or whether he will have to give to receive.

He pronounced himself to be "moving the process along" on Social Security by proposing that future benefits grow faster for people who are less affluent than for those who are better off (a delicate way of suggesting benefit cuts for the wealthy). But he gave no ground on his insistence that any overhaul must include private investment accounts— which Democrats uniformly oppose.

Mr. Bush spoke calmly, confidently, but was less exuberant than in his first news conference after his re-election.

New York Times, 29 April 2005.

He fired a direct shot at some prominent figures in his party who have couched Democratic opposition to his conservative judicial nominees as a question of hostility to the religious faithful, declaring: "I think people are opposing my nominees because they don't like the judicial philosophy of the people I've nominated."

That may well be because the president knows he could earn political points with his base even if his judicial nominees should be defeated. It would be much harder, however, for Mr. Bush to claim victory on overhauling Social Security if he cannot win adoption of some kind of personal retirement savings accounts in the program. The prospects for that seem dimmer at the end of his campaign to build public support for the idea than they did at the beginning.

"In his defense, I would judge it much too early to determine whether it's dead or not," said Charles O. Jones, a senior fellow at the Brookings Institution. "But it certainly in the short run looks bad. The one thing this guy has in his own mind, post-9/11, as part of his leadership, is persistence. Now, you can also characterize it as stubbornness, and it's very easy to go from there to arrogance." . . .

Mr. Bush said several times that he would listen to good ideas from either party, would seek solutions regardless of partisan advantage. But he also made it clear that his fundamental conviction about how he conducts his presidency has not changed.

It would be foolish to count out anyone so determined.

"Among the things the president has going for him is that he's still the president," said former senator Bob Kerrey of Nebraska. . . .

ESSENCE OF THE STORY

- Just three months into his second term, most of President Bush's policy initiatives seem stalled. So Bush held a press conference, just the fourth of his presidency, in order to take his case directly to the American people.

- Bush succeeded during his first term by persevering, even in the face of opposition, and in almost all cases he won. But he is now in his second term and is a lame-duck president, and many question whether this same political strategy will work.

- The last time Bush was criticized for stubbornness was during the 2004 campaign, and Bush was re-elected.

POLITICAL ANALYSIS

- A news conference is one aspect of the president's ability to "go public," or appeal for direct popular support for his policies (other strategies include public speaking tours and high-profile public events). By going public, the president takes advantage of his position as the only political leader elected by, and presumably speaking for, the whole nation.

- Bush's ability to go public in his second term is hampered by his lame-duck status. What also hinders Bush's ability to rally political support is the lack of a clearly designated heir apparent. Unlike Reagan or Clinton, both of whom were presumably trying to craft policies to help the eventual election of their vice president, Bush has no clear successor. Therefore, many ambitious politicians—especially Republicans—have incentives to compete with Bush as a way to foster their own political ambitions.

CHAPTER

7

The Executive Branch: Bureaucracy in a Democracy

On March 1, 2003, twenty-two federal agencies with responsibilities for combating international terrorism in the United States were transferred to the Department of Homeland Security. By all accounts, this event marked the most dramatic reform of the federal bureaucracy since the establishment of the Department of Defense in 1947. However, that earlier transformation took forty years to be fully realized, a time frame that is unacceptable in the midst of a "hot" war on terrorism.

Political forces coalesced soon after the catastrophic events of September 11, 2001. Both Republicans and Democrats realized that the public was going to demand some ongoing response to the terrorist threat (beyond the immediate military response in Afghanistan). Politicians on both sides of the aisle, then, were in agreement on their primary political goal—do *something* about the terrorist threat. This agreement made it almost certain that significant political change would occur.[1]

---

[1] John W. Kingdon calls events that limit and focus our political options "windows of political opportunity." See his *Agendas, Alternatives, and Public Policies* (Boston: Little, Brown, 1984).

But why did we end up with this particular solution—a new cabinet level agency? Democrats were quick to call for the creation of a new Department of Homeland Security. Yet, with Republicans—a party traditionally averse to large-scale bureaucratic solutions—in control of the White House and Congress, one would have expected at most a call for beefing up the intelligence and defense budgets, along with an attempt to shift blame to the previous administration. A congressional investigation, however, quickly revealed that serious security lapses and a lack of coordination among the various agencies with responsibility for domestic and foreign intelligence had occurred under *both* Clinton's and Bush's watch. Both parties could be blamed if the government did not respond aggressively enough to the terrorist threat.

Furthermore, the major alternative solution—the creation of a Homeland Security "czar"—proved inadequate. Tom Ridge, ex-governor of Pennsylvania, did not have the power to hire and fire his subordinates. He did not have budgetary authority. He had little beyond his title. In this case, the *lack* of rules and procedures meant that Ridge had no power to shape bureaucratic outcomes; and, according to the same principles of politics, the government needed to institutionalize rules and procedures to make Ridge's leadership effective. In the end, no alternative seemed available to the president and members of Congress on both sides of the aisle. The path to a cabinet-level agency was clear.

Eventually, the Department of Homeland Security (DHS) was authorized by Congress. Did that mean that the coordination problems faced by Ridge withered away? The last time the federal government attempted such a significant reorganization was in 1947, when the National Security Act merged the Departments of Navy and War to create the Department of Defense.

CHAPTER OUTLINE

Why Bureaucracy?

- Bureaucratic Organization Enhances Efficiency
- Bureaucracies Allow Governments to Operate
- Bureaucrats Fulfill Important Roles
- Politics

How Is the Executive Branch Organized?

- Clientele Agencies Serve Particular Interests
- Agencies for Maintenance of the Union Keep the Government Going
- Regulatory Agencies Guide Individual Conduct
- Agencies of Redistribution Implement Fiscal/Monetary and Welfare Policies

The Problem of Bureaucratic Control

- Bureaucrats Have Their Own Motivational Considerations
- Control of the Bureaucracy Is a Principal-Agent Problem
- The President as Chief Executive Can Direct Agencies
- Congress Can Promote Responsible Bureaucracy through Oversight and Incentives

How Can Bureaucracy Be Reduced?

- Termination
- Devolution
- Privatization

PREVIEWING THE PRINCIPLES

Bureaucracy is necessary for implementing public policy. Implementing the laws and policies passed by elected officials, bureaucrats can be understood to be agents of Congress and the presidency. As is the case in any principal-agent relationship, the agent (the bureaucracy) is delegated authority and has a certain amount of leeway for independent action. Despite the efforts of elected officials (the principals) to check departments and agencies (the agents), bureaucrats have their own goals and thus exercise their own influence on policy. The problem of controlling bureaucracy is a central concern for democracies. Although controlling the growth of bureaucracy is a major concern, the size of the federal bureaucracy has in fact kept pace with the economy and the needs of society. And because most Americans benefit in some way from programs implemented by government agencies, they are reluctant to cut back on the size and scope of these programs.

Today, more than five decades after the passage of the act, the various military services combined under the Defense Department's roof continually maneuver for advantage. Secretary of Defense Donald Rumsfeld compares the Defense Department bureaucracy to Soviet central planning.[2]

Coordination becomes more difficult as the number of people and the diversity of goals or preferences grow. In the case of the DHS, the agencies brought under one umbrella are tremendously diverse (see Table 7.1). Each of these agencies has gone down a particular path. Some of these bureaus had developed a bureaucratic culture and esprit de corps over more than two centuries (for example, the Customs Service and the Coast Guard), while others had grown aggressively in response to new threats (the Drug Enforcement Agency). It is very difficult to set these agencies on a new course.

To take just one example, the most visible change for most Americans is the army of screeners who have appeared at airports around the country. But just as the DHS is encountering great difficulties in merging and coordinating twenty-two separate agencies, the new Transportation Security Administration (TSA) has discovered that its immediate goal—ensuring security at thousands of American airports—conflicts directly with the goal of a traveling population used to convenience and protective of its privacy. The TSA's new rules and procedures have run roughshod over an economically distressed airline industry accustomed to managing its own gates and monitoring its own security.

TSA officials found that dozens of their screeners had criminal histories. Many of their supervisory staff have resigned in frustration. And airlines continue to bicker with the agency over speed and convenience. Originally, the TSA projected that it could hire and train 55,000 airport screeners and establish new security protocols for $5.1 billion. By mid-2003, the agency had spent $9 billion and was still counting. And this is just a small part of the new, sprawling DHS. In January 2003, the Government Accountability Office listed

---

[2]Cited in the *Cato Handbook for Congress: Policy Recommendations for the 108th Congress*, p. 63 (available at www.cato.org/pubs/handbook/index.html).

TABLE 7.1

The Shape of a Domestic Security Department

DEPARTMENT OF HOMELAND SECURITY	THE AGENCIES AND DEPARTMENTS THAT WERE MOVED TO THE MAIN DIVISIONS OF THE DHS UNDER THE LEGISLATION CREATING THE NEW DEPARTMENT	DEPARTMENT OR AGENCY PREVIOUSLY UNDER	FROM PRESIDENT BUSH'S BUDGET FOR THE 2003 FISCAL YEAR	
			BUDGET REQUEST, IN MILLIONS	ESTIMATED NUMBER OF EMPLOYEES
Border and Transportation Security	Immigration and Naturalization Service enforcement functions*	Justice Dept.	$ 6,416	39, 459
	Transportation Security Administration	Transportation Dept.	4,800	41,300
	Customs Service	Treasury Dept.	3,796	21,743
	Federal Protective Services	General Services Administration	418	1,408
	Animal and Plant Health Inspection Service (parts)	Agriculture Dept.	402	3,974
Emergency Preparedness and Response	Federal Emergency Management Agency	(Independent agency)	$ 6,174	5,135
	Chemical, biological, radiological, and nuclear response units	Health and Human Services Dept.	2,104	150
	Nuclear incident response teams	Energy Dept.	91	†
	National Domestic Preparedness Office	FBI	2	15
	Office of Domestic Preparedness	Justice Dept.	§	§
	Domestic Emergency Support Teams	From various depts. and agencies	Not applicable	Not applicable
Science and Technology	Civilian biodefense research programs	Health and Human Services Dept.	$ 1,993	150
	National Biological Warfare Defense Analysis Center	(Proposed in fiscal 2003 budget)	420	Not available
	Plum Island Animal Disease Center	Agriculture Dept.	25	124
	Lawrence Livermore National Laboratory (parts)	Energy Dept.	Not available	Not available
Information Analysis and Infrastructure Protection	National Communications System	Defense Dept.	$ 155	91
	National Infrastructure Protection Center	FBI	151	795
	Critical Infrastructure Assurance Office	Commerce Dept.	27	65
	National Infrastructure Simulation and Analysis Center	Energy Dept.	20	2
	Federal Computer Incident Response Center	General Services Administration	11	23
Secret Service	Secret Service, including presidential protection units	Treasury Dept.	$ 1,248	6,111
Coast Guard	Coast Guard	Transportation Dept.	$ 7,274	43, 639
		TOTAL	$35,527	164,184

In creating a Department of Homeland Security, the government committed massive numbers of employees, financial resources, and police authority—some new and some reassigned from other parts of the federal bureaucracy.

*Immigration services became a separate bureau within the department.
†Classified.
§Included in FEMA budget request.
SOURCE: The White House.

the DHS as one of the departments most vulnerable to waste, fraud, and mismanagement.[3]

The birth pains of new government agencies are often traumatic. But agencies also suffer midlife crises and even the decrepitude of old age.[4] Yet, Americans depend on government bureaucracies to accomplish the most spectacular achievements as well as the most mundane. They often do not realize that public bureaucracies are essential for providing the services that they use every day and that they rely on in emergencies. On a typical day, a college student might check the weather forecast, drive on an interstate highway, mail the rent check, drink from a public water fountain, check the calories on the side of a yogurt container, attend a class, log on to the Internet, and meet a relative at the airport. Each of these activities is possible because of the work of a government bureaucracy: the U.S. Weather Service, the U.S. Department of Transportation, the U.S. Postal Service, the Environmental Protection Agency, the Food and Drug Administration, the student loan programs of the U.S. Department of Education, the Advanced Research Projects Agency (which developed the Internet in the 1960s), and the Federal Aviation Administration. Without the ongoing work of such agencies, many of these common activities would be impossible, unreliable, or more expensive. Even though bureaucracies provide essential services that all Americans rely on, they are often disparaged by politicians and the general public alike. Criticized as "big government," many federal bureaucracies come into public view only when they are charged with fraud, waste, and abuse.

In emergencies, the national perspective on bureaucracy and, indeed, on "big government" shifts. After the September 11 terrorist attacks, as we just noted, all eyes turned to Washington. The federal government responded by strengthening and reorganizing the bureaucracy to undertake a whole new set of responsibilities designed to keep America safe. The president created the new cabinet-level Department of Homeland Security. Law-enforcement agencies gained new powers and resources. Reflecting the shift in priorities from crime investigation to terrorism prevention, the Federal Bureau of Investigation (FBI) received new responsibilities for domestic intelligence. Many other agencies assumed new duties associated with the antiterrorism objectives. The Treasury Department, for example, was assigned to create a financial intelligence-gathering system designed to track terrorists' financial transactions. The Centers for Disease Control and Prevention (CDC) undertook a new set of activities designed to prevent bioterrorism. Congress created a new Transportation Security Administration within the Department of Transportation (subsequently moved to the Department of Homeland Security). Charged with making all forms of travel safe, the new agency presided over a significant expansion of the federal workforce as it hired the thousands of workers who screen passengers at airports.

---

[3]Government Accountability Office, *Major Management Challenges and Program Risks: A Government-wide Perspective* (January 2003); GAO-03-95 (available at www.gao.gov/pas/2003/d0395.pdf).
[4]The Interstate Commerce Commission, the oldest regulatory agency (created in 1887), was put out of its misery in 1995.

The war on terrorism has highlighted the extensive range of the tasks shouldered by the federal bureaucracy. Both routine and exceptional tasks require the organization, specialization, and expertise found in bureaucracies. Turn to Table 7.1, which identifies the range of functions and activities brought under the jurisdiction of Homeland Security. Note especially the huge financial and human resources committed to these activities. (And there has been further growth in the two fiscal years since 2003.)

To provide services, government bureaucracies employ specialists such as meteorologists, doctors, and scientists. To do their jobs effectively, these specialists require resources and tools (ranging from paper to blood samples); they have to coordinate their work with others (for example, the traffic engineers must communicate with construction engineers); and there must be effective outreach to the public (for example, private doctors must be made aware of health warnings). Bureaucracy provides a way to coordinate the many different parts that must work together to provide good services.

In this chapter, we focus on the federal bureaucracy—the administrative structure that on a day-by-day basis *is* the American government. We first define and describe bureaucracy as a social and political phenomenon. Second, we look in detail at American bureaucracy in action by examining the government's major administrative agencies, their role in the governmental process, and their political behavior. These details of administration are the very heart and soul of modern government.

We mean for the reader to keep an open mind about bureaucracy. It is often portrayed as "runaway" and "out of control." It is often thought of pejoratively as self-serving, bloated, and highly inefficient. In short, bureaucracy has a very serious public relations problem! But bureaucracy is created by legislation—that is, an agency's existence (both initial and continued) is approved by both houses of Congress and the president. A bureau's authority can be expanded or trimmed by legislative authorization, its budgets increased or decreased via the normal appropriations process, and its actions subjected to scrutiny by legislative oversight committees and executive watchdog agencies. In short, bureaus and agencies of the federal government are the *creatures* of Congress and the president. We should wonder, before castigating bureaus and agencies, whether our elected officials are as much to blame as are appointees and civil servants for the excesses laid at the door of the federal bureaucracy.

WHY BUREAUCRACY?

Bureaucracies are commonplace because they touch so many aspects of daily life. Government bureaucracies implement the decisions made by the political process. Bureaucracies are full of routine because that ensures the regular delivery of the services and ensures that each agency fulfills its mandate. For this reason students often conclude that a consideration of bureaucracy is mechanical, routinized, and just plain boring. But that is a big mistake. Bureaucracy is not just about collecting garbage, training police, or mailing Social Security checks. Mainly, it is a reflection of political deals consummated by elected politicians, of turf wars among government agents and private-sector suppliers and contractors, of policy-delivery successes and failures in the eyes of the public, and, to complete the circle, of reactions to these by the very same elected officials who cut the deals in the first place. It is politics, through and through.

Public bureaucracies are powerful because legislatures and chief executives—and, indeed, the people—delegate to them vast power to make sure a particular job is done, enabling the rest of us to be freer to pursue our private ends. The public sentiments that emerged after September 11 revealed this underlying appreciation of public bureaucracies. When faced with the challenge of making air travel safe again, the public strongly supported giving the federal government responsibility for airport security, even though this meant increasing the size of the federal bureaucracy by making the security screeners federal workers. House majority whip Tom DeLay sought to forestall this growth in the federal government, declaring that "the last thing we can afford to do is erect a new bureaucracy that is unaccountable and unable to protect the American public."[5] But the antibureaucratic language that had been so effective before September 11 no longer resonated with a fearful public. Instead, there was a widespread belief that a public bureaucracy would provide more effective protection than the cost-conscious private security companies that had been charged with airport security in the past. Bureaucrats across the federal government felt the new appreciation for their work. As one civil servant at the Pentagon put it, "The whole mood has changed. A couple of months ago we were part of the bloated bureaucracy. Now we're Washington's equivalent of the cops and firemen in New York."[6] Is this a brief honeymoon or something more enduring?

We can shed some systematic light on public attitudes toward government bureaucracy by examining one of the standard questions posed in election years by the National Election Studies (NES). As part of its survey of the American public, the NES asks a range of questions, among which is "Do you think that people in the government waste a lot of money we pay in taxes, waste some of it, or don't waste very much of it?" While not perfect for eliciting from the public a nuanced assessment of bureaucratic performance, the question allows respondents to register a blunt evaluation. Results from the past several decades are given in Figure 7.1.

Public unhappiness with bureaucratic inefficiency grew during the 1960s and 1970s and became one of Ronald Reagan's campaign themes in the 1980 election. During the administrations of Reagan, George H. W. Bush, and Bill Clinton, this unhappiness declined from nearly 80 percent of the survey respondents believing government "wastes a lot" in 1980 to just over 60 percent in

[5]Janet Hook, "U.S. Strikes Back; Political Landscape; GOP Bypasses the Bipartisan Truce," *Los Angeles Times,* 14 October 2001, p. A8.
[6]R. W. Apple Jr., "White House Letter: Big Government Is Back in Style," *New York Times,* 23 November 2001, p. B2.

FIGURE 7.1

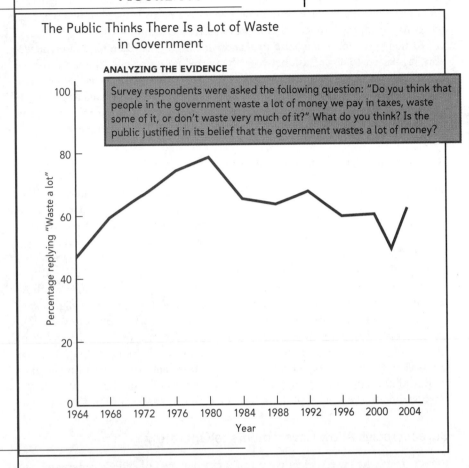

The Public Thinks There Is a Lot of Waste
in Government

ANALYZING THE EVIDENCE

Survey respondents were asked the following question: "Do you think that people in the government waste a lot of money we pay in taxes, waste some of it, or don't waste very much of it?" What do you think? Is the public justified in its belief that the government wastes a lot of money?

SOURCE: National Election Studies, 1948–2004 Cumulative Data File, conducted by the Center for Political Studies at the University of Michigan.

2004. This opinion has held steady in the low 60-percent range for twenty years, though there was a significant downward blip in 2002, just after September 11. But whatever honeymoon there might have been after the terror attacks, it appears that the public remains cynical about bureaucratic performance. The poor response of the Federal Emergency Management Agency (FEMA)—part of DHS—to the hurricane crises of the fall of 2005, and especially to charges of cronyism in personnel appointments, has surely contributed to further cynicism.

Despite this tendency to criticize bureaucracy because it is "bureaucratic," most Americans recognize that maintaining order in a large society is impossible without some sort of large governmental apparatus, staffed by professionals with some expertise in public administration. When we approve of what a government agency is doing, we give the phenomenon a positive name, *administration;* when we disapprove, we call the phenomenon *bureaucracy.*

Although the terms *administration* and *bureaucracy* are often used interchangeably, it is useful to distinguish between the two. *Administration* is the more general of the two terms; it refers to all the ways human beings might rationally coordinate their efforts to achieve a common goal. This applies to private as well as public organizations. ***Bureaucracy*** refers to the actual offices, tasks, and principles of organization that are employed in the most formal and sustained administration.

bureaucracy The complex structure of offices, tasks, rules, and principles of organization that are employed by all large-scale institutions to coordinate the work of their personnel.

Bureaucratic Organization Enhances Efficiency

The core of bureaucracy is the *division of labor.* The key to bureaucratic effectiveness is the coordination of experts performing complex tasks. If each job is specialized to gain efficiencies, then each worker must depend on the output of other workers, and that requires careful *allocation* of jobs and resources. Inevitably, bureaucracies become hierarchical, often approximating a pyramid in form. At the base of the organization are workers with the fewest skills and specializations; one supervisor can deal with a relatively large number of these workers. At the next level of the organization, where there are more highly specialized workers, the supervision and coordination of work involves fewer workers per supervisor. Toward the top of the organization, a very small number of high-level executives engages in the "management" of the organization, meaning the organization and reorganization of all the tasks and functions, plus the allocation of the appropriate supplies and the distribution of the outputs of the organization to the market (if it is a "private sector" organization) or to the public.

Bureaucracies Allow Governments to Operate

Bureaucracy, when used pejoratively, conjures up images of endless paperwork, red tape, and lazy, uncaring employees. But bureaucracy in fact represents a rather spectacular human achievement. By dividing up tasks, matching tasks to a labor force that develops appropriately specialized skills, routinizing procedure, and providing the incentive structure and oversight arrangements to get large numbers of people to operate in a coordinated, purposeful fashion, bureaucracies accomplish tasks and missions in a manner that would otherwise be unimaginable. The provision of "government goods" as broad as the defense of people, property, and national borders or as narrow as a subsidy to a wheat farmer, a beef rancher, or a manufacturer of specialty steel requires organization, routines, standards, and, at the end of the day, the authority for someone to cut a check and put it in the mail. Bureaucracies are created to do these things. No large organization would be larger than the sum of its parts, and many would be smaller, without bureaucratizing its activities.

Bureaucracy also consolidates a range of complementary programs and insulates them from the predatory ambitions of out-of-sympathy political forces. Nothing in

Rationality Principle

Bureaucracies are the instruments through which policy objectives are secured.

this world is permanent, but bureaucracies come close. By creating clienteles—in the legislature, the world of interest groups, and public opinion—a bureaucracy establishes a coalition of supporters, some of whom will fight to the end to keep it in place. It is a well-known rule of thumb that everyone in the political world cares deeply and intensely about a subset of policies and the agencies that produce them, and opposes other policies and agencies but not with nearly the same passion. Opponents, to succeed, must clear many hurdles, while proponents, to maintain the status quo, must marshall their forces only at a few veto points. In the final analysis, opponents typically meet obstacle after obstacle and eventually give up their uphill battles and concentrate on protecting and expanding what they care more deeply about. In a complex political system like that in the United States, it is much easier to do the latter. Politicians appreciate this fact of life. Consequently, both opponents and proponents of a particular set of government activities wage the fiercest battles at the time programs are enacted and a bureaucracy is created. Once created, these organizations assume a position of relative permanence.

So, in response to the question of how bureaucracy makes government possible, there is an *efficiency* part to the answer and a *credibility* part. The creation of a bureau is a way to deliver government goods efficiently *and* a device by which to "tie one's hands," thereby providing a credible commitment to the long-term existence of a policy.

Bureaucrats Fulfill Important Roles

"Government by offices and desks" conveys to most people a picture of hundreds of office workers shuffling millions of pieces of paper. There is a lot of truth in that image, but we have to look more closely at what papers are being shuffled and why. More than fifty years ago, an astute observer defined bureaucracy as "continuous routine business."[7] Almost any organization succeeds by reducing its work to routines, with each routine being given to a different specialist. But specialization separates people from each other; one worker's output becomes another worker's input. The timing of such relationships is essential, requiring these workers to stay in communication with each other. In fact, bureaucracy was the first information network. Voluminous routine came as bureaucracies grew and specialized. It's no small irony that, as bureaucracies have grown, the term *bureaucrat* now connotes sluggishness and inefficiency.

Bureaucrats Implement Laws Bureaucrats, whether in public or in private organizations, communicate with each other to coordinate all the specializations within their organization. This coordination is necessary to carry out the primary task of bureaucracy, which is ***implementation***—that is, implementing the objectives of the organization as laid down by its board of directors (if a private company) or by law (if a public agency). In government, the "bosses" are ultimately the legislature and

Collective-Action Principle

Coordination among bureaucrats is necessary to carry out the primary task of bureaucracy—implementation.

implementation
The efforts of departments and agencies to translate laws into specific bureaucratic routines.

---

[7]Arnold Brecht and Comstock Glaser, *The Art and Technique of Administration in German Ministries* (Cambridge, MA: Harvard University Press, 1940), p. 6.

the elected chief executive. As we saw in Chapter 1, in a principal-agent relationship, it is the principal who stipulates what he wants done, relying on the agent's concern for her reputation, appropriate incentives, and other control mechanisms to secure compliance with his wishes. Thus it may be argued that legislative principals establish bureaucratic agents—in departments, bureaus, agencies, institutes, and commissions of the federal government—to implement the policies promulgated by Congress and the president.

Institution Principle

Legislative principals establish bureaucratic agents to implement policies.

Bureaucrats Make and Enforce Rules   When the bosses—Congress, in particular, when it is making the law—are clear in their instructions to bureaucrats, implementation is a fairly straightforward process. Bureaucrats translate the law into specific routines for each of the employees of an agency. But what happens to routine administrative implementation when there are several bosses who disagree as to what the instructions ought to be? The agent of multiple principals who disagree often finds himself or herself in a real bind. The agent must chart a delicate course, seeking to do the best he or she can and trying not to offend any of the bosses too much. This requires yet another job for bureaucrats: interpretation. Interpretation is a form of implementation in that the bureaucrats still have to carry out what they believe to be the intentions of their superiors. But when bureaucrats have to interpret a law before implementing it, they are in effect engaging in *lawmaking*.[8] Congress often deliberately delegates to an administrative agency the responsibility of lawmaking. Members of Congress often conclude that some area of industry needs regulating or some area of the environment needs protection, but they are unwilling or unable to specify just how that should be done. In such situations, Congress delegates to the appropriate agency a broad authority within which the bureaucrats have to make law, through the procedures of ***rule making*** and ***administrative adjudication.***

rule making

A quasi-legislative administrative process that produces regulations by government agencies.

administrative adjudication

Applying rules and precedents to specific cases to settle disputes with regulated parties.

Rule making is exactly the same as legislation; in fact, it is often referred to as "quasi-legislation." The rules issued by government agencies provide more detailed and specific indications of what the policy actually will mean. For example, the Occupational Health and Safety Administration (OSHA) is charged with ensuring that our workplaces are safe. OSHA has regulated the use of chemicals and other well-known health hazards. In recent years, the widespread use of computers in the workplace has been associated with a growing number of cases of repetitive stress injury, which hurts the hands, arms, and neck. To respond to this new threat to workplace health, OSHA issued a new set of ergonomic rules in November 1999 that tell employers what they must do to prevent and address such injuries among their workers. Such rules take force only after a period of public comment. Reaction from the people or businesses that

[8]When bureaucrats engage in interpretation, the result is what political scientists call bureaucratic drift. Bureaucratic drift occurs because, as we've suggested, the "bosses" (in Congress) and the agents (within the bureaucracy) don't always share the same purposes. Bureaucrats also have their own agendas to fulfill. There exists a vast body of political-science literature on the relationship between Congress and the bureaucracy. For a review, see Kenneth A. Shepsle and Mark S. Bonchek, *Analyzing Politics: Rationality, Behavior, and Institutions* (New York: Norton, 1997), pp. 355–68.

are subject to the rules may cause an agency to modify the rules they first issue. The rule-making process is thus a highly political one. Once rules are approved, they are published in the *Federal Register* and have the force of law.

Bureaucrats Settle Disputes   Administrative adjudication is very similar to what the judiciary ordinarily does: applying rules and precedents to specific cases to settle disputes. In administrative adjudication, the agency charges the person or business suspected of violating the law. The ruling in an adjudication dispute applies only to the specific case being considered. Many regulatory agencies use administrative adjudication to make decisions about specific products or practices. For example, product recalls are often the result of adjudication. To take another instance, the National Labor Relations Board (NLRB) provides many examples of case-by-case administrative adjudication. One large class of cases involves union certification. Groups of workers seek the right to vote on creating a union, or to affiliate with an existing union as their bargaining agent, and are opposed by their employers, who assert that relevant provisions of labor law do not apply. The NLRB, case by case, takes testimony, considers evidence, and makes determinations for one side or the other, acting essentially like a court.

Institution Principle
Congress also delegates authority to bureaucrats to make law through the procedures of rule making and administrative adjudication.

In sum, government bureaucrats do essentially the same things that bureaucrats in large private organizations do, and neither type deserves the disrespect embodied in the term *bureaucrat*. But because of the authoritative, coercive nature of government, far more constraints are imposed on public bureaucrats than on private bureaucrats, even when their jobs are the same. Public bureaucrats are required to maintain a far more thorough paper trail. Public bureaucrats are also subject to a great deal more access from the public. Newspaper reporters, for example, have access to public bureaucrats. Public access has been vastly facilitated in the past thirty years; the adoption of the Freedom of Information Act (FOIA) in 1966 gave ordinary citizens the right of access to agency files and agency data to determine whether derogatory information exists in the file about citizens themselves and to learn about what the agency is doing in general.

And, finally, citizens are given far more opportunities to participate in the decision-making processes of public agencies. There are limits of time, money, and expertise to this kind of access, but it does exist, and it occupies a great deal of the time of mid-level and senior public bureaucrats. This public exposure and access serves a purpose, but it also cuts down significantly on the efficiency of public bureaucrats. Thus much of the lower efficiency of public agencies can be attributed to the political, judicial, legal, and publicity restraints put on public bureaucrats.

Politics

We have provided two main answers to the question "Why bureaucracy?": (1) bureaucracies enhance efficiency, and (2) they are the instruments of policy implementation. We would be remiss if we didn't include a third important answer: legislatures find it valuable to delegate.

In principle, the legislature could make all bureaucratic decisions itself, writing very detailed legislation each year, dotting every *i* and crossing every *t*. In some jurisdictions—tax policy, for example—this is in fact done. Tax policy is promulgated in significant detail by the House Ways and Means Committee, the Senate Finance Committee, and the Joint Committee on Taxation. The Internal Revenue Service, the administrative agency charged with implementation, engages in relatively less discretionary activity compared to many other regulatory and administrative agencies. But this is surely the exception.

The norm is for statutory authority to be delegated to the bureaucracy, sometimes with specificity but often in relatively vague terms. The bureaucracy is expected to "fill in the gaps." This, however, is not a blank check to exercise unconstrained discretion. The bureaucracy is expected to be guided by legislative intent, and it will be held to account by the legislature's oversight of bureaucratic performance. The latter is monitored by the staffs of relevant legislative committees, which also serve as repositories for complaints from affected parties.[9] Poor performance or the exercise of discretion inconsistent with the preferences of the important legislators invites sanctions ranging from the brow-beating of senior bureaucrats to the trimming of budgets and clipping of authority.

The delegation relationship will be revisited later in this chapter. For now, simply note that over and above the more conventional reasons for bureaucracy, politicians find it convenient to delegate many of the nuts-and-bolts decisions to bureaucratic agents. We will take up the reasons shortly.

HOW IS THE EXECUTIVE BRANCH ORGANIZED?

Cabinet departments, agencies, and bureaus are the operating parts of the bureaucratic whole. These parts can be separated into four general types: (1) cabinet departments, (2) independent agencies, (3) government corporations, and (4) independent regulatory commissions.

Although Figure 7.2 is an "organizational chart" of the Department of Agriculture, any other department could have been used as an illustration. At the top is the head of the department, called the "secretary" of the department. Below the department head are several top administrators, such as the deputy secretary, the general counsel, and the chief financial officer, whose responsibilities cut across the various departmental functions and provide the secretary with the ability to manage the entire organization. Of equal status are the under and assistant secretaries, each of whom has management responsibilities for a group of operating agencies, which are arranged vertically below each of the assistant secretaries.

The next tier, generally called the "bureau level," is the highest level of responsibility for specialized programs. The names of these "bureau-level agencies"

---

[9]See Matthew D. McCubbins and Thomas Schwartz, "Congressional Oversight Overlooked: Police Patrols versus Fire Alarms," *American Journal of Political Science* 28 (1984): 165–79.

FIGURE 7.2

Organizational Chart of the Department of Agriculture

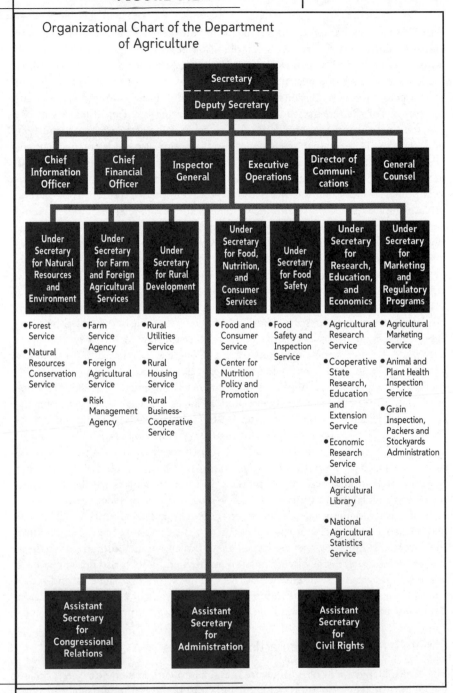

SOURCE: U.S. Department of Agriculture (www.usda.gov/img/content/org_chart_enlarged.jpg).

are often very well known to the public: the Forest Service and the Food Safety and Inspection Service are two examples. Sometimes they are officially called bureaus, as in the FBI, which is a bureau in the Department of Justice. Nevertheless, *bureau* is also the generic term for this level of administrative agency. Within the bureaus, there are divisions, offices, services, and units—sometimes designating agencies of the same status, sometimes designating agencies of lesser status.

Not all government agencies are part of cabinet departments. A second type of agency, the independent agency, is set up by Congress outside the departmental structure altogether, even though the president appoints and directs the head of this type of agency. Independent agencies usually have broad powers to provide public services that are either too expensive or too important to be left to private initiatives. Some examples of independent agencies are the National Aeronautics and Space Administration (NASA), the Central Intelligence Agency (CIA), and the Environmental Protection Agency (EPA). Government corporations are a third type of government agency but are more like private businesses performing and charging for a market service, such as delivering the mail (the United States Postal Service) or transporting railroad passengers (Amtrak).

Yet a fourth type of agency is the independent regulatory commission, given broad discretion to make rules. The first regulatory agencies established by Congress, beginning with the Interstate Commerce Commission in 1887, were set up as independent regulatory commissions because Congress recognized that regulatory agencies are "minilegislatures," whose rules are the same as legislation but require the kind of expertise and full-time attention that is beyond the capacity of Congress. Until the 1960s, most of the regulatory agencies that were set up by Congress, such as the Federal Trade Commission (1914) and the Federal Communications Commission (1934), were independent regulatory commissions. But beginning in the late 1960s and the early 1970s, all new regulatory programs, with two or three exceptions (such as the Federal Election Commission), were placed within existing departments and made directly responsible to the president. Since the 1970s, no major new regulatory programs have been established, independent or otherwise.

There are too many agencies in the executive branch to identify, much less to describe, so a simple classification of agencies will be helpful. Instead of dividing the bureaucracy into four general types, as we did above, an alternative classification organizes each agency by its mission, as defined by its jurisdiction: clientele agencies, agencies for maintenance of the Union, regulatory agencies, and redistributive agencies. We shall examine each of these types of agencies, focusing on both their formal structure and their place in the political process.

Clientele Agencies Serve Particular Interests

clientele agencies Departments or bureaus of government whose mission is to promote, serve, or represent a particular interest.

The entire Department of Agriculture is an example of a *clientele agency.* So are the Departments of the Interior, Labor, and Commerce. Although all administrative agencies have clientele, certain agencies are singled out and called by that name because they are directed by law to foster and promote the interests of their clientele. For example, the Department of Commerce and Labor was founded in 1903 as a single department "to foster, promote, and develop the foreign and domestic commerce, the mining, the manufacturing, the shipping, and fishing industries, and the transportation facilities of the United States."[10] It remained a single department until 1913, when the law created the two separate departments of Commerce and Labor, with each statute providing for the same obligation—to support and foster their respective clienteles.[11] The Department of Agriculture serves the many farming interests that, taken together, are the United States' largest economic sector (agriculture accounts for one fifth of the U.S. total domestic output).

Most clientele agencies locate a relatively large proportion of their total personnel in field offices dealing directly with the clientele. The Extension Service of the Department of Agriculture is among the most familiar, with its numerous local "extension agents" who consult with farmers on farm productivity. These same agencies also seek to foster the interests of their clientele by providing "functional representation"—that is, they try to learn what their clients' interests and needs are and then operate almost as a lobby in Washington on their behalf. In addition to the Department of Agriculture, other clientele agencies include the Department of the Interior and five of the newest cabinet departments: Housing and Urban Development (HUD), created in 1965; Transportation (DOT), created in 1966; Energy (DOE), created in 1977; Education (ED), created in 1979; and Health and Human Services (HHS), created in 1979.[12]

> **Policy Principle**
>
> The policies of clientele agencies promote the interests of their clientele.

Agencies for Maintenance of the Union Keep the Government Going

Agencies for maintenance of the Union could be called public-order agencies were it not for the fact that the Constitution entrusts so many of the vital functions of public order, such as the police, to the state governments. But some agencies vital to maintaining *national* bonds do exist in the national government, and they can be grouped for convenience into three categories: (1) agencies for control of the sources of government revenue, (2) agencies for control of conduct defined as a threat to internal national security, and (3) agencies for defending American security from external threats. The departments of greatest power in these three areas are Treasury, Justice, Defense, and State.

Revenue Agencies   The Internal Revenue Service (IRS) is the most important revenue agency. The IRS is also one of the federal government's largest bureaucracies. Over 100,000 employees are spread through four regions, sixty-three

---

[10]32 Stat. 825; 15 USC 1501.

[11]For a detailed account of the creation of the Department of Commerce and Labor and its split into two separate departments, see Theodore J. Lowi, *The End of Liberalism: The Second Republic of the United States*, 2nd ed. (New York: Norton, 1979), pp. 78–84.

[12]The Departments of Education and of Health and Human Services until 1979 were joined in a single department, the Department of Health, Education, and Welfare (HEW), which had been established by Congress in 1953.

districts, ten service centers, and hundreds of local offices. In 2001, the IRS processed more than 200 million tax returns and supplemental documents, with total collections amounting to $2,128,831,182. (It costs the IRS 41 cents to collect every $100 in taxes; this figure has dropped from 60 cents in 1993.) Nearly 17,500 IRS tax auditors and revenue agents are engaged in auditing tax returns, recommending additional taxes and penalties totaling billions of dollars in additional revenues.

Agencies for Internal Security   As long as the country is not in a state of insurrection, most of the task of maintaining the Union takes the form of legal work, and the main responsibility for that lies with the Department of Justice. It is indeed a luxury, and rare in the world, when national unity can be maintained by routines of civil law instead of imposed by a real army with guns. The largest and most important agency in the Justice Department is the Criminal Division, which is responsible for enforcing all the federal criminal laws, except for a few specifically assigned to other divisions. Criminal litigation is actually done by the U.S. attorneys. There is a presidentially appointed U.S. attorney assigned to each federal judicial district, and he or she supervises the work of assistant U.S. attorneys. The work or jurisdiction of the Antitrust and Civil Rights Divisions is described by their official names. Although it looms so very large in American folklore, the FBI is simply another bureau of the Department of Justice. The FBI handles no litigation but instead serves as the information-gathering agency for all the other divisions.

In 2002, Congress created the Department of Homeland Security to coordinate the nation's defense against the threat of terrorism. The new department is responsible for a number of tasks, including protecting commercial airlines from would-be hijackers.

Agencies for External National Security   Two departments occupy center stage here, State and Defense. There are a few key agencies outside State and Defense that have external national-security functions. They are treated in this chapter only as bureaucratic phenomena and as examples of the political problems relevant to administration.

Although diplomacy is generally considered the primary task of the State Department, diplomatic missions make up only one of its organizational dimensions. The State Department is also composed of geographic or regional bureaus concerned with all problems within a defined region of the world; "functional" bureaus, handling such things as economic and business affairs, intelligence and research; and international organizations and bureaus of internal affairs, which handle such areas as security, finance and management, and legal issues.

Despite the importance of the State Department in foreign affairs, fewer than 20 percent of all U.S. government employees working abroad are directly under its authority. By far the largest number of career government professionals working abroad are under the authority of the Defense Department.

The creation of the Department of Defense by legislation from 1947 to 1949 was an effort to unify the two historic military departments, the War Department and the Navy Department, and to integrate with them a new department, the Air Force Department. Real unification, however, did not occur. Instead, the Defense Department adds more pluralism to national security.

America's primary political problem with its military has not been the historic one of how to keep the military out of the politics of governing—a problem that has plagued so many countries in Europe and Latin America. The American military problem is one of the lower politics of the "pork barrel." President Clinton's long list of proposed military base closings, a major part of his budget-cutting drive for 1993, caused a firestorm of opposition even within his own party, including a number of members of Congress who were otherwise prominently in favor of significant reductions in the Pentagon budget. Emphasis on jobs rather than strategy and policy means pork-barrel use of the military for political purposes. This is a classic way for a bureaucracy to defend itself politically in a democracy. It is the distributive tendency, in which the bureaucracy ensures political support among elected officials by making sure to distribute things—military bases, contracts, facilities, and jobs—to the states and districts from which the legislators were elected. As is commonly known, it is hard to bite the hand that feeds you! Thus the best way to understand the military in American politics is to study it within the same bureaucratic framework used to explain the domestic agencies.

Policy Principle
The military pork barrel is an example of the distributive tendency in Congress.

Regulatory Agencies Guide Individual Conduct

As we saw in Chapter 3, our national government did not even begin to get involved in the regulation of economic and social affairs until the late nineteenth century. Until then, regulation was strictly a state and local affair. The federal *regulatory agencies* are, as a result, relatively new, most dating from the 1930s. But they have come to be extensive and important. In this section, we look at these regulatory agencies as an administrative phenomenon, with its attendant politics.

The United States has no "department of regulation" but has many regulatory agencies. Some of these are bureaus within departments, such as the Food and Drug Administration (FDA) in the Department of Health and Human Services, OSHA in the Department of Labor, and the Animal and Plant Health and Inspection Service (APHIS) in the Department of Agriculture. Other regulatory agencies are independent regulatory commissions—for example, the Federal Trade Commission (FTC). But whether departmental or independent, an agency or commission is regulatory if Congress delegates to it relatively broad powers over a sector of the economy or a type of commercial activity and authorizes it to make rules governing the conduct of people and businesses within that jurisdiction. Rules made by regulatory agencies have the force and effect of legislation; indeed, the rules they make are referred to as *administrative legislation.* And when these agencies make decisions or orders settling disputes between parties or between the government and a party, they are really acting like courts.

Because regulatory agencies exercise a tremendous amount of influence over the economy and because their rules are a form of legislation, Congress was at

regulatory agencies Departments, bureaus, or independent agencies whose primary mission is to eliminate or restrict certain behaviors defined as being negative in themselves or negative in their consequences.

administrative legislation Rules made by regulatory agencies and commissions.

first loath to turn them over to the executive branch as ordinary agencies under the control of the president. Consequently, most of the important regulatory programs were delegated to independent commissions with direct responsibility to Congress rather than to the White House. This is the basis of the 1930s reference to them as the "headless fourth branch."[13] With the rise of presidential government, most recent presidents have supported more regulatory programs but have successfully opposed the expansion of regulatory independence. The 1960s and 1970s witnessed adoption of an unprecedented number of new regulatory programs but only four new independent commissions.

Agencies of Redistribution Implement Fiscal/Monetary and Welfare Policies

Welfare agencies and fiscal/monetary agencies are responsible for the transfer of hundreds of billions of dollars annually between the public and the private spheres, and through such transfers these agencies influence how people and corporations spend and invest trillions of dollars annually. We call them agencies of redistribution because they influence the amount of money in the economy and because they directly influence who has money, who has credit, and whether people will want to invest or save their money rather than spend it.

Fiscal and Monetary Agencies   The best generic term for government activity affecting or relating to money is *fiscal* policy. However, we choose to make a further distinction, reserving *fiscal* for taxing and spending policies and using *monetary* for policies having to do with banks, credit, and currency. And the third, *welfare*, deserves to be treated as an equal member of this redistributive category.

Administration of fiscal policy is primarily performed in the Treasury Department. It is no contradiction to include the Treasury here and with the agencies for maintenance of the Union. This indicates (1) that the Treasury is a complex department, performing more than one function of government and (2) that traditional controls have had to be adapted to modern economic conditions and new technologies.

Today, in addition to administering and policing income tax and other tax collections, the Treasury is also responsible for managing the enormous federal debt.

The Treasury Department prints the currency that we use, but currency represents only a tiny proportion of the entire money economy. Most of the trillions of dollars used in the transactions that make up the private and public sectors of the U.S. economy exist on printed accounts and computers, not in currency.

Another important fiscal agency (although for technical reasons it is called an agency of monetary policy) is the **Federal Reserve System,** headed by the Federal Reserve Board. The Federal Reserve System (the Fed) has authority over the credit

Federal Reserve System (Fed)
Consisting of twelve Federal Reserve Banks, the Fed facilitates exchanges of cash, checks, and credit; it regulates member banks; and it uses monetary policies to fight inflation and deflation.

[13]*Final Report of the President's Committee on Administrative Management* (Washington, DC: Government Printing Office, 1937). The term *headless fourth branch* was invented by a member of the committee staff, Cornell University government professor Robert Cushman.

rates and lending activities of the nation's most important banks. Established by Congress in 1913, the Fed is responsible for adjusting the supply of money to the needs of banks in the different regions and of the commerce and industry in each. The Fed helps shift money from where there is too much to where it is needed. It also ensures that the banks do not overextend themselves by having lending policies that are too liberal, out of fear that if there is a sudden economic scare, a run on a few banks might be contagious and cause another terrible crash like the one in 1929. The Federal Reserve Board sits at the top of the pyramid of twelve district Federal Reserve Banks, which are "bankers' banks," serving the monetary needs of the hundreds of member banks in the national bank system.

Welfare Agencies   No single government agency is responsible for all the programs making up the "welfare state." The largest agency in this field is the Social Security Administration (SSA), which manages the social insurance aspects of Social Security and Supplemental Security Income (SSI). As the baby-boomer generation ages, a growing bloc of voters (and their children) have become concerned about the solvency of this system. It is a live political issue that figured prominently in the 2000 and 2004 presidential election campaigns. Many argue that without some adjustments in benefit schedules or taxes, the present population will begin drawing down the enormous amount of funds in the Social Security Trust Fund in two decades and exhaust it in forty years.

Other agencies in the Department of Health and Human Services administer Temporary Assistance to Needy Families (TANF) and Medicaid, and the Department of Agriculture is responsible for the Food Stamp Program. With the exception of Social Security, these are *means-tested* programs, requiring applicants to demonstrate that their total annual cash earnings fall below an officially defined poverty line. These public assistance programs create a large administrative burden.

In August 1996, virtually all of the means-tested public assistance programs were legally abolished as national programs and were "devolved" to the states (see also Chapter 3). However, for the five years between fiscal 1996 and 2001, there was still a great deal of national administrative responsibility because federal funding of these programs continued through large, discretionary block grants to each state. Other aspects of state welfare activity were policed by federal agencies, and all of that required about the same size of administrative capacity in welfare as existed before. Those who expected some kind of revolution after adoption of the Personal Responsibility and Work Opportunity Reconciliation Act of 1996 were in for a disappointment.

THE PROBLEM OF BUREAUCRATIC CONTROL

Two hundred years, millions of employees, and trillions of dollars after the founding, we must return to James Madison's observation that "you must first enable the government to control the governed; and in the next place oblige it to control itself."[14] Today the problem is the same, but the form has changed. Our problem today is bureaucracy and our inability to keep it accountable to elected political authorities.

Bureaucrats Have Their Own Motivational Considerations

Rationality Principle

One view of bureaucratic behavior is that bureaucrats are motivated to maximize their budgets.

The economist William A. Niskanen proposed that we consider a bureau or department of government as analogous to a division of a private firm and conceive of the bureaucrat just as we would the manager who runs that division.[15] In particular, Niskanen stipulates for the purposes of modeling bureaucratic behavior that a bureau chief or department head be thought of as a maximizer of his or her budget (just as the private-sector counterpart is a maximizer of his or her division's profits).

There are quite a number of different motivational bases on which bureaucratic budget maximizing might be justified. A cynical (though some would say realistic) basis for budget maximizing is that the bureaucrat's own compensation is often tied to the size of his or her budget. Not only might bureaus with large budgets have higher-salaried executives with more elaborate fringe benefits but also there may be enhanced opportunities for career advancement, travel, a poshly appointed office, possibly even a chauffeur-driven limousine.

A second, related motivation for large budgets is nonmaterial personal gratification. An individual understandably enjoys the prestige and respect that comes from running a major enterprise. You can't take these things to the bank or put them on your family's dinner table, but your sense of esteem and your stature are surely buoyed by the conspicuous fact that your bureau or division has a large budget. That you are also boss of a large number of subordinates, made possible by a large bureau budget, is another aspect of this sort of ego gratification.

But personal salary, "on-the-job consumption," and power-tripping are not the only forces driving a bureaucrat toward gaining as large a budget as possible. Some bureaucrats, perhaps most, actually *care* about their missions.[16] They initially choose to go into public safety, or the military, or health care, or social work, or education—as police officers, soldiers, hospital managers, social workers, and teachers, respectively—because they believe in the importance of helping people in their communities. As they rise through the ranks of a public bureaucracy into management responsibilities, they take this mission orientation with them. Thus, as chief of detectives in a big-city police department, as head of procurement in the air force, as director of nursing services in a public hospital, as supervisor of the social work division in a county welfare department, or as assistant superintendent of a town school system, individuals try to secure as large a budget as they can to succeed in achieving the missions to which they have devoted their professional lives.

[14]Clinton Rossiter, ed., *The Federalist Papers* (New York: New American Library, 1961), No. 51.
[15]William A. Niskanen Jr., *Bureaucracy and Representative Government* (Chicago: Aldine, 1971).
[16]John Brehm and Scott Gates, *Working, Shirking, and Sabotage: Bureaucratic Response to a Democratic Public* (Ann Arbor: University of Michigan Press, 1997).

Whether from cynical, self-serving motives or for the noblest of public purposes, it is entirely plausible that individual bureaucrats seek to persuade others (typically legislators or taxpayers) to provide them with as many resources as possible. Indeed, it is sometimes difficult to distinguish the saint from the sinner because each sincerely argues that he or she needs more to do more. This is one nice feature of Niskanen's assumption of budget maximizing: It doesn't really matter *why* a bureaucrat is interested in a big budget; what matters is simply that he or she wants more resources rather than less.

Critics of the budget-maximizing theory call into question its assumption about the passivity of the legislature. The legislature, the only customer of the bureau's product, in essence tells the bureau how much it is willing to pay for various production levels. The critics suggest that this is akin to a customer walking onto a used-car lot and telling the salesman precisely how much he or she is willing to spend for each vehicle.[17]

In a representative democracy, it may be difficult for the legislature to keep silent about its own willingness to pay. The bureau, at any rate, can do some research to judge the preferences of various legislators based on who their constituents are. But legislators can do research, too. Indeed, we suggested in Chapter 5 that the collection, evaluation, and dissemination of information—in this case information about the production costs of bureaucratic supply—are precisely the things in which specialized legislative committees engage. Committees hold hearings, request documentation on production, assign investigatory staff to various research tasks, and query bureau personnel on the veracity of their data and on whether they employ lowest-cost technologies (making it more difficult for the bureau to disguise on-the-job consumption). After the fact, the committees engage in oversight, making sure that what the legislature was told at the time that authorization and appropriations were voted actually holds in practice. In short, the legislature can be much more pro-active than the Niskanen budget-maximizing theory gives them credit for. And, in the real world, the legislature is more pro-active, as we shall see later in the chapter.

Before leaving motivational considerations, it should be remarked that budget maximizing is not the only objective that bureaucrats pursue. It needs to be emphasized and re-emphasized that career civil servants and high-level political appointees are *politicians*. They spend their professional lives pursuing political goals, bargaining, forming alliances and coalitions, solving cooperation and collective-action problems, making policy decisions, operating within and interfacing with political institutions—in short, doing what other politicians do. They do not have elections to win, but even elections affect their conditions of employment by determining the composition of the legislature and the partisan and ideological complexion of the chief executive. Bureaucrats are politicians beholden to other politicians for authority and resources. They are servants of many masters.

---

[17]This and other related points are drawn from Gary J. Miller and Terry M. Moe, "Bureaucrats, Legislators, and the Size of Government," *American Political Science Review* 77 (1983): 297–323.

As politicians subject to the oversight and authority of others, bureaucrats must make contingency plans. They must be strategic and forward thinking. Whichever party wins control of the House or Senate, whichever candidate wins the presidency, whoever becomes chair of the legislative committee with authorization or appropriation responsibility over their agency, life will go on and bureau chiefs will have to adjust to the prevailing political winds. To protect and expand authority and resources, bureaucratic politicians seek, in the form of *autonomy* and *discretion*, insurance against political change. They don't always succeed in acquiring this freedom, but they do try to insulate themselves from changes in the broader political world.[18] So bureaucratic motivations include budget-maximizing behavior, to be sure, but bureaucrats also seek the autonomy to weather changes in the political atmosphere and the discretion and flexibility to fine-tune their authority and resources toward the things they most want to achieve.

Control of the Bureaucracy Is a Principal-Agent Problem

Two broad categories of control mechanisms enable a principal to guard against opportunistic or incompetent agent behavior. They may be illustrated by a homeowner (the principal) who seeks out a contractor (the agent) to remodel a kitchen. The first category is employed before-the-fact and depends on the *reputation* an agent possesses. One guards against selecting an incompetent or corrupt agent by relying on various methods for authenticating the promises made by the agent. These include advice from people you trust (your neighbors who just had their kitchen remodeled), certification by various official boards (association of kitchen contractors), letters of recommendation and other testimonials, credentials (specialized training programs), and interviews. Before-the-fact protection relies on the assumption that an agent's reputation is a valuable asset that he or she does not want to depreciate.

The second class of control mechanisms operates after the fact. Payment may be made contingent on completion of various tasks by specific dates, so that it may be withheld for nonperformance. Alternatively, financial incentives (for example, bonuses) for early or on-time completion may be part of the arrangement. The agent may be required to post a bond that is forfeited for lack of performance. An inspection process, after the work is completed, may lead to financial penalties, bonuses, or possibly even legal action. Of course, the principal can always seek legal relief for breach of contract, either in the form of an injunction that the agent comply or an order that the agent pay damages.

How does the principal-agent problem apply to the president's and Congress's control of the bureaucracy?

---

[18]For an expanded view of bureaucratic autonomy and insulation, with historical application to the U.S. Department of Agriculture and the U.S. Post Office, see Daniel P. Carpenter, *The Forging of Bureaucratic Autonomy: Reputations, Networks, and Policy Innovation in Executive Agencies, 1862–1928* (Princeton, NJ: Princeton University Press, 2001).

Suppose the legislation that created the EPA required that after ten years new legislation be passed renewing its existence and mandate. The issue facing the House, the Senate, and the president in their consideration of renewal revolves around how much authority to give this agency and how much money to permit it to spend. Suppose the House is conservative on environmental issues and prefers limited authority and a limited budget. The Senate wants the agency to have wide-ranging authority but is prepared to give it only slightly more resources than the House (because of its concern with the budget deficit). The president is happy to split the difference between House and Senate on the matter of authority but feels beholden to environmental types and thus is prepared to shower the EPA with resources. Bureaucrats in the EPA want more authority than even the Senate is prepared to condone and more resources than even the president is willing to grant. Eventually, relevant majorities in the House and Senate (including the support of relevant committees) and the president agree on a policy reflecting a compromise among their various points of view.

The bureaucrats are not particularly pleased with this compromise because it gives them considerably less authority and funding than they had hoped for. If they flout the wishes of their principals and implement a policy exactly to their liking, they risk the unified wrath of the House, Senate, and president. Undoubtedly, the politicians would react with new legislation (and also presumably would find other political appointees and career bureaucrats at the EPA to replace the current bureaucratic leadership). If, however, the EPA implements some policy located between their own preferences and the preferences of their principals, they might be able to get away with it.

Thus we have a principal-agent relationship in which a political principal—a collective principal consisting of the president and coalitions in the House and Senate—formulates policy and creates an implementation agent to execute its details. The agent, however, has policy preferences of its own and, unless subjected to further controls, inevitably will implement a policy that drifts toward its ideal.

A variety of controls might conceivably restrict this **bureaucratic drift.** Indeed, legislative scholars often point to congressional hearings in which bureaucrats may be publicly humiliated; annual appropriations decisions that may be used to punish "out of control" bureaus; and the use of watchdog agents, like the Government Accounting Office, to monitor and scrutinize the bureau's performance. But these all come after the fact and may be only partially credible threats to the agency.

Before-the-Fact Controls

The most powerful before-the-fact political weapon is the *appointment process*. The adroit control of the political stance of a given bureau by the president and Congress, through their joint powers of nomination and confirmation (especially if they can arrange for appointees who more nearly share the political consensus on policy) is a self-enforcing mechanism for ensuring reliable agent performance.

A second powerful before-the-fact weapon is *procedural controls*. The general rules and regulations that direct the manner in which federal agencies conduct

bureaucratic drift The oft-observed phenomenon of bureaucratic implementation that produces policy more to the liking of the bureaucracy than originally legislated, but without triggering a political reaction from elected officials.

 Rationality Principle

Bureaucratic drift occurs because bureaucratic agents have different policy preferences from those of members of Congress or of the president.

their affairs are contained in the Administrative Procedures Act. This act is almost always the boilerplate of legislation creating and renewing every federal agency. It is not uncommon, however, for an agency's procedures to be tailored to suit particular circumstances.

Coalitional Drift as a Collective-Action Problem   Not only do politicians want the legislative deals that they strike to be faithfully implemented but they also want those deals to endure. This is especially problematic in American political life, with its shifting alignments and absence of permanent political cleavages. Today's coalition transforms itself overnight. Opponents today are partners tomorrow, and vice versa. A victory today, even one implemented in a favorable manner by the bureaucracy, may be undone tomorrow. What is to be done?

To some extent, legislative structure leans against undoing legislation. If such a coalition votes for handsome subsidies to grain farmers, say, it is very hard to reverse this policy without the gatekeeping and agenda-setting resources of members on the House and Senate Agricultural Committees; yet their members undoubtedly participated in the initial deal and are unlikely to turn against it. But even these structural units are unstable; old politicians depart and new ones are enlisted.

coalitional drift

The prospect that enacted policy will change because the composition of the enacting coalition is so temporary and provisional.

In short, legislatively formulated and bureaucratically implemented output is subject to ***coalitional drift.***[19] To prevent shifting coalitional patterns among politicians to endanger carefully fashioned policies, one thing the legislature might do is *insulate* the bureaucracy and its implementation activities from legislative interventions. If an enacting coalition makes it difficult for its *own* members to intervene in implementation, then it also makes it difficult for enemies of the policy to disrupt the flow of bureau output. This political insulation can be provided by giving bureaucratic agencies long lives, their political heads long terms of office and wide-ranging administrative authority, and other political appointees overlapping terms of office and secure sources of revenue. This insulation comes at a price, however. The civil servants and political appointees of bureaus insulated from political overseers are thereby empowered to pursue independent courses of action. Protection from coalitional drift comes at the price of an increased potential for bureaucratic drift. It is one of the great trade-offs in the field of intergovernmental relations.

The President as Chief Executive Can Direct Agencies

In 1937, President Franklin Roosevelt's Committee on Administrative Management gave official sanction to an idea that had been growing increasingly urgent:

---

[19]This idea, offered as a supplement to the analysis of bureaucratic drift, is found in Murray J. Horn and Kenneth A. Shepsle, "Administrative Process and Organizational Form as Legislative Responses to Agency Costs," *Virginia Law Review* 75 (1989): 499–509. It is further elaborated in Kenneth A. Shepsle, "Bureaucratic Drift, Coalitional Drift, and Time Consistency," *Journal of Law, Economics, and Organization* 8 (1992): 111–18.

"The president needs help." The national government had grown rapidly during the preceding twenty-five years, but the structures and procedures necessary to manage the burgeoning executive branch had not yet been established. The response to the call for help for the president initially took the form of three management policies: (1) all communications and decisions that related to executive policy decisions must pass through the White House; (2) to cope with such a flow, the White House must have adequate staffs of specialists in research, analysis, legislative and legal writing, and public affairs; and (3) the White House must have additional staff to follow through on presidential decisions—to ensure that those decisions are made, communicated to Congress, and carried out by the appropriate agency.

Establishing a management capacity for the presidency began in earnest with FDR, but it did not stop there. The story of the modern presidency can be told largely as a series of responses to the plea for managerial help. Indeed, each expansion of the national government into new policies and programs in the twentieth century was accompanied by a parallel expansion of the president's management authority. This pattern began even before FDR's presidency, with the policy innovations of President Woodrow Wilson between 1913 and 1920. Congress responded to Wilson's policies with the 1921 Budget and Accounting Act, which conferred agenda-setting power over budgeting on the White House. The president, in his annual budget message, transmits comprehensive budgetary recommendations to Congress. Because Congress retains ultimate legislative authority, a president's proposals are sometimes said to be "dead on arrival" on Capitol Hill. Nevertheless, the power to frame deliberations is potent and constitutes an important management tool. Each successive president has continued this pattern of setting the congressional agenda, creating what we now know as the "managerial presidency."

Institution Principle

In conferring budgetary agenda power on the president, the Budget and Accounting Act accelerated the development of the managerial presidency.

For example, though President Clinton was often criticized for the way he managed his administration (Clinton's easygoing approach led critics to liken his management style to college "bull sessions" complete with pizza and "all-nighters"), he also inaugurated one of the most systematic efforts "to change the way government does business" in his National Performance Review. Heavily influenced by the theories of management consultants who prized decentralization, customer responsiveness, and employee initiative, Clinton sought to infuse these new practices into government.[20]

George W. Bush was the first president with a degree in business. His management strategy followed a standard business-school dictum: select skilled subordinates and delegate responsibility to them. Bush followed this model closely in his appointment of highly experienced officials to cabinet positions. Especially noteworthy was his selection of Dick Cheney for vice president. Cheney was an old Washington hand with experience in Congress and previous administrations. (He was the first President Bush's chief of staff.) The second President Bush relied heavily on his vice president's insider abilities. Indeed, at the outset of his

[20]See John Micklethwait, "Managing to Look Attractive," *New Statesman* 125, 8 November 1996, p. 24.

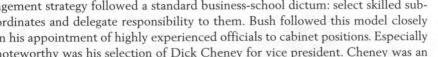

term, Bush often appeared overshadowed by these appointees (the vice president in particular). Many observers had the impression that Bush did not lead his own administration. The president's performance during the war in Afghanistan and the war on terrorism dispelled many doubts about his executive capabilities. These doubts were to reemerge as the results in Iraq came slowly and unevenly and the administration's handling of relief to New Orleans and the Gulf Coast after Hurricane Katrina was seen as incompetent.

The story of the modern presidency can be told largely as a series of responses to the rise of big government. *Each expansion of the national government in the twentieth century was accompanied by a parallel expansion of presidential management authority.* The executive bureaucracy and the institutional presidency are right in the middle of the separation-of-powers administrative state (Figure 7.3).

Congress Can Promote Responsible Bureaucracy through Oversight and Incentives

Congress is constitutionally essential to responsible bureaucracy because the key to government responsibility is legislation. When a law is passed and its intent is clear, then the president knows what to "faithfully execute" and the responsible agency understands what is expected of it. In our modern age, legislatures rarely make laws directly for citizens; most laws are really instructions to bureaucrats and their agencies. But when Congress enacts vague legislation, agencies are thrown back on their own interpretations. The president and the federal courts step in to tell them what the legislation intended. And so do intensely interested organized groups. But when everybody, from president to courts to interest groups, gets involved in the actual interpretation of legislative intent, to whom is the agency responsible? Even when it has the most sincere desire to behave responsibly, how shall this be accomplished?

The answer is *oversight.* The more legislative power Congress has delegated to the executive, the more it has sought to get back into the game through committee and subcommittee oversight of the agencies. The standing committee system in Congress is well suited for oversight, inasmuch as most of the congressional committees and subcommittees are organized with jurisdictions roughly parallel to one or more executive departments or agencies. Appropriations committees as well as authorization committees have oversight powers—as do their respective subcommittees. In addition to these, there is a committee on government operations both in the House and in the Senate, each with oversight powers not limited by departmental jurisdiction.

The best indication of Congress's oversight efforts is the use of public hearings, before which bureaucrats and other witnesses are summoned to discuss and defend agency budgets and past decisions. The data drawn from systematic studies of congressional committee and subcommittee hearings and meetings show dramatically that Congress has tried through oversight to keep pace with the expansion of the executive branch. Between 1950 and 1980, the annual number of committee

FIGURE 7.3

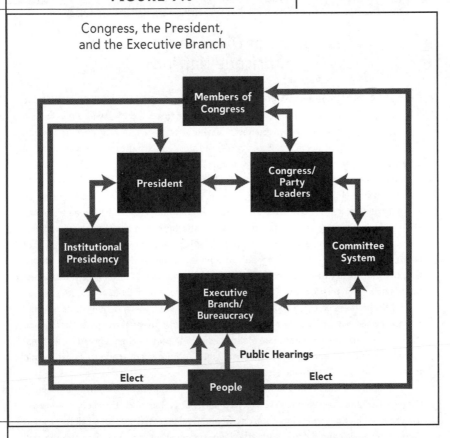

Congress, the President, and the Executive Branch

The separation of powers entails complex interrelationships among Congress, the president, and the bureaucracy. The "electoral connection" sits in the background, selecting politicians to govern and then holding them accountable for policy performance.

and subcommittee meetings in the House of Representatives rose steadily from 3,210 to 7,022 and in the Senate from 2,607 to 4,265 (in 1975–76). Beginning in 1980 in the House and 1978 in the Senate, the number of committee and sub-committee hearings and meetings slowly began to decline, reaching 4,222 in the House and 2,597 in the Senate by the mid-1980s. New questions about the ability of Congress to exercise oversight arose when the Republicans took over Congress in 1995. Reductions in committee staffing and an emphasis on using investigative oversight to uncover scandal meant much less time spent on programmatic over-sight. Moreover, congressional Republicans complained that they could not get

The Politics of Disaster: Terror and Hurricane Katrina

On March 1, 2003, in response to the terrorist attacks of September 11, 2001, twenty-two federal agencies, employing some 170,000 employees governed by seven different pay-roll and benefits systems and represented by seventeen different unions, were transferred to the Department of Homeland Security (DHS). Included in that group was the Federal Emergency Management Agency, better known as FEMA.

Two and a half years later, on August 29, 2005, FEMA faced its first major test after its absorption into DHS—responding to Hurricane Katrina, the third-strongest hurricane to make landfall in the United States since recordkeeping began in 1851. By all accounts, FEMA failed miserably. Although some charged the Bush administration with racism,[1] most agree that FEMA was simply unprepared.[2] What became clear after Katrina is that FEMA, a bureaucratic agency designed to prepare for natural disasters, did not fit well with DHS, an agency designed to coordinate efforts in the war on terror. The principles of politics help us understand why FEMA's failure was all too predictable.

Political forces coalesced soon after 9/11. Both Republicans and Democrats realized that the public was going to demand an ongoing response to the terrorist threat (beyond the military response in Afghanistan). Politicians in both parties, then, agreed on a prima-ry political goal—do *something* about terrorism. This agreement made it almost certain that significant political change would occur.[3]

Democrats were quick to call for the creation of a Department of Homeland Security. Yet with Republicans—traditionally averse to large-scale bureaucratic solutions—in con-trol of the White House and Congress, one would have expected at most a call for beefing up the intelligence and defense budgets, along with an attempt to shift blame to the pre-vious administration. A congressional investigation, however, revealed that serious securi-ty lapses and a lack of coordination among the agencies with responsibility for domestic and foreign intelligence had occurred under *both* Clinton and Bush. Both parties could be blamed if the government did not respond aggressively enough to the terrorist threat.

Furthermore, the major alternative solution—the creation of a Homeland Security "czar"—proved inadequate. Tom Ridge, ex-governor of Pennsylvania, did not have the power to hire and fire subordinates. He did not have budgetary authority. He had little beyond his title. In this case, a *lack* of rules and procedures meant that Ridge had no power to shape bureaucratic outcomes, and according to the same principle of politics, the government needed to institutionalize rules and procedures to make Ridge's leadership effective. In the end, for the president and Congress, no alternative seemed available. The path to a Cabinet-level agency was clear.

DHS immediately faced problems of coordination. The agencies that were brought under one umbrella are tremendously diverse (see Table 7.1). The history principle reminds us that each of these agencies has developed along its own path. Some had developed

Collective-Action Principle

In the midst of a political crisis, politi-cal differences of opin-ion can fade in the face of public pressure to address critical problems.

Policy Principle

Creation of a Cabinet-level Department of Homeland Security proved an attractive political solution to both Democrats and Republicans.

over more than two centuries (for example, the Customs Service or the Coast Guard), while others had grown aggressively in response to new threats (the Drug Enforcement Agency).

What about FEMA? The roots of FEMA are nearly as old as the nation—the first federal response to a local emergency occurred in 1803, when Congress passed legislation to assist a New Hampshire town struck by a fire. Thus, FEMA ought to be especially resistant to attempts to alter its bureaucratic mission. On the other hand, FEMA, in its current form, is relatively young. Federal programs dedicated to emergency response were not merged into a single agency until 1979, via an executive order by President Carter that created FEMA,[4] and only in 1993, under President Clinton, was a director of FEMA appointed who had emergency management experience. Thus, FEMA has not had much chance to develop a distinct bureaucratic culture and may be especially prone to mission "drift" when absorbed into the mammoth Department of Homeland Security.

In fact, many questioned the wisdom of folding FEMA into DHS. FEMA focuses on disaster response, while DHS focuses on terrorism prevention. Furthermore, the Secretary of DHS was given unusually strong powers by Congress. This proved to be problematic for the director of FEMA, who must respond rapidly during a national disaster.[5] As one observer wrote, FEMA officials have "responsibility without authority" and have suffered because of it.[6] Budgetary priorities were also altered. FEMA lost more than $800 million in grant money to the new Office of Disaster Preparedness, which deals solely with local and state preparations for terrorist attacks. And the money that had been allocated to FEMA was misspent—for instance, a grant to study evacuation plans for New Orleans was instead spent on studies for a new highway.[7] Finally, over the past two years, few of FEMA's disaster "scenarios"—a critical component of planning—dealt with natural disasters. Most were concerned with terrorist threats (biological, nuclear, or other types).

It's not clear what Congress will do with FEMA in the aftermath of Katrina. As one reporter noted, America's master plan for disasters, issued with much fanfare in January 2005, failed its first major test.[8] Another round of bureaucratic reorganization is sure to follow.

[1]Ken Herman, "Hurricane Katrina: Race Hot Issue for Bush in Storm's Wake," *Atlanta Journal-Constitution,* 17 September 2005.

[2]"Incompetence, Not Racism," Unsigned editorial, *Washington Post,* 20 September 2005.

[3]John Kingdon calls events that limit and focus our political options "windows of political opportunity," *Agendas, Alternatives, and Public Policies* (New York: Pearson, 1997).

[4]www.fema.gov/about/history.shtm.

[5]Jack Beerman, Ronald Cass, and Colin Diver, *Administrative Law: Cases and Materials,* 5th ed., (Aspen, CO: Aspen Law and Business, 2006), p. 117.

[6]Karen McPherson, "Has Terror Hurt? Some Say Bureaucracy Slows FEMA," *Pittsburgh Post-Gazette,* 3 September 2005.

[7]Gary Fields and David Rogers, "Disaster Renews Debate about Whether Agency Is Marginalized in War on Terror," *Wall Street Journal,* 1 September 2005.

[8]"After 9/11, a Master Plan for Disasters Was Drawn. It Didn't Weather the Storm," *Los Angeles Times,* 11 September 2005.

 History Principle

Over time, bureaucracies develop distinct cultures and workways that can make it difficult to coordinate their activities.

 Rationality Principle

With Republican and Democratic political leaders focused on terrorism, the government was relatively unprepared for a major natural disaster.

sufficient information about programs from the White House to conduct effective oversight. Congressional records show that in 1991–92, when Democrats controlled the House, they issued reports on fifty-five federal programs, while in 1997–98, the Republican Congress issued only fourteen.[21] On matters of major national importance, multiple committees may initiate oversight hearings simultaneously. No less than a dozen congressional committees (along with the Justice Department and the Securities and Exchange Commission) launched investigations into the collapse of the giant energy company Enron. Enron's close ties to the Bush administration and its campaign contributions to hundreds of politicians from both parties aroused intense public interest in the hearings, many of which were televised live. The investigations covered a broad range of issues, including secret partnerships, public utility laws, 401(k) retirement plans, accounting practices, and Enron's political influence.

Although congressional oversight is potent because of Congress's power to make—and, therefore, to change—the law, often the most effective and influential lever over bureaucratic accountability is "the power of the purse"—the ability of the House and Senate committees and subcommittees on appropriations to look at agency performance through the microscope of the annual appropriations process. This annual process makes bureaucrats attentive to Congress—especially members of the relevant authorizing committee and appropriations subcommittee—because they know that Congress has a chance each year to reduce their authority or funding.[22] A more recent evaluation of the budget and appropriations process by the National Performance Review expressed one serious concern about oversight through appropriation: Pressure to cut appropriations "has put a premium on preserving particular programs, projects, and activities from Executive Branch as well as congressional action."[23] This may be another explanation for why there may be some downsizing but almost no terminations of federal agencies.

Oversight can also be carried out by individual members of Congress. Such inquiries addressed to bureaucrats are considered standard congressional "casework" and can turn up significant questions of public responsibility even when the motivation is only to meet the demand of an individual constituent. Oversight also takes place very often through communications between congressional staff and agency staff. Congressional staff has been enlarged tremendously since the Legislative Reorganization Act of 1946, and the legislative staff, especially the staff of the committees, is just as professionalized and specialized as the staff of an executive agency. In addition, Congress has created for itself three quite large agencies whose obligations are to engage in constant research on problems taking place in the executive branch: the Government Accountability Office, the Congressional

[21]Richard E. Cohen, "Crackup of the Committees," *National Journal*, 31 July 1999, p. 2214.

[22]See Aaron Wildavsky, *The New Politics of the Budgetary Process*, 2nd ed. (New York: HarperCollins, 1992), pp. 15–16.

[23]National Performance Review, *From Red Tape to Results: Creating a Government That Works Better and Costs Less* (Washington, DC: U.S. Government Printing Office, 1993), p. 42.

Research Service, and the Congressional Budget Office. Each is designed to give Congress information independent of the information it can get through hearings and other communications directly from the executive branch.[24]

Congressional Oversight: Abdication or Strategic Delegation?

Congress often grants the executive-branch bureaucracies discretion in determining certain features of a policy during the implementation phase. Although the complexities of governing a modern industrialized democracy make the granting of discretion necessary, there are some who argue that Congress not only gives unelected bureaucrats too much discretion but also delegates too much policy-making authority to them. Congress, they say, has transferred so much power that it has created a "runaway bureaucracy" in which unelected officials accountable neither to the electorate nor to Congress make important policy decisions.[25] By enacting vague statutes that give bureaucrats broad discretion, so the argument goes, members of Congress effectively abdicated their constitutionally designated roles and effectively removed themselves from the policy-making process. The ultimate effect of this extreme delegation has left the legislative branch weak and ineffectual and has dire consequences for the health of our democracy.

Others claim that even though Congress may possess the tools to engage in effective oversight, it fails to do so simply because we do not see Congress actively engaging in much oversight activity.[26] However, Mathew D. McCubbins and Thomas Schwartz argue that these critics have focused on the wrong type of oversight and have missed a type of oversight that benefits members of Congress in their bids for re-election.[27] McCubbins and Schwartz distinguish between two types of oversight: *police patrol* and *fire alarm*. Under the police-patrol variety, Congress systematically initiates investigation into the activity of agencies. Under the fire-alarm variety, members of Congress do not initiate investigations but wait for adversely affected citizens or interest groups to bring bureaucratic perversions of legislative intent to the attention of the relevant congressional committee. To make sure that individuals and groups will bring these violations

---

[24]Until 1983, there was still another official tool of legislative oversight, the legislative veto. Each executive agency was obliged to submit to Congress proposed decisions or rules. These were to lie before both houses for thirty to sixty days; then, if Congress took no action by one-house or two-house resolution explicitly to veto a proposed measure, it became law. The legislative veto was declared unconstitutional by the Supreme Court in 1983 on the grounds that it violated the separation of powers because the resolutions Congress passed to exercise its veto were not subject to presidential veto, as required by the Constitution. See *Immigration and Naturalization Service v. Chadha*, 462 U.S. 919 (1983). On the congressional staff more generally, see Robert Salisbury and Kenneth A. Shepsle, "Congressman as Enterprise," *Legislative Studies Quarterly* 6 (1981): 559–76.

[25]Lowi, *The End of Liberalism*; and Lawrence C. Dodd and Richard L. Schott, *Congress and the Administrative State* (New York: Wiley, 1979).

[26]Morris S. Ogul, *Congress Oversees the Bureaucracy: Studies in Legislative Supervision* (Pittsburgh: University of Pittsburgh Press, 1976); Peter Woll, *American Bureaucracy*, 2nd ed. (New York: Norton, 1977).

[27]Mathew D. McCubbins and Thomas Schwartz, "Congressional Oversight Overlooked: Police Patrols versus Fire Alarms," *American Journal of Political Science* 28 (1984): 165–79.

to members' attention—to pull the fire alarm, so to speak—Congress passes laws that help individuals and groups make claims against the bureaucracy, including granting them legal standing before administrative agencies and federal courts.

McCubbins and Schwartz argue that fire-alarm oversight is more efficient than the police-patrol variety, given costs and the electoral incentives of members of Congress. Why should members spend their scarce resources (mainly time) to initiate investigations without having any evidence that they will reap electoral rewards? Police-patrol oversight can waste taxpayer dollars, too, because many investigations will not turn up any evidence on violations of legislative intent. It is much more cost-effective for members to conserve their resources and then claim credit for fixing the problem (and saving the day) after the fire alarms are pulled. McCubbins and Schwartz argue that given the incentives of elected officials, it makes sense that we would see Congress engaging more in fire-alarm oversight than police-patrol oversight.

On the other hand, bureaucratic drift might be contained if Congress spent more of its time clarifying its legislative intent and less of its time on oversight activity. If its original intent in the law were clearer, Congress could then afford to defer to presidential management to maintain bureaucratic responsibility. Bureaucrats are more responsive to clear legislative guidance than to anything else. But when Congress and the president are at odds (or coalitions within Congress are at odds), bureaucrats have an opportunity to evade responsibility by playing one branch off against the other.

Collective-Action Principle
When Congress and the president are at odds (or coalitions within Congress are at odds), bureaucrats have an opportunity to evade responsibility.

HOW CAN BUREAUCRACY BE REDUCED?

Americans like to complain about bureaucracy. Americans don't like Big Government because Big Government means Big Bureaucracy, and bureaucracy means *the federal service*—about 2.63 million civilian and 1.46 million military employees.[28] Promises to cut the bureaucracy are popular campaign appeals; "cutting out the fat" with big reductions in the number of federal employees is held out as a sure-fire way of cutting the deficit.

Despite fears of bureaucratic growth getting out of hand, however, the federal service has hardly grown at all during the past thirty years; it reached its peak postwar level in 1968 with 2.9 million civilian employees plus an additional 3.6 million military personnel (a figure swollen by Vietnam). The number of civilian federal executive-branch employees has since remained close to that figure. (In 2002, it was about 2,630,000.)[29] The growth of the federal service is

---

[28]This is just under 99 percent of all national government employees. About 1.4 percent work for the legislative branch and for the federal judiciary. See Office of Management and Budget, *Historical Tables, Budget of the United States Government, Fiscal Year 2004* (Washington, DC: Government Printing Office, 2003), Table 17.5, p. 306.

[29]Ibid.

even less imposing when placed in the context of the total workforce and when compared to the size of state and local public employment, which was 18,642,000 in 2002.[30] Figure 7.4 indicates that, since 1950, the ratio of federal service employment to the total workforce has been fairly steady, declining only slightly in the past twenty-five years. Another useful comparison is to be found in Figure 7.5. Although the dollar increase in federal spending shown by the bars looks impressive, the horizontal line indicates that even here the national government has simply kept pace with the growth of the economy.

In sum, the national government is indeed "very large," but the federal service has not been growing any faster than the economy or the society. The same is roughly true of the growth pattern of state and local public personnel. Bureaucracy keeps pace with our society, despite our seeming dislike for it, because we cannot operate the control towers, the prisons, the Social Security system, and other essential elements without bureaucracy. And we certainly could not conduct a war in Iraq without a gigantic military bureaucracy.

Nevertheless, some Americans continue to argue that bureaucracy is too big and that it should be reduced. In the 1990s, Americans seemed particularly enthusiastic about reducing (or to use the popular contemporary word, *downsizing*) the federal bureaucracy.

History Principle

The size of the federal bureaucracy has kept pace with the growth of the economy and the needs of society.

Termination

The only *certain* way to reduce the size of the bureaucracy is to eliminate programs. Variations in the levels of federal personnel and expenditures demonstrate the futility of trying to make permanent cuts in existing agencies. Furthermore, most agencies have a supportive constituency that will fight to reinstate any cuts that are made. Termination is the only way to ensure an agency's reduction, and it is a rare occurrence.

The Republican-led 104th Congress (1995–96) was committed to the termination of programs. Newt Gingrich, Speaker of the House, took Congress by storm with his promises of a virtual revolution in government. But when the dust had settled at the end of the first session of the first Gingrich-led Congress, no significant progress had been made toward downsizing through termination of agencies and programs.[31] The only two agencies eliminated were the Office of Technology Assessment, which provided research for Congress, and the Advisory Council on Intergovernmental Relations, which studied the relationship between the federal government and the state. Significantly, neither of these agencies had a strong constituency to defend it.[32]

[30]Ibid.

[31]A thorough review of the first session of the 104th Congress will be found in "Republican's Hopes for 1996 Lie in Unfinished Business," *Congressional Quarterly Weekly Report*, 6 January 1996, pp. 6–18.

[32]The Interstate Commerce Commission was also terminated in 1995. The ICC was the oldest regulatory commission, created in 1887. By 1995, however, many of its functions had been dispersed to other agencies. In that year, its remaining functions were transferred to the newly created National Surface Transportation Board.

FIGURE 7.4

Employees in the Federal Service—Total
Number as a Percentage of the Workforce*

Federal employment as a percentage of the total workforce has declined slightly, especially since 1970. Except for during the Vietnam era, military employment in relation to the total workforce has declined even more rapidly.

*Workforce includes unemployed persons.
SOURCE: Tax Foundation, *Facts & Figures on Government Finance* (Baltimore: Johns Hopkins University Press, 1990), pp. 22, 44; Office of Management and Budget, *Historical Tables, Budget of the United States Government, Fiscal Year 2002* (Washington, DC: Government Printing Office, 2001), p. 304; and U.S. Department of Labor, Bureau of Labor Statistics, Table A-1 at stats.bls.gov/webapps/legacy/cpsatab1.htm. Lines between 1939 and 1946 are broken because they connect the last prewar year with the first postwar year, disregarding the temporary ballooning of federal employees, especially military, during war years.

FIGURE 7.5

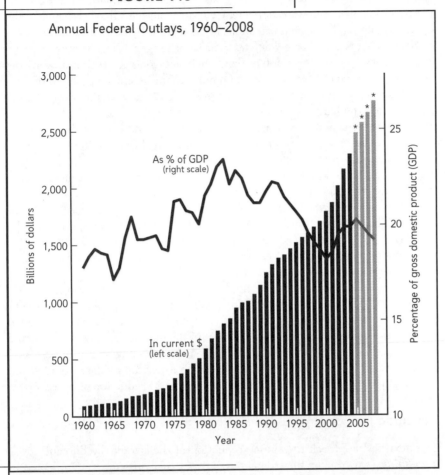

Annual Federal Outlays, 1960–2008

Real federal expenditures have increased each year for nearly fifty years. Since 1980, however, these expenditures are a declining proportion of total economic activity in the nation.

*Data from 2005–08 are estimated.
SOURCE: Office of Management and Budget, *Historical Tables, Budget of the United States Government, Fiscal Year 2004* (Washington, DC: Government Printing Office, 2003), p. 55.

The overall lack of success in terminating bureaucracy is a reflection of Americans' love/hate relationship with the national government. As antagonistic as Americans may be toward bureaucracy in general, they grow attached to the services being rendered and protections being offered by particular bureaucratic agencies—that is, they fiercely defend their favorite agencies while perceiving no inconsistency between that defense and their antagonistic attitude toward the bureaucracy in general. A good case in point was the agonizing problem of closing military bases in the wake of the end of the cold war with the former Soviet Union, when the United States no longer needed so many bases. Because every base is in some congressional member's district, it proved impossible for Congress to decide to close any of them. Consequently, between 1988 and 1990, Congress established the Defense Base Closure and Realignment Commission to decide on base closings, taking the matter out of Congress's hands altogether.[33] And even so, the process has been slow and agonizing.

Elected leaders have come to rely on a more incremental approach to downsizing the bureaucracy. Much has been done by budgetary means, reducing the budgets of all agencies across the board by small percentages, and cutting some less-supported agencies by larger amounts. Yet these changes are still incremental, leaving the existence of agencies unaddressed.

An additional approach has been taken to thwart the highly unpopular regulatory agencies, which are so small (relatively) that cutting their budgets contributes virtually nothing to reducing the deficit. This approach is called **deregulation,** simply defined as a reduction in the number of rules promulgated by regulatory agencies. But deregulation by rule reduction is still incremental and has certainly not satisfied the hunger of the American public in general and Washington representatives in particular for a genuine reduction of bureaucracy.

deregulation A policy of reducing or eliminating regulatory restraints on the conduct of individuals or private institutions.

Devolution

The next best approach to genuine reduction of the size of the bureaucracy is **devolution**—downsizing the federal bureaucracy by delegating the implementation of programs to state and local governments. Indirect evidence for this is seen in Figure 7.6, which shows the increase in state and local government employment against a backdrop of flat or declining federal employment. This suggests a growing share of government actions taking place on the state and local levels.

devolution
A policy to remove a program from one level of government by deregulating it or passing it down to a lower level of government, such as from the national government to the state and local governments.

Devolution often alters the pattern of who benefits most from government programs. In the early 1990s, a major devolution of transportation policy sought to open up decisions about transportation to a new set of interests. Since the 1920s, transportation policy had been dominated by road-building interests in the federal and state governments. Many advocates for cities and many environmentalists believed that the emphasis on road building hurt cities and harmed the environment. The 1992 reform, initiated by environmentalists, put more power in the hands of metropolitan planning organizations, and lifted many federal restrictions on how

---

[33]Public Law 101-510, Title XXIX, Sections 2,901 and 2,902 of Part A (Defense Base Closure and Realignment Commission).

FIGURE 7.6

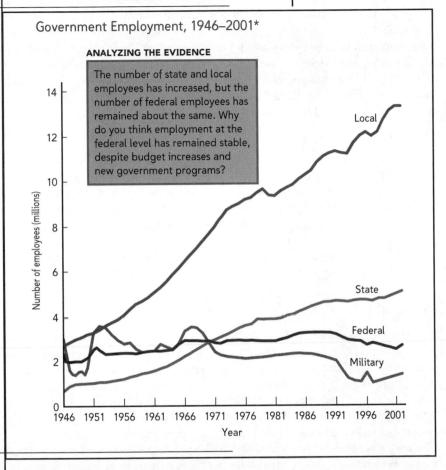

Government Employment, 1946–2001*

ANALYZING THE EVIDENCE

The number of state and local employees has increased, but the number of federal employees has remained about the same. Why do you think employment at the federal level has remained stable, despite budget increases and new government programs?

Local

State

Federal

Military

*Federal government employment figures include civilians only. Military employment figures include only active-duty personnel.

SOURCE: U.S. Bureau of the Census, *Historical Statistics of the United States: Colonial Times to 1970* (Washington, DC: Government Printing Office, 1975), pp. 1100, 1141; *Statistical Abstract of the United States, 1999.* Tables 534 and 578: U.S. Office of Personnel Management, *Pay Structure of the Federal Civil Service, 2001.* Table 1; and U.S. Postal Service, *Annual Report of the Postmaster General, 2000.* p. 68.

the money should be spent. Reformers hoped that these changes would open up the decision-making process so those advocating alternatives to road building, such as mass transit, bike paths, and walking, would have more influence over how federal transportation dollars were spent. Although the pace of change has been slow, devolution has indeed brought new voices into decisions about transportation spending, and alternatives to highways have received increasing attention.

Often the central aim of devolution is to provide more efficient and flexible government services. Yet, by its very nature, devolution entails variation across the states. In some states, government services may improve as a consequence of devolution. In other states, services may deteriorate as the states use devolution as an opportunity to cut spending and reduce services. This has been the pattern in the implementation of the welfare reform passed in 1996, the most significant devolution of federal government social programs in many decades. Some states, such as Wisconsin, have used the flexibility of the reform to design innovative programs that respond to clients' needs; other states, such as Idaho, have virtually dismantled their welfare programs. Because the legislation placed a five-year life-time limit on receiving welfare, the states will take on an even greater role in the future as existing clients lose their eligibility for federal benefits. Welfare reform has been praised by many for reducing welfare rolls and responding to the public desire that welfare be a temporary program. At the same time, it has placed more low-income women and their children at risk for being left with no form of as-sistance at all, depending on the state in which they live.

This is the dilemma that devolution poses. To a point, variation can be con-sidered one of the virtues of federalism. But there are dangers inherent in large variations in the provisions of services and benefits in a democracy.

Privatization

Privatization, another downsizing option, seems like a synonym for *termination*, but that is true only at the extreme. Most of what is called "privatization" is not termination at all but the provision of government goods and services by private contractors under direct government supervision. Except for top-secret strategic materials, virtually all of the production of military hardware, from boats to bul-lets, is done on a privatized basis by private contractors. Billions of dollars of research services are bought under contract by governments; these private contrac-tors are universities as well as ordinary industrial corporations and private "think tanks." **Privatization** simply means that a public purpose is provided under con-tract by a private company or companies. But such programs are still very much government programs; they are paid for by government and supervised by govern-ment. Privatization downsizes the government only in that the workers providing the service are no longer counted as part of the government bureaucracy.

The central aim of privatization is to reduce the cost of government. When pri-vate contractors can perform a task as well as government but for less money, tax-payers win. Government workers are generally unionized and, therefore, receive good pay and benefits. Private-sector workers are less likely to be unionized, and private firms often provide lower pay and fewer benefits. For this reason, public-sector unions have been one of the strongest voices arguing against privatization. Other critics of privatization observe that private firms may not be more efficient or less costly than government. This is especially likely when there is little competi-tion among private firms and when public bureaucracies are not granted a fair chance to bid in the contracting competition. When private firms have a monopoly on service provision, they may be more expensive than government.

privatization
Removing all or part of a program from the public sector to the private sector.

There are important questions about how private contractors can be held accountable. As one analyst of Pentagon spending put it, "The Pentagon is supposed to be representing the taxpayer and the public interest—its national security. So it's really important to have transparency, to be able to see these competitions and hold people accountable."[34] As security has become the nation's paramount concern, new worries about privatization have surfaced. Some Pentagon officials fear that too many tasks vital to national security may have already been contracted out and that national security might best be served by limiting privatization.

The new demands of domestic security have altered the thrust of bureaucratic reform. The emphasis on reducing the size of government that was so prominent during the previous two decades is gone. Instead, there is an acceptance that the federal government will grow as needed to ensure the safety of American citizens. The administration's security effort, focusing the entire federal bureaucracy on a single central mission, will require unprecedented levels of coordination among federal agencies. Despite the strong agreement on the goal of fighting terrorism, the effort to streamline the bureaucracy around a single purpose is likely to face considerable obstacles along the way. Reform of public bureaucracies is always complex because strong constituencies may attempt to block changes that they believe will harm them. Initiatives that aim to improve coordination among agencies can easily provoke political disputes if the proposed changes threaten to alter the access of groups to the bureaucracy. And groups that oppose bureaucratic changes can appeal to Congress to intervene on their behalf. As respected reform advocate Donald Kettl said of the effort to reinvent government, "Virtually no reform that really matters can be achieved without at least implicit congressional support."[35] In wartime, many obstacles to bureaucratic reform are lifted. But the war on terrorism is an unusual war that will be fought over an extended period of time. Whether the unique features of this war improve or limit the prospects for bureaucratic reform remains to be seen.

SUMMARY

Most American citizens possess less information and more misinformation about bureaucracy than about any other feature of government. We, therefore, began the chapter with an elementary definition of bureaucracy, identifying its key characteristics and demonstrating the extent to which bureaucracy is not only a phenomenon but an American phenomenon. In the second section of the chapter, we showed how all essential government services and controls are carried out by bureaucracies—or, to be more objective, administrative agencies. Following a very general description of the different types of bureaucratic agencies in the executive branch, we divided up the agencies of the executive branch into

---

[34]Ellen Nakashima, "Defense Balks at Contract Goals; Essential Services Should Not Be Privatized, Pentagon Tells OMB," *Washington Post*, 30 January 2002, p. A21.

[35]Quoted in Stephen Bar, "Midterm Exam for 'Reinvention': Study Cites 'Impressive Results' but Calls for Strategy to Win Congressional Support," *Washington Post*, 19 August 1994, p. A25.

Rationality Principle	Collective-Action Principle	Institution Principle	Policy Principle	History Principle
Bureaucracies are the instruments through which policy objectives are secured.	Coordination among bureaucrats is necessary to carry out the primary task of bureaucracy—implementation.	Legislative principals establish bureaucratic agents to implement policies.	The policies of clientele agencies promote the interests of their clientele.	Each expansion of the national government is accompanied by a parallel expansion of presidential management authority.
One view of bureaucratic behavior is that bureaucrats are motivated to maximize their budgets.	Coalitional drift makes the long-term implementation of policy more difficult.	Congress also delegates authority to bureaucrats to make law through the procedures of rule making and administrative adjudication.	The military pork barrel is an example of the distributive tendency in Congress.	The size of the federal bureaucracy has kept pace with the growth of the economy and the needs of society.
Bureaucratic drift occurs because bureaucratic agents have different policy preferences from those of members of Congress or of the president.	When Congress and the president are at odds (or coalitions within Congress are at odds), bureaucrats have an opportunity to evade responsibility.	The appointment process and procedural controls allow the president and Congress some before-the-fact control over bureaucratic agents.	Bureaucratic drift and coalitional drift are contrary tendencies. Fixing them often involves a trade-off.	Americans have grown attached to the programs implemented by government agencies and thus are reluctant to cut back on their size and scope.
		In conferring budgetary agenda power on the president, the Budget and Accounting Act accelerated the development of the managerial presidency.		

four categories according to mission: clientele agencies, agencies for maintaining the Union, regulatory agencies, and redistributive agencies. These illustrate the varieties of administrative experience in American government. Although the bureaucratic phenomenon is universal, not all the bureaucracies are the same in the way they are organized, in the degree of their responsiveness, or in the way they participate in the political process. "Bureaucracy in a Democracy" was the subtitle and theme of the chapter, not because we have succeeded in democratizing bureaucracies but because it is the never-ending challenge of politics in a democracy.

FOR FURTHER READING

Arnold, Peri E. *Making the Managerial Presidency: Comprehensive Reorganization Planning, 1905–1980.* Princeton, NJ: Princeton University Press, 1986.

Downs, Anthony. *Inside Bureaucracy.* Boston: Little, Brown, 1966.

Fesler, James W., and Donald F. Kettl. *The Politics of the Administrative Process.* 2nd ed. Chatham, NJ: Chatham House, 1996.

Heclo, Hugh. *A Government of Strangers: Executive Politics in Washington.* Washington, DC: Brookings Institution, 1977.

Skowronek, Stephen. *Building a New American State: The Expansion of National Administrative Capacities, 1877–1920.* New York: Cambridge University Press, 1982.

Wildavsky, Aaron, and Naomi Caiden. *The New Politics of the Budgetary Process.* 5th ed. New York: Longman, 2003.

Wilson, James Q. *Bureaucracy: What Government Agencies Do and Why They Do It.* New York: Basic Books, 1989.

Wood, Dan B. *Bureaucratic Dynamics: The Role of Bureaucracy in a Democracy.* Boulder, CO: Westview, 1994.

Politics in the News—
Reading between the Lines

U.S. Politics and Natural Disasters

At FEMA, Disasters and Politics Go Hand in Hand

By ALAN B. KRUEGER

"As we are all aware," James Lee Witt told Congress in April 1996, when he was director of the Federal Emergency Management Agency, "disasters are very political events."

There is much truth to Mr. Witt's statement. Research on the spending patterns of the emergency management agency shows that, to a significant degree, the agency is influenced by political concerns that are distinct from the suffering and destruction wrought by natural disasters, under both Democratic and Republican administrations.

Although declaring a disaster should be clear-cut and above politics, the legislation that governs FEMA gives the president much discretion to decide whether an event is a disaster that qualifies for assistance. Upon receiving a request by a state's governor, the president may declare a "major disaster" if a natural catastrophe "causes damage of sufficient severity and magnitude to warrant major disaster assistance."

While no one would doubt that a disaster of the magnitude of Hurricane

Katrina deserves the full commitment of the federal government, the language in the FEMA law is vague enough to count two feet of snow in Ohio as a major disaster, as was the case last December.

Indeed, the law specifically prohibits the use of an "arithmetic formula or sliding scale" to deny assistance. So, disaster requests are not evaluated based on standard quantitative evidence; instead, declarations involve subjective judgment.

Not surprisingly, in this vacuum presidents have displayed a tendency to declare more disasters in years when they face re-election. . . . Even after accounting for the amount of precipitation and flood damage each year, . . . the average number of flood-related disasters declared by the president was 46 percent higher in election years than in other years.

The tendency to declare more disasters during election years is not limited to floods. President Bill Clinton set a record by declaring 73 major disasters

New York Times, 15 September 2005, p. C2.

in 35 states and the District of Columbia in 1996, the year he was up for reelection.

When George W. Bush faced reelection in 2004, he declared 61 major disasters in 36 states—10 more than in 2003 and tied for the second highest number of major disaster declarations ever, according to data provided by FEMA.

The increase from 2003 to 2004 was particularly sharp in the 12 battleground states in which the election was decided by 5 percent or less; these states had 17 major disasters declared in 2004 but only 8 in 2003, and, therefore, accounted for 90 percent of the increase.

Congressional and presidential politics play an important role in allocating FEMA assistance. Most important, . . . the amount of disaster relief provided per incident increases with the number of representatives a state has on one of the FEMA oversight committees in the House of Representatives. Having an additional representative on either of the two main House oversight committees is associated with an extra $36.5 million of assistance from FEMA.

This figure may seem to overstate the role of politics because representatives from states prone to be hit by disasters probably seek out seats on FEMA oversight committees. But recall that the analysis simultaneously adjusts for the amount of Red Cross assistance and private insurance losses from disasters each year. So, having Congressional representation on an oversight committee appears to matter even when compared with disasters in other states that cause roughly the same amount of damage and suffering.

Interestingly, representation on a Senate oversight committee does not have a detectable effect on FEMA payments, perhaps because disasters are often local events that more intensely affect House members' constituents.

ESSENCE OF THE STORY

- Statistical analysis of federal spending during emergencies shows that politics, as much as disasters, influences the rate of spending. More disasters are declared during presidential election years, and battleground states seem to have more emergencies.

- The law mandating the creation of FEMA prohibits the use of any arithmetic formula to determine what constitutes a disaster, thus leaving this decision open to political considerations.

POLITICAL ANALYSIS

- As the primary federal agency devoted to emergency response, FEMA obviously fills an important governmental role. At the same time, a lack of clarity about what constitutes a disaster leaves FEMA open to political pressures from both the executive and the legislative branches.

- FEMA seems particularly prone to coalitional drift. New rulemaking, as suggested in this article, stimulated by real and perceived problems following Hurricane Katrina, may protect FEMA from coalitional drift in the future.

All told, . . . a third of FEMA payments are directly attributable to representation on one of the nine FEMA Congressional oversight committees, independent of the disaster's severity.

When Congress turns to evaluating the Hurricane Katrina disaster, it should also consider sharpening FEMA's mission. One helpful step would be to define more precisely the requirements necessary for the president to declare a disaster. For example, disaster payments could be restricted to events that cause damage exceeding a specified threshold or significant loss of life. Long before Hurricane Katrina, it should have been apparent that FEMA needed to focus more on alleviating and preventing suffering from major catastrophes and less on delivering pork to voters at election time.

CHAPTER

8

The Federal Courts:
Structure and Strategies

George W. Bush won the 2000 national presidential election. The final battle in the race, however, was not decided in the electoral arena and did not involve the participation of ordinary Americans. Instead, the battle was fought in the courts, in the Florida state legislature, and in the executive institutions of the Florida state government by small groups of attorneys and political activists. During the course of the dispute, some forty lawsuits were filed in the Florida circuit and supreme courts, the U.S. District Court, the U.S. Court of Appeals, and the U.S. Supreme Court.[1] Together, the two campaigns amassed nearly $10 million in legal fees during the month of litigation. In most of the courtroom battles, the Bush campaign prevailed. Despite two setbacks before the all-Democratic Florida supreme court, Bush attorneys won most of the circuit court cases and the ultimate clash before the U.S. Supreme Court in a narrow 5–4 vote.

During the arguments before the Supreme Court, it became clear that the conservative majority was determined to prevent a Gore victory. Conservative justices

---

[1]"In the Courts," *San Diego Union-Tribune*, 7 December 2000, p. A14.

were sharply critical of the arguments presented by Vice President Al Gore's lawyers, while openly sympathetic to the arguments made by Bush's lawyers. Conservative justice Antonin Scalia went so far as to intervene when Bush attorney Theodore Olson responded to a question from Justices David Souter and Ruth Bader Ginsburg. Scalia evidently sought to ensure that Olson did not concede too much to the Gore argument. "It's part of your submission, I think," Scalia said, "that there is no wrong when a machine does not count those ballots that it's not supposed to count?" Scalia was seeking to remind Olson that when voter error rendered a ballot unreadable by a tabulating machine, it was not appropriate for a court to order them counted by hand. "The voters are instructed to detach the chads entirely," Scalia said, "and if the machine does not count those chads where those instructions are not followed, there isn't any wrong." Olson was happy to accept Scalia's reminder.[2]

Liberal justice John Paul Stevens said the majority opinion smacked of partisan politics. The opinion, he said, "can only lend credence to the most cynical appraisal of the work of judges throughout the land." He concluded, "Although we may never know with complete certainty the identity of the winner of this year's presidential election, the identity of the loser is perfectly clear. It is the nation's confidence in the judge as an impartial guardian of the rule of law." Justice Stevens's eloquent dissent did not change the outcome.

[2]Linda Greenhouse, "U.S. Supreme Court Justices Grill Bush, Gore Lawyers in Effort to Close the Book on Presidential Race," *New Orleans Times-Picayune*, 12 December 2000, p. 1.

CHAPTER OUTLINE

The Judicial Process

The Organization of the Court System

- Types of Courts
- Federal Jurisdiction
- Federal Trial Courts
- Federal Appellate Courts
- The Supreme Court
- How Judges Are Appointed

How Do Courts Work as Political Institutions?

- Dispute Resolution
- Coordination
- Rule Interpretation

The Power of Judicial Review

- Judicial Review of Acts of Congress
- Judicial Review of State Actions
- Judicial Review of Federal Agency Actions
- Judicial Review and Presidential Power
- Judicial Review and Lawmaking

The Supreme Court in Action

- How Cases Reach the Supreme Court
- Controlling the Flow of Cases
- The Case Pattern
- The Supreme Court's Procedures

Judicial Decision Making

- The Supreme Court Justices
- Other Institutions of Government
- Implementation of Supreme Court Decisions
- Strategic Behavior in the Supreme Court

Judicial Power and Politics

- Traditional Limitations on the Federal Courts
- Two Judicial Revolutions

PREVIEWING THE PRINCIPLES

Although they are free from electoral considerations and constrained by precedents in ways that elected policy makers are not, federal judges and Supreme Court justices are politicians with political goals and preferences. In this sense, we can conceive of courts as political institutions. By treating courts as political institutions, we can understand them as dispute solvers, coordinators, and interpreters of rules. In deciding cases, judges and justices must seek to reconcile their policy goals and judicial philosophies on the one hand with existing precedents on the other.

Rationality Principle

Judges have political goals and policy preferences and act to achieve them.

Policy Principle

Courts are not legislative bodies, but many important policy issues are, nevertheless, decided by the judiciary.

Throughout the nation, Democrats saw the Supreme Court majority's opinion as a blatantly partisan decision. Nevertheless, the contest was over. The next day, Al Gore made a speech conceding the election, and on December 18, 2000, 271 presidential electors—the constitutionally prescribed majority—cast their votes for George W. Bush.

What does the court battle over Florida's twenty-five electoral votes reveal about the power of courts and judges in the American political system? First of all, this battle shows that judges are similar to other politicians in that they have political goals and policy preferences and they act accordingly so that those goals are realized. While thinking of judges as "legislators in robes" is antithetical to the view that judges rule according to a well-thought-out judicial philosophy based on constitutional law, there is evidence that strategic thinking on the part of judges is also a factor in their decision-making process. Second, this battle illustrates the political power that the courts now exercise. Over the past fifty years, the prominence of the courts has been heightened by the sharp increase in the number of major policy issues that have been fought and decided in the judicial realm. But since judges are not elected and accountable to the people, what does this shift in power mean for American democracy?

In this chapter, we first examine the judicial process, including the types of cases that the federal courts consider and the types of law with which they deal. Second, we assess the organization and structure of the federal court system as well as explain how judges are appointed to the courts. Third, we analyze courts as political institutions and consider their roles in the political system. Fourth, we consider judicial review and how it makes the Supreme Court a "lawmaking body." Fifth, we examine the flow of cases through the courts and various influences on the Supreme Court's decisions. Finally, we analyze the process of judicial decision making and the power of the federal courts in the American political process, looking in particular at the growth of judicial power in the United States.

THE JUDICIAL PROCESS

Originally, a "court" was the place where a sovereign ruled—where the king and his entourage governed. Settling disputes between citizens was part of governing. According to the Bible, King Solomon had to settle the dispute between two women over which of them was the mother of the child both claimed. Judging is the settling of disputes, a function that was slowly separated from the king and the king's court and made into a separate institution of government. Courts have taken over from kings the power to settle controversies by hearing the facts on both sides and deciding which side possesses the greater merit. But because judges are not kings, they must have a basis for their authority. That basis in the United States is the Constitution and the law. Courts decide cases by applying the relevant law or principle to the facts.

Court cases in the United States proceed under two broad categories of law: criminal law and civil law. One form of civil law, public law, is so important that we consider it as a separate category (Table 8.1).

Cases of *criminal law* are those in which the government charges an individual with violating a statute that has been enacted to protect the public health, safety, morals, or welfare. In criminal cases, the government is always the *plaintiff* (the party that brings charges) and alleges that a criminal violation has been committed by a named *defendant.* Most criminal cases arise in state and municipal courts and involve matters ranging from traffic offenses to robbery and murder. While the great bulk of criminal law is still a state matter, a large and growing body of federal criminal law deals with such matters as tax evasion, mail fraud, and the sale of narcotics. Defendants found guilty of criminal violations may be fined or sent to prison.

Cases of *civil law* involve disputes among individuals or between individuals and the government where no criminal violation is charged. Unlike criminal cases, the losers in civil cases cannot be fined or sent to prison, although they may be required to pay monetary damages for their actions. In a civil case, the one who brings a complaint is the plaintiff and the one against whom the complaint is brought is the defendant. The two most common types of civil cases involve contracts and torts. In a typical contract case, an individual or corporation charges that it has suffered because of another's violation of a specific agreement between the two. For example, the Smith Manufacturing Corporation may charge that Jones Distributors failed to honor an agreement to deliver raw materials at a specified time, causing Smith to lose business. Smith asks the court to order Jones to compensate it for the damage allegedly suffered. In a typical tort case, one individual charges that he or she has been injured by another's negligence or malfeasance. Medical malpractice suits are one example of tort cases.

In deciding cases, courts apply statutes (laws) and legal *precedents* (prior decisions). State and federal statutes often govern the conditions under which contracts are and are not legally binding. Jones Distributors might argue that it was not obliged to fulfill its contract with the Smith Corporation because actions by Smith—the failure to make promised payments—constituted fraud under state law. Attorneys for a physician being sued for malpractice, on the other hand, may search for prior instances in which courts ruled that actions similar to those of their client did not constitute negligence. Such precedents are applied under the doctrine of *stare decisis,* a Latin phrase meaning "let the decision stand."

A case becomes a matter of the third category, *public law,* when a plaintiff or defendant in a civil or criminal case seeks to show that their case involves the powers

criminal law The branch of law that deals with disputes or actions involving criminal penalties (as opposed to civil law). It regulates the conduct of individuals, defines crimes, and provides punishment for criminal acts.

plaintiff The individual or organization who brings a complaint in court.

defendant The individual or organization charged with a complaint in court.

civil law A system of jurisprudence, including private law and governmental actions, to settle disputes that do not involve criminal penalties.

precedents Prior cases whose principles are used by judges as the bases for their decisions in present cases.

stare decisis Literally, "let the decision stand." A previous decision by a court applies as a precedent in similar cases until that decision is overruled.

public law Cases involving the action of public agencies or officials.

TABLE 8.1

Types of Laws and Disputes

TYPE OF LAW	TYPE OF CASE OR DISPUTE	FORM OF CASE
Criminal law	Cases arising out of actions that violate laws protecting the health, safety, and morals of the community. The government is always the plaintiff.	*U.S. (or state) v. Jones* *Jones v. U.S. (or state),* if Jones lost and is appealing
Civil law	Law involving disputes between citizens or between government and citizen where no crime is alleged. Two general types are contract and tort. *Contract cases* are disputes that arise over voluntary actions. *Tort cases* are disputes that arise out of obligations inherent in social life. Negligence and slander are examples of torts.	*Smith v. Jones* *New York v. Jones* *U.S. v. Jones* *Jones v. New York*
Public law	All cases in which the powers of government or the rights of citizens are involved. The government is the defendant. *Constitutional law* involves judicial review of the basis of a government's action in relation to specific clauses of the Constitution as interpreted in Supreme Court cases. *Administrative law* involves disputes over the statutory authority, jurisdiction, or procedures of administrative agencies.	*Jones v. U.S. (or state)* *In re Jones* *Smith v. Jones,* if a license or statute is at issue in their private dispute

of government or rights of citizens as defined under the Constitution or by statute. One major form of public law is constitutional law, under which a court will examine the government's actions to see if they conform to the Constitution as it has been interpreted by the judiciary. Thus what began as an ordinary criminal case may enter the realm of public law if a defendant claims that his or her constitutional rights were violated by the police. Another important arena of public law is administrative law, which involves disputes over the jurisdiction, procedures, or authority of administrative agencies. Under this type of law, civil litigation between an individual and the government may become a matter of public law if the individual asserts that the government is violating a statute or abusing its power under the Constitution. For example, landowners have asserted that federal and state restrictions on land use constitute violations of the Fifth Amendment's restrictions on the government's ability to confiscate private property. Recently, the Supreme Court has been very sympathetic to such claims, which effectively transform an ordinary civil dispute into a major issue of public law.

Most of the Supreme Court cases we will examine in this chapter involve judgments concerning the constitutional or statutory basis of the actions of government agencies. As we shall see, it is in this arena of public law that Court decisions can have significant consequences for American politics and society.

THE ORGANIZATION OF THE COURT SYSTEM

Types of Courts

In the United States, systems of courts have been established both by the federal government and by the governments of the individual states. Both systems have several levels, as shown in Figure 8.1. Nearly 99 percent of all court cases in the United States are heard in state courts. The overwhelming majority of criminal cases, for example, involve violations of state laws prohibiting such actions as murder, robbery, fraud, theft, and assault. If such a case is brought to trial, it will be heard in a state *trial court* in front of a judge and sometimes a jury, who will determine whether the defendant violated state law. If the defendant is convicted, he or she may appeal the conviction to a higher court, such as a state *court of appeals,* and from there to a state's *supreme court.* Similarly, in civil cases, most litigation is brought in the courts established by the state in which the activity in question took place. For example, a patient bringing suit against a physician for malpractice would file the suit in the appropriate court in the state where the alleged malpractice occurred. The judge hearing the case would apply state law and state precedent to the matter at hand. (It should be noted that in both criminal and civil matters, most cases are settled before trial through negotiated agreements between the parties. In criminal cases, these agreements are called *plea bargains.*) Such bargains may affect the severity of the charge and/or the severity of the sentence.

trial court The first court to hear a criminal or civil case.

court of appeals A court that hears the appeals of trial-court decisions.

supreme court The highest court in a particular state or in the United States. This court primarily serves an appellate function.

plea bargains Negotiated agreements in criminal cases in which a defendant agrees to plead guilty in return for the state's agreement to reduce the severity of the criminal charge the defendant is facing.

FIGURE 8.1

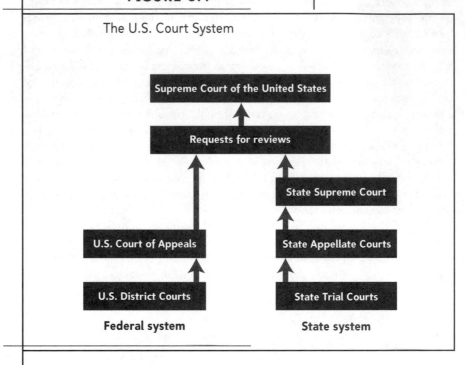

The U.S. Court System

There are fifty-one court systems in the United States—the federal system and fifty individual state systems, each with its own system of trial and appellate courts. State courts handle 99 percent of the cases heard in the United States.

In addition, the U.S. military operates its own court system under the Uniform Code of Military Justice, which governs the behavior of men and women in the armed services. On rare occasions, the government has constituted special military tribunals to hear cases deemed inappropriate for the civil courts. Such tribunals tried Nazi saboteurs apprehended in the United States during World War II. More recently, President Bush ordered the creation of military tribunals to try foreigners suspected of acts of terrorism against the United States.

Federal Jurisdiction

jurisdiction The sphere of a court's power and authority.

Cases are heard in the federal courts if they involve federal laws, treaties with other nations, or the U.S. Constitution; these areas are the official *jurisdiction* of the federal courts. In addition, any case in which the U.S. government is a party is heard in the federal courts. If, for example, an individual is charged with violating a federal criminal statute, such as evading the payment of income taxes, charges would be brought before a federal judge by a federal prosecutor. Civil cases involving the citizens of more than one state and in which more than seventy thousand dollars are at stake may be heard in either the federal or the state courts, usually depending on the preference of the plaintiff.

But even if a matter belongs in federal court, how do we know which federal court should exercise jurisdiction over the case? The answer to this seemingly simple question is somewhat complex. The jurisdiction of each federal court is derived from the U.S. Constitution and federal statutes. Article III of the Constitution gives the Supreme Court appellate jurisdiction in all federal cases and original jurisdiction in cases involving foreign ambassadors and issues in which a state is a party. Article III assigns original jurisdiction in all other federal cases to the lower courts that Congress was authorized to establish. Over the years, as Congress enacted statutes creating the federal judicial system, it specified the jurisdiction of each type of court it established. For the most part, Congress has assigned jurisdictions on the basis of geography. The nation is currently, by statute, divided into ninety-four judicial districts, including one court for each of three U.S. territories: Guam, the U.S. Virgin Islands, and the Northern Marianas. Each of the ninety-four U.S. district courts exercises jurisdiction over federal cases arising within its territorial domain. The judicial districts are, in turn, organized into eleven regional circuits and the D.C. circuit (Figure 8.2). Each circuit court exercises appellate jurisdiction over cases heard by the district courts within its region.

Geography is not the only basis for federal court jurisdiction. Congress has also established several specialized courts that have nationwide original jurisdiction in certain types of cases. These include the U.S. Court of International Trade, created to deal with trade and customs issues, and the U.S. Court of Federal Claims, which handles damage suits against the United States. Congress has, in addition, established a court with nationwide appellate jurisdiction. This is the U.S. Court of Appeals for the Federal Circuit, which hears appeals involving patent law and those arising from the decisions of the trade and claims courts. Other federal courts assigned specialized jurisdictions by Congress include the U.S. Court of Veterans Appeals, which exercises exclusive jurisdiction over cases involving veterans' claims, and the U.S. Court of Military Appeals, which deals with questions of law arising from trials by court-martial.

With the exception of the claims court and the Court of Appeals for the Federal Circuit, these specialized courts were created by Congress on the basis of the powers the legislature exercises under Article I, rather than Article III, of the Constitution. Article III is designed to protect judges from political pressure by granting them life tenure and prohibiting reduction of their salaries while they serve. The judges of Article I courts, by contrast, are appointed by the president for fixed terms of fifteen years and are not protected by the Constitution from salary reduction. As a result, these so-called "legislative courts" are generally

FIGURE 8.2

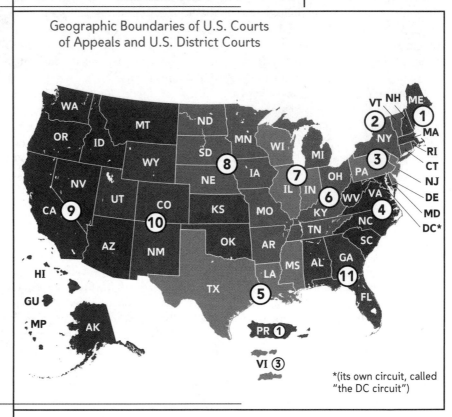

Geographic Boundaries of U.S. Courts of Appeals and U.S. District Courts

*(its own circuit, called "the DC circuit")

The United States is divided into eleven circuits plus the D.C. circuit and ninety-four judicial districts.

SOURCE: Office of the Federal Courts.

viewed as less independent than the courts established under Article III of the Constitution. The three territorial courts were also established under Article I, and their judges are appointed for ten-year terms.

The appellate jurisdiction of the federal courts also extends to cases originating in the state courts. In both civil and criminal cases, a decision of the highest state court can be appealed to the U.S. Supreme Court by raising a federal issue. Appellants might assert, for example, that they were denied the right to counsel or otherwise deprived of the **due process** guaranteed by the federal Constitution, or they might assert that important issues of federal law were at stake in the

due process The right of every citizen against arbitrary action by national or state governments.

case. The U.S. Supreme Court is not obligated to accept such appeals and will do so only if it believes that the matter has considerable national significance. We will return to this topic later in the chapter. In addition, in criminal cases, defendants who have been convicted in a state court may request a **writ of habeas corpus** from a federal district court. Sometimes known as the "Great Writ," *habeas corpus* is a court order to the authorities to release a prisoner deemed to be held in violation of his or her legal rights. In 1867, its distrust of southern courts led Congress to authorize federal district judges to issue such writs to prisoners whom they believed had been deprived of constitutional rights in state court. Generally speaking, state defendants seeking a federal writ of *habeas corpus* must show that they have exhausted all available state remedies and must raise issues not previously raised in their state appeals. Federal courts of appeals and, ultimately, the U.S. Supreme Court have appellate jurisdiction for federal district court *habeas* decisions.

Over the past three decades, the caseload of the federal courts has nearly tripled to more than 270,000 cases a year. This has come about because Congress has greatly expanded the number of federal crimes, particularly in the realm of drug possession and sale. Behavior that once was exclusively a state criminal question has, to some extent, come within the reach of federal law. In 1999, the late Chief Justice Rehnquist criticized Congress for federalizing too many offenses and intruding unnecessarily into areas that should be handled by the states.[3] About 80 percent of federal cases end in the district courts, and the remainder are appealed to the circuit courts. In a recent year, moreover, slightly more that 6,000 circuit court decisions were appealed to the Supreme Court. Most of the cases filed with the Supreme Court are dismissed without a ruling on their merits. The Court has broad latitude to decide what cases it will hear and generally listens only to those cases it deems to raise the most important issues. In 2003, for example, only ninety-four cases were given full-dress Supreme Court review (the nine justices actually sitting *en banc*—in full court—and hearing lawyers argue the case).[4]

Although the federal courts hear only a small fraction of all the civil and criminal cases decided each year in the United States, their decisions are extremely important. It is in the federal courts that the Constitution and federal laws that govern all Americans are interpreted and their meaning and significance established. Moreover, it is in the federal courts that the powers and limitations of the increasingly powerful national government are tested. Finally, through their power to review the decisions of the state courts, it is ultimately the federal courts that dominate the American judicial system.

writ of habeas corpus A court order demanding that an individual in custody be brought into court and shown the cause for detention. *Habeas corpus* is guaranteed by the Constitution and can be suspended only in cases of rebellion or invasion.

[3]Roberto Suro, "Rehnquist: Too Many Offenses Are Becoming Federal Crimes," *Washington Post*, 1 January 1999, p. A2.
[4]U.S. Bureau of the Census, *Statistical Abstract of the United States, 2002* (Washington, DC: Government Printing Office, 2002).

Federal Trial Courts

The federal district courts are trial courts of general jurisdiction, and their cases are, in form, indistinguishable from cases in the state trial courts.

There are eighty-nine district courts in the fifty states, plus one in the District of Columbia and one in Puerto Rico, and three territorial courts. There are 649 district judgeships. District judges are assigned to district courts according to the workload; the busiest of these courts may have as many as twenty-eight judges. Only one judge is assigned to each case, except where statutes provide for three-judge courts to deal with special issues. The routines and procedures of the federal district courts are essentially the same as those of the lower state courts, except that federal procedural requirements tend to be stricter. States, for example, do not have to provide a grand jury, a twelve-member trial jury, or a unanimous jury verdict. Federal courts must provide all these things. As we saw above, in addition to the district courts, cases are handled by several specialized courts, including the U.S. Tax Court, the Court of Federal Claims, and the Court of International Trade.

Federal Appellate Courts

Roughly 20 percent of all lower court cases, along with appeals from some federal agency decisions, are subsequently reviewed by a federal appeals court. As noted, the country is divided into twelve judicial circuits, each of which has a U.S. Court of Appeals. Every state and the District of Columbia are assigned to the circuit in the continental United States that is closest to it. A thirteenth appellate court, the U.S. Court of Appeals for the Federal Circuit, is defined by subject matter rather than geographical jurisdiction.

Except for cases selected for review by the Supreme Court, decisions made by the appeals courts are final. Because of this finality, certain safeguards have been built into the system. The most important is the provision of more than one judge for every appeals case. Each court of appeals has from three to twenty-eight permanent judgeships, depending on the workload of the circuit. Although normally three judges hear appealed cases, in some instances a larger number of judges sit together *en banc*.

Another safeguard is provided by the assignment of a Supreme Court justice as the circuit justice for each of the twelve circuits. The circuit justice deals with requests for special action by the Supreme Court. The most frequent and best-known action of circuit justices is that of reviewing requests for stays of execution when the full Court is unable to do so—mainly during the summer, when the Court is in recess.

The Supreme Court

The Supreme Court is America's highest court. Article III of the Constitution vests "the judicial Power of the United States" in the Supreme Court, and this court is supreme in fact as well as form. The Supreme Court is made up of a chief justice and eight associate justices. The *chief justice* presides over the Court's public sessions and conferences. In the Court's actual deliberations and decisions, however, the chief justice has no more authority than his or her colleagues. Each justice casts one vote. The chief justice, though, is always the first to speak and the last to vote when the justices deliberate. In addition, if the chief justice has voted with the majority, he decides which of the justices will write the formal opinion for the court. The character of the opinion can be an important means of influencing the evolution of the law beyond the mere affirmation or denial of the appeal at hand. To some extent, the influence of the chief justice is a function of his or her own leadership ability. Some chief justices, such as Earl Warren, have been able to lead the court in a new direction. In other instances, a forceful associate justice, such as Felix Frankfurter, is the dominant figure on the Court.

The Constitution does not specify the number of justices that should sit on the Supreme Court; Congress has the authority to change the Court's size. In the early nineteenth century, there were six Supreme Court justices; later there were seven. Congress set the number of justices at nine in 1869, and the Court has remained that size ever since. In 1937, President Franklin D. Roosevelt, infuriated by several Supreme Court decisions that struck down New Deal programs, asked Congress to enlarge the court so that he could add a few sympathetic justices to the bench. Although Congress balked at Roosevelt's "court-packing" plan, the Court gave in to FDR's pressure and began to take a more favorable view of his policy initiatives. The president, in turn, dropped his efforts to enlarge the Court. The Court's surrender to FDR came to be known as "the switch in time that saved nine."

How Judges Are Appointed

Federal judges are appointed by the president and are generally selected from among the more prominent or politically active members of the legal profession. Many federal judges previously served as state court judges or state or local prosecutors. Before the president makes a formal nomination, however, the senators from the candidate's own state must indicate that they support the nominee. This is an informal but seldom violated practice called *senatorial courtesy.* If one or both senators from a prospective nominee's home state belong to the president's political party, the president will almost invariably consult them and secure their blessing for the nomination. Because the president's party in the Senate will rarely support a nominee opposed by a home-state senator from their ranks, this arrangement gives these senators virtual veto power over appointments to the federal bench in their own states. Senators often see such a nomination as a way to reward important allies and contributors in their states. If the state has no senator from the president's party, the governor or members of the state's House delegation may make suggestions. In general, presidents endeavor to appoint judges who possess legal experience and good character and

whose partisan and ideological views are similar to the president's own. During the presidencies of Richard Nixon, Ronald Reagan, and George H. W. Bush, most federal judicial appointees were conservative Republicans. Indeed, Bush established an advisory committee to screen judicial nominees to make certain that their legal and political philosophies were sufficiently conservative. Bill Clinton's appointees to the federal bench, on the other hand, tended to be liberal Democrats. Following the example of Jimmy Carter, Clinton also made a major effort to appoint women and African Americans to the federal courts. Nearly half of his nominees were drawn from these groups.

Once the president has formally nominated an individual, the nominee must be considered by the Senate Judiciary Committee and confirmed by a majority vote in the full Senate. In recent years, the Senate Judiciary Committee has sought to signal the president when it has had qualms about a judicial nomination. After the Republicans won control of the Senate in 1994, for example, Judiciary Committee chair Orrin Hatch of Utah let President Clinton know that he considered two of Clinton's nominees to be too liberal. The president withdrew the nominations.

Federal appeals court nominations follow much the same pattern. Because appeals court judges preside over jurisdictions that include several states, however, senators do not have as strong a role in proposing potential candidates. Instead, potential appeals court candidates are generally suggested to the president by the Justice Department or by important members of the administration. The senators from the nominee's own state are still consulted before the president will formally act.

During President George W. Bush's first two years in office, Democrats controlled the Senate and used their majority on the Judiciary Committee to block eight of the president's first eleven federal court nominations. After the GOP won a narrow Senate majority in the 2002 national elections, Democrats used a filibuster to block action on several other Bush federal appeals court nominees. Both Democrats and Republicans saw struggles over lower court slots as practice and preparation for all-out partisan warfare over the next Supreme Court vacancy.

If political factors play an important role in the selection of district and appellate court judges, they are decisive when it comes to Supreme Court appointments. Because the high court has so much influence over American law and politics, virtually all presidents have made an effort to select justices who share their own political philosophies. Presidents Ronald Reagan and George H. W. Bush, for example, appointed five justices whom they believed to have conservative perspectives: Justices Sandra Day O'Connor, Antonin Scalia, Anthony M. Kennedy, David Hackett Souter, and Clarence Thomas. Reagan also elevated William Rehnquist to the position of chief justice. Reagan and Bush sought appointees who believed in reducing government intervention in the economy and who supported the moral positions taken by the Republican party in recent years, particularly opposition to abortion. However, not all the Reagan and Bush appointees have fulfilled their sponsors' expectations. Bush appointee Souter, for example, has been attacked by conservatives as a turncoat for his decisions on school prayer and abortion rights. Nevertheless, through their appointments, Reagan and Bush were able to create a far more conservative Supreme Court. For his part, President Bill Clinton endeavored to appoint liberal justices. Clinton named Ruth Bader Ginsburg and Stephen G. Breyer to the Court, hoping to counteract the influence of the Reagan and Bush appointees.

In 2005, President George W. Bush was given an opportunity to put his own stamp on the Supreme Court as Justice O'Connor announced her decision to retire and Chief Justice Rehnquist died of the cancer that had limited his judicial activities for a year (Table 8.2). Bush quickly nominated federal appeals court judge John G. Roberts, initially to replace O'Connor but then as Chief Justice when Rehnquist died while the Senate was still considering the appointment. Roberts, a moderate conservative with a brilliant legal record, provoked some Democratic opposition but was confirmed without much difficulty. Bush's next nominee, though, sparked an intense battle within the president's own party. To the surprise of most observers, the president named a long-time associate, White House Counsel Harriet Miers, to replace O'Connor. Many Republicans viewed Miers as merely a Bush crony who lacked judicial qualifications and was insufficiently supportive of conservative causes. Opposition to Miers within the GOP was so intense that Democrats remained gleefully silent as the president was forced to allow her to withdraw her name from consideration. In the wake of the Miers debacle, President Bush turned to a more conventional nominee, federal appeals court judge Samuel Alito. This nomination pleased conservative Republicans, who saw Alito as being in the mold of arch-conservative justice Antonin Scalia. But while Republicans were pleased, Democrats and liberal political forces promised an all-out battle to block the nomination. The Democratic opposition ultimately failed, and Alito was confirmed in February 2006.

In recent years, of course, Supreme Court nominations have come to involve intense partisan struggle. Typically, after the president has named a nominee, interest groups opposed to the nomination have mobilized opposition in the media, the public, and the Senate. When former president Bush proposed conservative judge Clarence Thomas for the Court, for example, liberal groups launched a campaign to discredit Thomas. After extensive research into his background, opponents of the nomination were able to produce evidence suggesting that Thomas had sexually harassed a former subordinate, Anita Hill. Thomas denied the charge. After contentious Senate Judiciary Committee hearings, highlighted by testimony from both Thomas and Hill, Thomas narrowly won confirmation.

Likewise, conservative interest groups carefully scrutinized Bill Clinton's somewhat more liberal nominees, hoping to find information about them that would sabotage their appointments. During his two opportunities to name Supreme Court justices, Clinton was compelled to drop several potential appointees because of information unearthed by political opponents.

TABLE 8.2

Supreme Court Justices, 2006

NAME	YEAR OF BIRTH	PRIOR EXPERIENCE	APPOINTED BY	YEAR OF APPOINTMENT
John G. Roberts, Jr.* *Chief Justice*	1955	Federal judge	Bush, G. W.	2005
John Paul Stevens	1920	Federal judge	Ford	1975
Antonin Scalia	1936	Law professor, federal judge	Reagan	1986
Anthony M. Kennedy	1936	Federal judge	Reagan	1988
David Hackett Souter	1939	Federal judge	Bush, G. H. W.	1990
Clarence Thomas	1948	Federal judge	Bush, G. H. W.	1991
Ruth Bader Ginsburg	1933	Federal judge	Clinton	1993
Stephen G. Breyer	1938	Federal judge	Clinton	1994
Samuel A. Alito, Jr.	1950	Federal judge	Bush, G. W.	2006

*Appointed chief justice by Bush in 2005.

These struggles over judicial appointments indicate the growing intensity of partisan struggle in the United States today. They also indicate how much importance competing political forces attach to Supreme Court appointments. Because these contending forces see the outcome as critical, they are willing to engage in a fierce struggle when Supreme Court appointments are at stake.

The matter of judicial appointments became an important issue in the 2000 and 2004 elections. Democrats charged that, if he were elected, George W. Bush would appoint conservative judges who might, among other things, reverse the *Roe v. Wade* decision and curb abortion rights. Bush would say only that he would seek judges who would uphold the Constitution without reading their own political biases into the document.

From the liberal perspective, the danger of a conservative judiciary was underlined by the Supreme Court's decision in the Florida election case, *Bush v. Gore*.

The Court's conservative bloc, in recent years, has argued that the states deserve considerable deference from the federal courts. In this instance, however, the Supreme Court overturned a decision of the Florida supreme court regarding Florida election law. The Court ruled that its Florida counterpart had ignored the U.S. Constitution's equal protection doctrine when it mandated recounts in some, but not all, Florida counties. By voting to overrule the Florida court, the Supreme Court's conservative justices appeared to disregard the logic of their own decisions—expanding the authority of the states—of the past two decades (see Chapter 3). To be sure, the same liberal justices who voted to uphold the Florida court's decision had frequently argued against deferring to the states in previous decisions. Ideological consistency notwithstanding, defenders of the decision argued that it was doctrinally sound and that it averted the chaos that might have ensued if a recount gave Gore the victory and the Florida legislature carried out its threat to appoint Bush electors. Two competing slates of electors might then have sought congressional certification. Critics of the decision, however, asserted that the Court was merely searching for a rubric under which it could ensure Bush's victory. As a result of the Florida contest, there can be little doubt that the next Supreme Court vacancy will generate sharp fighting in Washington.

HOW DO COURTS WORK AS POLITICAL INSTITUTIONS?

Judges are central players in important political institutions and this makes them politicians. To understand what animates judicial behavior, we thus need to place the judge or justice in context by briefly considering the role of the courts in the political system more generally. In doing so, we emphasize the role of courts as *dispute resolvers*, as *coordinators*, and as *interpreters of rules*.

Dispute Resolution

So much of the productive activity that occurs within families, among friends and associates, even between absolute strangers takes place because the participants do not have to devote substantial resources to protecting themselves and their property or monitoring compliance with agreements.[5] For any potential

---

[5]Naturally, some resources are devoted to protection and monitoring. However, if extraordinary resources had to be devoted, then their rising cost would cause the frequency of the productive activities alluded to in the text to decline, according to elementary economic theory. Indeed, because the costs of negotiating, monitoring, and enforcing agreements (what political economists call *transaction costs*) can be very high, they are a serious impediment to social interaction and productive activities of all sorts. Economizing on them—by providing the services of courts and judges, for example—is one of the great contributions of the modern state to social welfare.

violation of person or property, or defection from an agreement, all parties know in advance that an aggrieved party may take an alleged violator to court. The court, in turn, serves as a venue in which the facts of a case are established, punishment is meted out to violators, and compensation awarded to victims. The court, therefore, is an institution that engages in fact-finding and judgment.

In disputes between private parties, the court serves principally to determine whether claims of violation can be substantiated. An employee, for example, may sue his or her employer for allegedly violating the terms of a privately nego-tiated employment contract. Or a consumer may sue a producer for violating the terms of a product warranty. Or a tenant may sue a landlord for violating provi-sions of a lease. In all of these cases, some issue between private parties is in dis-pute. The court system provides the service of dispute resolution.

The examples in the preceding paragraph involve civil law. An entirely sepa-rate category of dispute, one in which the courts also have a role to play, involves criminal law. In these cases "the public" is a party to the dispute because the al-leged violation concerns not (only) something involving private parties but (also) a public law. This brings the public agencies of justice into play as parties to a dispute. When an individual embezzles funds from his partner, he not only vio-lates a privately negotiated agreement between them (namely, a promise of hon-est dealings), he also violates a public law prohibiting embezzlement generally. A court proceeding, in this case, determines not only whether a violation of a pri-vate arrangement has occurred but also whether the alleged perpetrator is inno-cent or guilty of violating a public law.

In all of these instances, the judge is responsible for managing the fact-finding and judgment phases of dispute resolution (sometimes in collaboration with a jury). Thus a large part of the daily life of a judge involves making an independ-ent, experienced assessment of the facts, determining whether the dispute in-volves a violation of a private agreement or a public law (or both), and finally rendering a judgment—a determination of which party (if either) is liable, and what compensation is in order (to the private party victimized and, if judged a criminal activity, to the larger public). Judging is a sophisticated blend of reading a mystery novel, solving a crossword puzzle, and providing wise counsel.

Coordination

Dispute resolution occurs after the fact—that is, after a dispute has already oc-curred. In a manner of speaking, it represents a failure of the legal system be-cause one function of law and its judicial institutions is to discourage such disputes in the first place. We may also think of courts and judges as before-the-fact *coordination mechanisms* inasmuch as the anticipation of what happens once their services are called on allows private parties to form rational expectations and thereby coordinate their actions in advance of possible disputes. A prospec-tive embezzler, estimating the odds of getting caught, prosecuted, and subse-quently punished, may think twice about cheating his partner. Surely, *some* prospective embezzlers are deterred from their crimes by these prospects. Conversely, the legal system can work as an incentive: Two acquaintances, for example, may confidently entertain the possibility of going into business together, knowing that the sword of justice hangs over their collaboration.

In this sense, the court system is as important for what it doesn't do as for what it does. The system of courts and law coordinates private behavior by providing incentives and disincentives for specific actions. To the extent that these work, there are fewer disputes to resolve and thus less after-the-fact dispute resolution for courts and judges to engage in. What makes the incentives and disincentives work is their power (are the rewards and penalties big or small?), their clarity, and the consistency with which judges administer them. Clear incentives, consistently employed, provide powerful motivations for private parties to resolve disputes ahead of time. This sort of advanced coordination, encouraged by a properly functioning legal system, economizes on the transaction costs that would diminish the frequency of, and otherwise discourage, socially desirable activity.

Collective-Action Principle

The legal system coordinates private behavior by providing incentives and disincentives for specific actions.

Rule Interpretation

Dispute resolution and coordination affect private behavior and the daily lives of ordinary citizens tremendously. Judges, however, are not entirely free agents (despite the fact that some of them are tyrants in their courtrooms). In matching the facts of a specific case to judicial principles and statutory guidelines, judges must engage in *interpretive* activity. They must determine what particular statutes or judicial principles mean, which of them fit the facts of a particular case, and then, having determined all this, they must ascertain the disposition of the case at hand. Does the statute of 1927 regulating the electronic transmission of radio waves apply to television, cellular phones, ship-to-shore radios, fax machines, and e-mail? Does the law governing the transportation of dangerous substances, passed in 1937, apply to nuclear fuels, infected animals, and artificially created biological hazards? Often, the enacting legislative body has not been crystal clear about the scope of the legislation it passes. Indeed, a legislature acting in 1927 or 1937 could not have anticipated technological developments to come. Nevertheless, cases such as these come up on a regular basis, and judges must make judgment calls, so to speak, on highly complex issues.

Interpreting the rules is probably the single most important activity in which higher courts engage. This is because the court system is *hierarchical* in the sense that judgments by higher courts constrain the discretion of judges in lower courts. If the Supreme Court rules that nuclear fuels are covered by the 1937 law on transporting dangerous substances, then lower courts must render subsequent judgments in a manner consistent with this ruling. The judge in a civil or criminal trial concerning the shipment of nuclear isotopes from a laboratory to a commercial user, for example, must make sure his or her ruling complies with the legal interpretations passed down by the higher courts. Also, because of the federal principle by which the American polity is organized, federal law and interpretations thereof often trump state and local laws.

As we shall see in the following section, courts and judges engage not only in *statutory interpretation* but in *constitutional interpretation* as well. Here they interpret the provisions of the U.S. Constitution, determining their scope and content. In determining, for example, whether the act of Congress regulating the transportation of dangerous substances from one state to another is constitutional, the justices of the Supreme Court might appeal to the commerce clause of the Constitution (allowing the federal government to regulate interstate commerce) to justify the constitutionality of that act. On the other hand, a Supreme Court majority might also rule that a shipment of spent fuel rods from a nuclear reactor in Kansas City to a nuclear waste facility outside of St. Louis is *not* covered by this law because the shipment took place entirely within the boundaries of a single state and thus did not constitute interstate commerce.

In short, judges and justices are continually engaged in elaborating, embellishing, even rewriting the rules by which private and public life are organized. In these interpretive acts they are conscious of the fact that their rulings not only will affect the participants in a specific case before them but also will carry interpretive weight in all similar cases that percolate down to the lower courts. Thus statutory and constitutional interpretations have authority over subsequent deliberations (and, in turn, are themselves influenced by earlier interpretations according to *stare decisis*).

However, judicial interpretation—elaboration, embellishment, and "redrafting"—of statutes is naturally subject to review. Statutory interpretation, even if it is conducted by the highest court in the land, is exposed to legislative review. If Congress is unhappy with a specific statutory interpretation—for example, suppose the current Congress does not like the idea of federal regulation of e-mail that a federal court claimed to be permissible under the 1927 act on electronic transmission—then it may amend the legislation so as to overcome the Court's objection or even to reverse the court ruling. In the same vein, in January 2005, the Supreme Court struck down the mandatory sentencing rules enacted by Congress in 1984.[6] The rules severely limited judicial discretion in the realm of sentencing and had long been resented by the bench. Members of Congress vowed to reinstate the guidelines through new legislation. Senator Jeff Sessions (R-Ala.) said, "The challenge will be to . . . re-create the guidelines in a way that will meet the court's test."[7] Of course, if the court makes a *constitutional* ruling, Congress cannot then abrogate that ruling through new legislation. Congress would need to commence the process of constitutional amendment to overturn a constitutional interpretation with which it disagreed.

[6] *United States v. Booker* (04–104) 2005.
[7] Carl Hulske and Adam Liptak, "New Fight over Controlling Punishments Is Widely Seen," *New York Times*, 13 January 2005, p. A27.

THE POWER OF JUDICIAL REVIEW

The phrase *judicial review* refers to the power of the judiciary to examine and, if necessary, invalidate actions undertaken by the legislative and executive branches. The phrase is sometimes also used to describe the scrutiny that appellate courts give to the actions of trial courts, but, strictly speaking, this is an improper usage. A higher court's examination of a lower court's decisions might be called "appellate review," but it is not judicial review (Figure 8.3).

judicial review
Power of the courts to declare actions of the legislative and executive branches invalid or unconstitutional. The Supreme Court asserted this power in *Marbury v. Madison.*

Judicial Review of Acts of Congress

Because the Constitution does not give the Supreme Court the power of judicial review of congressional enactments, the Court's exercise of it is something of a usurpation. Various proposals were debated at the Constitutional Convention. Among them was the proposal to create a council composed of the president and the judiciary that would share the veto power over legislation. Another proposal would have routed all legislation through the Court as well as through the president; a veto by either one would have required an overruling by a two-thirds vote of the House and Senate. Each proposal was rejected by the delegates, and no further effort was made to give the Supreme Court review power over the other branches.

This does not prove that the framers of the Constitution opposed judicial review, but it does indicate that "if they intended to provide for it in the Constitution, they did so in a most obscure fashion."[8] Disputes over the intentions of the framers were settled in 1803 in the case of *Marbury v. Madison.*[9] Although Congress and the president have often been at odds with the Court, its legal power to review acts of Congress has not been seriously questioned since 1803. One reason is that judicial power has been accepted as natural, if not intended. Another reason is that, during the early years of the Republic, the Supreme Court was careful to use its power sparingly, striking down only two pieces of legislation during the first seventy-five years of American history. One of these decisions was the 1857 *Dred Scott* ruling, which invalidated the Missouri Compromise and helped precipitate the Civil War. In recent years, with the power of judicial review securely accepted, the Court has been more willing to use it. Between 1986 and 2004, the Supreme Court struck down more than thirty-six acts of Congress.

History Principle
Since *Marbury v. Madison* (1803), the power of judicial review has not been in question.

Judicial Review of State Actions

The power of the Supreme Court to review state legislation or other state action and to determine its constitutionality is neither granted by the Constitution nor inherent in the federal system. But the logic of the *supremacy clause*

supremacy clause
Article VI of the Constitution, which states that all laws passed by the national government and all treaties are the supreme laws of the land and superior to all laws adopted by any state or any subdivision.

---

[8]C. Herman Pritchett, *The American Constitution* (New York: McGraw-Hill, 1959), p. 138.
[9]*Marbury v. Madison*, 1 Cr. 137 (1803).

FIGURE 8.3

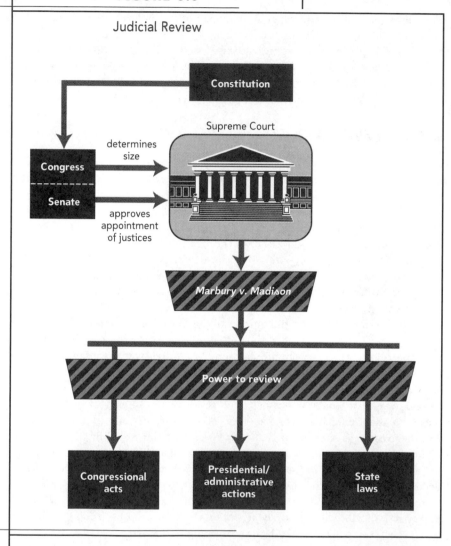

Judicial Review

Constitution

Supreme Court

Congress — determines size →

Senate — approves appointment of justices →

Marbury v. Madison

Power to review

Congressional acts

Presidential/ administrative actions

State laws

In the United States, courts can review the actions of the legislative and executive branches.

of Article VI of the Constitution, which declares it and laws made under its authority to be the supreme law of the land, is very strong. Furthermore, in the Judiciary Act of 1789, Congress conferred on the Supreme Court the power to reverse state constitutions and laws whenever they are clearly in conflict with the U.S. Constitution, federal laws, or treaties.[10] This power gives the Supreme Court jurisdiction over all of the millions of cases handled by American courts each year.

The supremacy clause of the Constitution not only established the federal Constitution, statutes, and treaties as the "supreme Law of the Land" but also provided that "the Judges in every State shall be bound thereby, any Thing in the Constitution or Laws of any State to the Contrary notwithstanding." Under this authority, the Supreme Court has frequently overturned state constitutional provisions or statutes and state court decisions it deems to contravene rights or privileges guaranteed under the federal Constitution or federal statutes.

The civil rights area abounds with examples of state laws that were overturned because the statutes violated guarantees of due process and equal protection contained in the Fourteenth Amendment to the Constitution. For example, in the 1954 case of *Brown v. Board of Education*, the Court overturned statutes from Kansas, South Carolina, Virginia, and Delaware that either required or permitted segregated public schools, on the basis that such statutes denied black schoolchildren equal protection of the law. In 1967, in *Loving v. Virginia*, the Court invalidated a Virginia statute prohibiting interracial marriages.[11]

State statutes in other subject-matter areas are equally subject to challenge. In *Griswold v. Connecticut*, the Court invalidated a Connecticut statute prohibiting the general distribution of contraceptives to married couples on the basis that the statute violated the couples' rights to marital privacy.[12] In *Brandenburg v. Ohio*, the Court overturned an Ohio statute forbidding any person from urging criminal acts as a means of inducing political reform or from joining any association that advocated such activities on the grounds that the statute punished "mere advocacy" and, therefore, violated the free-speech provisions of the Constitution.[13]

Judicial Review of Federal Agency Actions

Although Congress makes the law, as we saw in Chapters 5 and 7, Congress can hardly administer the thousands of programs it has enacted and must delegate power to the president and to a huge bureaucracy to achieve its purpose. For example, if Congress wishes to improve air quality, it cannot possibly anticipate all the conditions and circumstances that may arise over the years with respect to

---

[10]This review power was affirmed by the Supreme Court in *Martin v. Hunter's Lessee*, 1 Wheaton 304 (1816).

[11]*Brown v. Board of Education*, 347 U.S. 483 (1954); *Loving v. Virginia*, 388 U.S. 1 (1967).

[12]*Griswold v. Connecticut*, 381 U.S. 479 (1965).

[13]*Brandenburg v. Ohio*, 395 U.S. 444 (1969).

its general goal. Inevitably, Congress must delegate to the executive substantial discretionary power to make judgments about the best ways to bring about improved air quality in the face of changing circumstances. Thus, over the years, almost any congressional program will result in thousands and thousands of pages of administrative regulations developed by executive agencies nominally seeking to implement the will of Congress.

Such delegation is inescapable in the modern era. But the delegation of power to the executive poses a number of problems for Congress and the federal courts. If Congress delegates broad authority to the president, it risks seeing its goals subordinated to and subverted by those of the executive branch.[14] If Congress attempts to limit executive discretion by enacting precise rules and standards to govern the conduct of the president and the executive branch, it risks writing laws that do not conform to real-world conditions and that are too rigid to be adapted to changing circumstances.[15]

The issue of delegation of power has led to a number of court decisions over the past two centuries, generally revolving around the question of the scope of the delegation. Courts have also been called upon to decide whether the rules and regulations adopted by federal agencies are consistent with Congress's express or implied intent.

As presidential power expanded during the New Deal era, one measure of increased congressional subordination to the executive was the enactment of laws that contained few, if any, principles limiting executive discretion. Congress enacted legislation, often at the president's behest, that gave the executive virtually unfettered authority to address a particular concern. For example, the Emergency Price Control Act of 1942 authorized the executive to set "fair and equitable" prices without offering any indication of what those terms might mean.[16] Although the Court initially challenged these delegations of power to the president during the New Deal, a confrontation with President Franklin D. Roosevelt caused the Court to retreat from its position. Perhaps as a result no congressional delegation of power to the president has been struck down as impermissibly broad since then. In the last two decades in particular, the Supreme Court has found that so long as federal agencies developed rules and regulations "based upon a permissible construction" or "reasonable interpretation" of Congress's statute, the judiciary would accept the views of the executive branch. Generally, the courts give considerable deference to administrative agencies as long as those agencies have engaged in a formal rule-making process and can show that they have carried out the conditions prescribed by the various statutes governing agency rule-making. These include the 1946 Administrative

[14]See Theodore J. Lowi, *The End of Liberalism*, 2nd ed. (New York: Norton, 1979); also, David Schoenbrod, *Power without Responsibility: How Congress Abuses the People through Delegation* (New Haven, CT: Yale University Press, 1993).

[15]Kenneth Culp Davis, *Discretionary Justice* (Baton Rouge: Louisiana State University Press, 1969), pp. 15–21.

[16]56 Stat. 23 (30 January 1942).

Procedures Act, which requires agencies to notify parties affected by proposed rules as well as allow them ample time to comment on such rules before they go into effect.

Judicial Review and Presidential Power

The federal courts are also called on to review the actions of the president. As we saw in Chapter 6, presidents increasingly make use of unilateral executive powers rather than rely on congressional legislation to achieve their objectives. On many occasions, presidential orders and actions have been challenged in the federal courts by members of Congress and by individuals and groups opposing the president's policies. In recent years, assertions of presidential power in such realms as foreign policy, war and emergency powers, legislative power, and administrative authority have, more often than not, been upheld by the federal bench. Indeed, the federal judiciary has sometimes taken extraordinary presidential claims that were made for limited and temporary purposes and rationalized them—that is, converted them into routine and permanent instruments of presidential government. Take, for example, Richard Nixon's sweeping claims of executive privilege. In *United States v. Nixon*, the Court, to be sure, rejected the president's refusal to turn over tapes to congressional investigators.[17] For the first time, though, the justices also recognized the validity of the principle of executive privilege and discussed the situations in which such claims might be appropriate. This judicial recognition of the principle encouraged Presidents Bill Clinton and George W. Bush to make broad claims of executive privilege during their terms in office.[18] Executive privilege has been invoked to protect even the deliberations of the vice president from congressional scrutiny, in the case of Dick Cheney's consultations with representatives of the energy industry.

This pattern of judicial deference to presidential authority is also manifest in the Supreme Court's recent decisions regarding President Bush's war on terrorism. In June 2004, the Supreme Court ruled on three cases involving the president's antiterrorism initiatives and claims of executive power and in two of the three cases appeared to place some limits on presidential authority. Indeed, the justices had clearly been influenced by revelations that U.S. troops had abused prisoners in Iraq and sought in these cases to make a statement against the absolute denial of procedural rights to individuals in the custody of American military authorities. But, while the Court's decisions were widely hailed as reining in the executive branch, they actually fell far short of stopping presidential power in its tracks.

[17]*U.S. v. Nixon*, 418 U.S. 683 (1974).
[18]On Clinton, see Jonathan Turley, "Paradise Lost: The Clinton Administration and the Erosion of Executive Privilege," *Maryland Law Review* 60 (2001): 295. On Bush, see Jeffrey P. Carlin, *"Walker v. Cheney*: Politics, Posturing and Executive Privilege," *Southern California Law Review* 76 (November 2002): 235.

The most important case decided by the Court was *Hamdi v. Rumsfeld*.[19] Yaser Esam Hamdi, apparently a Taliban soldier, was captured by American forces in Afghanistan in late 2001 and brought to the United States, where he was incarcerated at the Norfolk Naval Station. Hamdi was classified as an enemy combatant and denied civil rights, including the right to counsel, despite the fact that he had been born in Louisiana and held American citizenship. A federal district court scheduled a hearing on Hamdi's *habeas* petition and ordered that he be given unmonitored access to counsel. This ruling, however, was reversed by the U.S. Court of Appeals for the Fourth Circuit. In its opinion, the court held that, in the national security realm, the president wields "plenary and exclusive power." This power was even greater, said the court, when the president acted with statutory authority from Congress. The court did not indicate which statute, in particular, might have authorized the president's actions, but went on to affirm the president's constitutional power, as supported in many prior rulings, to conduct military operations, decide who is and is not an enemy combatant, and determine the rules governing the treatment of such individuals. In essence, said the court, the president had virtually unfettered discretion to deal with emergencies, and it was inappropriate for the judiciary to saddle presidential decisions with what the court called the "panoply of encumbrances associated with civil litigation."

In June 2004, the Supreme Court ruled that Hamdi was entitled to a lawyer and "a fair opportunity to rebut the government's factual assertions." However, the Supreme Court affirmed that the president possessed the authority to declare a U.S. citizen to be an enemy combatant and to order that such an individual be held in federal detention. Several of the justices intimated that once designated an enemy combatant, a U.S. citizen might be tried before a military tribunal and the normal presumption of innocence be suspended. One government legal adviser indicated that the effect of the Court's decision was minimal. "They are basically upholding the whole combatant status and tweaking the evidence test," he said.[20]

Thus the Supreme Court did assert that presidential actions were subject to judicial scrutiny and placed some constraints on the president's power. But, at the same time, the Court affirmed the president's single most important claim—the unilateral power to declare individuals, including U.S. citizens, "enemy combatants" who could be detained by federal authorities under adverse legal circumstances. This hardly seems to threaten the foundations of the imperial presidency. Indeed, future presidents are likely to cite the Court's decisions as precedents for, rather than limits on, the exercise of executive power.

Policy Principle

By interpreting existing statutes as well as the Constitution, judges make law.

Judicial Review and Lawmaking

Much of the work of the courts involves the application of statutes to the particular case at hand. Over the centuries, however, judges have developed a body of

---

[19]542 (U.S. 507) 2004.

[20]Charles Lane, "Justices Back Detainee Access to U.S. Courts," *Washington Post*, 29 June 2004. p. 1.

rules and principles of interpretation that are not grounded in specific statutes. This body of judge-made law is called common law.

The appellate courts are in another realm. Their rulings can be considered laws, but they are laws governing the behavior only of the judiciary. They influence citizens' conduct only because, in the words of Justice Oliver Wendell Holmes, who served on the Supreme Court from 1902 to 1932, lawyers make "prophecies of what the courts will do in fact."[21]

The written opinion of an appellate court is about halfway between common law and statutory law. It is judge-made and draws heavily on the precedents of previous cases. But it tries to articulate the rule of law controlling the case in question and future cases like it. In this respect, it is like a statute. But it differs from a statute in that a statute addresses itself to the future conduct of citizens, whereas a written opinion addresses itself mainly to the willingness or ability of courts in the future to take cases and render favorable opinions. Decisions by appellate courts affect citizens by giving them a cause of action or by taking it away from them. That is, they open or close access to the courts.

Institution Principle

Because the court system is hierarchical, decisions by higher courts constrain the discretion of judges in lower courts.

A specific case may help clarify the distinction. Before World War II, one of the most insidious forms of racial discrimination was the "restrictive covenant," a clause in a contract whereby the purchasers of a house agreed that if they later decided to sell it, they would sell only to a white person. When a test case finally reached the Supreme Court in 1948, the Court ruled unanimously that citizens had a right to discriminate with restrictive covenants in their sales contracts but that the courts could not enforce these contracts. Its argument was that enforcement would constitute violation of the Fourteenth Amendment provision that no state shall "deny to any person within its jurisdiction equal protection under the law."[22] The Court was thereby predicting what it would and would not do in future cases of this sort. Most states have now forbidden homeowners to place such covenants in sales contracts.

Gideon v. Wainwright extends the point. When the Supreme Court ordered a new trial for Gideon because he had been denied the right to legal counsel, it said to all trial judges and prosecutors that henceforth they would be wasting their time if they cut corners in trials of indigent defendants.[23] It also invited thousands of prisoners to appeal their convictions.

Many areas of civil law have been constructed in the same way—by judicial messages to other judges, some of which are codified eventually into legislative enactments. An example of great concern to employees and employers is that of liability for injuries sustained at work. Courts have sided with employees so often that it has become virtually useless for employers to fight injury cases. It has become "the law" that employers are liable for such injuries, without regard to negligence. But the law in this instance is simply a series of messages to lawyers that they should advise their corporate clients not to appeal injury decisions.

[21] Oliver Wendell Holmes Jr., "The Path of the Law," *Harvard Law Review* 10 (1897): 457.
[22] *Shelley v. Kraemer*, 334 U.S. 1 (1948).
[23] *Gideon v. Wainwright*, 372 U.S. 335 (1963).

The appellate courts cannot decide what behavior will henceforth be a crime. They cannot directly prevent the police from forcing confessions or intimidating witnesses. In other words, they cannot directly change the behavior of citizens or eliminate abuses of power. What they can do, however, is make it easier for mistreated persons to gain redress.

In redressing wrongs, the appellate courts—and even the Supreme Court itself—often call for a radical change in legal principle. Changes in race relations, for example, would probably have taken a great deal longer if the Supreme Court had not rendered the 1954 *Brown* decision that redefined the rights of African Americans.

Similarly, the Supreme Court interpreted the separation of church and state doctrine so as to alter significantly the practice of religion in public institutions. For example, in a 1962 case, *Engel v. Vitale*, the Court declared that a once widely observed ritual—the recitation of a prayer by students in a public school—was unconstitutional under the establishment clause of the First Amendment. Almost all the dramatic changes in the treatment of criminals and of persons accused of crimes have been made by the appellate courts, especially the Supreme Court. The Supreme Court brought about a veritable revolution in the criminal process with three cases over less than five years: *Gideon v. Wainwright*, in 1963, was discussed above. *Escobedo v. Illinois*, in 1964, gave suspects the right to remain silent and the right to have counsel present during questioning. But the decision left confusions that allowed differing decisions to be made by lower courts. In *Miranda v. Arizona*, in 1966, the Supreme Court cleared up these confusions by setting forth what is known as the **Miranda rule**: arrested people have the right to remain silent, the right to be informed that anything they say can be held against them, and the right to counsel before and during police interrogation.[24]

One of the most significant changes brought about by the Supreme Court was the revolution in legislative representation unleashed by the 1962 case of *Baker v. Carr*.[25] In this landmark case, the Supreme Court held that it could no longer avoid reviewing complaints about the apportionment of seats in state legislatures. Following that decision, the federal courts went on to force reapportionment of all state, county, and local legislatures in the country.

Many experts on court history and constitutional law criticize the federal appellate courts for being too willing to introduce radical change, even when these experts agree with the general direction of the changes. Often they are troubled by the courts' (especially the Supreme Court's) willingness to jump into such cases prematurely—before the constitutional issues are fully clarified by many related cases through decisions by district and appeals courts in various parts of the country.[26] But from the perspective of the appellate judiciary, and especially

---

Miranda rule
Principles developed by the Supreme Court in the 1966 case of *Miranda v. Arizona* requiring that persons under arrest be informed of their legal rights, including their right to counsel, before police interrogation.

---

[24]*Engel v. Vitale*, 370 U.S. 421 (1962); *Gideon v. Wainwright*, 372 U.S. 335 (1963); *Escobedo v. Illinois*, 378 U.S. 478 (1964); and *Miranda v. Arizona*, 384 U.S. 436 (1966).

[25]*Baker v. Carr*, 369 U.S. 186 (1962).

[26]See Philip B. Kurland, *Politics, the Constitution, and the Warren Court* (Chicago: University of Chicago Press, 1970).

the Supreme Court, the situation is probably one of choosing between the lesser of two evils: They must take the cases as they come and then weigh the risks of opening new options against the risks of embracing the status quo.

THE SUPREME COURT IN ACTION

How Cases Reach the Supreme Court

Given the millions of disputes that arise every year, the job of the Supreme Court would be impossible if it were not able to control the flow of cases and its own caseload. The Supreme Court has original jurisdiction in a limited variety of cases defined by the Constitution. The original jurisdiction includes (1) cases between the United States and one of the fifty states, (2) cases between two or more states, (3) cases involving foreign ambassadors or other ministers, and (4) cases brought by one state against citizens of another state or against a foreign country. The most important of these cases are disputes between states over land, water, or old debts. Generally, the Supreme Court deals with these cases by appointing a "special master," usually a retired judge, to actually hear the case and present a report. The Supreme Court then allows the states involved in the dispute to present arguments for or against the master's opinion.[27]

Rules of Access   Over the years, the courts have developed specific rules that govern which cases within their jurisdiction they will and will not hear. To have access to the courts, cases must meet certain criteria that are initially applied by the trial court but may be reconsidered by appellate courts. These rules of access can be broken down into three major categories: case or controversy, standing, and mootness.

Article III of the Constitution and Supreme Court decisions define judicial power as extending only to "cases and controversies." This means that the case before a court must be an actual controversy, not a hypothetical one, with two truly adversarial parties. The courts have interpreted this language to mean that they do not have the power to render advisory opinions to legislatures or agencies about the constitutionality of proposed laws or regulations. Furthermore, even after a law is enacted, the courts will generally refuse to consider its constitutionality until it is actually applied.

Parties to a case must also have *standing*—that is, they must show that they have a substantial stake in the outcome of the case. The traditional requirement for standing has been to show injury to oneself; that injury can be personal, economic, or even aesthetic, for example. In order for a group or class of people to

Institution Principle
The courts have developed specific rules of access that govern which cases within their jurisdiction they will hear.

standing   The right of an individual or organization to initiate a court case.

[27]Walter F. Murphy, "The Supreme Court of the United States," in *Encyclopedia of the American Judicial System: Studies of the Principal Institutions and Processes of Law*, ed. Robert J. Janosik (New York: Scribner's, 1987).

have standing (as in class action suits), each member must show specific injury. This means that a general interest in the environment, for instance, does not provide a group with sufficient basis for standing.

The Supreme Court also uses a third criterion in determining whether it will hear a case: that of **mootness.** In theory, this requirement disqualifies cases that are brought too late—after the relevant facts have changed or the problem has been resolved by other means. The criterion of mootness, however, is subject to the discretion of the courts, which have begun to relax the rules of mootness, particularly in cases in which a situation that has been resolved is likely to come up again. In the abortion case *Roe v. Wade,* for example, the Supreme Court rejected the lower court's argument that because the pregnancy had already come to term, the case was moot. The Court agreed to hear the case because no pregnancy was likely to outlast the lengthy appeals process.

Putting aside the formal criteria, the Supreme Court is most likely to accept cases that involve conflicting decisions by the federal circuit courts, cases that present important questions of civil rights or civil liberties, and cases in which the federal government is the appellant.[28] Ultimately, however, the question of which cases to accept can come down to the preferences and priorities of the justices. If a group of justices believes that the Court should intervene in a particular area of policy or politics, these justices are likely to look for a case or cases that will serve as vehicles for judicial intervention. For many years, for example, the Court was not interested in considering challenges to affirmative action or other programs designed to provide particular benefits to minorities. In recent years, however, several of the Court's more conservative justices have been eager to push back the limits of affirmative action and racial preference, and have, therefore, accepted a number of cases that would allow them to do so. In 1995, the Court's decisions in *Adarand Constructors, Inc. v. Pena, Missouri v. Jenkins,* and *Miller v. Johnson* placed new restrictions on federal affirmative action programs, school desegregation efforts, and attempts to increase minority representation in Congress through the creation of "minority districts" (see Chapter 10).[29] Similarly, because some justices have felt that the Court had gone too far in the past in restricting public support for religious ideas, the Court accepted the case of *Rosenberger v. University of Virginia.* This case was brought by a Christian student group against the University of Virginia, which had refused to provide student activities fund support for the group's magazine, *Wide Awake.* Other student publications received subsidies from the activities fund, but university policy prohibited grants to religious groups. Lower courts supported the university, finding that support for the magazine would violate the Constitution's prohibition against government support for religion. The Supreme Court, however, ruled in favor of the students' assertion that the university's policies

mootness A criterion used by courts to screen cases that no longer require resolution.

Rationality Principle

The Supreme Court accepts cases based on the preferences and priorities of the justices.

[28]Gregory A. Caldeira and John R. Wright, "Organized Interests and Agenda Setting in the U.S. Supreme Court," *American Political Science Review* 82 (1988): 1109–27.

[29]*Adarand Constructors, Inc. v. Pena,* 115 S.Ct. 2038 (1995); *Missouri v. Jenkins,* 115 S.Ct. 2573 (1995); *Miller v. Johnson,* 115 S.Ct. 2475 (1995).

amounted to support for some ideas but not others. The Court said this violated the students' First Amendment right of freedom of expression.[30]

Most cases reach the Supreme Court through a ***writ of certiorari*** (Figure 8.4). Certiorari is an order to a lower court to deliver the records of a particular case to be reviewed for legal errors. The term *certiorari* is sometimes shortened to *cert*, and cases deemed to merit certiorari are referred to as "certworthy." An individual who loses in a lower federal court or state court and wants the Supreme Court to review the decision has 90 days to file a petition for a writ of certiorari with the clerk of the U.S. Supreme Court. There are two types of petitions, paid petitions and petitions *in forma pauperis* (in the form of a pauper). The former requires payment of filing fees, submission of a certain number of copies, and compliance with a variety of other rules. For ***in forma pauperis petitions***, usually filed by prison inmates, the Court waives the fees and most other requirements.

Since 1972, most of the justices have participated in a "certiorari pool" in which their law clerks work together to evaluate the petitions. Each petition is reviewed by one clerk who writes a memo for all the justices participating in the pool summarizing the facts and issues and making a recommendation. Clerks for the other justices add their comments to the memo. After the justices have reviewed the memos, any one of them may place any case on the ***discuss list***, which is circulated by the chief justice. If a case is not placed on the discuss list, it is automatically denied *certiorari*. Cases placed on the discuss list are considered and voted on during the justices' closed-door conference.

For *certiorari* to be granted, four justices must be convinced that the case satisfies Rule 10 of the Rules of the U.S. Supreme Court. Rule 10 states that *certiorari* is not a matter of right but is to be granted only when there are special and compelling reasons. These include conflicting decisions by two or more circuit courts, conflicts between circuit courts and state courts of last resort, conflicting decisions by two or more state courts of last resort, decisions by circuit courts on matters of federal law that should be settled by the Supreme Court, and a circuit court decision on an important question that conflicts with Supreme Court decisions. It should be clear from this list that the Court will usually take action under only the most compelling circumstances—when there are conflicts among the lower courts about what the law should be, when an important legal question has been raised in the lower courts but not definitively answered, and when a lower court deviates from the principles and precedents established by the high court. The support of four justices is needed for *certiorari*, and few cases are able to satisfy this requirement. In recent sessions, although thousands of petitions were filed (Figure 8.5), the Court has granted *certiorari* to hardly more than eighty petitioners each year—about 1 percent of those seeking a Supreme Court review.

A handful of cases reach the Supreme Court through avenues other than *certiorari*. One of these is the ***writ of certification.*** This writ can be used when a U.S. Court of Appeals asks the Supreme Court for instructions on a point of law that

writ of certiorari
A decision concurred in by at least four of the nine Supreme Court justices to review a decision of a lower court; from the Latin "to make more certain."

***in forma pauperis* petitions**
The fees and most other requirements are waived for indigent petitioners.

discuss list List circulated by the chief justice of all the petitions to be discussed and voted on at the Court's conference.

 **Collective-Action Principle**
Four of the nine Supreme Court justices need to agree to review a case.

writ of certification Writ issued when a U.S. Court of Appeals asks the Supreme Court for instructions on a point of law that has never been decided.

[30]*Rosenberger v. University of Virginia*, 115 S.Ct. 2510 (1995).

FIGURE 8.4

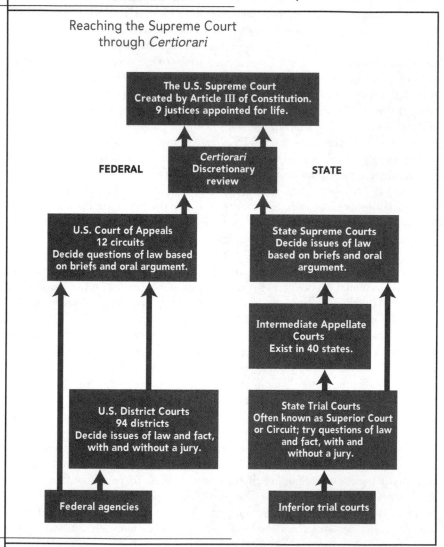

Reaching the Supreme Court through *Certiorari*

The U.S. Supreme Court
Created by Article III of Constitution.
9 justices appointed for life.

FEDERAL

Certiorari
Discretionary review

STATE

U.S. Court of Appeals
12 circuits
Decide questions of law based on briefs and oral argument.

State Supreme Courts
Decide issues of law based on briefs and oral argument.

Intermediate Appellate Courts
Exist in 40 states.

U.S. District Courts
94 districts
Decide issues of law and fact, with and without a jury.

State Trial Courts
Often known as Superior Court or Circuit; try questions of law and fact, with and without a jury.

Federal agencies

Inferior trial courts

Most cases reach the Supreme Court through a writ of *certiorari.*

FIGURE 8.5

Cases Filed in the U.S. Supreme Court,
1938–2002 Terms*

*Number of cases filed in term starting in year indicated.

SOURCE: Years 1938–69: successive volumes of U.S. Bureau of the Census, *Statistical Abstract of the United States* (Washington, DC: Government Printing Office); 1970–83: Office of the Clerk of the Supreme Court; 1984–99; reprinted with permission from *The United States Law Week* (Washington, DC: Bureau of National Affairs), vol. 56, 3102; vol. 59, 3064; vol. 61, 3098; vol. 63, 3134; vol. 65, 3100; vol. 67, 3167; vol. 69, 3134 (copyright © Bureau of National Affairs Inc.); 2000–2002: successive volumes of U.S. Bureau of the Census, *Statistical Abstract of the United States* (Washington, DC: Government Printing Office).

had never been decided. A second alternative avenue is the *writ of appeal,* which is used to appeal the decision of a three-judge district court.

Controlling the Flow of Cases

In addition to the judges themselves, two other actors play an important role in shaping the flow of cases through the federal courts: the solicitor general and federal law clerks.

The Solicitor General   If any single person has greater influence than the individual justices over the work of the Supreme Court, it is the solicitor general of the United States. The solicitor general is third in status in the Justice Department (below the attorney general and the deputy attorney general) but is the top government lawyer in virtually all cases before the appellate courts in which the government is a party. Although others can regulate the flow of cases, the solicitor general has the greatest control, with no review of his or her actions by any higher authority in the executive branch. More than half the Supreme Court's total workload consists of cases under the direct charge of the solicitor general.

The solicitor general exercises especially strong influence by screening cases long before they approach the Supreme Court; indeed, the justices rely on the solicitor general to "screen out undeserving litigation and furnish them with an agenda to hear government cases that deserve serious consideration."[31] Typically, more requests for appeals are rejected than are accepted by the solicitor general. Agency heads may lobby the president or otherwise try to circumvent the solicitor general, and a few of the independent agencies have a statutory right to make direct appeals, but without the solicitor general's support these are seldom reviewed by the Court; at best, they are doomed to *per curiam* ("by the court") rejection.

The solicitor general, by writing an *amicus curiae* ("friend of the court") brief, can enter a case even when the federal government is not a direct litigant. A "friend of the court" is not a direct party to a case but has a vital interest in its outcome. Thus, when the government has such an interest, the solicitor general can file as *amicus curiae,* or the Court can invite such a brief because it wants an opinion in writing. Other interested parties may file briefs as well.

In addition to exercising substantial control over the flow of cases, the solicitor general can shape the arguments used before the Court. Indeed, the Court tends to give special attention to the way the solicitor general characterizes the issues. The solicitor general is the person appearing most frequently before the Court and, theoretically at least, the most disinterested. The credibility of the solicitor general is not hurt when several times each year he or she comes to the Court to withdraw a case with the admission that the government has made an error.

---

[31]Robert Scigliano, *The Supreme Court and the Presidency* (New York: Free Press, 1971), p. 162. For an interesting critique of the solicitor general's role during the Reagan administration, see Lincoln Caplan, "Annals of the Law," *New Yorker,* 17 August 1987, pp. 30–62.

Law Clerks   Every federal judge employs law clerks to research legal issues and assist with the preparation of opinions. Each Supreme Court justice is assigned four clerks. The clerks are almost always honors graduates of the nation's most prestigious law schools. A clerkship with a Supreme Court justice is a great honor and generally indicates that the fortunate individual is likely to reach the very top of the legal profession. One of the most important roles performed by the clerks is to screen the thousands of petitions for writs of *certiorari* that come before the Court.[32] It is also likely that some justices rely heavily on their clerks for advice in writing opinions and in deciding whether an individual case ought to be heard by the Court. It is often rumored that certain opinions were actually written by a clerk rather than a justice.[33] Although such rumors are difficult to substantiate, it is clear that at the end of long judicial careers, justices such as William O. Douglas and Thurgood Marshall had become so infirm that they were compelled to rely on the judgments of their law clerks.

The Case Pattern

The Supreme Court has discretion over which case will be reviewed. The solicitor general can influence the Court's choice by giving advice and by encouraging particular cases and discouraging or suppressing others. But neither the court nor the solicitor general can suppress altogether the kinds of cases that individuals bring to court. Each new technology, such as computers and communications satellites, produces new disputes and the need for new principles of law. Newly awakened interest groups, such as the black community after World War II and the women's and the environmental movements in the 1970s, produce new legislation, new disputes, and new cases. Lawyers are professionally obligated to appeal their clients' cases to the highest possible court if an issue of law or constitutionality is involved.

The litigation that breaks out with virtually every social change produces a pattern of cases that eventually is recognized by the state and federal appellate courts. Appellate judges may at first resist trying such cases by ordering them remanded (returned) to their court of original jurisdiction for further trial. They may reject some appeals without giving any reason at all (*certiorari* denied *per curiam*). But eventually, one or more of the cases from the pattern may be reviewed and may indeed make new law.

Although some patterns of cases emerge spontaneously as new problems produce new litigation, many interest groups try to set a pattern as a strategy for expediting their cases through the appeals process. Lawyers representing these groups have to choose the proper client and the proper case, so that the issues in question are most dramatically and appropriately portrayed. They also have to pick the right district or jurisdiction in which to bring the case. Sometimes they even have to wait for an appropriate political climate.

[32]H. W. Perry Jr., *Deciding to Decide: Agenda Setting in the United States Supreme Court* (Cambridge, MA: Harvard University Press, 1991).

[33]Edward Lazarus, *Closed Chambers: The First Eyewitness Account of the Struggles inside the Supreme Court* (New York: Times Books, 1998).

Group litigants have to plan carefully when to use and when to avoid publicity. They must also attempt to develop a proper record at the trial-court level, one that includes some constitutional arguments and even, when possible, errors on the part of the trial court. One of the most effective litigation strategies used in getting cases accepted for review by the appellate courts is bringing the same type of suit in more than one circuit, in the hope that inconsistent treatment by two different courts will improve the chance of a Supreme Court review.

As we shall see more fully in Chapter 12, Congress will sometimes provide interest groups with legislation designed to facilitate their use of litigation. One important recent example is the 1990 Americans with Disabilities Act (ADA), enacted after intense lobbying by public interest and advocacy groups, which, in conjunction with the 1991 Civil Rights Acts, opened the way for disabled individuals to make extremely effective use of the courts to press their interests. As the sponsors of ADA had hoped, over time the courts have expanded the rights of the disabled as well as the definition of *disability*. In 1998, for example, the Supreme Court ruled that individuals with HIV were covered by the act.[34]

The two most notable users of the pattern-of-cases strategy in recent years have been the National Association for the Advancement of Colored People (NAACP) and the American Civil Liberties Union (ACLU). For many years, the NAACP (and its Defense Fund organization—now a separate group) has worked through local chapters and with many individuals to encourage litigation on issues of racial discrimination and segregation. Sometimes it distributes petitions to be signed by parents and filed with local school boards and courts, deliberately sowing the seeds of future litigation. The NAACP and the ACLU often encourage private parties to bring suit, then join the suit as *amici curiae*.

One illustration of an interest group employing a carefully crafted litigation strategy to pursue its goals through the judiciary was the Texas-based effort to establish a right to free public-school education for children of illegal aliens. The issue arose in 1977, when the Texas state legislature, responding to a sudden wave of fear about illegal immigration from Mexico, enacted a law permitting school districts to charge undocumented children a hefty tuition for the privilege of attending public school. A public interest law organization, the Mexican-American Legal Defense Fund, prepared to challenge the law in court after determining that public opposition precluded any chance of persuading the legislature to change its own law.

Part of the defense fund's litigation strategy was to bring a lawsuit in the northern section of Texas, far from the Mexican border, where illegal immigration would be at a minimum. Thus, in Tyler, Texas, where the complaint was initially filed, the trial court found only sixty undocumented alien students in a school district composed of 16,000. This strategy effectively contradicted the state's argument that the Texas law was necessary to reduce the burdens on educational resources created by masses of incoming aliens. Another useful litigation tactic was to select plaintiffs who, although illegal aliens, were nevertheless clearly planning to remain in Texas even without free public education for their children. Thus all of the plaintiffs came

---

[34]*Bragdon v. Abbott*, 118 S.Ct. 2186 (1998).

from families that had already lived in Tyler for several years and included at least one child who was an American citizen by virtue of birth in the United States. By emphasizing the stability of such families, the defense fund argued convincingly that the Texas law would not motivate families to return to the poverty in Mexico from which they had fled, but would more likely result in the creation of a subclass of illiterate people who would add to the state's unemployment and crime rates. Five years after the lawsuit on behalf of the Tyler children began, the U.S. Supreme Court, in the case of *Plyler v. Doe*, held that the Texas law was unconstitutional under the equal protection clause of the Fourteenth Amendment.[35]

Thus, regardless of the wishes of the Justice Department or the Supreme Court, many pathbreaking cases are eventually granted *certiorari* because continued refusal to review one or more of them would amount to a rule of law just as much as if the courts had handed down a written opinion. In this sense, the flow of cases, especially the pattern of significant cases, influences the behavior of the appellate judiciary.

More recently, a conservative advocacy group, the Washington, D.C.–based Center for Individual Rights has launched an active campaign of litigation to challenge affirmative action programs in college admissions and employment. In the case of *Hopwood v. Texas*, the center won a major victory against affirmative action, with the Fifth Circuit Court invalidating the University of Texas law school's program of preferential minority admissions.[36] In two important subsequent cases, the center challenged the University of Michigan's minority admissions programs, which gave preferential treatment to minority applicants to the college of arts and sciences and to the law school. In 2003, the U.S. Supreme Court upheld the law school's program with certain changes. But the justices struck down the affirmative action rules used by the undergraduate college.[37] In so doing, the Court forced colleges throughout the nation to place new restrictions on their affirmative action efforts. The center has also sued the University of Washington over minority admissions, Alabama State University (a historically black school) over preferential treatment for whites, and a school district in Minnesota over preferential treatment for minorities in magnet school admissions.[38] Through this pattern of suits in federal and state courts, the center has sought to challenge and undermine the legal underpinnings of affirmative action.

The Supreme Court's Procedures

The Preparation   The Supreme Court's decision to accept a case is the beginning of what can be a lengthy and complex process (Figure 8.6). First, the attorneys on both sides must prepare *briefs*—written documents in which the attorneys explain why the Court should rule in favor of their client. The document filed by the individual bringing the case is called the *petitioner's brief.* This

briefs Written documents in which attorneys explain— using case precedents—why the Court should rule in favor of their client.

petitioner's brief Document filed by the party bringing the appeal stating the facts of a case and reasons why the lower court's opinion should be overturned.

---

[35]*Plyler v. Doe*, 457 U.S. 202 (1982).
[36]*Hopwood v. State of Texas*, 78 F3d 932 (Fifth Circuit, 1996). 21 F3d 603 (Fifth Circuit, 1994).
[37]*Gratz v. Bollinger*, 123 S. Ct. 2411 (2003).
[38]*Jacobs v. Independent School District No. 625*, 99-CV-542 (D. Minn., filed April 6, 1999).

FIGURE 8.6

The Supreme Court's Decision-Making Process

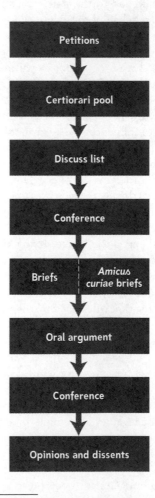

Thousands of petitions for *certiorari* are filed each year, but the Supreme Court accepts and decides only the handful of cases it deems to be especially important.

brief summarizes the facts of the case and presents the legal basis on which the Supreme Court is being asked to overturn the lower court's decision. The document filed by the side that prevailed in the lower court is called the **respondent's brief.** This brief explains why the Supreme Court should affirm the lower court's verdict. The petitioners then file a brief answering and attempting to refute the points made in the respondent's brief. This document is called the **petitioner's reply brief.** Briefs are filled with referrals to precedents specifically chosen to show that other courts have frequently ruled in the same way that the Supreme Court is being asked to rule. The attorneys for both sides muster the most compelling precedents they can in support of their arguments.

As the attorneys prepare their briefs, they often ask sympathetic interest groups for their help. Groups are asked to file *amicus curiae* briefs that support the claims of one or the other litigant. In a case involving separation of church and state, for example, liberal groups such as the ACLU and Citizens for the American Way are likely to be asked to file *amicus* briefs in support of strict separation, whereas conservative religious groups are likely to file *amicus* briefs advocating increased public support for religious ideas. Often, dozens of briefs will be filed on each side of a major case. *Amicus* filings are one of the primary methods used by interest groups to lobby the Court. By filing these briefs, groups indicate to the Court where their group stands and signal to the justices that they believe the case to be an important one.

Oral Argument The next stage of a case is *oral argument,* in which attorneys for both sides appear before the Court to present their positions and answer the justices' questions. Each attorney has only a half hour to present his or her case, and this time includes interruptions for questions. Certain members of the Court, such as Justice Antonin Scalia, are known to interrupt attorneys dozens of times. Others, such as Justice Clarence Thomas, seldom ask questions. For an attorney, the opportunity to argue a case before the Supreme Court is a singular honor and a mark of professional distinction. It can also be a harrowing experience, as justices interrupt a carefully prepared presentation. Nevertheless, oral argument can be very important to the outcome of a case. It allows justices to better understand the heart of the case and to raise questions that might not have been addressed in the opposing sides' briefs. It is not uncommon for justices to go beyond the strictly legal issues and ask opposing counsel to discuss the implications of the case for the Court and the nation at large.

The Conference After oral argument, the Court discusses the case in its Wednesday or Friday conference. The chief justice presides over the conference and speaks first; the other justices follow in order of seniority. The Court's conference is secret, and no outsiders are permitted to attend. The justices discuss the case and eventually reach a decision on the basis of a majority vote. As the case is discussed, justices may try to influence or change one another's opinions. At times, this may result in compromise decisions.

respondent's brief document filed by the party that won in the lower court explaining why that court's decision should not be overturned.

petitioner's reply brief Petitioner's answer to the respondent's brief.

 Institution Principle

Though the judiciary is normally above politics, the Supreme Court's procedures allow for various individuals and groups to influence the decision-making process.

oral argument Stage in Supreme Court proceedings in which attorneys for both sides appear before the Court to present their positions and answer questions posed by the justices.

Opinion Writing After a decision has been reached, one of the members of the majority is assigned to write the **opinion.** This assignment is made by the chief justice or by the most senior justice in the majority if the chief justice is on the losing side. The assignment of the opinion can make a significant difference to the interpretation of a decision. Every opinion of the Supreme Court sets a major precedent for future cases throughout the judicial system. Lawyers and judges in the lower courts will examine the opinion carefully to ascertain the Supreme Court's meaning. Differences in wording and emphasis can have important implications for future litigation. Thus, in assigning an opinion, the justices must give serious thought to the impression the case will make on lawyers and on the public, as well as to the probability that one justice's opinion will be more widely accepted than another's.

One of the more dramatic instances of this tactical consideration occurred in 1944, when Chief Justice Harlan F. Stone chose Justice Felix Frankfurter to write the opinion in the "white primary" case *Smith v. Allwright.* The chief justice believed that this sensitive case, which overturned the southern practice of prohibiting black participation in nominating primaries, required the efforts of the most brilliant and scholarly jurist on the Court. But the day after Stone made the assignment, Justice Robert H. Jackson wrote a letter to Stone urging a change of assignment. In his letter, Jackson argued that Frankfurter, a foreign-born Jew from New England, would not win the South with his opinion, regardless of its brilliance. Stone accepted the advice and substituted Justice Stanley F. Reed, an American-born Protestant from Kentucky and a southern Democrat in good standing.[39] Once the majority opinion is drafted, it is circulated to the other justices. Some members of the majority may agree with both the outcome and the rationale but wish to emphasize or highlight a particular point and so for that purpose draft a concurring opinion, called a *regular concurrence.* In other instances, one or more justices may agree with the majority but disagree with the rationale presented in the majority opinion. These justices may draft *special concurrences,* explaining their disagreements with the majority.

Dissent Justices who disagree with the majority decision of the Court may choose to publicize the character of their disagreement in the form of a *dissenting opinion.* The dissenting opinion is generally assigned by the senior justice among the dissenters. Dissents can be used to express irritation with an outcome or to signal to defeated political forces in the nation that their position is supported by at least some members of the Court. Ironically, the most dependable way an individual justice can exercise a direct and clear influence on the Court is to write a dissent. Because there is no need to please a majority, dissenting opinions can be more eloquent and less guarded than majority opinions. The current Supreme Court often produces 5–4 decisions, with dissenters writing long and detailed opinions that, they hope, will help them convince a swing justice to join their side on the next round of cases dealing with a similar topic. Thus, for example, Justice Souter wrote a thirty-four-page dissent in a 2002 case upholding the

[39]*Smith v. Allwright*, 321 U.S. 649 (1944).

use of government-funded school vouchers to pay for parochial school tuition. Souter called the decision "a dramatic departure from basic Establishment Clause principle" and went on to say that he hoped it would be reconsidered by a future court.[40]

Dissent plays a special role in the work and impact of the Court because it amounts to an appeal to lawyers all over the country to keep bringing cases of the sort at issue. Therefore, an effective dissent influences the flow of cases through the Court as well as the arguments that will be used by lawyers in later cases. Even more important, dissent emphasizes the fact that, although the Court speaks with a single opinion, it is the opinion only of the majority.

JUDICIAL DECISION MAKING

The judiciary is conservative in its procedures, but its effect on society can be radical. That effect depends on a variety of influences, two of which stand out above the rest. The first influence is the individual members of the Supreme Court, their attitudes and goals, and their relationships with each other. The second is the other branches of government, particularly Congress.

The Supreme Court Justices

The Supreme Court explains its decisions in terms of law and precedent. But although law and precedent do have an effect on the Court's deliberations and eventual decisions, it is the Supreme Court that decides what laws actually mean and what importance precedents will actually have. Throughout its history, the Court has shaped and reshaped the law. If any individual judges in the country influence the federal judiciary, they are the Supreme Court justices.

From the 1950s to the 1980s, the Supreme Court took an activist role in such areas as civil rights, civil liberties, abortion, voting rights, and police procedures. For example, the Supreme Court was more responsible than any other governmental institution for breaking down America's system of racial segregation. The Supreme Court virtually prohibited states from interfering with the right of a woman to seek an abortion and sharply curtailed state restrictions on voting rights. And it was the Supreme Court that placed restrictions on the behavior of local police and prosecutors in criminal cases.

But since the early 1980s, resignations, deaths, and new judicial appointments have led to many shifts in the mix of philosophies and ideologies represented on the Court. In a series of decisions between 1989 and 2001, the conservative justices appointed by Reagan and Bush were able to swing the Court to a more conservative position on civil rights, affirmative action, abortion rights, property rights, criminal procedure, voting rights, desegregation, and the power of the national government.

[40]Warren Richey, "Dissenting Opinions as a Window on Future Rulings," *Christian Science Monitor,* 1 July 2002, p. 1.

The importance of ideology was very clear during the Court's 2000–2001 term. In important decisions, the Court's most conservative justices—Scalia, Thomas, and Rehnquist, usually joined by Kennedy—generally voted as a bloc.[41] Indeed, Scalia and Thomas voted together in 99 percent of all cases. At the same time, the Court's most liberal justices—Breyer, Ginsburg, Souter, and Stevens—also generally formed a bloc, with Ginsburg and Breyer and Ginsburg and Souter voting together 94 percent of the time.[42] Justice O'Connor, a moderate conservative, was the swing vote in many important cases.[43] This ideological division led to a number of important 5–4 decisions. In the Florida election law case, *Bush v. Gore*, Justice O'Connor joined with the conservative bloc to give Bush a 5–4 victory.[44] Indeed, more than 33 percent of all the cases heard by the Court in its 2000–2001 term were decided 5–4. In the Court's 2003–04 term, nine of the fourteen most important cases were decided by a 5–4 margin (Table 8.3).

However, precisely because the Court has been so evenly split in recent years, the conservative bloc has not always prevailed. Among the justices serving at the beginning of 2005, Rehnquist, Scalia, and Thomas take conservative positions on most issues and are usually joined by O'Connor and Kennedy. Breyer, Ginsburg, Souter, and Stevens are reliably liberal. This has produced many 5–4 splits. On some issues, though, Justice O'Connor or Justice Kennedy will side with the liberal camp, producing a 5–4 and sometimes a 6–3 victory for the liberals. This pattern was very evident during the Court's 2003–04 term. In the case of *Missouri v. Siebert*, for example, Justice Kennedy joined a 5–4 majority to strengthen Miranda rights.[45] Similarly, in *McConnell v. Federal Election Commission*, Justice O'Connor joined the liberal bloc to uphold the validity of the Bipartisan Campaign Reform Act.[46] It remains to be seen how the departure of Rehnquist and O'Connor and their replacement by Roberts and, probably, Alito will affect the Court.

Activism and Restraint   One element of judicial philosophy is the issue of activism versus restraint. Over the years, some justices have believed that courts should interpret the Constitution according to the stated intentions of its framers and defer to the views of Congress when interpreting federal statutes. Justice Felix Frankfurter, for example, advocated judicial deference to legislative bodies and avoidance of the "political thicket," in which the Court would entangle itself by deciding questions that were essentially political rather than legal in character. Advocates of *judicial restraint* are sometimes called "strict constructionists" because they look strictly to the words of the Constitution in interpreting its meaning.

judicial restraint
Judicial philosophy whose adherents refuse to go beyond the set text of the Constitution in interpreting its meaning.

[41]Linda Greenhouse, "In Year of Florida Vote, Supreme Court Also Did Much Other Work," *New York Times*, 2 July 2001, p. A12.

[42]Charles E. Lane, "Laying Down the Law," *Washington Post*, 1 July 2001, p. A6.

[43]For an insightful discussion about how to figure out who the swing justice is on the Court, see Andrew D. Martin, Kevin M. Quinn, and Lee Epstein, "The Median Justice on the U.S. Supreme Court," *North Carolina Law Review*, in press.

[44]*Bush v. Gore*, 531 U.S. 98, 121 S.Ct. 525 (2000).

[45]*Missouri v. Siebert*, 124 S. Ct. 2601 (2004).

[46]*McConnell v. Federal Election Commission*, 540 U.S. 93 (2003).

The alternative to restraint is *judicial activism*. Activist judges such as former Chief Justice Earl Warren believed that the Court should go beyond the words of the Constitution or a statute to consider the broader societal implications of its decisions. Activist judges sometimes strike out in new directions, promulgating new interpretations or inventing new legal and constitutional concepts when they believe these to be socially desirable. For example, Justice Harry A. Blackmun's opinion in *Roe v. Wade* was based on a constitutional right to privacy that is not found in the words of the Constitution but was, rather, from the Court's prior decision in *Griswold v. Connecticut*.[47] Blackmun and the other members of the majority in the *Roe* case argued that the right to privacy was implied by other constitutional provisions. In this instance of judicial activism, the Court knew the result it wanted to achieve and was not afraid to make the law conform to the desired outcome.

Activism and restraint are sometimes confused with liberalism and conservatism. For example, conservative politicians often castigate "liberal activist" judges and call for the appointment of conservative jurists who will refrain from reinterpreting the law. To be sure, some liberal jurists are activists and some conservatives have been advocates of restraint, but the relationship is by no means one to one. Indeed, the Rehnquist Court, dominated by conservatives, has been among the most activist Courts in American history, striking out in new directions in such areas as federalism and election law.

Political Ideology The second component of judicial philosophy is political ideology. The liberal or conservative attitudes of justices play an important role in their decisions.[48] As just noted, the philosophy of activism versus restraint is sometimes a smokescreen for political ideology. In the past, liberal judges have been activists, willing to use the law to achieve social and political change, whereas conservatives have been associated with judicial restraint. It is interesting, however, that in recent years some conservative justices who have long called for restraint have actually become activists in seeking to undo some of the work of liberal jurists over the past three decades.

In our discussion of congressional politics in Chapter 5, we described legislators as *policy oriented*. In conceiving of judges as legislators in robes, we are effectively claiming that judges, like other politicians, have policy preferences they seek to implement. For example, in recent years, Justice O'Connor wrote a number of decisions that furthered her goal that Congress return authority to the states. The most recent of these decisions is the 2001 case of *Board of Trustees of the University of Alabama v. Garrett*, in which the Court held that state employees could not sue the states for alleged violations of the Americans with Disabilities Act.[49]

judicial activism
Judicial philosophy that posits that the Court should see beyond the text of the Constitution or a statute to consider broader societal implications for decisions.

[47]*Griswold v. Connecticut*, 381 U.S. 479 (1965).
[48]C. Herman Pritchett, *The Roosevelt Court: A Study in Judicial Politics and Values* (New York: Macmillan, 1948); Jeffrey A. Segal and Harold J. Spaeth, *The Supreme Court and the Attitudinal Model* (New York: Cambridge University Press, 1993).
[49]*Board of Trustees of the University of Alabama v. Garrett*, 531 U.S. 356 (2001).

TABLE 8.3

Major Rulings of the 2003–2004 Term

X = MAJORITY VOTE

	STEVENS	GINSBURG	SOUTER	BREYER	O'CONNOR	KENNEDY	REHNQUIST	SCALIA	THOMAS
Appointed by:	Ford	Clinton	G. H. W. Bush	Clinton	Reagan	Reagan	Nixon	Reagan	G. H. W. Bush
DETAINEES									
Rasul v. Bush — Foreign detainees at Guantanamo Bay, Cuba, may have access to federal court to challenge their detention.	X	X	X	X	X	X			
Hamdi v. Rumsfeld — Hamdi, a U.S. citizen, has the right to challenge his classification and detention as an "enemy combatant."	X	X	X	X	X	X	X	X	
Rumsfeld v. Padilla — Padilla, a U.S. citizen, brought his suit in the wrong federal court (New York) and must now file in South Carolina, where he is confined.					X	X	X	X	X
SENTENCING									
Blakely v. Washington — State sentencing guidelines give judges unconstitutional power.	X	X	X					X	X
FREE SPEECH									
Ashcroft v. American Civil Liberties Union — Government failed to justify the Child Online Protection Act, whose goal is to shield children from pornography on the Internet.	X	X	X			X			X
CAMPAIGN FINANCE									
McConnell v. Federal Election Commission — Upheld new limits on advertising and "soft money."	X	X	X	X	X				
FEDERALISM									
Tennessee v. Lane — States can be sued under the Americans with Disabilities Act for inaccessible courtrooms.	X	X	X	X	X				

MIRANDA RIGHTS *Missouri v. Seibert* Invalidated police tactic of trying to elicit confession by interrogating both before and after Miranda warnings.	X	X	X	X	X		X		
RELIGION *Locke v. Davey* States that give college scholarships do not have to subsidize training for the ministry.	X	X	X	X	X	X	X	X	
Elk Grove Unified School District v. Newdow Constitutional challenge to the words "under God" in the Pledge of Allegiance dismissed for lack of standing.	X	X	X	X		X	X	recused	
HEALTH CARE *Aetna Health v. Davila* Federal law pre-empts state laws that permit patients to sue HMOs.	X	X	X	X	X	X	X	X	X
GOVERNMENT SECRECY *Cheney v. United States District Court* Gave Vice President Cheney another chance to shield an energy task force from public disclosure.	X		X	X	X	X	X	X	X
PRIVACY *Hibel v. Sixth Judicial District Court* Police can require people suspected of wrongdoing to give their names.			X	X	X	X	X	X	X
REDISTRICTING *Vieth v. Jubelirer* Rejected Pennsylvania Democrats' claim of unconstitutional political gerrymander of congressional districts.				X	X	X	X	X	X

Many important Supreme Court decisions are decided by 5–4 margins, revealing defined liberal and conservative voting blocs.

SOURCE: Adapted from the *New York Times*, 5 July 2004, p. A12.

Other Institutions of Government

Congress At both the national and state level in the United States, courts and judges are "players" in the policy game because of the separation of powers. Essentially, this means that the legislative branch formulates policy (defined constitutionally and institutionally by a legislative process); that the executive branch implements policy (according to well-defined administrative procedures and subject to initial approval by the president or the legislative override of his veto); and that the courts, when asked, rule on the faithfulness of the legislated and executed policy either to the substance of the statute or to the Constitution itself. The courts, that is, may strike down an administrative action either because it exceeds the authority granted in the relevant statute (statutory rationale) or because the statute itself exceeds the authority granted the legislature by the Constitution (constitutional rationale).

If the court declares the administrative agent's act as outside the permissible bounds prescribed by the legislation, we suppose the court's majority opinion can declare whatever policy it wishes. If the legislature is unhappy with this judicial action, then it may either recraft the legislation (if the rationale for striking it down were statutory)[50] or initiate a constitutional amendment that would enable the stricken-down policy to pass constitutional muster (if the rationale for originally striking it down were constitutional).

In reaching their decisions, Supreme Court justices must anticipate Congress's response. As a result, judges will not always vote according to their true preferences because doing so may provoke Congress to enact legislation that moves the policy further away from what the judges prefer. By voting for a lesser preference, the justices can get something they prefer to the status quo without provoking congressional action to overturn their decision. The most famous example of this phenomenon is the "switch in time that saved nine," when two justices voted in favor of New Deal legislation, the constitutionality of which they doubted, to diminish congressional support for President Roosevelt's plan to "pack" the Court by increasing the number of justices. In short, the interactions between the Court and Congress are part of a complex strategic "game."[51]

The President The president's most direct influence on the Court is the power to nominate justices. Presidents typically nominate judges who they believe are close to their policy preferences and close enough to the preferences of a majority of senators, who must confirm the nomination.

Yet the efforts by presidents to reshape the federal judiciary are not always successful. Often in American history, judges have surprised and disappointed

---

[50] William N. Eskridge Jr., "Overriding Supreme Court Statutory Interpretation Decisions," *Yale Law Journal* 101 (1991): 331–55.

[51] A fully strategic analysis of the maneuvering among legislative, executive, and judicial branches in the separation-of-powers arrangement choreographed by the U.S. Constitution may be found in William Eskridge and John Ferejohn, "The Article I, Section 7 Game," *Georgetown Law Review* 80 (1992): 523–65. The entire issue of this journal is devoted to the theme of strategic behavior in American institutional politics.

the presidents who named them to the bench. Justice Souter, for example, has been far less conservative than President George H. W. Bush and the Republicans who supported Souter's appointment in 1990 thought he would be. Likewise, Justices O'Connor and Kennedy disappointed conservatives by opposing limitations on abortion.

Nevertheless, with a combined total of twelve years in office, both Reagan and Bush were able to exercise a good deal of influence on the composition of the federal district and appellate courts. By the end of Bush's term, he and Reagan together had appointed nearly half of all federal judges. Thus, whatever impact Reagan and Bush ultimately had on the Supreme Court, their federal appointments have certainly had a continuing influence on the temperament and behavior of the district and circuit courts.

President Clinton promised to appoint more liberal jurists to the district and appellate courts, as well as to increase the number of women and minorities serving on the federal bench. During his first two years in office, Clinton held to this promise (Figure 8.7). More than 50 percent of his 128 judicial nominees were women or members of minority groups.[52] A large number of judicial vacancies remained unfilled, however, when the Republicans took control of Congress at the end of 1994. Soon after the election, Senator Orrin Hatch of Utah, the new chair of the Senate Judiciary Committee, which confirms judicial nominations, indicated his intention to oppose any nominee whom he deemed to be too liberal. This prompted the Clinton White House to withdraw some nominations and to search for district and appellate nominees who would be more acceptable to the Republicans.[53]

During President George W. Bush's first term in office, Senate Democrats fought a pitched battle with the White House to block judicial nominees they deemed too conservative. Ten of Bush's nominees to the circuit courts were blocked by Democratic filibusters, though Bush infuriated Democrats by giving two of these individuals, Charles Pickering and William Pryor, temporary recess appointments. Democrats had hoped to block Bush's nominees until the 2004 elections, when, perhaps, a Democratic president would be chosen. After Bush's reelection, however, the battle resumed and Republicans threatened to change Senate rules to prevent a continuation of the Democrats' filibuster.

Implementation of Supreme Court Decisions

The president and executive branch, along with the Congress, the states, the lower courts, and a variety of private organizations and individuals also play key roles in the implementation of Supreme Court decisions. Once the high court has made a decision, a variety of other governmental agencies must put it into effect. The lower courts must understand and apply to new cases the principles asserted by the

[52]*Chicago Daily Law Bulletin*, 5 October 1994.
[53]R. W. Apple Jr., "A Divided Government Remains, and with It the Prospect of Further Combat," *New York Times*, 7 November 1996, p. B6.

FIGURE 8.7

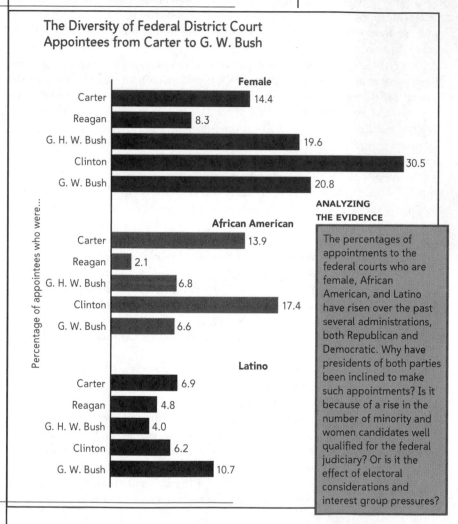

The Diversity of Federal District Court Appointees from Carter to G. W. Bush

Female

Carter	14.4
Reagan	8.3
G. H. W. Bush	19.6
Clinton	30.5
G. W. Bush	20.8

African American

Carter	13.9
Reagan	2.1
G. H. W. Bush	6.8
Clinton	17.4
G. W. Bush	6.6

Latino

Carter	6.9
Reagan	4.8
G. H. W. Bush	4.0
Clinton	6.2
G. W. Bush	10.7

Percentage of appointees who were...

ANALYZING THE EVIDENCE

The percentages of appointments to the federal courts who are female, African American, and Latino have risen over the past several administrations, both Republican and Democratic. Why have presidents of both parties been inclined to make such appointments? Is it because of a rise in the number of minority and women candidates well qualified for the federal judiciary? Or is it the effect of electoral considerations and interest group pressures?

SOURCE: Harold W. Stanley and Richard G. Niemi, *Vital Statistics on American Politics, 2001–2002* (Washington, DC: Congressional Quarterly Press, 2001), pp. 277–79, plus updates by the authors.

Supreme Court. The executive branch must enforce the Court's decision. State legislators and governors must implement the decision in their own jurisdictions. And, often, individuals and organizations must take action in the courts and in the political arena to demand that the Supreme Court's verdicts be fully implemented. At each of these stages, opposition on the part of the revelant actors, may delay full national implementation of a Supreme Court decision, sometimes for years.

For example, if lower court judges strongly disagree with a Supreme Court decision, they may use a variety of tactics to avoid fully implementing it. Lower court judges may, for example, avoid applying the case by disposing of similar cases on technical or procedural grounds. In a similar vein, they may apply the case as narrowly as possible or may declare that some portion of the Supreme Court's opinion was merely "dicta"—useful as guidance but not binding.

As to executive agencies, most Supreme Court decisions must be implemented by federal, state, and local agencies. If these agencies are unsympathetic to the Court's decision, they may obstruct, delay, or even refuse to accept them. In the nineteenth century, President Andrew Jackson famously refused to obey a Supreme Court decision, declaring, "[Chief Justice] John Marshall has made his decision. Now let him enforce it." While few executives or executive agencies have been as overtly defiant as Jackson, many have quietly ignored or sought to circumvent the Court. For example, many local school boards have, for years, searched for ways to circumvent the high court's various rulings prohibiting religious exercise in the public schools.

Strategic Behavior in the Supreme Court

In describing the role and effect of the Supreme Court, we have occasionally referred to the strategic opportunities the Court provides. It is useful to gather some of them in one place to stitch together a more consistent strategic interpretation. Let's divide this into three stages. Stage 1 begins with a period of "normal" politics—in legislatures (local or national), executive and regulatory agencies (local or national), political processes like elections, and the stuff of everyday life involving interactions among public and private entities (citizens, corporations, nonprofits, voluntary associations, governments). Conflict arises, and interested parties must decide what to do: live with the results, pursue normal political channels inside legislatures and agencies to resolve the conflict, or move the conflict into the courts. Stage 2 involves a court responding to its environment, with judges both reacting to demands from the outside and fashioning their own behavioral strategies inside the legal process. Stage 3 involves what happens once a court renders a decision and how the actors in stages 1 and 2 anticipate the decision and adjust their own behaviors to its expectations. While our discussion could be developed for all courts, we will focus on the U.S. Supreme Court. Indeed, we will narrow things even further by devoting the bulk of our remarks to the internal strategic environment of the Supreme Court at stage 2, when it both reacts to developments that have preceded its being drawn into a conflict (stage 1) and anticipates what will happen if it responds in a particular manner (stage 3).

Stage 1   Assume that a conflict has arisen, and appeals have been made through normal channels. Administrative and regulatory agencies, for example, often have well-defined procedures for appealing a ruling inside the agency, with the opportunity of a subsequent appeal to a court always being available. Unsatisfied

Judicial Decision-Making

How are judicial decisions made? In the criminal and civil courts—the courtrooms we've become accustomed to after a half-century of television drama, from *Perry Mason* to *Law and Order*—judges control rules of evidence and issue sentences. The judge seldom makes the wrong decision, and the guilty party is almost always exposed. These television shows may seem innocuous, but their impact on the public's view of our criminal justice system is real. The "CSI effect" has led prosecutors to question potential jurors about their television-viewing habits. Prosecutors have discovered that without the damning physical evidence produced by the technologically supercharged teams on the TV show, jurors believe that the prosecution's case must be weak.[1]

But the legal institutions that most interest scholars, the institutions that determine the scope of our rights and freedoms, and the ones that attract the most attention from political activists, politicians, and presidents are the *appellate courts* (including the Supreme Court). It is at the appellate levels, in both the state and the federal systems, that our most important legal decisions are made. Yet the rules and procedures of this level of the legal system are only dimly understood by the public, particularly how cases come under appellate jurisdiction.[2] Finally, because appellate court decisions are more about how evidence is collected and used than about *facts,* a judge's legal and philosophical inclinations, and perhaps personal ideological and partisan beliefs, come much more into play.

 Institution Principle

The Supreme Court reviews only a small percentage of the cases brought to it, and the decision to review a case or not has a major effect on lower courts.

In terms of appellate court judges, the most common distinction is between a "strict constructionist," who maintains fidelity to the language of the Founders, and a "noninterpretivist," who interprets the language and meaning of the Constitution in light of changing circumstances. Strict constructionists, or "originalists," look only to the language of the Constitution when determining the meaning of the Constitution. President George W. Bush, the Federalist Society (an influential activist group), and many conservative commentators are noted advocates of this position. Justice Clarence Thomas is often described as the most dedicated strict constructionist on today's Court.

Noninterpretivists view the Constitution in a very different light. Noninterpretivism implies that judges may go beyond what is stated in the document in order to best interpret law (thus the somewhat confusing label *non*interpretivist). Strict constructionism, they argue, is hopeless. More than two centuries of historical development have given different meanings to our rights and freedoms. To many noninterpretivists, strict constructionism is just traditional conservative ideology hidden under the guise of fidelity to a historical relic.[3]

The rallying cry for constructionists is the 1973 *Roe v. Wade* decision. The right to privacy, they claim, is not enshrined in the Constitution; thus, abortion is not a right that deserves Constitutional protection. The author of the *Roe* decision, Justice Harry A. Blackmun, argued that the right to privacy, although not explicitly mentioned in the Constitution, is embodied in the "concept of personal liberty" and the due process clause of the Fourteenth Amendment.[4]

The differences between constructionism and noninterpretivism animate much judicial debate, but many political scientists see three other models of judicial decision-making. The *attitudinal* approach places judges on relatively simply dimensions of policy preference (such as liberalism and conservatism) and predicts their votes based on that dimension.[5]

The *strategic* model posits that judges make decisions based on a game theoretic analysis of the judicial process. For example, even if a justice disagrees with a lower court decision, he or she may oppose reviewing a case because of the belief that it will be lost at the Supreme Court, a much more damaging outcome. As Harper and Rosenthal wrote more than a half century ago, "The work the Court doesn't do is as significant for the nation as the work which it does."[6]

Finally, advocates of the *legal* model argue that what may look like an ideological or strategic decision is actually the result of a process of legal decision making. "Fidelity to precedent," Justice Thurgood Marshall wrote, is essential to "the rule of law."[7]

These models help us understand general tendencies and trends in Court decision making, but it is also possible to find nuances that resist simple categorization. Justice Antonin Scalia, for example, is lauded by the right for being a strict constructionist, while many on the left accuse him of being a judicial "activist" who substitutes his own beliefs and values for longstanding Court precedent. Scalia believes that the Constitution is fundamentally a legal document that can be adapted to new circumstances via amendment. If, for example, citizens want to advocate a right to abortion, they should pass a law or promote a constitutional amendment. Even though Scalia may personally oppose abortion, he argues that political activists should pursue that right via other, more democratic venues. Otherwise, Scalia warns, we allow judges to "smuggle" new rights and deny old rights by fiat.[8] To judges like Scalia, our founding history matters—and in that respect he is a constructionist. On the other hand, Scalia is also a democrat (with a small "d"). According to his understanding of the American democratic game, legislatures, not courts, should be making the difficult decisions concerning a woman's right to choose.[9]

Regardless of their ideological positions, most Court observers agree that the tension between a democratic institution such as Congress and an undemocratic one such as the Court is perilous. If the Court does not defer to democratically elected branches of government, it will likely lose its political and legal authority relative to those other branches. For example, the Court's involvement in the election of George W. Bush in 2000 has led many to question the Court's legitimacy and independence.[10]

 Rationality Principle

Supreme Court justices decide some cases according to their own political preferences and sometimes *don't* review a case because it is likely that the case will be lost.

 History Principle

It may take decades for the Court to recover from the controversy over the 2000 election.

[1]"TV's Whodunit Effect," *Boston Globe Magazine,* 9 February 2003. *Picturing Justice: The Online Journal of Law and Popular Culture* examines these and other televised courtroom portrayals (www.usfca.edu/pj). See also "Picturing Justice,"*University of San Francisco Law Review* 30.4 (1996).

[2]A short and beautifully written introduction to judicial procedures is Benjamin Cardozo's *The Nature of the Judicial Process* (1921).

[3]See John Hart Ely, *Democracy and Distrust* (Cambridge: Harvard University Press, 1980).

[4]See www.oyez.org/oyez/resource/case/334/.

[5]Jeffery Segal and Harold Spaeth, *The Supreme Court and the Attitudinal Model Revisited* (Cambridge: Cambridge University Press, 2002).

[6]V. Harper Fowler and Alan S. Rosenthal, "What the Supreme Court Did Not Do in the 1949 Term—An Appraisal of Certiorari," *University of Pennsylvania Law Review* 293 (1950). See also H. W. Perry, *Deciding to Decide: Agenda Setting in the U.S. Supreme Court* (Cambridge: Harvard University Press, 1991), and Lee Epstein and Jack Knight, *The Choices Justices Make* (New York: Congressional Quarterly Press, 1997).

[7]Dissenting opinion in *Payne v. Tennessee* (1991). Reliance on precedent is also called *stare decisis.*

[8]See Antonin Scalia, *A Matter of Interpretation: Federal Courts and the Law* (Princeton: Princeton University Press, 1998).

[9]William Rehnquist, "The Notion of a Living Constitution," *Texas Law Review* 54 (1976).

[10]Cass Sunstein and Richard Epstein, *The Vote: Bush, Gore, and the Supreme Court* (Chicago: University of Chicago Press, 2001).

with the outcome, one of the parties moves the dispute to the courts, and, at some point in the process, the option of appeal to the U.S. Supreme Court is available. The aggrieved party has a decision to make. It is a calculated, strategic decision in three respects.

First, an appeal will consume resources that might otherwise be redeployed and used for different purposes. A prospective appellant must weigh an appeal against this "opportunity cost." The Sierra Club, for example, might use resources to appeal a lower court decision on environmental protection to the Supreme Court or, alternatively, devote some of those same resources to lobby Congress on other issues.

Second, a high court appeal sometimes competes with alternative political moves. An interest group like the Sierra Club that lost its lower court appeals might find it more sensible to focus on lobbying Congress for a change in the Environmental Protection Act to ameliorate the condition addressed in the legal proceedings.

Third, all options are uncertain propositions whose resolution stretches out over time. Regarding uncertainty, a prospective appellant must recognize that the probability of successfully getting to the Court is slim, and even if it succeeds in obtaining *cert*, it may not win on the merits of its case. Regarding the time dimension, even if the appellant wins, the process may take years, making the delayed victory bittersweet.

Ultimately these strategic calculations revolve around what an appellant can expect in pursuing an appeal—that is, what might happen in stages 2 and 3. Let us turn to them. [54]

Stage 2   As we have already reported, thousands of cases are appealed to the Supreme Court. This decision to appeal from a lower federal or state court is consummated in a petition for a writ of certiorari. The nine justices of the Supreme Court must sort through these petitions (more accurately, their clerks must) and, according to the **rule of four,** build their docket each session; a case is added to the docket if four justices vote to include it. The Court, in short, has the power to create its own agenda. Appellants for each session are competing with about 10,000 others to claim one of fewer than a hundred spots.

In building their docket for the current session of the Court, how do justices think about the available options? They support some cases undoubtedly out of a strong belief that an area is ripe for constitutional clarification. They support others out of an interest in the development of legal principles in a particular area of the law—criminal rights, privacy, First Amendment, abortion, affirmative action, federal-state relations, and so on—or in the belief that contradictory decisions in lower courts need to be sorted out. They may oppose certain appeals be-

rule of four
Certiorari will be granted only if four justices vote in favor of the petition.

---

[54]There are subtleties to the strategies of appellants. They may seek an appeal to the Supreme Court, for example, as a bluff to induce the winner in the lower court to accommodate in advance some of their preferences—in effect to "settle out of court." Why might the lower court winners be induced to do this? There are at least two reasons: first, to avoid the exorbitant costs of an appeal to the Supreme Court, and, second, to avoid the prospect of their victory in the lower court being reversed.

cause they believe a particular case will not provide a sufficiently clear-cut basis for clarifying a legal issue. That is, even though a case might attract the interest of a justice on substantive grounds or might be perceived by a justice as containing procedural errors that could lead to a reversal, he or she might not support *cert* because of a strategic calculation that it is not a particularly good vehicle or that it would be prudent to wait until a better vehicle comes up through the appeals process in a subsequent session.[55]

Once a case is included on the docket and oral arguments have been delivered by the attorneys for the litigants and written briefs filed by other interested parties (*amicus curiae* briefs), the case becomes the subject of two decisions. The first takes place after it is discussed by the justices in one of the regularly scheduled conferences during the Court's term. When discussion has concluded and all attempts at persuasion have come to an end, there is a *vote on the merits*—a vote in favor of the appeal or against it. In principle, this vote affects only the parties to the case, either affirming or reversing the lower court decision.

It is the second decision that has a wider bearing. Having decided one way or the other, the justices must now determine whether there is agreement on the *reasons* for their decision. The most senior justice on the winning side—the chief justice if he or she is in this group—assigns a colleague to write the majority opinion or keeps it for himself or herself to write. This is a highly strategic decision because the Court's impact over and above its effect on the contesting parties is through the reasons it gives for the decision at hand. The reasons of a *Court majority* set legal precedent for similar cases in the future, thus influencing litigation in lower courts. If the majority cannot agree among themselves on why they decided as they did, then there is no binding effect on other comparable cases. Drafting an opinion that can attract the signatures of at least five justices, therefore, is of pivotal significance. A justice on the winning side who stakes out an extreme position relative to the others is unlikely to be able to draft such an opinion, so moderate members of the Court usually do the heavy lifting of opinion drafting for especially controversial cases. Of course, in some cases, a majority may agree on the merits of a case but are unable to come to a consensus on the reasons. In such cases, there will be no majority opinion, though each justice is free to write his or her own opinion (possibly co-signed by others), either supporting or dissenting from the decision on the merits, giving his or her particular reasons. These opinions have no binding effect on future lower court cases, but they may still serve a strategic signaling role, conveying to the lower courts and the legal community where a justice stands on the issues involved in the case at hand.[56]

[55]An excellent discussion of this facet of Supreme Court decision making is found in H. W. Perry, *Deciding to Decide: Agenda Setting in the United States Supreme Court* (Cambridge, MA: Harvard University Press, 1991).

[56]For an insightful discussion of the strategic elements influencing how the senior justice in the winning coalitions assigns opinion writing, see David W. Rohde, "Policy Goals, Strategic Choice and Majority Opinion Assignments in the U.S. Supreme Court," *Midwest Journal of Political Science* 16 (1972): 652–82.

Stage 3 The Supreme Court is not an island unto itself. It is the top rung of one branch in a separation-of-powers system. Its decisions are not automatically implemented; it must depend on executive agencies for that and on lower courts to enforce its dicta. In fact, it ultimately depends on the willingness of others, especially ordinary citizens, to conform to its rulings. In some instances, the Court may worry about resistance. Throughout the 1940s and 1950s, for example, there were concerns that issues related to integration would meet with popular disapproval and defiance in the South. Indeed, in the famous *Brown* decision desegregating public schools in 1954, Chief Justice Earl Warren worried about precisely this. When he wrote the majority opinion for the Court, he strategically softened some of its language in order to attract the signatures of all nine justices. The 9–0 decision and opinion served as a signal to a potentially defiant South that the Court was united and that it would take a very long time (the time to replace at least four justices) before there was any prospect of reversal—that is, resistance would not pay off in the near or medium term.

In addition to compliance, enforcement, and resistance, the Court must also worry about reversal. On a decision taken by the court on a statutory issue—for example, on whether an existing law covers a particular situation—majorities in both houses of Congress and the president may pass a new statute reversing the court's interpretation. If, for example, the Court rules that the Radio Act of 1928 does not cover transmissions by cellular phones, and Congress and the president think otherwise, then Congress may pass legislation, and the president may sign it into law, amending the Radio Act of 1928 to allow for its provisions to govern the regulation of cell phones. The Court may well say "what the law is" (to quote Justice Oliver Wendell Holmes), but Congress and the president are free to change the law.[57]

For decisions taken by the Court on constitutional (as opposed to statutory) grounds, no mere revision of existing law is sufficient to reverse the Court. An amendment to the Constitution is required. President George W. Bush, for example, has given his blessing to efforts to amend the Constitution to reverse the *Roe v. Wade* decision permitting a woman to choose an abortion in the first two trimesters of her pregnancy.

At the end of the day, the Supreme Court is the final legal authority on whether governmental and interpersonal practices satisfy statutory or Constitutional scrutiny. But, as Yogi Berra put it, "It ain't over till it's over." The other branches of government must be taken into account as justices vote on cases and write legal opinions; the justices are not free agents. Hence strategic calculation cannot ever be far from their thinking.

JUDICIAL POWER AND POLITICS

One of the most important institutional changes to occur in the United States during the past half century has been the striking transformation of the role and

[57]On the strategic interaction between Court, Congress, and the President, see William Eskridge and John Ferejohn, "The Article I, Section 7 Game," *Georgetown Law Review* 80 (1992): 523–65.

power of the federal courts, and of the Supreme Court in particular. Understanding how this transformation came about is the key to understanding the contemporary role of the courts in America.

Traditional Limitations on the Federal Courts

For much of American history, the power of the federal courts was subject to five limitations.[58] First, courts were constrained by judicial rules of standing that limited access to the bench. Claimants who simply disagreed with governmental action or inaction could not obtain access. Access to the courts was limited to individuals who could show that they were particularly affected by the government's behavior in some area. This limitation on access to the courts diminished the judiciary's capacity to forge links with important political and social forces. Second, courts were traditionally limited in the character of the relief they could provide. In general, courts acted only to offer relief or assistance to individuals and not to broad social classes, again inhibiting the formation of alliances between the courts and important social forces. Third, courts lacked enforcement powers of their own and were compelled to rely on executive or state agencies to ensure compliance with their edicts. If the executive or state agencies were unwilling to assist the courts, judicial enactments could go unheeded.

Fourth, federal judges are, of course, appointed by the president (with the consent of the Senate). As a result, the president and Congress can shape the composition of the federal courts and ultimately, perhaps, the character of judicial decisions. Finally, Congress has the power to change both the size and jurisdiction of the Supreme Court and other federal courts. For example, Franklin Roosevelt's "court packing" plan encouraged the justices to drop their opposition to New Deal programs. In many areas, federal courts obtain their jurisdiction not from the Constitution but from congressional statutes. On a number of occasions, Congress has threatened to take matters out of the Court's hands when it was unhappy with the Court's policies.[59]

As a result of these five limitations on judicial power, through much of their history the chief function of the federal courts was to provide judicial support for executive agencies and to legitimate acts of Congress by declaring them to be consistent with constitutional principles. Only on rare occasions did the federal courts actually dare to challenge Congress or the executive.[60]

Two Judicial Revolutions

Since World War II, however, the role of the federal judiciary has been strengthened and expanded. There have actually been two judicial revolutions in the

[58]For limits on judicial power, see Alexander M. Bickel, *The Least Dangerous Branch: The Supreme Court at the Bar of Politics* (Indianapolis: Bobbs-Merrill, 1962).

[59]See Walter F. Murphy, *Congress and the Court: A Case Study in the American Political Process* (Chicago: University of Chicago Press, 1962).

[60]Robert Dahl, "The Supreme Court and National Policy Making," *Journal of Public Law* 6 (1958): 279.

United States since the war. The first and most visible of these was the substantive revolution in judicial policy. As we saw in Chapter 4, in policy areas—including school desegregation, legislative apportionment, and criminal procedure as well as obscenity, abortion, and voting rights—the Supreme Court was at the forefront of a series of sweeping changes in the role of the U.S. government and, ultimately, in the character of American society.[61]

But at the same time that the courts were introducing important policy innovations, they were also bringing about a second, less visible revolution. During the 1960s and 1970s, the Supreme Court and other federal courts began a series of institutional changes in judicial procedures that had major consequences by fundamentally expanding the power of the courts in the United States. First, the federal courts liberalized the concept of standing to permit almost any group that seeks to challenge the actions of an administrative agency to bring its case before the federal bench. In 1971, for example, the Supreme Court ruled that public interest groups could use the National Environmental Policy Act to challenge the actions of federal agencies by claiming that the agencies' activities might have adverse environmental consequences.[62] Congress helped make it even easier for groups dissatisfied with government policies to bring their cases to the courts by adopting Title 42, Section 1988, of the U.S. Code, which permits the practice of "fee shifting." Section 1988 allows citizens who successfully bring a suit against a public official for violating their constitutional rights to collect their attorneys' fees and costs from the government. Thus Section 1988 encourages individuals and groups to bring their problems to the courts rather than to Congress or the executive branch. These changes have given the courts a far greater role in the administrative process than ever before.

Second, the federal courts broadened the scope of relief to permit themselves to act on behalf of broad categories or classes of persons in "class action" cases, rather than just on behalf of individuals.[63] A **class action suit** is a procedural device that permits large numbers of persons with common interests to join together under a representative party to bring or defend a lawsuit. For example, in 1999, a consortium of several dozen law firms prepared to file a class action suit against firearms manufacturers on behalf of victims of gun violence. Claims could amount to billions of dollars. Some of the same law firms were involved earlier in the decade in a massive class action suit against cigarette manufacturers on behalf of the victims of tobacco-related illnesses. This suit eventually led to a settlement in which the tobacco companies agreed to pay out several billion dollars. The beneficiaries of the settlement included the treasuries of all fifty states, which received compensation for costs allegedly borne by the states in treating illnesses caused by tobacco use. Of course, the attorneys who brought the case also received an enormous settlement, splitting more than $1 billion. Continuing litigation against tobacco firms remains to be resolved.

Institution Principle

During the 1960s and 1970s, the courts liberalized the concept of standing.

class action suit
A lawsuit in which large numbers of persons with common interests join together under a representative party to bring or defend a lawsuit, such as hundreds of workers joining together to sue a company.

---

[61]Martin Shapiro, "The Supreme Court: From Warren to Burger," in *The New American Political System*, ed. Anthony King (Washington, DC: American Enterprise Institute, 1978).

[62]*Citizens to Preserve Overton Park v. Volpe*, 401 U.S. 402 (1971).

[63]See "Developments in the Law—Class Actions," *Harvard Law Review* 89 (1976): 1318.

Third, the federal courts began to employ so-called structural remedies, in effect retaining jurisdiction of cases until the court's mandate had actually been implemented to its satisfaction.[64] The best known of these instances was federal judge W. Arthur Garrity's effort to operate the Boston school system from his bench to ensure its desegregation. Between 1974 and 1985, Judge Garrity issued fourteen decisions relating to different aspects of the Boston school desegregation plan that had been developed under his authority and put into effect under his supervision.[65]

Through these three judicial mechanisms, the federal courts paved the way for an unprecedented expansion of national judicial power. In essence, liberalization of the rules of standing and expansion of the scope of judicial relief drew the federal courts into linkages with important social interests and classes, while the introduction of structural remedies enhanced the courts' ability to serve these constituencies. Thus, during the 1960s and 1970s, the power of the federal courts expanded in the same way the power of the executive expanded during the 1930s—through links with constituencies, such as civil rights, consumer, environmental, and feminist groups, that staunchly defended the Supreme Court in its battles with Congress, the executive, or other interest groups.

During the 1980s and early 1990s, the Reagan and George H. W. Bush administrations sought to end the relationship between the Court and liberal political forces. The conservative judges appointed by these Republican presidents modified the Court's position in areas such as abortion, affirmative action, and judicial procedure, though not as completely as some conservatives had hoped. In June 2003, for example, the Court handed down a series of decisions that pleased many liberals and outraged conservative advocacy groups. Within a period of one week, the Supreme Court affirmed the validity of affirmative action, reaffirmed abortion rights, strengthened gay rights, offered new protection to individuals facing the death penalty, and issued a ruling in favor of a congressional apportionment plan that dispersed minority voters across several districts—a practice that appeared to favor the Democrats.[66] It is interesting, however, that the current Court has not been eager to surrender the expanded powers carved out by earlier, liberal Courts. In a number of decisions during the 1980s and 1990s, the Court was willing to make use of its expanded powers on behalf of interests it favored.[67] In the 1992 case of *Lujan v. Defenders of Wildlife*, the Court seemed to retreat to a conception of standing more restrictive than that affirmed by liberal activist jurists.[68] Rather than representing an example of judicial restraint, however, the *Lujan* case was actually a direct judicial challenge to congressional power. The case involved an effort by an environmental group, the Defenders of Wildlife, to

History Principle

In the last fifty years, the power of the judiciary has been strengthened and expanded.

---

[64]See Donald L. Horowitz, *The Courts and Social Policy* (Washington, DC: Brookings Institution, 1977).

[65]*Moran v. McDonough*, 540 F. 2nd 527 (1 Cir., 1976; *cert denied* 429 U.S. 1042 [1977]).

[66]David Van Drehle, "Court That Liberals Savage Proves to Be Less of a Target," *Washington Post*, 29 June 2003, p. A18.

[67]Mark Silverstein and Benjamin Ginsberg, "The Supreme Court and the New Politics of Judicial Power," *Political Science Quarterly* 102 (Fall 1987): 371–88.

[68]*Lujan v. Defenders of Wildlife*, 112 S.Ct. 2130 (1992).

make use of the 1973 Endangered Species Act to block the expenditure of federal funds being used by the governments of Egypt and Sri Lanka for public works projects. Environmentalists charged that the projects threatened the habitats of several endangered species of birds and, therefore, that the expenditure of federal funds to support the projects violated the 1973 act. The Interior Department claimed that the act affected only domestic projects.[69]

The Endangered Species Act, like a number of other pieces of liberal environmental and consumer legislation enacted by Congress, encourages citizen suits—suits by activist groups not directly harmed by the action in question—to challenge government policies that they deem to be inconsistent with the act. Justice Scalia, however, writing for the Court's majority in the *Lujan* decision, reasserted a more traditional conception of standing, requiring those bringing suit against a government policy to show that the policy is likely to cause *them* direct and imminent injury.

Had Scalia stopped at this point, the case might have been seen as an example of judicial restraint. Scalia, however, went on to question the validity of any statutory provision for citizen suits. Such legislative provisions, according to Justice Scalia, violate Article III of the Constitution, which limits the federal courts to consideration of actual "Cases" and "Controversies." This interpretation would strip Congress of its capacity to promote the enforcement of regulatory statutes by encouraging activist groups not directly affected or injured to be on the lookout for violations that could provide the basis for lawsuits. This enforcement mechanism—which conservatives liken to bounty hunting—was an extremely important congressional instrument and played a prominent part in the enforcement of such pieces of legislation as the 1990 Americans with Disabilities Act. Thus the *Lujan* case offers an example of judicial activism rather than of judicial restraint; even the most conservative justices are reluctant to surrender the powers now wielded by the Court.

SUMMARY

Millions of cases come to trial every year in the United States. The great majority—nearly 99 percent—are tried in state and local courts. The types of law are civil law, criminal law, and public law. There are three types of courts that hear cases: trial court, appellate court, and (state) supreme court.

There are two kinds of federal cases: (1) civil cases involving disputes between individuals or between the government and an individual in which no criminal violation is charged, and (2) cases involving federal criminal statutes or state criminal cases that have been made issues of public law. Judicial power extends only to cases and controversies. Litigants must have standing to sue, and courts neither hand down opinions on hypothetical issues nor take the initiative.

[69]Linda Greenhouse, "Court Limits Legal Standing in Suits," *New York Times*, 13 June 1992, p. 12.

Rationality Principle	Collective-Action Principle	Institution Principle	Policy Principle	History Principle
Judges have political goals and policy preferences and act to achieve them.	Appointments to the federal bench involve informal bargaining (senatorial courtesy) as well as formal bargaining (Senate confirmation).	Because the court system is hierarchical, decisions by higher courts constrain the discretion of judges in lower courts.	Courts are not legislative bodies, but many important policy issues are, nevertheless, decided by the judiciary.	Since *Marbury v. Madison* (1803), the power of judicial review has not been in question.
The Supreme Court accepts cases based on the preferences and priorities of the justices.	The legal system coordinates private behavior by providing incentives and disincentives for specific actions.	The courts have developed specific rules of access that govern which cases within their jurisdiction they will hear.	By interpreting existing statutes as well as the Constitution, judges make law.	In the last fifty years, the power of the judiciary has been strengthened and expanded.
Groups will often file more than one suit in the hope that this will increase their chances of being heard in Court.	Four of the nine Supreme Court justices need to agree to review a case.	Though the judiciary is normally above politics, the Supreme Court's procedures allow for various individuals and groups to influence the decision-making process.		
	In reaching their decisions, Supreme Court judges must anticipate Congress's response.	During the 1960s and 1970s the courts liberalized the concept of standing.		

Sometimes appellate courts even return cases to the lower courts for further trial. They may also decline to decide cases by invoking the doctrine of political questions, although this is seldom done today.

The organization of the federal judiciary provides for original jurisdiction in the federal district courts, specialized courts, and federal regulatory agencies.

Each district court is in one of the twelve appellate districts, called circuits, presided over by a court of appeals. Appellate courts admit no new evidence; their rulings are based solely on the records of the court proceedings or agency hearings that led to the original decision. Appeals court rulings are final unless the Supreme Court chooses to review them.

The Supreme Court has some original jurisdiction, but its major job is to review lower court decisions involving substantial issues of public law. There is no explicit constitutional authority for the Supreme Court to review acts of Congress. Nonetheless, the 1803 case of *Marbury v. Madison* established the Court's right to review congressional acts. The supremacy clause of Article VI and the Judiciary Act of 1789 give the Court the power to review state constitutions and laws. Cases reach the Court mainly through the writ of *certiorari*. The Supreme Court controls its caseload by issuing few writs and by handing down clear leading opinions that enable lower courts to resolve future cases without further review.

Both appellate and Supreme Court decisions, including the decision not to review a case, make law. The effect of such law usually favors the status quo. Yet, many revolutionary changes in the law have come about through appellate court and Supreme Court rulings—in the criminal process, in apportionment, and in civil rights.

The judiciary as a whole is subject to two major influences: (1) the individual members of the Supreme Court, who have lifetime tenure, and (2) the other branches of government, particularly Congress.

The influence of the individual member of the Supreme Court is limited when the Court is polarized, and close votes in a polarized Court impair the value of the decision rendered. Writing the majority opinion for a case is an opportunity for a justice to influence the judiciary. But the need to frame an opinion in such a way as to develop majority support on the Court may limit such opportunities. Dissenting opinions can have more effect than the majority opinion; they stimulate a continued flow of cases around that issue. The solicitor general is the most important single influence outside the Court itself because he or she controls the flow of cases brought by the Justice Department and also shapes the argument in those cases. But the flow of cases is a force in itself, which the Department of Justice cannot entirely control. Social problems give rise to similar cases that ultimately must be adjudicated and appealed. Some interest groups try to develop such case patterns as a means of gaining power through the courts.

In recent years, the importance of the federal judiciary—the Supreme Court in particular—has increased substantially as the courts have developed new tools of judicial power and forged alliances with important forces in American society.

FOR FURTHER READING

Abraham, Henry J. *The Judicial Process: An Introductory Analysis of the Courts of the United States, England, and France.* 7th ed. New York: Oxford University Press, 1998.

Baum, Lawrence. *The Puzzle of Judicial Behavior.* Ann Arbor: University of Michigan Press, 1997.

Bickel, Alexander M. *The Least Dangerous Branch: The Supreme Court at the Bar of Politics.* Indianapolis: Bobbs-Merrill, 1962.

Epstein, Lee, and Jack Knight. *The Choices Justices Make.* Washington, DC: Congressional Quarterly Press, 1998.

Kahn, Ronald. *The Supreme Court and Constitutional Theory, 1953–1993.* Lawrence: University Press of Kansas, 1994.

O'Brien, David M. *Storm Center: The Supreme Court in American Politics.* 7th ed. New York: Norton, 2005.

Perry, H. W., Jr. *Deciding to Decide: Agenda Setting in the United States Supreme Court.* Cambridge, MA: Harvard University Press, 1991.

Segal, Jeffrey A., and Harold J. Spaeth. *The Supreme Court and the Attitudinal Model.* New York: Cambridge University Press, 1993.

Silverstein, Mark. *Judicious Choices: The New Politics of Supreme Court Confirmations.* New York: Norton, 1994.

Tribe, Laurence H. *Constitutional Choices.* Cambridge, MA: Harvard University Press, 1985.

Politics in the News—
Reading between the Lines

John Roberts and the Constitution

Chief Justice Nominee Speaks Volumes, While Saying Little

By ADAM LIPTAK

For someone accused of saying very little, Judge John G. Roberts Jr. revealed a great deal about how he will approach his work if confirmed as the 17th chief justice of the United States.

Over three days of testimony, between declining to answer questions on specific cases and legal issues, Judge Roberts made clear that his approach to interpreting the Constitution is more varied and flexible than the originalism subscribed to by Justices Clarence Thomas and Antonin Scalia. President Bush has singled them out as models for the sorts of justices he planned to appoint.

"I think the framers, when they used broad language like 'liberty,' like 'due process,' like 'unreasonable' with respect to search and seizures, they were crafting a document that they intended to apply in a meaningful way down the ages," Judge Roberts said Wednesday.

He said he would consider not only how the framers of the Constitution understood those words, but also how courts have interpreted them and how they apply to evolving societal conditions.

New York Times, 16 September 2005.

That approach disappointed some conservative legal scholars.

"He is not in the mold of Scalia and Thomas," said Steven G. Calabresi, a law professor at Northwestern and a chairman of the Federalist Society, the conservative legal group. "They have more of a theory of how to decide cases, and they look to text and original meaning. Roberts will look at text and original meaning, but he will also look to precedent and the consequences of his decisions."

Judge Roberts, for his part, said his approach would be pragmatic and case-specific. That approach places Judge Roberts closer to Justice Sandra Day O'Connor, who has often provided the swing vote in important cases. . . .

Judge Roberts disappointed some conservatives in the way he answered questions concerning the scope of Congressional power. In a series of decisions, the late Chief Justice William H. Rehnquist endorsed significant limitations on the ability of Congress to legislate on local matters.

"Roberts will be very deferential to Congress," Professor Calabresi said, "more so than Rehnquist."

Judge Roberts also made clear that it is not the role of the courts to interpret statutes more broadly than warranted. If Congress wants to allow certain kinds of lawsuits, he said, the legislation it passes should say so plainly and directly.

Judge Roberts provided substantial information, at least at the level of theory, about the right to privacy. He said it existed, located it in various constitutional provisions including the 14th Amendment and gave some examples of what it requires. He endorsed a 1965 decision of the Supreme Court holding that the right to privacy guarantees that married couples may use contraceptives.

But his adamant refusal to answer other questions frustrated Democratic senators and liberal scholars.

"From Bush v. Gore to the Second Amendment to separation of church and state to abortion," Erwin Chemerinsky, a law professor at Duke University, said of Judge Roberts, "he was masterful at saying a lot but avoiding answering the key questions." . . .

Senator Charles E. Schumer, Democrat of New York, summed up what he called the pros and cons of the Roberts nomination on Thursday.

The pros, Mr. Schumer said, are that Judge Roberts is brilliant, is "a lawyer above all" and is devoted to "a judicial philosophy of modesty and stability" that "respects precedent, the Congress and other judges' opinions."

On the negative side, Mr. Schumer said, were the questions Judge Roberts would not answer, the White House's refusal to release documents from his years as a more senior lawyer in the first Bush administration and what Mr. Schumer called "the question of compassion and humanity."

Judge Roberts, for his part, summed up his philosophy on Thursday.

ESSENCE OF THE STORY

- In his testimony before the U.S. Senate, Chief Justice John Roberts was criticized for not revealing his personal views about the Constitution.

- Roberts was praised, however, for his willingness to defer to precedent and legislative intent, in contrast with current justices Scalia and Thomas.

- Ultimately, Roberts's mastery of constitutional law and nonideological legal philosophy led to overwhelming bipartisan approval by the Senate.

POLITICAL ANALYSIS

- Roberts was initially nominated to replace Justice O'Connor. However, when William Rehnquist died, Roberts was the obvious candidate for Chief Justice. His nomination had already navigated most of the political minefields, so there was no reason for Bush to start over with a new candidate.

- By avoiding major areas of partisan disagreement such as the right to privacy or racial and gender discrimination, Roberts assured that Democrats would not oppose his nomination as Chief Justice.

- The Roberts nomination disappointed some of President Bush's conservative allies. However, Bush's public approval was declining due to the war in Iraq and government failings in responding to Hurricane Katrina. This made it unlikely that Bush would take on the political battle over a strongly conservative nominee.

"Somebody asked me, you know, 'Are you going to be on the side of the little guy?' "he said. "And you obviously want to give an immediate answer, but, as you reflect on it, if the Constitution says that the little guy should win, the little guy's going to win in court before me. But if the Constitution says that the big guy should win, well, then the big guy's going to win, because my obligation is to the Constitution. That's the oath."

three

Politics

CHAPTER

9

Public Opinion

In March 2003, American and British military forces invaded Iraq with the express intent of disarming Iraq's military and driving Iraqi president Saddam Hussein from power. The invasion followed months of diplomatic wrangling and an ultimately unsuccessful effort by President George W. Bush and British Prime Minister Tony Blair to win UN support for military action against Iraq. Bush and Blair charged that the Iraqi regime was hiding weapons of mass destruction and had failed to cooperate with weapons inspectors sent by the UN Security Council. In the months before the war, many Americans were dubious about the need to attack Iraq and uncertain about President Bush's foreign-policy leadership. For example, according to a CBS News poll taken during the first week of March 2003, only 50 percent of those responding thought removing Saddam from power was worth the potential costs of war, while 43 percent thought it was not worth it. The same poll reported that only 55 percent of Americans approved of the way President Bush was handling the situation with Iraq. Once the American and British invasion of Iraq began, however, popular support for U.S. military action rose by twenty-four points to 77 percent.

Many commentators attributed support for the war to a "rally round the flag" effect that is commonly seen when the president leads Americans into battle. Pundits predicted that support for the war and the president would drop if fighting were prolonged or inconclusive. It also quickly became apparent that support for the president and his war policy varied considerably with demographic and political factors. Men were more supportive than women of the president's policies, indicating a continuation of the "gender gap" that has been a persistent feature of American public opinion. Race was also a factor, with African Americans much more critical than whites of President Bush and his goals. In addition, partisanship was important. Republicans were nearly unanimous in their approval of President Bush's policies, while Democrats were more closely divided on the wisdom of going to war. Partisan politics, it seemed, did not stop at the water's edge.

After American forces destroyed the Iraqi army and occupied the country, many Americans who had once supported the war began to question the administration's policies. President Bush had told the nation that Saddam Hussein had to be overthrown because he possessed and sought to produce weapons of mass destruction (WMDs) that would ultimately threaten the United States. Bush had also suggested that Saddam was linked to the al-Qaeda terrorists who had attacked New York and Washington on September 11, 2001. Most Americans did not know enough about Iraq to evaluate the president's assertions. Indeed, Americans know little enough about the programs and policies of their own government, much less the plans of a dictatorial regime thousands of miles from home.[1] And, as is so often the case, even the experts to whom Americans might have looked for guidance seemed divided, with some pundits declaring that Iraq posed an imminent threat to the United States, and others declaring that it posed little or no danger.

As American occupation forces sifted through the wreckage of Iraq's military and intelligence programs, it soon

CHAPTER OUTLINE

What Are the Origins of Public Opinion?

- Common Fundamental Values
- Political Socialization
- Political Ideology

Public Opinion and Political Knowledge

Shaping of Opinion: The Influence of Political Leaders, Private Groups, and the Media

- Government and the Shaping of Public Opinion
- Private Groups and the Shaping of Public Opinion
- The Media and Public Opinion

Measuring Public Opinion

- Constructing Public Opinion from Surveys
- Public Opinion, Political Knowledge, and the Political Uncertainty Principle

How Does Public Opinion Influence Government Policy?

[1] Carroll J. Glynn, Susan Herbst, Garrett J. O'Keefe, Robert Y. Shapiro, and Mark Lindeman, *Public Opinion*, 2nd ed. (New York: Westview, 2004), Chapter 8.

became apparent that Iraq had no active WMD program and that there was little or no evidence pointing to Iraqi cooperation with al-Qaeda. To make matters worse from the president's perspective, early in 2004 Iraqi insurgents began to inflict a steady stream of casualties on American troops, so that by the end of 2004, more Americans had been killed and wounded during the occupation than in actual combat operations. Democrats highlighted these problems throughout the 2004 presidential campaign. Democratic presidential candidate John Kerry and his running mate, John Edwards, frequently pointed to the president's erroneous claims and lamented the unnecessary loss of American lives. Not surprisingly, by the end of 2004, popular approval of the president's policies in Iraq had dropped more than thirty points from its peak at what had seemed to be America's moment of military triumph a year earlier (Figure 9.1). By the end of 2005, Bush's standing in the polls had fallen even more precipitously.

PREVIEWING THE PRINCIPLES

Underlying political beliefs formed through political socialization often cohere into a political ideology. As a result, ideology can work as an information shortcut by allowing an individual to form an opinion on an issue or candidate while economizing on the costs of becoming informed of the details. Thus some analysts consider it rational for citizens to be ignorant or only partially informed about politics and to form political opinions by following the cues of others, such as government officials, leaders of interest groups, and members of the media. This creates a dilemma, however, because those who have more knowledge of politics also tend to have more influence on political outcomes. This dilemma contributes to a gulf between public opinion and public policy. This gulf is explained, in part, by how institutions shape outcomes. An institutional framework based on representative government limits the extent to which public opinion affects policy outcomes.

Even as popular support for his policies eroded, President Bush remained steadfast. The president won re-election despite doubts about his handling of the Iraq situation, and he was determined to bring about the creation of a pro-American regime in that nation. The president attempted to halt the downward trend of popular approval for his policies by hinting that American forces might be reduced after the 2005 Iraqi elections and continually restating the need to promote democracy in the Middle East. At the same time, though, President Bush made it clear that his policies would not respond to shifts in popular opinion. The president reminded Americans that he planned to do his duty as he saw it, regardless of the vicissitudes of public sentiment

These events underline many issues raised in this chapter. Do Americans know enough to form meaningful opinions about important policy issues? What factors account for differences in opinion? To what extent can the government manipulate popular sentiment? To what extent do—or should—the government's policies respond to public opinion?

public opinion
Citizens' attitudes about political issues, leaders, institutions, and events.

Public opinion is the term used to denote the values and attitudes that people have about issues, events, and personalities. Although the terms are sometimes used interchangeably, it is useful to distinguish between values and beliefs on the one

FIGURE 9.1

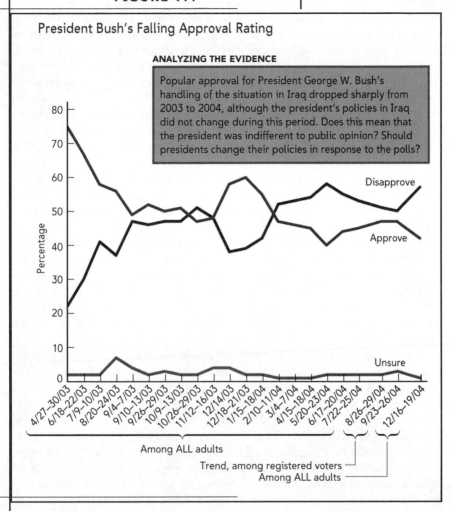

President Bush's Falling Approval Rating

ANALYZING THE EVIDENCE

Popular approval for President George W. Bush's handling of the situation in Iraq dropped sharply from 2003 to 2004, although the president's policies in Iraq did not change during this period. Does this mean that the president was indifferent to public opinion? Should presidents change their policies in response to the polls?

*N = 1,004 adults nationwide. Margin of error ±3.
SOURCE: ABC News/*Washington Post* poll, 16–19 December 2004 (www.pollingreport.com/iraq/htm). Fieldwork by TNS.

values (or beliefs) Basic principles that shape a person's opinions about political issues and events.

political ideology A cohesive set of beliefs that form a general philosophy about the role of government.

hand, and attitudes or opinions on the other. ***Values (or beliefs)*** are a person's basic orientations to politics. Values represent deep-rooted goals, aspirations, and ideals that shape an individual's perceptions of political issues and events. Liberty, equality, and democracy are basic political values that most Americans hold. Another useful term for understanding public opinion is *ideology*. ***Political ideology*** refers to a complex and interrelated set of beliefs and values that, as a whole, form a general philosophy about government. As we shall see, liberalism and conservatism are important ideologies in America today. For example, the idea that governmental solutions to problems are inherently inferior to solutions offered by the private sector is a belief also held by many Americans. This general belief, in turn, may lead individuals to have negative views of specific government programs even before they know much about them. An ***attitude (or opinion)*** is a specific view about a particular issue, personality, or event. An individual may have an opinion about George W. Bush or an attitude toward American policy in Iraq. The attitude or opinion may have emerged from a broad belief about Republicans or military intervention, but an attitude itself is very specific. Some attitudes may be short lived.

In this chapter, we examine the role of public opinion in American politics. First, we examine the political values and beliefs that help Americans form their perceptions of the political process. After reviewing basic American political values, we analyze how values and beliefs are formed and how certain processes and institutions influence their formation. We conclude this first section by considering the ways in which values and beliefs can cumulate to create political ideologies. Second, we see how general values and beliefs help shape more specific attitudes and opinions. In this discussion we consider the role of political knowledge and the influence of political leaders, private groups, and the media. We see why there appear to be so many differences of opinion among Americans. Third, we assess the science of gathering and measuring public opinion. Finally, we assess the effect of public opinion on the government and its policies. Is the U.S. government responsive to public opinion? Should it be?

One reason that public policy and public opinion may not always coincide is, of course, that ours is a representative government, not a direct democracy. The framers of the Constitution thought that our nation would be best served by a system of government that allowed the elected representatives of the people an opportunity to reflect and consider their decisions rather than one that bowed immediately to shifts in popular sentiment. A century after the founding, however, the populist movement averred that government was too far removed from the people and introduced procedures for direct popular legislation through the initiative and referendum. A number of states allow policy issues to be placed on the ballot, where they are resolved by a popular vote. Some modern-day populists believe that initiative and referendum processes should be adopted at the national level as well. Whether this would lead to greater responsiveness, however, is an open question to which we shall return.

attitude (or opinion) A specific preference on a specific issue.

Institution Principle

One reason why policy and opinion may not be consistent is that the United States is a representative government, not a direct democracy.

WHAT ARE THE ORIGINS OF PUBLIC OPINION?

Opinions are products of an individual's personality, social characteristics, and interests. But opinions are also shaped by institutional, political, and governmental forces that make it more likely that citizens will hold some beliefs and less likely that they will hold others.

Common Fundamental Values

Today most Americans share a common set of political beliefs. First, Americans generally believe in *equality of opportunity*—that is, they assume that all individuals should be allowed to seek personal and material success. Moreover, Americans generally believe that such success should be linked to personal effort and ability rather than family "connections" or other forms of special privilege. Second, Americans strongly believe in individual freedom. They typically support the notion that governmental interference with individuals' lives and property should be kept to the minimum consistent with the general welfare (although in recent years Americans have grown accustomed to greater levels of governmental intervention than would have been deemed appropriate by the founders of liberal theory). Third, most Americans believe in *democracy*. They presume that everyone should have the opportunity to take part in the nation's governmental and policy-making processes and to have some "say" in determining how they are governed (see Figure 9.2).[2]

Of course, support for abstract principles does not always carry over to affirmation of these same principles in concrete situations. For example, Americans who believe in individual freedom in the abstract may still support policies that limit freedom, especially if such policies are said to be necessary to combat crime or thwart terrorism. Nevertheless, widespread acceptance of a principle establishes a general benchmark or standard that can be difficult to dispute. During the 1960s, for instance, one reason that the civil rights movement focused on the issue of voting rights was that principle of access to the ballot box was so firmly established in the United States that opponents of voting rights for African Americans found it virtually impossible to find an intellectual basis from which to defend their position.

One indication that Americans of all political stripes share fundamental political values is the content of the acceptance speeches delivered by John Kerry and George W. Bush upon receiving their parties' presidential nominations in 2004. Kerry and Bush differed on many specific issues and policies. Yet the political visions they presented reveal an underlying similarity. A major emphasis of both candidates was equality of opportunity.

Kerry declared, "We believe that what millions want is not narrow appeals masquerading as values . . . but the shared values that unite us: family, faith, hard work, opportunity . . . so that every child, every adult, every parent, every worker in America has an equal shot at living up to their God-given potential." And, in a similar vein, Bush said, "We seek to provide not just a government program but a path to greater opportunity [and] more freedom." Thus, however much the two candidates differed on means and specifics, their understandings of the fundamental goals of government were quite similar.

Agreement on fundamental political values, though certainly not absolute, is probably more widespread in the United States than anywhere else in the Western world. During the course of Western political history, competing economic, social,

equality of opportunity A universally shared American ideal that all have the freedom to use whatever talents and wealth they have to reach their fullest potential.

---

[2]For a discussion of the political beliefs of Americans, see Everett Carll Ladd, *The American Ideology* (Storrs, CT: Roper Center, 1994).

FIGURE 9.2

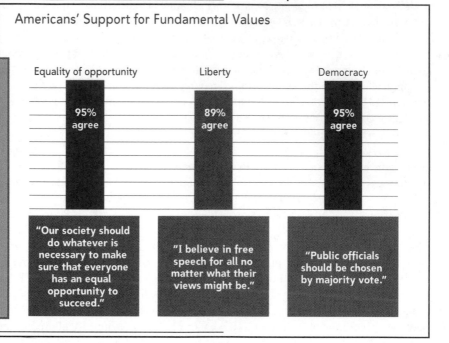

Americans' Support for Fundamental Values

Equality of opportunity

95% agree

"Our society should do whatever is necessary to make sure that everyone has an equal opportunity to succeed."

Liberty

89% agree

"I believe in free speech for all no matter what their views might be."

Democracy

95% agree

"Public officials should be chosen by majority vote."

SOURCE: 1992 American National Election Studies; Herbert McCloskey and John Zaller, *The American Ethos: Public Attitudes toward Capitalism and Democracy* (Cambridge, MA: Harvard University Press, 1984), p. 25; and Robert S. Erikson, Norman R. Luttbeg, and Kent L. Tedin, *American Public Opinion: Its Origins, Content, and Impact*, 4th ed. (New York: Macmillan, 1991), p. 108.

and political groups put forward a variety of radically divergent views, opinions, and political philosophies. America was never socially or economically homogeneous. But two forces that were extremely powerful and important sources of ideas and beliefs elsewhere in the world were relatively weak or absent in the United States. First, the United States never had the feudal aristocracy that dominated so much of European history. Second, for reasons including America's prosperity and the early availability of political rights, no Socialist movements comparable to those that developed in nineteenth-century Europe were ever able to establish themselves in the United States. As a result, during the course of American history, there existed neither an aristocracy to assert the virtues of inequality, special privilege, and a rigid class structure nor a powerful American Communist or Socialist party to seriously challenge the desirability of limited government and individualism.[3]

[3]See Louis Hartz, *The Liberal Tradition in America: An Interpretation of American Political Thought since the Revolution* (New York: Harcourt, Brace, 1955).

Obviously, the principles that Americans espouse have not always been put into practice. For 200 years, Americans were able to believe in the principles of equality of opportunity and individual liberty while denying them in practice to generations of African Americans. Yet, as we observed earlier, the strength of the principles ultimately helped overcome practices that deviated from those principles. Proponents of slavery and, later, of segregation were defeated in the arena of public opinion because their practices differed so sharply from the fundamental principles accepted by most Americans. Ironically, in contemporary politics, Americans' fundamental commitment to equality of opportunity has led to divisions over racial policy. In particular, both proponents and opponents of affirmative action programs cite their belief in equality of opportunity as the justification for their position. Proponents see these programs as necessary to ensure equality of opportunity, while opponents believe that affirmative action constitutes preferential treatment for some groups—a clear violation of the principle of equality of opportunity.[4]

Political Socialization

The attitudes that individuals hold about political issues and personalities tend to be shaped by their underlying political beliefs and values. For example, an individual who has basically negative feelings about government intervention into America's economy and society would probably be predisposed to oppose the development of new health care and social programs. Similarly, someone who distrusts the military would likely be suspicious of any call for the use of American troops. The processes through which these underlying political beliefs and values are formed are collectively called *political socialization*.

The process of political socialization is important. Probably no nation, and certainly no democracy, could survive if its citizens did not share some fundamental beliefs. If Americans had few common values or perspectives, it would be very difficult for them to reach agreement on particular issues. In contemporary America, some elements of the socialization process tend to produce differences in outlook, whereas others promote similarities. Four of the most important *agents of socialization* that foster differences in political perspectives are the family, membership in social groups, education, and prevailing political conditions.

No inventory of agencies of socialization can fully explain the development of a given individual's basic political beliefs. In addition to the factors that are important for everyone, forces that are unique to each individual play a role in shaping political orientations. For one person, the character of an early encounter with a member of another racial group can have a lasting impact on that individual's view of the world. For another, a highly salient political event, such as the Vietnam War, can leave an indelible mark on that person's political consciousness. For a third person, some deep-seated personality characteristic, such as paranoia, for example, may strongly influence the formation of political beliefs.

political socialization
The induction of individuals into the political culture; learning the underlying beliefs and values on which the political system is based.

agents of socialization
Social institutions, including families and schools, that help shape individuals' basic political beliefs and values.

[4]Paul M. Sniderman and Edward G. Carmines, *Reaching beyond Race* (Cambridge, MA: Harvard University Press, 1997).

Nevertheless, knowing that we cannot fully explain the development of any given individual's political outlook, let us look at some of the most important agencies of socialization that do affect one's beliefs.

The Family   Most people acquire their initial orientation to politics from their families. As might be expected, differences in family background tend to produce divergent political outlooks. Although relatively few parents spend much time teaching their children about politics, political conversations occur in many households and children tend to absorb the political views of parents and other caregivers, perhaps without realizing it. Studies have suggested, for example, that party preferences are initially acquired at home. Children raised in households in which the primary caregivers are Democrats tend to become Democrats themselves, whereas children raised in homes where their caregivers are Republicans tend to favor the GOP (Grand Old Party, a traditional nickname for the Republican party).[5] Similarly, children reared in politically liberal households are more likely than not to develop a liberal outlook, whereas children raised in politically conservative settings are prone to see the world through conservative lenses. Obviously, not all children absorb their parents' political views. Two of former conservative Republican president Ronald Reagan's three children, for instance, rejected their parents' conservative values. The late president's son, Ron, supported Democrat John Kerry in the 2004 presidential race. Moreover, even those children whose views are initially shaped by parental values may change their minds as they mature and experience political life for themselves. Nevertheless, the family is an important initial source of political orientation for everyone.

Social Groups   Another important source of divergent political orientations and values are the social groups to which individuals belong. Social groups include those to which individuals belong involuntarily—gender and racial groups, for example—as well as those to which people belong voluntarily—such as political parties, labor unions, and educational and occupational groups. Some social groups have both voluntary and involuntary attributes. For example, individuals are born with a particular social-class background, but as a result of their own efforts, people may move up—or down—the class structure.

Membership in social groups can affect political values in a variety of ways. Membership in a particular group can give individuals important experiences and perspectives that shape their view of political and social life. In American society, for example, the experiences of blacks and whites can differ significantly. Blacks are a minority and have been victims of persecution and discrimination throughout American history. Blacks and whites also have different educational and occupational opportunities, often live in separate communities, and may attend separate schools. Such differences tend to produce distinctive political out-

[5]See Angus Campbell, Philip E. Converse, Warren E. Miller, and Donald E. Stokes, *The American Voter* (New York: Wiley, 1960), p. 147.

looks. For example, in 1995 blacks and whites had very different reactions to the murder trial of former football star O. J. Simpson, who was accused of killing his ex-wife and one of her friends. Approximately 70 percent of the white Americans surveyed believed that Simpson was guilty, based on the evidence presented by the police and prosecutors. But an identical 70 percent of the black Americans surveyed immediately after the trial believed that the police had fabricated evidence and had sought to convict Simpson of a crime he had not committed; these beliefs were presumably based on blacks' experiences with and perceptions of the criminal justice system.[6] In a similar vein, the Reverend Al Sharpton's 2003–04 campaign for the Democratic presidential nomination was not taken seriously by most white voters and received little attention from the mainstream news media. Black voters, on the other hand, were quite attuned to Sharpton's candidacy, which received considerable coverage in the African American news media. Indeed, Sharpton received considerable financial backing from black media executives.[7]

According to other recent surveys, blacks and whites in the United States differ on a number of issues. For example, among middle-income Americans (defined as those earning between $30,000 and $75,000 per year), 65 percent of black respondents and only 35 percent of white respondents thought racism was a major problem in the United States today. Within this same group of respondents, 63 percent of blacks and only 39 percent of whites thought the federal government should provide more services even at the cost of higher taxes.[8] Other issues show a similar pattern of disagreement, reflecting the differences in experience, background, and interests between blacks and whites in America (see Figure 9.3).

Of course, disagreements between blacks and whites are not the only important racial or ethnic differences to be found in contemporary America. Latinos are another major American subgroup with distinctive opinions on some public issues. For example, 54 percent of Latinos surveyed in 2004 by the Pew Hispanic Center viewed education as the most important issue facing America. In the general population, however, only 5 percent of those surveyed attached such importance to education. Often immigrants or the children of immigrants, Hispanics view education as the ticket to a better life in America and attach great value to educational opportunity. As a population currently moving to the United States, Latinos also have a distinctive view of immigration. The 2004 Pew Hispanic survey found that more than 60 percent of Latinos believe that immigration is good for America. Among non-Latinos, though, more than 60 percent believe that immigration poses a major threat to the country. It is interesting that the Latino community is itself divided into subgroups based on national origin. Latinos of Mexican, Puerto Rican, Cuban, and Central American descent have distinct opinions and even partisan loyalties (Table 9.1) Cuban Americans, for example,

[6]Richard Morin, "Poll Reflects Division over Simpson Case," *Washington Post*, 8 October 1995, p. A31.
[7]"Paul Farhi, "Black Media Barons Back Sharpton Bid," *Washington Post*, 9 November 2003, p. A4.
[8]"Middle-Class Views in Black and White," *Washington Post*, 9 October 1995, p. A22.

FIGURE 9.3

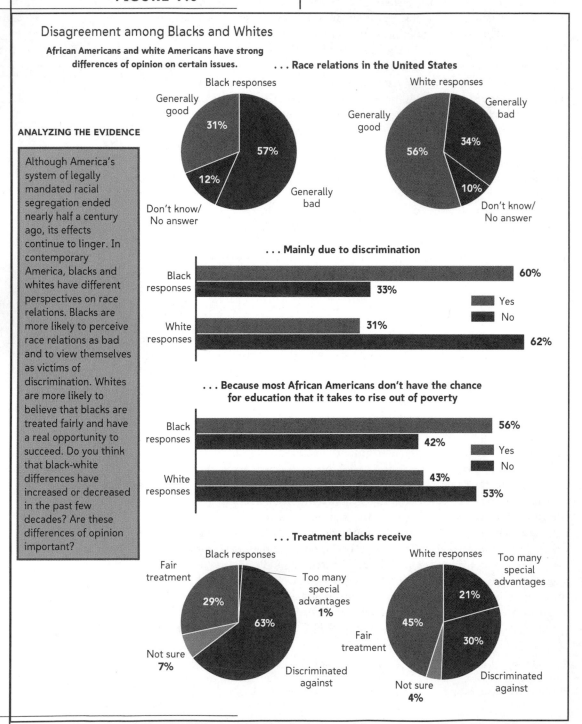

Disagreement among Blacks and Whites

African Americans and white Americans have strong differences of opinion on certain issues.

... Race relations in the United States

Black responses
- Generally good 31%
- Generally bad 57%
- Don't know/No answer 12%

White responses
- Generally good 56%
- Generally bad 34%
- Don't know/No answer 10%

... Mainly due to discrimination

Black responses: Yes 60%, No 33%
White responses: Yes 31%, No 62%

Yes / No

... Because most African Americans don't have the chance for education that it takes to rise out of poverty

Black responses: Yes 56%, No 42%
White responses: Yes 43%, No 53%

Yes / No

... Treatment blacks receive

Black responses
- Fair treatment 29%
- Too many special advantages 1%
- Discriminated against 63%
- Not sure 7%

White responses
- Too many special advantages 21%
- Discriminated against 30%
- Fair treatment 45%
- Not sure 4%

ANALYZING THE EVIDENCE

Although America's system of legally mandated racial segregation ended nearly half a century ago, its effects continue to linger. In contemporary America, blacks and whites have different perspectives on race relations. Blacks are more likely to perceive race relations as bad and to view themselves as victims of discrimination. Whites are more likely to believe that blacks are treated fairly and have a real opportunity to succeed. Do you think that black-white differences have increased or decreased in the past few decades? Are these differences of opinion important?

SOURCES: Survey by CBS News, 6–10 February 2000; survey by the National Opinion Research Center—General Social Survey, 1 February–25 June 2000; survey by NBC News/*Wall Street Journal*, 2–5 March 2000.

TABLE 9.1

Partisan Division in the Latino Community, 2004		
BACKGROUND	DEMOCRATIC (PERCENT)	REPUBLICAN (PERCENT)
Cuban	17	52
Mexican	47	18
Puerto Rican	50	17

Members of America's Latino community share a linguistic and cultural heritage, but they are not politically homogeneous. For example, most Mexican Americans and Puerto Ricans are staunchly Democratic, whereas most Cuban Americans are loyal Republicans. What factors might account for these differences?

SOURCE: Pew Hispanic Center/Kaiser Family Foundation, 2004 National Survey of Hispanics.

tend to be Republican and conservative, whereas Puerto Rican Americans are more likely to be liberal and Democratic. These differences, in turn, are related to the group's level of education, economic status, and history. Cubans tend to be wealthier and better educated than other Latinos and have traditionally viewed the Republican party as a foe of the Communist regime that forced them to flee Cuba. Puerto Ricans, by contrast, tend to be poorer and depend more on the social services championed by the Democratic party.

Religion has become another important source of variation in opinion. In recent years, contending political forces have placed a number of religious and moral issues on the national political agenda. The Republican party, in particular, has emphasized its support for traditional "family values" and its opposition to abortion, same-sex marriage, and other practices opposed by more conservative religious leaders. It is not surprising that public opinion on these issues differs along religious lines, with evangelical Protestants being most supportive of traditional values and respondents identifying themselves as "secular" manifesting the least support for these positions. Take the issue of same-sex marriage, for example (Table 9.2).

Men and women have important differences of opinion as well. Reflecting differences in social roles, political experience, and occupational patterns, women tend to be less militaristic than men on issues of war and peace, more likely than men to favor measures to protect the environment, and more supportive than men of government social and health-care programs (Table 9.3). Perhaps because of these differences on issues, women are more likely than men to vote for Democratic candidates, while men have become increasingly supportive of the GOP.[9] This tendency for men's and women's opinions to differ is called the *gender gap.*

gender gap
A distinctive pattern of voting behavior reflecting the differences in views between women and men.

[9]For data, see Rutgers University, Eagleton Institute of Politics, Center for the American Woman in Politics, "Sex Differences in Voter Turnout," August 1994.

TABLE 9.2

Should Same-Sex Marriage Be Legalized?

RELIGIOUS GROUP	FAVOR (PERCENT)	OPPOSE (PERCENT)
White Protestant evangelical	12	81
White Protestant nonevangelical	37	54
White Catholic	33	59
Black Protestant	22	67
Secular	64	28

SOURCE: Pew Research Center, October 2003.

Political party membership can be another factor affecting political orientation. Partisans tend to rely on party leaders and spokespersons for cues on the appropriate positions to take on major political issues. In recent years, congressional redistricting and partisan realignment in the South have reduced the number of conservative Democrats and all but eliminated liberal Republicans from Congress and positions of prominence in the party. As a result, the leadership of the Republican party has become increasingly conservative and that of the Democratic party has become more and more liberal. These changes in the positions of party leaders have been reflected in the views of party adherents and sympathizers in the general public. According to recent studies, differences between Democratic and Republican partisans on a variety of political and policy questions are greater today than during any other period for which data are available. On issues of national security, for example, Republicans have become very "hawkish," whereas Democrats have become quite "dovish." This was most evident in October 2003, when 85 percent of Republicans and only 39 percent of Democrats surveyed thought America's war against Iraq had been a good idea. Gaps on domestic social and economic issues were nearly as broad.[10]

Membership in a social group can affect individuals' political orientations in another way: through the efforts of groups themselves to influence their members. Labor unions, for example, often seek to "educate" their members through meetings,

[10]David S. Broder, "Partisan Gap Is at a High, Poll Finds," *Washington Post*, 9 November 2003, p. A6.

TABLE 9.3

Disagreements among Men and Women on Issues of War and Peace

GOVERNMENT ACTION	PERCENTAGE APPROVING OF ACTION	
	MEN	WOMEN
Going to war against Iraq (2003)	66	50
Prefer cease-fire over NATO air strikes on Yugoslavia (1999)	44	51
Ending ban on homosexuals in military (1993)	34	51
Military operation against Somali warlord (1993)	72	60
Going to war against Iraq (1991)	72	53

SOURCE: Gallup Poll, 1991, 1993, 1998, 1999; *Washington Post*, 2003.

rallies, and literature. These activities are designed to shape union members' understanding of politics and to make them more amenable to supporting the political positions favored by union leaders. Similarly, organization can sharpen the effect of membership in an involuntary group. Women's groups, black groups, religious groups, and the like usually endeavor to structure their members' political views through intensive educational programs. The importance of such group efforts can be seen from the impact of group membership on political opinion. Women who belong to women's organizations, for example, are likely to differ more from men in their political views than women without such group affiliation.[11] Other analysts have found that African Americans who belong to black organizations are likely to differ more from whites in their political orientations than blacks who lack such affiliations.[12]

In many cases, no particular efforts are required by groups to affect their members' beliefs and opinions. Often, individuals will consciously or unconsciously adapt their views to those of the groups with which they identify. For

[11]Pamela Johnston Conover, "The Role of Social Groups in Political Thinking," *British Journal of Political Science* 18 (1988): 51–78.

[12]See Michael C. Dawson, "Structure and Ideology: The Shaping of Black Opinion," paper presented at the 1995 annual meeting of the Midwest Political Science Association, Chicago, 7–9 April. See also Michael C. Dawson, *Behind the Mule: Race and Class in African-American Politics* (Princeton, NJ: Princeton University Press, 1994).

example, an African American who is dubious about affirmative action is likely to come under considerable peer pressure and internal pressure to modify his or her views. In this and other cases, dissenters are likely to gradually shift their own views to conform to those of the group. Political psychologist Elisabeth Noelle-Neumann has called this process the "spiral of silence."[13]

 Rationality Principle

Objective political interests fuel individuals' political beliefs.

A third way that membership in social groups can affect political beliefs is through what might be called objective political interests. On many economic issues, for example, the interests of the rich and poor differ significantly. Inevitably, these differences of interest will produce differences of political outlook. James Madison and other framers of the Constitution thought that the inherent gulf between the rich and the poor would always be the most important source of conflict in political life. Certainly today, struggles over tax policy, welfare policy, health-care policy, and so forth are fueled by differences of interest between wealthier and poorer Americans. In a similar vein, objective differences of interest between "senior citizens" and younger Americans can lead to very different views on such diverse issues as health-care policy, Social Security, and criminal justice. To take another example, in recent decades major differences of opinion and political orientation have developed between American civilians and members of the armed services. Military officers, in particular, are far more conservative in their domestic and foreign-policy views than the public at large and are heavily Republican in their political leanings.[14] It is interesting that support for the Republicans among military officers climbed sharply during the 1980s and 1990s, decades in which the GOP championed large military budgets. Could this be another case of objective interests swaying ideology?

It is worth pointing out again that, like the other agencies of socialization, group membership can never fully explain a given individual's political views. One's unique personality and life experiences may produce political views very different from those of the group to which one might nominally belong. This is why some African Americans are conservative Republicans and why an occasional wealthy industrialist is also a socialist. Group membership is conducive to particular outlooks, but it is not determinative.

Differences in Education   A third important source of differences in political perspectives comes from a person's education. In some respects, of course, schooling is a great equalizer. Governments use public education to try to teach all children a common set of civic values. It is mainly in school that Americans acquire their basic belief in liberty, equality, and democracy. In history classes, students are taught that the Founders fought for the principle of liberty. Through participation in class elections and student government, stu-

---

[13]Elisabeth Noelle-Neumann, *The Spiral of Silence: Public Opinion, Our Social Skin* (Chicago: University of Chicago Press, 1984).

[14]Ole R. Holsti, "A Widening Gap between the Military and Society?" in *Some Evidence, 1976–1996*, John M. Olin Institute for Strategic Studies, Harvard University, Working Paper no. 13 (October 1997).

dents are taught the virtues of democracy. In the course of studying such topics as the Constitution, the Civil War, and the civil rights movement, students are taught the importance of equality. These lessons are repeated in every grade in a variety of contexts. No wonder they are such an important element in Americans' beliefs.

At the same time, however, differences in educational attainment are strongly associated with differences in political outlook. In particular, those who attend college are often exposed to philosophies and modes of thought that will forever distinguish them from their friends and neighbors who do not pursue college diplomas. Table 9.4 outlines some general differences of opinion that are found between college graduates and other Americans.

In recent years, conservatives have charged that liberal college professors indoctrinate their students with liberal ideas. College does seem to have some "liberalizing" effect on students, but, more significant, college seems to convince students of the importance of political participation and of their own capacity to have an effect on politics and policy. Thus one of the major differences between college graduates and other Americans can be seen in levels of political participation. College graduates vote, write letters to the editor, join campaigns, take part in protests, and, generally, make their voices heard.

Political Conditions   A fourth set of factors that shape political orientations and values are the conditions under which individuals and groups are recruited into and involved in political life. Although political beliefs are influenced by family background and group membership, the precise content and character of these views is, to a large extent, determined by political circumstances. For example, many Americans who came of political age during the Great Depression and World War II developed an intense loyalty to President Franklin D. Roosevelt and became permanently attached to his Democratic party. In a similar vein, the Vietnam War and social upheavals of the 1960s produced lasting divisions among Americans of the baby boomer generation. Indeed, arguments over Vietnam persisted into the 2004 presidential election, some thirty years after American troops left Southeast Asia. Perhaps the September 11 terrorist attacks and ongoing threats to America's security will have a lasting impact on the political orientations of contemporary Americans.

In a similar vein, the views held by members of a particular group can shift drastically over time, as political circumstances change. For example, American white southerners were staunch members of the Democratic party from the Civil War through the 1960s. As members of this political group, they became key supporters of liberal New Deal and post–New Deal social programs that greatly expanded the size and power of the American national government. Since the 1960s, however, southern whites have shifted in large numbers to the Republican party. Now they provide a major base of support for efforts to scale back social programs and to sharply reduce the size and power of the national government. The South's move from the Democratic to the Republican camp took place because of white southern opposition to the Democratic party's racial

History Principle

Since the 1960s, southern whites have become a major source of support for the Republican party.

TABLE 9.4

Education and Public Opinion in 2000

The figures show the percentage of respondents in each
category agreeing with the statement.

**ANALYZING THE
EVIDENCE**

What factors might
explain the
relationship between
education and
opinion? Some
commentators believe
that many college
courses have a liberal
political orientation.
Do you agree? How
have your college
courses affected your
opinions on social and
political issues?

ISSUE	EDUCATION			
	DROP-OUT	HIGH SCHOOL	SOME COLLEGE	COLLEGE GRAD
Women and men should have equal roles.	45	72	84	85
Abortion should never be allowed.	31	16	11	5
The government should adopt national health insurance.	50	43	38	37
The United States should not concern itself with other nations' problems.	27	34	27	12
Government should see to fair treatment in jobs for African Americans.	24	33	32	43
Government should provide fewer services to reduce government spending.	18	13	19	31

SOURCE: The American National Election Studies, 2000 data, provided by the Inter-University Consortium for Political and Social Research, University of Michigan.

policies and because of determined Republican efforts to win white southern support. It was not a change in the character of white southerners but a change in the political circumstances in which they found themselves that induced this major shift in political allegiances and outlooks in the South.

The moral of this story is that a group's views cannot be inferred simply from the character of the group. College students are not inherently radical or inherently conservative. Jews are not inherently liberal. Southerners are not inherently conservative. Men are not inherently supportive of the military. Any group's political outlooks and orientations are shaped by the political circumstances in which that group finds itself, and those outlooks can change as circumstances change. Quite probably, the generation of American students now coming of political age will have a very different view of the use of American military power than their parents—members of a generation that reached political consciousness during the 1960s, when opposition to the Vietnam War and military conscription were important political phenomena.

Agreement on fundamental values, however, by no means implies that Americans do not differ with one another on a wide variety of issues. As we shall see, American political life is characterized by vigorous debate on economic, foreign policy, and social policy issues; race relations; environmental affairs; and a host of other matters.

Political Ideology

As we have seen, people's beliefs about government can vary widely. But for some individuals, this set of beliefs can fit together into a coherent philosophy about government. This set of underlying orientations, ideas, and beliefs through which we come to understand and interpret politics is called a political ideology.

In America today, people often describe themselves as liberals or conservatives. Liberalism and conservatism are political ideologies that include beliefs about the role of the government, ideas about public policies, and notions about which groups in society should properly exercise power. Historically, these terms were defined somewhat differently from the way they are today. As recently as the nineteenth century, a liberal was an individual who favored freedom from state control, while a conservative was someone who supported the use of governmental power and favored continuation of the influence of church and aristocracy in national life.

Today, the term *liberal* has come to imply support for political and social reform; extensive governmental intervention in the economy; the expansion of federal social services; more vigorous efforts on behalf of the poor, minorities, and women; and greater concern for consumers and the environment. In social and cultural areas, liberals generally support abortion rights and oppose state involvement with religious institutions and religious expression. In international affairs, liberal positions are usually seen as including support for arms control, opposition to the development and testing of nuclear weapons, support for aid to poor nations, opposition to the use of American troops to influence the domestic affairs of developing nations, and support for international organizations such as the United Nations. Of course, liberalism is not monolithic. For example, among individuals who view themselves as liberal, many support American military intervention when it is tied to a humanitarian purpose, as in the case of America's military action in Kosovo in 1998–99. Most liberals supported President George W. Bush's war on terrorism, even when some of the president's actions seemed to curtail civil liberties.

By contrast, the term *conservative* today is used to describe those who generally support the social and economic status quo and are suspicious of efforts to introduce new political formulas and economic arrangements. Conservatives believe strongly that a large and powerful government poses a threat to citizens' freedom. Thus, in the domestic arena, conservatives generally oppose the expansion of

 Rationality Principle

Ideologies serve as informational shortcuts, allowing individuals to arrive at a view on an issue or a candidate while economizing on the costs of becoming informed of the details.

liberal A liberal today generally supports political and social reform; extensive governmental intervention in the economy; the expansion of federal social services; more vigorous efforts on behalf of the poor, minorities, and women; and greater concern for consumers and the environment.

conservative Today this term refers to those who generally support the social and economic status quo and are suspicious of efforts to introduce new political formulas and economic arrangements. Many conservatives also believe that a large and powerful government poses a threat to citizens' freedoms.

governmental activity, asserting that solutions to social and economic problems can be developed in the private sector. Conservatives particularly oppose efforts to impose government regulation on business, pointing out that such regulation is frequently economically inefficient and costly and can ultimately lower the entire nation's standard of living. As to social and cultural positions, many conservatives oppose abortion and support school prayer. In international affairs, conservatism has come to mean support for the maintenance of American military power. Like liberalism, conservatism is far from a monolithic ideology. Some conservatives support many government social programs. Republican George W. Bush calls himself a "compassionate conservative" to indicate that he favors programs that assist the poor and needy. Other conservatives oppose efforts to outlaw abortion, arguing that government intrusion in this area is as misguided as government intervention in the economy. Such a position is sometimes called "libertarian." The real political world is far too complex to be seen in terms of a simple struggle between liberals and conservatives.

Liberal and conservative differences manifest themselves in a variety of contexts. For example, the liberal approach to increasing airline safety in October 2001 was to create a workforce of federal employees that would screen and inspect passenger luggage. The conservative approach was to call for better training of existing employees and supervision of private sector screeners. To some extent, contemporary liberalism and conservatism can be seen as differences of emphasis in regard to the fundamental American political values of liberty and equality. For liberals, equality is the most important of the core values. Liberals are willing to tolerate government intervention in such areas as college admissions and business decisions when these seem to result in high levels of race, class, or gender inequality. For conservatives, on the other hand, liberty is the core value. Conservatives oppose most efforts by the government, however well intentioned, to intrude into private life or the marketplace. This simple formula for distinguishing liberalism and conservatism is, of course, not always accurate because political ideologies seldom lend themselves to neat or logical characterizations.

Often political observers search for logical connections among the various positions identified with liberalism or with conservatism, and they are disappointed or puzzled when they are unable to find a set of coherent philosophical principles that define and unite the several elements of either of these sets of beliefs. On the liberal side, for example, what is the logical connection between opposition to U.S. government intervention in the affairs of foreign nations and calls for greater intervention in America's economy and society? On the conservative side, what is the logical relationship between opposition to governmental regulation of business and support for a ban on abortion? Indeed, the latter would seem to be just the sort of regulation of private conduct that conservatives claim to abhor.

Frequently, the relationships among the various elements of liberalism or the several aspects of conservatism are *political* rather than *logical*. One underlying basis of liberal views is that all or most represent criticisms of or attacks on the foreign and domestic policies and cultural values of the business and commercial strata that have been prominent in the United States for the past century. In some measure, the tenets of contemporary conservatism represent this elite's defense of its positions against its enemies, who include organized labor, minority groups, and some intellectuals and professionals. Thus liberals attack business and commercial elites by advocating more governmental regulation, including consumer protection and environmental regulation, opposition to military weapons programs, and support for expensive social programs. Conservatives counterattack by asserting that governmental regulation of the economy is ruinous and that military weapons are needed in a changing world.

Of course, it is important to note that many people who call themselves liberals or conservatives accept only part of the liberal or conservative ideology. Although it appears that Americans have adopted more conservative outlooks on some issues, their views in other areas have remained largely unchanged or even have become more liberal in recent years (see Table 9.5). Thus many individuals who are liberal on social issues are conservative on economic issues. There is certainly nothing illogical about these mixed positions. They simply indicate the relatively open and fluid character of American political debate.

PUBLIC OPINION AND POLITICAL KNOWLEDGE

As they read the newspapers, listen to the radio, watch television, and chat with their friends and associates, citizens are constantly confronted by new political events, issues, and personalities. Often, they will be asked what they think about a particular issue or whether they plan to support a particular candidate. Indeed, in our democracy, we expect every citizen to have views about the major problems of the day as well as opinions about who should be entrusted with the nation's leadership.

Some Americans know quite a bit about politics, and many have general views and hold opinions on several issues. Few Americans, though, devote sufficient time, energy, or attention to politics to really understand or evaluate the myriad issues with which they are bombarded on a regular basis. In fact, many studies have shown that the average American knows very little about politics. In one major study, for example, only 25 percent of respondents could name their two senators, only 29 percent could name their U.S. representative, and fewer than half knew that the Constitution's first ten amendments were called the Bill of Rights.[15] Evidence that half of America's citizens—particularly those who have not attended college—are so unaware of the nation's history and politics is troubling. And yet ignorance is probably a predictable and inevitable fact of political life. Some analysts have argued that political attentiveness is costly; it means spending time at the very least, and often money as well, to collect, organize, and digest political information.[16]

---

[15]Michael X. Delli Carpini and Scott Keeter, *What Americans Know about Politics and Why It Matters* (New Haven, CT: Yale University Press, 1996), pp. 307–28.

[16]Anthony Downs, *An Economic Theory of Democracy* (New York: Harper, 1957).

TABLE 9.5

Have Americans Become More Conservative?

How have Americans' political attitudes changed over time? How does people's liberalism or conservatism help shape their views of issues, events, or personalities? Can liberals and conservatives hold meaningful discussions?

QUESTION	PERCENTAGE RESPONDING YES										
	1972	1978	1980	1982	1984	1986	1988	1992	1996	1998	2000
Should the government help minority groups?	30	25	16	21	27	26	13	27	18	26	17
Should the government see to it that everyone has a job and a guaranteed standard of living?	27	17	22	25	28	25	24	30	24	30	22
Should abortion never be permitted?	9	10	8	13	13	13	12	12	13	12	12
Should the government provide fewer services and reduce spending?	NA*	NA	27	32	28	24	25	33	31	26	18

*NA: Not asked.

SOURCE: Center for Political Studies of the Institute for Social Research, University of Michigan. Data were made available through the Inter-University Consortium for Political and Social Research.

Rationality Principle

Some argue that the relatively high cost of political-information gathering makes staying uninformed rational and not surprising.

Balanced against this cost to an individual is the very low probability that he or she will, on the basis of this costly information, take an action that would not otherwise have been taken *and* that this departure in behavior will make a beneficial difference to him or her *and* that difference, if it exists, will exceed the cost of acquiring the information in the first place. That is, because individuals anticipate that informed actions taken by them will rarely make much difference while the costs of informing oneself are often not trivial, especially for those with little education to begin with, it is rational to remain ignorant. A more moderate version of "rational" ignorance recognizes that some kinds of information are inexpensive to acquire, such as sound bites from the evening news, or actually pleasant, such as reading the front page of the newspaper while drinking a cup of coffee. In these cases, an individual may become partially informed, but usually not in detail.

Precisely because becoming truly knowledgeable about politics requires a substantial investment of time and energy, many Americans seek to acquire political information and to make political decisions on the cheap, using shortcuts that seem to relieve them of having to engage in information gathering and evaluation. One "inexpensive" way to become informed is to take cues from trusted others—the local minister, the television commentator or newspaper editorialist, an interest-group leader, friends, and relatives.[17] Along the same lines, a common shortcut for political evaluation and decision making is to assess new issues and events through the lenses of one's general beliefs and orientations. Thus, if a conservative learns of a plan to expand federal social programs, he or she might express opposition to the endeavor without pondering the specific proposal. Similarly, if a liberal is told that President George W. Bush is backing a major overhaul of the Social Security system, he or she will probably not read thousands of pages of economic projections before asserting disapproval of the president's efforts.

Neither of these shortcuts, however, is entirely reliable. Taking cues from others may lead individuals to accept positions they would not support if they had more information. And general ideological orientations are usually poor guides to decision making in concrete instances. For one thing, especially when applied to discrete issues, most individuals' beliefs turn out to be filled with contradictions. For example, what position should a liberal take on immigration? Should a liberal favor keeping America's borders open to poor people from all over the world, or should a liberal be concerned that America's open borders create a pool of surplus labor that permits giant corporations to drive down the wages of poor American workers? Many other issues defy easy ideological characterization. What should liberals think about the intelligence reforms enacted by Congress in 2004? How should conservatives view America's military actions in Iraq? Each of these policies combines a mix of issues and is too complex to lend itself to simple ideological interpretation.

While understandable and, perhaps, inevitable, widespread inattentiveness to politics weakens American democracy in two ways. First, those who lack political information or resort to inadequate shortcuts to acquire and assess information cannot effectively defend their own political interests and can easily become victims or losers in political struggles. Second, the presence of large numbers of politically inattentive or ignorant individuals means that the political process can be more easily manipulated by the various institutions and forces that seek to shape public opinion.

As to the first of these problems, in our democracy, millions of ordinary citizens take part in political life, at least to the extent of voting in national elections. Those with little knowledge of the election's issues or candidates or procedures can find themselves acting against their own preferences and interests. One example is U.S.

[17]For a discussion of the role of information in democratic politics, see Arthur Lupia and Matthew D. McCubbins, *The Democratic Dilemma: Can Citizens Learn What They Need to Know?* (New York: Cambridge University Press, 1998).

America the Moderate?

Alexis de Tocqueville wrote in 1831 that "[t]he great advantage of Americans is that they have arrived at a state of democracy without having to endure a democratic revolution; and that they are born equal instead of becoming so."[1] America lacked feudalism and monarchy. It experienced neither conservative, reactionary movements nor radical social revolutionary movements. According to one classic description, American politics and American public opinion are essentially moderate, based on deep and lasting consensus about the essentials of American political and social life.[2] Today, however, the public is most often described as the "red and blue America," the "two Americas," and "one nation—divided."[3]

Which of these two pictures of the American public is most accurate? Do Americans continue to agree with each other on most political issues? Or have we become a nation divided against ourselves, hardened into opposing camps of rock-ribbed conservatives and left-wing liberals? The answer, as usual with public opinion, depends on *what issues* you are asking about and *whom you are asking.*

On the fundamental, core issues of democracy, Americans remain in substantial agreement. The vast majority endorse basic freedoms such as speech, religion, and nondiscrimination and the basic outlines of our capitalist economic system and democratic political system. While many Americans lack confidence in our current political leaders, overwhelming majorities endorse our major political and social institutions, such as Congress, the Presidency, the Supreme Court, and even the military. And most Americans agree that our political system is democratic and fair and that our political institutions are not in need of major reform.[4] All this lends an inherent stability to American politics.

But what of the "red and blue America"? Perhaps Americans agree on the fundamentals, but when it comes to current political issues, such as the budget deficit, the war in Iraq, or oil drilling in Alaska, isn't public opinion deeply divided? Not according to political scientist Morris Fiorina. Fiorina compares public opinion in the red and blue states across a wide variety of political and social issues and finds, perhaps surprisingly, that there are few statistically significant differences. Most Americans—blue and red—wish taxes were lower and are skeptical of government spending. Most—blue and red—support the death penalty and English as the official language and oppose job discrimination on the basis of sexual preference. In Fiorina's words, "[T]here are numerous similarities . . . some differences . . . but little that calls to mind the portrait of a culture war between these states."[5]

But even if American public opinion is not divided, American election results are. According to one political scientist, "The two political parties in Congress are as ideologically divergent as they have been at any point in the last three decades."[6] The red and blue map, especially when examined by county, paints a picture of a deeply divided nation.[7] Still, some challenge even this picture. Princeton computer scientist Robert Van-

History Principle

Americans' moderate political beliefs reflect the essentially egalitarian history of our society.

Collective-Action Principle

There has never been much support for radical changes to American democracy because the vast majority of Americans approve of the system.

derbei produced a "purple" map that shows that there are few sections in America which voted overwhelmingly for Bush or Kerry and that most were divided relatively evenly.[8]

Finally, *whom* you ask matters as well. Here the portrait of a divided America is more apparent. African Americans continue to be substantially more liberal than white Americans and voted for Kerry at an 88 percent clip. In contrast, white Americans who identify themselves as evangelical Christians and who attend church regularly are far more conservative, particularly on social issues. Eighty-four percent of these citizens voted for George W. Bush. And citizens who call themselves "strong" Democrats or Republicans—the same citizens who make up the bulk of voters in primaries and who supply the activist pool for candidates during elections—have become far more divided on a host of political and social issues.[9]

For some, the problem with American politics today stems from the distance between a polarized, divided set of political elites and a moderate but increasingly disaffected mainstream. This has led to suggestions for electoral reforms, such as open primaries, proportional representation or public financing of elections, or the emergence of a "radical center" that would reshape the direction of American politics.[10] The problem with these suggestions is that Americans, dissatisfied though they may be with current political debate, remain resolutely in favor of the status quo. There is little evidence that this moderate America is due for a change.

 Rationality Principle
Partisan divides between African Americans and white Americans or between more and less religious Americans can be traced to their differing policy beliefs.

Policy Principle
Election rules in America encourage political elites to highlight differences as a way to win elections

[1]Alexis de Tocqueville, *Democracy in America* (1831).

[2]Louis Hartz, *The Liberal Tradition in America* (1955).

[3]After the 2000 presidential contest, it became popular to categorize regions of the nation as "red" (Republican) and "blue" (Democratic) and to produce maps that illustrated the differences. See Liz Mariantes, "Inside Red and Blue America: A Look at America's Polarized Electorate," *Christian Science Monitor,* 14–18 July 2004; Stanley Greenberg, *The Two Americas: Our Current Political Deadlock and How to Break It* (New York: Thomas Dunne, 2004); and Mike Litwin, "One Nation—Divided under Bush," *Rocky Mountain News,* 20 January 2005.

[4]See John Hibbing and Elizabeth Theiss-Morse, *What Is It about Government That Americans Dislike?* (New York: Cambridge University Press, 2001).

[5]Morris Fiorina, *Culture War? The Myth of a Polarized America* (New York: Longman, 2005).

[6]Sean Theriault, "The Case of the Vanishing Moderates." Paper presented at the Annual Meeting of the Midwest Political Science Association, April 2003.

[7]The county-level red and blue map is available at www.usatoday.com/news/politicselections/vote2004/countymap.htm.

[8]Robert Vanderbei's "purple" map can be viewed at www.princeton.edu/~rvdb/JAVA/election2004/.

[9]Geoffrey Layman, "Culture Wars in the American Party System: Religious and Cultural Change among Party Activists since 1972," *American Politics Quarterly* 27.1.

[10]Ted Halstead and Michael Lind, *The Radical Center* (New York: Anchor Books, 2001).

tax policy. Over the past several decades, the United States has substantially reduced the rate of taxation paid by its wealthiest citizens. Most recently, tax cuts signed into law by President Bush in 2001 provided a tax break mainly for the top 1 percent of the nation's wage earners while further tax cuts proposed by the president offer additional benefits to this privileged stratum. It is surprising, however, that polling data show that millions of middle-class and lower-middle-class Americans who do not stand to benefit from the president's tax cuts seem to favor them, nonetheless. The explanation for this odd statement of affairs appears to be lack of political knowledge. Millions of individuals who are unlikely to derive much advantage from President Bush's tax policy think they will. Political scientist Larry Bartels has called this phenomenon "misplaced self-interest."[18] Upper-bracket taxpayers, who are usually served by an army of financial advisers, are unlikely to suffer from this problem. Knowledge may not always translate into political power, but lack of knowledge is almost certain to translate into political weakness.

Policy Principle

Government policies disproportionately reflect the goals and interests of those with higher levels of income and education because these individuals tend to have more knowledge of politics and are more willing to act on it.

SHAPING OF OPINION: THE INFLUENCE OF POLITICAL LEADERS, PRIVATE GROUPS, AND THE MEDIA

The fact that many Americans are inattentive to politics and lack even basic political information renders public opinion and the political process more easily susceptible to manipulation. Three forces play especially important roles in shaping opinion. These are the government, organized groups, and the news media.

Collective-Action Principle

Widely held political ideas are usually the products of orchestrated campaigns by government, organized groups, or the media.

Government and the Shaping of Public Opinion

All governments attempt, to a greater or lesser extent, to influence, manipulate, or manage their citizens' beliefs. But the extent to which public opinion is actually affected by governmental public relations efforts is probably limited. The government—despite its size and relations efforts is probably limited. The government—despite its size and power—is only one source of information and evaluation in the United States. Very often, governmental claims are disputed by the media, by interest groups, and at times by opposing forces within the government itself. Often, too, governmental efforts to manipulate public opinion backfire when the public is made aware of the government's tactics. Thus, in 1971, the United States government's efforts to build popular support for the Vietnam War were hurt when CBS News aired its documentary *The Selling of the Pentagon*, which purported to reveal the extent and character of governmental efforts to sway popular sentiment. In this documentary, CBS demonstrated the tech-

[18]Larry M. Bartels, "Homer Gets a Tax Cut: Inequality and Public Policy in the American Mind, " paper prepared for presentation at the 2003 annual meeting of the American Political Science Association, Philadelphia, August.

niques, including planted news stories and faked film footage, that the government had used to misrepresent its activities in Vietnam. These revelations, of course, undermined popular trust in all governmental claims.

A hallmark of the Clinton administration was the steady use of techniques like those used in election campaigns to bolster popular enthusiasm for White House initiatives. The president established a political "war room," similar to the one that operated in his campaign headquarters, where representatives from all departments met daily to discuss and coordinate the president's public relations efforts. Many of the same consultants and pollsters who directed the successful Clinton campaign were also employed in the selling of the president's programs.[19]

Indeed, the Clinton White House made more sustained and systematic use of public-opinion polling than by previous administration. For example, during his presidency, Bill Clinton relied heavily on the polling firm of Penn & Schoen to help him decide which issues to emphasize and what strategies to adopt. During the 1995–96 budget battle with Congress, the White House commissioned polls almost every night to chart changes in public perceptions about the struggle. Poll data suggested to Clinton that he should present himself as struggling to save Medicare from Republican cuts. Clinton responded by launching a media attack against what he claimed were GOP efforts to hurt the elderly. This proved to be a successful strategy and helped Clinton defeat the Republican budget.[20]

After he assumed office in 2001, President George W. Bush asserted that political leaders should base their programs on their own conception of the public interest rather than the polls. This, however, did not mean that Bush ignored public opinion. Bush has relied on pollster Jan van Lohuizen to conduct a low-key operation, sufficiently removed from the limelight to allow the president to renounce polling while continuing to make use of survey data.[21] At the same time, the Bush White House developed an extensive public relations program, led by former presidential aide Karen P. Hughes, to bolster popular support for the president's policies. Hughes, working with conservative TV personality Mary Matalin, coordinated White House efforts to maintain popular support for the administration's war against terrorism. These efforts included presidential speeches, media appearances by administration officials, numerous press conferences, and thousands of press releases presenting the administration's views.[22] The White House also made a substantial effort to sway opinion in foreign countries, even sending officials to present the administration's views on television networks serving the Arab world.

Another example of a Bush administration effort to shape public opinion is a series of commercials it produced at taxpayer expense in 2004 to promote the

[19]Gerald F. Seib and Michael K. Frisby, "Selling Sacrifice," *Wall Street Journal*, 5 February 1993, p. 1.

[20]Michael K. Frisby, "Clinton Seeks Strategic Edge with Opinion Polls," *Wall Street Journal*, 24 June 1996, p. A16.

[21]Joshua Green, "The Other War Room," *Washington Monthly*, April 2002.

[22]Peter Marks, "Adept in Politics and Advertising, Four Women Shape a Campaign," *New York Times*, 11 November 2001, p. B6.

new Medicare prescription drug program. The commercials, prominently featuring the president, were designed to look like actual news stories and were aired in English and Spanish by hundreds of local television stations. Called a "video news release," this type of commercial is designed to give viewers the impression that they are watching a real news story. The presumption is that viewers are more likely to believe what they think is news coverage than material they know to be advertising. Democrats, of course, accused the administration of conducting a partisan propaganda campaign with public funds, but Republicans pointed out that the Clinton administration had engaged in similar practices.

In January 2005, it was revealed that the administration had paid conservative African American radio pundit Armstrong Williams to comment favorably on its education policies. Williams received $240,000 in taxpayer dollars for touting the administration's programs but never indicated that he had been paid for his support. Presumably, listeners were never aware that they were hearing what amounted to government propaganda disguised as editorial commentary.

Private Groups and the Shaping of Public Opinion

Collective-Action Principle

Part of the "job description" of leaders of well-organized interest groups is to seek out issues around which they can mobilize group members. Organized interests are decidedly at an advantage in this respect, compared to latent, unorganized interests.

We have already seen how the government tries to shape public opinion. But the ideas that become prominent in political life are also developed and spread by important economic and political groups searching for issues that will advance their causes. In some instances, private groups espouse values in which they truly believe in the hope of bringing others over to their side. Take, for example, the recent campaign against so-called partial birth abortion that resulted in the Partial Birth Abortion Ban Act of 2003. Proponents of the act believed that prohibiting particular sorts of abortions would be a first step toward eliminating all abortions—something they viewed as a moral imperative.[23] In other cases, however, groups will promote principles designed mainly to further hidden agendas of political and economic interests. One famous example is the campaign against cheap, imported handguns—the so-called Saturday night specials—covertly financed by the domestic manufacturers of more expensive firearms. The campaign's organizers claimed that cheap handguns pose a grave risk to the public and should be outlawed. The real goal, though, was not safeguarding the public but protecting the economic well-being of the domestic gun industry. A more recent example is the campaign against the alleged "sweatshop" practices of some American companies manufacturing their products in third world countries. This campaign is mainly financed by U.S. labor unions seeking to protect their members' jobs by discouraging American firms from manufacturing their products abroad.

Typically, ideas are marketed most effectively by groups with access to financial resources, public or private institutional support, and sufficient skill or education to select, develop, and draft ideas that will attract interest and support. Thus the development and promotion of conservative themes and ideas in recent years

[23]Cynthia Gorney, "Gambling with Abortion," *Harper's* (November 2004): 33–46.

have been greatly facilitated by the millions of dollars that conservative corporations and business organizations such as the Chamber of Commerce and the Public Affairs Council spend each year on public information and what is now called in corporate circles "issues management." In addition, conservative business leaders have contributed millions of dollars to such conservative institutions as the Heritage Foundation, the Hoover Institution, and the American Enterprise Institute.[24] Many of the ideas that helped those on the right influence political debate were first developed and articulated by scholars associated with institutions such as these.

Although they do not usually have access to financial assets that match those available to their conservative opponents, liberal intellectuals and professionals have ample organizational skills; access to the media; and practice in creating, communicating, and using ideas. During the past three decades, the chief vehicle through which liberal intellectuals and professionals have advanced their ideas has been the "public interest group," an institution that relies heavily on voluntary contributions of time, effort, and interest on the part of its members. Through groups like Common Cause, the National Organization for Women, the Sierra Club, Friends of the Earth, and Physicians for Social Responsibility, intellectuals and professionals have been able to use their organizational skills and educational resources to develop and promote ideas.[25] Often, research conducted in universities and in liberal "think tanks" such as the Brookings Institution provides the ideas on which liberal politicians rely. For example, the welfare reform plan introduced by the Clinton administration in 1994 originated with the work of former Harvard professor David Ellwood. Ellwood's academic research led him to the conclusion that the nation's welfare system would be improved if services to the poor were expanded in scope but limited in duration. His idea was adopted by the 1992 Clinton campaign, which was searching for a position on welfare that would appeal to both liberal and conservative Democrats. The Ellwood plan seemed perfect: It promised liberals an immediate expansion of welfare benefits, yet it held out to conservatives the idea that welfare recipients would receive benefits for only a limited time. The Clinton welfare reform plan even borrowed phrases from Ellwood's book *Poor Support*.[26]

Journalist and author Joe Queenan has correctly observed that although political ideas can erupt spontaneously, they almost never do. Instead, he says,

> issues are usually manufactured by tenured professors and obscure employees of think tanks. . . . It is inconceivable that the American people, all by themselves, could independently arrive at the conclusion that the depletion of the ozone

[24]See David Vogel, "The Power of Business in America: A Reappraisal," *British Journal of Political Science* 13 (January 1983), pp. 19–44.

[25]See David Vogel, "The Public Interest Movement and the American Reform Tradition," *Political Science Quarterly* 96 (winter 1980), pp. 607–27.

[26]Jason DeParle, "The Clinton Welfare Bill Begins Trek in Congress," *New York Times*, 15 July 1994, p. 1.

layer poses a dire threat to our national well-being, or that an immediate, across-the-board cut in the capital-gains tax is the only thing that stands between us and the economic abyss. The American people do not have that kind of sophistication. *They have to have help.*[27]

The Media and Public Opinion

The communications media are among the most powerful forces operating in the marketplace of ideas. The mass media are not simply neutral messengers for ideas developed by others. Instead, the media have an enormous effect on popular attitudes and opinions. Over time, the ways in which the mass media report political events help shape the underlying attitudes and beliefs from which opinions emerge.[28] For example, for the past thirty years, the national news media have relentlessly investigated personal and official wrongdoing on the part of politicians and public officials. This continual media presentation of corruption in government and venality in politics has undoubtedly fostered the general attitude of cynicism and distrust that exists in the general public.

At the same time, the ways in which media coverage interprets or frames specific events can have a major impact on popular responses and opinions about these events.[29] Because media framing can be important, the Bush administration sought to persuade broadcasters to follow its lead in its coverage of terrorism and America's response to terrorism in the months after the September 11 attacks. Broadcasters, who found themselves targets of anthrax-contaminated letters apparently mailed by terrorists, needed little persuasion. For the most part, the media praised the president for his leadership and presented the administration's military campaign in Afghanistan and domestic antiterrorist efforts in a positive light. Even newspapers like the *New York Times*, which had strongly opposed Bush in the 2000 election and questioned his fitness for the presidency, asserted that he had grown into the job. In the aftermath of the 2003 Iraq war, however, media coverage of the Bush administration became more critical. Formerly supportive media accused the president of failing both to anticipate the chaos and violence of postwar Iraq and to develop a strategy that would allow America to extricate itself from its involvement in Iraq. The president, for his part, accused the media of failing to present an accurate picture of his administration's success in Iraq.

The extent to which some journalists opposed the president became apparent during the 2004 presidential election. Long-time CBS anchor Dan Rather presented a report charging that years earlier President Bush had shirked his Air National Guard duties and allowed evidence of this fact to be concealed. The re-

[27]Joe Queenan, "Birth of a Notion," *Washington Post*, 20 September 1992, p. C1.
[28]John Zaller, *The Nature and Origins of Mass Opinion* (New York: Cambridge University Press, 1992).
[29]See Shanto Iyengar, *Is Anyone Responsible? How Television Frames Political Issues* (Chicago: University of Chicago Press, 1991); Shanto Iyengar, *Do the Media Govern?* (Thousand Oaks, CA: Sage, 1997).

port was aired just before the election and was almost certainly calculated to damage the president's political fortunes. It soon emerged, however, that Rather and CBS had failed to verify the account they presented and, indeed, could not substantiate the charges against Bush. Rather had apparently been so anxious to attack the president before the election that he rushed in front of the cameras without checking his sources. Subsequently, Rather announced his retirement and several CBS news executives were fired. Though the extent to which this situation helped or hindered his campaign cannot be measured, Bush, of course, was reelected.

The efforts of the government, private groups, and the media would almost certainly affect public opinion even if Americans were knowledgeable about politics and possessed the analytic abilities of philosophers. But widespread political ignorance makes the task of those who wish to manipulate opinion all the easier. Perhaps even a more sophisticated public might have believed the government's false claims that Iraq possessed weapons of mass destruction, but an uninformed public was easily persuaded. Indeed, tens of millions of Americans continued to believe Iraq had WMDs even after this claim had been definitively disproved.[30] Perhaps a more attentive public would have understood that most Americans would not benefit from recently enacted tax changes, but a naive public was easily misled. Perhaps a more astute public would see through efforts by interest groups and the media to mask hidden agendas and selfish interests behind campaigns purporting to serve higher goals, but a credulous public was easily deceived. All in all, Americans' lack of political interest and awareness makes public opinion an easy target for manipulation.

MEASURING PUBLIC OPINION

As recently as fifty years ago, American political leaders gauged public opinion by people's applause and by the presence of crowds at meetings. This direct exposure to the people's views did not necessarily produce accurate knowledge of public opinion. It did, however, give political leaders confidence in their public support—and therefore confidence in their ability to govern by consent.

Abraham Lincoln and Stephen Douglas debated each other seven times in the summer and autumn of 1858, two years before they became presidential nominees. Their debates took place before audiences in parched cornfields and courthouse squares. A century later, most presidential debates, although seen by millions, take place before a few reporters and technicians in television studios that might as well be on the moon. The public's response cannot be experienced directly. This distance between leaders and followers is one of the agonizing problems of modern democracy. The media send information to millions of people, but they are not yet as efficient at getting information back to leaders. Is government by consent possible

---

[30]Mark Danner, "How Bush Really Won," *New York Review*, 13 January 2005, p. 51.

where the scale of communication is so large and impersonal? To compensate for the decline in their ability to experience public opinion for themselves, leaders have turned to science, in particular to the science of opinion polling.

It is no secret that politicians and public officials make extensive use of **public opinion polls** to help them decide whether to run for office, what policies to support, how to vote on important legislation, and what types of appeals to make in their campaigns. President Lyndon Johnson was famous for carrying the latest Gallup and Roper poll results in his pocket, and it is widely believed that he began to withdraw from politics because the polls reported losses in public support. All recent presidents and other major political figures have worked closely with polls and pollsters.

Constructing Public Opinion from Surveys

The population in which pollsters are interested is usually quite large. To conduct their polls, they first choose a **sample** of the total population. The selection of this sample is important. Above all, it must be representative. The views of those in the sample must accurately and proportionately reflect the views of the whole. To a large extent, the validity of the poll's results depends on the sampling procedure used.

Sampling Techniques and Selection Bias   The most common techniques for choosing such a sample are probability sampling and random digit dialing. In the case of **probability sampling**, the pollster begins with a listing of the population to be surveyed. This listing is called the "sampling frame." After each member of the population is assigned a number, a table of random numbers or a computerized random selection process is used to pick those to be surveyed. This technique is appropriate when the entire population can be identified. For example, all students registered at Texas colleges and universities can be identified from college records, and a sample of them can easily be drawn. When the pollster is interested in a national sample of Americans, however, this technique is not feasible, as no complete list of Americans exists.[31] National samples are usually drawn using a technique called **random digit dialing**. A computer random number generator is used to produce a list of as many ten-digit numbers as the pollster deems necessary. Given that more than 95 percent of American households have telephones, this technique usually results in a random national sample.

The importance of sampling was brought home early in the history of political polling. A 1936 *Literary Digest* poll predicted that Republican presidential candidate Alf Landon would defeat Democrat Franklin D. Roosevelt in that year's presidential election. The actual election, of course, ended in a Roosevelt landslide. The main problem with the survey was what it called **selection bias** in drawing the sample. The pollsters had relied on telephone directories and automobile registration rosters to produce a sampling frame. During the Great Depression, only wealthier

---

[31]Herbert Asher, *Polling and the Public* (Washington, DC: Congressional Quarterly Press, 2001), p. 64.

public opinion polls   Scientific instruments for measuring public opinion.

sample   A small group selected by researchers to represent the most important characteristics of an entire population.

probability sampling   A method used by pollsters to select a representative sample in which every individual in the population has an equal probability of being selected as a respondent.

random digit dialing   Polls in which respondents are selected at random from a list of ten-digit telephone numbers, with every effort made to avoid bias in the construction of the sample.

Americans owned telephones and automobiles. Thus the millions of working-class Americans who constituted Roosevelt's principle base of support were excluded from the sample. A more recent instance of polling error caused by selection bias was the 1998 Minnesota gubernatorial election. A poll conducted by the *Minneapolis Star Tribune* just six weeks before the election showed Jesse Ventura running a distant third to Democratic candidate Hubert Humphrey III, who seemed to have the support of 49 percent of the electorate, and the Republican Norm Coleman, whose support stood at 29 percent. Only 10 percent of those polled said they were planning to vote for Ventura. On election day, of course, Ventura outpolled both Humphrey and Coleman. Analysis of exit-poll data showed why the preelection polls had been so wrong. In an effort to be more accurate, preelection pollsters' predictions often take account of the likelihood that respondents will actually vote. This is accomplished by polling only people who have voted in the past or correcting for past frequency of voting. The *Star Tribune* poll was conducted only among individuals who had voted in the previous election. Ventura, however, brought to the polls not only individuals who had not voted in the last election but many people who had never voted before in their lives. Approximately 12 percent of Minnesota's voters in 1998 said they came to the polls only because Ventura was on the ballot. This surge in turnout was facilitated by the fact that Minnesota permits same-day voter registration. Thus the pollsters were wrong because Ventura changed the composition of the electorate.[32]

In recent years, the issue of selection bias has been further complicated by the fact that growing numbers of individuals refuse to answer pollsters' questions or use such devices as answering machines and Caller ID to screen unwanted callers. If pollsters could be certain that those who responded to their surveys simply reflected the views of those who refused to respond, there would be no problem. Some studies, however, suggest that the views of respondents and nonrespondents can differ, especially along social class lines. Middle- and upper-middle-class individuals are more likely to be willing to respond to surveys than their working-class counterparts.[33] Thus far, "nonresponse bias" has not undermined a major national survey, but the possibility of a future *Literary Digest* fiasco should not be ignored.

Sample Size   The degree of reliability in polling is also a function of sample size. The same sample is needed to represent a small population as to represent a large population. The typical size of a sample ranges from 450 to 1,500 respondents. This number, however, reflects a trade-off between cost and degree of precision desired. The degree of accuracy that can be achieved with even a small sample can be seen from the polls' success in predicting election outcomes. The chance that the sample used does not accurately represent the population from which it is drawn is called the ***sampling error*** or *margin of error*. A typical survey

selection bias
Polling error that arises when the sample is not representative of the population being studied, creating errors by over-representing or underrepresenting some opinions.

sampling error
Polling error that arises based on the small size of the sample.

[32]Carl Cannon, "A Pox on Both Our Parties," in *The Enduring Debate*, ed. David C. Canon et al. (New York: Norton, 2000), p. 389.

[33]John Goyder, Keith Warriner, and Susan Miller, "Evaluating Socio-Economic Status Bias in Survey Nonresponse," *Journal of Official Statistics* 18, no. 1 (2002).

of 1,500 respondents will have a sampling error of approximately 3 percent. When a preelection poll indicates 51 percent of voters surveyed favor the Republican candidate and 49 percent support the Democratic candidate, the outcome is too close to call because it is within the margin of error of the survey. A figure of 51 percent means that between 54 and 48 percent of voters in the population favor the Republicans, while a figure of 49 percent indicates that between 52 and 46 percent of all voters support the Democrats. Thus, in this example, a 52–48 percent Democratic victory would still be consistent with polls predicting a 51–49 percent Republican triumph.

Table 9.6 shows how accurate two of the major national polling organizations have been in predicting the outcomes of presidential elections. Pollsters have been mostly correct in their predictions.

Survey Design   Even with reliable sample procedures, surveys may fail to reflect the true distribution of opinion within a target population. One frequent source of *measurement error* is the wording of survey questions. The precise words used in a question can have an enormous effect on the answers it elicits. The validity of survey results can also be adversely affected by poor question format, faulty ordering of questions, inappropriate vocabulary, ambiguity of questions, or questions with built-in biases. Often, seemingly minor differences in the wording of a question can convey vastly different meanings to respondents and thus produce quite different response patterns (see Figure 9.4). For example, for many years the University of Chicago's National Opinion Research Center has asked respondents whether they think the federal government is spending too much, too little, or about the right amount of money on "assistance for the poor." Answering the question posed this way, about two thirds of all respondents seem to believe that the government is spending too little. However, the same survey also asks whether the government spends too much, too little, or about the right amount for "welfare." When the word *welfare* is substituted for *assistance for the poor*, about half of all respondents indicate that too much is being spent.[34]

Push Polling   In recent years, a new form of bias has been introduced into surveys by the use of a technique called *push polling*. This technique involves asking a respondent a loaded question about a political candidate designed to elicit the response sought by the pollster and, simultaneously, to shape the respondent's perception of the candidate in question. For example, during the 1996 New Hampshire presidential primary, push pollsters employed by the campaign of one of Lamar Alexander's rivals called thousands of voters to ask, "If you knew that Lamar Alexander had raised taxes six times in Tennessee, would you be less inclined or more inclined to support him?"[35] More than 100 consulting firms

measurement error   Failure to identify the true distribution of opinion within a population because of errors such as ambiguous or poorly worded questions.

push polling   A polling technique in which the questions are designed to shape the respondent's opinion.

[34]Michael Kagay and Janet Elder, "Numbers Are No Problem for Pollsters, Words Are," *New York Times*, 9 August 1992, p. E6.

[35]Donn Tibbetts, "Draft Bill Requires Notice of Push Polling," *Manchester Union Leader*, 3 October 1996, p. A6.

TABLE 9.6

Two Pollsters and Their Records, 1948–2004*			
	HARRIS	GALLUP	ACTUAL OUTCOME
2004			
Bush, G. W.	49%	49%	51%
Kerry	48	49	48
Nader	1	1	0
2000			
Bush	47%	48%	48%
Gore	47	46	49
Nader	5	4	3
1996			
Clinton	51%	52%	49%
Dole	39	41	41
Perot	9	7	8
1992			
Clinton	44%	44%	43%
Bush, G. H. W.	38	37	38
Perot	17	14	19
1988			
Bush, G. H. W.	51%	53%	54%
Dukakis	47	42	46
1984			
Reagan	56%	59%	59%
Mondale	44	41	41
1980			
Reagan	48%	47%	51%
Carter	43	44	41
Anderson		8	
1976			
Carter	48%	48%	51%
Ford	45	49	48
1972			
Nixon	59%	62%	61%
McGovern	35	38	38
1968			
Nixon	40%	43%	43%
Humphrey	43	42	43
Wallace	13	15	14
1964			
Johnson	62%	64%	61%
Goldwater	33	36	39
1960			
Kennedy	49%	51%	50%
Nixon	41	49	49
1956			
Eisenhower	NA	60%	58%
Stevenson		41	42
1952			
Eisenhower	47%	51%	55%
Stevenson	42	49	44
1948			
Truman	NA	44.5%	49.6%
Dewey		49.5	45.1

*All figures except those for 1948 are rounded. NA = Not asked.
SOURCE: Data from the Gallup Poll and the Harris Survey (New York: Chicago Tribune–New York News Syndicate, various press releases, 1964–2004). Courtesy of the Gallup Organization and Louis Harris Associates.

FIGURE 9.4

It Depends on How You Ask

The Question
President Clinton has proposed setting aside approximately two thirds of an expected budget surplus to fix the Social Security system. What do you think the leaders in Washington should do with the remainder of the surplus?

Variation 1: Should the money be used for a tax cut or should it be used to fund new government programs?

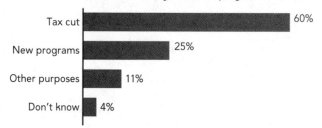

Tax cut	60%
New programs	25%
Other purposes	11%
Don't know	4%

Variation 2: Should the money be used for a tax cut or should it be spent on programs for education, the environment, health care, crime fighting, and military defense?

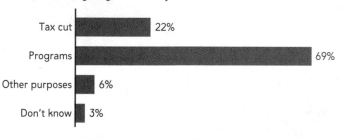

Tax cut	22%
Programs	69%
Other purposes	6%
Don't know	3%

SOURCE: Pew Research Center, reported in the *New York Times*, 30 January 2000.

across the nation now specialize in push polling.[36] Calling push polling the "political equivalent of a drive-by shooting," Representative Joe Barton (R-Tex.) launched a congressional investigation into the practice.[37] Push polls may be one reason that Americans are becoming increasingly skeptical about the practice of polling and increasingly unwilling to answers pollsters' questions.[38]

[36]"Dial S for Smear," *Memphis Commercial Appeal*, 22 September 1996, p. 6B.
[37]Amy Keller, "Subcommittee Launches Investigation of Push Polls," *Roll Call*, 3 October 1996, p. 1.
[38]For a discussion of the growing difficulty of persuading people to respond to surveys, see John Brehm, *Phantom Respondents* (Ann Arbor: University of Michigan Press, 1993).

Illusion of Saliency   In the early days of a political campaign when voters are asked which candidates they do, or do not, support, the answer they give often has little significance, because the choice is not yet important to them. Their preferences may change many times before the actual election. This is part of the explanation for the phenomenon of the postconvention "bounce" in the popularity of presidential candidates, which was observed after the Democratic and Republican national conventions in 1992 and 1996.[39] Respondents' preferences reflected the amount of attention a candidate had received during the conventions rather than strongly held views.

Salient interests are interests that stand out beyond others, that are of more than ordinary concern to respondents in a survey or to voters in the electorate. Politicians, social scientists, journalists, or pollsters who assume something is important to the public when in fact it is not are creating an ***illusion of saliency.*** This illusion can be created and fostered by polls despite careful controls over sampling, interviewing, and data analysis. In fact, the illusion is strengthened by the credibility that science gives survey results.

The problem of saliency has become especially acute as a result of the proliferation of media polls. The television networks and major national newspapers all make heavy use of opinion polls. Increasingly, polls are being commissioned by local television stations and local and regional newspapers as well.[40] On the positive side, polls allow journalists to make independent assessments of political realities—assessments not influenced by the partisan claims of politicians.

At the same time, however, media polls can allow journalists to make news when none really exists. Polling diminishes journalists' dependence on news makers. A poll commissioned by a news agency can provide the basis for a good story even when candidates, politicians, and other news makers refuse to cooperate by engaging in newsworthy activities. Thus on days when little or nothing is actually taking place in a political campaign, poll results, especially apparent changes in candidate popularity margins, can provide exciting news. Several times during the 2004 presidential campaign, for example, small changes in the relative standing of the Democratic and Republican candidates produced banner headlines around the country. Stories about what the candidates actually did or said often took second place to reporting the "horse race."

Because rapid and dramatic shifts in candidate margins tend to take place when voters' preferences are least fully formed, it is interesting that horse-race news is most likely to make the headlines when it is actually least significant.[41] In other words, media interest in poll results is inversely related to the actual salience of voters' opinions and the significance of the polls' findings. However, by influencing perceptions, especially those of major contributors, media polls can influence political realities.

salient interests
Attitudes and views that are especially important to the individual holding them.

illusion of saliency   The impression conveyed by polls that something is important to the public when actually it is not.

---

[39]See Richard Morin, "Is Bush's Bounce a Boom or a Bust?" *Washington Post National Weekly Edition*, 31 August–6 September 1992, p. 37.

[40]See Thomas E. Mann and Gary Orren, eds., *Media Polls in American Politics* (Washington, DC: Brookings, 1992).

[41]For an excellent and reflective discussion by a journalist, see Richard Morin, "Clinton Slide in Survey Shows Perils of Polling," *Washington Post*, 29 August 1992, p. A6.

Bandwagon Effect   The most noted, but least serious, of polling problems is the *bandwagon effect,* which occurs when polling results influence people to support the candidate marked as the probable victor. Some scholars argue that this bandwagon effect can be offset by an "underdog effect" in favor of the candidate who is trailing in the polls.[42] However, a candidate who demonstrates a lead in the polls usually finds it considerably easier to raise campaign funds than a candidate whose poll standing is poor. With these additional funds, poll leaders can often afford to pay for television time and other campaign activities that will cement their advantage.

Public Opinion, Political Knowledge, and the Political Uncertainty Principle

Many people are distressed to find public opinion polls not only unable to discover public opinion but unable to avoid producing unintentional distortions of their own. No matter how hard pollsters try, no matter how mature the science of opinion polling becomes, politicians forever may remain largely ignorant of public opinion.

Although knowledge is good for its own sake, and knowledge of public opinion may sometimes produce better government, ignorance also has its uses. It can, for example, operate as a restraint on the use of power. Leaders who think they know what the public wants are often autocratic rulers. Leaders who realize that they are always partially in the dark about the public are likely to be more modest in their claims, less intense in their demands, and more uncertain in their uses of power. Their uncertainty may make them more accountable to their constituencies because they will be more likely to continue searching for consent.

One of the most valuable benefits of survey research is actually "negative knowledge"—knowledge that pierces through irresponsible claims about the breadth of opinion or the solidarity of group or mass support. Because this sort of knowledge reveals the complexity and uncertainty of public opinion, it can help make citizens less gullible, group leaders less strident, and politicians less deceitful. This alone gives public opinion research, despite its great limitations, an important place in the future of American politics.[43]

HOW DOES PUBLIC OPINION INFLUENCE GOVERNMENT POLICY?

One of the fundamental notions on which the U.S. government was founded is that "the public" should not be trusted when it comes to governing. The framers designed institutions that, although democratic, somewhat insulated government

---

[42]See Michael Traugott, "The Impact of Media Polls on the Public," in *Media Polls in American Politics,* ed. Mann and Orren, pp. 125–49.

[43]For a fuller discussion of the uses of polling and the role of public opinion in American politics, see Benjamin Ginsberg, *The Captive Public: How Mass Opinion Promotes State Power* (New York: Basic Books, 1986).

decision making from popular pressure. For example, the indirect elections of senators and presidents were supposed to prevent the government from being too dependent on the vagaries of public opinion.

Research from the 1950s and 1960s indicates that the framers' concerns were well founded. Individual-level survey analysis reveals that the respondents lacked fundamental political knowledge and had ill-formed opinions about government and public policy.[44] Their answers seemed nothing more than "doorstep opinions"—opinions given off the top of their heads. When an individual was asked the same questions at different times, he or she often gave different answers. The dramatic and unpredictable changes seemed to imply that the public was indeed unreliable as a guide for political decisions.

Benjamin I. Page and Robert Y. Shapiro take issue with the notion that the public should not be trusted when it comes to policy making.[45] They contend that public opinion at the aggregate level is coherent and stable, and that it moves in a predictable fashion in response to changing political, economic, and social circumstances.

How is this possible, given what previous studies have found? Page and Shapiro hypothesize that the individual-level responses are plagued with various types of errors that make the people's opinions seem incoherent and unstable. However, when a large number of individual-level responses to survey questions are added up to produce an aggregate public opinion, the errors or "noise" in the individual responses, if more or less random, will cancel each other out, revealing a collective opinion that is stable, coherent, and meaningful. From their results, Page and Shapiro conclude that the general public can indeed be trusted when it comes to governing.

In democratic nations, leaders should pay heed to public opinion, and most evidence suggests that they do. There are many instances in which public policy and public opinion do not coincide, but in general the government's actions are consistent with citizens' preferences. One study, for example, found that between 1935 and 1979, in about two thirds of all cases, significant changes in public opinion were followed within one year by changes in government policy consistent with the shift in the popular mood.[46] Other studies have come to similar conclusions about public opinion and government policy at the state level.[47] Do these results imply that elected leaders merely pander to public opinion? The answer is no.

A recent study on the role that public opinion played during the failed attempt to enact health-care reform during 1993–94 found that public opinion polls had very little influence on individual members of Congress, who used these polls first to justify positions they had already adopted and then to shape public thinking on the issue. In other words, opinion and policy were related because policy makers

---

[44]Campbell et al., *The American Voter;* Philip E. Converse, "The Nature of Belief Systems in Mass Publics," in *Ideology and Discontent*, ed. David E. Apter (New York: Free Press, 1964).

[45]Benjamin I. Page and Robert Y. Shapiro, *The Rational Public: Fifty Years of Trends in Americans' Policy Preferences* (Chicago: University of Chicago Press, 1992).

[46]Benjamin I. Page and Robert Y. Shapiro, "Effects of Public Opinion on Policy," *American Political Science Review* 77 (March 1983): 175–90.

[47]Robert S. Erikson, Gerald C. Wright, and John P. McIver, *Statehouse Democracy: Public Opinion and Policy in the American States* (New York: Cambridge University Press, 1993).

shaped opinion to support paths they already planned to take. This pattern is consistent with the opinion-manipulation efforts we examined earlier in the chapter. However, the study also found that congressional party leaders designed their health-care legislation strategies based on their concerns about the effects of public opinion on the electoral fortunes of individual members. Leaders' concerns about public opinion thus help explain why the congressional policy-making process follows public opinion, even though individual members of Congress do not.[48]

There are always areas of disagreement between opinion and policy. For example, the majority of Americans favored stricter governmental control of handguns for years before Congress finally adopted the modest restrictions on firearms purchases embodied in the 1994 Brady Bill and the Omnibus Crime Control Act. Similarly, most Americans—blacks as well as whites—oppose school busing to achieve racial balance, yet such busing continues to be used in many parts of the nation. Most Americans are far less concerned with the rights of the accused than the federal courts seem to be. Most Americans oppose U.S. military intervention in other nations' affairs, yet such interventions continue to take place and often win public approval after the fact.

Several factors can contribute to a lack of consistency between opinion and governmental policy. First, the nominal majority on a particular issue may not be as intensely committed to its preference as the adherents of the minority viewpoint. An intensely committed minority may often be more willing to commit its time, energy, efforts, and resources to the affirmation of its opinions than an apathetic, even if large, majority. In the case of firearms, for example, although the proponents of gun control are by a wide margin in the majority, most do not regard the issue as one of critical importance to themselves and are not willing to commit much effort to advancing their cause. The opponents of gun control, by contrast, are intensely committed, well organized, and well financed and as a result are usually able to carry the day.

A second important reason that public policy and public opinion may not coincide has to do with the character and structure of the American system of government. The framers of the American Constitution, as we saw in Chapter 2, sought to create a system of government that was based on popular consent but that did not invariably and automatically translate shifting popular sentiments into public policies. As a result, the American governmental process includes arrangements such as an appointed judiciary that can produce policy decisions that may run contrary to prevailing popular sentiment—at least for a time.

Perhaps the inconsistencies between opinion and policy could be resolved if we made broader use of a mechanism currently employed by a number of states—the ballot initiative. This procedure allows propositions to be placed on the ballot and voted into law by the electorate, bypassing most of the normal machinery of representative government. In recent years, several important propositions sponsored by business and conservative groups have been enacted.[49] For example, California's

Institution Principle

Policy and opinion are not always consistent because policy is the product of institutional processes and public opinion is but one of many influences on these.

[48]Lawrence R. Jacobs, Eric D. Lawrence, Robert Y. Shapiro, and Steven S. Smith, "Congressional Leadership of Public Opinion," *Political Science Quarterly* 113 (1998): 21–41.

[49]David S. Broder, *Democracy Derailed: Initiative Campaigns and the Power of Money* (New York: Harcourt, 2000).

Proposition 209, approved by the state's voters in 1996, prohibited the state and local government agencies in California from using race or gender preferences in hiring, contracting, or university admissions decisions. Responding to conservatives' success, liberal groups launched a number of ballot initiatives in 2000. For example, in Washington State, voters were asked to consider propositions sponsored by teachers unions that would have required annual cost-of-living raises for teachers and more than $1.8 billion in additional state spending over the next six years.[50]

Initiatives such as these seem to provide the public with an opportunity to express its will. The major problem, however, is that government by initiative offers little opportunity for reflection and compromise. Voters are presented with a proposition, usually sponsored by a special interest group, and are asked to take it or leave it. Perhaps the true will of the people, not to mention their best interest, might lie somewhere between the positions taken by various interest groups. Perhaps, for example, California voters might have wanted affirmative action programs to be modified, but not scrapped altogether as Proposition 209 mandated. In a representative assembly, as opposed to a referendum campaign, a compromise position might have been achieved that was more satisfactory to all the residents of the state. This is one reason the framers of the U.S. Constitution strongly favored representative government rather than direct democracy.[51]

When all is said and done, however, there can be little doubt that in general the actions of the American government do not remain out of line with popular sentiment for very long. A major reason for this is, of course, the electoral process, to which we shall next turn. Lest we become too complacent, however, we should not forget that the close relationship between government and opinion in America may also partly be a result of the government's success in molding opinion.

SUMMARY

All governments claim to obey public opinion, and in the democracies politicians and political leaders actually try to do so.

The American government does not directly regulate opinions and beliefs in the sense that dictatorial regimes often do. Opinion is regulated by an institution that the government constructed and that it maintains—the marketplace of ideas. In this marketplace, opinions and ideas compete for support. In general, opinions supported by upper-class groups have a better chance of succeeding than those views that are mainly advanced by the lower classes.

Americans share a number of values and viewpoints but often classify themselves as liberal or conservative in their basic orientations. The meaning of these terms has changed greatly over the past century. Once liberalism meant opposition to big government. Today, liberals favor an expanded role for the government.

[50]Robert Tomsho, "Liberals Take a Cue from Conservatives: This Election, the Left Tries to Make Policy with Ballot Initiatives," *Wall Street Journal*, 6 November 2000, p. A12.

[51]For the classic treatment of take-it-or-leave-it referendums and initiatives, see Thomas Romer and Howard Rosenthal, "Political Resource Allocation, Controlled Agendas, and the Status Quo," *Public Choice* 33 (1978): 27–44.

Rationality Principle	Collective-Action Principle	Institution Principle	Policy Principle	History Principle
Objective political interests fuel individuals' political beliefs.

Ideologies serve as informational shortcuts, allowing individuals to arrive at a view on an issue or a candidate while economizing on the costs of becoming informed of the details.

Some argue that the relatively high cost of political-information gathering makes staying uninformed rational and not surprising. | Widely held political ideas are usually the products of orchestrated campaigns by government, organized groups, or the media.

Part of the "job description" of leaders of well-organized interest groups is to seek out issues around which they can mobilize group members. Organized interests are decidedly at an advantage in this respect, compared to latent, unorganized interests. | One reason why policy and opinion may not be consistent is that the United States is a representative government, not a direct democracy.

Policy and opinion are not always consistent because policy is the product of institutional processes and public opinion is but one of many influences on these. | Government policies disproportionately reflect the goals and interests of those with higher levels of income and education because these individuals tend to have more knowledge of politics and are more willing to act on it. | Since the 1960s, southern whites have become a major source of support for the Republican party. |

Once conservatism meant support for state power and aristocratic rule. Today, conservatives oppose government regulation, at least of business affairs.

Although the United States relies mainly on market mechanisms to regulate opinion, even our government intervenes to some extent, seeking to influence both particular opinions and, more important, the general climate of political opinion. Political leaders' increased distance from the public makes it difficult for them to gauge public opinion. Until recently, public opinion on some issues could be gauged better by studying mass behavior than by studying polls. Population characteristics are also useful in estimating public opinion on some subjects. Another approach is to go directly to the people. Two techniques are used: the impressionistic and the scientific. The impressionistic method relies on person-to-person communication, selective polling, or the use of bellwether districts. A person-to-person approach is quick, efficient, and inexpensive; but because it often depends on an immediate circle of associates, it can also limit awareness of new issues or unpleasant information. Selective polling usually involves interviewing a few people from different walks of life. Although risky, it has been used successfully to gauge public opinion. Bellwether districts are a popular means of predicting election outcomes. They are used by the media as well as by some candidates.

The scientific approach to learning public opinion is random sample polling. One advantage of random sample polling is that elections can be very accurately predicted; using a model of behavior, pollsters are often able to predict how voters will mark their ballots better than the voters themselves can predict. A second advantage is that polls provide information on the bases and conditions of voting decisions. They make it possible to assess trends in attitudes and the influence of ideology on attitudes.

There are also problems with polling, however. An illusion of central tendency can encourage politicians not to confront issues. The illusion of saliency, on the other hand, can encourage politicians to confront too many trivial issues. Even with scientific polling, politicians cannot be certain that they understand public opinion. Their recognition of this limitation, however, may function as a valuable restraint.

FOR FURTHER READING

Erikson, Robert S., and Kent L. Tedin. *American Public Opinion: Its Origins, Content, and Impact.* 6th ed. New York: Longman, 2001.

Gallup, George, and Saul Forbes Rae. *The Pulse of Democracy: The Public-Opinion Poll and How It Works.* New York: Simon & Schuster, 1940.

Ginsberg, Benjamin. *The Captive Public: How Mass Opinion Promotes State Power.* New York: Basic Books, 1986.

Herbst, Susan. *Numbered Voices: How Opinion Polling Has Shaped American Politics.* Chicago: University of Chicago Press, 1993.

Key, V. O. *Public Opinion and American Democracy.* New York: Knopf, 1961.

Lippmann, Walter. *Public Opinion.* New York: Harcourt, Brace, 1922.

Mueller, John. *Policy and Opinion in the Gulf War.* Chicago: University of Chicago Press, 1994.

Neuman, W. Russell. *The Paradox of Mass Politics: Knowledge and Opinion in the American Electorate.* Cambridge, MA.: Harvard University Press, 1986.

Page, Benjamin I., and Robert Y. Shapiro. *The Rational Public: Fifty Years of Trends in Americans' Policy Preferences.* Chicago: University of Chicago Press, 1992.

Roll, Charles W., and Albert H. Cantril. *Polls: Their Use and Misuse in Politics.* New York: Basic Books, 1972.

Stimson, James A. *Public Opinion in America: Moods, Cycles, and Swings.* 2nd ed. Boulder, CO.: Westview, 1998.

Sussman, Barry. *What Americans Really Think: And Why Our Politicians Pay No Attention.* New York: Pantheon, 1988.

Zaller, John R. *The Nature and Origins of Mass Opinion.* New York: Cambridge University Press, 1992.

Politics in the News— Reading between the Lines

Deliberative Polling

Taking the Town-Hall Pulse, for the Election and Beyond

By JOHN TIERNEY

As an undecided "security mom" in a battleground state, Kim Garcia was already one of America's most intensely scrutinized voters when she sat down in a classroom at Carnegie Mellon University on Saturday morning. But Mrs. Garcia, a nurse in Pittsburgh, was about to experience a whole new level of attention.

She was one of more than 1,500 randomly chosen voters in 17 cities participating in what was probably the largest, and certainly the most scientific, town-hall meeting of any presidential campaign. It may also have been the longest: eight hours of discussing the issues, watching informational videos, questioning experts and filling out surveys.

To the political scientists running this "deliberative poll," the results showed that Americans could transcend the bitter partisan rhetoric this year to become more tolerant of others' views, better informed about issues and possibly more inclined to vote for Senator John Kerry.

To some skeptics, in academia as well as in Mrs. Garcia's group, it was mainly a chance for the loudest and most articu-

New York Times, 20 October 2004, p. A22.

late to sound off to a captive audience of voters not about to change their minds. But even the skeptics acknowledged that this new form of polling could be a promising technique for resolving issues less complex than the presidency.

Mrs. Garcia, who is 44 and has two daughters, started the day as the lone undecided voter in a group with five favoring Mr. Kerry and four favoring President Bush. When they discussed the economy, she sided with the Kerry voters who criticized outsourcing. Complaining about the lack of jobs in Pittsburgh, she said that her husband, a mechanic at the struggling US Airways, could soon be out of work.

But when terrorism and the war in Iraq were discussed, she sided with the Bush voters.

Mrs. Garcia's views on the war moderated, though, after she and the other voters put questions to a panel of academic experts. It was an ideological mix of experts, but those favoring a Kerry multinational approach were the most outspoken, and at the end of the day Mrs. Garcia said their remarks left her inclined to vote for Mr. Kerry.

That was typical of the results among the other undecided voters in the national sample, who were significantly more likely to move toward Mr. Kerry than Mr. Bush, said James Fishkin, a political science professor at Stanford University who directed the experiment. But Professor Fishkin warned against reading too much into that result, because there were a disproportionate number of Republican no-shows, and the preponderance of Democrats might have swayed the undecideds.

The most important results, Professor Fishkin said, were other changes measured in before-and-after surveys of the 1,535 voters. Across the political spectrum, he said, voters became more knowledgeable on specific issues, like the outsourcing of jobs and how Mr. Kerry voted on the resolution authorizing the use of force in Iraq, and their views became more moderate on most issues.

"We've shown that even during a highly polarized election, people can actually reach some mutual understanding when they spend some time learning about the issues and talking to people very different from themselves," Professor Fishkin said. "This is a picture of what democracy could be like if people had a dialogue and heard more than the usual campaign sound bites." . . .

Some, though, questioned how useful this exercise was for a presidential election. Arthur Lupia, a political science professor at the University of Michigan, said that deliberative polling worked best when applied to relatively simple local issues, like how to run a public utility or whether to expand an airport—situations where a representative sample of the public could learn enough to reach a consensus more useful than a poll of voters who knew little about an issue.

"If you and I have some basic values in common and there's a problem, then

coming together and sharing information works great," Professor Lupia said. "But when people fundamentally disagree on what they're trying to accomplish, as Democrats and Republicans do today about the direction of the country, then coming together and talking doesn't change their minds. They commonly just tune each other out." . . .

ESSENCE OF THE STORY

- Fifteen hundred voters in seventeen cities took part in a "deliberative poll" during the 2004 campaign, a poll designed to examine how opinions might change after extended political discussion and debate.

- In the poll, more voters moved toward Kerry than toward Bush, but this may have been because of the mix of academic experts who answered questions posed by the participants.

- One researcher believes deliberative polling shows us how important discussion is in a democracy, while another suggests such extended debate can only be productive when we are in partisan and ideological agreement.

POLITICAL ANALYSIS

- The deliberative poll is another way to measure public opinion. It is different from a random sample survey because respondents experience hours of learning, discussion, and debate. It is similar to a sample survey because the respondents are randomly selected.

- The most important finding from the study is that voters may be able to bridge the partisan divide that seems to separate many Americans if they wrestle with opposing viewpoints in a calm and dispassionate forum.

- Like other research into individual political action, this study shows that citizens may be more likely to participate if they feel informed.

CHAPTER

10

Elections

Over the past two centuries, elections have come to play a significant role in the political processes of most nations. The forms that elections take and the purposes they serve, however, vary greatly from nation to nation. The most important difference among national electoral systems is that some provide the opportunity for opposition while others do not. Democratic electoral systems, such as those that have evolved in the United States and western Europe, allow opposing forces to compete against and even to replace current officeholders. Authoritarian electoral systems, by contrast, do not allow the defeat of those in power. In the authoritarian context, elections are used primarily to mobilize popular enthusiasm for the government, to provide an outlet for popular discontent, and to persuade foreigners that the regime is legitimate—that it has the support of the people. In the former Soviet Union, for example, citizens were required to vote even though no opposition to Communist party candidates was allowed.

In democracies, elections can also serve as institutions of legitimation and as safety valves for social discontent. But beyond these functions, democratic elections facilitate popular influence, promote leadership accountability, and offer groups in society a measure of protection from the abuse of governmental power. Citizens exercise influence through elections by determining who should control the government. The chance to decide who will govern is an opportunity for ordinary citizens to make choices about the policies, programs, and directions of government action. In the United States, for example, recent Democratic and Republican candidates have differed significantly on issues of taxing, social spending, and governmental regulation. As American voters have chosen between the two parties' candidates, they have also made choices about these issues.

Nominally, of course, a democratic election is the collective selection of leaders and representatives. In terms now familiar to the reader, elections are occasions in which multiple *principals*—the citizens—choose political *agents* to act on their behalf. There are two kinds of problems that face even the most rational of citizen-principals in these circumstances. Electoral rules and arrangements may be characterized and ultimately assessed as mechanisms for coming to grips with these.

The first is known as the adverse selection problem. The ***adverse selection problem*** is a consequence of *hidden information*. When selecting one alternative over another, we often are incompletely informed about just what we are choosing. Many aspects or features of our choices are hidden from view and become apparent only long after the choice has been made. Thus, by choosing Candidate A over Candidate B, exactly what are we getting? To some degree, candidates for office are "pigs in a poke." We may know some things about them and some other things about their opponents, but even in a world of investigative reporters, paparazzi, and Drudge reports on the Internet, we can't always know what we've selected. It may turn out badly, but then

CHAPTER OUTLINE

How Does Government Regulate the Electoral Process?

- Electoral Composition
- Translating Voters' Choices into Electoral Outcomes
- Insulating Decision-Making Processes
- Direct Democracy: The Referendum and Recall

How Do Voters Decide?

- Partisan Loyalty
- Issues
- Candidate Characteristics

The 2004 Elections

- Democratic Opportunities
- Republican Strategies
- The End Game

Campaign Finance

- Sources of Campaign Funds
- Campaign Finance Reform
- Implications for Democracy

Do Elections Matter?

- Why Is There a Decline in Voter Turnout?
- Why Do Elections Matter as Political Institutions?

adverse selection problem The problem of incomplete information—of choosing alternatives without knowing fully the details of available options.

PREVIEWING THE PRINCIPLES

Elections can be perceived as institutional opportunities for multiple principals—the citizenry—to select agents—their elected officials—to act on their behalf, even though citizens usually have imperfect information about candidates and don't know how their agents will act once in office. Like any institutional arrangement, the electoral process is subject to rules and regulations that affect outcomes. In addition to the composition of the electorate, the "rules of the game"—what it takes to win and the size and composition of electoral districts—as well as the means of limiting popular involvement in elections—like the electoral college—all play important roles in translating popular sentiment and votes into electoral outcomes. Voters decide, based on multiple criteria, including partisan loyalty, issues, and candidate characteristics. When issues dominate a campaign, candidates tend to converge toward the median voter. Voter turnout in the United States is low because candidates and parties often fail to mobilize voters and institutional barriers to participation—such as registration requirements—are too high for many Americans. But on the whole, elections remain important because they socialize and institutionalize political participation to actions within the system.

again it may not.[1] The candidates themselves affect, in large measure, what we know about them, and it is often in their interest to hide or shroud in ambiguity items about themselves that, though possibly highly relevant to the choices of citizens, might harm their electoral prospects. The solution to this problem is openness and transparency—a wide-open and freewheeling electoral process, a well-heeled political opposition, and an activist press. The latter may at times be perceived as crossing the line between the public and the private—as many felt was the case in the intense scrutiny of former president Clinton's private life—but much better this than a press easily cowed and constrained, because the public depends on an independent press to counter the otherwise self-serving information that is offered up by the candidates themselves.

The second problem is known as ***moral hazard.*** If adverse selection is a problem caused by hidden *information*, then moral hazard is a problem produced by hidden *action*. It is the problem of agents who, once selected, cannot easily be monitored in their behavior. Political leaders do many things that are public, such as making speeches, attaching their names as sponsors of legislation,

---

[1]A classic example of adverse selection is presidential selection of Supreme Court justices. Often a president finds that these men and women turn out much differently than expected. It is unlikely, for example, that President Eisenhower would have chosen Earl Warren, the former governor of California and 1948 Republican vice-presidential candidate, to be chief justice of the Supreme Court had he known of Warren's liberal leanings. Nor would he have appointed Justice William J. Brennan Jr., who turned out to be among the most liberal justices on the Court in the twentieth century. In Eisenhower's final press conference, he was asked by a reporter if he had made any mistakes while president. He said, "Two, and they're both sitting on the Supreme Court." President Nixon, to give another example, appointed Harry Blackmun to the Court, the justice who later crafted the famous pro-choice opinion *Roe v. Wade*. Finally, there was the near-fateful decision of the first President Bush in his elevation of Federal District Court Judge David Souter to the Supreme Court. Souter, in December 2000, joined the minority (only one vote short of a majority) that would have ordered the popular vote in Florida recounted—an action that might well have denied the second President Bush his presidency.

and voting on legislative motions. But behind this public visibility are many private acts that are imperfectly observed at best. These veiled encounters used to take place in the proverbial "smoke-filled rooms" of Washington; but today they take place in the private dining rooms of Capitol Hill, where deals are struck between legislators and special interests, or in the "wink and nod" conversations between presidents and large donors (who may get to spend a night in the Lincoln bedroom of the White House or hitch a ride on *Air Force One*).[2] Political agents can use their political power and the bully pulpits that public office provides to advance these special interests without a more general public awareness. Moral hazard makes the public vulnerable to abuses of the power delegated to elected agents. The solution to moral hazard is found in the way elections are conducted. If agents have strong incentives to want to renew their contracts—to be re-elected or to advance to a higher office—then they will take care not to abuse their delegated power, or at least not to take big risks that, if discovered, could damage their political reputations. Giving incumbents the incentive of possible re-election—indeed, tolerating small advantages that incumbency gives in electoral contests—will encourage them to moderate the inclination to strike private deals. The incentives that elections provide for agents are enhanced by other factors mitigating moral hazard, especially transparency and publicity. Moving the places where real decisions get made to more visible venues, opening these venues to public scrutiny, and empowering publicizers (the press, the political opposition) both dampen the motive and diminish the opportunities for hidden actions contrary to more public purposes. For example, congressional procedures have become more transparent—committee hearings and bill-drafting sessions are open, legislative votes in committee and on the floor are recorded, and records of campaign contributions are publicly available—thus providing increased visibility of an incumbent's record in office to his or her electoral constituency.

Elections thus promote leadership accountability because the threat of defeat at the polls exerts pressure on those in power to conduct themselves in a responsible manner and to take account of popular interests and wishes when they make their decisions. As James Madison observed in the *Federalist Papers*, elected leaders are "compelled to anticipate the moment when their power is to cease, when their exercise of it is to be reviewed, and when they must descend to the level from which they were raised, there forever to remain unless a faithful discharge of their trust shall have established their title to a renewal of it."[3]

In this chapter, we look first at the formal structure and setting of American elections. Second, we will see how—and what—voters decide when they take part in elections. Third, we will focus on recent national elections, including the 2004 presidential race. Fourth, we will discuss the role of money in the election process,

moral hazard
Not knowing all aspects of the actions taken by an agent (nominally on behalf of the principal but potentially at the principal's expense).

 Rationality Principle

Elections allow multiple principals—citizens—to choose political agents to act on their behalf. But citizens usually have imperfect information about candidates and don't know how agents will act once in office.

---

[2]Clinton's secretary of commerce, the late Ron Brown, a former head of the Democratic National Committee, used the frequent occasions of foreign travel required of his cabinet post to bring along many a Democratic fat cat. Republican officeholders, of course, are no less vigilant in rewarding their fat-cat contributors.

[3]Clinton Rossiter, ed., *The Federalist Papers* (New York: New American Library, 1961), No. 57, p. 352.

particularly in recent elections. Finally, we will assess the place of elections in the American political process, raising the important question, "Do elections matter?"

HOW DOES GOVERNMENT REGULATE THE ELECTORAL PROCESS?

Collective-Action Principle

Elections are a mechanism to channel and limit political participation to actions within the system.

In earlier chapters (see Chapter 1) we suggested that the relationship between citizens and elected politicians is an instance of a principal-agent relationship. There are two basic approaches to this relationship: the consent approach and the agency approach. The consent approach emphasizes the historical reality that the right of the citizen to participate in his or her own governance, mainly through the act of voting or other forms of consent, arises from an existing governmental order aimed at making it *easier* for the governors to govern by legitimizing their rule. By giving their consent, citizens provide this legitimization. The agency approach treats the typical citizen as someone who would much rather devote scarce time and effort to his or her own private affairs instead of spending that time and effort on governance. Therefore, he or she chooses to delegate governance to agents—politicians—controlled through election. In this approach, the control of agents is emphasized.

Whether to control their delegates (agency approach) or legitimize governance by politicians (consent approach), elections allow citizens to participate in political life on a routine and peaceful basis. Indeed, American voters have the opportunity to select and, if they so desire, depose some of their most important leaders. In this way, Americans have a chance to intervene in and to influence the government's programs and policies. Yet it is important to recall that elections are not spontaneous affairs. Instead, they are formal government institutions. Although elections allow citizens a chance to participate in politics, they also allow the government a chance to exert a good deal of control over when, where, how, and which of its citizens will participate. Electoral processes are governed by a variety of rules and procedures that allow those in power a significant opportunity to regulate the character—and perhaps also the consequences—of mass political participation.

Institution Principle

The electoral process is governed by a variety of rules and procedures that allow those in power an opportunity to regulate the character and consequences of political participation.

Thus elections provide governments with an excellent opportunity to regulate and control popular involvement. Three general forms of regulation have played especially important roles in the electoral history of the Western democracies. First, governments often attempt to regulate the composition of the electorate to diminish the electoral weight of groups they deem to be undesirable. Second, governments frequently seek to manipulate the translation of voters' choices into electoral outcomes. Third, virtually all governments attempt to insulate policy-making processes from electoral intervention through regulation of the relationship between electoral decisions and the composition or organization of the government.

Electoral Composition

Perhaps the oldest and most obvious device used to regulate voting and its consequences is manipulation of the electorate's composition. In the earliest elections in western Europe, for example, the suffrage was generally limited to property owners and others who could be trusted to vote in a manner acceptable to those in power. To cite just one illustration, property qualifications in France before 1848 limited the electorate to 240,000 of some 7 million men over the age of twenty-one.[4] Of course, no women were permitted to vote. During the same era, other nations manipulated the electorate's composition by assigning unequal electoral weights to different classes of voters. The 1831 Belgian constitution, for example, assigned individuals anywhere from one to three votes, depending on their property holdings, education, and position.[5] But even in the context of America's ostensibly universal and equal suffrage in the twentieth century, the composition of the electorate is still subject to manipulation. Until recent years, some states manipulated the vote by the discriminatory use of poll taxes and literacy tests or by such practices as the placement of polls and the scheduling of voting hours to depress participation by one or another group.[6] Today the most important example of the regulation of the American electorate's composition is our unique personal registration requirements.

Levels of voter participation in twentieth-century American elections were quite low compared to those of the other Western democracies (see Figure 10.1).[7] Indeed, voter participation in presidential elections in the United States has barely averaged 50 percent recently (see Figure 10.2). Turnout in the 2000 presidential election was 51 percent of voting-age Americans; in 2004 it was approximately 55 percent. During the nineteenth century, by contrast, voter turnout in the United States was extremely high, considerably larger than it is today.[8]

Before delving too deeply into the quantitative data, a few qualifying remarks are in order. A turnout rate is a ratio comparing the number of people who voted to some baseline population. The numerator of this ratio is relatively uncontroversial— it is the number of individuals who present themselves at a polling station or submit an absentee ballot. (There may be some ambiguity because some people do not vote for every office on the ballot, so the actual voting rate for president, for example, is usually higher than that for county recorder or town sheriff. But this is a relatively minor ambiguity. Walter Burnham calls this the "fall-off rate."[9])

[4]Stein Rokkan, *Citizens, Elections, Parties: Approaches to the Comparative Study of the Processes of Development* (New York: David McKay, 1970), p. 149. Also see Daron Acemoglu and James A. Robinson, "Why Did the West Extend the Franchise? Democracy, Inequality, and Growth in Historical Perspective," *Quarterly Journal of Economics* 115 (2000): 1167–99.

[5]John A. Hawgood, *Modern Constitutions since 1787* (New York: Van Nostrand, 1939), p. 148.

[6]In the aftermath of the 2004 presidential election, in which Ohio proved a pivotal state in George W. Bush's victory, it has been alleged that Republicans engaged in this sort of manipulation. In the county in which Kent State University (a Democratic stronghold) is located, very few voting machines were made available, producing long lines and up to nine-hour waiting times. Republican-leaning suburban locations, on the other hand, were adequately provisioned with voting machines. Similar stories about Democratic manipulations also circulated after the election.

[7]See Walter Dean Burnham, "The Changing Shape of the American Political Universe," *American Political Science Review* 59 (1965): 7–28. It should be noted that other democracies, like India and Switzerland, have even lower turnout rates, as do some of the new democracies in eastern Europe.

[8]See statistics of the U.S. Bureau of the Census and the Federal Election Commission. For voting statistics since 1960, see "National Voter Turnout in Federal Elections: 1960–2004," at www.infoplease.com/ipa/A0781453.html.

[9]Burnham, "The Changing Shape of the American Political Universe."

FIGURE 10.1

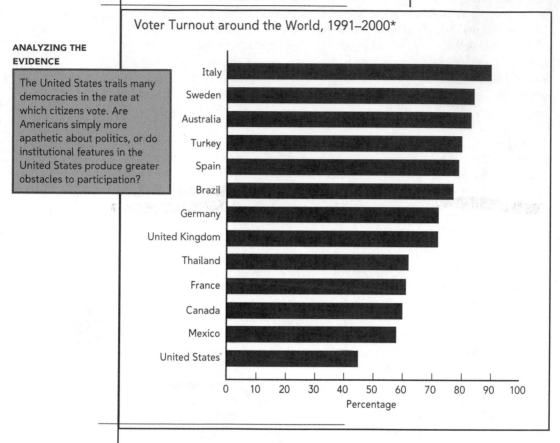

Voter Turnout around the World, 1991–2000*

ANALYZING THE EVIDENCE

The United States trails many democracies in the rate at which citizens vote. Are Americans simply more apathetic about politics, or do institutional features in the United States produce greater obstacles to participation?

*Average during the 1990s.

SOURCE: Voting and Democracy Research Center (www.fairvote.org/turnout).

The real problem with quantitative presentations is how to define the baseline population—the denominator of the turnout ratio. Some use the voting-age population, which is those eighteen years or older residing in the United States. (Of course, this voting age was set by the Twenty-sixth Amendment, ratified in 1971.) But this figure may be misleading in at least two ways. It incorrectly *includes* noncitizens and ineligible felons as well as eligible citizens who have failed to register. Furthermore, it incorrectly *excludes* overseas eligible voters. Other analysts use the eligible-voting population, certainly the more relevant denominator of the turnout ratio. But there are problems here as well. Cross-national comparisons may be misleading because eligibility requirements differ among

FIGURE 10.2

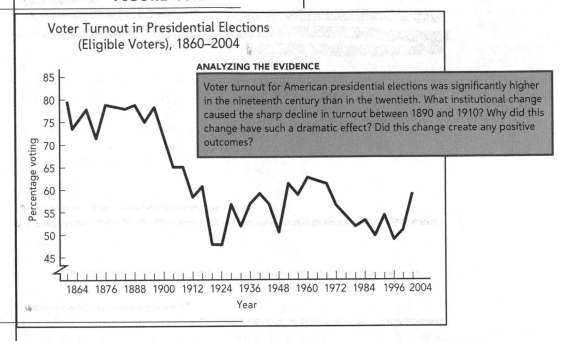

Voter Turnout in Presidential Elections
(Eligible Voters), 1860–2004

ANALYZING THE EVIDENCE

Voter turnout for American presidential elections was significantly higher in the nineteenth century than in the twentieth. What institutional change caused the sharp decline in turnout between 1890 and 1910? Why did this change have such a dramatic effect? Did this change create any positive outcomes?

SOURCES: For 1860–1928, U.S. Bureau of the Census, *Historical Statistics of the United States, Colonial Times to 1970*, Pt. 2, p. 1071. For 1932–92, U.S. Bureau of the Census, *Statistical Abstract of the United States, 1993* (Washington, DC: Government Printing Office, 1993), p. 284. For 1996–2004, Federal Election Commission data. Note that this data reflects voting-eligible population; the percentage of voting-age population that voted would be smaller.

countries. Over-time comparisons may also be misleading because eligibility criteria within the same country change over time. In the United States, for example, the Nineteenth Amendment, ratified in 1920, extended the vote to women, and the Twenty-sixth Amendment lowered the voting age to eighteen; both amendments changed the denominator of the turnout ratio.

Finally, we should point out that some turnout rates, such as those calculated for a series of elections in a country, are often reported as an average over several years (as in Figure 10.1). Such averages often pool different kinds of elections. In the United States, such measures include elections during presidential years as well as those of off-years (just congressional elections). Because off-year turnout is low, this practice pulls down the U.S. average compared to that of countries in which only national elections are counted.[10]

[10]For an excellent discussion of these and related issues, consult Michael P. M. McDonald and Samuel Popkin, "The Myth of the Vanishing Voter," *American Political Science Review* 95 (2001): 963–74.

As Figure 10.2 indicates, the critical years during which voter turnout declined across the United States were between 1890 and 1910. These years coincide with the adoption of laws across much of the nation requiring eligible citizens to appear personally at a registrar's office to register to vote some time before the actual date of an election. Personal registration was one of several "Progressive" reforms of political practices initiated at the turn of the twentieth century. The ostensible purpose of registration was to discourage fraud and corruption. But to many Progressive reformers, *corruption* was a code word, referring to the type of politics practiced in the large cities, where political parties had organized immigrant and ethnic populations. Reformers not only objected to the corruption that surely was a facet of party politics in this period but also opposed the growing political power of urban populations and their leaders.

Personal registration imposed a new burden on potential voters and altered the format of American elections. Under the registration systems adopted after 1890, it became the duty of individual voters to secure their own eligibility. This duty could prove to be a significant burden for potential voters. During a personal appearance before the registrar, individuals seeking to vote were (and are) required to furnish proof of identity, residence, and citizenship. While the inconvenience of registration varied from state to state, usually voters could register only during business hours on weekdays. Many potential voters could not afford to lose a day's pay in order to register. Second, voters were usually required to register well before the next election, in some states up to several months earlier. Third, because most personal registration laws required a periodic purge of the election rolls, ostensibly to keep them up to date, voters often had to re-register to maintain their eligibility. Thus, although personal registration requirements helped diminish the widespread electoral corruption that accompanied a completely open voting process, they also made it much more difficult for citizens to participate in the electoral process. Rational citizens with busy lives might well be expected to forgo political participation as its complications and costs go up.

Registration requirements particularly depress the participation of those with little education and low incomes because registration requires a greater degree of political involvement and interest than does the act of voting itself. To vote, a person need only be concerned with the particular election campaign at hand. Yet requiring individuals to register before the next election forces them to make a decision to participate on the basis of an abstract interest in the electoral process rather than a simple concern with a specific campaign. Such an abstract interest in electoral politics is largely a product of education. Those with relatively little education may become interested in political events once the stimuli of a particular campaign become salient, but by that time it may be too late to register. As a result, personal registration requirements not only diminish the size of the electorate but also tend to create an electorate that is, in the aggregate, less representative of the voting-age population. The electorate is better educated, higher in income and social status, and includes fewer African Americans and other minorities than the citizenry as a whole (Figure 10.3).

FIGURE 10.3

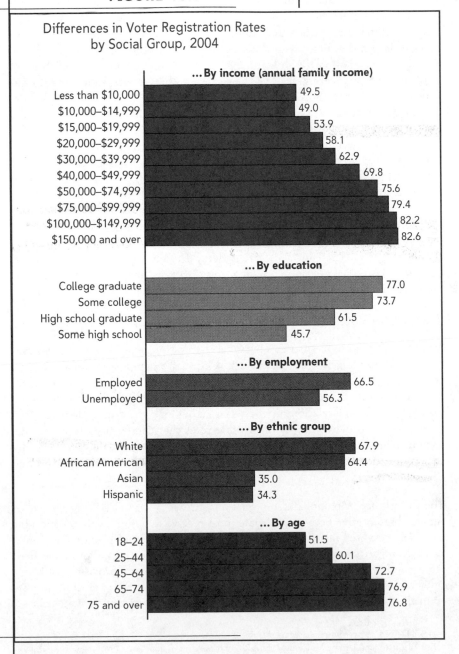

Differences in Voter Registration Rates
by Social Group, 2004

...By income (annual family income)

Income	Rate
Less than $10,000	49.5
$10,000–$14,999	49.0
$15,000–$19,999	53.9
$20,000–$29,999	58.1
$30,000–$39,999	62.9
$40,000–$49,999	69.8
$50,000–$74,999	75.6
$75,000–$99,999	79.4
$100,000–$149,999	82.2
$150,000 and over	82.6

...By education

Education	Rate
College graduate	77.0
Some college	73.7
High school graduate	61.5
Some high school	45.7

...By employment

Employment	Rate
Employed	66.5
Unemployed	56.3

...By ethnic group

Ethnic group	Rate
White	67.9
African American	64.4
Asian	35.0
Hispanic	34.3

...By age

Age	Rate
18–24	51.5
25–44	60.1
45–64	72.7
65–74	76.9
75 and over	76.8

The percentage of Americans who are registered to vote varies according to education level, employment status, ethnic group, and age.

SOURCE: U.S. Bureau of the Census, Population Division, Education & Social Stratification Branch, "Voting and Registration in the Election of November 2004" (April 2005), www.census.gov/population/www/socdemo/voting/cps2004.

Over the years, voter registration restrictions have been modified somewhat to make registration easier. In 1993, for example, Congress approved and President Clinton signed the "Motor Voter" bill to ease voter registration by allowing individuals to register when they applied for driver's licenses, as well as in public assistance and military recruitment offices.[11] In Europe, there is typically no registration burden on the individual voter; voter registration is handled automatically by the government. This is one reason that voter turnout rates in Europe are higher than those in the United States.

Another factor explaining low rates of voter turnout in the United States is the weakness of the American party system. During the nineteenth century, American political party machines employed hundreds of thousands of workers to organize and mobilize voters and bring them to the polls. The result was an extremely high rate of turnout, typically more than 90 percent of eligible voters.[12] But political party machines began to decline in strength in the early twentieth century and by now have largely disappeared. Without party workers to encourage them to go to the polls and even to bring them there if necessary, many eligible voters will not participate. In the absence of strong parties, participation rates drop the most among poorer and less-educated citizens. Because of the absence of strong political parties, the American electorate is smaller and skewed more toward the middle class than toward the population of all those potentially eligible to vote.[13]

Translating Voters' Choices into Electoral Outcomes

With the exception of America's personal registration requirements, contemporary governments generally do not try to limit the composition of their electorates. Instead, they prefer to allow everyone to vote, and then to manipulate the outcome of the election. This is possible because there is more than one way to decide the relationship between individual votes and electoral outcomes. There are any number of possible rules that can be used to determine how individual votes will be translated. Two types of regulations are especially important: the rules that set the criteria for victory and the rules that define electoral districts.

majority system
A type of electoral system in which, to win a seat in the parliament or other representative body, a candidate must receive a majority (50 percent plus 1) of all the votes cast in the relevant district.

The Criteria for Winning   In some nations, to win a seat in the parliament or other representative body, a candidate must receive a majority (50 percent plus 1) of all the votes cast in the relevant district. This type of electoral system is called a *majority system* and was used in the primary elections of most southern states until recent years. Generally, majority systems have a provision for a second or "runoff" election among the two top candidates if the initial contest drew so many contestants that none received an absolute majority of the votes cast.

[11] Helen Dewar, "'Motor Voter' Agreement Is Reached," *Washington Post*, 28 April 1993, p. A6.

[12] Erik W. Austin and Jerome M. Clubb, *Political Facts of the United States since 1789* (New York: Columbia University Press, 1986), pp. 378–79.

[13] Reports on the 2004 election suggest that both parties devoted considerable resources to targeting potential new voters, helping them register, and mobilizing them on Election Day. Elevated turnout in the election reflects this effort.

In other nations, candidates for office need not receive an absolute majority of the votes cast to win an election. Instead, victory is awarded to the candidate who receives the greatest number of votes in a given election regardless of the actual percentage of votes this represents. Thus a candidate who received 40 percent of the votes cast may win the contest so long as no rival receives more votes. This type of electoral process is called a ***plurality system,*** and it is the system used in almost all general elections in the United States.[14]

In some electoral systems, multiple representatives are selected from each district, constituency, or region. This is true in most European nations that employ a third electoral system, called ***proportional representation.*** Under proportional rules, competing political parties are awarded legislative seats roughly in proportion to the percentage of the popular vote that they receive. For example, a party that won 30 percent of the votes would receive roughly 30 percent of the seats in the parliament or other representative body. In the United States, proportional representation is used by many states in presidential primary elections. In these primaries, candidates for the Democratic and Republican nominations are awarded convention delegates in rough proportion to the percentage of the popular vote that they received in the primary. Early in the twentieth century, proportional representation systems were employed in many American cities, including New York, to elect city councils. Today these systems have nearly disappeared. Cambridge, Massachusetts, is one of the last cities to use such a system in city-council elections. Elections to the New York City school board are also still conducted using a proportional representation system.

Generally, systems of proportional representation work to the electoral advantage of smaller political parties, while majority and plurality systems tend to help larger and more powerful forces. This is because in legislative elections, proportional representation reduces, whereas majority and plurality rules increase, the number of votes that political parties must receive to win legislative seats. For instance, in European parliamentary elections, a Green party that wins 10 percent of the national vote will also receive approximately 10 percent of the parliamentary seats. In American congressional elections, by contrast, a Green party winning only 10 percent of the popular vote would probably receive no congressional seats at all.[15] Obviously,

plurality system
A type of electoral system in which victory goes to the individual who gets the most votes in an election, not necessarily a majority of votes cast.

proportional representation
A multiple-member district system that allows each political party representation in proportion to its percentage of the vote.

 **Institution Principle**
The rules that set the criteria for winning an election have an effect on the outcome.

---

[14]There are different types of plurality systems. The one currently used in the United States in congressional and presidential elections is single-member districts and first-past-the-post. For an accessible analysis of the different types of plurality systems and a model for analyzing electoral systems, see Kenneth A. Shepsle and Mark S. Bonchek, *Analyzing Politics: Rationality, Behavior, and Institutions* (New York: Norton, 1997), pp. 178–87.

[15]For an argument that plurality systems are governance oriented, whereas proportional systems are representation oriented, see Shepsle and Bonchek, *Analyzing Politics*, pp. 188–91. This argument derives from the famous Duverger's Law—an argument that plurality systems encourage two-party competition (with one party or the other securing a majority of seats in the legislature), whereas proportional systems encourage multiparty competition (with many parties holding seats in the legislature, with the very frequent outcome that no party commands a majority on its own, and thus parties must build coalitions). Thus plurality systems "manufacture" government (majority legislative parties) but squeeze out a lot of political diversity. Proportional systems encourage diversity but require majority coalitions to be "built" after the election. The law was first described systematically by the French political scientist Maurice Duverger in his *Political Parties, Their Organization and Activity in the Modern State,* trans. Barbara North and Robert North (New York: Wiley, 1954).

choices among types of electoral systems can have important political consequences. Competing forces often seek to establish an electoral system they believe will serve their political interests while undermining the fortunes of their opponents. For example, in 1937, New York City Council seats were awarded on the basis of proportional representation. This led to the selection of several Communist party council members. During the 1940s, to prevent the election of Communists, the city adopted a plurality system. Under the new rule, the tiny Communist party was unable to muster enough votes to secure a council seat. In a similar vein, the introduction of proportional representation for the selection of delegates to the Democratic party's 1972 national convention was designed in part to maximize the voting strength of minority groups and, not entirely coincidentally, to improve the electoral chances of the candidates they were most likely to favor.[16]

Electoral Districts   Despite the occasional use of proportional representation and majority voting systems, most electoral contests in the United States are decided on the basis of plurality rules. Rather than seeking to manipulate the criteria for victory, American politicians have usually sought to influence electoral outcomes by manipulating the organization of electoral districts. Congressional district boundaries in the United States are redrawn by governors and state legislatures every ten years, after the decennial census determines the number of House seats to which each state is entitled (Figure 10.4). The manipulation of electoral districts to increase the likelihood of one or another outcome is called *gerrymandering*, in honor of nineteenth-century Massachusetts governor Elbridge Gerry, who was alleged to have designed a district in the shape of a salamander to promote his party's interests. The principle is a simple one. Different distributions of voters among districts produce different electoral outcomes; those in a position to control the arrangements of districts are also in a position to manipulate the results. For example, until recent years, gerrymandering to dilute the voting strength of racial minorities was employed by many state legislatures. One of the more common strategies involved redrawing congressional boundary lines in such a way as to divide and disperse a black population that would have otherwise constituted a majority within the original district.

    This form of racial gerrymandering, sometimes called "cracking," was used in Mississippi during the 1960s and 1970s to prevent the election of a black congressman. Historically, the black population in Mississippi was clustered in the western half of the state, along the Mississippi Delta. From 1882 until 1966, the delta was one congressional district. Although blacks constituted a clear majority within the district (66 percent in 1960), the continuing election of white congressmen was ensured simply because blacks were denied the right to register and vote. With Congress's passage of the Voting Rights Act of 1965, however, the Mississippi state legislature moved swiftly to minimize the potential voting power of blacks by redrawing congressional district lines in such a way as

gerrymandering
Apportionment of voters in districts in such a way as to give unfair advantage to one political party.

[16]See Nelson W. Polsby and Aaron Wildavsky, *Presidential Elections: Strategies of American Electoral Politics*, 5th ed. (New York: Scribners, 1980).

FIGURE 10.4

Congressional Redistricting

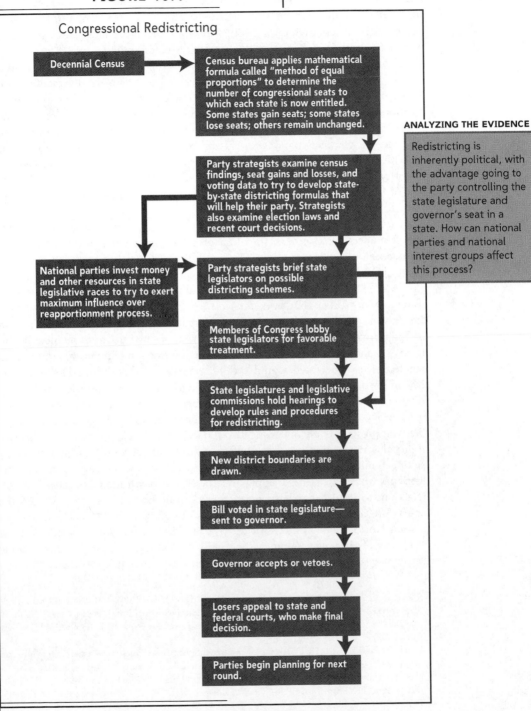

Decennial Census

Census bureau applies mathematical formula called "method of equal proportions" to determine the number of congressional seats to which each state is now entitled. Some states gain seats; some states lose seats; others remain unchanged.

Party strategists examine census findings, seat gains and losses, and voting data to try to develop state-by-state districting formulas that will help their party. Strategists also examine election laws and recent court decisions.

National parties invest money and other resources in state legislative races to try to exert maximum influence over reapportionment process.

Party strategists brief state legislators on possible districting schemes.

Members of Congress lobby state legislators for favorable treatment.

State legislatures and legislative commissions hold hearings to develop rules and procedures for redistricting.

New district boundaries are drawn.

Bill voted in state legislature—sent to governor.

Governor accepts or vetoes.

Losers appeal to state and federal courts, who make final decision.

Parties begin planning for next round.

ANALYZING THE EVIDENCE

Redistricting is inherently political, with the advantage going to the party controlling the state legislature and governor's seat in a state. How can national parties and national interest groups affect this process?

to fragment the black population in the delta into four of the state's five congressional districts. Mississippi's gerrymandering scheme was preserved in the state's redistricting plans in 1972 and 1981 and helped prevent the election of any black representative until 1986, when Mike Espy became the first African American since Reconstruction to represent Mississippi in Congress.

In recent years, the federal government has encouraged what is sometimes called "benign gerrymandering," designed to increase minority representation in Congress. The 1982 amendments to the Voting Rights Act of 1965 encourage the creation of legislative districts with predominantly African American or Hispanic American populations by requiring states, when possible, to draw district lines that take account of concentrations of African American and Hispanic American voters. These amendments were initially supported by Democrats who assumed that minority-controlled districts would guarantee the election of Democratic members of Congress. However, Republicans have championed these efforts, reasoning that if minority voters were concentrated in their own districts, Republican prospects in other districts would be enhanced.[17] Moreover, Republicans hoped some Democratic incumbents might be forced from office to make way for minority representatives. In some cases, the Republicans' theory has proved correct. As a result of the creation of a number of new minority districts in 1991, several long-term white Democrats lost their congressional seats. The 1993 Supreme Court decision in *Shaw v. Reno*, however, opened the way for challenges by white voters to the drawing of these districts. In the 5–4 majority opinion, Justice Sandra Day O'Connor wrote that if district boundaries were so "bizarre" as to be inexplicable on any grounds other than an effort to ensure the election of minority group members to office, white voters would have reason to assert that they had been the victims of unconstitutional racial gerrymandering.[18] In its 1995 decision in *Miller v. Johnson*, the Court questioned the entire concept of benign racial gerrymandering by asserting that the use of race as a "predominant factor" in the drawing of district lines was presumptively unconstitutional. However, the Court held open the possibility that race could be *one* of the factors taken into account in legislative redistricting. Similarly, in *Bush v. Vera*, the Court ruled that three Texas congressional districts with black or Hispanic majorities were unconstitutional because state officials put too much emphasis on race in drawing boundaries. "Voters," said the Court, "are more than mere racial statistics." In *Shaw v. Hunt*, the Court struck down a North Carolina black-majority voting district for similar reasons. In the 1997 case of *Abrams v. Johnson*, the Court upheld a new Georgia congressional district map that eliminated two of the state's three black-majority districts.[19]

[17]Roberto Suro, "In Redistricting, New Rules and New Prizes," *New York Times*, 6 May 1990, sec. 4, p. 5. A more recent examination is found in Gary W. Cox and Jonathan N. Katz, *Elbridge Gerry's Salamander: The Electoral Consequences of the Reapportionment Revolution* (New York: Cambridge University Press, 2002).

[18]*Shaw v. Reno*, 113 S.Ct. 2816 (1993); Linda Greenhouse, "Court Questions Districts Drawn to Aid Minorities," *New York Times*, 29 June 1993, p. 1. See also Joan Biskupic, "Court's Conservatism Unlikely to Be Shifted by a New Justice," *Washington Post*, 30 June 1993, p. 1.

[19]*Bush v. Vera*, 116 S.Ct. 1941 (1996); *Shaw v. Hunt*, 64 USLW 4437 (1996); *Abrams v. Johnson*, 95-1425 (1997).

Traditionally, district boundaries have been redrawn only once a decade, following the decennial national census. In recent years, however, the Republican party has adopted an extremely aggressive reapportionment strategy, in some instances not waiting for a new census before launching a redistricting effort that could serve its political interests. In Texas, for example, after the GOP took control of both houses of the state legislature in the 2002 elections, Republican lawmakers sought to enact a redistricting plan that promised to shift as many as five congressional seats to the Republican column. This Republican effort was masterminded by U.S. House Majority Leader Tom DeLay, who is himself a Texan. DeLay saw an opportunity to increase the Republican majority in the House and reduce Democratic prospects for regaining control of Congress. In an effort to block DeLay's plan, a group of fifty-one Democratic legislators refused to attend state legislative sessions, leaving the Texas legislature without a quorum and unable to conduct its business. The legislature's Republican leadership ordered the state police to apprehend the missing Democrats and to return them to the Capitol. The Democrats responded by escaping to Oklahoma, beyond the jurisdiction of the Texas police. Eventually, the Democrats capitulated, and the GOP was able to enact its redistricting plan. In the 2004 election, the first under the new plan, the Republicans defeated four Democratic incumbents and won three of the five seats in which no incumbent was running. This is equal to the total Republican gain in the House nationally. A similar GOP redistricting effort in Colorado failed when it was ruled unconstitutional by the state's supreme court. The court declared that the Colorado constitution permitted the legislature to redistrict the state only once every ten years.

Insulating Decision-Making Processes

Virtually all governments attempt at least partially to insulate decision-making processes from electoral intervention. The most obvious forms of insulation are the confinement of popular election to only some governmental positions, various modes of indirect election, and lengthy tenure in office. In the United States, the framers of the Constitution intended that only members of the House of Representatives would be subject to direct popular selection. The president and members of the Senate were to be indirectly elected for rather long terms to allow them, as the *Federalist Papers* put it, to avoid "an unqualified complaisance to every sudden breeze of passion, or to every transient impulse which the people may receive."[20]

The Electoral College In the early history of popular voting, nations often made use of indirect elections. In these elections, voters would choose the members of an intermediate body. These members would, in turn, select public officials. The assumption underlying such processes was that ordinary citizens were not really qualified to choose their leaders and could not be trusted to do

---

[20]Rossiter, ed., *The Federalist Papers*, No. 71, p. 432.

electoral college
The presidential electors from each state who meet in their respective state capitals after the popular election to cast ballots for president and vice president.

so directly. The last vestige of this procedure in America is the *electoral college,* the group of electors who formally select the president and vice president of the United States.

When Americans go to the polls on Election Day, they are technically not voting directly for presidential candidates. Instead, voters within each state are choosing among slates of electors who have been nominated by political parties some months earlier. The electors who are chosen in the presidential race are pledged to support their own party's presidential candidate. In each state (except for Maine and Nebraska), the slate that wins casts all the state's electoral votes for its party's candidate.[21] Each state is entitled to a number of electoral votes equal to the number of the state's senators and representatives combined, for a total of 538 electoral votes for the fifty states and the District of Columbia. Occasionally, an elector breaks his or her pledge and votes for the other party's candidate. For example, in 1976, when the Republicans carried the state of Washington, one Republican elector from that state refused to vote for Gerald Ford, the Republican presidential nominee. More recently, a Gore elector from Washington, D.C., refused to vote for him in 2000 because he believed Gore to be insufficiently supportive of D.C. statehood. Many states have now enacted statutes formally binding electors to their pledges, but some constitutional authorities doubt whether such statutes are enforceable.

In each state, the electors whose slate has won proceed to the state's capital on the Monday after the second Wednesday in December and formally cast their ballots. These are sent to Washington, tallied by the Congress in January, and the name of the winner is formally announced. If no candidate received a majority of all electoral votes, the names of the top three candidates would be submitted to the House, where each state would be able to cast one vote. Whether a state's vote would be decided by a majority, plurality, or some other fraction of the state's delegates would be determined under rules established by the House.

In 1800 and 1824, the electoral college failed to produce a majority for any candidate. In the election of 1800, Thomas Jefferson, the Jeffersonian Republican party's presidential candidate, and Aaron Burr, that party's vice-presidential candidate, received an equal number of votes in the electoral college, throwing the election into the House of Representatives. (The Constitution at that time made no distinction between presidential and vice-presidential candidates, specifying only that the individual receiving a majority of electoral votes would be named president.) Some members of the Federalist party in Congress suggested that they should seize the opportunity to damage the Republican cause by supporting Burr and denying Jefferson the presidency. Federalist leader Alexander Hamilton put a stop to this mischievous notion, however, and made certain that his party sup-

---

[21]State legislatures determine the system by which electors are selected, and almost all states use this "winner take all" system. Maine and Nebraska, however, provide that one electoral vote goes to the winner in each congressional district and two electoral votes go to the winner statewide. In 2004, a proposition of the Colorado ballot to divide electoral votes as in Maine and Nebraska was defeated two to one.

ported Jefferson. Hamilton's actions enraged Burr and helped lead to the infamous duel between the two men, in which Hamilton was killed. The Twelfth Amendment, ratified in 1804, was designed to prevent a repetition of such a situation by providing for separate electoral-college votes for president and vice president.

In the 1824 election, four candidates—John Quincy Adams, Andrew Jackson, Henry Clay, and William H. Crawford—divided the electoral vote; no one of them received a majority. The House of Representatives eventually chose Adams over the others, even though Jackson won more electoral and popular votes. This choice resulted from the famous "corrupt bargain" in which Clay threw his support to Adams, the eventual winner, and was subsequently named secretary of state. After 1824, the two major political parties had begun to dominate presidential politics to such an extent that by December of each election year, only two candidates remained for the electors to choose between, thus ensuring that one would receive a majority. This freed the parties and the candidates from having to plan their campaigns to culminate in Congress, and Congress very quickly ceased to dominate the presidential selection process.

On all but three occasions since 1824, the electoral vote has simply ratified the nationwide popular vote. Because electoral votes are won on a state-by-state basis, it is mathematically possible for a candidate who receives a nationwide popular plurality to fail to carry states whose electoral votes would add up to a majority. Thus, in 1876, Rutherford B. Hayes was the winner in the electoral college despite receiving fewer popular votes than his rival, Samuel Tilden. In 1888, Grover Cleveland received more popular votes than Benjamin Harrison, but received fewer electoral votes. And in 2000, Al Gore outpolled his opponent, George W. Bush, but lost the electoral college by a mere four electoral votes. In 2004, President Bush won both the popular vote and an electoral majority in his successful reelection bid. In doing so, Bush was the first candidate since Ronald Reagan in 1984 to win a clear majority of the popular vote.

In the modern era the electoral college has a profound effect on the nature of campaigning. Imagine no electoral college, so that the popular vote winner is elected. Campaigns in this scenario focus on votes *wherever they may be found*. Resources—for television ads, candidate visits, or securing local endorsements—are invested wherever the vote yield is expected to be fruitful. In a world *with* an electoral college, on the other hand, votes in a state matter only if they can move that state into the candidate's column. There was no point in 2004, for example, for either Bush or Kerry to devote scarce campaign resources to Massachusetts (a sure Kerry state) or Texas (a sure Bush state); instead, they focused on places that were contestable: Ohio, Florida, and Colorado. A contest with no electoral college would entail a wide-open national campaign with votes sought out everywhere. A contest with an electoral college, in contrast, concentrates campaign activity in contestable states.

Frequency of Elections Less obvious are the insulating effects of electoral arrangements that permit direct, and even frequent, popular election of public officials but tend to fragment the impact of elections on the government's composition. In the

United States, for example, the constitutional provision of staggered terms of service in the Senate was designed to diminish the effect of shifts in electoral sentiment on the Senate as an institution. Because only one third of its members were to be selected at any given point in time, the composition of the institution would be partially protected from changes in electoral preferences. This would prevent what the *Federalist Papers* called "mutability in the public councils arising from a rapid succession of new members."[22]

Size of Electoral Districts   The division of the nation into relatively small, geographically based constituencies for the purpose of selecting members of the House of Representatives was, in part, designed to have a similar effect. Representatives were to be chosen frequently. And although not prescribed by the Constitution, the fact that each was to be selected by a discrete constituency was thought by Madison and others to diminish the government's vulnerability to mass popular movements.

In a sense, the House of Representatives was compartmentalized. First, by dividing the national electorate into small districts, the importance of local issues would increase. Second, the salience of local issues would mean that a representative's electoral fortunes would be more closely tied to factors peculiar to his or her own district than to national responses to issues. Third, given a geographical principle of representation, national groups would be somewhat fragmented while the formation of local forces that might or might not share common underlying attitudes would be encouraged. No matter how well represented individual constituencies might be, the influence of voters on national policy questions would be fragmented. In Madison's terms, the influence of "faction" would thus become "less likely to pervade the whole body than some particular portion of it."[23]

The Ballot   Another example of an American electoral arrangement that tends to fragment the impact of mass elections on the government's composition is the Australian ballot (named for its country of origin). Before the introduction of this official ballot in the 1890s, voters cast ballots according to political parties. Each party printed its own ballots, listed only its own candidates for each office, and employed party workers to distribute its ballots at the polls. This ballot format had two important consequences. First, the party ballot precluded secrecy in voting. Because each party's ballot was distinctive in size and color, it was not difficult for party workers to determine how individuals intended to vote. This, of course, facilitated the intimidation and bribery of voters. Second, the format of the ballot prevented split-ticket voting. Because only one party's candidates appeared on any ballot, it was difficult for a voter to cast anything other than a straight party vote.

The official ***Australian ballot*** represented a significant change in electoral procedure. The new ballot was prepared and administered by the state rather

Australian ballot
An electoral format that presents the names of all the candidates for any given office on the same ballot. Introduced at the turn of the century, the Australian ballot replaced the partisan ballot and facilitated split-ticket voting.

[22]Rossiter, ed., *The Federalist Papers,* No. 62.
[23]Ibid., No. 10.

than the parties. Each ballot was identical and included the names of all candidates for office. This reform, of course, increased the secrecy of voting and reduced the possibility for voter intimidation and bribery. Because all ballots were identical in appearance, even the voter who had been threatened or bribed might still vote as he or she wished, without the knowledge of party workers. But perhaps even more important, the Australian-ballot reform made it possible for voters to make their choices on the basis of the individual rather than the collective merits of a party's candidates. Because all candidates for the same office now appeared on the same ballot, voters were no longer forced to choose a straight party ticket. It was indeed the introduction of the Australian ballot that gave rise to the phenomenon of split-ticket voting in American elections.[24] Ticket splitting is especially prevalent in states that use the "office block" ballot format, which does not group candidates by their partisan affiliations. By contrast, the "party column" format places all the candidates affiliated with a given party in the same row or column. The former facilitates ticket splitting, whereas the latter encourages straight-ticket voting.

It is this second consequence of the Australian-ballot reform that tends to fragment the impact of American elections on the government's composition. Before the reform of the ballot, it was not uncommon for an entire incumbent administration to be swept from office and replaced by an entirely new set of officials. In the absence of a real possibility of split-ticket voting, any desire on the part of the electorate for change could be expressed only as a vote against all candidates of the party in power. Because of this, there always existed the possibility, particularly at the state and local levels, that an insurgent slate committed to policy change could be swept into power. The party ballot thus increased the potential effect of elections on the government's composition. Although this potential may not always have been realized, the party ballot at least increased the chance that electoral decisions could lead to policy changes. By contrast, because it permitted choice on the basis of candidates' individual appeals, the Australian ballot lessened the likelihood that the electorate would sweep an entirely new administration into power. Ticket splitting led to increasingly divided partisan control of government.

The ballots used in the United States are a mix of forms developed as long ago as the 1890s, when the states took over the printing of ballots from the political parties. These were modified during the 1940s and 1950s, when voting machines and punch-card ballots were introduced, and ballots were further updated in some jurisdictions during the 1990s, when more modern and accurate computerized voting methods were introduced. The choice of ballot format is a county decision, and, within any state, various counties may use different formats, depending on local resources and preferences. For example, the Palm Beach County butterfly ballot, which in 2000 seemed to confuse many voters, was selected by Democratic election officials who thought its larger print would

[24]Jerold G. Rusk, "The Effect of the Australian Ballot Reform on Split Ticket Voting: 1876–1908," *American Political Science Review* 64 (December 1970): 1220–38.

help elderly, predominantly Democratic voters read the names of the candidates. Often, as turned out to be the case in Florida, neighboring counties use completely different ballot systems. For example, the city of Baltimore, Maryland, introduced voting machines many years ago and continues to use them. Baltimore County, Maryland, uses more modern ballots that are optically scanned by computers. Neighboring Montgomery County, Maryland, employs a cumbersome punch-card system that requires voters to punch several different cards on both sides—a bewildering process that usually results in large numbers of spoiled ballots. In some states, including Florida, different precincts within the same county may use different voting methods, causing still more confusion.

As became only too evident during the struggle over Florida's votes in 2000, America's overall balloting process is awkward, confusing, riddled with likely sources of error and bias, and, in cases of close races, incapable of producing a result that will stand up to close scrutiny. Results can take several days to process, and every recount appears to produce a slightly different result. Often, too, the process of counting and recounting is directed by state and county officials with political axes to grind. The Votomatic punch-card machines used in a number of Florida counties are notoriously unreliable. The Votomatics are popular with many county governments because they are inexpensive. About 37 percent of the precincts in America's 3,140 counties use Votomatics or similar machines.[25] However, voters often find it difficult to insert the punch cards properly, frequently punch the wrong hole, or do not sufficiently perforate one or more chads to allow the punch cards to be read by the counting machine. Votomatics and other punch-card voting devices generally yield a much higher rate of spoiled votes than other voting methods. Indeed, a 1988 Florida Senate race was won by Republican Connie Mack in part because of thousands of spoiled Votomatic ballots. To make matters worse, precinct-level election officials—often elderly volunteers—may not understand the rules themselves, and they are, therefore, unable to help voters with questions. These difficulties would not have been subject to public scrutiny as long as they affected only local races. In 2000, however, America's antiquated electoral machinery collapsed under the weight of a presidential election, revealing its flaws for all to see. Despite these problems, electoral officials are often reluctant to change voting methods because changes can affect the outcome of the next election perhaps in ways that run against officials' preferences.

Institution Principle

The electoral college and the Australian ballot are two instances of how changes in electoral rules can affect the outcomes of elections.

referendum The practice of referring a measure proposed or passed by a legislature to the vote of the electorate for approval or rejection.

Direct Democracy: The Referendum and Recall

In addition to voting for candidates, twenty-four states also provide for referendum voting. The ***referendum*** process allows citizens to vote directly on proposed laws or other governmental actions. In recent years, voters in several states have voted to set limits on tax rates, to block state and local spending proposals, and

---

[25]Chad Terhune and Joni James, "Presidential Race Brings Attention to Business of Voting Machines," *Wall Street Journal*, 16 November 2000, p. A16.

to prohibit social services for illegal immigrants. Although it involves voting, a referendum is not an election. The election is an institution of representative government. Through an election, voters choose officials to act for them. The referendum, by contrast, is an institution of direct democracy; it allows voters to govern directly without intervention by government officials. The validity of referendum results, however, are subject to judicial action. If a court finds that a referendum outcome violates the state or national constitution, it can overturn the result. This happened in the case of a 1995 California referendum curtailing social services to illegal aliens.[26] It should be emphasized that the issues that emerge as referendum subjects are of the "hot button" variety. It is not clear that these often emotional issues, which require deliberation and reflection, are the ones best dealt with by direct democracy. In other words, referendum issues are often adversely selected.

Twenty-four states permit various forms of the initiative. Whereas the referendum described above allows citizens to affirm or reject a policy produced by legislative action, the **initiative** provides citizens with a way forward in the face of legislative *inaction*. This is done by placing a policy proposal (legislative or state constitutional amendment) on the ballot to be approved or disapproved by the electorate. To have a place on the ballot, a petition must be accompanied by a minimum number of voter signatures—a requirement that varies from state to state—that are certified by the state's secretary of state.

initiative A process by which citizens may petition to place a policy proposal on the ballot for public vote.

The initiative is also vulnerable to adverse selection. Ballot propositions involve policies the state legislative cannot (or does not want to) resolve. Like referendum issues, these are often highly emotional and, consequently, not always well suited to resolution in the electoral arena. One of the "virtues" of the initiative is that it may be *action forcing*. Legislative leaders can induce recalcitrant legislators to move ahead on controversial issues in the knowledge that a possibly worse outcome will result from inaction.[27]

Eighteen states also have legal provisions for **recall** elections. The recall is an electoral device introduced by turn-of-the-twentieth-century Populists to allow voters to remove governors and other state officials from office before the expiration of their terms. Federal officials such as the president and members of Congress are not subject to recall. Generally speaking, a recall effort begins with a petition campaign. For example, in California, the site of a tumultuous recall battle in 2003, if 12 percent of those who voted in the last general election sign petitions demanding a special recall election, one must be scheduled by the state board of elections. Such petition campaigns are relatively common, but most fail to garner enough signatures to bring the matter to a statewide vote. In the California case, however, a conservative Republican member of Congress, Darrell Issa, led a successful effort to recall Democratic governor Gray Davis. Voters were unhappy about the state's economy and dissatisfied with Davis's performance; they

recall Removal of a public official by popular vote.

---

[26]*League of United Latin American Citizens v. Wilson*, CV-94-7569 (C.D. Calif.) (1995).

[27]This point is developed in Morton Bennedsen and Sven Feldmann, "Lobbying Legislatures," *Journal of Political Economy* 110 (2002): 919–46.

blamed Davis for the state's $38 billion budget deficit. Issa and his followers were able to secure enough signatures to force a vote, and in October 2003 Davis became the second governor in American history to be recalled by his state's electorate (the first was North Dakota governor Lynn Frazier, who was recalled in 1921). Under California law, voters in a special recall election are also asked to choose a replacement for the official whom they dismiss. Californians in 2003 elected movie star Arnold Schwarzenegger to be their governor. While critics charged that the Davis recall had been a "political circus," the campaign had the effect of greatly increasing voter interest and involvement in the political process. More than 400,000 new voters registered in California in 2003, many drawn into the political arena by the opportunity to participate in the recall campaign.

The referendum, initiative, and recall all entail shifts in agenda-setting power. The referendum gives an impassioned electoral majority the opportunity to reverse legislation that displeases them, thus affecting the initial strategic calculations of institutional agenda setters (who want to get as much of what they want *without* its being subsequently reversed). The initiative has a similar effect on institutional agenda setters, but here it inclines them toward action rather than inaction. Combining the two, an institutional agenda setter is caught between the two horns of an institutional dilemma—do I act, risking reversal via referendum, or do I maintain the status quo, risking being overruled via initiative? The recall complements both of these, keeping institutional agenda setters on their toes to avoid being ousted.

HOW DO VOTERS DECIDE?

Thus far, we have focused on the election as an institution. But the election is also a process in which millions of individuals make decisions and choices. Three types of factors influence voters' decisions at the polls: partisan loyalty, issue and policy concerns, and candidate characteristics.

Partisan Loyalty

Many studies have shown that most Americans identify more or less strongly with one of the two major political parties. Partisan loyalty was considerably stronger during the 1940s and 1950s than it is today. But even now most voters feel a certain sense of identification or kinship with the Democratic or Republican party. This sense of identification is often handed down from parents to children and is reinforced by social and cultural ties. Partisan identification predisposes voters in favor of their party's candidates and against those of the opposing party. Partisanship is most likely to assert itself in the less-visible races, where issues and the candidates are not very well known. State legislative races, for example, are often decided by voters' party ties. However, even at the level of the presidential contest, in which issues and candidate personalities become very important, many Americans supported George W. Bush or John Kerry largely because of partisan loyalty (Figure 10.5). Once formed, partisan loyalties are resistant to change. But

FIGURE 10.5

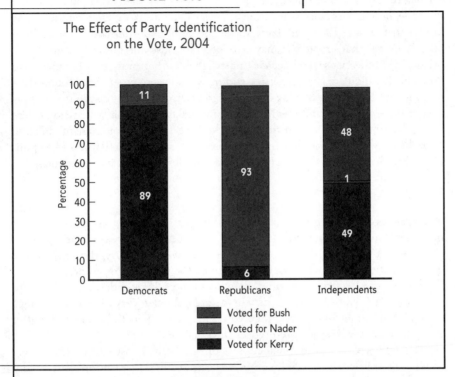

The Effect of Party Identification on the Vote, 2004

Voted for Bush
Voted for Nader
Voted for Kerry

sufficiently strong events and experiences may have the effect of eroding or even reversing them. White males in the South, for example, have, over the last fifty years, been transformed from strong partisans of the Democratic party to independents and even supporters of the Republican party. Voters tend to keep their party affiliations unless some crisis causes them to re-examine the bases of their loyalties and to conclude that they have not given their support to the appropriate party. During these relatively infrequent periods of electoral change, millions of voters can change their party ties. For example, at the beginning of the New Deal era between 1932 and 1936, millions of former Republicans transferred their allegiance to Franklin Roosevelt and the Democrats.

Partisan loyalty should be understood as more than a psychological attachment (although it certainly is that as well). It is also an informational shortcut—a way for voters to economize on information collection and processing. In many circumstances, it may be "enough" simply to know what party label a particular candidate wears. Any extra information—issue positions or personal attributes—may not influence the voter's choice once the partisan content has been taken on board. For example, once a particular voter learns that a candidate is a Democrat, he or she knows that this candidate is likely to be the preferred alternative; for another voter, however, that simple fact may be enough to cause him or her to vote for the other guy! In the last several decades, party label has begun to lose its capacity to signal likely candidate characteristics, and more and more voters have found their partisan attachments weakening or disappearing altogether. The rise in the proportion of the electorate who now identify only weakly with a party or who declare themselves independents is testimony to this fact.[28] (In the next chapter, Figure 11.2 shows the relative decline in Democratic partisanship, the flatness of Republican identification, and the steep rise in those professing to be independents.)

Issues

Issues and policy preferences are a second factor influencing voters' choices at the polls. Voters may cast their ballots for the candidate whose position on economic issues they believe to be closest to their own. Similarly, they may select the candidate who has what they believe to be the best record on foreign policy. Issues are more important in some races than others. If candidates actually "take issue" with one another—that is, articulate and publicize very different positions on important public questions—then voters are more likely to be able to identify and act on whatever policy preferences they may have.[29]

The ability of voters to make choices on the basis of issue or policy preferences is diminished, however, if competing candidates do not differ substantially or do not focus their campaigns on policy matters. Very often, candidates deliberately take the safe course and emphasize topics that will not be offensive to any voters. Thus candidates often trumpet their opposition to corruption, crime, and inflation. Presumably, few voters favor these things. While it may be perfectly reasonable for candidates to take the safe course and remain as inoffensive as possible, this candidate strategy makes it extremely difficult for voters to make their issue or policy preferences the bases for their choices at the polls.

Similarly, a paucity of useful and discriminating information during a campaign can induce the "wrong" decision by "knowledge-challenged" voters. Some

---

[28] For a detailed assessment of the political use of information-economizing devices like party labels, see Arthur Lupia and Mathew D. McCubbins, *The Democratic Dilemma: Can Citizens Learn What They Need to Know?* (New York: Cambridge University Press, 1998). For the classic argument that party loyalty is a *variable*, not a constant, and that the voter updates party loyalty on the basis of his or her experience with the parties and their candidates, see Morris P. Fiorina, *Retrospective Voting in American National Elections* (New Haven, CT: Yale University Press, 1981).

[29] Issue preferences and partisan loyalty are often suggested as separate factors influencing the voter's decision. Along with Morris Fiorina, however, let us reiterate that partisan identification is not merely a psychological attachment (like Boston's love affair with the Red Sox). There is a heavy dose of issue content to party identification. If a party consistently moves away from issue positions important to voters, then partisan attachment weakens. Voters are subsequently less likely to use the partisan label as an informational shortcut.

analysts claimed that in 2000 Al Gore snatched defeat from the jaws of victory in just this way. In his efforts to distance himself from his scandal-plagued predecessor, he also failed to remind voters of his great successes—eight years of peace and prosperity as Clinton's vice president. Consequently, voters, such as moderate Republicans, who may have been prepared to overlook Gore's party label because of his achievements were not given much opportunity to do so.[30] An example from the most recent campaign also illustrates this. During the 2004 campaign, John Kerry provided abundant information about his views on the war in Iraq, but they straddled so many different sides of the issue as to confuse rather than inform voters. At one point he began emphasizing in campaign speeches that he had voted against a war appropriation in Senate deliberation but had voted for it a few minutes later. Analysts believe his straddling was an attempt to establish his credentials with antiwar voters while not alienating those who supported the war. This "mixed" strategy earned Kerry the label of "flip-flopper" in Republican campaign advertising.

Voters' issue choices usually involve a mix of their judgments about the past behavior of competing parties and candidates, with their hopes and fears about candidates' future behavior. Political scientists call choices that focus on future behavior ***prospective voting,*** and those based on past performance are called ***retrospective voting.*** To some extent, whether prospective or retrospective evaluation is more important in a particular election depends on the strategies of competing candidates. Candidates always endeavor to define the issues of an election in terms that will serve their interests. Incumbents running during a period of prosperity will seek to take credit for the economy's happy state and define the election as revolving around their record of success. This strategy encourages voters to make retrospective judgments. By contrast, an insurgent running during a period of economic uncertainty will tell voters it is time for a change and ask them to make prospective judgments. Thus Bill Clinton focused on change in 1992 and prosperity in 1996 and through well-crafted media campaigns was able to define voters' agenda of choices.

In 2004, President Bush emphasized his efforts to protect the nation from terrorists and his strong commitment to religious and moral values. Democratic candidate John Kerry, on the other hand, attacked Bush's decision to invade Iraq, questioned the president's leadership in the war on terror, and charged that the president's economic policies had failed to produce prosperity. When asked by exit pollsters which issue mattered most in deciding how they voted for president, 22 percent of all voters cited moral values as their chief concern. More than 80 percent of these voters supported President Bush. The economy was cited as the most important issue by 20 percent of those who voted and 80 percent of these Americans voted for Senator Kerry. Terrorism ranked third in terms of the percentage of voters who indicated it was the most important issue for

prospective voting Voting based on the imagined future performance of a candidate.

retrospective voting Voting based on the past performance of a candidate.

[30]This argument is spelled out in Morris Fiorina, Samuel Abrams, and Jeremy Pope, "The 2000 U.S. Presidential Election: Can Retrospective Voting Be Saved?" *British Journal of Political Science* 33 (2003): 163–87.

them. President Bush received more than 80 percent of the votes of those Americans concerned mainly with terrorism.

Rationality Principle

Issue voting motivates candidates to converge toward the median voter.

When voters engage in issue voting, competition between the two candidates has the effect of pushing the candidate issue positions toward the middle of the distribution of voter preferences. This is known as the *median voter theorem*, made famous by Duncan Black and Anthony Downs.[31] To see the logic of this claim, imagine a series of possible stances on a policy issue as points along a line, stretching from 0 to 100 (Figure 10.6). A voter is represented by an "ideal" policy and preferences, which decline as policy moves away from this ideal. Thus voters in Group 1 prefer policy X_1 most, and their preference declines as the policy moves to the left or right of X_1. Voters whose ideal policy lies between, say, 0 and 25 are said to be liberal on this policy (Groups 1 and 2), those whose ideal lies between 75 and 100 are conservative (Groups 4 and 5), and those whose favorite policy is between 25 and 75 are moderate (Group 3). An issue voter cares only about issue positions, not partisan loyalty or candidate characteristics, and would, therefore, vote for the candidate whose announced policy is closest to his or her own most preferred policy.

Policy Principle

The median voter theorem predicts policy moderation on the part of candidates.

Consider now an electorate of 125 voters evenly distributed among the five groups shown in Figure 10.6. The middle group contains the median voter because half or more of this electorate has an ideal policy at or to the left of X_3 (Groups 1, 2, and 3) and half or more has an ideal policy at or to the right of X_3 (Groups 3, 4, and 5). Group 3 is in the driver's seat, as the following reasoning suggests. If a candidate announces X_3 as his policy—the most preferred alternative of the median voter—and if his opponent picks any point to the right, then the median voter and all those with ideal policies to the left of the median voter's (Groups 1–3) will support the first candidate. They constitute a majority, by definition of the median, so this candidate will win. Suppose instead that the opponent chose as her policy some point to the left of the median ideal policy. Then the median voter and all those with ideal policies to the right of the median voter's (Groups 3–5) will support the first candidate—and he wins, again. In short, the median voter theorem says that the candidate whose policy position is closest to the ideal policy of the median voter will defeat the other candidate in a majority contest. We can conclude from this brief analysis that issue voting encourages *candidate convergence* (both candidates move toward the center to cozy up to the position of the median voter). Even when voters are not exclusively issue voters, two-candidate competition still encourages a tendency toward convergence, although it may not fully run its course.[32]

[31]See Duncan Black, *The Theory of Committees and Elections*, rev. 2nd ed. (Boston: Kluwer, 1998), and Anthony Downs, *An Economic Theory of Democracy* (New York: Harper, 1957). A general, accessible treatment of this subject is found in Shepsle and Bonchek, *Analyzing Politics*, Chapter 5.

[32]This convergence will also be a moderating force as candidates move toward what they believe will appeal to voters in the middle. But if the middle of the voter distribution of preferences tilts toward the right or toward the left, it may not be very "moderate"—if X_3, for example, was barely to the left of X_4.

FIGURE 10.6

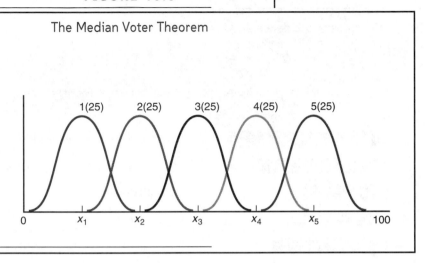

The Median Voter Theorem

Politicians competing to win a majority of the 125 votes will tend to move their policy position to the location of the median voter (a member of group 3 with most-preferred-policy x_3).

The Economy   As we identify the strategies and tactics employed by opposing political candidates and parties, we should keep in mind that the best-laid plans of politicians often go awry. Election outcomes are affected by a variety of forces that candidates for office cannot fully control. Among the most important of these forces is the condition of the economy. If voters are satisfied with their economic prospects, they tend to support the party in power, while voter unease about the economy tends to favor the opposition. Thus George H. W. Bush lost in 1992 during an economic downturn, even though his victory in the Middle East had briefly given him a 90 percent favorable rating in the polls. And Bill Clinton won in 1996 during an economic boom, even though voters had serious concerns about his moral fiber. Over the past quarter-century, the Consumer Confidence Index, calculated by the Conference Board, a business research group, has been a fairly accurate predictor of presidential outcomes. The index is based on surveys asking voters how optimistic they are about the future of the economy. It would appear that a generally rosy view, indicated by a score greater than 100, augers well for the party in power. An index score less than 100, suggesting that voters are pessimistic about the economy's trend, suggests that incumbents should worry about their own job prospects (Figure 10.7).

FIGURE 10.7

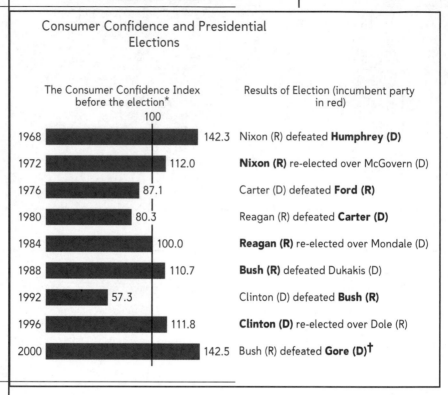

Consumer Confidence and Presidential Elections

The Consumer Confidence Index before the election*	Results of Election (incumbent party in red)
1968 — 142.3	Nixon (R) defeated **Humphrey (D)**
1972 — 112.0	**Nixon (R)** re-elected over McGovern (D)
1976 — 87.1	Carter (D) defeated **Ford (R)**
1980 — 80.3	Reagan (R) defeated **Carter (D)**
1984 — 100.0	**Reagan (R)** re-elected over Mondale (D)
1988 — 110.7	**Bush (R)** defeated Dukakis (D)
1992 — 57.3	Clinton (D) defeated **Bush (R)**
1996 — 111.8	**Clinton (D)** re-elected over Dole (R)
2000 — 142.5	Bush (R) defeated **Gore (D)**[†]

*Survey was bimonthly before 1977, so figures for 1968, 1972, and 1976 are for October; they are for September from 1980 on.

[†]Gore won the popular vote but Bush was elected by the Electoral College.

SOURCE: Bloomberg Financial Markets.

Candidate Characteristics

Candidates' personal attributes always influence voters' decisions. Some analysts claim that voters prefer tall candidates to short ones, candidates with shorter names to candidates with longer names, and candidates with lighter hair to candidates with darker hair. Perhaps these rather frivolous criteria do play some role. But the more important candidate characteristics that affect voters' choices are race, ethnicity, religion, gender, geography, and social background. In general, voters prefer candidates who are closer to themselves in terms of these categories. Voters presume that such candidates are likely to have views and perspectives close to their own. Moreover, they may be proud to see someone of their ethnic, religious, or geographic background in a position of leadership. This is why, for many years, politicians sought to "balance the ticket," making certain that their party's ticket included members of as many important groups as possible.

Just as a candidate's personal characteristics may attract some voters, so they may repel others. Many voters are prejudiced against candidates of certain ethnic, racial, or religious groups. And for many years, voters were reluctant to support the political candidacies of women, although this appears to be changing.

Voters also pay attention to candidates' personality characteristics, such as their "decisiveness," "honesty," and "vigor." In recent years, integrity has become a key election issue. In the 2000 presidential race, Al Gore chose Joe Lieberman as his running mate in part because Lieberman had been sharply critical of Bill Clinton's moral lapses. The senator's presence on the Democratic ticket thus helped defuse the GOP's efforts to link Gore to Clinton's questionable character. In the 2004 presidential race, President Bush and the Republicans accused Senator Kerry of being inconsistent, a "flip-flopper" who continually changed his positions when it was expedient to do so. Bush, on the other hand, emphasized his own constancy. "I say what I mean and I do what I say" was the president's frequent refrain. The president also pointed to his strong religious commitment as evidence of exemplary character. For their part, Democrats emphasized Senator Kerry's intelligence, empathy for ordinary Americans, and record of wartime heroism, which, they said, stood in sharp contrast to Bush's own somewhat blemished military record. In the end, the GOP's characterization of Kerry as a "flip-flopper" and Bush as an individual with deep moral and religious commitments seemed to resonate with voters. Among those who said that it was important for the president to take a clear stand on issues, 80 percent voted for President Bush; among those for whom strong religious faith was important, 90 percent voted for Bush; and among those who cited honesty as the candidate quality that mattered most, more than 70 percent gave their votes to Bush. On the other hand, among Americans who thought a president should be empathic and care about people like them, Kerry received 75 percent support, and among those who thought intelligence was the most important personal characteristic of a president, 91 percent voted for Kerry and only 9 percent for Bush.

All candidates seek, through polling and other mechanisms, to determine the best image to project to the electorate. At the same time, the communications media—television in particular—exercise a good deal of control over how voters perceive candidates. In recent years, the candidates have developed a number of techniques designed to wrest control of the image-making process away from the media. Among the chief instruments of this "spin control" are candidate talk-show appearances, used quite effectively by both Al Gore and George W. Bush. During one appearance, Bush gave Oprah Winfrey a big kiss to show that he was friendly and not "stiff" like his opponent, Al Gore.

THE 2004 ELECTIONS

In 2004, President George W. Bush led the Republican party to a solid electoral victory, winning 51 percent of the popular vote versus Senator John Kerry's 48 percent, a 286–252 majority in the electoral college (Figure 10.8), and helping solidify what had been shaky Republican control of both houses of Congress. Republicans added four seats in the Senate, giving them a 55–44 majority (with one independent) and five seats in the House of Representatives, to gain a 234–200 majority in the lower chamber (with one independent). To embarrass the Democrats further, Senate Democratic leader Tom Daschle was defeated by his Republican opponent in a hard-fought South Dakota campaign.

Bush's political strategists, led by senior adviser Karl Rove, believed that three ingredients would combine to solidify the president's political strength and ensure his re-election in 2004. The first of these was an expansive economic policy. The Bush administration pursued a program of tax cuts and low interest rates that it hoped would produce a booming economy by election time. Generally, presidents who preside during times of economic decline are not returned to office (Figure 10.7) The second ingredient was money. Early in his term, President Bush embarked on an unprecedented fund-raising effort, building a $100-million campaign chest before the Democrats were even close to nominating a candidate.

The final ingredient was the war on terrorism. The war on terrorism entailed new risks but, politically speaking, also produced new opportunities. A war of indefinite duration would mean that on a permanent and ongoing basis the American public would look to its government, especially to its president, for protection and reassurance. So long as the public remained convinced that President Bush was making an effective effort to safeguard the nation, it would be unlikely to deprive him of office.

Democratic Opportunities

In the aftermath of September 11, 2001, President Bush seemed to have developed a formula that virtually guaranteed political success. A new set of political circumstances, however, emerged to diminish the president's political standing and to threaten his grip on power. The first of these was the economy. Despite the administration's efforts, economic growth was slow and job growth anemic through Bush's first term in office. The sluggish economy allowed Democrats to declare that Bush was the only president in recent history to preside over a net loss of jobs during his administration. Ultimately, more important than the economy was the Iraq war. Most Americans initially supported the war, and early battlefield success seemed to bolster President Bush's standing. It soon became apparent, however, that any Iraqi weapons of mass destruction program that might have once existed had been largely abandoned by Saddam Hussein's regime. The administration, moreover, failed to prove a connection between Sad-

FIGURE 10.8

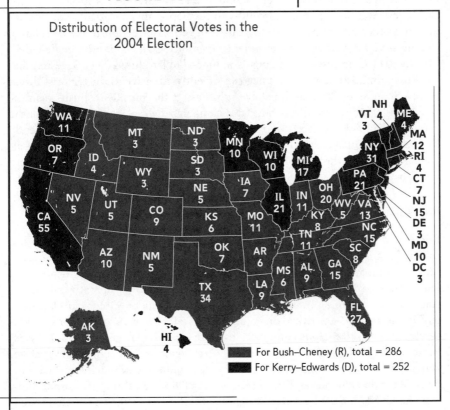

Distribution of Electoral Votes in the 2004 Election

For Bush–Cheney (R), total = 286
For Kerry–Edwards (D), total = 252

dam and terrorism. Thus the president's stated war aims seemed to have been mistaken. To make matters worse, armed resistance to the American occupation of Iraq gradually stiffened, producing a steady drumbeat of American casualties. The Iraq war, though militarily successful, appeared to have been pointless and suddenly made Bush politically vulnerable.

Adding to the president's problems and to the Democrats' opportunities was the effort by rich liberal activists—George Soros, for example—to form independent groups, known as *527 committees*, specifically to defeat President Bush. Beyond raising millions of dollars to defeat Bush, these independent groups also registered millions of new Democratic voters. This influx of registrants posed a substantial threat to the GOP, not only at the presidential level but in congressional and local races as well.

527 committees
Tax-exempt organizations that engage in political activities, often through unlimited "soft-money" contributions. They're not restricted by current law on campaign finance, exploiting a loophole in the Internal Revenue Service code.

Still, Democrats understood that to have any serious chance of defeating President Bush, they must somehow undermine the president's strongest political claim—that he responded forcefully to the September 11 attacks and continued to protect the country from the threat of terrorism. As Bush had calculated, so long as voters accepted the president's contentions, he could not be defeated. But the 9/11 Commission's findings, announced in late July 2004, suggested that the Bush administration had not been sufficiently attentive to the terrorist threat before September 2001 and deeply embarrassed the president. Bush was now clearly vulnerable, and throughout the campaign Democrats charged that the president had failed to heed warnings of a terrorist attack and had subsequently focused on an imaginary threat from Iraq rather than the real danger from al-Qaeda. This was a theme emphasized by Senator Kerry during all three presidential debates.

Republican Strategies

Republicans were hardly idle while their Democratic foes enrolled voters and castigated the president. To deal with the threat posed by newly registered Democratic voters, the GOP began its own voter-registration campaign. Armed with data on millions of voters and potential voters, GOP operatives in every state—especially in so-called battleground states such as Ohio, Florida, Iowa, and Pennsylvania—embarked on an ambitious effort to register millions of conservative voters. Religious conservatives were a particular target of GOP registration efforts. To ensure that the growing legion of religious conservatives actually went to the polls on November 2, Republican campaign materials emphasized moral themes and the president's religious and moral commitments, and the GOP launched a series of ballot initiatives on such "hot-button" issues as same-sex marriage and abortion. Republicans calculated that these initiatives in closely contested Ohio and Florida would bring religious conservatives to the polls. Once at their polling places, they would also vote for President Bush. This strategy seems to have been especially successful in Ohio, where religious conservatives mobilized furiously behind an initiative to ban same-sex marriage. Ohio turned out to be essential to Bush's re-election.

Ultimately, competitive Democratic and Republican registration efforts produced the highest level of voter turnout in nearly four decades. About 55 percent of voting-age Americans went to the polls in 2004, an increase of almost five percentage points over 2000. In the end, more new voters supported Kerry than Bush, but the margin was not overwhelming. The Democratic effort to overwhelm the GOP with new registrants had been blunted.

In addition to enrolling their own new voters and emphasizing the religious themes deemed important to these voters, Republicans worked to discredit Kerry as a plausible president. Bush and other Republican campaigners accused Kerry of continually "flip-flopping" on important issues. Republicans also sought to undermine one of Kerry's strongest moral claims, his record during the Vietnam war. Just as Democrats had raised questions about Bush's leadership after the September 11 attacks, so Republicans raised questions about Kerry's military record. The GOP organized a group of conservative veterans called "Swift Boat Veterans for Truth" who succeeded in airing doubts about the truth of Kerry's wartime heroism. The GOP's efforts seemed to bear fruit. Throughout the early fall 2004, President Bush maintained a solid lead in the polls, despite months of Democratic attacks.

The End Game

In October, however, Bush's lead appeared to evaporate in the wake of the presidential debates. In most national elections, the first debate is crucial. Much of the nation watches or listens to the first debate while the audience diminishes in size during the ensuing debates. Most observers agreed that President Bush's performance in the first debate was a political disaster. The president appeared ill-at-ease and some commentators described him as irritable, whereas Senator Kerry was articulate and quite presidential in demeanor. The national news media, generally unfriendly to Bush, declared the debate a major Kerry victory. Republicans were stunned and Democrats elated. Bush rallied in the subsequent two debates, but most of the media declared Kerry the victor in each one and awarded John Edwards the victory in the vice-presidential clash. In the aftermath of the debates, the polls indicated that the two tickets were running neck and neck.

As the election approached, each side realized that success would depend on its ability to produce high levels of turnout among its most loyal partisans in the ten or so states that could swing to either party. Democrats relied on their traditional allies, such as labor unions and African American churches, and sought to ensure high levels of turnout among their new registrants. For example, to encourage newly registered college students to go to the polls, the Kerry campaign charged that President Bush was planning to reinstitute military conscription—a factually baseless but politically useful claim. For their part, Republicans relied heavily on such conservative groups as the Home School Legal Defense Fund and a host of religious organizations to bring out their voters. In this so-called ground game, each party made use of enormous computer data banks to identify likely voters and volunteers.

In the end, the GOP's superior on-the-ground organization prevailed. Republicans registered and brought to the polls tens of millions of religious conservatives who gave President Bush the margin of victory in such key states as Florida, Ohio, and Missouri. The importance of religious conservatives is manifest in the exit poll data, which indicate that on a national basis 22 percent of all voters cited moral values as the issue that mattered most to them—more voters than cited the economy, terrorism, the Iraq war, or any other issue. Of these morally committed Americans, an overwhelming proportion gave their votes to President Bush.[33]

---

[33]These exit polls indicate voter sentiment but are not of the highest scientific merit. What *is* impressive is not that "moral values" was the single most important issue in the campaign—it probably was not— but that many Americans found it important, and of these, overwhelming proportions voted for Bush.

The 2004 Election: The Minimax Regret Strategy of Presidential Campaigning

According to the median voter theorem, competition in our political system—with a winner-take-all election system and two political parties—forces the major contenders to moderate their policies and converge toward the middle of the ideological spectrum.

Yet in the 2004 election, chief Republican political strategist Karl Rove openly disdained a strategy of moderation. He focused the Bush candidacy squarely on the Republican base, assuming that turning out the base, plus drawing into the election the 4 million self-identified evangelical Christians who did not vote in 2000, would be enough to push the president to victory.[1] In contrast to the "compassionate conservative" Bush of 2000, who tried to appeal on education, health care, and national service,[2] the "wartime" Bush of 2004 focused on terrorism, an extension of his already controversial tax cuts, a ban on gay marriage, and attacks on his opponent's credibility and character.

Did Karl Rove disprove the median voter theorem in 2004? If we consider that the candidates converged in most respects on how the government ought to manage the economy, then the answer is no. Traditionally in the United States, "liberals" have advocated for a larger role for government in reducing the inequalities that inevitably accompany capitalism, while "conservatives" believe that the economy, and society, functions better if government plays a smaller, if not minimal, role.[3] Yet Democratic candidate Bill Clinton called for an "end to welfare as we know it" during his 1992 acceptance speech and near the end of his first term signed legislation that essentially ended welfare. By 1997, Clinton had positioned the Democratic Party as the party of fiscal responsibility and small government. Candidates Bush and Kerry differed dramatically on how well the economy had been managed, but neither proposed dramatic changes to what government ought to do for the next four years.[4]

But what the last quarter-century of presidential elections have made clear is that Americans don't evaluate presidential candidates solely on the basis of traditional notions of "liberal" and "conservative." Political scientist Morris Fiorina argues that candidate competition occurs along two dimensions, the first being economic and the second being moral. Thomas Franks, in *What's the Matter with Kansas?,* argues that Kansans (and, by implication, working-class voters nationwide) are no longer voting their economic self-interest, but instead are voting on the basis of their moral interests.[5]

It is certainly hard to think of "morality" in the same way that we think of proposals to raise or lower taxes or spend more or less on defense. But psychologists have known for decades that our perception of other people relies heavily on emotions and on personality assessments. Essentially, how we evaluate a presidential candidate may depend as much on whether we *like* that person as on what we think he or she will do for us.[6]

Did Bush and Kerry differ on morality—or more importantly, did voters *think* they differed? We've already seen that the Bush campaign became quite active on gay marriage, endorsing a constitutional amendment banning gay marriage and encouraging

Policy Principle

As predicted by the median voter theorem, both parties converged on a small-government, low-deficit policy during the 1990s.

Rationality Principle

When voters don't perceive differences between the parties on economics, they may substitute moral concerns for more traditional economic policy concerns.

state initiatives.[7] In exit polls, 80 percent of respondents who placed "moral issues" at the top of their concerns voted for Bush.[8] Voters who said they regularly attended church voted for Bush 65–35 percent, while those who said they never or seldom attended church voted for Kerry 65–35 percent. And, as Karl Rove predicted, evangelical voters turned out at much higher rates in 2004 than in 2000, and these new voters went overwhelmingly for George Bush. Gay marriage played a key role in turnout among evangelicals.[9] Kerry, it seems, was never able to convince voters most focused on moral issues that he shared their concerns.

But there is another advantage that Bush had over Kerry, one that has something to do with personality but fits much better into theories of rational behavior. Some theories of rational behavior don't focus as much on maximizing utility as on minimizing the possibility of loss (often called "minimax regret"). One way to minimize the chances of loss is to reduce uncertainty. Put your money on a sure bet, even if it's not the best choice, because you know what the payoff will be.

How does this apply to voting? Political scientist R. Michael Alvarez has shown that presidential voters are risk averse—they don't like uncertainty.[10] This is completely rational. The presidency is far too important to give to an unknown or uncertain quantity.

Such behavior hurt John Kerry badly. For millions of voters, the 2004 election was all about reducing uncertainty—uncertainty about the war in Iraq, about the economy, and about America's future in the world. And for these Americans, George Bush, while maybe not the ideal candidate, was a known quantity. Kerry, by contrast, was a relative unknown. The more you believed that terrorists were an ongoing threat and the more fearful you were about the future, the more likely you were to vote for Bush.

Kerry knew that many voters disapproved of Bush's handling of the economy and thought that this would bring him victory. But Karl Rove knew that many more voters cared about morality and leadership. So in one respect, Rove *did* disprove the median voter theorem by finding dimensions on which Kerry could not "converge" with Bush. In another respect, however, Rove only showed us that rationality is more complicated than we think it is and that reducing *uncertainty* can be as important to voters as any single issue.

 Rationality Principle

Minimax regret [a theory of rationality where you minimize possible loss] shows us that presidential voters often choose the known quantity— an incumbent— during uncertain times.

[1]For an account of Rove's strategy, see Chris Suellentrop, "The Vanishing Non Voter," *Slate,* 20 October 2004 (slate.msn.com/id/2108924/), and Stephen Koff and Bill Sloat, "Bush Targets GOP Base," *Cleveland Plain Dealer,* 16 October 2004.

[2]Allison Mitchell, "Bush Campaign Draws Theme from More Than the Heart," *New York Times,* 11 June 2000.

[3]Theodore Lowi, *The End of Liberalism,* 2nd ed. (New York: Norton, 1979).

[4]Kerry did argue against an extension of Bush's 2001 tax cuts, but even those extensions were not scheduled to take place until 2010, well after either candidate's term would have ended.

[5]Morris Fiorina, *Culture War? The Myth of a Polarized America* (New York: Longman, 2005). Thomas Franks, *What's the Matter with Kansas?* (New York: Metropolitan Books, 2004).

[6]Carolyn Funk, "Bringing the Candidate into Models of Candidate Evaluation," *Journal of Politics* 61.3 (1999).

[7]Peter Brownfield, "Gay Marriage: A Campaign Wedge Issue," Fox News, 5 October 2004. Available at www.foxnews.com/story/0,2933,134442,00.html.

[8]Alan Borshuk and Nahal Toosi, "Election 2004: Focus on Values Drove Many Bush Voters," *Milwaukee Journal Sentinel,* 4 November 2004.

[9]Debra Rosenberg and Karen Breslau, "Culture Wars: Winning the Values Vote," *Newsweek,* 15 November 2004.

[10]R. Michael Alvarez, *Information and Elections* (Ann Arbor: University of Michigan Press, 2000).

For the most part, each candidate ran well among voters who normally support his party. Kerry won the support of union members, Jews, African Americans, and women. Bush was successful among white males, upper-income wage earners, and southerners. Neither candidate reached much beyond his political base, though Bush was somewhat more successful in 2004 than in 2000 among women, Hispanics, and Catholics. After hundreds of millions of dollars in expenditures and years of planning and maneuvering, the key to victory was old-fashioned voter turnout. After the issues had been debated, charges made and answered, and claims made and debunked, Bush and the GOP prevailed because a record number of Republicans went to the polls on November 2—a democratic conclusion to an untidy but thoroughly democratic process.

CAMPAIGN FINANCE

Modern national political campaigns are fueled by enormous amounts of money. In a national race, millions of dollars are spent on media time as well as on public opinion polls and media consultants. In 2000, political candidates and independent groups spent more than $3 billion on election campaigns. The average winning candidate in a campaign for a seat in the House of Representatives spent more than $500,000; the average winner in a senatorial campaign spent $4.5 million.[34] The 2004 Democratic and Republican presidential candidates were eligible to receive a total of $150 million in public funds to run their campaigns.[35] Each presidential candidate was also helped by tens of millions of dollars in so-called independent expenditures on the part of corporate and ideological political action committees. As long as such political expenditures are not formally coordinated with a candidate's campaign, they are considered to be constitutionally protected free speech and are not subject to legal limitation or even reporting requirements.[36]

Sources of Campaign Funds

Federal Election Commission data suggest that approximately a quarter of the private funds spent on political campaigns in the United States is raised through small, direct-mail contributions from ordinary citizens; another quarter is provided by large, individual gifts; another comes from contributions from political action committees (PACs). The remaining quarter is drawn from the political parties and from candidates' personal or family resources.[37] Another source of campaign funds that are not required to be reported to the Federal Election Commission is independent expenditures by interest groups and parties.

[34]Jonathan Salant, "Million-Dollar Campaigns Proliferate in 105th," *Congressional Quarterly Weekly Report*, 21 December 1996, pp. 3448–51.
[35]U.S. Federal Election Commission.
[36]It is likely, however, that Congress or the courts will attempt to rein in spending by 527 committees.
[37]Federal Election Commission reports.

Individual Donors   Direct mail serves both as a vehicle for communicating with voters and as a mechanism for raising funds. Direct-mail fund-raising efforts begin with the purchase or rental of computerized mailing lists of voters deemed likely to support the candidate because of their partisan ties, interests, or ideology. Candidates send out pamphlets, letters, and brochures describing their views and appealing for funds. Tens of millions of dollars are raised by national, state, and local candidates through direct mail each year, usually in $25 and $50 contributions, although in 2000, Bush and Gore collected about three quarters of their donor contributions from individuals giving the then-$1,000 maximum amount.[38]

Political Action and 527 Committees   *Political action committees (PACs)* are organizations established by corporations, labor unions, or interest groups to channel the contributions of their members into political campaigns. Under the terms of the 1971 Federal Elections Campaign Act, which governs campaign finance in the United States, PACs are permitted to make larger contributions to any given candidate than individuals are allowed to make. Individuals may donate a maximum of $2,000 to any single candidate, but a PAC may donate as much as $5,000 to each candidate. Moreover, allied or related PACs often coordinate their campaign contributions, greatly increasing the amount of money a candidate actually receives from the same interest group. As a result, PACs have become central to campaign finance in the United States. Many critics assert that PACs corrupt the political process by allowing corporations and other interests to influence politicians with large contributions. It is by no means clear, however, that PACs corrupt the political process any more than large, individual contributions.

More than 4,500 PACs are registered with the Federal Election Commission (FEC), which oversees campaign finance practices in the United States. Nearly two thirds of all PACs represent corporations, trade associations, and other business and professional groups. Alliances of bankers, lawyers, doctors, and merchants all sponsor PACs. One example is the National Beer Wholesaler's Association PAC, which, for many years, was known as "SixPAC." Labor unions also sponsor PACs, as do ideological, public interest, and nonprofit groups. For example, the National Rifle Association sponsors a PAC, as does the Sierra Club. Many congressional and party leaders have also established PACs, known as leadership PACs, to provide funding for their political allies.

In recent years, PACs and individual contributions—so-called hard money—have amounted to hundreds of millions of dollars for political campaigns. But, while they have been important fund-raising tools, they have been overshadowed by so-called soft money contributed to the political parties and then recycled into campaigns. Soft money is not contributed directly to a candidate and is thus not subject to the limitations of the Federal Elections Campaign Act. As a result, well-heeled individuals and interests often preferred to make large,

political action committees (PACs)   Private groups that raise and distribute funds for use in election campaigns.

---

[38]Ibid. In 2004, Howard Dean, the governor of Vermont, emerged as a major contestant for the Democratic presidential nomination in large part because he mastered campaign fund-raising via the Internet.

anonymous soft-money contributions to parties rather than—or in addition to—relatively small and publicly recorded contributions directly to PACs and candidates. By 2000, as many as three soft-money dollars were spent for every dollar of hard money given directly and thus subject to FEC regulation. The 2002 campaign finance reform act outlawed many, albeit not all, forms of soft money and thus potentially will increase the importance of political action committees in the funding process.

The 527 committees have been another important source of soft money. Expenditures by these committees are "soft" because they are not given to or coordinated with any specific candidate's campaign. Indeed, 527 committee advertisements cannot directly endorse a candidate. But by registering voters with serious Democratic propensities in 2004, as did the 527 committee financed by billionaire George Soros, or by attacking John Kerry's Vietnam service record, as did the Swift Boat Veterans for Truth, these soft money expenditures had clear and significant candidate- and party-specific effects.

The Candidates   On the basis of the Supreme Court's 1976 decision in *Buckley v. Valeo*,[39] the right of individual candidates to spend their *own* money on their campaigns for office is a constitutionally protected matter of free speech and is not subject to limitation. Thus extremely wealthy candidates often contribute millions of dollars to their own campaigns. Jon Corzine, for example, spent approximately $60 million of his own funds in a successful New Jersey Senate bid in 2000.

Independent Spending   As was noted above, some forms of spending is also free from regulation; private groups, political parties, and wealthy individuals, engaging in what is called *issue advocacy,* may spend as much as they wish to help elect one candidate or defeat another, as long as these expenditures are not coordinated with any candidate's campaign. Many business and ideological groups engage in such activities. Some estimates suggest that groups and individuals spent as much as $509 million on issue advocacy—generally through television advertising—during the 2000 elections.[40] The National Rifle Association, for example, spent $3 million to remind voters of the importance of the right to bear arms, while the National Abortion and Reproductive Rights League spent nearly $5 million to express its support for Al Gore.

Some groups are careful not to mention particular candidates in their issue ads to avoid any suggestion that they might merely be fronts for a candidate's campaign committee. Most issue ads, however, are attacks on the opposing candidate's record or character. Organized labor spent more than $35 million in 1996 to attack a number of Republican candidates for the House of Representatives. Business groups launched their own multimillion-dollar issues campaign to defend the

issue advocacy
Independent spending by individuals or interest groups on a campaign issue but not directly tied to a particular candidate.

---

[39] *Buckley v. Valeo*, 424 U.S. 1 (1976).

[40] Kathleen Hall Jamieson, "Issue Advertising in the 1999–2000 Election Cycle," Annenberg Public Policy Center, University of Pennsylvania, 1 February 2001.

GOP House members targeted by labor.[41] In 2000, liberal groups ran ads bashing Bush's record on capital punishment, tax reform, and Social Security. Conservative groups attacked Gore's views on gun ownership, abortion, and environmental regulation. In 2004, many of these same groups attacked Bush and Kerry, respectively.

Public Funding The Federal Elections Campaign Act also provides for public funding of presidential campaigns. As they seek a major party presidential nomination, candidates become eligible for public funds by raising at least $5,000 in individual contributions of $250 or less in each of twenty states. Candidates who reach this threshold may apply for federal funds to match, on a dollar-for-dollar basis, all individual contributions of $250 or less they receive. The funds are drawn from the Presidential Election Campaign Fund. Taxpayers can contribute $1 to this fund, at no additional cost to themselves, by checking a box on the first page of their federal income tax returns. Major party presidential candidates receive a lump sum (currently nearly $90 million) during the summer before the general election. They must meet all their campaign expenses from this money—that is, they may not accept other contributions. Under current law, no candidate is required to accept public funding for either the nominating races or general presidential election. Candidates who do not accept public funding are not affected by any expenditure limits. Thus in 1992 Ross Perot financed his own presidential bid and was not bound by the $55 million limit to which the Democratic and Republican candidates were held that year. Perot accepted public funding in 1996. In 2000, George W. Bush refused public funding and raised enough money to finance his own primary campaign. Eventually, Bush raised and spent nearly $200 million—twice the limit to which matching funds would have subjected him. Al Gore accepted federal funding and was nominally bound by the associated spending limitations. Soft money and independent spending, however, not limited by election law at the time, allowed Gore to close the gap with his Republican opponent.

Third-party candidates are eligible for public funding only if they received at least 5 percent of the vote in the previous presidential race. This stipulation effectively blocks pre-election funding for third-party or independent candidates, although a third party that wins more than 5 percent of the vote can receive public funding after the election. In 1980, John Anderson convinced banks to loan him money for an independent candidacy on the strength of poll data showing that he would receive more than 5 percent of the vote and thus would obtain public funds with which to repay the loans.

Campaign Finance Reform

The United States is one of the few advanced industrial nations that permit individual candidates to accept large private contributions from individual or corporate

[41]David Broder and Ruth Marcus, "Wielding Third Force in Politics," *Washington Post*, 20 September 1997, p. 1.

BOX 10.1

Federal Campaign Finance Regulation

The Rules for Campaign Contributions

WHO	CAN CONTRIBUTE . . .	TO . . .	IF . . .
Individuals	up to $2,000 ("hard money)	a candidate	they are contributing to a single candidate in a single election
Individuals	up to $25,000	a national party committee	
Individuals	up to $5,000	a PAC	
PACs	up to $5,000	a candidate	they contribute to the campaigns of at least five different candidates
Individuals and PACs	unlimited funds	a 527 committee	these funds are used for issue advocacy and the 527 committee's efforts are not coordinated with any political campaign
Individuals and PACs	up to $10,000 (soft money)	a state party committee	the money is used for voter registration and get-out-the-vote efforts

The Rules for Campaign Advertising

WHO	CANNOT . . .	IF . . .
Unions, corporations, and nonprofit organizations	broadcast issue ads mentioning federal candidates	they occur within sixty days of a general election or thirty days of a primary

The Rules for Funding Presidential Elections

CANDIDATES	MAY RECEIVE . . .	IF . . .
In presidential primaries	federal matching funds, dollar for dollar, up to $5 million	they raise at least $5,000 in each of twenty states, from contributions of $250 or less
In general elections	full federal funding (they can spend no more than their federal funding)	they are from a major party (minor-party candidates may receive partial funding)
In any election	money from independent groups (PACs and 527 committees)	the group's efforts are not tied directly to the official campaign

Important Definitions for Campaign Finance Regulation

- *Political action committee (PAC):* Private group that raises and distributes funds for use in election campaigns.
- *527 committee:* Tax-exempt organization that engages in political activities, often through unlimited "soft-money" contributions. It is not restricted by current law on campaign finance, exploiting a loophole in the Internal Revenue Service code.
- *Soft money:* Unregulated contributions to the national parties nominally to assist in party-building or voter-registration efforts rather than for particular campaigns.
- *Hard money:* Contributions by individuals and PACs that are specified for a particular political campaign. These contributions are subject to federal regulation.
- *Federal matching funds:* Federal funds that match, dollar for dollar, all individual contributions a candidate receives of $250 or less. To qualify, the candidate must raise at least $5,000 in individual contributions of $250 or less in each of twenty states.
- *Federal Election Commission:* The commission that oversees campaign finance practices in the United States.

donors. Most other countries mandate either public funding of campaigns or, as in the case of Britain, require that large private donations be made to political parties rather than to individual candidates. The logic of such a requirement is that a contribution that might seem very large to an individual candidate would weigh much less heavily if made to a national party. Thus the chance that a donor could buy influence would be reduced.

After both the 1996 and 2000 national elections, efforts were made to enact reform measures, but these failed. In 2002, however, a scandal involving contributions made by Enron, a giant Texas energy company, which subsequently went bankrupt in a climate of scandal, gave reformers the ammunition they needed to bring about a set of changes in election law in the form of the Bipartisan Campaign Reform Act (BCRA). One of the changes brought about by BCRA was a ban on campaign spending by the national party organizations, which had previously used hundreds of millions of dollars in soft money contributions from corporations, unions, and individuals to influence electoral contests. The long-term effects of this reform remain to be seen. Perhaps banning soft money will reduce the influence of wealthy donors; but, at the same time, eliminating soft money is likely to weaken the national parties—now among the few sources of coherence in America's fragmented political process. In the short term, at least, the Democratic party seems to be suffering most from the soft money ban. The Democratic party had come to depend on a relatively small number of well-heeled contributors who wrote large checks to the national party. Republicans, on the other hand, have developed a broader base of smaller contributors who are accustomed to sending money directly to individual candidates. These hard money contributions are not affected by the new law.[42] In the 2004 election, 527 committees, though not able to spend directly on particular campaigns, took up some of this slack, with Democrats outspending Republicans via this route.

Implications for Democracy

The important role played by private funds in American politics affects the balance of power among contending social groups. Politicians need large amounts of money to campaign successfully for major offices. This fact inevitably ties their interests to the interests of the groups and forces that can provide this money. In a nation as large and diverse as the United States, to be sure, campaign contributors represent many different groups and often represent clashing interests. Business groups, labor groups, environmental groups, and pro-choice and right-to-life forces all contribute millions of dollars to political campaigns. Through such PACs as EMILY's List, women's groups contribute millions of dollars to women running for political office. One set of trade associations may contribute millions to win politicians' support for telecommuni-

---

[42]Adam Nagourney, "McCain Feingold School Finds Many Bewildered," *New York Times*, 19 February 2003, p. A23.

cations reform, while another set may contribute just as much to block the same reform efforts. Insurance companies may contribute millions of dollars to Democrats to win their support for changes in the health-care system, while physicians may contribute equal amounts to prevent the same changes from becoming law.

Interests that donate large amounts of money to campaigns expect, and often receive, favorable treatment from the beneficiaries of their largesse. For example, in 2000, a number of major interest groups with specific policy goals made substantial donations to the Bush presidential campaign. These interests included airlines, energy producers, banks, tobacco companies, and a number of others.

After Bush's election, these interests pressed the new president to promote their legislative and regulatory agendas. For example, MBNA America was a major donor to the 2000 Bush campaign. The bank and its executives gave Bush $1.3 million. The bank's president helped raise millions more for Bush and personally gave an additional $100,000 to the president's inaugural committee after the election. All told, MBNA and other banking companies donated $26 million to the GOP in 2000. Within weeks of his election, President Bush signed legislation providing MBNA and the others with something they had sought for years—bankruptcy laws making it more difficult for consumers to escape credit-card debts. Such laws could potentially enhance the earnings of large credit-card issuers like MBNA by tens of millions of dollars every year.

In a similar vein, a coalition of manufacturers led by the U.S. Chamber of Commerce and the National Association of Manufacturers also provided considerable support for Bush's 2000 campaign. This coalition sought, among other things, the repeal of federal rules, promulgated in 2000 by the federal Occupational Safety and Health Administration (OSHA), that were designed to protect workers from repetitive-motion injuries. Again, within weeks of his election, the president approved a resolution rejecting the rules. In March 2001, the House and Senate both voted to kill the ergonomic regulations.

In a like manner Democrat-inclined groups, such as trial lawyers, were generous contributors to Clinton's campaigns in 1992 and 1996, Gore's in 2000, and Kerry's in 2004. They are keen to allow jurisdiction over tort damages to remain with state courts rather than federal courts because the former have been more sympathetic toward large damage awards (which is how trial lawyers make their money). In early 2005 the Bush administration began to have some modest success in shifting some of these cases to federal court dockets.

Despite the diversity of contributors, however, not all interests play a role in financing political campaigns. Only those interests that have a good deal of money to spend can make their interests known in this way. These interests are not monolithic, but they do not completely reflect the diversity of American society. The poor, the destitute, and the downtrodden also live in America and have an interest in the outcome of political campaigns. Who speaks for them?

DO ELECTIONS MATTER?

What is the place of elections in the American political process? Unfortunately, recent political trends, such as the increasing importance of money, raise real questions about the continuing ability of ordinary Americans to influence their government through electoral politics.

Why Is There a Decline in Voter Turnout?

Despite the sound and fury of contemporary American politics, one very important fact stands out: participation in the American political process is abysmally low. For every registered voter who voted in the 2000 elections, for example, one stayed home. However, there was a slight increase in voter turnout in 2004.

 Rationality Principle
At least until recent years, political parties have been the primary agents for giving citizens the motivation and incentive to vote.

Competition and Voter Turnout Throughout much of American history, the major parties have been the principal agents responsible for giving citizens the motivation and incentive to vote. One of the most interesting pieces of testimony to the lengths to which parties have been willing to go to induce citizens to vote is a list of Chicago precinct captains' activities in the 1920s and 1930s. Among other matters, these party workers helped constituents obtain food, coal, and money for rent; gave advice in dealing with juvenile and domestic problems; helped constituents obtain government and private jobs; adjusted taxes; aided with permits, zoning, and building-code problems; served as liaisons with social, relief, and medical agencies; provided legal assistance and help in dealing with government agencies; handed out Christmas baskets; and attended weddings and funerals.[43] Obviously, all these services were provided in the hope of winning voters' support at election time. And this, in turn, becomes even more compelling as the competition between parties heated up. Hence party competition has long been known to be a key factor in stimulating voting. As political scientists Stanley Kelley, Richard Ayres, and William Bowen note, competition not only gives citizens an incentive to vote but also gives politicians an incentive to get them to vote.[44]

The parties' competitive efforts to attract citizens to the polls are not their only influence on voting. Individual voters, as we have seen, tend to form psychological ties with parties. Although the strength of partisan ties in the United States has declined in recent years, a majority of Americans continue to identify with either the Republican or the Democratic party. Party loyalty gives citizens a stake in election outcomes that encourages them to take part with considerably greater regularity than those lacking partisan ties.[45] Even when both legal facilitation and competitiveness are weak, party loyalists vote with great regularity.

[43]Harold F. Gosnell, *Machine Politics, Chicago Model*, rev. ed. (Chicago: University of Chicago Press, 1968), Chapter 4.

[44]Stanley Kelley, Jr., Richard E. Ayres, and William G. Bowen, "Registration and Voting: Putting First Things First," *American Political Science Review* 61 (June 1967): 359–70.

[45]See Angus Campbell et al., *The American Voter* (New York: Wiley, 1960).

In recent decades, as we will see in Chapter 11, the importance of party as a political force in the United States has diminished considerably. The decline of party is undoubtedly one of the factors responsible for the relatively low rates of voter turnout that characterize American national elections. To an extent, the federal and state governments, and even more recently PACs and 527 committees, have directly assumed some of the burden of voter mobilization once assigned to the parties.

For example, the 1993 Motor Voter Bill was a step, though a hesitant one, in the direction of expanded voter participation. This act requires all states to allow voters to register by mail when they renew their driver's licenses (twenty-eight states already had similar mail-in procedures) and provides for the placement of voter registration forms in motor vehicle, public assistance, and military recruitment offices. Motor Voter did result in some increases in voter registration. Thus far, however, few of these newly registered individuals have actually gone to the polls to cast their ballots. After 1996, the percentage of newly registered voters who appeared at the polls actually dropped.[46]

A number of other simple institutional reforms could increase voter turnout. Same-day registration—currently used in several states, including Minnesota—could boost turnout by several percentage points. Weekend voting or, alternatively, making Election Day a federal holiday would make it easier for Americans to go to the polls. Weekend voting in a number of European nations has increased turnout by up to 10 percentage points. Still, these "fixes" do not ensure increased turnout, and evidence to date is not strong one way or the other.

Institution Principle

Instituting new election laws, such as same-day voter registration, could increase turnout.

Diminished turnout in the United States may be due in part to the way we structure elections. The median voter theorem suggests that, with only one winner in a winner-takes-all system, candidates head for the center and toward one another, much as Bill Clinton succeeded in doing in 1992 and 1996, and George W. Bush in 2000. This sometimes produces disillusionment, even disgust, in voters who find, in the immortal words of former third-party candidate George Wallace, that "there ain't a dime's worth of difference" between the candidates. Many citizens conclude there is not much point to going to the polls. Turnout, according to this view, is a consequence not only of candidates failing to mobilize voters but also of their failure, via the inexorable pull of the median voter, to differentiate themselves and thus inspire voters.

Is It Rational to Vote?   Compared to other democracies, voter turnout in national elections is extremely low in the United States (see Figure 10.1). It is usually around 50 percent for presidential elections and between 30 and 40 percent for midterm elections. In other Western democracies, turnout regularly exceeds 80 percent. In defense of American citizens, it should be pointed out that occasions for voting as a form of civic activity occur more frequently in the United States than in other democracies. There are more offices filled by election in the United

---

[46]Peter Baker, "Motor Voter Apparently Didn't Drive Up Turnout," *Washington Post*, 6 November 1996, p. B7.

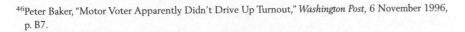

States than elsewhere—indeed, more offices per capita, which is somewhat startling given how large a democracy the United States is. Many of these are posts that are filled by appointment in other democracies. Especially unusual in this respect are elected judges in many jurisdictions and elected local "bureaucrats" (like the local sheriff and the proverbial town dog catcher). In addition, there are primaries as well as general elections; and, in many states, there are initiatives and referendums to vote on, too. It is a wonder that American citizens don't suffer from some form of democratic fatigue! Though many scholars have tried to answer the question "Why is turnout so low?" others have argued that the real question should be "Why is turnout so high?" That is, why does anyone turn out to vote at all?

If we think of voter turnout in terms of cost-benefit analysis, then it isn't obvious why people vote.[47] There are many costs to voting. People must take time out of their busy schedules, possibly incurring a loss of wages, to show up at the polls. In many states, voters have to overcome numerous hurdles just to register. If an individual wants to cast an informed vote, he or she must also spend time learning about the candidates and their positions.

Voters must bear these costs no matter what the outcome of the election, yet it is extremely unlikely that an individual's vote will actually affect the outcome, unless the vote makes or breaks a tie. Just making a close election one vote closer by voting for the loser, or the winner one vote more secure by voting for her, doesn't matter much. As the saying goes, "Closeness only counts in horseshoes and dancing." It is almost certain that if an individual did not incur the costs of voting and stayed home instead, the election results would be the same. The probability of a single vote being decisive in a presidential election is about 1 in 10 million.[48] Given the tiny probability that an individual's vote will determine whether or not the candidate he or she prefers is elected, it seems as if those who turn out to vote are behaving irrationally.[49]

One possible solution to this puzzle is that people are motivated by more than just their preferences for electing a particular candidate—they are, in fact,

Rationality Principle

Because the chance of affecting an election is low, it is not plainly irrational to stay home and not participate.

[47]William H. Riker and Peter C. Ordeshook, "A Theory of the Calculus of Voting," *American Political Science Review* 62 (1968): 25–42. Riker and Ordeshook conclude that someone caring only about the relative *benefits* from securing the victory of his or her favorite candidate over the opponent, net of the *costs* of voting, will want to weigh the likelihood that his or her vote is decisive. Because this probability is bound to be low—indeed, infinitesimal in a moderately large electorate (as we discuss in the text shortly)—the benefits will have to be extraordinary, relative to the costs to motivate participation. Hence, Riker and Ordeshook wonder why turnout is "so high" and look to reasons other than the simple (some say, "simplistic") cost-benefit analysis for the explanation.

[48]Andrew Gelman, Gary King, and John Boscardin, "Estimating the Probability of Events That Have Never Occurred: When Is Your Vote Decisive?" *Journal of the American Statistical Association* 93, no. 441 (March 1998): 1–9.

[49]A *strategic* cost-benefit analysis plays out the following reasonable argument: "If everyone determines that his or her vote doesn't matter, and no one votes, then *my* vote will determine the outcome!" This kind of strategic conjecturing has been analyzed in Thomas Palfrey and Howard Rosenthal, "Voter Participation and Strategic Uncertainty," *American Political Science Review* 79 (March 1985): 62–79. They conclude that once all the back-and-forth conjecturing is done, the question of why anyone participates remains.

satisfying their duty as citizens, and this benefit exceeds the costs of voting.[50] Yet this hypothesis still does not provide an adequate answer to the rationality of voting—it only speaks to the fact that people value the *act of voting* itself. That is, people have a "taste" for voting. But the rational-choice approach cannot say where tastes come from[51] and, therefore, cannot say much about voter turnout.

John Aldrich offers another possible solution: He looks at the question from the politician's point of view.[52] Candidates calculate how much to invest in campaigns based on their probability of winning. In the unlikely event that an incumbent appears beatable, the challengers often invest heavily in their own campaigns because they believe the investment has a good chance of paying off. In response to these strong challenges, incumbents not only will work harder to raise campaign funds but will also spend more of what they raise.[53] Parties seeking to maximize the number of positions in the government they control may also shift resources to help out the candidates in these close races.

More vigorous campaigns will generally lead to increased turnout. The increase is not necessarily due to citizens reacting to the closeness of the race (that is, the perception that their vote may affect the outcome) but to the greater effort and resources that candidates put into close races, which, in turn, reduce the costs of voting. Candidates share some of the costs of voting by helping citizens register and by getting them to the polls on Election Day. Heated advertising campaigns reduce the voters' costs of becoming informed (because candidates flood the public with information about themselves). This decrease in costs to individual voters in what strategic politicians perceive to be a close race at least partially explains why rational individuals would turn out to vote. Thus the incredible registration and mobilization efforts by politicians and 527 committees in 2004 produced an increase in turnout. By the same token, lower effort in non-presidential-election years is associated with much lower turnout.

 Rationality Principle

Given the tiny probability that an individual's vote will determine the winner of an election, candidates need to reduce the cost of voting for citizens in order to mobilize them.

Why Do Elections Matter as Political Institutions?

Voting choices and electoral outcomes can be extremely important in the United States. Yet observing the relationships among voters' choices, leadership selection, and policy decisions is only part of the significance of democratic elections. Important as they are, voters' choices and electoral results may still be less consequential for government and politics than the simple fact of voting itself. The fact of mass electoral participation can be more significant than what or how citizens

---

[50]This was Riker and Ordeshook's line of argument. They claim, in effect, that there is an *experiential* as well as an *instrumental* rationale for voting. In more economic terms, this is the view that voting is a form of consumption as much as it is a type of investment. For a brief and user-friendly development of this logic, see Shepsle and Bonchek, *Analyzing Politics*, pp. 251–59.

[51]Brian Barry, *Sociologists, Economists, and Democracy* (London: Collier-Macmillan, 1970).

[52]John H. Aldrich, "Rational Choice and Turnout," *American Journal of Political Science* 37 (February 1993): 246–78.

[53]Gary C. Jacobson and Samuel Kernell, *Strategy and Choice in Congressional Elections*, 2nd ed. (New Haven, CT: Yale University Press, 1983).

decide once they participate. Thus electoral participation has important consequences in that it socializes and institutionalizes political action.

First, democratic elections socialize political activity. Voting is not a natural or spontaneous phenomenon. It is an institutionalized form of mass political involvement. That individuals vote rather than engage in some other form of political behavior is a result of national policies that create the opportunity to vote and discourage other political activities relative to voting. Elections transform what might otherwise consist of sporadic, citizen-initiated acts into a routine public function. This transformation expands and democratizes mass political involvement. At the same time, however, elections help preserve the government's stability by containing and channeling away potentially more disruptive or dangerous forms of mass political activity. By establishing formal avenues for mass participation and accustoming citizens to their use, government reduces the threat that volatile, unorganized political involvement can pose to the established order.

Second, elections bolster the government's power and authority. Elections help increase popular support for political leaders and for the regime itself. The formal opportunity to participate in elections serves to convince citizens that the government is responsive to their needs and wishes. Moreover, elections help persuade citizens to obey. Electoral participation increases popular acceptance of taxes and military service on which the government depends. Even if popular voting can influence the behavior of those in power, voting serves simultaneously as a form of co-optation. Elections—particularly democratic elections—substitute consent for coercion as the foundation of governmental power.

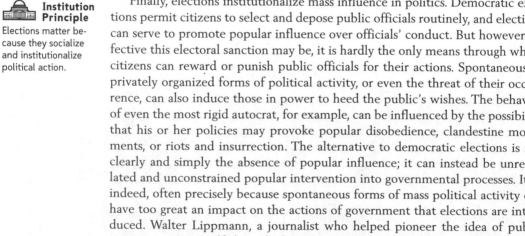

Institution Principle

Elections matter because they socialize and institutionalize political action.

Finally, elections institutionalize mass influence in politics. Democratic elections permit citizens to select and depose public officials routinely, and elections can serve to promote popular influence over officials' conduct. But however effective this electoral sanction may be, it is hardly the only means through which citizens can reward or punish public officials for their actions. Spontaneous or privately organized forms of political activity, or even the threat of their occurrence, can also induce those in power to heed the public's wishes. The behavior of even the most rigid autocrat, for example, can be influenced by the possibility that his or her policies may provoke popular disobedience, clandestine movements, or riots and insurrection. The alternative to democratic elections is not clearly and simply the absence of popular influence; it can instead be unregulated and unconstrained popular intervention into governmental processes. It is, indeed, often precisely because spontaneous forms of mass political activity can have too great an impact on the actions of government that elections are introduced. Walter Lippmann, a journalist who helped pioneer the idea of public opinion voicing itself through the press via the op-ed page, once observed that "new numbers were enfranchised because they had power, and giving them the vote was the least disturbing way of letting them exercise their power."[54] The

[54]Walter Lippmann, *The Essential Lippmann*, ed. Clinton Rossiter and James Lare (New York: Random House, 1965), p. 12.

vote can provide the "least disturbing way" of allowing ordinary people to exercise power. If the people had been powerless to begin with, elections would never have been introduced.

Thus, although citizens can secure enormous benefits from their right to vote, governments secure equally significant benefits from allowing them to do so.

SUMMARY

Allowing citizens to vote represents a calculated risk on the part of power holders. On the one hand, popular participation can generate consent and support for the government. On the other hand, the right to vote may give ordinary citizens more influence in the governmental process than political elites would like.

Voting is only one of many possible types of political participation. The significance of voting is that it is an institutional and formal mode of political activity. Voting is organized and subsidized by the government. This makes voting both more limited and more democratic than other forms of participation.

All governments regulate voting to influence its effects. The most important forms of regulation include regulation of the electorate's composition, regulation of the translation of voters' choices into electoral outcomes, and insulation of policy-making processes from electoral intervention.

Voters' choices themselves are based on partisanship, issues, and candidates' personalities. Which of these criteria will be most important varies over time and depends on the factors that opposing candidates choose to emphasize in their campaigns.

Campaign funds in the United States are provided by small, direct-mail contributions, large gifts, PACs, 527 committees, political parties, candidates' personal resources, and public funding. Campaign finance is regulated by the Federal Elections Campaign Act of 1971. There have been continuing efforts since then to dampen the influence money has on elections.

Whatever voters decide, elections are important institutions because they socialize political activity, increase governmental authority, and institutionalize popular influence in political life.

FOR FURTHER READING

Black, Earl, and Merle Black. *The Vital South: How Presidents Are Elected.* Cambridge, MA: Harvard University Press, 1992.

Brady, David W. *Critical Elections and Congressional Policy Making.* Stanford, CA: Stanford University Press, 1988.

Carmines, Edward G., and James A. Stimson. *Issue Evolution: Race and the Transformation of American Politics.* Princeton, NJ: Princeton University Press, 1989.

Rationality Principle	Collective-Action Principle	Institution Principle	Policy Principle	History Principle
Elections allow multiple principals—citizens—to choose political agents to act on their behalf. But citizens usually have imperfect information about candidates and don't know how agents will act once in office.	Elections are a mechanism to channel and limit political participation to actions within the system.	The electoral process is governed by a variety of rules and procedures that allow those in power an opportunity to regulate the character and consequences of political participation.	The median voter theorem predicts policy moderation on the part of candidates.	Between 1890 and 1910, voter turnout declined in the United States as a result of new registration requirements. Since that time, turnout has remained low in comparison with the nineteenth century.
As registration costs rise, the number of citizens participating may be expected to decrease.		The rules that set the criteria for winning an election have an effect on the outcome.		
Issue voting motivates candidates to converge toward the median voter.		The electoral college and the Australian ballot are two instances of how changes in electoral rules can affect the outcomes of elections.		
At least until recent years, political parties have been the primary agents for giving citizens the motivation and incentive to vote.		Instituting new election laws, such as same-day voter registration, could increase turnout.		
Because the chance of affecting an election is low, it is not plainly irrational to stay home and not participate.		Elections matter because they socialize and institutionalize political action.		
Given the tiny probability that an individual's vote will determine the winner of an election, candidates need to reduce the cost of voting for citizens in order to mobilize them.				

Conway, M. Margaret. *Political Participation in the United States.* 3rd ed. Washington, DC: Congressional Quarterly Press, 2000.

Fowler, Linda L. *Candidates, Congress, and the American Democracy.* Ann Arbor: University of Michigan Press, 1994.

Fowler, Linda L., and Robert D. McClure. *Political Ambition: Who Decides to Run for Congress.* New Haven, CT: Yale University Press, 1989.

Ginsberg, Benjamin, and Martin Shefter. *Politics by Other Means: Politicians, Prosecutors, and the Press from Watergate to Whitewater.* 3rd ed. New York: Norton, 2002.

Jackson, Brooks. *Honest Graft: Big Money and the American Political Process.* Rev. ed. New York: Knopf, 1990.

Piven, Frances Fox, and Richard A. Cloward. *Why Americans Don't Vote.* New York: Pantheon, 1988.

Reed, Adolph L., Jr. *The Jesse Jackson Phenomenon: The Crisis of Purpose in Afro-American Politics.* New Haven, CT: Yale University Press, 1987.

Reichley, A. James, ed. *Elections American Style.* Washington, DC: Brookings Institution, 1987.

Sorauf, Frank J. *Inside Campaign Finance: Myths and Realities.* New Haven, CT: Yale University Press, 1992.

Tate, Katherine. *From Protest to Politics: The New Black Voters in American Elections.* Cambridge, MA: Harvard University Press, 1994.

Witt, Linda, Karen M. Paget, and Glenna Matthews. *Running as a Woman: Gender and Power in American Politics.* New York: Free Press, 1994.

Why Vote?

By STEPHEN J. DUBNER and STEVEN D. LEVITT

. . . The odds that your vote will actually affect the outcome of a given election are very slim. Even in the closest elections, it is almost never the case that a single vote is pivotal. Of the more than 16,000 Congressional elections, only one election in the past 100 years—a 1910 race in Buffalo—was decided by a single vote.

Still, people do continue to vote, in the millions. Why? Here are three possibilities:

1. Perhaps we are just not very bright and therefore wrongly believe that our votes will affect the outcome.
2. Perhaps we vote in the same spirit in which we buy lottery tickets. From a financial perspective, playing the lottery is a bad investment. But it's fun and relatively cheap: for the price of a ticket, you buy the right to fantasize how you'd spend the winnings—much as you get to fantasize that your vote will have some impact on policy.
3. Perhaps we have been socialized into the voting-as-civic-duty idea,

believing that it's a good thing for society if people vote, even if it's not particularly good for the individual. And thus we feel guilty for not voting.

But wait a minute, you say. If everyone thought about voting the way economists do, we might have no elections at all.

This is indeed a slippery slope—the seemingly meaningless behavior of an individual, which, in aggregate, becomes quite meaningful. Here's a similar example in reverse. Imagine that you and your 8-year-old daughter are taking a walk through a botanical garden when she suddenly pulls a bright blossom off a tree.

"You shouldn't do that," you find yourself saying.

"Why not?" she asks.

"Well," you reason, "because if everyone picked one, there wouldn't be any flowers left at all."

"Yeah, but everybody isn't picking them," she says with a look. "Only me."

. . . [O]nly slightly more than half of eligible voters participated in the last

New York Times, 6 November 2005.

presidential election—but it might be . . . worthwhile to stand this problem on its head and instead ask a different question: considering that an individual's vote almost never matters, why do so many people bother to vote at all?

The answer may lie in Switzerland.

The Swiss love to vote—on parliamentary elections, on plebiscites, on whatever may arise. But voter participation had begun to slip over the years (maybe they stopped handing out live pigs there too), so a new option was introduced: the mail-in ballot. Whereas each voter in the U.S. must register, that isn't the case in Switzerland. Every eligible Swiss citizen began to automatically receive a ballot in the mail, which could then be completed and returned by mail.

From a social scientist's perspective, there was beauty in the setup of this postal voting scheme: because it was introduced in different cantons (the 26 statelike districts that make up Switzerland) in different years, it allowed for a sophisticated measurement of its effects over time.

Never again would any Swiss voter have to tromp to the polls during a rainstorm; the cost of casting a ballot had been lowered significantly. An economic model would therefore predict voter turnout to increase substantially. Is that what happened?

Not at all. In fact, voter turnout often decreased, especially in smaller cantons and in the smaller communities within cantons. . . .

But why is this the case? Why on earth would fewer people vote when the cost of doing so is lowered?

It goes back to the incentives behind voting. If a given citizen doesn't stand a chance of having her vote affect the outcome, why does she bother? In Switzerland, as in the U.S., "there exists a fairly strong social norm that a good citizen should go to the polls," Funk writes. "As long as poll-voting was the only option,

ESSENCE OF THE STORY

• According to the economist's rational-choice analysis, no one should vote. Yet millions do vote in every national election.

• Election reforms instituted in Switzerland, where each citizen was automatically sent a ballot and could mail the ballot back, should have increased turnout, since the costs of voting were reduced. Instead, turnout declined.

• The authors speculate that the social rewards of voting are what actually motivate us to turn out.

POLITICAL ANALYSIS

• Voter turnout has been studied by rational-choice scholars—and also by critics of rational choice—as a way to test their theories.

• In many areas of the United States, new methods of voting are being introduced, such as by-mail voting, relaxed absentee balloting, and even Internet voting, all under the assumption that they will increase turnout. But it is possible that removing the community aspect of voting will actually cause turnout to decline.

• Taking into account social norms of participation may be as important as focusing on measurable financial gains in stimulating all sorts of collective action (including voting).

there was an incentive (or pressure) to go to the polls only to be seen handing in the vote. The motivation could be hope for social esteem, or just the avoidance of informal sanctions. Since in small communities, people know each other better and gossip about who fulfills civic duties and who doesn't, the benefits of norm adherence were particularly high in this type of community."

In other words, we do vote out of self-interest but not necessarily the same self-interest as indicated by our actual ballot choice. For all the talk of how people "vote their pocketbooks," we may be driven to vote less by a financial incentive than a social one. . . .

CHAPTER

11

Political Parties

We often refer to the United States as a nation with a "two-party system." By this we mean that in the United States the Democratic and Republican parties compete for office and power. Most Americans believe that party competition contributes to the health of the democratic process. Certainly, we are more than just a bit suspicious of those nations that claim to be ruled by their people but do not tolerate the existence of opposing parties.

The idea of party competition was not always accepted in the United States. In the early years of the Republic, parties were seen as threats to the social order. In his 1796 "Farewell Address," President George Washington admonished his countrymen to shun partisan politics:

> Let me . . . warn you in the most solemn manner against the baneful effects of the spirit of party, generally. This spirit . . . exists under different shapes in all governments, more or less stifled, controlled, or repressed; but in those of the popular form it is seen in its greatest rankness and is truly their worst enemy.

Often, those in power viewed the formation of political parties by their opponents as acts of treason that merited severe punishment. Thus, in 1798, the Federalist party, which controlled the national government, in effect sought to outlaw its Democratic-Republican opponents through the infamous Alien and Sedition Acts, which, among other things, made it a crime to publish or say anything that might tend to defame or bring into disrepute either the president or the Congress. Under this law, twenty-five individuals—including several Republican newspaper editors—were arrested and convicted.[1]

These efforts to outlaw political parties obviously failed. By the mid-nineteenth century, American politics was dominated by powerful "machines" that inspired enormous voter loyalty; controlled electoral politics; and, through elections, exercised immense influence over government and policy in the United States. In recent years, these party machines have all but disappeared. Electoral politics has become a "candidate-centered" affair in which individual candidates for office build their own campaign organizations, while voters make choices based more on their reactions to the candidates than on loyalty to the parties. Party organization, as we saw in Chapter 5, continues to be an important factor in Congress. Even in Congress, however, the influence of party leaders is based more on ideological affinity than any real power over party members. The

[1]See Richard Hofstadter, *The Idea of a Party System: The Rise of Legitimate Opposition in the United States, 1780–1840* (Berkeley: University of California Press, 1969).

CHAPTER OUTLINE

Why Do Political Parties Form?

- To Facilitate Collective Action in the Electoral Process

- To Resolve Collective Choice in the Policy-Making Process

- To Deal with the Problem of Ambition

What Functions Do Parties Perform?

- Recruiting Candidates

- Nominations

- Getting Out the Vote

- Facilitating Mass Electoral Choice

- Influencing National Government

Parties and the Electorate

- Group Affiliations

Party Systems

- The First Party System: Federalists and Democratic-Republicans

- The Second Party System: Democrats and Whigs

- The Third Party System: Republicans and Democrats, 1860–96

- The Fourth Party System, 1896–1932

- The Fifth Party System: The New Deal Coalition, 1932–68

- The Sixth Party System?

- American Third Parties

How Strong Are Political Parties Today?

- High-Tech Politics and the Rise of Candidate-Centered and Capital-Intensive Politics

- Labor-Intensive to Capital-Intensive Politics

- Contemporary Party Organizations

- The Contemporary Party as Service Provider to Candidates

- Parties and Democracy

weakness of the party system is an important factor in understanding contemporary American political patterns.[2]

In this chapter, we examine the realities underlying the changing conceptions of political parties. As long as political parties have existed, they have been criticized for introducing selfish, "partisan" concerns into public debate and national policy. Yet political parties are extremely important to the proper functioning of a democracy. As we shall see, parties expand popular political participation, promote more effective choice in elections, and smooth the flow of public business in the Congress. Our problem in America today is not that political life is too partisan but that our parties are not strong enough to function effectively. This is one reason that America has such low levels of popular political involvement. Parties continue to play an important role in the American political process. For one thing, tens of millions of Americans identify strongly with one or the other major party. Many Republican partisans would not dream of voting for a Democrat, and many Democratic partisans viewed the 2004 re-election of George W. Bush as a national tragedy. In recent years, a growing ideological gulf between the two parties has translated into rancorous debate on many policy issues in Congress and in the state legislatures. And yet, contemporary American political parties lack the discipline and organizational coherence of their nineteenth-century forebears. Once, parties dominated the electoral process, but today's party leaders control neither candidate nominations nor campaigns for political office. For the most part, modern-day candidates are self-selected and manage and finance their own campaigns. At one time, powered party barons ruled Capitol Hill, dispensing rewards and punishments and imposing discipline on the legislative process. Today, congressional party leaders depend mainly on the voluntary cooperation of their legislative troops. Reforms enacted in 2002, such as the elimination of soft money, will likely further erode party strength in America.

PREVIEWING THE PRINCIPLES

Political parties act as solutions to collective-action problems in terms of electoral choice, collective choice in the policy-making process, and problems related to the ambitions of politicians. In elections, parties facilitate collection action by helping candidates attract campaign funds, assemble campaign workers, and mobilize voters. Parties also facilitate a voter's choice by providing cues or brand names to simplify the complex choices voters are given. In terms of policy making, parties work as permanent coalitions of individuals with shared goals and interests and thus facilitate cooperation in Congress. Finally, parties help regulate ambition by resolving competition among party members. Parties represent evolving coalitions of different groups in society; and over time, the nature of those coalitions, and thus the nature of party politics, have changed. That is, the collective-action problems that parties seek to overcome are historically determined.

[2]For an excellent discussion of the fluctuating role of political parties in the United States and the influence of government on that role, see John J. Coleman, *Party Decline in America: Policy, Politics, and the Fiscal State* (Princeton, NJ: Princeton University Press, 1996).

We look first at party formation and organization and at the place of parties in the American political process. Second, we discuss the role of parties in election campaigns and the policy process. Third, we consider why America has a two-party system, trace the history of each of the major parties, and look at some of the third parties that have come and gone over the past two centuries. Finally, we address the significance and changing role of parties in American politics today and answer the question "Is the party over?"

WHY DO POLITICAL PARTIES FORM?

Political parties, like interest groups, are organizations seeking influence over government. Ordinarily, they can be distinguished from interest groups on the basis of their orientation. A party seeks to control the entire government by electing its members to office, thereby controlling the government's personnel. Interest groups, through campaign contributions and other forms of electoral assistance, are also concerned with electing politicians—in particular, those who are inclined in their policy direction. But interest groups ordinarily do not sponsor candidates directly, and between elections, they usually accept government and its personnel as given and try to influence government policies through them. They are *benefit seekers*, whereas parties are composed mainly of *office seekers*.[3]

Political parties organize because of three problems with which politicians and other political activists must cope. The first is the problem of collective action. This is chiefly an outgrowth of elections in which a candidate for office must attract campaign funds, assemble a group of activists and workers, and mobilize and persuade prospective voters to vote for him or her. Collective action is also a problem *inside* government, where kindred spirits in a legislature must arrange for, and then engage in, cooperation. The second problem for which parties are sometimes the solution is the problem of collective choice of policy.[4] The give-and-take within a legislature and between the legislature and the executive can make or break policy success and subsequent electoral success. The third problem follows from the fact that fellow politicians, like members of any organization, simultaneously seek success for the organization and success for themselves. This problem of ambition can undermine the collective aspirations of fellow partisans unless astutely managed. We briefly examine each of these three problems below.

---

[3]This distinction is from John H. Aldrich, *Why Parties? The Origin and Transformation of Party Politics in America* (Chicago: University of Chicago Press, 1995).

[4]A slight variation on this theme is emphasized by Gary W. Cox and Mathew D. McCubbins in *Legislative Leviathan: Party Government in the House* (Berkeley: University of California Press, 1993). They suggest that parties in the legislature are electoral machines whose purpose is to preserve and enhance party reputation, thereby giving meaning to the party labels when elections are contested. By keeping order within their ranks, parties make certain that individual actions by members do not discredit the party label. This is an especially challenging task for party leaders when there is diversity within each party, as has often been the case in American political history.

To Facilitate Collective Action in the Electoral Process

Collective-Action Principle

Parties facilitate collective action in the electoral process by helping candidates attract campaign funds, assembling campaign workers, and mobilizing voters.

Political parties as they are known today developed along with the expansion of suffrage and can be understood only in the context of elections. The two are so intertwined that American parties actually take their structure from the electoral process. The shape of party organization in the United States has followed a simple rule: For every district where an election is held, there should be some kind of party unit. These units provide the brand name, the resources—both human and financial—the "buzz," and the link to the larger national organization, which all help the party's candidates arouse interest in their candidacies, stimulate commitment, and ultimately overcome the free riding that diminishes turnout in general elections.

Party organization is also generally an essential ingredient for effective electoral competition by groups lacking substantial economic or institutional resources. Party building has typically been the strategy pursued by groups that must organize the collective energies of large numbers of individuals to counter their opponents' superior material means or institutional standing. Historically, disciplined and coherent party organizations were generally developed first by groups representing the political aspirations of the working classes. Parties, French political scientist Maurice Duverger notes, "are always more developed on the Left than on the Right because they are always more necessary on the Left than on the Right."[5] Compared to political parties in Europe, parties in the United States have always seemed weak. They have no criteria for party membership—no cards for their members to carry, no dues to pay, no obligatory participation in any activity, no notion of exclusiveness. Today, they seem weaker than ever as they are less able to control nominations, campaigns, or the legislative process.

To Resolve Collective Choice in the Policy-Making Process

Policy Principle

Parties help resolve collective choice in the policy-making process by acting as permanent coalitions of individuals with similar policy goals.

Political parties are also essential elements in the process of making policy. Within the government, parties are coalitions of individuals with shared or overlapping interests who, as a rule, will support one another's programs and initiatives. Even though there may be areas of disagreement within each party, a common party label in and of itself gives party members a reason to cooperate. Because they are permanent coalitions, parties greatly facilitate the policy-making process. If alliances had to be formed from scratch for each legislative proposal, the business of government would slow to a crawl or would halt altogether. Parties create a basis for coalition and thus sharply reduce the time, energy, and effort needed to advance a legislative proposal. For example, in January 1998, when President Bill Clinton considered a series of new policy initiatives, he met first with the House and Senate leaders of the Democratic party. Although some congressional Democrats disagreed with the pres-

---

[5]See Maurice Duverger, *Political Parties: Their Organization and Activity in the Modern State*, trans. Barbara North and Robert North (New York: Wiley, 1954), p. 426.

ident's approach to a number of issues, all felt they had a stake in cooperating with Clinton to burnish the party's image in preparation for the next round of national elections. Without the support of a party, the president would be compelled to undertake the daunting and probably impossible task of forming a completely new coalition for each and every policy proposal—a virtually impossible task.

To Deal with the Problem of Ambition

To the extent that politicians share principles, causes, and constituencies, there is a basis for coordination, common cause, cooperation, and joint enterprise. But individual ambition, sometimes in the background but often in the foreground, constantly threatens to undermine any bases for cooperation. Political parties, by regulating career advancement, by providing for the orderly resolution of ambitious competition, and by attending to the post-career care of elected and appointed party officials, do much to rescue coordination and cooperation and permit fellow partisans to pursue common causes where feasible. Simple devices like primaries, for example, provide a context in which clashing electoral ambitions may be resolved. Representative partisan bodies, like the Democratic Committee on Committees in the House (with comparable bodies in the Senate and for the Republicans), resolve competing claims for power positions. In short, politics does not consist of foot soldiers walking in lockstep but rather of ambitious and autonomous individuals seeking power. The unchecked and unregulated burnishing of individual careers is a formula for chaos and destructive competition in which the dividends of cooperation are rarely reaped. Political parties constitute organizations of relatively kindred spirits that try to capture some of those dividends by providing a structure in which ambition is not suppressed altogether, but is not so destructive either.

Rationality Principle

Parties help deal with the threat to cooperation posed by ambitious individuals by regulating career advancement and resolving competition.

WHAT FUNCTIONS DO PARTIES PERFORM?

Parties perform a wide variety of functions. They are mainly involved in nominations and elections—providing the candidates for office, getting out the vote, and facilitating mass electoral choice. That is, they help solve the problems of collective action and ambition to which we alluded earlier. They also influence the institutions of government—providing the leadership and organization of the various congressional committees. That is, they help solve the problem of collective choice concerning institutional arrangements and policy formulation that we also noted earlier.

Recruiting Candidates

One of the most important but least noticed party activities is the recruitment of candidates for local, state, and national office. Each election year, candidates must be found for thousands of state and local offices as well as for congressional seats. Where they do not have an incumbent running for re-election, party leaders attempt to identify strong candidates and to interest them in entering the campaign.

An ideal candidate will have an unblemished record and the capacity to raise enough money to mount a serious campaign. Party leaders are usually not willing to provide financial backing to candidates who are unable to raise substantial funds on their own. For a House seat, this can mean several hundred thousand dollars; for a Senate seat, a serious candidate must be able to raise several million dollars. Often, party leaders have difficulty finding attractive candidates and persuading them to run. In recent years, party leaders in several states have reported that many potential congressional candidates declined the opportunity to run for office, saying they were reluctant to leave their homes and families for the hectic life of a member of Congress. Candidate recruitment has become particularly difficult in an era when political campaigns often involve mudslinging and candidates must assume that their personal lives will be intensely scrutinized in the press.[6]

Nominations

Article I, Section 4, of the Constitution makes only a few provisions for elections. It delegates to the states the power to set the "Times, Places and Manner" of holding elections, even for U.S. senators and representatives. It does, however, reserve to Congress the power to make such laws if it chooses to do so. The Constitution has been amended from time to time to expand the right to participate in elections. Congress has also occasionally passed laws about elections, congressional districting, and campaign practices. But the Constitution and the laws are almost completely silent on nominations, setting only citizenship and age requirements for candidates. The president must be at least thirty-five years of age, a natural-born citizen, and a resident of the United States for fourteen years. A senator must be at least thirty, a U.S. citizen for at least nine years, and a resident of the state he or she represents. A member of the House must be at least twenty-five, a U.S. citizen for seven years, and a resident of the state he or she represents.

nomination
The process through which political parties select their candidates for election to public office.

Nomination is the process by which a party selects a single candidate to run for each elective office. Nomination is the parties' most serious and difficult business. The nominating process can precede the election by many months (Figure 11.1), as it does when the many candidates for the presidency are eliminated from consideration through a grueling series of debates and state primaries until there is only one survivor in each party—the party's nominee.

[6]For an excellent analysis of parties' role in recruitment, see Paul S. Herrnson, *Congressional Elections: Campaigning at Home and in Washington* (Washington, DC: Congressional Quarterly Press, 1995).

FIGURE 11.1

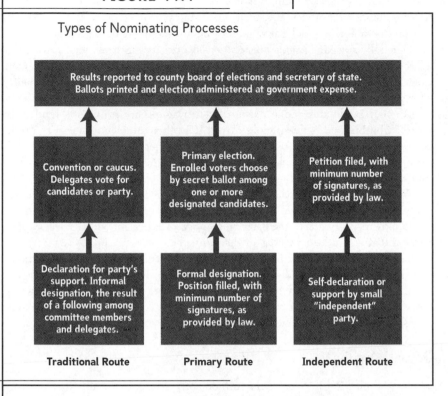

Types of Nominating Processes

Results reported to county board of elections and secretary of state. Ballots printed and election administered at government expense.

| Convention or caucus. Delegates vote for candidates or party. | Primary election. Enrolled voters choose by secret ballot among one or more designated candidates. | Petition filed, with minimum number of signatures, as provided by law. |

| Declaration for party's support. Informal designation, the result of a following among committee members and delegates. | Formal designation. Position filled, with minimum number of signatures, as provided by law. | Self-declaration or support by small "independent" party. |

Traditional Route   **Primary Route**   **Independent Route**

Nomination by Convention   A nominating convention is a formal caucus bound by a number of rules that govern participation and nominating procedures. Conventions are meetings of delegates elected by party members from the relevant county (county convention) or state (state convention). Delegates to each party's national convention (which nominates the party's presidential candidate) are chosen by party members on a state-by-state basis, for there is no single national delegate selection process.

Nomination by Primary Election   In primary elections, party members select the party's nominees directly rather than selecting convention delegates who then select the nominees. Primaries are far from perfect replacements for conventions because it is rare that more than 25 percent of the enrolled voters participate in them. Nevertheless, they are replacing conventions as the dominant method of nomination.[7] At the present time, only a small number of states, including Connecticut, Delaware, and Utah, provide for state conventions to nominate candidates for statewide offices, and even those states also use primaries whenever a substantial minority of delegates vote for one of the defeated aspirants.

Generally speaking, candidates chosen in primary elections tend to be more aggressive and ambitious individuals, whereas those selected by party conventions are more likely to have mastered the arts of compromise and collegiality. The shift from party conventions to primary elections for the nomination of presidential candidates is one reason that contemporary presidents tend to be more ambitious and, indeed, more driven than their nineteenth-century predecessors. Party conventions tend to choose candidates who can get along, while primary elections tend to favor politicians with the energy and enterprise to mount a public campaign.[8]

Primary elections are mainly of two types—closed and open. In a **_closed primary,_** participation is limited to individuals who have previously declared their affiliation by registering with the party. In an **_open primary,_** individuals declare their party affiliation on the actual day of the primary election. To do so, they simply go to the polling place and ask for the ballot of a particular party. The open primary allows each voter to consider candidates and issues before deciding whether to participate and in which party's contest to participate. Open primaries, therefore, are less conducive to strong political parties. But in either case, primaries are more open than conventions or caucuses to new issues and new types of candidates.

Getting Out the Vote

The actual election period begins immediately after the nominations. Historically, this has been a time of glory for the political parties, whose popular base of support is fully displayed. All the paraphernalia of party committees and all the committee members are activated into local party workforces.

The first step in the electoral process involves voter registration. This aspect of the process takes place all year round. There was a time when party workers were responsible for virtually all of this kind of electoral activity, but they have been supplemented (and in many states virtually displaced) by civic groups such as the League of Women Voters, unions, and chambers of commerce.

Those who have registered have to decide on Election Day whether to go to the polling place, stand in line, and actually vote for the various candidates and referenda on the ballot. Political parties, candidates, and campaigning can make a big difference in convincing the voters to vote. Because it is costly for voters to participate in elections and because many of the benefits that winning parties

 Institution Principle

Primary elections tend to favor aggressive and ambitious politicians, whereas conventions tend to favor those who have mastered the arts of compromise and collegiality.

closed primary
A primary election in which voters can participate in the nomination of candidates, but only of the party in which they have been enrolled for a period of time before primary day.

open primary
A primary election in which voters can wait until the day of the primary to choose which party to enroll in to select candidates for the general election.

[7]For a discussion of some of the effects of primary elections, see Peter F. Galderisi and Benjamin Ginsberg, "Primary Elections and the Evanescence of Third Party Activity in the United States," in *Do Elections Matter?*, ed. Benjamin Ginsberg and Alan Stone (Armonk, NY: Sharpe, 1986), pp. 115–30.

[8]Matthew A. Crenson and Benjamin Ginsberg, *How the White House Conquered America* (New York: Norton, 2006).

bestow are public goods (i.e., parties cannot exclude any individual from enjoying them), people will try to free-ride by enjoying the benefits without incurring the costs of electing the party that provided the benefits. This is the *free-rider problem* (see Chapter 1), and parties are important because they help overcome this by mobilizing the voters to support the candidates.

Collective-Action Principle

Parties can help mobilize voters who are potential free riders.

In recent years, not-for-profit groups like Americans Coming Together (ACT) have made an effort to register and mobilize voters. To comply with election law, these groups are nominally independent of the political parties. In reality, though, such not-for-profits are shadow appendages of the two parties, with liberal groups working to mobilize Democratic voters and conservative groups laboring to mobilize Republicans. In 2004, Republican and conservative registration and get-out-the-vote efforts helped secure George W. Bush's re-election.

On any general election ballot, there are likely to be only two or three candidacies for which the nature of the office and the characteristics and positions of the candidates are well known to voters. But what about the choices for judges, the state comptroller, the state attorney general, and many other elective positions? Without partisan cues, voters are likely to find it extremely difficult to make informed choices about these candidates. And what about referenda? This method of making policy choices is being used more and more as a means of direct democracy. A referendum may ask: Should there be a new bond issue for financing the local schools? Should there be a constitutional amendment to increase the number of county judges? The typical referendum question is one on which few voters have clear and knowledgeable positions. Parties and campaigns help most by giving information when voters must choose among obscure candidates and vote on unclear referenda.

Facilitating Mass Electoral Choice

Parties facilitate mass electoral choice. It is often argued that we should vote for the "best person" regardless of his or her party affiliation. But, as the late Harvard political scientist V. O. Key pointed out, in the absence of party labels, voters would be constantly confronted by a bewildering array of "new faces, new choices" and might have considerable difficulty making informed decisions. Without a doubt, their own party identifications and candidates' party affiliations help voters make reasonable choices.

Rationality Principle

Parties can lower the cost of voting by facilitating a voter's choice.

Parties lower information costs of participating by providing a kind of "brand name" recognizability—that is, voters know with a substantial degree of accuracy what positions a candidate will take just by identifying the candidate's party affiliation. In addition, parties give elections a kind of sporting-event atmosphere, with voters treating parties like teams that they can support and cheer on to victory. This enhances the entertainment value of participating in elections. Parties also direct the flow of government benefits, such as patronage jobs, to those who put the party in power. These and other activities encourage individuals to identify with and support one of the two parties.

Although political parties continue to be significant in the United States, the role of party organizations in electoral politics has clearly declined over the past three decades. This decline, and the partial replacement of the party by new forms of electoral technology (discussed later in this chapter), is one of the most important developments in twentieth- and twenty-first-century American politics.

Influencing National Government

The ultimate test of the party system is its relationship to and influence on the institutions of government and the policy-making process. Thus it is important to examine the party system in relation to Congress and the president.

Policy Principle

Policies typically reflect the goals of whichever party is in power.

Parties and Policy   One of the most familiar observations about American politics is that the two major parties try to be all things to all people and are, therefore, indistinguishable from each other. Data and experience give some support to this observation. Parties in the United States are not programmatic or ideological, as they have sometimes been in Britain or other parts of Europe. But this does not mean that there are no differences between them. During the Reagan era, important differences emerged between the positions of Democratic and Republican party leaders on a number of key issues, and these differences are still apparent today. For example, the national leadership of the Republican party supports maintaining high levels of military spending, cuts in social programs, tax relief for middle- and upper-income voters, tax incentives to businesses, and the "social agenda" backed by members of conservative religious denominations. The national Democratic leadership, on the other hand, supports expanded social welfare spending, cuts in military spending, increased regulation of business, and a variety of consumer and environmental programs.

These positions reflect differences in philosophy as well as in the core constituencies to which the parties seek to appeal. The Democratic party at the national level seeks to unite organized labor, the poor, members of racial minorities, and liberal upper-middle-class professionals. The Republicans, by contrast, appeal to business, upper-middle- and upper-class groups in the private sector, and social conservatives. Often, party leaders will seek to develop issues that they hope will add new groups to their party's constituent base. During the 1980s, for example, under the leadership of Ronald Reagan, the Republicans devised a series of "social issues," including support for school prayer, opposition to abortion, and opposition to affirmative action, designed to cultivate the support of white southerners. This effort was extremely successful in increasing Republican strength in the once solidly Democratic South. In the 1990s, under the leadership of Bill Clinton, who called himself a "new Democrat," the Democratic party sought to develop new social programs designed to solidify the party's base among working-class and poor voters, and new, somewhat more conservative economic programs aimed at attracting the votes of middle- and upper-middle-class voters.

As these examples suggest, parties do not always support policies because they are favored by their constituents. Instead, party leaders can play the role of policy entrepreneurs, seeking ideas and programs that will expand their party's base of support while eroding that of the opposition. In recent years, for example, leaders of both major political parties have sought to develop ideas and programs they hoped would appeal to America's most rapidly growing electoral bloc—Latino voters. Thus President George W. Bush has recommended a number of proposals designed to help Latinos secure U.S. residence and employment. Democrats, for their part, have proposed education and social service programs designed to appeal to the needs of Latino immigrants. Both parties promoted their ideas extensively within the Latino community in the 2004 presidential campaign; and though the Democrats won more Latino votes in 2004, each party claimed to be satisfied with its long-term strategy for building Latino support.

It is one of the essential characteristics of party politics in America that a party's programs and policies often lead, rather than follow, public opinion. Like their counterparts in the business world, party leaders seek to identify and develop "products" (programs and policies) that will appeal to the public. The public, of course, has the ultimate voice. With its votes, it decides whether or not to "buy" new policy offerings.

Through members elected to office, both parties have made efforts to translate their general goals into concrete policies. Republicans, for example, implemented tax cuts, increased defense spending, cut social spending, and enacted restrictions on abortion during the 1980s and 1990s. Democrats were able to defend consumer and environmental programs against GOP attacks and sought to expand domestic social programs in the late 1990s. During his two terms in office, President Bush has sought substantial cuts in federal taxes, "privatization" of the Social Security system, and a larger role for Republican-allied faith-based organizations in the administration of federal social programs. In the context of the nation's campaign against terrorism, Bush also sought to shift America's defense posture from an emphasis on deterrence to a doctrine of preemptive strikes against perceived threats.

The Parties and Congress   Congress, in particular, depends more on the party system than is generally recognized. First, the speakership of the House is essentially a party office. All the members of the House take part in the election of the Speaker. But the actual selection is made by the ***majority party.*** When the majority party caucus presents a nominee to the entire House, its choice is then invariably ratified in a straight party-line vote.

The committee system of both houses of Congress is also a product of the two-party system. Although the rules organizing committees and the rules defining the jurisdiction of each are adopted like ordinary legislation by the whole membership, all other features of the committees are shaped by parties. For example, each party is assigned a quota of members for each committee, depending on the percentage of total seats held by the party. On the rare occasions when an independent or third-party candidate is elected, the leaders of the two parties must agree against whose quota this member's committee assignments will count. Presumably, the member will not be able to serve on any committee until the question of quota is settled.

majority party
Party that holds the majority of legislative seats in either the House or the Senate.

Collective-Action Principle
Cooperation in Congress is facilitated by the party system.

The Causes and Effects of Party Polarization in the United States

Party polarization has been blamed for many of America's problems in recent years, including distrust of government, policy gridlock in Congress, and even the impeachment of President Bill Clinton. But what is party polarization? Can party polarization be *measured*?

The answer is yes, we can measure polarization, and by almost any measure it has increased. One place to look is at political elites. According to Sean Theriault, "The two political parties in Congress are as ideologically divergent as they have been at any point in the last three decades."[1] Presidential candidates are also increasingly drawn from the ideological wings of their respective parties.[2] And the gulf between Republican and Democratic activists has also grown.[3]

Another place to look is at the public. Here, the picture is more complicated. Morris Fiorina argues that Americans have not become more polarized, on either ideological or partisan grounds.[4] However, when we look only at those who call themselves "strong" partisans, these people—those who volunteer for campaigns, give money, and vote more frequently—are becoming increasingly conservative and liberal.[5]

Yet even if we can show that parties have polarized, what does it mean? Party polarization may be *caused* by strategic political actors at the same time that it is an *effect* of those actors responding to changes in the behavior of citizens.

A political party is fundamentally an organization used by candidates and party activists to gain and hold onto political power.[6] Party leaders, their activist supporters, and their candidates may find it advantageous to distinguish themselves from their opponents. As long as voters remain loyal to the party, or are constrained to choose among party candidates (as in a primary), then party polarization is *caused* by party elites.

But voters don't follow parties blindly. Parties mobilize voters and facilitate voter choice, but parties must follow public opinion if they want to retain support. It may be that the policy beliefs of Americans who say they are Republicans and Democrats have changed—become more polarized—and that these voters are selecting more extreme candidates. From this perspective, party polarization is the *effect* and a changing American public is the cause.

There is a third, more subtle possibility, however. Party polarization may be a combination of strategic political actors and citizen voters acting according to a set of rules and procedures. The *policy principle* directs us to ways in which changes in electoral politics in the last quarter-century may have encouraged extremism on the part of candidates and extreme choice on the part of voters.

Two of the most important changes to the rules of the electoral game that may have caused polarization are gerrymandering and the rise of primary elections.

Not surprisingly, the computer has radically changed how we draw the lines for congressional and state legislative seats. Computers allow politicians a new degree of sophistication when redistricting. Party members—both officeholders and party officials—know

Rationality Principle

Competing candidates want to carve out distinctive policy positions in order to garner political support.

Policy Principle

Party polarization is a result of the interaction of rational behavior by candidates and voters within a changing set of election rules.

that control of redistricting can lead to control of the legislature. Map drawers are now fairly confident about the "safety" of electoral districts and have systematically eliminated "swing districts" (which favor moderate candidates) and replaced them with districts that are more homogeneous in both ideology and partisanship.

The use of primary elections to select candidates increased after both parties reformed their internal rules in the late 1960s and early 1970s. Historically, most candidates were nominated by a combination of county and state party committees, party caucuses, and, for the president, a national convention. Party leaders and their loyalists controlled the nomination process, and candidates were beholden to the party. Primaries, on the other hand, allowed voters to participate more broadly in nominating candidates, and it was the candidate (not the party) who decided to run and who competed for votes.

How did the increase in primaries polarize American politics? Primary voters are more ideologically extreme and more committed partisans than their general election counterparts. Unlike party officials, primary voters are less interested in moderates who can win in the general election and more interested in candidates who represent a particular ideological position. As a result, state legislatures and Congress are filled with members from the extremes of their party rather than from the center.

Political deadlock may be a consequence of the increase in political polarization. With increased partisanship, the opportunity for the type of compromises necessary for lawmaking decreases. The outcome can be substantial, as shown by recent controversies in the U.S. Senate about judicial nominations. There seems to be no middle ground between the Republicans and the Democrats. The decline of moderate members also represents a loss of natural mediators between the two parties. As a result, the legislative process slows and disputes over major policies become more rancorous. The polarization of parties may also be depressing voter turnout. An absence of moderate candidates may alienate moderate voters. Presented with a choice between competing ideologues, moderate voters may simply be opting out of elections altogether.

 History Principle
Increasingly sophisticated gerrymanders after each decennial census have eliminated many competitive seats.

 Policy Principle
The rise of primary elections, combined with the ideological attitudes of primary voters, has pushed party candidates to the extremes of both parties.

 Collective-Action Principle
Party polarization makes cooperation between parties difficult.

[1]Sean Theriault, "The Case of the Vanishing Moderates." Paper presented at the Midwest Political Science Association, April 2003.

[2]Charles Cameron, "Studying the Polarized Presidency," *Presidential Studies Quarterly* 32.4 (2002).

[3]See Thomas M. Carsey and Geoffrey C. Layman, "Party Activists and the Ideological Polarization of American Politics: A Dynamic Model." Paper presented at the Midwest Political Science Association, April 2002.

[4]Morris Fiorina, *Culture War? The Myth of a Polarized America* (New York: Longman, 2005).

[5]David King, "The Polarization of Political Parties and Mistrust of Government," in Joseph S. Nye, Philip Zelikow, and David C. King, eds., *Why People Don't Trust Government* (Cambridge: Harvard University Press, 1997).

[6]John Aldrich, "Political Parties Can Be Seen as Coalitions of Elites Used to Capture and Use Political Office," in *Why Parties? The Origin and Transformation of Political Parties in America* (Chicago: University of Chicago Press, 1995).

As we saw in Chapter 5, the assignment of individual members to committees is a party decision. Each party has a "committee on committees" to make such decisions. Permission to transfer to another committee is also a party decision. Moreover, advancement up the committee ladder toward the chair is a party decision. Since the late nineteenth century, most advancements have been automatic—based on the length of continuous service on the committee. This seniority system has existed only because of the support of the two parties, and each party can depart from it by a simple vote. During the 1970s, both parties reinstituted the practice of reviewing each chairmanship—voting anew every two years on whether each chair would be continued. In 2001, Republicans lived up to their 1995 pledge to limit House committee chairs to three terms. Existing chairmen were forced to step down but were generally replaced by the next most senior Republican member of each committee.

President and Party   As we saw earlier, the party that wins the White House is always led, in title anyway, by the president. The president normally depends on fellow party members in Congress to support legislative initiatives. At the same time, members of the party in Congress hope that the president's programs and personal prestige will help them raise campaign funds and secure re-election. During his two terms in office, President Bill Clinton had a mixed record as party leader. In the realm of trade policy, Clinton sometimes found more support among Republicans than among Democrats. In addition, although Clinton proved to be an extremely successful fund-raiser, congressional Democrats often complained that he failed to share his largesse with them. At the same time, however, a number of Clinton's policy initiatives seemed calculated to strengthen the Democratic party as a whole. Clinton's early health-care initiative would have linked millions of voters to the Democrats for years to come, much as FDR's Social Security program had done in a previous era. But by the middle of Clinton's second term, the president's acknowledgement of his sexual affair with a White House intern threatened his position as party leader. Initially, Democratic candidates nationwide feared that the scandal would undermine their own chances for election, and many moved to distance themselves from the president. The Democrats' surprisingly good showing in the 1998 elections, however, strengthened Clinton's position and gave him another chance to shape the Democratic agenda.

Between the 1998 and 2000 elections, however, the president's initiatives on Social Security and nuclear disarmament failed to make much headway in a Republican-controlled Congress. The GOP was not prepared to give Clinton anything for which Democrats could claim credit in the 2000 elections. Lacking strong congressional leadership, however, the GOP did agree to many of Clinton's budgetary proposals in 1999 and dropped its own plan for large-scale cuts in federal taxes.

When he assumed office in 2001, President George W. Bush called for a new era of bipartisan cooperation, and the new president did receive the support of some Democratic conservatives. Generally, however, Bush depended on near-unanimous backing from his own party in Congress to implement his plans for cutting taxes as well as other elements of his program. After September 11, both parties united behind Bush's military response. By the end of the president's first term, however, the parties were sharply divided on the administration's policies in Iraq, on economic policy, on Social Security reform, on abortion and other social issues, and on the need for enhanced governmental law-enforcement powers to combat terrorism. Ultimately, Bush relied mainly on Republican support to achieve his goals.

PARTIES AND THE ELECTORATE

Political parties are more than just organizations and leaders; they are made up of millions of rank-and-file members. Individual voters tend to develop *party identification* with one of the political parties. Although it is a psychological tie, party identification also has a rational component. Voters generally form attachments to parties that reflect their views and interests. Once those attachments are formed, however, they are likely to persist and even to be handed down to children, unless some very strong factors convince individuals that their party is no longer an appropriate object for their affections. In some sense, party identification is similar to brand loyalty in the marketplace: consumers choose a brand of automobile for its appearance or mechanical characteristics and stick with it out of loyalty, habit, and unwillingness to constantly reexamine their choices; but they may eventually change if the old brand no longer serves their interests.

party identification An individual voter's psychological ties to one party or another.

Although the strength of partisan ties in the United States has declined in recent years, most Americans continue to identify with either the Republican Party or the Democratic Party (see Figure 11.2). Party identification gives citizens a stake in election outcomes that goes beyond the particular race at hand. This is why strong party identifiers are more likely than other Americans to go to the polls and, of course, are more likely than others to support the party with which they identify. *Party activists* are drawn from the ranks of the strong identifiers. Activists are those who not only vote but also contribute their time, energy, and effort to party affairs. Activists ring doorbells, stuff envelopes, attend meetings, and contribute money to the party cause. No party could succeed without the thousands of volunteers who undertake the mundane tasks needed to keep the organization going.

party activists Partisans who contribute time, energy, and effort to support their party and its candidates.

Group Affiliations

The Democratic and Republican parties are America's only national parties. They are the only political organizations that draw support from most regions of the country and from Americans of every racial, economic, religious, and ethnic group. The two parties do not draw equal support from members of every social stratum, however. When we refer to the Democratic or Republican "coalition," we mean the groups that generally support one or the other party. In the United States today, a variety of group characteristics are associated with party identification. These include race and ethnicity, gender, religion, class, ideology, and region.

FIGURE 11.2

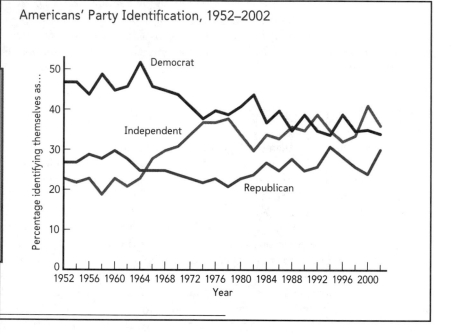

Americans' Party Identification, 1952–2002

SOURCE: Harold W. Stanley and Richard G. Niemi, *Vital Statistics on American Politics, 2001–2002* (Washington, DC: Congressional Quarterly Press, 2001), p. 115, and *National Election Studies Guide to Public Opinion and Electoral Behavior.*

Race and Ethnicity   Since the 1930s and Franklin Roosevelt's New Deal, African Americans have been overwhelmingly Democratic in their party identification. More than 90 percent of African Americans describe themselves as Democrats and support Democratic candidates in national, state, and local elections. Approximately 25 percent of the Democratic party's support in presidential races comes from African American voters.

Latino voters do not form a monolithic bloc, by contrast. Cuban Americans are generally Republican in their party affiliations, whereas Mexican Americans favor the Democrats by a small margin. Other Latino voters, including those from Puerto Rico, are overwhelmingly Democratic. Asian Americans tend to be divided as well, but along class lines. The Asian American community's influential business and professional stratum identifies with the Republicans, but less-affluent Asian Americans tend to support the Democrats.

Gender   Women are somewhat more likely to support Democrats, and men are somewhat more likely to support Republicans, in surveys of party affiliation. This difference is known as the *gender gap.* In the 1992 presidential election, women gave Bill Clinton 47 percent of their votes, whereas only 41 percent of the men who voted supported Clinton. In 1996, the gender gap was even more pronounced: women voted for Clinton 54 percent of the time, and only 43 percent of voting men did so. In the 2000 election, the gender gap closed, but only slightly.

gender gap
A distinctive pattern of voting behavior reflecting the differences in views between women and men.

Religion Jews are among the Democratic party's most loyal constituent groups and have been since the New Deal. Nearly 90 percent of all Jewish Americans describe themselves as Democrats. Catholics were also once a strongly pro-Democratic group but have been shifting toward the Republican party since the 1970s, when the GOP began to focus on abortion and other social issues deemed to be important to Catholics. Protestants are more likely to identify with the Republicans than with the Democrats. Protestant fundamentalists, in particular, have been drawn to the GOP's conservative stands on social issues, such as school prayer and abortion. The importance of religious conservatives to the Republican party became quite evident in 2001. After his victory in the November 2000 presidential election, George W. Bush announced that his administration would seek to award federal grants and contracts to religious groups. By using so-called faith-based groups as federal contractors, Bush was seeking to reward religious conservatives for their past loyalty to the GOP and to ensure that these groups would have a continuing stake in Republican success.

Class Upper-income Americans are considerably more likely to affiliate with the Republicans, whereas lower-income Americans are far more likely to identify with the Democrats. This divide is reflected by the differences between the two parties on economic issues. In general, the Republicans support cutting taxes and social spending—positions that reflect the interests of the wealthy. The Democrats, however, favor increasing social spending, even if this requires increasing taxes—a position consistent with the interests of less-affluent Americans. One important exception to this principle is that relatively affluent individuals who work in the public sector or such related institutions as foundations and universities also tend to affiliate with the Democrats. Such individuals are likely to appreciate the Democratic party's support for an expanded governmental role and high levels of public spending.

Ideology Ideology and party identification are very closely linked. Most individuals who describe themselves as conservatives identify with the Republican party, whereas most who call themselves liberals support the Democrats. This division has increased in recent years as the two parties have taken very different positions on social and economic issues. Before the 1970s, when party differences were more blurred, it was not uncommon to find Democratic conservatives and Republican liberals. Both of these species are rare today.

Region Between the Civil War and the 1960s, the "Solid South" was a Democratic bastion. Today, the South is becoming solidly Republican, as is much of the West and Southwest. The area of greatest Democratic party strength is the Northeast. The Midwest is a battleground, more or less evenly divided between the two parties.

The explanations for these regional variations are complex. Southern Republicanism has come about because conservative white southerners identify the Democratic party with the civil rights movement and with liberal positions on abortion, school prayer, and other social issues. Republican strength in the South and in the West is also related to the weakness of organized labor in these regions, as well as to the dependence of the two regions on military programs supported by the Republicans. Democratic strength in the Northeast is a function of the continuing influence of organized labor in the large cities of this region, as well as of the region's large population of minority and elderly voters, who benefit from Democratic social programs.

Age Age is another factor associated with partisanship. At the present time, individuals younger than fifty or older than sixty-five are fairly evenly divided between Democrats and Republicans, whereas those between the ages of fifty and sixty-four are much more likely to be Democrats. There is nothing about a particular numerical age that leads to a particular party loyalty. Instead, individuals from the same age cohort are likely to have experienced a similar set of events during the period when their party loyalties were formed. Thus Americans between the ages of fifty and sixty-four came of political age during the cold war, Vietnam, and civil rights eras. Apparently among voters whose initial perceptions of politics were shaped during this period, more responded favorably to the role played by the Democrats than to the actions of the Republicans. It is interesting that among the youngest group of Americans, a group that came of age during an era of political scandals that tainted both parties, the majority describe themselves as independents.

Figure 11.3 indicates the relationship between party identification and a number of social criteria. Race, religion, and income seem to have the greatest influence on Americans' party affiliations. None of these social characteristics is inevitably linked to partisan identification, however. There are black Republicans, southern white Democrats, Jewish Republicans, and even an occasional conservative Democrat. The general party identifications just discussed are broad tendencies that both reflect and reinforce the issue and policy positions the two parties take in the national and local political arenas.

PARTY SYSTEMS

History Principle

Parties are products of their own histories and of the history of their interactions with their rivals.

Our understanding of political parties would be incomplete if we considered only their composition and roles. America's political parties compete with one another over offices, policies, and power, and, as malleable institutions, have adapted to the demands of the time and age. In short, the history of each party is inextricably linked to that of its major rival. Historians often call the constellation of parties that are important at any given moment a nation's "party system." The most obvious feature of a party system is the number of major parties competing for power. Usually, the United States has had a two-party system, meaning that only

FIGURE 11.3

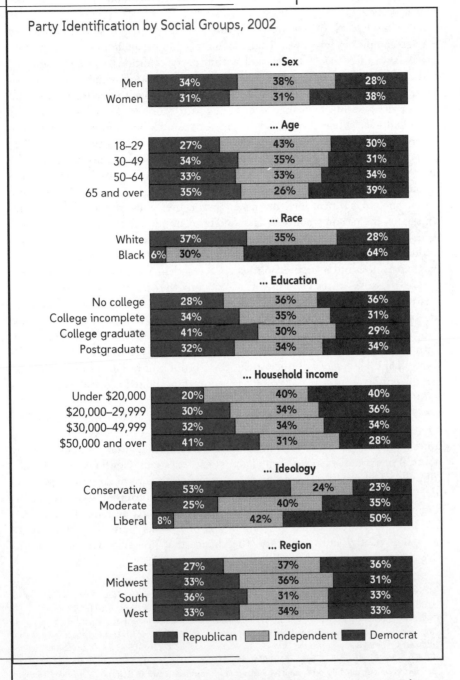

Party Identification by Social Groups, 2002

... Sex

	Republican	Independent	Democrat
Men	34%	38%	28%
Women	31%	31%	38%

... Age

	Republican	Independent	Democrat
18–29	27%	43%	30%
30–49	34%	35%	31%
50–64	33%	33%	34%
65 and over	35%	26%	39%

... Race

	Republican	Independent	Democrat
White	37%	35%	28%
Black	6%	30%	64%

... Education

	Republican	Independent	Democrat
No college	28%	36%	36%
College incomplete	34%	35%	31%
College graduate	41%	30%	29%
Postgraduate	32%	34%	34%

... Household income

	Republican	Independent	Democrat
Under $20,000	20%	40%	40%
$20,000–29,999	30%	34%	36%
$30,000–49,999	32%	34%	34%
$50,000 and over	41%	31%	28%

... Ideology

	Republican	Independent	Democrat
Conservative	53%	24%	23%
Moderate	25%	40%	35%
Liberal	8%	42%	50%

... Region

	Republican	Independent	Democrat
East	27%	37%	36%
Midwest	33%	36%	31%
South	36%	31%	33%
West	33%	34%	33%

■ Republican   ☐ Independent   ■ Democrat

SOURCE: Harold W. Stanley and Richard G. Niemi, *Vital Statistics on American Politics, 2003–2004* (Washington, DC: Congressional Quarterly Press, 2003), Table 3-2, p. 119.

two parties have a serious chance to win national elections. Of course, we have not always had the same two parties, and, as we shall see, minor parties often put forward candidates.

The term *party system*, however, refers to more than just the number of parties competing for power. It also connotes the organization of the parties, the balance of power between and within party coalitions, the parties' social and institutional bases, and the issues and policies around which party competition is organized. Seen from this broader perspective, the character of a nation's party system can change, even though the number of parties remains the same and even when the same two parties seem to be competing for power. Today's American party system is very different from the party system of fifty years ago, even though the Democrats and Republicans continue to be the major competing forces (Figure 11.4). The character of a nation's party system can have profound consequences for the relative influence of social forces, the importance of political institutions, and even the types of issues and policies that reach the nation's political agenda. For example, the contemporary American political parties mainly compete for the support of different groups of middle-class Americans. One reason for this is that less-affluent Americans participate less often in the political process than wealthier Americans (see Figure 10.3). As a result, issues that concern the middle and upper-middle classes, such as the environment, health care, retirement benefits, and taxation, are very much on the political agenda, while issues that concern working-class and poorer Americans, such as welfare and housing, receive short shrift from both parties.[9] Of course, throughout America's history, the creation of new issues did not just *happen*. Rather, it was the fruit of political entrepreneurs looking for opportunities to undermine the prevailing political orthodoxy and its political beneficiaries.[10]

Over the course of American history, changes in political forces and alignments have produced six party systems, each with distinctive political institutions, issues, and patterns of political power and participation. Of course, some political phenomena have persisted across party systems. Conflicts over the distribution of wealth, for example, are an enduring feature of American political life. But even such phenomena manifest themselves in different ways during different political eras. For example, the contemporary party system, characterized by weak party organization and low levels of popular participation, tends to favor the wealthy and to diminish the chance that poorer Americans will improve their fortunes via the political process.

---

[9]See Matthew A. Crenson and Benjamin Ginsberg, *Downsizing Democracy: How America Sidelined Its Citizens and Privatized Its Public* (Baltimore: Johns Hopkins University Press, 2002).
[10]Such entrepreneurial efforts are not always successful; history tends mainly to remember the successful ones. For an intriguing development of this notion, see William H. Riker, *Liberalism against Populism: A Confrontation between the Theory of Democracy and the Theory of Social Choice* (San Francisco: Freeman, 1982), especially Chapters 8 and 9. See also Andrew J. Polsky, "When Business Speaks: Political Entrepreneurship, Discourse, and Mobilization in American Partisan Regimes," *Journal of Theoretical Politics* 12 (2002): 451–72.

FIGURE 11.4

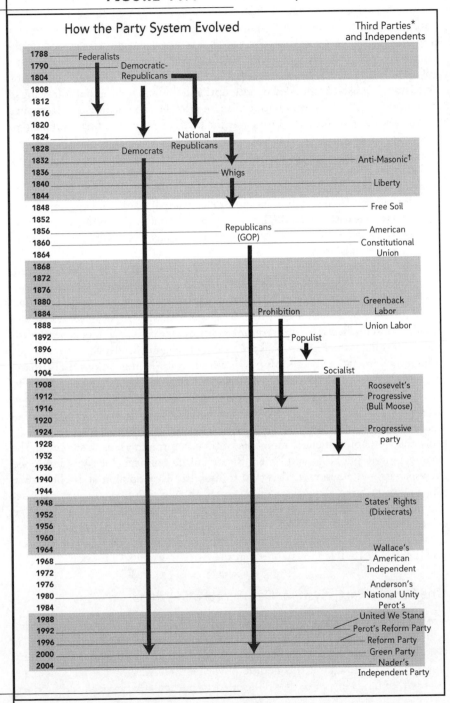

How the Party System Evolved

Third Parties* and Independents

*Or, in some cases, fourth party; most of these are one-term parties.

†The Anti-Masonics not only had the distinction of being the first third party but also were the first party to hold a national nominating convention and the first to announce a party platform.

The First Party System: Federalists and Democratic-Republicans

Although George Washington and, in fact, many leaders of the time deplored partisan politics, the two-party system emerged early in the history of the new Republic. Competition in Congress between northeastern mercantile and southern agrarian factions led Alexander Hamilton and the northeasterners to form a cohesive voting bloc within Congress. The southerners, led by Thomas Jefferson and James Madison, responded by attempting to organize a popular following to change the balance of power within Congress. When the northeasterners replied to this southern strategy, the result was the birth of America's first national parties—the Democratic-Republicans, whose primary base was in the South, and the Federalists, whose strength was greatest in the New England states. The Federalists spoke mainly for New England mercantile groups and supported a program of protective tariffs to encourage manufacturers, assumption of the states' Revolutionary War debts, the creation of a national bank, and resumption of commercial ties with England. The Democratic-Republicans opposed these policies, favoring instead free trade, the promotion of agrarian over commercial interests, and friendship with France.

Collective-Action Principle

The first American political parties were formed mainly to overcome collective-action problems in Congress.

The rationale behind the formation of both parties was primarily as a means to institutionalize existing voting blocs in Congress around a cohesive policy agenda. While the Federalists and Democratic-Republicans competed in elections, their ties to the electorate were loose. In 1800, the American electorate was small, and deference was an important political factor, with voters generally expected to follow the lead of local political and religious leaders and community notables. Nominations were informal without rules or regulations. Local party leaders would simply gather all the party elites, and they would agree on the person, usually from among themselves, who would be the candidate. The meetings where candidates were nominated were generally called caucuses. In this era before the introduction of the secret ballot, many voters were reluctant to publicly defy the views of influential members of their communities. In this context, the Democratic-Republicans and Federalists organized political clubs and developed newspapers and newsletters designed to mobilize elite opinion and relied upon local elites to bring along their followers. In the election of 1800, Jefferson defeated incumbent Federalist president John Adams and led his party to power. Over the ensuing years, the Federalists gradually weakened. The party disappeared altogether after the pro-British sympathies of some Federalist leaders during the War of 1812 led to charges that the party was guilty of treason.

The Second Party System: Democrats and Whigs

From the collapse of the Federalists until the 1830s, America had only one political party, the Democratic-Republicans. This period of one-party politics is sometimes known as the "era of good feelings," to indicate the absence of party competition. Throughout this period, however, there was intense factional conflict within the Democratic-Republican party, particularly between the supporters and opponents of General Andrew Jackson, America's great military hero of the War of 1812. Jackson was one of five serious party candidates for president in 1824 and won the most popular and electoral votes but a majority of neither, thus throwing the election into the House of Representatives. Jackson's opponents united to deny him the presidency in 1824, but Jackson won election in 1828 and again in 1832.

Jackson was greatly admired by millions of ordinary Americans living in the nation's farms and villages, and the Jacksonians made the most of the general's appeal to the common people by embarking on a program of suffrage expansion that would give Jackson's impecunious but numerous supporters the right to vote. To bring growing numbers of voters to the polls, the Jacksonians built political clubs and held mass rallies and parades, laying the groundwork for a new and more popular politics. Jackson's vice president and eventual successor, Martin Van Buren, was the organizational genius behind the Jacksonian movement, establishing a party central committee, state party organizations, and party newspapers. In response to widespread complaints about cliques of party leaders dominating all the nominations at party caucuses and leaving no place for the other party members who wanted to participate, the Jacksonians also established the state and national party convention as the forums for nominating presidential candidates. The conventions gave control over the presidential nominating process to the new state party organizations that the Jacksonians had created and expected to control. As political scientist John Aldrich has argued, unlike any political leader before him, Van Buren appreciated the possibilities for mass mobilization and the necessity of a well-oiled national organization to overcome free riding and other collective action problems.[11]

The Jacksonians, who came to be known as the Democratic party, were not without opponents, however, especially in the New England states; and during the 1830s, groups opposing Jackson for reasons of personality and politics united to form a new political force—the Whig party—thus giving rise to the second American party system. During the 1830s and 1840s, the Democrats and Whigs built party organizations throughout the nation, and both sought to enlarge their bases of support by expanding the suffrage through the elimination of property restrictions and other barriers to voting—at least voting by white males. This would not be the last time that party competition paved the way for expansion of the electorate. Support for the new Whig party was stronger in the Northeast than in the South and the West and stronger among mercantile groups than among small farmers. Hence, in some measure, the Whigs were the successors of the Federalists. Many, though not all, Whigs favored a national bank, a protective tariff, and federally sponsored internal improvements. The Jacksonians opposed all three policies. Yet conflict between the two parties revolved as much around personalities as policies. The Whigs were a diverse group, united more by opposition to the Democrats than by agreement on programs. In 1840, the Whigs won their first presidential election under the leadership of General William Henry

[11]See Aldrich, *Why Parties?*, Chapter 4.

Harrison, a military hero known as "Old Tippecanoe." The 1840 election marked the first time in American history that two parties competed for the presidency in every state in the Union. The Whig campaign carefully avoided issues—because different party factions disagreed on most matters—and emphasized the personal qualities and heroism of the candidate. The Whigs also invested heavily in campaign rallies and entertainment to win the hearts, if not exactly the minds, of the voters. The 1840 campaign came to be called the "hard cider" campaign to denote the then-common practice of using food and, especially, drink to elicit electoral favor.

In the late 1840s and early 1850s, conflicts over slavery produced sharp divisions within both the Whig and Democratic parties, despite the efforts of party leaders like Henry Clay and Stephen Douglas to develop sectional compromises that would bridge the increasing gulf between the North and the South. By 1856, the Whig party had all but disintegrated under the strain. The 1854 Kansas-Nebraska Act overturned the Missouri Compromise of 1820 and the Compromise of 1850, which together had hindered the expansion of slavery in the American territories. The Kansas-Nebraska Act gave each territory the right to decide whether or not to permit slavery. Opposition to this policy led to the formation of a number of antislavery parties, with the Republicans emerging as the strongest of these new forces.[12] It drew its membership from existing political groups—former Whigs, Know-Nothings, Free-Soilers, and antislavery Democrats. In 1856, the party's first presidential candidate, John C. Frémont, won one third of the popular vote and carried eleven states.

The early Republican platforms appealed to commercial as well as antislavery interests. The Republicans favored homesteading, internal improvements, the construction of a transcontinental railroad, and protective tariffs, as well as the containment of slavery. In 1858, the Republican party won control of the House of Representatives; in 1860, the Republican presidential candidate, Abraham Lincoln, was victorious. Lincoln's victory strengthened Southern calls for secession from the Union and led, soon thereafter, to all-out civil war.

The Third Party System: Republicans and Democrats, 1860–96

During the course of the war, President Lincoln depended heavily on Republican governors and state legislatures to raise troops, provide funding, and maintain popular support for a long and bloody military conflict. The secession of the South had stripped the Democratic party of many of its leaders and supporters, but, nevertheless, the Democrats remained politically competitive throughout the war and nearly won the 1864 presidential election because of war weariness on the part of the Northern public. With the defeat of the Confederacy in 1865, some congressional Republicans sought to convert the South into a Republican bastion through a program of reconstruction that enfran-

[12]See William E. Gienapp, *The Origins of the Republican Party, 1852–1856* (New York: Oxford University Press, 1994).

chised newly freed slaves while disenfranchising many white voters and disqualifying many white politicians from seeking office. This reconstruction program collapsed in the 1870s as a result of divisions within the Republican party in Congress and violent resistance to Reconstruction by Southern whites. With the end of Reconstruction, the former Confederate states regained full membership in the Union and full control of their internal affairs. Throughout the South, African Americans were deprived of political rights, including the right to vote, despite post–Civil War constitutional guarantees to the contrary. The post–Civil War South was solidly Democratic in its political affiliation and, with a firm Southern base, the national Democratic party was able to confront the Republicans on a more or less equal basis. From the end of the Civil War to the 1890s, the Republican party remained the party of the North, with strong business and middle-class support, while the Democratic party was the party of the South, with support from working-class and immigrant groups in the North. Republican candidates campaigned by waving the "bloody shirt" of the Civil War and urging their supporters to "vote the way you shot." Democrats emphasized the issue of the tariff, which they claimed was ruinous to agricultural interests.

Party Machines as a Strategic Innovation   It was during the third party system that party entrepreneurs were most successful in making party organizations well-oiled machines. In the nineteenth and early twentieth centuries, many cities and counties, and even a few states on occasion, had such well organized parties that they were called *party machines* and their leaders were bosses. Party machines depended heavily on the patronage of the spoils system, the party's power to control government jobs. Patronage worked as a selective benefit with anyone the party wished to attract to its side. With thousands of jobs to dispense to the party faithful, party bosses were able to recruit armies of political workers, who, in turn, mobilized millions of voters. During the height of party machines, party and government were virtually interchangeable.

> **party machines**
> In the late nineteenth and early twentieth centuries, local party organizations that controlled local politics through patronage and control of nominations.

Many critics condemned party machines as antidemocratic and corrupt. They argued that machines served the interests of powerful businesses and did not help the working people who voted for them. But one of the most notorious machine leaders in American political history, George Washington Plunkitt of New York City's Tammany Hall, considered machine politics and the spoils system to be "patriotic." Plunkitt grasped a simple, central fact about purposeful behavior and overcoming the collective-action problem. To create and retain political influence and power, "you must study human nature and act accordin'." He argued with some acumen that the country was built by political parties, that the parties needed such patronage to operate and thrive, and that if patronage was withdrawn, the parties would "go to pieces." As we will see next, he was somewhat prescient in making this observation.

Institutional Reforms of the Progressives   Around the turn of the twentieth century, the excessive powers and abuses of party machines and their bosses led to one of the great reform movements in American history, the so-called Progressive era. Many Progressive reformers were undoubtedly motivated by a sincere desire to rid politics of corruption and to improve the quality and efficiency of government in the United States. But, simultaneously, from the perspective of middle- and upper-class Progressives and the financial, commercial, and industrial elites with whom they were often associated, the weakening or elimination of party organization would also mean that power could more readily be acquired and retained by the "best men"—that is, those with wealth, position, and education.

The list of anti-party reforms of the Progressive era is a familiar one. As we saw in Chapter 10, voter registration laws were introduced that required eligible voters to register in person well before the actual election. The Australian-ballot reform took away the parties' privilege of printing and distributing ballots and thus introduced the possibility of split-ticket voting (see also Chapter 10). The introduction of nonpartisan local elections eroded grassroots party organization. The extension of "merit systems" for administrative appointments stripped party organizations of their vitally important access to patronage and thus reduced party leaders' capacity to control candidate nominations.

These reforms obviously did not destroy political parties as entities, but taken together they did substantially weaken party organizations in the United States. After the turn of the twentieth century, the strength of American political parties gradually diminished, and voter turnout declined precipitously. Between the two world wars, organization remained the major tool available to contending electoral forces, but in most areas of the country the "reformed" state and local parties that survived the Progressive era gradually lost their organizational vitality and coherence, and became less effective campaign tools. While most areas of the nation continued to boast Democratic and Republican party groupings, reform did mean the elimination of the permanent mass organizations that had been the parties' principal campaign weapons.

The Fourth Party System, 1896–1932

During the 1890s, profound and rapid social and economic changes led to the emergence of a variety of protest parties, including the Populist party, which won the support of hundreds of thousands of voters in the South and West. The Populists appealed mainly to small farmers but also attracted western mining interests and urban workers as well. In the 1892 presidential election, the Populist party carried four states and elected governors in eight states. In 1896, the Democrats in effect adopted the Populist party platform and nominated William Jennings Bryan, a Democratic senator with pronounced Populist sympathies, for the presidency. The Republicans nominated conservative senator William McKinley. In the ensuing campaign, northern and midwestern business made an all-out effort to defeat what it saw as a radical threat from the Populist-Democratic alliance. When the dust settled, the Republicans had won a resounding victory. In the nation's metropolitan regions, especially in the Northeast and upper Midwest, workers became convinced that the Populist-Democratic alliance threatened the industries that provided their jobs, while immigrants were frightened by the nativist rhetoric employed by some Populist orators and writers. The GOP had carried the northern and midwestern states and confined the Democrats to their bastions in the South and Far West. For the next thirty-six years, the Republicans were the nation's majority party, carrying seven of nine presidential elections and controlling both houses of Congress in fifteen of eighteen contests. The Republican party of this era was very much the party of American business, advocating low taxes, high tariffs, and a minimum of government regulation. The Democrats were far too weak to offer much opposition. Southern Democrats, moreover, were more concerned with maintaining the region's autonomy on issues of race to challenge the Republicans on other fronts.

The Fifth Party System: The New Deal Coalition, 1932–68

Soon after Republican presidential candidate Herbert Hoover won the 1928 presidential election, the nation's economy collapsed. The Great Depression, which produced unprecedented economic hardship, stemmed from a variety of causes; but from the perspective of millions of Americans, the Republican party had not done enough to promote economic recovery. In 1932, Americans elected Franklin D. Roosevelt and a solidly Democratic Congress. FDR developed a program for economic recovery that he dubbed the "New Deal." Under the auspices of the New Deal, the size and reach of America's national government was substantially increased. The federal government took responsibility for economic management and social welfare to an extent that was unprecedented in American history. Roosevelt designed many of his programs specifically to expand the political base of the Democratic party. He rebuilt the party around a nucleus of unionized workers, upper-middle-class intellectuals and professionals, southern farmers, Jews, Catholics, and northern African Americans (few blacks in the South could vote) that made the Democrats the nation's majority party for the next thirty-six years. Republicans groped for a response to the New Deal and often wound up supporting popular New Deal programs like Social Security in what was sometimes derided as "me too" Republicanism.

The New Deal coalition was severely strained during the 1960s by conflicts over President Lyndon Johnson's Great Society initiative, civil rights, and the Vietnam War. A number of Johnson's Great Society programs, designed to fight poverty and racial discrimination, involved the empowerment of local groups that were often at odds with established city and county governments. These programs touched off battles between local Democratic political machines and the national administration that split the Democratic coalition. For its part, the struggle over civil rights initially divided northern Democrats, who supported the civil rights cause, from white southern Democrats, who defended the system of racial segregation. Subsequently, as the civil rights movement launched a northern campaign aimed at securing access to jobs and education and an end to racial discrimination in such realms as housing, northern Democrats also split, often along class lines, with more blue-collar workers voting Republican. The struggle over the Vietnam War further divided the Democrats, with upper-income liberal Democrats strongly opposing the Johnson administration's decision to send U.S. forces to fight in Southeast Asia. These schisms within the Democratic party provided an opportunity for the GOP to return to power, which it did in 1968 under the leadership of Richard Nixon.

The Sixth Party System?

In the 1960s, conservative Republicans argued that "me-tooism" was a recipe for continual failure and sought to reposition the GOP as a genuine alternative to the Democrats. In 1964, for example, Republican presidential candidate Barry Goldwater, author of a book titled *The Conscience of a Conservative* (1960), argued in favor of substantially reduced levels of taxation and spending, less government regulation of the economy, and the elimination of many federal social programs. Although Goldwater was defeated by Lyndon Johnson, the ideas he espoused continue to be major themes for the Republican party. The Goldwater message, however, was not enough to lead Republicans to victory. It took Richard Nixon's "southern strategy" to give the GOP the votes it needed to end Democratic dominance of the political process. Nixon appealed strongly to disaffected white southerners and, with the help of independent candidate and former Alabama governor George Wallace, sparked the shift of voters that eventually gave the once-hated "party of Lincoln" a strong position in all the states of the former Confederacy. In the 1980s, under the leadership of Ronald Reagan, Republicans added another important group to their coalition—religious conservatives who were offended by Democratic support for abortion rights as well as alleged Democratic disdain for traditional cultural and religious values.

While Republicans built a political base around economic and social conservatives and white southerners, the Democratic party maintained its support among unionized workers and upper-middle-class intellectuals and professionals. Democrats also appealed strongly to racial minorities. The 1965 Voting Rights Act had greatly increased black voter participation in the South and helped the Democratic party retain some congressional and Senate seats in the South. And, while the GOP appealed to social conservatives, the Democrats appealed strongly to Americans concerned with abortion rights, gay rights, feminism, environmentalism, and other progressive social causes. The result so far has been a small but growing edge for the GOP. Three of the last four U.S. presidents have been Republicans; and during the Clinton era, Republicans took control of the House of Representatives for the first time in decades. The 2000 presidential election ended in a virtual tie, with Democratic presidential candidate Al Gore outpolling George W. Bush by a handful of votes. But Republicans, nevertheless, captured the White House and both houses of Congress. In 2004, Bush defeated Democratic challenger John Kerry by more than 5 million votes and Republicans increased their majorities in the House and Senate.

The shift of much of the South from the Democratic to the Republican camp along with the other developments mentioned above also meant that each political party became ideologically more homogeneous after the 1980s. Today, there are few liberal Republicans or conservative Democrats. One consequence of this development is that party loyalty in Congress, which had been weak between the 1950s and 1970s, became a more potent force. Battles over such matters as the Clinton impeachment, for example, resulted in nearly straight party-line voting in the House and Senate. On other matters, including budgetary priorities, judicial appointments, and foreign policy, party-line voting has become far more common than in prior years (see Chapter 5).

To some extent, ideology has replaced organization as the glue holding together each party's coalition. But, in the long run, ideology is often an unreliable basis for party unity. Though the activists within each party grouping are united by some beliefs, ideological divisions also plague both camps. Within the Republican coalition, social conservatives are often at odds with economic conservatives; whereas among Democrats, proponents of regulatory reform and economic internationalism are frequently at odds with traditional liberal Democrats, who favor big government and protecting American workers from foreign competition. The party workers of yesteryear supported the leadership almost no matter what. Today's more ideologically motivated party activists, though, give their leaders only very conditional backing and feel perfectly free to withhold support if they disagree with the leadership's goals and plans. Because of internal divisions in the Republican party, for example, GOP congressional leaders have adopted a strategy of avoiding votes on the many issues that might split the party.[13] The price of unity through ideology can be inability to act.

The ideological gap between the two parties has been exacerbated by two other factors: each party's dependence on ideologically motivated activists, and the changes in the presidential nominating system that were introduced during the 1970s. As to the first of these factors, Democratic political candidates depend heavily on the support of liberal activists, such as feminists, environmentalists, and civil libertarians, to organize and finance their campaigns, while Republican political candidates depend equally upon the support of conservative activists, including religious fundamentalists. In the nineteenth century, political activists were motivated more by party loyalty and political patronage than by programmatic concerns. Today's issue-oriented activists, by contrast, demand that politicians demonstrate strong commitments to moral principles and political causes in exchange for the activists' support. The demands of party activists have tended to push Democrats further to the political Left and Republicans further to the political Right. Often, efforts by politicians to reach compromises on key issues are attacked by party activists as "sellouts," leading to stalemates on such matters as the budget and judicial appointments.

The parties' ideological split has also been exacerbated by the changes in the presidential nominating system that developed during the 1970s. After the

---

[13]Isaiah J. Poole, "Votes Echo Electoral Themes," *Congressional Quarterly Weekly Report*, 11 December 2004, pp. 2906–08.

Democratic party's defeat in 1968, liberal forces, through the so-called McGovern-Fraser Commission on party reform, succeeded in changing the rules governing Democratic presidential nominations to reduce the power of party officials and professionals while increasing the role of issue-oriented activists. Among other changes, the new Democratic rules required national convention delegates to be chosen in primaries and caucuses rather than by the state party central committees, as had previously been the practice in many states. Subsequently, Republican activists were able to bring about similar changes in the GOP's rules so that today, in both parties, presidential nominating processes are strongly influenced by precisely the sorts of grassroots activists who are often inclined to oppose centrist or pragmatic politicians in favor of those appearing to manifest ideological purity. As a result, elections have tended to pit liberal Democrats against conservative Republicans. Observers of post–World War II American political parties often dubbed them "Tweedledum and Tweedledee," but the two parties today differ sharply on a number of social, economic, and foreign policy issues. Compare, for example, Democratic and Republican legislative priorities at the opening of the 109th Congress in January 2005 (Figure 11.5). Republicans emphasized tax cuts, tort reform, the overhaul of Social Security, and new laws to strengthen marriage and discourage abortion. The Democrats emphasized expanding social programs, protecting the jobs of unionized workers, and strengthening abortion rights. These competing agendas set the stage for a contentious legislative session.

American Third Parties

third parties
Parties that organize to compete against the two major American political parties.

Although the United States is said to possess a two-party system, we have always had more than two parties. Typically, *third parties* in the United States have represented social and economic protests that, for one or another reason, were not given voice by the two major parties.[14] Such parties have had a good deal of influence on ideas and elections in the United States. The Populists, a party centered in the rural areas of the West and Midwest, and the Progressives, spokesmen for the urban middle classes in the late nineteenth and early twentieth centuries, are the most important examples in the past hundred years. More recently, Ross Perot, who ran in 1992 and 1996 as an independent, impressed some voters with his folksy style in the presidential debates and garnered almost 19 percent of the votes cast in the 1992 presidential election.

Table 11.1 shows a listing of all the parties that offered candidates in one or more states in the presidential election of 2004 as well as independent candidates. The third-party and independent candidates together polled barely 1 million votes. They gained no electoral votes for president, and most of them disappeared immediately after the presidential election. The significance of the table is that it demonstrates the large number of third parties running candidates and appealing to voters. Third-party candidacies also arise at the state and local levels. In New York, the Liberal and Conservative parties have been on the ballot

---

[14]For a discussion of third parties in the United States, see Daniel A. Mazmanian, *Third Parties in Presidential Elections* (Washington, DC: Brookings Institution, 1974).

FIGURE 11.5

Dueling Agendas*

Republicans' priorities	Democrats' priorities
1. Social Security overhaul	**1.** Increase active-duty troop strength and expand benefits for troops and their families
2. Tax-code overhaul	**2.** Increase military special forces and prevent proliferation of weapons of mass destruction
3. Improve homeland security and crisis response, coupled with increased benefits for families of troops killed in action	**3.** Boost benefits for veterans
4. Expand health-care coverage and affordability	**4.** Discard the president's overtime-labor rules, raise the minimum wage, and protect U.S. workers in trade agreements
5. Overhaul the class-action lawsuit system	**5.** Fully fund and make changes to the No Child Left Behind Law
6. Offer incentives for marriage, including welfare provisions and permanently ending the marriage penalty	**6.** Offer tax cuts to encourage companies to provide medical coverage, allow reimportation of drugs, and expand Medicaid coverage
7. Make most 2001 and 2003 tax cuts permanent	**7.** Election reform law to prevent voting problems
8. Prevent minors from being taken across state lines to circumvent parental-notification laws when getting abortions	**8.** Expand the 2003 Medicare prescription-drug law and hold down Medicare premium increases
9. Expand the president's No Child Left Behind law	**9.** Enforce budget rules on the Senate to control spending
10. Set a new national energy policy	**10.** Expand access to contraception and family-planning services

ANALYZING THE EVIDENCE

In recent years the Democratic and Republican parties have taken sharply different positions on major social, economic, and foreign policy issues. These differences reflect the parties' divergent constituent bases, the philosophical differences between the leaders of the coalitions, and questions of political strategy. Is our nation better served by political parties that express strong disagreements or by parties whose differences are more muted?

*The top ten legislative priorities for the 109th Congress, announced by Democratic and Republican senators.
SOURCE: *Washington Times*, 25 January 2005, p. A4.

for decades. In 1998, Minnesota elected a third-party governor, former professional wrestler Jesse Ventura.

Although the Republican party, founded as a third party in the 1850s, was only the third American political party ever to make itself permanent (by replacing the Whigs and becoming the Democrats' major competitor), other third parties have enjoyed an influence far beyond their electoral size. This was because

TABLE 11.1

Though the Democrats and Republicans are America's dominant political forces, many minor parties nominate candidates for the presidency. Why are there so many minor parties? Why don't these parties represent much of a threat to the major parties?

Parties and Candidates in 2004

CANDIDATE	PARTY	VOTE TOTAL*	PERCENTAGE OF VOTE*
George W. Bush	Republican	58,978,616	51
John F. Kerry	Democrat	55,384,497	48
Ralph Nader	Independent	394,578	0
Michael Badnarik	Libertarian	377,940	0
Michael A. Peroutka	Constitution	129,842	0
David Cobb	Green	105,525	0
Leonard Peltier	Peace and Freedom	21,616	0
Walter F. Brown	Independent	10,258	0
James Harris	Socialist Workers	6,699	0
Roger Calero	Socialist Workers	5,274	0
Thomas J. Harens	Other	2,395	0
Bill Van Auken	Independent	2,078	0
Gene Amondson	Libertarian	1,896	0
John Parker	Liberty Union	1,159	0
Charles Jay	Personal Choice	867	0
Stanford "Andy" E. Andress	Unaffiliated	720	0
Earl F. Dodge	Prohibition	122	0
None of the above	–	3,646	0

*With 99 percent of votes tallied.
SOURCE: www.washingtonpost.com/wp-srv/elections/2004/page/295001 (accessed 8 November 2004).

large parts of their programs were adopted by one or both of the major parties, who sought to appeal to the voters mobilized by the new party and so expand their own electoral strength. The Democratic party, for example, became a great deal more liberal when it adopted most of the Progressive program early in the twentieth century. Many Socialists felt that President Roosevelt's New Deal had adopted most of their party's program, including old-age pensions, unemployment compensation, an agricultural marketing program, and laws guaranteeing workers the right to organize into unions.

This kind of influence explains the short lives of third parties. Their causes are usually eliminated by the ability of the major parties to absorb their programs and to draw their supporters into the mainstream. There are, of course, additional reasons for the short duration of most third parties. One is the usual limitation of their electoral support to one or two regions. Populist support, for example, was primarily midwestern. The 1948 Progressive party, with Henry Wallace as its candidate, drew nearly half its votes from the state of New York. The American Independent party polled nearly 10 million popular votes and 45 electoral votes for George Wallace in 1968—the most electoral votes ever polled by a third-party candidate. But all of Wallace's electoral votes and the majority of his popular vote came from the states of the Deep South.

Americans usually assume that only the candidates nominated by one of the two major parties have any chance of winning an election. Thus a vote cast for a third-party or independent candidate is often seen as a wasted vote. Voters who would prefer a third-party candidate may feel compelled to vote for the major-party candidate who they regard as the "lesser of two evils" to avoid wasting their vote in a futile gesture. Third-party candidates must struggle—usually without success—to overcome the perception that they cannot win. Thus in 2004, many liberals who admired Ralph Nader nevertheless urged him not to mount an independent bid for the presidency for fear that he would siphon liberal votes away from the Democrats as he did in 2000. Some former Naderites participated in efforts to keep Nader off the ballot in a number of states. Ultimately Nader did mount a presidential campaign but received 2.5 million fewer votes in 2004 than in 2000. Most of his former adherents, knowing he could not win, voted for John Kerry.

As many scholars have pointed out, third-party prospects are also hampered by America's *single-member-district* plurality election system. In many other nations, several individuals can be elected to represent each legislative district. This is called a system of *multiple-member districts.* With this type of system, the candidates of weaker parties have a better chance of winning at least some seats. For their part, voters are less concerned about wasting ballots and usually more willing to support minor-party candidates.

Reinforcing the effects of the single-member district, plurality voting rules (as was noted in Chapter 10) generally have the effect of setting what could be called a high threshold for victory. To win a plurality race, candidates usually must secure many more votes than they would need under most European systems of proportional representation. For example, to win an American plurality election in a single-member district where there are only two candidates, a

single-member district An electorate that is allowed to elect only one representative from each district; the normal method of representation in the United States.

multiple-member district Electorate that selects several candidates at large from the whole district; each voter is given the number of votes equivalent to the number of seats to be filled.

politician must win more than 50 percent of the votes cast. To win a seat from a European multimember district under proportional rules, a candidate may need to win only 15 or 20 percent of the votes cast. This high American threshold discourages minor parties and encourages the various political factions that might otherwise form minor parties to minimize their differences and remain within the major-party coalitions.[15]

It would nevertheless be incorrect to assert (as some scholars have maintained) that America's single-member plurality election system guarantees that only two parties will compete for power in all regions of the country. All that can be said is that American election law depresses the number of parties likely to survive over long periods of time in the United States. There is nothing magical about two. Indeed, the single-member plurality system of election can also discourage second parties. After all, if one party consistently receives a large plurality of the vote, people may eventually come to see their vote *even for the second party* as a wasted effort. This happened to the Republican party in the Deep South before World War II.

Institution Principle

Third-party prospects for electoral success are hampered by America's single-member-district plurality election system.

HOW STRONG ARE POLITICAL PARTIES TODAY?

As a result of Progressive reform, American party organizations entered the twentieth century with rickety substructures. As the use of civil service, primary elections, and the other Progressive innovations spread during the period between the two world wars, the strength of party organizations continued to be eroded. By the end of World War II, political scientists were already bemoaning the absence of party discipline and "party responsibility" in the United States.

High-Tech Politics and the Rise of Candidate-Centered and Capital-Intensive Politics

History Principle

The erosion of the strength of party organizations set the stage for the introduction of new political campaign techniques and the rise of candidate-centered campaigns.

This erosion of the parties' organizational strength set the stage for the introduction of new political techniques. These new methods represented radical departures from the campaign practices perfected during the nineteenth century. In place of manpower and organization, contending forces began to employ intricate electronic communications techniques to attract electoral support. This new political technology includes six basic elements: polling, the broadcast media, phone banks, direct mail, professional public relations, and the Internet.

Polling Surveys of voter opinion provide the information that candidates and their staffs use to craft campaign strategies. Candidates employ polls to select issues, to assess their own strengths and weaknesses (as well as those of the oppo-

---

[15]See Duverger, *Political Parties.*

sition), to check voter response to the campaign, and to determine the degree to which various constituent groups are susceptible to campaign appeals. Virtually all contemporary campaigns for national and statewide office as well as many local campaigns make extensive use of opinion surveys. As we saw in Chapter 9, President Clinton made extensive use of polling data both during and after the 1996 presidential election to shape his rhetoric and guide his policy initiatives.

The Broadcast Media Extensive use of the electronic media, television in particular, has become the hallmark of the modern political campaign. One commonly used broadcast technique is the 30- or 60-second television spot advertisement—such as George H. W. Bush's "Willie Horton" ad in 1988 or Lyndon Johnson's famous "daisy girl" ad in 1964—which permits the candidate's message to be delivered to a target audience before uninterested or hostile viewers can psychologically, or physically, tune it out. Television spot ads and other media techniques are designed to establish candidate name recognition, to create a favorable image of the candidate and a negative image of the opponent, to link the candidate with desirable groups in the community, and to communicate the candidate's stands on selected issues. These spot ads can have an important electoral impact. Generally, media campaigns attempt to follow the guidelines indicated by a candidate's polls, emphasizing issues and personal characteristics that appear important in the poll data. The broadcast media are now so central to modern campaigns that most candidates' activities are tied to their media strategies. Candidate activities are designed expressly to stimulate television news coverage. For instance, members of Congress running for re-election or for president almost always sponsor committee or subcommittee hearings to generate publicity.

Phone Banks Through the broadcast media, candidates communicate with voters en masse and impersonally. Phone banks, on the other hand, allow campaign workers to make personal contact with hundreds of thousands of voters. Personal contacts of this sort are thought to be extremely effective. Again, poll data serve to identify the groups that will be targeted for phone calls. Computers select phone numbers from areas in which members of these groups are concentrated. Staffs of paid or volunteer callers, using computer-assisted dialing systems and prepared scripts, then place calls to deliver the candidate's message. The targeted groups are generally those identified by polls as either uncommitted or weakly committed, as well as strong supporters of the candidate who are contacted simply to encourage them to vote.

Direct Mail Direct mail serves both as a vehicle for communicating with voters and as a mechanism for raising funds. The first step in a direct mail campaign is the purchase or rental of a computerized mailing list of voters deemed to have some particular perspective or social characteristic. Often, sets of magazine subscription lists or lists of donors to various causes are employed. For example, a candidate interested in reaching conservative voters might rent subscription lists from the *National Review;* a candidate interested in appealing to liberals might rent subscription lists from the *New York Review of Books* or from the *New Republic.* Considerable fine-tuning is possible. After obtaining the appropriate mailing lists, candidates usually send pamphlets, letters, and brochures describing themselves and their views to voters believed to be sympathetic. Different types of mail appeals are made to different electoral subgroups. Often the letters sent to voters are personalized. The recipient is addressed by name in the text and the letter appears actually to have been signed by the candidate. Of course, these "personal" letters are written and even signed by a computer.

In addition to its use as a political advertising medium, direct mail has also become an important source of campaign funds. Computerized mailing lists permit campaign strategists to pinpoint individuals whose interests, background, and activities suggest that they may be potential donors to the campaign. Letters of solicitation are sent to these potential donors. Some of the money raised is then used to purchase additional mailing lists. Direct-mail solicitation can be enormously effective.

Professional Public Relations   Modern campaigns and the complex technology on which they rely are typically directed by professional public relations consultants. Virtually all serious contenders for national and statewide office retain the services of professional campaign consultants.[16] Increasingly, candidates for local office, too, have come to rely on professional campaign managers. Consultants offer candidates the expertise necessary to conduct accurate opinion polls, produce television commercials, organize direct-mail campaigns, and make use of sophisticated computer analyses.

The Internet   A more recent form of new technology has been the Internet. Most candidates for office set up a Web site as an inexpensive means of establishing a public presence. The 1998 election saw increased use of the Internet by political candidates. Virtually all statewide candidates, as well as many candidates for Congress and local offices, developed Web sites providing contact information, press releases, speeches, photos, and information on how to volunteer, contact the candidate, or donate money to the campaign. During his campaign, Florida governor Jeb Bush sold "Jebware," articles of clothing emblazoned with his name, through his Web site. In the 2000 contest, the politician who made the most extensive use of the Internet was John McCain. McCain used his Web site to mobilize volunteers and to raise hundreds of thousands of dollars for his unsuccessful bid for the Republican presidential nomination. In the future, all politicians will use the Web to collect information about potential voters and supporters, which, in turn, will allow them to personalize mailings and calls as well as e-mail advertising. One consultant now refers to politics on the Internet as "netwar," and asserts that "small, smart attackers" can defeat more powerful opponents in the new, information-age

---

[16]Larry Sabato, *The Rise of Political Consultants: New Ways of Winning Elections* (New York: Basic Books, 1981).

"battlespace."[17] Although the Internet has not yet become a dominant force in political campaigns, most politicians and consultants believe that its full potential for customizing political appeals is only now beginning to be realized.

During the 2004 presidential primaries, Democratic hopeful Howard Dean made extensive use of the Internet as a communication and fund-raising tool. Thousands of bloggers maintained discussion forums that promoted Dean's candidacy and solicited funds. By the end of 2003, Dean had amassed a war chest of more than $15 million, much of it raised on the Internet, for his presidential bid. Dean Internet guru Joe Trippi hoped to persuade 2 million Americans to each give "one hundred dollars online," to match the funds President Bush was expected to accumulate through traditional fund-raising methods. In the general election, both Kerry and Bush used the Internet to raise money and mobilize voters. Liberal advocacy groups tied to the Democratic party, like Americans Coming Together, also made use of the Internet to boost voter registration among young people and others thought to have Democratic leanings.

Labor-Intensive to Capital-Intensive Politics

The displacement of organizational methods by the new political technology is, in essence, a shift from labor-intensive to capital-intensive competitive electoral practices. Campaign tasks were once performed by masses of party workers with some cash. These tasks now require fewer personnel but a great deal more money, for the new political campaign depends on polls, computers, and other electronic paraphernalia. This shift has given the advantage to groups with the ability to raise a great deal of money. This has served the political interests of the GOP and those of wealthy donors within the Democratic party. The harsh logic of fund-raising is another reason why neither party cares much about issues that affect the poor.

Contemporary Party Organizations

In the United States, party organizations exist at virtually every level of government (Figure 11.6). These organizations are usually committees made up of a number of active party members. State law and party rules prescribe how such committees are constituted. Usually, committee members are elected at local party meetings—called *caucuses*—or as part of the regular primary election. The best-known examples of these committees are at the national level—the Democratic National Committee and the Republican National Committee.

National Convention   At the national level, the party's most important institution is the national convention. The convention is attended by delegates from each of the states; as a group, they nominate the party's presidential and vice-presidential candidates, draft the party's campaign platform for the presidential

caucuses (political)
Normally closed meetings of a political or legislative group to select candidates, plan strategy, or make decisions regarding legislative matters.

---

[17]Dana Milbanks, "Virtual Politics," *New Republic*, 5 July 1999, p. 22.

FIGURE 11.6

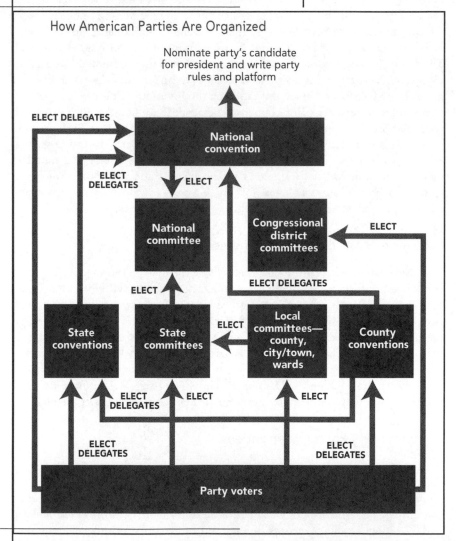

How American Parties Are Organized

Nominate party's candidate
for president and write party
rules and platform

ELECT DELEGATES

National
convention

ELECT
DELEGATES   ELECT

National
committee

Congressional
district
committees   ELECT

ELECT

ELECT DELEGATES

State
conventions

State
committees   ELECT   Local
committees—
county,
city/town,
wards   County
conventions

ELECT
DELEGATES   ELECT   ELECT   ELECT

ELECT
DELEGATES   ELECT
DELEGATES

Party voters

race, and approve changes in the rules and regulations governing party procedures. Before World War II, presidential nominations occupied most of the time,
energy, and effort expended at the national convention. The nomination process
required days of negotiation and compromise among state party leaders and
often required many ballots before a nominee was selected. In recent years,
however, presidential candidates have essentially nominated themselves by win-

ning enough delegate support in primary elections to win the official nomination on the first ballot. The actual convention has played little or no role in selecting the candidates.

The convention's other two tasks, establishing the party's rules and platform, remain important. Party rules can determine the relative influence of competing factions within the party and can also increase or decrease the party's chances for electoral success. In 1972, for example, the Democratic National Convention adopted a new set of rules favored by the party's liberal wing. Under these rules, state delegations to the Democratic convention were required to include women and members of minority groups in rough proportion to those groups' representation among the party's membership in that state. Liberals correctly calculated that women and African Americans would generally support liberal ideas and candidates. The rules also called for the use of proportional representation—a voting system liberals thought would give them an advantage by allowing the election of more women and minority delegates. (Although Republican rules do not require proportional representation for selecting delegates, some state legislatures have moved to compel both parties to use this system in all their presidential primaries.)

Institution Principle

Party rules can determine the relative influence of competing factions within the party and can also increase or decrease the party's chances for electoral success.

The convention also approves the party platform. Platforms are often dismissed as documents filled with platitudes that are seldom read by voters. To some extent this criticism is well founded. Not one voter in a thousand so much as glances at the party platform, and even the news media pay little attention to the documents. Furthermore, the parties' presidential candidates make little use of the platforms in their campaigns; usually they prefer to develop and promote their own themes. Occasionally, nominees even disavow their party's platform. In 1864, for example, Democratic presidential nominee General George McClellan repudiated his party's peace platform. Nonetheless, the platform can be an important document. The platform should be understood as a contract in which the various party factions attending the convention state their terms for supporting the ticket. For one faction, welfare reform may be a key issue. For another faction, tax reduction may be more important. For a third, the critical issue may be deficit reduction. When one of these "planks" is included in the platform, its promoters are asserting that this is what they want in exchange for their support of the ticket, while other party factions are agreeing that the position seems reasonable and appropriate.

National Committee Between conventions, each national political party is technically headed by its national committee. For the Democrats and Republicans, these are called the Democratic National Committee (DNC) and the Republican National Committee (RNC), respectively. These national committees raise campaign funds, head off factional disputes within the party, and endeavor to enhance the party's media image. Since 1972, the size of staff and the amount of money raised have increased substantially for both national committees. The actual work of each national committee is overseen by its chairperson. Other committee members are generally major party contributors or fund-raisers and serve in a largely ceremonial capacity.

For the party that controls the White House, the national committee chair is appointed by the president. Typically, this means that that party's national committee becomes little more than an adjunct to the White House staff. For a first-term president, the committee devotes the bulk of its energy to the re-election campaign. The national committee chair of the party not in control of the White House is selected by the committee itself and usually takes a broader view of the party's needs, raising money and performing other activities on behalf of the party's members in Congress and in the state legislatures.

Congressional Campaign Committees Each party forms House and Senate campaign committees to raise funds for House and Senate election campaigns. Their efforts may or may not be coordinated with the activities of the national committees. For the party that controls the White House, the national committee and the congressional campaign committees are often rivals because both groups are seeking donations from the same people but for different candidates: the national committee seeks funds for the presidential race while the congressional campaign committees approach the same contributors for support for the congressional contests. In recent years, the Republican party has attempted to coordinate the fund-raising activities of all its committees. Republicans have sought to give the GOP's national institutions the capacity to invest funds in those close congressional, state, and local races where they can do the most good. The Democrats have been slower to coordinate their various committee activities, and this may have placed them at a disadvantage in recent congressional and local races. The efforts of the parties to centralize and coordinate fund-raising activities have helped bring about greater party unity in Congress. As members have come to rely on the leadership for campaign funds, they have become more likely to vote with the leadership on major issues. All in all, campaign committees have begun to resemble large-scale campaign consulting firms, hiring full-time political operatives and evolving into professional organizations.

State and Local Party Organizations Each of the two major parties has a central committee in each state. The parties traditionally also have county committees and, in some instances, state senate district committees, judicial district committees, and, in the case of larger cities, city-wide party committees and local assembly district "ward" committees as well. Congressional districts also may have party committees.

Some cities also have precinct committees. Precincts are not districts from which any representative is elected but instead are legally defined subdivisions of wards that are used to register voters and set up ballot boxes or voting machines. A precinct is typically composed of 300 to 600 voters. Well-organized political parties—especially the famous old machines of New York, Chicago, and Boston—provide for "precinct captains" and a fairly tight group of party members around them. Precinct captains were usually members of long standing in neighborhood party clubhouses, which were important social centers as well as places for distributing favors to constituents.

Nevertheless, state and local party organizations are very active in recruiting candidates, conducting voter registration drives, and providing financial assistance to candidates. In many respects, federal election law has given state and local party organizations new life. Under current law, state and local party organizations can spend unlimited amounts of money on "party-building" activities such as voter registration and get-out-the-vote drives. As a result, the national party organizations, which have enormous fund-raising abilities but are limited by law in how much they can spend on candidates, each year transfer millions of dollars to the state and local organizations. The state and local parties, in turn, spend these funds, sometimes called soft money, to promote the candidacies of national, as well as state and local, candidates. In this process, as local organizations have become linked financially to the national parties, American political parties have become somewhat more integrated and nationalized than ever before. At the same time, the state and local party organizations have come to control large financial resources and play important roles in elections despite the collapse of the old patronage machines.[18]

The Contemporary Party as Service Provider to Candidates

Party leaders have adapted parties to the modern age. Parties-as-organizations are more professional, better financed, and more organized than ever before.[19] Political scientists argue that parties have evolved into "service organizations," which, though they no longer hold a monopoly over campaigns, still provide services to candidates, without which it would be extremely difficult for candidates to win and hold office.

Many politicians, however, are able to raise funds, attract volunteers, and win office without much help from local party organizations. Once in office, these politicians often refuse to submit to party discipline; instead they steer independent courses. They are often supported by voters who see independence as a virtue and party discipline as "boss rule." Analysts refer to this pattern as a "candidate-centered" politics to distinguish it from a political process in which parties are the dominant forces. The problem with a candidate-centered politics is that it tends to be associated with low turnout, high levels of special-interest influence, and a lack of effective decision making. In short, many of the problems that have plagued American politics in recent years can be traced directly to the independence of American voters and politicians, and the candidate-centered nature of American national politics.

Parties and Democracy

Political parties make democratic government possible. We often do not appreciate that democratic government is a contradiction in terms. Government implies policies, programs, and decisive action. Democracy, on the other hand, implies an

---

[18]For a useful discussion, see John Bibby and Thomas Holbrook, "Parties and Elections," in *Politics in the American States: A Comparative Analysis*, ed. Virginia Gray and Herbert Jacob, 6th ed. (Washington, DC: Congressional Quarterly Press, 1996), pp. 78–121.

[19]See Aldrich, *Why Parties?*, Chapter 8.

opportunity for all citizens to participate fully in the governmental process. The contradiction is that full participation by everyone is often inconsistent with getting anything done. At what point should participation stop and governance begin? How can we make certain that popular participation will result in a government capable of making decisions and developing needed policies?

Strong political parties are a partial antidote to the inherent contradiction between participation and government. Strong parties can both encourage popular involvement and convert participation into effective government. More than fifty years ago, a committee of the academic American Political Science Association (APSA) called for the development of a more "responsible" party government. By responsible party government, the committee meant political parties that mobilized voters and were sufficiently well organized to develop and implement coherent programs and policies after the election. Strong parties can link democratic participation and government.

SUMMARY

Political parties seek to control government by controlling its personnel. Elections are one means to this end. Thus parties take shape from the electoral process. The formal principle of party organization is this: For every district in which an election is held—from the entire nation to the local district, county, or precinct—there should be some kind of party unit.

Nominating and electing are the basic functions of parties. Originally, nominations were made in party caucuses, and individuals who ran as independents had a difficult time getting on the ballot. In the 1830s, dissatisfaction with the cliquish caucuses led to nominating conventions. Although these ended the "King Caucus" that controlled the nomination of presidential candidates and thereby gave the presidency a popular base, they, too, proved unsatisfactory. Primaries now have more or less replaced the conventions. There are both closed and open primaries. The former are more supportive of strong political parties than the latter. Contested primaries sap party strength and financial resources, but they nonetheless serve to resolve important social conflicts and recognize new interest groups. Winning at the top of a party ticket usually depends on the party regulars at the bottom getting out the vote. At all levels, the mass communications media are important. Mass mailings, too, are vital in campaigning. Thus campaign funds are crucial to success.

Congress is organized around the two-party system. The House speakership is a party office. Parties determine the makeup of congressional committees, including their chairs, which are no longer based entirely on seniority.

The two-party system dominates U.S. politics. While the two parties agree on some major issues, the Democrats generally favor higher levels of social spending funded by higher levels of taxation than the GOP is willing to support. Republicans favor lower levels of domestic activity on the part of the federal government, but also support federal action on a number of social and moral issues such as abortion. Even though party affiliation means less to Americans than it once did, partisanship remains important. What ticket splitting there is occurs mainly at the presidential level.

Third parties are short-lived for several reasons. They have limited electoral support, the tradition of the two-party system is strong, and a major party often adopts their platforms. Single-member districts with two competing parties also discourage third parties.

In recent years, the role of parties in political campaigns has been partially supplanted by the use of new political technologies. These include polling, the broadcast media, phone banks, direct-mail fund-raising and advertising, professional public relations, and the Internet. These techniques are enormously expensive and have led to a shift from labor-intensive to capital-intensive politics. This shift works to the advantage of political forces representing the well-to-do.

Rationality Principle	Collective-Action Principle	Institution Principle	Policy Principle	History Principle
Parties help deal with the threat to cooperation posed by ambitious individuals by regulating career advancement and resolving competition.	Parties facilitate collective action in the electoral process by helping candidates attract campaign funds, assembling campaign workers, and mobilizing voters.	Primary elections tend to favor aggressive and ambitious politicians, whereas conventions tend to favor those who have mastered the arts of compromise and collegiality.	Parties help resolve collective choice in the policy-making process by acting as permanent coalitions of individuals with similar policy goals.	Parties are products of their own histories and of the history of their interactions with their rivals.
Parties can lower the cost of voting by facilitating a voter's choice.	Parties can help mobilize voters who are potential free riders.	Third-party prospects for electoral success are hampered by America's single-member-district plurality election system.	Policies typically reflect the goals of whichever party is in power.	The erosion of the strength of party organizations set the stage for the introduction of new political campaign techniques and the rise of candidate-centered campaigns.
	Cooperation in Congress is facilitated by the party system.	Party rules can determine the relative influence of competing factions within the party and can also increase or decrease the party's chances for electoral success.		
	The first American political parties were formed mainly to overcome collective-action problems in Congress.			
	The efforts of the parties to centralize and coordinate fund-raising activities have helped bring about greater party unity in Congress.			

FOR FURTHER READING

Aldrich, John H. *Why Parties? The Origin and Transformation of Party Politics in America.* Chicago: University of Chicago Press, 1995.

Beck, Paul Allen, and Marjorie Randon Hershey. *Party Politics in America.* 10th ed. New York: Longman, 2003.

Chambers, William N., and Walter Dean Burnham, eds. *The American Party Systems: Stages of Political Development.* 2nd ed. New York: Oxford University Press, 1975.

Coleman, John J. *Party Decline in America: Policy, Politics, and the Fiscal State.* Princeton, NJ: Princeton University Press, 1996.

Grimshaw, William J. *Bitter Fruit: Black Politics and the Chicago Machine, 1931–1991.* Chicago: University of Chicago Press, 1992.

Hofstadter, Richard. *The Idea of a Party System: The Rise of Legitimate Opposition in the United States, 1780–1840.* Berkeley: University of California Press, 1969.

Kayden, Xandra, and Eddie Mahe Jr. *The Party Goes On: The Persistence of the Two-Party System in the United States.* New York: Basic Books, 1985.

Lawson, Kay, and Peter H. Merkl. *When Parties Fail: Emerging Alternative Organizations.* Princeton, NJ: Princeton University Press, 1988.

Milkis, Sidney M. *The President and the Parties: The Transformation of the American Party System since the New Deal.* New York: Oxford University Press, 1993.

Polsby, Nelson W. *Consequences of Party Reform.* New York: Oxford University Press, 1983.

Shafer, Byron, ed. *Beyond Realignment? Interpreting American Electoral Eras.* Madison: University of Wisconsin Press, 1991.

Smith, Eric R. A. N. *The Unchanging American Voter.* Berkeley: University of California Press, 1989.

Sundquist, James L. *Dynamics of the Party System: Alignment and Realignment of Political Parties in the United States.* Washington, DC: Brookings Institution, 1983.

Wattenberg, Martin P. *The Decline of American Political Parties, 1952–1996.* Cambridge, MA: Harvard University Press, 1998.

Politics in the News— Reading between the Lines

ACT and the Post-Party World

Machine Dreams

By MATT BAI

If you needed any more proof that Democratic politics were in a profound state of upheaval, consider this: on the eve of the 2004 election, there were three especially powerful groups, aside from the Kerry campaign itself, working to turn out votes for the party in critical states, and those were the Democratic National Committee, the A.F.L.-C.I.O. and a lavishly endowed start-up known as America Coming Together. Nine months later, not one of these institutions has emerged entirely intact. First, Howard Dean staged a hostile takeover of the D.N.C. Then big labor unraveled on its 50th birthday. And finally, earlier this month, ACT announced that it was suspending most of its operations and closing down its state offices, effectively shuttering the largest independently financed turnout drive in history after a single outing.

It was hard not to think of ACT's demise as a kind of political version of "Titanic"—a story of hubris and oversize ambition. It was a saga that began in 2002, when Congress tightened the nation's campaign-finance laws, making it illegal to contribute unlimited amounts of money to national political parties.

The law did, however, leave donors a loophole: they could contribute as much as they pleased to outside groups known as "527's," named for a section of the tax code. That's when three of the Democratic Party's smartest and most influential strategists—Steve Rosenthal, the former political director of the A.F.L.-C.I.O.; Ellen Malcolm, the founder of Emily's List; and the longtime liberal power broker Harold Ickes—had the idea to raise money for a giant turnout machine that would essentially supplant the party's efforts. A couple of sympathetic billionaires, the financier George Soros and the insurance magnate Peter Lewis, liked the idea enough to contribute about $20 million each to ACT. Other donors then kicked in millions more. For wealthy Democrats, ACT was the best available vehicle for dethroning George W. Bush. . . .

Just how it is that ACT failed in this mission is a question no one seems able to answer. After all, ACT exceeded its own goals for voter turnout, and in most of the Democratic urban counties on which it focused, John Kerry received more votes than any Democrat before

New York Times, 21 August 2005, section 6, p. 11.

him. ACT didn't do much to change the balance in more conservative rural and exurban areas, but then persuading undecided voters was (and always has been) the candidate's job; blaming ACT for the loss of Ohio or Florida would be like firing the Yankees' grounds crew because Derek Jeter failed to get on base.

Even so, ACT wasn't supposed to simply increase the vote count—it was supposed to win—and in those grim months after the election, some of ACT's supporters turned their fury on the organizational monster they had helped bring to life. . . .

There is an important twist, however, to this story. It's true, perhaps, that the organizers who ran ACT were working off an outdated playbook, written when the great urban machines of the 20th century were able to dominate almost any state or national election. The nation's demography no longer confers such power on a handful of manufacturing centers.

But to cast ACT as the last breath of a dying party establishment is to miss its significance. In fact, ACT represented the first serious challenge to the industrial-age structure of the modern political party. Before Soros and Lewis plunked down all that cash for ACT, liberal donors had assumed that their only avenue into the political system was through supporting the party and its candidates, both of whom seemed to regard them as little more than a cash machine with some annoying voice commands. Through ACT, Soros and Lewis showed that there was a new way of doing business, and it didn't require fealty to an inefficient party apparatus. From this revelation—no matter how Congress or the Federal Elections Commission may try to yet again amend the campaign-finance rules—there is probably no going back.

In this way, ACT helped to usher us into the post-party world. We are now confronting a period in which the power and the innovation in American

ESSENCE OF THE STORY

- America Coming Together, the largest organization ever dedicated to getting out the Democratic vote, disbanded less than a year after the 2004 election.

- Even though ACT failed to deliver John Kerry to the White House, it did succeed in increasing Democratic turnout in all of the urban areas in which it dedicated resources.

- Dispite its disbandment, ACT shows that the future of political organizing rests less in traditional party organizations and more in loosely affiliated groups organized by "Internet impresarios" and funded by deep-pocketed donors.

POLITICAL ANALYSIS

- ACT may represent not only the end of the traditional political party but also the rebirth of the party both as a coordinating mechanism for campaigns and as a fulcrum around which affiliated groups can organize their efforts.

- The birth and death of ACT show how important the Internet is going to be for all types of political organizations, including parties, if they intend to win elections.

- However, political parties have traditionally provided a path of "political ambition" for individuals, even if they did not have wealth or education. All one needed to do was work hard. The new era of technological, money-driven politics may exacerbate the tendency of our political system to represent the wealthy and the well-educated.

politics will reside not in some party headquarters on Capitol Hill but in a decentralized network of grass-roots groups, donors and Internet impresarios, all of whom seem to be increasingly entwined with one another.

There's peril in this trend—it would seem to favor millionaires over workers, and ideologues over pragmatists—but it was probably inevitable. . . .

CHAPTER

12

Groups and Interests

For more than two decades, lobbyists for senior citizens, led by AARP (formerly called the American Association of Retired Persons), have sought to add a prescription drug benefit to the Medicare program on which most seniors depend for their health care. Many members of Congress have opposed such a benefit because it would cost hundreds of billions of dollars. The pharmaceutical industry also feared that such a Medicare prescription plan would open the way for governmental regulation of drug prices as well as other aspects of the industry. Through its political arm, the Pharmaceutical Research and Manufacturers of America (PhRMA), the pharmaceutical industry is one of the most powerful lobby groups in Washington. Drug company executives and corporate political action committees (PACs) have contributed more than $60 million to political campaigns since 2000, and a number of drug industry lobbyists and executives were major donors to and fund-raisers for George W. Bush's presidential campaigns. The drug industry's political clout was, for years, an enormous impediment to the enactment of a Medicare prescription drug plan.

By the early 2000s, however, the industry had begun to face a number of economic and political problems. To begin with, the high prices charged for prescription drugs were producing enormous pressure in Congress to reduce the patient protection enjoyed by drug company products; this would allow cheaper generic drugs to enter the marketplace more rapidly. Second, many consumers had discovered that they could purchase drugs in Canada and Europe for as much as 75 percent less than what they cost in the United States. These foreign purchases, while illegal, are difficult to monitor and are costing the drug companies millions of dollars in profits. Finally, growing numbers of senior citizens were not able to afford their prescription drugs at all and so were simply not buying medicine—another source of lost profit for the industry.

In the face of these problems, PhRMA changed its lobbying strategy. Rather than continue to resist a Medicare drug plan, the industry moved to craft a plan of its own. In 2002, the pharmaceutical industry formed an alliance with several other health industry groups, including nursing home and hospital interests, to develop a new Medicare bill. AARP had a number of misgivings about the bill but lent its support, calculating that once a law was enacted, the "senior lobby" could secure favorable amendments over the ensuing years. The resulting legislation, enacted by Congress in November 2003, after the drug industry spent nearly $40 million lobbying on its behalf, appeared to be perfectly tailored to suit the industry's needs. Under the new plan, Medicare will subsidize drug purchases for all seniors who agree to pay a modest monthly fee. The plan prohibits the government from attempting to force the companies to lower drug prices, leaves in place the ban on imported drugs, and does not address the issue of generic drugs. Once in place in 2006, the Medicare prescription plan is expected to lead to substantially higher drug purchases and to increase industry profits by as much as $13 billion a year at a cost of tens of billions of dollars a year to the federal treasury.[1] PhRMA's nursing home

[1]Ceci Connolly, "Drugmakers Protect Their Turf," *Washington Post*, 21 November 2003, p. A4.

CHAPTER OUTLINE

What Are the Characteristics of Interest Groups?

• Interest Groups Enhance Democracy . . .

• . . . But Also Represent the Evils of Faction

• Organized Interests Are Predominantly Economic

• All Groups Require Money and Leadership, and Most Need Members

• Group Membership Has an Upper-Class Bias

• Groups Form in Response to Changes in the Political Environment

How and Why Do Interest Groups Form?

• Interest Groups Facilitate Cooperation

• Selective Benefits: A Solution to the Collective-Action Problem

• Political Entrepreneurs Organize and Maintain Groups

How Do Interest Groups Influence Policy?

• Direct Lobbying

• Using the Courts

• Mobilizing Public Opinion

• Using Electoral Politics

• Interest Groups: Are They Effective?

Groups and Interests: The Dilemma of Reform

and hospital allies also won favorable treatment under the plan.[2] Seniors at long last will get their drug plan but in a form that will cost the nation an enormous amount of money, funds that will be transferred from the pockets of hard-pressed middle-class taxpayers into the coffers of an already fabulously wealthy industry.

The story of the pharmaceutical industry suggests the answers to three questions. First, the story suggests why individuals and interests form groups. Second, the story indicates some of the tactics and coalition-building strategies that groups use to get what they want. Third, the story shows that in a democracy, political struggle has its own logic and does not always lead to the most sensible outcomes. High-minded Americans have been complaining about the role of interest groups since the nation's founding. We should remember, however, that vigorous interest-group activity is a consequence and reflection of a free society. As James Madison put it so well in *The Federalist Papers*, No. 10, "Liberty is to faction what air is to fire."[3]

In this chapter, we examine some of the antecedents and consequences of interest-group politics in the United States. We analyze the group basis of politics, the problems that result from collective action, and some solutions to these problems. We seek to understand the character of the interests promoted by interest groups. We assess the growth of interest-group activity in recent American political history, including the emergence of "public interest" groups. We review and evaluate the strategies that competing groups use in their struggle for influence. Finally, we assess the question: Are interest groups too influential in the political process?

PREVIEWING THE PRINCIPLES

Inasmuch as an interest group is an organization in which a group of individuals works to achieve common policy-related goals, the difficulties associated with collective action are particularly acute. To overcome the obstacles to collective action, groups must provide individuals with incentives to join. Group politics is also organized, in part, through the goal-oriented activities of political entrepreneurs. Despite the obstacles to collective action, the number and types of interest groups in American politics proliferated throughout the twentieth century. Moreover, recognizing the importance of institutions in influencing political outcomes, groups strategically seek out institutional venues they believe will be most hospitable to their goals and interests.

WHAT ARE THE CHARACTERISTICS OF INTEREST GROUPS?

An ***interest group*** is an organized group of people that makes policy-related appeals to government. This definition of interest groups includes membership organizations but also businesses, corporations, universities, and other institutions

[2]Thomas B. Edsall, "2 Bills Would Benefit Top Bush Fundraisers," *Washington Post*, 22 November 2003, p. 1.
[3]Clinton Rossiter, ed., *The Federalist Papers* (New York: New American Library, 1961), No. 10, p. 78.

that do not accept members. Individuals form groups to increase the chance that their views will be heard and their interests treated favorably by the government. Interest groups are organized to influence governmental decisions.

Interest groups are sometimes referred to as "lobbies." Interest groups are also sometimes confused with political action committees. These committees focus on winning elections. Interest groups focus on influencing the elected. One final distinction that we should make is that interest groups are also different from political parties: interest groups tend to concern themselves with the *policies* of government; parties tend to concern themselves with the *personnel* of government.

<aside>
interest group
An organized group of people that makes policy-related appeals to government.
</aside>

Interest Groups Enhance Democracy . . .

There are an enormous number of interest groups in the United States, and millions of Americans are members of one or more groups, at least to the extent of paying dues or attending an occasional meeting. By representing the interests of such large numbers of people and encouraging political participation, organized groups can and do enhance American democracy. Organized groups educate their members about issues that affect them. Groups lobby members of Congress and the executive branch, engage in litigation, and generally represent their members' interests in the political arena. Groups mobilize their members for elections and grassroots lobbying efforts, thus encouraging participation. Interest groups also monitor government programs to make certain that their members are not adversely affected. In all these ways, organized interests can be said to promote democratic politics.

. . . But Also Represent the Evils of Faction

The framers of the American Constitution feared the power that could be wielded by organized interests. Madison wrote: "The public good is disregarded in the conflict of rival [factions], . . . citizens . . . who are united and actuated by some common impulse of passion, or of interest, adverse to the rights of other citizens, or to the permanent and aggregate interests of the community."[4] Yet, the Founding Fathers believed that interest groups thrived because of freedom— the freedom that all Americans enjoyed to organize and express their views. To the framers, this problem presented a dilemma. If the government were given the power to regulate or in any way to forbid efforts by organized interests to interfere in the political process, the government would in effect have the power to suppress freedom. The solution to this dilemma was presented by Madison:

> Take in a greater variety of parties and interest [and] you make it less probable that a majority of the whole will have a common motive to invade the rights of other citizens. . . . [Hence the advantage] enjoyed by a large over a small republic.[5]

[4]Ibid.
[5]Ibid., p. 83.

According to the Madisonian theory, a good constitution encourages multitudes of interests so that no single interest can ever tyrannize the others. The basic assumption is that competition among interests will produce balance and compromise, with all the interests regulating each other.[6] Today, this Madisonian principle of regulation is called *pluralism*. According to pluralist theory, all interests are and should be free to compete for influence in the United States. Moreover, according to pluralist doctrine, the outcome of this competition is compromise and moderation, because no group is likely to be able to achieve any of its goals without accommodating itself to some of the views of its many competitors.[7]

There are tens of thousands of organized groups in the United States, but the huge number of *interest groups* competing for influence in the United States does not mean that all *interests* are fully and equally represented in the American political process. As we shall see, the political deck is heavily stacked in favor of those interests able to organize and to wield substantial economic, social, and institutional resources on behalf of their cause. This means that within the universe of interest-group politics, it is political power—not some abstract conception of the public good—that is likely to prevail. Moreover, this means that interest-group politics, taken as a whole, is a political format that works more to the advantage of some types of interests than others. In general, a politics in which interest groups predominate is a politics with a distinctly upper-class bias.

pluralism The theory that all interests are and should be free to compete for influence in the government. The outcome of this competition is compromise and moderation.

Organized Interests Are Predominantly Economic

When most people think about interest groups, they immediately think of groups with a direct and private economic interest in governmental actions. These groups are generally supported by groups of producers or manufacturers in a particular economic sector. Examples of this type of group include the National Petroleum Refiners Association, the American Farm Bureau Federation, and the National Federation of Independent Business, which represents small-business owners. At the same time that broadly representative groups like these are active in Washington, specific companies, like Disney, Shell Oil, IBM, and General Motors, may be active on certain issues that are of particular concern to them.

Labor organizations are equally active lobbyists. The AFL-CIO, the United Mine Workers, and the Teamsters are all groups that lobby on behalf of organized labor. In recent years, lobbies have arisen to further the interests of public employees, the most significant among these being the American Federation of State, County, and Municipal Employees.

Professional lobbies like the American Bar Association and the American Medical Association have been particularly successful in furthering their own in-

[6]Ibid.

[7]The best statement of the pluralist view is in David Truman, *The Governmental Process: Political Interests and Public Opinion* (New York: Knopf, 1951), Chapter 2.

terests in state and federal legislatures. Financial institutions, represented by organizations like the American Bankers Association and the National Savings & Loan League, although often less visible than other lobbies, also play an important role in shaping legislative policy.

Recent years have witnessed the growth of a powerful "public interest" lobby purporting to represent interests whose concerns are not addressed by traditional lobbies. These groups have been most visible in the consumer protection and environmental policy areas, although public interest groups cover a broad range of issues. The Natural Resources Defense Council, the Union of Concerned Scientists, and Common Cause are all examples of public interest groups.

The perceived need for representation on Capitol Hill has generated a public-sector lobby in the past several years, including the National League of Cities and the "research" lobby. The latter group comprises think tanks and universities that have an interest in obtaining government funds for research and support, such as Harvard University, the Brookings Institution, and the American Enterprise Institute. Indeed, universities have expanded their lobbying efforts even as they have reduced faculty positions and course offerings and increased tuition.[8]

All Groups Require Money and Leadership, and Most Need Members

Although there are many interest groups, most share certain key organizational components. First, most groups must attract and keep members. Usually, groups appeal to members not only by promoting political goals or policies that they favor but also by providing them with direct economic or social benefits. Thus, for example, AARP, which promotes the interests of senior citizens, at the same time offers members a variety of insurance benefits and commercial discounts. Similarly, many groups whose goals are chiefly economic or political also seek to attract members through social interaction and good fellowship. Thus the local chapters of many national groups provide their members with a congenial social environment, while collecting dues that finance the national office's political efforts.

Second, every group must build a financial structure capable of sustaining an organization and funding the group's activities. Most interest groups rely on yearly membership dues and voluntary contributions from sympathizers. Many also sell some ancillary services, such as insurance and vacation tours, to members. Third, every group must have a leadership and decision-making structure. For some groups, this structure is very simple. For others, it can be quite elaborate and involve hundreds of local chapters that are melded into a national apparatus. Finally, most groups include an agency that actually carries out the group's tasks. This may be a research organization, a public relations office, or a lobbying office in Washington or a state capital.

[8]Betsy Wagner and David Bowermaster, "B.S. Economics," *Washington Monthly* (November 1992): 19–21.

Group Membership Has an Upper-Class Bias

Membership in interest groups is not randomly distributed in the population. People with higher incomes, higher levels of education, and management or professional occupations are much more likely to become members of groups than those who occupy the lower rungs on the socioeconomic ladder.[9] Well-educated, upper-income business and professional people are more likely to have the time and the money, and to have acquired through the educational process the concerns and skills, needed to play a role in a group or association. Moreover, for business and professional people, group membership may provide personal contacts and access to information that can help advance their careers. At the same time, corporate entities—businesses and the like—usually have ample resources to form or participate in groups that seek to advance their causes.

The result is that interest-group politics in the United States tends to have a very pronounced upper-class bias. Certainly, there are many interest groups and political associations that have a working-class or lower-class membership—labor organizations or welfare-rights organizations, for example—but the great majority of interest groups and their members are drawn from the middle and upper-middle classes. In general, the "interests" served by interest groups are the interests of society's "haves." Even when interest groups take opposing positions on issues and policies, the conflicting positions they espouse usually reflect divisions among upper-income strata rather than conflicts between the upper and lower classes.

In general, to obtain adequate political representation, forces from the bottom rungs of the socioeconomic ladder must be organized on the massive scale associated with political parties. Parties can organize and mobilize the collective energies of large numbers of people who, as individuals, may have very limited resources. Interest groups, on the other hand, generally organize smaller numbers of the better-to-do. Thus the relative importance of political parties and interest groups in American politics has far-ranging implications for the distribution of political power in the United States. As we saw in Chapter 11, political parties have declined in influence in recent years. Interest groups, on the other hand, as we shall see shortly, have become much more numerous, more active, and more influential in American politics.

Groups Form in Response to Changes in the Political Environment

If interest groups and our concerns about them were a new phenomenon, we would not have begun this chapter with Madison in the eighteenth century. As long as there is government, as long as government makes policies that add value or impose costs, and as long as there is liberty to organize, interest groups will abound; and if government expands, so will interest groups. There was, for exam-

---

[9]Kay Lehman Schlozman and John T. Tierney, *Organized Interests and American Democracy* (New York: Harper & Row, 1986), p. 60.

ple, a spurt of growth in the national government during the 1880s and 1890s, arising largely from the first governmental efforts at economic intervention to fight large monopolies and to regulate some aspects of interstate commerce. In the latter decade, a parallel spurt of growth occurred in national interest groups, including the imposing National Association of Manufacturers (NAM) and numerous other trade associations. Many groups organized around specific agricultural commodities, as well. This period also marked the beginning of the expansion of trade unions as interest groups. Later, in the 1930s, interest groups with headquarters and representation in Washington began to grow significantly, concurrent with that decade's expansion of the national government.

Over the past thirty-five years, there has been an enormous increase both in the number of interest groups seeking to play a role in the American political process and in the extent of their opportunity to influence that process. The total number of interest groups in the United States today is not known. There are certainly tens of thousands of groups at the national, state, and local levels. One indication of the proliferation of such groups' activity is the growth over time in the number of PACs attempting to influence U.S. elections. Nearly six times as many PACs operated in 2004 as in the 1970s (Figure 12.1). A *New York Times* report, for example, noted that during the 1970s, expanded federal regulation of the automobile, oil, gas, education, and health-care industries impelled each of these interests to increase substantially its efforts to influence the government's behavior. These efforts, in turn, had the effect of spurring the organization of other groups to augment or counter the activities of the first.[10] Similarly, federal social programs have occasionally sparked political organization and action on the part of clientele groups seeking to influence the distribution of benefits and, in turn, the organization of groups opposed to the programs or their cost. For example, federal programs and court decisions in such areas as abortion and school prayer were the stimuli for political action and organization by fundamentalist religious groups. The Christian Coalition, for instance, whose major focus is opposition to abortion, has nearly 2 million active members organized in local chapters in every state. Twenty of the state chapters have full-time staff and fifteen have annual budgets over $200,000.[11] The ongoing struggles over abortion and school prayer have helped the Christian Coalition, the Family Research Council, and other organizations making up the Christian Right to expand the membership rolls of their state and local organizations. Anti-abortion forces, in particular, are organized at the local level throughout the United States and are prepared to participate in political campaigns and legislative battles. The importance of religious conservatives to the Republican party became quite evident in 2001. After his victory in the November 2000 presidential election, George W. Bush announced that his administration would seek to award federal grants and contracts to religious groups. By using so-called faith-based groups as

History Principle

The explosion of interest-group activity has its origins in the expansion of the role of government, especially since the 1960s.

[10]John Herbers, "Special Interests Gaining Power as Voter Disillusionment Grows," *New York Times*, 14 November 1978.

[11]Rich Lowry, "How the Right Rose," *National Review* 66, 11 December 1995, pp. 64–76.

FIGURE 12.1

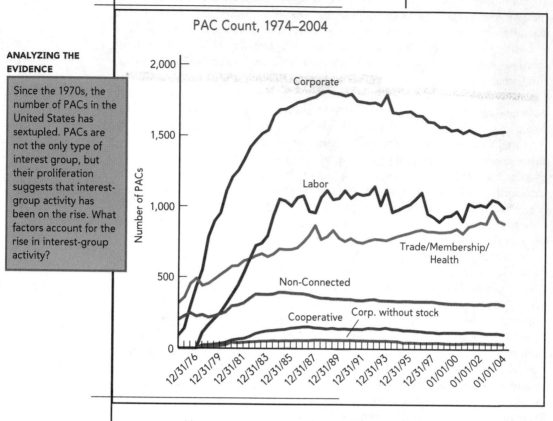

PAC Count, 1974–2004

SOURCE: Federal Election Commission (fecweb1.fec.gov/press/paccnt_grph.html).

ANALYZING THE EVIDENCE

Since the 1970s, the number of PACs in the United States has sextupled. PACs are not the only type of interest group, but their proliferation suggests that interest-group activity has been on the rise. What factors account for the rise in interest-group activity?

federal contractors, Bush was seeking to reward religious conservatives for their past loyalty to the GOP and to ensure that these groups would have a continuing stake in Republican success. Thus the expansion of government in recent decades has also stimulated increased group activity and organization.

Another factor accounting for the explosion of interest-group activity in recent years was the emergence of a new set of forces in American politics that can collectively be called the New Politics movement.

The New Politics movement is made up of upper-middle-class professionals and intellectuals for whom the civil rights and antiwar movements were formative experiences, just as the Great Depression and World War II had been for their parents. The crusade against racial discrimination and the Vietnam War led these young men and women to see themselves as a political force in opposition to the public policies and politicians associated with the nation's postwar regime. In more recent years, the forces of New Politics have focused their attention on such issues as environmental protection, women's rights, and nuclear disarmament.

Members of the New Politics movement constructed or strengthened "public interest" groups such as Common Cause, the Sierra Club, the Environmental Defense Fund, Physicians for Social Responsibility, the National Organization for Women, and the various organizations formed by consumer activist Ralph Nader. Through these groups, New Politics forces were able to influence the media, Congress, and even the judiciary, and enjoyed a remarkable degree of success during the late 1960s and early 1970s in securing the enactment of policies they favored. New Politics activists also played a major role in securing the enactment of environmental, consumer, and occupational health and safety legislation.

Among the factors contributing to the rise and success of New Politics forces was technology. In the 1970s and 1980s, computerized direct-mail campaigns allowed public interest groups to reach hundreds of thousands of potential sympathizers and contributors. Today, the Internet and e-mail serve the same function. Electronic communication allows relatively small groups to efficiently identify and mobilize their adherents throughout the nation. Individuals with perspectives that might be in the minority everywhere can become conscious of one another and mobilize for national political action through the magic of electronic politics.

HOW AND WHY DO INTEREST GROUPS FORM?

Pluralist theory argues that, because individuals in the United States are free to join or form groups that reflect their common interests, interest groups should easily form whenever a change in the political environment warrants their formation. If this argument is correct, groups should form roughly in proportion to people's interests. We should find a greater number of organizations around interests shared by a greater number of people. The evidence for this pluralist hypothesis, however, is weak. Kay Schlozman and John Tierney examined interest groups that represent people's occupations and economic roles.[12] Using census data and listings of interest groups, they compared how many people in the United States have particular economic roles and how many organizations represent those roles in Washington. For example, they found that (in the mid-1980s) 4 percent of the population was looking for work, but only a handful of organizations actually represented the unemployed in Washington.[13]

There is a considerable disparity in Washington representation across categories of individuals in the population, as Table 12.1 suggests. Schlozman and

[12]Schlozman and Tierney, *Organized Interests and American Democracy.*
[13]Of course, the *number* of organizations is at best only a rough measure of the extent to which various categories of citizen are represented in the interest-group world of Washington.

TABLE 12.1

Who Is Represented by Organized Interests?

ANALYZING THE EVIDENCE

What types of interests are most likely to be represented by interest groups? If interest-group politics is biased in favor of the wealthy and powerful, should we curb group politics? What was James Madison's answer? Do you agree with Madison?

ECONOMIC ROLE OF INDIVIDUAL	% OF U.S. ADULTS	% OF ORGS.	TYPE OF ORG. IN WASHINGTON, DC	RATIO OF ORGS. TO ADULTS
Managerial/administrative	7	71.0	Business association	10.10
Professional/technical	9	17.0	Professional association	1.90
Student/teacher	4	4.0	Educational organization	1.00
Farm workers	2	1.5	Agricultural organization	0.75
Unable to work	2	0.6	Handicapped organization	0.30
Other non–farm workers	41	4.0	Union	0.10
At home	19	1.8	Women's organizations	0.09
Retired	12	0.8	Senior-citizens organization	0.07
Looking for work	4	0.1	Unemployment organization	0.03

Tierney note, for example, that there are at least a dozen groups representing senior citizens, but none for the middle-aged. Ducks Unlimited is an organization dedicated to the preservation of ducks and their habitats; turkeys, on the other hand, have no one working on their behalf. The pluralists' inability to explain why groups form around some interests and not others led some scholars to investigate the dynamics of collective action. Mancur Olson's work, mentioned in Chapter 1 and discussed later in this chapter, is the most well-known challenge to the pluralists. It is in Olson's insights that we find the basis for interest-group formation.

Interest Groups Facilitate Cooperation

Groups of individuals pursuing some common interest or shared objective—maintenance of a hunting and fishing habitat, creation of a network for sharing computer software, lobbying for favorable legislation, playing a Beethoven symphony, etc.—consist of individuals who bear some cost or make some contribution on behalf of the joint goal. Each member of the Possum Hollow Rod and Gun Club may, for example, pay annual dues and devote one weekend a year to cleaning up the rivers and forests of the club-owned game preserve.

We can think of this in an analytical fashion, somewhat removed from any of these specific examples, as an instance of two-person cooperation writ large. Accordingly, each of a very large number of individuals has, in the simplest situation, two options in his or her behavioral repertoire: "contribute" or "don't contribute" to achieving the jointly shared objective. If the number of contributors to the group enterprise is sufficiently large, then a group goal is achieved. However, just as in the swamp-clearing example in Chapter 1, there is a twist. If the group goal is achieved, then *every member of the group enjoys its benefits, whether he or she contributed to its achievement or not.*

The Prisoners' Dilemma   Researchers often rely on the metaphor of the *prisoners' dilemma* when theorizing about social situations of collective action, like the swamp-clearing example of Chapter 1. According to this metaphor, two prisoners (A and B) who are accused of jointly committing a crime are kept in separate interview rooms. The arresting officers do not have enough evidence for a judge to give the prisoners the maximum sentence, so the officers hope that one of the prisoners will provide the additional evidence they require. The prisoners know that the officers have scant evidence against them and that they will probably receive a less severe sentence or escape punishment altogether if they remain silent. Each prisoner is offered the same plea bargain: "Testify against the other prisoner in exchange for freedom, provided that your accomplice does not also testify against you. Remain silent and you will possibly get the maximum sentence if your accomplice testifies against you."

If you assume that prisoners A and B are self-interested, rational actors (who, given the choice between two alternatives, will choose the one that offers the best deal) and that they prefer less jail time to more, then they will face an unpleasant choice. Notice that in Figure 12.2, prisoner A is better off choosing to "snitch," no matter what prisoner B does. If B chooses to snitch, then A's choice to snitch gets A a three-year jail term, but a "don't snitch" choice by A would have resulted in six years for A—clearly worse. On the other hand, if B chooses not to snitch, then A gets no jail time if he snitches instead of one year if he also chooses not to snitch. In short, A is always better off snitching. But this situation is symmetrical, so it follows that B is better off snitching, too. If both prisoners snitch, the prosecutor is able to convict both of them, and they would each serve three years. If they had both been *irrational* and kept silent, they would only have gotten one year each! In terms of game theory (from which the prisoners' dilemma is drawn), each player has a *dominant strategy*—snitching is best no matter what the other player does—and this leads paradoxically to an outcome in which each player is *worse* off.

The prisoners' dilemma provides the insight that rational individual behavior does not always lead to rational collective results. The logic of this situation is very compelling—if A appreciates the dilemma and realizes that B appreciates

Collective-Action Principle

The prisoners' dilemma, an example of a collective-action problem, explains why cooperation in groups can be difficult to achieve.

FIGURE 12.2

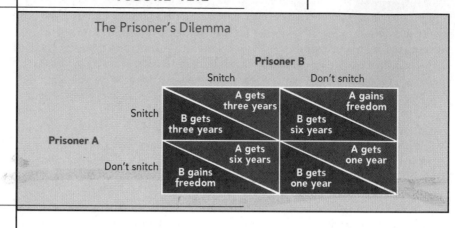

The Prisoner's Dilemma

the dilemma, then A will still be drawn to the choice of snitching. The reasons for this are the temptation to get off scot-free (if he testifies and his accomplice doesn't) and the *fear* of being "suckered." The dilemma is brilliant because it applies to a wide range of circumstances.

 Rationality Principle

In a group setting, rational individuals have an incentive to free-ride.

Consider again the swamp-clearing example in which each person benefits from a drained swamp, even if he or she does not provide the required effort. As long as enough other people do so, any individual can "ride free" on the efforts of the others. This is a multiperson prisoners' dilemma because not providing effort, like snitching, is a dominant strategy, yet it is one that, if everyone avails himself or herself of it, leads to an unwanted outcome—a mosquito-infested swamp. The prospect of free riding, as we shall see next, is the bane of collective action.

The Logic of Collective Action   Mancur Olson, writing in 1965, essentially took on the political-science establishment by noting that the pluralist assumption of the time, that common interests among individuals are automatically transformed into group organization and collective action, was problematic. Individuals are tempted to free-ride on the efforts of others, have difficulty coordinating multiple objectives, and may even have differences of opinion about which common interest to pursue (conflicts of interest).

Olson is at his most persuasive when talking about large groups and mass collective action, like many of the antiwar demonstrations and civil rights rallies of the 1960s. In these circumstances, the world of politics is a bit like the swamp-clearing example, where each individual has a rational strategy of not contributing. The logic of collective action makes it difficult to induce participation in and contribution to collective goals.

Olson claims that this difficulty is severest in large groups, for three reasons. First, large groups tend to be anonymous. Each household in a city is a taxpaying unit and may share the wish to see property taxes lowered. It is difficult, however, to forge a group identity or induce households to contribute effort or activity for the cause of lower taxes on such a basis. Second, in the anonymity of the large-group context, it is especially plausible to claim that no one individual's contribution makes much difference. Should the head of a household kill the better part of a morning writing a letter to his city council member in support of lower property taxes? Will it make much difference? If hardly anyone else writes, then the council member is unlikely to pay much heed to this one letter; on the other hand, if the council member is inundated with letters, would one more have a significant additional effect? Finally, there is the problem of enforcement. In a large group, are other group members going to punish a slacker? By definition, they cannot prevent the slacker from receiving the benefits of collective action, should those benefits materialize. (Every property owner's taxes will be lowered if anyone's is.) But, more to the point, in a large, anonymous group it is often hard to know who has and who has not contributed, and, because there is only the most limited sort of group identity, it is hard for contributors to identify, much less take action against, slackers. As a consequence, many large groups that share common interests fail to mobilize at all—they remain *latent*.

This same problem plagues small groups, too, as the swamp-clearing problem in Chapter 1 reveals. But Olson argues that small groups manage to overcome the problem of collective action more frequently and to a greater extent than their larger counterparts. Small groups are more personal, and their members are, therefore, more vulnerable to interpersonal persuasion. In small groups, individual contributions may make a more noticeable difference so that individuals feel that their contributions are more essential. Contributors in small groups, moreover, often know who they are and who the slackers are. Thus punishment, ranging from subtle judgmental pressure to social ostracism, is easier to effect.

In contrast to large groups that often remain latent, Olson calls these small groups *privileged* because of their advantage in overcoming the free-riding, coordination, and conflict-of-interest problems of collective action. It is for these perhaps counterintuitive reasons that small groups often prevail over, or enjoy greater privileges relative to, larger groups. These reasons, therefore, help explain why we so often see producers win out over consumers, owners of capital over owners of labor, and a party's elite over its mass members.

Selective Benefits: A Solution to the Collective-Action Problem

Despite the free-rider problem, interest groups offer numerous incentives to join. Most important, as Olson shrewdly noted in a profound theoretical insight, they make various "selective benefits" available only to group members (see Chapter 1). These benefits can be informational, material, solidary, or purposive. Table 12.2 gives some examples of the range of benefits in each of these categories.

TABLE 12.2

Selective Benefits of Interest-Group Membership

CATEGORY	BENEFITS
Informational benefits	Conferences Professional contacts Training programs Publications Coordination among organizations Research Legal help Professional codes Collective bargaining
Material benefits	Travel packages Insurance Discounts on consumer goods
Solidary benefits	Friendship Networking opportunities
Purposive benefits	Advocacy Representation before government Participation in public affairs

Belonging to an interest group may provide an individual with several types of benefits.

SOURCE: Adapted from Jack L. Walker Jr., *Mobilizing Interest Groups in America: Patrons, Professions, and Social Movements* (Ann Arbor: University of Michigan Press, 1991), p. 86.

informational benefits Special newsletters, periodicals, training programs, conferences, and other information provided to members of groups to entice others to join.

material benefits Special goods, services, or money provided to members of groups to entice others to join.

Informational benefits are the most widespread and important category of selective benefits offered to group members. Information is provided through conferences, training programs, and newsletters and other periodicals sent automatically to those who have paid membership dues.

Material benefits include anything that can be measured monetarily, such as special services, goods, and even money. A broad range of material benefits can be offered by groups to attract members. These benefits often include discount purchasing, shared advertising, and, perhaps most valuable of all, health and retirement insurance.

Another option identified in Table 12.2 is that of *solidary benefits.* The most notable of this class of benefits are the friendship and "networking" opportunities that membership provides. Another benefit that has become extremely important to many of the newer nonprofit and citizen groups is what has come to be called "consciousness-raising." One example of this can be seen in the claims of many women's organizations that active participation conveys to each member of the organization an enhanced sense of her own value and a stronger ability to advance individual as well as collective civil rights. A similar solidary or psychological benefit has been the mainstay of the appeal of group membership to discouraged and disillusioned African Americans since their emergence as a constitutionally free and equal people.

A fourth type of benefit involves the appeal of the purpose of an interest group. The benefits of religious interest groups provide us with the best examples of such *purposive benefits.* The Christian Right is a powerful movement made up of a number of interest groups that offer virtually no material benefits to their members. The growth and success of these groups depends on the religious identifications and affirmations of their members. Many such religiously based interest groups have arisen, especially at state and local levels, throughout American history. For example, both the abolition and the prohibition movements were driven by religious interest groups whose main attractions were nonmaterial benefits.

Ideology itself, or the sharing of a commonly developed ideology, is another important nonmaterial benefit. Many of the most successful interest groups of the past twenty years have been citizen groups or public interest groups, whose members are brought together largely around shared ideological goals, including government reform, election and campaign reform, civil rights, economic equality, "family values," or even opposition to government itself.

Political Entrepreneurs Organize and Maintain Groups

In a review of Olson's book,[14] Richard Wagner noticed that Olson's arguments about groups and politics in general, and his theory of selective incentives in particular, had very little to say about the internal workings of groups. In Wagner's experience, however, groups often came into being and then were maintained in good working order, not only because of selective incentives but also because of the extraordinary efforts of specific individuals—leaders, in ordinary language, or *political entrepreneurs* in Wagner's more colorful expression.

Wagner was motivated to raise the issue of group leaders because, in his view, Olson's theory was too pessimistic. Mass organizations in the real world—labor unions, consumer associations, senior-citizen groups, environmental organizations—all exist, some persisting and prospering over long periods. Contrary to Olson's suggestions, they seem to get jump-started somehow in the real world.

[14]Richard Wagner, "Pressure Groups and Political Entrepreneurs," *Papers on Non-Market Decision Making I* (1966): 161–70.

solidary benefits Selective benefits of group membership that emphasize friendship, networking, and consciousness-raising.

Collective-Action Principle Selective benefits are one solution to the collective-action problem.

purposive benefits Selective benefits of group membership that emphasize the purpose and accomplishments of the group.

Wagner suggests that a special kind of theory of selective incentives is called for. Specifically, he argues that certain selective benefits may accrue to *those who organize and maintain otherwise latent groups.*

Senator Robert Wagner (no relation) in the 1930s and Congressman Claude Pepper in the 1970s each had *private reasons*—electoral incentives—to try to organize laborers and the elderly, respectively. Wagner, a Democrat from New York, had a large constituency of working men and women who would reward him by re-electing him—a private, conditional payment—if he bore the cost of organizing (or at least of facilitating the organization of) workers. And this he did. The law that bears his name, the Wagner Act of 1935, made it much easier for unions to organize in the industrial North.[15] Likewise, Claude Pepper, a Democratic congressman with a large number of elderly constituents in his south Miami district, saw it as serving his own electoral interests to provide the initial investment of effort for the organization of the elderly as a political force.

Rationality Principle

Organizing collective action can provide private benefits to a political entrepreneur.

In general, a political entrepreneur is someone who sees a prospective cooperation dividend that is currently not being enjoyed. This is another way of saying that there is a latent group that, if it were to become manifest, would enjoy the fruits of collective action. For a price, whether in votes (as in the cases of Wagner and Pepper), a percentage of the dividend, nonmaterial glory, or other perks, the entrepreneur bears the costs of organizing, expends effort to monitor individuals for slacker behavior, and sometimes even imposes punishment on slackers (such as expelling them from the group and denying them any of its selective benefits).

To illustrate this phenomenon, there is a story about a British tourist who visited China in the late nineteenth century. She was shocked and appalled to see teams of men pulling barges along the Yangtze River, overseen by whip-wielding masters. She remarked to her guide that such an uncivilized state of affairs would never be tolerated in modern societies like those in the West. The guide, anxious to please but concerned that his employer had come to a wildly erroneous conclusion, hastily responded, "Madam, I think you misunderstand. The man carrying the whip is *employed* by those pulling the barge. He noticed that it is generally difficult, if you are pulling your weight along a tow path, to detect whether any of your team members are pulling theirs or, instead, whether they are 'free-riding' on your labors. He convinced the workers that his entrepreneurial services were required and that they should hire him. For an agreed-on compensation, he monitors each team member's effort level, whipping those who shirk in their responsibilities. Notice, madam, that he rarely ever uses the whip. His mere presence is sufficient to get the group to accomplish the task."

Thus political entrepreneurs, such as the whip-wielding driver, may be thought of as complements to Olsonian selective incentives in that both are ways

---

[15]The Wagner Act made it possible for unions to organize by legalizing the so-called closed shop. If a worker took a job in a closed shop or plant, he or she was *required* to join the union there. "Do not contribute" was no longer an option, so that workers in closed shops could not free-ride on the efforts made by others to improve wages and working conditions.

Can the Internet Help Americans "Meet Up" and Cooperate?

In the 2004 presidential election, a new tool for political organization burst onto the scene. Advocates claimed that it could triple campaign donations, could produce a flood of volunteers, and was cheap and easy to use. This new tool was not the much-maligned "527" organizations, nor was it a new kind of campaign commercial or a new campaign theme. Instead, this tool appealed to one of the most basic of human instincts—the desire to socialize with likeminded people and make friends—but it did so with a high-tech twist.

"Meetups" (named for a popular Web site, www.meetup.com) are online communities of likeminded individuals, organized around a bewildering diversity of interests. There are scrapbookers in Singapore, Harley-Davidson owners in Houston, and pug owners in Colorado. Howard Dean's presidential campaign recognized the potential of meetups early on, in December 2002. Such groups rapidly multiplied, until "politics and activism" became the largest category on meetup.com.[1]

Dean set the standard for Internet organizing in 2004. Through his ability to harness the power of the Internet, Dean raised the astonishing sum of $40 million before the Iowa caucus and recruited hundreds of thousands of volunteers. By mid-2005, more than eighteen months after the election, there were still 925 "Democracy for America" meetup groups (the inheritors of the Dean campaign), with nearly 150,000 members.

Dean is only the most prominent example of the new world of Internet organizing. On September 12, 2001, Eli Pariser organized three hundred peace activists and garnered media attention from as far away as Romania simply by emailing a few friends his views on war.[2] Eventually, Pariser spawned indymedia.org, an "alternative" media outlet that encourages individuals to post their own version of the news. Moveon.org, which began in 1998 as a Web page to fight the impeachment of President Clinton, grew by the 2004 campaign into a clearinghouse for liberal activists and one of the largest political action committees in the Democratic Party.

What all these examples illustrate is the potential of the Internet for overcoming one of the central problems in politics, the basis of the second principle of politics, and the central lesson of this chapter—Mancur Olson's "logic of collective action." Stripped to its bare essentials, Olson's formulation argues that, for most individuals, it is not rational to work toward the provision of a public good. The individual's contribution is unlikely to make a difference, and individuals can enjoy the public good anyway. So why participate?

Olson provides some solutions to the collective action problem, among them keep groups small and intimate. So how can we explain the success of meetups? These groups seem to contradict Olson. They are large (national and even international in scope) and anonymous (most individuals know each other only electronically). Has the Internet changed the logic of collective action?

The answer is no. The Internet has simply made it easier to overcome the barriers to collective action.

History Principle

New types of interest groups formed when the Internet became an easy way for individuals to interact and communicate.

One way that groups recruit and maintain members is by providing them selective benefits. When we think of selective benefits, most of us think of material benefits such as reduced prescription drug prices (AARP), auto insurance (American Automobile Association), and magazines (Sierra Club). But another important benefit is *solidary:* the friendship and sense of belonging that come with membership in a group.

This is clearly part of what is happening with meetup.com. The Internet makes it easier for groups to provide solidary benefits. Chat rooms, email lists, and bulletin boards provide cheap and easy venues for interpersonal interaction. Emailing a newsletter or maintaining a Web site is far less expensive than maintaining local chapters. From the perspective of the individual, these technologies decrease the costs of membership, further bolstering participation.

Still, electronic communities have the same class bias that traditional interest groups display—again showing that the Internet has not radically changed the nature of many political organizations. One study showed that most "meetup" members in the 2004 campaign were white, middle class, and well-educated.[3]

Another way that groups form is through the efforts of political entrepreneurs. These are individuals who have private incentives to organize a group. The Internet is unlikely to affect the number of entrepreneurs, but because the Internet lowers costs, it is likely to increase the possibility that they can organize a group.[4] The leaders of the American Revolution had to rely on horse-drawn mail and pamphlets to coordinate their actions and popularize their views. Modern activists can communicate their views through email, weblogs, and Web sites, reaching more people and at a lower cost.

What benefits do these entrepreneurs receive? An important one is that they can satisfy their own political ambitions. Moveon.org started when a few wealthy Silicon Valley entrepreneurs developed a Web site because they were angry about Republican attempts to impeach Clinton. Once the site grew dramatically (and unexpectedly), it became a logical vehicle to organize liberal political interests.[5] And ironically, Eli Pariser, the founder of the anti-establishment indymedia, now serves as executive director of that most insider of political organizations, Moveon.org.

Collective-Action Principle

Solidary benefits—interacting with like-minded people—can be just as important as material benefits for many people and can help explain many forms of collective action.

Rationality Principle

Even though it is still rational for individuals to free-ride, it may be rational for political entrepreneurs to organize groups, because their personal benefits exceed the costs.

[1]Chris Gray, "Meetup.com Working to Become a Force in Local, State Politics," *Philadelphia Inquirer,* 12 February 2004.

[2]George Packer, "Smart-Mobbing the War," *New York Times Magazine,* 9 March 2003.

[3]Christine Williams and Jesse Gordon, "The Meetup Presidency," *Campaigns and Elections,* July 2004.

[4]Recall that political entrepreneurs gain only if their private benefits exceed the costs of organizing the group. Thus, if you lower the costs of organizing a group, you increase the number of entrepreneurs who will find it profitable.

[5]See Michael Falcone, "Dear Campaign Diary: Seizing the Day, Online," *New York Times,* 11 September 2003, and Josh Richman, "MoveOn.org Redefines Art of Activism, Fund Raising," *Alameda Times-Star,* 26 February 2003.

of motivating groups to accomplish collective objectives. Indeed, if selective incentives *resolve* the paradox of collective action, then political entrepreneurs *dissolve* the paradox. Both are helpful, and sometimes both are needed to initiate and maintain collective action. Groups that manage, perhaps on their own, to get themselves organized at a low level of activity often take the next step of *creating* leaders and leadership institutions to increase the activity level and resulting cooperation dividends. Wagner, in other words, took Olson's theory of selective incentives and suggested an alternative explanation, one that made room for institutional solutions to the problem of collective action.

HOW DO INTEREST GROUPS INFLUENCE POLICY?

Interest groups work to improve the probability that they and their policy interests will be heard and treated favorably by all branches and levels of the government. The quest for political influence or power takes many forms. Insider strategies include access to key decision makers and using the courts. Outsider strategies include going public and using electoral politics. These strategies do not exhaust all the possibilities, but they paint a broad picture of ways that groups use their resources in the fierce competition for power.

Many groups employ a mix of insider and outsider strategies. For example, environmental groups like the Sierra Club lobby members of Congress and key congressional staff members; participate in bureaucratic rule making by offering comments and suggestions to agencies on new environmental rules; and bring lawsuits under various environmental acts like the Endangered Species Act, which authorizes groups and citizens to come to court if they believe the act is being violated. At the same time, the Sierra Club attempts to influence public opinion through media campaigns and to influence electoral politics by supporting candidates who they believe to share their environmental views and opposing candidates who they view as foes of environmentalism.

Direct Lobbying

Lobbying is an attempt by a group to influence the policy process through persuasion of government officials. Most Americans tend to believe that interest groups exert their influence through direct contact with members of Congress, but lobbying encompasses a broad range of activities that groups engage in with all sorts of government officials and the public as a whole.

The 1946 Federal Regulation of Lobbying Act defines a lobbyist as "any person who shall engage himself for pay or any consideration for the purpose of attempting to influence the passage or defeat of any legislation of the Congress of the United States." The 1995 Lobbying Disclosure Act requires all organizations employing lobbyists to register with Congress and to disclose whom they represent, whom they lobby, what they are lobbying for, and how much they are paid.

lobbying An attempt by a group to influence the policy process through persuasion of government officials.

More than 7,000 organizations, collectively employing many thousands of lobbyists, are currently registered.

Lobbying involves a great deal of activity on the part of someone speaking for an interest. Lobbyists badger and buttonhole legislators, administrators, and committee staff members with facts about pertinent issues and facts or claims about public support of them.[16] Lobbyists can serve a useful purpose in the legislative and administrative process by providing this kind of information. In 1978, during debate on a bill to expand the requirement for lobbying disclosures, Democratic senators Edward Kennedy of Massachusetts and Dick Clark of Iowa joined with Republican senator Robert Stafford of Vermont to issue the following statement: "Government without lobbying could not function. The flow of information to Congress and to every federal agency is a vital part of our democratic system."[17]

Lobbying Members of Congress   Interest groups also have substantial influence in setting the legislative agenda and in helping craft specific language in legislation (Figure 12.3). Today, sophisticated lobbyists win influence by providing information about policies to busy members of Congress. As one lobbyist noted, "You can't get access without knowledge. . . . I can go in to see [former Energy and Commerce Committee chair] John Dingell, but if I have nothing to offer or nothing to say, he's not going to want to see me."[18] In recent years, interest groups have also begun to build broader coalitions and comprehensive campaigns around particular policy issues.[19] These coalitions do not rise from the grassroots, but instead are put together by Washington lobbyists who launch comprehensive lobbying campaigns that combine stimulated grassroots activity with information and campaign funding for members of Congress. In recent years, the Republican leadership worked so closely with lobbyists that critics charged that the boundaries between lobbyists and legislators had been erased, and that lobbyists had become "adjunct staff to the Republican leadership."[20]

In many instances, the influence of lobbyists is based on networks of personal relationships and behind-the-scenes services that they are able to perform for lawmakers. For example, one of Washington's most successful lobbyists is J. Steven Hart, a senior partner at Williams & Jensen, a well-known Washington, DC, lobbying and law firm. Hart's roster of clients includes such firms as Dell Inc. and Bass Enterprises. What does Hart offer such clients? The most important service Hart

[16]For discussions of lobbying, see Jeffrey M. Berry, *Lobbying for the People: The Political Behavior of Public Interest Groups* (Princeton, NJ: Princeton University Press, 1977); and John R. Wright, *Interest Groups and Congress: Lobbying, Contributions, and Influence* (Boston: Allyn & Bacon, 1996).

[17]"The Swarming Lobbyists," *Time*, 7 August 1978, p. 15.

[18]Daniel Franklin, "Tommy Boggs and the Death of Health Care Reform," *Washington Monthly* (April 1995): 36.

[19]Marie Hojnacki, "Interest Groups' Decisions to Join Alliances or Work Alone," *American Journal of Political Science* 41(1997): 61–87; Kevin W. Hula, *Lobbying Together: Interest Group Coalitions in Legislative Politics* (Washington, DC: Georgetown University Press, 1999).

[20]Peter H. Stone, "Follow the Leaders," *National Journal*, 24 June 1995, p. 1641.

FIGURE 12.3

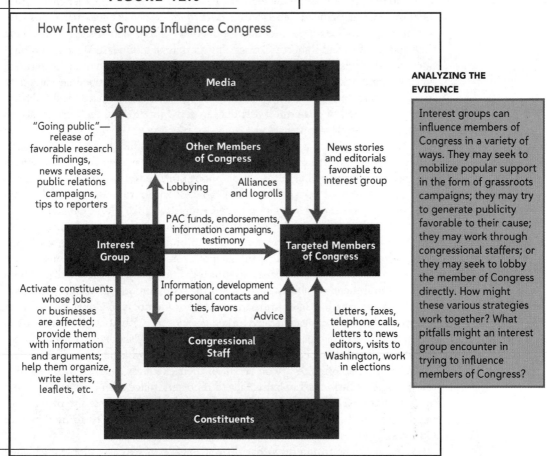

How Interest Groups Influence Congress

Media

"Going public"—release of favorable research findings, news releases, public relations campaigns, tips to reporters

Other Members of Congress

Lobbying   Alliances and logrolls

News stories and editorials favorable to interest group

Interest Group

PAC funds, endorsements, information campaigns, testimony

Targeted Members of Congress

Activate constituents whose jobs or businesses are affected; provide them with information and arguments; help them organize, write letters, leaflets, etc.

Information, development of personal contacts and ties, favors

Advice

Letters, faxes, telephone calls, letters to news editors, visits to Washington, work in elections

Congressional Staff

Constituents

ANALYZING THE EVIDENCE

Interest groups can influence members of Congress in a variety of ways. They may seek to mobilize popular support in the form of grassroots campaigns; they may try to generate publicity favorable to their cause; they may work through congressional staffers; or they may seek to lobby the member of Congress directly. How might these various strategies work together? What pitfalls might an interest group encounter in trying to influence members of Congress?

provides is direct access to the leadership of Congress. Hart, as it happens, serves as the personal attorney for former House majority leader Tom DeLay as well as a number of other members of the House leadership. Often, this legal work is performed at a nominal fee, as a "loss leader" to encourage others to send their business to the firm.[21] As a result of this personal relationship with the majority leader, Hart is able to promise clients that their case will be heard by the nation's most important officials. Hart, for example, organized a meeting in DeLay's office in September 2001 in which airline executives were able to convince congressional leaders of

[21]Steven Brill, *After: How America Confronted the September 12 Era* (New York: Simon & Shuster, 2003).

the need for an airline bailout package in the wake of September 11. On the whole, about 50 percent of Washington lobbyists have prior government experience. Other lobbyists present included Rebecca Cox, wife of influential congressman Chris Cox of California. Ms. Cox is counsel for Continental Airlines, one of the firms seeking the bailout. Chris and Rebecca Cox are an example of a standard Washington phenomenon—a legislator married to a lobbyist. For instance, Hadassah Lieberman, wife of Connecticut senator and former Democratic vice-presidential candidate Joseph Lieberman, was for many years a lobbyist for the pharmaceutical industry. Lobbyists married to powerful legislators can certainly promise their clients access to the highest levels of government.

Interest groups also have substantial influence in setting the legislative agenda and in helping craft specific language in legislation. Today, sophisticated lobbyists win influence by providing information about policies to busy members of Congress. As one lobbyist noted, "You can't get access without knowledge. . . . I can go in to see [former Energy and Commerce Committee chair] John Dingell, but if I have nothing to offer or nothing to say, he's not going to want to see me.[22] In recent years, interest groups have also begun to build broader coalitions and comprehensive campaigns around particular policy issues.[23] These coalitions do not rise from the grassroots but instead are put together by Washington lobbyists who launch comprehensive lobbying campaigns that combine stimulated grassroots activity with information and campaign funding for members of Congress. In recent years, the Republican leadership worked so closely with lobbyists that critics charged that the boundaries between lobbyists and legislators had been erased, and that lobbyists had become "adjunct staff to the Republican leadership."[24]

Lobbyists also often testify on behalf of their clients at congressional committee and agency hearings. Lobbyists talk to reporters, place ads in newspapers, and organize letter-writing, e-mail, and telegram campaigns. Lobbyists also play an important role in fund-raising, helping direct clients' contributions to members of Congress and presidential candidates.

What happens to interests that do not engage in extensive lobbying? They often find themselves "Microsofted." In 1998, the software giant was facing antitrust action from the Justice Department and had few friends in Congress. One member of the House, Representative Billy Tauzin (R-La.), told Microsoft chairman Bill Gates that without an extensive investment in lobbying, the corporation would continue to be "demonized." Gates responded by quadrupling Microsoft's lobbying expenditures and hiring a group of lobbyists with strong ties to Congress. The result was congressional pressure on the Justice Department, resulting in a settlement of the Microsoft suit on terms favorable to the company. Similarly,

---

[22]Daniel Franklin, "Tommy Boggs and the Death of Health Care Reform," *Washington Monthly* (April 1995): 36.

[23]Majie Hojnacki, "Interest Groups' Decisions to Join Alliances or Work Alone," *American Journal of Political Science* 41 (1997): 61–87; Kevin W. Hula, *Lobbying Together: Interest Groups Coalitions in Legislative Politics* (Washington, DC: Georgetown University Press, 1999).

[24]Peter H. Stone, "Follow the Leaders," *National Journal*, 24 June 1995, p. 1641.

in 1999, members of Congress advised Wal-Mart that its efforts to win approval to operate savings and loans in its stores were doomed to failure if the retailer did not greatly increase its lobbying efforts. "They don't give money. They don't have congressional representation—so nobody here cares about them," said one influential member. Like Microsoft, Wal-Mart learned its lesson, hired more lobbyists, and got what it wanted.[25]

Providing access is only one of the many services lobbyists perform. Lobbyists often testify on behalf of their clients at congressional committee and agency hearings; lobbyists sometimes help their clients identify potential allies with whom to construct coalitions; lobbyists provide research and information to government officials; lobbyists often draft proposed legislation or regulations to be introduced by friendly lawmakers; lobbyists talk to reporters, place ads in newspapers, and organize letter-writing, e-mail, and telegram campaigns. Lobbyists also play an important role in fund-raising, helping direct clients' contributions to members of Congress and presidential candidates.

Lobbying the President   All these efforts and more are needed when the target of a lobbying campaign is the president of the United States. So many individuals and groups clamor for the president's time and attention that only the most skilled and well-connected members of the lobbying community can hope to influence presidential decisions. One Washington lobbyist who fills this bill is Tom Kuhn, president of the Edison Electric Institute, a lobbying organization representing the electric power industry. Kuhn is a friend and former college classmate of President George W. Bush. In 2000, Kuhn was among the leading "Pioneers"—individuals who raised at least $100,000 for the Bush election campaign. Later, the electric power companies represented by Kuhn gave nearly $20 million to congressional candidates in the 2001–02 election cycle. Kuhn's close relationship with the president and his efforts on behalf of the president's election have given Kuhn enormous leverage with the White House. During the 2000 transition, candidates for a presidential nomination to head the EPA felt compelled to pay "courtesy calls" to Kuhn. Subsequently, Kuhn led a successful effort to delay and weaken proposed new EPA controls on electric-power-plant emissions of mercury, a toxic substance linked to neurological damage, especially in children.[26] This was a victory for the electric power industry that promised to save the industry hundreds of millions of dollars a year and illustrates the influence that can be brought to bear by a powerful lobbyist.

Lobbying the Executive Branch   Even when an interest group is very successful at getting its bill passed by Congress and signed by the president, the prospect of full and faithful implementation of that law is not guaranteed. Often, a group and

[25]"The Microsoft Playbook: A Report from Common Cause," 25 Sept. 2000 (www.commoncause.org).
[26]"Edison Electric Institute Lobbying to Weaken Toxic Mercury Standards," http://tristatenews.com, 28 February 2003.

its allies do not pack up and go home as soon as the president turns their lobbied-for new law over to the appropriate agency. On average, 40 percent of interest-group representatives regularly contact both legislative and executive branch organizations, while 13 percent contact only the legislature and 16 percent only the executive branch.[27]

In some respects, interest-group access to the executive branch is promoted by federal law. The Administrative Procedures Act, first enacted in 1946 and frequently amended in subsequent years, requires most federal agencies to provide notice and an opportunity for comment before implementing proposed new rules and regulations. So-called "notice and comment rule-making" is designed to allow interests an opportunity to make their views known and to participate in the implementation of federal legislation that affects them. In 1990, Congress enacted the Negotiated Rulemaking Act to encourage administrative agencies to engage in direct and open negotiations with affected interests when developing new regulations. These two pieces of legislation—which have been strongly enforced by the federal courts—have played an important role in opening the bureaucratic process to interest-group influence. Today, few federal agencies would consider attempting to implement a new rule without consulting affected interests, who are sometimes known as "stakeholders" in Washington.[28]

Policy Principle
Public policy can reveal the impact of lobbying.

Cultivating Access Exerting influence on Congress or government agencies by providing their members with information about issues, support, and even threats of retaliation requires easy and constant access to decision makers. One interesting example of why groups need to cultivate and maintain access is the dairy farmers. Through the 1960s, dairy farmers were part of the powerful coalition of agricultural interests that had full access to Congress and to the Department of Agriculture. During the 1960s, a series of disputes broke out between the dairy farmers and the producers of corn, grain, and other agricultural commodities over commodities prices. Dairy farmers, whose cows consume grain, prefer low commodities prices, whereas grain producers obviously prefer to receive high prices. The commodities producers won the battle, and Congress raised commodities prices, in part at the expense of the dairy farmers. In the 1970s, the dairy farmers left the agriculture coalition, set up their own lobby and political action groups, and became heavily involved in public relations campaigns and both congressional and presidential elections. Thus the dairy farmers lost their traditional access and had to pursue an "outsider" strategy. Indeed, the political fortunes of the dairy operations were badly hurt when they were accused of making illegal contributions to President Nixon's re-election campaign in 1972.

Collective-Action Principle
Lobbying and cultivating access require coordination across the legislative and executive branches.

Access is usually a result of time and effort spent cultivating a position within the inner councils of government. This method of gaining access often requires

[27] John P. Heinz et al., *The Hollow Core: Private Interests in National Policy Making* (Cambridge, MA: Harvard University Press, 1993).

[28] For an excellent discussion of the political origins of the Administrative Procedure Act, see Martin Shapiro, "APA: Past, Present, Future," 72 *Virginia Law Review* 377 (March 1986): 447–92.

the sacrifice of short-run influence. For example, many of the most important organized interests in agriculture devote far more time and resources cultivating the staff and trustees of state agriculture schools and county agents back home than buttonholing members of Congress or bureaucrats in Washington.

Regulations on Lobbying As a result of the constant access to important decision makers that lobbyists seek out and require, stricter guidelines regulating the actions of lobbyists have been adopted in the last decade. For example, as of 1993, businesses may no longer deduct lobbying costs as a business expense. Trade associations must report to members the proportion of their dues that goes to lobbying, and that proportion of the dues may not be reported as a business expense. The most important attempt to limit the influence of lobbyists was the 1995 Lobbying Disclosure Act, which significantly broadened the definition of people and organizations that must register as lobbyists. According to the filings under the act, there were almost 11,500 lobbyists working the halls of Congress.

In 1996, Congress passed legislation limiting the size of gifts to $50 and no more than $100 annually from a single source. It also banned the practice of honoraria, which had been used by special interests to supplement congressional salaries. But Congress did not limit the travel of representatives, senators, their wives, or congressional staff members. Interest groups can pay for congressional travel as long as a trip is related to legislative business and is disclosed on congressional reports within thirty days. On these trips, meals and entertainment expenses are not limited to $50 per event and $100 annually. The rules of Congress allow its members to travel on corporate jets as long as they pay an amount equal to first-class airfare.

Using the Courts

Interest groups sometimes turn to the courts to augment other avenues of access. They can use the courts to affect public policy in at least three ways: (1) by bringing suit directly on behalf of the group itself, (2) by financing suits brought by individuals, and (3) by filing a companion brief as *amicus curiae* (literally "friend of the court") to an existing court case.

Among the most significant modern illustrations of the use of the courts as a strategy for political influence are those that accompanied the "sexual revolution" of the 1960s and the emergence of the movement for women's rights. Beginning in the mid-1960s, a series of cases was brought into the federal courts in an effort to force definition of a right to privacy in sexual matters. The effort began with a challenge to state restrictions on obtaining contraceptives for nonmedical purposes, a challenge that was effectively made in *Griswold v. Connecticut*, in which the Supreme Court held that states could neither prohibit the dissemination of information about nor prohibit the actual use of contraceptives by married couples. That case was soon followed by *Eisenstadt v. Baird*, in which the Court held that the states could not prohibit the use of contraceptives by single persons any more than it could prohibit their use by married

Institution Principle

Groups can turn to the courts if they are not successful in the legislative and executive branches.

couples. One year later, the Court held, in the 1973 case of *Roe v. Wade*, that states could not impose an absolute ban on voluntary abortions. Each of these cases, as well as others, were part of the Court's enunciation of a constitutional doctrine of privacy.[29]

The 1973 abortion case sparked a controversy that brought conservatives to the fore on a national level. These conservative groups made extensive use of the courts to whittle away the scope of the privacy doctrine. They obtained rulings, for example, that prohibit the use of federal funds to pay for voluntary abortions. And in 1989, right-to-life groups were able to use a strategy of litigation that significantly undermined the *Roe v. Wade* decision—namely, in the case of *Webster v. Reproductive Health Services*, which restored the right of states to place restrictions on abortion.[30]

Another extremely significant set of contemporary illustrations of the use of the courts as a strategy for political influence are those found in the history of the National Association for the Advancement of Colored People (NAACP). The most important of these court cases was *Brown v. Board of Education*, in which the U.S. Supreme Court held that legal segregation of the schools was unconstitutional.[31]

Business groups are also frequent users of the courts because of the number of government programs applied to them. Litigation involving large businesses is most mountainous in such areas as taxation, antitrust, interstate transportation, patents, and product quality and standardization. Often a business is brought to litigation against its will by virtue of initiatives taken against it by other businesses or by government agencies. But many individual businesses bring suit themselves to influence government policy. Major corporations and their trade associations pay tremendous amounts of money each year in fees to the most prestigious Washington law firms. Some of this money is expended in gaining access. A great proportion of it, however, is used to keep the best and most experienced lawyers prepared to represent the corporations in court or before administrative agencies when necessary.

New Politics forces made significant use of the courts during the 1970s and 1980s, and judicial decisions were instrumental in advancing their goals. Facilitated by rules changes on access to the courts (the rules of standing are discussed in Chapter 8), the New Politics agenda was clearly visible in court decisions handed down in several key policy areas. In the environmental policy area, New Politics groups were able to force federal agencies to pay attention to environmental issues, even when the agency was not directly involved in activities related to environmental quality.

Mobilizing Public Opinion

going public
Launching a media campaign to build popular support.

Going public is a strategy that attempts to mobilize the widest and most favorable climate of opinion. Many groups consider it imperative to maintain this cli-

---

[29]*Griswold v. Connecticut*, 381 U.S. 479 (1965); *Eisenstadt v. Baird*, 405 U.S. 438 (1972); *Roe v. Wade*, 410 U.S. 113 (1973).

[30]*Webster v. Reproductive Health Services*, 109 S.Ct. 3049 (1989).

[31]*Brown v. Board of Education*, 347 U.S. 483 (1954).

mate at all times, even when they have no issue to fight about. An increased use of this kind of strategy is usually associated with modern advertising. As early as the 1930s, political analysts were distinguishing between the "old lobby" of direct group representation before Congress and the "new lobby" of public relations professionals addressing the public at large to reach Congress.[32]

One of the best-known ways of going public is the use of institutional advertising. A casual scanning of important mass-circulation magazines and newspapers will provide numerous examples of expensive and well-designed ads by the major oil companies, automobile and steel companies, other large corporations, and trade associations. The ads show how much these organizations are doing for the country, for the protection of the environment, or for the defense of the American way of life. Their purpose is to create and maintain a strongly positive association between the organization and the community at large in the hope that these favorable feelings can be drawn on as needed for specific political campaigns later on.

During one month in 2005, for example, members of the radio or television audience might have been exposed to an advertisement sponsored by a consortium of defense contractors touting the virtues of the F/A-22 Raptor jet fighter. Presumably few members of the audience would be interested in purchasing a Raptor, but positive feelings among constituents might encourage members of Congress to support the purchase of this expensive weapons system. During the same month, viewers and listeners might have been treated to ads touting the virtues of pork, poultry, and dairy products, all sponsored by consortia of producers. The purpose of such ads is to give Americans a positive feeling toward the products—a positive feeling that can be harnessed by the industry in the event of health scares or other problems that might arise in the future.

Many groups resort to protest because they lack the resources, the contacts, or the experience to use other political strategies. The sponsorship of boycotts, sit-ins, mass rallies, and marches by Martin Luther King's Southern Christian Leadership Conference (SCLC) and related organizations in the 1950s and 1960s is one of the most significant and successful cases of going public to create a more favorable climate of opinion by calling attention to abuses. The success of these events inspired similar efforts on the part of women. Organizations such as the National Organization for Women (NOW) used public strategies in their drive for legislation and in their efforts to gain ratification of the Equal Rights Amendment. In 1993, gay rights groups organized a mass rally in their effort to eliminate restrictions on military service and other forms of discrimination against individuals based on their sexual preference.

Another form of going public is the grassroots lobbying campaign. In such a campaign, a lobby group mobilizes ordinary citizens throughout the country to write their representatives in support of the group's position. A grassroots campaign

Collective-Action Principle

One means groups use to overcome collective-action problems is to mobilize public opinion in their support.

---

[32]Pendleton Herring, *Group Representation before Congress* (1928; reissue New York: Russell & Russell, 1967). See also Ken Kollman, *Outside Lobbying: Public Opinion and Interest Group Strategies* (Princeton, NJ: Princeton University Press, 1998).

can cost anywhere from $40,000 to sway the votes of one or two crucial members of a committee or subcommittee, to millions of dollars to mount a national effort aimed at the Congress as a whole. During the past several years, grassroots lobbying campaigns have played an important role in battles over presidential appointments. In 2005, President George W. Bush was presented with an opportunity to fill two Supreme Court vacancies, one occasioned by the death of Chief Justice William Rehnquist and the other by the retirement of Justice Sandra Day O'Connor. Immediately, liberal and conservative advocacy groups mobilized for battle. In particular, pro-choice and pro-life groups saw the two Supreme Court appointments as a decisive point in the long-standing national struggle over abortion. Pro-choice groups feared that Bush would appoint justices hostile to abortion rights while pro-life groups feared that he would not. As each side urged its members to pressure Congress, hundreds of thousands of calls, letters, telegrams, and emails flooded Capitol Hill. These campaigns had a major impact upon the appointment process, forcing President Bush to withdraw the name of one nominee, Harriet Miers, and very nearly derailing a second Bush nominee, Samuel Alito.

Grassroots lobbying campaigns have been so effective in recent years that a number of Washington consulting firms specialize in this area. Firms such as Bonner & Associates, for example, will generate grassroots telephone campaigns on behalf of or in opposition to important legislative proposals.

Grassroots lobbying has become more prevalent in Washington over the last couple of decades because the adoption of congressional rules limiting gifts to members has made traditional lobbying more difficult. This circumstance makes all the more compelling the question of whether grassroots campaigning has reached an intolerable extreme. One case in particular may have tipped it over: in 1992, ten giant companies in the financial services, manufacturing, and high-tech industries began a grassroots campaign and spent millions of dollars to influence a decision in Congress to limit the ability of investors to sue for fraud. Retaining an expensive consulting firm, these corporations paid for the use of specialized computer software to persuade Congress that there was "an outpouring of popular support for the proposal." Thousands of letters from individuals flooded Capitol Hill. Many of those letters were written and sent by people who sincerely believed that investor lawsuits are often frivolous and should be curtailed. But much of the mail was phony, generated by the Washington-based campaign consultants; the letters came from people who had no strong feelings or even no opinion at all about the issue. More and more people, including leading members of Congress, are becoming quite skeptical of such methods, charging that these are not genuine grassroots campaigns but instead represent "Astroturf lobbying" (a play on the brand name of an artificial grass used on many sports fields). Such "Astroturf" campaigns have increased in frequency in recent years as members of Congress grow more and more skeptical of Washington lobbyists and far more concerned about demonstrations of support for a particular issue by their constituents. But after the firms mentioned above spent millions of dollars and generated thousands of letters to members of Congress, they came to the somber conclusion that "it's more effective to have 100 letters from your district where constituents took the time to write and understand the issue," because "Congress is sophisticated enough to know the difference."[33]

The White House Office of Management and Budget (OMB) estimates that the total cost of lobbying activities at the federal level in 2004 was more than $2 billion. This figure includes grassroots groups that spent a few thousand dollars and organizations like AARP that spent more than $21 million. The OMB estimate does not include lobbying at the state and local levels, but the amount spent to influence state legislatures and city and county councils is staggering. For example, in 2003, a New York State commission estimated that $120 million was spent lobbying the state legislature. The largest single spender was the teachers union, which spent $2.3 million opposing school voucher and charter school plans. The New York State commission also revealed that a number of organizations had violated the state's lobbying laws and had been fined by state authorities. The New York Yankees paid a fine of $75,000, and the Correction Corporation of America (CCA), an operator of private prisons that holds a number of state contracts to house inmates, was fined $300,000 for illegal activities. Fortunately for CCA executives, they were not forced to spend time in their own facilities.

Using Electoral Politics

In addition to attempting to influence members of Congress and other government officials, interest groups also seek to use the electoral process to elect the right legislators in the first place and to ensure that those who are elected will owe them a debt of gratitude for their support. To put matters into perspective, groups invest far more resources in lobbying than in electoral politics. Nevertheless, financial support and campaign activism can be important tools for organized interests.

Political Action Committees By far the most common electoral strategy employed by interest groups is that of giving financial support to the parties or to particular candidates. But such support can easily cross the threshold into outright bribery. Therefore, Congress has occasionally made an effort to regulate this strategy. For example, the Federal Elections Campaign Act of 1971 (amended in 1974) limits campaign contributions and requires that each candidate or campaign committee itemize the full name and address, occupation, and principal business of each person who contributes more than $100. These provisions have been effective up to a point, considering the rather large number of embarrassments, indictments, resignations, and criminal convictions in the aftermath of the Watergate scandal.

The Watergate scandal itself was triggered by the illegal entry of Republican workers into the office of the Democratic National Committee in the Watergate

[33]Jane Fritsch, "The Grass Roots, Just a Free Phone Call Away," *New York Times*, 23 June 1995, pp. A1 and A22.

apartment complex. But an investigation quickly revealed numerous violations of campaign finance laws, involving millions of dollars in unregistered cash from corporate executives to President Nixon's re-election committee. Many of these revelations were made by the famous Ervin Committee, whose official name and jurisdiction was the Senate Select Committee to Investigate the 1972 Presidential Campaign Activities.

Reaction to Watergate produced further legislation on campaign finance in 1974 and 1976, but the effect has been to restrict individual rather than interest-group campaign activity. Individuals may now contribute no more than $2,000 to any candidate for federal office in any primary or general election. A political action committee, however, can contribute $5,000, provided it contributes to at least five different federal candidates each year. Beyond this, the laws permit corporations, unions, and other interest groups to form *political action committees (PACs)* and to pay the costs of soliciting funds from private citizens for the PACs.

political action committees
Private groups that raise and distribute funds for use in election campaigns.

Electoral spending by interest groups has been increasing steadily despite the flurry of reform following Watergate. Table 12.3 presents a dramatic picture of the growth of PACs as the source of campaign contributions. The dollar amounts for each year indicate the growth in electoral spending. The number of PACs has also increased significantly—from 608 in 1974 to nearly 4,000 in 2004 (Figure 12.1). Although the reform legislation of the early and mid-1970s attempted to reduce the influence of special interests over elections, the effect has been almost the exact opposite. Opportunities for legally influencing campaigns are now widespread.

Given the enormous costs of television commercials, polls, computers, and other elements of the new political technology (see Chapter 11), most politicians are eager to receive PAC contributions and are at least willing to give a friendly hearing to the needs and interests of contributors. It is probably not the case that most politicians simply sell their votes to the interests that fund their campaigns. But there is considerable evidence to support the contention that interest groups' campaign contributions do influence the overall pattern of political behavior in Congress and in the state legislatures.

Indeed, PACs and campaign contributions provide organized interests with such a useful tool for gaining access to the political process that calls to abolish PACs have been quite frequent among political reformers. Concern about PACs grew through the 1980s and 1990s, creating a constant drumbeat for reform of federal election laws. Proposals were introduced in Congress on many occasions, perhaps the most celebrated being the McCain-Feingold bill. When it was originally proposed in 1996, the bill was aimed at reducing or eliminating PACs. But, in a stunning about-face, when campaign finance reform was adopted in 2002 as the Bipartisan Campaign Reform Act (BCRA), it did not restrict PACs in any significant way. Rather, it eliminated unrestricted "soft money" donations to the national political parties (see Chapter 10). One consequence of this reform was the creation of a host of new organizations, called 527 committees after the section of the tax code that defines them, often directed by former party officials but nominally unaffiliated with the two parties. These organizations are free to raise

TABLE 12.3

Presidential Campaign Receipts for PAC Contributions (in millions of dollars)

ANALYZING THE EVIDENCE

Political action committees contributed more than $1 billion to the Democratic and Republican campaign efforts in 2004. This is nearly $400,000 more than their total contributions in 2000. Why do PACs contribute so much money to political candidates? On what other sources of funding do candidates rely?

	2004		2000		1996
Primary campaigns					
Bush	$269.6	Bush	$95.5	Clinton	$42.5
Kerry	$234.6	Gore	$48.1	Dole	$44.9
All others	$169.7	All others	$208.0	All others	$160.9
General election campaigns					
Major party grants	$149.2	Major party grants	$135.2	Major party grants	$123.6
Bush legal/accounting	$12.2	Bush legal/accounting	$9.0	Clinton legal/accounting	$4.2
Kerry legal/accounting	$8.9	Gore legal/accounting	$11.5	Dole legal/accounting	$3.5
		Reform grant	$12.6		
Conventions					
Major party grants	$29.8	Major party grants	$27.0	Major party grants	$24.7
Boston host (Dem)	$56.8	Los Angeles host (Dem)	$29.3	Chicago host (Dem)	$20.4
NY host (Rep)	$85.7	Philadelphia host (Rep)	$70.8	San Diego host (Rep)	$24.2
		Reform grant	$2.5		
Total	$1,016.5		$649.5		$449.0
Independent expenditures for	$85.7		$12.7		$0.6
Independent expenditures against	$106.7		$2.0		$0.8
Communication costs for	$11.9		$10.9		$2.4
Communication costs against	$0.4		$0.6		$0.3
Electioneering communications	$40.8				

SOURCE: Federal Election Commission.

and spend as much money as they are able. In addition to 527 committees, issue advocacy groups (501C3 and 501C4) are also permitted to engage in political spending under BCRA. Thus contemporary reforms may have weakened political parties and strengthened interest groups.

The campaign spending of activist groups is carefully kept separate from party and candidate organizations to avoid the restrictions of federal campaign finance laws. As long as a group's campaign expenditures are not coordinated with those of a candidate's own campaign, the group is free to spend as much money as it wishes. Such expenditures are viewed as "issue advocacy" and are protected by the First Amendment. This view was recently reaffirmed by the Federal Election Commission, which ruled in May 2004 that spending by 527 committees was not limited by the BCRA. In 2004, 527s and 501s gave nearly $1 billion to candidates for political office.

Campaign Activism Financial support is not the only way that organized groups seek influence through electoral politics. Sometimes, activism can be even more important than campaign contributions.

In 2004, a number of advocacy groups supporting the Democratic party made a concerted effort to register and mobilize millions of new voters they hoped would support Democratic candidates. Organized labor, of course, targeted union households. Civil rights groups worked to register African Americans. And a number of new groups, including MoveOn.org labored to reach young people via the Internet. Their presumption was that young voters would disproportionately favor the Democrats.

Republicans, for their part, worked with church groups and such advocates of conservative causes as the National Rifle Association and the National Federation of Independent Business to register and mobilize voters likely to support the GOP. Ultimately, Republicans were more successful than their Democratic counterparts. In such key states as Ohio and Florida, hundreds of thousands of religious conservatives, inflamed by social issues like gay marriage and abortion, trooped to the polls and helped hand the GOP a solid victory.

The Initiative Another political tactic sometimes used by interest groups is sponsorship of ballot initiatives at the state level. The *initiative,* a device adopted by a number of states around 1900, allows proposed laws to be placed on the general election ballot and submitted directly to the state's voters. This procedure bypasses the state legislature and governor. The initiative was originally promoted by late nineteenth-century Populists as a mechanism that would allow the people to govern directly. Populists saw the initiative as an antidote to interest-group influence in the legislative process.

initiative The process that allows citizens to propose new laws and submit them for approval by the state's voters.

Ironically, many studies have suggested that most initiative campaigns today are actually sponsored by interest groups seeking to circumvent legislative opposition to their goals. In recent years, for example, initiative campaigns have been sponsored by the insurance industry, trial lawyers' associations, and tobacco companies.[34] The role of interest groups in initiative campaigns should come as no surprise since such campaigns can cost millions of dollars.

Interest Groups: Are They Effective?

Do interest groups have an effect on government and policy? The short answer is yes. One of the best academic studies of the impact of lobbying was conducted

[34]Elisabeth R. Gerber, *The Populist Paradox: Interest Group Influence and the Promise of Direct Legislation* (Princeton, NJ: Princeton University Press, 1999), p. 6.

in 2001 by John de Figueiredo of MIT and Brian Silverman of the University of Toronto.[35] Figueiredo and Silverman focused on a particular form of lobbying: efforts by lobbyists for colleges and universities to obtain "earmarks," special, often disguised, congressional appropriations for their institutions. Millions of dollars in earmarks are written into law every year.

The authors discovered that lobbying had an impact. The more money schools spent on lobbying activities, the larger the total quantity of earmarked funds they received. The extent of lobbying's effect, however, varied with institutional factors. Schools in states with a senator on the Senate Appropriations Committee received $18 to $29 in earmarks for every dollar spent on lobbying. Schools in congressional districts whose representative served on the House Appropriations Committee received between $49 and $55 for every dollar spent on lobbying. On the other hand, schools lacking such representation averaged only about $1 for every dollar spent on lobbying—hardly worth the effort.

These results suggest, as is so often the case, that institutions and politics are profoundly related. Schools without access to members of Congress in positions to help them cannot gain much from lobbying. Schools with such access still need to lobby to take advantage of the potential that representation on the Senate and House appropriations committees can give them. But, if they do so, the potential return from lobbying is substantial.

GROUPS AND INTERESTS: THE DILEMMA OF REFORM

We would like to think that policies are products of legislators' concepts of the public interest. Yet in reality few programs and policies ever reach the public agenda without the vigorous support of important national interest groups. In the realm of economic policy, social policy, international trade policy, and even such seemingly interest-free areas as criminal justice policy, where, in fact, private prison corporations lobby for longer sentences for lawbreakers, interest-group activity is a central feature of American politics and public policy. But before we throw up our hands in dismay, it is worth remembering that the untidy process and sometimes undesirable outcomes of interest-group politics are virtually inherent aspects of democratic politics. At times, our larger interest in maintaining a vigorous and democratic politics may require us to tolerate such foolish things as tax subsidies for chicken poop.

When Madison wrote that "liberty is to faction what air is to fire,"[36] he meant that the organization and proliferation of interests was inevitable in a free society. To seek to place limits on the organization of interests, in Madison's view, would be to limit liberty itself. Madison believed that interests should be permitted to regulate themselves by competing with one another. As long as competition among

---

[35]"Academic Earmarks and the Returns to Lobbying," available online (hal-law.usc.edu/cleo/workshops/01-02/defigueiredo.pdf).

[36]*The Federalist Papers*, No. 10.

interests was free, open, and vigorous, there would be some balance of power among them, and none would be able to dominate the political or governmental process.

There is considerable competition among organized groups in the United States. Nevertheless, interest-group politics is not as free of bias as Madisonian theory might suggest. Although the weak and poor do occasionally become organized to assert their rights, interest-group politics is generally a form of political competition in which the wealthy and powerful are best able to engage.

Moreover, although groups sometimes organize to promote broad public concerns, interest groups more often represent relatively narrow, selfish interests. Small, self-interested groups can be organized much more easily than large and more diffuse collectives. For one thing, the members of a relatively small group—say, bankers or hunting enthusiasts—are usually able to recognize their shared interests and the need to pursue them in the political arena. Members of large and more diffuse groups—say, consumers or potential victims of firearms— often find it difficult to recognize their shared interests or the need to engage in collective action to achieve them.[37] This is why causes presented as public interests by their proponents often turn out, upon examination, to be private interests wrapped in a public mantle.

Thus we have a dilemma to which there is no ideal answer. To regulate interest-group politics is, as Madison warned, to limit freedom and to expand governmental power. Not to regulate interest-group politics, on the other hand, may be to ignore justice. Those who believe that there are simple solutions to the issues of political life would do well to ponder this problem.

---

[37]Mancur Olson Jr., *The Logic of Collective Action: Public Goods and the Theory of Groups* (Cambridge, MA: Harvard University Press, 1971).

SUMMARY

Efforts by organized groups to influence government and policy are becoming an increasingly important part of American politics. Such interest groups use a number of strategies to gain power.

Lobbying is the attempt to influence the policy process through persuasion of government officials. Lobbyists—individuals who receive some form of compensation for lobbying—are required to register with the House and Senate. In spite of an undeserved reputation for corruption, lobbyists serve a useful function, providing members of Congress and other government officials with a vital flow of information.

Access is participation in government. Most groups build up access over time through great effort. They work years to get their members into positions of influence on congressional committees.

Litigation sometimes serves interest groups when other strategies fail. Groups may bring suit on their own behalf, finance suits brought by individuals, or file *amicus curiae* briefs.

Going public is an effort to mobilize the widest and most favorable climate of opinion. Advertising is a common technique in this strategy. Others are boycotts, strikes, rallies, and marches.

Groups engage in electoral politics either by embracing one of the major parties, usually through financial support, or through a nonpartisan strategy. Interest groups' campaign contributions now seem to be flowing into the coffers of candidates at a faster rate than ever before.

The group basis of politics, present since the founding, is both a curse and a blessing. In overcoming the hurdles of collective action, groups are an important means by which Americans participate in the political process and influence its outcomes. But participation in group life does not draw representatively from the population. So while it increases citizen involvement, influence is not evenly distributed. Collective action thus remains a dilemma.

PRINCIPLES OF POLITICS IN REVIEW

Rationality Principle	Collective-Action Principle	Institution Principle	Policy Principle	History Principle
In a group setting, rational individuals have an incentive to free-ride.	The prisoners' dilemma, an example of a collective-action problem, explains why cooperation in groups can be difficult to achieve.	Groups can turn to the courts if they are not successful in the legislative and executive branches.	Public policy can reveal the impact of lobbying.	The explosion of interest-group activity has its origins in the expansion of the role of government, especially since the 1960s.
Organizing collective action can provide private benefits to a political entrepreneur.	Selective benefits are one solution to the collective-action problem.			
	Lobbying and cultivating access require coordination across the legislative and executive branches.			
	One means groups use to overcome collective-action problems is to mobilize public opinion in their support.			

FOR FURTHER READING

Cigler, Allan J., and Burdett A. Loomis, eds. *Interest Group Politics*. 6th ed. Washington, DC: Congressional Quarterly Press, 2002.

Clawson, Dan, Alan Neustadtl, and Denise Scott. *Money Talks: Corporate PACs and Political Influence*. New York: Basic Books, 1992.

Hansen, John Mark. *Gaining Access: Congress and the Farm Lobby, 1919–1981*. Chicago: University of Chicago Press, 1991.

Heinz, John P., et al. *The Hollow Core: Private Interests in National Policy Making*. Cambridge, MA: Harvard University Press, 1993.

Lowi, Theodore J. *The End of Liberalism: The Second Republic of the United States*. 2nd ed. New York: Norton, 1979.

Moe, Terry M. *The Organization of Interests: Incentives and the Internal Dynamics of Political Interest Groups*. Chicago: University of Chicago Press, 1980.

Olson, Mancur, Jr. *The Logic of Collective Action: Public Goods and the Theory of Groups*. Cambridge, MA: Harvard University Press, 1965, 1971.

Petracca, Mark P., ed. *The Politics of Interests: Interest Groups Transformed*. Boulder, CO: Westview, 1992.

Salisbury, Robert H. *Interests and Institutions: Substance and Structure in American Politics*. Pittsburgh: University of Pittsburgh Press, 1992.

Schlozman, Kay Lehman, and John T. Tierney. *Organized Interests and American Democracy*. New York: Harper & Row, 1986.

Truman, David B. *The Governmental Process: Political Interests and Public Opinion*. New York: Knopf, 1951.

Vogel, David. *Fluctuating Fortunes: The Political Power of Business in America*. New York: Basic Books, 1989.

Wright, John R. *Interest Groups and Congress: Lobbying, Contributions, and Influence*. Boston: Allyn & Bacon, 1996.

Flush with Victory, Grass-Roots Crusader Against Same-Sex Marriage Thinks Big

By JAMES DAO

The warning call came in December 1995. "Do you folks on the mainland know what is going on here?" a friend from Hawaii asked Phil Burress, an anti-pornography crusader from the suburbs of Cincinnati.

Mr. Burress confessed that he did not. "They're going to legalize gay marriage here, and it's coming your way," the friend said, referring to a case before the Hawaii Supreme Court dealing with the right of same-sex couples to marry.

Mr. Burress, a self-described former pornography addict, had spent much of the 1990's fighting strip clubs and X-rated bookstores. But here was something he saw as a potentially greater threat to his fundamentalist Christian beliefs and traditional family values: something he called the "gay agenda." . . .

And so Mr. Burress became a Paul Revere for the movement against same-sex marriage. . . . By January 1996, he had helped organize a meeting of Christian conservatives where a program to combat

same-sex marriage was devised. By that fall, they had persuaded Congress and President Bill Clinton to enact legislation defining marriage as between a man and a woman. Within four years, more than 30 state legislatures had followed suit. And on Election Day this month, voters in 11 states, including Ohio, overwhelmingly passed constitutional amendments banning same-sex marriage.

Mr. Burress's organization gathered 575,000 signatures to put the Ohio measure on the ballot in fewer than 90 days, then helped turn out thousands of conservative voters on Election Day. Their support is widely viewed as having been crucial to President Bush's narrow victory in that swing state. . . .

Just days after their thundering victories in the fall elections, Mr. Burress and other Christian conservative leaders met in Washington to discuss next year's constitutional amendment battles, which will focus on about 10 states, including Arizona, Florida and Kansas. They hope

New York Times, 26 November 2004, p. A28.

those fights will be the prelude to their real goal: amending the United States Constitution to prohibit same-sex marriage, which could take years.

Beyond that, Mr. Burress plans to take his grass-roots movement in Ohio to a new level, using a computer database of 1.5 million voters to build a network of Christian conservative officials, candidates and political advocates. . . .

"I'm building an army," Mr. Burress said. "We can't just let people go back to the pews and go to sleep."

For someone who can sound so combative, Mr. Burress comes across as anything but. Tall, with thinning gray hair, he exudes a folksy, earnest charm. But he also has an inner toughness developed from years as a union negotiator for truck drivers, and he is clearly willing to play political hardball. . . .

His opponents praise Mr. Burress for shaping issues in ways that are clear and compelling for the average voter. But they also say he distorts those issues, and they say he is closed-minded and intolerant of dissenting views, not to mention alternative ways of life.

"He is pretty frightening, because he and other spokesmen for the campaign believe that if you don't subscribe to their view, there is something morally wrong with you," said Alan Melamed, who managed the Ohio campaign against the constitutional amendment.

Mr. Burress disagrees with such descriptions. "I don't have a homophobic bone in my body," he said. "What I'm concerned about is having these things forced on our culture."

For anyone who assumes Mr. Burress's political plans will be a boon to all Republicans, Mr. Burress says think again.

Though he strongly supported Mr. Bush's re-election, Mr. Burress says he is furious that powerful Republicans like Governor Taft, Attorney General Jim Petro and Senators George V. Voinovich and Mike DeWine opposed Ohio's

ESSENCE OF THE STORY

- Ohioan Phil Burress, a fundamentalist Christian, has created a very successful grassroots political movement against gay marriage. His group currently lists more than 1.5 million members.

- Burress's group is credited with convincing thirty legislatures to enact laws defining marriage as between a man and a woman and, in the 2004 election, helping to pass constitutional amendments in eleven states.

POLITICAL ANALYSIS

- Gay marriage has become a lightning rod for Christian conservatives, perhaps the most powerful force for group mobilization since *Roe v. Wade*.

- The widespread adoption of rules allowing referendum and initiatives has stimulated the growth of citizen groups at the state and local levels; many of these groups focus on amending the Constitution or passing laws that bypass what they view as politically corrupt legislatures.

marriage amendment. (They asserted that the amendment would harm Ohio businesses by prohibiting employee benefits for domestic partners.)

Mr. Burress attacked those Republicans as "enablers" of what he calls the homosexual agenda, and he has vowed to run candidates against them and anyone else who opposes what he considers pro-family, antiabortion or anti-gay-rights policies.

"I'm not an R or a D," he said. "Both parties are driven by selfishness. They are run by people who are Republican or Democrat because it benefits them or their jobs. Our movement will be built on passion, on values, on fire-in-the-belly morals."

CHAPTER

13

The Media

In March 2003, American and British forces attacked Iraq to oust long-time Iraqi dictator Saddam Hussein. For the first time in history, reporters accompanied the troops into battle and provided real-time broadcasts from the battlefront twenty-four hours a day, seven days a week. As the U.S. military had hoped, these so-called embedded journalists quickly identified with the troops they accompanied and often used the pronoun *we* when discussing military operations.

While the embedded reporters generally provided favorable accounts of U.S. military activities, their colleagues behind the lines reporting from U.S. headquarters in Kuwait or commenting from New York and Washington were not always as kind. Before the war, there had been clear divisions within the media regarding the desirability of attacking Iraq. Generally speaking, the more liberal and Democratic press, led by the *New York Times* and several of the networks, had been sharply critical of President Bush's diplomatic efforts and his intention to oust Saddam Hussein. For the most part, the more conservative and Republican media, led by such publications as the *Washington Times* and the *Weekly Standard* and by Fox Network News, staunchly supported the president's policies. Some divisions on the war, to be sure, manifested themselves even within these two camps. For example, the normally liberal and pro-Democratic *Washington Post* and *New Republic* backed the war, whereas Pat Buchanan's *American Conservative* opposed American intervention in Iraq.

American forces had barely crossed the Iraqi border when journalists—particularly those who had been critical of President Bush's policies—began questioning the conduct of the American campaign. Some journalists and commentators, including several retired military officers employed by the networks, suggested that not enough troops had been committed to the battle, that supplies were inadequate, that Iraqi resistance had been underestimated, and that the war could easily become a Vietnam-style "quagmire." Defense Secretary Donald Rumsfeld and military briefers were subjected to withering questioning from journalists, who clearly doubted the veracity of the answers they were given. Some commentators, again resorting to Vietnam-era imagery, referred to a "credibility gap."

The gap became an ever-widening chasm when Iraqi resistance to the U.S. occupation began to produce a steady stream of American casualties and nightly newscasts featuring violence and mayhem in Iraq's cities and villages. The media also gave enormous coverage to charges that U.S. forces had abused Iraqi prisoners at the Abu Ghraib facility near Baghdad. Night after night, images of cowering Iraqi inmates mistreated by smiling American guards dominated the news. Even the apparently successful January 2005 Iraqi elections did not fully reverse the negative tone of the media coverage.

One feature of American journalism highlighted by these events is the tendency of the press to criticize programs, policies, and public officials. This tendency, sometimes called "adversarial journalism," has become commonplace in America. While this form of journalism sometimes irritates many Americans, it should probably be seen as a positive feature of American press coverage. A number of critics, to be sure, have suggested that the media have contributed to popular cynicism and the low levels of citizen participation that characterize American political processes. But before we begin

CHAPTER OUTLINE

The Media Industry and Government

- Types of Media
- Regulation of the Broadcast and Electronic Media
- Freedom of the Press
- Organization and Ownership of the Media
- Nationalization of the News

What Affects News Coverage?

- Journalists
- Politicians
- Consumers

What Are the Sources of Media Power in American Politics?

- Agenda Setting
- Priming
- Framing
- The Media and Elections
- The Rise of Adversarial Journalism

Media Power and Responsibility

PREVIEWING THE PRINCIPLES

Media coverage can be analyzed in terms of the interests of members of the media, politicians, and consumers. The conflicting goals of politicians and
members of the media help explain their adversarial
relationship. This relationship can be analyzed as a
Prisoner's Dilemma. Both politicians and members of
the media benefit from mutual cooperation but are
tempted to defect on occasion to secure even larger
gains. The historical relationship between government and media in the United States differs from that
in other democracies because of the freedom of the
press, guaranteed by the Constitution. This has led
the United States away from public ownership and
more toward regulation.

**Rationality
Principle**

Media coverage can
be analyzed in terms
of the interests of
members of the
media, politicians,
and consumers.

to think about means of compelling the media to adopt a more cheerful view of politicians and political issues, we should consider the possibility that media criti-cism is one of the major mechanism+s of political accountability in the Ameri-can political process. Without aggressive media coverage, would we have known of Bill Clinton's misdeeds or, for that matter, those of Richard Nixon? Without aggressive media coverage, would impor-tant questions be raised about the con-duct of American foreign and domestic policy? It is easy to criticize the media for their aggressive tactics, but would our democracy function effectively without the critical role of the press?

We should also evaluate the some-times adversarial relationship between the media and politicians in terms of the interests each has. Politicians want to sell their policy agenda to citizens and mobi-lize support for it, but they need the media to help communicate their message. Politicians would prefer to control the content of the news, but because the media have different goals and interests—market share, professional prestige, and, in some cases, political influence—news journalists and elected leaders often come into con-flict with another. Finally, we should take into account the interests of citizens—the consumers of the news—and how their demands for certain types and amounts of political news influence the adversarial nature of media politics.[1]

In this chapter, we examine the role and increasing power of the media in Amer-ican politics. First, we look at the media industry and government. Second, we dis-cuss the factors that help determine "what's news"—that is, the factors that shape media coverage of events and personalities. Third, we examine the scope of media power in politics. Finally, we address the question of responsibility: In a democracy, to whom are the media accountable for the use of their formidable power?

THE MEDIA INDUSTRY
AND GOVERNMENT

The freedom to speak one's mind is one of the most cherished of American politi-cal values—one that is jealously safeguarded by the media. As we mentioned

---

[1]John Zaller, "A Theory of Media Politics: How the Interests of Politicians, Journalists, and Citizens Shape the News" (unpublished manuscript).

above, a wide variety of newspapers, news magazines, broadcast media, and Web sites regularly present information that is at odds with the government's claims and write editorial opinions that are sharply critical of high-ranking officials. Yet even though thousands of media companies exist across the United States, surprisingly little variety appears in what is reported about national events and issues.

Types of Media

Americans obtain their news from three main sources: broadcast media (radio, television), print media (newspapers and magazines), and, increasingly, the Internet. Each of these sources has distinctive characteristics. Television news reaches more Americans than any other single news source. Tens of millions of individuals watch national and local news programs every day. Television news, however, covers relatively few topics and provides little depth of coverage. Television news is more like a series of newspaper headlines connected to pictures. It serves the extremely important function of alerting viewers to issues and events but provides little else.

The twenty-four-hour news stations like Cable News Network (CNN) offer more detail and commentary than the networks' half-hour evening news shows. During the 2003 Iraq war, CNN, Fox, and MSNBC provided twenty-four-hour-a-day coverage of the war, including on-the-scene reports from embedded reporters, expert commentary, and interviews with government officials. In this instance, these networks' depth of coverage rivaled that of the print media. Normally, however, CNN and the others offer more headlines than analysis, especially during their prime-time broadcasts. In recent years cable has been growing in importance as a news source (Table 13.1).

Politicians generally view the local broadcast news as a friendlier venue than the national news. National reporters are often inclined to criticize and question, whereas local reporters often accept the pronouncements of national leaders at face value. For this reason, presidents often introduce new proposals in a series of short visits to a number of cities—indeed, sometimes flying from airport stop to airport stop—in addition to or instead of making a national presentation. For example, in February 2002, President Bush introduced his idea for a new national volunteer corps during his State of the Union message and then made a number of local speeches around the country promoting the same theme. While national reporters questioned the president's plans, local news coverage was overwhelmingly positive.

Radio news is also essentially a headline service but without pictures. In the short time—usually five minutes per hour—that they devote to news, radio stations announce the day's major events without providing much detail. In major cities, all-news stations provide a bit more coverage of major stories, but for the most part these stations fill the day with repetition rather than detail. All-news stations like WTOP (Washington, D.C.) and WCBS (New York City) assume that most listeners are in their cars and that, as a result, the people in the audience change markedly throughout the day as listeners reach their destinations. Thus, rather than use their time to flesh out a given set of stories, they repeat the

TABLE 13.1

Trend in Regular News Consumption

	MAY 1993 (%)	APRIL 1996 (%)	APRIL 1998 (%)	APRIL 2000 (%)	APRIL 2002 (%)	DECEMBER 2004 (%)
Local TV news	77	65	64	56	57	51
Cable TV news	—	—	—	—	33	38
Nightly network news	60	42	38	30	32	36
Radio[*]	47[†]	44	49	43	41	NA
Newspaper[*]	58[†]	50	48	47	41	44
Online news[‡]	—	2[§]	13	23	25	20

[*]Based on use "yesterday."
[†]From February 1994.
[‡]At least three days per week.
[§]From June 1995.
SOURCES: Pew Research Center: 1993–2002; Gallop Poll: 2004.

ANALYZING THE EVIDENCE

The percentage of Americans who say they regularly watch the broadcast news or read newspapers has declined, whereas cable TV and the Internet have grown in importance. Does this matter? How might online news content differ from print and broadcast news? Will everyone see the same news online?

same stories each hour to present them to new listeners. In recent years, radio talk shows have become important sources of commentary and opinion. A number of conservative radio hosts such as Rush Limbaugh have huge audiences and have helped mobilize support for conservative political causes and candidates. Liberals have had less success in the world of talk radio and have complained that biased coverage helped bring about Democratic defeats in 2000 and 2002. In 2003, however, a group of wealthy liberal political activists led by Anita Drobny, a major Democratic party donor, announced plans for the creation of a liberal talk-radio network designed to combat conservative dominance of this important medium. One executive of the nascent network said, "There are so many right-wing talk shows, we think it created a hole in the market you could drive a truck through." Liberals hoped their network would be entertaining as well as informative, specializing in parody and political satire.[2]

The most important source of news is the old-fashioned newspaper. Newspapers remain critically important even though they are not the primary news sources for most Americans. The print media are important for two reasons. First, as we shall see later in this chapter, the broadcast media rely on leading

[2]CNN.com/Inside Politics, 18 February 2003.

newspapers such as the *New York Times* and the *Washington Post* to set their news agenda. The broadcast media engage in very little actual reporting; they primarily cover stories that have been "broken," or initially reported, by the print media. For example, sensational charges that President Bill Clinton had an affair with a White House intern were reported first by the *Washington Post* and *Newsweek* before being trumpeted around the world by the broadcast media. It is only a slight exaggeration to observe that if an event is not covered in the *New York Times*, it is not likely to appear on the *CBS Evening News*. One important exception, obviously, is the case of "breaking" news, which can be carried by the broadcast media as it unfolds or soon after, while the print media are forced to catch up later in the day. Recall the dramatic real-time videos of the collapsing Twin Towers seen by tens of millions of Americans. Second, the print media provide more detailed and complete information, offering a better context for analysis. Third, the print media are also important because they are the prime source of news for educated and influential individuals. The nation's economic, social, and political elites rely on the detailed coverage provided by the print media to inform and influence their views about important public matters. The print media may have a smaller audience than their cousins in broadcasting, but they have an audience that matters.

A relatively new source of news is the Internet. Every day, several million Americans, especially younger Americans, scan one of many news sites on the Internet for coverage of current events. For the most part, however, the Internet provides electronic versions of coverage offered by print sources. One great advantage of the Internet is that it allows frequent updating. It potentially can combine the depth of coverage of a newspaper with the timeliness of television and radio, and probably will become a major news source in the next decade. Already, most political candidates and many interest groups have created sites on the World Wide Web. Some of the more sensational aspects of President Clinton's relationship with Monica Lewinsky were first reported on a Web site maintained by Matt Drudge, an individual who specializes in posting sensational charges about public figures. Though many deny it, most reporters scan Drudge's site regularly, hoping to pick up a bit of salacious gossip. In recent years, many Americans have relied on Web sites such as CNN.com for up-to-the-minute election news during the campaign, the dramatic post-election battle in Florida, the terrorist attacks on New York City and Washington, D.C., and the war in Iraq.[3] Acknowledging the growing importance of the Internet as a political communications medium, the U.S. Supreme Court posted its decisions in the Florida election cases as soon as they were issued. Online magazines such as *Slate* have a growing audience and often feature the work of major political writers such as Christopher Hitchens and Ed Finn. Also, a number of political entrepreneurs have sought to organize online advocacy groups that would be able to raise money, make their positions known

[3]For discussions of the growing role of the Internet, see Leslie Wayne, "On Web, Voters Reinvent Grass-Roots Activism," *New York Times*, 21 May 2000, p. 22. See also James Fallows, "Internet Illusions," *New York Review of Books*, 16 November 2000, p. 28.

through e-mail and letter campaigns, and provide support for politicians who accepted their views. One of the most successful of these enterprises is MoveOn.org, founded by two liberal Silicon Valley entrepreneurs. MoveOn seeks to build electronic advocacy groups, allowing members to propose issues and strategies and acting on behalf of those that appear to have the highest level of member support.

In addition, hundreds of thousands of readers turn to more informal sources of Internet news and commentary called Web logs, or "blogs." Blogs are intermittently published online by thousands of individuals and generally feature personal opinion and commentary on national and world events. Some "bloggers," as the authors of blogs are called, occasionally achieve fame or, at least, notoriety among online readers for their political and social views. Many blogs invite readers to post comments and can become online discussion forums. In 2002 and 2003, the Howard Dean presidential campaign relied on hundreds of friendly bloggers to publicize the candidate's views and tout his virtues. Bloggers also helped Dean raise tens of millions of dollars in small contributions to finance his presidential bid. The Dean campaign's own blog posted 160,000 comments between June and November 2003. The Bush campaign also developed a blog but did not post comments from readers.[4] As online access becomes simpler and faster, the Internet could give Americans access to unprecedented quantities of information.

In recent years, much of the content of the news, especially local news, has shifted away from politics and public affairs toward "soft news"—that is, coverage focusing on celebrities, health tips, advice to consumers, and other topics more likely to provide entertainment than enlightenment. Even a good deal of political coverage is soft. For example, media coverage of the 2005 presidential inauguration devoted nearly as much attention to the dresses worn by President Bush's daughters as to the content of his address.

Softer even than soft news is a category of programming sometimes called "infotainment." This neologism refers to material that purports to combine information with entertainment. For example, in 2003 Arnold Schwarzenegger appeared on the *Tonight Show*, exchanged jokes and insults with host Jay Leno, and announced that he would be a candidate for governor of California. A currently popular infotainment program is *The Daily Show*, which presents comedic parodies of political figures and calls itself America's "most trusted name in fake news." While purveyors of the "true" news often sneer at *The Daily Show* and other infotainment programs, one recent survey suggests that *Daily Show* viewers do receive a surprising quantity of correct information along with their fake news (Table 13.2). Perhaps the *Daily Show* producers are right—we understand politicians better when we see how funny they are.

Regulation of the Broadcast and Electronic Media

In some countries, the government controls media content. In other countries, the government owns the broadcast media (e.g., the BBC in Britain), but it does

---

[4]Brian Faler, "Add 'Blog' to the Campaign Lexicon," *Washington Post*, 15 November 2003, p. A4.

TABLE 13.2

Six-Question Political Knowledge Test[*]	
TELEVISION PROGRAM	**ITEMS ANSWERED CORRECTLY**
No late-night comedy	2.62
Letterman	2.91
Leno	2.95
Daily Show with Jon Stewart	3.59

[*]Results are based on 19,013 telephone interviews conducted between July 15 and September 19, 2004. The phone numbers were selected randomly and results were weighed to adjust for geographical region, sex, race, age, and education.

SOURCE: Annenberg Public Policy Center of the University of Pennsylvania, NAES04.

not tell the media what to say. In the United States, the government neither owns nor controls the communications networks, but it does regulate the content and ownership of the broadcast media.

In the United States, the print media are essentially free from government interference. The broadcast media, on the other hand, are subject to federal regulation. American radio and television are regulated by the Federal Communications Commission (FCC), an independent regulatory agency established in 1934. Radio and TV stations must renew their FCC licenses every five years. Licensing provides a mechanism for allocating radio and TV frequencies to prevent broadcasts from interfering with and garbling one another. License renewals are almost always granted automatically by the FCC. Indeed, renewal requests are now filed by postcard.

Through regulations prohibiting obscenity, indecency, and profanity, the FCC has also sought to prohibit radio and television stations from airing explicit sexual and excretory references between 6 A.M. and 10 P.M. These are the hours when children are most likely to be in the audience. The FCC has enforced these rules haphazardly. Since 1990, nearly half the $5 million in fines levied by the agency have involved Howard Stern, a "shock jock" whose programs are built around sexually explicit material. In 2004, after another set of FCC fines, Stern's program was dropped by a major outlet, Clear Channel Communications. Stern charged that the Bush administration had singled him out for censure because of his known opposition to the president.

For more than sixty years, the FCC also sought to regulate and promote competition in the broadcast industry, but in 1996 Congress passed the Telecommunications Act, a broad effort to do away with most regulations in effect since

1934. The act loosened restrictions on media ownership and allowed for telephone companies, cable television providers, and broadcasters to compete with one another for telecommunication services. Following the passage of the act, several mergers between telephone and cable companies and between different segments of the entertainment media produced an even greater concentration of media ownership.

The Telecommunications Act of 1996 also included an attempt to regulate the content of material transmitted over the Internet. This law, known as the Communications Decency Act, made it illegal to make "indecent" sexual material on the Internet accessible to those under eighteen years of age. The act was immediately denounced by civil libertarians and brought to court as an infringement of free speech. The case reached the Supreme Court in 1997 and the act was ruled an unconstitutional infringement of the First Amendment's right to freedom of speech.

Although the government's ability to regulate the content of the electronic media on the Internet has been questioned, the federal government has used its licensing power to impose several regulations that can affect the political content of radio and TV broadcasts. The first of these is the *equal time rule,* under which broadcasters must provide candidates for the same political office equal opportunities to communicate their messages to the public. If, for example, a television station sells commercial time to a state's Republican gubernatorial candidate, it may not refuse to sell time to the Democratic candidate for the same position.

The second regulation affecting the content of broadcasts is the *right of rebuttal,* which requires that individuals must be given the opportunity to respond to personal attacks. In the 1969 case of *Red Lion Broadcasting Company v. FCC,* for example, the U.S. Supreme Court upheld the FCC's determination that a radio station was required to provide a liberal author with an opportunity to respond to an attack from a conservative commentator that the station had aired.[5]

For many years, a third important federal regulation was the *fairness doctrine.* Under this doctrine, broadcasters who aired programs on controversial issues were required to provide time for opposing views. In 1985, the FCC stopped enforcing the fairness doctrine on the grounds that there were so many radio and television stations—to say nothing of newspapers and news magazines—that in all likelihood many different viewpoints were already being presented without having to require each station to try to present all sides of an argument. Critics of this FCC decision charge that in many media markets the number of competing viewpoints is small. Nevertheless, a congressional effort to require the FCC to enforce the fairness doctrine was blocked by the Reagan administration in 1987.

Freedom of the Press

Unlike the broadcast media, the print media are not subject to federal regulation. Indeed, the great principle underlying the federal government's relationship with the press is the doctrine against *prior restraint.* Beginning with the land-

equal time rule
The requirement that broadcasters provide candidates for the same political office an equal opportunity to communicate their messages to the public.

right of rebuttal
A Federal Communications Commission regulation giving individuals the right to have the opportunity to respond to personal attacks made on a radio or TV broadcast.

fairness doctrine
A Federal Communications Commission requirement for broadcasters who air programs on controversial issues to provide time for opposing views.

[5]*Red Lion Broadcasting Company v. Federal Communications Commission,* 395 U.S. 367 (1969).

mark 1931 case of *Near v. Minnesota*, the U.S. Supreme Court has held that, except under the most extraordinary circumstances, the First Amendment of the U.S. Constitution prohibits government agencies from seeking to prevent newspapers or magazines from publishing whatever they wish.[6] Indeed, in the case of *New York Times v. United States*, the so-called *Pentagon Papers* case, the Supreme Court ruled that the government could not even block publication of secret Defense Department documents furnished to the *New York Times* by a liberal opponent of the Vietnam War who had obtained the documents illegally.[7] In a 1990 case, however, the Supreme Court upheld a lower-court order restraining CNN from broadcasting tapes of conversations between former Panamanian leader Manuel Noriega and his lawyer, supposedly recorded by the U.S. government. By a vote of 7 to 2, the Court held that CNN could be restrained from broadcasting the tapes until the trial court in the Noriega case had listened to the tapes and had decided whether their broadcast would violate Noriega's right to a fair trial. This case would seem to weaken the "no prior restraint" doctrine. But whether the same standard will apply to the print media has yet to be tested in the courts. In 1994, the Supreme Court ruled that cable television systems were entitled to essentially the same First Amendment protections as the print media.[8]

Even though newspapers may not be restrained from publishing whatever they want, they may be subject to sanctions after the fact. Historically, newspapers were subject to the law of libel, which provided that newspapers that printed false and malicious stories could be compelled to pay damages to those they defamed. In recent years, however, American courts have greatly narrowed the meaning of libel and made it extremely difficult, particularly for politicians or other public figures, to win a libel case against a newspaper. The most important case on this topic is the 1964 U.S. Supreme Court case of *New York Times Co. v. Sullivan*, in which the Court held that to be deemed libelous a story about a public official not only had to be untrue but had to result from "actual malice" or "reckless disregard" for the truth.[9] In other words, the newspaper had to deliberately print false and malicious material. In practice, it is nearly impossible to prove that a paper deliberately printed false and damaging information, and, as conservatives discovered in the 1980s, it is very difficult for a politician or other public figure to win a libel case. Libel suits against CBS News by General William Westmoreland and against *Time* magazine by General Ariel Sharon of Israel, both financed by conservative legal foundations who hoped to embarrass the media, were both defeated in court because they failed to show "actual malice." In the 1991 case of *Masson v. New Yorker Magazine, Inc.*, this tradition again affirmed the Court's opinion that fabricated quotations attributed to a public figure were libelous only if the fabricated account "materially changed" the

prior restraint
An effort by a governmental agency to block the publication of material it deems libelous or harmful in some other way; censorship. In the United States, the courts forbid prior restraint except under the most extraordinary circumstances.

---

[6]*Near v. Minnesota*, 283 U.S. 697 (1931).
[7]*New York Times v. United States*, 403 U.S. 731 (1971).
[8]*Cable News Network v. Noriega*, 111 S.Ct. 451 (1990); *Turner Broadcasting System, Inc. v. Federal Communications Commission*, 93-44 (1994).
[9]*New York Times Co. v. Sullivan*, 376 U.S. 254 (1964).

The Press and Politicians: Caught in a Prisoner's Dilemma

"You won't have Nixon to kick around anymore, because, gentlemen, this is my last press conference." —Richard Nixon, Los Angeles, California, November 7, 1962

Just six years after accusing the media of sabotaging his 1962 gubernatorial campaign, Richard Nixon won the 1968 presidential contest. Apparently media bias was not sufficient to curtail his political ambitions. Nixon realized, as do almost all politicians, that the press and political leadership are in an uneasy symbiosis: often adversarial, seldom mutually supportive, but always locked into a set of complicated strategic interactions.

But what is the nature of this game? Is it a cooperative game, where the gains to the press, such as more viewers for their news programs, are also gains to the politician, such as a high-profile public appearance? If so, the press and the politicians ought to get along famously. Or is it a competitive game, where gains to the press in terms of market share or ratings may come at the cost of a politician's reputation or even lower confidence in government as a whole?[1] The truth is a little bit of both, and this is what makes the relationship between the press and politicians so complicated.

The press needs politicians—and the institutions that they lead—to provide a daily dose of newsworthy items. Classic portrayals of the press corps, such as that in Timothy Crouse's *The Boys on the Bus,* show how reliant reporters are on "official sources." Press spokespersons provide daily quotes; government press offices supply reporters with details; and anonymous "leaks" and "off the record" interviews help fill the daily byline.[2] By citing "official" sources, journalists can maintain the fiction that they are independent of the government, even while they rely heavily on the government for their long-term viability and profitability.[3]

Collective-Action Principle

The press will cooperate with politicians only if the cooperation results in some sort of gain.

Politicians need the press just as badly. Mass democracy is impossible, some argue, without a well-functioning and independent media. Almost all of our political information is "mediated" through one or another source, and the mass media is the most common source in advanced industrialized nations. At a more strategic level, competing political actors use the press to promote their policies to the public. Politicians float "trial balloons," attack rival policies, and try to muster public support. In the 1930s, President Roosevelt battled Republican opposition to his New Deal policies through a series of "fireside chats" that were broadcast on the radio. Fast-forward to President George W. Bush flying in a fighter jet, touching down on the *U.S.S. Abraham Lincoln,* and announcing that "major combat operations have ended" in Iraq. Within a few days of this May 1, 2003, event, Bush's landing was being criticized as a "stunt" by some of his political opponents. And just as the landing was "news," so was the criticism.

Institution Principle

In complex societies, a mass media is necessary so that the public and the government can communicate with one another.

In the language of the principles of politics, the press and the politicians are in a prisoner's dilemma. Both benefit from mutual cooperation. The politicians benefit from having their message conveyed to the public, and the press benefits from obtaining useful information.

Yet cooperation in a prisoner's dilemma is an unstable equilibrium: each party has an incentive to defect—and gain an extra advantage. Journalists show an overwhelming preference for "conflict," stories that present two sides of an issue.[4] The press may choose to use only part, or none, of what was provided by a politician. Or a journalist may seek out opposing voices in an attempt to provide "balance." After all, the interests of the media, as an institution, and the preferences of reporters, as political actors, are certainly not met by simply parroting official sources. Politicians also have an incentive to defect—that is, to not provide the full details of a story to the media "player." The politicians use the media to sell a particular story and manage public opinion, not necessarily to make sure the public is fully informed.

So when things backfire, they backfire badly, as in a 2005 scandal that captured Washington's attention: the "outing" of covert CIA agent Valerie Plame.

In the Plame affair, reporters for *Time* magazine and the *New York Times* and Robert Novak, a commentator for CNN, revealed the name of a CIA operative who was married to ex-diplomat Joseph Wilson—Wilson had been publicly questioning the rationale for the invasion of Iraq for more than a year.

What appears to have happened is that high-level administration officials, including chief presidential advisor Karl Rove, helped direct journalists to Plame by suggesting that a trip that Wilson took to Niger was a junket organized by his wife, who also happened to work for the CIA. At first, this seemed like just another inside-the-Beltway battle, albeit a somewhat mean-spirited one: journalists got their front-page story and administration officials got their pound of flesh.

However, revealing the identity of a CIA operative is illegal. Once a special prosecutor got on the case, both those who leaked the information from the White House and the journalists who used the information fell over themselves blaming each other.

Who ended up worse off? Perhaps none suffered as much as then–*New York Times* reporter Judith Miller. Ironically, Miller never actually wrote about Wilson or Plame, but her refusal to divulge her sources landed her in jail. (*Time* reporter Matthew Cooper, with the approval of his employer, testified before a grand jury.) Perhaps worse than jail time, however, was the damage to Miller's reputation. Miller was castigated on liberal blogs as an "apologist" for the administration and even criticized by her own former editor as a "risk taker" who sometimes willingly served as a conduit for administration propaganda regarding the war in Iraq.[5] Cooper testified in front of a grand jury, and the president appears unwilling to fire his close friend and advisor Karl Rove (nor is it clear that Rove broke any law). In round 1 of this prisoner's dilemma, it appears that only one player had no "get out of jail free" card, and that was Judith Miller.

Policy Principle

Political actors use the media to promote their own policy interests.

[1]David Niven, *Tilt: The Search for Media Bias* (Westport, CT: Greenwood Publishing, 2002). Patricia Moy and Michael Pfau, *With Malice Toward All: The Media and Public Confidence in Democratic Institutions* (Westport, CT: Greenwood Publishing, 2000).

[2]Crouse's *The Boys on the Bus* (New York: Random House, 1973) portrays the ways of the press during the Nixon administration. See also Timothy Cook, *Governing the News* (Chicago: University of Chicago Press, 1998), and Curtis Gans, *Deciding What's News* (New York: Vintage, 1980), for a discussion of how the media relies on government officials to help decide what is newsworthy.

[3]Robert McChesney, *Rich Media, Poor Democracy* (New York: The New Press, 1999).

[4]Cook, chs. 1 and 5.

[5]"Jailed Reporter Miller Described as Risk Taker," NPR, "Morning Edition," 3 August 2005.

meaning of what the person actually said.[10] For all intents and purposes, the print media can publish anything they want about a public figure.

Organization and Ownership of the Media

The United States boasts more than 1,000 television stations, approximately 1,800 daily newspapers, and more than 9,000 radio stations. Even though the number of TV and radio stations and daily newspapers reporting news in the United States is enormous, and local coverage varies greatly from place to place, the number of sources of national news is actually quite small—one wire service, four broadcast networks, public radio and TV, two elite newspapers, three news magazines, and a scattering of other sources such as the national correspondents of a few large local papers, and the small independent radio networks. Most of the national news that is published by local newspapers is provided by the one wire service, the Associated Press. More than 500 of the nation's TV stations are affiliated with one of the four networks and carry its evening news reports. Dozens of others carry Public Broadcasting System (PBS) news. Several hundred local radio stations also carry network news or National Public Radio (NPR) news broadcasts. At the same time, although there are only three truly national newspapers, the *Wall Street Journal*, the *Christian Science Monitor*, and *USA Today*, two other papers, the *New York Times* and the *Washington Post*, are read by political leaders and other influential Americans throughout the nation. Such is the influence of these two "elite" newspapers that their news coverage sets the standard for virtually all other news outlets. Stories carried in the *New York Times* or the *Washington Post* influence the content of many other papers as well as the network news. Note how often this text, like most others, relies on *New York Times* and *Washington Post* stories as sources for contemporary events.

National news is also carried to millions of Americans by the three major news magazines—*Time, Newsweek*, and *U.S. News & World Report*. Beginning in the late 1980s, CNN became another major news source. The importance of CNN increased dramatically after its spectacular coverage of the Persian Gulf War. At one point, CNN was able to provide live coverage of American bombing raids on Baghdad after the major networks' correspondents had been forced to flee to bomb shelters. By 2003, Fox had displaced CNN as the nation's primary cable news source. The rise of Fox had important political implications because its coverage and commentators are considerably more conservative than CNN's. Even the availability of new electronic media on the Internet has failed to expand the number of news sources. Most national news available on the World Wide Web, for example, consists of electronic versions of the conventional print or broadcast media.

The trend toward homogenization of national news has been hastened by dramatic changes in media ownership, which became possible in part due to the

---

[10]*Masson v. New Yorker Magazine, Inc.*, 111 S.Ct. 2419 (1991).

relaxation of government regulations since the 1980s. The enactment of the 1996 Telecommunications Act opened the way for further consolidation in the media industry, and a wave of mergers and consolidations has further reduced the field of independent media across the country. Since that time, among the major news networks, ABC was bought by the Walt Disney Company; CBS was bought by Westinghouse Electric and later merged with Viacom, the owner of MTV and Paramount Studios; and CNN was bought by Time Warner. NBC has been owned by General Electric since 1986. Australian press baron Rupert Murdoch owns the Fox network plus a host of radio, television, and newspaper properties around the world. A small number of giant corporations now controls a wide swath of media holdings, including television networks, movie studios, record companies, cable channels and local cable providers, book publishers, magazines, and newspapers. These developments have prompted questions about whether enough competition exists among the media to produce a diverse set of views on political and corporate matters or whether the United States has become the prisoner of media monopolies (Figure 13.1 and Table 13.3).[11]

In June 2003, the FCC announced a set of new rules that seemed to pave the way to even more concentration in the media industry. The FCC mandated that the major networks could own TV stations that collectively reached 45 percent of all viewers, up from 35 percent under the old rule. The new FCC rule also permits a single company to own the leading newspaper as well as multiple television and radio outlets in a single market. In the largest cities, this could include a newspaper, three television stations, and as many as eight radio stations.[12] Major media companies, which had long lobbied for the right to expand their activities, welcomed the new FCC rule. Critics, however, expressed grave concern that the decision would result in a narrowing of the range of views and issues presented to the general public. Congressional opponents of the FCC's action sought to overturn the rule but were stymied by opposition from the House Republican leadership as well as a threatened presidential veto. However, a federal appeals court placed the new regulation on hold; and in January 2005, the Bush administration decided not to appeal the case to Supreme Court. The FCC may opt to attempt to write new rules or drop the effort altogether.

Nationalization of the News

In general, the national news media cover more or less the same sets of events, present similar information, and emphasize similar issues and problems. Indeed, the national news services watch one another carefully. It is unlikely that a major story carried by one will not soon find its way into the pages or programming of the others. As a result, we have developed in the United States a centralized national news through which a relatively similar picture of events, issues, and problems is

[11]For a criticism of the increasing consolidation of the media, see the essays in Patricia Aufderheide et al., *Conglomerates and the Media* (New York: New Press, 1997).

[12]David Lieberman, "How Will FCC's Action Affect Consumers?" *USA Today*, 4 June 2003, p. 48.

FIGURE 13.1

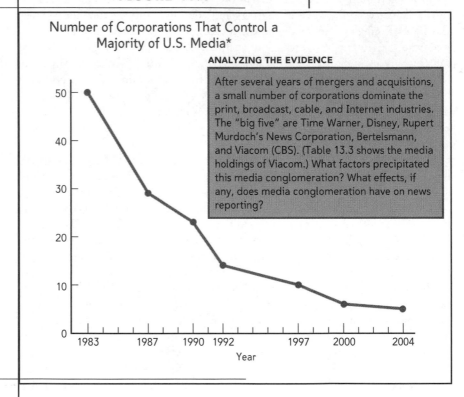

Number of Corporations That Control a
Majority of U.S. Media*

ANALYZING THE EVIDENCE

After several years of mergers and acquisitions, a small number of corporations dominate the print, broadcast, cable, and Internet industries. The "big five" are Time Warner, Disney, Rupert Murdoch's News Corporation, Bertelsmann, and Viacom (CBS). (Table 13.3 shows the media holdings of Viacom.) What factors precipitated this media conglomeration? What effects, if any, does media conglomeration have on news reporting?

*Newspapers, magazines, TV and radio stations, books, music, movies, videos, wire services, and photo agencies.

SOURCE: Media Reform Information Center.

presented to the entire nation.[13] The nationalization of the news was accelerated by the development of radio networks in the 1920s and 1930s, and was brought to a peak by the creation of the television networks after the 1950s. This nationalization of news content has very important consequences for American politics.

Nationalization of the news has contributed greatly to the nationalization of politics and of political perspectives in the United States. Before the development of the national media and the nationalization of news coverage, the news traveled very slowly. Every region and city saw national issues and problems mainly through its own local lens. Concerns and perspectives varied greatly from

[13]See Leo Bogart, "Newspapers in Transition," *Wilson Quarterly*, special issue (1982); and Richard Harwood, "The Golden Age of Press Diversity," *Washington Post*, 22 July 1994, p. A23.

TABLE 13.3

Who Owns What? VIACOM

TELEVISION	CBS STATIONS	UPN STATIONS	OTHER LOCAL STATIONS
	17 Stations	18 Stations	5 Stations

CABLE	STATIONS		TELEVISION PRODUCTION AND DISTRIBUTION
	• MTV	• Spike TV	• Spelling Television
	• MTV2	• CMT	• Big Ticket Television
	• Nickelodeon	• Comedy Central	• King World Productions
	• BET	• Showtime	
	• Nick at Nite	• The Movie Channel	
	• TV Land	• Flix	
	• NOGGIN	• Sundance Channel	
	• VH1		

RADIO	INFINITY BROADCASTING				THE VIACOM OUTDOOR GROUP
	NORTHEAST	SOUTH	MIDWEST	WEST	
	42 Stations	42 Stations	34 Stations	58 Stations	2 Stations

FILM

• Paramount Pictures
• Paramount Home Entertainment

PUBLISHING	SIMON & SCHUSTER	
	ADULT PUBLISHING GROUP	CHILDREN'S PUBLISHING
	• Atria Books	• Aladdin Paperbacks
	• Kaplan	• Atheneum Books for Young Readers
	• Pocket Books	• Little Simon
	• Scribner	• Margaret K. McElderry Books
	• Simon & Schuster	• Simon & Schuster Books for Young Readers
	• The Free Press	• Simon Pulse
	• The Touchstone	• Simon Spotlight
	• Fireside Group	
	Simon & Schuster New Media	
	Simon & Schuster Online	
	Simon & Schuster UK	
	Simon & Schuster Australia	
	MTV Books	

SOURCE: *Columbia Journalism Review* at Columbia University's Graduate School of Journalism.

region to region, city to city, and village to village. Today, in large measure as a result of the nationalization of the media, residents of all parts of the country share similar ideas and perspectives.[14] They may not agree on everything, but they at least see the world in similar ways.

WHAT AFFECTS NEWS COVERAGE?

Because of the important role the media can play in national politics, it is essential to understand the factors that affect media coverage.[15] What accounts for the media's agenda of issues and topics? What explains the character of coverage—why does a politician receive good or bad press? What factors determine the interpretation or "spin" that a particular story will receive? Although a host of minor factors play a role, there are three major factors: (1) journalists or producers of the news; (2) politicians, who are usually the sources or topics of the news; and (3) citizens, the audience for the news.

Journalists

First, media content and news coverage are inevitably affected by the views, ideals, and interests of the individuals who seek out, write, and produce news and other stories. At one time, newspaper publishers exercised a great deal of influence over their papers' news content. Publishers such as William Randolph Hearst and Joseph Pulitzer became political powers through their manipulation of news coverage. Hearst, for example, almost single-handedly pushed the United States into war with Spain in 1898 through his newspapers' relentless coverage of the alleged brutality employed by Spain in its efforts to suppress a rebellion in Cuba, then a Spanish colony. The sinking of the American battleship *Maine* in Havana Harbor under mysterious circumstances gave Hearst the ammunition he needed to force a reluctant President McKinley to lead the nation into war. Today, few publishers have that kind of power. Most publishers are more concerned with the business end of the paper than its editorial content, although a few continue to impose their interests and tastes on the news.

 **Rationality Principle**

The goals and incentives of journalists—such as ratings, career success, and prestige—influence what is created and reported as news.

More important than publishers, for the most part, are the reporters. The goals and incentives of journalists are varied, but they often include considerations of ratings, career success and professional prestige, and political influence. For all of these reasons, journalists seek not only to *report* the news but also to *interpret* the news. Journalists' goals have a good deal of influence on what is created and reported as news.

[14]See Benjamin Ginsberg, *The Captive Public: How Mass Opinion Promotes State Power* (New York: Basic Books, 1986).

[15]See the discussions in Michael Parenti, *Inventing Reality: The Politics of the Mass Media* (New York: St. Martin's Press, 1986); Herbert Gans, *Deciding What's News: A Study of CBS Evening News, NBC Nightly News, Newsweek, and Time* (New York: Vintage, 1980); and W. Lance Bennett, *News: The Politics of Illusion*, 5th ed. (New York: Longman, 2002).

Those who cover the news for the national media generally have a lot of discretion or freedom to interpret stories and, as a result, have an opportunity to interject their own views and ideals into news stories. For example, the personal friendship and respect that some reporters felt for Franklin Roosevelt and John F. Kennedy helped generate more favorable news coverage for these presidents. On the other hand, the dislike and distrust felt by many reporters for Richard Nixon was also communicated to the public. In the case of Ronald Reagan, the disdain that many journalists felt for the president was communicated in stories suggesting that he was often asleep or inattentive when important decisions were made.

Conservatives have long charged that the liberal biases of reporters and journalists result in distorted news coverage. A 1996 survey of Washington newspaper bureau chiefs and correspondents seems to support this charge. The study, conducted by the Roper Center and the Freedom Forum, a conservative foundation, found that 61 percent of the bureau chiefs and correspondents polled called themselves "liberal" or "liberal to moderate." Only 9 percent called themselves "conservative" or "conservative to moderate." In a similar vein, 89 percent said that they had voted for Bill Clinton in 1992, while only 7 percent indicated that they had voted for George Bush. Approximately 50 percent said they were Democrats, and only 4 percent claimed to be Republicans.[16] Another survey has indicated that even among the radio talk-show hosts lambasted by President Clinton, Democrats outnumber Republicans by a wide margin: of 112 hosts surveyed, 39 percent had voted for Clinton in 1992, and only 23 percent had supported George Bush.[17] Generally speaking, reporters for major national news outlets tend to be more liberal than their local counterparts who often profess moderate or even conservative views.

One major instance of what appeared to be ideologically or personally biased reporting on the part of a major network figure occurred just before the 2004 presidential election. Dan Rather, longtime anchor of the CBS Evening News, aired a story on another CBS program charging that President Bush had shirked his duties years earlier while serving in the Texas Air National Guard and then participated in a coverup of the facts. Because Bush's opponent, John Kerry, was a decorated war hero, the story was potentially very damaging to the president. Soon after the program aired, however, it became apparent that Rather and his producers had made little or no effort to check their facts or sources. They apparently had been so anxious to damage Bush's standing that they had rushed to present as fact a series of undocumented rumors and accusations. CBS launched an internal investigation and terminated several executives. Rather announced his retirement.

The linkage between journalists and liberal ideas is by no means absolute. While the most important national newspapers, such as the New York Times and

---

[16]Rowan Scarborough, "Leftist Press? Reporters Working in Washington Acknowledge Liberal Leanings in Poll," Washington Times, 18 April 1996, p. 1.

[17]Michael Kinsley, "Bias and Baloney," Washington Post, 26 November 1992, p. A29; and John H. Fund, "Why Clinton Shouldn't Be Steamed at Talk Radio," Wall Street Journal, 7 July 1994, p. A12.

Washington Post, are liberal and Democratic in their orientation, many smaller papers support the Republicans. Indeed, in recent years, more newspapers have endorsed GOP presidential candidates than have supported their Democratic rivals, though in 2004 Kerry received slightly more endorsements (51 percent) than Bush (Figure 13.2). Predictably, Kerry was endorsed by 60 percent of the papers with circulations above 250,000, whereas Bush won support of 54 percent of the papers with circulations between 15,000 and 30,000. One notable exception was the weekly paper serving President Bush's hometown of Crawford, Texas, which endorsed John Kerry in 2004.

In addition, most reporters attempt to maintain some measure of balance or objectivity, whatever their personal views. Moreover, over the past several years a conservative media complex has emerged in opposition to the liberal media. This complex includes two major newspapers, the *Wall Street Journal* and the *Washington Times*, several magazines such as the *American Spectator* and the *Weekly Standard*, and a host of conservative radio and television talk programs. Also important is media baron Rupert Murdoch, creator of Fox Network News and the financial force behind the *Weekly Standard*. The emergence of this conservative media complex has meant that liberal policies and politicians are virtually certain to come under attack even when the "liberal media" are sympathetic to them.

selection bias (in the media) The predisposition to choose particular types of stories.

Probably more important than ideological bias is a ***selection bias (in the media)*** in favor of news that the media view as having a great deal of audience appeal because of its dramatic or entertainment value. In practice, this bias often results in news coverage that focuses on crimes and scandals, especially those involving prominent individuals, despite the fact that the public obviously looks to the media for information about important political debates.[18] For example, even though most journalists may be Democrats, this partisan predisposition did not prevent an enormous media frenzy in January 1998 when reports surfaced that President Clinton may have had an affair with Lewinsky. Once a hint of blood appeared in the water, partisanship and ideology were swept away by the piranha-like instincts often manifested by journalists.

Politicians

Rationality Principle

News coverage is influenced by the interests of politicians.

News coverage is also influenced by politicians and public officials, who are subjects of the news and whose interests and activities are actual or potential news topics. Politicians want to be seen by the public as trustworthy, energetic, caring, and generally able to discharge the public duties with which they have been or hope to be entrusted. Accordingly, most politicians will seize or, if necessary, create opportunities for media coverage they deem likely to contribute to the public image they wish to fashion. Presidents, for example, know that their speeches on vitally important topics will be televised throughout the nation. This provides

[18]See Joseph N. Cappella and Kathleen Hall Jamieson, *Spiral of Cynicism: The Press and the Public Good* (New York: Oxford University Press, 1997).

FIGURE 13.2

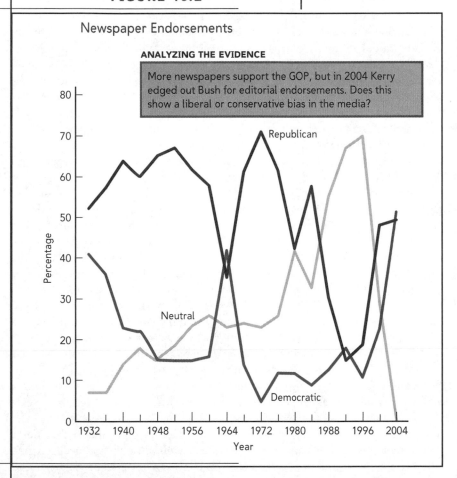

Newspaper Endorsements

ANALYZING THE EVIDENCE

More newspapers support the GOP, but in 2004 Kerry edged out Bush for editorial endorsements. Does this show a liberal or conservative bias in the media?

SOURCE: Harold Stanley and Richard Niemi, *Vital Statistics of American Politics, 2001–2002* (Washington, D.C.: Congressional Quarterly Press, 2001), pp. 194–95; 2004 data by Jacobian.org, compiled from *Editor and Publisher*.

them with an opportunity to use the media to demonstrate that they possess strong leadership qualities and fully understand the problems and issues facing the nation. President Bush's speech in the wake of the September 11 terrorist attacks, for example, was designed to reassure Americans and demonstrate that he was firmly in command. In a similar vein, presidents and other politicians know that the media will give considerable coverage to floods, hurricanes, earthquakes, and other natural disasters. Thus, as a general rule, politicians are drawn to natural disasters like bees to honey. Indeed, the televised official inspection tour is a staple of American politics. This tour consists of the president, governor, senator, or other politician, trailed by staff and reporters: first flying over the scene of the disaster, then landing—at a safe location—to offer condolences to survivors, and finally pledging to devote the resources of the government to make things right. Politicians hope that viewers will see them as compassionate problem solvers, certainly worthy of the public's trust. Politicians use many other techniques to develop favorable media images. President John F. Kennedy sought to develop strong relationships with influential journalists. Bill Clinton thought that appearances on soft news and entertainment programs allowed him to connect with ordinary Americans and show them that their president was not aloof or out of touch. Thus Clinton famously tooted his saxophone on a late-night entertainment program and discussed his choice of underwear with teenage reporters on MTV.

But, of course, while politicians try to use the media for their purposes, reporters often have their own agendas. Often enough, hostile or merely determined journalists will break through the smoke screens thrown up by the politicians and report annoying truths. Thus, for example, despite the Bush administration's best efforts to manage the news from Iraq, throughout 2004 journalists were filing accounts of Iraqi resistance, abuse of Iraqi prisoners, and other unpleasant facts the administration might have preferred to keep off the table.

Collective-Action Principle

The relationship between media members and politicians is a Prisoner's Dilemma. Each participant benefits from mutual cooperation but finds himself or herself tempted to defect on occasion to secure even larger gains.

More generally, the relationship between a politician and a member of the media may be characterized as a Prisoner's Dilemma (see Chapter 12). The two can cooperate—the politician leaking juicy news to the reporter in exchange for the reporter casting the politician in a favorable light. But each may be tempted to defect. A reporter may decide to turn against his trusted political friend because the opportunity is just "too juicy." The politician may decide to leak a newsworthy tidbit to a competing journalist in exchange for favorable consideration from him or her as a form of insurance. Both the (first) reporter and the politician are worse off as a result of defection; but they fear that if they don't defect, then they will be taken advantage of. So, while "sweetheart" arrangements between the media and the political class certainly do exist, the participants find themselves constantly tempted to defect. The best journalists and the shrewdest politicians resist these temptations and are willing to forgo the immediate windfall resulting from defection in exchange for a long-term relationship of cooperation. But some journalists are neither long-run oriented nor particularly scrupulous. Nor are some politicians.

These issues were highlighted by the 2005 Valerie Plame affair. Plame was a CIA analyst married to former ambassador Joseph Wilson, a vocal critic of the Bush administration's Iraq policy. In 2005, a federal grand jury convened by Special Prosecutor Patrick Fitzgerald investigated charges that Plame's identity had been revealed to reporters—in violation of federal law protecting covert operatives—by one or more high-ranking administration officials seeking to discredit her husband. Suspicions centered on presidential adviser Karl Rove and on Vice President Cheney's chief of staff, Lewis "Scooter" Libby, who was indicted for lying in his testimony before the grand jury. As the investigation proceeded, it became clear that a number of prominent Washington journalists, including Judith Miller of the *New York Times* and Bob Woodward of the *Washington Post*, regularly exchanged sensitive information with important politicians and public officials. Indeed, while some journalists learned of Plame's covert activities from government officials, some officials claimed to have learned the secret from the journalists. The journalists were as furious as the politicians when Fitzgerald's inquiries revealed these relationships. Bob Woodward called the special prosecutor a "junkyard dog" and deemed his investigation "disgraceful," before admitting that he, himself, had been told of Plame's identity.[19]

Some politicians become extremely adept image makers—or at least skilled at hiring publicists who are skillful image makers. Indeed, press releases drafted by skillful publicists often become the basis for reporters' stories. A substantial percentage of the news stories published every day were initially drafted by publicists and later rewritten only slightly, if at all, by busy reporters and editors. Furthermore, political candidates often endeavor to tailor their images for specific audiences. For example, to cultivate a favorable image among younger voters during his 1992 campaign, Bill Clinton made several appearances on MTV, and he continued to grant interviews to MTV after his election. His MTV forays came to an end, however, when he was severely criticized for discussing his preferred type of underwear with members of an MTV audience.

During his presidency, Bill Clinton was able to survive repeated revelations of sexual improprieties, financial irregularities, lying to the public, and illegal campaign fund-raising activities. Clinton and his advisers crafted what the *Washington Post* called a "toolkit" for dealing with potentially damaging media revelations. This toolkit included techniques such as chiding the press, browbeating reporters, referring inquiries quickly to lawyers who would not comment, and acting quickly to change the agenda. These techniques helped Clinton maintain a favorable public image despite the Monica Lewinsky scandal and even the humiliation of a formal impeachment and trial.

President George W. Bush's administration has developed a highly sophisticated communications office, initially under the leadership of former presidential aide Karen Hughes. Hughes, who resigned in April 2002, and her staff endeavored to craft a new media message every few days to continually shape the nation's press coverage. For example, Bush's reference to nations supporting terrorist groups as an "axis of evil" in February 2002 was designed to give the media a catch phrase that would dominate the headlines and provide **sound bites**—short, attention-grabbing summaries of a story—for the broadcast media for days. By the time the media tired of the "axis of evil," the White House hoped to have developed a new sound bite for the reporters.

During the Iraq War, the White House sent James Wilkinson, one of the heads of its communications office, to direct communications for military forces in the Persian Gulf region. Wilkinson helped shape a number of communications strategies for American forces. After the dramatic rescue of American POW Jessica

sound bites
Short snippets of information aimed at dramatizing a story rather than explaining its substantive meaning.

[19]Howard Kurtz, "Woodward Talks of Admission, Apology," *Washington Post*, 22 November 2005, p. A9.

Lynch, Wilkinson coined the slogan "America does not leave its heroes behind." This sound bite was repeated by the networks for days.

The Bush team also pays enormous attention to the visual elements of a story. For example, in summer 2002, the president delivered a speech at Mount Rushmore. His media advisers positioned the platform for television crews off to one side so that the cameras would show the president in profile, perfectly aligned with the statues of the four presidents carved into the mountain. In a similar vein, in May 2003 the president spoke in Indiana on his economic plan. Staffers asked people in the audience who might be seen on camera to remove their ties so that they would look like the ordinary individuals the president said would benefit from his tax cuts.[20]

In 2005, revelations surfaced of still another Bush administration media strategy. It appeared that the administration had hired several friendly journalists to promote its programs and initiatives in their stories and columns. Thus, for example, the Department of Education paid conservative African American pundit Armstrong Williams $240,000 to tout the president's No Child Left Behind initiative in his columns and television appearances. Williams never indicated that he was a paid pitchman but, instead, allowed readers and viewers to assume that he was merely presenting his own editorial commentary. Similarly, columnists Michael McManus and Maggie Gallagher were paid to write columns promoting the administration's views on gay marriage, again without indicating that their work was anything other than their own editorial commentary. It is not surprising that critics have charged the Bush administration with using taxpayer dollars to fund political propaganda. Cynics might say that many of the media techniques used by politicians are vulnerable to the same charge.

Individual politicians are not the only ones trying to influence news coverage. As we saw in Chapter 9, by using media consultants and "issues managers," many social, economic, and political groups vigorously promote their ideas and interests through speeches, articles, books, news releases, research reports, and other mechanisms designed to attract favorable media coverage. Typically, competing forces seek to present—and to persuade the media to present—their own interests as more general or "public" interests. In recent years, for example, liberals have been very successful in inducing the media to present their environmental, consumer, and political reform proposals as matters of the public interest. Indeed, the advocates of these goals are organized in "public interest" groups. Seldom do the national media ever question a public interest group's equation of its goals with the general interest of all.

The capacity of politicians and groups to influence the news is hardly unlimited. Media consultants and issues managers may shape the news for a time, but it is generally not difficult for the media to penetrate the smoke screens thrown up by the news sources if they have a reason to do so. Thus, for example, despite the administration's media management, by fall 2003 reporters in Iraq were fil-

[20]Elisabeth Bumiller, "Keepers of Bush Image Lift Stagecraft to New Heights," *New York Times*, 16 May 2003, p. 1.

ing numerous accounts of the resistance American occupation forces were encountering. Unfavorable media coverage placed President Bush under enormous pressure to modify his policies in Iraq, and in November 2003 the president intimated that he would speed up efforts to return control of Iraqi affairs to an interim local government. Indeed, media coverage is sometimes shaped by the third and most important factor influencing news content—the audience.

Consumers

The print and broadcast media are businesses that, in general, seek to show a profit. This means that, like any other business, they must cater to the preferences of consumers. This has very important consequences for the content and character of the news media.

Rationality Principle
Consumer preferences, such as those of the affluent or those of people who watch news for its entertainment value, influence news content.

Catering to the Upscale Audience In general, and especially in the political realm, the print and broadcast media and the publishing industry are not only responsive to the interests of consumers generally but are particularly responsive to the interests and views of the better educated and more affluent segments of the audience. The preferences of these audience segments have a profound effect on the content and orientation of the press, of radio and television programming, and of books, especially in the areas of news and public affairs.[21]

Although affluent consumers do watch television programs and read periodicals whose contents are designed simply to amuse or entertain, the one area that most directly appeals to the upscale audience is that of news and public affairs. The affluent—who are also typically well educated—are the core audience of news magazines, journals of opinion, books dealing with public affairs, serious newspapers like the *New York Times* and the *Washington Post*, and broadcast news and weekend and evening public-affairs programming. While other segments of the public also read newspapers and watch the television news, their level of interest in world events, national political issues, and the like is closely related to their level of education (Table 13.4). As a result, upscale Americans are overrepresented in the news and public-affairs audience. The concentration of these strata in the audience makes news, politics, and public affairs potentially very attractive topics to advertisers, publishers, radio broadcasters, and television executives.

Entire categories of events, issues, and phenomena of interest to lower-, middle-, and working-class Americans receive scant attention from the national print and broadcast media. For example, trade-union news and events are discussed only in the context of major strikes or revelations of corruption. No network or national periodical routinely covers labor organizations. Religious and church affairs receive little coverage (unless scandal is involved, as was the case in 2002

[21]See Tom Burnes, "The Organization of Public Opinion," in *Mass Communication and Society*, ed. James Curran et al. (Beverly Hills, CA: Sage, 1979), pp. 44–230. See also David L. Altheide, *Creating Reality: How TV News Distorts Events* (Beverly Hills, CA: Sage, 1976).

TABLE 13.4

Education and Attention to the News

Educated Americans
are far more
attentive to news
programming than
their less-well-
educated fellow
citizens. How does
this affect the type
of news reported?
Which issues are
more likely to
receive attention?
Which issues are
more likely to be
overlooked?

LEVEL OF EDUCATION	LEVEL OF ATTENTION TO HARD NEWS *		
	HIGH (%)	MEDIUM (%)	LOW (%)
College graduate	43	53	4
Some college	33	57	10
High school graduate	28	57	15
Less than high school	16	58	26

*High: follows international, national, local, and business news closely; low: does not follow the news.
SOURCE: Pew Research Center, June 2004.

and 2003 in many dioceses of the Roman Catholic Church). The activities of veterans', fraternal, ethnic, and patriotic organizations are also generally ignored.

The Media and Conflict   While the media respond most to the upscale audience, groups who cannot afford the services of media consultants and issues managers can publicize their views and interests through protest. Frequently, the media are accused of encouraging conflict and even violence as a result of the fact that the audience mostly watches news for the entertainment value that conflict can provide. Clearly, conflict can be an important vehicle for attracting the attention and interest of the media, and thus may provide an opportunity for media attention to groups otherwise lacking the financial or organizational resources to broadcast their views. But while conflict and protest can succeed in drawing media attention, these methods ultimately do not allow groups from the bottom of the social ladder to compete effectively in the media.

The chief problem with protest as a media technique is that, in general, the media on which the protesters depend have considerable discretion in reporting and interpreting the events they cover. For example, should the media focus on the conflict itself, rather than the issues or concerns created by the conflict? The answer to this question is typically determined by the media, not by the protesters. This means that media interpretation of protest activities is more a reflection of the views of the groups and forces to which the media are responsive—as we have seen, usually segments of the upper-middle class—than it is a function of the wishes of the protesters themselves. It is worth noting that civil rights protesters received their most favorable media coverage when a segment of the white upper-middle class saw blacks as potential political allies in the Democratic party.

Typically, upper-middle-class protesters—student demonstrators and the like—have little difficulty securing favorable publicity for themselves and their causes. Upper-middle-class protesters are often more skilled than their lower-class counterparts in the techniques of media manipulation. That is, they typically have a better sense—often as a result of formal courses on the subject—of how to package messages for media consumption. For example, it is important to know what time of day a protest should occur if it is to be carried on the evening news. Similarly, the setting, definition of the issues, character of the rhetoric used, and so on all help determine whether a protest will receive favorable media coverage, unfavorable coverage, or no coverage at all. Moreover, upper-middle-class protesters can often produce their own media coverage through "underground" newspapers, college papers, student radio and television stations, and, now, the Internet. The same resources and skills that generally allow upper-middle-class people to publicize their ideas are usually not left behind when segments of this class choose to engage in disruptive forms of political action. Note the media attention given antiwar protesters in 2003 even though polls indicated that such groups were a minor force in American politics.

WHAT ARE THE SOURCES OF MEDIA POWER IN AMERICAN POLITICS?

The content and character of news and public-affairs programming—what the media choose to present and how they present it—can have far-reaching political consequences. Media disclosures can greatly enhance—or fatally damage—the careers of public officials. Media coverage can rally support for—or intensify opposition to—national policies. The media can shape and modify, if not fully form, public perceptions of events, issues, and institutions.

In recent American political history, the media have played a central role in at least three major events. First, the media were critically important factors in the civil rights movement of the 1950s and 1960s. Television photos showing peaceful civil rights marchers attacked by club-swinging police helped generate sympathy among northern whites for the civil rights struggle and greatly increased the pressure on Congress to bring an end to segregation.[22] Second, the media were instrumental in compelling the government to negotiate an end to the Vietnam War. Beginning in 1967, the national media, reacting in part to a shift in elite opinion, portrayed the war as misguided and unwinnable, and, as a result, helped turn popular sentiment against continued American involvement.[23] Finally, the media were central actors in the Watergate affair, which ultimately forced President Richard Nixon, landslide victor in the 1972 presidential election, to resign from office in

---

[22]David J. Garrow, *Protest at Selma: Martin Luther King, Jr., and the Voting Rights Act of 1965* (New Haven, CT: Yale University Press, 1978).

[23]See Todd Gitlin, *The Whole World Is Watching: Mass Media in the Making and Unmaking of the New Left* (Berkeley: University of California Press, 2003). See also William M. Hammond, *Reporting Vietnam: Media and Military at War* (Lawrence: University Press of Kansas, 1998).

disgrace. It was the relentless series of investigations launched by the *Washington Post*, the *New York Times*, and the television networks that led to the disclosures of the various abuses of which Nixon was guilty and ultimately forced Nixon to choose between resignation and almost certain impeachment.

Agenda Setting

agenda setting
Activities that help determine which issues are taken up by political actors and institutions.

The power of the media stems from several sources. The first is *agenda setting,* which means the media help determine which political issues become part of the public debate. Groups and forces that wish to bring their ideas before the public to generate support for policy proposals or political candidacies must somehow secure media coverage. If the media are persuaded that an idea is newsworthy, then they may declare it an "issue" that must be resolved or a "problem" to be solved, thus clearing the first hurdle in the policy-making process. On the other hand, if an idea lacks or loses media appeal, its chance of resulting in new programs or policies is diminished. Some ideas seem to surface, gain media support for a time, lose media appeal, and then resurface.

In most instances, the media serve as conduits for agenda-setting efforts by competing groups and forces. Occasionally, however, journalists themselves play an important role in setting the agenda of political discussion. For example, whereas many of the scandals and investigations surrounding President Clinton were initiated by his political opponents, the Watergate scandal that destroyed Nixon's presidency was in some measure initiated and driven by the *Washington Post* and the national television networks.

Priming

priming A process of preparing the public to take a particular view of an event or a political actor.

A second important media power is *priming.* This occurs when media coverage affects the way the public evaluates political leaders or candidates for office. For example, nearly unanimous media praise for President Bush's speeches to the nation in the wake of the September 11 terrorist attacks prepared, or "primed," the public to view Bush's subsequent response to terrorism in an extremely positive light, even though some aspects of the administration's efforts were problematic.

In the case of political candidates, the media have considerable influence over whether or not a particular individual will receive public attention, whether or not a particular individual will be taken seriously as a viable contender, and whether the public will evaluate a candidate's performance favorably. Thus, if the media find a candidate interesting, they may treat him or her as a serious contender even though the facts of the matter seem to suggest otherwise. In a similar vein, the media may declare that a candidate has "momentum," a mythical property that the media confer on candidates, if the candidates happen to exceed the media's expectations. Momentum has no substantive meaning—it is simply a media prediction that a particular candidate will do even better in the future than in the past. Such media prophecies can become self-fulfilling as contributors and supporters jump on the bandwagon of the candidate possessing this "momentum." In 1992, when Bill Clinton's poll standings surged in the wake of the Democratic National Convention, the media determined that Clinton had enormous momentum. In fact, nothing that happened during the remainder of the race led the media to change its collective judgment.

Framing

A third source of the media's power, known as *framing,* is their power to decide how political events and results are interpreted by the American people. For example, during the 1995–1996 struggle between President Clinton and congressional Republicans over the nation's budget—a struggle that led to several partial shutdowns of the federal government—the media's interpretation of events forced the Republicans to back down and agree to a budget on Clinton's terms. At the beginning of the crisis, congressional Republicans, led by then-House Speaker Newt Gingrich, were confident that they could compel Clinton to accept their budget, which called for substantial cuts in domestic social programs. Republicans calculated that Clinton would fear being blamed for lengthy government shutdowns and would quickly accede to their demands, and that once Americans saw that life went on with government agencies closed, they would support the Republicans in asserting that the United States could get along with less government.

For the most part, however, the media did not cooperate with the GOP's plans. Media coverage of the several government shutdowns during this period emphasized the hardships imposed on federal workers who were being furloughed in the weeks before Christmas. Indeed, Speaker Gingrich, who was generally portrayed as the villain who caused the crisis, came to be called the "Gin*grinch*" who stole Christmas from the children of hundreds of thousands of federal workers. Rather than suggest that the shutdown demonstrated that America could carry on with less government, media accounts focused on the difficulties encountered by Washington tourists unable to visit the capital's monuments, museums, and galleries. The woes of American travelers whose passports were delayed were given considerable attention. This sort of coverage eventually convinced most Americans that the government shutdown was bad for the country. In the end, Gingrich and the congressional Republicans were forced to surrender and to accept a new budget reflecting many of Clinton's priorities. The Republicans' defeat in the budget showdown contributed to the unraveling of the GOP's legislative program and, ultimately, to the Republicans' poor showing in the 1996 presidential elections. The character of media coverage of an event thus had enormous repercussions of how Americans interpreted it.

In 2001, the Bush White House especially recognized the importance of framing when presidential aides held extensive discussions with television networks and Hollywood filmmakers about the portrayal of America's war on terrorism. The White House asked the media to sound a patriotic note and frame the war as a patriotic duty. By all accounts the media responded favorably, especially after several network news anchors became the targets of anthrax-laden letters that were possibly sent by terrorists.

framing The power of the media to influence how events and issues are interpreted.

The Media and Elections

Because of its power to influence the political agenda—primarily the public's perceptions of issues and candidates—and to frame the political debate, the mass media can have considerable influence in national elections. In the 2004 presidential contest, the national print and broadcast media were firmly convinced that national and homeland security issues were the top items on the national political agenda. Other issues received less attention, if they got any attention at all. This media perspective served the interests of the GOP, which is generally seen by most Americans as the party best able to protect the country from its foreign foes. Indeed, President Bush had positioned himself as a strong military leader who responded to the challenge of terrorism with overwhelming military might. This agenda played an important role in the Democratic party's nominating process. Many leading Democrats were convinced that only a candidate with strong national security credentials would have any chance against Bush. Of course, Democrats eventually turned to Senator John Kerry, a decorated Vietnam veteran, whose combat record could be contrasted favorably with Bush's "stateside" service in the National Guard. Republicans, nevertheless, were delighted that security issues would be the focus of the contest as far as the national media were concerned. They were convinced that security was the GOP's strong suit, despite setbacks in Iraq and Democratic efforts to chip away at Bush's military credentials.

While the major media focused on national security, another important media segment saw the 2004 political agenda in somewhat different terms. For religious print and broadcast outlets associated with conservative religious denominations, the chief agenda items in 2004 were moral issues, particularly abortion and gay marriage, the question of whether same-sex unions should receive legal sanction. GOP strategists worked hard to keep these issues on the political agenda, sponsoring referenda on gay marriage in a number of hotly contested "battleground" states like Ohio. What was later called a "stealth" agenda, this also worked to the advantage of Bush and the Republicans in the general election.

Though the 2004 election was fought on issues that provided favorable terrain for the Republicans, media priming and important media frames tended to be more helpful to the Democrats. In particular, the media presented Kerry as considerably more intelligent than Bush. Bush's alleged lack of intelligence had been a media theme since the 2000 contest. The president was generally described as lacking a firm command of policy issues, depending heavily on his vice president and close advisers and generally being unable even to construct a coherent English sentence without the help of speech writers. Senator Kerry, on the other hand, was usually portrayed as intelligent, articulate, and cultured. Even the "haughty" French were said to respect him.

These depictions of the candidates primed Americans for the way in which the media framed many campaign events, especially the all-important presidential debates. Before the debates, Bush had led in the polls by a solid margin. The national media, however, almost unanimously declared Kerry the winner of the debates and devoted considerable air and print time to discussing the magnitude and meaning of Kerry's forensic victory. In subsequent polling, even Americans who had not seen or heard the actual debates asserted that Kerry had won. The media frame became a fact, Bush's commanding lead evaporated, and the election remained too close to call until the final hours of Election Day.

The Rise of Adversarial Journalism

The political power of the news media has increased greatly in recent years through the growing prominence of "adversarial journalism"—a form of journalism in which the media adopt a hostile posture toward the government and public officials.

During the nineteenth century, American newspapers were completely subordinate to the political parties. Newspapers depended on official patronage—legal notice and party subsidies—for their financial survival and were controlled by party leaders. (A vestige of that era survived into the twentieth century in such newspaper names as the *Springfield Republican* and the *St. Louis Globe-Democrat*.) At the turn of the century, with the development of commercial advertising, newspapers became financially independent. This made possible the emergence of a formally nonpartisan press.

Presidents were the first national officials to see the opportunities in this development. By communicating directly to the electorate through newspapers and magazines, Theodore Roosevelt and Woodrow Wilson established political constituencies independent of party organizations and strengthened their own power relative to Congress. President Franklin Roosevelt used the radio, most notably in his famous fireside chats, to reach out to voters and to make himself the center of American politics. FDR was also adept at developing close personal relationships with reporters, which enabled him to obtain favorable news coverage despite the fact that in his day a majority of newspaper owners and publishers were staunch conservatives. Following Roosevelt's example, subsequent presidents have sought to use the media to enhance their popularity and power. For example, through televised news conferences, President John F. Kennedy mobilized public support for his domestic and foreign policy initiatives.

During the 1950s and early 1960s, a few members of Congress also made successful use of the media—especially television—to mobilize national support for their causes. Senator Estes Kefauver of Tennessee became a major contender for the presidency and won a place on the 1956 Democratic national ticket as a result of his dramatic televised hearings on organized crime. Senator Joseph McCarthy of Wisconsin made himself a powerful national figure through his well-publicized investigations of alleged Communist infiltration of key American institutions. These senators, however, were more exceptional than typical. Through the mid-1960s, the executive branch continued to generate the bulk of news coverage, and the media served as a cornerstone of presidential power.

The Vietnam War shattered this relationship between the press and the presidency. During the early stages of U.S. involvement, American officials in Vietnam

History Principle

The Vietnam War shattered the favorable relationship between the news media and elected leaders.

who disapproved of the way the war was being conducted leaked information critical of administrative policy to reporters. Publication of this material infuriated the White House, which pressured publishers to block its release; on one occasion, President Kennedy went so far as to ask the *New York Times* to reassign its Saigon correspondent. The national print and broadcast media discovered, however, that there was an audience for critical coverage and investigative reporting among segments of the public skeptical of administration policy. As the Vietnam conflict dragged on, critical media coverage fanned antiwar sentiment. Moreover, growing opposition to the war among liberals encouraged some members of Congress, most notably Senator J. William Fulbright, chair of the Senate Foreign Relations Committee, to break with the president. In turn, these shifts in popular and congressional sentiment emboldened journalists and publishers to continue to present critical news reports. Through this process, journalists developed a commitment to adversarial journalism, while a constituency emerged that would rally to the defense of the media when it came under White House attack.

This pattern endured through the 1970s and into the present. Political forces opposed to presidential policies, many members of Congress, and the national news media began to find that their interests often overlapped. Adversarial, or "attack," journalism has become commonplace in America, and some critics have suggested that the media have contributed to popular cynicism and the low levels of citizen participation that characterize contemporary American political processes. But before we begin to think about means of compelling the media to adopt a more positive view of politicians and political issues, we should consider the possibility that media criticism is one of the major mechanisms of political accountability in the American political process. Without aggressive media coverage, would we have known of Bill Clinton's misdeeds or, for that matter, those of Richard Nixon? Without aggressive media coverage, would important questions be raised about the conduct of American foreign and domestic policy? It is easy to criticize the media for their aggressive tactics, but would our democracy function effectively without the critical role of the press? A vigorous and critical media are needed as the "watchdogs" of American politics. Of course, in October 2001, the adversarial relationship between the government and the media was at least temporarily transformed into a much more supportive association as the media helped rally the American people for the fight against terrorism. And, indeed, some commentators have suggested that segments of the media, the more conservative media in particular, have become far less adversarial in their tone during the Bush presidency than in prior years.

The adversarial relationship between the government and segments of the press, however, resumed in the wake of the 2002–03 Iraq War. Such newspapers as the *Washington Post* and the *New York Times* castigated President Bush for going to war without winning the support of some of America's major allies. When American forces failed to uncover evidence that Iraq possessed weapons of mass destruction—a major reason cited by the administration for launching the war—these newspapers intimated that the war had been based on intelligence failures, if not outright presidential deceptions. The president, as noted earlier, denounced the media for distorting his record. Thus, after a brief interlude of post–September 11 harmony, the customary hostilities between the government and the press seemed to manifest themselves once again.

MEDIA POWER AND RESPONSIBILITY

The free media are absolutely essential to democratic government. We depend on the media to investigate wrongdoing, to publicize and explain governmental actions, to evaluate programs and politicians, and to bring to light matters that might otherwise be known only to a handful of governmental insiders. In short, without free and active media, popular government would be virtually impossible. Citizens would have few means by which to know or assess the government's actions—other than the claims or pronouncements of the government itself. Moreover, without active—indeed, aggressive—media, citizens would be hard pressed to make informed choices among competing candidates at the polls. Often enough, the media reveal discrepancies between candidates' claims and their actual records, and between the images that candidates seek to project and the underlying realities.

At the same time, the increasing decay of party organizations (see Chapter 11) has made politicians ever more dependent on favorable media coverage. National political leaders and journalists have had symbiotic relationships, at least since FDR's presidency, but initially politicians were the senior partners. They benefited from media publicity, but they did not totally depend on it as long as they could still rely on party organizations to mobilize votes. Journalists, on the other hand, depended on their relationships with politicians for access to information and would hesitate to report stories that might antagonize valuable sources. News reporters feared exclusion from the flow of information in retaliation. Thus, for example, reporters did not publicize potentially embarrassing information, widely known in Washington, about the personal lives of such figures as Franklin Roosevelt and John F. Kennedy.

With the decline of party, the balance of power between politicians and journalists has been reversed. Now that politicians have become heavily dependent on the media to reach their constituents, journalists no longer need fear that their access to information can be restricted in retaliation for negative coverage.

Freedom gives the media enormous power. The media can make or break reputations, help launch or destroy political careers, and build support for or rally opposition against programs and institutions.[24] Wherever there is so much power, there exists at least the potential for its abuse or overly zealous use. All things considered, free media are so critically important to the maintenance of a democratic society that we must be prepared to take the risk that the media will occasionally abuse their power. The forms of governmental control that would prevent the media from misusing their power would also certainly destroy our freedom.

 History Principle

The increasing decay of party organizations over the past fifty years has made politicians more dependent on the media.

---

[24]See Martin Linsky, *Impact: How the Press Affects Federal Policy Making* (New York: Norton, 1991).

Rationality Principle	Collective-Action Principle	Institution Principle	Policy Principle	History Principle
Media coverage can be analyzed in terms of the interests of members of the media, politicians, and consumers.

The goals and incentives of journalists—such as ratings, career success, and prestige— influence what is created and reported as news.

News coverage is influenced by the interests of politicians.

Consumer preferences, such as those of the affluent or those of people who watch news for its entertainment value, influence news content. | The relationship between media members and politicians is a Prisoner's Dilemma. Each participant benefits from mutual cooperation but finds himself or herself tempted to defect on occasion to secure even larger gains. | | | The Vietnam War shattered the favorable relationship between the news media and elected leaders.

The increasing decay of party organizations over the past fifty years has made politicians more dependent on the media. |

SUMMARY

The American news media are among the world's freest. The print and broadcast media regularly present information and opinions critical of the government, political leaders, and policies.

The media help determine the agenda or focus of political debate in the United States, shape popular understanding of political events and results, and influence popular judgments of politicians and leaders.

Over the past century, the media have helped nationalize American political perspectives. Media coverage is influenced by the perspectives of journalists, politicians, and upscale audiences. The attention that the media give to protest and conflict is also a function of audience factors.

Free media are an essential ingredient of popular government.

FOR FURTHER READING

Cook, Timothy E. *Making Laws and Making News: Media Strategies in the U.S. House of Representatives.* Washington, DC: Brookings Institution, 1989.

Gans, Herbert. *Deciding What's News: A Study of CBS Evening News, NBC Nightly News, Newsweek, and Time.* New York: Vintage, 1980.

Graber, Doris A. *Mass Media and American Politics.* 6th ed. Washington, DC: Congressional Quarterly Press, 2002.

Hallin, Daniel C. *The Uncensored War: The Media and Vietnam.* Berkeley: University of California Press, 1986.

Hart, Roderick P. *Seducing America: How Television Charms the Modern Voter.* Rev. ed. Thousand Oaks, CA: Sage, 1999.

Hess, Stephen. *Live From Capitol Hill!: Studies of Congress and the Media.* Washington, DC: Brookings Institution, 1991.

Nacos, Brigitte L. *The Press, Presidents, and Crises.* New York: Columbia University Press, 1990.

Owen, Diana. *Media Messages in American Presidential Elections.* New York: Greenwood, 1991.

Spitzer, Robert J., ed. *Media and Public Policy.* Westport, CT: Praeger, 1993.

West, Darrell M. *Air Wars: Television Advertising in Election Campaigns, 1952–2000.* 3rd ed. Washington, DC: Congressional Quarterly Press, 2001.

Winfield, Betty Houchin. *FDR and the News Media.* Urbana: University of Illinois Press, 1990.

Courts Grow Increasingly Skeptical of Any Special Protections for the Press

By ADAM LIPTAK

Reporters frequently maintain that they are just representatives of the public, and that any special legal protections they claim for themselves are for the good of society generally.

Courts were for a time receptive to that argument. But a pileup of recent cases and judicial decisions, including the Supreme Court's refusal yesterday to hear the cases of two reporters facing jail, suggests a new hostility, one fueled by skepticism about the very value of the institutional press.

"We're seeing outright contempt for an independent press in a free society," said Jane Kirtley, who teaches media ethics and law at the University of Minnesota. . . .

The courts' reluctance to grant reporters special rights may reflect a broader dissatisfaction by politicians and the public about the role the news media have come to play. The press has increasingly found itself a target of politically charged attacks, particularly from conser-

vatives, who tend to view the mainstream media as liberal and out of touch with the concerns of many Americans. To at least some extent, the press has also wounded itself with a series of scandals that have undermined its credibility and with what many journalists acknowledge is an over-reliance on confidential sources.

"We're in an era of great judicial skepticism regarding the reliability and professionalism of the media generally," said Rodney A. Smolla, dean of the University of Richmond School of Law, "and that atmosphere, I think, makes courts reluctant to recognize any special First Amendment protection."

Professor Kirtley said the legal turning point came in 2003 with a decision written by Richard A. Posner, an influential federal appeals court judge in Chicago. Judge Posner wrote that lower courts had often misread and failed to follow the holding of a 1972 Supreme Court decision, *Branzburg v. Hayes*, which rejected First Amendment pro-

New York Times, 28 June 2005, p. A16.

tection for reporters facing grand jury subpoenas.

Professor Smolla said news organizations had for 30 years managed to convince lower courts that *Branzburg,* decided on a vote of 5 to 4, held the opposite of what its majority had decided. While the majority opinion had been fairly clear, lawyers for news organizations had seized on a brief and enigmatic concurrence by Justice Lewis F. Powell Jr. to convince the courts that they should recognize some level of protection.

That seemed to end yesterday in the Supreme Court, which upheld without comment lower court decisions ordering that Judith Miller of the *New York Times* and Matthew Cooper of *Time* magazine be jailed for refusing to testify about their sources in an investigation into the disclosure of a covert C.I.A. officer's identity. . . .

Since Judge Posner's decision, the floodgates have opened:

Ms. Miller and Mr. Cooper may soon be in jail.

Several other reporters have been held in contempt for refusing to identify their sources in a lawsuit brought by Wen Ho Lee. Dr. Lee, a scientist at the Los Alamos National Laboratory, was suspected of espionage in 1999 but ultimately pleaded guilty to a lesser charge.

A television reporter in Rhode Island recently completed four months of home confinement for refusing to say who had given him a surveillance tape in a political corruption case.

Those cases point to a split between federal law and the laws of 49 states, which all afford substantial protection to reporters. The attorneys general of 34 states and the District of Columbia had urged the Supreme Court to address that split in the cases of Mr. Cooper and Ms. Miller.

The conflict over First Amendment protection is likely to grow more complicated, given the rising influence of the Internet.

ESSENCE OF THE STORY

- Recent Court decisions have essentially eliminated the media's claim of special protection—whereby they need not reveal the names of confidential sources even if withholding them impedes a civil or criminal proceeding.

- Recent cases, such as those involving reporters in the Valerie Plame or Wen Ho Lee affairs, have further eroded the credibility of the press.

- The growth of the Internet and blogs, by blurring the distinction between reporters and others who disseminate information, may make it even harder for reporters to protect their sources.

POLITICAL ANALYSIS

- If the media and government officials are caught in a "Prisoner's Dilemma," changing legal doctrine may ultimately break up this relationship.

- The era of the "adversarial journalist" began after Vietnam and exposed many cases of government wrongdoing, but public confidence in the press also declined during this period. This is making it hard for the media to gain public sympathy and support during its legal struggles.

"The federal judiciary, from the Supreme Court down, has grown very skeptical of any claim that the institutional press is deserving of First Amendment protection over and above those of ordinary citizens," Professor Smolla said. "The rise of the Internet and blogger culture may have contributed to that. It makes it more difficult to draw lines between the traditional professional press and those who disseminate information from their home computers."

Whatever the reason, said Lucy Dalglish, executive director of the Reporters Committee for Freedom of the Press, the press's arguments lately have been falling on deaf ears. . . .

CHAPTER

14

Government in Action:
Public Policy and the Economy

Until 1929, most Americans believed that the government had little role to play in managing the economy. The world was guided by Adam Smith's theory that the economy, if left to its own devices, would produce full employment and maximum production. But the government was not entirely uninvolved with the economy. During the nineteenth and early twentieth centuries, it regulated banks; coined and printed money; directed trade through tariffs; and engaged in public works such as building roads, canals, and railroads. Nevertheless, the public philosophy of early-twentieth-century America emphasized economic self-reliance and personal effort, with the government playing a secondary role at most. This traditional view of the relationship between government and the economy crumbled with the stark reality of the Great Depression of 1929–33. Some misfortune befell nearly everyone. Around 20 percent of the workforce became unemployed, and few of these individuals had any monetary resources or the old family farm to fall back on. Banks failed, wiping out the savings of millions who had been prudent enough or fortunate enough to have any.

Thousands of businesses failed, throwing middle-class Americans onto the bread lines alongside unemployed laborers and dispossessed farmers. The Great Depression had finally proven to Americans that imperfections in the economic system could exist.

Demands mounted for the federal government to take action. In Congress, some Democrats proposed that the federal government finance public works at an accelerated rate to aid the economy and put people back to work. Other members of Congress introduced legislation to provide federal grants to the states to assist them in their relief efforts.

When President Franklin D. Roosevelt took office in 1933, he energetically threw the federal government into the business of fighting the Depression. He proposed a variety of temporary measures to provide federal relief and work programs. Most of the programs he proposed were financed by the federal government but administered by the states. In addition to these temporary measures, Roosevelt presided over the creation of several important federal programs designed to provide future economic security for Americans. Since that time, the government has been instrumental in ensuring that the economy will never again collapse as it did during the Depression.

For example, just two weeks after the September 11 attacks, Congress enacted a $15-billion financial package designed to prop up the airline industry. Already hurting from a weak economy, the airlines faced a grim future after the terrorist attacks. With the nation's air fleet entirely grounded for three days after the attacks and predictions of sharply reduced business in the weeks and months to come, multiple bankruptcies loomed on the horizon. Congress's swift and nearly unanimous decision to provide assistance underscored the importance of the airline industry to the American economy. It also reflected the widely shared expectation that the federal government would act to address so grave an economic problem.

The airline-industry bailout package and the accompanying air-safety measures revealed the many purposes that drive government involvement in the economy. First and foremost is the goal of ensuring a healthy economy. As they debated the legislation, many members of Congress pointed to the strategic importance of the airlines to the entire economy. Government also routinely intervenes in the economy to protect individual welfare and promote the public good. Air-safety measures, which included posting National Guardsmen in airports in the months after the attacks and the subsequent federal takeover of

CHAPTER OUTLINE

How Does Government Make a Market Economy Possible?

- Prerequisites for a Market Economy

- The Bases of Government Involvement

What are the Goals, Tools, and Politics of Economic Policy?

- Public Order and Private Property

- Business Development

- Maintaining a Stable and Strong Economy

airport security, were the key measures designed to achieve these goals. Such government action is critical because heightened security requires expensive equipment, personnel training, and safety procedures that the airlines had avoided implementing due to cost considerations. After September 11, critics of the air security system charged that industry pressure to reduce costs had created lax security that allowed the attacks to occur in the first place. A final objective of government economic policy is to regulate competition. In 1979, the government deregulated the airline industry, removing federal control over ticket prices and airline routes. The results benefited many consumers because the increased competition produced lower fares. (They also resulted in a less desirable outcome—more cramped seats.) Even in the era of deregulation, however, the federal government continued to subsidize and regulate airline activity to provide service to small or remote places. The post–September 11 airline bailout package included special provisions to ensure ongoing service to these less profitable routes.

Government involvement in the economy is now routine and widespread, touching practically every aspect of economic life. Nonetheless, specific decisions about government action in the economy often provoke heated controversy over who benefits (and who does not) from government activity. The airline bailout package was no exception. Despite strong support for the measure, there was considerable dissatisfaction among some Democrats, who wanted the package to include specific provisions to help the thousands of laid-off airline workers. The package ensured that airline executives could continue to receive salaries up to $300,000 but did nothing to assist workers. As one frustrated Democrat shouted during the deliberations in the House of Representatives, "Why in this chamber do the big dogs always eat first?"[1] In addition to these divisions within the airline industry, representatives from other industries hard hit by the terrorist attacks, including travel agents, restaurants, hotels, and the insurance industry, descended on Washington to lobby for special assistance. As Congress considered (and largely rejected) these claimants, it was effectively drawing a line between policies that would serve the larger public interest and policies that would benefit only small segments of the economy.

The job of this and the succeeding two chapters is to look at the *purposive* actions of government—the policies. **Public policy** can be defined simply as an officially expressed intention backed by a sanction, which can be a reward or a punishment. Thus a public policy is a law, a rule, a statute, an edict, a regulation, or an order. Its purpose is to provide incentives, whether carrot-like rewards or stick-like punishments, to induce people either to change what they are currently doing and do something else or to do more or less of what they are currently doing. In the first section of this chapter, we discuss the rationale for government's involvement in the economy. In the next section, we look at the goals of national economic policies. These policies have been organized into three categories: (1) policies that protect public order and private property, (2) policies that

public policy
A governmental law, rule, statute, or edict that expresses the government's goals and provides for rewards and punishments to promote their attainment.

 **Rationality Principle**
Public policies create incentives for people to alter the direction or intensity of their behavior.

[1] Frank Swoboda and Martha McNeil Hamilton, "Congress Clears $15 Billion to Aid Airlines," *Washington Post*, 23 September 2001, p. A1.

control or influence markets, and (3) policies that are designed to defend or enhance the vitality of our capitalist economy.

As we said in Chapter 1 and emphasized in other chapters, governments do what they do in part because of the concerns, ambitions, and purposes of politicians and other government officials and the institutional contexts in which these concerns, ambitions, and purposes get played out. Since the policy-making process allows many opportunities to change the purposes of government, politicians and officials constantly take advantage of their capacities as *agenda setters*. But policy change requires success at every step of the rather lengthy and intricate policy-making process. The institutional arrangements of a government create hurdles that a proposed change in policy must clear. This often means that change is nearly impossible. Because change is difficult, policies—once put in place—possess a degree of *durability*. This durability, in turn, provides a semblance of order and predictability in an otherwise uncertain world.

PREVIEWING THE PRINCIPLES

Public policies create incentives for people to alter the direction or intensity of their behavior. With regard to economic policy, government can play an important role in establishing the rules and institutions that allow a free market to function. Government has lots of tools to affect the economy, but there is considerable political conflict over which tools to use, how to use them, and when to use them. And because institutional arrangements and historical precedent make change difficult, public policies are durable. Nevertheless, historical events such as the Great Depression or September 11 can motivate government officials to adopt new policies.

Policy Principle

Because institutional arrangements make change difficult, public policies are durable.

History Principle

Historical events can motivate government officials to adopt new policies.

This emphasis on analyzing policy as the product of individual preferences and institutional procedures is, however, only part of the story. Historical events, sometimes appearing out of the blue, add another source of motivation for governments to act. This should be more obvious from reflecting on the aftermath of the events of September 11, 2001, a fateful day of terrorist activity in New York City, Washington, D.C., and Pennsylvania. That massive blow to our sense of national security was also an economic blow; policy makers had to begin to cope with the threatened safety of all Americans and an economy pushed into recession. After that historic day, national, state, and local agencies crafted responses to and new policy initiatives for the rapidly changing social and economic environment.

HOW DOES GOVERNMENT MAKE A MARKET ECONOMY POSSIBLE?

Government makes a market economy possible. Government sets the rules that allow markets to function. Government also develops and sustains the institutions necessary to support a market economy. By doing so, government lowers the costs of doing business. In the United States, certain arrangements facilitated the emergence of the modern market economy. These arrangements are institutions that gave participants guarantees or rules of the game that induced them to "enter the market." Our objective here is to examine what these arrangements are and what role government plays in establishing them.

Prerequisites for a Market Economy

Establishing Law and Order   As we saw in Chapter 1, the first feature is inherent in the very idea of government. There must be a minimal degree of predictability about the basic rules of social interaction. In other words, there must be a system of law and order. Participants in the market must be able to assume not only that they can get to the market safely—that they won't be robbed on the way—but also that, having arrived, the people with whom they are dealing will behave predictably and will be bound by some number of calculable laws.

Defining Rules of Property   The second feature that encourages people to participate in the market focuses on defining and dealing with property. If the market involves exchanges of ownership, there must be clear laws about what constitutes property. Property may be many things—your labor or your ideas or the bed you sleep in—but the very concept of property is inconceivable without laws that define what you can call your own.

Institution Principle

Government can play an important role in establishing the rules and institutions that allow a market economy to function.

Property ownership means that we can exercise dominion over something that we have declared our own, and it is defined by laws that enable us to exercise that dominion. Something is not our own unless we can be reasonably certain that someone else cannot walk away with it. Trespass laws, for example, give concrete meaning to what constitutes property: a trespass law confers on us a legal right to keep others away from certain kinds of property. It is clear, then, that laws or rules that define property are an essential part of the political economy. Before we can enter a market and participate in an exchange, we must be able to expect not only that we can lay claim to something but that those around us will respect that claim. In this sense, private property has a public component. The probability of enjoying property would be remote unless there were laws that were widely enforced and accepted.

Enforcing Contracts   A third prerequisite that must be met before a market economy can operate involves rules governing the enforcement of contracts. There are, of course, societies that do not have a recognizable concept of contract, but our Western economy is highly dependent on contract notions.

Contracts are closely related to property because contracts are necessary only in connection with exchanges of property, broadly construed. A contract refers to a voluntary agreement between two or more private persons that governs future conduct. And while the agreement may be private, it has a distinctively public component: A contract must be enforceable, or it is meaningless.

Governing Rules of Exchange   The fourth prerequisite for the emergence or creation of a market economy is closely tied to the contract requirement. A market exists only when exchanges occur, and there must be rules governing exchange itself. Laws of exchange structure how, when, and under what conditions you can sell your property. You might think that once the laws of property have defined what you own you ought to be able to transfer it, but that transfer is surrounded by rules that govern the transfer itself.

Certain kinds of exchanges are deemed off-limits altogether. For example, you own your own body, but under what conditions can you sell it? Laws about prostitution limit the selling or renting of one's body.

Setting Market Standards

The fifth prerequisite for the emergence of the modern free market is related to the fourth. When people engage in exchanges that are not face to face—where they can't point to a good and say "I want that tomato or that fish"—both parties must have some way of understanding what the goods are that they are bargaining over. To do that, terminology must be standardized, and one of the essential acts any government does is to establish standard weights and measures.

With modern products, the standards must go beyond weights and measures; buyers and sellers must be able to specify both quantities and qualities of goods before they enter into their contracts. These buyers and sellers must know, for example, what is meant by long- and short-staple cotton, and everything in between; they must know what they are getting when they order automobile tires of a particular quality. Many of these standards today are developed by private-sector trade associations, of course; but those standards are often incorporated into government regulations, and so they acquire governmental status—or, more important, they are protected by government action through the courts. If a member of the porcelain enamel association, for example, agrees to produce a certain type of enamel according to the trade association's specifications, the member can be sued if he or she cuts corners and evades those standards.

Providing Public Goods

The sixth prerequisite to the operation of a market economy involves the provision of *public goods.* As we saw in Chapter 1, this term refers to facilities that the government may provide because no single participant can afford or is willing to provide those facilities itself. The provision of public goods extends from supplying the physical marketplace itself—like the commons in New England towns—to an interstate highway system to stimulate the trucking industry. The provision of public goods is essential to market operation, and the manner in which the government provides those goods affects the market's character.

public goods
Goods that (1) may be enjoyed by anyone if they are provided and (2) may not be denied to anyone once they have been provided.

Creating a Labor Force

The seventh prerequisite to the emergence of a market economy is the creation of a labor force. Every society has provisions that force people to work. One of the best, albeit most recent, examples of these provisions is the requirement for universal compulsory education in this society: People are educated so that they can learn the skills necessary to function in the market. Long before education laws, however, we had poorhouses, vagrancy laws, and other more police-oriented means of forcing people to work; these rules meant that people could starve or be punished if they failed to earn their own keep. Our welfare system today serves the same purpose: We adjust the welfare system in cycles to be sure that the support we give is uncomfortable enough that people will prefer working to retiring on the low income that they will get from welfare.

Ameliorating Externalities   Another prerequisite is not always obvious, but it is nonetheless critical to creating the conditions for a market economy. To allow the market economy to operate, there must be provisions for allocating responsibility when the social cost of some behavior far exceeds the private cost. For instance, the cost of driving a gas-guzzling car is more than the total of the monthly payments, insurance, and gasoline. The cost also includes the widely distributed impact of smog and the effects of carbon monoxide emissions. Negative external effects, such as pollution, that can result from market activities are called ***externalities.*** Such externalities, when individuals or firms engage in private behavior that has broader social consequences, provide government an additional rationale to regulate the economy.

Promoting Competition   Finally, once markets emerge, they must be maintained. This means that it should be reasonably easy for a producer to enter and freely compete in the market. If this is not the case, such as when one company has established a ***monopoly,*** the efficiency of the market and the equitable distribution of its benefits are threatened. Decreased competition provides government another reason for getting involved in the economy by functioning as a watchdog over potential monopoly control.

The Bases of Government Involvement

It should now be obvious that governments—national, state, and local—are deeply embedded in the operation of a market economy. They provide rules (of property, exchange, liability); they enforce contracts and deliver law and order more generally; they supply public goods; they underwrite market standards and regulate the conditions of work; and they generally oversee the multiple aspects of competition that sustain a market economy. In short, the bases of a market economy are also the *opportunities* for government agents—elected politicians, bureaucrats, judges—to influence economic outcomes.

A benign and not altogether inaccurate perspective on government involvement in the economy begins with the idea of ***market failure.*** Markets sometimes fail to deliver all they promise—the efficient allocation of society's economic resources—because of imperfections of various sorts. A seller, for example, may possess information about his or her product of which a prospective buyer is unaware. (This is known as the *problem of incomplete information.*) This may cause the buyer to buy the product when, if he or she were fully informed, there would have been no purchase. Or this may lead to too many (or too few) transactions compared to what would have transpired under conditions of full and

externalities
The differences between the private costs and the social costs of economic behavior.

monopoly   The existence in a market of a single firm that provides all the goods and services of that market; the absence of competition.

Policy Principle
The market economy provides opportunities for government agents to intervene by formulating and implementing policies.

market failure
An instance when the market fails to produce an efficient outcome.

complete information. In this instance the market has misallocated resources, so to speak, because the incomplete information has misled market participants.

If incomplete information is one way the market may fail, then imperfections in the assignment of property rights is another. Thus the market may fail to induce appropriate safeguarding of the environment because of a failure to assign property rights in a complete and/or uncontested way. (This is known as the *problem of incomplete property rights*.) Because of the incomplete assignment of rights, no one "owns" the air, and so anyone may use it as dumping ground for pollutants (from their automobile exhaust, from their hairspray aerosol cans, from their chimney). Except to an environmental extremist, *some* air pollution is acceptable (since with none it is impossible to imagine any productive activities at all taking place—no cars, no hairspray, no chimneys); but markets, unaided, do not necessarily encourage "optimal" levels of pollution.

The benign view of government involvement in the economy is one of government as an agent to correct (or at least to ameliorate) these kinds of market failures (and there are others). By providing and enforcing market standards for instance, as mentioned in the previous section, government helps alleviate information asymmetries between prospective buyers and sellers, thereby correcting an imbalance and a prospective failure to consummate market deals. Imposing a fair-labeling requirement on a manufacturer is an instance of this. So is an obligation of a butcher shop to have a properly working scale. (Aware that the butcher's scale will be inspected from time to time by a government agent, consumers will be more confident about doing business in that shop.) Or, as in the second example above, by establishing (partial and limited) property rights to the air—say, "pollution permits" giving its holders the right to deposit a certain specified amount of particulate matter into the atmosphere—governments in the Los Angeles air basin have controlled pollution levels and improved smog conditions in this locale without abolishing pollution-producing activities altogether (activities like manufacturing, driving autos, barbecuing in the backyard).

Institution Principle

Government institutions—most notably courts and regulatory agencies—engage in market interventions to alleviate (not always successfully) market failures.

Part one, then, of the benign rationale for government involvement in the economy is the reduction of market failures. A second part of the benign view of government involvement involves the production of public goods. As we described earlier, some goods have the property that they may be enjoyed by anyone once they are provided, regardless of whether a person has contributed to their provision or not and regardless of how many other people are enjoying the good. This produces an incentive problem—namely, too few people have an incentive to contribute to the production of this good—and thus it will be undersupplied in the marketplace. (This is known as the *problem of free riding*.) Consequently, it is argued, governments, because they possess the ability to coerce contribution through the imposition of taxes, are the natural provider of goods like defense, transportation infrastructure, clean air and water. They can provide these public goods by taxing citizens and then, with the revenue that these taxes provide, go out and hire the necessary inputs to make them available.

Some think the benign interpretation is a fairy tale. True, market failures and undersupplied public goods provide an opportunity for a well-intentioned government to step in, take charge, and do good. The same may be said for the provision of property, exchange, and liability rules; for contract enforcement; and for the regulation of work conditions. All these constitute occasions in which markets underperform and thus opportunities for social improvement. The portentous and less benign prospect, however, is that it also provides opportunities for self-interested political actors to intervene.

Consider the following example. Senator Robert Byrd of West Virginia, in his previous role as the powerful majority leader of the U.S. Senate in the 1980s and 1990s, was a vigilant defender of the West Virginia coal industry. This industry produces high-sulfur coal, the kind that generates much more serious pollution than low-sulfur coal from the West. Byrd has been very successful in making certain that environmental laws do not adversely affect high-sulfur coal. Specifically, he has made it possible to burn high-sulfur coal while reducing the environmental damage it causes by writing into environmental legislation that coal-fired furnaces must have *scrubbers* installed on their smokestacks (to clean the pollution residue from the smoke after the coal is burned). This is a more expensive environmental "fix" than simply requiring that only low-sulfur (western) coal be burned. The result is that West Virginia coal miners and owners of coal mines are protected at the expense of their fellow miners and owners out West. So, even as the national government uses its powers to provide a public good—clean air—it does so in a manner that nevertheless is advantageous to some and disadvantageous to others.[2]

⊕ **Rationality Principle**

Even if governments seek to "do good," this does not prevent rational politicians from searching for opportunities to take care of their constituents.

It should come as no surprise, then, that even when there is consensus over ends, like cleaning up the environment or protecting the nation from terrorism or getting Americans back to work, there is considerable conflict over means. Even when policies produce similar results, they may have different effects on different parts of the economy or regions of the country. One policy may clean up the environment by requiring scrubbers on all plants using coal-fired furnaces (to eliminate sulfur emissions at the smokestack). Another policy might have precisely the same environmental effect but produce it by requiring that coal-fired furnaces burn only low-sulfur western coal (so that far fewer sulfur particulates are emitted in the first place). The first policy protects the jobs and profits of West Virginians; the second policy threatens them. Consensus on ends, in other words, does not guarantee consensus on means. Agreement on goals is often accompanied by disagreements about tools. Collective action, then, is not only about achieving a shared vision, a common policy, or a joint objective. It is also about "how to get from here to there."

You might wonder how decisions over means get made. This is what politics is all about—and this is why some shadows of doubt accompany the benign rationale for government involvement in the economy. There is no gainsaying the central

---

[2]On the clever manner in which Byrd helped West Virginia coal producers, see Bruce A. Ackerman and William T. Hassler, *Clean Coal/Dirty Air: Or How the Clean Air Act Became a Multi-Billion-Dollar Bail-Out for High-Sulfur Coal Producers and What Should Be Done About It* (New Haven, CT: Yale University Press, 1981).

pieces of the benign rationale—market failures and undersupplied public goods are very real problems for any advanced industrial society. But there is also no gainsaying the existence of clever politicians looking for ways to "take care of their own," even at the expense of others—that is, the benign rationale requires qualification. Markets create problems for sure. But once we open the door to government, economic and social groups, through their political representatives, will jockey for advantage, looking for ways to get ahead or to hobble their competitors.

To summarize, it is difficult to understand why the modern economy has its present shape without understanding what factors regularly affected its development. The structure of the capitalist economy and every other economic system depends highly on a series of government actions that make it possible for that economy to maintain itself in one form or another.

Governments are neither aloof nor separate from the economy but are inextricably bound up in its activities. Governments provide a structure and a framework—standards, rules, laws—as well as substantive support in the form of subsidies, regulations, and taxes, all of which allow the economy to operate. Through politics, however, governments and their agents create winners and losers. The winners may think of government's policies as benign; the losers do not.

WHAT ARE THE GOALS, TOOLS, AND POLITICS OF ECONOMIC POLICY?

The goals of economic policy often shift as a new administration takes power in Washington, but such shifts are usually a matter of emphasis. Political leaders realize that the public expects the government to achieve multiple goals in its economic policy. Public expectations about what government economic policy can and should do have expanded over the course of our nation's history. This growth in public expectations has made economic policy more complex as government strives to achieve multiple goals, some of which may conflict with one another.

Three major goals have guided government involvement in the economy since the early years of our nation's history: promoting a strong and stable economy, encouraging business development, and maintaining public order. Over time, the federal government has taken on greater responsibility for meeting each of these goals. The Great Depression of the 1930s marked a decisive turning point. As Washington created new agencies and new measures to monitor the nation's economic health, it transformed public expectations about the federal role in the economy. The federal government assumed primary responsibility for achieving established goals, and it faced heightened expectations about its ability to reach those goals.

Public Order and Private Property

We begin our discussion with public order policies for two reasons. First, these policies lay and maintain the foundations of the economy. Second, because so many of these policies are old and established state government policies, most people don't appreciate them as policies and go on believing that the U.S. economy was once "unregulated" by the government.

Federalism and Public Order   Under the American federalist system, there is no national police force, there is no national criminal law, there is no national common law, there are no national property laws. The national government does have a few policies directly concerned with public order, however, most of which are mandated by the Constitution itself. These include laws against counterfeiting, against using the mails to defraud, and against crossing state lines to avoid arrest for a violation of state laws. A few other offenses against public order have simply been presumed to be interstate crimes against which federal statutes have been enacted, mainly in the twentieth century. Important examples include kidnapping, narcotics dealing, and political subversion. But virtually all of the multitudes of other policies dealing with public order and the foundations of the economy are left to the states and their local governments.

In the wake of the terrorist attacks of September 11, 2001, the federal role in public order increased. President George W. Bush, in one of his first acts in response to the attacks, announced the creation of a new cabinet-level agency named the Office of Homeland Defense, which later became the Department of Homeland Security. Its mission is to coordinate the federal government's role in the preservation of public order.

Private Property   Another unique feature of the American approach to public order is the emphasis placed on *private property*. Private property is valued in most of the cultures of the world but not as centrally as in the United States, where it is embodied in the Constitution. Seizing private property for a public use, or ***expropriation,*** is widely used in the United States, especially in land-use regulation. Almost all public works, from highways to parks to government office buildings, involve the forceful taking of some private property to assemble sufficient land and the correct distribution of land for the necessary construction. The vast Interstate Highway Program required expropriation of thousands of narrow strips of private land. Urban redevelopment projects often require city governments to use the powers of seizure in the service of private developers, who actually build the urban projects on the land that would be far too expensive if purchased on the open market.[3] Private utilities that supply electricity and gas to individual subscribers are given powers to take private property whenever a new facility or a right-of-way is needed.

We generally call the power to expropriate ***eminent domain,*** and the eminent-domain power is recognized as inherent in any government. The Fifth Amendment

expropriation
Confiscation of property with or without compensation.

eminent domain
The right of government to take private property for public use, with reasonable compensation awarded for the property.

---

[3]At the end of its 2005 term, the Supreme Court, in *Kelo v. New London*, sustained actions by the redevelopment authority of the city of New London, Connecticut, to use expropriation authority to seize private property and make it available to developers, not for public projects but for private commercial developments.

of the U.S. Constitution surrounds this expropriation power with important safeguards against abuse, so that government agencies in the United States are not permitted to use that power except through a strict due process, and they must offer "fair market value" for the land sought.[4]

Not all the policies toward property are policies that regulate the conduct of people who would take property. Many policies positively encourage property ownership on the theory that property owners are better citizens and, therefore, more respectful of public order. One of the most important national policies in American history was ***homesteading,*** otherwise called "squatting," which permitted people to gain ownership of property by occupying public or unclaimed lands, living on the land for a specified period of time, and making certain minimal improvements on that land.

Many other policies encourage homeownership today, the most significant being that part of the tax code that permits homeowners to deduct interest paid on mortgage loans from their taxes. In addition, three large federal agencies—the Federal Housing Administration (FHA), the Farmers Home Administration (FMHA), and the Veterans Administration (VA)—encourage homeownership by making mortgage loans available at interest rates below the market rate. The Farm Credit Administration (FCA) operates the extensive Farm Credit System, whose primary function is to make long-term and short-term loans to improve farm and rural real estate, loans available only to bona fide farm operators and farm-related companies who are members of the farm credit system. Many of these agencies make direct loans at below-market rates. Some of them (in particular the FHA and the VA) also insure or guarantee loans so that private commercial banks have less risk and can charge proportionately lower interest rates.

homesteading
A national policy that permitted people to gain ownership of property by occupying public or unclaimed lands, living on the land for a specified period of time, and making certain minimal improvements on that land. Also known as squatting.

Business Development

Promoting Business Development through Promotional Policies During the nineteenth century, the national government was almost exclusively a promoter of markets. National roads and canals were built to tie states and regions together. National tariff policies promoted domestic markets by restricting imported goods; a tax on an import raised its price and weakened its ability to compete with similar domestic products. The national government also heavily subsidized the railroad. Until the 1840s, railroads were thought to be of limited commercial value. But between 1850 and 1872, Congress granted over 100 million acres of public-domain land to railroad interests, and state and local governments pitched in an estimated $280 million in cash and credit. Before the end of the century, 35,000 miles of track existed—almost half the world's total.

Railroads were not the only clients of federal support aimed at fostering the expansion of private markets. Many sectors of agriculture received federal subsidies

---

[4]For an evaluation of the politics of eminent domain, see Theodore J. Lowi et al., *Poliscide: Big Government, Big Science, Lilliputian Politics* (Lanham, MD: University Press of America, 1990), p. 235 and *passim*, and especially Chapters 11 and 12, written by Julia Vitullo-Martin and Thomas Vitullo-Martin.

during the nineteenth century. Agriculture remains highly subsidized. In 2001, an environmental group caused a stir by putting the exact amounts of subsidies received by individual farmers on a widely publicized Web site (www.ewg.org/farm). The top recipient of government aid in Texas, for example, received $1.3 million in 2001. President Bush continued the tradition of generous agricultural subsidies, approving a 2002 law that increased federal payments to farmers by 80 percent.

In the twentieth century, traditional promotional techniques were expanded, and some new ones were invented. For example, a great proportion of the promotional activities of the national government are now done indirectly through *categorical grants-in-aid* (see Chapter 3). The national government offers grants to states on condition that the state (or local) government undertake a particular activity. Thus to use motor transportation to improve national markets, a national highway system of 900,000 miles was built during the 1930s, based on a formula whereby the national government would pay 50 percent of the cost if the state would provide the other 50 percent. And then for over twenty years, beginning in the late 1950s, the federal government constructed over 45,000 miles of interstate highways. This was brought about through a program whereby the national government agreed to pay 90 percent of the construction costs on the condition that each state provide for 10 percent of the costs of any portion of a highway built within its boundaries.[5] More recently the federal government has been involved in the subsidization of urban mass transit, airport construction and modernization, and port improvements—a combination of promotional and security concerns at work.

Tools for Promotional Policy   Subsidies and contracting are the carrots of public policy. Their purpose is to encourage people to do something they might not otherwise do or to get people to do more of what they are already doing. Sometimes the purpose is merely to compensate people for something done in the past.

Subsidies are simply government grants of cash or other valuable commodities, such as land. Although subsidies are often denounced as "giveaways," they have played a fundamental role in the history of government in the United States. Subsidies were the dominant form of public policy of the national government and the state and local governments throughout the nineteenth century. They continue to be an important category of public policy at all levels of government. The first planning document ever written for the national government, Alexander Hamilton's *Report on Manufactures*, was based almost entirely on Hamilton's assumption that American industry could be encouraged by federal subsidies and that these were not only desirable but constitutional.

The thrust of Hamilton's plan was not lost on later policy makers. Subsidies in the form of land grants were given to farmers and to railroad companies to encourage western settlement. Substantial cash subsidies have traditionally been

categorical grants-in-aid
Funds given by Congress to states and localities, earmarked by law for specific categories such as education or crime prevention.

subsidies
Governmental grants of cash or other valuable commodities such as land to individuals or organizations. Subsidies can be used to promote activities desired by the government, to reward political support, or to buy off political opposition.

---

[5]The act of 1955 officially designated the interstate highways as the National System of Interstate and Defense Highways. It was indirectly a major part of President Eisenhower's defense program. But it was just as obviously a pork-barrel policy as any rivers and harbors legislation.

given to commercial shipbuilders to help build the commercial fleet and to guarantee the use of the ships as military-personnel carriers in time of war.

Subsidies have always been a technique favored by politicians because subsidies can be treated as "benefits" that can be spread widely in response to many demands that might otherwise produce profound political conflict. Subsidies can, in other words, be used to buy off the opposition.

Contracting Like any corporation, a government agency must purchase goods and services by contract. The law requires open bidding for a substantial proportion of these contracts because government contracts are extremely valuable to businesses in the private sector and because the opportunities and incentives for abuse are very great. But contracting is more than a method of buying goods and services. Contracting is also an important technique of policy because government agencies are often authorized to use their ***contracting power*** as a means of encouraging corporations to improve themselves, as a means of helping build up whole sectors of the economy and as a means of encouraging certain desirable goals or behavior, such as equal employment opportunity. For example, the infant airline industry of the 1930s was nurtured by the national government's lucrative contracts to carry airmail. A more recent example is the use of government contracting to encourage industries, universities, and other organizations to engage in research and development.

contracting power The power of government to set conditions on companies seeking to sell goods or services to government agencies.

Military contracting has long been a major element in government spending. So tight was the connection between defense contractors and the federal government during the cold war that, as he was leaving office, President Eisenhower warned the nation to beware of the powerful "military-industrial complex." After the cold war, as military spending and production declined, major defense contractors began to look for alternative business activities to supplement the reduced demand for weapons. For example, Lockheed Martin, the nation's largest defense contractor, began to bid on contracts related to welfare reform. Since September 11, however, the military budget has been awash in new funds, and military contractors are flooded with business. President Bush proposed to increase the Pentagon budget by $48 billion (14.3 percent), requesting so many weapons systems that one observer called the budget a "weapons smorgasbord."[6] Military contractors geared up to produce not only weapons for foreign warfare but also surveillance systems to enhance domestic security.

 Rationality Principle

Contracting may be used instrumentally as a tool to encourage particular sectors of the economy.

Promotional Policy and Logrolling Politics Promotional policies work largely through encouragement of individuals in the private sector. The government acts like any patron, such as a patron of the arts or a private foundation. A patronage policy simply authorizes a government agency to take whatever funds are budgeted to it and dispense them to individuals, companies, or groups to encourage new building, to pay for the provision of a particular service, or as an incentive

 Policy Principle

In promotional policies, political actors seek to distribute funds and projects to their political supporters.

[6]James Dao, "The Nation; Big Bucks Trip Up the Lean New Army," *New York Times*, 10 February 2002, sec. 4, p. 5.

for a private individual to take an initiative that he or she might not otherwise take. Sometimes these funds are distributed according to a contract for work to be done or goods to be bought, as in a contract with a private construction company to build a bridge. At other times, these funds are in the form of a grant to an individual to engage in research or to support an artistic project.

Promotional policy was the dominant type of policy adopted by Congress during the nineteenth century, and it played an important role in our discussion of federalism in Chapter 3. These policies are called "pork-barrel" policies because they can be broken up into smaller pieces of resources and distributed to a maximum number of the people (that is, voters) who are clamoring for a piece of the pork (i.e., government benefits). Just as *pork-barrel* best describes these policies, so *logrolling* best describes the *politics* of these policies. **Logrolling** is a political relationship between two or more persons who have nothing in common. Their understanding is that "if you will support me on issue A, I will support you on any other issue you want; just tell me when and how you want me to vote. I don't need to know the particulars."[7] These logrolling relationships found a hospitable environment in Congress in the nineteenth century, and congressional committees and political parties flourished through their ability to gain and maintain political support by means of logrolling relationships. Indeed, political scientist Samuel Beer found that most of the nineteenth century was a period of pork-barrel coalitions, in which the members of these coalitions held no common interests but were joined together by the prospect of each member of the coalition being "able to get from the central government the action it needs."[8]

Drawing on these patterns of the past, we can make an informed guess about the power structure of politics in the category of promotional policy today. The following, by the political scientist John Ferejohn, is a brief description of the pattern, written for today but clearly connected to its nineteenth-century ancestry:

> . . . If a bill calling for improvements in a single district is [proposed], it will not pass since all the districts must pay and only one will benefit. Consequently, only an omnibus bill proposing expenditures in at least a majority of the districts has a chance of passage.[9]

"Omnibus" is the name given a bill or act that is composed of many sections with little substantive or logical connection among them. Each rivers and harbors bill, for example, is a collection of dozens of separate projects. For example, the Water Resources Development Act of 2003 is a true omnibus act with five separate substantive titles, three of which actually provide approvals for specific proj-

logrolling A legislative practice wherein reciprocal agreements are made between legislators, usually in voting for or against a bill. In contrast to bargaining, logrolling unites parties that have nothing in common but their desire to exchange support.

Institution Principle

American political institutions, particularly Congress, allow promotional policies to take the form of pork-barrel legislation through vote trading, logrolling, and omnibus bills.

---

[7]These policy categories and their associated political patterns were first laid out by Theodore J. Lowi in "American Business, Public Policy, Case Studies and Political Theory," *World Politics* 16.4 (July 1964).

[8]Samuel Beer, "The Modernization of American Federalism," *Public Administration Review* 3.2 (Fall 1973): 59, citing Lowi, "American Business, Public Policies, Case Studies and Political Theory."

[9]John A. Ferejohn, *Pork Barrel Politics: Rivers and Harbors Legislation, 1947–1968* (Stanford, CA: Stanford University Press, 1974), p. 235. See also Clem Miller, *Member of the House: Letters of a Congressman*, ed. John W. Baker (New York: Scribner, 1962), especially pp. 16–17.

ects (Title III), authorizations for initial studies and research for future projects (Title IV), and provisions for extensions, repairs, and reports of progress (Title V). All in all, in these three titles, 237 separate sections provide authorization for specific projects. Some of the sections cover reauthorizations and deauthorizations, and some apply to more than one district. But the named projects, each given a section number, amount to exactly 54 percent of the 435 districts of the House of Representatives. This is spectacularly close to the perfect combination in Ferejohn's "law" of pork-barrel policies. Each project is of intense interest to one district and of little interest elsewhere. Supporters of each project agree to support all the other projects in return for the support their own project will receive. Thus promotional policy has a distinctive pattern of politics.[10]

Promoting Business Development by Regulating Competition   Americans have long been suspicious of concentrations of economic power. Federal economic regulation aims to protect the public against potential abuses by concentrated economic power in two ways. First, the federal government can establish conditions that govern the operation of big businesses to ensure fair competition. For example, it can require business to make information about its activities and account books available to the public. Second, the federal government can force large businesses to break up into smaller companies if it finds that the company has established a monopoly. This is called *antitrust policy.* In addition to economic regulation, the federal government engages in social regulation. Social regulation establishes conditions on businesses to protect workers, the environment, and consumers.

antitrust policy
Government regulation of large businesses that have established monopolies.

Federal regulatory policy was a reaction to public demands. As the American economy prospered throughout the nineteenth century, some companies grew so large that they were recognized as possessing "market power." This meant that they were powerful enough to eliminate competitors and to impose conditions on consumers rather than cater to consumer demand. The growth of billion-dollar corporations led to collusion among companies to control prices, much to the dismay of smaller businesses and ordinary consumers. Moreover, the expanding economy was more mechanized, and this involved greater dangers to employees as well as to consumers. Small businesses, laborers, farmers, and consumers all began to clamor for protective regulation from the federal government. If markets were national, there would have to be national regulation.[11]

[10]For more on this distinctive pattern of politics that builds on the notion of distributive politics developed in Lowi, "American Business, Public Policies, Case Studies and Political Theory," see Kenneth A. Shepsle and Barry R. Weingast, "Political Preferences for the Pork Barrel," *American Journal of Political Science* 25 (1981): 96–111; Barry R. Weingast, Kenneth A. Shepsle, and Christopher Johnsen, "The Political Economy of Benefits and Costs: A Neoclassical Approach to Distributive Politics," *Journal of Political Economy* 89 (1981): 642–64; and Robert M. Stein and Kenneth N. Bickers, *Perpetuating the Pork Barrel: Policy Subsystems and American Democracy* (New York: Cambridge University Press, 1995).

[11]For an account of the relationship between mechanization and law, see Lawrence M. Friedman, *A History of American Law* (New York: Simon & Schuster, 1973), pp. 409–29.

The first national regulatory policy was the Interstate Commerce Act of 1887, which created the first national independent regulatory commission, the Interstate Commerce Commission (ICC), designed to control the monopolistic practices of the railroads. Two years later, the Sherman Antitrust Act extended regulatory power to cover all monopolistic practices. These were strengthened in 1914 with the enactment of the Federal Trade Act (creating the Federal Trade Commission, or FTC) and the Clayton Act. The only significant addition of national regulatory policy beyond interstate regulation of trade, however, was the establishment of the Federal Reserve System in 1913, which was given powers to regulate the banking industry along with its general monetary powers.

The modern epoch of comprehensive national regulation began in the 1930s. Most of the regulatory programs of the 1930s were established to regulate the conduct of companies within specifically designated sectors of American industry. For example, the jurisdiction of one agency was the securities industry; the jurisdiction of another was the radio (and eventually television) industry. When Congress turned once again toward regulatory policies in the 1970s, it became still more bold, moving beyond the effort to regulate specific sectors of industry toward regulating some aspect of the entire economy. The scope or jurisdiction of agencies such as the Occupational Safety & Health Administration (OSHA), the Consumer Product Safety Commission (CPSC), and the Environmental Protection Agency (EPA) is as broad and as wide as the entire economy, indeed the entire society.

By the late 1970s, a reaction against regulation set in. Businesses complained about the burden of the new regulations they confronted, and many economists began to argue that excessive regulation was hurting the economy. Congress and the president responded with a wave of *deregulation.* President Ford's and President Carter's accomplishments include the Securities Act Amendment of 1975, the Railroad Revitalization Act of 1976, the Airline Deregulation Act of 1978, the Staggers Rail Deregulation Act of 1980, the Depository Institution Deregulation and Monetary Control Act of 1980, and the Motor Carrier Act of 1980. President Reagan went about the task of changing the direction of regulation by way of "presidential oversight." One of his first actions after taking office was Executive Order 12291, issued February 17, 1981, which gave the Office of Management and Budget (OMB) the authority to review all proposals by all executive-branch agencies for new regulations to be applied to companies or people within their jurisdiction. By this means, President Reagan succeeded in reducing the total number of regulations issued by federal agencies to such an extent that the number of pages in the *Federal Register* dropped from 74,000 in 1980 to 49,600 in 1987.[12] During the 1990s, substantial deregulation in the telecommunications industry and in agriculture and officially supported relaxation of regulatory activity in civil rights, pollution control, protection of endangered species, and natural resources suggest a further retreat from regulation. But by 2000, the *Federal Register* had crept up to a record 74,258 pages.

History Principle

The scope of national regulatory policies expanded during the 1930s, 1960s, and early 1970s but contracted during the late 1970s to mid-1990s.

deregulation

A policy of reducing or eliminating regulatory restraints on the conduct of individuals or private institutions.

---

[12]The *Federal Register* is the daily publication of all official acts of Congress, the president, and the administrative agencies. A law or executive order is not legally binding until published in the *Federal Register.*

Regulatory Tools   If promotional tools are the carrots of public policy, regulatory tools can be considered the sticks. ***Regulation*** comes in several forms, but every regulatory technique shares a common trait: direct government control of conduct. When conduct is said to be regulated, the purpose is rarely to eliminate the conduct but rather to influence it toward more appropriate channels, toward more appropriate locations, or toward certain qualified types of persons all for the purpose of minimizing injuries or inconveniences. This type of regulated conduct is sometimes called ***administrative regulation*** because the controls are given over to administrative agencies rather than to the police. Each regulatory agency has extensive powers to keep a sector of the economy under surveillance as well as powers to make rules dealing with the behavior of individual companies and people. But these administrative agencies have fewer powers of punishment than the police and the courts have, and the administrative agencies generally rely on the courts to issue orders enforcing the rules and decisions made by the agencies.

Sometimes a government will adopt administrative regulation if an economic activity is considered so important that it is not to be entrusted to competition among several companies in the private sector. This is the rationale for the regulation of local or regional power companies. A single company, traditionally called a "utility," is given an exclusive license (or franchise) to offer these services, but because the one company is made a legal monopoly and is protected from competition by other companies, the government gives an administrative agency the power to regulate the quality of the services rendered, the rates charged for those services, and the margin of profit that the company is permitted to make.

At other times, administrative regulation is the chosen technique because the legislature decides that the economy needs protection from itself—that is, it may set up a regulatory agency to protect companies from destructive or predatory competition on the assumption that economic competition is not always its own solution. This is the rationale behind the Federal Trade Commission, which has the responsibility of watching over such practices as price discrimination or pooling agreements between two or more companies when their purpose is to eliminate competitors.

Regulatory Policy and Pluralist Politics   The key characteristic of regulatory policy is control of individual conduct by directly coercive techniques. Regulatory techniques are used to impose obligations, duties, or restrictions on conduct. The *politics* of regulation follows from this directly coercive character of regulatory *policy*.

The best way to define the politics of regulatory policy, thus distinguishing it from the politics of promotional policy, is to compare the politics of nineteenth-century states to the politics of the nineteenth-century national government. Nineteenth-century national government economic policies were almost exclusively promotional. And the politics of the national government was very stable. It was dominated by political parties, and the individual and sectional conflicts that emerged could be settled peacefully, by logrolling, through the parties in Congress. The national government could expand and could subdivide government resources to meet the demands of individuals and groups. Thus political conflict

regulation   A particular use of government power in which the government adopts rules imposing restrictions on the conduct of private citizens.

administrative regulation   Rules made by regulatory agencies and commissions.

could be bought off or tabled until a future time. In contrast, the states in the nine-teenth century were doing all of the regulating, and the political patterns of the states were highly unstable, constantly upset by demonstrations, large social move-ments, and frequent violence. In the less volatile moments, the politics of the states was dominated by interest groups, especially corporate interest groups.[13]

Group politics is the essence of "pluralism," and pluralism is the key to the poli-tics of modern regulatory policy.[14] In *The Federalist* No. 10, James Madison noted that, in popular government, people divide into "factions," with each faction seeking its own satisfaction without any regard for the public interest. As long as there are many groups, with no one group or coalition of groups consistently dominating all the others, power will not become too concentrated, and all groups will be willing to conduct themselves within the constraints of the Constitution. Today these fac-tions are called groups, interests, and power centers, and the competition among them leads to demands so that policies are adopted to mediate the conflicts. Groups seek to expand their power through lobbying Congress and through form-ing larger coalitions with other groups, either to dominate the political parties by overpowering electoral support with economic force or by making special arrange-ments with the parties.[15] Thus while political parties and local districts have been at the very core of the politics of promotional policy, they have been far less impor-tant in the politics of regulatory policy. For example, groups organized around the steel interest, the cotton interest, small business, the trade unions, etc., cross elec-toral constituencies and, therefore, blur the lines of party politics and elections.

Policy Principle

The politics of regulatory policy tends to be dominated by interest groups, especially those interests that might be regulated by government.

Maintaining a Stable and Strong Economy

A stable and strong economy is the basic goal of all economic policy. What makes reaching this goal so difficult is that the key elements of a strong economy—economic growth, full employment, and low inflation—often appear to conflict with one another. Economic policy must manage the trade-offs among these goals. This is a complicated task because there is much disagreement about whether pur-

[13]Good accounts of the politics of the states in the nineteenth century will be found in V. O. Key, *American State Politics* (Westport, CT: Greenwood, 1983; orig. published 1956); V. O. Key, *Southern Politics in State and Nation*, 2nd ed. (Knoxville: University of Tennessee Press, 1984); Bernard L. Hyink and David H. Provost, *Politics and Government in California*, 16th ed. (New York: Longman, 2003); and Frances Fox Piven and Richard A. Cloward, *Poor People's Movements: Why They Succeed, How They Fail* (New York: Pantheon, 1977). For studies of political violence that show the particular affinity of vio-lence to state politics, see Phillip Taft and Phillip Ross, "American Labor Violence: Its Causes, Charac-ter, and Outcome," in *The History of Violence in America: Historical and Comparative Perspectives*, ed. Hugh Davis Graham and Ted Robert Gurr (New York: Praeger, 1969); Robert Fogelson, "Violence as Protest," *Proceedings of the Academy of Political Science* 29.1 (1968); on vigilantism, see Friedman, *A History of American Law*, pp. 318–22.

[14]For a brief intellectual history of the rise of pluralism as a theory and as an ideology, see Theodore J. Lowi, *The End of Liberalism: The Second Republic of the United States*, 2nd ed. (New York: Norton, 1979), Chapter 3.

[15]For the best theoretical statements of pluralism, see Robert A. Dahl, *A Preface to Democratic Theory* (Chicago: University of Chicago Press, 1956); and Robert A. Dahl and Charles E. Lindblom, *Politics, Economics and Welfare: Planning and Politico-economic Systems Resolved into Basic Social Processes* (New York: Harper, 1953).

suing one of these economic goals really does mean sacrificing the others. Moreover, the trade-offs among these goals appear to change over time. The expansion of the American economy in the latter half of the 1990s defied all previous expectations about the relationship between growth, employment, and inflation. The fast pace of economic growth, combined with low inflation and very high employment, suggested that it was now possible to combine all three central goals of economic policy.[16] In 2001, an economic downturn reminded policy makers how difficult it is to sustain such high levels of growth. Let us now turn to the actual policies designed to accomplish economic stability and growth.

Monetary Policies   *Monetary policies* manipulate the growth of the entire economy by controlling the availability of money to banks. With a very few exceptions cited below, banks in the United States are privately owned and locally operated. Until well into the twentieth century, banks were regulated, if at all, by state legislatures. Each bank was granted a charter, giving it permission to make loans, hold deposits, and make investments. Although more than 25,000 banks continue to be state-chartered banks, they are less important than they used to be in the overall financial picture, as the most important banks now are members of the "federal system."

But banks did not become the core of American capitalism without intense political controversy. The Federalist majority in Congress, led by Alexander Hamilton, did in fact establish a Bank of the United States in 1791, but it was vigorously opposed by agrarian interests led by Thomas Jefferson, based on the fear that the interests of urban, industrial capitalism would dominate such a bank. The Bank of the United States was terminated during the administration of Andrew Jackson; but the fear of a central, *public* bank still existed eight decades later, when Congress in 1913 established an institution—the *Federal Reserve System*—to integrate private banks into a single system. The Federal Reserve System did not become a central bank in the European tradition but rather is composed of twelve Federal Reserve banks, each located in a major commercial city. The Federal Reserve banks are not ordinary banks; they are banker's banks, which make loans to other banks, clear checks, and supply the economy with currency and coins. They also play a regulatory role over the member banks. Every national bank must be a member of the Federal Reserve System; each must follow national banking rules and must purchase stock in the Federal Reserve System (which helps make the system self-financing). State banks and savings and loan associations may also join if they accept national rules. At the top of the system is the Federal Reserve Board ("the Fed"), made up of seven members appointed by the president (with Senate confirmation) for fourteen-year terms. The chairman of the Fed is selected by the president from among the seven members of the board for a four-year term. In all other concerns, however, the Fed is an independent agency inasmuch as its members cannot be removed during their terms except "for cause," and the president's executive power does not extend to them or their policies.

The major advantage of belonging to the federal system is that each member bank can borrow money from the Fed, using as collateral the notes on loans already

monetary policies Efforts to regulate the economy through manipulation of the supply of money and credit. America's most powerful institution in the area of monetary policy is the Federal Reserve Board.

Federal Reserve System (Fed) Consisting of twelve Federal Reserve Banks, the Fed facilitates exchanges of cash, checks, and credit; it regulates member banks; and it uses monetary policies to fight inflation and deflation.

[16]Louis Uchitelle, "107 Months, and Counting," *New York Times*, 30 January 2000, sec. 3, p. 1.

made. This enables them to expand their loan operations continually, as long as there is demand for new loans. This ability of a member bank to borrow money from the Fed is a profoundly important monetary policy. The Fed charges interest, called a ***discount rate,*** on its loans to member banks.

If the Fed significantly decreases the discount rate—that is, the interest it charges member banks when they come for new credit—that can be a very good shot in the arm of a sagging economy. During 2001, the Fed cut interest rates eleven times to combat the combined effects of recession and the terrorist attacks. If the Fed adopts a policy of higher discount rates, that will serve as a brake on the economy if it is expanding too fast, because the higher rate pushes up the interest rates charged by leading private banks to their customers. In 2004 and 2005, the Fed reversed course and raised interest rates to keep inflation in check.

Another monetary policy is one of increasing or decreasing the ***reserve requirement,*** which sets the actual proportion of deposited money that a bank must keep "on demand" as it makes all the rest of the deposits available as new loans.

A third important technique used by the Fed is ***open-market operations***—the buying and selling of Treasury securities to absorb excess dollars or to release more dollars into the economy.

Finally, a fourth power is derived from one of the important services rendered by the Federal Reserve System, which is the opportunity for member banks to borrow from each other. One of the original reasons for creating the Federal Reserve System was to balance regions of the country that might be vigorously expanding with other areas that might be fairly dormant: The national system would enable the banks in a growing region, facing lots of demand for credit, to borrow money from banks in regions of the country where the demand for credit was much lower. This exchange is called the "federal funds market," and the interest rate charged by one bank to another, the ***federal funds rate,*** can be manipulated just like the discount rate, to expand or contract credit.

The federal government also provides insurance to foster credit and encourage private capital investment. The Federal Deposit Insurance Corporation (FDIC) protects bank deposits up to $100,000. Another important promoter of investment is the federal insurance of home mortgages through the Department of Housing and Urban Development (HUD). By federally guaranteeing mortgages, the government reduces the risks that banks run in making such loans, thus allowing banks to lower their interest rates and make such loans more affordable to middle- and lower-income families. These programs have enabled millions of families who could not have otherwise afforded it to finance the purchase of a home.

Fiscal Policies ***Fiscal policies*** include the government's taxing and spending powers. Personal and corporate income taxes, which raise most government revenues, are the most prominent examples. Although the direct purpose of an income tax is to raise revenue, each tax has a different impact on the economy, and government can plan for that impact (see Figure 14.1). For example, although the main reason favoring a significant increase in the Social Security tax (which is an income tax) under President Carter was to keep Social Security solvent, a big reason for it in

FIGURE 14.1

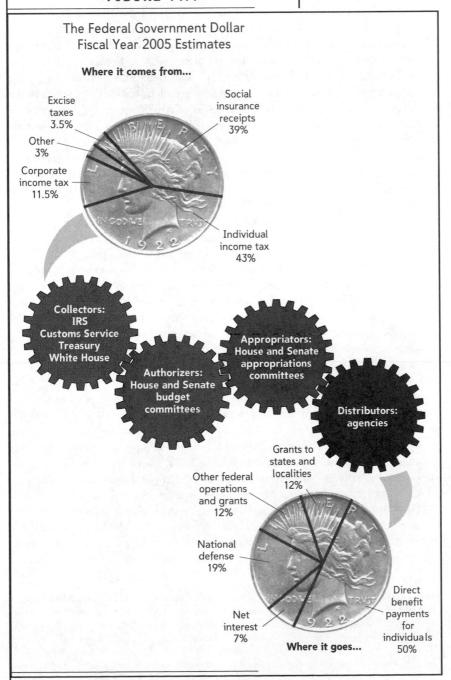

The Federal Government Dollar
Fiscal Year 2005 Estimates

Where it comes from...

Excise taxes 3.5%

Other 3%

Corporate income tax 11.5%

Social insurance receipts 39%

Individual income tax 43%

Collectors:
IRS
Customs Service
Treasury
White House

Authorizers:
House and Senate budget committees

Appropriators:
House and Senate appropriations committees

Distributors:
agencies

Grants to states and localities 12%

Other federal operations and grants 12%

National defense 19%

Net interest 7%

Direct benefit payments for individuals 50%

Where it goes...

SOURCE: Office of Management and Budget, *Budget of the United States Government, Fiscal Year 2005* (Washington, D.C.: Government Printing Office, 2003), pp. 32, 117.

Institution Principle

The autonomy of the Federal Reserve System is a significant design feature of this institution, allowing it either to stimulate or to put a brake on the economy, depending on economic circumstances, without the explicit concurrence of other branches of government.

the minds of many legislators was that it would reduce inflation by shrinking the amount of money people had in their hands to buy more goods and services.

Likewise, President Clinton's commitment in his 1992 campaign to a "middle-class tax cut" was motivated by the goal of encouraging economic growth through increased consumption. Soon after the election, upon learning that the deficit would be far larger than had been earlier reported to him, he confessed he would have to break his promise of such a tax cut. Nevertheless, the idea of a middle-class tax cut is an example of a fiscal policy aimed at increased consumption because of the theory that people in middle-income brackets tend to spend a high proportion of unexpected earnings or windfalls, rather than saving or investing them.[17]

In 2001, the newly elected Republican administration pursued a program of massive tax cuts. This occurred in a context of several years of vigorous economic growth under Clinton, which had produced large revenue surpluses (which the proposed tax cuts would diminish). The Bush administration's policy increased the income threshold for paying taxes, thus relieving some of the poorest taxpayers of any tax obligations at all. But the bulk of the reduction was enjoyed by wealthier taxpayers. The Republicans thus were able to reward their natural electoral constituency and demonstrate their ideological commitment to a smaller role for government. However, a subsequent economic recession, combined with the huge outlays required by September 11 and the wars in Afghanistan and Iraq, rendered the tax cuts aimed at reducing the surplus into one producing record deficits. On top of all this, the requirements of the Social Security program in light of retiring baby boomers were made more problematic by the tax cut. By 2005, some experts had concluded that the Bush tax cuts were fiscally reckless.

Taxation   All taxes discriminate, leaving to public policy the question of *what kind* of discrimination is called for. The tariff—a tax on imported goods—was the most important tax of the nineteenth century, and the "tax policy" of the tariff put most of the burden of raising revenue on foreigners seeking to export their goods to America. This policy was designed to protect our "infant industries" against the more advanced foreign competitors of the day, the implicit assumption being that the tariff would disappear once our industries were no longer in their infancy.

The most important tax of the twentieth century, and indeed the most important choice Congress ever made about taxation (or about any policy, for that matter), was the decision to raise revenue by taxing personal and corporate incomes—the "income tax."[18] The second most important policy choice

[17]For a fascinating behind-the-scenes look at how and why President Clinton abandoned his campaign commitment to tax cuts and economic stimulus and instead accepted the fiscal conservatism advocated by the Federal Reserve and its chairman, Alan Greenspan, see Bob Woodward, *The Agenda: Inside the Clinton White House* (New York: Simon & Schuster, 1994).

[18]The U.S. government imposed an income tax during the Civil War that remained in effect until 1872. In 1894, Congress enacted a modest 2 percent tax on all incomes over $4,000. This $4,000 exemption was in fact fairly high, excluding all working-class people. But in 1895, the Supreme Court declared it unconstitutional, citing the provision of Article I, Section 9, that any direct tax would have to be proportional to the population in each state. See *Pollock v. Farmers' Loan and Trust Company*, 158 U.S. 601 (1895). In 1913, the Sixteenth Amendment was ratified, effectively reversing the *Pollock* case.

624   CH. 14 Government in Action

Congress made was that the income tax be "progressive" or "graduated," with the heaviest burden carried by those most able to pay. A tax is called *progressive* if the rate of taxation goes up with each higher income bracket. A tax is called *regressive* if people in lower income brackets pay a higher proportion of their income toward the tax than people in higher income brackets. For example, a sales tax is deemed regressive because everybody pays at the same rate, so that the proportion of total income paid in taxes goes down as the total income goes up (assuming, as is generally the case, that as total income goes up the amount spent on sales-taxable purchases increases at a lower rate). The Social Security tax is another example of a regressive tax. Current law applies a tax of 6.2 percent on the first $87,900 of income for the retirement program and an additional 1.45 percent on all income (without limit) for Medicare benefits, for a total of 7.65 percent in Social Security taxes. This means that a person earning an income of $87,900 pays $6,724.35 in Social Security taxes, a rate of 7.65 percent. But someone earning nearly twice that income, $150,000, pays a total of $7,624.80 in Social Security taxes, the equivalent of a 5.1 percent rate on the entire income. As income continues to rise, the amount of Social Security taxes also rises, but the *rate*, or the percentage of income that goes to taxes, declines.

> **progressive taxation** Taxation that hits the upper-income brackets more heavily.

> **regressive taxation** Taxation that hits the lower-income brackets more heavily.

The graduated income tax is a moderately progressive tax; in other words, as it collects revenue, it pursues a deliberate *policy of redistribution,* although moderately redistributive. Table 14.1 demonstrates the success of this policy. Before genuine progressive income taxation was instituted in the 1930s, the disparity between the lowest income bracket and the highest reached its widest stretch, almost 46 percentage points. From the 1930s through the 1970s, this gap was reduced. Beginning in the 1980s, however, the gap began to increase again, and it is no coincidence that big across-the-board income tax cuts were adopted in 1981 and 1986. The tax cuts of 2001 and 2003 will accelerate this trend.[19]

> **policy of redistribution** An objective of the graduated income tax—to raise revenue in such a way as to reduce the disparities of wealth between the lowest- and the highest-income brackets.

Redistribution of wealth is not the only policy being pursued by the American personal and corporate income tax. Another important policy imbedded in that tax is the encouragement of the capitalist economy. When the tax law allows individuals or companies to deduct from their taxable income any money they can justify as an investment or as a "business expense," that is an incentive to individuals and companies to spend money to expand their production, their advertising, or their staff, and it reduces the income taxes they pay. These kinds of deductions are called incentives or "equity" by those who support them. For others, they might be called "loopholes." The tax laws of the 1980s actually closed a number of important loopholes. But others still exist—on home mortgages, including second homes, and on business expenses, for example—and others will return, because there is a strong consensus among members of Congress that businesses often need such incentives. They may differ on which incentives

---

[19]The redistributive effect of the income tax would probably have been even more marked if it had not been neutralized to an extent by other regressive taxes such as Social Security taxes, state sales taxes, many federal excise taxes, and tariffs.

TABLE 14.1

The gap between
the richest and
poorest segment of
the population
diminished as the
effects of the
progressive income
tax were felt
beginning in the
1930s. By the
1970s, the gap had
begun to increase.
Do you think tax
cuts had something
to do with this?

Income Distribution in the United States
(1929–2002): The Proportion of Money Income
Going to Each Fifth of the Population[*]

FAMILY INCOME BRACKET	1929	1934	1944	1950	1960	1970	1980	1990	2002
Lowest fifth	5.4	5.9	4.9	4.5	4.8	4.1	4.3	3.9	3.5
Second fifth	10.1	11.5	10.9	12.0	12.2	10.8	10.3	9.6	8.8
Third fifth	14.4	15.5	16.2	17.4	17.8	17.4	16.9	15.9	14.8
Fourth fifth	18.8	20.4	22.2	23.5	24.0	24.5	24.9	24.0	23.3
Highest fifth	51.3	49.7	45.8	42.6	41.3	43.3	43.7	46.6	49.7
Gap between lowest and highest fifths	45.9	43.8	40.9	38.1	36.5	39.2	39.4	42.7	46.2

[*]Figures are not strictly comparable because of differences in calculating procedures.
SOURCES: Data for 1929–50: Allan Rosenbaum, "State Government, Political Power, and Public
Policy: The Case of Illinois" (Ph.D. diss., University of Chicago, 1974), Chapters 10–11, used by
permission; 1960–2002: U.S. Department of Commerce, Bureau of the Census, *Income in the
United States Current Population Reports, 2002* Series P-60 (Washington, DC: Government
Printing Office, 2003).

are best, but there is almost universal agreement in government that some incentives are justifiable.[20]

In every presidential election year, both Democrats and Republicans try to woo voters with pledges of tax cuts. In 2001, George W. Bush made good on his promise to introduce major tax cuts. Although congressional Democrats believed that the administration's proposal benefited the wealthy and jeopardized the budget surplus, they eventually agreed on a compromise bill. The bill reduced taxes at all levels of income (although less than Bush had initially proposed),

[20]For a systematic account of the role of government in providing incentives and inducements to business, see Charles E. Lindblom, *Politics and Markets: The World's Political Economic Systems* (New York: Basic Books, 1977), Chapter 13. For a detailed account of the dramatic Reagan tax cuts and reforms, see Jeffrey H. Birnbaum and Alan S. Murray, *Showdown at Gucci Gulch: Lawmakers, Lobbyists, and the Unlikely Triumph of Tax Reform* (New York: Random House, 1987).

creating a new bottom bracket of 10 percent and reducing the tax rate in each of the other five brackets. In the highest bracket, taxes were cut from 39.6 percent to 35 percent. Most controversial was the provision to repeal the estate tax, a tax that has historically been seen as a way to prevent the emergence of a monied aristocracy in the United States. Reflecting the uneasy compromise that allowed the bill to pass, many of the provisions were slated to phase in over time. The estate tax repeal, for example, does not take effect until 2010. Moreover, all the provisions were subject to a "sunset" provision that automatically repeals the legislation in 2010 unless Congress renews it. Faced with the new budgetary demands of the war on terrorism and a budget deficit, congressional Democrats argued that the Bush tax reform had left the government with insufficient resources. Some urged that the reform be repealed, but Democratic leaders held back, fearing that they would be charged with raising taxes.

Government Spending   The federal government's power to spend is one of the most important tools of economic policy. Decisions about how much to spend affect the overall health of the economy. They also affect every aspect of American life from the distribution of income through the availability of different modes of transportation to the level of education in society. It is not surprising that the fight for control over spending is one of the most contentious in Washington, as interest groups and politicians strive to determine the priorities and appropriate levels of spending. Decisions about spending are made as part of the annual budget process. During the 1990s, when the federal *budget deficit* became a major political issue and when parties were deeply split on spending, the budget process became the focal point of the entire policy-making process. Even though the budget deficit disappeared in the late 1990s, the budget continued to dominate the attention of policy makers. With the deficit on the rise again after September 11, budget politics are sure to remain on the national agenda.

budget deficit
Amount by which government spending exceeds government revenue in a fiscal year.

The president and Congress have each created institutions to assert control over the budget process. The OMB in the Executive Office of the President is responsible for preparing the president's budget. This budget contains the president's spending priorities and the estimated costs of the president's policy proposals. It is viewed as the starting point for the annual debate over the budget. When different parties control the presidency and Congress, the president's budget may have little influence on the budget that is ultimately adopted. Members of the president's own party also may have different priorities. In 2002, members of Congress from both parties resisted the president's efforts to cut spending for domestic programs. A key Republican staffer defended congressional prerogatives to shape the budget, declaring, "Our job is not to rubber-stamp what OMB says."[21]

Congress has its own budget institutions. Congress created the Congressional Budget Office (CBO) in 1974 so that it could have reliable information about the costs and economic impact of the policies it considers. At the same time,

[21]Karen Masterson, "Bush's Budget Promise Goes Bust," *Houston Chronicle*, 7 May 2002, p. A1.

The Federal Reserve Board as a Political Institution

Alan Greenspan, chairman of the Federal Reserve from 1987 to 2006 (when he stepped down and was replaced by Ben S. Bernanke), was one of those rare political actors who are praised by both liberals and conservatives. He was appointed by Ronald Reagan and reappointed by Republicans George H. W. Bush and George W. Bush and Democrat Bill Clinton. Economists from the Right, such as Milton Friedman, and from the Left, such as James Tobin, have sung his praises.[1] What can Greenspan's long and successful political career teach us about the principles of politics?

The fifth principle of politics teaches us that a series of coincidental events can easily build an irreversible historical path. Part of Greenspan's political success is due to sheer luck. He was chairman of the Fed during the 1990s, a period of unprecedented economic expansion. And he was head of the central bank in the world's largest and most powerful capitalist nation when other competing economic systems seemed to fade away as historical relics.

Economic growth during the 1990s was so impressive that it led the *New York Times* to argue in 2003 for Greenspan's reappointment to a *fifth* term, describing him as the architect of one of the great economic booms in American history.

But is Greenspan really a "political" success? What is "political" about the Federal Reserve? The rules and procedures governing the Federal Reserve are supposed to shield it from politics, but in practice these same rules have made the Fed a powerful political institution.

The authors of the 1913 legislation that set up the Federal Reserve felt that it was vital to insulate monetary policy from undue pressure and influence by partisan politicians obsessed with their own short-range re-election prospects. The Federal Reserve was set up along the lines of an independent regulatory commission, not as just one more agency under the direction of the president and supervised by Congress.

The Federal Reserve System's highest decision-making body is the Board of Governors, consisting of seven members. Members are nominated for their positions by the president of the United States and must be confirmed by the Senate. The members serve long terms (fourteen years) and, once appointed, may not be removed from office except through a cumbersome process of impeachment for personal violations of criminal law. The people selected have nearly always been professional bankers, executives of Wall Street brokerage houses, or occasionally professional economists.[2]

These rules by themselves make the Fed and its chair politically powerful. Economic policy, as you are learning in this chapter, is inseparable from politics. The members of the Board of Governors can ignore short-run political pressures; after all, they are in office for fourteen years. The chair is more prone to pressure. Still, his appointment is for four years, purposely designed to be distinct from the presidential and congressional election calendars. Finally, many political institutions struggle with the principal-agent problem, but it is not clear that

History Principle

The strong economic growth of the 1990s solidified Greenspan's position as Fed chairman.

Institution Principle

The long terms of the Federal Reserve Board of Governors insulate them from political pressures.

the Fed is the agent for anyone. In both theory and practice, the Federal Reserve represents the interests of the "economy." This gives the Fed a great deal of autonomy.

The internal rules of the Fed strengthen its hand vis-à-vis other political institutions. The Federal Reserve Board is a small group of generally like-minded economic experts who benefit from all the advantages of a small, homogeneous group. And, unlike the executive branch and especially Congress, the deliberations of the Federal Reserve are purposely kept secret. This is done for good economic reasons: If the deliberations of the board were made public too soon, they could roil economic markets. But secrecy is a powerful tool. As we know from the second principle of politics, homogeneity, small size, and confidentiality make it far easier for a group to bargain, negotiate, and reach a collective decision.

Contrast this with the annual debate over the federal budget. Budget politics in recent years have put Congress on display before the American people, and the picture has not been pretty. In the 2003 session of Congress, only one defense bill managed to pass both the Senate and the House. It was only the specter of another government shutdown that convinced members in both chambers to pass a reconciliation bill that kept the government running for another year. Whom would you trust with your money—Alan Greenspan, with his owlish glasses, confident demeanor, and nonpartisan pose, or 535 argumentative, noisy, and partisan members of Congress?

But don't believe that Alan Greenspan, Ben Bernanke, or the Board of Governors of the Federal Reserve are not political actors, despite Bernanke's pledge to be "independent of all political influences."[3] Like the Supreme Court, the Federal Reserve Board and its chairman are acutely sensitive to political currents. In 1992, Greenspan, who refused to cut interest rates rapidly enough to encourage an economic recovery, was blamed for George H. W. Bush's defeat. But Greenspan, a lifelong Republican, quickly warmed to Bill Clinton and convinced the president to become a deficit hawk in the mid-1990s, even if it meant increasing taxes. In early 2001, however, Greenspan suddenly became an advocate of lowered tax rates, conveniently the same policy promoted by the newly elected George W. Bush.

The rules and procedures of the Fed insulate it from rapid political changes. Combine this with historical events over the past two decades and the adroit political antenna of former chairman Greenspan, and the Federal Reserve has quietly become one of the most powerful institutions in the American government, if not in the world economy.

Collective-Action Principle

The makeup of the Fed's Board of Governors facilitates collective decision-making.

[1]You can learn more about Greenspan's life and career in Bob Woodward, *Maestro: Greenspan's Fed and the American Boom* (New York: Simon & Schuster, 2000); and Justin Martin, *Greenspan: The Man behind the Money* (Cambridge, MA: Perseus, 2001).

[2]Federal Reserve Act of 1913. See also James Livingston, *Origins of the Federal Reserve System: Money, Class, and Corporate Capitalism, 1890–1913* (Ithaca, NY: Cornell University Press, 1986); and William Greider, *Secrets of the Temple: How the Federal Reserve Runs the Country* (New York: Simon & Schuster, 1987).

[3]msnbc.msn.com, 15 November 2005.

History Principle

The budget not only reflects future policy priorities but mirrors past decisions as well. The historical accumulation of policy promises is ultimately reflected in the cumulative debt that must be "serviced" each year by interest payments.

Congress set up a budget process designed to establish spending priorities and to consider individual expenditures in light of the entire budget. A key element of the process is the annual budget resolution, which designates broad targets for spending. By estimating the costs of policy proposals, Congress hoped to control spending and to reduce deficits. When the congressional budget process proved unable to hold down deficits in the 1980s, Congress instituted stricter measures to control spending, including "spending caps" that limit spending on some types of programs.

A very large and growing proportion of the annual federal budget is *mandatory spending,* expenditures that are, in the words of the OMB, "relatively uncontrollable." Interest payments on the national debt, for example, are determined by the actual size of the national debt. Legislation has mandated payment rates for such programs as retirement under Social Security, retirement for federal employees, unemployment assistance, Medicare, and farm price supports (see Figure 14.2). These payments increase with the cost of living; they increase as the average age of the population goes up; they increase as national and world agricultural surpluses go up. In 1970, 38.6 percent of the total federal budget was made up of these *uncontrollables;* in 1975, 52.5 percent fell into that category; and by 2001, around 64.7 percent was in the uncontrollable category. This means that the national government now has very little *discretionary spending* to increase or decrease spending to counteract fluctuations in the business cycle.

This has a profound political implication. With mandatory, or relatively uncontrollable, spending on the rise, there is less scope for the exercise of discretion. If a budget has to be cut and categories of mandatory spending are taken off the table, then the cuts will disproportionately fall on what remains. With the pain of cutting "available" programs, the prospects for distributing the cuts in a manner acceptable to all interested parties grow dim. Thus the politics will be more intense and dirty; groups will be more highly mobilized, energized, and at one another's throats; Congress and the president will be eyeball to eyeball as they seek to protect their different constituencies; and political partisans will not be in the mood for compromise.[22]

Government spending as a fiscal policy works fairly well when deliberate deficit spending is used to stop a recession and to speed up the recovery period. But it does not work very well in fighting inflation because elected politicians are politically unable to make the drastic expenditure cuts necessary to balance the budget, much less to produce a budgetary surplus.

---

[22]Of course, it should be underscored that "relatively uncontrollable" is itself a policy decision taken by the president and Congress. It is not carved in granite; it can be undone. To undo some things, like not making a promised payment on the national debt, would have horrible consequences in credit markets. A modest across-the-board reduction in outlays for hospital assistance under Medicare, on the other hand, while painful (literally and figuratively), might nevertheless be accommodated (with hospitals and patients sharing the burden in various ways—for example, deferral of elective procedures or delaying a salary increase). That is, things that are alleged to be "off the table" can be put right back on the table.

FIGURE 14.2

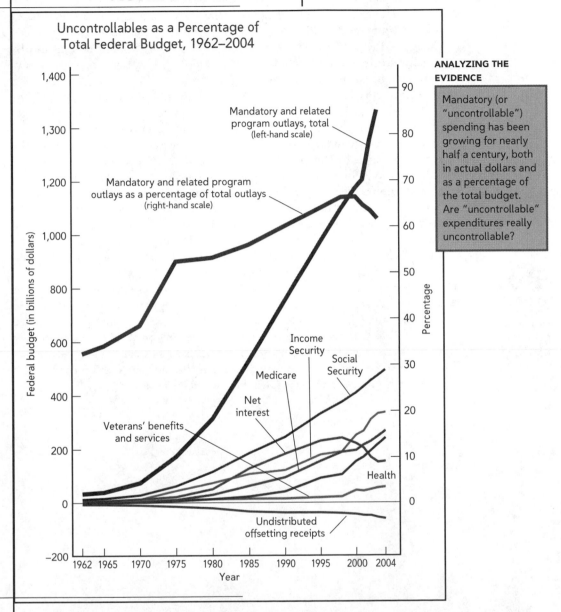

Uncontrollables as a Percentage of
Total Federal Budget, 1962–2004

ANALYZING THE EVIDENCE

Mandatory (or "uncontrollable") spending has been growing for nearly half a century, both in actual dollars and as a percentage of the total budget. Are "uncontrollable" expenditures really uncontrollable?

SOURCE: Office of Management and Budget, *Budget of the U.S. Government, Fiscal Year 2005. Historical Tables* (Washington, DC: Government Printing Office, 2004), pp. 45, 125, 129.

The Politics of Redistributive Policy   Redistributive policies seek to control citizens by manipulating their environment rather than by attempting to control their conduct directly. For example, a small percentage change in the interest rate can immediately affect millions of potential homeowners or investors; a change of the top income-tax rate from 39.6 percent to 35.0 percent can be equally effective. Yet in neither of these examples do citizens have to "do" anything to come within the jurisdiction of the law.

One theory describing the politics of redistributive policy is called the "power elite" theory. Offered by many social scientists as a general theory of power in a capitalist nation, it has turned out to be unconvincing as a general theory. According to the power-elite theory, the most important decisions for the society are made by a small political elite, generally composed of individuals and families who enjoy the highest incomes and status of the society. These individuals and families tend to be drawn from corporate leadership, the occupants of the highest political positions, and the highest echelons of the defense establishment. Although these may appear to be distinct sectors of society, power-elite theory holds that they constitute a single elite because these people tend to know each other, go to the same elite schools, and share a general consensus on long-range objectives for the society.[23]

The power-elite theory of redistributive politics, however, begs the obvious question: What motivates the power elite? An alternative answer more in line with the rationality principle is that tax policy reflects the interests of elected politicians in being re-elected. If politicians deciding on tax rates are motivated by re-election and the median voter's income is more than the average, the tax system will be less redistributive. Likewise, if the median voter's income is less than the average, the tax system will be more redistributive.[24]

> **Policy Principle**
>
> Redistributive policies reflect the interests of elected leaders in getting re-elected.

---

[23]C. Wright Mills, *The Power Elite* (New York: Oxford University Press, 1956); Kenneth Prewitt and Alan Stone, *The Ruling Elites: Elite Theory, Power, and American Democracy* (New York: Harper & Row, 1973); G. William Domhoff, *Who Rules America Now? A View for the '80s* (Englewood Cliffs, NJ: Prentice Hall, 1983).

[24]See Allan H. Meltzer and Scott F. Richard, "A Rational Theory of the Size of Government," *Journal of Political Economy* 89 (1981): 914–27.

SUMMARY

To study public policy is to understand government in action, to see how government seeks to control the population by creating incentives for people to alter their behavior. Public policy is a synonym for law, and the use of public policy has become more widespread over the years, probably because it seems more reciprocal, humane, and changeable in response to demands—in a word, democratic.

The first major section of this chapter defined market economy and the conditions needed for creating a modern free market. This was followed by a discussion of the substantive goals of public policies within a market economy—that is, the objectives people seek through government—the tools government uses to achieve these goals, and the political patterns typically at work in achieving them. We began with the most fundamental type of policy: public order and private property. Virtually everyone supports these policies, even though people may differ on how much they want and how they want the policies implemented. We went on to another policy also widely and strongly defended in the United States: supporting and maintaining business development. This includes regulating the market, a restrictive approach but one motivated by the goal of making markets more stable and more competitive, not eliminating them. Deregulation is, of course, an aspect of regulation. All of these policies have one major objective—to maintain not only a market economy but also a sound and fiscally responsible capitalist economy.

Rationality Principle	Collective-Action Principle	Institution Principle	Policy Principle	History Principle
Public policies create incentives for people to alter the direction or intensity of their behavior.	Government has lots of tools that affect the economy, but there is considerable political conflict over which tools to use, how to use them, and when to use them. Government involvement in the economy thus provides opportunities for groups to mobilize in order to become winners or to avoid becoming losers.	Government can play an important role in establishing the rules and institutions that allow a market economy to function.	Because institutional arrangements make change difficult, public policies are durable.	Historical events can motivate government officials to adopt new policies.
Even if governments seek to "do good," this does not prevent rational politicians from searching for opportunities to take care of their constituents.		Government institutions—most notably courts and regulatory agencies—engage in market interventions to alleviate (not always successfully) market failures.	The market economy provides opportunities for government agents to intervene by formulating and implementing policies.	The scope of national regulatory policies expanded during the 1930s, 1960s, and early 1970s but contracted during the late 1970s to mid-1990s.
Contracting may be used instrumentally as a tool to encourage particular sectors of the economy.		American political institutions, particularly Congress, allow promotional policies to take the form of pork-barrel legislation through vote trading, logrolling, and omnibus bills.	In promotional policies, political actors seek to distribute funds and projects to their political supporters.	The budget not only reflects future policy priorities but mirrors past decisions as well. The historical accumulation of policy promises is ultimately reflected in the cumulative debt that must be "serviced" each year by interest payments.
		The autonomy of the Federal Reserve System is a significant design feature of this institution, allowing it either to stimulate or to put a brake on the economy, depending on economic circumstances, without the explicit concurrence of other branches of government.	The politics of regulatory policy tends to be dominated by interest groups, especially those interests that might be regulated by government.	
			Redistributive policies reflect the interests of elected leaders in getting re-elected.	

FOR FURTHER READING

Birnbaum, Jeffrey H., and Alan S. Murray. *Showdown at Gucci Gulch: Lawmakers, Lobbyists, and the Unlikely Triumph of Tax Reform*. New York: Random House, 1987.

Cochran, Clarke E., Lawrence C. Mayer, T. R. Curr, and N. Joseph Cayer. *American Public Policy: An Introduction*, 7th ed. New York: St. Martin's Press, 2003.

Derthick, Martha, and Paul J. Quirk. *The Politics of Deregulation*. Washington, DC: Brookings Institution, 1985.

Greider, William. *Secrets of the Temple: How the Federal Reserve Runs the Country*. New York: Simon & Schuster, 1987.

Heilbroner, Robert L. *The Nature and Logic of Capitalism*. New York: Norton, 1985.

Holmes, Stephen, and Cass R. Sunstein. *The Cost of Rights: Why Liberty Depends on Taxes*. New York: Norton, 1999.

Krugman, Paul R. *Peddling Prosperity: Economic Sense and Nonsense in the Age of Diminished Expectations*. New York: Norton, 1994.

Levy, Frank. *The New Dollars and Dreams: American Incomes and Economic Change*. New York: Russell Sage Foundation, 1998.

Lindblom, Charles. *Politics and Markets: The World's Political Economic Systems*. New York: Basic Books, 1977.

Suskind, Ron. *The Price of Loyalty: George W. Bush, the White House, and the Education of Paul O'Neill*. New York: Simon & Schuster, 2004.

Vogel, David. *Fluctuating Fortunes: The Political Power of Business in America*. New York: Basic Books, 1989.

Tax Reform and Special Interests

Echoes of 1986? Not in Bush's Tax Reform Panel

By EDMUND L. ANDREWS

Twenty years ago, President Ronald Reagan found himself politically weakened by large budget deficits, the Nicaraguan contra imbroglio and a Congress that was partly controlled by his Democratic opponents.

Yet Mr. Reagan managed to push through a sweeping overhaul of the tax code that, at least for a few years, stood as a victory of bipartisan common sense over high-priced special interests. . . .

Could President Bush achieve a comparable breakthrough? Not unless he changes his modus operandi in fundamental ways.

Mr. Bush took a first step toward tax overhaul on Tuesday, when his hand-picked advisory panel delivered two broad proposals for again purging the tax code of its complexity, corruption and cost to the economy.

But cleaning up the tax code creates winners and losers, and Mr. Bush has shown little appetite for confronting losers. . . . Mr. Bush's biggest obstacle has little to do with uncompromising opposition by Democrats. Rather, Mr.

Bush's effort is more likely to die as a result of constraints he put on his own tax panel and, by extension, on himself. At the same time, the panel's recommendations would provoke opposition from armies of special-interest groups with something to lose.

Under Mr. Bush's explicit marching orders, the panel's proposals had to be "revenue neutral" and to assume that his tax cuts would be made permanent. He also ordered the panel to retain homeowners' tax breaks, one of the most expensive tax expenditures in the entire code, and to protect tax breaks for charities.

Not surprisingly, the resulting plan was sober but uninspiring.

The panel would eliminate the alternative minimum tax, or A.M.T., a parallel tax originally aimed at the very rich that is now set to engulf millions of middle-income families every year. . . .

The panel's main proposal would indeed simplify many aspects of the tax code. It would greatly benefit wealthy taxpayers by sharply reducing taxes on

New York Times, 6 November 2005, section 3, p. 3.

investment income, but it would also cut back on tax breaks that primarily benefit the rich.

However sensible those ideas may be, they fall far short of a radical overhaul. Neither of the proposals would have replaced today's system with a flat tax or a pure consumption tax, the goal of many Republican conservatives. More important, neither of the proposals would significantly lower existing tax rates—a crucial attraction of the 1986 overhaul. . . .

At the same time, both proposals immediately provoked opposition from industry groups and their well-paid lobbyists. Mortgage lenders immediately lashed out at the panel's recommendation to trim back the huge tax deduction for interest payments on home mortgages. . . .

Such complaints are inevitable when tax breaks are up for debate. The problem is that special-interest pleaders have extraordinary political leverage if there isn't a big idea animating the overall project.

One of the panel's boldest ideas, for example, is to scale back the huge tax deduction on mortgage interest, and to use that money to offset the cost of losing the alternative minimum tax. The mortgage deduction has been sacrosanct ever since the income tax was created almost a century ago. It benefits tens of millions of families and is supposed to make homeownership more affordable and thus more widespread.

But the panel . . . noted that the rate of homeownership in the United States is the same or lower than it is in Britain and Australia, which have no mortgage interest deduction. If there were no tax deduction for mortgage interest, house prices would almost certainly be lower.

The panel also noted that 70 percent of American tax filers received no benefit from the mortgage deduction in 2002, even though nearly 69 percent of families were homeowners. Fifty-five

ESSENCE OF THE STORY

- In 1986, President Reagan, though under political attack, pushed through sweeping reforms of the tax code. In 2005, President Bush shows no similar willingness to take on the political risks of reforming the tax code.

- Bush placed two major restrictions on the panel: first, assume that the 2001 tax cuts were going to be made permanent, and second, protect the home mortgage deduction. These restrictions so hampered the panel that only modest reforms were proposed.

- Republicans who are in favor of sweeping reforms, such as a national sales tax, are unenthusiastic, while interest groups such as the homebuilders association are strongly opposed to any large-scale reform.

POLITICAL ANALYSIS

- Tax reformers face a classic collective action problem. Millions of individual taxpayers benefit from reform, but simplifying the code results in unclear savings and perhaps a small amount of tax reduction. Each individual tax break, however, is fiercely defended by small, homogeneous, and highly organized interests.

- Politically, President Bush is caught between one part of the Republican Party, which advocates a dramatic overhaul of the tax code, and the main financial supporters of his party, which tend to be the interests that benefit from the current code.

- The home mortgage deduction highlights a common complaint about the tax code—many provisions, though promoting laudable goals like home ownership, benefit wealthier citizens.

percent of the tax benefits went to the top 12 percent of taxpayers who earned more than $100,000 a year.

Given that critique, the truly bold approach would have been to scrap the mortgage deduction altogether.

But the panel could not do that, because Mr. Bush had ordered it to protect incentives for homeownership.

CHAPTER

15

Government and Society

Social policies promote a range of public goals. The first is to protect against the risks and insecurities that most people face over the course of their lives. These include illness, disability, temporary unemployment, and the reduced earning capability that comes with old age. Most spending on social welfare in the United States goes to programs such as Social Security and medical insurance for the elderly that serve these purposes. These are widely regarded as successful and popular programs. They are the least controversial areas of social spending, although the debates about funding Social Security reveal that even widely-agreed-on policies can generate conflict. Such conflicts over how to achieve security against risks have prevented the United States from adopting universal health insurance. Despite the fact that most Americans support a public role in guaranteeing health coverage, disputes over how this should be done have blocked repeated efforts at health reform.

More controversial have been the other two goals of social policy: promoting *equality of opportunity* and assisting the poor. Although Americans admire the ideal of equal opportunity, there is no general agreement about what govern-

equality of opportunity
The American ideal that all have the freedom to use whatever talents and wealth they possess to reach their fullest potential.

ment should do to address inequalities of results: groups that have suffered from past inequality generally support much more extensive government action to promote equality of opportunity than do others. Yet most Americans favor some government action, especially in the area of education.

The third goal of social policy—to alleviate poverty—has long generated controversy in the United States. Americans take pride in their strong work ethic and prize the value of self-sufficiency. As a result, the majority of Americans express suspicions that the able-bodied poor will not try hard enough to support themselves if they are offered too much assistance or if they receive the wrong kind of assistance. Yet there is also recognition that poverty may be the product of past inequality of opportunity. Since the 1960s, a variety of educational programs and income assistance policies have sought to end poverty and promote equal opportunity. Much progress has been made toward these goals. However, the disproportionate rates of poverty among minorities suggest that our policies have not solved the problem of unequal opportunity. Likewise, the high rates of child poverty challenge us to find new ways to assist the poor.

There is no way to know precisely when the government ought to be called on and what the government ought to do to help individuals secure the right to pursue their own happiness. Economic and social transformations pose new challenges and often alter public views about what government should do. In the 1930s, a deep and widespread economic depression created broad public support for new programs such as federal unemployment insurance. Today, the increased numbers of women in the labor force and the growth in single-parent households have prompted calls for more government assistance to help people combine work and family responsibilities more effectively. Yet there is no agreement on what government should do. Likewise, as the economy has changed, inequality among working people has grown. Should the government address such inequality? If so, with what measures? Shifting patterns of risk and opportunity provoke new demands from citizens and, in so doing, place social-policy issues at the center of national politics.

The first two sections of the chapter deal with the politics and history of social policy. We start with this because the politics of redistributing wealth, status, and security is a special politics.

CHAPTER OUTLINE

The Politics of Social Policy

The History of the Social Welfare System

What Are the Foundations of the Social Welfare System?

• Social Security

• Medicare

• Welfare: Means-Tested Public Assistance Policy

Analyzing the Welfare System

• Arguments against It

• Arguments for It

How Can Government Create Opportunity?

• Education Policies and Their Politics

• Health Policies and Their Politics

Who Is Poor? What Can Government Do?

The third section deals with policies concerned with increasing security by reducing the risk of poverty and dependency. Most of these policies come under the conventional label of "Social Security" or "social insurance," which concerns the *contributory* part of the welfare state (discussed immediately below). The fourth section focuses on welfare or the welfare system, which is also concerned with alleviation of poverty and dependency but is the *noncontributory*, or "means-tested" dimension; eligibility to receive benefits is based on demonstrated need. The two dimensions together—contributory and noncontributory—make up the "welfare state," a name that became popular in the United States in the late 1930s to distinguish welfare state from warfare state. This section concludes with recent efforts to reform the system. The fifth section deals with social policies other than civil rights policies that are concerned primarily with increasing opportunities for the poor and the underprivileged. The final section provides a debate or dialogue on the welfare state, including efforts at reform by its supporters and the opposition throughout its history.

THE POLITICS OF SOCIAL POLICY

There is no way to predict when political leaders will get the message and put an issue on the policy agenda. This is especially difficult when issues involve questions of rights. The unprecedented Great Depression was enough to put Social Security and the welfare state on the policy agenda. The foundations of the welfare state were in place by 1935. But ten years later, after World War II and the emergence of women and African Americans as true participants in American society, not a single social policy had been produced. The postwar economy broke all records for growth; but increased poverty and minority unrest also grew—without a single step toward addressing the expectations and demands that these new groups were bringing forward. One of the most important documents in the history of social policy in the United States was composed by President Truman's Committee on Civil Rights, *To Secure These Rights*, published in 1949. It set the terms of discourse for the ensuing five years and helped spur the litigation by the

National Association for the Advancement of Colored People (NAACP) and its famous special counsel, Thurgood Marshall, who would take *Brown v. Board*[1] to the Supreme Court in 1954. He was later nominated to the Supreme Court and became the first black justice. But that stunning and unusually well-written Truman committee document, coupled with the brilliant legal maneuverings of Marshall and associates, did not put civil rights and equal opportunity directly on any public policy agenda. A sense of urgency did not produce widespread agreement on what the government ought to do. Should we address inequality at all? If so, with what measures and techniques? What to do and when to do it? How to do it? To what end?

All of this sounds like the household noise of democratic politics: interest groups, mass opinions, political parties, and public appeals interact at all levels with representative institutions, culminating with legislation that passes into the agencies of the executive branch for implementation. However, social policies are *redistributive* policies. This is a special category of public policy, which we identified and discussed, along with promotional and regulatory policies, toward the end of Chapter 14. Here are some examples of the redistributive type of policy: A tiny increase in the tax liability of the top income earners or a tiny increase in Social Security benefits for those with the lowest incomes can result in a quite significant transfer of income from the upper-income brackets to the lower. Or a tiny boost or reduction in interest rates can redistribute economic opportunities as well as hard cash to or from the investing classes to the mortgaging and construction classes, where both classes are in the *higher* income brackets. Because of their potential redistributive effect, it is extremely difficult to get social policies on the agenda of the president and Congress; and, for the same reason, once a social policy is adopted, it tends to remain on the statute books as though untouchable. This is why in recent years social policies have often been referred to as the "third rail" of American politics.

To repeat, for the sake of clarity, *redistributive policies are special because their effect cuts across class lines.* "Class" is not limited to rich versus poor or employees versus employers. There are other major cleavages in society that are worthy of the term "class," such as labor-intensive industries versus capital-intensive industries; other significant class cleavages are age versus youth, female versus male, white versus black, agricultural versus commercial, and even, very generally, seaboard (blue) versus interior (red). Many critics of social policy raise the specter of "class warfare" whenever a new social policy is proposed. But class cleavage does not have to be warfare. In fact, the *interest-group politics* that tends to be the prevailing pattern around regulatory and promotional policies can be a lot more intense than class politics. For example, on issues of the regulation and sale of guns and the registration of gun owners, the formidable National Rifle Association (NRA)—probably the second most influential interest group in the country—rises up as if going into battle, arguing that even the smallest intrusion on "the right to bear arms" would destroy the Constitution and our society itself. In contrast, on Social Security reform,

[1] *Brown v. Board of Education*, Topeka, Kansas, 347 U.S. 483 (1954).

the American Association of Retired Persons (AARP)—probably the *most* influential and largest of all interest groups—speaks with a single voice, "as a class," for all retired persons and those soon to retire. AARP is the leading foe of President Bush's Social Security reforms. In the last two weeks of March 2005, AARP reportedly spent $5 million on anti-Bush ads, nearly three times as much as all expenditures of all groups supporting President Bush on Social Security. AARP was, of course, denounced by the other side, yet key White House aides worked with AARP in an effort to find "common ground," and AARP officials let it be known that they were not averse to changing Social Security but were mainly opposing the Bush plan for private accounts. AARP's size and distribution throughout many critical congressional districts may kill the entire Bush proposal, but that will be due to stalemate and not because of intimidation and other strategies of political warfare.[2]

It is also fair to compare recent Social Security–type issues with the politics of President Bush's proposal for caps on the fees that tort lawyers can charge for winning product-liability, doctor-negligence, and other damage suits, especially class action suits. In response, tort lawyers mobilized around their national association and became the leading interest group opposing caps, pitting their own efforts against those of other divisions of the American Bar Association, the insurance companies, doctors (especially gynecologists and obstetricians), hospital associations, and so on. Another case of the politics of regulatory economic policy, the regulation of pharmaceuticals, is one subset of the larger issue of product liability. Manufacturers of medications such as Vioxx and Celebrex are a formidable interest group battling the trial lawyers and a variety of consumer groups and alternate drug producers to keep Congress from tightening safety measures, especially expensive and time-consuming testing procedures. Competition among interest groups often comes close to warfare.

Care should be taken here not to let the politics of policy making overshadow a prior phase: the *agenda*. Policy *making* is the end of a long process. Chapter 5 lays out how a bill becomes a law; but before that, and just as important, is how a bill becomes a bill. Any member of Congress can propose a bill. It is read once by the presiding officer and then referred to a committee, where it can die after a long waiting period. To survive it has to be moved up to a higher priority, the real agenda of Congress.

Agenda is simply "a list of things to be done." Many people call their appointment book their agenda. But in collective decision making, an agenda remains a list of things to be done, and getting on the policy agenda of a legislature or a president is difficult—and probably the most creative phase of the entire policy-making process. In this institutional context, the agenda is the current list of *agreements on what to disagree about.*

Lacking a capacity to agree on what to disagree about, a legislative assembly is doomed. The popular picture of representative government is a legislature made

[2]See especially Jeffrey Birnbaum, "Listen to the Wallet—AARP Has Become a Formidable Foe of President Bush's Social Security Plan," *Washington Post National Weekly Edition*, 4–10 April 2005, pp. 11–12.

up of representatives, all equal in having been elected from a "constituency," who debate for as long as necessary, then call for a vote of passage or failure of the bill. But if the legislature is to be what the name implies, a giver of the laws, it must depart from that ideal of equality among representatives and organize itself in a way that it can control the order of which items comes first, second, and third; the rules of debate and amendment; and the terms of when the debate has to be closed and the vote taken. Moreover, the "yea–nay" vote after formal debate is the end process; important issues are not born in simple two-part debate format. It is a prime function of the two major parties, probably their most important function, to compose the agenda, to enforce the order of priority, to control the time allotted, and to provide and police the procedures governing debate and passage. None of this has anything to do with which side of the issue one is on. The two major parties have to operate in virtual unanimity to make the legislative process work, largely because the agenda requires nonpartisan, bipartisan, virtual unanimous agreement.

We oversimplify politics and make bad judgments about political power by adding up "who got what" in the policies produced by government. We also have to take into account what kinds of issues are *kept off the agenda* and never come up for any attention whatsoever.[3] For example, it took the 1954 Supreme Court decision and ten years of mass movements coupled with the assassination of John F. Kennedy to get the first serious civil rights bill on Congress's agenda. For another, more complex example, it takes a majority of members to get a controversial issue of any sort assigned to a congressional committee agenda and then to get it placed on Congress's formal agenda (the Calendar); but, given the filibuster rule in the Senate, it takes a three-fifths (60) vote to get it on the *real* agenda for debate and an up-or-down roll-call vote. Republicans kept many of President Bill Clinton's judicial nominees off the agenda by bottling up their names in the Senate Judiciary Committee; and Democrats paid them back, keeping a number of President George W. Bush's judicial nominees off the agenda by threatening to filibuster any nominee reported from the Republican-controlled Judiciary Committee to a Senate with a majority of Republicans but lacking the votes to overcome the filibuster. There is a lot of power at stake in that workaday word *agenda*.

Agenda is equally a presidential concern. The president's party and indeed the entire membership of Congress depend on the president to mobilize the public around key issues. This is part of what we called "presidential initiative" in Chapter 6. The presidential initiative is not only the mobilization of one issue and one proposal at a time; Congress depends on the president to coordinate and prioritize issues. Since the 1950s, this has come to be called "the president's program." That

---

[3]A classic argument on this point is Peter Bachrach and M. S. Baratz, "Two Faces of Power," *American Political Science Review* (1962): 947–52. On the basis of their research, Bachrach and Baratz conclude that pluralism is not very democratic because, despite vigorous competition among interest groups and the universalization of suffrage, groups representing lower or less-respected classes do not have power because their demands rarely get on the agenda at all.

concept was virtually the first insight that led to recognition of the transformation of the "new American state" from a "congressional government" to a "presidential government."[4]

Presidential initiative is most important when the policy at issue is a redistributive social policy, because mass support on either side of that issue is so much more difficult to mobilize than the already mobilized and well-organized interest groups that dominate in the regulatory and promotion field of public policy. An entire class of people is too large and too diffuse to become suddenly organized when an issue arises. This is why issues like Social Security and welfare and income tax structure get on the national agenda only once in ten or twenty years. It has been nearly twenty years since Social Security was last up for serious reconsideration. And, despite the fact that President Bush made Social Security reform a major campaign issue in 2004 and gave it high priority in his State of the Union address of 2005, coupled with an intensive nationwide campaign for Social Security reform in early 2005, it did not reach the agenda for full consideration in the House and Senate that year. Moreover, many of his own Republican leaders in Congress are doubtful that it will reach Congress at all because 2006 is an election year, during which members hate to touch that third rail. Another factor is that President Bush is a lame duck (one who cannot run for office again). For another example, the "noncontributory" welfare programs (discussed below) had *never* been on Congress's agenda for fundamental reform until 1996, and only then because Republicans broke all modern records by winning control of Congress in 1994 and convincing President Clinton that cooperation with conservatives was the only way to survive the 1996 election. Finally, Medicare reform was put on the agenda in 2004 for the first time since 1972–73.

In contrast, regulatory and promotional policy issues in such important economic areas as energy, the environment, communications, agriculture, and international trade get regular airings, because virtually every sector of the economy is represented by highly specialized interest groups. Their proposals are not always adopted as new law; but interest groups represented by prominent Washington lobbyists can get their issues on the agenda, accompanied by thorough research documents, participation in hearings by congressional committees, and on to the floor for debate.

THE HISTORY OF THE SOCIAL WELFARE SYSTEM

Americans do not have a long history of taking public responsibility for inequalities of opportunity. We were, in fact, the last of the Western democracies to

---

[4]Two classic articles on this development of the president's program were published by Richard Neustadt in 1952: "Presidency and Legislation: Planning the President's Program" and "Presidency and Legislation: The Growth of Central Clearance," in *American Political Science Review* (September 1954 and December 1955, respectively).

enter this realm of social policy. First, our faith in individualism was extremely strong. Second, this was fed by the existence of the frontier, which was so enticing that poverty was seen as a temporary condition that could be alleviated by moving westward. Third, Americans conceived of poverty as belonging in two separate classes: the "deserving poor" and the "undeserving poor." The deserving poor were the widows, orphans, and others rendered dependent by some misfortune beyond their control, such as national disaster, injury in the course of honest labor, or effects of war. The undeserving poor were able-bodied persons unwilling to work; transients from their communities; or others of whom, for various reasons, the community did not approve. An extensive system of private charity developed during the nineteenth century on the basis of this distinction between the deserving poor and the undeserving poor. Most of this kind of welfare came from churches, related religious groups, and, to an extent, ethnic and fraternal societies. This was called charity, or "Christian love," which was often coupled with a high moral sense of obligation.

Until the end of the nineteenth century, government involvement in charitable activities, or what we today call welfare, was slight, not only because of America's preference for individual endeavors and for private and voluntary approaches to charity but also because Americans believed that all of the deserving poor would be taken care of by private efforts. Congress did enact pensions for Civil War veterans and their dependents; and for its day, this was considered a generous social policy. But those pension policies were badly undercut by a patronage-ridden administration of the benefits, thus damaging the system and depriving a large segment of American citizens of federal aid.[5] Congress also attempted to reach the lower-income groups with policies that would eliminate child labor, and a number of states joined in with attempts to eliminate the most egregiously dangerous and unsanitary working conditions. But these efforts were soon declared unconstitutional by the Supreme Court. Other efforts, such as the experiment with mothers' pensions and additional protective labor policies, were adopted by a few progressive states. But even as late as 1928, only 11.6 percent of all relief granted in fifteen of the largest cities came from public funds.[6]

The traditional approach, dominated by the private sector with its severe distinction between deserving and undeserving poor, crumbled in 1929 before the stark reality of the Great Depression. During the Depression, misfortune became so widespread and private wealth shrank so drastically that private charity was out of the question, and the distinction between deserving and undeserving became impossible to draw. The Great Depression proved to Americans that poverty could be a result of imperfections in the economic system rather than of individual irresponsibility. Americans held to their distinction between the deserving and the

 History Principle

The Great Depression was a turning point in the national government's decision to be involved in improving the welfare of the poor.

[5]See Suzanne Mettler, *Divided Citizens: Gender and Federalism in New Deal Public Policy* (Ithaca, NY: Cornell University Press, 1998), p. 2. See also Theda Skocpol, *Protecting Soldiers and Mothers: The Political Origins of Social Policy in the United States* (Cambridge, MA: Harvard University Press, 1992).
[6]Merle Fainsod, Lincoln Gordon, and Joseph C. Palamountain Jr., *Government and the American Economy*, 3rd ed. (New York: Norton, 1959), p. 769, based on a WPA study by Ann E. Geddes.

undeserving poor but significantly altered their standards regarding who was deserving and who was not.

Once poverty and dependency were accepted as problems inherent in the economy, a large-scale public policy approach became practical. Indeed, there was no longer any real question about whether the national government would assume a major responsibility for poverty; from that time forward, it was a question of how generous or restrictive the government was going to be about the welfare of the poor. The national government's efforts to improve the welfare of the poor can be divided into two responses. First, it instituted policies that attempted to change the economic rules about the condition of work for those who were working and could work. Second, it set in place policies seeking to change the economic rules determining the quality of life of those who could not (and in some cases, would not) work. The first response comes under the heading of policies for labor regulation. We dealt with some of these policies in Chapter 3, showing how the Constitution itself, especially the commerce clause, had to be interpreted in a fundamentally different way to reach into local plants and firms to improve the conditions and rewards of work. Since the adoption of the 1935 National Labor Relations (Wagner) Act, there have been revisions (e.g., the Taft-Hartley Act of 1947 and the Landrum-Griffin Labor Management Act of 1959), but no real change of the economic rules established in 1935. These rules were designed to protect laborers so that they could organize and bargain collectively with their employers rather than (according to the older economic rules) negotiating as individuals under vastly unequal conditions.

That same year, 1935, Congress also adopted the historical Social Security Act. As defined and detailed in the next section, the program applied to a far larger segment of the population than the Wagner Act, which applied almost exclusively to wage workers in heavy industry represented by trade unions. Social Security programs at the start, and as later expanded, covered the vast majority of Americans: all wage earners, temporarily unemployed workers seeking work, survivors of eligible workers, the elderly, and disabled persons. Another expression outside the Social Security Act was the minimum wage, which had a modest beginning in the Fair Labor Standards Act of 1938. Efforts were made several times, including an ambitious effort by President Richard Nixon, to establish a minimum annual income. Although all these efforts failed, a program accomplishing part of the same objective, the Earned Income Tax Credit (EITC), was adopted in 1975. Aimed at working families near the officially recognized poverty line, EITC gives a tax credit fore each dollar earned, up to a certain point, and then the payments are phased out as the worker's income rises. As of 2004 the income level set for eligibility for EITC payments was $11,490.

We turn now to the most important of policies that seek to change the rules regarding (1) who shall be poor; (2) how poor they shall be allowed to be; and (3) who, for whatever reason, cannot work or otherwise find means to provide for themselves. All these policies together make up what we have come to call the welfare state.

WHAT ARE THE FOUNDATIONS OF THE SOCIAL WELFARE SYSTEM?

The foundations of the American welfare system were established by the Social Security Act of 1935. Table 15.1 is an outline of the key programs in the social welfare system.

Social Security

Contributory programs are financed by taxation, which justifiably can be called "forced savings." These contributory programs are what most people have in mind when they refer to **Social Security** or social insurance. Under the original retirement program, old-age insurance, the employer and the employee were each required to pay equal amounts, which in 1937 was set at 1 percent of the first $3,000 of wages, to be deducted from the paycheck of each employee and matched by the same amount from the employer. This percentage has increased over the years; the total contribution is now 7.65 percent, subdivided as follows: 6.2 percent on the first $87,900 of income for Social Security benefits, plus 1.45 percent on all earnings for Medicare.[7]

Social Security is a rather conservative approach to welfare. In effect, the Social Security (FICA) tax, as a forced saving, sends a message that people cannot be trusted to save voluntarily to take care of their own retirement needs. But in another sense, it is quite radical. Social Security is not real insurance; workers' contributions do not accumulate in a personal account like an annuity. Consequently, contributors do not receive benefits in proportion to their own contributions, and this means that there is a redistribution of wealth. In brief, contributory Social Security mildly redistributes wealth from higher- to lower-income people; and it quite significantly redistributes wealth from younger workers to older retirees. Since 1972, Social Security benefits and costs have been adjusted through *indexing,* whereby benefits paid out under contributory programs are modified annually by cost-of-living adjustments (COLAs) based on changes in the Consumer Price Index, so that benefits increase automatically as the cost of living rises. And to pay for these automatic adjustments, Social Security taxes (contributions) also increased. This made Social Security, in the words of one observer, "a politically ideal program. It bridged partisan conflict by providing liberal benefits under conservative financial auspices."[8] In other words, conservatives could more readily yield to the demands of the well-organized and

contributory programs
Social programs financed in whole or in part by taxation or other mandatory contributions by their present or future recipients. The most important example is Social Security, which is financed by a payroll tax.

Social Security
A contributory welfare program into which working Americans place a percentage of their wages and from which they receive cash benefits after retirement.

indexing Periodic process of adjusting social benefits or wages to account for increases in the cost of living.

---

[7]The figures cited are for 2004. Although on paper the employer is taxed, this is all part of forced savings because in reality the employer's contribution is nothing more than a mandatory wage supplement that the employee never sees or touches before it goes into the trust funds held exclusively for the contributory programs.

[8]Edward J. Harpham, "Fiscal Crisis and the Politics of Social Security Reform," in *The Attack on the Welfare State,* ed. Anthony Champagne and Edward J. Harpham (Prospect Heights, IL.: Waveland Press, 1984), p. 13.

TABLE 15.1

Public Welfare Programs	YEAR ENACTED	FEDERAL OUTLAYS IN 2004 (IN BILLIONS)	FEDERAL OUTLAYS (2005 ESTIMATE IN BILLIONS)	FEDERAL OUTLAYS (2006 ESTIMATE IN BILLIONS)
CONTRIBUTORY				
Old Age, Survivors', and Disability Insurance (Social Security)	1935	414.8	432.4	451.4
Medicare	1965	295.9	327.0	394.6
Unemployment Compensation	1935	43.1	36.2	37.4
NONCONTRIBUTORY				
Medicaid	1965	176.2	188.5	192.7
Food Stamps	1964	28.6	34.2	37.6
Supplemental Security Income	1974	31.2	36.5	35.7
School Lunch Program (listed as Child Nutrition and special milk programs)	1946	11.2	12.2	12.5
Temporary Assistance to Needy Families (listed as Family Support Payments to States and TANF)	1996	21.5	22.0	22.2

SOURCE: Office of Management and Budget, *Budget of the United States Government, Fiscal Year 2006, Historical Tables* (Washington, DC: Government Printing Office, 2005), Table 11.3; and www.whitehouse.gov/omb/budget/fy2006/budget.html.

expanding constituency of elderly voters if benefit increases were guaranteed and automatic; and liberals could cement conservative support by agreeing to finance the expanded benefits through increases in the regressive Social Security tax rather than out of general revenues coming from the more progressive income tax.

The Politics of Reforming Social Security In 2004, an estimated 47.7 million Americans received an estimated $506 billion in Social Security benefits, distributed to 40 million retirees and dependents or survivors and to 8 million disabled people—up by nearly a million since 2003.[9] For more than half of all American workers, this is their only pension plan. And if there were no Social Security, half of all senior citizens would be living below the poverty line. No wonder Social Security is called the untouchable "third rail" of American politics.

Social Security has had its moments of potential crisis, but the only real crisis was in the late 1970s, triggered by the earlier decision to index benefits to the cost of living. The historic (for America) inflation of the 1970s caused the crisis, and it was readily "fixed" by increasing the payroll tax and the level of earnings (the cap) to which the tax applied. But a more fundamental reform would have to come as the ratio between contributing workers and retirees declined, from a comfortable sixteen contributors to one retiree downward toward three contributors per one retiree. With the record-breaking retirement of the baby boomers to begin around 2010, the ratio of contributors to workers will drop toward two to one. Fear is therefore growing in all circles that contributions today will not pay for the retirements of tomorrow. Up to now the system has run with a surplus. But the low ratio of contributors to retirees coupled with projected higher life expectancies could bankrupt the system. That is, without reform.

Bankruptcy will never be permitted, not only because that would be a national moment of shame but because retired persons are already too large a class to permit it, and their political clout will be greater still as baby boomers retire. All contributions are to be deposited in a Social Security Trust Fund, which officially earns interest at the average level for U.S. government securities. But that is a myth. The U.S. Treasury regularly borrows money from the trust fund and leaves IOUs to hide—or soften the impression—of the true national debt in this country. Thus the Social Security system, through no fault of its own but due to the irresponsibility of successive Democratic and Republican administrations, turned out to be a pay-as-you-go program in which today's youth take care of today's aged. That is what we meant by the redistribution of some wealth from the youth to the elderly.

Reforms have been proposed but tossed aside. One of the best ideas, and certainly the earliest back in the 1940s when the system was just beginning to take hold, was to safeguard the reserve (trust fund) by having the Treasury invest the contributions in *private* securities, earning interest and at the same time keeping the reserve safely away from the politics and government. One of the elder statesmen of that time retorted, "Why that would be socialism!" A more recent reform, on which Al Gore staked his 2000 presidential campaign, was to simply respect the trust fund by keeping it in interest-bearing government securities but in a "locked box" unavailable to serve as a hidden part of the national debt. Gore's position was ridiculed.

Social Security got its boost to the top of the domestic policy agenda from President George Bush, not during his first term but after his re-election in 2004. And he pushed reform all the more intensely because of his awareness that 2005

[9]See www.socialsecurity.gov\budget\2005bud.htm\.

might be his only chance to succeed—since AARP was campaigning to make 2006 an election year that would frighten a large number of Republican representatives in whose districts there were a significant number of retired persons, who are the most likely voters. As *The Economist* put it, "If [Social Security is] the third rail of American politics, the AARP generates much of the lethal current."[10] That threat called for equal intensity in return from Bush. He began with a warning that unless something drastic is done now, the system will be paying out more than it takes in by 2018 and will certainly end up in bankruptcy by the 2040s. This stark warning appeared to have the same objective as his proclamation in 2003 of imminent nuclear capacity in Iraq—galvanizing the country to action through fear. That projection of Social Security doom, especially in his February 2005 State of the Union address, was followed by a cross-country campaign blitz, mainly in the "red states." He was showing his willingness to "spend the political capital" that he claimed to have earned by reelection.

Oddly enough, his campaign contained no new and startling changes in Social Security itself. The radical part of his reform was his commitment to "the ownership society," which had no bearing whatsoever on the operating parts of the Social Security system. The ownership society was, instead, an effort to alter the principle of Social Security itself, which was governmentally guaranteed security. The ownership society was his name for the proposal to permit employees to voluntarily divert up to about one third of their payroll tax into an individual private account (a maximum of about $1,000 per year). That money would be invested in any of three options and would be converted into a personal annuity on retirement (ending with the death of the owner). The proponents claimed that the private account would return significantly higher earnings than those of the government accounts and would more than compensate for the cut in benefits that makes up the second and less-publicized part of President Bush's plan.

Those who oppose the Bush reform argue first that the private account would outperform the government's account only during a sustained bull market and could yield a punishing reduction in the value of the annuity if retirement should come during a bad market. The opponents also argue that the government would have to go into stupendous additional debt to make up for the money diverted from the contributions into the private accounts. Payment would have to come the same old way, by raising payroll taxes and increasing the cap, both of which Bush opposes, or reducing the retirement benefits, which Bush supports, on faith that growth in the value of the personal retirement accounts would more than make up the difference in the reduced benefits.

There are merits on both sides, even though the reform proponents are not offering many details while inviting doubters to come forward and bargain with alternatives. Bush's partially hidden agenda is to get the principle of personal investment accounts adopted so that it might become a first step toward a completely privatized retirement pension system. In other words, this 30 percent

[10]"The AARP—Still the Biggest Bruiser?", *The Economist* 5 February 2005, p. 26.

diversion in contributions could jumpstart the most radical social policy idea since Social Security was conceived, because it aims to alter the entire principle of the Social Security system. President Bush's campaign blitz of 2005 was not only a measure of the strength of his commitment but also another indication of the scale and difficulty of the politics of redistributive policies. If Bush succeeds in mobilizing mass support for a 30 percent step toward privatization, he will have won his side of what conservatives have called "class warfare." If he falls short of the sixty votes he will need to beat the Senate filibuster by those on the other side (Democrats and Republicans) of class politics, we might not hear drumbeats for Social Security reform for another decade or more.

All this means back to the drawing board to develop a menu of increased taxes, raised caps, and the change "whose name may not be spoken": elevation of the age of retirement eligibility. A combination of these is going to be necessary if Social Security is to take us through the rest of the twenty-first century.

Medicare

In February 2005, as President Bush was kicking off his nationwide campaign for Social Security reform, the semiofficial and ordinarily restrained periodical *Congressional Quarterly* led off its cover story with the following headline: The Real Crisis Waits Its Turn: Looming Medicare Crunch Dwarfs the . . . Social Security Shortfall."[11]

Medicare was the biggest expansion in contributory programs after 1935. Established in 1965, it was set up to provide substantial medical services to elderly persons. Like Social Security, Medicare is not means tested (means-tested non-contributory programs are discussed in the next section). Medicare was set up to provide substantial medical services to elderly persons who are already eligible to receive old-age survivors and disability insurance through their contributions under the original Social Security system. Medicare provides hospital insurance but allows beneficiaries to choose whether or not to participate in the government-assisted program to cover doctors' fees. A major role is given to the private health-care industry by essentially limiting Medicare to the role of third-party payer. In other words, program recipients purchase all their health services in the free market, and then they or their doctors and hospitals are reimbursed by Medicare. As a result, there is little government control over the quality of the services and the level of fees that health-care providers charge. That is definitely a major reason why Medicare costs expanded to such a degree.

Medicare
National health insurance for the elderly and the disabled.

Today, more than 41 million senior citizens are covered by Medicare. However, the spectacular increase in the cost of Medicare is only partly attributable to the growing number of participants; much of the increase is due to the rising cost of health care, whose rate has gone up much more sharply than inflation.

Another more recent boost in the cost of health care was provided by none other than President Bush and his Republican party control of Congress. As the

[11]*Congressional Quarterly* 21 February 2005, p. 446.

Congressional Quarterly put it, "Far from trimming Medicare's spending, the legislation that Congress passed in 2003 may have made the program better for seniors, but it piled on billions of dollars in new spending and trillions of dollars in long-term liabilities."[12] But even if the drug benefit had not been added to the program in 2003, there would be a crisis in Medicare costs because of the revolution in health care. The drug benefit was recognition of the medical revolution, but nobody anticipated the change in the health-care industry itself. Back when Medicare was established, hospitalization was a much more common part of the health-care process. Then along came new drugs and new methods and therefore new expectations of disease prevention, and this became the preferred form of medical care for seniors.

As a consequence, while Social Security can anticipate a $3.7 trillion gap during the next seventy-five years between the benefits promised and the cost of those benefits, Medicare confronts a $27.8 trillion gap. The liabilities added by the Bush Medicare prescription drug benefit alone come to an estimated $8.1 trillion.[13]

The Politics of Medicare Reform   Having dealt with Medicare in late 2003 to their satisfaction, the Bush administration not only opposed further action but hoped to discourage further Democratic efforts by moving as quickly as possible to Social Security reform. Democratic leaders complained bitterly about the arm twisting to get prescription drug benefits, accusing the Republicans of softening the sticker shock of added costs to the program by providing drug discount cards, which were available for purchase for $30 per year with savings projected up to 10 percent and possibly 20 percent. Democrats screamed foul also on Republican rosy estimates and demanded amendments, including elimination of tax breaks for health savings accounts, expansion of drugs covered in the program, reduced payments to private plans, and permission to import prescription drugs from Canada, which promised substantial savings. In fact there were fears among many in Congress, Republican as well as Democratic, that if Medicare were not fully confronted now, it would be off the agenda for years. Others, including then–Fed chairman Alan Greenspan, favored postponement of further treatment of Medicare in hopes that the science and technology of pharmaceuticals might produce still another revolution in treatment as well as in reduced cost. Moreover, Bush's prescription drug program was not to go into effect until 2006.

Meanwhile, the states were getting into the act. Since 2001, about half the states were adopting a policy of demanding rebates from drug companies beyond those required by federal law. Some states went further to form consortiums to allow large-lot or wholesale purchase at discounted prices. The National Conference of State Legislatures reported that in 2004 alone over 320 bills and resolutions were introduced in state legislatures to adopt policies aimed at generating

[12]Ibid.
[13]Ibid., p. 447.

and negotiating discounts, subsidies, and other cost-reducing and cost-containing results. And there is a growing movement among state governors and mayors to find ways of sponsoring and facilitating imports of lower-cost drugs from Canada.

The Pharmaceutical Research Manufacturers of America (PhRMA), the trade association of the drug industry, has, of course, mobilized in response. Always a major contributor to federal congressional campaigns, PhRMA has more recently been dumping unprecedented amounts of money into state legislative elections and into state lobbying. In 2004 alone, PhRMA budgeted $78.7 million for "state advocacy."[14]

Welfare: Means-Tested Public Assistance Policy

Programs to which beneficiaries do not have to contribute—*noncontributory programs*—are also known as *public assistance programs*, or, derisively, as "welfare." Until 1996, the most important noncontributory program was **Aid to Families with Dependent Children (AFDC,** originally called Aid to Dependent Children, or ADC), which was founded in 1935 by the original Social Security Act. In 1996, Congress abolished AFDC and replaced it with the Temporary Assistance to Needy Families (TANF) block grant. Eligibility for public assistance is determined by *means testing,* a procedure that requires applicants to show a financial need for assistance. Between 1935 and 1965, the government created programs to provide housing assistance, school lunches, and food stamps to other needy Americans.

As with contributory programs, the noncontributory public assistance programs also made their most significant advances in the 1960s and 1970s. The largest single category of expansion was the establishment in 1965 of **Medicaid,** a program that provides extended medical services to all low-income persons who have already established eligibility through means testing under AFDC or TANF. Noncontributory programs underwent another major transformation in the 1970s in the level of benefits they provide. Besides being means tested, noncontributory programs are federal rather than national; grants-in-aid are provided by the national government to the states as incentives to establish the programs (see Chapter 3). Thus, from the beginning, there were considerable disparities in benefits from state to state. The national government sought to rectify the disparities in levels of old-age benefits in 1974 by creating the **Supplemental Security Income (SSI)** program to augment benefits for the aged, the blind, and the disabled. SSI provides uniform minimum benefits across the entire nation and includes mandatory COLAs. States are allowed to be more generous if they wish, but no state is permitted to provide benefits below the minimum level set by the national government. As a result, twenty-five states increased their own SSI benefits to the mandated level.

The new TANF program is also administered by the states, and, like the old-age benefits just discussed, benefit levels vary widely from state to state (Figure 15.1). For example, the states' monthly TANF benefits varied from $170 in Mississippi to

[14]Barbara Dreyfuss, "Almost Heaven? The Pharmaceutical Lobby Is Taking Its Fight to the States," *The American Prospect* (February 2005): 26.

noncontributory programs Social programs that assist people based on demonstrated need rather than contributions they have made. Also known as "public assistance programs."

Aid to Families with Dependent Children (AFDC) Federal funds for children in families that fall below state standards of need. The largest federal cash transfer program. In 1996, Congress abolished AFDC and replaced it with the Temporary Assistance to Needy Families (TANF) block grant.

means testing A procedure that determines eligibility for government public assistance programs. A potential beneficiary must show a need and an inability to provide for it.

Medicaid A federally financed, state-operated program for medical services to low-income people.

Supplemental Security Income (SSI) A program providing a minimum monthly income to people who pass a means test and are sixty-five years or older, blind, or disabled. Financed from general revenues that are not Social Security contributions.

FIGURE 15.1

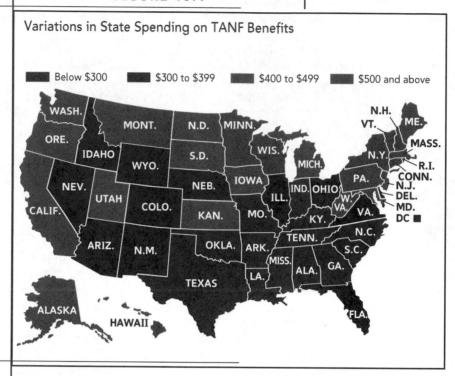

Variations in State Spending on TANF Benefits

■ Below $300　■ $300 to $399　■ $400 to $499　■ $500 and above

SOURCE: Ways and Means Committee Print. WMCP: 108-16, *2003 Green Book*, at waysandmeans.house.gov/media/pdf/greenbook2003/section7.pdf.

food stamps
The largest in-kind benefits program, administered by the Department of Agriculture, providing coupons to individuals and families who satisfy a means test; the food stamps can be exchanged for food at most grocery stores.

$923 in Alaska.[15] Even the most generous TANF payments are well below the federal poverty line. In 2002, the poverty level for a family of three included those earning less than $14,496, or $1,208 a month.

The number of people receiving AFDC benefits expanded in the 1970s, in part because new welfare programs had been established in the mid-1960s: Medicaid (discussed earlier) and *food stamps,* which are coupons that can be exchanged for food at most grocery stores. These programs provide what are called *in-kind benefits*—noncash goods and services that would otherwise have to be paid for in cash by the beneficiary. In addition to simply adding on the cost of medical services and food to the level of benefits given to AFDC recipients, the possibility of receiving Medicaid benefits provided an incentive for many poor

[15]Ways and Means Committee, *Greenbook 2003* [WMCP: 108–16]. Available at waysandmeans.house.gov/media/pdf/greenbook2003/section7.pdf.

Americans to establish their eligibility for AFDC, which would also establish their eligibility to receive Medicaid. At the same time, the government significantly expanded its publicity efforts to encourage the dependent unemployed to establish their eligibility for these various programs.

Another, more complex reason for the growth of AFDC in the 1970s was that it became more difficult for the government to terminate people's AFDC benefits for lack of eligibility. In the 1970 case of *Goldberg v. Kelly*, the Supreme Court held that the financial benefits of AFDC could not be revoked without due process—that is, a hearing at which evidence is presented.[16] This ruling inaugurated the concept of **entitlement**, a class of government benefits with a status similar to that of property (which, according to the Fourteenth Amendment, cannot be taken from people "without due process of law"). *Goldberg v. Kelly* did not provide that the beneficiary had a "right" to government benefits; it provided that once a person's eligibility for AFDC was established, and as long as the program was still in effect, that person could not be denied benefits without due process. The decision left open the possibility that Congress could terminate the program and its benefits by passing a piece of legislation. If the welfare benefit were truly a property right, Congress would have no authority to deny it by a mere majority vote.

Thus, the establishment of in-kind benefit programs and the legal obstacles involved in terminating benefits contributed to the growth of the welfare state. But it is important to note that real federal spending on AFDC itself did not rise after the mid-1970s. Unlike Social Security, AFDC was not indexed to inflation; without COLAs, the value of AFDC benefits fell by more than one third. Moreover, the largest noncontributory welfare program, Medicaid (see Table 15.1), actually devotes less than one third of its expenditures to poor families; the rest goes to the disabled and the elderly in nursing homes.[17] Together, these programs have significantly increased the security of the poor and the vulnerable, and must be included in a genuine assessment of the redistributive influence and the cost of the welfare system today.

The Politics of Welfare Reform The unpopularity of welfare led to widespread calls for reform as early as the 1960s. Public opinion polls consistently showed that Americans disliked welfare more than any other government program. Although a series of modest reforms were implemented starting in the late 1960s, it took thirty years for Congress to enact a major transformation in the program. Why did welfare become so unpopular, and why was it so hard to reform? How has the 1996 law that replaced AFDC with TANF changed welfare?

From the 1960s to the 1990s, opinion polls consistently showed that the public viewed welfare beneficiaries as "undeserving."[18] Underlying that judgment was the belief that welfare recipients did not want to work. The Progressive era reformers

in-kind benefits
Goods and services provided to needy individuals and families by the federal government, as contrasted with cash benefits. The largest in-kind federal welfare program is food stamps.

History Principle
The number of people receiving welfare benefits expanded in the 1970s because of the creation of new programs, such as Medicaid and food stamps, in the mid-1960s.

entitlement
Eligibility for benefits by virtue of a category defined by law. Category can be changed only by legislation. Deprivation of individual benefits can be determined only through due process in court.

History Principle
The Supreme Court's decision in *Goldberg v. Kelly* established the concept of entitlement and created legal obstacles to terminating welfare benefits.

[16]*Goldberg v. Kelly*, 397 U.S. 254 (1970).

[17]See U.S. House of Representatives, Committee on Ways and Means, *Where Your Money Goes: The 1994–95 Greenbook* (Washington, DC: Brassey's, 1994), pp. 325, 802.

[18]See Martin Gilens, *Why Americans Hate Welfare: Race, Media, and the Politics of Antipoverty Policy* (Chicago: University of Chicago Press, 1999), Chapters 3–4.

who first designed AFDC wanted single mothers to stay at home with their children. Motivated by horror stories of children killed in accidents while their mothers were off working or of children tied up at home all day to keep them safe, these reformers believed that it was better for the child if the mother did not work. By the 1960s, as more women entered the labor force and as welfare rolls rose, welfare recipients appeared in a more unfavorable light. Common criticisms charged that welfare recipients were taking advantage of the system; that they were irresponsible people who refused to work. These negative assessments were amplified by racial stereotypes. By 1973, approximately 46 percent of welfare recipients were African American. Although the majority of recipients were white, media portrayals helped create the widespread perception that the vast majority of welfare recipients were black. A careful study by Martin Gilens has shown how racial stereotypes of blacks as uncommitted to the work ethic reinforced public opposition to welfare.[19]

Despite public opposition, it proved difficult to reform welfare. Congress added modest work requirements in 1967, but little changed in the administration of welfare. A more significant reform in 1988 imposed stricter work requirements but also provided additional support services such as child care and transportation assistance. This compromise legislation reflected a growing consensus that effective reform entailed a combination of sticks (work requirements) and carrots (extra services to make work possible). The 1988 reform also created a new system to identify the absent parent (usually the father) and enforce child-support payments.

These reforms were barely implemented when welfare rolls rose again with the recession of the early 1990s, reaching an all-time high in 1994. Sensing continuing public frustration with welfare, presidential candidate Bill Clinton vowed "to end welfare as we know it," an unusual promise for a Democrat. Once in office, Clinton found it difficult to design a plan that would provide an adequate safety net for recipients who were unable to find work. One possibility—to provide government jobs as a last resort—was rejected as too expensive. Clinton's major achievement in the welfare field was to increase the Earned Income Tax Credit. This credit allows working parents whose annual income falls below approximately $32,000 to file through their income tax return for an income supplement of up to $4,000, depending on their family size. It was a first step toward realizing Clinton's campaign promise to ensure that "if you work, you shouldn't be poor."

Congressional Republicans proposed a much more dramatic reform of welfare, which Clinton, faced with re-election in 1996, signed. The Personal Responsibility and Work Opportunity Reconciliation Act (PRWORA) repealed AFDC. In place of the individual entitlement to assistance, the new law created block grants to the states and allowed states much more discretion in designing their cash-assistance programs to needy families. The new law also established time limits, restricting recipients to two years of assistance and creating a lifetime limit of five years. It imposed new work requirements on those receiving welfare, and it

[19]Ibid.

restricted most legal immigrants from receiving benefits. The aim of the new law was to reduce welfare caseloads, promote work, and reduce out-of-wedlock births. Notably, reducing poverty was not one of its stated objectives.

After this law was enacted, the number of families receiving assistance dropped by 58 percent nationwide (Figure 15.2). The sharp decline in the number of recipients was widely hailed as a sign that welfare reform was working. Indeed, former welfare recipients have been more successful at finding and keeping jobs than many critics of the law predicted. The law has been less successful in other respects: researchers have found no evidence that it has helped reduce out-of-wedlock births. And critics point out that most former welfare recipients are not paid enough to pull their families out of poverty. Moreover, many families eligible for food stamps and Medicaid stopped receiving these benefits when they left the welfare rolls. The law has helped reduce welfare caseloads, but it has done little to reduce poverty.[20]

As Congress prepared to reauthorize the welfare law in 2002, two different perspectives emerged. Democrats proposed changes that would make the welfare law "an antipoverty weapon."[21] They sought to increase spending on child care, allow more education and training, and relax time limits for those working and receiving welfare benefits. Republicans, by contrast, proposed stricter work requirements and advocated programs designed to promote marriage among welfare recipients.[22] Neither party challenged the basic features of the 1996 reform. Nonetheless, as caseloads began to rise again in 2001 due to the combined effects of the recession and the terrorist attacks, both sides were attentive to new problems. Enacted in a period of low unemployment and economic prosperity, welfare reform has yet to confront the consequences of a prolonged economic downturn.

ANALYZING THE WELFARE SYSTEM

Arguments against It

1. The first argument is the simplest: the welfare state costs too much. The contributory programs will sooner (Republican) or later (Democratic) come into their second or third financial crisis. But both parties agree that the crisis will come because too little account has been taken for demographic factors, with a ratio of workers to retirees approaching two to one. And that does not take into account increased life expectancy. Another factor affecting cost is the indexing of benefits to the cost-of-living index. This reflects inflation and in fact contributes to inflation.

[20]See the discussion of the law and the data presented in House Ways and Means Committee, *Greenbook 2000* [WMCP: 106-14]. Available at www.access.gpo.gov/congress/wm001.html.

[21]Robert Pear, "House Democrats Propose Making the '96 Welfare Law an Antipoverty Weapon," *New York Times*, 24 January 2002, p. A22.

[22]Robin Toner, "Welfare Chief Is Hoping to Promote Marriage," *New York Times*, 19 February 2002, p. A1.

FIGURE 15.2

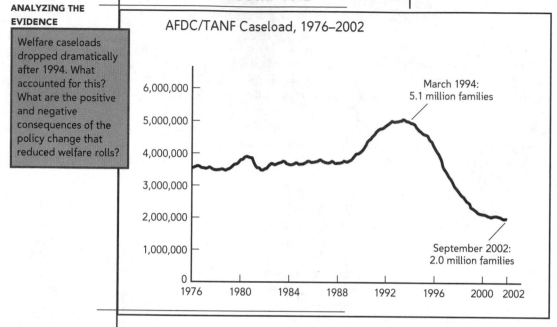

AFDC/TANF Caseload, 1976–2002

March 1994:
5.1 million families

September 2002:
2.0 million families

SOURCE: Figure prepared by the Congressional Research Service on the basis of data from the U.S. Department of Health and Human Services.

ANALYZING THE EVIDENCE

Welfare caseloads dropped dramatically after 1994. What accounted for this? What are the positive and negative consequences of the policy change that reduced welfare rolls?

2. A major factor contributing to cost escalation especially in health care, both Medicare and Medicaid, was adoption of a third-party structure of repayment. Once the systems were set up so that doctors and patients could establish their relationship with the fees being paid by the government, this relieved both doctors and patients from almost any concern at all for cost of services.

3. The welfare state is too paternalistic. The contributory programs are based on forced savings, leaving all individuals to some degree of concern for their own future. The noncontributory programs are also paternalistic even though it is true that people in poverty usually have no choice to save.

4. The welfare state is an example of moral hazard. *Moral hazard* is "the danger of probability that a policy will encourage the behavior or bring about the problem that it is supposed to ward off." For example, many people whose cars are insured will take less care to prevent their cars from being damaged or stolen. Another example is the increase of safety factors in automobiles and in contact-sports equipment. The tendency is to push the envelope with higher speeds, faster turns, and the use of often-ineffective headgear and

Rationality Principle

Some critics of the welfare state argue that it creates a moral hazard by providing the wrong incentives to welfare recipients.

other pads in violent sports. But the safety net might tend to be a moral hazard if it can be shown to weaken self-reliance and individual responsibility. That is why the sponsors of the 1996 welfare reform included "personal responsibility" in the title. A second argument is that entitlement to benefits weakens the work incentive. Even the strong supporters of noncontributory public assistance agree that care has to be taken to keep the benefits high enough for subsistence but not so high that people will prefer to stay on benefits rather than take a job. Finally, entitlement to child support, so the argument goes, "brings more babies into the world."[23]

5. The welfare system lays most of the blame for society's woes on "the system." Consequently, it removed the morality (or immorality) from poverty and relieved employers of a large part of their traditional responsibility to take care of their employees. Meanwhile the welfare employees are relieved to a large extent from personal responsibility.

These critiques are not subject to scientific proof or disproof. Like a good lawyer preparing a case for court, the welfare state critic is summoning up the best examples and logic available in the hope that "the preponderance of evidence" will convince the jury—that is, the public and the policy makers. But the strength of those arguments is that they are based more on moral principles than on science and empirical demonstration.

Arguments for It

1. The welfare system is good fiscal policy. As discussed in the previous chapter, the welfare system is one of the "automatic stabilizers." When the economy is declining, welfare payments go up enough to help maintain consumer demand. In contrast, during inflationary periods, welfare taxes take an extra bite out of consumer dollars, thereby dampening inflation somewhat (Figure 15.3).

2. The welfare system *is* paternalistic. A vice to the critics of welfare, paternalism is a virtue to its supporters, because it is a notorious fact that Americans don't save enough. Welfare taxation has produced a system of universal saving, which is a safety net for employers just as much as for employees. Social Security, unemployment compensation, disability benefits, and other features of contributory and noncontributory welfare have cushioned employers, especially those operating on narrow profit margins in our globalizing economy. It is no paradox that the employers who at first opposed the welfare state quickly accepted it once it was established.

3. As a consequence of the first and second arguments, the welfare system is believed by many to be the savior of capitalism. Each and every title in the orig-

[23]The strongest arguments in all these points is probably that of Charles Murray, *Losing Ground: American Social Policy, 1950–1980* (New York: Basic Books, 1994); and Murray, "Does Welfare Bring More Babies?", *Public Interest* 114 (Spring 1994): 17–31. Another influential critic of the welfare state is George Guilder, *Wealth and Poverty* (New York: Basic Books, 1981), Chapter 10.

FIGURE 15.3

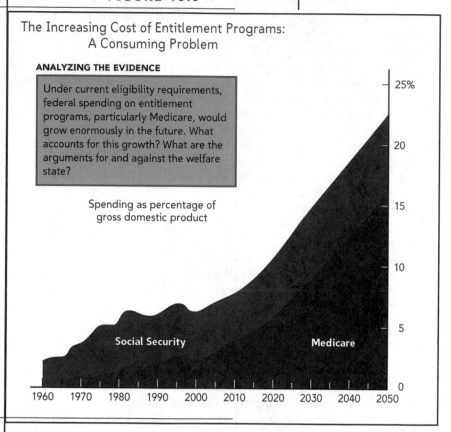

The Increasing Cost of Entitlement Programs:
A Consuming Problem

ANALYZING THE EVIDENCE

Under current eligibility requirements, federal spending on entitlement programs, particularly Medicare, would grow enormously in the future. What accounts for this growth? What are the arguments for and against the welfare state?

Spending as percentage of gross domestic product

Social Security

Medicare

1960 1970 1980 1990 2000 2010 2020 2030 2040 2050

25%

20

15

10

5

0

SOURCE: Congressional Budget Office.

inal Social Security Act creating the welfare system identified a particular imperfection of capitalism and sought to cope with it: age, unemployment, widowhood, disability for injury, illness, birth defects, inadequate education/training, and so on. The welfare system is not anticapitalist. It recognizes that capitalism is neither perfect nor self-perfecting and, therefore, needs various deliberate, public means of dealing with its imperfections.

4. The welfare system lays most of the blame for society's woes on the system. In other words, it removes the morality (or immorality) from poverty and also relieves employers from a large part of their traditional responsibility to take care of their own employees. This is the brighter side of the "personal

responsibility" complaint covered by arguments 2 and 3 made by the critics. Welfare system proponents have to agree that there are many chiselers and abusers in the contributory and noncontributory parts of the welfare system; but cheating abounds in the private sector as well and need not discredit welfare any more than it discredits business. Roughly half the people on welfare at any one time are off it within one year. It should also be noted that a large proportion of recipients of the more respectable Social Security retirement system receive far more in benefits than they contribute in taxes, especially if they live ten or more years beyond their retirement. This gives rise to an interesting question: Which of us isn't taking "welfare"?[24]

5. The welfare system is politically essential. As pro–welfare system conservative George Will put the case:

> Two conservatives (Disraeli and Bismarck) pioneered the welfare state, and did so for impeccably conservative reasons: to reconcile the masses to the vicissitudes and hazards of a dynamic and hierarchical industrial economy. They acted on the principle of "economy of exertion," using government power judiciously to prevent less discriminating, more disruptive uses of power.[25]

In Bismarck's own words, in a speech to the Reichstag in 1899:

> I will consider it a great advantage when we have 700,000 small pensioners drawing their annuities from the state, especially if they belong to those classes who otherwise do not have much to lose by an upheaval and erroneously believe they can actually gain much by it.[26]

If this appears to be cynical, so be it. It may be difficult to sympathize in this epoch of relative prosperity and stability, but the likelihood of great social and political disorder, if not revolution, was very much in the minds of the American political leaders in 1933–35 leading up to the passage of the Social Security Act. In the spring of 1933, for example, Secretary of Labor Frances Perkins was urged by an influential friend to leave Washington for the summer if she possibly could because of expectations of widespread violence in Washington and New York.[27]

---

[24]Ruth Rosen, "Which of Us Isn't Taking 'Welfare'?" *Los Angeles Times*, 27 December 1994, p. B5; sources of data: U.S. Department of Commerce; "Who Gets Assistance?" *Current Population Reports* [Household Economic Studies], July 1996.

[25]George F. Will, *Statecraft as Soulcraft: What Government Does* (New York: Simon & Schuster, 1983), p. 126.

[26]Quoted in Gaston V. Rimlinger, *Welfare Policy and Industrialization in Europe, America, and Russia* (New York: Wiley, 1971), p. 121.

[27]Episode reported in Theodore J. Lowi, *The End of Liberalism: Ideology, Policy, and the Crisis of Public Authority* (New York: Norton, 1969), p. 200. For an entirely different view of the same political phenomenon, see Frances Fox Piven and Richard A. Cloward; *The New Class War: Reagan's Attack on the Welfare State and Its Consequences* (New York: Pantheon, 1982).

Social Welfare and the Politics of Collective Action

In 1992, presidential candidate Bill Clinton promised to "end welfare as we know it." President Bill Clinton held fast to his promise in 1996, signing the Personal Responsibility and Work Opportunity Act, and basically ended many of the social welfare protections in place since the New Deal.

That a Democratic president ended welfare "as we know it" should come as no surprise. The American welfare system has been under attack for decades, from both the Right and the Left. From both sides of the political aisle, critics, bemoaning "welfare queens," believed that the welfare system had failed and advocated reforms such as time limits, work requirements, and taking advantage of market incentives, all in the name of getting "tough with the poor."

The irony of the American debate over welfare is how misdirected it all was. Non-means-tested social insurance programs (primarily Medicare and Social Security but also unemployment insurance, farm-price supports, and other retirement and disability programs) constitute $910 billion in federal spending as of fiscal year 2002, while means-tested programs, what we typically think of as welfare spending, are less than a third that amount ($286 billion). Thus, more than 75 percent of "welfare" spending is in non-means-tested social insurance programs, received by more than 40 million Americans. They constitute the real "welfare state."[1]

The principles of politics provide a ready guide to this debate. Collective action does not just require a shared set of preferences; it also requires organizational and individual resources.

The poor, of course, are often at a disadvantage in terms of organization and resources. Still, poor people who are concentrated in urban areas can use their voting power to their advantage, possibly to influence politicians to support welfare spending. They have historically organized (or have been organized by political entrepreneurs) via political parties and churches. However, many of our less-well-off are scattered throughout rural America. They are small in numbers relative to large congressional districts. They control few financial or organizational resources. The "intimacy" required to start many collective-action movements seldom exists among the rural poor. As a result, their political influence is minimal.

The elderly, farmers, and veterans groups, in contrast, are very well organized. Retired citizens live in electorally important parts of the country (Florida, Texas, California), and they vote far more regularly than younger and poorer Americans. The largest interest group in the United States—the AARP—spends millions every year lobbying for the interests of older Americans.

Farmers are disadvantaged in some of the same ways as the rural poor are, but because of their business relationships, farmers have regular interactions with other farmers at Grange halls and agricultural commodity-distribution points.

Collective-Action Principle

The poor often face barriers to collective action, such as living in far-flung rural areas and controlling few financial or organizational resources.

More important, though, is the third principle of politics: the impact of institutions on individual behavior. Members of these groups exist within a web of government rules, regulations, and benefits. The health-care and retirement income of most elderly Americans is partially or fully funded by the government. Agriculture in this country has been heavily subsidized by the government since the 1930s. And veterans receive health benefits and pensions (depending on their length of service) from the government. It is no surprise, then, that these groups are well organized. Governmental institutions *encourage* them to organize.

The result is that the social welfare system in America is heavily skewed toward providing social *insurance* but not much social *welfare*. Over the last decade of reforms, the elderly and veterans continued to receive significant benefits without any means testing. Farm subsidies continued apace even though they have caused serious frictions with our trading partners. Welfare spending to help the most destitute, on the other hand, has been substantially cut.

This may or may not constitute social justice. But it does reflect the realities of the principles of politics. As long as our political system relies on individualized political efforts, self-funded candidates, and well-financed interest groups, and does not have strong political parties (institutions that have incentives to organize as many potential voters as possible), it is likely that the poor will receive the short end of the social welfare stick.

[1]See Theodore R. Marmor, Jerry L. Mashaw, and Philip L. Harvey, *America's Misunderstood Welfare State: Persistent Myths, Enduring Realities* (New York: Basic Books, 1990).

Institution Principle

People strongly served by government are more likely to organize than those who lack effective government services.

Policy Principle

The welfare system is skewed toward the people who are able to organize.

There is obviously no simple solution to the welfare system. Most critics and defenders make cogent arguments for their side largely because they emphasize different aspects of the beast.[28] The welfare system was not a solution in the first place. It was a series of improvisations to some intractable problems that every nation faces when it tries, in George Will's words, "to reconcile the masses to the . . . hazards of . . . industrial economy," especially when those come to a head as quickly as they did in the early 1930s.[29] The welfare state is an institution of many parts, and no single approach to the whole will work.

[28]From the Right, the most serious academic critique is Lawrence M. Mead, *The New Politics of Poverty: The Nonworking Poor in America* (New York: Basic Books, 1992). The best academic defense of the welfare system, in our opinion, is John E. Schwarz and Thomas J. Volgy, *The Forgotten Americans: Thirty Million Working Poor in the Land of Opportunity* (New York: Norton, 1993); to that must be added an outstanding evaluation of the implications of welfare reform for federalism by Demetrios Caraley, "Dismantling the Federal Safety Net: Fictions versus Realities," *Political Science Quarterly* (Summer 1996): 225–58.

[29]Will; *Statecraft as Soulcraft.*

HOW CAN GOVERNMENT CREATE OPPORTUNITY?

The welfare system not only supplies a measure of economic security but also provides opportunity. The American belief in equality of opportunity makes such programs particularly important. Programs that provide opportunity keep people from falling into poverty, and they offer a hand up to those who are poor. At their best, opportunity policies allow all individuals to rise as high as their talents will take them. Two types of policy stand out as most effective in opening opportunity: education policy and health policy.

Education Policies and Their Politics

Most education of the American people is provided by the public policies of state and local governments. What may be less obvious is that these education policies—especially the policy of universal compulsory public education—are the most important single force in the distribution and redistribution of opportunity in America.

Compared with state and local efforts, the role of *national* education policy pales. With just a few exceptions, the national government did not involve itself at all in education for the first century of its existence as an independent republic (Table 15.2). The first two of these exceptions preceded the Constitution—the Land Ordinance of 1785 followed by the Northwest Ordinance of 1787. These provided for a survey of all the public lands in the Northwest Territory and required that four sections of the thirty-six sections in each township be reserved for public schools and their maintenance. It was not until 1862, with adoption of the Morrill Act, that Congress took a third step, establishing the land-grant colleges and universities. Later in the nineteenth century, more federal programs were created for the education of farmers and other rural residents. But the most important national education policies have come only since World War II: the GI Bill of Rights of 1944, the National Defense Education Act (NDEA) of 1958, the Elementary and Secondary Education Act (ESEA) of 1965, and various youth and adult vocational training acts since 1958. Note, however, that since the GI Bill was aimed almost entirely at postsecondary schooling, the national government did not really enter the field of elementary education until after 1957.[30]

What finally brought the national government into elementary education was embarrassment over the fact that the Soviets had beaten us into space with the launching of *Sputnik*. The national policy under NDEA was aimed specifi-

---

[30]There were a couple of minor precedents. One was the Smith-Hughes Act of 1917, which made federal funds available to the states for vocational education at the elementary and secondary levels. Second, the Lanham Act of 1940 made federal funds available to schools in "federally impacted areas"—that is, areas with an unusually large number of government employees and/or where the local tax base was reduced by large amounts of government-owned property.

TABLE 15.2

Growth of the Welfare System

	WELFARE	EDUCATION	HEALTH AND HOUSING
State era (1789–1935)	Private and local charity	Northwest Ordinance of 1787 (federal)	Local public health ordinances
	State child labor laws	Local academies	
	State unemployment and injury compensation	Local public schools	
	State mothers' pensions	State compulsory education laws	
		Morrill Act of 1862 for land-grant colleges (federal)	
Federal era (1935–present)	Social Security (federal)	GI Bill	Public housing
	Disability insurance	National Defense Act of 1958	Hospital construction
	VISTA, OEO*	Elementary and Secondary Education Act of 1965	School lunch program
	Supplemental Security Income	School desegregation	Food stamps
	Cost-of-living adjustment (indexing)	Head Start	Medicare
			Medicaid

*VISTA, Volunteers in Service to America; OEO, Office of Economic Opportunity.

cally at improving education in science and mathematics. General federal aid for education did not come until ESEA was passed in 1965, which allocated funds to school districts with substantial numbers of children from families who were unemployed or earning less than $2,000 a year.

Reagan's administration signaled a new focus for federal education policy: the pursuit of higher standards. In 1983, the Department of Education issued *A Nation at Risk*, an influential report that identified low educational standards as the cause of America's declining international economic competitiveness. The report did not suggest any changes in federal policy, but it urged states to make excellence in education their primary goal. This theme was picked up again by President George H. W. Bush. Calling himself the "education president," Bush convened the nation's governors for a highly publicized retreat designed to promote the development of state educational standards. Because

Republicans have historically opposed a strong federal role in education, the initiatives of Reagan and Bush remained primarily advisory. But they were very influential in focusing educational reform on standards and testing, now widely practiced across the states.

Both Bill Clinton and George W. Bush further energized the movement for educational achievement. The standards remained voluntary, however; the federal government restricted its role to providing grants to states that developed standards programs.[31] The federal role was substantially increased by President George W. Bush's signature education act, the No Child Left Behind Act of 2001. This act created stronger federal requirements for testing and school accountability. It required that every child in grades 3 through 8 be tested yearly for proficiency in math and reading. Individual schools are judged on the basis of how well their students perform on these tests. Parents whose child is in a failing school will have the right to transfer the child to a better school. Students in failing schools can also get access to special funds for tutoring and summer programs. Because there was strong congressional opposition to creating a national test, the states are responsible for setting standards and devising appropriate tests.

Although there was strong bipartisan support for the program, the act was a madhouse to implement. Many states were just plainly unable to move to a new system of standards and testing. But the big problem was that the federal government was demanding big improvements without providing sufficient funding to pay for such changes. There was some embarrassment in Republican party circles because of the fact that they had for years complained against "unfunded mandates" that Democratic Congresses were imposing on the states. Now they found themselves doing the same thing in the area of education.

Despite the compromises and confusions in the new program, federal money aimed at the poorest students did increase by a third. Local educators argue that that is not enough to meet the high standard the law requires, but money was at least forthcoming. In addition, many education experts contend that yearly test results are too volatile to provide a good measure of school performance and that failing schools have been made weaker as more-motivated parents transfer their children out of them.[32]

The federal program got a boost after the 2004 reelection, because Bush saw his reelection as a vindication, indeed a mandate, for the program that had been so prominent on his agenda. In early 2005, Bush requested $1.3 billion to extend the coverage of the law to the high schools up to the eleventh grade and to expand and improve college preparatory courses and programs aimed at keeping students from dropping out. Through 2005 there continued to be doubt that

[31]See Diane Ravitch, *National Standards in American Education: A Citizen's Guide* (Washington, DC: Brookings Institution, 1995).

[32]A summary and overview of the act can be found at www.ed.gov/offices/OESE/esea/summary.html; for a critique of the act's provisions, see Thomas Toch, "Bush's Big Test," *Washington Monthly* 33.11 (November 2001): 12–18.

Bush would get the increase he sought, first because many thought the problem of inadequate high schools and of dropping out still rested with the weaknesses in the primary schools and second because of the embarrassment over the mushrooming general budget deficits.

Hesitation and doubt in Washington despite the strong rhetoric and the promise of some financial backing put the question of primary and secondary education back in the hands of the states—in particular in the hands of the governors. Having been the two-term governor of Texas and a Republican for states' rights, President Bush could hardly go against initiatives the governors were prepared to take. Moreover, the governors were not only acting independently for their own states; there was sufficient bipartisanship among the governors to be able to act through their own "interest group," the National Governors Association. In their first meeting in 2005 after the Bush request for the $1.5 billion addition, the National Governors Association released a report concluding that although graduation requirements are lax and four in ten graduates are not adequately prepared for college or the job market, billions of dollars in remedial schooling would be required to address the situation and much of that would have to come from the national government. This was not a happy message for the conservative wing of the Republican party. As recently as the mid-1990s in the inspirational moment of the Gingrich revolution and the Contract with America, their message of smaller government, states rights, and the abolition of the Department of Education was one of the most popular songs being sung in the 1990s. Thus, despite the "political capital" that President Bush was willing to spend on No Child Left Behind, education policy in his second term was stalemated, due to cleavages within the Republican party and a deeply partisan cleavage between the Republican and the Democratic parties.[33]

Another political volcano in education policy is the issue of "school choice." Here again the political cleavages occur within and between the major parties and also within the well-established ideological groups. One issue of school choice is the simple one of permitting parents to move their children from the local public school that has been defined as "failing" into a public school of another district, anywhere in the area. A far more controversial issue is the school voucher movement, in which parents would be given vouchers to enroll their children in the school of their choice, *whether public or private*. The vouchers would help defray the cost of the tuition in the chosen private school. Supporters of vouchers claim that the public education system is too bureaucratic to provide quality education and does not give the parents enough control over the education of their own children. After several years of trial use, vouchers remain fairly popular in principle, but the data on comparative success of vouchers are not clear enough to provide a verdict one way or the other.

Finally, there is still another issue of school choice and vouchers, the "charter school." Charter schools are publicly funded schools that are free from bureaucratic

[33]Good coverage of the politics of education policy in Bush's second term is found in Bill Swindell, "States Eager to Retake Lead in School Policy," *Congressional Quarterly* 28 February 2005, pp. 492–93.

rules and regulations of the school district in which they are located. They are called charter schools because there must be an organization to form one, it must present its proposal to state authorities, and it must receive a charter as a kind of corporation that gives it the legal opportunity to operate. Charter schools are free to design specialized curricula and to use resources in ways that they think most effective. Since the creation of the first charter schools in Minnesota in 1990, states across the country have passed legislation to allow charter schools. But here again, there are many charges against vouchers and against charter schools as being "class biased." The fear persists that the opportunity for school choice would skim away the best students in the problem schools and would thus doom those schools to continued mediocrity or failure.

One can safely predict that the politics of education policy in the immense area of primary and secondary schooling will continue to be heated, as long as the technological revolutions and globalized markets in the new economy push far ahead of the education and training that the schools can provide. (We had a similar national curriculum crisis after World War I and another after World War II, when we finally got serious about equal education opportunities for minorities.) And the politics of education policy continues to resemble the politics of redistributive policy that we already encountered in the politics of the welfare state.

Health Policies and Their Politics

Until recently, no government in the United States—national, state, or local—concerned itself directly with individual health. But public responsibility was always accepted for *public* health. After New York City's newly created Board of Health was credited with holding down a cholera epidemic in 1867, most states followed with the creation of statewide public health agencies. Within a decade, the results were obvious. Between 1884 and 1894, for example, Massachusetts's rate of infant mortality dropped from 161.3 per 1,000 to 141.4 per 1,000.[34] Reductions in mortality rates produced by local public health programs during the late nineteenth century may be the most significant contribution ever made by government to human welfare.

The U.S. Public Health Service (USPHS) has been in existence since 1798 but was a small part of public health policy until after World War II. Created in 1937 but little noticed for twenty years was the National Institutes of Health (NIH), an agency within USPHS created to do biomedical research. Between 1950 and 2002, NIH expenditures by the national government increased from $160 million to $23.3 billion. NIH research on the link between smoking and disease led to one of the most visible public health campaigns in American history. The NIH's focus then turned to cancer and AIDS. As with smoking, its work on AIDS resulted in massive public health education as well as new products and regulations.

[34]Morton Keller, *Affairs of State: Public Life in Late Nineteenth Century America* (Cambridge, MA: Belknap Press of Harvard University Press, 1977), p. 500.

More recent commitments to the improvement of public health are the numerous laws, now housed mainly in the Environmental Protection Agency (1970), addressing hazardous air and water pollutants along with degradation of the natural environment. The Occupational Safety and Health Administration (OSHA) was created in 1970 to make the workplace safer from air pollutants as well as threats from machinery and operations. Laws that attempted to improve the health and safety of consumer products were created in 1972 and housed in the Consumer Product Safety Commission (CPSC).

But by far the most important commitments to public health were made in 1965, with the creation of Medicare and Medicaid. Medicare services are available to all persons already eligible under the Social Security Insurance Program (and it becomes automatic for retired persons when they reach the age of sixty-five). Although there are nutritional programs for the poor, particularly food stamps and the school lunch program, Medicaid is far and away the most important health program for this group.

But public health is only half the health policy area. The other half is the health-care system—that is, delivery of services between individual doctors and individual patients. Early in his administration, Clinton announced a plan with two key objectives: (1) to limit the rising costs of the American health-care system and (2) to provide universal health insurance coverage for all Americans (almost 40 million Americans lacked health insurance at that time). Clinton's plan at first garnered enormous public support and seemed likely to win congressional approval in some form. But the plan, which entailed a major expansion of federal administration of the health-care system, gradually lost momentum as resistance to it took root among those who feared changes in a system that worked well for them. Though Clinton attempted to make health care the centerpiece of his 1994 legislative agenda, no health-care bill even came up for a full congressional vote in 1994. After the president's failure on health care, Congress passed a much smaller program expanding health-insurance coverage for low-income children not already receiving Medicaid. Called the State Children's Health Insurance Program, the law provides federal funds to states so that they can offer health insurance to more low-income children. The results have been uneven: some states have greatly expanded coverage of uninsured children and have even sought to insure their parents. Other states have been far less aggressive and have not significantly increased the number of insured children. With the recession of 2002, all states had to cut back on plans for broader coverage as their budgets grew tighter.

WHO IS POOR? WHAT CAN GOVERNMENT DO?

When we study social policies from a group perspective, we see that minorities, women, and children are disproportionately poor. Much of this poverty is the result of disadvantages that stem from the position of these groups in the labor market.

African Americans and Latinos tend to be economically less well off than the rest of the American population. Much of this economic inequality stems from the fact that minority workers tend to have low-wage jobs. Minorities are also more likely to become unemployed and to remain unemployed for longer periods of time than are white Americans. African Americans, for example, typically have experienced twice as much unemployment as other Americans. The combination of low-wage jobs and unemployment often means that minorities are less likely to have jobs that give them access to the shadow welfare state. They are more likely to fall into the precarious categories of the working poor or the nonworking poor.

In the past several decades, policy analysts have begun to talk about the "feminization of poverty," or the fact that women are more likely to be poor than men are. This problem is particularly acute for single mothers, who are more than twice as likely to fall below the poverty line as the average American. When the Social Security Act was passed in 1935, the main programs for poor women were ADC and survivors' insurance for widows. The framers of the act believed that ADC would gradually disappear as more women became eligible for survivors' insurance. The social model behind the Social Security Act was that of a male breadwinner with a wife and children. Women were not expected to work; and if a woman's husband died, ADC or survivors' insurance would help her stay at home and raise her children. The framers of Social Security did not envision today's large number of single women heading families. At the same time, they did not envision that so many women with children would also be working. This combination of changes helped make AFDC (the successor program to ADC) more controversial. Many people ask, Why shouldn't welfare recipients work, if the majority of women who are not on welfare work?

Controversies over the welfare state have led to adaptations in welfare policy in recent years. Similar controversies over affirmative action policies—those that partially determine "who shall be poor"—have led to gradual changes in civil rights policies. But, as we concluded in Chapter 4, although the problems of rights in America are agonizing, they can be looked at optimistically. The United States has a long way to go before it constructs a truly just, "equally protected" society. But it also has come very far in a relatively short time. Groups pressing for equality have been able to use government to change a variety of discriminatory practices. The federal government has become an active partner in ensuring civil rights and political equality. All explicit *de jure* barriers to minorities have been dismantled. Many *de facto* barriers have also been dismantled, and thousands upon thousands of new opportunities have been opened.

Madison set the tone for this chapter in *The Federalist*, No. 51, in prose that has more the character of poetry:

> Justice is the end of government.
>> It is the end of civil society.
>> It ever has been and ever will be pursued
>>> Until it be obtained,
>> Or until liberty be lost in the pursuit.

Equality of opportunity has produced unequal results, and the unequal results of one generation can be visited upon later generations. Considerable inequality is accepted unless the advantages are maintained through laws and rules that favor those already in positions of power and through prejudices that tend to develop against any group that has long been on the lower rungs of society. Yet efforts to reduce the inequalities or to eliminate the consequences of prejudice can produce their own injustices if government intervention is poorly planned or is too heavy-handed.

SUMMARY

The capitalist system is the most productive type of economy on Earth, but it is not perfect. Poverty amid plenty continues. Many policies have emerged to deal with these imperfections.

The first section of this chapter discussed the welfare system and gave an account of how Americans came to recognize extremes of poverty and dependency and how Congress then attempted to reduce these extremes with policies that moderately redistribute opportunity.

Welfare policies are subdivided into several categories. First there are the contributory programs. Virtually all employed persons are required to contribute a portion of their wages into welfare trust funds; and later on, when workers retire or are disabled, they have a right, or entitlement, to draw on those contributions. Another category of welfare is composed of noncontributory programs, also called "public assistance." These programs provide benefits and supports for people who can demonstrate need by passing a "means test." Noncontributory programs can involve either cash benefits or in-kind benefits. All of the contributory programs are implemented through cash benefits. Spending on social policies, especially Social Security and Medicare, has increased dramatically in recent decades, raising concerns about how entitlement programs will be paid for in future decades.

Education and health policies are two ways to break this cycle and redistribute opportunities. The education policies of state and local governments are the most important single force in the distribution and redistribution of opportunity in America. Although states have taken the early lead in the arena of public health policy, the federal government also adopted policies in the early 1900s to protect citizens from the effects of pollution and other health hazards.

FOR FURTHER READING

Bryner, Gary. *Politics and Public Morality: The Great American Welfare Reform Debate.* New York: Norton, 1998.

Katz, Michael B. *In the Shadow of the Poorhouse: A Social History of Welfare in America.* Rev. ed. New York: Basic Books, 1996.

Lemann, Nicholas. *The Promised Land: The Great Black Migration and How It Changed America.* New York: Knopf, 1991.

Levy, Frank. *The New Dollars and Dreams: American Incomes and Economic Change.* New York: Russell Sage Foundation, 1998.

Marmor, Theodore R., Jerry L. Mashaw, and Philip L. Harvey. *America's Misunderstood Welfare State: Persistent Myths, Enduring Realities.* New York: Basic Books, 1990.

Mink, Gwendolyn. *Welfare's End.* Rev. ed. Ithaca, NY: Cornell University Press, 2002.

Murray, Charles. *Losing Ground: American Social Policy, 1950–1980.* 2nd ed. New York: Basic Books, 1994.

Piven, Frances Fox, and Richard A. Cloward. *Regulating the Poor: The Functions of Public Welfare.* Updated ed. New York: Vintage, 1993.

Schwarz, John E. *America's Hidden Success: A Reassessment of Public Policy from Kennedy to Reagan.* Rev. ed. New York: Norton, 1988.

Self, Peter. *Government by the Market? The Politics of Public Choice.* Boulder, CO: Westview, 1993.

Weir, Margaret, Ann S. Orloff, and Theda Skocpol, eds. *The Politics of Social Policy in the United States.* Princeton, NJ: Princeton University Press, 1988.

PRINCIPLES OF POLITICS IN REVIEW

Rationality Principle	Collective-Action Principle	Institution Principle	Policy Principle	History Principle
Some critics of the welfare state argue that it creates a moral hazard by providing the wrong incentives to welfare recipients.				The Great Depression was a turning point in the national government's decision to be involved in improving the welfare of the poor.

The number of people receiving welfare benefits expanded in the 1970s because of the creation of new programs, such as Medicaid and food stamps, in the mid-1960s.

The Supreme Court's decision in *Goldberg v. Kelly* established the concept of entitlement and created legal obstacles to terminating welfare benefits. |

Politics in the News—
Reading between the Lines

The Politics of Social Security Reform

Flare-Ups in Battle to Push or Bury Bush Social Security Plan

By SHERYL GAY STOLBERG, RICHARD W. STEVENSON,

and GLEN JUSTICE

The public relations war over President Bush's Social Security plan escalated on Wednesday, as a liberal advocacy group attacked the Republican chairman of the House Social Security subcommittee, and conservative groups fought among themselves over strategy.

The advocacy group, Campaign for America's Future, accused the subcommittee chairman, Representative Jim McCrery of Louisiana, of conflict of interest, saying he had accepted nearly $200,000 in contributions over four years from securities firms and commercial banks that could benefit from Mr. Bush's plan to let workers invest in retirement accounts.

Mr. McCrery responded by accusing the group, which is backed by labor unions and left-leaning philanthropists, including George Soros, of "extreme liberal bias."

As Mr. McCrery and his detractors traded barbs, supporters of Mr. Bush's plan battled among themselves. The

Cato Institute, the libertarian research organization that has long been a leader in pushing for private Social Security accounts, lashed out at USA Next, a conservative lobbying group that says it plans to spend up to $10 million on commercials and other tactics attacking AARP, the retirees' organization.

"This is not very bright politics," Michael Tanner, the director of health and welfare studies at Cato, said in a telephone interview. In particular, he objected to an Internet advertisement by USA Next that tries to paint AARP as an advocate of same-sex marriage. "Introducing homophobia and other things that are not relevant to Social Security reform is not helpful," Mr. Tanner said.

But Charlie Jarvis, the president of USA Next, said his group would not back down. "We are going to make sure their members know their position on that and every other issue," he said of AARP, adding, "They can run, but they cannot hide." . . .

New York Times, 24 February 2005, p. A14.

On Capitol Hill, there are deep splits among supporters of personal accounts over issues like how big the accounts should be, whether to include deep benefit cuts in any overhaul of the retirement system and whether Mr. Bush needs to put forth more details. Now, outside the Capitol, USA Next is exposing fissures in strategy as well as substance.

The group has hired some of the same consultants who worked for Swift Vets and P.O.W.'s for Truth, the group that orchestrated the advertisements attacking Senator John Kerry's military record in last year's presidential campaign. USA Next's Internet advertisement, which ran on Monday as part of a test campaign, featured a photograph of a soldier in camouflage, crossed out by a red X, juxtaposed against a green check mark over two tuxedo-clad men kissing. The caption reads, "The real AARP agenda."

"You need to build a coalition to win this fight," Mr. Tanner of the Cato Institute said. "You're not going to get Social Security reform passed just through the right wing of the Republican Party. Groups like gays are disadvantaged by the current system, and I'd think we would want to bring them into the campaign, not insult them." . . .

ESSENCE OF THE STORY

- The political battle over President Bush's Social Security reform package continues unabated. Liberal interest groups are attacking members of Congress who are working to pass the legislation, while conservative groups cannot agree upon what position to take on the bill.

- The Republican chair of the Social Security subcommittee has been accused of taking large campaign donations from industry PACs that will benefit from the reform. AARP, which opposes the bill, has been accused of having a pro gay-rights agenda.

- Some supporters of Bush's proposals argue that conservative groups need to focus more on coalition-building, and less on attack politics, if the reform bill is to have any chance of passage.

POLITICAL ANALYSIS

- Well-funded interest groups are playing an important role in shaping public debate over Social Security reform.

- Altering Social Security is difficult even during calm political times. The program overwhelmingly benefits senior Americans, who constitute a minority of the population but vote at high rates and are clustered in politically influential states. The current system seems unsustainable financially, but the most severe problems are decades away, making it easy for politicians to avoid the issue.

- It is not surprising that conservative groups are split. Some oppose Social Security in principle, preferring that individuals take responsibility for their own future. Others are thinking more short-term. The Republican Party is already suffering in the public's eye due to the war in Iraq and a series of administration scandals, so why risk their political future on this issue?

CHAPTER

16

Foreign Policy and Democracy

Ever since George Washington, in his Farewell Address, warned the American people "to have . . . as little political connection as possible" with foreign nations and to "steer clear of permanent alliances," Americans have been distrustful of foreign policy. Despite this distrust, the United States has been forced to pursue its national interests in the world, even when this has meant fighting a war. As a result of its foreign entanglements, the United States emerged as a world power, but not without maintaining some misgivings about foreign policy. As Alexis de Tocqueville noted in the 1830s, democracies lack the best qualities for the successful pursuit of foreign-policy goals:

> Foreign policies demand scarcely any of those qualities which are peculiar to a democracy; they require, on the contrary, the perfect use of almost all those in which it is deficient. . . . A democracy can only with great difficulty regulate the details of an important undertaking, persevere in a fixed design, and work out its execution in spite of serious obstacles. It cannot combine its measures with secrecy or await their consequences with patience.[1]

[1] Alexis de Tocqueville, *Democracy in America*, trans. Phillips Bradley, 2 vols. (1835; New York: Vintage, 1945), I, p. 243.

Fear and antagonism toward foreign entanglements became a revered American tradition. Only the most extraordinary affront to American sovereignty or American interest could mobilize the American people behind a sustained involvement in foreign affairs, and the mobilization, when it did occur, was usually for war, which required complete demonization of the adversary. Mere conflicts of interest between nations were rarely enough to mobilize Americans.

The cold war, which lasted from 1946 to 1989, seemed to put an end to that tradition. The term itself was coined in 1946 to distinguish America's emerging confrontation with the Soviet Union from a "hot war," or "shooting war," to total mobilization for war to prevent war.[2] Division of the world into two antagonistic camps, each armed with enough nuclear weapons to annihilate the other, redefined (or "escalated") what had once been considered incidental threats into serious challenges. Investment in total military preparedness became a race to deter the other side from any expansion, with each side attributing to the other an overriding commitment to arms' expansion.

Each of the leading nations in the cold war—the United States and the Soviet Union—developed what we call a "cold war culture." This cold war culture was built on a policy in which (1) the United States must prepare for war to prevent war; (2) each day that war did not occur was further confirmation of America's commitment to preparedness and deterrence because American leaders believed that the Soviet Union was aggressive and would expand communist influence wherever weaknesses were detected; and (3) the United States must continually increase its capabilities because whatever prevented Soviet expansion today could be inadequate tomorrow, especially considering that the Soviets, like the United States, were continuing to invest in military power.

[2]William Safire provides a brief and informative account of the history of the term in his *Safire's Political Dictionary* (New York: Random House, 1978), pp. 127–29.

CHAPTER OUTLINE

Who Makes and Shapes Foreign Policy?

- The President
- The Bureaucracy
- Congress
- Interest Groups
- The Media
- Putting It Together

What Are the Values in American Foreign Policy?

- Legacies of the Traditional System
- The Great Leap to World Power

What Are the Instruments of Modern American Foreign Policy?

- Diplomacy
- The United Nations
- The International Monetary Structure
- Economic Aid
- Collective Security
- Military Deterrence

Roles Nations Play

- Choosing a Role
- Choice of Roles for America Today

Those were simpler days. The U.S. role in the world was clear and its enemy was well known. The cold war ended in 1989, and its culture would pass away in its wake.

Without a clear-cut enemy, the American fear of foreign entanglements seemed to return during the 1990s, as the United States was initially reluctant to get involved with politically troubled countries like Somalia, Bosnia, and Kosovo. But September 11, 2001, changed that. September 11 and its aftermath led to a revision of America's view of its place in the world. America went to war, but not only in Afghanistan and Iraq. In the years since September 11, 2001, the United States has been engaged in a "war on terrorism," with American servicemen and women "deployed across the world." This was an international, multicountry conspiracy of evil against good, whose "terrorists continue to plot against America and the civilized world."[3] In his 2004 State of the Union address, President George W. Bush justified this ongoing war as necessary for homeland security, a war that would have to be fought in distant places or else in our own communities.

In this same speech, President Bush went beyond military security to identify still another major goal of foreign policy—a very new and unprecedented goal—the "building a new Iraq" as part of "a mission . . . pursuing a forward strategy of freedom in the greater Middle East." The principal means of achieving this is the military, but with a twist. President Bush envisioned in his message an America leading "a coalition of the willing" of thirty or more nation-states. However, this coalition was not to operate under United Nations (UN) auspices: "There is a difference . . . between leading a coalition of many nations and submitting to the objections of a few. America will never seek a permission slip to defend the security of our people." This alliance of the willing has minimal military value because, except for the United Kingdom, the members were expected to contribute virtually zero manpower in troops on the ground. They were included to give a form of "moral support," the purpose being to add legitimacy to the worldwide effort. Diplomatic methods were also identified in Bush's message, but they were explicitly limited to keeping the UN informed and working out a role for the UN in humanitarian aspects of nation building. The president's message also included commitment to a significantly increased role to be played by the Voice of America and other broadcast services aimed at the region, in Arabic and Persian languages. Another propaganda channel to be enhanced, by the doubling of its budget, was the National Endowment for Democracy, "to focus its new work on the development of free elections, free markets, free press, and free labor unions in the Middle East." Bush underlined the rebuilding of Middle Eastern countries along American lines with the remark that "it is mistaken and condescending to assume that whole cultures and great religions are incompatible with liberty and self-government." This is part of a general and widely held theory that countries with similar systems of government will not go to war against each other. Consequently, "as long as the Middle East remains a place of tyranny . . . it will continue to produce men and movements that threaten the safety of America and our friends."

[3] All quotations are from George W. Bush's 2004 State of the Union address.

Finally, state building itself is the ultimate method with Iraq and Afghanistan as only the start. For the Bush administration, state building has less to do with the apparatus of government—it is much more concerned with a new constitution; a new, directly elected assembly; a bill of rights; and the embrace of the values of freedom. After peace and freedom are established, "full sovereignty" would be restored to Iraq; and after that, the Iraq regime will be imitated in other countries. All of this would come to pass without "any desire to dominate" and without any "ambitions of empire." Only time will tell if the Bush administration is successful in its ultimate goal of a democratic Iraq and Afghanistan. But the issues that the Bush team faces, such as overcoming much of the world's antipathy toward the U.S. power, will certainly outlast the administration.

The Bush administration's conduct of foreign policy, as expressed by Bush in his 2004 State of the Union address, reveals the many tensions evident in the conduct of foreign policy in U.S. history. Should the United States fear foreign entanglements or be engaged in world affairs? What are the foreign-policy goals of the United States? Economic self-interest, the spread of democracy around the world, or both? What is the best means for the United States to achieve its goals? The military, diplomacy, or both? Should the United States act unilaterally or multilaterally?

As the Iraqi insurgency persisted and then intensified in 2005 and 2006, with attacks focused on Iraqi efforts to form a government—hitting police stations and other governmental, civic, and religious activities to discredit the American efforts and discourage Iraqi cooperation—American representatives in Iraq pushed harder and harder to get the new Iraqi constitution adopted by national referendum. The constitution had become the principal means of stabilizing the country through democratization. Supporters and critics in large numbers were beginning to call the Bush Doctrine a form of "democratic imperialism." But if democratization succeeds even modestly in Iraq, democratic imperialism will strengthen the real Bush foreign policy and will become a strong appeal to many other democracies in the world.

Iraq is only one of the many foreign-policy issues the United States will confront during the last years of the Bush administration and the years of his successors. The conduct of foreign policy is so complex that no single approach, even if

PREVIEWING THE PRINCIPLES

Foreign-policy interests are pursued through both domestic infighting and strategic interaction with other foreign "players." The one consistent influence on the making of foreign policy is the president as "coordinator in chief," who strategically deploys an array of instruments and coordinates an array of officials and institutions to conduct foreign policy. In addition, international institutions such as the United Nations and collective security organizations such as the North Atlantic Treaty Organization (NATO) can be used by the United States to conduct its foreign policy, but these institutions and organizations can also work as constraints on American foreign policy. Two historical legacies that continue to influence the conduct of American foreign policy are the intermingling of domestic and foreign policy and unilateralism.

rational, will be sufficient to meet the many problems facing the United States. Democratization could well be an important one; but to be rational, American foreign policy must have a well-balanced analysis of international problems and a well-considered menu of foreign-policy approaches. The search for rational and effective foreign policy must treat at least four dimensions of foreign policy, which make up the four main sections of this chapter. We begin by asking who makes and shapes foreign policy in the United States. From there, we cover American values: What does the United States want? What are its national interests, if any? What counts as success? In the third section, we identify and examine the main instruments of foreign policy, such as administrative arrangements, institutions, laws, and programs. Finally, we discuss how the United States behaves in world politics. Are its roles consistent with its values?

WHO MAKES AND SHAPES AMERICAN FOREIGN POLICY?

As in domestic policy, foreign-policy making is a highly pluralistic arena. First there are the official players, those who make up the "foreign-policy establishment"; these players and the agencies they head can be called the actual "makers" of foreign policy: the president and his advisers, the bureaucracy, and Congress. But there are other major players, less official but still influential. We call these the "shapers": interest groups and the media.

The President

History Principle

Most American presidents have come to office focused primarily on domestic policies and issues.

Most American presidents have been domestic politicians who set out to make their place in history through achievements in domestic policy. This is consistent with the traditional role of foreign policy, which has been treated as virtually an extension of domestic policies. The standard joke during Bill Clinton's 1992 campaign, extending well into his first year, was that he had learned his foreign policy at the International House of Pancakes! Thus it was not shockingly unusual that President George W. Bush had virtually no foreign-policy preparation. He had traveled very little outside the United States, and he had had virtually no foreign experience as governor of Texas, even though that state has the largest international border of any state in the United States. But, like his immediate predecessor, Bush displayed very soon after his inauguration that he was a quick learner. He stacked his cabinet and subcabinet with foreign- and defense-policy experts of extraordinary training, experience, and knowledge gained in years of service for previous Republican administrations. For example, Vice President Richard Cheney served as President Gerald Ford's chief of staff, spent twelve years in Congress, served as President George H. W. Bush's secretary of defense, and left government to serve as the chief executive officer of the international corporation Halliburton. Donald Rumsfeld served as Richard Nixon's ambassador to the North Atlantic Treaty Organization (NATO) and as Ford's secretary of defense, and he had major international corporate experience before becoming George W. Bush's secretary of defense. Colin Powell, a career military officer, served as national security adviser to President Ronald Reagan, as chair of the Joint Chiefs of Staff under the first President Bush as well as President Clinton, before being appointed secretary of state by George W. Bush. And Condoleezza Rice had been a specialist on the Soviet Union during her academic career, before serving as a National Security Council staff specialist on the Soviet Union for the first President Bush. She served as national security adviser for George W. Bush, who then appointed her secretary of state in his second administration. And Bush was quick to appreciate the significant foreign-policy powers —constitutional and traditional—that accompany the multiple official roles a president plays, as commander in chief, head of state, head of government, head of his party, and as the single most important legislative leader. Table 16.1 lays out the constitutional powers of president and Congress in the making and shaping of foreign policy; but traditional and more recent informal powers have accrued to presidents, providing still greater superiority over Congress in foreign policy, as we shall see.

Bush's first major foreign-policy actions were to bomb Afghanistan and then Iraq—a fairly safe and inexpensive way to convey the impression that he was determined to be an effective commander in chief. And, whether right or wrong, he was decisive in the initiatives he took to define America's national interest for his administration. Examples include revival of the controversial nuclear missile shield ("Star Wars"); his readiness to abandon the Anti-Ballistic Missile (ABM) Treaty, which meant a serious and ugly confrontation with the Russians; changes in policy priorities away from humanitarian and environmental goals with a far stronger emphasis on goals more directly within the realm of national security; and turning America's concerns (by degree or emphasis) away from Europe and toward an "Asia first" policy. His first real test of leadership—the imbroglio with China over the emergency landing of a U.S. spy plane—was almost universally praised for patience and finesse.

Thus, even during his first eight months as president, Bush had already learned most of what he was going to use in the aftermath of September 11. He learned, for example, that any conceivable event that had an international dimension to it is an occasion when the president can take the initiative, make a public commitment, defend it in the national interest, and bring the public along, knowing that Congress will follow with the appropriate legal and budgetary support. In earlier times, the cynical view of realists about the head of state was as follows: Mobilize the elite and you mobilize the electorate. Modern presidents have more or less turned that on its head: Mobilize the electorate and you mobilize the elite. Congress follows a presidential foreign-policy initiative because the typical representatives see they have no choice due to fear that inaction would leave ships or troops stranded in some ocean, desert, or forest. For example, Congress approved and financed the escalation of the Vietnam War immediately after the deceitful allegation that North Vietnamese had bombed our ship in the Gulf of Tonkin. Congress was at the ready again in 2003, after the

 Rationality Principle

Foreign-policy initiatives by the president are taken in light of the domestic political landscape.

TABLE 16.1

Presidential and Congressional Powers and Roles in Foreign Policy

	CONSTITUTIONAL PROVISION		INFORMAL ROLES	
	PRESIDENT	CONGRESS	PRESIDENT	CONGRESS
War power	Commander in chief	Declare war; "provide for common defense"	Preemptive military commitment; threat of war; secret agreements	Refusal to appropriate; investigation and exposure; threat to impeach
Treaty power	Negotiate treaties	Treaty ratification (by two-thirds Senate vote)	Executive agreements	Resolution condemning refusal to appropriate
Appointment power	Select and nominate ambassadors	Majority Senate vote	Recess appointment	Resolutions condemning; reject later appointment
Foreign commerce power	Treaty negotiation	"to regulate foreign commerce"	Executive agreements; foreign aid	Cut or reduce aid
Recognition power	Receiving ambassadors	No explicit power	Friendly visits; negotiation	Symbolic visits; resolution

announcement of the allegation, again unfounded, of Iraq's capacity to deliver weapons of mass destruction (WMD) within less than three weeks. Not only was the budget authorized but unlimited executive power was authorized. The 1964 Gulf of Tonkin Resolution was passed unanimously in the House and with only two negative votes in the Senate, despite the fact that the resolution provided that the United States was "prepared, *as the president determines*, to take all necessary steps, including armed forces" [emphasis added]. Almost in identical terms, the September 11 resolution was passed by Congress with only one dissenting vote and provided that the president could "use all necessary and appropriate force against those nations, organizations or persons he determines planned, authorized, committed, or aided the terrorist attacks that occurred on September 11, 2001, or harbored such organizations or persons."

September 11, 2001, and its aftermath immensely accentuated the president's role and place in foreign policy. By 2002, foreign policy was the centerpiece of the Bush administration's agenda. In a June 1 speech at West Point, the ***"Bush Doctrine"*** of preemptive war was announced. Bush argued that "our security will require all Americans . . . to be ready for preemptive action when necessary to defend our liberty and to defend our lives." Bush's statement was clearly intended to justify his administration's plans to invade Iraq, but it had much wider implications for international relations (as we shall explore at the end of the chapter), including the central role of the American president in guiding foreign policy.

Bush Doctrine
Foreign policy based on the idea that the United States should take preemptive action against threats to its national security.

The Bureaucracy

The major foreign-policy players in the bureaucracy are the secretaries of the Departments of State, Defense, and the Treasury; the Joint Chiefs of Staff (JCOS), especially the chair of the JCOS; and the director of the Central Intelligence Agency (CIA). During the entire cold war, from 1947 on, a separate unit in the White House oversaw the vast foreign-policy establishment for the purpose of synthesizing all the messages arising out of the bureaucracy and helping the president make his own foreign policy. This is the National Security Council (NSC). It is a "subcabinet" made up of the major players just listed, plus two or three others each president was given the authority to add. Since the profound shake-up of September 11, two additional key players have been added. The first of these was the secretary of the new Department of Homeland Security (DHS), composed of twenty-two existing agencies relocated from all over the executive branch on the theory that their expertise could be better coordinated, more rational, and more efficient in a single organization designed to fight international terrorism and domestic natural disasters (Chapter 10). The second was imposed at the top as the war in Iraq was becoming a quagmire: a director of central intelligence, to collate and coordinate intelligence coming in from multiple sources and to report a synthesis of all this to the president, on a daily basis. This implied a demotion of the CIA and its director (whose job it had been to make the daily intelligence reports to the president), causing "considerable turmoil . . . within the agency."[4] All this indicates the difficulty a president has in creating clarity and consistency in his pursuit of national interest.

Coordinating the diverse missions of a single agency is a challenge; coordinating the efforts of multiple agencies is especially problematic. American foreign policy is replete with instances of the CIA heading in one direction while the Department of State or Defense or the Joint Chiefs of Staff head in another. The National Security Council and now the Department of Homeland Security attempt to keep the

Collective-Action Principle
Coordinating the efforts of the many agencies of the foreign-policy establishment is especially difficult.

[4]*New York Times*, 23 September 2005, p. A12.

various players on the same page. But will these agencies—each with its own authority, interests, and priorities—follow the same protocol? It should be understood that this is not merely a matter of coordinating different players on the same team. Each player has his or her own ax to grind. Agencies have different policy priorities and budgetary aspirations.

The problem of integrating the Department of Homeland Security hit with great force in its first important homeland crisis; hurricane Katrina laid waste to New Orleans and the nearby ocean-front of Mississippi and parts of Alabama. The most specific organization failure was in the one agency in the DHS most responsible for quick and effective reaction, the Federal Emergency Management Agency (FEMA). The DHS reorganization had demoted FEMA from an independent cabinet-level agency to a conventional bureau within the new department and, in the process, reduced the stature of the head of the agency to such an extent that the director appointed by President Bush was basically a patronage appointee, a FOG (friend of George), a crony with no experience in management at all, let alone crisis management, which required the ability to harness federal resources and use them as leverage to concentrate the assistance and recovery effort of local and state agencies, the National Guard, and military and police officials sent from neighboring cities and states to provide law and order. (All this was to be run by the FEMA director, whose prior experience was ten years as a commissioner for the International Arabian Horse Association!)

Institution Principle

Institutions such as the National Security Council and Department of Homeland Security attempt to keep the various foreign-policy players on the same page.

In addition to top cabinet-level officials, key lower-level staff members have policy-making influence as strong as that of the cabinet secretaries—some may occasionally exceed cabinet influence. These include the two or three specialized national security advisers in the White House, the staff of the NSC (headed by the national security adviser), and a few other career bureaucrats in the Departments of State and Defense, whose influence varies according to their specialty and to the foreign policy at hand.

Many intelligence agencies have come in for heavy criticism since the September 11 attacks. Top among these is the CIA, set up in 1947 to be the supervisor, coordinator, assimilator, and final integrator of all the other agencies in the intelligence community, including the National Security Agency (NSA), which breaks codes and performs electronic eavesdropping, the latter of which has come under heavy criticism in early 2006; the National Reconnaissance Office (NRO), which coordinates satellite research and development; the Central Imaging Office (CIO), which supervises photographic surveillance; the Defense Intelligence Agency (DIA, in the Defense Department), which performs military intelligence analysis; and the intelligence services of each of the armed-services divisions within the Defense Department. There are also a few civilian intelligence agencies, the most important of which are the Federal Bureau of Investigation (FBI), the U.S. Citizenship and Immigration Services (USCIS, formerly the Immigration and Naturalization Service, or INS), and the Internal Revenue Service (IRS). Although the names of these agencies are familiar to the public, in many respects they are "secret agencies," even down to their actual budgets, not to mention their espionage and sabotage operations.[5] After World War II, the CIA began to keep strictly to activities outside the United States, and the FBI (in particular) limited itself to the domestic United States. That separation of jurisdiction no longer makes sense in our globalized world. One of the consequences of the creation of the Office (and then Department) of Homeland Security is that central coordination might make these agencies a bit more transparent.

The urgency of the need for reorganization of the entire foreign-policy establishment, especially the intelligence functions, was highlighted by Katrina, because turf wars and split authority and responsibility can bring the most pressing actions to a halt. However, another insight was produced by September 11 but not fully appreciated until Katrina. It should be applied to foreign policy, especially to control of terrorism. A historic catastrophe like Katrina could not be prevented. No amount of good intelligence could have alerted us to the scale or the precise location of that "attack" on our homeland. The same is actually true of catastrophic attacks on our homeland by hostile human action. No amount of reorganization for coordination will guarantee "victory," if victory is defined as absolute assurance that no attack will be made on our homeland. This was put well by *Newsweek* columnist Fareed Zakaria:

> All [the] tough tactics and all the intelligence in the world will not change the fact that in today's open societies, terrorism is easy to carry out. . . . Real victory is not about preventing all attacks everywhere. No one can guarantee that. It's really about preventing the worst kinds of attacks, and responding well to others. . . . Our leaders remain unwilling to speak honestly about the world we live in and to help people develop the mentality of response that is essential to prevailing.[6]

Congress

While the Constitution gives Congress the power to declare war, Congress has exercised this power on only five occasions: the War of 1812, the Mexican War (1846), the Spanish-American War (1898), World War I, and World War II. For the first 150 years of American history, Congress's role was limited because, as we will see, the United States's role in world affairs was limited. During this time, the Senate was the only important congressional foreign-policy player because of its constitutional role in reviewing and approving treaties. The treaty power is still the primary entrée of the Senate into foreign-policy making. But since World War II and the continual involvement of the United States in international security and foreign aid, Congress as a whole has become a major foreign-policy maker because most modern foreign policies require financing, which requires both the House of Representatives and the Senate. For example, Congress's first action after September 11 was to authorize the president to use "all necessary and appropriate force,"

[5]Loch K. Johnson, *Secret Agencies: U.S. Intelligence in a Hostile World* (New Haven, CT: Yale University Press, 1996).

[6]Fareed Zakaria, "How We Can Prevail," *Newsweek*, 18 July 2005, p. 41.

coupled with a $40 billion emergency appropriations bill for homeland defense. And while Bush believed he possessed the constitutional authority to invade Iraq, he still first sought congressional approval, which he received in October 2002. Congress has also become increasingly involved in foreign-policy making because of the increasing use by the president of *executive agreements* to conduct foreign policy. Executive agreements have the force of treaties but do not require prior approval by the Senate. But, according to political scientist Loch K. Johnson, about 95 percent of executive agreements are made before or pursuant to congressional authorization. For example, many executive agreements are made to pursue, fulfill, or clear up details of treaties already adopted. Others are carried out under a prior legislative act or are covered by later legislation. This gives both the House and the Senate a genuine institutional role in foreign policy.[7] Another opening for congressional involvement in foreign policy is the fact that, although executive agreements have the force of treaties and do not require prior approval by the Senate, they can in fact be revoked by action of both chambers of Congress. Such action is by "joint resolution," a form of legislative disapproval that the president cannot veto. Yet another aspect of Congress's role in foreign policy is that the Senate has the power to confirm the president's nominations for cabinet members, ambassadors, and other high-ranking officials (such as the director of the CIA, but not the director of the NSC). A final constitutional power for Congress is to "regulate commerce with foreign nations."

Other congressional players are the foreign-policy and military-policy committees: in the Senate these are the Foreign Relations Committee, the Armed Services Committee, and the Intelligence Committee; in the House, these are the International Relations Committee, the Armed Services Committee, and the Intelligence Committee. Usually, a few members of these committees who have spent years specializing in foreign affairs become trusted members of the foreign-policy establishment and are actually makers rather than mere shapers of foreign policy. In fact, several members of Congress have left to become key foreign-affairs cabinet members. After September 11, congressional committees conducted hearings on the failure of the intelligence agencies, but most members of Congress were reluctant to take on these agencies or a popular president.

Interest Groups

Although the president, the executive branch "bureaucracy," and Congress are the makers of foreign policy, the "foreign-policy establishment" is a much larger arena, including what can properly be called the shapers of foreign policy—a host of unofficial, informal players, people in groups, who possess varying degrees of influence, depending on their prestige, their reputation, their socioeconomic standing, and—most important—the party and ideology that is dominant at a given moment.

---

executive agreement An agreement between the president and another country that has the force of a treaty but does not require the Senate's "advice and consent."

---

[7]Loch K. Johnson, *The Making of International Agreements: Congress Confronts the Executive* (New York: New York University Press, 1984).

By far the most important category of nonofficial player is the interest group—that is, the interest group to whom one or more foreign-policy issues are of long-standing and vital relevance. The type of interest group with the reputation for the most influence is the economic interest group. Yet the myths about this group's influence far outnumber and outweigh the realities. The actual influence of organized economic interest groups in foreign policy varies enormously from issue to issue and year to year. Most of these groups are "single-issue" groups and are, therefore, most active when their particular issue is on the agenda. On many of the broader and more sustained policy issues, such as the North American Free Trade Agreement (NAFTA) or the general question of American involvement in international trade, the larger interest groups, sometimes called "peak associations," find it difficult to maintain tight enough control of their many members to speak with a single voice. The most systematic study of international trade policies and their interest groups concluded that the leaders of these large, economic interest groups spend more time maintaining consensus among their members than they do actually lobbying Congress or pressuring major players in the executive branch.[8] The more successful economic-interest groups, in terms of influencing foreign policy, are the narrower, single-issue groups such as the tobacco industry, which over the years has successfully kept American foreign policy from putting heavy restrictions on international trade in and advertising of tobacco products, and the computer hardware and software industries, which have successfully hardened the American attitude toward Chinese piracy of intellectual property rights.

Another type of interest group with a well-founded reputation for influence in foreign policy is made up of people with strong attachments and identifications to their country of national origin. The interest group with the reputation for greatest influence is Jewish Americans, whose family and emotional ties to Israel make them one of the most alert and active interest groups in the whole field of foreign policy. But note once again how narrowly specialized that interest is—it focuses almost entirely on policies toward Israel. Similarly, Americans of Irish heritage, despite having lived in the United States for two, three, or four generations, still maintain a vigilance about American policies toward Ireland and Northern Ireland; some even contribute to the Irish Republican Army. Many other ethnic and national interest groups wield similar influence over American foreign policy.

These ethnic or national-origin interest groups are more influential than counterpart groups in other democratic countries. This is a kind of "dual loyalty" that Americans generally welcome as a worthy sentiment. But there are limits, especially when national origin is coupled with or tied to countries in which a single religion is dominant. For example, Jews with strong ties to Israel and Catholics with connections to Ireland have on occasion been blocked from group influence on foreign policy because "dual loyalty" can be taken by other groups as "doubtful loyalty."[9]

[8]Raymond A. Bauer, Ithiel de Sola Pool, and Lewis Anthony Dexter, *American Business and Public Policy: The Politics of Foreign Trade*, 2nd ed. (Chicago: Aldine-Atherton, 1972).
[9]For a good treatment of this in regard to Irish Catholics and Catholics in general, see Timothy Byrnes, *Catholic Bishops and American Politics* (Princeton, NJ: Princeton University Press, 1991).

Nevertheless, Irish and Jewish groups as well as a variety of other ethnic American interest groups are vigorously involved in salient aspects of foreign policy, and it is an irrational or nonrational elected politician who disregards their signals. It is quite possible that the "electoral connection"[10] and the politics of representation in Congress (and the White House) are at their most intense when national origin is linked to a foreign-policy issue. Many will argue that the rationality principle "need not . . . be equated with such narrowly self-serving actions."[11] However, the nationality interest is often the strongest electoral connection.

A third type of interest group, one with a reputation that has been growing in the past two decades, is the human rights interest group. Such groups are made up of people who, instead of having self-serving economic or ethnic interests in foreign policy, are genuinely concerned for the welfare and treatment of people throughout the world—particularly those who suffer under harsh political regimes. A relatively small but often quite influential example is Amnesty International, whose exposés of human-rights abuses have altered the practices of many regimes around the world. In recent years, the Christian Right has also been a vocal advocate for the human rights of Christians who are persecuted in other parts of the world, most notably in China, for their religious beliefs. For example, the Christian Coalition joined groups like Amnesty International in lobbying Congress to cut trade with countries that permit attacks against religious believers.

A related type of group with a fast-growing influence is the ecological or environmental group, sometimes called the "greens." Groups of this nature often depend more on demonstrations than on the usual forms and strategies of influence in Washington—lobbying and using electoral politics, for example. Demonstrations in strategically located areas can have significant influence on American foreign policy. The most recent examples are the 1999 protests in Seattle and the 2001 protest in Genoa, Italy, against the World Trade Organization (WTO) and its authority to impose limits and restrictions on sovereign nations (even the United States).

The Media

Each part of the media has its own character and mode of operations; and as a consequence, each may pose a different source of anguish and of opportunity in making and implementing foreign policy. This makes the media a very special problem for each president because—as George Washington warned—once we become "entangled" with other nations, the media has to be "managed" to a certain extent to present a single, national voice. And managing can come close to violation of the

[10]This felicitous term is from David Mayhew, *Congress: The Electoral Connection* (New Haven, CT: Yale University Press, 1974).
[11]John Aldrich, *Why Parties? The Origin and Transformation of Political Parties in America* (Chicago: University of Chicago Press, 1995), p. 278.

First Amendment's "freedom of the press" guarantee. This becomes an overwhelming problem during times of war, cold war, or any other sustained threat to national security, including after September 11.

The balancing of security against freedom of the press has become increasingly difficult with the increased power of the media that follows upon significant developments in communications and information technology. Iraq is, of course, the most important case in point. During the first few weeks of the invasion in 2003, nearly 600 embedded journalists (plus a number of "free-floating" U.S. and non-U.S. journalists) provided the most intensive coverage in the history of war; and, without any question, for the first time, the coverage was instantaneous, visual, annotated, and in color—not only on TV but on the front pages of all the major newspapers.

Take special note of the key word *embedded*. No matter how delicately put, this involved the management of the journalists in a deal to provide access and protection in return for "responsible" reporting, leading to widespread suspicion and fear that not only the journalists but the news itself was being managed. The suspicion grew as the war changed after the deposing of the Saddam Hussein regime, the dispersal of the Iraqi armed forces, and the decommissioning of the entire civil government that had been dominated by the Hussein Baathist party. Quite simply, the situation changed from a conventional, organized war to an ambiguous, insurgent war. This was the end of any practice of embedding and the beginning of fewer but more free-floating journalists, which also meant the expansion of dissent and open criticism accompanying the reports. "News management" of whatever extent was certainly no longer possible.

As casualties mounted and the insurgency dragged on, reporting from Iraq (and the entire Middle East) began to demonstrate the true plurality of the term *media*. There remained considerable support—of Americans and of journalists reporting from the scene—for maintaining Iraq commitment and for sustaining and increasing American support. But as reports critical of the policy and, even more, of its implementation expanded in number, scale, and intensity, the reaction against this unmanaged reporting also increased. Inevitably charges were being made by self-designated conservatives and neoconservatives that ideology was driving the opposition to the war and that the media—especially certain national newspapers, periodicals, and television syndicates—were nothing more than channels for "liberal bias."

There is ample, varied bias in every division (medium) of the media. But it would be impossible to sustain an argument that prowar is conservative and antiwar is liberal. For example, the so-called liberals of the Harry S. Truman administration were the "cold warriors" who initiated the Korean War and the Vietnam War. And many of those very supporters became the neoconservatives as a reaction against Democrats who were moved toward opposition to Vietnam in particular and to the cold war commitment in general. (It is important to stress here that the very term *neoconservative* was invented by the liberals who had turned against the cold war and was meant to be applied to those liberals who had maintained their strong cold war foreign policy commitment.)

Putting It Together

Collective-Action Principle

The one influence toward consistency in the making of foreign policy is the president as "coordinator in chief," or the "legal dictator." But coordination fails without clear presidential communication.

Policy Principle

Because the number of participants in making foreign policy is limited, foreign policy reflects the goals of the president and his circle of advisers.

Rationality Principle

Foreign-policy interests are pursued through both domestic infighting and strategic interaction with foreign "players."

What can we say about who really makes American foreign policy? First, except for the president, the influence of players and shapers varies from case to case—that is a good reason to look with some care at each example of foreign policy in this chapter. Second, because the one constant influence is the centrality of the president in foreign policy making, it is best to evaluate other actors and factors as they interact with the president.[12] Third, the reason influence varies from case to case is that each case arises under different conditions and with vastly different time constraints: for issues that arise and are resolved quickly, the opportunity for influence is limited. Fourth, foreign-policy experts will usually disagree about the level of influence any player or type of player has on policy making.

But just to get started, let's make a few tentative generalizations and then put them to the test with the substance and experience reported in the remainder of this chapter. First, when an important foreign-policy decision has to be made under conditions of crisis—where time is of the essence—the influence of the presidency is at its strongest. Second, within those time constraints, access to the decision is limited almost exclusively to the narrowest definition of the foreign-policy establishment. The arena for participation is tiny; any discussion at all is limited to the officially and constitutionally designated players. To put this another way, in a crisis, the foreign-policy establishment works as it is supposed to.[13] As time becomes less restricted, even when the decision to be made is of great importance, the arena of participation expands to include more government players and more nonofficial, informal players—the most concerned interest groups and the most important journalists. In other words, the arena becomes more pluralistic and, therefore, less distinguishable from the politics of domestic policy making. Third, because there are so many other countries with power and interests on any given issue, there are severe limits on the choices the United States can make. That is, in sharp contrast to domestic politics, U.S. policy makers in the foreign-policy realm are engaged not only in infighting but also in strategic interaction with those in other nations; their choices are made both in reaction to and in anticipation of these strategic interactions. As one author concludes, in foreign affairs, "policy takes precedence over politics."[14] Thus, even though foreign-policy making in noncrisis situations may more closely resemble the pluralistic politics of domestic policy making, foreign-policy making is still a narrower arena with fewer participants.

---

[12]A very good brief outline of the centrality of the president in foreign policy is found in Paul E. Peterson, "The President's Dominance in Foreign Policy Making," *Political Science Quarterly* 109.2 (Summer 1994): 215, 234.

[13]One confirmation of this is found in Theodore Lowi, *The End of Liberalism: The Second Republic of the United States,* 2nd ed. (New York: Norton, 1979), pp. 127–30; another is found in Stephen Krasner, "Are Bureaucracies Important?" *Foreign Policy* 7 (Summer 1972): 159–79. However, it should be added that Krasner was writing his article in disagreement with Graham T. Allison, "Conceptual Models and the Cuban Missile Crisis," *American Political Science Review* 63, no. 3 (September 1969): 689–718.

[14]Peterson, "The President's Dominance in Foreign Policy Making," 232.

WHAT ARE THE VALUES IN AMERICAN FOREIGN POLICY?

When President Washington was preparing to leave office in 1796, he crafted with great care, and with the help of Alexander Hamilton and James Madison, a farewell address that is one of the most memorable documents in American history. We have already had occasion to look at a portion of Washington's Farewell Address because in it he gave some stern warnings against political parties (see Chapter 11). But Washington's greater concern was to warn the nation against foreign influence:

> History and experience prove that foreign influence is one of the most baneful foes of republican government. . . . The great rule of conduct for us in regard to foreign nations is, in extending our commercial relations to have with them as little *political* connection as possible. So far as we have already formed engagements let them be fulfilled with perfect good faith. Here let us stop. . . . There can be no greater error than to expect or calculate upon real favors from nation to nation. . . . Trust to temporary alliances for extraordinary emergencies, [but in all other instances] steer clear of permanent alliances with any portion of the foreign world. . . . Such an attachment of a small or weak toward a great and powerful nation dooms the former to be the satellite of the latter. [Emphasis in original.][15]

With the exception of a few leaders such as Thomas Jefferson and Thomas Paine, who were eager to take sides with the French against all others, Washington was probably expressing sentiments shared by most Americans. In fact, during most of the nineteenth century, American foreign policy was to a large extent nonexistent. But Americans were never isolationists, if isolationism means the refusal to have any associations with the outside world. Americans were eager for trade and for treaties and contracts facilitating trade. Americans were also expansionists, but their vision of expansionism was limited to the North American continent only.

Three familiar historical factors help explain why Washington's sentiments became the tradition and the source of American foreign-policy values. The first was a deep and abiding opposition to strong national government. Although some of that sentiment exists today in the form of demands for tax relief; deregulation; privatization; and, in general, to "get the government off our backs," it was far stronger throughout the nineteenth century and on into the first third of the twentieth century. A second, and highly reinforcing factor was federalism—defense of "states' rights." We had no standing army and no national "general staff." We mobilized a national army for war but demobilized it as soon after as possible.

---

[15]A full version of the text of the Farewell Address, along with a discussion of the contribution to it made by Hamilton and Madison, is found in Daniel J. Boorstin, ed., *An American Primer*, 2 vols. (Chicago: University of Chicago Press, 1966), I, pp. 192–210. This editing is by Richard B. Morris.

In the lengthy interim between wars, the states had their militias, which Congress had the constitutional power (under Article I, Section 8) to "call forth" when necessary. That is the way it happened, until after World War II. The third factor was the position of the United States in world affairs as a *client state*—that is, as a state with the capacity to pursue its own foreign interests most of the time, but, one that had to depend on one or more of the major powers to maintain international relations in general. Most nineteenth-century Americans recognized that if the United States became entangled in foreign affairs, national power would naturally grow at the expense of the states, and so would the presidency at the expense of Congress. Why? Because foreign policy meant having a professional diplomatic corps, professional armed forces with a general staff—and secrets. This meant professionalism, elitism, and remoteness from citizens. Being a client state allowed America to keep its foreign policy to a minimum. Moreover, maintaining American sovereignty was in the interest of the European powers because it prevented any one of them from gaining an advantage over the others in the Western Hemisphere.

Legacies of the Traditional System

Two identifiable legacies flowed from the long tradition based on antistatism, federalism, and client status. One is the intermingling of domestic and foreign-policy institutions. The second is unilateralism—America's willingness to go it alone. Each of these reveals a great deal about the values behind today's conduct of foreign policy.

Intermingling of Domestic and Foreign Policy Because the major European powers once policed the world, American political leaders could treat foreign policy as a mere extension of domestic policy. The tariff is the best example. A tax on one category of imported goods as a favor to interests in one section of the country would directly cause friction elsewhere in the country. But the demands of those adversely affected could be met without directly compromising the original tariff, by adding a tariff to still other goods that would placate those who were complaining about the original tariff. In this manner, Congress was continually adding and adjusting tariffs on more and more classes of commodities.

An important aspect of the treatment of foreign affairs as an extension of domestic policy was amateurism. Unlike many other countries, Americans refused to develop a tradition of a separate foreign service composed of professional people who spent much of their adult lives in foreign countries, learning foreign languages, absorbing foreign cultures, and developing a sympathy for foreign points of view. Instead, Americans have tended to be highly suspicious of any American diplomat or entrepreneur who spoke sympathetically of any foreign viewpoints.[16] No systematic progress was made to create a professional diplomatic corps until after the passage of the Foreign Service Act of 1946.

---

[16]E. E. Schattschneider, *Politics, Pressures and the Tariff* (Englewood Cliffs, NJ: Prentice-Hall, 1935).

Unilateralism Unilateralism, not isolationism, was the American posture toward the world until the middle of the twentieth century. Isolationism means trying to cut off contacts with the outside, to be a self-sufficient fortress. America was never isolationist; it preferred *unilateralism,* or "going it alone." Americans have always been more likely to rally around the president in support of direct action rather than for a sustained, diplomatic involvement.

The Great Leap to World Power

The traditional era of U.S. foreign policy came to an end with World War I for several important reasons. First, the "balance of power" system[17] that had kept the major European powers from world war for a hundred years had collapsed.[18] In fact, the great powers themselves had collapsed internally. The most devastating of all wars up to that time had ruined their economies; their empires; and, in most cases, their political systems. Second, the United States was no longer a client state but in fact one of the great powers. Third, as we saw in earlier chapters, the United States was soon to shed its traditional domestic system of federalism with its national government of almost pure promotional policy. Thus, virtually all the conditions that contributed to the traditional system of American foreign policy had disappeared. Yet there was no discernible change in America's approach to foreign policy in the period between World War I and World War II. After World War I, as one foreign-policy analyst put it, "the United States withdrew once more into its insularity. Since America was unwilling to use its power, that power, for purposes of foreign policy, did not really exist."[19]

The Great Leap in foreign policy was finally made thirty years after conditions demanded it and only then after another world war. After World War II, pressure for a new tradition came into direct conflict with the old. The new tradition required foreign entanglements; the old tradition feared them deeply. The new tradition required diplomacy; the old distrusted it. The new tradition required acceptance of antagonistic political systems; the old embraced democracy and was aloof from all else.

The values of the new tradition were all apparent during the cold war. Instead of unilateralism, the United States pursued *multilateralism,* entering into treaties with other nations to achieve its foreign-policy goals. The most notable of these treaties is that which formed NATO in 1948, allying the United States, Canada, and most of western Europe. With its NATO allies, the United States

---

unilateralism
A foreign policy that avoids international alliances, entanglements, and permanent commitments in favor of independence, neutrality, and freedom of action.

 History Principle
Once the United States became a world power after World War II, its foreign policy focused on mutilateralism, containment, and deterrence.

multilateralism
A foreign policy that encourages the involvement of several nation-states in coordinated action, usually in relation to a common adversary, with terms and conditions usually specified in a multicountry treaty, such as NATO.

---

[17]"Balance of power" was the primary foreign-policy role played by the major European powers during the nineteenth century, and it is a role available to the United States in contemporary foreign affairs, a role occasionally adopted but not on a world scale. This is the third of the four roles identified and discussed later in this chapter.

[18]The best analysis of what he calls the "100 years' peace" will be found in Karl Polanyi, *The Great Transformation* (Boston: Beacon, 1944, rpt. ed. 1957), pp. 5ff.

[19]John G. Stoessinger, *Crusaders and Pragmatists: Movers of Modern American Foreign Policy,* 2nd ed. (New York: Norton, 1985), pp. 21, 34.

containment
The primary cold war foreign policy of the United States during the 1950s and 1960s, whereby the United States used its political, economic, and military power to prevent the spread of communism to developing or unstable countries.

deterrence
The development and maintenance of military strength for the purpose of discouraging attack.

practiced a two-pronged policy in dealing with its rival, the Soviet Union: *containment* and *deterrence*. Fearing that the Soviet Union was bent on world domination, the United States fought wars in Korea and Vietnam to "contain" Soviet power. And to deter a direct attack against itself or its NATO allies, the United States developed a multibillion-dollar nuclear arsenal capable of destroying the Soviet Union many times over.

An arms race between the United States and the Soviet Union was extremely difficult, if not impossible, to avoid because there was no way for either side to know when it had enough deterrent to continue preventing aggression by the other side. As we mentioned in the beginning of this chapter, the cold war ended abruptly in 1989, after the Soviet Union had spent itself into oblivion and allowed its empire to collapse. Many observers called the end of the cold war a victory for democracy. But more important, it was a victory for capitalism over communism, a vindication of the free market as the best way to produce the greatest wealth of nations. Furthering capitalism has long been one of the values guiding American foreign policy, and this might be more true now than ever before.

WHAT ARE THE INSTRUMENTS OF MODERN AMERICAN FOREIGN POLICY?

 Rationality Principle
The instruments of foreign policy— economic, diplomatic, institutional, military—are deployed to serve strategic purposes.

Any nation-state has at hand certain instruments, or tools, to use in implementing its foreign policy. There have been many instruments of American foreign policy, and we can deal here only with those instruments we deem to be most important in the modern epoch: diplomacy, the United Nations, the international monetary structure, economic aid, collective security, and military deterrence. Each of these instruments is evaluated in this section for its utility in the conduct of American foreign policy, and each is assessed in light of the history and development of American values.

Diplomacy

We begin this treatment of instruments with diplomacy because it is the instrument to which all other instruments should be subordinated, although they seldom are. Diplomacy is the representation of a government to other foreign governments. Its purpose is to promote national values or interests by peaceful means. According to Hans Morgenthau, "a diplomacy that ends in war has failed in its primary objective."[20]

The first effort to create a modern diplomatic service in the United States was made through the Rogers Act of 1924, which established the initial framework for a professional foreign service staff. But it took World War II and the Foreign Service Act of 1946 to forge the foreign service into a fully professional diplomatic corps.

---

[20]Hans J. Morgenthau, *Politics among Nations*, 2nd ed. (New York: Knopf, 1956), p. 505.

Diplomacy, by its very nature, is overshadowed by spectacular international events, dramatic initiatives, and meetings among heads of state or their direct personal representatives. The traditional American distrust of diplomacy continues today, although in weaker form. Impatience with or downright distrust of diplomacy has been built not only into all the other instruments of foreign policy but also into the modern presidential system itself.[21] So much personal responsibility has been heaped on the presidency that it is difficult for presidents to entrust any of their authority or responsibility in foreign policy to professional diplomats in the State Department and other bureaucracies.

Distrust of diplomacy has also produced a tendency among all recent presidents to turn frequently to military and civilian personnel outside the State Department to take on a special diplomatic role as direct personal representatives of the president. As discouraging as it is to those who have dedicated their careers to foreign service to have political hacks appointed over their heads, it is probably even more discouraging when they are displaced from a foreign-policy issue as soon as relations with the country they are posted in begin to heat up. When a special personal representative is sent abroad to represent the president, that envoy holds a status higher than that of the local ambassador, and the embassy becomes the envoy's temporary residence and base of operation. Despite the impressive professionalization of the American foreign service—with advanced training, competitive exams, language requirements, and career commitment—this practice of displacing career ambassadors with political appointees and with special personal presidential representatives continues. For instance, when President Clinton in 1998, sought to boost the peace process in Northern Ireland, he called on former senator George J. Mitchell. Mitchell received almost unanimous praise for his skill and patience in chairing the Northern Ireland peace talks. The caliber of his work in Northern Ireland led to Senator Mitchell's becoming involved in another of the world's apparently unsolvable conflicts— that between the Israelis and the Palestinians.

Diplomacy was once again put to the test in the months following the terrorist attacks of September 11, 2001. Although September 11 itself was quickly traced back to Osama bin Laden and his headquarters in Afghanistan, terrorist networks were known to exist in a number of countries and to be receiving financial support by still other countries. Getting access to these terrorist sources directly and through alliances required diplomatic, not military means. Secretary of State Colin Powell extracted pledges from dozens of countries, but keeping those pledges when sympathy for American suffering waned required constant diplomatic effort by Powell and the entire State Department as well as by other leading players, including President Bush himself.

Diplomacy began losing its promise by summer 2002, with the Bush Doctrine, asserting a national right and determination to engage in preemptive attacks when and where our vital interests were at stake. This meant that Powell's

[21]See Theodore J. Lowi, *The Personal President: Power Invested, Promise Unfulfilled* (Ithaca, NY: Cornell University Press, 1985), pp. 167–69.

diplomatic approach to multilateral containment of terrorism was losing out to a more military-driven approach, led by Vice President Cheney, Secretary of Defense Rumsfeld a host of highly committed deputy and assistant secretaries of defense, and the influential National Security Adviser Condoleezza Rice, who would replace Powell as secretary of state after the 2004 election.

Powell pushed mightily for diplomacy and, in particular, for diplomacy through the United Nations, whose inspection programs would help contain Saddam Hussein's expansionist tendencies and would justify political, economic, and military sanctions if Iraq persisted in developing weapons of mass destruction (WMD). Powell's approach prevailed during the many months of UN debate; but through all the debate and negotiation, the United States made it clear that military measures would be triggered by diplomatic failure. In fact, the Bush Doctrine contributed to the decision by many allied powers to resist entering an alliance against Iraq that would, in their opinion, almost certainly end in "preemptive war."

The significance of diplomacy and its vulnerability to domestic politics may be better appreciated as we proceed to the other instruments. Diplomacy was an instrument more or less imposed on Americans as the prevailing method of dealing among nation-states in the nineteenth century. The other instruments to be identified and assessed below are instruments that Americans self-consciously crafted for themselves to take care of their own chosen place in the world affairs of the second half of the twentieth century. They are, therefore, more reflective of American culture and values than is diplomacy.

The United Nations

United Nations (UN) An organization of nations founded in 1945 to serve as a channel for negotiation and a means of settling international disputes peaceably.

The utility of the *United Nations (UN)* to the United States as an instrument of foreign policy can be too easily underestimated because the United Nations is a very large and unwieldly institution with few powers and no armed forces to implement its rules and resolutions. Its supreme body is the UN General Assembly, composed of one representative of each of the 191 member states, and each member representative has one vote, regardless of the size of the country. Important issues require a two-thirds majority vote, and the annual session of the General Assembly runs only from September to December (although it can call extra sessions). It has little organization that can make it an effective decision-making body, with only six standing committees, few tight rules of procedure, and no political parties to provide priorities and discipline. Its defenders are quick to add that, although it lacks armed forces, it relies on the power of world opinion; and this is not to be taken lightly. The powers of the United Nations devolve mainly to its "executive committee," the UN Security Council, which alone has the real power to make decisions and rulings that member states are obligated by the UN Charter to implement. The Security Council may be called into session at any time, and each member (or a designated alternate) must be present at UN headquarters in New York at all times. It is composed of fifteen members: five are permanent, and ten are elected by the General Assembly for two-year, nonrepeatable terms. The five permanent members are China, France, Russia, the United Kingdom, and the United States. Each of the fifteen members has only one vote, and a nine-vote majority of the fifteen is required on all substantive matters. But each of the five permanent members also has a negative vote, a "veto," and one veto is sufficient to reject any substantive proposal.

During the first decade or more after its founding in 1945, the United Nations was a fairly consistent servant of American interests. The most spectacular example of its use as an instrument of American foreign policy was the official UN authorization and sponsorship of intervention in Korea with an international "peacekeeping force" in 1950. The Soviet Union was boycotting the United Nations at that time, and that deprived it of its ability to use its veto in the Security Council. Consequently, the United States was able to get its legitimizing resolution from the Security Council and to conduct the Korean War under the auspices of the United Nations.

The United States provided 40 percent of the UN budget in 1946 (its first full year of operation) and 26 percent of the $1.2 billion UN budget in 1997–98.[22] Many Americans feel that the United Nations does not give good value for the investment. But any evaluation of the United Nations must take into account the purpose for which the United States sought to create it: to achieve *power without diplomacy*. After World War II, when the United States could no longer remain aloof from foreign policy, the nation's leaders sought to use our power to create an international structure that could be run with a minimum of diplomatic involvement—so that Americans could return to their normal domestic pursuits.

The UN gained a new lease on life in the post–cold war era, especially with its performance in the 1991 Persian Gulf War. Although President George H. W. Bush's immediate reaction to Iraq's invasion of Kuwait was unilateral, he quickly turned to the UN for sponsorship. The UN General Assembly initially adopted resolutions condemning the invasion and approving the full blockade of Iraq. Once the blockade was seen as having failed to achieve the unconditional withdrawal demanded by the UN, the General Assembly adopted further resolutions authorizing the twenty-nine-nation coalition to use force if, by January 15, 1991, the resolutions were not observed. As foreign-policy expert Richard Haass put it, "The UN Security Council's authorization enhanced the undertaking's political and legal appeal, making it easier for the governments [of the twenty-nine-nation alliance] to join the common effort."[23] The Gulf War victory was a UN victory just as much as it was a victory for the United States and the twenty-nine-nation alliance. The cost of the operation was estimated at $61.1 billion.

---

[22]In 1997, the next five biggest contributors were Japan (16.0 percent), Germany (9.0 percent), France (6.7 percent), the United Kingdom (5.6 percent), and the Russian federation (4.4 percent). These figures do not include many specific UN operations and organizations or the U.S. contributions to these programs. See the 1998 *Information Please Almanac* (Boston: Houghton Mifflin, 1998), pp. 348–49.

[23]Richard N. Haass, *The Reluctant Sheriff: The United States after the Cold War* (New York: Council on Foreign Relations Press, 1997), p. 94.

First authorized by the U.S. Congress, actual U.S. outlays were offset by pledges from the other participants—the largest shares coming from Saudi Arabia ($15.6 billion), Kuwait ($16 billion), Japan ($10 billion), and Germany ($6.5 billion). The final U.S. costs were estimated at a maximum of $8 billion.[24]

Of course not all UN-sponsored actions are clear-cut victories. When Yugoslavia's communist regime collapsed in the early 1990s, the country broke apart into war among the ethnically distinct regions. The war concentrated in Bosnia, where fierce fighting broke out among Muslims, Croatians, and Serbians, each fearing they would lose their identity if one of the others dominated Bosnia. The United States and its NATO allies pushed toward peace by creating "safe havens" in several cities and towns. But the United States and its NATO allies turned the maintenance of those "safe havens" over to UN troops. President Clinton criticized President George H. W. Bush for not doing more, but Clinton turned out to be politically unable to muster any more support for the failing UN mission. After this failure of the international community to prevent Serbs from waging a war of aggression, which they themselves called "ethnic cleansing," UN peacekeepers and aid workers were again given the same thankless task in Kosovo immediately after the pullout of hostile Serbian troops in 1999. Despite the difficulty of restoring peace, the UN and its peacekeeping troops did an extraordinary job in the former Yugoslavia, dealing both with the intransigence of the warring parties and with the disagreement among the European powers about how to deal with a vicious and destructive civil war.

September 11, 2001, also involved the UN. Less than three weeks afterward, the UN Security Council unanimously (15 to 0) approved a U.S.-sponsored resolution requiring all countries to deny safe haven to anyone financing or committing a terrorist act. The resolution actually criminalized the financing of terrorist activity and extended its coverage beyond countries to individuals and "entities" within countries. The UN also created a committee of the Security Council members to monitor implementation of the resolution, which included freezing all monetary assets available to terrorists and passing tougher laws to detain suspected terrorists as well as to share intelligence regarding terrorism. Moreover, although this resolution stresses economic rather than military means, it does not prohibit "use of force," which the UN Charter allows, as long as force is used for self-defense and not for "armed reprisals" after the fact.

The UN Security Council was also central in the debate over the U.S. potential invasion of Iraq during the fall of 2002. At first, President George W. Bush was reluctant to seek UN approval because he believed that he already had enough UN authority based on past Security Council resolutions that Saddam Hussein had so egregiously disregarded. But growing opposition to unilateral U.S. action against Iraq on the part of several Security Council members produced second thoughts and led Bush to appear at the United Nations and

---

[24]There was, in fact, an angry dispute over a "surplus" of at least $2.2 billion, on the basis of which Japan and others demanded a rebate. *Report of the Secretary of Defense to the President and Congress* (Washington, DC: Government Printing Office, 1992), p. 26.

request a renewed and more authoritative, unconditional resolution. In response to this renewed U.S. cooperativeness, the Security Council unanimously adopted a resolution, calling on Iraq's president, Saddam Hussein, to disarm and to allow weapons inspectors into Iraq. Peacekeeping and diplomacy may be the preferred UN modus operandi, but the organization has shown that it is willing even to support war as long as prescribed procedures are followed and appropriate international support is evident. This proved not to be the case in early 2003. Following authorization for weapons inspections, the Bush administration pressured the UN Security Council to support military action in Iraq but met resistance from France, Russia, and others. Knowing it faced a veto by France and possibly Russia, the Bush administration ultimately decided to go to war without another UN Security Council vote.

This and other recent UN interventions show the promise and the limits of the UN in the post–cold war era. Although the United States can no longer control UN decisions, as it could in the UN's early days, the UN continues to function as a useful instrument of American foreign policy.

The International Monetary Structure

Fear of a repeat of the economic devastation that followed World War I brought the United States together with its allies (except the U.S.S.R.) to Bretton Woods, New Hampshire, in 1944 to create a new international economic structure for the postwar world. The result was two institutions: the International Bank for Reconstruction and Development (commonly called the World Bank) and the International Monetary Fund.

The World Bank was set up to finance long-term capital. Leading nations took on the obligation of contributing funds to enable the World Bank to make loans to capital-hungry countries. (The U.S. quota has been about one third of the total.)

The International Monetary Fund (IMF) was set up to provide for the short-term flow of money. After the war, the dollar, instead of gold, was the chief means by which the currencies of one country would be "changed into" currencies of another country for purposes of making international transactions. To permit debtor countries with no international balances to make purchases and investments, the IMF was set up to lend dollars or other appropriate currencies to needy member countries to help them overcome temporary trade deficits. For many years after World War II, the IMF, along with U.S. foreign aid, in effect constituted the only international medium of exchange.

During the 1990s, the IMF returned to a position of enhanced importance through its efforts to reform some of the largest debtor nations and former communist countries and to bring them more completely into the global capitalist economy. For example, Russia and thirteen other former Soviet republics were invited to join the IMF and the World Bank, with the expectation of receiving $10.5 billion from these two agencies, primarily for a ruble-stabilization fund. Each republic was to get a permanent IMF representative, and the IMF increased

Rationality Principle

The United States typically incorporates the UN into its international engagements (such as the one in Iraq) as long as the collective body does not block or frustrate U.S. purposes.

its staff by at least 10 percent to provide the expertise necessary to cope with the problems of these emerging capitalist economies.[25]

Policy Principle

The lending policies of the IMF reflect the interests of its leading shareholders, most notably the United States.

The IMF, with $93 billion, has more money to lend poor countries than the United States, Europe, or Japan (the three leading IMF shareholders) do individually, and it makes its policy decisions in ways that are generally consonant with the interests of the leading shareholders.[26] As an international institution, the IMF plays an important role in inducing cooperation among member countries. Two weeks after September 11, 2001, the IMF had approved a $135 million loan to economically troubled Pakistan, a key player in the war against the Taliban government of Afghanistan because of its strategic location. Turkey, with its strategic location in the Middle East, was also put back in the IMF pipeline.[27]

These activities of the IMF indicate just how effectively it is committed to the extension of capitalist victory. The reforms imposed on poorer countries—imposed as conditions to be met before receiving IMF loans—are reforms that commit a troubled country to joining or maintaining membership in the system of global capital exchange that allows investment to seek the highest profits, without restraint. This goal can ignite a boom—as it did in South Korea, Indonesia, Singapore, and Thailand—but that boom can terminate just as abruptly, leaving the economy in question defenseless.

The future of the IMF, the World Bank, and all other private sources of international investment will depend in part on extension of more credit to the Third World and other developing countries because credit means investment and productivity. But the future may depend even more on reducing the debt that is already there from previous extensions of credit. "Debt relief" is becoming a more acceptable foreign-policy option. The most spectacular (and some say the most effective) champion and lobbyist for debt relief is Bono, lead singer of the rock band U2. In May 2002, in what may turn out to have been a culmination of his efforts, Bono made a two-week tour of Equatorial Africa with Paul O'Neill, U.S. Secretary of the Treasury, to address investment needs as well as poverty and the AIDS epidemic. Debt relief, however, seemed highest on the agenda of this "odd couple," who seemed to view it as a kind of prerequisite for the advancement of other social and cultural goals.

Economic Aid

Commitment to rebuilding war-torn countries came as easily as commitment to the basic postwar international monetary structure. This is the way President

[25]"IMF: Sleeve-Rolling Time," *Economist*, 2 May 1992, pp. 98–99.

[26]James Dao and Patrick E. Tyler, "U.S. Says Military Strikes Are Just a Part of Big Plan," *The Alliance* 27 September 2001; and Joseph Kahn, "A Nation Challenged: Global Dollars," *New York Times*, 20 September 2001, p. B1.

[27]Turkey was desperate for help to extricate its economy from its worst recession since 1945. The Afghanistan crisis was going to hurt Turkey all the more; its strategic location helped its case with the IMF. "Official Says Turkey Is Advancing in Drive for I.M.F. Financing," *New York Times*, 6 October 2001, p. A7.

Franklin Roosevelt put the case in a press conference in November 1942, less than one year after the United States entered World War II:

> Sure, we are going to rehabilitate [other nations after the war]. Why? . . . Not only from the humanitarian point of view . . . but from the viewpoint of our own pocketbooks, and our safety from future war.[28]

The particular form and timing for enacting American foreign aid was heavily influenced by Great Britain's sudden decision in 1947 that it would no longer be able to maintain its commitments to Greece and Turkey (full proof that America would now have to *have* clients rather than *be* one). Within three weeks of that announcement, President Truman recommended a $400 million direct-aid program for Greece and Turkey, and by mid-May of 1947, Congress approved it. Since President Truman had placed the Greece-Turkey action within the larger context of a commitment to help rebuild and defend all countries the world over, wherever the leadership wished to develop democratic systems or to ward off communism, the Greek-Turkish aid was followed quickly by the historically unprecedented program that came to be known as the Marshall Plan, named in honor of Secretary of State (and former five-star general) George C. Marshall.[29]

The Marshall Plan—officially known as the European Recovery Program (ERP)—was essential for the rebuilding of war-ravaged Europe. By 1952, the United States had spent over $34 billion for the relief, reconstruction, and economic recovery of Western Europe. The emphasis was shifted in 1951, with passage of the Mutual Security Act, to building up European military capacity. Of the $48 billion appropriated between 1952 and 1961, over half went for military assistance, the rest for continuing economic aid. Over those years, the geographic emphasis of U.S. aid also shifted, toward South Korea, Taiwan, the Philippines, Vietnam, Iran, Greece, and Turkey—that is, toward the rim of communism. In the 1960s, the emphasis shifted once again, toward what became known as the Third World. From 1962 to 1975, over $100 billion was sent, mainly to Latin America for economic assistance. Other countries of Africa and Asia were also brought in.[30]

Many critics have argued that foreign aid is really aid for political and economic elites, not for the people. Although this is to a large extent true, it needs to be understood in a broader context. If a country's leaders oppose distributing food or any other form of assistance to its people, there is little that the United States, or any aid organization, can do, short of terminating the assistance. Goods have to be exchanged across national borders before they can reach the people

 History Principle

The United States was drawn from isolation to internationalism by the failure of Great Britain and the rise of an atomic-powered Soviet Union.

---

[28]Quoted in John Lewis Gaddis, *The United States and the Origins of the Cold War, 1941–1947* (New York: Columbia University Press, 1972), p. 21.

[29]The best account of the decision and its purposes will be found in Joseph Jones, *The Fifteen Weeks (February 21–June 4, 1947)* (New York: Viking, 1955).

[30]Robert A. Pastor, *Congress and the Politics of U.S. Foreign Economic Policy, 1929–1976* (Berkeley: University of California Press, 1980), pp. 256–80.

who need them. Needy people would probably be worse off if the United States cut off aid altogether. The lines of international communication must be kept open. That is why diplomacy exists, and foreign aid can facilitate diplomacy, just as diplomacy is necessary to help get foreign aid where it is most needed.

Another important criticism of U.S. foreign-aid policy is that it has not been tied closely enough to U.S. diplomacy. This is precisely the kind of coordination failure we mentioned earlier in this chapter—a case in which one hand did not know or could not control what the other hand was doing. The original Marshall Plan was set up as an independent program outside the State Department and had its own separate missions in each participating country. Essentially, "ERP became a Second State Department."[31] This did not change until the program was reorganized as the Agency for International Development (AID) in the early 1960s. Meanwhile, the Defense Department has always had principal jurisdiction over the substantial proportion of economic aid that goes to military assistance. The Department of Agriculture administers the commodity aid programs, such as Food for Peace. Each department has in effect been able to conduct its own foreign policy, leaving many foreign diplomats to ask, "Who's in charge here?"

That brings us back to the history of U.S. efforts to balance traditional values with the modern needs of world leadership. Economic assistance is an instrument of American foreign policy, but it has been less effective than it might have been because of the inability of American politics to overcome its traditional opposition to foreign entanglements and build a unified foreign policy—something that the older nation-states would call a foreign ministry. The United States has undoubtedly made progress, but other countries still often wonder who is in charge.

Collective Security

In 1947, most Americans hoped that the United States could meet its world obligations through the United Nations and economic structures alone. But most foreign-policy makers recognized that it was a vain hope even as they were permitting and encouraging Americans to believe it. They had anticipated the need for military entanglements at the time of drafting the original UN charter by insisting on language that recognized the right of all nations to provide for their mutual defense independently of the United Nations. And almost immediately after enactment of the Marshall Plan, the White House and a parade of State and Defense Department officials followed up with an urgent request to the Senate to ratify and to Congress to finance mutual defense alliances.

At first quite reluctant to approve treaties providing for national security alliances, the Senate ultimately agreed with the executive branch. The first collective security agreement was the Rio Treaty (ratified by the Senate in September 1947), which created the Organization of American States (OAS). This was the

[31]Quoted in Lowi, *The End of Liberalism*, p. 162.

model treaty, anticipating all succeeding collective security treaties by providing that an armed attack against any of its members "shall be considered as an attack against all the American States," including the United States. A more significant break with U.S. tradition against peacetime entanglements came with the North Atlantic Treaty (signed in April 1949), which created NATO. ANZUS, a treaty tying Australia and New Zealand to the United States, was signed in September 1951. Three years later, the Southeast Asia Treaty created the Southeast Asia Treaty Organization (SEATO).

In addition to these ***multilateral treaties,*** the United States entered into a number of ***bilateral treaties***—treaties between two countries. As one author has observed, the United States has been a *producer* of security while most of its allies have been *consumers* of security.[32] Figure 16.1 demonstrates that the United States has consistently devoted a greater percentage of its gross domestic product (GDP) to defense than have its NATO allies and Japan.

This pattern has continued in the post–cold war era, and its best illustration is the Persian Gulf War, in which the United States provided the initiative, the leadership, and most of the armed forces, even though its allies were obliged to reimburse over 90 percent of the cost.

It is difficult to evaluate collective security and its treaties because the purpose of collective security as an instrument of foreign policy is prevention, and success of this kind has to be measured according to what did *not* happen. The critics have argued that U.S. collective security treaties posed a threat of encirclement to the Soviet Union, forcing it to produce its own collective security, particularly the Warsaw Pact.[33] Nevertheless, no one can deny the counterargument that the planet has enjoyed almost sixty years without world war.

In 1998 the expansion of NATO took its first steps toward former Warsaw Pact members, extending membership to Poland, Hungary, and the Czech Republic. Most of Washington embraced this expansion as the true and fitting end of the cold war, and the U.S. Senate echoed this with a resounding 80–19 vote to induct these three former Soviet satellites into NATO. The expansion was also welcomed among European member nations, who quickly approved the move, which was hailed as the final closing of the book on Yalta, the 1945 treaty that divided Europe into Western and Soviet spheres of influence after the defeat of Germany. Expanded membership seems to have made NATO less threatening and more acceptable to Russia. Russia became a partner when the NATO-Russia Council was formed in 2002. Finally, although the expanded NATO membership (now nineteen countries) reduces the threat to Russia, it also reduces the utility of NATO as a military alliance. The September 11 attacks on the United States represented the first time in its fifty-plus year history that Article 5 of the

multilateral treaty A treaty among more than two nations.

bilateral treaty A treaty made between two nations.

Institution Principle

Mutual security organizations like NATO persist as institutional vehicles for solving collective-action dilemmas involving mutual defense, economic issues, environmental problems, and human rights.

---

[32] George H. Quester, *The Continuing Problem of International Politics* (Hinsdale, IL.: Dryden Press, 1974), p. 229.

[33] The Warsaw Pact was signed in 1955 by the Soviet Union, the German Democratic Republic (East Germany), Poland, Hungary, Czechoslovakia, Romania, Bulgaria, and Albania. Albania later dropped out. The Warsaw Pact was terminated in 1991.

FIGURE 16.1

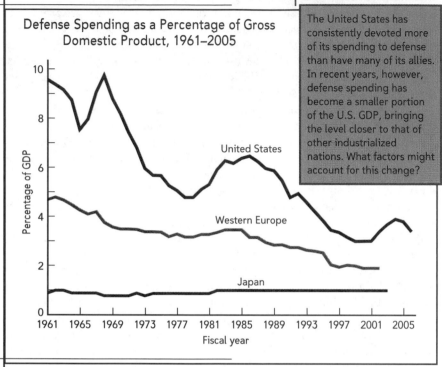

Defense Spending as a Percentage of Gross Domestic Product, 1961–2005

The United States has consistently devoted more of its spending to defense than have many of its allies. In recent years, however, defense spending has become a smaller portion of the U.S. GDP, bringing the level closer to that of other industrialized nations. What factors might account for this change?

SOURCES: Office of Management and Budget, *Budget of the United States Government, Fiscal Year 2006, Historical Tables* (Washington, DC: Government Printing Office, 2005), p. 128; Stockholm International Peace Research Institute, *SIPRI Yearbook 2003* (New York: Oxford University Press, 2003), p. 303.

North Atlantic Treaty had to be invoked; it provides that an attack on one country is an attack on all the member countries.

In fighting the war on terrorism, the Bush administration recognized that no matter how preponderant American power was, some aspects of its foreign policy could not be achieved without multilateral cooperation. On the other hand, the United States did not want to be constrained by its alliances. The global coalition initially forged after September 11 numbered over 170 countries. Although only a few joined the Afghan War in 2001, and still fewer the Iraq War of March 2003, they supported economic sanctions; they shared to varying degrees their intelligence sources; and most important, they lent an element of legitimacy to both campaigns. However, because the Iraq War was preemptive and was initiated despite the lack of proof of the presence of WMD and after rejection of relevant resolutions in the UN, the large, hoped-for coalition became a "coalition of the willing," with substantial moral and military support coming only from the United Kingdom. It was at this point that President Bush concluded that America possessed enough military force to maintain its world leadership, including unilateral containment of terrorism.

Military Deterrence

For the first century and a half of its existence as an independent republic, the United States held strongly to a "Minuteman" theory of defense: maintain a small corps of professional officers, a few flagships, and a small contingent of marines; leave the rest of defense to the state militias. In case of war, mobilize as quickly as possible, taking advantage of the country's immense size and its separation from Europe to gain time to mobilize; and between wars, demobilize.

The United States applied this policy as recently as the post–World War I years and was beginning to apply it after World War II. The cycle of demobilization–remobilization was broken, and in its place the United States adopted a new policy of constant mobilization and preparedness: *deterrence*, or the development and maintenance of military strength as a means of preventing attack. After World War II, military deterrence against the Soviet Union became the fundamental American foreign-policy objective, requiring a vast commitment of national resources. Figure 16.1 suggests a steady decline of defense spending during the build-up and the phasing out of the Vietnam segment of the cold war; but that conveys the wrong impression because the figures are percentages of the GDP. Those years were in fact a period of such persistent economic growth that continued defense expenditures at a high level were easily justified for that evasive goal called deterrence.[34]

The end of the cold war and the collapse of the Soviet Union raised public expectations for a "peace dividend" after nearly a decade (1981–91) of unprecedented defense budget increases. But that was not to be. The decline of the defense budget profile after 1992 (Fig. 16.1) was again the product of renewed economic growth, because actual defense expenditures continued at a very high level. Why? One factor was the Gulf War. A second and probably more important factor was fear that a shrinkage of investment in new military technology by the United States would dry up the American defense industry, and foreign customers would turn to military industries in other countries "to buy the winning weaponry." The Soviet Union, once the leading competitor of the United States in the world arms market, was succeeded by Russia and other post-Soviet republics because there are no longer any "ideological limitations" in the competition for customers.[35] After the United States and Russia, the list of top arms

---

[34]On the theory of deterrence, the classic arguments are developed in Robert Powell, *Nuclear Deterrence Theory: The Search for Credibility* (New York: Cambridge University Press, 1990).

[35]"Arms for Sale," *Newsweek*, 8 April 1991. See also Isaiah Wilson, "Unintended Consequences" (Ph.D. dissertation, Cornell University, 2004).

The Bush Doctrine: Unilateralism in a Unipolar World

The problems of competition and lack of collective action that underlie the principles of politics are endemic in the international arena. There is no world government, and thus there are few if any established rules, procedures, and norms to bind nations into cooperative arrangements. According to the traditional "realist" model of international politics, nothing but a nation's self-interest matters in foreign policy.[1]

An alternative viewpoint, called liberalism, argues that, even lacking an international "policeman," international institutions such as the UN do shape the behavior of nations (much in the spirit of the third principle of politics: institutions shape politics). Some scholars formulate this argument using the same rational-choice language favored by realists. Nations understand that unbridled international competition can result in tariff conflicts, arms races, and eventually wars. Nations realize that they are not, in fact, completely autonomous. Something of an international "society" does exist, and therefore it is in a country's long-term self-interest to give up some powers to an international institution.[2]

One important way to think about the difference between "realism" and "liberalism" is to consider whether the United States should act in concert with other nations (multilateralism) or go it alone (unilateralism). At least as understood by President Bush's foreign policy team, in its formulation of the "Bush Doctrine," the answer is clear. President Bush, in a speech at West Point on June 1, 2002, outlined the Bush Doctrine: pre-emptive war, preeminent U.S. military strength, the promotion of liberal democracy worldwide, and the right of the United States to pursue unilateral military action where necessary.[3]

Contrast George W. Bush's policy with that of his father. Influenced by the peaceful end of the Cold War, the reunification of Germany, the breakup of the Soviet Union, and the international response to the Iraqi invasion of Kuwait, President George H. W. Bush placed a new emphasis on the UN as the key to a "new world order." What happened to change U.S. policy so significantly in just one decade?

The world of George W. Bush is very different from that of his father. Many neoconservatives, such as former Deputy Defense Secretary Paul Wolfowitz, *Weekly Standard* editor William Kristol, and columnist Charles Krauthammer, advocate a diminished role for the United Nations. The UN's role must be marginalized, they say, because the UN has failed to protect America's security interests (as shown by the 9/11 attack) and failed to promote collective action between states (as shown by the UN's unwillingness to support military action against Afghanistan and Iraq). The UN's treatment of weak and strong states as equal is an obstacle to cooperation among the great powers. Wolfowitz argues that the United States should take the opportunity to promote democracy and, in doing so, ensure its own security (something he has been promoting since the early 1990s).[4]

In the language of the principles of politics, the collective action game has changed dramatically since 1992. During most of the postwar era, the United States had a powerful competitor—the Soviet Union. In fact, the "prisoner's dilemma," one of the most widely

Collective-Action Principle

Over the long run, nations may find it in their self-interest to cooperate, and not compete, in the international arena.

Policy Principle

U.S. foreign policy under George W. Bush reflects the long-held policy positions of his advisers.

known game theory models, was made famous by its application to nuclear competition between the two nations.[5]

Now, the United States has no clear competitor—in game theoretic terms, we are the only player. From this perspective—the perspective of George W. Bush and his advisers—the United States should not work within the context of the UN because the UN can provide a means for other nations to restrict American power.

There are also good historical reasons to expect the United States to act unilaterally. Americans have long believed that their nation is "exceptional," as exemplified by the popular image of our nation as a "city on a hill" providing a beacon of freedom and democracy to the world.[6] Our Founders revolted against the European order; we grew up as a nation outside of European feuds; and we believe that our institutions and values are superior to those of the "old world." American exceptionalism argues that the United States must actively promote its values worldwide. This was the foreign-policy position of the United States for much of the nineteenth century, and it was only the realities of superpower conflict that forced us to act multilaterally.[7]

Given the convergence of strategy and history, it is not surprising that our pro-UN era was so short-lived. Republican president George H. W. Bush was willing to work outside the UN during the first Gulf War. Democratic president Bill Clinton acted unilaterally during U.S. actions in Bosnia and Herzegovina and Kosovo. To many, the American success in replacing the Afghani and Iraqi governments only strengthens the unilateral position.

Liberals dispute these conclusions. They point to the limits of American power and to the value of the UN in solving a growing variety of international problems. For liberals, American victories in the Middle East are irrelevant; these are a function of our overwhelming military power. The ongoing difficulties in establishing stable states in Afghanistan and Iraq, and what many perceive as a growing terrorist threat, demonstrate that American self-interest still lies within a set of healthy international institutions.

Rationality Principle

In a world with just one superpower, some argue that the United States does not have to cooperate with other nations.

History Principle

American "exceptionalism"—our social, political, and geographical separation from the great powers in Europe—has shaped American foreign policy since our founding and has encouraged unilateralism.

[1]For statements of foreign policy realism, see Hans Morgenthau, *Politics Among Nations* (1948), and Kenneth Waltz, *Theory of International Politics* (1979).

[2]See Robert Keohane and Joseph Nye, *Power and Interdependence,* 3rd ed. (2000).

[3]Bush's speech is available at www.whitehouse.gov/news/releases/2002/06/20020601-3.html.

[4]Patrick E. Tyler, "Seven Hypothetical Conflicts Foreseen by the Pentagon," *New York Times,* 16 February 1992.

[5]Thomas Schelling, *The Strategy of Conflict* (Cambridge: Harvard University Press, 1980).

[6]Ronald Reagan made particularly powerful use of this symbolism.

[7]Jonathan Monten, "The Roots of the Bush Doctrine," *International Security* (Spring 2005).

sales competitors includes France, the United Kingdom, and China. Each can defend this tragic practice by saying simply, "if not from us, customers will go elsewhere"; and in the process, the United States not only loses high-paying jobs but, of greater importance, we impair or close down private companies that produce most of the research and development (R&D) to maintain our technological superiority. Figure 16.2 not only provides a picture of the scale and size of the arms market but dramatically indicates the interdependence of the players. In sum, we all maintain higher arm sales to support our defense habit.

Support for continuation of cold war theories of deterrence was significantly strengthened by the sudden emergency (because undetected by our intelligence gatherers) of two new members of the Nuclear Club and at least two prospective members, who did not bother to keep their commitment secret. The first two were India and Pakistan, both of whom tested their nuclear devices in May and June of 1998. Long-standing conflicts between these two countries over religion, ethnic rights, and territories made resorting to atomic warfare a distinct possibility, especially a few years later when war threatened to break out over control of Kashmir. Of equal and possibly greater import was the shocking advance of nuclear capacity in Iran and North Korea. Both countries have serious problems with their neighbors, and any nation-state considers acquisition of any weapon of deterrence a right and an obligation of national sovereignty. Moreover, both see this nuclear capacity as the only way to bargain for influence with its hostile neighbors as well as with the great American superpower. Another serious feature of this turn of events is the interdependence and potential friendship of North Korea and Pakistan, based on North Korea's extensive acquisition of essential nuclear technology by the illegal (but consciously tolerated) purchase from Pakistan's top nuclear scientists. There is hope these otherwise severely weak countries are simply seeking good chips for bargaining (i.e., diplomacy). But these chips are only credible if they are real and can be delivered as WMDs. And credibility does not require long-range missile delivery capacity. One small nuclear (or the appropriate biological or chemical) device delivered in a suitcase, a shipping carton, or a suicide bomber's waistband might be sufficient to bring a powerful nation-state to its knees. Here is deterrence put to its ultimate test.

Indeed, it is this new political reality that served as the impetus for the Bush Doctrine of preemptive use of force. *Preemption* means "striking first," based on credible evidence that the adversary is likely to attack you. *Deterrence* is based on "striking back," on the logic that the threat of second-strike capacity will stop an adversary from striking first. Although deterrence held up well during the cold war, the nature of the enemy and of the threat has changed in the war on terrorism, requiring, at least according to the Bush Doctrine, a different kind of response. Theoretically, preemption can strengthen deterrence as long as there is a definable adversary, usually a nation-state, that has a stake in its own survival, that of its rulers, their system of rule, and even their population. As Condoleezza Rice put it when she was national security adviser to President Bush, there are times when "you can't wait to be attacked to respond." And as long as the White House

FIGURE 16.2

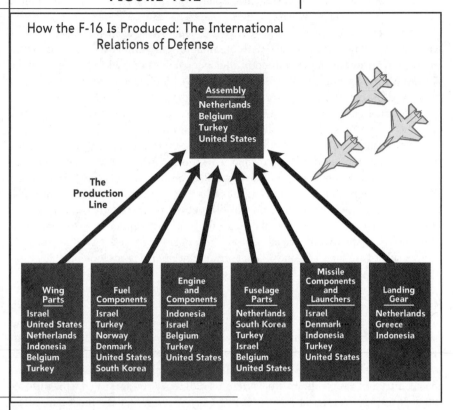

How the F-16 Is Produced: The International Relations of Defense

The Production Line

Assembly
Netherlands
Belgium
Turkey
United States

Wing Parts	Fuel Components	Engine and Components	Fuselage Parts	Missile Components and Launchers	Landing Gear
Israel	Israel	Indonesia	Netherlands	Israel	Netherlands
United States	Turkey	Israel	South Korea	Denmark	Greece
Netherlands	Norway	Belgium	Turkey	Indonesia	Indonesia
Indonesia	Denmark	Turkey	Israel	Turkey	
Belgium	United States	United States	Belgium	United States	
Turkey	South Korea		United States		

SOURCE: U.S. Congress, Office of Technology Assessment, *Arming Our Allies: Cooperation and Competition in Defense Technology*, OTA-ICS-449 (Washington, DC: Government Printing Office, May 1990), pp. 42–43, which is an extremely elaborate diagram of at least seventy-five separate parts of the F-16. The information was provided by the primary manufacturer, General Dynamics Corporation.

believed, or claimed to believe, that Iraq had WMDs and delivery capacity, the time factor was compelling. Anti-Americanism, a lust for expansion, and a potential conspiracy with Osama bin Laden seemed like a lot of evidence for motive. However, terrorism without a nation-state—which would be true of bin Laden *without* Iraq or some other sponsoring nation-state—is a completely unanticipated and untheorized problem for American foreign policy. Terrorism is a strategy used by an extremely weak adversary against an overwhelmingly strong adversary, using violence against the innocent and the nonbelligerent to change the power relationships enough to get the attention and the concessions of the stronger force. It was used successfully by Israelis to establish their nation-state and unsuccessfully by Basques against Spain and the Corsicans against France. Many examples lie in-between.

Critics can argue that President Bush turned to war against Iraq because it was a real nation-state adversary with a palpable stake in its own survival, while "world terrorism," even personified in the spectacular enemy bin Laden, is as invisible as an oncoming pandemic for which we don't yet have a vaccine or a cure. And, just perhaps, a victory in Iraq, coupled with spectacular success in constitutional government and economic reconstruction, could be the best vaccine and cure against the invisible world terrorism.

Critics can argue that the United States cannot win the war unless it also wins the peace: An Iraqi political system that is legitimate in the eyes of the Iraqi people, strong enough to ensure political stability and economic prosperity for its people, and impressive enough to "start a prairie fire" of democratization throughout the region. Meanwhile, does the Bush Doctrine of preemptive war make the world a safer place? An answer will take far longer than merely a second Bush term in office. Meanwhile, we all have the responsibility to ask two questions: "Is there a substitute for war?" and, "What would *preemptive peace* look like?"

ROLES NATIONS PLAY

Although each president has hundreds of small foreign fires to fight and can choose whichever instruments of policy best fit each particular situation, the primary foreign-policy problem any president faces is choosing an overall role for the country in foreign affairs. Roles help us define a situation to control the element of surprise in international relations. Surprise is in fact the most dangerous aspect of international relations, especially in a world made smaller and more fragile by advances in and the proliferation of military technology.

Napoleonic role
A strategy pursued by a powerful nation to prevent aggressive actions against itself by improving the internal state of affairs of a particular country, even if this means encouraging revolution in that country. This strategy is based on the assumption that countries with comparable political systems will never go to war against each other.

Choosing a Role

The problem of choosing a role can be understood by identifying a limited number of roles played by nation-states in the past. Four such roles are drawn from history—the Napoleonic, the Holy Alliance, the balance-of-power, and the economic expansionist roles. Although the definitions given here are exaggerations of the real world, they do capture in broad outline the basic choices available.

The Napoleonic Role The *Napoleonic role* takes its name from the role played by postrevolutionary France under Napoleon Bonaparte. The French at that time felt not only that their new democratic system of government was the best on earth but also that France would not be safe until democracy was adopted universally. If this meant intervention into the internal affairs of France's neighbors, and if that meant warlike reactions, then so be it. President Woodrow Wilson expressed a similar viewpoint when he supported the U.S.

declaration of war in 1917 with his argument that "the world must be made safe for democracy." Obviously such a position can be adopted by any powerful nation as a rationalization for intervening at its convenience in the internal affairs of another country. But it can also be sincerely espoused, and in the United States it has from time to time enjoyed broad popular consensus. The United States played the Napoleonic role in ousting Philippine dictator Ferdinand Marcos (February 1986), Panamanian leader Manuel Noriega (December 1989), the Sandinista government of Nicaragua (February 1990), and the military rulers of Haiti (September 1994).

The Holy Alliance Role   The concept of the *Holy Alliance role* emerged out of the defeat of Napoleon and the agreement by the leaders of Great Britain, Russia, Austria, and Prussia to preserve the social order against *all* revolution, including democratic revolution, at whatever cost. (Post-Napoleonic France also joined it.) The Holy Alliance made use of every kind of political instrument available—including political suppression, espionage, sabotage, and outright military intervention—to keep existing governments in power. The Holy Alliance role is comparable to the Napoleonic role in that each operates on the assumption that intervention into the internal affairs of other countries is justified for the maintenance of peace. But Napoleonic intervention is motivated by fear of dictatorship, and it can accept and even encourage revolution. In contrast, Holy Alliance intervention is antagonistic to any form of political change, even when this means supporting an existing dictatorship.[36] Because the Holy Alliance role became more important after the cold war ended, illustrations of this role will be given later in the chapter.

The Balance-of-Power Role   The *balance-of-power role* is basically an effort by the major powers to play off against each other so that no great power or combination of great and lesser powers can impose conditions on others. The most relevant example of the use of this strategy is found in the nineteenth century, especially the latter half. The feature of the balance-of-power role that is most distinct from the two previously identified roles is that this role accepts the political system of each country, asking no questions except whether the country will join an alliance and will use its resources to ensure that each country will respect the borders and interests of all the others.[37]

The Economic Expansionist Role   The *economic expansionist role,* also called the capitalist role, shares with the balance-of-power role the attitude that the

Holy Alliance role   A strategy pursued by a superpower to prevent any change in the existing distribution of power among nation-states, even if this requires intervention into the internal affairs of the country in order to keep an authoritarian ruler from being overturned.

balance-of-power role   The strategy whereby countries form alliances with one country or several other countries to counterbalance the behavior of other, usually more powerful, nation-states.

economic expansionist role   The strategy often pursued by capitalist countries to adopt foreign policies that will maximize the success of domestic corporations in their dealings with other countries.

[36]For a thorough and instructive exposition of the original Holy Alliance pattern, see Paul M. Kennedy, *The Rise and Fall of the Great Powers: Economic Change and Military Conflict from 1500 to 2000* (New York: Random House, 1987), pp. 159–60. And for a comparison of the Holy Alliance role with the balance-of-power role, to be discussed next, see Polanyi, *The Great Transformation*, pp. 5–11 and 259–62.

[37]Felix Gilbert et al., *The Norton History of Modern Europe* (New York: Norton, 1971), pp. 1222–24.

political system or ideology of a country is irrelevant; the only question is whether a country has anything to buy or sell and whether its entrepreneurs, corporations, and government agencies will honor their contracts. Governments and their armies are occasionally drawn into economic expansionist relationships to establish, reopen, or expand trade relationships and to keep the lines of commerce open. But the role is political, too. The point can be made that the economic expansionist role was the role consistently played by the United States in Latin and Central America until the cold war (perhaps in the 1960s and beyond) pushed us toward the Holy Alliance role with most of those countries.

Like arms control, however, economic expansion does not happen spontaneously. In the past, economic expansion owed a great deal to military backing because contracts do not enforce themselves, trade deficits are not paid automatically, and new regimes do not always honor the commitments made by regimes they replace. The only way to expand economic relationships is through diplomacy.

Choice of Roles for America Today

These four roles should not be literally translated into models that heads of state or foreign-policy establishments consciously adopt. They are names of patterns of policy conduct that have prevailed during certain important points in history. These labels were actually used by key participants during those points in history, or by historians, to capture and evaluate the patterns of conduct. In our time, they remain useful descriptions of patterns, and the labels enable us to compare an important pattern of conduct today with real moments in the past. The sequence of these roles in post–World War II history is not precisely the same as the sequence in real historical time. They do, however, capture the highlights of our own epoch, and the comparisons do give us a better basis for evaluation.

A new alliance with a new purpose was struck in response to the terrorist attacks of September 11, 2001. Such a great-power alliance for international order has not been seen since the mid-nineteenth century, when the threat came from middle-class revolutionaries rather than religious fanatics. But even though the enemies are different, the goals and strategies are about the same. All countries in the West are vulnerable because al-Qaeda and its associated groups are anti-West. All capitalist and developing countries are susceptible because terrorism is intensely anticapitalist. And all moderate Arab regimes are vulnerable because they are seen by al-Qaeda as traitors and collaborators with the West. All of these vulnerable nation-states need each other to deprive terrorists of the turf they need for safe havens, headquarters, training, and communication, not to mention financing. Even though the war against the Taliban regime was almost entirely conducted by the United States, there was no hope for a sustained campaign without the substantial cooperation and participation of many other countries. Pakistan was most vital, and its participation came at the risk of undermining its own regime. Russia and several other former Soviet republics on the northern border of Afghanistan were vital as well. The NATO nations were contractually an important part of the alliance, if only because the NATO charter was built on a solemn promise that an attack on any member was tantamount to an attack on all the members.

Yet once the Afghan phase of the war on world terrorism began quieting down, the United States confronted a new challenge: the resurgence of Iraq and the possibility that the weapons of mass destruction Saddam possessed would be used against the United States or one of its allies. President Bush's response, the Bush Doctrine, was a significant departure from the Holy Alliance model and movement toward a Napoleonic role. The tenets of the doctrine allowed the United States (1) to take preemptive action against a hostile state without waiting for an attack on us, (2) to eliminate permanently the threat of WMDs, (3) to eliminate the regime itself, and (4) to remain as an occupying power in Iraq long enough to rebuild the country into a modern democratic state.

Although the Holy Alliance role continues to be the principal role among the four historically and conventionally defined roles, it is not the only role America plays; and, more to the point, it is never played exactly the same in all cases. Even in Afghanistan, the alliance to defeat the Taliban and contain terrorism was accompanied by a genuine, albeit secondary, version of the Napoleonic role. The Bush administration seemed determined not to "hit and run" as the United States had done when it fought *with* the Taliban against the Russians in the early 1980s. American policy is strongly committed both to rebuilding the Afghan economy along capitalist lines and to moving the Afghan regime toward some form of democratization. But in the short run at least, the United States quickly settled for an imposed national leader presiding over a domestic coalition of mutually distrustful warlords, with only the barest hint of any kind of democratic process. That is the underlying Holy Alliance at work. Moreover, the Bush administration is just as committed as its predecessors to a balance-of-power role in the perennial Middle East hot spot, the Israel-Palestine conflict. The United States has succeeded in keeping the neighboring Arab countries from forming their own anti-Israel (therefore anti–United States) alliance. (Keeping antagonistic alliances from forming is an essential feature of the balance-of-power role—like spokes on a wheel, keeping each country dependent on the United States at the hub while keeping each country apart from one another.) But the use of terrorism by the Palestinians has prevented the United States from playing the balance-of-power role of "honest broker."

No foreign-policy role—however the roles are categorized—can ever relieve the United States of the need for sustained diplomacy. In fact, diplomacy has become all the more important because despotic regimes eventually fail and, in their failure, create instability. Since September 11, it has also become clear that failing regimes can become the breeding grounds for world terrorism. This is not to argue that war is never justifiable or that peace can always be achieved through discussions among professional diplomats. It is only to argue that there are limits to any role a country chooses to play and that failure will come faster and will be more serious if the choice of role is not made with patience, deliberation, rationality, and, most important, a knowledge of and sensitivity to history.

SUMMARY

This chapter began by raising some dilemmas about forming foreign policy in a democracy like the United States. Skepticism about foreign entanglements and the secrecy surrounding many foreign-policy issues form the basis of these dilemmas. Although we cannot provide solutions to the foreign-policy issues that the United States faces, we can provide a well-balanced analysis of the problems of foreign policy. This analysis is based on the four basic dimensions of foreign policy: the players, the values, the instruments, and the roles.

The first section of this chapter looked at the players in foreign policy: the makers and shapers. The influence of institutions and groups varies from case to case, with the important exception of the president. Since the president is central to all foreign policy, it is best to assess how other actors interact with the president. In most instances, this interaction involves only the narrowest element of the foreign-policy establishment. The American people have an opportunity to influence foreign policy, but primarily through Congress or interest groups.

The next section, on values, traced the history of American values that had a particular relevance to American perspectives on the outside world. We found that the American fear of a big government applied to foreign as well as domestic governmental powers. The founders and the active public of the founding period all recognized that foreign policy was a special element, that the national government had special powers in its dealings with foreigners, and that presidential supremacy was justified in the conduct of foreign affairs. The only way to avoid the big national government and presidential supremacy was to avoid the foreign entanglements that made foreign policy, diplomacy, secrecy, and presidential discretion necessary. Americans held on to their "anti-statist" tradition until World War II, long after world conditions cried out for American involvement. And even as it became involved in world affairs, the United States held on tightly to the legacies of 150 years of tradition: the intermingling of domestic and foreign-policy institutions as well as unilateralism, or the tendency to go it alone when confronted with foreign conflicts.

We then looked at the instruments—the tools—of American foreign policy. These are the basic statutes and the institutions by which foreign policy has been conducted since World War II: diplomacy, the United Nations, the international monetary structure, economic aid, collective security, and military deterrence. Although Republicans and Democrats look at the world somewhat differently, and although each president has tried to impose a distinctive flavor on foreign policy, they have all made use of these basic instruments, and that has given foreign policy a certain continuity. When Congress created these instruments after World War II, the old tradition was still so strong that it moved Congress to try to create instruments that would do their international work with a minimum of diplomacy—a minimum of human involvement. This is what we called power without diplomacy.

The next section concentrated on the role or roles the president and Congress have sought to play in the world. To help simplify the tremendous variety of tactics and strategies that foreign-policy leaders can select, we narrowed the field down to four categories of roles nations play, suggesting that there is a certain amount of consistency and stability in the conduct of a nation-state in its dealings with other nation-states. These were labeled according to actual roles that diplomatic historians have identified in the history of major Western nation-states: the Napoleonic, Holy Alliance, balance-of-power, and economic expansionist roles. We also attempted to identify and assess the role of the United States in the post–cold war era, essentially the Holy Alliance role. But whatever its advantages may be, the Holy Alliance approach will never allow the United States to conduct foreign policy without diplomacy. America is tied inextricably to the perils and ambiguities of international relationships, and diplomacy is still the monarch of all available instruments of foreign policy.

Rationality Principle	Collective-Action Principle	Institution Principle	Policy Principle	History Principle
Foreign-policy initiatives by the president are taken in light of the domestic political landscape.	American foreign-policy making demonstrates that there are costs as well as gains from pluralism in politics. Agency pluralism approximates "the paradox of collective choice."	Institutions such as the National Security Council and Department of Homeland Security attempt to keep the various foreign-policy players on the same page.	Because the number of participants in making foreign policy is limited, foreign policy reflects the goals of the president and his circle of advisers.	Most American presidents have come to office focused primarily on domestic policies and issues.
Foreign-policy interests are pursued through both domestic infighting and strategic interaction with foreign "players."	Coordinating the efforts of the many agencies of the foreign-policy establishment is especially difficult.	Mutual security organizations like NATO persist as institutional vehicles for solving collective-action dilemmas involving mutual defense, economic issues, environmental problems, and human rights.	The lending policies of the IMF reflect the interests of its leading shareholders, most notably the United States.	The legacies of the United States' traditional system of foreign policy include the intermingling of domestic and foreign policy and unilateralism.
The instruments of foreign policy—economic, diplomatic, institutional, military—are deployed to serve strategic purposes.	The one influence toward consistency in the making of foreign policy is the president as "coordinator in chief," or "legal dictator." But the coordination fails without clear presidential communication.	Persistence of insurgency in Iraq demonstrates the difficulty of creating institutions.	The only hope for consistency and coordination among the pluralism of agencies is clear policy articulation from the top.	Once the United States became a world power after World War II, its foreign policy focused on multilateralism, containment, and deterrence.
Diplomatic and military instruments may be thought of as complements to be used in tandem. The military option is the "club behind the door," to be used when diplomacy fails.		The automatic response element in mutual security enhances credibility as deterrent.		The United States was drawn from isolation to internationalism by the failure of Great Britain and the rise of an atomic-powered Soviet Union.
The United States typically incorporates the UN into its international engagements (such as the one in Iraq) as long as the collective body does not block or frustrate U.S. purposes.				

FOR FURTHER READING

Berman, Paul. *Terror and Liberalism*. New York: Norton, 2004.

Daalder, Ivo H., and James M. Lindsay. *America Unbound—The Bush Revolution in Foreign Policy*. Washington: The Brookings Institution Press, 2003.

Gilpin, Robert. *The Political Economy of International Relations*. Princeton, NJ: Princeton University Press, 1987.

Greenfeld, Liah. *Nationalism: Five Roads to Modernity*. Cambridge, MA.: Harvard University Press, 1993.

Haass, Richard N. *The Reluctant Sheriff—The United States after the Cold War*. New York: Council on Foreign Relations Book, 1997.

Jentleson, Bruce. *American Foreign Policy—The Dynamics of Choice in the Twenty-First Century*. 2nd ed. New York: Norton, 2004.

Keller, William W. *Arm in Arm: The Political Economy of the Global Arms Trade*. New York: Basic Books, 1995.

Kennan, George F. *Around the Cragged Hill: A Personal and Political Philosophy*. New York: Norton, 1993.

Kennedy, Paul M. *The Rise and Fall of the Great Powers: Economic Change and Military Conflict from 1500 to 2000*. New York: Random House, 1987.

LaFeber, Walter. *The American Age: United States Foreign Policy at Home and Abroad since 1750*. 2nd ed. 2 vols. New York: W. W. Norton, 1994.

Reid, T. R. *The United States of Europe—The New Superpower and the End of American Supremacy*. New York: Penguin Press, 2004.

Smist, Frank J. Jr. *Congress Oversees the United States Intelligence Community, 1947–1994*. 2nd ed. Knoxville: University of Tennessee Press, 1994.

U.S. Congress. *Report of the Congressional Committees Investigating the Iran-Contra Affair*. Washington, DC: Government Printing Office, 1987.

Politics in the News— Reading between the Lines

Country Coalitions and U.S. Foreign Policy

The New Global Dance Card

By DAVID E. SANGER

. . . When Mr. Bush started coalition-building after the Sept. 11 attacks, he expected the United States to be the linchpin. But now, . . . the president is increasingly facing what might be called coalitions of the unwilling, pursuing their own interests or pushing back American goals around the world, issue by issue, in search of oil or regional influence. . . .

China, Russia and India
The effort to adopt sanctions against Iran has failed so far, mostly because of this troika. China and India are growing at rates that have made them voracious consumers of oil—and thus friends of the Iranians. Russia has been a key supplier to Iran's multibillion-dollar effort to build a large nuclear reactor.

None wants to jeopardize its relations with Iran over a nuclear weapons program that Tehran denies exists.

Russia and China could veto any sanctions in the Security Council. So Mr. Bush is reluctant to force a vote he could lose, perhaps emboldening Iran to speed ahead with its nuclear development.

The Iranian case has created another unlikely partnership-of-the-moment: In-dia and Pakistan. Both spent decades building secret nuclear arsenals. Three years ago the United States was trying to stop the two countries from blowing each other up in their dispute over Kashmir. . . .

And no one understands where, if anywhere, this new detente may be going.

China and South Korea vs. the United States and Japan
The cold war kept alliances simple. In the Pacific, the United States stood with Japan and South Korea. North Korea's lifeline was China. Then came the 1990's boom, when the Chinese decided that capitalism wasn't all bad and opened diplomatic relations with South Korea.

Now, in the negotiations over dis-arming North Korea, the relationship between Seoul and Beijing goes far beyond sharing the secrets of making microprocessors.

To Washington and Tokyo, disarming North Korea—believed to have upward of six or eight weapons—is job one.

But the South Koreans and Chinese desperately want stability first.

"Our biggest fear is that if the central government collapses, we will have

New York Times, 18 September 2005, section 4, p. 3.

CH. 16 Foreign Policy and Democracy

millions of angry, hungry Koreans coming over our border," a senior Chinese official said.

The South Koreans have a similar fear. So they are happy to have talks, talks and more talks, so long as they head off any risk that the United States will take unilateral action. . . .

In two recent speeches, President Roh Moo Hyun talked openly about a new role. South Korea, he said, would play a "balancing role" in the region.

That set off alarm bells in Washington. "We told the South Koreans that the Chinese were not going to stick their necks out for them if things get ugly," a senior American official said.

But when South Korea was caught a year ago secretly toying with some nuclear experiments, American intelligence officials questioned whether the country is once again thinking about building the bomb. The South Koreans deny that this was their goal.

Russia and Europe

Standing in the East Room with Vladimir Putin on Friday afternoon, President Bush said he's stopped counting how many times he's met the Russian leader "because I've run out of fingers on my hands." And he never fails to praise Mr. Putin as a partner in the war on terror.

But the reality is that many in the White House are deeply suspicious of his motives and his centralization of power.

So at key moments Mr. Putin has sought succor in Europe, particularly on issues that the Europeans and the Bush administration see very differently: the war in Iraq, the Middle East and global warming, to name three.

And, like many Europeans, Mr. Putin has not exactly embraced Mr. Bush's call for spreading democracy around the world.

ESSENCE OF THE STORY

- After 9/11, the Bush administration was able to build broad coalitions that supported U.S. policies against terrorism. Now, several years later, a number of countries, including U.S. allies, are forming coalitions and partnerships that oppose U.S. initiatives.

- On the issue of Iran's nuclear program, two countries with a U.N. veto (China and Russia) object to attempts to penalize Iran. India and Pakistan, long-time adversaries, are also opposed to the effort.

- In another region of the world, China and South Korea are working together to resist U.S. efforts to pressure North Korea.

- Finally, Russia and the European Union are finding common ground on issues.

POLITICAL ANALYSIS

- The United States has been criticized for acting unilaterally, not taking into account the positions of our allies, and otherwise acting as the world's policeman. While the United States remains the world's only superpower, overwhelming military force may not help resolve the war on terror, which is as much a diplomatic and cultural battle as a military one.

- Because the United States has undermined international institutions such as the U.N. by acting outside U.N. authority in Afghanistan and Iraq, other nations may have seen it as rational to behave the same way, pursuing their own self-interested alliances.

- In addition, as we move further in time from 9/11, countries are looking to their shared economic interests, even if this means cooperating less with the United States on military matters.

Earlier this year he gave Mr. Bush a 40-minute lecture in Slovakia about the imperfections in American democracy.

"It was a brush-back pitch," a White House aide said. "And you can imagine, the boss didn't enjoy it."

Appendix

The Declaration of Independence

In Congress, July 4, 1776

When in the course of human events, it becomes necessary for one people to dissolve the political bands which have connected them with another, and to assume among the Powers of the earth, the separate and equal station to which the Laws of Nature and of Nature's God entitle them, a decent respect to the opinions of mankind requires that they should declare the causes which impel them to the separation.

We hold these truths to be self-evident, that all men are created equal, that they are endowed by their Creator with certain unalienable rights, that among these are Life, Liberty, and the pursuit of Happiness. That to secure these rights, Governments are instituted among Men, deriving their just powers from the consent of the governed. That whenever any Form of Government becomes destructive of these ends, it is the Right of the People to alter or to abolish it, and to institute new Government, laying its foundation on such principles and organizing its powers in such form, as to them shall seem most likely to effect their Safety and Happiness. Prudence, indeed, will dictate that Governments long established should not be changed for light and transient causes; and accordingly all experience hath shown, that mankind are more disposed to suffer, while evils are sufferable, than to right themselves by abolishing the forms to which they are accustomed. But when a long train of abuses and usurpations, pursuing invariably the same Object evinces a design to reduce them under absolute Despotism, it is their right, it is their duty, to throw off such Government, and to provide new Guards for their future security.—Such has been the patient sufferance of these Colonies; and such is now the necessity which constrains them to alter their former Systems of Government. The history of the present King of Great Britain is a history of repeated injuries and usurpations, all having in direct object the establishment of an absolute Tyranny over these States. To prove this, let Facts be submitted to a candid world.

He has refused his Assent to Laws, the most wholesome and necessary for the public good.

He has forbidden his Governors to pass Laws of immediate and pressing importance, unless suspended in their operation till his Assent should be obtained; and when so suspended, he has utterly neglected to attend to them.

He has refused to pass other Laws for the accommodation of large districts of people, unless those people would relinquish the right of Representation in the Legislature, a right inestimable to them and formidable to tyrants only.

He has called together legislative bodies at places unusual, uncomfortable, and distant from the depository of their public Records, for the sole purpose of fatiguing them into compliance with his measures.

He has dissolved Representative Houses repeatedly, for opposing with manly firmness his invasions on the rights of the people.

He has refused for a long time, after such dissolutions, to cause others to be elected; whereby the Legislative powers, incapable of Annihilation, have returned to the People at large for their exercise; the State remaining in the mean time exposed to all dangers of invasion from without, and convulsions within.

He has endeavored to prevent the population of these States; for that purpose obstructing the Laws of Naturalization of Foreigners; refusing to pass others to encourage their migrations hither, and raising the conditions of new Appropriations of Lands.

He has obstructed the Administration of Justice, by refusing his Assent to Laws for establishing Judiciary powers.

He has made Judges dependent on his Will alone, for the tenure of their offices, and the amount and payment of their salaries.

He has erected a multitude of New Offices, and sent hither swarms of Officers to harass our People, and eat out their substance.

He has kept among us, in times of peace, Standing Armies without the Consent of our legislature.

He has affected to render the Military independent of and superior to the Civil Power.

He has combined with others to subject us to a jurisdiction foreign to our constitution, and unacknowledged by our laws; giving his Assent to their Acts of pretended Legislation:

For quartering large bodies of armed troops among us:

For protecting them, by a mock Trial, from Punishment for any Murders which they should commit on the Inhabitants of these States:

For cutting off our Trade with all parts of the world:

For imposing taxes on us without our Consent:

For depriving us in many cases, of the benefits of Trial by jury:

For transporting us beyond Seas to be tried for pretended offences:

For abolishing the free System of English Laws in a neighboring Province, establishing therein an Arbitrary government, and enlarging its Boundaries so as to render it at once an example and fit instrument for introducing the same absolute rule into these Colonies:

For taking away our Charters, abolishing our most valuable Laws, and altering fundamentally the Forms of our Governments:

For suspending our own Legislatures, and declaring themselves invested with Power to legislate for us in all cases whatsoever.

He has abdicated Government here, by declaring us out of his Protection and waging War against us.

He has plundered our seas, ravaged our Coasts, burnt our towns, and destroyed the lives of our people.

He is at this time transporting large armies of foreign mercenaries to compleat the works of death, desolation, and tyranny, already begun with circumstances of Cruelty & perfidy scarcely paralleled in the most barbarous ages, and totally unworthy the Head of a civilized nation.

He has constrained our fellow Citizens taken Captive on the high Seas to bear Arms against their Country, to become the executioners of their friends and Brethren, or to fall themselves by their Hands.

He has excited domestic insurrections amongst us, and has endeavored to bring on the inhabitants of our frontiers, the merciless Indian Savages, whose known rule of warfare, is an undistinguished destruction of all ages, sexes, and conditions.

In every stage of these Oppressions We have Petitioned for Redress in the most humble terms: Our repeated Petitions have been answered only by repeated injury. A Prince, whose character is thus marked by every act which may define a Tyrant, is unfit to be the ruler of a free people.

Nor have We been wanting in attention to our British brethren. We have warned them from time to time of attempts by their legislature to extend an unwarrantable jurisdiction over us. We have reminded them of the circumstances of our emigration and settlement here. We have appealed to their native justice and magnanimity, and we have conjured them by the ties of our common kindred to disavow these usurpations, which, would inevitably interrupt our connections and correspondence. They too must have been deaf to the voice of justice and of consanguinity. We must, therefore, acquiesce in the necessity, which denounces our Separation, and hold them, as we hold the rest of mankind, Enemies in War, in Peace Friends.

WE, THEREFORE, the Representatives of the UNITED STATES OF AMERICA, in General Congress, Assembled, appealing to the Supreme Judge of the world for the rectitude of our intentions, do, in the Name, and by Authority of the good People of these Colonies, solemnly publish and declare, That these United Colonies are, and of Right ought to be FREE AND INDEPENDENT STATES; that they are Absolved from all Allegiance to the British Crown, and that all political connection between them and the State of Great Britain, is and ought to be totally dissolved; and that as Free and Independent States, they have full Power to levy War, conclude Peace, contract Alliances, establish Commerce, and to do all other Acts and Things which Independent States may of right do. And for the support of this Declaration, with a firm reliance on the Protection of Divine Providence, we mutually pledge to each other our Lives, our Fortunes, and our sacred Honor.

The foregoing Declaration was, by order of Congress, engrossed, and signed by the following members:

John Hancock

NEW HAMPSHIRE
Josiah Bartlett
William Whipple
Matthew Thornton

MASSACHUSETTS BAY
Samuel Adams
John Adams
Robert Treat Paine
Elbridge Gerry

RHODE ISLAND
Stephen Hopkins
William Ellery

CONNECTICUT
Roger Sherman
Samuel Huntington
William Williams
Oliver Wolcott

NEW YORK
William Floyd
Philip Livingston
Francis Lewis
Lewis Morris

NEW JERSEY
Richard Stockton
John Witherspoon
Francis Hopkinson
John Hart
Abraham Clark

PENNSYLVANIA
Robert Morris
Benjamin Rush
Benjamin Franklin
John Morton
George Clymer
James Smith
George Taylor
James Wilson
George Ross

DELAWARE
Caesar Rodney
George Read
Thomas M'Kean

MARYLAND
Samuel Chase
William Paca
Thomas Stone
Charles Carroll,
* of Carrollton*

VIRGINIA
George Wythe
Richard Henry Lee
Thomas Jefferson
Benjamin Harrison
Thomas Nelson, Jr.
Francis Lightfoot Lee
Carter Braxton

NORTH CAROLINA
William Hooper
Joseph Hewes
John Penn

SOUTH CAROLINA
Edward Rutledge
Thomas Heyward, Jr.
Thomas Lynch, Jr.
Arthur Middleton

GEORGIA
Button Gwinnett
Lyman Hall
George Walton

Resolved, That copies of the Declaration be sent to the several assemblies, conventions, and committees, or councils of safety, and to the several commanding officers of the continental troops; that it be proclaimed in each of the United States, at the head of the army.

The Articles of Confederation

Agreed to by Congress November 15, 1777; ratified and in force
March 1, 1781

To all whom these Presents shall come, we the undersigned Delegates of the
States affixed to our Names send greeting. Whereas the Delegates of the United
States of America in Congress assembled did on the fifteenth day of November
in the Year of our Lord One Thousand Seven Hundred and Seventy seven, and
in the Second Year of the Independence of America agree to certain articles of
Confederation and perpetual Union between the States of Newhampshire,
Massachusetts-bay, Rhodeisland and Providence Plantations, Connecticut, New-
York, New-Jersey, Pennsylvania, Delaware, Maryland, Virginia, North-Carolina,
South-Carolina and Georgia in the Words following, viz. "Articles of
Confederation and perpetual Union between the states of Newhampshire,
Massachusetts-bay, Rhodeisland and Providence Plantations, Connecticut, New-
York, New-Jersey, Pennsylvania, Delaware, Maryland, Virginia, North-Carolina,
South-Carolina and Georgia.

Art. I. The Stile of this confederacy shall be "The United States of America."

Art. II. Each state retains its sovereignty, freedom and independence, and
every Power, Jurisdiction and right, which is not by this confederation expressly
delegated to the United States, in Congress assembled.

Art. III. The said states hereby severally enter into a firm league of friendship
with each other, for their common defence, the security of their Liberties, and
their mutual and general welfare, binding themselves to assist each other, against
all force offered to, or attacks made upon them, or any of them, on account of religion, sovereignty, trade, or any other pretence whatever.

Art. IV. The better to secure and perpetuate mutual friendship and inter-
course among the people of the different states in this union, the free inhabitants
of each of these states, paupers, vagabonds and fugitives from Justice excepted,
shall be entitled to all privileges and immunities of free citizens in the several
states; and the people of each state shall have free ingress and regress to and from
any other state, and shall enjoy therein all the privileges of trade and commerce,
subject to the same duties, impositions and restrictions as the inhabitants thereof
respectively, provided that such restriction shall not extend so far as to prevent
the removal of property imported into any state, to any other state of which the
Owner is an inhabitant; provided also that no imposition, duties or restriction
shall be laid by any state, on the property of the united states, or either of them.

If any Person guilty of, or charged with treason, felony, or other high misde-
meanor in any state, shall flee from Justice, and be found in any of the united

states, he shall upon demand of the Governor or executive power, of the state from which he fled, be delivered up and removed to the state having jurisdiction of his offence.

Full faith and credit shall be given in each of these states to the records, acts and judicial proceedings of the courts and magistrates of every other state.

Art. V. For the more convenient management of the general interests of the united states, delegates shall be annually appointed in such manner as the legislature of each state shall direct, to meet in Congress on the first Monday in November, in every year, with a power reserved to each state, to recall its delegates, or any of them, at any time within the year, and to send others in their stead, for the remainder of the Year.

No state shall be represented in Congress by less than two, nor by more than seven Members; and no person shall be capable of being a delegate for more than three years in any term of six years; nor shall any person, being a delegate, be capable of holding any office under the united states, for which he, or another for his benefit receives any salary, fees or emolument of any kind.

Each state shall maintain its own delegates in a meeting of the states, and while they act as members of the committee of the states.

In determining questions in the united states, in Congress assembled, each state shall have one vote.

Freedom of speech and debate in Congress shall not be impeached or questioned in any Court, or place out of Congress, and the members of congress shall be protected in their persons from arrests and imprisonments, during the time of their going to and from, and attendance on congress, except for treason, felony, or breach of the peace.

Art. VI. No state without the Consent of the united states in congress assembled, shall send any embassy to, or receive any embassy from, or enter into any conference, agreement, or alliance or treaty with any King, prince or state; nor shall any person holding any office or profit or trust under the united states, or any of them, accept of any present, emolument, office or title of any kind whatever from any king, prince or foreign state; nor shall the united states in congress assembled, or any of them, grant any title of nobility.

No two or more states shall enter into any treaty, confederation or alliance whatever between them, without the consent of the united states in congress assembled, specifying accurately the purposes for which the same is to be entered into, and how long it shall continue.

No state shall lay any imposts or duties, which may interfere with any stipulations in treaties, entered into by the united states in congress assembled, with any king, prince or state, in pursuance of any treaties already proposed by congress, to the courts of France and Spain.

No vessels of war shall be kept up in time of peace by any state, except such number only, as shall be deemed necessary by the united states in congress assembled, for the defence of such state, or its trade; nor shall any body of forces be kept up by any state, in time of peace, except such number only, as in the judgment of the united states, in congress assembled, shall be deemed requisite to garrison the forts necessary for the defence of such state; but every state shall always keep up a well regulated and disciplined militia, sufficiently armed and accoutred, and shall provide and constantly have ready for use, in public stores, a due number of field pieces and tents, and a proper quantity of arms, ammunition and camp equipage.

No state shall engage in any war without the consent of the united states in congress assembled, unless such state be actually invaded by enemies, or shall have received certain advice of a resolution being formed by some nation of Indians to invade such state, and the danger is so imminent as not to admit of a delay, till the united states in congress asssembled can be consulted; nor shall any state grant commissions to any ships or vessels of war, nor letters of marque or reprisal, except it be after a declaration of war by the united states in congress assembled, and then only against the kingdom or state and the subjects thereof, against which war has been so declared, and under such regulations as shall be established by the united states in congress assembled, unless such state be infested by pirates; in which case vessels of war may be fitted out for that occasion, and kept so long as the danger shall continue, or until the united states in congress assembled shall determine otherwise.

Art. VII. When land-forces are raised by any state for the common defence, all officers of or under the rank of colonel, shall be appointed by the legislature of each state respectively by whom such forces shall be raised, or in such manner as such state shall direct, and all vacancies shall be filled up by the state which first made the appointment.

Art. VIII. All charges of war, and all other expences that shall be incurred for the common defence or general welfare, and allowed by the united states in congress assembled, shall be defrayed out of a common treasury, which shall be supplied by the several states, in proportion to the value of all land within each state, granted to or surveyed for any Person, as such land and the buildings and improvements thereon shall be estimated according to such mode as the united states in congress assembled, shall from time to time direct and appoint. The taxes for paying that proportion shall be laid and levied by the authority and direction of the legislatures of the several states within the time agreed upon by the united states in congress assembled.

Art. IX. The united states in congress assembled, shall have the sole and exclusive right and power of determining on peace and war, except in the cases mentioned in the sixth article—of sending and receiving ambassadors—entering into treaties and alliances, provided that no treaty of commerce shall be made whereby the legislative power of the respective states shall be restrained from imposing such imposts and duties on foreigners, as their own people are subjected to, or from prohibiting the exportation of any species of goods or commodities whatsoever—of establishing rules for deciding in all cases, what captures on land or water shall be legal, and in what manner prizes taken by land or naval forces in the service of the united states shall be divided or appropriated—of granting letters of marque and reprisal in times of peace—appointing courts for the trial of piracies and felonies committed on the high seas and establishing courts for receiving and determining finally appeals in all cases of captures, provided that no member of congress shall be appointed a judge of any of the said courts.

The united states in congress assembled shall also be the last resort on appeal in all disputes and differences now subsisting or that hereafter may arise between two or more states concerning boundary, jurisdiction or any other cause whatever; which authority shall always be exercised in the manner following. Whenever the legislative or executive authority or lawful agent of any state in controversy with another shall present a petition to congress stating the matter in question and praying for a hearing, notice thereof shall be given by order of congress to the legislative or executive authority of the other state in controversy, and a day assigned for the appearance of the parties by their lawful agents, who shall then be directed to appoint by joint consent, commissioners or judges to constitute a court for hearing and determining the matter in question: but if they cannot agree, congress shall name three persons out of each of the united states, and from the list of such persons each party shall alternately strike out one, the petitioners beginning, until the number shall be reduced to thirteen; and from that number not less than seven, nor more than nine names as congress shall direct, shall in the presence of congress be drawn out by lot, and the persons whose names shall be so drawn or any five of them, shall be commissioners or judges, to hear and finally determine the controversy, so always as a major part of the judges who shall hear the cause shall agree in the determination: and if either party shall neglect to attend at the day appointed, without shewing reasons, which congress shall judge sufficient, or being present shall refuse to strike, the congress shall proceed to nominate three persons out of each state, and the secretary of congress shall strike in behalf of such party absent or refusing; and the judgment and sentence of the court to be appointed, in the manner before prescribed, shall be final and conclusive; and if any of the parties shall refuse to submit to the authority of such court, or to appear to defend their claim or cause, the court shall nevertheless proceed to pronounce sentence, or judgment, which shall in like manner be final and decisive, the judgment or sentence and other proceedings being in either case transmitted to congress, and lodged among the acts of congress for the security of the parties concerned: provided that every commissioner, before he sits in judgment, shall take an oath to be administered by one of the judges of the supreme or superior court of the state, where the cause shall be tried, "well and truly to hear and determine the matter in question, according to the best of his judgment, without favour, affection or hope of reward:" provided also that no state shall be deprived of territory for the benefit of the united states.

All controversies concerning the private right of soil claimed under different grants of two or more states, whose jurisdictions as they may respect such lands, and the states which passed such grants are adjusted, the said grants or either of them being at the same time claimed to have originated antecedent to such settlement of jurisdiction, shall on the petition of either party to the congress of the united states, be finally determined as near as may be in the same manner as is before prescribed for deciding disputes respecting territorial jurisdiction between different states.

The united states in congress assembled shall also have the sole and exclusive right and power of regulating the alloy and value of coin struck by their own authority, or by that of the respective states—fixing the standard of weights and measures throughout the united states—regulating the trade and managing all affairs with the Indians, not members of any of the states, provided that the legislative right of any state within its own limits be not infringed or violated—establishing and regulating post-offices from one state to another, throughout all the united states, and exacting such postage on the papers passing thro' the same as may be requisite to defray the expences of the said office—appointing all officers of the land forces, in the service of the united states, except regimental officers—appointing all the officers of the united states—making rules for the government and regulation of the said land and naval forces, and directing their operations.

The united states in congress assembled shall have the authority to appoint a committee, to sit in the recess of congress, to be denominated "A Committee of the States," and to consist of one delegate from each state; and to appoint such other committees and civil officers as may be necessary for managing the general affairs of the united states under their direction—to appoint one of their number to preside, provided that no person be allowed to serve in the office of president more than one year in any term of three years; to ascertain the necessary sums of Money to be raised for the service of the united states, and to appropriate and apply the same for defraying the public expences—to borrow money, or emit bills on the credit of the united states, transmitting every half year to the respective states an account of the sums of money so borrowed or emitted,—to build and equip a navy—to agree upon the number of land forces, and to make requisitions from each state for its quota, in proportion to the number of white inhabitants in such state; which requisition shall be binding, and thereupon the legislature of each state shall appoint the regimental officers, raise the men and cloath, arm and equip them in a soldier like manner, at the expence of the united states, and the officers and men so cloathed, armed and equipped shall march to the place appointed, and within the time agreed on by the united states in congress assembled: But if the united states in congress assembled shall, on consideration of circumstances judge proper that any state should not raise men, or should raise a smaller number than its quota, and that any other state should raise a greater number of men than the quota thereof, such extra number shall be raised, officered, cloathed, armed and equipped in the same manner as the quota of such state, unless the legislature of such state shall judge that such extra number cannot be safely spared out of the same, in which case they shall raise, officer, cloath, arm and equip as many of such extra number as they judge can be safely spared. And the officers and men so cloathed, armed and equipped, shall march to the place appointed, and within the time agreed on by the united states in congress assembled.

The united states in congress assembled shall never engage in a war, nor grant letters of marque and reprisal in time of peace, nor enter into any treaties or alliances, nor coin money, nor regulate the value thereof, nor ascertain the sums and expences necessary for the defence and welfare of the united states, or any of them, nor emit bills, nor borrow money on the credit of the united states, nor appropriate money, nor agree upon the number of vessels of war, to be built or purchased, or the number of land or sea forces to be raised, nor appoint a commander in chief of the army or navy, unless nine states assent to the same: nor shall a question on any other point, except for adjourning from day to day be determined, unless by the votes of a majority of the united states in congress assembled.

The congress of the united states shall have power to adjourn to any time within the year, and to any place within the united states, so that no period of adjournment be for a longer duration than the space of six Months, and shall publish the Journal of their proceedings monthly, except such parts thereof relating to treaties, alliances or military operations as in their judgment require secresy; and the yeas and nays of the delegates of each state on any question shall be entered on the Journal, when it is desired by any delegate; and the delegates of a state, or any of them, at his or their request shall be furnished with a transcript of the said Journal, except such parts as are above excepted to lay before the legislatures of the several states.

Art. X. The committee of the states, or any nine of them, shall be authorised to execute, in the recess of congress, such of the powers of congress as the united states in congress assembled, by the consent of nine states, shall from time to time think expedient to vest them with; provided that no power be delegated to the said committee, for the exercise of which, by the articles of confederation, the voice of nine states in the congress of the united states assembled is requisite.

Art. XI. Canada acceding to this confederation, and joining in the measures of the united states, shall be admitted into, and entitled to all the advantages of this union: but no other colony shall be admitted into the same, unless such admission be agreed to by nine states.

Art. XII. All bills of credit emitted, monies borrowed and debts contracted by, or under the authority of congress, before the assembling of the united states, in pursuance of the present confederation, shall be deemed and considered as a charge against the united states, for payment and satisfaction whereof the said united states and the public faith are hereby solemnly pledged.

Art. XIII. Every state shall abide by the determinations of the united states in congress assembled, on all questions which by this confederation are submitted to them. And the Articles of this confederation shall be inviolably observed by every state, and the union shall be perpetual; nor shall any alteration at any time hereafter be made in any of them; unless such alteration be agreed to in a congress of the united states, and be afterwards confirmed by the legislatures of every state.

AND WHEREAS it hath pleased the Great Governor of the World to incline the hearts of the legislatures we respectively represent in congress, to approve of, and to authorize us to ratify the said articles of confederation and perpetual union. KNOW YE that we the undersigned delegates, by virtue of the power and authority to us given for that purpose, do by these presents, in the name and in behalf of our respective constituents, fully and entirely ratify and confirm each and every of the said articles of confederation and perpetual union, and all and singular the matters and things therein contained: And we do further solemnly plight and engage the faith of our respective constituents, that they shall abide by the determination of the united states in congress assembled, on all questions, which by the said confederation are submitted to them. And that the articles thereof shall be inviolably observed by the states we respectively represent, and that the union shall be perpetual. In Witness whereof we have hereunto set our hands in Congress. Done at Philadelphia in the state of Pennsylvania the ninth Day of July in the Year of our Lord one Thousand seven Hundred and Seventy-eight and in the third year of the independence of America.

The Constitution of the United States of America

Annotated with references to *The Federalist Papers*

*Federalist Paper
Number (Author)*

[PREAMBLE]

We the People of the United States, in Order to form a more perfect Union, estab-   84 (Hamilton)
lish Justice, insure domestic Tranquility, provide for the common defence, promote
the general Welfare, and secure the Blessings of Liberty to ourselves and our
Posterity, do ordain and establish this Constitution for the United States of America.

ARTICLE I

Section 1
[LEGISLATIVE POWERS]

All legislative Powers herein granted shall be vested in a Congress of the   10, 45 (Madison)
United States, which shall consist of a Senate and House of Representatives.

Section 2
[HOUSE OF REPRESENTATIVES, HOW CONSTITUTED, POWER OF IMPEACHMENT]

The House of Representatives shall be composed of Members chosen every   39, 45, 52–53, 57
second Year by the People of the several States, and the Electors in each State   (Madison)
shall have the Qualifications requisite for Electors of the most numerous Branch
of the State Legislature.

No Person shall be a Representative who shall not have attained to the Age of   52 (Madison)
twenty-five Years, and been seven Years a Citizen of the United States, and who
shall not, when elected, be an inhabitant of that State in which he shall be chosen.   60 (Hamilton)

Representatives and *direct Taxes*[1] shall be apportioned among the several   54, 58 (Madison)
States which may be included within this Union, according to their respective
Numbers, *which shall be determined by adding to the whole Number of free Persons,
including those bound to Service for a Term of Years, and excluding Indians not
taxed, three-fifths of all other Persons.*[2] The actual Enumeration shall be made
within three Years after the first Meeting of the Congress of the United States,
and within every subsequent Term of ten Years, in such Manner as they shall by
Law direct. The Number of Representatives shall not exceed one for every thirty

[1]Modified by Sixteenth Amendment.
[2]Modified by Fourteenth Amendment.

55–56 (Madison)

Thousand, but each State shall have at Least one Representative; *and until such enumeration shall be made, the State of New Hampshire shall be entitled to chuse three, Massachusetts eight, Rhode-Island and Providence Plantations one, Connecticut five, New-York six, New Jersey four, Pennsylvania eight, Delaware one, Maryland six, Virginia ten, North Carolina five, South Carolina five, and Georgia three.*[3]

When vacancies happen in the Representation from any State, the Executive Authority thereof shall issue Writs of Election to fill such Vacancies.

79 (Hamilton)

The House of Representatives shall chuse their Speaker and other Officers; and shall have the sole Power of Impeachment.

Section 3
[THE SENATE, HOW CONSTITUTED, IMPEACHMENT TRIALS]

39, 45 (Madison)
60 (Hamilton)

The Senate of the United States shall be composed of two Senators from each State, *chosen by the Legislature thereof,*[4] for six Years; and each Senator shall have one Vote.

62–63 (Madison)
59, 68 (Hamilton)

Immediately after they shall be assembled in Consequence of the first Election, they shall be divided as equally as may be into three Classes. The Seats of the Senators of the first Class shall be vacated at the Expiration of the second Year, of the second Class at the Expiration of the fourth Year, and of the third Class at the Expiration of the sixth Year, so that one third may be chosen every second Year: *and if vacancies happen by Resignation, or otherwise, during the Recess of the Legislature of any State, the Executive thereof may make temporary Appointments until the next Meeting of the Legislature, which shall then fill such Vacancies.*[5]

62 (Madison)
64 (Jay)

No person shall be a Senator who shall not have attained to the Age of thirty Years, and been nine Years a Citizen of the United States, and who shall not, when elected, be an Inhabitant of that State for which he shall be chosen.

The Vice-President of the United States shall be President of the Senate, but shall have no Vote, unless they be equally divided.

The Senate shall chuse their other Officers, and also a President pro tempore, in the Absence of the Vice-President, or when he shall exercise the Office of President of the United States.

39 (Madison)
65–67, 79
(Hamilton)

The Senate shall have the sole Power to try all Impeachments. When sitting for that Purpose, they shall be on Oath or Affirmation. When the President of the United States is tried, the Chief Justice shall preside: And no Person shall be convicted without the Concurrence of two-thirds of the Members present.

84 (Hamilton)

Judgment in Cases of Impeachment shall not extend further than to removal from Office, and disqualification to hold and enjoy any Office of honor, Trust or Profit under the United States: but the Party convicted shall nevertheless be liable and subject to Indictment, Trial, Judgment and Punishment, according to Law.

[3]Temporary provision.
[4]Modified by Seventeenth Amendment.
[5]Modified by Seventeenth Amendment.

Section 4
[ELECTION OF SENATORS AND REPRESENTATIVES]

The Times, Places and Manner of holding Elections for Senators and Representatives, shall be prescribed in each State by the Legislature thereof; but the Congress may at any time by Law make or alter such Regulations, except as to the Places of chusing Senators.

The Congress shall assemble at least once in every Year, and such Meeting shall be on the first Monday in December, unless they shall by Law appoint a different Day.[6]

59–61 (Hamilton)

Section 5
[QUORUM, JOURNALS, MEETINGS, ADJOURNMENTS]

Each House shall be the Judge of the Elections, Returns and Qualifications of its own Members, and a Majority of each shall constitute a Quorum to do Business; but a smaller Number may adjourn from day to day, and may be authorized to compel the Attendance of absent Members, in such Manner, and under the Penalties as each House may provide.

Each House may determine the Rules of its Proceedings, punish its Members for disorderly Behavior, and, with the Concurrence of two-thirds, expel a Member.

Each House shall keep a Journal of its Proceedings, and from time to time publish the same, excepting such Parts as may in their Judgment require Secrecy; and the Yeas and Nays of the Members of either House on any questions shall, at the Desire of one-fifth of the present, be entered on the Journal.

Neither House, during the Session of Congress, shall, without the Consent of the other, adjourn for more than three days, nor to any other Place than that in which the two Houses shall be sitting.

Section 6
[COMPENSATION, PRIVILEGES, DISABILITIES]

The Senators and Representatives shall receive a Compensation for their Services, to be ascertained by Law, and paid out of the Treasury of the United States. They shall in all Cases, except Treason, Felony and Breach of the Peace, be privileged from Arrest during their Attendance at the Session of their respective Houses, and in going to and returning from the same; and for any Speech or Debate in either House, they shall not be questioned in any other Place.

No Senator or Representative shall, during the time for which he was elected, be appointed to any civil Office under the authority of the United States, which shall have been created, or the Emoluments whereof shall have been encreased during such time; and no Person holding any Office under the United States, shall be a Member of either House during his Continuance in Office.

55 (Madison)
76 (Hamilton)

[6]Modified by Twentieth Amendment.

Section 7
[PROCEDURE IN PASSING BILLS AND RESOLUTIONS]

66 (Hamilton)

All Bills for raising Revenue shall originate in the House of Representatives; but the Senate may propose or concur with Amendments as on other Bills.

69, 73 (Hamilton)

Every Bill which shall have passed the House of Representatives and the Senate, shall, before it become a Law, be presented to the President of the United States; if he approve he shall sign it, but if not he shall return it, with his Objections to that House in which it shall have originated, who shall enter the Objections at large on their Journal, and proceed to reconsider it. If after such Reconsideration two-thirds of that House shall agree to pass the Bill, it shall be sent, together with the Objections, to the other House, by which it shall likewise be reconsidered, and if approved by two-thirds of that House it shall become a Law. But in all such Cases the Votes of both Houses shall be determined by Yeas and Nays, and the Names of the Persons voting for and against the Bill shall be entered on the Journal of each House respectively. If any Bill shall not be returned by the President within ten Days (Sundays excepted) after it shall have been presented to him, the Same shall be a Law, in like Manner as if he had signed it, unless the Congress by their Adjournment prevent its Return, in which Case it shall not be a Law.

69, 73 (Hamilton)

Every Order, Resolution, or Vote to which the Concurrence of the Senate and House of Representatives may be necessary (except on a question of Adjournment) shall be presented to the President of the United States; and before the Same shall take Effect, shall be approved by him, or being disapproved by him, shall be repassed by two-thirds of the Senate and House of Representatives, according to the Rules and Limitations prescribed in the Case of a Bill.

Section 8
[POWERS OF CONGRESS]

The Congress shall have Power

To lay and collect Taxes, Duties, Imposts and Excises, to pay the Debts and provide for the common Defence and general Welfare of the United States; but all Duties, Imposts and excises shall be uniform throughout the United States;

30–36 (Hamilton)
41 (Madison)

To borrow Money on the Credit of the United States;

56 (Madison)

To regulate Commerce with foreign Nations, and among the several States, and with the Indian Tribes;

42, 45, 56
(Madison)

To establish an uniform Rule of Naturalization, and uniform Laws on the subject of Bankruptcies throughout the United States;

32 (Hamilton)

To coin Money, regulate the Value thereof, and of foreign Coin, and fix the Standard of Weights and Measures;

42 (Madison)

To provide for the Punishment of counterfeiting the Securities and current Coin of the United States;

42 (Madison)

To establish Post Offices and post Roads;

42 (Madison)

To promote the Progress of Science and useful Arts, by securing for limited Times to Authors and Inventors the exclusive Right to their respective Writings and Discoveries;

42, 43 (Madison)

To constitute Tribunals inferior to the supreme Court;

81 (Hamilton)

To define and Punish Piracies and Felonies committed on the high Seas, and Offences against the Law of Nations;

42 (Madison)

To declare War, grant Letters of Marque and Reprisal, and make Rules concerning Captures on Land and Water;

41 (Madison)

To raise and support Armies, but no Appropriation of Money to that Use shall be for a longer Term than two Years;

23, 24, 26 (Hamilton)

To provide and maintain a Navy;

41 (Madison)

To make Rules for the Government and Regulation of the land and naval forces;

To provide for calling for the Militia to execute the Laws of the Union, suppress Insurrections and repel Invasions;

29 (Hamilton)

To provide for organizing, arming, and disciplining, the Militia, and for governing such Part of them as may be employed in the Service of the United States, reserving to the States respectively, the Appointment of the Officers, and the Authority of training the Militia according to the discipline prescribed by Congress;

29 (Hamilton)
56 (Madison)

To exercise exclusive Legislation in all Cases whatsoever, over such District (not exceeding ten Miles square) as may, by Cession of particular States, and the Acceptance of Congress, become the Seat of the Government of the United States, and to exercise like Authority over all Places purchased by the Consent of the Legislature of the State in which the Same shall be, for the Erection of Forts, Magazines, Arsenals, dock-Yards, and other needful Buildings;—And

32 (Hamilton)
43 (Madison)

To make all Laws which shall be necessary and proper for carrying into Execution the foregoing Powers, and all other Powers vested by this Constitution in the Government of the United States, or in any Department or Officer thereof.

29, 33 (Hamilton)
44 (Madison)

Section 9
[SOME RESTRICTIONS ON FEDERAL POWER]

The Migration or Importation of such Persons as any of the States now existing shall think proper to admit, shall not be prohibited by the Congress prior to the Year one thousand eight hundred and eight, but a Tax or Duty may be imposed on such Importation, not exceeding ten dollars for each Person.[7]

42 (Madison)

The privilege of the Writ of *Habeas Corpus* shall not be suspended, unless when in Cases of Rebellion or Invasion the public Safety may require it.

83, 84 (Hamilton)

No Bill of Attainder or ex post facto Law shall be passed.

84 (Hamilton)

No Capitation, or other direct, Tax shall be laid, unless in Proportion to the Census or Enumeration herein before directed to be taken.[8]

No Tax or Duty shall be laid on Articles exported from any State.

No Preference shall be given by any Regulation of Commerce or Revenue to the Ports of one State over those of another; nor shall vessels bound to, or from, one State, be obliged to enter, clear, or pay Duties in another.

32 (Hamilton)

No Money shall be drawn from the Treasury, but in Consequence of Appropriations made by Law; and a regular Statement and Account of the Receipts and Expenditures of all public Money shall be published from time to time.

[7]Temporary provision.
[8]Modified by Sixteenth Amendment.

No Title of Nobility shall be granted by the United States: And no Person holding any Office of Profit or Trust under them, shall, without the Consent of the Congress, accept of any present, Emolument, Office or Title, of any kind whatever, from any King, Prince, or foreign State.

Section 10
[RESTRICTIONS UPON POWERS OF STATES]

No State shall enter into any Treaty, Alliance, or Confederation; grant Letters of Marque and Reprisal; coin Money; emit Bills of Credit; make any Thing but gold and silver Coin a Tender in Payment of Debts; pass any Bill of Attainder, ex post facto Law, or Law impairing the Obligation of Contracts, or grant any Title of Nobility.

No State shall, without the Consent of the Congress, lay any Imposts or Duties on Imports or Exports, except what may be absolutely necessary for executing its inspection Laws: and the net Produce of all Duties and Imposts, laid by any State on Imports or Exports, shall be for the Use of the Treasury of the United States; and all such Laws shall be subject to the Revision and Control of the Congress.

No State shall, without the Consent of Congress, lay any Duty of Tonnage, keep Troops, or Ships of War in time of Peace, enter into any Agreement or Compact with another State, or with a foreign Power, or engage in War, unless actually invaded, or in such imminent Danger as will not admit of Delay.

ARTICLE II

Section 1
[EXECUTIVE POWER, ELECTION, QUALIFICATIONS OF THE PRESIDENT]

The executive Power shall be vested in a President of the United States of America. *He shall hold his Office during the Term of four years and, together with the Vice-President, chosen for the same Term, be elected, as follows:*[9]

Each State shall appoint, in such Manner as the Legislature thereof may direct, a Number of Electors, equal to the whole Number of Senators and Representatives to which the State may be entitled in the Congress: but no Senator or Representative, or Person holding an Office of Trust or Profit under the United States, shall be appointed an Elector.

The electors shall meet in their respective States, and vote by ballot for two Persons, of whom one at least shall not be an Inhabitant of the same State with themselves. And they shall make a List of all the Persons voted for, and of the Number of Votes for each; which List they shall sign and certify, and transmit sealed to the Seat of the Government of the United States, directed to the President of the Senate. The President of the Senate shall, in the Presence of the Senate and House of Representatives, open all the Certificates, and the Votes shall then be counted. The Person having the greatest Number of Votes shall be the

---

[9]Number of terms limited to two by Twenty-second Amendment.

39 (Madison)
84 (Hamilton)

33 (Hamilton)
44 (Madison)

32 (Hamilton)
44 (Madison)

39 (Madison)
70, 71, 84
(Hamilton)

68, 69, 71, 77
(Hamilton)
39, 45 (Madison)

66 (Hamilton)

President, if such Number be a Majority of the whole Number of Electors appointed; and if there be more than one who have such Majority and have an equal Number of Votes, then the House of Representatives shall immediately chuse by Ballot one of them for President; and if no person have a Majority, then from the five highest on the List the said House shall in like Manner chuse the President. But in chusing the President, the Votes shall be taken by States, the Representation from each State having one Vote; A quorum for this Purpose shall consist of a Member or Members from two-thirds of the States, and a Majority of all the States shall be necessary to a Choice. In every Case, after the Choice of the President, the person having the greatest Number of Votes of the Electors shall be the Vice-President. But if there should remain two or more who have equal vote, the Senate shall chuse from them by Ballot the Vice-President.[10]

The Congress may determine the Time of chusing the Electors, and the Day on which they shall give their Votes; which Day shall be the same throughout the United States.

No Person except a natural born Citizen, or a Citizen of the United States, at the time of the Adoption of this Constitution, shall be eligible to the Office of President; neither shall any Person be eligible to that Office who shall not have attained to the Age of thirty-five Years, and been fourteen Years a Resident within the United States. 64 (Jay)

In Case of the Removal of the President from Office, or his Death, Resignation, or Inability to discharge the Powers and Duties of the said Office, the same shall devolve on the Vice-President, and the Congress may by Law provide for the Case of Removal, Death, Resignation, or Inability, both of the President and Vice-President, declaring what Officer shall then act as President, and such Officer shall act accordingly, until the Disability be removed, or a President shall be elected.

The President shall, at stated Times, receive for his Services, a Compensation, which shall neither be encreased nor diminished during the Period for which he shall have been elected, and he shall not receive within that Period any other Emolument from the United States, or any of them. 73, 79 (Hamilton)

Before he enter on the Execution of his Office, he shall take the following Oath or Affirmation:—"I do solemnly swear (or affirm) that I will faithfully execute the Office of President of the United States, and will to the best of my Ability, preserve, protect and defend the Constitution of the United States."

Section 2
[POWERS OF THE PRESIDENT]

The President shall be Commander in Chief of the Army and Navy of the United States, and of the Militia of the several States, when called into the actual Service of the United States; he may require the Opinion, in writing, of the principal Officer in each of the executive Departments, upon any Subject relating to the Duties of their respective Offices, and he shall have Power to grant Reprieves and Pardons for Offences against the United States, except in Cases of Impeachment. 69, 74 (Hamilton)

[10]Modified by Twelfth and Twentieth Amendments.

42 (Madison)
64 (Jay)
66, 69, 76, 77
(Hamilton)

He shall have Power, by and with the Advice and Consent of the Senate, to make Treaties, provided two-thirds of the Senators present concur; and he shall nominate, and by and with the Advice and Consent of the Senate, shall appoint Ambassadors, other public Ministers and Consuls, Judges of the Supreme Court, and all other Officers of the United States, whose Appointments are not herein otherwise provided for, and which shall be established by Law: but the Congress may by Law vest the Appointment of such inferior Officers, as they think proper, in the President alone, in the Courts of Law, or in the Heads of Departments.

67, 76
(Hamilton)

The President shall have Power to fill up all Vacancies that may happen during the Recess of the Senate, by granting Commissions which shall expire at the End of their next Session.

Section 3
[POWERS AND DUTIES OF THE PRESIDENT]

69, 77, 78
(Hamilton)
42 (Madison)

He shall from time to time give to the Congress Information of the State of the Union, and recommend to their Consideration such Measures as he shall judge necessary and expedient; he may, on extraordinary Occasions, convene both Houses, or either of them, and in Case of Disagreement between them, with Respect to the Time of Adjournment, he may adjourn them to such Time as he shall think proper; he shall receive Ambassadors and other public Ministers; he shall take Care that the Laws be faithfully executed, and shall Commission all the Officers of the United States.

Section 4
[IMPEACHMENT]

39 (Madison)
69 (Hamilton)

The President, Vice-President and all civil Officers of the United States shall be removed from Office on Impeachment for, and Conviction of, Treason, Bribery, or other high Crimes and Misdemeanors.

ARTICLE III

Section 1
[JUDICIAL POWER, TENURE OF OFFICE]

65, 78, 79, 81, 82
(Hamilton)

The judicial Power of the United States, shall be vested in one supreme Court, and in such inferior Courts as the Congress may from time to time ordain and establish. The Judges, both of the supreme and inferior Courts, shall hold their Offices during good Behavior, and shall, at stated Times, receive for their Services, a Compensation, which shall not be diminished during their Continuance in Office.

Section 2
[JURISDICTION]

80 (Hamilton)

The judicial Power shall extend to all Cases, in Law and Equity, arising under this Constitution, the Laws of the United States, and Treaties made, or which shall be made, under their Authority;—to all Cases affecting Ambassadors, other public Ministers and Consuls;—to all Cases of admiralty and maritime Jurisdiction;—to Controversies to which the United States shall be a party;—to Controversies between two or more States;—*between a State and Citizens of another State;*—between Citizens of different States,—between Citizens of the same State claiming Lands under Grants of different States, *and between a State,* or the Citizens thereof, *and foreign States, Citizens or Subjects.*[11]

In all Cases affecting Ambassadors, other public Ministers and Consuls, and those in which a State shall be Party, the supreme Court shall have original Jurisdiction. In all the other Cases before mentioned, the supreme Court shall have appellate Jurisdiction, both as to Law and Fact, with such Exceptions, and under such Regulations as Congress shall make.

81 (Hamilton)

The Trial of all Crimes, except in Cases of Impeachment, shall be by Jury; and such Trial shall be held in the State where the said Crimes shall have been committed; but when not committed within any State, the Trial shall be at such Place or Places as the Congress may by Law have directed.

83, 84 (Hamilton)

Section 3
[TREASON, PROOF, AND PUNISHMENT]

Treason against the United States, shall consist only in levying War against them, or in adhering to their Enemies, giving them Aid and Comfort. No Person shall be convicted of Treason unless on the Testimony of two Witnesses to the same overt Act, or on Confession in open Court.

43 (Madison)
84 (Hamilton)

The Congress shall have Power to declare the Punishment of Treason, but no Attainder of Treason shall work Corruption of Blood, or Forfeiture except during the Life of the Person attained.

43 (Madison)
84 (Hamilton)

ARTICLE IV

Section 1
[FAITH AND CREDIT AMONG STATES]

Full Faith and Credit shall be given in each State to the public Acts, Records, and judicial Proceedings of every other State. And the Congress may by general Laws prescribe the Manner in which such Acts, Records and Proceedings shall be proved, and the Effect thereof.

42 (Madison)

Section 2
[PRIVILEGES AND IMMUNITIES, FUGITIVES]

The Citizens of each State shall be entitled to all Privileges and Immunities of Citizens in the several States.

80 (Hamilton)

A person charged in any State with Treason, Felony or other Crime, who shall flee from Justice, and be found in another State, shall on Demand of the executive

[11]Modified by Eleventh Amendment.

Authority of the State from which he fled, be delivered up to be removed to the State having Jurisdiction of the Crime.

No person held to Service or Labour in one State, under the Laws thereof, escaping into another, shall, in Consequence of any Law or Regulation therein, be discharged from such Service or Labour, but shall be delivered up on Claim of the Party to whom such Service or Labour may be due.[12]

Section 3
[ADMISSION OF NEW STATES]

43 (Madison)

New States may be admitted by the Congress into this Union; but no new State shall be formed or erected within the Jurisdiction of any other State; nor any State be formed by the Junction of two or more States, or Parts of States, without the Consent of the Legislatures of the States concerned as well as of the Congress.

43 (Madison)

The Congress shall have Power to dispose of and make all needful Rules and Regulations respecting the Territory or other Property belonging to the United States; and nothing in this Constitution shall be so construed as to Prejudice any Claims of the United States, or of any particular State.

Section 4
[GUARANTEE OF REPUBLICAN GOVERNMENT]

39, 43
(Madison)

The United States shall guarantee to every State in this Union a Republican Form of Government, and shall protect each of them against Invasion; and on Application of the Legislature, or of the Executive (when the Legislature cannot be convened) against domestic Violence.

ARTICLE V

[AMENDMENT OF THE CONSTITUTION]

39, 43 (Madison)
85 (Hamilton)

The Congress, whenever two-thirds of both Houses shall deem it necessary, shall propose Amendments to this Constitution, or, on the Application of the Legislatures of two-thirds of the several States, shall call a Convention for proposing Amendments, which, in either Case, shall be valid to all Intents and Purposes, as Part of this Constitution, when ratified by the Legislatures of three-fourths of the several States, or by Conventions in three-fourths thereof, as the one or the other Mode of Ratification may be proposed by the Congress; *Provided that no Amendment which may be made prior to the Year One thousand eight hundred and eight shall in any Manner affect the first and fourth Clauses in the Ninth Section of the first Article;*[13] and that no State, without its Consent, shall be deprived of its equal Suffrage in the Senate.

[12]Repealed by Thirteenth Amendment.
[13]Temporary provision.

ARTICLE VI

[DEBTS, SUPREMACY, OATH]

All Debts contracted and Engagements entered into, before the Adoption of this Constitution, shall be as valid against the United States under this Constitution, as under the Confederation.

43 (Madison)

This Constitution, and the Laws of the United States which shall be made in Pursuance thereof; and all Treaties made, or which shall be made, under the Authority of the United States, shall be the supreme Law of the Land; and the Judges in every State shall be bound thereby, any Thing in the Constitution or Laws of any State to the Contrary notwithstanding.

27, 33 (Hamilton)
39, 44 (Madison)

The Senators and Representatives before mentioned, and the Members of the several State Legislatures, and all executive and judicial Officers, both of the United States and of the several States, shall be bound by Oath or Affirmation, to support this Constitution; but no religious Test shall be required as a Qualification to any Office or public Trust under the United States.

27 (Hamilton)
44 (Madison)

ARTICLE VII

[RATIFICATION AND ESTABLISHMENT]

The Ratification of the Conventions of nine States, shall be sufficient for the Establishment of this Constitution between the States so ratifying the Same.[14]

39, 40, 43
(Madison)

Done in Convention by the Unanimous Consent of the States present the Seventeenth Day of September in the Year of our Lord one thousand seven hundred and Eighty seven and of the Independence of the United States of America the Twelfth. *In Witness* whereof We have hereunto subscribed our Names,

G:⁰ WASHINGTON—
*Presidt, and Deputy
from Virginia*

New Hampshire	JOHN LANGDON	New York	ALEXANDER HAMILTON
	NICHOLAS GILMAN	New Jersey	WIL: LIVINGSTON
Massachusetts	NATHANIEL GORHAM		DAVID BREARLEY
	RUFUS KING		WM PATERSON
			JONA: DAYTON
Connecticut	WM SAML JOHNSON		
	ROGER SHERMAN		

[14]The Constitution was submitted on September 17, 1787, by the Constitutional Convention, was ratified by the conventions of several states at various dates up to May 29, 1790, and became effective on March 4, 1789.

Pennsylvania	B FRANKLIN
	THOMAS MIFFLIN
	ROBT MORRIS
	GEO. CLYMER
	THOS. FITZSIMONS
	JARED INGERSOLL
	JAMES WILSON
	GOUV MORRIS
Delaware	GEO READ
	GUNNING BEDFOR JUN
	JOHN DICKINSON
	RICHARD BASSETT
	JACO: BROOM
Maryland	JAMES MCHENRY
	DAN OF ST THOS. JENIFER
	DANL CARROLL

Virginia	JOHN BLAIR—
	JAMES MADISON JR.
North Carolina	WM BLOUNT
	RICHD DOBBS SPAIGHT
	HU WILLIAMSON
South Carolina	J. RUTLEDGE
	CHARLES COTESWORTH PINCKNEY
	CHARLES PINCKNEY
	PIERCE BUTLER
Georgia	WILLIAM FEW
	ABR BALDWIN

Amendments to the Constitution

*Proposed by Congress and Ratified by the Legislatures of the
Several States, Pursuant to Article V of the Original Constitution.*

Amendments I–X, known as the Bill of Rights, were proposed by Congress on September 25, 1789, and ratified on December 15, 1791. *The Federalist Papers* comments, mainly in opposition to a Bill of Rights, can be found in number 84 (Hamilton).

AMENDMENT I

[FREEDOM OF RELIGION, OF SPEECH, AND OF THE PRESS]

Congress shall make no law respecting an establishment of religion, or prohibiting the free exercise thereof; or abridging the freedom of speech, or of the press; or the right of the people peaceably to assemble, and to petition the Government for a redress of grievances.

AMENDMENT II

[RIGHT TO KEEP AND BEAR ARMS]

A well regulated Militia, being necessary to the security of a free State, the right of the people to keep and bear Arms, shall not be infringed.

AMENDMENT III

[QUARTERING OF SOLDIERS]

No Soldier shall, in time of peace be quartered in any house, without the consent of the Owner, nor in time of war, but in a manner to be prescribed by law.

AMENDMENT IV

[SECURITY FROM UNWARRANTABLE SEARCH AND SEIZURE]

The right of the people to be secure in their persons, houses, papers, and effects, against unreasonable searches and seizures, shall not be violated, and no Warrants shall issue, but upon probable cause, supported by Oath or affirmation, and particularly describing the place to be searched, and the persons or things to be seized.

AMENDMENT V

[RIGHTS OF ACCUSED PERSONS IN CRIMINAL PROCEEDINGS]

No person shall be held to answer for a capital, or otherwise infamous crime, unless on a presentment or indictment of a Grand Jury, except in cases arising in the land or naval forces, or in the Militia, when in actual service in time of War or in public danger; nor shall any person be subject for the same offence to be twice put in jeopardy of life or limb; nor shall be compelled in any Criminal Case to be a witness against himself, nor be deprived of life, liberty, or property, without due process of law; nor shall private property be taken for public use, without just compensation.

AMENDMENT VI
[RIGHT TO SPEEDY TRIAL, WITNESSES, ETC.]

In all criminal prosecutions, the accused shall enjoy the right to a speedy and public trial, by an impartial jury of the State and district wherein the crime shall have been committed, which district shall have been previously ascertained by law, and to be informed of the nature and cause of the accusation; to be confronted with the witnesses against him; to have compulsory process for obtaining Witnesses in his favor, and to have the Assistance of Counsel for his defence.

AMENDMENT VII
[TRIAL BY JURY IN CIVIL CASES]

In suits at common law, where the value in controversy shall exceed twenty dollars, the right of trial by jury shall be preserved, and no fact tried by a jury shall be otherwise re-examined in any Court of the United States, than according to the rules of the common law.

AMENDMENT VIII
[BAILS, FINES, PUNISHMENTS]

Excessive bail shall not be required, nor excessive fines imposed, nor cruel and unusual punishments inflicted.

AMENDMENT IX
[RESERVATION OF RIGHTS OF PEOPLE]

The enumeration in the Constitution, of certain rights, shall not be construed to deny or disparage others retained by the people.

AMENDMENT X
[POWERS RESERVED TO STATES OR PEOPLE]

The powers not delegated to the United States by the Constitution, nor prohibited by it to the States, are reserved to the States respectively, or to the people.

AMENDMENT XI
[Proposed by Congress on March 4, 1794; declared ratified on January 8, 1798.]

[RESTRICTION OF JUDICIAL POWER]

The Judicial power of the United States shall not be construed to extend to any suit in law or equity, commenced or prosecuted against one of the United States by Citizens of another State, or by Citizens or Subjects of any Foreign State.

AMENDMENT XII

[Proposed by Congress on December 9, 1803; declared ratified on September 25, 1804.]

[ELECTION OF PRESIDENT AND VICE-PRESIDENT]

The Electors shall meet in their respective states, and vote by ballot for President and Vice-President, one of whom, at least, shall not be an inhabitant of the same state with themselves; they shall name in their ballots the person voted for as President, and in distinct ballots the person voted for as Vice-President, and they shall make distinct lists of all persons voted for as President, and of all persons voted for as Vice-President, and of the number of votes for each, which lists they shall sign and certify, and transmit sealed to the seat of the government of the United States, directed to the President of the Senate;—The President of the Senate shall, in presence of the Senate and House of Representatives, open all the certificates and the votes shall then be counted;—The person having the greatest number of votes for President, shall be the President, if such number be a majority of the whole number of Electors appointed; and if no person have such majority, then from the persons having the highest numbers not exceeding three on the list of those voted for as President, the House of Representatives shall choose immediately, by ballot, the President. But in choosing the President, the votes shall be taken by states, the representation from each state having one vote; a quorum for this purpose shall consist of a member or members from two-thirds of the states, and a majority of all states shall be necessary to a choice. And if the House of Representatives shall not choose a President whenever the right of choice shall devolve upon them, before the fourth day of March next following, then the Vice-President, shall act as President, as in the case of the death or other constitutional disability of the President. The person having the greatest number of votes as Vice-President, shall be the Vice-President, if such a number be a majority of the whole number of Electors appointed, and if no person have a majority, then from the two highest numbers on the list, the Senate shall choose the Vice-President; a quorum for the purpose shall consist of two-thirds of the whole number of Senators, and a majority of the whole number shall be necessary to a choice. But no person constitutionally ineligible to the office of President shall be eligible to that of Vice-President of the United States.

AMENDMENT XIII

[Proposed by Congress on January 31, 1865; declared ratified on December 18, 1865.]

Section 1
[ABOLITION OF SLAVERY]

Neither slavery nor involuntary servitude, except as a punishment for crime whereof the party shall have been duly convicted, shall exist within the United States, or any place subject to their jurisdiction.

Section 2
[POWER TO ENFORCE THIS ARTICLE]

Congress shall have power to enforce this article by appropriate legislation.

AMENDMENT XIV
[Proposed by Congress on June 13, 1866; declared ratified on July 28, 1868.]

Section 1
[CITIZENSHIP RIGHTS NOT TO BE ABRIDGED BY STATES]

All persons born or naturalized in the United States, and subject to the jurisdiction thereof, are citizens of the United States and of the State wherein they reside. No state shall make or enforce any law which shall abridge the privileges or immunities of citizens of the United States; nor shall any State deprive any person of life, liberty, or property, without due process of law; nor deny to any person within its jurisdiction the equal protection of the laws.

Section 2
[APPORTIONMENT OF REPRESENTATIVES IN CONGRESS]

Representatives shall be apportioned among the several States according to their respective numbers, counting the whole number of persons in each State, excluding Indians not taxed. But when the right to vote at any election for the choice of electors for President and Vice-President of the United States, Representatives in Congress, the Executive and Judicial officers of a State, or the members of the Legislature thereof, is denied to any of the male inhabitants of such State, being twenty-one years of age, and citizens of the United States, or in any way abridged, except for participation in rebellion, or other crime, the basis of representation therein shall be reduced in the proportion which the number of such male citizens shall bear to the whole number of male citizens twenty-one years of age in such State.

Section 3
[PERSONS DISQUALIFIED FROM HOLDING OFFICE]

No person shall be a Senator or Representative in Congress, or elector of President and Vice-President, or hold any office, civil or military, under the United States, or under any State, who, having previously taken an oath, as a member of Congress, or as an officer of the United States, or as a member of any State legislature, or as an executive or judicial officer of any State, to support the Constitution of the United States, shall have engaged in insurrection or rebellion against the same, or given aid or comfort to the enemies thereof. But Congress may by a vote of two-thirds of each House, remove such disability.

Section 4
[WHAT PUBLIC DEBTS ARE VALID]

The validity of the public debt of the United States, authorized by law, including debts incurred for payment of pensions and bounties for services in suppressing insurrection or rebellion, shall not be questioned. But neither the United States nor any State shall assume or pay any debt or obligation incurred in aid of insurrection or rebellion against the United States, or any claim for the loss or emancipation of any slave; but all such debts, obligations and claims shall be held illegal and void.

Section 5
[POWER TO ENFORCE THIS ARTICLE]

The Congress shall have power to enforce, by appropriate legislation, the provisions of this article.

AMENDMENT XV

[Proposed by Congress on February 26, 1869; declared ratified on March 30, 1870.]

Section 1
[NEGRO SUFFRAGE]

The right of citizens of the United States to vote shall not be denied or abridged by the United States or by any State on account of race, color, or previous condition of servitude.

Section 2
[POWER TO ENFORCE THIS ARTICLE]

The Congress shall have power to enforce this article by appropriate legislation.

AMENDMENT XVI

[Proposed by Congress on July 12, 1909; declared ratified on February 25, 1913.]
[AUTHORIZING INCOME TAXES]

The Congress shall have power to lay and collect taxes on incomes, from whatever source derived, without apportionment among the several States, and without regard to any census or enumeration.

AMENDMENT XVII

[Proposed by Congress on May 13, 1912; declared ratified on May 31, 1913.]
[POPULAR ELECTION OF SENATORS]

The Senate of the United States shall be composed of two Senators from each State, elected by the people thereof, for six years; and each Senator shall have one vote. The electors in each State shall have the qualifications requisite for electors of the most numerous branch of the State Legislature.

When vacancies happen in the representation of any State in the Senate, the executive authority of such State shall issue writs of election to fill such vacancies:

Provided, That the Legislature of any State may empower the executive thereof to make temporary appointment until the people fill the vacancies by election as the Legislature may direct.

This amendment shall not be so construed as to affect the election or term of any Senator chosen before it becomes valid as part of the Constitution.

AMENDMENT XVIII

[Proposed by Congress December 18, 1917; declared ratified on January 29, 1919.]

Section 1
[NATIONAL LIQUOR PROHIBITION]

After one year from the ratification of this article the manufacture, sale, or transportation of intoxicating liquors within, the importation thereof into, or the exportation thereof from the United States and all territory subject to the jurisdiction thereof for beverage purposes is hereby prohibited.

Section 2
[POWER TO ENFORCE THIS ARTICLE]

The Congress and the several states shall have concurrent power to enforce this article by appropriate legislation.

Section 3
[RATIFICATION WITHIN SEVEN YEARS]

This article shall be inoperative unless it shall have been ratified as an amendment to the Constitution by the legislatures of the several states, as provided in the Constitution, within seven years from the date of the submission hereof to the states by the Congress.[15]

AMENDMENT XIX

[Proposed by Congress on June 4, 1919; declared ratified on August 26, 1920.]
[WOMAN SUFFRAGE]

The right of the citizens of the United States to vote shall not be denied or abridged by the United States or by any state on account of sex.

Congress shall have power to enforce this article by appropriate legislation.

AMENDMENT XX

[Proposed by Congress on March 2, 1932; declared ratified on February 6, 1933.]

Section 1
[TERMS OF OFFICE]

The terms of the President and Vice-President shall end at noon on the 20th day of January, and the terms of the Senators and Representatives at noon on the

[15]Repealed by Twenty-first Amendment.

3rd day of January, of the years in which such terms would have ended if this article had not been ratified; and the terms of their successors shall then begin.

Section 2
[TIME OF CONVENING CONGRESS]

The Congress shall assemble at least once in every year, and such meeting shall begin at noon on the 3rd day of January, unless they shall by law appoint a different day.

Section 3
[DEATH OF PRESIDENT-ELECT]

If, at the time fixed for the beginning of the term of the President, the President-elect shall have died, the Vice-President-elect shall become President. If a President shall not have been chosen before the time fixed for the beginning of his term, or if the President-elect shall have failed to qualify, then the Vice-President-elect shall act as President until a President shall have qualified; and the Congress may by law provide for the case wherein neither a President-elect nor a Vice-President-elect shall have qualified, declaring who shall then act as President, or the manner in which one who is to act shall be selected, and such person shall act accordingly until a President or Vice President shall have qualified.

Section 4
[ELECTION OF THE PRESIDENT]

The Congress may by law provide for the case of the death of any of the persons from whom the House of Representatives may choose a President whenever the right of choice shall have devolved upon them, and for the case of the death of any of the persons from whom the Senate may choose a Vice-President whenever the right of choice shall have devolved upon them.

Section 5
[AMENDMENT TAKES EFFECT]

Sections 1 and 2 shall take effect on the 15th day of October following ratification of this article.

Section 6
[RATIFICATION WITHIN SEVEN YEARS]

This article shall be inoperative unless it shall have been ratified as an amendment to the Constitution by the legislatures of three-fourths of the several States within seven years from the date of its submission.

AMENDMENT XXI
[Proposed by Congress on February 20, 1933; declared ratified on December 5, 1933.]

Section 1
[NATIONAL LIQUOR PROHIBITION REPEALED]

The eighteenth article of amendment to the Constitution of the United States is hereby repealed.

Section 2
[TRANSPORTATION OF LIQUOR INTO "DRY" STATES]

The transportation or importation into any State, Territory, or Possession of the United States for delivery or use therein of intoxicating liquors, in violation of the laws thereof, is hereby prohibited.

Section 3
[RATIFICATION WITHIN SEVEN YEARS]

This article shall be inoperative unless it shall have been ratified as an amendment to the Constitution by conventions in the several States, as provided in the Constitution, within seven years from the date of the submission hereof to the States by the Congress.

AMENDMENT XXII

[Proposed by Congress on March 21, 1947; declared ratified on February 26, 1951.]

Section 1
[TENURE OF PRESIDENT LIMITED]

No person shall be elected to the office of President more than twice, and no person who has held the office of President or acted as President for more than two years of a term to which some other person was elected President shall be elected to the Office of the President more than once. But this Article shall not apply to any person holding the office of President when this Article was proposed by the Congress, and shall not prevent any person who may be holding the office of President, or acting as President, during the term within which this Article becomes operative from holding the office of President or acting as President during the remainder of such term.

Section 2
[RATIFICATION WITHIN SEVEN YEARS]

This Article shall be inoperative unless it shall have been ratified as an amendment to the Constitution by the legislatures of three-fourths of the several states within seven years from the date of its submission to the States by the Congress.

AMENDMENT XXIII

[Proposed by Congress on June 21, 1960; declared ratified on March 29, 1961.]

Section 1
[ELECTORAL COLLEGE VOTES FOR THE DISTRICT OF COLUMBIA]

The District constituting the seat of Government of the United States shall appoint in such manner as the Congress may direct:

A number of electors of President and Vice-President equal to the whole number of Senators and Representatives in Congress to which the District would be entitled if it were a State, but in no event more than the least populous State;

they shall be in addition to those appointed by the States, but they shall be considered, for the purposes of the election of President and Vice-President, to be electors appointed by a State; and they shall meet in the District and perform such duties as provided by the twelfth article of amendment.

Section 2
[POWER TO ENFORCE THIS ARTICLE]

The Congress shall have power to enforce this article by appropriate legislation.

AMENDMENT XXIV

[Proposed by Congress on August 27, 1963; declared ratified on January 23, 1964.]

Section 1
[ANTI-POLL TAX]

The right of citizens of the United States to vote in any primary or other election for President or Vice-President, for electors for President or Vice-President, or for Senator or Representative of Congress, shall not be denied or abridged by the United States or any State by reasons of failure to pay any poll tax or other tax.

Section 2
[POWER TO ENFORCE THIS ARTICLE]

The Congress shall have power to enforce this article by appropriate legislation.

AMENDMENT XXV

[Proposed by Congress on July 7, 1965; declared ratified on February 10, 1967.]

Section 1
[VICE-PRESIDENT TO BECOME PRESIDENT]

In case of the removal of the President from office or his death or resignation, the Vice-President shall become President.

Section 2
[CHOICE OF A NEW VICE-PRESIDENT]

Whenever there is a vacancy in the office of the Vice-President, the President shall nominate a Vice-President who shall take the office upon confirmation by a majority vote of both houses of Congress.

Section 3
[PRESIDENT MAY DECLARE OWN DISABILITY]

Whenever the President transmits to the President pro tempore of the Senate and the Speaker of the House of Representatives his written declaration that he is unable to discharge the powers and duties of his office, and until he transmits to them a written declaration to the contrary, such powers and duties shall be discharged by the Vice-President as Acting President.

Section 4
[ALTERNATE PROCEDURES TO DECLARE AND TO END PRESIDENTIAL DISABILITY]

Whenever the Vice-President and a majority of either the principal officers of the executive departments, or of such other body as Congress may by law provide, transmit to the President pro tempore of the Senate and the Speaker of the House of Representatives their written declaration that the President is unable to discharge the powers and duties of his office, the Vice-President shall immediately assume the powers and duties of the office as Acting President.

Thereafter, when the President transmits to the President pro tempore of the Senate and the Speaker of the House of Representatives his written declaration that no inability exists, he shall resume the powers and duties of his office unless the Vice-President and a majority of either the principal officers of the executive departments, or of such other body as Congress may by law provide, transmit within four days to the President pro tempore of the Senate and the Speaker of the House of Representatives their written declaration that the President is unable to discharge the powers and duties of his office. Thereupon Congress shall decide the issue, assembling within 48 hours for that purpose if not in session. If the Congress, within 21 days after receipt of the latter written declaration, or, if Congress is not in session, within 21 days after Congress is required to assemble, determines by two-thirds vote of both houses that the President is unable to discharge the powers and duties of his office, the Vice-President shall continue to discharge the same as Acting President; otherwise, the President shall resume the powers and duties of his office.

AMENDMENT XXVI

[Proposed by Congress on March 23, 1971; declared ratified on June 30, 1971.]

Section 1
[EIGHTEEN-YEAR-OLD VOTE]

The right of citizens of the United States, who are eighteen years of age or older, to vote shall not be denied or abridged by the United States or by any State on account of age.

Section 2
[POWER TO ENFORCE THIS ARTICLE]

The Congress shall have power to enforce this article by appropriate legislation.

AMENDMENT XXVII

[Proposed by Congress on September 25, 1789; ratified on May 7, 1992.]

No law varying the compensation for the services of the Senators and Representatives shall take effect until an election of Representatives shall have intervened.

Federalist Papers

NO. 10: MADISON

Among the numerous advantages promised by a well-constructed Union, none deserves to be more accurately developed than its tendency to break and control the violence of faction. The friend of popular governments never finds himself so much alarmed for their character and fate as when he contemplates their propensity to this dangerous vice. He will not fail, therefore, to set a due value on any plan which, without violating the principles to which he is attached, provides a proper cure for it. The instability, injustice, and confusion introduced into the public councils have, in truth, been the mortal diseases under which popular governments have everywhere perished, as they continue to be the favorite and fruitful topics from which the adversaries to liberty derive their most specious declamations. The valuable improvements made by the American constitutions on the popular models, both ancient and modern, cannot certainly be too much admired; but it would be an unwarrantable partiality to contend that they have as effectually obviated the danger on this side, as was wished and expected. Complaints are everywhere heard from our most considerate and virtuous citizens, equally the friends of public and private faith and of public and personal liberty, that our governments are too unstable, that the public good is disregarded in the conflicts of rival parties, and that measures are too often decided, not according to the rules of justice and the rights of the minor party, but by the superior force of an interested and overbearing majority. However anxiously we may wish that these complaints had no foundation, the evidence of known facts will not permit us to deny that they are in some degree true. It will be found, indeed, on a candid review of our situation, that some of the distresses under which we labor have been erroneously charged on the operation of our governments; but it will be found, at the same time, that other causes will not alone account for many of our heaviest misfortunes; and, particularly, for that prevailing and increasing distrust of public engagements and alarm for private rights which are echoed from one end of the continent to the other. These must be chiefly, if not wholly, effects of the unsteadiness and injustice with which a factious spirit has tainted our public administration.

By a faction I understand a number of citizens, whether amounting to a majority or minority of the whole, who are united and actuated by some common impulse of passion, or of interest, adverse to the rights of other citizens, or to the permanent and aggregate interests of the community.

There are two methods of curing the mischiefs of faction: the one, by removing its causes; the other, by controlling its effects.

There are again two methods of removing the causes of faction: the one, by destroying the liberty which is essential to its existence; the other, by giving to every citizen the same opinions, the same passions, and the same interests.

It could never be more truly said than of the first remedy that it was worse than the disease. Liberty is to faction what air is to fire, an aliment without which it instantly expires. But it could not be a less folly to abolish liberty, which is essential to political life, because it nourishes faction than it would be to wish the annihilation of air, which is essential to animal life, because it imparts to fire its destructive agency.

The second expedient is as impracticable as the first would be unwise. As long as the reason of man continues fallible, and he is at liberty to exercise it, different opinions will be formed. As long as the connection subsists between his reason and his self-love, his opinions and his passions will have a reciprocal influence on each other; and the former will be objects to which the latter will attach themselves. The diversity in the faculties of men, from which the rights of property originate, is not less an insuperable obstacle to a uniformity of interests. The protection of these faculties is the first object of government. From the protection of different and unequal faculties of acquiring property, the possession of different degrees and kinds of property immediately results; and from the influence of these on the sentiments and views of the respective proprietors ensues a division of the society into different interests and parties.

The latent causes of faction are thus sown in the nature of man; and we see them everywhere brought into different degrees of activity, according to the different circumstances of civil society. A zeal for different opinions concerning religion, concerning government, and many other points, as well of speculation as of practice; an attachment to different leaders ambitiously contending for preeminence and power; or to persons of other descriptions whose fortunes have been interesting to the human passions, have, in turn, divided mankind into parties, inflamed them with mutual animosity, and rendered them much more disposed to vex and oppress each other than to co-operate for their common good. So strong is this propensity of mankind to fall into mutual animosities that where no substantial occasion presents itself the most frivolous and fanciful distinctions have been sufficient to kindle their unfriendly passions and excite their most violent conflicts. But the most common and durable source of factions has been the various and unequal distribution of property. Those who hold and those who are without property have ever formed distinct interests in society. Those who are creditors, and those who are debtors, fall under a like discrimination. A landed interest, a manufacturing interest, a mercantile interest, a moneyed interest, with many lesser interests, grow up of necessity in civilized nations, and divide them into different classes, actuated by different sentiments and views. The regulation of these various and interfering interests forms the principal task of modern legislation and involves the spirit of party and faction in the necessary and ordinary operations of government.

No man is allowed to be judge in his own cause, because his interest would certainly bias his judgment and, not improbably, corrupt his integrity. With equal, nay with greater reason, a body of men are unfit to be both judges and parties at the same time; yet what are many of the most important acts of legislation but so many judicial determinations, not indeed concerning the rights of single persons, but concerning the rights of large bodies of citizens? And what are the different classes of legislators but advocates and parties to the causes which they determine? Is a law proposed concerning private debts? It is a question to which the creditors are parties on one side and the debtors on the other. Justice ought to hold the balance between them. Yet the parties are, and must be, themselves the judges; and the most numerous party, or in other words, the most powerful faction must be expected to prevail. Shall domestic manufacturers be encouraged, and in what degree, by restrictions on foreign manufacturers? are questions which would be differently decided by the landed and the manufacturing classes, and probably by neither with a sole regard to justice and the public good. The apportionment of taxes on the various descriptions of property is an act which seems to require the most exact impartiality; yet there is, perhaps, no legislative act in which greater opportunity and temptation are given to a predominant party to trample on the rules of justice. Every shilling with which they overburden the inferior number is a shilling saved to their own pockets.

It is in vain to say that enlightened statesmen will be able to adjust these clashing interests and render them all subservient to the public good. Enlightened statesmen will not always be at the helm. Nor, in many cases, can such an adjustment be made at all without taking into view indirect and remote considerations, which will rarely prevail over the immediate interest which one party may find in disregarding the rights of another or the good of the whole.

The inference to which we are brought is that the *causes* of faction cannot be removed and that relief is only to be sought in the means of controlling its *effects*.

If a faction consists of less than a majority, relief is supplied by the republican principle, which enables the majority to defeat its sinister views by regular vote. It may clog the administration, it may convulse the society; but it will be unable to execute and mask its violence under the forms of the Constitution. When a majority is included in a faction, the form of popular government, on the other hand, enables it to sacrifice to its ruling passion or interest both the public good and the rights of other citizens. To secure the public good and private rights against the danger of such a faction, and at the same time to preserve the spirit and the form of popular government, is then the great object to which our inquiries are directed. Let me add that it is the great desideratum by which alone this form of government can be rescued from the opprobrium under which it has so long labored and be recommended to the esteem and adoption of mankind.

By what means is this object attainable? Evidently by one of two only. Either the existence of the same passion or interest in a majority at the same time must be prevented, or the majority, having such coexistent passion or interest, must be rendered, by their number and local situation, unable to concert and carry into effect schemes of oppression. If the impulse and the opportunity be suffered to coincide, we well know that neither moral nor religious motives can be relied on as an adequate control. They are not found to be such on the injustice and violence of individuals, and lose their efficacy in proportion to the number combined together, that is, in proportion as their efficacy becomes needful.

From this view of the subject it may be concluded that a pure democracy, by which I mean a society consisting of a small number of citizens, who assemble and administer the government in person, can admit of no cure for the mischiefs of faction. A common passion or interest will, in almost every case, be felt by a majority of the whole; a communication and concert results from the form of government itself; and there is nothing to check the inducements to sacrifice the weaker party or an obnoxious individual. Hence it is that such democracies have ever been spectacles of turbulence and contention; have ever been found incompatible with personal security or the rights of property; and have in general been as short in their lives as they have been violent in their deaths. Theoretic politicians, who have patronized this species of government, have erroneously supposed that by reducing mankind to a perfect equality in their political rights, they would at the same time be perfectly equalized and assimilated in their possessions, their opinions, and their passions.

A republic, by which I mean a government in which the scheme of representation takes place, opens a different prospect and promises the cure for which we are seeking. Let us examine the points in which it varies from pure democracy, and we shall comprehend both the nature of the cure and the efficacy which it must derive from the Union.

The two great points of difference between a democracy and a republic are: first, the delegation of the government, in the latter, to a small number of citizens elected by the rest; secondly, the greater number of citizens and greater sphere of country over which the latter may be extended.

The effect of the first difference is, on the one hand, to refine and enlarge the public views by passing them through the medium of a chosen body of citizens, whose wisdom may best discern the true interest of their country and whose patriotism and love of justice will be least likely to sacrifice it to temporary or partial considerations. Under such a regulation it may well happen that the public voice, pronounced by the representatives of the people, will be more consonant to the public good than if pronounced by the people themselves, convened for the purpose. On the other hand, the effect may be inverted. Men of factious tempers, of local prejudices, or of sinister designs, may, by intrigue, by corruption, or by other means, first obtain the suffrages, and then betray the interests of the people. The question resulting is, whether small or extensive republics are most favorable to the election of proper guardians of the public weal; and it is clearly decided in favor of the latter by two obvious considerations.

In the first place it is to be remarked that however small the republic may be the representatives must be raised to a certain number in order to guard against the cabals of a few; and that however large it may be they must be limited to a certain number in order to guard against the confusion of a multitude. Hence, the number of representatives in the two cases not being in proportion to that of the constituents, and being proportionally greatest in the small republic, it follows that if the proportion of fit characters be not less in the large than in the small republic, the former will present a greater option, and consequently a greater probability of a fit choice.

In the next place, as each representative will be chosen by a greater number of citizens in the large than in the small republic, it will be more difficult for unworthy candidates to practise with success the vicious arts by which elections are too often carried; and the suffrages of the people being more free, will be more likely to center on men who possess the most attractive merit and the most diffusive and established characters.

It must be confessed that in this, as in most other cases, there is a mean, on both sides of which inconveniencies will be found to lie. By enlarging too much the number of electors, you render the representative too little acquainted with all their local circumstances and lesser interests; as by reducing it too much, you render him unduly attached to these, and too little fit to comprehend and pursue great and national objects. The federal Constitution forms a happy combination in this respect; the great and aggregate interests being referred to the national, the local and particular to the State legislatures.

The other point of difference is the greater number of citizens and extent of territory which may be brought within the compass of republican than of democratic government; and it is this circumstance principally which renders factious combinations less to be dreaded in the former than in the latter. The smaller the society, the fewer probably will be the distinct parties and interests composing it; the fewer the distinct parties and interests, the more frequently will a majority be found of the same party; and the smaller the number of individuals composing a majority, and the smaller the compass within which they are placed, the more easily will they concert and execute their plans of oppression. Extend the sphere and you take in a greater variety of parties and interests; you make it less probable that a majority of the whole will have a common motive to invade the rights of other citizens; or if such a common motive exists, it will be more difficult for all who feel it to discover their own strength and to act in unison with each other. Besides other impediments, it may be remarked that, where there is a consciousness of unjust or dishonorable purposes, communication is always checked by distrust in proportion to the number whose concurrence is necessary.

Hence, it clearly appears that the same advantage which a republic has over a democracy in controlling the effects of faction is enjoyed by a large over a small republic—is enjoyed by the Union over the States composing it. Does this advantage consist in the substitution of representatives whose enlightened views and virtuous sentiments render them superior to local prejudices and to schemes of injustice? It will not be denied that the representation of the Union will be most likely to possess these requisite endowments. Does it consist in the greater security afforded by a greater variety of parties, against the event of any one party being able to outnumber and oppress the rest? In an equal degree does the increased variety of parties comprised within the Union increase this security? Does it, in fine, consist in the greater obstacles opposed to the concert and accomplishment of the secret wishes of an unjust and interested majority? Here again the extent of the Union gives it the most palpable advantage.

The influence of factious leaders may kindle a flame within their particular States but will be unable to spread a general conflagration through the other States. A religious sect may degenerate into a political faction in a part of the Confederacy; but the variety of sects dispersed over the entire face of it must secure the national councils against any danger from that source. A rage for paper money, for an abolition of debts, for an equal division of property, or for any other improper or wicked project, will be less apt to pervade the whole body of the Union than a particular member of it, in the same proportion as such a malady is more likely to taint a particular county or district than an entire State.

In the extent and proper structure of the Union, therefore, we behold a republican remedy for the diseases most incident to republican government. And according to the degree of pleasure and pride we feel in being republicans ought to be our zeal in cherishing the spirit and supporting the character of federalist.

PUBLIUS

NO. 51: MADISON

To what expedient, then, shall we finally resort, for maintaining in practice the necessary partition of power among the several departments as laid down in the Constitution? The only answer that can be given is that as all these exterior provisions are found to be inadequate the defect must be supplied, by so contriving the interior structure of the government as that its several constituent parts may, by their mutual relations, be the means of keeping each other in their proper places. Without presuming to undertake a full development of this important idea I will hazard a few general observations which may perhaps place it in a clearer light, and enable us to form a more correct judgment of the principles and structure of the government planned by the convention.

In order to lay a due foundation for that separate and distinct exercise of the different powers of government, which to a certain extent is admitted on all hands to be essential to the preservation of liberty, it is evident that each department should have a will of its own; and consequently should be so constituted that the members of each should have as little agency as possible in the appointment of the members of the others. Were this principle rigorously adhered to, it would require that all the appointments for the supreme executive, legislative, and judiciary magistracies should be drawn from the same fountain of authority, the people, through channels having no communication whatever with one another. Perhaps such a plan of constructing the several departments would be less difficult in practice than it may in contemplation appear. Some difficulties, however, and some additional expense would attend the execution of it. Some deviations, therefore, from the principle must be admitted. In the constitution of the judiciary department in particular, it might be inexpedient to insist rigorously on the principle: first, because peculiar qualifications being essential in the members, the primary consideration ought to be to select that mode of choice which best secures these qualifications; second, because the permanent tenure by which the appointments are held in that department must soon destroy all sense of dependence on the authority conferring them.

It is equally evident that the members of each department should be as little dependent as possible on those of the others for the emoluments annexed to their offices. Were the executive magistrate, or the judges, not independent of the legislature in this particular, their independence in every other would be merely nominal.

But the great security against a gradual concentration of the several powers in the same department consists in giving to those who administer each department the necessary constitutional means and personal motives to resist encroachments of the others. The provision for defense must in this, as in all other cases, be made commensurate to the danger of attack. Ambition must be made to counteract ambition. The interest of the man must be connected with the constitutional rights of the place. It may be a reflection on human nature that such devices should be necessary to control the abuses of government. But what is government itself but the greatest of all reflections on human nature? If men were angels, no government would be necessary. If angels were to govern men, neither external nor internal controls on government would be necessary. In framing a government which is to be administered by men over men, the great difficulty lies in this: you must first enable the government to control the governed; and in the next place oblige it to control itself. A dependence on the people is, no doubt, the primary control on the government; but experience has taught mankind the necessity of auxiliary precautions.

This policy of supplying, by opposite and rival interests, the defect of better motives, might be traced through the whole system of human affairs, private as well as public. We see it particularly displayed in all the subordinate distributions of power, where the constant aim is to divide and arrange the several offices in such a manner as that each may be a check on the other—that the private interest of every individual may be a sentinel over the public rights. These inventions of prudence cannot be less requisite in the distribution of the supreme powers of the State.

But it is not possible to give to each department an equal power of self-defense. In republican government, the legislative authority necessarily predominates. The remedy for this inconveniency is to divide the legislature into different branches; and to render them, by different modes of election and different principles of action, as little connected with each other as the nature of their common functions and their common dependence on the society will admit. It may even be necessary to guard against dangerous encroachments by still further precautions. As the weight of the legislative authority requires that it should be thus divided, the weakness of the executive may require, on the other hand, that it should be fortified. An absolute negative on the legislature appears, at first view, to be the natural defense with which the executive magistrate should be armed. But perhaps it would be neither altogether safe nor alone sufficient. On ordinary occasions it might not be exerted with the requisite firmness, and on extraordinary occasions it might be perfidiously abused. May not this defect of an absolute negative be supplied by some qualified connection between this weaker branch of the stronger department, by which the latter may be led to support the constitutional rights of the former, without being too much detached from the rights of its own department?

If the principles on which these observations are founded be just, as I persuade myself they are, and they be applied as a criterion to the several State constitutions, and to the federal Constitution, it will be found that if the latter does not perfectly correspond with them, the former are infinitely less able to bear such a test.

There are, moreover, two considerations particularly applicable to the federal system of America, which place that system in a very interesting point of view.

First. In a single republic, all the power surrendered by the people is submitted to the administration of a single government; and the usurpations are guarded against by a division of the government into distinct and separate departments. In the compound republic of America, the power surrendered by the people is first divided between two distinct governments, and then the portion allotted to each subdivided among distinct and separate departments. Hence a double security arises to the rights of the people. The different governments will control each other, at the same time that each will be controlled by itself.

Second. It is of great importance in a republic not only to guard the society against the oppression of its rulers, but to guard one part of the society against the injustice of the other part. Different interests necessarily exist in different classes of citizens. If a majority be united by a common interest, the rights of the minority will be insecure. There are but two methods of providing against this evil: the one by creating a will in the community independent of the majority—that is, of the society itself; the other, by comprehending in the society so many separate descriptions of citizens as will render an unjust combination of a majority of the whole very improbable, if not impracticable. The first method prevails in all governments possessing an hereditary or self-appointed authority. This, at best, is but a precarious security; because a power independent of the society may as well espouse the unjust views of the major as the rightful interests of the minor party, and may possibly be turned against both parties. The second method will be exemplified in the federal republic of the United States. Whilst all authority in it will be derived from and dependent on the society, the society itself will be broken into so many parts, interests and classes of citizens, that the rights of individuals, or of the minority, will be in little danger from interested combinations of the majority. In a free government the security for civil rights must be the same as that for religious rights. It consists in the one case in the multiplicity of interests, and in the other in the multiplicity of sects. The degree of security in both cases will depend on the number of interests and sects; and this may be presumed to depend on the extent of country and number of people comprehended under the same government. This view of the subject must particularly recommend a proper federal system to all the sincere and considerate friends of republican government, since it shows that in exact proportion as the territory of the Union may be formed into more circumscribed Confederacies, or States, oppressive combinations of a majority will be facilitated; the best security, under the republican forms, for the rights of every class of citizen, will be diminished; and consequently the stability and independence of some member of the government, the only other security, must be proportionally increased. Justice is the end of government. It is the end of civil society. It ever has been and ever will be pursued until it be obtained, or until liberty be lost in the pursuit. In a society under the forms of which the stronger faction can readily unite and oppress the weaker, anarchy may as truly be said to reign as in a state of nature, where the weaker individual is not secured against the violence of the stronger; and as, in the latter state, even the stronger individuals are prompted, by the uncertainty of their condition, to submit to a government which may protect the weak as well as themselves; so, in the former state, will the more powerful factions or parties be gradually induced, by a like motive, to wish for a government which will protect all parties, the weaker as well as the more powerful. It can be little doubted that if the State of Rhode Island was separated from the Confederacy and left to itself, the insecurity of rights under the popular form of government within such narrow limits would be displayed by such reiterated oppressions of factious majorities that some power altogether independent of the people would soon be called for by the voice of the very factions whose misrule had proved the necessity of it. In the extended republic of the United States, and among the great variety of interests, parties, and sects which it embraces, a coalition of a majority of the whole society could seldom take place on any other principles than those of justice and the general good; whilst there being thus less danger to a minor from the will of a major party, there must be less pretext, also, to provide for the security of the former, by introducing into the government a will not dependent on the latter, or, in other words, a will independent of the society itself. It is no less certain than it is important, notwithstanding the contrary opinions which have been entertained, that the larger the society, provided it lie within a practicable sphere, the more duly capable it will be of self-government. And happily for the *republican cause*, the practicable sphere may be carried to a very great extent by a judicious modification and mixture of the *federal principle*.

PUBLIUS

Glossary of Terms

administrative adjudication Applying rules and precedents to specific cases to settle disputes with regulated parties.

administrative legislation Rules made by **regulatory agencies** and commissions.

administrative regulation Rules made by **regulatory agencies** and commissions.

adverse selection problem The problem of incomplete information—of choosing alternatives without knowing fully the details of available options.

affirmative action A policy or program designed to redress historic injustices committed against specific groups by making special efforts to provide members of these groups with access to educational and employment opportunities.

after-the-fact authority The authority to follow up on the fate of a proposal once it has been approved by the full chamber.

agents of socialization Social institutions, including families and schools, that help shape individuals' basic political **beliefs** and **values.**

agency loss The difference between what a principal would like an agent to do and the agent's actual performance.

agency representation The type of representation by which representatives are held accountable to their constituents if they fail to represent them properly; that is, constituents have the power to hire and fire their representatives. This is the incentive for good representation when the personal backgrounds, views, and interests of the representatives differ from their constituents'.

agenda power Control over what the group will consider for discussion.

agenda setting Activities that help determine which issues are taken up by political actors and institutions.

Aid to Families with Dependent Children (AFDC) Federal funds for children in families that fall below state standards of need. The largest federal cash transfer program. In 1996, Congress abolished AFDC and replaced it with the **Temporary Assistance to Needy Families (TANF) block grant.**

amicus curiae "Friend of the court"; individuals or groups who are not parties to a lawsuit but who seek to assist the court in reaching a decision by presenting additional **briefs.**

antitrust policy Government regulation of large businesses that have established monopolies.

appellate court A court that hears the appeals of **trial court** decisions.

Articles of Confederation and Perpetual Union America's first written constitution. Adopted by the Continental Congress in 1777, the Articles of Confederation and Perpetual Union was the formal basis for America's national **government** until 1789, when it was supplanted by the Constitution.

attitude (or opinion) A specific preference on a specific issue.

Australian ballot An electoral format that presents the names of all the candidates for any given office on the same ballot. Introduced at the turn of the twentieth century, the Australian ballot replaced the partisan ballot and facilitated split-ticket voting.

authoritarian government A system of rule in which the **government** recognizes no formal limits but may nevertheless be restrained by the power of other social institutions.

autocracy A form of **government** in which a single individual rules.

balance-of-power role The strategy whereby many countries form alliances with one country or several other countries in order to counterbalance the behavior of other, usually more powerful, nation-states.

bandwagon effect A shift in electoral support to the candidate whom public opinion polls report as the frontrunner.

bicameralism The division of a legislative assembly into two chambers or houses.

bicameral legislature A legislative assembly composed of two chambers or houses.

bilateral treaty A treaty made between two nations.

Bill of Rights The first ten amendments to the U.S. Constitution, ratified in 1791. They ensure certain rights and liberties to the people.

block grants Federal funds given to state **governments** to pay for goods, services, or programs, with relatively few restrictions on how the funds may be spent.

briefs Written documents in which attorneys explain—using case precedents—why the Court should rule in favor of their client.

budget deficit Amount by which **government** spending exceeds government revenue in a fiscal year.

bureaucracy The complex structure of offices, tasks, rules, and principles of organization that are employed by all large-scale institutions to coordinate the work of their personnel.

bureaucratic drift The oft-observed phenomenon of bureaucratic implementation that produces policy more to the liking of the **bureaucracy** than originally legislated, but without triggering a political reaction from elected officials.

Bush Doctrine   Foreign policy based on the idea that the United States should take preemptive action against threats to its national security.

by-product theory   The idea that groups provide members with private benefits to attract membership; the possibility of group **collective action** emerges as a consequence.

cabinet   The secretaries, or chief administrators, of the major departments of the federal **government.** Cabinet secretaries are appointed by the president with the consent of the Senate.

casework   An effort by members of Congress to gain the trust and support of constituents by providing them with personal service. One important type of casework consists of helping constituents obtain favorable treatment from the federal **bureaucracy.**

categorical grants-in-aid   Funds given by Congress to states and localities, earmarked by law for specific categories such as education or crime prevention.

caucus   An association of members of Congress based on party, interest, or social characteristics such as gender or race; also, a normally closed meeting of a political or legislative group to select candidates, plan strategy, or make decisions regarding legislative matters.

checks and balances   Mechanisms through which each branch of **government** is able to participate in and influence the activities of the other branches.

chief justice   Justice on the **Supreme Court** who presides over the Court's public sessions.

civil law   A system of jurisprudence, including private law and governmental actions, to settle disputes that do not involve criminal penalties.

civil liberties   Protections of citizens from improper **government** action.

civil rights   Legal or moral claims that citizens are entitled to make on the **government.**

class action suit   A lawsuit in which large numbers of persons with common interests join together under a representative party to bring or defend a lawsuit, such as hundreds of workers joining together to sue a company.

clientele agencies   Departments or bureaus of **government** whose mission is to promote, serve, or represent a particular interest.

client state   A nation-state whose foreign policy is subordinated to that of another nation.

closed primary   A primary election in which voters can participate in the nomination of candidates, but only of the party in which they are enrolled for a period of time prior to primary day. Contrast with **open primary.**

closed rule   Provision by the House Rules Committee prohibiting the introduction of amendments during debate.

cloture A rule allowing a supermajority of the members in a legislative body to set a time limit on debate over a given bill.

coalitional drift The prospect that enacted policy will change because the composition of the enacting coalition is so temporary and provisional.

collective action The pooling of resources and coordination of effort and activity by a group of people (often a large one) to achieve common goals.

commander in chief The power of the president as commander of the national military and the state national guard units (when called into service).

commerce clause Article I, Section 8, of the Constitution, which delegates to Congress the power "to regulate Commerce with foreign Nations, and among the several States, and with the Indian Tribes." This clause was interpreted by the **Supreme Court** in favor of national power over the economy.

concurrent powers Authority possessed by *both* state and national **governments,** such as the power to levy taxes.

conference committee A joint committee created to work out a compromise for House and Senate versions of a piece of legislation.

conscription Compulsory military service, usually for a prescribed period or for the duration of a war; the draft.

conservative Today this term refers to those who generally support the social and economic status quo and are suspicious of efforts to introduce new political formulas and economic arrangements. Many conservatives also believe that a large and powerful **government** poses a threat to citizens' freedoms.

constituency The district making up the area from which an official is elected.

constitutionalism (constitutional rule) A system of rule in which formal and effective limits are placed on the powers of the **government.**

containment The primary cold war foreign policy of the United States during the 1950s and 1960s, whereby the United States used its political, economic, and military power to prevent the spread of communism to developing or unstable countries.

contracting power The power of **government** to set conditions on companies seeking to sell goods or services to government agencies.

contributory programs Social programs financed in whole or in part by taxation or other mandatory contributions by their present or future recipients. The most important example is **Social Security,** which is financed by a payroll tax.

cooperative federalism A type of **federalism** existing since the New Deal era in which **grants-in-aid** have been used strategically to encourage states and localities (without commanding them) to pursue nationally defined goals. Also known as intergovernmental cooperation.

court of appeals   A court that hears the appeals of trial-court decisions.

criminal law   The branch of law that deals with disputes or actions involving criminal penalties (as opposed to **civil law**). It regulates the conduct of individuals, defines crimes, and provides punishment for criminal acts.

***de facto* segregation**   Racial segregation that is not a direct result of law or **government** policy but is, instead, a reflection of residential patterns, income distributions, or other social factors.

defendant   The individual or organization charged with a complaint in court.

***de jure* segregation**   Racial segregation that is a direct result of law or official policy.

delegate   A representative who votes according to the preferences of his or her constituency.

delegated powers   Constitutional powers assigned to one governmental agency that are exercised by another agency with the express permission of the first.

delegation   Transmitting authority to some other official or body for the latter's use (though often with the right of review and revision).

democracy   A system of rule that permits citizens to play a significant part in the governmental process, usually through the selection of key public officials.

deregulation   A policy of reducing or eliminating regulatory restraints on the conduct of individuals or private institutions.

deterrence   The development and maintenance of military strength for the purpose of discouraging attack.

devolution   A policy to remove a program from one level of **government** by deregulating it or passing it down to a lower level of government, such as from the national government to the state and local governments.

discount rate   The interest rate charged by the **Federal Reserve** when commercial banks borrow in order to expand their lending operations. An effective tool of monetary policy.

discretionary spending   Federal spending on programs that are controlled through the regular budget process.

discuss list   List circulated by the chief justice of all the petitions to be discussed and voted on at the Supreme Court's conference.

dissenting opinion   Decision written by a justice with the minority opinion in a particular case, in which the justice fully explains the reasoning behind his or her opinion.

distributive tendency   The tendency of Congress to spread the benefits of a policy over a wide range of members' districts.

divided government   The condition in American **government** when the presidency is controlled by one party while the opposing party controls one or both houses of Congress.

double jeopardy Being tried more than once for the same crime. The Constitution guarantees that no one shall be subjected to double jeopardy.

dual federalism The system of **government** that prevailed in the United States from 1789 to 1937 in which most fundamental governmental powers were shared between the federal and state governments. Compare with **cooperative federalism.**

due process The right of every citizen against arbitrary action by national or state **governments.**

economic expansionist role The strategy often pursued by capitalist countries to adopt foreign policies that will maximize the success of domestic corporations in their dealings with other countries.

electoral college The presidential electors from each state who meet in their respective state capitals after the popular election to cast ballots for president and vice president.

eminent domain The right of **government** to take private property for public use, with reasonable compensation rewarded for the property.

entitlement Eligibility for benefits by virtue of a category of benefits defined by law. The category can only be changed by legislation. Deprivation of individual benefits can be determined only through **due process** in court.

equality of opportunity A universally shared American ideal that all have the freedom to use whatever talents and wealth they have to reach their fullest potential.

equal protection clause Provision of the Fourteenth Amendment guaranteeing citizens "the equal protection of the laws." This clause has served as the basis for the **civil rights** of African Americans, women, and other groups.

equal time rule The requirement that broadcasters provide candidates for the same political office an equal opportunity to communicate their messages to the public.

executive agreement An agreement between the president and another country that has the force of a treaty but does not require the Senate's "advice and consent."

Executive Office of the President (EOP) The permanent agencies that perform defined management tasks for the president. Created in 1939, the EOP includes the Office of Management and Budget, the Council of Economic Advisers, the National Security Council, and other agencies.

executive orders Rules or regulations issued by the president that have the effect and formal status of legislation.

executive privilege The claim that confidential communications between a president and close advisers should not be revealed without the consent of the president.

expressed powers The notion that the Constitution grants to the federal government only those powers specifically named in its text.

expropriation Confiscation of property with or without compensation.

externalities The differences between the private costs and the social costs of economic behavior.

fairness doctrine A Federal Communications Commission requirement for broadcasters who air programs on controversial issues to provide time for opposing views.

federal funds rate The interest rate on loans between banks that the Federal Reserve Board influences by affecting the supply of money available.

federalism System of **government** in which a constitution divides power between a central government and regional governments.

Federal Reserve System (Fed) Consisting of twelve Federal Reserve Banks, the Fed facilitates exchanges of cash, checks, and credit; it regulates member banks; and it uses monetary policies to fight inflation and deflation.

filibuster A tactic used by members of the Senate to prevent action on legislation they oppose by continuously holding the floor and speaking until the majority backs down. Once given the floor, senators have unlimited time to speak, and it requires a **cloture** vote of three-fifths of the Senate to end the filibuster.

fiscal policies The use of taxing, monetary, and spending powers to manipulate the economy.

527 committees Tax-exempt organizations that engage in political activities, often through unlimited "soft-money" contributions. They are not restricted by current law on campaign finance, exploiting a loophole in the Internal Revenue Service code.

food stamps The largest **in-kind benefits** program, administered by the Department of Agriculture, providing coupons to individuals and families who satisfy a **means test;** the food stamps can be exchanged for food at most grocery stores.

formula grants Grants-in-aid in which a formula is used to determine the amount of federal funds a state or local **government** will receive.

framing The power of the media to influence how events and issues are interpreted.

free riding Enjoying the benefits of some good or action and letting others bear the costs. See also **public good.**

full faith and credit clause Provision from Article IV, Section I, of the Constitution requiring that the states normally honor the public acts and judicial decisions that take place in another state.

gatekeeping authority The right and power to decide if a change in policy will be considered.

gender gap A distinctive pattern of voting behavior reflecting the differences in views between men and women.

gerrymandering Apportionment of voters in districts in such a way as to give unfair advantage to one political party.

going public Launching a media campaign to build popular support.

government Institutions and procedures through which a land and its people are ruled.

grants-in-aid A general term for funds given by Congress to state and local **governments**. See also **categorical grants-in-aid**.

Great Compromise Agreement reached at the Constitutional Convention of 1787 that gave each state an equal number of senators regardless of its population but linked representation in the House of Representatives to population.

Holy Alliance role A strategy pursued by a superpower to prevent any change in the existing distribution of power among nation-states, even if this requires intervention into the internal affairs of the country in order to keep an authoritarian ruler from being overturned.

home rule Power delegated by the state to a local unit of **government** to manage its own affairs.

homesteading A national policy that permitted people to gain ownership of property by occupying public or unclaimed land, living on the land for a specified period of time, and making certain minimal improvements on that land. Also known as squatting.

illusion of saliency The impression conveyed by polls that something is important to the public when actually it is not.

impeachment The charging of a governmental official (president or otherwise) with "Treason, Bribery, or other high Crimes and Misdemeanors" and bringing of him or her before Congress to determine guilt.

implementation The efforts of departments and agencies to translate laws into specific bureaucratic routines.

implied powers Powers derived from the **necessary and proper clause** of Article I, Section 8, of the Constitution. Such powers are not specifically **expressed** but are **implied** through the expansive interpretation of **delegated powers**.

incumbency Holding a political office for which one is running.

indexing Periodic process of adjusting social benefits or wages to account for increases in the cost of living.

***in forma pauperis* petitions** Requests to waive most rules and fees for indigent petitioners.

informational benefits Special newsletters, periodicals, training programs, conferences, and other information provided to members of groups to entice others to join.

inherent powers Powers claimed by a president that are not expressed in the Constitution but are inferred from it.

initiative A process by which citizens may petition to place a policy proposal on the ballot for public vote.

in-kind benefits Goods and services provided to needy individuals and families by the federal **government,** as contrasted with cash benefits. The largest in-kind federal welfare program is **food stamps.**

institutions Rules and procedures that provide incentives for political behavior, thereby shaping politics.

instrumental Done with purpose, sometimes forethought and even calculation.

interest group An organized group of people that makes policy-related appeals to **government.**

issue advocacy Independent spending by individuals or **interest groups** on a campaign issue but not directly tied to a particular candidate.

judicial activism Judicial philosophy that posits that the Court should see beyond the text of the Constitution or a statute to consider broader societal implications for decisions.

judicial restraint Judicial philosophy whose adherents refuse to go beyond the set text of the Constitution in interpreting its meaning.

judicial review Power of the courts to declare actions of the legislative and executive branches invalid or unconstitutional. The **Supreme Court** asserted this power in *Marbury v. Madison.*

jurisdiction The sphere of a court's power and authority.

Kitchen Cabinet An informal group of advisers to whom the president turns for counsel and guidance. Members of the official **cabinet** may or may not also be members of the Kitchen Cabinet.

legislative clearance The power given to the president to require all agencies of the executive branch to submit through the budget director all requests for new legislation along with estimates of their budgetary needs.

legislative initiative The president's inherent power to bring a legislative agenda before Congress.

legislative supremacy The preeminent position assigned to Congress by the Constitution.

liberal A liberal today generally supports political and social reform; extensive governmental intervention in the economy; the expansion of federal social services; more vigorous efforts on behalf of the poor, minorities, and women; and greater concern for consumers and the environment.

line-item veto The power of the executive to veto specific provisions (lines) of a bill passed by the legislature.

lobbying An attempt by a group to influence the policy process through persuasion of **government** officials.

logrolling A legislative practice wherein reciprocal agreements are made between legislators, usually in voting for or against a bill. In contrast to bargaining, logrolling unites parties that have nothing in common but their desire to exchange support.

majority leader The elected leader of the party holding a majority of the seats in the House of Representatives or in the Senate. In the House, the majority leader is subordinate in the party hierarchy to the Speaker.

majority party The party that holds the majority of legislative seats in either the House or the Senate.

majority system A type of electoral system in which, to win a seat in the parliament or other representative body, a candidate must receive a majority (50 percent plus 1) of all the votes cast in the relevant district.

mandate (electoral) A claim by a victorious candidate that the electorate has given him or her special authority to carry out promises made during the campaign.

mandatory spending Federal spending that is made up of **"uncontrollables,"** budget items that cannot be controlled through the regular budget process.

market failure An instance when the market fails to produce an efficient outcome.

material benefits Special goods, services, or money provided to members of groups to entice others to join.

means testing A procedure that determines eligibility for **government** public assistance programs. A potential beneficiary must show a need and an inability to provide for it.

measurement error Failure to identify the true distribution of opinion within a population because of errors such as ambiguous or poorly worded questions.

Medicaid A federally financed, state-operated program for medical services to low-income people.

Medicare National health insurance for the elderly and the disabled.

minority leader The elected leader of the party holding less than a majority of the seats in the House or Senate.

Miranda rule Principles developed by the **Supreme Court** in the 1966 case of *Miranda v. Arizona* requiring that persons under arrest be informed of their legal rights, including their right to counsel, prior to police interrogation.

monetary policies Efforts to regulate the economy through manipulation of the supply of money and credit. America's most powerful institution in the area of monetary policy is the Federal Reserve Board.

monopoly The existence in a market of a single firm that provides all the goods and services of that market; the absence of competition.

mootness A criterion used by courts to screen cases that no longer require resolution.

moral hazard   Not knowing all aspects of the actions taken by an agent (nominally on behalf of the principal but potentially at the principal's expense).

multilateralism   A foreign policy that seeks to encourage the involvement of several nation-states in coordinated action, usually in relation to a common adversary, with terms and conditions usually specified in a multicountry treaty, such as NATO.

multilateral treaty   A treaty among more than two nations.

multiple-member district   Electorate that selects several candidates at large from the whole district; each voter is given the number of votes equivalent to the number of seats to be filled.

Napoleonic role   A strategy pursued by a powerful nation to prevent aggressive actions against it by improving the internal state of affairs of a particular country, even if this means encouraging revolution in that country. This strategy is based on the assumption that countries with comparable political systems will never go to war against each other.

National Security Council (NSC)   A presidential foreign policy advisory council composed of the president; the vice president; the secretaries of state, defense, and the treasury; the attorney general; and other officials invited by the president.

necessary and proper clause   Article I, Section 8, of the Constitution, which enumerates the powers of Congress and provides Congress with the authority to make all laws "necessary and proper" to carry them out; also referred to as the "elastic clause."

nomination   The process through which political parties select their candidates for election to public office.

noncontributory programs   Social programs that assist people based on demonstrated need rather than contributions they have made. Also known as *public assistance programs.*

oligarchy   A form of **government** in which a small group of landowners, military officers, or wealthy merchants controls most of the governing decisions.

open-market operations   The process whereby the Open Market Committee of the **Federal Reserve** buys and sells **government** securities and the like to help finance government operations and to loosen or tighten the total amount of credit circulating in the economy.

open primary   A primary election in which the voter can wait until the day of the primary to choose which party to enroll in to select candidates for the general election. Contrast with **closed primary**.

open rule   Provision by the House Rules Committee that permits floor debate and the addition of new amendments to a bill.

opinion   The written explanation of the **Supreme Court**'s decision in a particular case.

oral argument Stage in **Supreme Court** proceedings in which attorneys for both sides appear before the Court to present their positions and answer questions posed by the justices.

oversight The effort by Congress, through hearings, investigations, and other techniques, to exercise control over the activities of executive agencies.

party activists Partisans who contribute time, energy, and effort to support their party and its candidates.

party caucus A normally closed meeting of a political or legislative group to select candidates, plan strategy, or make decisions regarding legislative matters.

party identification An individual voter's psychological ties to one party or another.

party machines In the late nineteenth and early twentieth centuries, local party organizations that controlled local politics through patronage and control of nominations.

party vote A **roll-call vote** in the House or Senate in which at least 50 percent of the members of one party take a particular position and are opposed by at least 50 percent of the members of the other party. Party votes are rare today, although they were fairly common in the nineteenth century.

path dependency The idea that certain possibilities are made more or less likely because of the historical path taken.

patronage The resources available to higher officials, usually opportunities to make partisan appointments to offices and to confer grants, licenses, or special favors to supporters.

per curiam A brief unsigned decision by an appellate court, usually rejecting petition to review the decision of a lower court.

permanent campaign A description of presidential politics in which all presidential actions are taken with re-election in mind.

petitioner's brief Document filed by the party bringing an appeal stating the facts of a case and reasons why the lower court's opinion should be overturned.

petitioner's reply brief Petitioner's answer to the respondent's brief.

plaintiff The individual or organization who brings a complaint in court.

plea bargains Negotiated agreements in criminal cases in which a **defendant** agrees to plead guilty in return for the state's agreement to reduce the severity of the criminal charge the defendant is facing.

pluralism The theory that all interests are and should be free to compete for influence in the **government.** The outcome of this competition is compromise and moderation.

plurality system A type of electoral system in which victory goes to the individual who gets the most votes in an election, not necessarily a majority of votes cast.

pocket veto A method by which the president vetoes a bill by taking no action on it when Congress has adjourned. See also **veto.**

police power Power reserved to the **government** to regulate the health, safety, and morals of its citizens.

policy of redistribution An objective of the graduated income tax—to raise revenue in such a way as to reduce the disparities of wealth between the lowest and the highest income brackets.

political action committees (PACs) Private groups that raise and distribute funds for use in election campaigns.

political ideology A cohesive set of beliefs that form a general philosophy about the role of **government.**

political socialization The induction of individuals into the political culture; learning the underlying **beliefs** and **values** upon which the political system is based.

pork-barrel legislation Appropriations made by legislative bodies for local projects that are often not needed but that are created so that local representatives can carry their home district in the next election.

precedents Prior cases whose principles are used by judges as the bases for their decisions in present cases.

priming A process of preparing the public to take a particular view of an event or a political actor.

principal-agent relationship The relationship between a principal and his or her agent; this relationship may be affected by the fact that each is motivated by self-interest, yet their interests may not be well aligned.

prior restraint An effort by a governmental agency to block the publication of material it deems libelous or harmful in some way; censorship. In the United States, the courts forbid prior restraint except under the most extraordinary circumstances.

privatization Removing all or part of a program from the public sector to the private sector.

privileges and immunities clause Provision from Article IV, Section 2, of the Constitution that a state cannot discriminate against someone from another state or give its own residents special privileges.

probability sampling A method used by pollsters to select a sample in which every individual in the population has a known (usually equal) probability of being selected as a respondent so that the correct weight can be given to all segments of the population.

professional legislature A legislature with members that serve full-time for multiple terms.

progressive taxation Taxation that hits the upper-income brackets more heavily.

project grants Grant programs in which state and local **governments** submit proposals to federal agencies and for which funding is provided on a competitive basis.

proportional representation A multiple-member district system that allows each political party representation in proportion to its percentage of the vote.

proposal power The capacity to present a proposal to the full legislature.

prospective voting Voting based on the imagined future performance of a candidate.

public good A good (1) that may be enjoyed by anyone if it is provided and (2) that may not be denied to anyone once it has been provided. See also **free riding**.

public law Cases involving the actions of public agencies or officials.

public opinion Citizens' attitudes about political issues, leaders, institutions, and events.

public opinion polls Scientific instruments for measuring public opinion.

public policy A governmental law, rule, statute, or edict that expresses the **government's** goals and provides for rewards and punishments to promote their attainment.

purposive benefits **Selective benefits** of group membership that emphasize the purpose and accomplishments of the group.

push polling A polling technique in which the questions are designed to shape the respondent's opinion.

random digit dialing Polls in which respondents are selected at random from a list of ten-digit telephone numbers, with every effort made to avoid bias in the construction of the sample.

random sampling Polls in which respondents are chosen mathematically, at random, with every effort made to avoid bias in the construction of the sample.

recall Removal of a public official by popular vote.

referendum The practice of referring a measure proposed or passed by a legislature to the vote of the electorate for approval or rejection.

regressive taxation Taxation that hits the lower-income brackets more heavily.

regular concurrence Concurring Court opinion that agrees with the outcome and majority's rationale but highlights a particular legal point.

regulation A particular use of **government** power in which the government adopts rules imposing restrictions on the conduct of private citizens.

regulatory agencies Departments, bureaus, or independent agencies whose primary mission is to eliminate or restrict certain behaviors defined as being negative in themselves or negative in their consequences.

reserved powers Powers, derived from the Tenth Amendment to the Constitution, that are not specifically **delegated** to the national government or denied to the states.

reserve requirement The amount of liquid assets and ready cash that the **Federal Reserve** requires banks to hold to meet depositors' demands for their money. The ratio revolves above or below 20 percent of all deposits, with the rest being available for new loans.

respondent's brief Document filed by the party that won in the lower court explaining why that court's decision should not be overturned.

retrospective voting Voting based on the past performance of a candidate.

right of rebuttal A Federal Communications Commission regulation giving individuals the right to have the opportunity to respond to personal attacks made on a radio or TV broadcast.

roll-call votes A vote in which each legislator's yes or no vote is recorded.

rule-making A quasi-legislative administrative process that produces regulations by **government** agencies.

rule of four *Certiorari* will be granted only if four justices vote in favor of the petition.

salient interests Attitudes and views that are especially important to the individual holding them.

sample A small group selected by researchers to represent the most important characteristics of an entire population.

sampling error Polling error that arises based on the small size of the sample.

selection bias (media) The predisposition to choose particular types of stories.

selection bias (polling) Polling error that arises when the sample is not representative of the population being studied, creating errors by overrepresenting or underrepresenting some opinions.

selective benefits Benefits that do not go to everyone, but rather are distributed selectively—only to those who contribute to the group enterprise.

senatorial courtesy The practice whereby the president, before formally nominating a person for a federal judgeship, checks on whether the senators from the candidate's state support the nomination.

seniority Priority or status ranking given to an individual on the basis of length of continuous service on a congressional committee.

"separate but equal" rule Doctrine that public accommodations could be segregated by race but still be equal.

separation of powers The division of governmental power among several institutions that must cooperate in decision making.

single-member district An electorate that is allowed to elect only one representative from each district; the normal method of representation in the United States.

Social Security   A **contributory** welfare **program** into which working Americans place a percentage of their wages and from which they receive cash benefits after retirement.

solidary benefits   Selective benefits of group membership that emphasize friendship, networking, and consciousness-raising.

sound bites   Short snippets of information aimed at dramatizing a story, rather than explaining its substantive meaning.

sovereignty   Supreme and independent political authority.

Speaker of the House   The chief presiding officer of the House of Representatives. The Speaker is elected at the beginning of every Congress on a straight **party vote.** The Speaker is the most important party and House leader, and can influence the legislative agenda, the fate of individual pieces of legislation, and members' positions within the House.

special concurrences   Concurring opinions that agree with the outcome but disagree with the rationale presented by the majority opinion.

staff agencies   Agencies responsible for providing Congress with independent expertise, administration, and **oversight** capability.

standing   The right of an individual or organization to initiate a court case.

standing committee   A permanent legislative committee that considers legislation within its designated subject area; the basic unit of deliberation in the House and Senate.

stare decisis   Literally "let the decision stand." A previous decision by a court applies as a precedent in similar cases until that decision is overruled.

state sovereign immunity   Legal doctrine that holds that states cannot be sued for violating an act of Congress.

states' rights   The principle that states should oppose increasing authority of the national **government.** This view was most popular before the Civil War.

subsidies   Governmental grants of cash or other valuable commodities such as land to individuals or organizations. Subsidies can be used to promote activities desired by the **government,** to reward political support, or to buy off political opposition.

Supplemental Security Income (SSI)   A program providing a minimum monthly income to people who pass a **means test** and are sixty-five years old or older, blind, or disabled. Financed from general revenues that are not **Social Security** contributions.

supremacy clause   Article VI of the Constitution, which states that all laws passed by the national **government** and all treaties are the supreme laws of the land and superior to all laws adopted by any state or any subdivision.

supreme court   The highest court in a particular state or in the United States. This court primarily serves an appellate function.

Temporary Assistance to Needy Families (TANF) *See* Aid to Families with Dependent Children (AFDC).

third parties Parties that organize to compete against the two major American political parties.

Three-fifths Compromise Agreement reached at the Constitutional Convention of 1787 stipulating that for purposes of the apportionment of congressional seats, every slave would be counted as three-fifths of a person.

totalitarian government A system of rule in which the **government** recognizes no formal limits on its power and seeks to absorb or eliminate other social institutions that might challenge it.

transaction costs The cost of clarifying each aspect of a principal-agent relationship and monitoring it to make sure arrangements are complied with.

trial court The first court to hear a criminal or civil case.

trustee A representative who votes based on what he or she thinks is best for his or her **constituency.**

tyranny Oppressive and unjust **government** that employs the cruel and unjust use of power and authority.

uncontrollables Budgetary items that are beyond the control of budgetary committees and can be controlled only by substantive legislative action in Congress. Some uncontrollables are beyond the power of Congress because the terms of payments are set in contracts, such as interest on the debt.

unfunded mandates National standards or programs imposed on state and local **governments** by the federal government without accompanying funding or reimbursement.

unilateralism A foreign policy that seeks to avoid international alliances, entanglements, and permanent commitments in favor of independence, neutrality, and freedom of action.

United Nations (UN) An organization of nations founded in 1945 to serve as a channel for negotiation and a means of settling international disputes peaceably. The UN has had frequent successes in providing a forum for negotiation and on some occasions a means of preventing international conflicts from spreading. On a number of occasions, the UN has been a convenient cover for U.S. foreign-policy goals.

values (or beliefs) Basic principles that shape a person's opinions about political issues and events.

veto The president's constitutional power to turn down acts of Congress. A presidential veto may be overridden by a two-thirds vote of each house of Congress.

veto power The ability to defeat something, even if it has made it onto the agenda of an institution.

War Powers Resolution A resolution of Congress that the president can send troops into action abroad only by authorization of Congress or if American troops are already under attack or serious threat.

whip system A communications network in each house of Congress; whips poll the membership to learn their intentions on specific legislative issues and to assist the **majority** and **minority leaders** in various tasks.

White House staff Analysts and advisers to the president, often given the title "special assistant."

writ of appeal Writ that may be issued to accept appeals, mainly from the decision of a three-judge district court.

writ of certification Writ issued when a U.S. Court of Appeals asks the Supreme Court for instructions on a point of law that has never been decided.

writ of *certiorari* A decision concurred in by at least four of the nine **Supreme Court** justices to review a decision of a lower court; from the Latin "to make more certain."

writ of *habeas corpus* A court order demanding that an individual in custody be brought into court and shown the cause for detention. *Habeas corpus* is guaranteed by the Constitution and can be suspended only in cases of rebellion or invasion.

Index

Page numbers in *italics* refer to figures and tables.

AAA (American Automobile Association), 542
AARP (American Association of Retired Persons), 22, 23, 524–25, 529, 542, 553, 642, 650, 662
ABC, 577
ABM (Anti-Ballistic Missile) Treaty, 681
abortion, 129–30, 135, 326–27, 353, 364, 396, 556
  Democratic support for, 494, 504
  G. W. Bush's opposition to, 366
  G. W. Bush's Supreme Court appointees and, 552
  1989 undermining of, 550
  O'Connor and, 129, 359
  partial-birth, 195
  Reagan's opposition to, 486, 504
  religious conservative opposition to, 556
  Republican opposition to, 504
  2003 ruling on, 369
  see also Roe v. Wade
Abraham Lincoln, U.S.S., 574
absentee ballots, 427
Abu Ghraib, 565
ACLU (American Civil Liberties Union), 348
ACT (Americans Coming Together), 513, 522–23
action-forcing, 443
activism, political parties and, 491, 505
ADA (Americans with Disabilities Act), 348, 370
Adams, John, 40, 42, 43, 234
Adams, John Quincy, 234, 439

Adams, Samuel, 40, 41
Adarand Constructors v. Pena, 151, 153, 342
administrative adjudication, 280–81
administrative law, 319
administrative legislation, 287
Administrative Procedure Act (1946), 294, 336–37, 548
administrative regulation, 619
Advanced Research Protection Agency, 274
adverse selection problem, 423
Advisory Council on Intergovernmental Relations, 303
AFDC (Aid to Families with Dependent Children), 98, 653–56, *658*, 670
affirmative action, 149–54
  equality of opportunity and, 385
  executive orders and, 261
  Proposition 209 and, 153–54, 416–17
  Republican opposition to, 486
  spiral of silence and, 392
  Supreme Court and, 150–53, 342, 353, 364, 369
  see also Roe v. Wade
Afghanistan, 224, 225, 256, 338, 712
  bin Laden in, 695
  state building in, 679, 707
Afghanistan war, 24, 25, 29, 30, 270, 296, 678, 681, 700, 704, 713
  communication office and, 256
  as discretionary war, 27
  outlays for, 624
  see also War on Terror
AFL-CIO, 528
Africa, 700

authoritarian governments in, 5
U.S. aid to, 701
African Americans, 133, 392
  civil rights groups for, 556
  Congressional Black Caucus and, 192, 212
  and Democratic Party, 588
  Eleanor Roosevelt and, 250
  election registration and, 430
  gerrymandering in Mississippi of, 434–36
  as interest group, 347
  Iraq War and, 379
  Kerry supported by, 458
  party identity of, 492
  in post-World War II U.S., 640
  poverty and, 670
  as Republicans, 392
  solidary benefits and, 539
  Voting Rights Act and, 434, 436
  welfare and, 656
  whites' disagreements with, 386–87, *388*, 391
  see also affirmative action; slavery
after-the-fact authority, 188
age, in party identity, 494
Agency for International Development (AID), 702
agency representation, 165–66
agenda, 642
agenda power, 17–18, 19
agenda setting, 590
agents, 18
Agostini v. Felton, 131
Agricultural Adjustment Act (1938), 239
agriculture, 19–20, 168, 208, 618, 644, 662–63
  in colonial America, 39, 40
  federal subsidies to, 603, 614, 630, 662, 663
  price supports and, 4
  in South Dakota, 29

Agriculture Department, U.S., 226, 287, 292*n*, 702
  as clientele agency, 284–85
  Extension Service of, 285
  organization of, 282, *283*
AID (Agency for International Development), 702
AIDS, 668, 700
Aid to Families with Dependent Children (AFDC), 98, 653–56, *658*, 670
Air Force Department, U.S., 287
Airline Deregulation Act (1978), 618
airlines:
  regulation of, 603–4, 618
  September 11 and, 545–46, 603
Alabama, 87, 684
  Hurricane Katrina, 31
  privacy rights in, 128
  same sex marriage and, 86
Alabama State University, 349
Alaska, 87
  "bridge to nowhere" in, 172–73
  oil drilling in, 400
  same-sex marriage banned in, 149
Alcorn, George, 207
Aldrich, John, 469, 499
Alexander, Lamar, 410
Alien and Sedition Acts (1798), 477
Alito, Samuel, 30, 209, 327, 552
  Roe v. Wade and, 129–30
allocation, 278
al Qaeda, 379, 454, 712
AMA (American Medical Association), 22, 528
ambition, political party control of, 479, 481
American Association of Retired Persons (AARP), 22, 23, 524–25, 529, 542, 553, 642, 650, 662
American Automobile Association (AAA), 542
American Bankers Association, 529
American Bar Association, 528, 642
American Civil Liberties Union (ACLU), 348
American Conservative, 565
American Enterprise Institute, 405, 529
American Farm Bureau Federation, 528

American Federation of State, County, and Municipal Employees, 528
American Independent Party, 509
American Medical Association (AMA), 22, 528
American Petroleum Institute, 263
American Political Science Association (APSA), 518
American Revolution, 37–38, 39, 43
Americans Coming Together (ACT), 513, 522–23
American Spectator, 582
American with Disabilities Act (ADA; 1990), 148, 348, 370
amicus curiae, 346, 348, 365
Amtrak, 284
Anderson, John, 461
Animal and Plant Health and Inspection Service (APHIS), 287
Annapolis Convention, 44, 45, 84
Anti-Ballistic Missile (ABM) Treaty, 681
Antifederalists, 38, 59–65, *60*, 73, 85, 118–19, 134
antitrust policies, 617
ANZUS (Australia, New Zealand and United States treaty), 703
APHIS (Animal and Plant Health and Inspection Service), 287
appellate courts, 339–40, 362
APSA (American Political Science Association), 518
Arizona, House seats gained by, 176
Armey, Dick, 184
Army Corps of Engineers, 226
Articles of Confederation, 42–45, 84
  adoption of, 42, 74
  Constitution vs., 56, 59, 72, 79
  flaws of, 43–44, 52, 78
artisans, 39, 40
Asbestos Hazard Emergency Act (1986), 97
Ashcroft, John, 28
Asia:
  authoritarian governments in, 5
  Bush's foreign policy and, 681
Asian Americans, party identity of, 492

Astroturf lobbying, 552
"At FEMA, Disaster and Politics Go Hand in Hand" (*New York Times*), 312–13
attitudes, 382
Australia, 703
  in coalition of the willing, 25
Australia ballot, 440–41
Austria, 711
authoritarian governments, 5
autocracy, 5
Ayres, Richard, 466

Baathist Party, 25–26, 688
Bai, Matt, 522–23
Baker, James, 250
Baker v. Carr, 340
Bakke, Allan, 150
Bakke case, 150, 153
balance of power, 693
balance-of-power role, 711, 713, 716
bandwagon effect, 414
Bank of the United States, 89, 621
banks, 602
banks, Federal Reserve, 289
bargaining, 12–13
Barron v. Baltimore, 122–23, 124–26, 133, 154
Bartels, Larry, 402
Barton, Joe, 412
Basques, 710
Bass Enterprises, 544
BCRA (Bipartisan Campaign Reform Act; 2002), 354, 464, 554–56
Beard, Charles, 46
Bedford, Gunning, 47
Beer, Samuel, 616
"Behind-The-Scenes Battle on Tracking Data Mining" (*New York Times*), 158–59
Belgium, elections in, 427
beliefs, 381
"benign" gerrymandering, 436
Benton v. Maryland, 128
Bernanke, Ben S., 628, 629
Bible, 316
bicameralism, 51, 64, 167–69
bilateral treaties, 703
Bill of Rights, 56, 59, 61, 66, 118–22
  Antifederalist demand for, 65, 134
  basis of, 52
  denationalization of, 130–32
  nationalization of, 127–30, 154

purpose of, 68, 69
state v.national, 122–27
see also specific amendments
bills, 18, 195, *196*
see also specific bills
bin Laden, Osama, 695, 709
Bipartisan Campaign Reform
Act (BCRA; 2002), 354,
464, 554–56
Bismark, Otto von, 661
Black, Duncan, 448
Blackmun, Harry, 355, 362,
424*n*
blacks, *see* African Americans
Blair, Tony, 378
block grants, 100
blogs (Web logs), 570
blue states, 400
Blunt, Roy, 183
Board of Health, New York, 668
Bonner and Associates, 552
Bono, 700
border security, 399
Bosnia, 224, 225, 678, 698, 707
Boston, Mass., Stamp Act in,
36
Boston Massacre, 40
Boston Tea Party, 37, 41,
44–45
Bowen, William, 466
Bowers v. Hardwick, 148
Brady Handgun Violence
Prevention Act (1993),
104, 416
Brandeis, Louis, 100*n*
branding, in political parties,
479*n*, 480, 491
Brennan, William J., 424*n*
Bretton Woods, N.H., 699
Breyer, Stephen, 30, 133, 327,
354
broadcast media, 567
Brookings Institution, 112, 529
Brown, Linda, 137
Brown, Oliver, 137
Brown University, 146
Brown v. Board of Education,
127, 136–38, 156, 340,
550, 641
threat to, 144
Warren's fears about, 366
"Brutus," 62, 65
Bryan, William Jennings, 502
Buchanan, Pat, 565
Buckley v. Valeo, 460
budget:
Congress and, 163, 627
president and, 627
Budget and Accounting Act
(1921), 295
Budget and Impoundment
Control Act (1974),
228*n*

budget deficit, 400, 627, 630,
667
bureaucracy, 270–313
appointment process and,
293
Congress and, 280–81,
296–97, 300–302
control of, 289–302
credibility of, 279
Defense Department and,
271–72
efficiency of, 279, 308–10
of executive branch,
282–89
foreign policy and, 683–85,
686, 695
Homeland Security
Department and,
270–72
motivational considerations
of, 290–92
possible reduction of, 302–8
principle-agent problem
and, 292–93
procedural control and,
293–94
war on terrorism and, 275
bureaucratic drift, 293, 302
Burger, Warren, 105, 133, 145
Burnham, Walter, 427
Burr, Aaron, 438
Bush, George H. W., 99, 152,
203, 295
Cheney as secretary of defense for, 249, 680
Congress and, 214
education policies of,
665–66
Greenspan reappointed by,
628
Gulf War waged by, 25, 697
Iraq War and, 698–99
Joint Chiefs of Staff and,
249
judicial appointees of,
326–27, 328, 353, 369
1992 election loss of, 449,
629
NSC and, 249
OMB under, 249
Panama invasion ordered by,
224
partisan struggles and, 202
Powell's work for, 681
public appearances of, 256
regulatory review used by, 4
reporters and, 581
Rice's work for, 681
UN and, 706–7
as vice president, 250
Bush, George W.:
abortion ban desired by, 366
ads for, 460

agricultural subsidies increased by, 614
appointments by, 246
approval ratings, 256
bipartisanship requested by,
490
"Bush Doctrine" of, 219,
679, 683, 695, 696,
706–7, 708, 710
cabinet of, 246
Cheney as vice president of,
249–50
communication skills of,
263
as compassionate conservative, 396
Congress and, 214
diplomacy of, 695
drug company funding of,
524–25
education policies of,
666–67
in election of 2000,
314–16, 363, 424*n*, 439,
451, 461, 493, 504, 531
in election of 2004, 23, 25,
27, 383, 401, 427*n*, 439,
447–48, 451, 452–58,
465, 470, 504, 592
ergonomics standard and,
265
executive offices and, 260
executive orders issued by,
262–63
executive privilege claimed
by, 337
faith based initiatives policy
of, 531–32
federalism of, 100–101
filibuster threat and, 253
foreign policy inexperience
of, 680
framing and, 591
Greenspan reappointed by,
628
Homeland Security
Department created by,
233, 258, 612
hurricanes and, 226
"intelligence czar" and,
28–29
Internet as campaign tool
of, 513
Iraq War and, 25–26, 225,
378–80, 564–65,
594–95, 678, 705
judicial nominations of,
208–9, 326, 359, 643
Kuhn as friend of, 547
management strategy of,
295
media portrayal of, 406–7,
582

Bush, George W.: *(cont.)*
    Medicare bill signed by, 22,
        252, 253
    Medicare spending of, 651
    Miers nomination and, 327,
        552
    military tribunals set up by,
        320
    national protection and, 223
    No Child Left Behind Act
        and, 99, 102
    nomination acceptance
        speech of, 383
    partisanship and, 202–3,
        444
    Pentagon budget increased
        by, 615
    policies of, 487
    public appearances of, 256
    public opinion and, 403–4
    regulatory review used by, 4
    Roe v. Wade and, 129
    Rumsfeld as secretary of de-
        fense for, 681
    same sex marriage and, 86
    senate partisanship and, 169
    September 11 terrorist at-
        tacks and, 271, 583
    Social Security reform and,
        164, 192, 399, 642, 644,
        649–51, 674–75
    Soros's donations against,
        464
    as strict constructionist, 362
    Supreme Court nominees
        of, 30, 552
    tax policies of, 26, 402, 625,
        626, 629, 636–37
    Terri Schiavo and, 81
    U.S.S. *Abraham Lincoln*
        speech of, 574
    veto and, 229, 232, 234–35
    war on terrorism of, 251,
        337–38, 395
    White House Office of
        Legislative Affairs cre-
        ated by, 114
Bush, Jeb, 80–81, 512
Bush, Laura, 251, 256
Bush Doctrine, 219, 679, 683,
    695, 696, 706–7, 708,
    710
Bush v. Gore, 328–29
business development, 613–14
Butler, Pierce, 49
by-product theory, 14–15
Byrd, Robert, 206n, 610

cabinet, 3, 246, 282
Cable News Network (CNN),
    567, 573, 575, 577
Calendar, Congressional, 643
California:

gerrymandering in, 177–78
House districts in, 198
illegal alien referendum in,
    443
Proposition 209 in, 416–17
recall election in, 443–44
retirees in, 662
same sex marriage and, 86
welfare in, 100
California, University of, 150
California Civil Rights
    Initiative, 153
Cameron, Charles M., 240, 251
campaign contributions, 10n
campaign finance, 458
Canada, 44
    in NATO, 693
    prescription drugs from,
        652, 653
canals, 602, 613
cancer, 668
capitalism, 660
    Cold War and, 694
    tax laws and, 625–26
    see also market economy
Cardozo, Benjamin, 126
Carter, Jimmy, 30, 250, 618,
    622
    draft evaders pardoned by,
        226
Carter, Rosalynn, 250
Case Act (1972), 210
casework, 172
categorical grants-in-aid, 92,
    94, 614
Catholics, 686
caucuses, 182, 183, 192, 212,
    513–16
CBO (Congressional Budget
    Office), 98, 192, 627
CBS Evening News, 569, 581
CBS News, 402–3, 573, 577
CCA (Correction Corporation
    of America), 553
CDA (Communication
    Decency Act) (1996),
    134, 572
CDC (Centers for Disease
    Control), 274
CEA (Council of Economic
    Advisers), 245–46,
    248–49
Celebrex, 642
Center for Individual Rights,
    349
Centers for Disease Control
    (CDC), 274
Central Imaging Office (CIO),
    684
Central Intelligence Agency
    (CIA), 28, 224, 249,
    263, 284, 683, 684, 685,
    686

Chamber of Commerce, 405
charities, 645
Chase, Samuel, 198
checks and balances, *58, 107*
    and deference to president,
        111
    definition of, 58, 106
    executive privilege and, 228
    Federalists on, 65
    McCarthyism and, 73
Cheney, Dick, 246, 249–50,
    295–96, 337, 594, 696
    experience of, 680
Cheney, Lynne, 249
Chicago, University of,
    National Opinion
    Research Center, 410
Children and Families
    Department, 81
China, 708
    Christians in, 686
    intellectual theft in, 686
    Internet in, 135
    in UN, 697
Christian Coalition, 531, 688
Christian Right, 531, 539
    lobbying by, 688
Christian Science Monitor, 576
CIA (Central Intelligence
    Agency), 28, 224, 249,
    263, 284, 683, 684, 685,
    686
CIO (Central Imaging Office),
    684
city-council elections, 433, 434
City of Boerne v. Flores, 104
civil law, 317, *318*
civil liberties, 73, 120, 130–33
    Brown v. Board of Education,
        127
    definition of, 154, 156
    nationalization of, 124
    Plessy v. Ferguson, 127
    right to privacy as, 128–29
    in war, 218
    see also Bill of Rights
civil rights, 73, 97, 120–21,
    133–56, *143*, 353, 393,
    494, 503–4, 536, 539
    Brown v. Board of Education,
        127
    controversies regarding,
        121–22
    definition of, 156
    Fourteenth Amendment
        and, 133, 135–36
Civil Rights Act (1875), 101,
    133
Civil Rights Act (1964), 142,
    261
    Title VII, 144–45, 147
Civil Rights Act (1991), 151,
    348

Civil Rights Commission, 142
civil rights movement, 588,
    589
Civil War, U.S., 82, 123, 211,
    223, 393, 500
    draft during, 6
    pensions for veterans of,
        645
    taxes in, 624n
Clark, Dick, 544
class, in party identity, 493,
    494
class action suits, 368, 642
Clay, Henry, 439, 500
Clayton Act (1914), 618
Cleveland, Grover, 439
clientele agency, 284–85
client state, 692
Clinton, Bill, 251, 504, 624
    affirmative action and, 151,
        152
    approval ratings of, 256
    budget victories of, 263
    cabinet of, 246
    campaigns of, 447
    "Contract with America"
        and, 73
    Democratic support for,
        480–81
    "Don't ask, don't tell" policy
        of, 148, 237
    elections of, 202, 493
    executive agencies and, 260
    executive orders issued by,
        261–62
    executive privilege claimed
        by, 337
    fiscal responsibility and, 456
    foreign policy inexperience
        of, 680
    gay rights and, 237
    Gore as vice president of,
        250
    Greenspan reappointed by,
        628
    Greenspan's advice to, 629
    health care initiative of, 22,
        201, 207, 490, 669
    impeachment of, 169, 210,
        488, 505
    judicial nominees of, 326,
        327, 643
    line-item veto used by, 229
    management strategy of,
        295
    Medicare reform vetoed by,
        22–23
    military base closings pro-
        posed by, 287
    "momentum" and, 591
    Motor Voter bill signed by,
        432
    MoveOn.org and, 541, 542

    on MTV, 585
    as "new Democrat," 486
    new federalism and, 100
    Northern Ireland and, 695
    partial-birth abortion bill
        vetoed by, 195
    as party leader, 490
    polls taken by, 511
    Powell's work for, 681
    regulatory review used by,
        4, 265
    reporters and, 581, 582, 584
    scandals of, 109, 228, 566,
        569, 582, 585, 590, 594
    scrutiny of private life of,
        424, 451
    September 11 terrorist at-
        tacks and, 271
    Supreme Court appoint-
        ments of, 133
    veto and, 229
    welfare reform of, 644, 656,
        662
Clinton, George, 61
Clinton, Hillary, 31, 251
Clinton administration, public
    relations efforts of, 403
closed primary, 484
closed rule, 193
cloture, 194
CNN (Cable News Network),
    567, 573, 577
CNN.com, 569
coalitional drift, 294
coalition of the willing, 25–26,
    678
coal mines, 610
Coast Guard, 226
    in DHS, 3, 272
Cochran, Thad, 200
coercion, 6, 7, 85
coinage, 602
COLAs (cost-of-living adjust-
    ments), 647, 653, 655
Cold War, 677–78, 683, 694,
    705, 706, 708, 712
    American unilateralism
        ended by, 677
collective action, 11–15, 22,
    198, 610
    benefits of, 537–39, 538,
        540
    Internet as overcoming bar-
        riers to, 541–42
    logic of, 536–37
    see also interest groups
collective action principle, 11,
    22, 24, 31, 32
    American Revolution and,
        40–41
    bargaining and, 325
    benefits as solutions in, 539,
        542

    Bill of Rights and, 119, 155
    Brown v. Board of Education
        and, 139, 155
    bureaucracy and, 279, 310
    civil rights movement and,
        139, 155
    coalitional drift and, 294,
        310
    Congress and, 164, 180,
        182, 195, 206, 207, 213,
        234, 253, 264, 302, 310
    at Constitutional
        Convention, 49
    coordination across
        branches for lobbying in,
        548
    crises and, 298, 310
    Fed's Board of Governor's
        and, 629, 633
    foreign policy and, 683,
        690, 706, 715
    and government involve-
        ment in economy, 611,
        633
    grants-in-aid and, 92, 113
    G. W. Bush and, 27–28
    interest groups and, 201,
        404
    lack of support for radical
        change in, 400
    legal system and, 330
    logrolling and, 207
    media and, 574, 584, 596
    No Child Left Behind and,
        103
    orchestrated campaigns for
        political ideas in, 402
    parties and, 182, 479–80,
        485, 487, 489, 498, 516,
        520
    political participation chan-
        neled into elections in,
        426
    poverty and, 662
    president and, 234, 239,
        240, 251, 253, 264
    prisoner's dilemma and, 535
    public opinion and over-
        coming problems in,
        551
    state competition and, 100,
        113
    Supreme Court and, 31,
        343, 371
    veto and, 232
    whip system and, 206
Colorado:
    attempted redistricting in,
        437
    constitution of, 148–49
    presidential election of
        2004 in, 439
    commander in chief, 223–24

commerce, 60, 91–92
  in Constitution, 53, 73
  state power and, 75
Commerce and Labor
    Department, U.S.,
    284–85
commerce clause, 89, 686
Commerce Department, U.S.,
    226
Committee on Administrative
    Management, 294–95
Committee on Civil Rights,
    640
Committee on Committees,
    481
committee system, 17, 182,
    184–91, 204, 212, 214
  authority of, 187–88
  conference committees,
    194–95
  deliberation in, 193
  discharge petition in, 190
  gatekeeping authority of,
    187
  hierarchy in, 189
  interest groups and, 201–2
  jurisdiction of, 186–87
  oversight of, 188
  proposal power of, 187–88
  reform of, 191
  see also specific committees
Common Cause, 405, 533
common law, 339
commons, 16
Communication Decency Act
    (CDA) (1996), 134, 572
communications, 644
communism, Cold War and,
    694
Communist Party, 389, 422,
    434
companies, regulation and, 619
compassionate conservatism,
    100, 102
Compromise of 1850, 500
Concerned Senators for the
    Arts, 192
Concord, battle of, 37
concurrent powers, 85
Conference Board, 449
conference committee, 188,
    194–95
Congress, U.S., 212, 214, 221,
    303, 400
  AFDC and, 655
  affirmative action strength-
    ened by, 151
  agenda of, 642–43
  airline assistance of, 603, 604
  under Articles of
    Confederation, 42–45
  Bank of the United States
    and, 89

budget and, 248, 630
bureaucracy and, 280–81,
    296–97, 300–302,
    309–10
cabinet departments cre-
    ated by, 3
Case Act passed by, 210
Cheney in, 249, 680
Civil War pensions enacted
    by, 645
Clinton's proposed military
    base closings and, 287
Committee on Committees
    in, 490
committee system, 185–91
compliance and, 181–82
in Connecticut Plan, 47
constituency in, 200–201
constitutional amendments
    and, 67
constitutional powers of,
    83, 89
constitutional principles
    and, 21
Contract with America and,
    98
decision-making process of,
    200–208
delegated powers and,
    222–23
deliberations of, 629
distributive tendency in,
    197, 199–200
districts of, 176–78
economic policy and, 243
effect of polls on, 415–16
electoral system and,
    169–78
electoral votes and, 438–39
executive branch vs., 164,
    179, 237, 238–39,
    263–64, 297
Fed created by, 289
First Amendment and, 68
foreign policy and, 163,
    234, 681, 682, 685–86,
    714
grants-in-aid and, 92, 94
grassroots campaigns and,
    551–53
Great Depression and, 603
gridlock of, 264
Homeland Security
    Department creation
    and, 233
impeachment power of, 210
incumbency and, 170–76
information and, 181
interest groups and, 527,
    545, 548–49, 686
interstate commerce and,
    91, 130
judicial review and, 333

legislative priorities of, 506,
    507
lobbying of, 545–46
logrolling in, 206–7
loss of power by, 245
Medicare spending of, 652
in nineteenth century, 211
Nixon and, 228
No Child Left Behind Act
    and, 99
103rd, 202
104th, 183, 191
107th, 191
108th, 25
109th, 183
organization of, 167–69,
    182–92
oversight and, 296–97,
    300–302
party loyalty in, 505–6
party system and, 476, 477,
    487–90
political struggles in, 4
"presidential government"
    and, 245
presidential nomination by,
    221–22
presidential power and, 18,
    163–64, 252
problems of legislation by,
    178–82
procedural rules of,
    192–200, 212
promotional policy and, 616
representation in, 165–67,
    166
Republican control of, 504
seniority rule in, 189
and separation of powers,
    80
September 11 terrorist at-
    tacks and, 30, 203, 219
social policies and, 641
Social Security reform of,
    164, 644
staff system in, 182, 191–92
standing committees in, 17
Supreme Court size de-
    cided by, 325
Supreme Court's relation-
    ship with, 354, 355,
    358, 367
term limits proposed for,
    164
Terri Schiavo and, 80–82
terrorism resolution passed
    by, 111
2004 farm bill of, 29
uncontrollable spending
    and, 630
U.S. budget and, 295
veto and, 198, 229, 232–33
Vietnam War and, 209–10

war powers of, 224–25
welfare reform and, 656, 657
whip system in, 206
see also House of Representatives, U.S.; Senate, U.S.
Congressional Black Caucus, 192, 212
Congressional Budget Office (CBO), 98, 192, 627
Congressional Caucus for Women's Issues, 192
Congressional Government (Wilson), 240
Congressional Quarterly, 651–52
Congressional Research Service, 192
Congressional Review Act (CRA), 265
congressional staff, 182, 191–92
Connecticut:
 Palko case in, 126
 privacy rights in, 128–29
 Virginia Plan opposition of, 47
Connecticut Compromise, 47
Conscience of a Conservative, The (Goldwater), 504
conscription, 6
Conservative Party, 506–7
conservatives, conservatism, 382, 395–97, 398, 417–18
 on college professors, 393
 "Contract with America" and, 73
 defining of, 395
 Greenspan approved by, 628
 in media, 564
 Medicare reform and, 23
 as Republican base, 454, 486, 493, 504
 Social Security and, 647–48
 Tenth Amendment and, 101
 war and, 688
constituency, 165
Constitution, U.S., 2–3, 37, 38, 39, 56, 75, 82–83, 317, 416, 527
 amendments to, 55–56, 65–71, 67, 70, 71, 72, 86, 358
 Article I, 18n, 52, 53, 57, 68, 73, 75, 88, 89, 91, 109, 127, 162, 228, 240–41, 321–22, 692
 Article II, 53, 57, 75, 220–21, 222–24, 227, 228

Article III, 54–55, 57, 68, 75, 321–22, 341, 370
Article IV, 55, 75, 84, 85, 87–88, 225
Article V, 55, 66, 75
Article VI, 55, 75, 333, 335
Article VII, 56, 75
commerce clause in, 89, 646
Congress in, 83, 89, 168, 212
as contract, 79
direct elections in, 437
equality and, 393
executive branch in, 53–54, 220–25, 237, 240, 265–66
expressed powers in, 84
House of Representatives in, 168
impeachment power of, 210
implied powers in, 84
institutions in, 16, 19
interest and principle in, 45–46
judicial branch in, 54–55, 325, 333–35, 341
legislative branch in, 53, 162, 224–25
national government restrained by, 109
necessary and proper clause in, 53, 64, 84
Nineteenth amendment to, 429
president in, 261
privileges and immunities clause in, 87
public order in, 612
ratification of, 59–62
representation in, 62–63
Senate in, 168, 208
slavery in, 47–49
state sovereignty in, 2
supremacy clause in, 55, 64, 333, 335
Supreme Court and, 83
Twenty-sixth amendment to, 429
vice presidency in, 249
war powers in, 224–25, 684
writing of, 118–20
see also Antifederalists; Bill of Rights; federalism; Federalists; separation of powers; *specific amendments*
constitutional amendments:
 First, 121–22, 126, 128, 131, 156, 342–43, 364, 556, 572, 573, 688
 Second, 68, 121
 Third, 68, 129

Fourth, 68, 128, 129
Fifth, 68, 121, 122, 125, 129, 319, 612–13
Sixth, 68
Seventh, 68
Eighth, 68
Ninth, 129, 130
Tenth, 85, 101, 103
Eleventh, 69, 103–4
Twelfth, 439
Thirteenth, 66, 69, 70, 133
Fourteenth, 66, 69n, 70, 81, 123–26, 127–28, 128n, 133, 135–36, 137–38, 154, 156, 339, 362, 655
Fifteenth, 66, 133, 136
Sixteenth, 70
Seventeenth, 52
Eighteenth, 66, 70
Twentieth, 68–69
Twenty-first, 66
Twenty-second, 69
Twenty-fifth, 69
Twenty-seventh, 70
Constitutional Convention, 44, 48, 72, 84, 118
constitutional governments, 5
constitutional interpretation, 332
constitutionalism, 79
Consumer Confidence Index, 449
Consumer Price Index, 647
Consumer Product Safety Act (1972), 239
Consumer Product Safety Commission (CPSC), 239, 618, 669
containment, 694
Continental Airlines, 546
Continental Congress, First, 41–42
Continental Congress, Second, 42
contract cases, 317
contracting power, 615
contracts, 79, 606
Contract with America, 73, 98, 103
contributory welfare programs, 640, 647, 657
conventions, national, 513–15
 see also Democratic National Conventions; Republican National Conventions
Cooper, Matthew, 575
cooperative federalism, 91–95
Cooper v. Aaron, 141n
Correction Corporation of America (CCA), 553
"corrupt bargain," 439
Corsicans, 710

Corzine, Jon, 170, 460
cost-of-living adjustments
        (COLAs), 647, 653, 655
Council of Economic Advisers
        (CEA), 245–46,
        248–49
Council on Environmental
        Quality, 248–49
court appeals, 319
Court of Appeals, U.S., 314,
        324, 343
    Eleventh Circuit, 81
    Fifth Circuit, 151
Court of Appeals for the
        Federal Circuit, U.S.,
        321
Court of Federal Claims, U.S.,
        321
Court of International Trade,
        U.S., 321
Court of Military Appeals,
        U.S., 321
Court of Veterans Appeals,
        U.S., 321
courts, 314–75
    appellate, 339–40
    decision-making in, 362–63
    dispute resolution and,
        329–32
    interest groups and, 549–50
    political struggles in, 4
    regulation and, 619
    see also judicial branch;
        Supreme Court, U.S.
court system, 319–29, 320
Cox, Chris, 546
Cox, Gary W., 479n
Cox, Rebecca, 546
CPSC (Consumer Product
        Safety Commission),
        239, 618, 669
CRA (Congressional Review
        Act), 265
Crawford, William H., 439
Crime Control Act (1994),
        416
criminal law, 317, 318, 353
Croatia, 698
Cuba, 389, 580
Cuban Americans, 387, 388
Customs Service, in DHS, 3,
        272
Czech Republic, 703

Daily Show, The, 570
Daschle, Tom, 29, 170, 173,
        174, 184, 452
Davie, William R., 49
Davis, Gray, 443–44
Dean, Howard, 513, 541, 570
Debs, Eugene, 134
debt relief, 700
decentralization, 18

decisiveness, 17, 19
Declaration of Independence,
        42, 74
defendants, 317
Defenders of Wildlife, 369–70
defense, 8–9, 609
Defense Base Closure and
        Realignment
        Commission, 306
Defense Department, U.S.,
        271–72, 285, 286–87,
        573, 683, 684, 702
    creation of, 3, 270
    in war on terrorism, 27
Defense Intelligence Agency
        (DIA), 28, 684
Defense of Marriage Act
        (1996), 86
Delaware, 198
    school segregation in, 137
    Virginia Plan opposition of,
        47
DeLay, Tom, 183n, 204, 276,
        437, 545
delegated powers, 222–23
delegates, 165
delegation, 18, 19
deliberative polling, 420–21
Dell, Inc., 544
democracy, 5
    Cold War and, 694
    representative, 18
    as weakened by political
        inattentiveness, 399
Democratic Forum, 192
Democratic National
        Committee (DNC),
        515, 553
Democratic National
        Conventions:
    of 1972, 515
    of 1992, 413
    of 1996, 413
Democratic Party, 182
    ads for, 460, 461
    advocacy groups for, 556
    African Americans and, 588
    airline bailout and, 604
    "benign" gerrymandering
        and, 436
    Bush's judicial nominees
        and, 359
    Bush's proposed Social
        Security reform and, 651
    California gerrymandering
        and, 177–78
    candidate image and, 451
    civil rights movement and,
        503–4
    Clinton's impeachment
        and, 169
    collective action favored by,
        22

    on contributory programs,
        657
    divisions within, 503–4
    as doveish, 390
    1864 peace platform of, 515
    filibuster threat and, 253
    funding of, 458
    Great Depression and, 503,
        603
    GWB's court appointees
        and, 326, 327
    history of, 498–506
    Iraq War and, 380
    Jackson's founding of, 241,
        499
    Latino support for, 389
    legislative priorities of, 506,
        507
    liberalism in, 504, 509
    loyalty to, 393
    Lyndon Johnson and, 234
    media and, 582
    Medicare and, 652
    members of, 202, 203–4
    neoconservatives' reaction
        to, 689
    New Deal and, 503
    "new Democrats" in, 486
    1968 election and, 506
    1972 national convention
        of, 434
    in 1994 election, 173–74
    No Child Left Behind and,
        99, 103
    opportunities in 2004 elec-
        tions of, 452–54
    PACs and, 541, 555
    partisanship and, 30–31,
        203, 205
    reporters in, 581
    Republicans' differences
        with, 423, 486
    Social Security irresponsi-
        bility of, 649
    tax cuts pledged by, 626
    Terri Schiavo and, 81
    Texas gerrymandering and,
        178
    in 2004 election, 27, 427n
    welfare reform and, 657,
        662
    white southerners in,
        393–94, 500–501, 503
Democratic-Republican party,
        see Republican party
        (Jeffersonian)
Democratic Study Group, 192
Depository Institution
        Deregulation and
        Monetary Control Act
        (1980), 618
Depression, Great, 220, 242,
        393, 408–9, 503, 532

deregulation, 306, 618, 691
Deschler's Procedures, 17
desegregation, 140–44
deterrence, 694, 705, 708–10
devolution, 100, 111–12,
    306–8
DHS, *see* Homeland Security
    Department, U.S.
DIA (Defense Intelligence
    Agency), 684
Diet, Japanese, 163
Dingell, John, 544, 546
diplomacy, 694–96, 702, 708
direct mail, 511–12
discount rate, 622
discretionary spending, 630
discrimination, 133
Disney, 528
dispute resolution, 329–32
Disraeli, Benjamin, 661
distributive tendency, 199
District Court, U.S., 81, 314,
    371
divided government, 108
division of labor, 278
DNC (Democratic National
    Committee), 515, 553
DOE, *see* Energy Department,
    U.S.
Dole, Bob, 103
"Don't ask, don't tell" policy,
    237
DOT, *see* Transportation
    Department, U.S.
double jeopardy, 126, 128
Douglas, Stephen, 407, 500
Douglas, William O., 129, 347
Downs, Anthony, 448
Dred Scott case, 108
Drobny, Anita, 568
Drudge, Matt, 569
Drug Enforcement Agency,
    272
dual federalism, 89–90, 111
dual loyalty, 686
Ducks Unlimited, 534
due process of law, 126,
    322–23
Duke Power Company, 145
Duncan v. Louisiana, 128*n*
duties, 163
Duverger, Maurice, 433*n*, 480
Duverger's Law, 433*n*

Early, Stephen, 255
earmarks, 172, 556
Earned Income Tax Credit
    (EITC), 646, 656
East India Company, 41
"Echoes of 1986? Not in
    Bush's Tax Reform
    Panel" (*New York Times*),
    636–37

economic aid, 700–702
economic class, in party iden-
    tity, 493, 494
economic expansion role,
    711–12, 716
economics, economy, 452, 455,
    496, 602–37
    business development and,
        613–14
    capitalist, 611
    Congress and, 243
    election outcomes affected
        by, 449
    executive branch and,
        243–44
    fiscal policies and, 622, 624
    government spending and,
        627, 630
    market, 605–11, 632, 634
    monetary policies and,
        621–22
    public order and, 612
    taxation and, 624–27
    see also Federal Reserve
        System; taxes
Economist, 650
Edison Electric Institute,
    547
education, 392–93, *394*, 398,
    404, 553, 665–66, 671
    and equality of opportunity,
        639
    for illegal aliens, 348–49
    labor force and, 607–8
    vouchers for, 667–68
    see also No Child Left
        Behind Act
Education Act (1972), 146,
    263, 274
Education Department, U.S.,
    102, 263–64, 285, 586,
    665
    Office for Civil Rights, 146
Edwards, John, 249–50, 380,
    455
Egypt, 370
Eighteenth Amendment, 66,
    70
Eighth Amendment, 68
Eisenhower, Dwight D., 141,
    225, 424*n*, 614*n*
    on "military-industrial com-
        plex," 615
Eisenstadt v Baird, 549–50
EITC (Earned Income Tax
    Credit), 646, 656
elastic clause, 53
Election Day, 467, 469,
    484–85
election of 2004, 23, 24, 25,
    26–27, 30, 252, 328,
    452–58, 478, *508*
    Daschle's loss in, 173, 174

Dean in, 513
    Democratic opportunities
        in, 452–54
    distribution of electoral
        votes in, *453*
    incumbency and, 173
    judicial appointments and,
        328
    media and, 592
    Nader in, 509
    outcomes and results of,
        455, 458
    presidential debates in, 455
    Republican strategies for,
        454–55
election outcomes, candidates'
    personal attributes and,
    450–51
election reform, 539
elections, U.S., 4, 11, 30,
    249–50, 361, 422–75,
    481–82
    of 1800, 438–39, 498
    of 1824, 438–39, 499
    of 1828, 499
    of 1832, 499
    of 1840, 499–500
    of 1856, 500
    of 1858, 500
    of 1860, 500
    of 1864, 515
    of 1876, 439
    of 1888, 439
    of 1892, 502
    of 1896, 502
    of 1928, 503
    of 1932, 220, 503
    of 1936, 408
    of 1948, 509
    of 1964, 504
    of 1968, 504, 506, 509
    of 1972, 589
    of 1992, 173, 176, 202,
        493, 506, 629
    of 1994, 22, 173–74, 176,
        198–99, 208, 234
    of 1996, 493, 506
    of 1998, 490, 512
    of 2000, 328, 439, 493,
        504, 509, 512
    of 2002, 25
    campaign finance in, 458,
        478
    criteria for victory in, 433
    electoral composition and,
        427–28, 432
    frequency of, 439–40
    funding for, 458
    issues, 447
    media and, 592–93
    midterm, 467
    nominations for, 482–84,
        489, 505–6

elections, U.S., *(cont.)*
partisan loyalty in, 444–46, 479*n*, 480
primary, 483–84, 488–89
rational behavior and, 474–75
registration for, 427, 430–32
turnout of, 425–32, *428*, 432
voters' decisions in, 444–51
see also voting rights
electoral college, 221, 437–39, 468
electoral system, 169–78
Elementary and Secondary Education Act (ESEA) (1965), 664–65
Eleventh Amendment, 69, 103–4
Ellsworth, Oliver, 47
Emergency Price Control Act (1942), 336
EMILY's List, 170, 464
eminent domain, 612–13
employment, discrimination in, 144
Endangered Species Act (1973), 370, 543
energy, 644
Energy Department, U.S., 226, 285
Engel v. Vitale, 340
England, 246
Enron, 300
entitlement, 655
environment, 73, 97, 180, 461, 608, 609, 610, 617, 644
Environmental Defense Fund, 533
environmental groups, 347, 688
Environmental Impact Statement, 237
Environmental Protection Agency (EPA), 237, 238, 261, 274, 547, 618, 669
EOP (Executive Office of the President), 248–49, 255, 259, 263
EPA (Environmental Protection Agency), 237, 238, 261, 274, 547, 618, 669
equality of opportunity, 383, 638–39
equal protection clause, 133
Equal Rights Amendments (ERA), 551
equal time rule, 572
ERA (Equal Rights Amendments), 551

"era of good feelings," 498
ERP (European Recovery Program), 701, 702
Ervin committee, 554
Escobedo v. Illinois, 340
ESEA (Elementary and Secondary Education Act) (1965), 664–65
Espy, Mike, 436
Establishment Clause, 353
ethnic cleansing, 698
Europe:
American sovereignty and, 692
authoritarian governments in, 5
balance of power in, 693
Bush's foreign policy and, 681
commons in, 16
in IMF, 700
in NATO, 693
proportional representation in, 433
European Recovery Program (ERP), 701, 702
exclusionary rule, 128
exclusive powers, 54
executive agreements, 209, 227, 686
executive branch, 270–313
Congress vs., 164, 179, 237, 238–39, *297*
in Constitution, 53–54, 220–25, 237, 240, 265–66
deliberations of, 629
economy and, 243–44
foreign policy and, 234
interest groups' lobbying of, 547–48, 686
judicial branch vs., *58*
legislative branch vs., *58*, 195, 211
organization of, 282–89
oversight and, 188
political struggles in, 4
Supreme Court decisions and, 359
see also presidency
Executive Office of the President (EOP), 248–49, 255, 259, 263
Executive Order No. 8248, 237
Executive Order No. 11246, 261
Executive Order No. 12291, 237, 618
executive orders, 235, 236–37, 260–63, *262*
executive privilege, 109, 227–28

expressed powers, 53, 84, 222
expropriation, 612
externalities, of market activities, 608

factions, 620
Fair Deal, 211
Fair Labor Standards Act (1938), 646
fairness doctrine, 572
Family Research Council, 531
Farewell Address (Washington), 676, 688, 691
Farm Credit Administration (FCA), 613
Farm Credit System, 613
farmers:
in colonial America, 39, 40
price supports and, 4
subsidies and, 168, 208, 603, 614, 630, 662, 663
Farmers Home Administration (FMHA), 613
Faubus, Orval, 141, 225
Faulkner, Shannon, 146
FBI (Federal Bureau of Investigation), 224, 274, 284, 286, 684, 685
FCA (Farm Credit Administration), 613
FCC (Federal Communications Commission), 284, 572, 577
FDA (Food and Drug Administration), 112, 260, 261, 274, 287
FDIC (Federal Deposit Insurance Corporation), 622
FEC (Federal Election Commission), 284, 458, 460, 556
federal appellate courts, 324
Federal Aviation Administration, 274
Federal Bureau of Investigation (FBI), 224, 274, 284, 286, 684, 685
Federal Campaign Finance Regulation, *462–63*
Federal Communications Commission (FCC), 284, 572, 577
Federal Deposit Insurance Corporation (FDIC), 622
Federal Election Campaign Act (1971), 459, 553
Federal Election Commission (FEC), 284, 458, 460, 556

Federal Elections Campaign
  Act (1972), 461
Federal Emergency
  Management Agency
  (FEMA), 198–99, 226,
  312–13
  in DHS, 3
  Hurricane Katrina and,
    298–99, 684
"Federal Farmer," 62, 65
federal funds rate, 622
Federal Housing
  Administration (FHA),
  613
federalism, 59, 80, *90, 110,*
  240–41, 691–92, 693
  in Constitution, 84–88
  cooperative, 92–95
  definition of, 56, 79, 83
  dual, 89–92, 111
  grants-in-aid, 91–95
  layer cake v. marble cake,
    94, *95*
  new, 100
  No Child Left Behind and,
    102
  regulated, 97–99
  separation of powers and,
    82–88, 111–12, 114
  Supreme Court and, 101,
    103–5, 128
Federalist Papers, 38, 61–62,
  425, 437, 526
  No. 10, 620
  No. 51, 240–41, 670
Federalist party, 438, 477, 498,
  499
Federalists, 38, 59–65, *60,* 85,
  118–19, 198
Federalist Society, 362
federal jurisdiction, 320–23
Federal Occupation Safety and
  Health, 98
Federal Register, 281, 618
Federal Regulation of
  Lobbying Act, 543
Federal Reserve banks, 289
Federal Reserve Board,
  289–90, 621–22,
  628–29, 633
Federal Reserve System, 243*n,*
  288–89, 618, 621–22,
  628–29
federal service, 302–3
Federal Trade Act (1914),
  243*n,* 618
Federal Trade Commission
  (FTC), 284, 287, 618,
  619
federal trial courts, 324
FEMA (Federal Emergency
  Management Agency),
  199–99, 226, 312–13

in DHS, 3
  Hurricane Katrina and,
    298–99, 684
Ferejohn, John, 616–17
FHA (Federal Housing
  Administration), 613
FICA tax, 647
  see also Social Security tax
Fifteenth Amendment, 66,
  133, 136
Fifth Amendment, 68, 121,
  122, 125, 129, 319,
  612–13
Fifth Circuit Court, 349
Figueiredo, John de, 557
filibuster, 194, 199, 214, 233,
  253
Fillmore, Millard, 234
Finn, Ed, 569
Fiorina, Morris, 400, 456, 488
fire alarm oversight, 301–2
fireside chats, 574
First Amendment, 364, 688
  establishment clause of, 131
  freedom of the press and,
    572, 573
  issue advocacy and, 556
  national government and,
    121–22
  nationalization of, 126, 128,
    156
  religious ideas and, 342–43
First Continental Congress,
  41–42
First Hundred Days, 242
first lady, 250–51
fiscal policies, 622, 624
Fitzgerald, Patrick, 584–85
527 committees, 460, 464,
  541, 554–56
"Flare-Ups in Battle to Push or
  Bury Bush Social
  Security Plan" (*New York
  Times*), 674–75
Florida, 329, 424*n,* 439,
  441–42, 454, 455, 569
  House districts in, 198
  House seats gained by, 176
  retirees in, 662
  storm in, 225
Florida legislature, 315
FMHA (Farmers Home
  Administration), 613
FOIA (Freedom of
  Information Act)
  (1966), 281
Food and Drug Administration
  (FDA), 112, 260, 261,
  274, 287
Food for Peace, 702
Food Safety and Inspection
  Service, 284
food stamps, 23*n,* 654, 657

Ford, Gerald, 226, 438, 618,
  680
foreign entanglements, 676,
  678
foreign policy, 163, 676–716
  balance-of-power role, 711,
    713, 716
  bureaucracy and, 683–85,
    686, 695
  collective security and,
    702–5
  Congress and, 681, *682,*
    685–86, 714
  deterrence and, 694, 705,
    708–10
  diplomacy and, 694–96,
    702, 708
  economic aid and, 700–702
  economic expansion role in,
    711–12, 716
  Great Leap in, 693–94
  Holy Alliance role in, 711,
    712, 713, 716
  interest groups and, 686–88
  media and, 688–89
  Napoleonic role in, 710–11,
    713, 716
  president and, *602,* 680–83,
    686, 690, 695, 714
  values of, 691–94
Foreign Relations Committee,
  Senate, 686
Foreign Service Act (1946),
  692, 694
Forest Service, 284
formal bargaining, 12–13
formula grants, 94
Fourteenth Amendment, 66, 70,
  123–26, 133, 339, 655
  Barron v. Baltimore and,
    154, 156
  Bill of Rights and, 69*n,*
    127–28
  Brown v. Board of Education
    and, 137–38
  Plessy v. Ferguson and,
    135–36
  "right to privacy" and, 362
  Terri Schiavo and, 81
Fourth Amendment, 68, 128,
  129
Fourth Circuit Court of
  Appeals, 338
Fox Network News, 564, 567,
  576, 582
framework, 79
framing, 591
France, 38, 87, 227, 708, 710
  elections in, 427
  Iraq War and, 25, 699
  Paine's and Jefferson's sup-
    port for, 691
  in UN, 697

Frankfurter, Felix, 325, 352, 354
Franklin, Benjamin, 42
Franklin v. Gwinnett County Public Schools, 146
Franks, Thomas, 456
Frazier, Lynn, 444
Freedom Forum, 580
freedom of assembly, Supreme Court and, 126
Freedom of Information Act (FOIA) (1966), 281
freedom of speech, 566–67, 572
   Supreme Court and, 126
   see also First Amendment
freedom of the press, 572–73, 576
   Supreme Court and, 126
free riding, 8–9, 14
Free-Soilers, 500
Frémont, John C., 500
French and Indian wars, 39
Friedman, Milton, 628
Friends of the Earth, 405
Frist, Bill, 23, 184, 209
frontier, 645
FTC (Federal Trade Commission), 284, 287, 618, 619
Fulbright, J. William, 594
full faith and credit clause, 85–86
Fulton, Robert, 91

Gallagher, Maggie, 586
Gallup polls, 408, *411*
Garfield, James A., 234
Garrity, W. Arthur, 369
gatekeeping, 17–18, 187
Gates, Bill, 546
gay and lesbian movement, 148, 369, 456, 551, 556, 562
gender discrimination, 145–47
gender gap, 389
   in party identity, 492–93
General Accounting Office, 192
General Electric, 577
General Motors, 87, 528
General Services Administration, 226
Genêt, Edmond, 227
Genoa, Italy, WTO protest in, 688
geographical region, in party identity, 493–94
Georgia:
   House seats gained by, 176
   same sex marriage of, 86
   slavery in, 48
   Virginia Plan and, 47

Gephardt, Richard, 183, 208
Germany:
   Gulf War sponsored by, 698
   reunification of, 706
Germany, Nazi, 5
Gerry, Elbridge, 434
gerrymandering, 177–78, 434–36, 488
Gibbons v. Ogden, 91
GI Bill of Rights (1944), 64
Gideon v. Wainwright, 128, 339, 340
Gilens, Martin, 656
Gingrich, Newt, 303, 591
   education policies of, 667
   Medicare reform urged by, 22
   as Republican leader, 184
Ginsburg, Ruth Bader, 133, 315, 327, 354
going public strategy, 550–53
Goldberg, Arthur, 129
Goldberg v. Kelly, 655
Goldwater, Barry, 204*n*, 504
Gonzales v. Raich, 130
Gore, Al, 102, 250, 329, 438, 439, 447, 451, 460, 461, 504
   Social Security plan of, 649
government, U.S., 9
   American skepticism of, 9
   complexity of, 2–4
   definition of, 5
   divided, 108
   forms of, 5
   foundations of, 5–7
   media's disputes with, 402–3
   necessity of, 7–9
   responsible party, 518
   as restrained by Constitution, 109
   unified vs. divided, 251
   see also bureaucracy; federalism; *specific branches*
Government Accountability Office, 272–73
government spending, 400
Gramm-Rudman Act, 108–9
grants-in-aid, 91–95, 102, 111, 114
grassroots lobbying, 551–53
Gratz v. Bollinger, 152–53
Great Britain, *see* United Kingdom
Great Compromise, 47–48
Great Depression, 220, 242, 393, 408–9, 503, 532, 602–3, 611, 639, 640, 645
Great Society, 22, 23*n*, 211, 251, 503
Greece, 701
Green parties, 433

greens, 688
Greenspan, Alan, 628–29
   Medicare and, 652
Griffin v. Prince Edward County School Board, 141*n*
Griswold V. Connecticut, 128–29, 549
Grodzins, Morton, 94
Grutter v. Bollinger, 153
Guam, 321
   abortion laws in, 131*n*
Guantánamo Bay Naval Base, 109, 111
Gulf of Tonkin Resolution, 681
Gulf War, 25, 30, 449, 697, 703, 705, 707
gun laws, 404, 416, 460, 461
   see also Second Amendment

habeas corpus, 109, 111, 223, 323, 338
Hadley, Stephen, 246
Haiti, 711
Halliburton, 680
Hamdi, Yaser Esam, 338
Hamdi v. Rumsfeld, 338
Hamilton, Alexander, 44, 45, 52–53, 61, 62, 63, 65, 118, 119, 438–39, 498, 614–15, 621
   Washington's Farewell Address and, 691
Harrison, Benjamin, 439
Harrison, William Henry, 234, 499–500
Harris polls, *411*
Hart, J. Steven, 544, 546
Harvard University, 529
Hastert, Dennis, 28, 183
Hatch, Orrin, 326
Hawaii, same-sex marriage banned in, 149
Hawaii Supreme Court, 86
Hayes, Rutherford B., 439
Head Start, 23*n*
Health and Human Services Department, U.S., 226, 285, 287, 289
Hearst, William Randolph, 580
Heritage Foundation, 405
hidden information, 423
Highway Trust Fund, 173
Hill, Anita, 327
Hispanic Caucus, 192
history principle, 21, 23, 24, 31, 32
   American "exceptionalism" and, 707, 715
   bicameralism and, 168
   Brown v. Board of Education and, 138, 155
   budget and, 630, 633

bureaucracies and, 299, 303
civil rights movement and, 147, 155
committee system and, 185
Congress and, 164, 185, 211, 213
Constitution and, 83, 113
cooperative federalism and, 112
domestic policy and, 680
economy and, 244, 264
education and, 102, 113
egalitarian U.S. society as, 400
executive branch and, 221
executive orders and, 235, 264
foreign policy and, 692, 693, 701, 715
Goldberg v. Kelly and, 655, 673
government agencies and, 306
government expansion as, 531
Greenspan and, 628, 633
growth of interest group activity and, 531
G. W. Bush and, 29–30
Internet-based interest groups and, 541
judicial review and, 333
judiciary expansion and, 369, 371
media and, 593, 595, 596
national regulatory policies and, 618, 633
New Deal and, 244, 264
parties and, 489, 494, 520
presidency and, 242, 264, 296
public policy and, 605, 633
rights and, 134, 155
Roe v. Wade and, 129, 155
Shays's Rebellion and, 45, 74
of Southern support of GOP, 393
Stamp Act and, 38, 74
Supreme Court and, 31, 92, 113, 363
veto and, 234, 264
Vietnam War, 593, 596
voter turnout declines tied to registration requirements as, 430
welfare and, 645, 655, 673
Hitchens, Christopher, 569
HIV, 348
Hobbes, Thomas, 7–8
holds, 194, 208
Holmes, Oliver Wendell, 339, 366

Holy Alliance role, 711, 712, 716
Homeland Security Department, U.S., 31, 226, 285, 683–84, 685
creation of, 3, 25, 26, 28, 101, 233, 237, 251, 258, 270–72, 273, 274, 298, 612, 683
funding for, 99
Hurricane Katrina and, 28*n*, 298–99
war on terrorism and, 26, 27–28
home rule, 88
Home School Legal Defense Fund, 455
homesteading (squatting), 613
Hoover, Herbert, 503
executive orders of, 235
Hoover Institution, 405
Hopwood v. Texas, 151–52, 349
House of Commons, British, 41, 162
House of Representatives, U.S.:
Agriculture Committee of, 19, 183, 187, 189–90
airline bailout and, 604
Appropriations Committee of, 183, 184, 185, 197, 557
Armed Services Committee of, 186–87, 686
bicameralism and, 167–69
bills per session of, 187
Budget Committee of, 183
California gerrymandering and, 177–78
campaign committees of, 516
campaign expenditures for, *175*, 458, 482
checks and balances and, 106
Clinton's impeachment and, 169
committee meetings in, 297
committees reduced in, 164
in Connecticut Plan, 47
in Constitution, 48, 52
Constitutional amendments and, 66, 67
debate in, 193–94
defense bill passed by, 629
discharge petition in, 190
elections and, 68, 437
electoral college and, 438–39
electoral districts of, 439, 488–89
electoral system and, 169–78

Energy and Commerce Committee of, 187, 204*n*
ergonomics regulations and, 465
Ethics Committee of, 183, 204
Feedgrains Subcommittee of, 189
foreign policy and, 685
Gulf of Tonkin Resolution passed by, 682
impeachment power of, 210
"intelligence czar" and, 28
lawmaking ability of, 18*n*, 167–69
Medicare Act (2003) passed by, 22
organization of, 167–69, 183–84
organized labor and, 460–61
oversight and, 296
partisanship in, 169
party leadership in, 167–68
presidential elections and, 221
Republican control of, 504
rulebook for, 17
Rules Committee of, 185, 193, 194, 197, 199, 214
Science and Technology Committee of, 187
Senate vs., 216–17
seniority rule in, 189, 191
Social Security reform and, 644
subcommittees in, 188–89
Supreme Court judges and, 325–26
terms of, 52
Texas gerrymandering and, 178
turnovers in, 176
in 2004 elections, 25, 452
vetos overridden by, 195, 229
Washington's refusal of request by, 228
Water Resources Development Act and, 617
Ways and Means Committee of, 23, 184, 187
whip system in, 206
see also Congress, U.S.; Senate, U.S.; Speaker of the House
Housing and Urban Development Department (HUD), U.S., 23*n*, 285, 622

Hoyer, Steny, 183
HUD (Housing and Urban Development Department), 622
Hughes, Charles Evans, 83
Hughes, Karen P., 255–56, 403, 585
Hulse, Carl, 216–17
Human Rights Campaign Fund, 148
Hume, David, 8
Hungary, 703
hurricanes, 24
Hussein, Saddam, 25–26, 29, 225, 263, 378, 452–53, 564, 689, 696, 698–99

ICC (Interstate Commerce Commission), 284, 618
Idaho, 308
ideology, 539
    in party identity, 493
    in political parties, 505
"I Have a Dream" speech, 139
illusion of saliency, 413
IMF (International Monetary Fund), 699–700
immigrants, immigration, 387, 389, 399
    public opinion and, 387, 389
Immigration and Naturalization Services (INS), 226, 684
impeachment, 210
    see also Clinton, Bill, impeachment of; Johnson, Andrew, impeachment of
implementation, 279
implied power, 84
income distribution, 626
incumbency, 169, 170–76, 174
Independents with Disabilities Act, 99
indexing, 647
India, 708
individual rights, 79–80
Indonesia, 700
inflation, 624, 649
    contributory programs and, 657
    Medicare and, 651
informal bargaining, 12
informational benefits, 538
infotainment, 570
inherent powers, 223
initiatives, 443, 444
in-kind benefits, 654
In Re Oliver, 128n
INS (Immigration and Naturalization Services), 226, 684

institutional analysis, 198
institution principle, 15, 22, 24, 31, 32
    Articles of Confederation and, 44, 74
    Bill of Rights and, 128, 155
    Brown v. Board of Education and, 138, 155
    Budget and Accounting Act and, 295
    bureaucracies and, 280, 281
    and checks and balances, 105, 113
    committee system and, 185, 190, 193
    Congress and, 164, 165, 184, 185, 188, 190, 193, 213, 245, 264, 281, 294
    Constitution and, 83, 113
    courts and, 339, 341, 351
    election outcome effected by process as, 433, 442
    electoral college and, 221
    federalism and, 89, 113
    Federal Reserve Board and, 628, 633
    Federal Reserve System and, 624, 633
    foreign policy and, 684, 715
    government services and, 663
    G. W. Bush and, 28–29
    increasing voter turnout and, 467
    interest groups use of judicial branch and, 549
    Internet speech and, 134
    market economy and, 606, 609, 633
    media and, 574
    NATO and, 703, 715
    party rules and, 515, 520
    policy inconsistent with public opinion as, 416
    political participation regulated by electoral process as, 426
    pork-barrel legislation and, 616, 633
    presidency and, 223, 228, 229, 245, 263, 294
    primary elections and, 484, 520
    of representative government, 382
    separation-of-power and, 225
    and socialization and institutionalization of political action, 470
    Supreme Court and, 31, 362, 371
    third parties and, 510, 520

institutions, 15–19, 20–21
instrumental actions, 11
Intelligence Committee, House, 686
Intelligence Committee, Senate, 686
intelligence czar, 28–29
interest-group politics, 641
interest groups, 201–2, 207–8, 347, 404, 455, 526–60, 641–42
    access cultivated by, 548–49
    Congress and, 527, 545, 548–49
    cooperation facilitated by, 534–35
    courts and, 549–50
    economy and, 644
    foreign policy and, 686–88
    formation of, 530–34
    groups represented by, 534
    House of Representatives and, 168, 169
    increase in activity of, 531
    individual's contribution to, 537
    latent, 537
    organization of, 529
    PACs and, 10n, 553–56
    policy influence and, 543–56
    political struggles and, 4
    privileged, 537
    pros and cons of, 557–58
    upper class bias of members of, 530
    see also AARP; lobbies, lobbying
Interior Department, U.S., 284, 285, 370
Internal Relations Committee, 686
Internal Revenue Service (IRS), 238, 285–86, 684
International Arabian Horse Association, 684
International Bank for Reconstruction and Development, 699
International Business Machines, 528
International Monetary Fund (IMF), 699–700
International Relations Committee, House, 686
international trade, 644
Internet, 134–35, 274, 512–13, 519, 567, 569, 572
    political activism and, 541–42
Interstate Commerce Act (1887), 242, 243n, 618

Interstate Commerce
    Commission (ICC),
    284, 618
Interstate Highway Program,
    612
interstate highways, 97, 612,
    614
Iowa, 454
Iran, 25, 701, 708
    hostage crisis in, 30
    Internet in, 135
Iraq, 696, 707
    Internet in, 135
    Kuwait invaded by, 697
    nuclear capability of, 650
    state building in, 679
Iraq War, 24, 25–27, 29, 30,
    101, 678, 681, 689,
    698–99, 704–5
    bureaucracy and, 303
    Bush's popularity and, 256,
        378, 452
    casualties of, 256
    Constitution and, 686
    doubts over, 296
    Kerry on, 380, 447, 454
    in media, 564–65, 567,
        569, 584, 586–87,
        594–95
    outlays for, 624
    party division over, 380,
        460
    pork barrel politics and, 200
    public opinion and,
        378–80, 400, 452–53,
        455
    race and, 379
    Senate partisanship and,
        169, 203
    War Powers Resolution and,
        225
    WMDs and, 380
Ireland, Irish Americans and,
    686–87
Irish Americans, Ireland and,
    686–87
Irish Republican Army, 686
irreversibilities, 21, 24
IRS (Internal Revenue
    Service), 238, 285–86,
    684
isolationism, 691, 693
Israel, 695, 710, 713
    Jewish Americans and,
        686–87
Issa, Darrell, 443–44
issue advocacy, 460
Italy, totalitarian government
    in, 5

Jackson, Andrew, 361, 439
    Democratic party founded
        by, 241, 499

as strong president, 241
Jackson, Robert, 352
Jacksonian period, 498–500
Japan, 703
    in coalition of the willing,
        25
    Gulf War sponsored by, 698
    in IMF, 700
    totalitarian government in,
        5
Japanese Americans, intern-
    ment of, 218–19, 261
Jay, John, 61, 62
JCOS (Joint Chiefs of Staff),
    249, 680, 683
Jebware, 512
Jefferson, Thomas, 42, 89, 118,
    120, 198, 234, 621, 691
    electoral college and,
        438–39
    executive branch under, 241
Jeffords, James, 23
Jewish Americans, 458
    Israel and, 686–87
Johnson, Andrew, 253–54
    Confederate amnesty given
        by, 226
    impeachment of, 210, 211,
        254
Johnson, Lady Bird, 250
Johnson, Loch K., 686
Johnson, Lyndon B., 234–35,
    250, 503–4
    affirmative action imple-
        mented by, 149
    Civil Rights Act order of,
        261
    Great Society of, 23n, 211,
        251, 503
    polls and, 408
    vice presidency of, 249
    Vietnam War and, 30
Johnston, J. Bennett, 207
Joint Chiefs of Staff (JCOS),
    249, 680, 683
Jones, Charles, 256
Jones & Laughlin Steel
    Corporation, 243
judges, 317
    appointment of, 325–26,
        489
judicial activism, 355
judicial branch, 314–75
    in Constitution, 54–55,
        325, 333–35, 341
    executive vs., 58
    legislative vs., 58
    see also Supreme Court,
        U.S.
judicial restraint, 354
judicial review, 55, 109,
    333–41, 334
    of Congress, 333

of federal agency action,
    335–37
lawmaking and, 338–41
presidential power and, 337
Judiciary Act (1789), 335, 372
jurisdiction, 16–17, 19, 83,
    320–23
Justice Department, U.S., 152,
    226, 284, 285, 286, 300,
    326, 346, 349
    creation of, 3
    Microsoft antitrust suits
        and, 546
    war on terrorism and, 26,
        27

Kansas, 456
    school segregation in, 137
Kansas-Nebraska Act (1854),
    500
Kashmir, 708
Katrina, Hurricane, 3, 27, 28n,
    31, 101, 226, 235, 296,
    298–99, 684, 685
Kefauver, Estes, 593
Kelley, Stanley, 466
Kelo v. New London, 612n
Kennedy, Anthony, 326, 354,
    359
Kennedy, Edward, 99, 544
Kennedy, John F.:
    assassination of, 643
    election of, 249
    New Frontier of, 211
    news conferences of, 593
    personal life of, 595
    reporters and, 580, 584,
        594, 595
Kent State University, 427n
Kentucky, same sex marriage
    and, 86
Kernell, Samuel, 240
Kerry, John, 26–27, 454–58
    African Americans and, 401
    campaign contributions to,
        465
    Edwards and, 249, 380
    "flip-flopper" accusations
        and, 451
    Internet and, 513
    on Iraq War, 380, 447, 454
    media endorsements of,
        582, 592–93
    Nader and, 509
    nomination acceptance
        speech of, 383
    partisan loyalty and, 444
    popular vote and, 452, 504
    Swift Boat Veterans for
        Truth and, 460
    as war hero, 581
Kettl, Donald, 309
Key, V. O., 485

King, Martin Luther, Jr., 139
King Caucus, 221
Kissinger, Henry, 249
Kitchen Cabinet, 248
Know-nothings, 500
Korean War, 109, 224, 689,
    694, 697
    draft in, 6
    Truman and, 30
Korematsu v. United States, 153
Kosovo, 395, 678, 707
Krauthammer, Charles, 706
Kristol, William, 706
Kuhn, Tom, 547
Kuwait, 25, 564, 697, 706
    Gulf War sponsored by, 698

Labor Department, U.S., 287
laborers, 39, 40
labor unions, 5, 168, 390–91,
    458, 486, 494, 504, 539,
    553, 556
    campaign against sweat-
      shops by, 404
    FDR and, 503, 509
    outsourcing opposed by, 4
    PACs created by, 10n
La Guardia, Fiorello, 255
Lambda Legal Defense and
    Education Fund, 148
Landon, Alfred M., 408
Land Ordinance (1785), 664
Landrum-Griffin Labor
    Management Act
    (1959), 646
Lanham Act (1940), 664n
Lansing, John, 47
Lasswell, Harold, 9
Latino Americans, 387, 389
    poverty and, 670
Latinos, party identity of, 492
law, statutory, 339
Law and Order (TV show),
    362
law clerks, 347
Lawrence v. Texas, 149
lawsuits, 317
League of Women Voters, 484
Lee, Richard Henry, 62
Legal Defense Fund, 137
legislative branch:
    agenda of, 642–43
    in Constitution, 53
    from 1800–1933, 240–42
    executive branch vs., *58*,
      195, 211
    executive orders and,
      236–37
    judicial vs., *58*
    oversight in, 188
    see also Congress, U.S.
legislative initiative, 233,
    235–36

Legislative Leviathan (Cox and
    McCubbins), 479n
legislative supremacy, 106,
    108, 241
legislative veto, 301n
Leno, Jay, 570
Lewinsky, Monica, 210, 569,
    582, 585
Lexington, battle of, 37
Libby, Lewis "Scooter," 584
Liberal Party, 506–7
liberals, liberalism, 382,
    395–97, 417
    civil rights movement and,
      73
    collective action favored by,
      22
    in college, 393
    defining of, 395
    as Democratic base, 486,
      494
    Greenspan approved by,
      628
    in media, 568, 586
    party identity of, 493
    Social Security and, 647–48
    war and, 689
libertarians, 396
    small government favored
      by, 22
liberty, *see specific freedoms*
Lieberman, Hadassah, 546
Lieberman, Joseph, 451, 546
Limbaugh, Rush, 568
Lincoln, Abraham, 218, 500
    Douglas's debates with, 407
    executive orders of, 223
    as strong president, 241
line-item veto, 109, 229
Line-Item Veto Act (1996),
    109
Lippmann, Walter, 470
Literary Digest poll (1936),
    408
Little Rock, Ark., 141, 225
Livingston, Robert, 42, 183
lobbies, lobbying, 543–49,
    604, 686
    of Congress, 545–46
    of executive branch, 547–48
    going public strategy of,
      550–53
    grassroots, 551–53
    of president, 547
    see also interest groups
Lobbying Disclosure Act
    (1995), 549
Locke, John, 8
Lockheed Martin, 615
logrolling, 206–7, 616
London, 38
Los Angeles, Calif., riots in,
    226

Los Angeles, pollution in, 609
Louisiana:
    abortion laws in, 131n
    affirmative action in, 151
    Hurricane Katrina in, 31
    same-sex marriage banned
      in, 149
Louisiana Purchase, 260
Lujan v. Defenders of Wildlife,
    369–70
Lynch, Jessica, 585–86

MacArthur, Douglas, 198
McCain, John, 512
McCain-Feingold Act (2002),
    see Bipartisan Campaign
    Reform Act
McCarthy, Joseph, 593
McClellan, George, 515
*McConnell v. Federal Election
    Commission*, 354
McCubbins, Mathew D.,
    301–2, 479n
McCulloch v. Maryland, 89, 91
McGovern-Fraser
    Commission, 506
McKinley, William, 502, 580
Mack v. United States, 104
McManus, Michael, 586
Madison, James, 38, 61, 62, 64,
    119, 240–41, 289–90,
    425, 498, 530
    on class conflict, 392
    on constitutional amend-
      ments, 66
    on factions, 557–58, 620
    on legislative branch,
      240–41
    on liberty, 526, 557–58
    on pluralism, 527–28
    on Senate, 53
    on separation of powers, 65,
      105
    on slavery, 48
    Washington's Farewell
      Address and, 691
    see also Marbury v. Madison
Maine, 580
Maine, electoral college in, 438
majority leader, 183, 212, 214
majority party, 487
majority system, 432
managerial presidency, 295
mandate, 252
Mandate Monitor, 99
mandates, 111
    unfunded, 98
mandatory spending, 630
manufacturing, 614–15
Mapp v. Ohio, 128
Marbury v. Madison, 108, 333,
    372
March on Washington, 139

Marcos, Ferdinand, 711
market economy, 605–11, 617, 632, 634
   failure of, 608–11
marriage, same sex, 86
Marshall, John, 108, 131
   Bill of Rights and, 122
   on Commerce clause, 89, 91
   on implied powers, 89
   Jackson and, 361
   nationalizing court of, 105
Marshall, Thurgood, 347, 641
Marshall Plan, 701, 702
Maryland:
   bank tax and, 89, 91
   slavery in, 48
Mason, George, 118
Massachusetts, 433, 439
   cholera in, 668
   Federalists in, 118
   same-sex marriage in, 86, 149
   Virginia Plan and, 47
Masson v. New Yorker Magazine, Inc., 573, 576
mass popularity, 256–57
Matalin, Mary, 403
material benefits, 538
MBNA America, 465
"means-tested" part of welfare state, 640, 651, 653, 662
media, 404, 406–7, 564–99
   broadcast, 567
   candidates image as portrayed in, 451
   consumers of, 587–89
   elections and, 592–93
   foreign policy and, 688–89
   government's disputes with, 402–3
   nationalization of, 578–80
   political campaigns and, 511
   political struggles and, 4
   politicians and, 582–87
   presidential debates and, 455
   print, 567, 568–69, 572–73
   radio, 567–68
   regulation of, 570–72
   selection bias in, 582
   types of, 567–68
median voter theorem, 448, 456, 457
Medicaid, 640, 653, 655, 657, 658, 669
medical insurance, 638
Medicare, 22–23, 86, 116–17, 252, 253, 403–4, 524–25, 630, 647, 651–53, 654–55, 658, 669, 674
   cost of, 662

Greenspan and, 652
   increasing cost of, *660*
   reform of, 644
   tax for, 615
Medicare Prescription Drug, Improvement, and Modernization Act (2003), 22–23
meetup.com, 541
meet ups, 541–42
membership associations, 529
merchants, New England, 38, 39, 40, 46, 48, 60
Mexican-American Legal Defense Fund, 348–49
Mexican War, 685
Michigan:
   No Child Left Behind in, 102
   same sex marriage and, 86
Microsoft, 546
Middle East, 678, 707
mid-term elections, 429
Miers, Harriet, 30, 209, 327, 552
military, 163, 677, 684
military-industrial complex, 615
Milkis, Sydney, 254–55
Miller, Dan, 173–74
Miller, Judith, 575, 585
Miller v. Johnson, 436
Milliken v. Bradley, 143–44
minimum wage, 100
Minnesota:
   abortion laws in, 131*n*
   charter schools in, 668
   welfare in, 100
minority leader, 183, 214
Miranda rule, 128, 340
Miranda v. Arizona, 340
"misplaced self-interest," 402
Mississippi, 684
   affirmative action in, 151
   Hurricane Katrina in, 31
   racial gerrymandering in, 434–36
Missouri, 87, 455
   abortion laws in, 131*n*
   same-sex marriage banned in, 149
   in 2004 election, 455
Missouri Compromise of 1820, 500
Missouri v. Jenkins, 144, 342
Missouri v. Siebert, 354
Mitchell, George J., 695
Moe, Terry, 245*n*, 265
"momentum," 590–91
monetary policies, 621–22
monopolies, 608
Montana, same sex marriage and, 86

Montesquieu, Baron de, 56–57, 105
moral hazard, 424, 425, 658–59
Morgenthau, Hans, 694
Morrill Act (1862), 664
Motor Carrier Act (1980), 618
Motor Voter bill (1993), 432, 467
MoveOn.org, 541, 542, 556, 570
Mr. Smith Goes to Washington (film), 199
MSNBC, 567
MTV, 577, 585
multilateralism, 693–94, 703
multilateral treaties, 703
multiple-member-district, 509–10
multiple referral, 184–85
Murdoch, Rupert, 577, 582
Mushroom Caucus, 192
Muslims, 698
Mutual Security Act (1951), 701
Myanmar, 135

NAACP (National Association for the Advancement of Colored People), 128, 137, 348, 550, 641
Nader, Ralph, 509, 533
NAFTA (North American Free Trade Agreement), 687
NAM (National Association of Manufacturers), 531
Napoleonic role, 710–11, 716
National Abortion and Reproductive Rights League, 460
National Aeronautics and Space Administration (NASA), 284
National Association for the Advancement of Colored People (NAACP), 128, 137, 348, 550, 641
National Association of Manufacturers (NAM), 531
National Beer Wholesalers' Association, 459
National Conference of State Legislature, 99
National Conference of State Legislatures, 652–53
National Defense Education Act (NDEA) (1958), 664–65
National Education Association, 103
National Endowment for Democracy, 678

National Endowment for the Arts, 207
National Federation of Independent Business (NFIB), 528, 556
National Guard, 603, 684
Arkansas, 225
National Industrial Recovery Act (1933), 108n, 239
National Institutes of Health (NIH), 668
National Labor Relations (Wagner) Act (1935), 646
National Labor Relations Board (NLRB), 243
National Labor Relations Board v. Jones & Laughlin Steel Corporation, 243
National League of Cities, 529
National Organization for Women (NOW), 405, 533, 551
National Performance Review (NPR), 250, 295, 300
National Petroleum Refiners Association, 528
National Public Radio (NPR), 576
National Reconnaissance Office (NRO), 684
National Resources Defense Council, 529
National Review, 512
National Rifle Association (NRA), 459, 460, 556, 641
National Savings & Loan League, 529
national security, 452
public opinion and, 390
National Security Act (1947), 271–72
National Security Agency, 28
National Security Council (NSC), 224, 246, 249, 681, 683, 684
Nation at Risk, A, 665
Native Americans, 104
NATO (North Atlantic Treaty Organization), 679, 703–4, 712–13
creation of, 703
in former Yugoslavia, 698
multilateralism and, 693–94
Navy Department, U.S., 287
NBC, 577
NCLB (No Child Left Behind Act; 2001), 28, 99, 101, 102–3, 112, 586, 666, 667

NDEA (National Defense Education Act) (1958), 664–65
Near v. Minnesota, 573
Nebraska:
electoral college in, 438
same-sex marriage banned in, 149
necessary and proper clause, 53, 64, 84
Negotiated Rulemaking Act (1990), 548
Negroponte, John, 29
neoconservatives, 689
Neumann, Mark, 183
Nevada, same-sex marriage banned in, 149
New Deal, 109, 130, 211, 222, 503, 603, 640, 662
Democratic Party and, 445, 492
federalism and, 111
presidency and, 242–43, 245, 251, 336
Republican opposition to, 574
Socialists and, 509
Supreme Court and, 105, 336, 358
new federalism, 100
New Frontier, 211
New Hampshire, Federalists in, 118
New Jersey:
Corzine in, 170
Virginia Plan opposition of, 47
New Jersey Plan, 47
New Orleans, 3, 31, 684
New Politics movement, 532–33, 550
New Republic, 512, 565
New State Ice Co. v. Lieberman, 100n
Newsweek, 569, 685
New York:
Federalists in, 119
House seats lost by, 176
Virginia Plan opposition, 47
New York City, N.Y., 433, 434, 605
Board of Health in, 668
New York Journal, 62
New York Review of Books, 512
New York State, 553
New York Times, 28, 76–77, 158–59, 216–17, 374–75, 406, 420–21, 474–75, 531, 562–63, 564, 569, 575, 576, 581, 585, 587, 590, 594, 598–99, 628, 636–37, 674–75

New York Times Co. v Sullivan, 573
New York Times v. United States, 573
New York Yankees, 553
New Zealand, 703
NFIB (National Federation of Independent Business, 528, 556
Nicaragua, 711
NIH (National Institutes of Health), 668
9/11 Commission, 28, 454
Ninth Amendment, 129, 130
Niskanen, William A., 290, 291
Nixon, Richard, 109, 210, 224, 424n, 504, 566, 574, 594, 646
Congress and, 228
Environmental Protection Agency created by, 237
executive privilege claimed by, 337
NSC and, 248, 249
pardon of, 226
reporters and, 580
resignation of, 589–90
Rumsfeld as NATO ambassador of, 680
Vietnam War and, 30
NLRB (National Labor Relations Board), 243
No Child Left Behind Act (NCLB; 2001), 28, 99, 101, 102–3, 112, 586, 666, 667
Noelle-Neumann, Elisabeth, 392
noncontributory welfare programs, 640, 644, 653, 655
noninterpretivists, 362–63
Noriega, Manuel, 573, 711
North American Free Trade Agreement (NAFTA), 687
North Atlantic Treaty Organization (NATO), 679, 703–4, 712–13
creation of, 703
in former Yugoslavia, 698
multilateralism and, 693–94
North Carolina:
racial lawsuit in, 145
slavery in, 48
Virginia Plan, 47
North Dakota, same sex marriage and, 86
Northern Ireland, 686, 695
Northern Marianas, 321
North Korea, 224, 708

North Vietnam, 681
Northwest Ordinance (1787), 664
Northwest Territory, 664
"no taxation without representation" slogan, 36, 38, 40
Novak, Robert, 575
NOW (National Organization for Women), 405, 533, 551
NPR (National Performance Review), 250, 295, 300
NPR (National Public Radio), 576
NRA (National Rifle Association), 459, 460, 556, 641
NRO (National Reconnaissance Office), 684
NSC (National Security Council), 224, 246, 249, 681, 683, 684
Nuclear Club, 708
nuclear missile shield ("Star Wars"), 681

OAS (Organization of American States), 702
Occupational Safety and Health Administration (OSHA), 238, 265, 280, 287, 465, 618, 669
O'Connor, Sandra Day, 326
   abortion and, 129, 359
   Bush v. Gore and, 354
   on gerrymandering, 436
   Guantánamo Bay prison and, 111
   retirement of, 30, 209, 327, 552
   Roe v. Wade and, 129
   as swing vote, 354
OEO (Office of Economic Opportunity), 665n
Office of Civil Defense, 250
Office of Disaster Preparedness, 299
Office of Economic Opportunity (OEO), 665n
Office of Information and Regulatory Affairs (OIRA), 4
Office of Management and Budget (OMB), *see* White House Office of Management and Budget
Office of Technology Assessment, 303
Ohio, 427n, 439, 454, 455, 592

abortion laws in, 131n
   same sex marriage and, 86
   in 2000 election, 455
OIRA (Office of Information and Regulatory Affairs), 4
Oklahoma, 178
   same sex marriage and, 86
oligarchy, 5
Olson, Mancur, 14–15, 534, 536–37, 539, 541, 543
Olson, Theodore, 315
OMB (Office of Management and Budget), *see* White House Office of Management and Budget
O'Neill, Paul, 700
open-market operations, 622
open primary, 484
open rule, 193
Orange Revolution, 135
order, 7–8
Organization of American States (OAS), 702
OSHA (Occupational Safety and Health Administration), 238, 265, 280, 287, 465, 618, 669
outsourcing, union opposition to, 4
oversight, 188, 296–97, 300–302
ownership society, 650

PACs (political action committees), 10, 148, 459–60, 464, 513, 524, 527, 531, 532, 553–56, 555
Page, Benjamin I., 415
Paine, Thomas, 691
Pakistan, 708, 712
   IMF loan to, 700
Palestinians, 695, 713
Palko case, 126, 128
Panama, 224
Panama Refining Co. v. Ryan, 108n
Paramount Studio, 577
Pariser, Eli, 541, 542
Parliament, British, 36
Parliamentarian's Office, 187
parliamentary rules, 182
Partial Birth Abortion Ban Act (2003), 404
parties, political, *see* political parties
partisanship, public opinion and, 390, 401
party caucus, 183
party conference, 183
party identity, 479n, 480, 485, 491–94, 492n, 495

party labels, *see* branding
party machines, 501
party systems, 476, 496–510
   balance of power in, 496
   evolution of, 497
   fifth, 503–4
   first, 498
   fourth, 502–3
   second, 498–500
   third, 500–502
   strength of, 478
   two-party, 494, 496
   see also political parties
party vote, 202
Paterson, William, 47
path dependency, 24
Patriot Act (2001), 29, 134, 251–52
   see also USA PATRIOT Act
patronage, 172
   in political parties, 401
PBS (Public Broadcasting System), 576
Peace Corps, 261
peak associations, 687
Pearl Harbor attack, 30
Pelosi, Nancy, 183
Penn & Schoen, 403
Pennsylvania, 454
   abortion laws in, 131n
   House seats lost by, 176
   radical control of, 44
   September 11 attack in, 605
   Virginia Plan and, 47
Pentagon, 276
Pentagon Papers, 573
Pepper, Claude, 540
per curiam rejection, 346
Perkins, Frances, 661
permanent campaign, 256
Perot, Ross, 461, 506
Perry Mason (TV show), 362
Persian Gulf War, 25, 30
Personal Responsibility and Work Opportunity Reconciliation Act (PRWORA), 100, 289, 656, 662
Pew Hispanic Center, 387
Pharmaceutical Research and Manufactures of America (PhRMA), 524–26, 653
Philadelphia, 45
Philippines, 701, 711
phone banks, 511
Physicians for Social Responsibility, 405, 533
Pickering, Charles, 359
Pinellas County, 80
"Pioneers," 547
plaintiffs, 317
Plame, Valerie, 575, 584

Planned Parenthood League of
 Connecticut, 128
Planned Parenthood v. Casey,
 131–32
planters, southern, 39, 40, 46,
 48, 60
plea bargains, 319
Plessy, Homer, 135–36
Plessy v. Ferguson, 127, 133,
 135–36
Plunkett, George Washington,
 19, 501
pluralism, 528, 620
plurality, 533
plurality systems, 433–34
Plyler v. Doe, 349
pocket veto, 195, 229
Poland, 703
polarization, of political parties, 488–89, 505–6
police patrol oversight, 301–2
police power, 85
policy, public opinion driven
 by, 415
policy entrepreneurs, 486–87
policy-making powers, 243–44
policy of redistribution, 625
policy principle, 19–21, 23, 24,
 31, 32
  bureaucracy and, 294
  clientele agencies and, 285
  Congress and, 155, 164,
   198, 200, 213, 239, 264
  courts and, 316, 338, 371
  devolution and, 100, 113
  DHS and, 298
  executive branch and, 239,
   264
  foreign policy and, 690,
   706, 715
  G. W. Bush and, 29
  highlighting differences to
   win elections as, 401
  IMF and, 700, 715
  impact of lobbying on public policy, 548
  market economy and, 608,
   633
  media and, 575
  median voter theorem and,
   448, 456
  military pork barrel and,
   287
  parties and, 479, 480, 486,
   488, 489, 520
  political knowledge translated into power as, 402
  pork-barrel legislation and,
   173
  promotional policies and,
   615, 633
  public policies and, 605,
   633

  redistributive policies and,
   632, 633
  regulated federalism and,
   102
  regulatory policy and, 620,
   633
  Supreme Court appointees
   and, 31
  veto and, 232, 234, 264
  welfare and, 663
political action committees
 (PACs), 10, 148, 179,
 459–60, 464, 524, 527,
 531, *532*, 553–56, *555*
 Congress and, 170, 184,
  201–2
political attentiveness, cost of,
 397–99
political behavior, purpose of,
 10–11
political entrepreneurs, 15*n*,
 539–40, 543
political ideology, 381–82
 as informational shortcut,
  395, 399
political opinions, formation
 of, 397–407
political parties, 182–83, 212,
 516–19
 activism and, 491, 505
 ambition controlled by, 479,
  481
 branding and, 479*n*, 480,
  491
 campaign contributions for,
  10*n*
 candidate recruitment by,
  481–82
 collective action principle
  and, 479–80, 485, 487,
  489, 498
 and Congress, 477, 487–90
 constitutional principles
  and, 21
 declining influence of, 530
 development, 476–81
 formation of, 479–81
 functions of, 481–91
 history principle and, 489,
  494
 ideology in, 505
 interest groups and, 479
 as machines, 477
 machines in, 501
 nomination for, 482–84, *483*
 organization of, 477, 480,
  496, 499, 501–2, 505,
  513–17, *514*
 patronage in, 501
 polarization of, 488–89,
  505–6
 policy entrepreneurs of,
  486–87

 policy principle and, 179,
  486, 488, 489
 political struggles and, 4
 presidential power and, 253
 in Progressive era, 502
 rationality principle and,
  481, 485, 488
 reform in, 502
 strength of, 477, 480, 510
 technology used by, 510–13
 third parties and, 506–10
 2004 election and, *508*
 see also party identity; party
  systems
political socialization, 385–95
politics, 9
 as collective action, 11–15
 complexity of, 9
 five key principles of, 9–21,
  24
 purpose and, 10–11
 "retail," 11
 "wholesale," 11
politics, U.S., complexity of, 21
polls, polling, 408–9, 418–19,
 448, 454
 deliberative, 420–21
 design of, 410
 measurement error of,
  409–10
 negative knowledge pro-
  duced by, 414
 probability sampling in, 408
 push polling and, 410, 412
 random digital dialing in,
  408
 sample size of, 409–10
 selection bias in, 408
Populist movement, 556
Populist party, 502–3
pork-barrel legislation, 21,
 101, 172–73, 200, 287,
 614*n*
 promotional policy as,
  616–17
Postal Service, U.S., 274, 284,
 292*n*
poverty, 639, 645, 669–71
poverty programs, 97
Powell, Colin, 25, 28, 249
 diplomacy of, 695–96
 experience of, 681
Powell, Lewis, 153
"power elite" theory, 632
PRA (Personal Responsibility
 and Work Opportunity
 Reconciliation Act, 100,
 289
precedents, legal, 317
precinct captains, 516
preemptive action, 683, 708
presidency, 207, 218–69, *247*,
 400

administrative state and, 259–64, 265
budget and, 295
Congress and, 18, 212, 218–20, 297
congressional powers given to, 163–64
in Constitution, 220–22
constitutional principles and, 21
of 1800–1933, 240–42
elections and, 437–38
executive office of, 259
executive orders and, 236–37, 260–63
expressed powers of, 223–28
Federal Reserve and, 628
foreign policy and, 680–83, 682, 686, 690, 695, 713
formal resources of power by, 245–52
lawmaking ability of, 18n
lobbying of, 547
performance ratings of, 258
policy and, 251–52
post-New Deal power gain by, 242–43, 245
power bases of, 252
public and, 253–59
regulatory review and, 260
Senate vs., 112–13
and separation of powers, 80
social policies and, 641
Supreme Court's relationship with, 54, 358–59
veto power of, 18, 195
see also executive branch
presidential debates, in election of 2004, 455
Presidential Election Campaign Fund, 461
presidential initiative, 643
presidential oversight, 618
presidential power, 243–44
presidential program, 643–44
press, freedom of, 572–73, 576
see also First Amendment
primary elections, 483–85, 488–89
priming, 590–91
principal relationship, 18–19
principals, 18
print media, 567, 568–69
Printz v. United States, 104
prior restraint, 572–73
Prisoner's Dilemma, 535–37, 584, 706
privacy, right to, 128–29, 130, 135, 362
privatization, 308–9, 691

privileges and immunities clause, 87
professional legislature, 171
Progressive era, 501–2, 510, 655–56
Progressive Party, 509
Progressive reformers, 430, 509
progressive taxation, 625
Prohibition, 66, 70, 75
project grants, 94
promotional policies, 615–16
property, 8, 60, 606, 607, 610, 612–13
proportional representation, 433
proposal power, 187–88
Proposition 22, 86
Proposition 209, 153–54, 416–17
prospective voting, 447
Prussia, 711
PRWORA (Personal Responsibility and Work Opportunity Reconciliation Act), 656, 662
Pryor, William, 359
Public Affairs Council, 405
public assistance programs, 653
see also noncontributory welfare programs
Public Broadcasting System (PBS), 576
public economy, 607
public goods, 8–9
Public Health Service, U.S. (USPHS), 668
public interest groups, 529
public law, 317–19, 318
public opinion, 256, 380–81, 397–407
depth of division in, 400
origins of, 382–97
policy influenced by, 414–17
political ideology and, 395–97
political socialization and, 385–95
polls of, 408–9
public order, 606, 612
public policy, 604, 632, 634
Publius, 61, 62
Pulitzer, Joseph, 580
purposive benefits, 539
push polling, 412

Quayle, Dan, 250
Queenan, Joe, 405–6

race, in party identity, 492, 494
racial gerrymandering, 434–36

racism, 386–87
radio, 567–68, 572, 578, 618
Radio Act (1928), 366
Railroad Revitalization Act (1976), 618
railroads, 602, 613, 614, 618
rallying effect, 256
Randolph, Edmund, 46, 49
Rather, Dan, 581
rationality principle, 23, 24, 31, 32
beliefs driven by objective political interests, 392
Bill of Rights and, 119, 155
bureaucracy and, 278, 290, 293, 310
candidates converge toward median voters as, 448
compassionate conservatism and, 102
Congress and, 164, 167, 170, 180, 184, 213, 245, 264
constituencies and, 610, 633
Constitution and, 52, 74, 83
contracting and, 615, 633
of cost in political information gathering, 398
disasters and, 299
elections and, 170
federalism and, 83, 113
Federalists vs. Antifederalists and, 60, 74
foreign policy and, 683, 690, 694, 696, 699, 715
free-ride incentive and, 536, 542
of ideologies as informational shortcuts, 395
impact of a single vote and, 468, 469
incumbents as likely winners in uncertain times as, 457
judges and, 316
lack of voter participation and, 468
media and, 566, 582, 587, 596
of moral concerns substituted for economic concerns, 456
parties and, 481, 485, 520
of partisan divides on policy beliefs, 401
and political entrepreneurs, 540
political participation impacted by registration cost, 430

rationality principle, *(cont.)*
 presidency and, 223, 228,
  245, 264
 public policy and, 604, 633
 rights and, 134
 selection of political agents
  and, 425
 separation of powers and,
  83, 113
 Supreme Court and, 30–31,
  342, 348, 363, 371
 unilateralism and, 707, 715
 veto and, 232, 233
 voter mobilization, 466,
  469
 voter motivation by political parties, 466
 welfare and, 658, 673
Rayburn, Sam, 204*n*
Reagan, Nancy, 250–51
Reagan, Ronald, 250, 326, 439,
  504, 618
 children of, 386
 Congress and, 214
 deregulation and, 237
 education policy of, 665–66
 fairness doctrine and, 572
 Greenspan appointed by,
  628
 judicial appointees of,
  326–27, 353, 369
 partisan struggles and, 202
 Powell as national security
  adviser of, 680
 public appearances of, 256
 regulatory review used by, 4
 reporters and, 580
 small government favored
  by, 100–101
 social issues and, 486
 tax cuts and, 263
recall elections, 443–44
recession (2002), 669
Reconstruction, 210, 211,
  500–502
redistributive policies, 632,
  641
redistricting, 176–78
*Red Lion Broadcasting
 Company v. FCC*, 572
red states, 400
Reed, Stanley, 352
referendums, 442–43, 444
regressive taxation, 625
regulated federalism, 97–99
regulation, 618, 619
regulatory agencies, 287–88
regulatory policy, 619–20
regulatory review, 4, 260
Rehnquist, William H., 30,
  105, 109, 130–33, 209,
  323, 328, 354, 552
 Roe v. Wade and, 129

Rehnquist Court, 355
Reid, Harry, 184
religion:
 in party identity, 493
 public opinion and, 389
religious conservatives, 504
religious Right, *see* Christian
  Right
Report on Manufactures
 (Hamilton), 614–15
representative government,
  382, 425
Republican National
 Committee (RNC),
  515
Republican National
 Conventions:
 of 1992, 413
 of 1996, 413
Republican Party, 182, 542
 African Americans as, 392
 "benign" gerrymandering
  and, 436
 "bridge to nowhere" and,
  172
 budget and, 627
 Bush's cabinet and, 680
 Bush's proposed Social
  Security reform and,
  651
 candidate image and, 451
 Clinton's impeachment
  and, 169
 Clinton's judicial nominees
  and, 643
 Clinton supported by, 490
 conservative base of, 504
 "Contract with America" of,
  73
 on contributory programs,
  657
 Democrats' differences
  with, 423, 485
 devolution revolution of,
  112
 education policies of, 666
 funding of, 458, 516
 Gingrich's support by, 184
 Greenspan in, 629
 G. W. Bush and, 234,
  326–27
 as hawkish, 390
 history of, 500–506
 House committee pledge of,
  490
 House committee system
  reformed by, 191
 Iraq War and, 380
 Johnson's impeachment
  and, 210
 Latino support for, 389
 legislative priorities of, 506,
  507

Lincoln's leadership of, 241
 lobbyists and, 546
 media and, 582
 Medicare Act (2003) passed
  by, 22–23
 Medicare and, 651, 652
 members of, 202, 203–4
 military officers' support
  for, 392
 1994 election victories of,
  22, 173–74, 198–99,
  208, 211–12, 234
 1994 mobility of, 176
 1995 government shutdown
  and, 23, 591
 No Child Left Behind and,
  103
 in 104th Congress, 191
 PACs and, 541, *555*
 partisanship and, 30–31,
  203, *205*
 religious conservatives in,
  504
 reporters in, 581
 Roe v. Wade and, 129
 small government favored
  by, 22
 social issues of, 486
 Social Security irresponsibility of, 649
 strategies for 2004 elections
  of, 454–55
 tax cuts engineered by, 26,
  624, 626
 Terri Schiavo and, 31,
  80–81
 Texas redistricting by, 178,
  437
 2002 election victories of,
  25
 in 2004 election, 27, 592
 voter manipulation in 2004
  by, 427*n*
 welfare reform and, 657
 white southerners in,
  393–94, 494, 504
Republican party
 (Jeffersonian), 477,
  498–99
reserved powers amendment,
  85
reserve requirement, 622
responsible party government,
  518
restrictive covenant, 339
"retail" politics, 11
retrospective voting, 447
revenue collection, 6–7
revenue sharing, 100
Rhode Island, 56
 Constitutional Convention
  and, 45
 radical control of, 44, 51

Rice, Condoleezza, 28, 696, 708
experience of, 681
Ridge, Tom, 26, 28, 233, 271, 298
right of rebuttal, 572
right to privacy, 128–29, 130, 135
Rio Treaty (1947), 702
Rita, Hurricane, 226
RNC (Republican National Committee), 515
roads, 602, 613
Roberts, John G., 30, 133, 209, 327, 374–75
Roe v. Wade and, 130
Robinson, Donald, 49
Roe v. Wade, 129–30, 550
Blackmun's opinion in, 355, 362, 427*n*
Bush's opposition to, 129, 366
constructionists and, 362
mootness and, 342
right to privacy and, 135, 355
Rogers Act (1924), 694
roll-call vote, 202
Roman Catholic Church, 588
Romer v. Evans, 148
Roosevelt, Eleanor, 250, 251
Roosevelt, Franklin D., 218–19, 250
Committee on Administrative Management of, 294–95
court packing plan of, 198, 325, 336, 358, 367
election of, 503
executive orders of, 235
fireside chats of, 574, 593
on foreign aid, 701
loyalty towards, 393
national protection and, 223
New Deal of, 105, 211, 222, 242–43, 245, 251, 492, 503, 509, 574, 603, 640, 662
in 1932 election, 220
1936 poll and, 407
Pearl Harbor and, 30
personal life of, 595
proposals for legislative action by, 229
public appeals used by, 254–55
reporters and, 581
Republican support for, 445
Social Security, 490
White House staff of, 248
Roosevelt, Theodore:
constituency of, 593

popular mobilization and, 253
Roper Center, 580
Roper polls, 407
Rosenberger v. University of Virginia, 131, 342–43
Rove, Karl, 452, 456, 457, 575
royalists, 39, 40
Rule 10, 343
rulemaking, 280–81
rule of four, 364
Rumsfeld, Donald, 28, 246, 272, 565, 696
experience of, 680–81
Russia, 703, 711, 712, 713
ABM Treaty and, 681
in IMF and World Bank, 699
Iraq War and, 25, 699
in UN, 697
see also Soviet Union
Rutledge, John, 65

St. Louis Globe Democrat, 593
sales tax, 625
saliency, 413, 419
same-sex marriage, 86, 149, 389, *390*, 562–63
Sandinistas, 711
San Francisco Superior Court, 86
Saudi Arabia, Gulf War sponsored by, 698
Scalia, Antonin, 315, 327, 328, 351, 354, 363, 370
Schecter Poultry Co. v. United States, 108*n*
Schiavo, Terri, 31, 80–82, 112
Schlozman, Kay, 533–34
school board elections, 433
Schwartz, Thomas, 301–2
Schwarzenegger, Arnold, 444, 570
SCLC (Southern Christian Leadership Conference), 139, 551
SEATO (South East Asia Treaty Organization), 703
Seattle, Wash., WTO protest in, 688
secession, 123
Second Amendment, 68, 121
Second Continental Congress, 42
Securities Act Amendment (1975), 618
Securities and Exchange Commission, 300
securities industry, 618
segregation, 133, 135–44, 353, 368, 385, 550, 589
selection bias (in the media), 582

selective benefits, 14–15
"Selling of the Pentagon, The" (documentary), 402–3
Seminoles, 104
Senate, U.S.:
Agriculture Committee of, 189–90
Appropriations Committee of, 185, 197, 557
Armed Services Committee of, 186–87, 686
bicameralism, 167–69
cabinet approved by, 246
campaign committees of, 516
campaign costs in, 482
campaign expenditures for, *175*
checks and balances and, 106
Clinton's impeachment and, 169
committees in, 297
in Connecticut Plan, 47
in Constitution, 52
Constitutional amendments and, 66, 67
debate in, 194, 198
defense bill passed by, 629
elections and, 68, 437
ergonomics regulations and, 465
executive agreements and, 686
executive appointments approved by, 227
Federal Reserve board confirmed by, 621, 628
filibuster in, 643
foreign policy and, 685
Foreign Relations Committee of, 594
Gulf of Tonkin Resolution passed by, 682
Hillary Clinton's election to, 251
impeachment power of, 210
"intelligence czar," 28
judicial nominations and, 208–9, 489
Judiciary Committee of, 326, 327, 643
lawmaking ability of, 18*n*
Medicare Act (2003) passed by, 22
organization of, 167–69, 184–85
oversight and, 296
partisanship in, 169
party leadership in, 168
president vs., 112–13, 253
rulebook for, 17
Rules Committee of, 185

Senate, U.S.: *(cont.)*
  Select Committee to
    Investigate the 1972
    Presidential Campaign
    Activities of, 554
  Social Security reform and,
    644
  Supreme Court appointees
    and, 31
  Supreme Court judges and,
    54, 325–26
  terms of, 53
  treaties and, 54, 163
  in 2004 election, 25, 452
  veto overridden by, 195,
    229
  vice president and, 249
  vs. House, 216–17
senatorial courtesy, 325
senior citizens, 534
seniority rule, 189
"separate but equal" rule, 136
separation of powers, 56–57,
    57, 79, 80, 82–83, 105,
    110–12, 114
September 11, 2001, terrorist
    attacks of, 24, 26, 29,
    30, 101, 109, 113, 203,
    226, 256, 270, 274, 379,
    452, 454, 583, 590, 681,
    685–86, 695, 704, 712,
    713
  airline bailout for, 545–46,
    603
  budget deficits and, 627
  bureaucracy and, 276
  Bush's leadership after, 25
  Congress on, 219, 682–83
  foreign entanglements and,
    678
  IMF and, 700
  in media, 569
  military budget increased
    by, 615
  9/11 commission and, 28
  outlays for, 624
  possible impact of, 393
  public order and, 612
  2004 elections and, 27
  UN and, 698
Serbia, 225, 698
Sessions, Jeff, 332
Seventeenth Amendment, 52
Seventh Amendment, 68
sexual revolution, 549–50
Shapiro, Robert Y., 415
Sharon, Ariel, 573
Shaw v. Reno, 436
Shays, Daniel, 45
Shays's Rebellion, 44–45, 52,
    84
Shelley v. Kraemer, 136
Shell Oil, 528

Sherman, Roger, 42
Sherman Antitrust Act (1890),
    242, 243n, 618
shopkeepers, 39, 40
*Shuttlesworth v. Birmingham
    Board of Education*, 142n
Sierra Club, 180, 364, 405,
    459, 533, 543
Silicon Valley, 570
Silverman, Brian, 557
Simpson, O. J., 387
Singapore, 700
single-member-district,
    509–10
SixPAC, 459
Sixteenth Amendment, 70
Sixth Amendment, 68
Slate (online magazine), 569
slavery, 82, 105
  in Constitution, 47–49
  Democrats split by, 500
  emancipation of, 260
  as political issue, 500
  public opinion and, 385
  as state law, 123
Smith, Adam, 18–19, 602
Smith-Hughes Act (1917),
    664n
Smith v. Allwright, 352
socialization:
  agencies of, 385, 386–95
  political, 385–95
Social Security, 100, 392, 399,
    490, 503, 630, 638, 640,
    644, 647, 652, 671
  bureaucracy, 303
  Bush and, 461
  Clinton and, 490
  cost of, 662
  gay marriage and, 86
  G. W. Bush's reform plan
    for, 164, 192, 642, 644,
    649–51, 674–75
  history of, 646
  increasing cost of, *660*
  indexing of, 647
  liberal defense of, 22
  reform of, 641–42, 644,
    648–51
Social Security Act (1935),
    646, 647, 653, 661, 670
Social Security Administration
    (SSA), 289
Social Security Insurance
    Program, 669
Social Security tax, 622, 624,
    625, 647
Social Security Trust Fund, 649
soft money, 459–60, 554
solicitor general, 346
solidary benefits, 539, 542
Solomon, King, 316
Somalia, 678

sophomore surge, 173
Soros, George, 460, 464
sound bites, 585
Souter, David, 315, 327,
    352–53, 354, 359, 424n
South:
  American Independent
    Party in, 509
  move to Republican camp
    by, 393–94, 493–94,
    504, 505
South America, authoritarian
    governments in, 5
South Carolina, 146
  abortion laws in, 131n
  Constitution ratified by, 65
  Federalists in, 118
  school segregation in, 137
  slavery in, 48
South Dakota, 29, 174, 198
South East Asia Treaty
    Organization (SEATO),
    703
Southern Christian Leadership
    Conference (SCLC),
    139, 551
South Korea, 224
  IMF loan to, 700
  U.S. aid to, 701
South Vietnam, 209
sovereignty, 78–79
Soviet Union, 5, 306, 664,
    677, 703, 705
  breakup of, 706
  elections in, 422
  NATO and, 694
  Rice's experience with, 681
  see also Russia
Spain, 710
  in coalition of the willing,
    25
  U.S. war against, 580
Spanish-American War, 685
Speaker of the House, 183,
    184, 193, 206, 211, 212,
    487
specialization of labor, 18
spin control, 451
Spirit of the Laws, The
    (Montesquieu), 56–57
split-ticket voting, 441
Springfield Republican, 593
Sputnik, 664
squatting (homesteading), 613
Sri Lanka, 370
SSA (Social Security
    Administration), 289
staff agencies, 191–92
Stafford, Robert, 544
staff system, 191–92, 212
Staggers Rail Deregulation Act
    (1980), 618
stakeholders, 548

Stalin, Joseph, 5
Stamp Act (1765), 36–37,
     39–40
Stamp Act Congress, 37
standing committees, 17, 185,
     186
     see also committee system
stare decisis, 317
"Star Wars" (nuclear missile
     shield), 681
state building, 679
State Children's Health insur-
     ance Plan, 669
State Department, U.S., 285,
     286, 683, 684, 695, 702
     creation of, 3
     war on terrorism and, 26
State Drug Costs for the Dual-
     Eligibles, 99
state legislatures, 60–61, 84,
     176
State of the Union, 228–29,
     567, 644, 650, 678, 679
states, U.S.:
     creation of, 78–79
     No Child Left Behind and,
          102
     sovereignty of, 2
     supreme courts of, 319
state sovereign immunity, 104
states' power, 85
     see also federalism
states' rights, 101, 105, 691–92
statutory interpretation, 332
statutory law, 339
Steel Caucus, 192
Steel Seizure, 109
Stevens, John Paul, 315, 354
Stone, Harlan Fiske, 101, 352
straight party vote, 441
strict constructionists, 362–63
strict scrutiny, 127
Student nonviolent
     Coordinating
     Committee, 139
subcommittees, 188–89, 191,
     193, 197
subsidies, 603, 614–15, 630,
     662, 663
suffrage, *see* voting rights
Sugar Act (1764), 40
Sunni Triangle, 26
Supplemental Security Income
     (SSI), 653
supremacy clause, 55, 64
Supreme Court, Hawaii, 86
supreme court, state, 319
Supreme Court, U.S., *345,*
     350, 400, 424*n*, 552
     affirmative action in,
          149–54
     Bill of Rights and, 122–23
     briefs of, 349–51

cases heard by, 341–57,
     344, 356–57
certiorari and, *344,* 349
changes in, 30
chief justice of, 325
civil rights and, 643
Communications Decency
     Act and, 572
Congress's relationship
     with, 355, 358, 367
Constitution and, 54–55, 83
criticism of, 129
denationalizing trend of,
     131–33
dissenting opinion in,
     352–53
eminent domain upheld by,
     612*n*
entitlement and, 640
on executive agreements,
     209
FDR's court packing plan
     and, 325, 336
federalism and, 89, 91–92,
     101, 103–5
Fourteenth Amendment
     and, 123–26, 154, 156
gays rights and, 148
gender discrimination and,
     145–47
Guantánamo Bay prison
     and, 109, 111
implementation of decisions
     by, 359–61
on income tax, 624*n*
interstate commerce and,
     243
Japanese-American intern-
     ment and, 219
justices, *328*
law clerks and, 347
line-item veto struck down
     by, 228
nationalized rights and,
     123–26
nomination to, 208–9,
     240
obscenity laws and, 134–35
opinion writing by, 352–53
oral arguments in, 351
presidential nominees to,
     325
president's relationship
     with, 358–59
restrictive covenants and,
     339
revolutions of, 367–70
right to privacy and,
     128–30
Rules of, 343
segregation and, 133,
     135–38, 142–44, 550
Senate and, 208–9

separation of powers and,
     108–9, 111
state sovereignty and, 2
strategic behavior in, 361,
     364–66
Tenth Amendment and, 101
Terri Schiavo and, 81
2000 presidential election
     decided by, 314–16
in 2005, 27
war on terrorism and,
     337–38
     see also judicial review; *spe-
     cific cases*
Supreme Court, Vermont, 86
Supreme Judicial Court,
     Massachusetts, 149
*Swann v. Charlotte-
     Mecklenburg Board of
     Education,* 142–43,
     142*n*
"Swift Boat Veterans for
     Truth," 455, 460

Taft-Hartley Act (1947), 646
Taiwan, 701
Taliban, 25, 29, 225, 256, 338,
     700, 713
Tammany Hall, 19, 501
Taney, Roger, 105
TANF (Temporary Assistance
     to Needy Families), 100,
     289, 653–54, *654, 658*
tariffs, 238, 602, 613, 624, 692
Tauzin, Billy, 546
tax cuts, 402, *412,* 452
taxes, 6–7, 624–27, 692
     breaks in, 4, 203
     Bush and, 461, 487
     in colonial America, 39, 40
     Congress and, 238
     congressional responsibility
          for, 184
     in Constitution, 53, 163
     cuts for middle-class, 624
     Greenspan and, 629
     G. W. Bush's cuts in, 625,
          626, 636–37
     on imports, 613
     income, 70–71, 624–25,
          632, 644
     partisanship and, 203
     Republican cuts of, 624
     Social Security, 622, 624
     between states, 84
     welfare and, 647
tax relief, 691
Taylor, Zachary, 234
Tea Act (1773), 41
Teamsters, 528
telecommunications, 618
Telecommunications Act
     (1996), 572, 577

television, 567, 572, 578, 618
Temporary Assistance to
    Needy Families (TANF),
    100, 289, 653–54, *654*,
    658
Tenth Amendment, 85, 101,
    103
terrorism, 28, 101, 309,
    447–48, 452–53, 455,
    610, 695, 698, 705, 709,
    712, 713
    public defense and, 9
    see also Al Qaeda;
        September 11, 2001,
        terrorist attacks of; War
        on Terror
Terrorism Information
    Awareness Program,
    134–35
Texas, 680
    affirmative action in,
        151–52
    annexation of, 260
    gerrymandering in, 178
    House districts in, 198
    House seats gained by, 176
    No Child Left Behind in,
        102
    presidential election of
        2004 in, 439
    redistricting in, 437
    retirees in, 662
Texas, University of, Law
    School of, 136
Texas Air National Guard, 581
Thailand, 700
Theriault, Sean, 488
Third Amendment, 68, 129
third parties, 506–10
Thirteenth Amendment, 66,
    69, 70, 133
Thomas, Bill, 23
Thomas, Clarence, 326, 327,
    351, 354, 362
Three-fifths Compromise,
    47–49
Thune, John, 170
Tierney, John, 533–34
Tilden, Samuel, 439
Time, 573, 575, 576
Time Warner, 577
Tobin, James, 628
Tocqueville, Alexis de, 400,
    676
Tonight Show, 570
tort cases, 317
To Secure These Rights, 640–41
totalitarian governments, 5
trade, 687
    international, 644
"tragedy of the commons, the,"
    15

transaction cost, 19
transparency, 425
transportation, 609
Transportation Act (2005), 101
Transportation Department,
    U.S., 226, 274, 285
Transportation Safety
    Administration, 226
Transportation Security
    Administration (TSA),
    272, 274
Travel and Tourism Caucus,
    192
Treasury Department, U.S.,
    285, 288, 683
    creation of, 3
    September 11 and, 274
treaties, 52
trial court, 317
Trippi, Joe, 513
Truman, Harry S., 109, 207,
    224, 227, 701
    Fair Deal of, 211
    Korean War and, 30
    MacArthur fired by, 198
    World War II and, 30
trustees, 165
TSA (Transportation Security
    Administration), 272,
    274
Turkey, 700, 701
Twelfth Amendment, 439
Twentieth Amendment, 68–69
Twenty-first Amendment, 66
Twenty-second Amendment,
    69
Twenty-fifth Amendment, 69
Twenty-seventh Amendment,
    70
Tyler, Texas, 348–49
tyranny, 63

U2, 700
Ukraine, 135
uncontrollables, 630, *631*
unemployment, 660
    of African Americans, 670
    cost of insurance for, 662
    federal insurance for, 639
unfunded mandates, 98
Unfunded Mandates Reform
    Act (UMRA), 98
Uniform Code of Military
    Justice, 320
unilateralism, 679, 693
Union of Concerned Scientists,
    529
unions, 4, 5, 10*n*, 168, 390–91,
    404, 458, 486, 494, 503,
    504, 509, 539, 553, 556
United Kingdom, 25, 564, 701,
    705, 708, 711

Iraq War and, 678
    in UN, 697
United Mine Workers, 528
United Nations, 378, 395, 694,
    696–99, 706
    Charter of, 696, 698
    General Assembly of,
        696–97
    G. H. W. Bush and, 706–7
    Iraq War and, 678, 698–99
    Security Council of, 25,
        696, 697, 698, 699
    weapons inspectors, 25
United States:
    in IMF, 700
    in UN, 697
United States v. Lopez, 104
United States v. Morrison,
    104
United States v. Nixon, 109,
    228, 337
universalization of rights, 145
upper income wage earners,
    tax breaks supported
    by, 4
USA PATRIOT Act (2002),
    226, 251–52
USA Today, 576
U.S. Citizenship and
    Immigration Services
    (USCIS), 684
U.S. News & World Report,
    576
USPHS (U.S. Public Health
    Service), 668
U.S. v. Lopez, 130
U.S. v. Morrison, 130
Utah:
    No Child Left Behind in,
        102
    same sex marriage and, 86

VA (Veterans Administration),
    613
Valley Forge, 37
values, 381
Van Buren, Martin, 499
van Lohuizen, Jan, 403
Venderbei, Robert, 400–401
Ventura, Jesse, 507
Vermont, No Child Left
    Behind in, 102
Vermont Supreme Court, 86
Veterans Administration (VA),
    613
veto, 195, 229, *230*, 231, *231*,
    232–33, 234–35
veto points, 198
veto power, 18, 19
Viacom, 577
vice presidency, 249–50
Vietnam, 701

Vietnam War, 134, 209–10, 224, 228, 302, 454, 532, 589, 593–94, 689, 694, 705
Congress and, 681–82
draft evaders of, 226
draft in, 6
media and, 402–3
social upheaval caused by, 393, 395
Violence against Women Act (1994), 104, 130, 147
Vioxx, 642
Virginia:
Federalists in, 118
school segregation in, 137
slavery in, 48
Virginia Plan and, 47
Virginia, University of, 342–43
Virginia Military Institute, 146
Virginia Plan, 46–47
Virgin Islands, 321
VISTA (Volunteers in Service to America), 665n
Voice of America, 678
volunteer activists, 179
Volunteers in Service to America (VISTA), 665n
voter registration:
differences in rate of, 431
drives to increase, 454
voter turnout, 429
measuring, 427
voting, see elections, U.S.
voting rights, 52, 147, 353, 429, 434, 436
Voting Rights Act (1965), 178, 434, 436, 504
"Votomatic" machines, 442
vouchers, for education, 667–68

Wabash, St. Louis, and Pacific Railway Company v. Illinois, 91n
Wagner, Richard, 539–40, 543
Wagner, Robert, 540
Wagner Act (1935), 243, 540, 646
Wallace, George, 504, 509
Wallace, Henry, 509
Wall Street Journal, 576, 582
Wal-Mart, 547
Walt Disney Company, 577
war:
civil liberties in, 218
in Constitution, 53
declaration of, 84, 163
public defense and, 9
see also specific wars

War Department, U.S., 286–87
see also Defense Department, U.S.
Wards Cove v. Atonio, 150
War of 1812, 211, 498–99, 685
War on Terror, 24, 26–27, 29, 113, 134, 251, 275, 337–38, 395, 452–53, 455, 627, 704
see also Afghanistan; Iraq War
War Powers Resolution (1973), 224–25
Warren, Earl, 109, 133, 325, 355, 366, 424n
Warsaw Pact, 703
Washington, D.C., September 11 attack in, 605
Washington, George, 44
farewell address of, 476, 676, 688, 691
Genêt received by, 227
House request refused by, 228
political parties deplored by, 476, 498
on Shays's Rebellion, 45
Washington, University of, 349
Washington Post, 565, 569, 576, 581, 585, 587, 590, 594
Washington State, 417
Washington Times, 564, 582
Watergate scandal, 210, 228, 228n, 553–54, 589–90
Water Resources Development Act (2003), 616–17
Watson, Albert, 204n
WCBS (radio stop), 567
Wealth of Nations (Smith), 19
weapons of mass destruction (WMDs), 25, 378, 380, 407, 696, 705, 708, 709, 713
Weather Service, U.S., 274
Web logs (blogs), 570
Webster v. Reproductive Health Services, 131, 550
Weekly Standard, 564, 582, 706
welfare, 289, 607, 640, 644, 648, 662–63, 671
arguments against, 657–59
arguments for, 659–61, 663
decrease of, 658
foundations of, 647–57
growth of, 665
history of, 644–46
in polls, 410
reform plan of 1996, 111

see also Personal Responsibility and Work Opportunity Reconciliation Act
welfare reform, 308, 615, 655–57, 658, 662
Westinghouse Electric, 577
Westmoreland, William, 573
West Point, 683, 706
West Virginia, coal mining in, 610
What's the Matter With Kansas (Franks), 456
Whig party, 499–500, 507
whip, 183, 214
whip system, 206
White House Communications Office, 255–56, 258
White House Office of Legislative Affairs, 114
White House Office of Management and Budget (OMB), 4, 248, 259, 553, 618, 627, 630
White House staff, 248
whites, 386–87, 388
Iraq War and, 379
"wholesale" politics, 11
"Why Vote," 474
Wide Awake (magazine), 342
Wilkinson, James, 585–86
Will, George, 101n, 661, 663
Williams, Armstrong, 404, 586
Williams, John Bell, 204n
Williams & Jensen, 544
Wilson, James, 47, 49
Wilson, Joseph, 575
Wilson, Pete, 154
Wilson, Woodrow, 240, 243n, 295
constituency of, 593
popular mobilization and, 253
Winfrey, Oprah, 451
Wisconsin, 308
WMDs (weapons of mass destruction), 25, 378, 380, 407, 696, 705, 708, 709, 713
Wolfowitz, Paul, 706
women, 347
in labor force, 639
in post-World War II U.S., 640
see also gender discrimination; gender gap; League of Women Voters; Violence Against Women Act
women's rights, 539

Woodward, Bob, 585
World bank, 699
World Trade Organization
        (WTO), protests against,
        688
World War I, 134, 668, 685,
        693
    draft in, 6
    as presidential war, 211
World War II, 393, 532, 640,
        668, 685, 694, 699, 705,
        714
    civil liberties in, 218–19
    draft in, 6

grants-in-aid and, 92
    as presidential war, 211
    Truman and, 30
World Wide Web, 576
writ of appeal, 346
writ of certification, 343
writ of *certiorari*, 343, *344*,
        347, 372
writ of habeas corpus, 109,
        111, 323
WTO (World Trade Organiza-
        tion), protests against,
        688
WTOP (radio station), 567

www.ewg.org/farm, 614
Wyoming, 198

Yalta treaty, 703
Yates, Robert, 47, 62
*Youngstown Sheet & Tube Co. v.
        Sawyer*, 261
Yugoslavia, 698

Zakaria, Fareed, 685